Fourteenth Edition

The LAW *and* BUSINESS ADMINISTRATION *in* CANADA

J. E. SMYTH
LATE PROFESSOR OF COMMERCE,
FACULTY OF MANAGEMENT STUDIES,
UNIVERSITY OF TORONTO

D. A. SOBERMAN
LATE PROFESSOR OF LAW,
FACULTY OF LAW,
QUEEN'S UNIVERSITY

A. J. EASSON
LATE PROFESSOR OF LAW,
FACULTY OF LAW,
QUEEN'S UNIVERSITY

S. A. MCGILL
SCHOOL OF BUSINESS & ECONOMICS,
WILFRID LAURIER UNIVERSITY

PEARSON

Toronto

Vice-President, CMPS: Gary Bennett
Editorial Director: Claudine O'Donnell
Acquisitions Editor: Megan Farrell
Marketing Manager: Jessica Saso
Project Manager: Kimberley Blakey
Developmental Editor: Jill Renaud
Manager Content Development: Suzanne Schaan
Media Editor: Daniella Balabuk
Media Developer: Bogdan Kosenko
Production Services: Cenveo
Permissions Project Manager: Joanne Tang
Text Permissions Research: Lumina Datamatics, Inc.
Interior Designer: Anthony Leung
Cover Designer: Anthony Leung
Cover Image: © Iurii Sokolov / Fotolia

Credits and acknowledgments for material borrowed from other sources and reproduced, with permission, in this textbook appear on the appropriate page within the text.

Original edition published by Pearson Education, Inc., Upper Saddle River, New Jersey, USA. Copyright © [2016] Pearson Education, Inc. This edition is authorized for sale only in Canada.

If you purchased this book outside the United States or Canada, you should be aware that it has been imported without the approval of the publisher or the author.

This book offers a general discussion of legal principles relevant to business students. It is not intended to provide legal advice nor address specific situations. The law discussed in this book was compiled between January and June of 2014. Subsequent changes in the law will not be reflected in the text.

10 9 8 7 6 5 4 3 2 1 [EBM]

Library and Archives Canada Cataloguing in Publication

Smyth, J. E. (James Everil), 1920-, author
     The law and business administration in Canada / J.E. Smyth
(Late Professor of Commerce, Faculty of Management Studies,
University of Toronto), D.A. Soberman (Late Professor of Law, Faculty
of Law, Queen's University), A.J. Easson (Late Professor of Law, Faculty
of Law, Queen's University), S.A. McGill (School of Business & Economics,
Wilfrid Laurier University).—Fourteenth edition.

Includes bibliographical references and index.
ISBN 978-0-13-325167-8 (bound)

     1. Commercial law—Canada—Textbooks. 2. Commercial law—Canada —
Cases. I. Easson, A. J., author II. Soberman, D. A., 1929-, author III. McGill,
S. A. (Shelley A.), author IV. Title.

KE919.S69 2015   346.7107   C2014-907370-4

ISBN 978-0-13325167-8

Brief Table of Contents

Detailed Table of Contents

Part VIII The Modern Legal Environment for Business 705

About the Authors

J.E. Smyth

James Everil (Ev) Smyth (1920–1983) studied commerce at the University of Toronto, where he earned a B.A. and an M.A. He also became a Chartered Accountant and a Fellow of the Institute of Chartered Accountants. He taught at Queen's University from 1946 to 1963, and then returned to the University of Toronto where he taught until 1983. He was an outstanding teacher and also served a term as head of the Department of Political Economy and then as head of the School of Business at the University of Toronto. He was the author of *Introduction to Accounting Methods* (Kingston: Jackson Press, 1951) and *The Basis of Accounting* (Toronto: Ryerson Press, 1954). In 1983, he was posthumously given the L.S. Rosen Award for Outstanding Contribution to Canadian Accounting Education by the Canadian Academic Accounting Association.

Dan Soberman

Dan Soberman (1929–2010) studied law at Dalhousie University and Harvard University. He began teaching at Dalhousie in 1955, and in 1957 moved to Queen's University to help start the law faculty. He was dean of the faculty from 1968 to 1977, taught full-time until retirement in 1993, and continued to teach part-time there and in the School of Business until 1999. In the late 1960s, he was a member of the federal Business Corporations Task Force that drafted the Canada Business Corporations Act. In the autumn term of 2000, he was visiting professor at Kwansai Gakuin University in Japan. From 1977 until 2000, he was an adjudicator on human rights tribunals in Ontario and federally, and also acted as an arbitrator in labour disputes. He authored, or co-authored, chapters in various legal books and articles in law journals.

Alex Easson

Alex Easson (1936–2007) studied law in England, at Oxford University and the London School of Economics. Prior to coming to Canada, he practised law as a solicitor in London and taught at the University of Southampton. He was appointed professor of law at Queen's University in 1976 and remained at Queen's until he retired from full-time teaching in 2000. He then concentrated on his consulting practice, working principally for international organizations such as the IMF and the OECD, and specializing in international taxation, foreign investment, and economic reform. His work took him to more than forty countries on five continents. He authored, or co-authored, more than a dozen books, the most recent being *Tax Incentives for Foreign Direct Investment* (The Hague: Kluwer Law International, 2004). We at Pearson Canada appreciate his contributions to several editions of this highly acclaimed text.

Shelley McGill

Shelley McGill received her LL.B. from the University of Western Ontario and her LL.M. from Osgoode Hall Law School at York University. She is an associate professor of business law at Wilfrid Laurier University's School of Business and Economics, where she teaches law to graduate and undergraduate business students. She is also a deputy judge of the Ontario Small Claims Court where she presides on a part-time basis. Prior to joining Laurier, Professor McGill was a partner in the Ontario law firm of Sims Clement Eastman. Her research focuses on consumer protection issues and has been published in a variety of Canadian and international law journals, including the *Canadian Business Law Journal* and the *American Business Law Journal*.

Preface

We are excited to introduce the 14th edition of *The Law and Business Administration in Canada!* Over the past five decades, this text has been studied by thousands of business students. It has shaped today's business leaders and given them an introduction to the integral relationship between law and business.

More today than ever before, law plays a part in every facet of day-to-day business activities. Although contractual relationships remain the foundation of most business dealings with customers, suppliers, and lenders, other pressing legal issues continually emerge. Throughout the previous 13 editions, this text has responded to the quick pace of change in the business and educational environments with new content, features, and resources. The 14th edition responds to the needs of today's business students by streamlining the traditional study of contractual principles, emphasizing current legal topics involving government regulation of business, corporate governance, ecommerce, privacy, and globalization, and adding continuity to the discussion of strategies to manage businesses' legal risks by asking students to consider the legal issues facing a single business as it evolves through each chapter.

The 14th edition is a perfect fit for the current business education environment, maximizing both print and online resources. It expands the available online resources students have come to rely upon. In addition to legal content available in print, each chapter has supplemental detail and/or topics available on the Companion Website, giving instructors greater flexibility in the depth in which they cover certain topics.

As in previous editions, the 14th edition combines an unsurpassed commitment to in-depth legal content with an integrated practical approach to legal risk management. Each chapter identifies relevant international and ethical issues and highlights strategies to manage the legal risks identified in the chapter.

In this edition, we continue to streamline the contract content to make it more manageable and student friendly. The former Chapters 9 and 10 are combined to deal with writing and contractual interpretation in a consolidated manner. The Sale of Goods chapter in the specialty contracts part of the book is expanded to include consumer contracts, giving it a broader appeal. Government regulation of business continues to grow in importance, so this topic is given new priority in the 14th edition. The former Chapter 30 is revised and moved to the first part of the book; now, as Chapter 3, it rounds out the introductory material. Content in Chapters 1 and 2 was redistributed to guide the reader through the sources of law into a more detailed discussion of administrative law issues in the new Chapter 3. As a result of all of these changes, the 14th edition contains 32 rather than 33 chapters and the early tort and contract chapter numbers have changed.

As always, the new edition incorporates recent developments in the law into all chapters. Significant changes to copyright legislation, as well as new anti-spam legislation, are discussed in the relevant chapters. Landmark Supreme Court judgments involving copyright, international jurisdiction, and secured creditor priority are also incorporated into this edition. We completed the research supporting the revisions in the spring of 2014 so subsequent changes in the law will be reflected in the next edition.

In sum, the 14th edition presents a comprehensive overview of traditional and current business law topics in a readable, practical, multiplatform format with expanded online content and resources.

Shelley McGill
July 2014

SUMMARY OF CHANGES TO THIS EDITION

We set three key goals for this edition:

- streamlining and integrating print material with online resources
- reorganizing Part 1 to incorporate government regulation of business
- improving the organization and delivery of the contract content

A multiplatform delivery of content in both print and online formats benefits both instructors and students. In addition to the province-specific material that has been available online for some time, the Companion Website for the 14th edition offers supplemental material for each chapter including some of the detail and historical content offered in previous editions of the print book as well as expanded coverage of difficult or new topics. This online resource gives instructors greater flexibility in their approach to individual topics; those wishing more background, depth, or examples can incorporate the online material into class content, while those taking a more general approach may omit it. Students' reading assignments can be more easily customized to instructor priorities and students with particular interests may access additional material on their own. An added benefit of this coordinated use of resources is that the print text is considerably shorter than the 13th edition. We continue to make every effort to simplify the writing style while maintaining the in-depth coverage and level of explanation.

Part 1, entitled "The Law in Its Social and Business Context," sets the stage for the more in-depth study of law that follows it. In this edition, a new chapter is added to this part that naturally follows the Chapter 2 content on the "Sources of Law" discussion of the legislative process with "Government Regulation of Business" content from the former Chapter 30. Expanded content on administrative law is also offered at this point, giving students a more complete description of procedural law before they confront the substantive principles in the balance of the book.

Contracts are the cornerstone of business activity, and therefore contract law is the heart of every business law course. Unfortunately, the detailed rules and exceptions can be confusing and overlapping. To improve student comprehension, we have consolidated the discussion of the requirement of writing with contractual interpretation by combining the former Chapters 9 and 10 into one comprehensive chapter. Detailed content is provided online. Chapter 14, formerly covering only specialty contracts involving the Sale of Goods Act, has been expanded to cover consumer contracts as well.

All chapters have been thoroughly updated and the Cases and Problems in each chapter now include a continuing scenario. A simple start-up business is introduced in Chapter 2 and followed through successive chapters as it confronts chapter relevant legal issues or challenges. Students will see how common it is for a single business to repeatedly encounter different legal issues as it evolves.

Extensive revisions made to particular chapters are summarized below.

Part 1: The Law in Its Social and Business Context

This part has undergone significant organizational and content changes to coordinate and consolidate the procedural and administrative law content from the former Chapter 30 with the existing Chapters 1 and 2.

Chapter 1: Law, Society, and Business

- **Moved** historic content online.
- **Added** legal profession content formerly in Chapter 2 as part of the "Legal Risk Management" content.

Chapter 2: The Machinery of Justice

- **Revised and moved** the administrative law content to Chapter 3 and supported it with additional content online.
- **Moved** the historic description of House of Lords and Privy Council online and describe the new (now independent) UK Supreme Court.

- **Moved** the discussion of the legal profession to Chapter 1.
- **Introduced** the continuing business scenario that will appear in each successive chapter's Cases and Problems.

Chapter 3: Government Regulation of Business

As noted earlier, this chapter was moved to Part 1 so that it follows naturally after the description of legislation, constitutional powers, and the Charter in Chapters 1 and 2 and eliminates the duplication of this material (needed to refresh the reader by the time they got to the former Chapter 30). In response to reviewer demand, this chapter is substantively changed to increase the emphasis on procedural enforcement of government regulations by adding "Administrative Law" as a stand-out section.

- **Revised and reduced** the content in "The Legal Framework for Doing Business in Canada" and "The Power to Regulate Business" to avoid repetition with Chapters 1 and 2.
- **Deleted** Case 30.1 repeated from Chapter 1 and added online examples.
- **Added** "Administrative Law" section before "Judicial Review of Government Regulation" discussing how regulatory boards monitor compliance with government regulations.
- **Reordered** the "Competition" content for a detailed description of the regulatory scheme complete with investigative and adjudicative components.
- **Reduced** content on "Regulation of Business Conduct Toward Consumers," moving most to the new Chapter 14, "Sale of Goods and Consumer Contracts," and some online.
- **Deleted** content under "The Common Law" heading as students will not have studied this yet.
- **Added** "Environmental Protection" content to the print and online resource referencing the new Canadian Environmental Assessment Act, 2012, and new Supreme Court decisions as well as the new Foreign Corrupt Practices Act.

Part 2: Torts

Chapter 4: The Law of Torts

- **Added** content on the new Supreme Court of Canada cases addressing key intentional torts such as nuisance, malicious prosecution, and unlawful interference with economic relations.
- **Added** content on the new tort of intrusion on seclusion; greater detail is offered in Chapter 32, "Privacy."
- **Revised** the negligence content to separate causation and damage topics and simplify the discussion of remoteness.
- **Moved** some footnote detail, historic content on res ipsa loquitor, and policy discussions about the relevance of insurance to the Companion Website.

Chapter 5: Professional Liability: The Legal Challenges

- **Revised** the content on fiduciary duty to incorporate the new criteria set by the Supreme Court in 2011.
- **Reordered** the material on negligent misrepresentation, moving some of the history of its development online.

Part 3: Contracts

All contract chapters were revised to streamline and update content and remove duplication. Two chapters were consolidated.

Chapter 10: Writing and Interpretation

- **Combined** the content of the 13th edition's Chapters 9 and 10 into one chapter.
- **Revised** the subsection on "The Benefits of a Written Record" to incorporate a condensed version of "The Relationship Between Formation and Interpretation of Contracts" in the 13th edition's Chapter 10.
- **Revised** the subsection on "Types of Contract Affected by the Statute of Frauds" in the 13th edition to a list format with shorter descriptions, moving some content online.
- **Reduced** detail on "Requirements of the Sale of Goods Act," moving some detail to the new Chapter 14 and some to the Companion Website.
- **Reduced** the detail of "Consumer Protection Legislation" to a list format, moving the details to the new Chapter 14, "Sale of Goods and Consumer Contracts."
- **Added** 13th edition's Chapter 10 content on "The Interpretation of Express Terms" beginning with the former Illustration 10.1.
- **Revised** the former Ethical Issue "Can Judges Really Assess Credibility?" under a new heading, "Conflicting Testimony and Credibility."
- **Consolidated** material under "How the Courts Apply the Approaches" with content under "Predicting the Likely Outcome of the Court" and "The Goal of the Courts: Giving Validity to Contracts."
- **Updated** content on "Implied Terms" to include reference to terms implied by statutes, specifically the Sale of Goods Act and Consumer Protection Act (referring readers to Chapter 14).

Part 4: Special Types of Contracts

Chapter 14: Sale of Goods and Consumer Contracts

- **Moved** excess detail on risk of loss online.
- **Added to,** revised, and updated Sale of Goods Act and consumer contract content from the former Chapters 9, 10, and 30.

Chapter 19: Negotiable Instruments

- **Updated** content on Canadian Payments Association and Canadian Payments Act.
- **Added** online content on electronic cheque cashing.

Part 5: Property

The chapters in this part have undergone some modifications to incorporate key legislative changes including the Copyright Act and multiple Supreme Court of Canada decisions.

Chapter 20: Intellectual Property

- **Revised** copyright content to reflect the passage of the new Copyright Act.
- **Added** discussion of six new Supreme Court of Canada copyright cases.

Part 8: The Modern Legal Environment for Business

Chapter 30: International Business Transactions

- **Updated** the discussion of jurisdiction and forum non conveniens arising from new Supreme Court of Canada decisions.
- **Expanded** the NAFTA content on the Companion Website.

Chapter 31: Electronic Commerce

- **Updated** the discussion of Canadian anti-spam legislation.
- **Added** content on internet defamation arising from new Supreme Court of Canada decisions.
- **Updated** content on the new copyright legislation and Supreme Court of Canada decisions.
- **Expanded** discussion of forum non conveniens as it relates to internet contracts.

Chapter 32: Privacy (added in the 12th edition)

- **Added** discussion of new invasion of privacy tort called "intrusion on seclusion."
- **Added** new content on three Supreme Court of Canada decisions on privacy.

FEATURES

A careful effort has been made to standardize features in each chapter that will facilitate learning and enhance an understanding of business applications:

- An Explanation of Abbreviations is printed on the inside back cover.
- A Table of Statutes and a Table of Cases are provided on pages xxv and xxx, respectively.
- Case and illustration boxes throughout each chapter in the book and on the Companion Website provide examples based on actual cases.
- The opening section of each chapter summarizes the focus of the material to follow and lists some of the questions that will be considered.
- Definitions of key terms are included in the margins of each page.
- A continuing scenario involving the same business is included in the Cases and Problems section of each chapter.
- For convenience, an explanation of How to Read a Citation is printed on the inside back cover.

SUPPLEMENTS

Companion Website (www.pearsoncanada.ca/smyth)

The Companion Website provides students with an assortment of tools to help enrich the learning experience, including

- self-assessment quizzes,
- mini-cases with assessment questions,
- province-specific legal material, and
- supplemental content for each chapter.

An access code for the Companion Website may be packaged with the printed text or may be purchased separately.

Instructor Supplements

The following instructor supplements are available for downloading from a password-protected section of Pearson Education Canada's online catalogue (**www.pearsoncanada.ca/highered**). Navigate to your book's catalogue page to view a list of those supplements that are available. See your local sales representative for details and access.

- **Instructor's Resource Manual:** This manual provides lecture suggestions, a summary of the major changes from the 13th edition, additional information about the cases cited in the text, notes on the various Issue boxes, and suggested answers to all the Questions for Review and Cases and Problems.

- **Computerized Test Bank:** Pearson's computerized test banks allow instructors to filter and select questions to create quizzes, tests, or homework. Instructors can revise questions or add their own, and may be able to choose print or online options. The test bank for *The Law and Business Administration*, 14th edition, includes over 1800 questions in multiple choice, true–false, short answer, and essay format.
- **Test Item File:** This test bank includes all the questions from the computerized version in Microsoft Word format.
- **PowerPoints:** Chapter-by-chapter presentations complement the text chapter content.

CourseSmart for Instructors. CourseSmart goes beyond traditional expectations—providing instant, online access to the textbooks and course materials you need at a lower cost for students. And even as students save money, you can save time and hassle with a digital eTextbook that allows you to search for the most relevant content at the very moment you need it. Whether it's evaluating textbooks or creating lecture notes to help students with difficult concepts, CourseSmart can make life a little easier. See how when you visit **www.coursesmart.com**.

Pearson Custom Library. For enrollments of at least 25 students, you can create your own textbook by choosing the chapters that best suit your own course needs. To begin building your custom text, visit **www.pearsoncustomlibrary.com**. You may also work with a dedicated Pearson Custom editor to create your ideal text—publishing your own original content or mixing and matching Pearson content. Contact your local Pearson representative to get started.

Learning Solutions Managers. Pearson's Learning Solutions Managers work with faculty and campus course designers to ensure that Pearson technology products, assessment tools, and online course materials are tailored to meet your specific needs. This highly qualified team is dedicated to helping schools take full advantage of a wide range of educational resources by assisting in the integration of a variety of instructional materials and media formats. Your local Pearson Education sales representative can provide you with more details on this service program.

Authors' Acknowledgments

Over the years we have been fortunate to receive helpful advice and encouragement from many of our colleagues. In particular, our thanks are due to Stuart Ryan, Hugh Lawford, Richard Gosse, Donald Wood, David Bonham, Bruce McDonald, Gordon Simmons, Marvin Baer, David Mullan, Kenneth Swan, William Lederman, Robert Land, Nicholas Bala, Stanley Sadinsky, and Donald Stuart. We have also had the assistance of a number of excellent student researchers, notably Ib Petersen, Don Luck, Darryl Aarbo, Colleen Dempsey, Rebecca Lovelace, Grace Pereira, Ryan Mills, Samia Alam, Allison Ostafew McLure, Michelle Frigon, Brendan McGill, and Scott Buchanan. Additionally, we have had the benefit of the many helpful and constructive suggestions that have been passed on to us by our publishers from the reviewers of each new edition. To all of these people we express our thanks.

We appreciate the insights and suggestions of the following individuals—as well as others who choose to remain anonymous—who provided feedback on the 13th edition or reviewed the manuscript for the 14th edition:

Michael Begg, Capilano University
Nancy Breen, Nova Scotia Community College, Strait Area Campus
Robert L. Malach, University of Calgary
Gerald Palmer, University of the Fraser Valley

We would also like to thank all those at Pearson Education Canada who worked so diligently to bring this text into print. Among others, thanks go to Megan Farrell, Senior Acquisitions Editor; Patti Altridge, Senior Developmental Editor; Jill Renaud, Associate Editor; Jessica Saso, Marketing Manager; Kim Blakey, Project Manager; and Laurel Sparrow, Copy Editor.

Table of Statutes

Table of Cases

Chapter 1

Law, Society, and Business

What do we mean when we use the word "law"? Simple definitions are not enough. We begin by examining the role of law in society, how law relates to morals and ethics, and how it applies to the business environment.

In this chapter we examine such issues as:

- How does law reflect society's attitudes?

- What is the significance of the law to the business environment?

- How should business approach the management of legal risks?

- What is the relationship between the law and business ethics?

- Who makes law?

- How do courts decide whether the legislation is valid under the Constitution?

- What else do courts do?

- How does the Charter of Rights and Freedoms protect our human rights?

- Why is the Charter relevant for business?

- What is the purpose of a code of conduct?

- How does law impact international business activities?

THE ROLE OF LAW

How Is Law Defined?

A simple definition would be misleading because law is so diverse and complex. Beginning with a brief description of what law does is helpful: the law sets basic standards of behaviour that are enforced by government and also by individuals and groups with the help of government. The law binds all of us; we cannot opt out of the legal system as we may from a club's rules by simply resigning—a club's rules are not law. Who makes law and how it is made are discussed later in this chapter and in Chapter 2.

Why do we have—and need—law? First, law is needed to protect persons, property, and society as a whole; it prohibits conduct that society believes to be harmful to others, such as assaulting another person or stealing that person's property. The law punishes someone who commits illegal conduct. However, it does much more than forbid harmful conduct: It also prescribes simple but vital rules that allow us to get on with our everyday lives—for example, requiring motor vehicles to drive on the right-hand side of the road. There is no moral reason to drive on the right side rather than on the left, as a number of countries require. But clearly, we must have just one rule about this in a particular country that all drivers obey.

Second, law gives government the power to act for the benefit of society as a whole. It authorizes government to provide policing, fire fighting, education, and health care—and to raise taxes to pay for those activities. We expect our government to operate in accordance with the **rule of law**. Law involving the government is labelled **public law**.

Third, law regulates individuals' interaction with each other; for example, it enables us to make legally binding agreements enforceable in the courts. This is known as **private law**, also sometimes referred to as civil law. It allows us to plan and organize our affairs, and we can bargain with others for mutual advantages. The essential feature is that we can rely on such arrangements because they are enforceable: We can book in advance a flight across the Pacific, accept a long-term employment contract or a lease of business offices, or buy an interest in a partnership or a corporation. The law provides certainty in determining contractual and property rights—something that is essential for business to carry on efficiently.

rule of law established legal principles that treat all persons equally and that government itself obeys

public law law that regulates the conduct of government and the relations between government and private persons

private law law that regulates the relations between private persons and groups of private persons

---

CHECKLIST
What Does Law Do?

- It influences and controls the behaviour of individuals in society.
- It empowers, influences, and controls the actions of government.
- It influences and controls interaction between individuals.

How Is Law Linked to Morals and Ethics?

Law, morals, and ethics are interrelated. Individuals "must" comply with the law—doing so is not optional. Therefore, laws must be just so that most of society views them as fair and therefore voluntarily complies. Most laws naturally evolve from basic moral principles that all people accept. For more information on this topic, see the Companion Website. Still, law often reflects only a minimum standard acceptable to most people. Morals and ethics, on the other hand, are optional standards of behaviour that people "ought" to observe even though doing so is not compulsory. They are considered to be a higher standard than the law, involving concepts of integrity, trust, and honour. Although legal philosophers try to create clear distinctions, the categories overlap. For more information on this topic, see the Companion Website. For example, lying is always unethical and immoral, and sometimes against the law. The law imposes ethical obligations of trust and integrity on some positions, such as directors of corporations, lawyers, and doctors. When unethical and immoral behaviour is recognized by most of society as unacceptable, it is likely that a law will be introduced to regulate the unethical conduct. Therefore, the moral and ethical values of society as a whole shape the development and direction of the law. An ethical issue is highlighted in each chapter of this book.

Is It Ever Right to Break the Law?

Even an effective, democratic legal system still leaves us with a number of difficult issues: Is it ever right to break the law? Is "law" the same thing as "justice"? What if a law is unjust? Intelligent, moderate men and women generally agree that there are times when an individual is justified in breaking the law, although they would add that, generally speaking, the law should be obeyed. They would also agree that there are unjust laws, but even these ought to be obeyed because of the chaotic consequences for society if many people fail to obey them. Even while trying to get unjust laws changed by normal, lawful means, we should still comply with them.

ILLUSTRATION 1.1

Mary Brown was at home tending her sick 18-month-old baby. He had a high temperature caused by an undetermined virus. Suddenly she realized that the child had lapsed into a coma. Fearing that he was in a state of convulsion and might die, she rushed him to her car and drove to the nearest hospital. Within a few moments she was driving 110 km/h in a 50 km/h zone. On arrival at the hospital, the child was placed in emergency care, and the doctor commended her for having saved the life of her child. A police officer arrived on the scene and presented her with a summons for dangerous driving.

Mary Brown drove her car far in excess of the speed limit—a speed limit designed to promote safety. She endangered the lives of other users of the streets, but she did so in order to save the life of her own child. She would not argue that the 50 km/h speed limit was unreasonable or unjust, but only that, in the circumstances, she was justified in breaking the law or, possibly, that the law should not apply to that particular situation. Nonetheless, the law was apparently broken.

Law and justice, may not always coincide. But, one may ask, "Is an unjust law really law?" In some rare circumstances, it has been argued that a law is so terribly unjust that it need not be obeyed by anyone. Conversely, is there any point in having a law that no one will obey, such as prohibition of unauthorized music downloading? These perplexing questions demonstrate the link between law and ethics. Law must be rooted in the ethical and moral values of the society in order to be effective.

How Does Law Influence Behaviour?

First, we hope that individuals voluntarily comply with the law simply because it is the law, and the vast majority of us instinctively understand the need to obey the rules.

However, to further encourage compliance, most laws, if broken, trigger penalties or consequences. When a person breaks the law, he or she is held responsible for the consequences; this is often described as **legal liability**. How offensive society finds the conduct determines how severe the consequence of the conduct will be. If lawmakers view the

legal liability responsibility for the consequences of breaking the law conduct as extremely offensive to society as a whole, as with murder, they will consider it a matter of public law, require the government to enforce the law, and impose the most serious consequence, that of **criminal liability**. If society views the conduct as less offensive but still necessary for an orderly society, as with proper driving habits, then the conduct might be exposed only to **regulatory or quasi-criminal liability**, and the government will generally ticket offenders. Alternatively, if lawmakers designate the conduct as primarily a private matter affecting only the parties involved, such as when a tenant fails to pay rent, it will be considered a matter of private law, and persons harmed by the conduct will be responsible for enforcing the law through private or civil lawsuits. This type of liability is known as **civil liability**. These three forms of legal liability are the tools used by lawmakers to encourage people to abide by the law.

criminal liability responsibility arising from commission of an offence against the government or society as a whole

regulatory or quasi-criminal liability responsibility arising from breaches of less serious rules of public law, often enforced through specialized regulatory tribunals set up by the government for specific purposes

civil liability responsibility arising from a breach of a private law, enforced through a lawsuit initiated by the victim

Tickets

CHECKLIST

Forms of Legal Liability

Lawmakers use three forms of liability to influence individual behaviour:
- Criminal liability
- Regulatory or quasi-criminal liability
- Civil liability

ILLUSTRATION 1.2

In 2004, the federal government announced plans to decriminalize possession of recreational-use marijuana. This sparked a debate about whether society's attitude toward marijuana use had changed. Some people misunderstood the plan as one that would legalize marijuana use when, in fact, the conduct would remain illegal as a regulatory offence.

ILLUSTRATION 1.3

A business releases chemicals into the groundwater, contrary to the environmental emissions standards. Local residents drink the contaminated water and die. The company would face criminal liability if charged by the government with the offence of criminal negligence causing death. It could also face regulatory liability if fined for breach of the particular environmental regulations, and it would also face civil liability when sued by the victims' families for the losses associated with the deaths of their loved ones.

It is possible for one event to attract all three types of liability.

LAW AND BUSINESS

The Significance of Law for the Business Environment

Law is part of every facet of doing business and is central to a business's interaction with its customers, suppliers, competitors, and government. Law outlines what to do, how to do it, and what not to do. Businesses may face criminal, regulatory, and/or civil liability if they do not comply. Some say that there are too many laws—that business is overregulated: Laws may be resented because they add to the cost of doing business. Too much regulation can restrict economic freedom and make a country's businesses less competitive.

There is no doubt, however, that modern society cannot function without laws, and businesses cannot succeed without understanding those laws. Indeed, business executives identify legal certainty as one of the key factors that determine whether or not to invest in a particular country. To have a good environment for business, a country must provide an adequate legal infrastructure that clearly defines rights and responsibilities and properly enforces them. Overregulation may be a severe inconvenience—but it is far less of an obstacle to business than is the complete absence of regulation.

Law and International Business

Generally, law regulates conduct within a country's jurisdictional boundaries, but business is not restricted to the borders of a single country. Increasingly, the world is becoming a single giant marketplace in which firms from different countries carry on business; they make agreements, and they compete against and sometimes cooperate with each other. For Canada, more than for most countries, the international dimension of business is especially important; foreign trade and foreign investment result in a wide variety of legal relationships between parties in two or more countries. Accordingly, the law is a significant element in the international business environment.

Businesses may be faced with different rules for each country in which they operate. Determining which laws apply to any given situation can lead to a conflict of laws. As will be discussed in later chapters, governments and non-governmental organizations are trying to harmonize laws in order to address these conflicts through the use of treaties, conventions, and model laws. Model laws are recommended templates for domestic laws that are developed by advisory organizations such as law reform commissions. Treaties and conventions are international agreements between governments in which countries agree to pass similar laws. These agreements are often brokered through **super-governmental organizations** such as the United Nations. The success of these initiatives depends on the willingness of countries to implement the agreed-upon treaty rules. Each chapter of this book will identify an international issue where countries take differing legal positions.

super-governmental organizations non-profit associations of governments from around the world working to find common approaches to international issues, such as the World Trade Organization or the United Nations

LEGAL RISK MANAGEMENT

Businesses must understand the laws that affect them, the relevant compliance requirements, and the risks of legal liability associated with their activities. Some may question why business managers need to familiarize themselves with the law, correctly suggesting that lawyers are the experts in this field. However, business managers are the experts in the activities of their businesses, and they must understand the **legal risk** associated with the everyday choices they make. Business managers cannot effectively use lawyers unless the managers know what to ask and when to ask it—and then understand the advice they receive.

Early identification of a legal risk is vital to effective management. Businesses must develop a **legal risk management plan** that anticipates possible legal liability and provides preventive and remedial strategies. The involvement of lawyers is only part of the overall plan.

legal risk business activities, conduct, events, or scenarios that could expose a business to any type of legal liability

legal risk management plan a plan developed by a business that identifies potential legal liability and provides preventive and remedial strategies

Developing a Legal Risk Management Plan

Developing a legal risk management plan requires five distinct steps involving every facet of the organization, as well as experts in law, finance, and insurance. The process is continuous and includes ongoing revision as law evolves, business expands and diversifies, and personnel changes.

First, managers must undertake a **legal audit** of the operation, which involves an examination of every area, action, and interaction of the business in order to identify potential legal liability and legal compliance risks. This audit requires the participation of those most familiar with the functional areas of the business, and these managers must be conversant in the principles of legal liability. This book focuses on the important business law principles of legal liability.

legal audit a review of each area, action, and interaction of the business to identify potential legal liability and legal compliance risks

Second, after a comprehensive list of legal risks is developed, the risks must be prioritized. What is the most serious legal risk facing the business? Prioritization involves assessing the likelihood or frequency of the event occurring and the magnitude of the consequences if the event occurs. Risks should be addressed in order of their priority. This book reviews important business law cases that will help value and assess risks.

Third, managers must develop effective strategies to deal with each risk. The strategy must have proactive and reactive elements; in other words, there must be a plan to prevent the risk from occurring and also a plan to deal with the risk in a way that minimizes its consequences if it does occur. Prevention is important because there are consequences even with a successful legal dispute. A legal dispute is expensive and time-consuming to process, it drains energy, focus, and resources from other areas of the business, and it attracts negative publicity. Reaction is important because you cannot prevent every eventuality. For example, a nuclear power plant puts safety measures in place to prevent an accident, but must still have an evacuation plan in case an accident occurs. Each chapter in this book will conclude with legal strategies for risk management.

Fourth, the business must implement the plan. Implementation involves more than just announcing the plan. There must be education, training, testing, and monitoring. Employees must be aware of the plan and capable of complying with it. Management must undertake regular monitoring to ensure that the plan is followed. Having a plan and not following it is worse for a business than having no plan at all.

Fifth and finally, the plan must be revised regularly. New legal risks must be added to the plan. Legal risks change every day as new laws are introduced and cases are decided. As businesses expand to new jurisdictions, different laws apply. New products and processes bring new risks. Personnel restructuring means responsibilities may shift. A legal risk management plan must reflect current organizational structures so everyone performs their responsibilities.

CHECKLIST

Steps in the Development of a Legal Risk Management Plan

- Identify potential legal risks.
- Assess and prioritize each legal risk based on likelihood and magnitude.
- Develop a strategy to address each risk from both proactive and reactive perspectives.
- Implement the plan.
- Regularly review and update the plan.

Strategies to Manage Legal Risks

As noted, every legal risk management plan involves preventive and reactive strategies. Four general strategies exist for managing legal risk:

- Avoid the risk: This strategy involves discontinuing the conduct or finding another way to achieve the result.
- Reduce the risk: This strategy includes quality control initiatives that decrease the likelihood of the risk or minimize its damage.
- Transfer the risk: This strategy accepts that the risk may occur and shifts the consequences to someone else—an insurance company or a consumer who, through contracts, assumes responsibility.

■ Absorb the risk: This strategy accepts that the risk may occur and budgets for the expenses. This strategy is used with remote risks or small-valued risks. The potential cost is factored into the price of the product, and the strategy is known as "self-insuring."

A business will use all of these strategies in combination.

Subsequent chapters will conclude with suggested strategies to manage the legal risks discussed in the chapter.

ILLUSTRATION 1.4

Illustration 1.3 describes the legal liability risks associated with water contamination. A manufacturing business can avoid the most serious risks by selecting the safest chemicals for its manufacturing process. It will further reduce the likelihood of the risk by implementing strong quality control measures and warning those nearby of the use of chemicals. Naturally, it will also carry insurance to transfer the costs of an environmental cleanup. However, this insurance is very expensive, so the business may absorb some of the risk by choosing a high deductible.

The Legal Profession

Every legal risk management plan involves the use of legal experts. In England, the legal profession is divided into two groups: solicitors and barristers. A **solicitor** is an "office" lawyer whose time is mostly spent interviewing clients and carrying on the legal aspects of business and family affairs. Solicitors also prepare cases for trial. A **barrister** takes cases assigned by solicitors—and presents them in court. Barristers also give opinions with respect to potential litigation and are consulted by solicitors on a wide variety of more complex legal issues such as corporate mergers and tax planning.

In the Canadian common law provinces, all lawyers are qualified as both barristers and solicitors; they may carry out the duties of both professions and often do so, especially in smaller cities and towns. In larger cities, lawyers tend to specialize in particular areas of the law; lawyers who specialize in private (civil) trials are known as "litigation" lawyers. Under the civil law of Quebec, the profession is divided in approximately the same way as in England. Quebec recognizes the designations of **notary** (solicitor) and **advocate** (barrister). In the United States the distinction has broken down completely. A lawyer is not even called "barrister and solicitor" as in Canada, but is simply an **attorney**.

The Canadian legal profession is organized on a provincial basis. Each province has its own "bar" (barristers' society or law society), and one must qualify and be licensed as a member in order to practise law. Law societies set professional standards of behaviour for all their members and discipline lawyers who violate the standards. The standards—including honesty, integrity, confidentiality, and competency—govern the lawyer's relationship with clients, the courts, the administration of justice, and the public. The most serious violations result in a lawyer's being **disbarred**—expelled from the law society and losing the privilege of practising law. The National Mobility Agreement (signed by all the provincial law societies) sets the rules for temporary and permanent movement of lawyers between provinces.[1] A member in one province must meet the standards and pay the fees of the provincial bar in another province before practising in that province permanently. Out-of-province lawyers may carry on some minor (temporary) activity within another province without fees or licensing. A member of any provincial bar, however, may appear before the Supreme Court of Canada.

solicitor an "office" lawyer in England who interviews clients, carries on legal aspects of business and family affairs, and prepares cases for trial

barrister a lawyer in England who accepts cases from solicitors and presents them in court, and also acts as consultant in complex legal issues

notary a solicitor in Quebec

advocate a barrister in Quebec

attorney a lawyer in the United States, encompassing the roles of both barrister and solicitor

disbarred expelled from the law society and deprived of the privilege of practising law

---

[1] National Mobility Agreement, 2013, Federation of Law Societies of Canada, www.flsc.ca.

When a client hires a lawyer, the relationship is governed by the professional standards of their law society as well as the historic protection of **solicitor–client privilege**. This privilege requires the lawyer to keep confidential all communications between the lawyer and the client. The lawyer cannot be forced to reveal such communication to a court unless the client approves. This privilege protects the client and allows the client to speak candidly to the lawyer, ultimately ensuring the best possible legal advice.

The most recent development affecting the legal profession is the emergence of the **paralegal**—a non-lawyer who provides some form of legal service. For many years, lawyers have hired non-lawyers, trained them in a specific area, and then delegated clerical responsibilities to the paralegal. In this model, they work under the supervision of a lawyer and the lawyer is responsible to the client for the work. As lawyers' fees increased, paralegals began offering clerical services directly to the public in such areas as incorporations, uncontested divorces, and simple wills. Now paralegals are regulated and licensed in some provinces to assist people in all minor court matters such as highway traffic tickets, landlord and tenant disputes, and Small Claims Court matters. Although some paralegals offer exceptional service, unregulated paralegals present risks to the public: The quality of service varies widely; they are not subject to educational requirements, licensing, professional standards, or discipline; and they do not have to carry liability insurance. Ontario was the first jurisdiction in North America to regulate paralegals. In order to offer services directly to the public, Ontario and Alberta require paralegals to be licensed by the law societies, carry insurance, meet competency standards, and be subject to discipline.[2] The Law Society of British Columbia approved new regulations of paralegals in 2013.

Business and the Legal Profession

Should a business hire a lawyer to deal with a problem when it arises, or should it reserve the services of a lawyer through paying a **retainer** in advance of any particular need? Should a business hire or retain one lawyer or law firm to handle all its needs? Should the business retain multiple lawyers with specific specialties? Is the best solution an in-house lawyer? Are paralegals best for some problems? These are difficult questions that every business must answer. The answer depends on the size of the business, the types of legal risks, and the resources available. The development of a legal risk management plan, as discussed above, will help the business to identify its legal needs.

Most businesses use some **outside counsel**—self-employed lawyers who work alone, in small partnerships, or in large national firms, and bill the business for services rendered. Using this type of lawyer allows a business to select the specific specialty needed for the job. However, it is also valuable for a business to have a long-term relationship with one lawyer or firm that becomes familiar with its business and legal needs. Sometimes this is accomplished by hiring a large firm, building a relationship with one contact lawyer, and referring work as needed to various lawyers within the firm.

Businesses with regular legal needs sometimes hire a lawyer, known as **in-house counsel**, as a full-time employee of the business. The in-house counsel might need to hire outside counsel for matters beyond his or her capabilities, but in such circumstances the in-house counsel can communicate with and supervise the outside counsel in a way that minimizes the cost. In addition, the in-house counsel often supervises a team of paralegals working as compliance officers in various areas of the business. A **compliance officer** monitors regulatory and legislative requirements applicable to the business and ensures that the business complies. The role of in-house counsel is expanding to include a proactive role

solicitor–client privilege a client's right to have all communications with his or her lawyer kept confidential

paralegal a non-lawyer who provides some form of legal service to the public

retainer the contract between a lawyer and client that describes the work that will be done and the fee that will be charged

outside counsel self-employed lawyers who work alone, in small partnerships, or in large national firms, and bill the business for services rendered

in-house counsel a lawyer who provides legal services to a business as a full-time employee of the business

compliance officer an employee that monitors regulatory and legislative requirements applicable to the business and ensures that the business complies

---

[2] See, for example, Law Society Act, R.S.O. 1990, c. L-8 as amen. See also the criticism of the Ontario model contained in Chapter 4 of the Federal Competition Bureau Report Self-Regulated Professions Balancing Competition and Regulation, December 2007, www.competitionbureau.gc.ca/epic/site/cb-bc.nsf/en/02523e.html (accessed February 13, 2008).

in the management and strategy of the business. An in-house counsel can be a valuable member of the management team, and the decision to hire such a lawyer should not be undertaken as a purely mathematical calculation of saved legal fees.

LAW AND BUSINESS ETHICS

Business Ethics

Earlier we discussed whether breaking the law can ever be right. We should also consider whether merely abiding by the law is always sufficient: are there occasions when a higher standard of behaviour is required? In a commercial context, this question raises the issue of business ethics and **corporate social responsibility**. As shown in Figure 1.1, corporate social responsibility can be thought to have three domains: ethical, legal, and economic. In the wake of recent corporate scandals, businesses are encouraged to live up to a higher ethical standard than is imposed on them by law. One way to promote an ethical climate in a business is to introduce a **code of conduct** that requires behaviour in line with ethical values such as honesty, trust, loyalty, and responsibility.[3]

Why should a firm commit itself to observing a higher ethical standard than the law requires? The answer may be quite straightforward: A firm behaves ethically because that is how its owners or managers believe it should behave. More often, however, ethical behaviour is a matter of enlightened self-interest. A firm that respects its employees is more likely to have a stable, contented, and productive work force; a firm that operates a liberal "returns" policy is more likely to create consumer loyalty; a firm that shows concern for the environment and the community in which it is located will benefit from an improved public image; and a firm with transparent and independent leadership will benefit from the trust and confidence of the public investor. Finally, as we have noted, the ethical values of society shape the development of the law; proactive legal risk management anticipates where the law may go in the future and prepares for it now. Today's voluntary ethical standard may be tomorrow's mandatory obligation. Most chapters of this book will identify an ethical issue.

corporate social responsibility a concept that suggests business decision makers consider ethical issues—including the interests of customers, employees, creditors, the public, and other stakeholders—in addition to legal and financial concerns

code of conduct a common standard of behaviour that may take the form of a values statement or a prescribed set of rules often used by a professional organization setting out the duties and appropriate standards of behaviour to be observed by its members

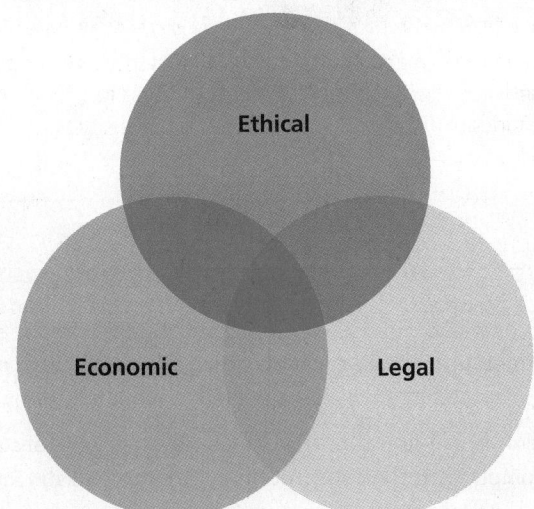

Figure 1.1 Corporate Social Responsibility: A Three Domain Approach

Source: Mark S. Schwartz and Archie B. Carroll, "Corporate Social Responsibility: A Three Domain Approach" (2003), 13(4) *Business Ethics Quarterly* 509.

---

[3] Mark S. Schwartz, "A Code of Ethics for Corporate Codes of Ethics" (2002), 41 *Journal of Business Ethics* 27–43; Mark S. Schwartz and Archie B. Carroll, "Corporate Social Responsibility: A Three Domain Approach" (2003), 13(4) *Business Ethics Quarterly* 503–30.

Codes of Conduct

Codes of conduct take a variety of forms and can fill gaps that law cannot reach:

Binding Codes Some activities, particularly of professionals, are regulated by a code of conduct, or a similar set of rules laid down by a governing body or trade association. Professional codes of conduct are considered further in Chapter 5.

Although these rules are not law, their effect is often similar. A member of a profession or trade association who breaches the code of conduct may face disciplinary proceedings and may even be expelled from that body—a very severe sanction, since often expulsion will deprive the offender of the right to work in the profession. These bodies can cross jurisdictional boundaries that the law does not.

Voluntary Codes Some industries have established voluntary codes of conduct for their activities. Although voluntary, these codes often have a strong persuasive effect. A voluntary code may even be used as a substitute for government regulation, the implicit threat being that, if an industry—for example, the advertising industry—does not regulate itself satisfactorily, the government will step in and legislate standards. In other cases, voluntary codes are adopted where no effective power to legislate exists. A well known example is the United Nations Code of Conduct on Transnational Corporations. Multinational enterprises are urged to observe certain minimum standards—for example, on employment of child labour—even though there are no legal restrictions in countries in which they operate.

Self-Imposed Codes Some firms have adopted and published their own codes of conduct, especially in relation to employment conditions and environmental protection. Codes may be a response to public criticism—for example, to criticism of working conditions in overseas factories of manufacturers of clothing and sporting goods. Sometimes they may be used to impress and attract particular groups of consumers. In other cases, they simply reflect the philosophy of the owners or managers of the firm. The contents of the code may form part of employment contracts, and employees may be disciplined for violations.

ILLUSTRATION 1.5

Students attending a university are governed by an academic code of conduct that forbids cheating. Cheating is unethical. The code allows the university to expel or suspend a student for cheating. The university does not have to establish that the student broke the law, only that he or she violated the academic code of conduct that forms part of the contractual relationship between the university and the student.

WHO MAKES LAW?

Law comes from a variety of sources:

basic law a constitution that lists the founding legal principles accepted by the citizens of a country and that they regard as legitimate and binding

(a) The constitution—the **basic law** from which all other laws draw their power. This law might be created by a sovereign, such as a monarch, or by a government.

A constitution is a "higher" law by which all other laws are governed; all other laws must comply with the constitution in order to be valid and enforceable.

statutes pieces of legislation passed by government

(b) Legislation—also known as statute law, **statutes**, or acts—is passed by Parliament and by provincial legislatures under the authority of and in compliance with Canada's Constitution.

(i) Subordinate legislation—rules passed under authorization of a statute by a body designated in the statute, such as the federal or a provincial cabinet, or by a cabinet minister, or by an administrative body such as the Canadian Radio-television and Telecommunications Commission. These rules are referred to as **regulations**.

regulations administrative rules implemented by government as a result of authorization given in a statute

(ii) Administrative rulings—rulings handed down by administrative regulatory bodies created by the legislation to hear complaints and applications by individuals and groups, according to the terms of the legislation. We will discuss regulatory law in Chapter 3.

(c) Court decisions—judgments handed down by single judges or a panel of judges after hearing a case before the court. These decisions are collectively referred to as **case law**. Sometimes a decision impacts only the parties involved, but other times the decision includes explanations and opinions that shape the law and have relevance beyond the specific parties. We will deal with this type of law in more detail in Chapter 2.

case law a collection of individual cases decided by the courts that develop and shape legal principles

Courts play a very special role in our society: Whenever the government itself or any private citizen or group believes another person has broken the law, the complaining party may resort to the courts. Courts are central to law enforcement. Under a legal system such as ours, derived from the English common law, legislation has historically played only a small part in resolving legal disputes between private parties—individuals, corporations, or other organized groups not connected with the government. Large areas of the law are unaffected by legislation. In these areas, the courts apply principles from case law that they themselves have developed in their long history of delivering written decisions, and in novel situations of developing new principles. These activities of the courts are important and complex. We will discuss the evolution and continuing importance of court decisions based on principles developed by the courts themselves in Chapter 2. This chapter will review the relationship between legislation and the courts.

CHECKLIST

What Do Courts Do?

- They determine the validity of legislation.
- They interpret legislation.
- They protect human rights.
- They develop case law, creating new principles to be applied to resolve disputes without court intervention.
- They determine disputes for the parties before the courts.

THE COURTS AND LEGISLATION

Even in areas where there is legislation, courts play an important role. It will be the court that decides if a statute is valid and enforceable. If it is valid, the court must decide what the words of the statute mean and whether that interpretation covers the subject of the dispute. In Canada, validity depends on the Constitution.

Federalism and the Constitution

In a federal country such as Canada (and also the United States), there are two distinct levels of government: federal and provincial (or state in the United States). Under the Constitution Act, 1867,[4] each level has an independent existence and its own sphere of authority. Our national Parliament cannot alter the structure of provincial governments.[5]

---

[4] This act was formerly known as the British North America Act, but was officially renamed The Constitution Act, 1867 by the Constitution Act, 1982. Both of these acts and all intervening amendments are now referred to as the Constitution.

[5] Such changes may be done only by amending the Constitution, a difficult task that requires approval of the provinces themselves.

The division of legislative power, mainly under sections 91 and 92 of the Constitution, allocates certain areas to the federal Parliament and others (including power over municipalities) to the provincial legislatures. When conflict arises, the courts determine if legislation is within the jurisdiction of the enacting government. Whenever an act—or any provision in an act—is found by the court to be outside the legislature's jurisdiction and therefore beyond its powers (**ultra vires**), that act or provision is void. The Constitution also gives **residual powers** to the federal government, so that all fields not expressly allocated to the provinces are within federal jurisdiction. Examples are new activities developed after 1867, such as air traffic and radio and television broadcasting.

ultra vires beyond the powers and therefore void

residual powers powers that fall within federal jurisdiction because they are not expressly allocated to the provinces by the Constitution

Sometimes practical problems do not fit neatly into well defined subjects that fall clearly within either federal or provincial jurisdiction. The courts must resolve these jurisdictional disputes. In fact, the Canadian Supreme Court has become the constitution's jurisdiction umpire.

Courts follow a two-step process when deciding jurisdictional disputes between federal and provincial powers. First, they look at the law itself—what does the law do and why? The primary topic or dominant feature known as the "pith and substance" of the law is identified. Second, the court decides under which delegated power the identified topic falls—where does this *primary* subject matter fit?

If the court places the topic under a power of the other government, the law will be found invalid.[6] Minor infringements for incidental matters will not defeat a law whose primary purpose falls within the power of the enacting government.

CASE 1.1

The Quebec Consumer Protection Act prohibits advertising directed at persons under the age of 13. The provisions of the Act apply to all forms of advertising—including newspapers, magazines, and television. Extensive federal regulations of television broadcasting already existed. After receiving warnings from the Quebec government about its television advertising for children, Irwin Toys Limited asked that the court declare the provisions in the provincial act to be void because they interfered with the federal government's jurisdiction to regulate television. The court disagreed; it found that the purpose of the Act was to protect children, "a valid provincial objective," and while it did have an "incidental" effect on television advertising, it was not incompatible with existing federal regulations. "Neither television broadcasters nor advertisers are put into a position of defying one set of standards by complying with the other."[7] Consequently, the court held that the provisions of the Quebec Consumer Protection Act were not in conflict with federal regulations and, so, not void.

The court's decision was consistent with the principle that it should not easily strike down legislation—that it should respect the intent of the legislatures—unless the legislation was clearly inconsistent with the constitutional division of powers.

concurrent powers overlapping powers of both levels of government to regulate the same activities

Many problems overlap both jurisdictions, and often, both levels of government seem to have **concurrent powers** to regulate an activity. Section 95 is an example where the Constitution actually grants shared jurisdiction over agriculture and immigration. More often, both levels of government will have passed laws in the same area, relying on their own respective powers in section 91 and section 92. The court may find that the subject matter has a "double aspect"—that is, it clearly falls within both a federal and a provincial head of power. If there is no conflict between the federal and provincial laws, then both are valid.[8]

---

[6] *Reference Re Assisted Human Reproduction Act*, [2010] S.C.J. No. 61 at para. 19 (S.C.C.); *R. v. Van Kessel Estate*, 2013 BCCA 221.

[7] *Irwin Toy Ltd. v. Quebec (Attorney-General)*, [1989] 1 S.C.R. 927 at 964. This case raised other issues under the Canadian Charter of Rights and Freedoms, noted later in this chapter.

[8] See, for example, *Multiple Access v. McCutcheon*, [1982] 2 S.C.R. 161. The court found no conflict between federal and provincial laws concerning insider trading in corporate securities and both laws could coexist. See also *Rothmans, Benson & Hedges Inc. v. Saskatchewan*, [2005] 1 S.C.R. 188.

But what if there is a conflict? In that event, the principle of **federal paramountcy** applies. In order to preserve the same law across the country in an area of federal jurisdiction, the federal law prevails over a contrary provincial law.[9]

federal paramountcy   the principle that a federal law prevails over a conflicting provincial law

THE CHARTER OF RIGHTS AND FREEDOMS

A constitution often does more than allocate jurisdiction between levels of government: It might also prohibit all government interference in certain areas, or it might remove those areas from the legislative power of both levels. In 1982, the Charter of Rights and Freedoms became part of the Constitution; it places limits on many aspects of government action and protects **human rights**.[10]

human rights   recognized entitlements encompassing traditional freedoms associated with civil liberty and basic human necessities

The Charter refers to a variety of "rights and freedoms" that we will collectively refer to as "human rights" and it has important ramifications for business as well as individuals. First, we should note that the Charter is entrenched in the Constitution: It cannot be repealed by an ordinary act of Parliament or of provincial legislatures in each of the areas where formerly they were able to pass and repeal laws at their will. Section 52(1) states:

> The Constitution of Canada is the supreme law of Canada, and any law that is inconsistent with the provisions of the Constitution is, to the extent of the inconsistency, of no force or effect.[10A]

Any change in the Charter can only occur by way of amendment as provided for in the Constitution Act—that is, by consent of the Parliament of Canada and the legislatures of at least two-thirds of the provinces containing at least 50 percent of the population of all the provinces. We can see then that the Charter is much more difficult to change than is an ordinary statute.

Second, subject to the important qualifications in the following paragraphs, rights entrenched in the Charter cannot be infringed upon by ordinary legislation: To the extent that a statute offends a right in the Charter, the statute will be declared invalid. The legislature cannot interfere with those rights that are founded on the "higher law" of the Constitution. The idea of rights based on a higher law was a major departure from British parliamentary supremacy, and is more like the theory of the Constitution of the United States.

Although prior to the Charter our courts had not dealt with entrenched human rights, they did have wide experience in deciding whether a piece of legislation was within the competence of the federal Parliament or of provincial legislatures under section 91 or 92 of the Constitution; they struck down legislation when they concluded that it went beyond the powers granted. The Supreme Court of Canada has shown that it is prepared to strike down those provisions in statutes that offend the rights and freedoms guaranteed in the Charter.[11] Indeed, the Supreme Court has gone further: It has "read into" a human rights act (rather than striking down a part of the act) words prohibiting discrimination on the basis of sexual orientation, words that the legislature had not chosen to include as part of the act.[12]

Third, the Charter includes section 33, which permits a legislature to override certain other sections. That is, if a statute states expressly that it "shall operate notwithstanding"

---

[9] See, for example, *Bank of Montreal v. Hall*, [1990] 1 S.C.R. 121, which considered the interaction between the federal Bank Act and the provincial PPSA legislation as discussed in Chapter 28. Both were jurisdictionally valid, but if there was a conflict, the federal legislation prevailed. In another case it was held that, since the federal government has exclusive jurisdiction over aeronautics, provincial building code legislation and municipal zoning bylaws were not applicable to the construction of airport buildings: *Greater Toronto Airports Authority v. City of Mississauga* (2000), 192 D.L.R. (4th) 443.

[10] The terms "human rights," "civil liberties," and "civil rights" are synonyms.

[10A] Section 52(1), Section 52 - Constitution Act, 1982.

[11] See, for example: *R. v. Big M Drug Mart Ltd.* (1985), 18 D.L.R. (4th) 321, striking down the Lord's Day Act of Canada as a form of compulsory religious practice; and *A.G. of Quebec v. Quebec Association of Protestant School Boards et al.* (1984), 10 D.L.R. (4th) 321, nullifying certain sections of Quebec's Charter of the French Language as violating minority language rights under section 23 of the Charter of Rights and Freedoms.

[12] *Vriend et al. v. The Queen in the Right of Alberta et al.* (1998), 156 D.L.R. (4th) 385.

those specified sections, a legislature may infringe some of the most important rights guaranteed by the Charter. Section 33 also contains a so-called sunset clause: The overriding section of the statute expires five years after it comes into force unless it is re-enacted by the legislature—and continues to expire after each further five years. The reasoning behind these provisions seems to be as follows: The declaration of certain rights in our Constitution gives them great moral and political force; governments will rarely dare to pass legislation expressly overriding the Charter, and very likely for only limited purposes—and they will have to produce strong reasons for continuing the override beyond the first five years. In the years since the Charter, legislatures have operated within these constraints; in general they have not found it politically easy to avoid the Charter and to use the override section.

Fourth, none of the rights set out in the Charter is absolute: section 1 states that they are all subject "to such reasonable limits prescribed by law as can be demonstrably justified in a free and democratic society."[12A] The problem of what amounts to "reasonable limits" arises whenever a complainant claims that a right entrenched in the Charter, such as the freedom of expression, has been infringed.

In general, a statute is presumed to be valid (that is, to be within the power of a legislature passing it): A person attacking it must show why it is invalid. However, a person need show only that one of his constitutionally guaranteed rights has been infringed by a provision in a statute; the provision would then be presumed invalid unless the government could persuade the court that the infringement was "demonstrably justified." So the **burden** shifts to the government to show that the section of a statute that interferes with constitutional rights is justified. It is difficult to predict in a general way how deferential the courts will be to the legislatures. In what circumstances will judges say, "Since the elected majority think this infringement is justified, we will not interfere," rather than "The will of the majority does not justify this interference with individual rights"?

Fifth, the Charter applies to governments and governmental activities; it has limited application between private persons. In the private sector, the protection of human rights has been a matter for human rights codes passed by each of the provinces and by Parliament (to cover those activities that are under federal jurisdiction). These codes are not entrenched and may be amended from time to time by the legislature, or even repealed entirely, although complete repeal is highly unlikely. The Charter itself states that it applies "in respect of all matters within the authority of Parliament . . . [and] . . . of the legislature of each province."[12B] These words make the Charter applicable to all statutes, to regulations under statute law, to municipal laws, and to Crown corporations. However, the Supreme Court of Canada has refused to extend Charter requirements to corporations and even to our publicly funded universities because they are considered to be independent of the government.[13] This matter has been left to human rights codes.

The Rights and Freedoms Protected by the Charter

Several of the most important protections given by the Charter are reproduced here beginning with those rights and freedoms that may be overridden by Parliament or a provincial legislature through use of section 33.

Fundamental Freedoms

2. Everyone has the following fundamental freedoms:
    (a) freedom of conscience and religion;

[12A] Section 1 - Constitution Act, 1982.

[12B] Application of Charter, Section Thirty-two of the Canadian Charter of Rights and Freedoms.

[13] *McKinney v. University of Guelph*, [1990] 3 S.C.R. 229, at 266, "the mere fact that an entity is a creature of statute . . . is in no way sufficient to make its actions subject to the Charter."

---

burden   the requirement that, unless a party can establish facts and law to prove its case, it will lose

(b) freedom of thought, belief, opinion and expression, including freedom of the press and other media of communication;

(c) freedom of peaceful assembly; and

(d) freedom of association.[13A]

Legal Rights

7. Everyone has the right to life, liberty and security of the person and the right not to be deprived thereof except in accordance with the principles of fundamental justice.[13B]

8. Everyone has the right to be secure against unreasonable search or seizure.[13C]

9. Everyone has the right not to be arbitrarily detained or imprisoned.[13D]

10. Everyone has the right on arrest or detention.

(a) to be informed promptly of the reasons therefor;

(b) to retain and instruct counsel without delay and to be informed of that right; and

(c) to have the validity of the detention determined by way of habeas corpus and to be released if the detention is not lawful.[13E]

Sections 11 to 14 deal in detail with the rights of persons accused of crimes during criminal proceedings against them.

Equality Rights

15. (1) Every individual is equal before and under the law and has the right to the equal protection and equal benefit of the law without discrimination and, in particular, without discrimination based on race, national or ethnic origin, colour, religion, sex, age or mental or physical disability.

(2) Subsection (1) does not preclude any law, program or activity that has as its object the amelioration of conditions of disadvantaged individuals or groups including those that are disadvantaged because of race, national or ethnic origin, colour, religion, sex, age or mental or physical disability.[13F]

Two aspects of section 15 deserve comment. First, subsection (2) permits "affirmative action" (or "reverse discrimination")—that is, programs aimed at assisting disadvantaged people such as the aged, those who have disabilities, or those who, because of racial or ethnic background, have lived in impoverished conditions. Without such a provision, it might have been possible for a person not a member of a disadvantaged group to complain that he was not receiving equality of treatment if a disadvantaged person were given an extra benefit such as special funding to obtain higher education or training for a job.

Second, section 28 of the Charter states:

Notwithstanding anything in this Charter, the rights and freedoms referred to in it are guaranteed equally to male and female persons.[13G]

This section is not subject to being overridden by Parliament or a legislature; it deals with equality of treatment between the sexes—as does section 15(2)—and it states that equality is guaranteed "notwithstanding anything in the Charter" including, presumably, section 15(2).

[13A] Section Two of the Canadian Charter of Rights and Freedoms, Constitution Act, 1982.

[13B] Section Seven of the Canadian Charter of Rights and Freedoms, Constitution Act, 1982.

[13C] Section Eight of the Canadian Charter of Rights and Freedoms, Constitution Act, 1982.

[13D] Section Nine of the Canadian Charter of Rights and Freedoms, Constitution Act, 1982.

[13E] Section Ten of the Canadian Charter of Rights and Freedoms, Constitution Act, 1982.

[13F] Section Fifteen of the Canadian Charter of Rights and Freedoms, Constitution Act, 1982.

[13G] Section Twenty-eight of the Canadian Charter of Rights and Freedoms, Constitution Act, 1982.

Does this phrase then mean that affirmative action for the benefit of women offends section 28, so that a man may complain of unequal treatment if a woman is given special benefit?

The Significance of the Charter for Business

As noted above, the Charter of Rights and Freedoms applies to government behaviour and not the private sector, so why is it relevant to business? The answer lies in the fact that government regulates and controls the business environment through legislation. If that legislation violates the Charter of Rights and Freedoms, it can be declared invalid, and business will be free of the regulation. The retail industry was revolutionized by just such a Charter argument.

CASE 1.2

The Lord's Day Act was a federal statute dating back to 1906 that required businesses to remain closed on Sundays. In 1982, an Alberta-based pharmacy, Big M Drug Mart Ltd., remained open on a Sunday and was charged with a violation of the act. In defence, the company claimed that the law was invalid because it violated the Charter of Rights and Freedoms, specifically freedom of religion. They felt the Lord's Day Act forced non-Christians to honour the Christian religious practice of not working on Sunday. The Supreme Court agreed, held the Lord's Day Act invalid for offending the Charter, and found Big M Drug Mart Ltd. not guilty because no one can be convicted of an offence under an unconstitutional law.[14]

The societal and business impact of this change in the law was profound. Now Sunday shopping is the rule rather than the exception and the retail industry is forever changed. Employment in the retail industry rose between 5 and 12 percent, depending upon the province, because of the increased hours of operation.[15]

CHALLENGING THE VALIDITY OF A STATUTE

As we have seen, the court will declare a statute invalid if

- the subject matter is outside the constitutional jurisdiction of the government, or
- the statute violates the Charter of Rights and Freedoms.

In order to make this determination, the court must investigate the purpose and effect of the statute. What does it do and why? What do the words mean? Interpreting the legislation in a narrow way may mean that it falls inside the power of the government, while a broad interpretation may lead to invalidity.

ILLUSTRATION 1.6

The Canadian Parliament receives a report of a special study of abuses in the stock market that cause investors to lose their savings. In response, it passes a statute prohibiting as misleading certain kinds of advertising of securities and making them criminal offences. A broker who specializes in these transactions claims that his activity is lawful, and carries on in defiance of the statute. He is charged with an offence and raises the following arguments in defence: (a) that the law is unconstitutional because it purports to make changes in an area that is exclusively within the jurisdiction of the provinces under the Constitution Act, 1867; and (b) that even if his first argument is wrong, the government as prosecuting authority has placed an unreasonable interpretation upon the statute and has applied it too broadly in charging him with an offence. He argues, in other words, that under any reasonable interpretation of the statute his activity would remain lawful.

We can see from Illustration 1.6 that a legislature faces a double problem in attempting any type of reform. First, it knows that if its entire statute is ruled unconstitutional, the statute will be void and make no change at all in the law. (The broker in the illustration would then be subject to no new regulation whatsoever.) Indeed, even were the Supreme Court

---

[14] R. v. Big M Drug Mart Ltd., supra, n. 13.

[15] Mikal Skuterud, "The Impact of Sunday Shopping on Employment and Hours of Work in the Retail Industry: The Canadian Experience" (2005) 49 (8) *European Economic Rev.* 1953 available at http://economics.-uwaterloo.-ca/-~skuterud/-eer.-pdf

to interpret the statute as not being completely beyond federal powers, it might still restrict its application to areas within federal jurisdiction and so limit the statute that it would fail to accomplish the desired reform. In effect, the court would be saying: "If these words were given a broad meaning, they would attempt to regulate activity beyond the powers of the federal Parliament. Clearly, Parliament could not have meant to do such a thing. If, however, we restrict their meaning to 'such and such,' the regulation will be within federal jurisdiction and valid. We will assume that Parliament meant to do only what is possible under the Constitution, and accordingly find that these words have a restricted meaning." (Once again the broker would escape regulation if his activity were outside federal jurisdiction.)

Second, and apart from the constitutional hurdle, courts have sometimes been criticized for interpreting statutes narrowly so as to interfere as little as possible with existing **private rights**. Such an interpretation may in large measure frustrate an intended reform. (Again, in this event, the broker might be saved by the narrow interpretation of the statute.)

private rights individual rights arising from private law

We can see that a constitutional defeat in the courts is more serious than a narrow interpretation. Parliament cannot overcome a decision by the Supreme Court that a statute is unconstitutional unless the Constitution itself is amended—a process that requires a high degree of provincial agreement as well as the consent of Parliament.[16] However, if the problem is simply one of interpretation, the government can then introduce an amendment to broaden the application of the statute. The trouble with relying on the ability to amend legislation is that, except for emergencies or extraordinary pressure on government, the wheels of Parliament "grind exceedingly slow," and a year or several years might pass in the normal course of events before an amendment is enacted.

When the Supreme Court nullifies legislation on constitutional grounds, it can arouse strong feelings and sometimes vehement attacks, both for and against the judges as individuals and the idea that a court can have so much authority. A variety of cries can be heard: "The Court is a reactionary bastion standing in the way of badly needed reform"; "The Court is nine elderly lawyers, neither elected nor representative of the people, defeating the wishes of a democratically elected legislature"; "The Court has prevented one level of government from running roughshod over the jurisdiction of the other"; "The Court has stopped the government from making an unwarranted intrusion on individual liberties." Judges of the Supreme Court cannot escape making decisions that play a critical role in political, social, and economic change. As a result, the role and the personality of Supreme Court judges in particular, and of judges generally, have become subjects of great interest to legal theorists, sociologists, psychologists, and the media, as well as to the practising lawyers who appear before them.

CHECKLIST

Three Ways to Challenge a Statute

- Argue that the statute is invalid because the subject matter of the legislation is not within the jurisdiction of the relevant government.

- Argue that the statute is invalid because the legislation violates the Charter of Rights and Freedoms.

- Argue that the interpretation of the legislation is wrong and the statute does not apply to the particular conduct.

---

[16] A constitution, whether it is of a small social club or a large nation, almost always contains provisions for its own amendment. A "simple majority"—that is, any number more than 50 percent (for example, 50.01 percent)—may pass an appropriate motion to change any earlier motion or law also passed by a simple majority. But the provisions of a constitution are usually "entrenched": only a "special majority" may amend them. Typically a special majority is two-thirds or three-quarters of the ballots cast, but sometimes there are quite complex special majorities, giving a specified group the power of veto. Unless that group, even if it comprises a very small minority, approves of a proposed amendment, the amendment will be lost.

Have judges become too "political"? Are they "usurping" the powers of Parliament and the provincial legislatures? Should the political views of judges be explored during appointment? The very public and politicized confirmation process for United States Supreme Court judges is a stark contrast to the private appointment of Canadian Supreme Court judges.

Earlier in this chapter, we discussed the role of our courts in interpreting the Constitution. The traditional role of the courts in a federation has been to act as umpire in jurisdictional disputes involving legislation affecting levels of government. However, since the Charter of Rights and Freedoms became part of our Constitution in 1982, increasingly the courts have been asked to interpret and strike down legislation of both levels as being inconsistent with rights entrenched in the Charter. Two cases, in 1998 and 1999, added to the controversy about whether our courts have become too "activist."

In *Vriend v. Alberta*[17] in 1998, the Supreme Court of Canada went further than simply striking down a provision in a statute; it in effect ordered the legislature of Alberta to amend its human rights legislation to prohibit discrimination based on a person's sexual orientation. In 1999, our courts upheld the decision of a federal Human Rights Tribunal.[18] The Tribunal had ordered the federal government to pay several billion dollars in compensation to current federal employees and to former employees—almost entirely women—who were discriminated against because they were not paid fairly for work of equal value usually performed by male counterparts.

Some critics have complained that such court activism is depriving elected legislators of the power to make policy decisions and to enact legislation based on their value judgments and what they believe their constituents want. Others have defended the courts on the basis that our federal and provincial governments together made a basic decision in 1981–82 to entrench Charter rights: Ever since, legislatures must abide by the consequences because the courts have no alternative but to interpret statutes in the light of the Charter. In response, the critics claim that the courts have not shown enough deference to legislatures and to their values as

implemented in statutes; instead the courts are imposing their own values. This has led to calls for the reform of the judicial appointment process.

In 2004, the Supreme Court handed down two decisions that appeared to recognize the central role of legislatures.[19] In October 2004, the Court deferred to a decision by the government of Newfoundland and Labrador not to honour a deal reached in 1988 with its public sector workers to end pay discrimination against female hospital workers. By 1991, the government claimed it could not deliver on the deal because of the "severe" fiscal crisis hitting the province. The Court agreed that such a denial of Charter rights could only be justified by "extraordinary" circumstances, but it accepted the position taken by the province. This decision has generated criticism that the Supreme Court has become too deferential to government decisions.

In December 2004, the Supreme Court gave its opinion in the reference on the controversial subject of same-sex marriages,[20] in which it stated that the power to change the definition of marriage lies exclusively with the federal government. Although it appeared that the Court was showing deference to the legislature, it did declare that churches could not be forced to perform same-sex marriages. This was after the Ontario Court of Appeal had already effectively legalized same-sex marriage by striking down the marriage licence rules that prevented same-sex couples from obtaining a licence.[21] The Court refused to state whether it agreed with lower courts that the traditional man–woman definition of marriage offends the Charter rights of same-sex couples because the judgment was not appealed by the government.

In 2013, the Court made another decision that could transform Canadian society, by striking down the laws against prostitution. The laws against bawdy houses, soliciting on city streets, and living off of avails of prostitution were held to violate the Charter because they disproportionately endangered vulnerable women, actually making them less safe. The ruling was suspended for one year for the federal government to decide on a new strategy to regulate the sex worker industry.[22]

>

[17] *Vriend v. Alberta, supra,* n. 10.

[18] *Supra,* n. 10.

[19] *Newfoundland (Treasury Board) v. N.A.P.E.* (2004), 244 D.L.R. (4th) 294.

[20] *Reference re: Same-Sex Marriage* (2004), 246 D.L.R. (4th) 193.

[21] *Halpern v. Attorney General of Ontario et al.* (2003), 65 O.R. (3d) 161 (C.A.).

[22] *Canada (Attorney General) v. Bedford,* 2013 SCC 72; See also *Canada (Attorney General) v. Downtown Eastside Sex Workers United Against Violence,* 2012 SCC 46.

QUESTIONS FOR REVIEW

1. Describe the three main roles of law in our society.

2. How is the legal infrastructure of a country significant for business?

3. What is legal liability?

4. Distinguish between criminal liability and civil liability.

5. Are law and ethics the same thing?

6. What are the features of a legal risk management plan?

7. Why have business enterprises adopted codes of conduct?

8. What is the special role of the courts in a federal country?

9. What are residual powers? Concurrent powers?

10. What makes a "constitutional defeat" before the courts so serious for a legislature?

11. What strategies does business use to manage legal risk?

12. What is the special meaning of "public law" as distinct from "private law"?

13. Describe the special significance of sections 91 and 92 of the Constitution Act. What problems do these sections encompass?

14. If a citizen claims a provision in a statute to be unconstitutional because it is contrary to the Canadian Charter of Rights and Freedoms, must the government then show it is constitutional? Explain.

15. Which activities are governed by the Charter and which are not? Describe the distinction.

16. "We have a parliament to pass laws, a government to administer laws, and a police department to enforce laws. Ironically, these potent instruments for the restriction of liberty are necessary for the enjoyment of liberty." (A.A. Borovoy, The Fundamentals of Our Fundamental Freedoms [Toronto: The Canadian Civil Liberties Education Trust, 1974] at 5.) Comment on the meaning of this quotation.

Additional Resources for Chapter 1 on Companion Website

(www.pearsoncanada.ca/smyth)

In addition to pre- and post-tests, mini-cases, and application exercises, the Companion Website includes the following province-specific resources for Chapter 1:

- **Alberta:** Adult Interdependent Relationships Act; Alberta Human Rights Code
- **Atlantic Provinces:** Human Rights; Law Societies
- **British Columbia:** Administrative Tribunals; British Columbia's Electoral System; British Columbia's Legislative Process; Government Lobbyists; Judicial Review; Municipal Bylaws; Statutory Interpretation
- **Manitoba/Saskatchewan:** Lawyers and Ethics; Government Made Law—Statutes; Ethics and the Law; Charter Cases; Human Rights
- **Ontario:** Agreements to Share Power; Business Ethics; Corporate Social Responsibility; Corporate Codes of Ethics; Charter of Rights and Freedoms; Human Rights Legislation; Jurisdiction; Legislation; Same-Sex Marriage

Chapter 2
The Machinery of Justice

This chapter provides the basic information needed to use the legal system and to develop risk management strategies. Chapter 1 introduced the sources of law and considered the key role of the Constitution. In this chapter, we identify the various ways in which law is classified. We revisit the sources of law—judge-made law, legislation, and administrative rulings—and examine how each type develops and evolves over time.

In this chapter we examine such questions as:

■ What is the difference between substantive and procedural law? Public and private law? The civil and common law legal systems?

■ How does the theory of precedent balance the need for both certainty and flexibility?

■ How are the systems of courts organized?

■ What are the procedures for using the courts and making out-of-court settlements?

■ What costs are associated with going to court and who pays them?

■ What alternative methods of resolving disputes are available?

■ What is a class action?

■ How is legislative policy implemented?

CLASSIFYING LAW

Dividing law into broad categories helps us understand and organize the many laws that govern us. In Chapter 1, we explained that laws fall into two basic categories: public law (dealing with government actions) and private law (dealing with non-government relationships). Each of these categories is subdivided into more specific topics. Subcategories of public law include constitutional law, criminal law, and taxation. Private law covers topics such as contracts, torts, and property law. Business law draws on topics from both public and private law. This book emphasizes contract law, as it is the foundation of every business transaction.

substantive law the rights and duties that each person has in society

procedural law rules that deal with how substantive rights and duties may be enforced

Laws are also divided into two other categories: **substantive law** and **procedural law**. When lawmakers decide to address particular conduct, they define acceptable conduct and then identify a process to enforce it. The rules that define the acceptable conduct or the rights and duties of each person are substantive laws. Some examples are the right to own property, to vote, to enter into contracts, and to sell or give away property; the duty to avoid injuring others and to perform contractual obligations. Rules that deal with how the rights and duties may be protected and enforced are procedural laws. Put more simply, substantive law is "what" the law is and procedural law deals with "how" the law is enforced.

WHO MAKES LAW?

Chapter 1 identified two key sources of law:

- the courts through case decisions; and
- the government through legislation.

Legislation is made by federal, provincial, and even local governments and includes, for instance, regulations passed by a licence committee of a town council. The committee's authority can be traced to provincial legislation, but as a practical matter, the committee is creating new law. The Constitution is the foundation of all legislation, and its role in establishing and enforcing the law was introduced in Chapter 1. This chapter will examine how case law and legislation develop. Chapter 3 will look specifically at how government uses legislation to regulate business. The relative importance of case law and legislation vary from country to country depending on the legal system adopted by the jurisdiction.

LEGAL SYSTEMS: CIVIL LAW AND COMMON LAW

Regions of the World under Each System

civil law the system of law involving a comprehensive legislated code, derived from Roman law that developed in continental Europe and greatly influenced by the Code Napoléon of 1804

Two major systems of law developed in Western Europe, and they have spread through most parts of the world colonized by European nations. The older of the two systems is the **civil law** system. It covers the whole of continental Europe and, to a large extent, Scotland, much of Africa, and the whole of South and Central America. In North America, it applies in Quebec, Mexico, and, to some degree, in some of the southern United States, such as Louisiana. When the English conquered French Canada, they guaranteed the people of Quebec the continued use of French civil law in most areas of private law. To this day, most of the private law of the province of Quebec operates under the civil law system. Civil law is based upon legislation and is derived from **Roman law**. A civil law system requires that all law be collected into a consolidated body of legislation known as the civil code, and this code is far more important than any case decision. The court always refers to the code to settle a dispute. If the code does not seem to cover a new problem, then the court is free to reason by analogy to settle the problem from general principles in the code. In theory,

Roman law the system of law codified by the Eastern Roman Emperor Justinian in the 6th century a later court need not follow the earlier reasoning in a similar case; the second court may decide that, in its view, a just result of the law ought to be the reverse of the earlier decision.

The other legal system is the **common law** system and it originated in England. The common law system is followed in most of the English-speaking world (including Canada, the United States, and Australia), and it is a significant part of the law of many non-English–speaking countries that were part of the British Empire (notably India, Pakistan, Bangladesh, and the former colonies in Africa and the Caribbean). The common law system favours case law—the recorded reasons given by courts for their decisions and applied by judges in later cases. This book focuses on common law, and we describe the basis of common law in the following sections entitled "The Theory of Precedent" and "The Sources of Law."

Simply put, civil law values legislation over case law, and common law gives case law the same or sometimes greater value than legislation. Although both civil and common law courts often reach similar conclusions, there are some important differences. Here, we deal only with principles of the common law. Much of what is written in this book does not necessarily apply to the civil law jurisdiction of Quebec.

> **common law**   the case-based system of law originating in England and covering most of the English-speaking world—based on the recorded reasons given by courts for their decisions

The Need for Consistency and Predictability

For consistency and fairness, we need like cases to be treated alike. This also reduces the number of disputes that go to court because parties can anticipate how a case will turn out based on prior outcomes.

ILLUSTRATION 2.1

A contracts to build a house for B but does not carry out the agreement. Their contract specifies that B is entitled to only $50 if A defaults. B sues A and collects only $50 for the breach. X makes a similar contract with Y and fails to carry out the contract. Y sues X for damages, but the court awards Y $10 000 in the suit, refusing to enforce the $50 cap on damages.

Either decision, examined entirely separately, might seem reasonable enough: Some people might well believe that the builder should pay only $50; others might favour the owner's true losses. But if we place the two decisions side by side, for example, in adjoining courtrooms on the same day, there would be two very unhappy litigants. X would complain because A, in a similar situation, escaped without paying any real damages; B would be angry because she obtained virtually nothing while Y got substantial damages for breach of a similar contract. X and B would both feel unjustly treated, and most people would agree with them—the law should be either one way or the other.

Equal and consistent treatment in like situations is an important part of justice. Therefore, whether in civil law or in common law countries, judges must be interested in, and influenced by, what other judges have decided in similar cases.

A second major element of law is predictability. Suppose, after the contrary decisions we have just discussed, P wishes to make a similar contract with Q. Q asks a lawyer whether the contractual limit on damages is a binding one: If P backs out, will he be liable to pay damages to Q for any loss caused by failing to carry out the bargain, or will he only need to pay $50? Q's lawyer would have to say, "Maybe yes, maybe no; it depends on whether the court prefers the result in the case of A against B or that in X against Y." One can imagine the state of confusion if this were the normal advice a client was to receive! People must be able to predict outcomes so like cases need to be decided alike.

In order to predict outcomes, judges give reasons and describe the principles applied in making their decisions—these principles are collected into a set of predictable rules that are applied to determine outcomes in other cases. In effect, these principles become law known as precedents.

COMMON LAW: THE THEORY OF PRECEDENT

Certainty versus Flexibility

stare decisis to stand by a previous decision

The Latin phrase **stare decisis**, meaning "to stand by a previous decision," defines the theory of precedent. It means decisions of higher courts must be followed by lower courts, most of the time.

There are limits to the stare decisis rule.

- First, although judges may be influenced by all prior decisions, they are only bound (required) to follow decisions of a higher level court. Decisions of lower courts have influential value only.

- Second, precedents bind only the exact same circumstances. No two sets of facts are identical in every respect—even when the same parties are involved, the time must be different. Judges can **distinguish** the current case from an earlier precedent by dwelling upon factual differences. In this way, they are able to adjust the law rather slowly to changing circumstances and values.

distinguish identify a factual difference that renders a precedent inapplicable to the case before the court

Still, the foundation of the common law system is the theory of precedent: We look to past decisions to find relevant principles and apply them to new situations. Accordingly, a large part of the study of law involves the study of previously decided cases.

The theory of precedent does make it difficult for judges to respond quickly to change in society. A decision that seemed quite acceptable in 1985 may be entirely out of step with current social standards. Changing an existing precedent is possible but takes time.

Accommodating Change

overrule declare an existing precedent no longer binding or effective

In order to **overrule** an established precedent, the same matter must be addressed by a court higher than the one establishing the initial precedent. As will be discussed under the sections on systems of courts, courts are organized into a hierarchy involving three basic levels: courts of first instance (trial courts); appeal courts that hear appeals from the trial courts; and the Supreme Court, which is the highest level of appeal and hears only "important" cases from the appeal courts. Courts are reluctant to overrule precedents established at the same level. The danger in overruling decided cases too freely is that doing so would undermine the needed consistency and predictability in law. Obviously, Supreme Courts must be able to overrule themselves; otherwise, old precedents could never change without legislative intervention; the Canadian Supreme Court often does this;[1] it is rarer for other courts to overrule themselves.[2]

THE SOURCES OF LAW

The Variety of Sources

Judge-made law is the oldest form of law, but it is important to remember that even in a common law legal system, the government also makes law.

---

[1] See statement by Cartwright, J., in *R. v. Binus*, [1968] 1 C.C.C. 227 at 229: "I do not doubt the power of the court to depart from a previous judgment of its own . . . ." It should be noted, however, that the court did not overrule itself in this case.

[2] In 2007, the Ontario Court of Appeal took the unusual step of overruling its own 2005 precedent on real-estate fraud, candidly describing the 2005 case as "incorrectly decided." See *Lawrence v. Maple Trust Co. et al.* (2007), 84 O.R. (3d) 94 overruled *Household Realty Corp. Ltd. v. Liu* (2005), 261 D.L.R. (4th) 679 (C.A.).

Case Law: Judge-Made Law

The Common Law[3] Case law precedents, not statutes, form the bulk of Canadian private law. A flow of reported cases from an organized national **system of courts** is needed to build precedents. This collection of case law precedents is also referred to as common law. Lawyers arguing a case may say to a judge, "At common law, the rule is . . . ," meaning that the existing precedents, taken together, give us this rule. Each court must have a recognized position within the system of courts in order to "rank" the importance of their decision in influencing judges in subsequent cases.

The earliest decisions were made, of course, without the benefit of previous precedent, so courts looked to a variety of outside sources for direction. Canadian courts looked to England's existing precedents when they had none of their own. English courts formed their earliest common law precedents by borrowing from **canon law**, Roman law, **feudal law**, and **merchant law**.

As the number of precedents increased, the need to draw on outside sources was reduced. English judges applied their precedents rigidly. Eventually, the common law became very formal, with much of its cumbersome procedure rooted in ancient customs and superstitions.

Equity The early rigidness of England's common law precedents led to the development of a completely separate system of courts: the **courts of chancery**. If the common law courts rejected a request, an unhappy party could ask for help from the courts of chancery. These early English courts created exceptions to the common law rules when they felt the precedent was too harsh. They became known as courts of equity, and the rules that they developed also created precedents called the principles of equity or, simply, **equity**. Equity and the common law contribute equally to the current legal system developed by today's judges.

The courts of common law offered very few remedies; they would award only money damages to a party injured by a breach of contract. Yet sometimes money alone was not adequate compensation.

By contrast, the courts of equity were prepared, if they thought fit, to grant **equitable remedies** such as specific performance—for example, in a situation such as Illustration 2.2, to order the defendant to convey the land. If the defendant refused, he would be jailed for **contempt of court** until he gave in and carried out the order. The threat of a medieval jail was highly persuasive!

system of courts the organization of courts into a hierarchy that designates the responsibilities of the court and determines the importance of the precedent; the standard system has three levels: trial, appeal, and final appeal

canon law law created by the Church, which had its own jurisdiction and courts in matters pertaining to itself, family law, and wills

feudal law a system of land ownership rooted in sovereign ownership: land was handed down to lords who gave possession of parcels of land to lesser "royals" in exchange for military service and loyalty

merchant law rules and trade practices developed by merchants in medieval trade guilds and administered by their own courts

courts of chancery a system of courts under the king's chancellor and vice-chancellors developed from the hearing of petitions to the king—courts of equity

equity rules developed by the courts of equity as exceptions to existing rules of common law

equitable remedies new remedies created by the courts of equity to address situations where money damages did not solve the problem

contempt of court a finding by a court that a person has willfully refused to obey a court order and therefore will be punished

---

ILLUSTRATION 2.2

B owned two separate lots of land and agreed to buy the middle lot between them from S in order to erect a large building on the three pieces once they were joined.

S changed his mind and refused to convey the middle lot. If B sued for breach of contract in a common law court, he would be awarded only money damages, an inadequate remedy since his building project would be frustrated.

In summary, the approach of the chancery courts was different from that of the common law courts. "Equity was a gloss on common law; it was a set of rules which could be invoked to supplement the deficiencies of common law or to ease the clumsy working of

---

[3] Confusingly, the term "common law" has three different meanings: (a) the legal system of a common law country as opposed to a civil law country; (b) judge-made law (including equity) as opposed to statute law; and (c) strict legal rules as opposed to equity (flexible principles of fairness).

common law actions and remedies."[4] Remedies in equity were discretionary: The relative innocence of the petitioner and the hardship he suffered determined whether the individual could hope for equity's special type of intervention. It was equity that pioneered key legal concepts of trust and loyalty, and it was equity that considered the relative positions of the parties when applying the law. As equity developed over many years, its principles became as important as those of the common law.

CHECKLIST

Three Meanings of Common Law

The phrase "common law" can be confusing. It refers to three interrelated topics:

1. The English-based legal system—common law system—as opposed to the French-based civil law system;
2. The original body of precedents developed by common law courts as opposed to the body of precedents known as equity, developed by the courts of chancery;
3. The entire collection of case law or judge-made law as opposed to statutes or legislation.

Merger of Law and Equity

In 1865, the British Parliament passed an act merging the courts of common law and equity into the single system we know today where one set of courts applies principles and precedents from both common law and equity.[5] The Canadian provinces passed similar acts shortly afterward.

Amalgamating the courts of common law and equity did not result in abandoning the philosophy of equity. The precedents also merged into one set of rules. Every judge now applies both sets of precedents. Judges exercise their discretion to apply an equitable principle when it appears warranted in the circumstances of a case. Today, equity provides a link between law and ethics.

THE SYSTEM OF COURTS

A major part of business law continues to be created by judges so we should be familiar with the system of courts and their rules of procedure. Figure 2.1 illustrates the simple framework of the English common law court system. It is a good starting place because England has a single government, and its system of courts is easier to grasp than the more complicated federal structure existing in Canada.

The role of the three levels—courts of first instance, appeal courts, final court of appeal—is much the same in England as in Canada.

The Courts of First Instance—Trial Courts

Courts of first instance are also sometimes called courts of original jurisdiction because actions begin and trials take place in this court. This is the place where witnesses are called and an initial judgment is rendered.

---

[4] R.M. Jackson, *The Machinery of Justice in England*, 8th ed., J.R. Spencer, ed. (Cambridge: Cambridge University Press, 1989) at 7.

[5] For convenience, the division of labour has been preserved in England by having two divisions within the High Court of Justice: a Chancery Division and a Queen's Bench Division.

Figure 2.1 Basic Court System

The Court of Appeal

The Court of Appeal is the next level. Actions do not start in this court, but a party who is dissatisfied with the decision of a court of first instance may appeal to the Court of Appeal to reconsider the decision. The party who petitions for an appeal is called the **appellant**; the other party is the **respondent**. The appeal is not a new trial and no witnesses are called: The court does not consider questions of fact because they were for the trial judge to decide. The Court of Appeal proceeds on the basis of the written trial record, and lawyers for each side argue only questions of law—with the appellant claiming that the trial judge erred in interpreting the law, and the respondent arguing to uphold the decision of the trial judge. The court may do one of four things:

appellant the party who petitions for an appeal

respondent the party who defends on an appeal

1. Agree with the trial judge and dismiss the appeal;
2. Agree with the appellant and reverse the trial judgment;
3. Vary the trial judgment in part; or
4. Declare that the trial judge erred in failing to consider certain facts and send the case back for a **new trial** in the lower court.

new trial a case sent back by the appeal court for retrial by the lower court

The Court of Appeal usually hears cases in a panel of three judges, but occasionally five judges may hear a very important case. The outcome is determined by a simple majority.

Final Court of Appeal—The Supreme Court

Parties dissatisfied with a decision of the Court of Appeal have one more chance—the ultimate court of appeal and the highest court in the land. Originally, the House of Lords (members of the peerage) had this responsibility. In 2009, an independent supreme court was formed in England with full-time salaried judges.

THE SYSTEM OF COURTS IN CANADA

The Canadian system of courts is a little more complicated than the basic English system. The Canadian Constitution divides legislative powers between the federal and provincial governments. It gives the provinces jurisdiction over the administration of justice—the organization and operation of police forces and the system of courts. It gives the federal government jurisdiction over trade and commerce, banking, bankruptcy, and criminal law—matters frequently litigated before the courts—as well as the exclusive right to appoint, and the obligation to pay, all Superior Court judges.[6] Therefore both levels of government must work together to operate a coordinated court system. For more information on this topic, see the Companion Website.

There are three tiers of courts in the Canadian system: the courts of first instance or trial divisions, the intermediate provincial courts of appeal, and the final court of appeal,

---

[6] The Constitution Act, 1867, ss. 91, 92, 96, and 100. In all provinces, superior and county courts have merged. Some provincial judges are appointed and paid by the province to do specific legislatively created tasks.

the Supreme Court of Canada. The names and jurisdictions of the courts differ somewhat from province to province, but in general they follow the same pattern as set out below. Figure 2.2 illustrates the structure of the Canadian Court System.

Figure 2.2   Canadian Court System

The Provincial Court System

This system is the primary system of courts that deals with most matters of private and public law. As will be noted below, a federal court system only exists to deal with a relatively small percentage of matters of federal jurisdiction including tax and intellectual property.

The Courts of First Instance   The courts of first instance are trial courts where witnesses give evidence and initial judgments are made. The subject matter of the dispute determines which trial court hears the dispute. There are two branches of trial courts. The inferior trial courts are courts created by provincial legislation for a particular purpose. The superior trial courts are the constitutionally created courts presided over by federally appointed judges and hear everything else. Individual provinces designate branches at each level to deal with specific topics. Most of the time, inferior trial court judgments are appealed to the superior trial court before they move to the intermediate appeal level.

Small Claims Court   This court handles private disputes for smaller amounts of money. The maximum amounts have been increased in recent years but may vary considerably from one province to another.[7] Its procedure is quite simple and informal, so that the cost of taking action is small. The court is important to business because most consumer or client disputes and collections are handled in this court. Despite its small monetary limit, it is the busiest civil court.

Provincial Division   This court decides very little, if any, private law. It hears criminal cases of almost every type except for the most serious offences such as murder, treason, sexual assault, and manslaughter. It may hold preliminary hearings in prosecution of these crimes to decide whether there is enough evidence to proceed to a Superior Court trial. No jury trials are held before Provincial Division judges. If an accused person elects (as one may) to have a jury trial, the case must be heard in Superior Court. Anyone charged with a criminal offence for which there can be a prison sentence of five years or more has the right to a trial by jury. In some cases where the prison sentence is less than five years, an accused person may also choose a jury.

---

[7] Alberta has the highest limit at $50,000; British Columbia, Nova Scotia, and Ontario limits are $25 000. In Ontario and Manitoba, Small Claims Court is a division of Superior Court, while other provinces maintain Small Claims Court as a civil division of the Provincial Court.

A different division of this court hears family questions of custody and support but not divorce. Some provinces set up a separate criminal division to act as a Youth Court where children and adolescents can be dealt with by special youth court judges rather than in the adult criminal courts.

Superior Trial Courts—Surrogate Court (or Probate Court)   This court supervises the estates of deceased persons. It appoints an administrator to wind up the affairs of anyone who dies intestate (without leaving a will), settles disputes over the validity of wills and the division of assets, and approves the accounts of executors and administrators. Some provinces have merged this court into the Superior Court system.[8]

Superior Trial Courts—Superior Court   This court has unlimited jurisdiction in civil (private) and criminal trials. It may be called the Court of Queen's Bench, Superior Court, or even Supreme Court depending upon the province. Federally appointed judges hear trials that deal with divorce and the most serious criminal matters, as well as all civil (private law) disputes above the jurisdiction of Small Claims Court. The court may also serve as a court of appeal for less serious criminal matters begun in Provincial Division. In Ontario, the Divisional Court is a branch of the Superior Court of Justice and it hears appeals from Small Claims Court and other administrative tribunals. Judges of the Superior Court of Justice also act as Divisional Court judges.

Intermediate Appellate Court—The Court of Appeal   Each province has one intermediate appellate court, usually called the Court of Appeal. It performs the same function as the Court of Appeal in England. All matters arising in all the courts of first instance are appealed to the provincial court of appeal. This is the highest level of court in each province. The final level of appeal is to the Supreme Court of Canada, which hears appeals from all provinces and brings all cases into the federal system.

The Federal Courts—Supreme Court of Canada

The Supreme Court of Canada is the final court of appeal in Canada. It consists of nine judges and hears appeals from both the provincial courts of appeal and the Federal Court of Canada. In addition, it has special jurisdiction under the Supreme Court Act[9] to rule on the constitutionality of federal and provincial statutes when they are referred to the court by the federal Cabinet. In private actions, the appellant must obtain special leave from the Supreme Court to appeal.[10] Relatively few private matters are granted leave, so for many disputes, the provincial Court of Appeal is the last resort.

The Federal Courts—Courts of First Instance

Tax Court of Canada   The Tax Court hears appeals of taxpayers against assessments by the Canada Revenue Agency. The court hears only tax appeals and with relatively simple procedures. Either the taxpayer or the department may appeal its decisions to the Federal Court of Appeal.

The Federal Court of Canada   The federal government maintains the Federal Court of Canada in two divisions: a Trial Division and an Appeal Division. The Federal Court has exclusive jurisdiction over such matters as disputes concerning ships and navigation and many sorts of lawsuits against the federal government itself. In the rather complicated areas of patents, copyright, and trademarks, the Federal Court has exclusive jurisdiction in some portions, but in others there is concurrent jurisdiction with provincial courts. A large area

---

[8] Alberta, New Brunswick, Nova Scotia, and Saskatchewan.

[9] R.S.C. 1985, c. S-26, s. 53.

[10] *Ibid.*, s. 40.

of concurrent jurisdiction remains, where a plaintiff may sue in either a provincial court or the Federal Court. For example, a person injured by the careless operation of a government motor vehicle may sue in a provincial court.

Intermediate Level Appeal

Federal Court of Appeal This court hears appeals from the Federal Tax Court and the Federal Court of Canada Trial Division. As noted above, matters from the Federal Court of Appeal are appealed to the Supreme Court of Canada.

INTERNATIONAL ISSUE

The System of Courts in the United States

Both Canada and the United States have federal systems of government and common law legal systems, but there are major differences between their constitutions. In the United States, the individual states—at least theoretically—have more autonomy, and have the residual power that in Canada rests with the federal government. Although under the Constitution the Canadian government has the power to create a full system of three-tier federal courts throughout Canada, Parliament has felt content to allow the provincial governments to organize one centralized set of provincial courts using their constitutional power over the administration of justice. The provincial courts decide cases of first instance (with the exception of the fields reserved exclusively to the federal and tax courts), with federally and provincially appointed judges deciding matters falling within their respective constitutional authorities.

On the other hand, the United States has two systems: a full system of federal courts—including a court of final appeal, the U.S. Supreme Court—that handles a large portion of litigation, although much less than the total handled by the state courts. Criminal law, for example, is a state matter, except in cases involving specific fields of federal jurisdiction, such as national defence, or in cases where an offence is committed in more than one state, such as moving stolen goods across state boundaries. The federal courts have jurisdiction in the following areas: bankruptcy; postal matters; federal banking laws; disputes concerning maritime contracts or wrongs; prosecution of crimes punishable under federal laws of the United States or committed at sea; actions requiring an interpretation of the U.S. Constitution, federal statutes, and treaties; and disputes between citizens of different states.

Most states also have an independent three-tier system of courts, with a final state appellate court. Unlike in Canada, there is no integration of the state and federal courts. Rarely, appeals are accepted by the U.S. Supreme Court when the appellant can convince the Supreme Court that a "substantial constitutional issue" is involved in a state matter.

Another fundamental difference between the two systems lies in their judicial selection processes. In Canada, all judges are appointed to a life term. Although the process varies somewhat for provincial and federal judges, most appointments begin with an application from a lawyer. The applicant is then screened by a selection committee; selected applicants are often interviewed by the committee. A list of acceptable candidates is then turned over to the Minister of Justice (or the provincial equivalent) who makes the final selection after consultation with Cabinet.

As noted in Chapter 1, the United States Supreme Court judges are appointed to a life term by the president, with a public confirmation process through the Senate. However, most state trial judges are elected for limited terms. In New York, the Democratic and Republican parties each select one candidate to represent their party in the state election so that only two names appear on the ballot. On January 16, 2008, the United States Supreme Court upheld this "partisan voting" process in *New York State Board of Elections v. Lopez Torres*.[11] In other states, any candidate may run, but the electoral district may be so wide that minority voices are suppressed. In other states, the governor appoints the judge for the first term and thereafter the judge must face the electorate to be renewed. This is known as retention election. Critics of retention elections worry that judges are tempted to make popular decisions in order to win re-election.

Questions to Consider

1. What are the arguments in favour of elected judges?

2. What are the disadvantages of judicial elections?

3. Discuss the pros and cons of life-term appointment.

4. In Chapter 1 we discussed the Ontario Court of Appeal decision that opened the door for same-sex marriage and the subsequent reference sent by Parliament to the Supreme Court of Canada. Why do you think the elected members of Parliament looked to the courts for direction on this issue?

Sources: Randolph N. Jonakait, *Checking Abuses of Power: The American Jury System* (New Haven, CT: Yale University Press, 2006) at Chapter 2; Gordon Van Kessell, "Adversary Excesses in the American Criminal Trial" (1992) 67 *Notre Dame Law Review* 427; Adam Liptak, "Rendering Justice, With One Eye on Re-election," *New York Times*, May 25, 2008, at 1, 13.

---

[11] 552 U.S. 196 (2008)

PROCEDURAL LAW: USING THE COURTS

The following is a general description of the procedures involved in a civil (private) lawsuit. Each province enacts regulations setting out the steps in a lawsuit, including forms, fees, and timelines. These regulations are known as the **rules of civil procedure**. Public law disputes have different procedures.

rules of civil procedure the provincial regulations that set out the steps in a private lawsuit, including forms, fees, and timelines

Who May Sue?

Not everyone has the capacity to start an action. An adult citizen of Canada has the broadest capacity—virtually unlimited access to the courts for any type of action. Generally speaking, non-Canadians may also sue as freely as citizens. A child (a person under the age of 18 or 19, depending on the province) is not permitted to bring an action alone but must be represented by an adult person. Similarly, an insane person cannot sue without a court-appointed representative.

Generally speaking, corporations may sue and be sued, although foreign corporations may be subject to strict regulation and be required to obtain a provincial licence before bringing an action. For this purpose, a corporation is considered to be a legal "person" or "entity."

Greater difficulties arise when an action is brought by or against an **unincorporated collectivity**, a group of persons such as a social club, a church, a political party, or, perhaps most important, a trade union. In most cases, unincorporated groups are not recognized by the courts and may not sue or be sued. The position of trade unions varies: In some jurisdictions, it is possible to sue and be sued by a trade union, while in others it is not.

unincorporated collectivity a group of persons that in most cases is not recognized by the courts and that may not sue or be sued

Standing to Sue

Who has the right to start a lawsuit? Generally speaking, only individuals whose rights are specifically affected have **standing** before the courts. The courts are concerned that especially litigious members of the public might clog the courts with matters in which they have no direct interest.

standing the right to bring a lawsuit

On the other hand, with growing awareness of damage to our environment through pollution and its impact on the safe supply of food and water, the risk of serious injury to large groups of persons has grown.

Some decisions of the Supreme Court of Canada have recognized the right of a taxpayer to sue when he believes public revenues are being improperly used, and the right of a movie viewer to bring an action when he believes his right to see a film has been taken away by a provincial censorship body.[12] Similarly, governments have invited the assistance of public interest plaintiffs in the enforcement of consumer protection standards.[13] The legislatures and the courts continue to work to achieve a balance between protecting the public interest and minimizing abuse of the judicial process.

Class Actions[14]

What if many people's interests are affected by the same conduct? Suppose the owner of a car wishes to sue the manufacturer to recover loss caused by a serious defect in the car, and the defect is known to exist in several thousand other cars of the same model. Who

---

[12] *Nova Scotia Board of Censors v. MacNeil* (1975), 55 D.L.R. (3d) 632; *Minister of Justice of Canada v. Borowski* (1981), 130 D.L.R. (3d) 588; *Finlay v. Minister of Finance*, [1986] 2 S.C.R. 607; *Canadian Council of Churches v. Canada*, [1992] 1 S.C.R. 236.

[13] See for example, Business Practices and Consumer Protection Act, S.B.C. 2004, c. 2, s. 172. The important role of the public interest plaintiff is recognized by Justice Binnie in *Siedel v. TELUS Communications*, 2011 S.C.C. 15.

[14] W.K. Branch, *Class Actions in Canada* (Vancouver: Western Legal Publications, 1996); C. Jones, *Theory of Class Actions* (Toronto: Irwin Law, 2003). Also called class proceedings: Class Proceedings Act, 1992, S.O. 1992, c. 6.

should sue? It would be unfortunate to clog the courts with hundreds, perhaps thousands, of repetitive claims in which all the essential facts and applicable laws had already been clearly established. Sometimes the amount in dispute is individually minor and not worth the cost of a lawsuit unless there is more than one **plaintiff** and the multiple plaintiffs can pool their resources. Grouping parties with similar claims into one action is known as a **class action** and the benefits include avoiding multiple actions and inconsistent results, allowing economic access to justice, and deterring wrongful behaviour of defendants.[15] Consumers often commence class actions against businesses.

A court must approve the basis of a class action before the class action can proceed. There must be an identifiable class or group and common issues, and a class action must be the preferable procedure. If the court so decides, then the class action is certified and the matter proceeds to trial as one action. The resulting judgment binds all members of the class; it makes the matter **res judicata** and the case cannot be brought before the court again to contest legal liability. In our example of the defective car, if liability has already been established, other owners still have the right to have the court assess the amount of damage if the parties could not settle on an amount.[16]

Specific rules about bringing class actions vary by province.[17] The British Columbia and Ontario acts permit either a plaintiff or a defendant to apply to a court to have himself and others in his group declared to be a "class." However, most class actions are brought by plaintiffs. Defendants complain that class actions encourage frivolous lawsuits that are so expensive to defend, even through just the certification process, that unfounded claims are often paid to settle.

Procedure Before Trial

An overall understanding of the steps in lawsuit is necessary for business administrators to work effectively with their legal advisers. Lawsuits progress through the courts in a form called an **action**, and most actions are begun by **issuing** and **serving** a **writ** or a statement of claim.[18] The statement of claim describes the reason for the action or the **cause of action**. A cause of action is an event or set of events that gives rise to legal liability. The statement of claim must describe both the facts and the legal principles that make up the cause of action.

plaintiff   the party that commences a private (civil) legal action against another party

class action   an action in which an individual represents a group of possible plaintiffs and the judgment decides the matter for all members of the class at once

res judicata   a case that has already been decided by a court and cannot be brought before a court again

action   lawsuit

issuing   commencing the lawsuit by filing a copy of the statement of claim with the court office

serving   providing a copy of the issued claim to each defendant

writ   an ancient form required in order to take a grievance to court

cause of action   an event or set of events that gives rise to legal liability

---

ILLUSTRATION 2.3

Tom buys an apple from a farmer, eats it, and becomes ill. Tom may commence an action for compensation for his suffering, lost time from work, and cost of medicine. The statement of claim must describe the facts of the event and the particulars of his loss. When, where, and from whom was the apple purchased? These would be the relevant facts. In addition, the claim must refer to the legal principles that apply to make the farmer responsible. In Tom's case, the claim would refer to the rules of contract law, product liability, and sale of goods that require a product to be fit for the purpose for which it was sold.

---

[15] In *Western Canadian Shopping Centres v. Dutton*, [2001] 2 S.C.R. 534, the goals of class actions are discussed.

[16] The difficulties in maintaining a class action in such circumstances are well illustrated by the decision of the Supreme Court of Canada in *Naken v. General Motors of Canada Ltd.* (1983), 144 D.L.R. (3d) 385. For comment, see Fox (1984), 6 S.C.L.R. 335.

[17] Class Proceedings Act, R.S.B.C. 1996, c. 50; C.C.S.M., c. C30; S.O. 1992, c. 6; S.S. 2001, c. 12.01.

[18] Several provinces have simplified the process by abolishing the writ as a means of starting an action. The process now begins with the issue of a statement of claim.

A trial does not automatically follow the start of an action. After a plaintiff has a statement of claim issued by the court, the document is served on the defendant. In this way, the defendant learns by whom and for what he is being sued, so that he can prepare to defend himself; the plaintiff cannot proceed until the notice has been served. It is obvious that as soon as one is served with a writ or statement of claim one should immediately consult a lawyer. It is a well-known saying that "he who acts on his own behalf has a fool for a client."

Once a plaintiff has formally commenced an action and served the required documents on the defendant, why should they not go to trial immediately? For one thing, court trials are expensive; the time of the plaintiff and defendant, their **counsel** (lawyers), the judge, and other officers of the court is valuable. It would be wasteful to use time in court before the issues and evidence have been fully investigated. Time is needed to find witnesses, check documents, and research the law. Pre-trial procedure attempts to narrow the trial issues to those matters on which the parties disagree. The necessary steps are as follows:

counsel lawyer representing a plaintiff or defendant

(a) In the statement of claim, the plaintiff sets out in detail the facts that she alleges have given rise to her cause of action and the damages suffered by her. The defendant who intends to contest the action commences by **entering (filing) an appearance** and replies with a **statement of defence**, admitting those facts not in dispute in the statement of claim and denying all others, and in addition setting out any other facts that the defendant intends to prove in court in support of his defence. Referring to Illustration 2.3, the farmer may admit to selling the apple but deny that it was the apple that made Tom sick. The statement of defence may also dispute the law. The plaintiff may then deliver a reply countering the added facts alleged by the defendant and adding any further facts believed necessary to cope with the defence. Often the defendant may have a claim of his own arising from the same facts. He will then **counterclaim** as well as defend. In turn the plaintiff will defend the counterclaim. Both claims will then be tried together. Collectively these documents are called the **pleadings** and they must tell the full story. Information left out of the pleadings will not be allowed into the trial.

entering (filing) an appearance filing notice of an intention to contest an action

statement of defence a reply to a statement of claim, admitting facts not in dispute, denying other facts, and setting out facts in support of the defence

counterclaim a claim by the defendant arising from the same facts as the original action by the plaintiff to be tried along with that action

pleadings documents filed by each party to an action providing information it intends to prove in court

(b) Depending upon the value of the claim, the next step is some form of **examination for discovery**, a process allowing either party to examine the other's evidence in order to narrow the issues further and to decide whether to proceed with a trial. Discovery allows a party to learn about the strength of the other party's case so that an informed decision about settlement can be made. Both parties must also produce their list of witnesses and relevant documents. Discovery of documents involves locating documents, preserving them, reviewing them for relevance, and producing them to the other side. Increasingly, relevant documents are in electronic form, and production of these documents has become known as ediscovery. Once both sides have satisfied themselves that the action should go to trial, they ask court officials to place the case on the docket for the next sitting of the court.

examination for discovery process allowing either party to examine the other in order to narrow the issues

(c) Most provinces require a pre-trial or settlement conference with a judge or mediator after discovery is complete. During this meeting, the issues in dispute are reviewed in an attempt to settle as many as possible or at least narrow the issues so that any eventual trial will be shorter.

The Trial

At trial the parties bring their evidence of all facts in dispute before the court. In private or civil actions, the burden of proof is on the plaintiff to prove her case. The standard of proof is the balance of probabilities—enough evidence to convince a judge that it is "more likely than not." This is done by bringing all the evidence of favourable facts before the court. The plaintiff asks the court to apply the law to the facts to come to a result favouring the plaintiff. The defendant, on the other hand, attempts to establish another version of the facts or at least to minimize the value of the evidence submitted by the plaintiff. The gap between the versions of the two parties is often astonishing. Sometimes the defendant will argue that even if the facts are as the plaintiff claims, the law has not been applied properly.

Evidence is brought before the court by examining witnesses who produce documents. Counsel for the plaintiff calls as witnesses those persons whose testimony is favourable to the client. Counsel for the defendant may then cross-examine those witnesses to bring out any aspects of their testimony that were neglected and that might serve the defendant's position. Counsel for the plaintiff may then re-examine the witnesses to clarify any points dealt with in the cross-examination. Counsel for the defendant may also call witnesses of his own.

An opposing party may object to evidence introduced by another party for a number of reasons. It may not be relevant or it may be unreliable. One type of evidence that is not **admissible evidence** because it is considered unreliable is **hearsay**; that is, words attributed by the witness to a person not before the court. The basis for the hearsay rule is the view that the credibility of oral evidence cannot be properly assessed when it is secondhand, and that one who is alleged to have made an assertion should testify in person and be subject to cross-examination and the scrutiny of the court. Witnesses must confine their evidence to the facts they know—they cannot give opinions about possible situations unless they are experts in the particular field. Although very technical, the rules of admissibility of evidence are intended to separate bad evidence from good.

After the court has heard all the evidence, counsel then present the arguments in law favouring their respective clients. In simple cases, the judge may give the decision at once or after a short recess, but in complicated and important cases, the judge will usually **reserve judgment** in order to have time to study the notes of the facts and legal arguments and to compare the opinions in decided cases and textbooks. The judgment may be given orally in the court; decisions in important cases are always given in written form as well and are reprinted in the law reports.

Appeals

If either or both parties wish to appeal, they must make up their minds and serve notice within a time limit, usually 30 days or less.

As we have seen, most appeals take the form of a review by an appeal court of the written transcript of the trial forwarded to it from the trial courts. An appeal court also reviews proceedings of the trial court when a party contends that the trial judge erred in applying the law or in admitting or excluding certain evidence. If the appeal court agrees, it may order the case sent back to a new trial, directing the judge to correct the shortcomings of the first trial.

Costs

Who Provides Funds for the Court System?
Quite apart from the time and effort of the parties who are adversaries in the court—their time away from employment and the lost energy—a lawsuit occupies the time of highly trained and expensive judges and court officials, lawyers, and their staffs.

In an important sense, the courts provide a public service, a forum for peacefully settling disputes with the aid of government supervision and enforcement. The courts provide an essential alternative to parties taking matters into their own hands, with the probable risks of violence. Our governments pay the expenses of sustaining the court system, including the salaries of judges, registrars, clerks, and other employees, as well as the maintenance of court buildings. Litigants pay a portion of these overhead **costs** through

admissible evidence evidence that is acceptable to the court

hearsay words attributed by a witness to a person who is not before the court

reserve judgment postpone giving a decision after the hearing ends

costs funds paid by litigants to cover a portion of the government's expenses in maintaining the court system charges made for specific items such as issuing a writ or registering a judgment against a losing defendant in order to enforce a claim.

Solicitor–Client Fees Litigants themselves pay the costs of hiring their own lawyers, although an important development in criminal and family disputes has been the system of **legal aid**, where the government pays for many legal services provided to low-income litigants. Legal aid is not particularly relevant to the business context. For more information on this topic, see the Companion Website.

legal aid a system where the government pays for many legal services provided to low-income litigants

A client pays a lawyer a **solicitor–client fee**: payment for time the lawyer spends discussing the case with the client, helping the client decide whether to pursue or defend the action, and agreeing to be retained—that is, to represent the client in negotiations to settle or in a court action. As well, there are usually various expenses associated with a court case, such as time required to prepare for trial, court charges, travel costs when the case is heard or when evidence must be obtained at another location, and the usual array of out-of-pocket costs, all of which must be paid by the litigant. These direct costs of litigation are often substantial, especially if the original hearing is followed by an appeal, and, as we shall discuss below, they play an important part in an individual's decision to proceed with a lawsuit or settle.

solicitor–client fee payment for the time and expenses of a lawyer in preparing a case and representing the client in negotiations to settle or in court

Party and Party Costs Suppose a person is sued and defends himself successfully, with the court dismissing the action brought by the plaintiff. Should he be left with all the expense of defending an action that the court rejected? Or suppose a party demands payment for an injury wrongfully inflicted on her: the other party denies any liability; she then sues successfully. Should she have to bear the expense of her successful court action to recover a sum that the other party was legally obligated to pay?

Canada applies the "loser pays" rule. This means that at least part of the winning party's legal costs should be paid by the losing side by an award known as **party and party costs**.[19] Each province has a published scale of costs, varying with the level of court in which the case is heard, setting monetary amounts for the preparation of court documents by the lawyer and for time spent preparing the case and for each appearance or day in court. Accordingly, when a plaintiff wins a case, the court will award "*x* dollars damages, plus costs" against the defendant. If the defendant successfully defends the action, the court will dismiss the claim "with costs"—that is, party and party costs against the plaintiff. If the result of the action is a mixed one—for example, a plaintiff's claim succeeds in part and is rejected in part—the costs may be apportioned, or each party may be left to pay its own costs.

party and party costs an award that shifts some of the costs of litigation to the losing side according to a published scale of fees

Total Costs of Litigation A solicitor–client fee (the actual lawyer's bill) is almost always greater than an award of party and party costs. Therefore, even when a client wins a case with an award of costs in her favour, these costs will ordinarily cover only a portion of the fee charged by her lawyer; she will have to pay an amount over and above the costs recovered from the losing side. But she is considerably better off than the losing side with respect to the costs of the litigation; the loser must pay both party and party costs to the other side and a solicitor–client fee to his own lawyer, in addition, of course, to the amount of the judgment. In rare cases, when a judge believes the losing party behaved unreasonably, solicitor–client costs will be awarded. This means that the loser must pay the winner's entire solicitor–client fees.

Occasionally a client may believe that his lawyer has charged too high a fee for representing him in a court action, and the two are unable to reach a satisfactory settlement of the bill. If necessary, the client can have the matter referred to an officer of the court to assess the bill—that is, to set a fair fee for the service rendered in the action.

---

[19] See G.D. Watson et al., *Civil Litigation*, 4th ed. (Toronto: Emond Montgomery, 1991) at Chapter 4.

The Economics of Civil Litigation

The subject of costs raises the question of the economics of litigation: is it worthwhile to start an action? This is a key business law risk management question. First, there is always a risk of losing: A plaintiff who loses is not only denied the remedy sought, but also must pay costs of the defendant. Even if the party seems certain of winning, it would generally be unwise to proceed with a claim that would occupy the time of the courts and incur heavy expenses in retaining a lawyer in order to collect a minor sum, to pursue a poor defendant, or, conversely, to defend an insignificant claim.[20]

Second, even apart from legal costs, businesses must examine the business costs of litigation. Often it may not be worth a business's time and effort to fight. For instance, a supplier of perishable goods such as potatoes might be offered payment of a reduced price by a buyer who claims that the potatoes had not arrived in as good condition as promised. The supply firm might decide that it is not worth the trouble to sue for the difference in price of, say, $200; nor, for that matter, would it wish to alienate the buyer, a good customer. It simply accepts the reduced price in full payment. On the other hand, the supply firm might think it necessary to fight the minor claim in order to discourage other claims.

A strategy should be developed considering the impact of the litigation on all segments of the business. If the supply firm has had several similar complaints from customers and is concerned that the carrier has been careless in transporting the potatoes, it may decide to change carriers or to claim against the carrier. If the carrier should deny liability, the supplier would find it necessary to sue the carrier and "join" the buyer in the same suit in order to obtain a ruling. In other words, a party may have additional reasons besides the actual recovery of an award of damages for bringing an action for a relatively small sum.

Contingent Fees

Origins in the United States
In the United States, most courts do not follow the "loser pays" rule; a party, whether winner or loser, is required to pay only his own lawyer's fees. As a result, the **contingency fee** was developed to give access to justice to poor litigants who might otherwise be denied the chance to pursue their claims.

> **contingency fee** a fee paid for a lawyer's services only if the client is successful; there is no charge if the client is unsuccessful

Critics argue that prospective litigants clog American courts with large claims even when the chances of success are poor; a plaintiff who fails does not risk having to pay the defendant's costs. At the same time, the American system of costs "fails to compensate justly the winner whose claim has been vindicated, and it discourages the litigation of small claims."[21]

Under a contingency fee arrangement, "the lawyer agrees to act on the basis that if the client is successful the lawyer will take as a fee a certain percentage of the judgment amount, and in the event that the client is unsuccessful the lawyer will make no charge for the services rendered."[22] From a prospective litigant's point of view—especially in a case where there may be a fairly poor chance of winning, but any award made will likely be for a large sum—a contingency fee arrangement might be the only practical way of bringing an action. A lawyer may take several cases and will be content to win one; the single contingency fee will cover his expenses in all the cases and leave him with substantial compensation for his work.

---

[20] For discussion about the costs of litigation, see P. Puri, "Financing of Litigation by Third-Party Investors: A Share of Justice?" (1998), 36 Osgoode Hall L.J. 515 (the Introduction).

[21] Warren K. Winkler, Evaluation of Civil Case Management in Toronto Region, 27 (Toronto, 2008), http://www.ontariocourts.ca/coa/en/ps/reports/rule78.pdf at p. 265.

[22] *Ibid.*, p. 253.

A is injured very seriously while skiing on an open slope. She complains that the accident was caused by an unmarked obstacle. Very likely, a court would find either that she accepted the risks voluntarily or that she was the author of her own misfortune through personal carelessness. Even so, if A is in a jurisdiction where a contingency fee agreement is available to her, she might well find it practical to bring an action on the small chance that the court would find the resort owner liable for the injury. She would probably not be able to afford the expense of litigation under the traditional solicitor–client way of charging fees.

The Use of Contingency Fees in Canada Canada was slow to adopt contingency fees as a result of concerns that such arrangements

- encourage unnecessary and even frivolous litigation;
- expose defendants to the costs of defending themselves against claims that have no merit;
- encourage some clients to agree to unconscionably large percentage fees demanded by their lawyers;
- drive up the cost of settlements and court awards and thus affect insurance premiums;
- cloud the judgment of the lawyer who becomes a stakeholder in the litigation.

However, access to justice arguments prevailed, and most Canadian provinces now accept contingency fee arrangements, subject to supervision by the courts.[23] In 2004, Ontario was the last province to endorse contingency fees; the cap in Ontario states that the fee cannot exceed the amount of the plaintiff's recovery.[24] Although no statistics are available, it is generally agreed that contingency fees are most often used in class actions, and the combination has led critics to lament the explosion of American-style litigation. Criticism has focused on class actions involving individually minor claims where it appears that the lawyers make millions.[25]

A class action was commenced against National Money Mart, a payday loan company, alleging that 210 000 Ontario borrowers were being charged a criminally high rate of interest contrary to s. 347 of the Criminal Code. The plaintiffs' lawyers were retained on a contingency fee basis with a written retainer that included a formula. Prior to trial, after multiple unsuccessful proceedings to have the action stayed and to block certification, National Money Mart settled the case. The settlement included a fee of $27.5 million for the class members' lawyers pursuant to the contingency fee agreement. Class action settlements require the approval of the court and when the Ontario Superior Court reviewed the terms of settlement, Justice Perell valued the settlement at $30 million in cash and $58 million in debt forgiveness and reduced the plaintiffs' lawyers' fees to $14.5 million.[26] The fact that the class action led to new payday loan legislation in Ontario was relevant to the assessment of counsel fee, but the relatively low cash recovery of the individual class members was also relevant. On appeal to the Ontario Court of Appeal, the $14.5 million counsel fee was found to be fair and reasonable in the circumstances.[27]

[23] Justice Statute Law Amendment Act, 2002, S.O. 2002, c. 24; O. Reg. 195/2004; Solicitors Act, R.S.O. 1990, c. S-15 as amen. See also: M. Trebilcock, "The Case for Contingent Fees: The Ontario Legal Profession Rethinks Its Position" (1985), 15 Can. Bar L.J. 360–8.

[24] "A Slice of the Settlement: Contingency Fees across Canada" *National* 13:9 (October 1986) 12.

[25] S.G. McKee, "The Canadian Challenge: Class Actions in Canada; A Potentially Momentous Change to Canadian Legislation," in J. Robson and O. Libbert, eds., *Law and Markets: Is Canada Inheriting America's Litigious Legacy* (Vancouver: Fraser Institute, 1997), http://oldfraser.lexi.net/publications/books/laws_markets/canadian_challenge.html (accessed February 13, 2008).

[26] *Smith v. National Money Mart*, 2010 ONSC 1334 (CanLII).

[27] *Smith v. National Money Mart*, [2011] O.J. No. 1321 (Ont. C.A.).

Settlement Out of Court

Advantages   Breaches of laws cause damage to a vast number of people, but only a small proportion of these claims are litigated. Even when parties start court proceedings, the disputes rarely go to trial. The great majority of claims are resolved by **settlement**, an out-of-court procedure where one party agrees to pay a sum of money or do certain things in return for a waiver from the other party of all rights claimed in the lawsuit. Ontario's settlement rate has been reported as high as 96 percent.[28]

Settlement provides quick compensation and avoids the expense of litigation. Those claims covered by insurance have immediate access to a claims process and settlement funds. Each party to a settlement also avoids the risk that the court will find against him. Since there are two sides to a story, there is some uncertainty in predicting which side will win. Of course, the stronger a person's claim appears to be, the more advantageous a settlement he will demand and usually obtain. Often a person starts legal proceedings to convince her adversary to seriously consider settlement. As a result, many actions are settled soon after they are started.

Why then are the courts and the relatively small body of decisions resulting from an enormous number of disputes so important? There are two main reasons. First, the decided cases create the law and supply the principles by which parties may gauge the relative merits of their claims, predict the outcome of a possible court action, and strike a value for their claims. Second, the court is the last resort, the decisive tribunal when all compromise fails. It settles the issue when the parties themselves cannot.

Growing Delay in the Court System   Despite the obvious advantages of settling disputes out of court, the number (not percentage) of cases going to trial has increased steadily over the years, indeed much faster than the growth in population. This might be because of the higher general level of education and the greater awareness of rights (especially since the Charter of Rights and Freedoms became part of our Constitution), the increased complexity of society, and the legal system generally. The large increase in the number of cases has led to a backlog causing very long delays in actually getting most cases heard. In 2000, claims issued in Toronto languished in the system for just under two years before being resolved.[29] Since then, most provinces have designed simplified procedures and case management systems to move matters to trial more quickly.[30]

Delay often creates hardship: A plaintiff who has suffered serious injury might wait many years to be compensated; it might become much more difficult for witnesses to recall evidence; indeed sometimes one of the parties will die before the case is heard. As a result, rules have been enacted to encourage settlement.[31]

1. Parties must attend mandatory settlement conferences as part of pre-trial procedures. At this conference, judges offer opinions on possible trial outcomes and settlement offers.

---

[28] Remarks of the Honourable Warren K. Winkler, "Civil Justice Reform—The Toronto Experience," University of Ottawa, Faculty of Law, September 12, 2007, available online at http://www.ontariocourts.ca/coa/en/ps/speeches/civiljusticereform.htm. See also Herbert N. Kritzer, "Disappearing Trials? A Comparative Prespective" (2004) 1(3) *J. Empirical L. Stud.* 735 at 751, Figure 8.

[29] Warren K. Winkler, *Evaluation of Civil Case Management in Toronto Region*, 27 (Toronto, 2008), http://www.ontariocourts.ca/coa/en/ps/reports/rule78.pdf

[30] Ontario has a simplified procedure for matters under $100 000. British Columbia has a pilot project testing a simplified procedure for Small Claims under $5000. Case management systems set timelines for completion of each step of the process, failing which the matter is dismissed. Toronto claims now average approximately one year in age before resolution.

[31] Rule 57 (18), B.C. Rules of the Supreme Court; Rule 49, Rules of Civil Procedure, Ont.; Rule 10, Rules of Court, N.S.

---

settlement   an out-of-court procedure by which one of the parties agrees to pay a sum of money or perform an act in return for a waiver by the other party of all rights arising from the grievance

2. The rules penalize parties who do not accept a reasonable offer of settlement. So, if a party rejects a reasonable offer to settle from the other party and the court's subsequent judgment shows that the offer was a good one—that is, it orders substantially the same remedy as the offer made—the first party will be ordered to pay the costs incurred by the other party.

3. The use of alternative dispute resolution processes is encouraged by the courts. Some systems require mediation before trial.

ALTERNATIVE DISPUTE RESOLUTION

There have always been informal ways to resolve disputes rather than resorting to the courts and, by the 1970s, the rising costs and delays involved in using the court system encouraged a new emphasis on the alternatives. Today, many parties to disputes agree not to go to court and instead to use the private procedures of alternative dispute resolution (ADR). The oldest form of ADR is **arbitration**—referring a dispute to an arbitrator who will **adjudicate** the matter; the arbitrator will hear the parties and their witnesses in private less formally and more promptly than a court, and will deliver a decision with reasons. The decisions bind only the parties involved and are confidential. Arbitration was developed specifically with the business disputant in mind. The cost is borne entirely by the parties. The goal is party autonomy: Parties design their own process by selecting the rules, the forum, the arbitrator, and even the law that will be applied to the dispute. Often parties agree, through a term in their original contract, to refer any future dispute that may arise to arbitration. In the absence of a pre-dispute term, they may agree to arbitration after a dispute arises. Arbitration is also used in public sector disputes, in such areas as labour relations, workers' compensation, and international commerce (as discussed in Chapter 30). Normally, the parties agree in advance to be bound by the arbitrator's decision, but under some plans, a party may appeal to the courts.[32]

> **arbitration** a form of ADR where a dispute is referred to an arbitrator who adjudicates the matter and the parties agree to be bound by the arbitrator's decision, although there may be a right to appeal to the courts

> **adjudicate** hear parties and deliver a decision with reasons

An increasingly important form of ADR is **mediation**. In mediation, a neutral third party acceptable to both sides acts as mediator during settlement negotiations. The mediator has no power to make a binding decision but assists the parties in reaching a settlement. This is the ultimate form of party autonomy where parties not only design the process, like arbitration, but also design their own settlement. The mediator hears both parties, identifies and clarifies the issues, and explores middle ground that might be acceptable. Mediation can be evaluative—where the mediator offers an opinion on the substance of the dispute—or it may be facilitative—where the mediator guides the process only. It may focus on the rights of the parties but it will often include an interest-based discussion. Mediation allows imaginative settlements not possible in courts and considers interests and factors beyond who would win in a courtroom.

> **mediation** a form of ADR where a neutral third party who is acceptable to both sides acts as a mediator, assisting the parties to reach a settlement

The process usually begins with the mediator and both sides present, and after preliminary remarks by the mediator, each side presents its position; the mediator usually asks questions and tries to clarify those areas where the parties agree and disagree. Separate meetings may be held with each side to explore the prospects of agreement. All parties must adhere to basic rules of respect and confidentiality for an effective mediation.

While informal mediation has been used to settle disputes for many years, in the last two decades it has developed into a sophisticated procedure, and the success rate of reaching settlement is relatively high. There is now a very large volume of literature

---

[32] John C. Carson, "Dispute Resolution, Negotiation, Mediation and Arbitration in Ontario" (1993) 10(1) Bus. and L. 1.

on the subject.[33] As well, training courses are available across Canada at universities and through associations of mediators.

To be effective, a mediator must have the respect and confidence of both parties; key qualities are impartiality, sensitivity to each side's concerns, the ability to understand and analyze the disagreement, and the ability to present a creative approach to suggesting solutions.

Mediation has become very attractive to parties in disputes, although sometimes it can be abused: A party who does not really want to settle the dispute may agree to mediation in order to gain time by delay. When mediation fails, the parties ordinarily resort to arbitration or the courts.

The advantages of ADR, both arbitration and mediation, are:

- speed—cases are resolved by mediation or arbitration much more promptly than through the courts;

- cost—promptness in itself saves money; in addition, since the parties themselves have chosen this method, they usually cooperate to avoid delays and keep the hearing as short as they can; parties do have to pay the arbitrator fees themselves;

- choice of adjudicator or mediator—unlike the courts, the parties can choose a person whom they believe to be especially suited to resolve the issue because of her experience and expertise in the area of the dispute;

- confidentiality—the parties can agree to keep the dispute private to minimize harm to their business through disclosure of confidential information or encouraging others to bring similar complaints;

- preservation of ongoing relations—since ADR is usually less adversarial than litigation, it is less likely to foster antagonism between the parties, and will allow them to continue to work together afterward.[34]

ADR has become important to legal risk management not only because of the foregoing advantages but also because of its wide availability and enforceability. The ADR movement—arbitration, in particular—grew out of commercial business disputes and was driven by the inability of domestic legal systems to handle international business disputes. Federal and provincial arbitration legislation was passed to promote arbitration and recognize and enforce arbitration awards through the courts.[35] Since the early 1990s, Canadian courts have followed a policy in favour of arbitration by upholding and enforcing arbitration agreements.[36] Organizations such as the International Chamber of Commerce facilitate arbitration among private sector international business partners. Domestically, private sector providers are widely available through organizations such as ADR Chambers

---

[33] The 2001 Ministry of the Attorney General Evaluation of the Ontario Mandatory Mediation Program reported a 40 percent settlement rate, www.attorneygeneral.us.gov.on.ca/english/courts/manmed/exec_summary _recommend.pdf (accessed February 13, 2008). The following four recent books are high-quality examples: G. Adams, *Mediating Justice: Legal Dispute Negotiations* (Toronto: CCH Canadian, 2003); R.M. Nelson, *Nelson on ADR* (Scarborough: Thomson Carswell, 2003); C. Picard et al., *The Art and Science of Mediation* (Toronto: Emond Montgomery, 2004); A.J. Pirie, *Alternative Dispute Resolution Skills, Science and the Law* (Toronto: Irwin Law, 2000).

[34] For a general overview, see D. Paul Emond, *Commercial Dispute Resolution: Alternatives to Litigation* (Aurora, ON: Canada Law Book, 1989) or A. J. Pirie, *supra* note 32.

[35] Arbitration Act, R.S.B.C. 1996, ch. 55 (CAA); Arbitration Act, R.S.A. 2000, c. A-43; Arbitration Act, 1992, S.S. 1992, c. A-24.1; Arbitration Act, C.C.S.M., c. A120; Arbitration Act, R.S.Y. 2002, c. 8; Arbitration Act, R.S.N.W.T. 1988, c. A-5; Arbitration Act, S.N.B. 1992, c. A-10.1; Arbitration Act, R.S.N.S. 1989, c.19; Arbitration Act, R.S.P.E.I. 1988, c. A-16; Arbitration Act, R.S.N.L. 1990, c. A-14; Quebec Code of Civil Procedure, R.S.Q. c. C-25, art. 940–51.2 (Arbitration legislation).

[36] *Ontario Hydro v. Denison Mines Ltd*, [1992] O.J. No. 2948 at para. 8; see *Deluce Holdings Inc. v. Air Canada*, [1992] O.J. No. 2382; *Buck Bros. Ltd. v. Frontenac Builders*, [1994] O.J. No. 37; *Onex Corp. v. Ball Corp.* (1994), 12 B.L.R. (2nd) 151; *Canadian National Railway Co. v. Lovat Tunnel Equipment Inc.* (1999), 174 D.L.R. (4th) 385 (Ont C.A.); *Diamond & Diamond v. Srebrolow*, [2003] O.J. No. 4004.

and American Arbitration Forum, to name just a couple. Better Business Bureaus around the country offer ADR services to their members. By placing an ADR clause in a business agreement, businesses can take a proactive approach to legal risk management and ensure that if a dispute does arise it will not be resolved in the courts.

Mediation is also being embraced by the court systems. In Ontario, every civil (private) and estate action commenced in Toronto, Ottawa, and Windsor must undergo a three-hour mandatory mediation session before it may be set for trial. Saskatchewan also has a mandatory mediation program for civil actions filed in the Court of Queen's Bench. In Alberta, all Small Claims Court actions are screened and selected actions must enter mandatory mediation; civil actions in the Alberta Court of Queen's Bench may be moved to mediation by either party upon the filing of a notice. These provinces maintain rosters of approved mediators.[37]

Still, ADR has its limits and its critics. It is not right for every dispute. Situations that involve an imbalance of power between the parties can result in abuse. Parties might be forced unwillingly into ADR or they might be bullied into undesirable settlements in mediation. Therefore, restrictions and protections have been put in place for certain types of conflicts. Family disputes cannot be arbitrated in Quebec, and Ontario has created a specially regulated and supervised form of family arbitration.[38] Consumers are another group that are being protected from mandatory ADR processes, with several provinces refusing to enforce pre-dispute arbitration clauses.[39]

Ethical Issue **Access to Justice**

One fundamental tenet in democratic nations is that all people should have access to justice, or, as one popular maxim states: "Everyone is entitled to their day in court." What does this mean? Is it enough that courts exist and are available for use? Are courts synonymous with justice? What about alternative dispute resolution processes? Several topics in this chapter raise questions such as "What is access to justice?" and "When has it been denied?" If courts and lawyers are too expensive, is access to justice denied?

Some of the provinces have taken steps to reduce the cost of litigation. For example, British Columbia has simplified rules of procedure for claims of $100 000 or less, and in 2010 Ontario raised its simplified procedure limit from $50 000 to $100 000. Simplified procedures expedite the path to trial with early disclosure requirements, limited pre-trial procedures, and reduction in the length of trials. Most Canadian provinces have Small Claims Court limits over $20 000 with

Alberta and Ontario at $25 000. Ontario has undertaken some mandatory mediation pilot projects. The hope is that many cases will be settled in mediation, at less cost to the parties and to the public. The Alberta Provincial Court may refer parties to mediation of its own accord or at a party's request. The British Columbia Superior Court promotes the use of settlement conferences conducted by a judge or a master (a judicial officer who presides over certain types of proceedings).

What if disputants cannot access these simplified initiatives? Over the last decade, it has become common for big companies to insert mandatory arbitration clauses and waivers of class actions into consumer contracts so that consumers must arbitrate their disputes. Dell Computers, TELUS Communications, and Rogers Cable have all had such clauses upheld by the courts, effectively preventing consumers from processing lawsuits against them.[40] Is this effective legal risk management or a denial of consumer

>

---

[37] Rule 24.1 and 75.1 Ontario Rules of Civil Procedure; Alberta Civil Practice Note No. 11; The Queen's Bench Act, 1998, S.S. 1998, c. Q-1.01, s. 42.

[38] Article 2639, Civil Code of Quebec, S.O. 1991, c. 64; Family Statute Law Amendment Act, 2006, S.O. 2006, c.1.; O. Reg. 134/07.

[39] Ontario banned pre-dispute consumer arbitration clauses and class action waivers: Consumer Protection Act, 2002, S.O. 2002, c. 30, ss. 7, 8. Quebec banned them on December 14, 2006: Consumer Protection Act, R.S.Q., c. P-40.1, s. 11.1. Alberta has legislation requiring government approval of consumer arbitration clauses: Fair Trading Act, R.S.A. 2000, c. F-2, s. 16. See also Shelley McGill, "Consumer Arbitration Clause Enforcement: A Balanced Legislative Response" (2010) Am. Bus. L.J. 361.

[40] *Dell Computers v. Union des consommateurs*, 2007 SCC 34; *Kanitz v. Rogers Cable Inc.* (2002), 58 O.R. (3d) 299 (ON. S.C.J.); *Seidel v. TELUS Communications*, 2011 S.C.C. 15. See also Shelley McGill, "Consumer Arbitration after Seidel v. TELUS" (2011), 51 Can. Bus. L.J. 187.

LEGISLATION: GOVERNMENT MADE LAW

The second source of law is made by government and referred to as legislation, statutes, or acts. Legislation may be passed by Parliament and by provincial legislatures. Cabinet, in its formal role of adviser to the monarch, can also "legislate" within certain limited areas by issuing orders-in-council.[41] Every province has passed statutes providing for the creation of municipal governments and for their supervision. These statutes give municipalities the power to make law and to raise revenue for the benefit of their citizens. Municipal bylaws and regulations are a form of statute law. There is a vast area of **subordinate legislation** usually known as administrative law: Statutes create various administrative agencies of government to make rules and regulations in order to carry out the specific purposes set out in the legislation. Chapter 3 focuses on the use of administrative law to regulate business.

subordinate legislation law created by administrative agencies whose authority is granted by statute in order to carry out the purposes of the legislation

Statutes

As already discussed in Chapter 1, sometimes legislatures enact statutes to **codify** existing case law precedents in an area rather than to change the laws, as, for example, in the passing of the Sale of Goods Act, and the Partnership Act. Before these acts were passed, the related law was found in a huge number of individual cases. The acts did away with the slow task of searching through many cases.

codify set down and summarize in a statute the existing common law rules governing a particular area of activity

Courts are often asked to decide what the words in a statute mean, or whether it applies to the facts of a case. Their decisions then form a precedent referred to in subsequent cases. Therefore, judge-made law and statutes are connected. However, the attitude of the courts toward case law is quite different from their attitude toward statutes. When deciding a case using case law, the courts regularly expand principles from earlier decisions, to cover new situations even though the facts are different. On the other hand, the courts will only apply the provisions of a statute when the facts of the case are covered specifically by the words in the statute; they respect the legislature's intention when passing the statute, expecting that words chosen reflect the intention of the legislature. This attitude of the courts is called the **strict interpretation** of statutes.

strict interpretation courts apply the provisions of a statute only where the facts of the case are covered specifically by the statute

Statutory interpretation takes a variety of approaches. Courts may take a literal approach by adopting the dictionary meaning of the word when the meaning appears plain and obvious. A **liberal approach to statutory interpretation** involves consideration of the context, the custom and trade usage of the language, as well as the intent or purpose of the government when it passed the law. This approach involves looking at the state of the law at the time of the passage of the statute and the language used when the bill was introduced and debated. The entire statute must be examined, as one section will not be given a meaning inconsistent with the express terms in another part of the statute.

liberal approach to statutory interpretation statutory interpretation that considers the legislative intent, purpose, and history of the statute, as well as the context of the language

---

[41] An order-in-council is issued by the Privy Council (in effect, the Cabinet) in the name of the monarch, either in exercise of the royal prerogative or under authority of a statute.

Canadian courts are encouraged to take a liberal approach to statutory interpretation. The federal Interpretation Act directs the court to take a "fair, liberal and large" interpretation of statutes.[42]

A farmer hired a contractor to level out the sand hills on his farm; the contractor removed the sand, sold it, and levelled the land with top soil. The contractor was charged with operating a pit without a licence as required by the Aggregate Resources Act. The Court of Appeal was asked to determine the meaning of the word "pit" used in the legislation. The Court found that the contractor's activities fit within the grammatical and ordinary meaning of the word "pit." As well, using the liberal approach, the Court held that the presence of exemption procedures in the legislation for those pits not producing aggregate demonstrates an intention of the legislature to include all excavating activities such as improvement of farmland in the meaning of the word "pit." The contractor was convicted.[43]

Legislation Framework

There are two main classes of legislation: passive and active. The first and simplest consists of those statutes that change the law: They prohibit an activity formerly permitted or else remove a prohibition, so enabling people to carry on a formerly illegal activity. This type of legislation is essentially passive because, although it provides a legal framework for people to go about their business, it does not presume to supervise and evaluate their activities. Passive legislation leaves it to an injured party or a law-enforcement official to complain about any activity that has violated a statute of this kind and to begin court proceedings.

"Active" Legislation: Administrative Law and Government

Programs The second class, "active" legislation, gives the government itself power to carry on a program and supervise compliance—to levy taxes and to provide revenue for the purpose stated in the statute, such as paying pensions to the elderly. The statute may authorize the government to offer subsidies to encourage a particular economic activity, and to create an agency to supervise and to regulate the related trade or activity. Parliament itself is not the right body to run any program requiring continual supervision. Its members from across the country have diverse talents and interests, and their primary responsibilities are to represent their ridings and to set policy through legislation.

Projects authorized by Parliament are executed by designated government officials—the term "executive" describes the agencies of government that carry out Parliament's will. This process requires that every government department, agency, and tribunal be established by the legislature in an authorizing statute. For example, the Canadian Radio-television and Telecommunications Commission is established under the Broadcasting Act, which sets out the Commission's purposes and grants it regulatory powers to carry them out.[44]

Subordinate Legislation In exercising its regulatory powers and acting in its executive capacity, an administrative agency creates new law, which we described earlier as regulations or "subordinate legislation." Some subordinate legislation sets down broad criteria, such as regulating the type of guarantee that a licence applicant must supply to carry on a particular activity, and the amount and type of investment required as a precondition. Other subordinate legislation may be detailed and technical (fees for applications).

---

[42] Interpretation Act, R.S.C. 1985, c. I-21, s. 12.

[43] *R. v. 311578 Ontario Corp.*, 2012 ONCA 604.

[44] Broadcasting Act, S.C. 1991, c. 11

Important regulations, such as those setting out broad standards, require the approval of the Cabinet in the form of an order-in-council. The agency itself drafts these regulations, and the minister responsible for the agency brings them before the Cabinet. Lesser regulations may be authorized by the minister, the head of the agency, or even a designated officer of the agency.

The constitutional validity of these regulations may be challenged in the same way as any other statute, and misinterpretation of the regulation by the agency responsible for its administration may also be appealed to the courts.

CASE 2.3

The Alcohol and Gaming Commission of Ontario supervises the granting of liquor licences to businesses under the authority of the Liquor Licence Act. The Registrar applied to revoke Famous Flesh Gordon's liquor licence because its proprietor was a member of the Hells Angels, a criminal organization. The administrative tribunal hearing the application refused to revoke the licence because the proprietor had no criminal record of his own. The Registrar appealed to the courts and won. The tribunal applied the wrong standard of evaluation and the revocation application was returned to the board for reconsideration.[45]

As we noted in Chapter 1, the growing complexity of society and government has increased the need for specialized knowledge and control in such areas as environmental protection, energy, transportation, communications, education, and welfare, and the list includes a growing number of business and professional activities that are believed to affect the public interest. Administrative law is an important tool used to regulate business behaviour in these areas, as will be apparent in Chapter 3 when we look at regulation of competition, consumer protection and the environment. Other administrative law topics such as labour relations and intellectual property will be discussed in later chapters.

Strategies to Manage the Legal Risks

This chapter addressed procedural rather than substantive laws, and strategies to reduce the legal risks associated with processing a dispute or court action can still be applied. Every business should have a protocol for managing disputes or complaints. Often, disputes wind up in court because they have been ignored. Similarly, once in the court system, timelines must be met or a party will lose its opportunity to be heard. Therefore, every business needs a system to manage complaints and monitor resolution or escalation. This system is important not only to the outcome of the specific dispute but also for business planning purposes. Data on the volume of disputes, their value, and resolution outcomes will help the business determine its legal resource needs and dispute resolution strategy.

The costs of legal services vary just as the needs of the business do. Written retainer agreements should define the scope of work and the basis upon which a fee will be charged. Relatively few types of claims are appropriate for contingency fee arrangements. The rest are billed on a fee-for-service basis. The hourly rate for time spent should be disclosed, as well as the number of hours expected. Similarly, disbursements for expert advice or assistance can be costly and should require pre-approval. Retention of legal help should not be only reactive— that is, after a dispute arises. Identified areas of risk should trigger proactive legal advice.

---

[45] *Ontario (Alcohol and Gaming Commission of Ontario) v. 751809 Ontario Inc.*, 2013 ONCA157.

Preferred methods of resolving disputes can be designated in advance in the contracts with suppliers, employees, and customers. The costs of defending a class action can be high, and, therefore, many businesses seek to avoid this risk by designating individual arbitration as the dispute resolution forum. This is done at the time of the original contract with the complainant and is most effective in business-to-business relationships. In business-to-consumer transactions, the effectiveness of this strategy will depend on the provincial legislation.

QUESTIONS FOR REVIEW

1. Distinguish the civil law system from the common law system.
2. Explain the theory of precedent and its values.
3. Describe the relationship between the courts of common law and equity.
4. What is the purpose of codifying law in a statute?
5. Why has subordinate legislation come to prominence?
6. How does the operation of an appeal court differ from that of a trial court?
7. Motion pictures and television programs are responsible for a misconception about the way in which trials proceed. Explain.
8. Describe the basic difference between the systems of courts in the United States and in Canada.
9. What are the advantages of a settlement over a court trial?
10. Define *appellant*; *respondent*; *counterclaim*; *counsel*; *bench*; *writ*; *settlement*; *pleadings*; *party and party costs*; *res judicata*.
11. What is a "class action" and when do parties use them?
12. How does a judge decide a case when there is no precedent available in earlier decisions?
13. Explain why a legal rule in one province may differ from that in another province.
14. One of the major purposes of private law is to settle disputes between businesses. How can the settlement of a particular private dispute make a contribution to the business community as a whole?
15. "I was never ruined but twice; once when I won a lawsuit and once when I lost one." How can a successful litigant lose?
16. Explain the nature of a "contingency fee." How are contingency fees used in Canada?
17. What are the advantages that make ADR an attractive means of settling disputes?

CASES AND PROBLEMS

Continuing Scenario

The topics covered in this book have been chosen because they raise common legal issues that regularly confront businesses. Businesses face legal challenges every day. In order to highlight the ongoing interaction between law and business, we will follow one business throughout this book as it deals with an applicable legal issue in each of the following chapters. We begin with simple facts.

Ashley graduated from George Brown Culinary School as a pastry chef. She is opening a restaurant in Toronto. She will face legal issues as she starts the business, leases space, seeks professional accounting advice, sets up a website, creates her menu, finances expansion, hires employees and deals with many other typical business issues. Follow Ashley as she grows her business in the Cases and Problems section at the end of each chapter.

Chapter 3

Government Regulation of Business

- THE LEGAL FRAMEWORK FOR DOING BUSINESS IN CANADA

- CHALLENGING GOVERNMENT REGULATION OF BUSINESS

- JUDICIAL REVIEW OF GOVERNMENT REGULATION

- COMPETITION

- CONSUMER PROTECTION

- ENVIRONMENTAL PROTECTION

- STRATEGIES TO MANAGE THE LEGAL RISKS

Government controls business activity through legislation and regulations; regulations are the detailed rules imposed under the general power of the authorizing legislation. Regulations are used to manage business relationships with key stakeholders such as customers, competitors, and the public. In this chapter, we examine the Canadian regulatory framework within which business must operate, concentrating on three general areas of regulation that apply to most businesses: competition, consumer protection, and the environment. Other areas of regulation will be dealt with in later chapters of this book.

We examine such questions as:

- Who has the power to regulate?

- How are specific business sectors regulated?

- How can business use the law to eliminate oppressive regulation?

- How does competition law affect business arrangements?

- What are the consequences of consumer protection law for the consumer and for business?

- What are the main elements of environmental protection law?

THE LEGAL FRAMEWORK FOR DOING BUSINESS IN CANADA

Regulation is another word for *control*. Governments control business behaviour through regulation. In the legal context, a regulation is a detailed rule adopted under the authority of an existing government statute; in Chapter 2, we referred to this as subordinate legislation. For business to operate fairly and efficiently, an adequate legal and regulatory framework must be in place. However, excessive regulation can impose heavy and unnecessary costs and inhibit business activity. The challenge is to strike an appropriate balance. Political parties are categorized as "left" or "right" based upon the level of government regulation that they support: Parties "on the left" favour lots of government regulation, and parties "on the right" support minimal regulation. Therefore, the emphasis on government regulation will vary depending upon which party forms the government of the day.

During the 1980s and early 1990s, "deregulation" was a popular notion—freeing business from existing (excessive) government control. In many instances, direct government interference was merely replaced by a different sort of regulation, social regulation. Direct regulation occurs when the government controls such matters as prices, rates of return, and production levels. Social regulation, on the other hand, lays down standards that businesses must observe while carrying on their activities, in such areas as health, safety, and the environment. Chapter 2 described how governments use their legislative powers to create legislation, subordinate legislation, and administrative tribunals.

In this chapter, we examine how regulatory schemes may be challenged and look at some direct and social regulatory regimes designed to protect three key stakeholders: consumers, competitors, and the public. Future chapters will examine other regulatory schemes protecting other stakeholders such as employees and public investors.

CHALLENGING GOVERNMENT REGULATION OF BUSINESS

Business does not always agree with the regulatory scheme imposed upon it by government. We saw in Chapter 1 that there are three general strategies that businesses may use to try to avoid complying with government regulation: They may ask a court to find that

- the statute is invalid because the subject matter of the legislation is not within the jurisdiction of the relevant government,

- the statute is invalid because the legislation violates the Charter of Rights and Freedoms, and/or

- the interpretation of the legislation is wrong and the statute does not apply to the particular conduct.

Jurisdiction over "Business Activities" under the Constitution

The Canadian Constitution Act, 1867 divides the power to regulate business between the federal and provincial governments. The checklist below identifies some of the powers often used to regulate business. Under the provincial power to regulate municipalities, provinces have delegated local business regulation power to municipal councils. As a result, all three levels of government—federal, provincial, and municipal—regulate business activities.

The Constitution Act, 1867: Constitutional Power to Regulate Business Activities

Federal Powers, Section 91

- Regulation of trade and commerce
- Specific industries such as banking, shipping and navigation, air transportation, and radio and television
- Taxation
- Intellectual property
- Interest, currency, and promissory notes

Provincial Powers, Section 92

- Property and civil rights
- Municipalities (this section allows a province to delegate the power to regulate to a municipality)
- Direct taxation within the province
- All matters of a private nature within the province
- Other specific industries such as road transportation, including trucking; and stock exchanges and securities trading

Inevitably there is overlap between the categories, and sometimes there are even conflicting rules, making it difficult for businesses and their lawyers to determine which regulations apply in a particular situation, especially when business is carried on in more than one province.[2]

When a business wishes to challenge a particular scheme, it begins by asking whether the legislature that passed the law had jurisdiction. This is not always an easy question for courts to answer, since some of the powers in section 91 overlap those listed in section 92. As we discussed in Chapter 1, questions about jurisdictional power are resolved by the courts using a two-step process that first identifies the primary subject matter of the law and then determines under which power that topic fits.[3] Broad interpretations of any power will shelter many laws.

CASE 3.1

The City of Toronto passed a bylaw prohibiting the selling or consuming of shark fins. Shark fin vendors complained that the bylaw was beyond the power of the city, it unfairly targeted/discriminated against the Chinese community as shark fins are part of a traditional Chinese delicacy, and it hurt those businesses that supply them. The bylaw was declared invalid because the City of Toronto Act only gave the city the power to regulate municipal issues. The inhumane treatment of sharks occurred oceans away from the city and the ecological threat was a global issue—neither of these purposes fell under social, environmental, or health needs of the city.[1]

The courts have very broadly interpreted the provincial power over "property and civil rights" giving the provinces control over virtually all of private law, including contracts and most business transactions—matters that arguably could also fall in federal jurisdiction over "trade and commerce." Alternatively, the federal power over "trade

---

[1] *Eng v. Toronto* 2012 ONSC 6818; on deference to be shown to municipal bylaws see *Friends of Landsdowne Inc. Ottawa (City)* 2012 ONCA 273.

[2] For example, section 95 provides that both the federal and provincial governments have concurrent jurisdiction over agriculture and immigration, and section 92A gives the provinces to make laws regulating the export of natural resources. The Supreme Court of Canada recently held the provincial consumer protection legislation also applied to federally regulated banks: *Bank of Montreal v. Marcotte* 2014 SCC 55.

[3] See Chapter 1; *Reference Re Assisted Human Reproduction Act*, [2010] S.C.J. No. 61 at para. 19 (S.C.C.).

and commerce" has been interpreted very narrowly to mean trade and commerce across borders.[4] Therefore, it applies to matters of interprovincial and international commerce and not to matters conducted wholly within a single province.[5] For example, section 91 has been interpreted to give the federal government exclusive jurisdiction over banks and banking; deep sea, coastal, and Great Lakes shipping and navigation; air transportation; radio and television broadcasting; and atomic energy. The production, storage, sale, and delivery of oats, barley, and wheat is in federal hands on the basis that its major activity is international.

On the other hand, two sectors with a large interprovincial element remain almost exclusively within regulatory schemes of the provinces—road transportation, including trucking; and stock exchanges and securities transactions in general. In 2011, the Supreme Court of Canada rejected a proposed national Securities Act as overreaching the national concern. It held that regulating publicly traded companies was a provincial power and did not fit under the federal government's trade and commerce power.[6]

Still, business activities in many sectors fall within both federal and provincial jurisdiction.

Government Regulation of Business and the Impact of the Charter

Even if a law is within the jurisdictional power of the government passing it, that law may still be challenged. As we noted in Chapter 1, the rights entrenched in the Canadian Charter of Rights and Freedoms cannot be infringed by legislation, federal or provincial, unless it is justifiable in a free and democratic society. Although Charter rights are essentially personal in nature, they still have an important application to some business situations. To the extent a law offends a right in the Charter, it will be declared invalid and this can have important business consequences. We saw in Chapter 1 that a provincial government law preventing businesses from operating on Sunday was declared invalid because it discriminated based on religion and therefore violated the charter.[7] The result was that businesses were free to operate seven days a week.

The fundamental freedoms of expression and association may also be invoked to protect business activities.[8] The Supreme Court of Canada has ruled on a number of occasions

---

[4] *Citizen's Insurance Co. v. Parsons* (1881), 7 App. Cas. 96: the Privy Council ruled that a provincial statute regulating fire insurance was within the provincial power; it did not affect the federal trade and commerce power because the federal power did not extend to matters wholly within the boundaries of a single province. The Supreme Court of Canada has continued to question the federal power to legislate in general commercial matters where the application of a law falls within the boundaries of a province. See, for example, *MacDonald v. Vapour Canada*, [1977] 2 S.C.R. 134, and *Labatt Breweries v. Attorney General of Canada*, [1980] 1 S.C.R. 914.

[5] It is interesting to note that the U.S. Constitution's equivalent to our trade and commerce provision is "commerce among the several states." The U.S. Supreme Court has given these words a much wider interpretation and has expanded the powers of Congress, despite the interstate requirement of the words themselves.

[6] *Reference re Security Act*, [2011] SCC 66.

[7] *R. v. Big M Drug Mart*, [1985] 1 S.C.R. 295. Subsequently, in *R. v. Edwards Books and Art*, [1986] 2 S.C.R. 713, the court held that an Ontario law prohibiting stores from opening on Sundays was a valid exercise of the province's power over property and civil rights, since the purpose of the law was to ensure that workers had a uniform day off each week. Sunday opening has since been legalized in Ontario.

[8] Charter of Rights and Freedoms, section 2(b) and (d). By contrast, in *Canadian Egg Marketing Agency v. Richardson*, [1998] 3 S.C.R. 157, the mobility rights (under section 6) were held to be essentially private in nature; they do not extend to the right to conduct one's business anywhere in Canada without restriction. See also *Archibald v. Canada* (2000), 188 D.L.R. (4th) 538, concerning the legality of restrictions on grain farmers under the Canadian Wheat Board Act, R.S.C. 1985, c. C-24.

that "commercial speech" is protected under section 2(b).[9] Restrictions on advertising of products or of professional services are at first glance contrary to the Charter, though such restrictions may be justified under section 1, provided they are reasonable and do not go beyond what is necessary to promote a legitimate objective.[10] Arbitrary or unreasonable restrictions will be struck down.[11]

CASE 3.2

In 1988, the federal government introduced legislation prohibiting all advertising and promotion of tobacco products. The prohibition was challenged by one of the leading cigarette manufacturers.

The Supreme Court of Canada held that the legislation violated section 2(b) of the Charter and was not justifiable under section 1. The objective of the legislation—to discourage the use of tobacco—was legitimate, but there was no direct scientific evidence showing a causal link between advertising bans and decreased tobacco consumption. The

government had failed to show that a partial advertising ban would be less effective than a total ban. The impairment of the complainant's rights was more than minimal, and the offending provisions of the legislation were declared to be of no force and effect.[12]

As a result of the court's ruling, the federal government adopted new legislation[13] restricting tobacco advertising, but in a way that is intended to be consistent with the ruling. The new law has, in turn, been challenged by the manufacturers, but has so far been found not to infringe the Charter.[14]

With respect to freedom of association, protected by section 2(d) of the Charter, Case 3.3 shows its business application.

CASE 3.3

Pursuant to the Optometrists Act, R.S.B.C. 1996, c. 342, the Board of Examiners in Optometry adopted rules prohibiting business associations between optometrists and non-optometrists. Two optometrists who had been cited by the board for violating the prohibition petitioned for judicial review of the validity of the board's rules. They argued that the rules violated their freedom of association guaranteed by section 2(d) of the Charter.

The court held that the rules were of a public nature. Section 2(d) applies to a wide range of associations, including

those of an economic nature, and a business relationship is an association protected under the section. The prohibition could not be justified under section 1 of the Charter. The board had failed to establish that the rules were proportional to the objective of maintaining high standards of professional conduct and independence free of any real or apparent conflicts of interest that would undermine the public's confidence in the profession. The absolute prohibition against any business relationship between optometrists and non-optometrists was excessively broad.[15]

---

[9] *Irwin Toy Ltd. v. Quebec* (1989), 58 D.L.R. (4th) 577; *Rocket v. Royal College of Dental Surgeons of Ontario* (1990), 71 D.L.R. (4th) 68. In *UL Canada Inc. v. Attorney General of Quebec* (2003), 234 D.L.R. (4th) 398, aff'd [2005] S.C.J. No. 11, the Quebec Court of Appeal held (and the Supreme Court of Canada agreed) that a ban on the sale of yellow-coloured margarine did not violate the Charter freedom of expression.

[10] See *Griffin v. College of Dental Surgeons of British Columbia* (1989), 64 D.L.R. (4th) 652; *Urban Outdoor Trans Ad v. City of Scarborough* (2001), 196 D.L.R. (4th) 304; *Vann Niagara Ltd. v. Town of Oakville* (2002), 214 D.L.R. (4th) 307; (2004), 234 D.L.R. (4th) 118 (S.C.C.).

[11] See the decision of the Supreme Court of Canada in *R. v. Guignard* (2002), 209 D.L.R. (4th) 549. See also *Carmichael v. Provincial Dental Board of Nova Scotia* (1998), 169 N.S.R. (2d) 294.

[12] *RJR-MacDonald Inc. v. Canada* (1995), 127 D.L.R. (4th) 1.

[13] Tobacco Act, S.C. 1997, c. 13.

[14] *J.Y.I. MacDonald Corp. v. Canada* (2002), 102 C.R.R. (2d) 189. See also *Rothmans, Benson & Hedges Inc. v. Saskatchewan*, [2005] 1 S.C.R. 188.

[15] *Costco Wholesale Canada Ltd. v. British Columbia* (1998), 157 D.L.R. (4th) 725.

To convince a court to apply the Charter to a business situation, the business must show more than just an economic impact:

> [B]ecause there is an economic aspect to a Charter claim does not, for that reason alone, disqualify it . . . there have been numerous Charter cases in which there was an economic component or implication to a claim. On the other hand, where a claim is based solely on economic grounds, it [is] unlikely that a Charter claim could succeed.[16]

Corporations may invoke the Charter's protection. In particular, a corporation should be allowed to rely on the Charter where it is charged with an offence or is the defendant in civil proceedings instigated by the government. Just as no one should be convicted of an offence under an unconstitutional law, no one should be subject to any proceedings or sanction authorized by an unconstitutional law.[17]

Administrative Law

Finally, a business may oppose the application of regulation on the basis that the regulation does not apply to its circumstances. This involves attacking the decision of whichever decision maker applied the regulation to the business. The decision maker could be a court or an administrative government commission, tribunal, or other official.

In 2013, the Chief Justice of the Supreme Court observed that the modern trend is for regulatory schemes to shift work away from the courts toward administrative tribunals with specialized adjudicators, not judges, ruling on those matters that fall under the specific authorizing legislation.[18] The decisions of administrative adjudicators must be made fairly, reasonably, and in accordance with the power given to them by the initiating legislation. This means that not only should the decision be right based upon the facts, it must be one that the administrator is allowed to make and is arrived at after following fair procedures. The law about the actions and operation of administrative tribunals and decision makers is known as **administrative law**.

administrative law law about actions and operations of government administrators and administrative tribunals

We saw in Chapter 2 that "active" legislative schemes are the foundation of administrative law and regulatory liability. The legislation outlines general principles and then delegates the power over the details to administrators named in the legislation itself. The administrators set specific standards, qualifying conditions, and procedures, and implement, enforce, and monitor compliance. As also noted in Chapter 2, the rules made by the administrators are called subordinate legislation.

Residential landlord and tenant law is regulated this way in most provinces. Disputes between landlords and tenants do not go to the courts, but to specialized adjudicators that only deal with residential tenancies. The Residential Tenancies Act of British Columbia creates a director who is then responsible for "the administration and management" of all matters under the Act including forms, fees, and dispute resolution.[19] Arbitrators appointed by the director decide landlord and tenant disputes according to the rules set by the director and the principles in the legislation. The Ontario Securities Commission is another example of an administrative agency which sets the rules for publicly trading stocks under

---

[16] *Archibald v. Canada*, *supra*, n. 8, at 545–6, per Rothstein, J.A.

[17] *Canadian Egg Marketing Agency v. Richardson*, *supra*, n. 8. In that case, a national egg marketing scheme was held (by the Supreme Court of Canada) not to be contrary to the Charter.

[18] Right Honourable Beverly McLachlin, Administrative Tribunals and The Courts: An Evolutionary Relationship, http://www.scc-csc.gc.ca/court-cour/judges/spe-dis/bm-2013-05-27-eng.aspx (May 27, 2013).

[19] S.B.C. 2002 c. 78, s. 9.

the authority of the provincial Securities Act and then monitors compliance of traders, issuing companies, and licensees.

Businesses are frequently subject to regulatory schemes with administrative bodies supervising their compliance. The environmental and competition regulatory schemes are examples examined in this chapter. If a business disagrees with the decision of an administrator, it may appeal the decision's correctness or it may attack the underlying authority or procedures followed to arrive at the decision through a process called judicial review. Both appeals and judicial review involve the courts.

JUDICIAL REVIEW OF GOVERNMENT REGULATION

It remains the court's job to make sure that administrative decision makers exercise their power properly, even when the legislation that creates regulatory powers says the decisions are final. Federal and provincial legislation gives the courts a power of review. The Federal Court has a general jurisdiction to review actions of federal boards and commissions,[20] and several of the provinces have enacted similar provisions with respect to provincial boards.[21] Even without such legislation, the courts have a general right to review the legality of administrative acts and decisions.

As mentioned above, an administrative act or decision may be challenged on a number of grounds:

- Lack of authority—although the relevant legislation itself may be valid, the official or agency acted outside the scope of the authority conferred by the statute.

- Procedural irregularity—the official or agency proceeded in a manner inconsistent with the requirements of the statute; for example, public meetings required by the legislation were not held, or the prescribed notice was not given.

- Procedural unfairness—even when the legislation does not prescribe appropriate procedures, an official or agency is not entitled to act in a purely arbitrary manner.

Procedural fairness means that persons likely to be affected have a right to be heard and to have access to relevant documents, that adequate notice must be given of any public hearings, and that the decision maker must act impartially and not have a personal interest in the subject matter.

When courts review decisions, they are careful to show respect for the special area of expertise of the administrative tribunal. Therefore the standard of review applied to evaluate administrative decisions is usually reasonableness: As long as the decision is one of the possible acceptable outcomes based on the facts and law, it will be allowed to stand. It need not be the same decision the court would have made. Only rarely, in matters of general law (outside the tribunal's area of expertise) will a standard of correctness be applied, meaning it must be the same decision the court would have made.[22] For more information on this topic, see the Companion Website.

---

[20] Federal Court Act, R.S.C. 1985, c. F-7, s. 18.

[21] See, for example, Judicial Review Procedure Act, R.S.B.C. 1996, c. 241; R.S.O. 1990, c. J.1.

[22] *Dunsmuir v. New Brunswick*, [2008] 1 S.C.R. 190, 2008 SCC 9. Even when determining if an administrative decision-maker has properly exercised his discretion in accordance with the Charter, the standard of review is reasonableness: *Dore v. Barreau du Quebec* 2012 SCC 12 para 58.

Next, we look at three regulatory regimes that affect most businesses: competition, consumer protection, and environmental protection.

COMPETITION

The essential characteristic of an efficient market economy is competition. If consumers and customers have a choice between the goods or services of competing firms, prices will be lower or quality better, or both. But an entirely unregulated market does not ensure competition. The most efficient firms will ultimately drive the less efficient out of business—at least in certain sectors of the market. They will then enjoy a monopoly, there will be no competition, and the benefits of a free market will be lost. The same might occur where two or more firms coordinate their actions and strategies in such a way as to divide up the market rather than compete for it. Where such market imperfections exist or are likely to occur, governments must intervene in order to preserve competition.

The Competition Act

The federal Competition Act[23] was enacted under the trade and commerce power to prevent unfair competition and abuse. It creates a regulatory regime that controls three main types of anti-competitive behaviour:

- conspiracies,
- monopolizing, and
- mergers.

Before examining these provisions, two aspects of the Act should be considered briefly: exemptions and administrative enforcement.

Exemptions   The Act does not apply to certain classes of persons or to certain types of restrictive practice with their own regulatory oversight. In particular, the basic prohibition against conspiracies generally does not apply to the professions. Governing bodies of professions such as law, medicine, and public accountancy may establish agreements among their members dealing with such matters as qualifications, provided they are reasonably necessary for the protection of the public. Also exempt are agreements or arrangements among underwriters and others involved in the distribution of securities.

Enforcement   The responsibility for administration of the Act is delegated to the Commissioner of Competition, as head of the Competition Bureau. Less serious regulatory offences known as civil matters or reviewable matters are managed by the Deputy

---

[23] R.S.C. 1985, c. C-34. References to section numbers in this part of the chapter are to this Act, as amended. It underwent significant revisions in 2010.

Commissioner–Civil Matters and are ultimately referred to the Competition Tribunal (see Figure 3.1). This specialized tribunal has the power to grant or impose a variety of civil remedies and penalties. More serious cases involving **criminal offences** are investigated by the Deputy Commissioner–Criminal Matters and prosecuted through the courts by the attorney general. The Act creates a number of criminal offences, punishable by heavy fines and by imprisonment for up to five years. In one criminal case, fines totalling almost $90 million were imposed on a number of producers of vitamins participating in an international price-fixing cartel (for more information on this topic, see the Companion Website); a Swiss businessman was personally fined $250 000.[24]

criminal offences most serious offences that require proof of mental intent with penalties imposed by the courts

Normally, a person who is adversely affected by conduct that is prohibited by the Act lodges a complaint, and then it is the commissioner's responsibility to investigate and take the appropriate procedure. However, section 36 also provides that an individual may bring a civil action for damages resulting from prohibited conduct or from contravention of an order of the tribunal.[25] This is rarely done because it is difficult and expensive to prove.

Conspiracies

The Competition Act prohibits competitors from entering into agreements that hurt competition in their industry, which are generally described as **conspiracies**. The Act divides these agreements into three categories. In the first group are agreements considered so harmful that they are subject to a blanket prohibition without requiring any proof that competition would actually be reduced. This type of conspiracy results in criminal liability through the courts. The second group is for less serious forms of conspiracies that are merely reviewable by the Competition Bureau. If the bureau determines that the agreement lessens competition, it will be subject to regulatory action by the tribunal. There is a third category of acceptable competitor agreements: the Competition Act has a registration process under which parties may seek regulatory approval of their proposed agreement and thereby avoid liability.

conspiracies agreements or arrangements between competitors to lessen competition

Figure 3.1 Competition Bureau Enforcement Process

---

[24] *Commissioner of Competition v. F. Hoffman La-Roche Ltd.* (1999) (guilty plea) see Competition Bureau – Penalties Imposed, http://www.competitionbureau.gc.ca/eic/site/cb-bc.nsf/eng/01144.html

[25] The constitutionality of this provision was upheld by the Supreme Court of Canada in *City National Leasing Ltd. v. General Motors of Canada*, [1989] 1 S.C.R. 641. For a recent example of such an action, see *Culhane v. ATP Aero Training Products Inc.* (2004), 238 D.L.R. (4th) 112, in which the plaintiff failed to substantiate a claim of predatory pricing.

Criminal Conspiracies: Section 45 of the Competition Act Section 45 of the Act is an absolute prohibition of the most serious conspiracies. The negative impact on competition is assumed. It states that

1. [e]very person commits an offence who, with a competitor of that person with respect to a product, conspires, agrees or arranges

   (a) to fix, maintain, increase or control the price for the supply of the product;

   (b) to allocate sales, territories, customers or markets for the production or supply of the product; or

   (c) to fix, maintain, control, prevent, lessen or eliminate the production or supply of the product[25A]

For these serious types of conspiracy (price fixing, market allocation, and output restrictions), the Act creates a criminal indictable offence that proceeds to court rather than the tribunal. Possible punishments include imprisonment for a term not exceeding 14 years or a fine not exceeding $25 million, or both.

"Conspires, Agrees or Arranges . . ." The essential requirement of section 45 is that two or more persons conspire together—that is, they enter into some sort of agreement. The great difficulty lies in proving the conspiracy. Restrictive agreements are rarely in writing. There would be little point in drawing up a formal written agreement since it would not be enforceable and would constitute damning evidence of a criminal conspiracy. When investigating suspected offences under the Competition Act, the Competition Bureau has wide powers to search premises and computer records, and to seize documents (sections 15 and 16), and authorizes the court to "infer the existence of a conspiracy, agreement or arrangement from circumstantial evidence, with or without direct evidence of communication between or among the alleged parties to it" (section 45(3)).[25B]

CASE 3.4

Members of the Canadian Steel Pipe Institute were concerned about the lack of price stability in their market, following a period during which there had been wide fluctuations and various attempts by some firms to undercut their competitors and fellow members. Public meetings were held and industry reports circulated, urging members to adopt an open pricing policy. The policy involved publication of price lists and notification of price changes.

The Institute emphasized that the policy was a voluntary one, and each member was free to adopt its own pricing policy. Nevertheless, the evidence was that after the open price policy was instituted, bids submitted by members of the Institute were frequently identical.

The evidence to support the existence of an actual agreement comprised the following:

1. the various public statements that had been made

2. the publication of price lists

3. the fact of identical pricing

4. a communication from one firm to another to the effect that a third firm, which had been awarded a contract at a substantially lower price, was "not playing ball"

On that evidence the court inferred that an agreement existed among the members of the Institute.[26]

---

parallel pricing the practice, among competing firms, of adopting similar pricing strategies

The fact that prices among competitors in a particular industry tend to go up or down at the same time, and by approximately the same amount, does not necessarily mean that there is a conspiracy or agreement. Within the industry, prices of competitors will tend to be similar for similar products, a practice called **parallel pricing**; otherwise, those with higher prices would lose sales. One firm may tend to be the "price leader," so that if it raised or reduced its prices, the others would quickly follow suit even though they had made no commitment to do so. Therefore, parallel pricing by itself is not evidence of conspiracy.

[25A] Section 45 of the Competition Act.

[25B] Section 45(3) of the Competition Act.

[26] R. v. Armco Canada Ltd. (1976), 70 D.L.R. (3d) 287.

Other Criminal Conspiracies   Apart from the activities listed above, the Act names three other agreements that constitute criminal conspiracy offences. In particular, it is an offence

bid-rigging   agreeing not to submit a bid or agreeing in advance what bids will be submitted in response to a call for bids or tenders

- to agree to withdraw or not submit a bid or to agree in advance on the details of bids to be submitted in response to a call for bids or tenders (**bid-rigging**) (section 47);

- to conspire to limit unreasonably the opportunities for any person to participate in professional sport or to play for the team of her or his choice in a professional league (s. 48); and

- to implement in Canada a directive or instruction from a person outside Canada, giving effect to a conspiracy that, if it had been entered into in Canada, would constitute an offence under the Act (s. 46).

Reviewable Conspiracies: Lessening of Competition   For this, less serious group of conspiracies, the Competition Act does not specify the types of agreements covered. Any agreement that lessens or has the potential to lessen competition may be reviewed by the Competition Bureau (section 90.1). Thereafter, the Commissioner of Competition may seek enforcement proceedings before the Competition Tribunal. The available remedies are a cease-and-desist order or an order requiring some other form of corrective or modifying action. There are no fines or imprisonment imposed on the parties unless they fail to comply with the tribunal's order, and no private cause of action for damages is allowed. Factors relevant to the determination that an agreement lessens competition include the impact of foreign competitors and the availability of substitute products.

Registered Agreements: Specialization Agreements   Where competitors freely enter into an agreement under which each will discontinue producing a current product, the agreement is known as a specialization agreement. If the efficiencies created for the market by the agreement make up for any lessening of competition, the competitors may apply to the Competition Tribunal for approval of the agreement (sections 84–90). If the tribunal approves the agreement, it will direct that the agreement be registered with the bureau for a specific period of time. Registration exempts the agreement from both the criminal and regulatory conspiracy rules. This registry may be searched by any member of the public.

Monopolizing

The offence of conspiracy requires that two or more persons agree to restrict competition. However, a single person or firm that enjoys a monopoly or even a very powerful position in a particular sector of the market may also abuse its power in a manner that inhibits competition. The Act identifies and restricts some improper distribution practices and labels

---

ILLUSTRATION 3.1

One of the most famous illustrations of improper distribution (tied selling) and abuse of market dominance is Microsoft's bundling of its Windows operating software with its internet browser and media player. Windows consumers could not get one product without the other. This had a devastating effect on other software suppliers. Microsoft's practice was challenged not only in the United States, but all around the world. In the European Union, Microsoft was ordered to separate the products, offer unbundled software, and share codes that would allow compatibility with other products. It was also fined $690 million plus costs. In February 2008, Microsoft was fined an additional $1.325 billion for failure to comply with the earlier rulings.[27]

---

[27] *United States v. Microsoft*, 87 F. Supp. 2d 30 (D.D.C. 2000) aff'd in part 253 F. 3d 34 (D.C. Cir. 2001) This action subsequently settled under terms approved at 2002 WL 31439450 (D.D.C. Nov. 1, 2002); Kevin O'Brien, "Microsoft Rejected in Antitrust Appeal," *International Herald Tribune*, September 17, 2007, www.iht.com /articles/2007/09/17/business/msft.php?page=2; Bo-Mi Lim, "Microsoft Loses Antitrust Case Before S.-Korean Regulator," *Washington Post*, December 7, 2005, www.washingtonpost.com/wpdyn/content/article/2005/12/07 /AR2005120700137.html; Steve Lohr, "Europe's Latest Blow to Microsoft," *New York Times*, September 17, 2007, http://www.nytimes.com/2007/09/17/europes-latest-blow-to-microsoft/?_php=true&type=blog&_r=0

abuse of dominant position
taking an unfair advantage of possessing a monopoly or dominant position in the marketplace

some anti-competitive behaviour as an **abuse of dominant position**, which, though not a criminal offence, may be reviewed and prohibited by order of the Tribunal.

Distribution Practices   Generally, a supplier is entitled to choose its customers and is free to decide whether to supply a particular person or not, except where that refusal is part of a conspiracy or is related to a pricing offence. However, in circumstances where a vendor refuses to deal with a customer even though there is plenty of product and the customer is willing to pay the usual price, the tribunal may order a supplier to supply that customer (section 75). This is done when the refusal is having a negative impact on the market.

Exclusive dealing, tied selling, and market restriction are also reviewable distribution practices. A supplier may make it a condition that the buyer deals only or primarily in the supplier's products (**exclusive dealing**); it may be a condition for the supply of one type of product that the buyer also deals in other products of the supplier (**tied selling**); or it may be a condition of supplying a customer that the customer markets the product only within a prescribed area (**market restriction**). Such practices are not forbidden, but section 77 provides that the tribunal may, on application by the commissioner, make an order prohibiting the practices or requiring them to be modified when they are lessening competition.

exclusive dealing   where a supplier of goods makes it a condition that the buyer should deal only or primarily in the supplier's products

tied selling   where a supplier makes it a condition that, to obtain one type of product, the buyer must also deal in other products of the supplier

market restriction   where a supplier makes it a condition that the buyer markets the product only within a prescribed area

predatory pricing   where a seller temporarily reduces prices to an unreasonably low level with the aim of driving competitors out of business

discriminatory pricing   where a seller makes a practice of discriminating between purchasers with respect to the price charged for goods or services

Abuse of Dominant Position   Also reviewable by the tribunal is conduct amounting to an abuse of a dominant position. Examples of suspect behaviour include **predatory pricing**, which involves selling products at unreasonably low prices to drive others out of the market, and **discriminatory pricing**, which involves differentiating pricing between purchasers to give one group an advantage. In one example of predatory pricing, a valium manufacturer supplied the drug free to Canadian hospitals for a period of one year; this was viewed as an attempt to prevent other manufacturers of tranquillizers from entering the market.[28]

To obtain an order remedying an abuse of dominant position, the commissioner must show that the firm against which the order is sought is in substantial control of a particular business sector and has engaged in an anti-competitive practice that has prevented, or is likely to prevent or substantially lessen, competition (section 79). Section 78 sets out a non-exhaustive list of practices that are regarded as anti-competitive, such as the buying up of products to prevent the erosion of existing price levels, the pre-emption of scarce facilities or resources, and the requirement that a supplier refrain from selling to a competitor or sell only to certain customers.

The applicability of section 79 depends largely upon the identification of the relevant product and market. The firm usually argues for a broad definition, while the commissioner proposes a narrower definition so that fewer products or a smaller geographic area will be taken into account.[29]

CASE 3.5

NutraSweet accounted for more than 95 percent of all Canadian sales of the sweetener aspartame—a product used mainly in the soft-drink industry. One other firm, Tosoh, accounted for the rest of the market.

Tosoh complained to the Competition Bureau that NutraSweet had entered into exclusive purchasing contracts with its customers: If they wished to buy aspartame from NutraSweet, they had to agree to buy only from NutraSweet.

This raised the question of defining the relevant market: Was it the market for aspartame or for sweeteners generally, and was the market Canada or the world?

The tribunal considered the evidence of cross-elasticity of demand between the various types of sweeteners and concluded that there was, at most, only weak evidence of competition between aspartame and other sweeteners. Customers were unlikely to switch to other sweeteners on account of the conditions imposed by NutraSweet. Similarly, although

>

---

[28] *R. v. Hoffman-LaRoche Ltd.* (1980), 28 O.R. (2d) 151, aff'd [1981] O.J. No. 3075.

[29] See, for example, *Canada (Director of Investigation and Research, Competition Act) v. Southam Inc.*, [1997] 1 S.C.R. 748 at paras. 14–20. See also *Canada (Commissioner of Competition) v. Canada Pipe Co.*, 2006 FCA 233; *(Canada) Commissioner of Competition v. Toronto Real Estate Board*, 2014 FCA 29 at para. 14.

aspartame was available in other countries, transportation costs were low, and there were no tariff barriers, the tribunal concluded that the relevant market was Canada. Prices in Canada differed significantly from prices in other countries, suggesting that Canada was a distinct geographic market and that customers were unlikely to switch to imported aspartame.

Having defined the market, the tribunal found that NutraSweet had used its market power to keep other suppliers out of Canada, with the effect of lessening competition significantly.[30]

For more information on this topic, see the Companion Website.

Mergers

One way to combat monopolizing is to try to prevent monopolies from coming into existence in the first place. To this end, section 92 of the Competition Act gives the tribunal power to prevent a merger from proceeding, in whole or in part, and to make various other orders, where it concludes that the merger is likely to prevent or significantly lessen competition in Canada. The tribunal may act only on a reference from the commissioner, after the commissioner has carried out a full investigation of a proposed merger or of one that has taken place. The initial review may be followed up with a second request for information in complex mergers.

Merger is broadly defined (by section 91) to include the acquisition, by the purchase of shares or assets, or by amalgamation, combination, or other means, of control over, or of a

merger the amalgamation of two or more businesses into a single business entity

---

[30] *Director of Investigation and Research v. NutraSweet Co.* (1990), 32 C.P.R. (3d) 1.

significant interest in, the business of a competitor (horizontal merger), supplier, customer (vertical merger), or other person (conglomerate or diversification merger). "Control" apparently means legal control—that is, ownership of more than 50 percent of the shares or voting rights of another corporation, but a "significant interest" may be something less than legal control.[31] Most likely to lessen competition are horizontal mergers between competing firms, since the number of competitors is effectively reduced when one such firm obtains control over another. But vertical mergers, where a firm takes control of its suppliers or its distributors, may also reduce competition by increasing the market control of large firms. Diversification will only rarely have an anti-competitive effect.

In determining whether a merger is likely to have a significant effect on competition, the tribunal is required (by section 93) to have regard to a variety of factors. In particular, it should consider whether

- the existence of foreign competition is likely to ensure that a reduction of competition within Canada will not have adverse consequences;

- the "target" firm is in poor economic health and would likely not have continued in business;

- acceptable substitutes exist for the products affected;

- there are barriers that might prevent new competitors from entering the market;

- effective competition will still exist after the merger; and

- the merger will eliminate a vigorous, effective, and innovative competitor.

Even where it is determined that a proposed merger will substantially and detrimentally lessen competition, it may still be justified on grounds of economic efficiency (section 96). The creation of a larger firm, pooling the assets and skills of the parties, may produce gains—such as improved products, increased exports, or reduced reliance on imports—that offset any detrimental effects resulting from a reduction in competition.[32]

Although the tribunal has the power to "unscramble" a completed merger within one year after closing, such an event is unlikely for two reasons. First, there are pre-notification requirements for large mergers involving firms whose combined revenues exceed $400 million per year, or whose assets exceed $70 million (section 110). A party proposing a large acquisition must inform the bureau before proceeding with the transaction.[33] Consequently, the mergers most likely to affect competition are reviewed before they take place. Second, where it is reasonably clear that a merger will not have anti-competitive consequences, the review process can be avoided by obtaining an advance ruling from the commissioner.

CASE 3.6

Bell (BCE Inc.) proposed a takeover of Astral Media Inc. for $3.38 billion. The Competition Bureau reviewed the proposed merger. To preserve consumer choice in television programming, Bell was required to sell several specialty television channels including The Family Channel, Teletoon, The Cartoon Network, Disney XD and others, in order to obtain Competition Bureau approval. The broadcasting regulator (Canadian Radio-television and Telecommunications Commission) was also free to impose other conditions on the deal.[34]

For more information on this topic, see the Companion Website.

---

[31] The Act does not define significant interest—the Bureau considers the qualitative and quantitative impact of the acquisition. See Competition Bureau, Merger Enforcement Guidelines, October 6, 2011, available on the Competition Bureau website.

[32] This involves a balancing of positive and negative effects: see *Commissioner of Competition v. Superior Propane Inc.* (2002), 18 C.P.R. (4th) 417, *aff'd* (2003) D.L.R. (4th) 55 (F.C.A.).

[33] S. 110. Under the Investment Canada Act, additional conditions apply in the case of acquisition of a Canadian firm by a foreign firm.

[34] *The Commissioner of Competition v. BCE Inc.* CT 2013-002 (Consent Agreement March 4, 2013).

CONSUMER PROTECTION

Consumers are broadly defined as individuals who purchase goods and services from a business for their personal use and enjoyment. The definition does not include organizations or individuals using goods or services for a business activity or resale. Consumer protection statutes apply to both the sale of goods and the supply of services such as home repairs, carpet cleaning, and the preparation of income tax returns. They regulate the behaviour of manufacturers, distributors, importers, advertisers, and retailers.

consumers individuals who purchase goods and services from a business for their personal use and enjoyment

Why Is Consumer Protection Legislation Necessary?

Protective legislation is necessary because modern business methods have increased risks for consumers. Figure 3.2 shows some of the ways modern developments have affected consumers.

Figure 3.2   The Modern Business Environment

*George Mitchell (Chesterhall) Ltd. v. Finney Lock Seeds Ltd., [1983] 1 All E.R. 108 at 113; in the words of Lord Denning: "The freedom was all on the side of the big concern. . . . The big concern said 'Take it or leave it.' The little man had no option but to take it."

Consumer protection is one of those topics that falls under concurrent jurisdiction of both federal and provincial governments; every Canadian province, as well as the federal government, has legislation. The result is a collection of individual statutes that often overlap. The federal government is trying to organize its legislation under a comprehensive Consumer Protection Action Plan,[35] beginning with the implementation of the Canada Consumer Product Safety Act (CCPSA) in 2011.[36] As we will discuss below, the CCPSA applies many of the existing consumer protection strategies to a wider range of products and adds some new initiatives. The two most important new CCPSA initiatives are mandatory recall power for Health Canada and regulatory and criminal liability for corporate directors and officers.[37]

---

[35] Health Canada, Harper Government's Canada Product Safety Act Comes into Force, News Release, June 20, 2011.

[36] S.C. 2010, c. 21.

[37] *Ibid.*, ss. 42, 43.

Principal Types of Consumer Legislation

Some consumer risks are contractual—arising from the one-sided agreement made with the business. Onerous terms, high cost of credit, and low negotiating power are contractual risks. Therefore, one type of consumer protection legislation regulates consumer contracts including pressure sales tactics, onerous terms, disclosure and cancellation rights; this type of legislation falls primarily under provincial jurisdiction and it generally takes a "passive" form where it is up to the consumer to enforce their rights. We address this type of legislation in the chapters dealing with contracts, and specifically in Chapter 14, Sale of Goods and Consumer Contracts.

In this chapter, we focus on the second type of consumer protection legislation. It is broader in scope, is typically "active" with an administrative agency to enforce it, and addresses behaviour of business with the public. This legislation is primarily federal, dealing with national concerns such as health, safety, and mass communication in the form of advertising and labelling; many of the statutes address more than one risk.

In this section, we provide an overview of the non-contractual issues in consumer protection. They are

- regulation of misleading advertising;
- regulation of quality standards affecting labelling, safety, performance, and availability of servicing and repairs;
- regulation of high risk industries that deal with the public through licensing, bonding, and inspection.

Misleading Advertising   More and more legislation addresses misleading representations by sellers of goods and services. Statutes create both regulatory and criminal offences to punish non-compliance. One act that addresses advertising of food, cosmetics, and **devices** is the Food and Drugs Act. It is administered by Health Canada and enforced by the Canadian Food Inspection Agency. It is a regulatory or even criminal offence to:

devices medical apparatus and test kits such as pregnancy tests

- label, package, treat, process, sell or advertise any food or drug in a manner that is false, misleading or deceptive or is likely to create an erroneous impression regarding its character, value, quantity, composition, merit or safety (s. 5, 9)[38]
- label, package, sell or advertise a product in a way that it is likely to be mistaken for a regulated cosmetic (s. 17)
- label, package, sell or advertise a device in a false, misleading or deceptive way (s. 19)

As already discussed, the federal Competition Act is the most comprehensive legislation regulating business conduct and so, not surprisingly, it also deals with advertising and false claims. It contains a general prohibition of misleading representations made for the purpose of promoting the supply or use of a product or of any business interest.[39] Specifically, the Act makes it an offence to make false or misleading representations about

- Qualities of a product
- Length of life
- Warranties[40]
- Guarantees

---

[38] R.S.C. 1985, c. F-27, s. 5(1). Other provisions regulating labels and advertising are found in the Weights and Measures Act, R.S.C. 1985, c. W-6. There are separate federal statutes regulating the sale of meat, livestock, fruit, vegetables, and honey.

[39] Competition Act, R.S.C. 1985, c. C-34, s. 52.

[40] *Ibid.*, s. 74.01.

- Performance claims
- Test results[41]

The Act defines the word "product" as referring equally to goods and services. Liability extends to importers of goods from outside Canada, even though the misrepresentation may have been made outside Canada. This is clearly aimed at American manufacturers who target Canadian consumers. Misleading advertising during telemarketing is addressed separately.

Misleading advertising is a **dual offence**. Depending upon the seriousness of the non-compliance, it may constitute either a criminal or a regulatory offence. The criminal offence carries a maximum penalty of 14 years' imprisonment, a substantial fine, or both. The regulatory penalty is a maximum fine of $200 000 and/or one year's imprisonment (s. 52(5)).

dual offence an offence of the Competition Act that may be either a criminal or a regulatory offence, depending upon the seriousness of the conduct

Several other advertising-related offences under the Act are exclusively regulatory offences included in a category of reviewable "deceptive market practices."[43] These include **bait-and-switch advertising**, making performance claims that lack proper substantiation, and making misleading savings claims and misrepresenting the original price of a sale item. Such practices are subject to review by the Competition Tribunal, which may order the offender to refrain from such conduct for up to 10 years and may impose fines of up to $10 000 000 on corporations (s. 74.1).

bait-and-switch advertising advertising a product at a bargain price but not supplying it in reasonable quantities

---

[41] *Ibid.*, s. 74.02.

[42] *Canada (Competition Bureau) v. Chatr Wireless Inc.* 2013 ONSC 5315 (CanLII).

[43] *Ibid.*, ss. 74.01–74.07.

[44] *R. v. Benlolo (2006), 81 O.R. (3d) 440 (On. C.A.). See also Canada (Competition Bureau) v. Yellow Pages Marketing B.V.* 2013 ONCA 71.

As noted above, the Canada Consumer Product Safety Act (CCPSA) focuses on harmful or dangerous products. It is an offence for a manufacturer or importer to advertise a product that is a danger to human health or safety or is the subject of a recall (s. 8). Retailers and advertisers may be convicted of an offence if they know the product is dangerous or recalled. Again, the CCPSA offences are dual offences that will be treated as criminal offences in the more serious circumstances.

The provinces also have legislation dealing with misleading advertising. In addition to prohibiting such advertising and imposing fines against sellers, consumers affected by misleading statements may start their own lawsuits. For instance, Ontario's Consumer Protection Act declares it to be an "unfair practice" to make "a false, misleading or deceptive consumer representation," which may include a wide variety of representations about the "sponsorship, approval, performance characteristics, accessories, uses, ingredients, benefits or quantities" that the goods or services do not have.[45] There is a long list of examples of deceptive representations. The Act also creates "an unconscionable consumer representation" as a type of unfair practice that includes such conduct as simply asking a price that "grossly exceeds the price at which similar goods or services are readily available to like consumers."[46] A consumer subjected to an unfair practice may terminate the contract and "where rescission is not possible . . . the consumer is entitled to recover any payment exceeding the fair value of the goods or services received under the agreement or damages, or both" (section 18(2)).[46A] In addition, the court may award exemplary or punitive damages against the business. Similar protection exists in other provinces.[47]

The above provisions demonstrate the overlap of federal and provincial jurisdictions in the Constitution; both levels of government seem to have concurrent powers to regulate these selling practices, and this has led to some confusion.

Ethical Issue Corporate Social Responsibility and Self-Regulation of Advertising

It can be difficult to determine when an ad is misleading, and, therefore, only the most obvious abuses are acted upon by the government. In an effort to raise the level of professionalism in advertising and foster public confidence, Advertising Standards Canada (ASC), an industry body formed in the 1960s, developed the Canadian Code of Advertising Standards. The code goes far beyond inaccurate or misleading ads, and addresses advertisements that:

- target children,
- contain violence,
- play on fears, or
- offend public decency.

This voluntary code of conduct is widely adopted by advertisers, advertising agencies, and the media. A dispute resolution process is also available to resolve consumer and competitor complaints.

Questions to Consider

1. How does compliance with the Canadian Code of Advertising Standards promote corporate social responsibility?

2. What are the arguments in favour of and against endorsing the ASC code?

3. When is an ad too violent or offensive to public decency?

Regulation of Labelling, Product Safety, and Performance Standards

There is a lot of federal legislation establishing public health and safety standards for consumer products. Some standards focus on the quality of the product itself, while other standards ensure that the consumer is informed about the product. For example, the Consumer

---

[45] Consumer Protection Act, 2002, S.O. 2002, c. C.30, s. 14.

[46] *Ibid.*, s. 15 (2)(b).

[46A] Consumer Protection Act, 2002, S.O. 2002, c. C.30, s.18(2).

[47] See, for example, Trade Practice Act, R.S.B.C. 1996, c. 457; Fair Trading Act, R.S.A. 2000, c. F-2.

Packaging and Labelling Act[48] sets out comprehensive rules for packaging and labelling consumer products, including requirements for identifying products by their generic names and stating the quantity of the contents. The Act also provides for standardized package sizes to avoid confusion.

The Textile Labelling Act[49] requires labels bearing the generic name of the fabric to be attached to all items of clothing. The federal care labelling program encourages manufacturers to include recommended procedures for cleaning and preserving the fabric. The Ministry of Labour administers this Act and offences are processed through the courts.[50]

The Hazardous Products Act[51] is one of many statutes that deal with harmful products. In 2010, control over products so dangerous that their manufacture is banned in Canada was transferred to the Canada Consumer Product Safety Act. This act deals with "controlled" products that must be manufactured and handled in conformity with regulations under the Act and includes such items as bleaches, hydrochloric acid, and various glues containing potent solvents. The Minister of Health[52] has broad discretion to regulate products deemed to be a threat to public health or safety which includes warning symbols and container type, and to appoint investigators. In British Columbia, the Workers' Compensation Board administers the requirements of this Act.

The Motor Vehicle Safety Act[53] provides for the adoption of regulations setting out national safety standards for motor vehicles (whether manufactured in Canada or imported) and accessories such as seat belts and booster seats. It also requires manufacturers to give notice of defects in vehicles to Transport Canada and to all purchasers of the defective vehicles. All of the above-described federal statutes create regulatory and/or criminal offences for non-compliance.

As discussed, the Food and Drugs Act[54] is a comprehensive statute regulating many aspects of foods and medical and cosmetic products, since virtually all of them, if improperly processed, manufactured, stored, or labelled, may adversely affect consumers' health or safety. Provisions deal with such matters as sanitary production, contamination prevention, the listing of ingredients contained in products, and the dating of products having a shelf life of less than 90 days. The Act is administered jointly by the Canadian Food Inspection Agency and Health Canada. They have the power to search, seize, examine, and recall products, including imports.

ILLUSTRATION 3.2

The 2008 tainted meat outbreak involving Maple Leaf Foods illustrates the importance of effective inspection and recall procedures. More than 30 people died from eating various products containing tainted meat, and a $100 million class action lawsuit was commenced.

The Canadian Food Inspection Agency came under heavy criticism when the contents of a 2005 report were made public. The report identified problems in the system, including irregular inspections, delays in warning the public, unclear recall protocols, and limited resources.[55]

>

---

[48] R.S.C. 1985, c. C-38.

[49] R.S.C. 1985, c. T-10.

[50] Department of Industry Act S.C. 1995 C. 1, s. 9 establishes the framework for the many regulatory regimes assigned to this government agency.

[51] R.S.C. 1985, c. H-3.

[52] *Ibid.*, s. 2, 20, 21.

[53] S.C. 1993, c. 16.

[54] R.S.C. 1985, c. F-27.

[55] Robert Cribb, "Food Alarms Rang in '05," TheStar.com, September 24, 2008, www.thestar.com/News/Canada/article /504671; Joanna Smith, "Two More Firms Jointly Launch Class Action Against Maple Leaf," TheSpec.com, August 27, 2008, www.thespec.com/news-story/2103464-two-more-firms-jointly-launch-class-action-against-maple-leaf/

The passage of the Canada Consumer Product Safety Act in 2010 addressed some of these issues.[56] It applies to manufacturing, importing, selling, and distributing a broad range of products that could pose a danger to health or safety of Canadians. It bans some unsafe products such as baby walkers, and sets standards for quality for others such as hockey helmets. Packaging and labelling must not misrepresent the safety of the product. The Act empowers Health Canada to inspect premises, products, and records and expands and clarifies mandatory recall power beyond food products:

32. (1) If an inspector believes on reasonable grounds that a consumer product is a danger to human health or safety, they may order a person who manufactures, imports or sells the product for commercial purposes to recall it.[56A]

If the business does not comply, Health Canada may carry out the recall itself and bill the business for the cost. The CCPSA also requires mandatory disclosure of defect incidents, increases penalties for non-compliance, and expands criminal liability to include corporate directors and officers. The process is now much more transparent and you can view the latest recalls and safety alerts on the Health Canada website.

Regulation of Specific Businesses by Licensing, Bonding, Inspection, or Other Regulation

Licensing of businesses is another common method of protecting consumers. We will discuss the licensing of professions in Chapter 5. Licensing is also used to regulate the providers of a variety of goods and services. A familiar example is the inspection and licensing of restaurants by municipal authorities to ensure sanitary conditions in the preparation of food.

Provincial consumer protection acts allow regulatory boards to suspend or revoke registration and to hear complaints. All provinces prohibit door-to-door traders from continuing to sell unless they are registered, so that sanctions, if actively pursued, can be effective. Collection agencies—often accused of using high-pressure tactics and harassment to collect outstanding debts—are also subject to similar registration requirements.

After some highly publicized failures of travel agencies in which consumers who had paid for holiday packages lost their money, some provinces passed legislation to license travel firms in much the same way as door-to-door sellers and collection agencies. In addition, travel agents must be bonded in order to guarantee consumers against loss of prepaid travel; industry-wide Travel Assurance Funds accomplish the same purpose.

ILLUSTRATION 3.3

The payday loan industry provides an interesting illustration of provincial and federal cooperation in consumer protection regulation. In 2004, the questionable lending practices of the payday loan industry caught the attention of the press. *The Toronto Star* reported that the combination of administrative charges, interest, and insurance fees typically collected on a two-week payday loan amounted to the equivalent of an annualized interest rate of 390–891 percent, even though it is a criminal offence to charge more than 60 percent per annum.

Since banking and interest are matters of federal jurisdiction, the federal government acted first by amending the Criminal Code to allow provinces to regulate this lending industry and set their own interest rate caps. Since then, British Columbia, Manitoba, Nova Scotia, Ontario, and Saskatchewan have passed legislation regulating the industry. Licensing, bonding, reporting, and disclosure requirements are common to most of the provincial schemes, but not all have capped the interest rates. Manitoba set an interest rate cap of 17 percent per annum. Ontario's legislation sets an actual cost-of-borrowing cap of $21 per $100 borrowed for loans of 62 days or less. This results in a higher rate of interest for shorter loans. Ontario also mandates disclosure and preserves the right to bring a class action.[57]

For more information on this topic, see the Companion Website.

---

[56] S.C.2010, c. 21.

[56A] Canada Consumer Product Safety Act S.C. 2010, s. 32. (1).

[57] Criminal Code, R.S.C. 1985, c. C-46, s. 347.1; Provincial payday lending regulations: B.C. Reg. 57/2009, Alta Reg. 1572009; NS Reg. 248/2009; Man. Reg. 99/2007, Man. Reg. 50/2010; Payday Loans Act, 2008, S.O. 2008, c. 9; O. Reg. 98/09. Joanna Smith and Robert Benzie, "Payday Loan Crackdown," TheStar.com, April 1, 2008, www.thestar.com/News/Ontario/article/407813

Federal Regulation of Consumer Protection

Topic	Legislation	Administrative Agency
Misleading Advertising	Food and Drugs Act	Health Canada Canadian Food Inspection Agency
	Competition Act	Commissioner of Competition Competition Bureau
	Canada Consumer Product Safety Act	Health Canada
Labelling, Product Safety, and Performance	Consumer Packaging and Labelling Act	Canadian Food Inspection Agency, Minister of Agriculture and Minister of Industry
	Food and Drugs Act	Health Canada Canadian Food Inspection Agency
	Textile Labelling Act	Minister of Industry
	Hazardous Products Act	Minister of Health
	Motor Vehicle Safety Act	Transport Canada

ENVIRONMENTAL PROTECTION

The environment is another area managed by government regulation. Most businesses need professional advice to navigate the complicated environmental regulatory schemes applicable to their industry. Non-compliance will trigger costly clean-up costs as well as fines and penalties.

The Legislative Framework

The federal parliament and provincial legislatures have concurrent jurisdiction over environmental law. The protection of the environment is clearly within the competence of the provinces, but matters such as air and water pollution are national problems and require national solutions. Municipalities also pass bylaws to provide local environmental protection and to restrict activities deemed to be harmful. All three levels of government need to be involved because environmental damage is not contained by borders.

CASE 3.9

Corporations operating in Manitoba, Ontario, and Saskatchewan were found to have improperly discharged mercury into rivers that drained into Manitoba. The Manitoba government passed a regulatory scheme requiring the companies to compensate fishermen for loss suffered as a result of mercury contamination. The Supreme Court of Canada held that, although creating a civil cause of action for damages caused by pollution was within provincial jurisdiction, Manitoba did not have power to impose liability in respect of acts done outside the province.[58]

---

[58] *Interprovincial Corp. Ltd. v. R.*, [1976] S.C.R. 477.

Federal Legislation The most important federal legislation is contained in the Canadian Environmental Protection Act (CEPA) administered by Environment Canada.[59] It is augmented by a number of separate statutes relating to particular types of pollution or dangers to the environment.[60]

The CEPA applies to all elements of the environment—air, land, and water, all layers of the atmosphere, all organic and inorganic matter and living organisms, and any interacting natural systems that include components of the foregoing. The Act contemplates a coordinated intergovernmental approach to environmental policy and requires the minister of the environment to create a national advisory committee with representatives from every province, territory, and Aboriginal government (section 6) The committee will advise on environmental quality objectives and recommend guidelines and codes of practice to the minister (section 54), taking a precautionary (preventive) strategy. To facilitate access to the many resulting policies, guidelines, and regulations, the minister must also create a public registry of all regulations, proposed regulations, and court proceedings (sections 12–14). Separate parts of the CEPA deal with subjects such as toxic substances, hazardous wastes, nutrients, international air pollution, and ocean dumping, as well as reactive measures for emergencies and clean-up. Any substance listed in Schedule 1 is considered toxic and subject to special controls. Substances not yet classified must be assessed by Health Canada and Environment Canada before they can be imported or manufactured.

In the case of an abnormal environmental event, the person who owns or controls the substance or activity has a duty to report and take remedial action. Environment Canada will investigate, issue emergency orders and clean-up orders, and may lay charges if it finds non-compliance with environmental standards.

Part 10 of the CEPA deals with enforcement and empowers enforcement officers to deal with polluters as peace officers with the power to search, seize, and arrest (sections 217–224). Any contravention of the CEPA or its regulation is a criminal offence with a minimum fine, as well as a maximum fine of $1 000 000 and three years of imprisonment, or both. Fines double for second offences. This is separate from the costs of the clean-up. The CEPA imposes a personal duty on officers and directors of corporations to comply with the Act, and they are subject to the same penalties (s. 280, 280.1). For more information on this topic, see the Companion Website.

CASE 3.10

During blasting of rock to widen a highway, rock debris escaped and flew 90 metres into the natural environment, damaging homes and cars in the area. This was a dangerous and abnormal result, so the contractor reported the incident to the Ministry of Labour and the Ministry of Transport, but failed to report the incident to the Ministry of Environment.

The contractor was convicted of the offence of failing to report an incident. It appealed all the way to the Supreme Court of Canada and the Court held that the event was out of the ordinary and not trivial, as it produced adverse effects; therefore, reporting was necessary.[61]

---

[59] S.C. 1999, c. 33. The Act consolidated a number of earlier statutes, among them the Clean Air Act, the Environmental Contaminants Act, the Ocean Dumping Control Act, and parts of the Canada Water Act.

[60] Most notably in the Nuclear Energy Act, R.S.C. 1985, c. A-16; the Fisheries Act, R.S.C. 1985, c. F-14; the Pest Control Products Act, S.C. 2002, c. 28; and the Transportation of Dangerous Goods Act, S.C. 1992, c. 34.

[61] *Castonguay Blasting Ltd. v. Ontario (Environment)* 2013 SCC 52.

Provincial Legislation All the provinces have a "general" environment protection law,[62] supplemented by various statutes referring to specific types of environmental protection. Examples are statutes relating to air pollution,[63] water conservation and pollution,[64] transportation of dangerous goods,[65] and waste management.[66]

Environmental Impact Assessment Review

It is much better to prevent injury to the environment than to try to remedy it after it has occurred and, as noted above, CEPA takes a precautionary approach. Environmental impact assessment review processes are required at the federal level by the Canadian Environmental Assessment Act (CEAA)[67] and in all provinces. Regulations under the CEAA identify specific types of projects that may require an environmental assessment. For these projects, the developer must submit a summary of the project to the Canadian Environmental Assessment Agency and the Agency has 45 days to decide if an assessment is required. Selected projects will be reviewed by a panel of independent experts. Public hearings are held in the communities likely to be affected. The review board submits its findings to the minister responsible or to the whole cabinet, which makes the final decision about the future of the project based upon whether or not it will have significant adverse environmental effect. The federal process is concerned about environmental effects on matters within federal jurisdiction (such as fishing), on federal land or on environments outside the project's host province or outside Canada, or on Aboriginal land, culture, health, or traditions.[68] Conditions may be attached to any approval. The process must be completed within 365 days. For more information on this topic, see the Companion Website.

The scope and the procedures of the review process vary from one jurisdiction to another. Where multiple jurisdictions are involved, the federal Minister of the Environment may substitute the provincial process for the federal one.

Enforcement and Liability

Although private enforcement of environmental standards is possible using the common law tort of nuisance or negligence, the enforcement of environmental laws is primarily a public matter. Legislation provides public authorities with a wide variety of enforcement tools. Polluters may be ordered to refrain from harmful activities, to remedy existing situations, and to pay for the costs of clean-up. Owners of contaminated property may be forbidden from dealing with that property, even where they were not responsible for causing the contamination. Most important, environmental legislation normally creates a number of offences, punishable by fines and, in serious cases, by imprisonment. Since most major polluters are corporations, which cannot be sent to prison, the statutes frequently provide for the punishment of corporate directors and officers who are personally responsible for pollution offences. For more information on this topic, see the Companion Website.

---

[62] See, for example, Environmental Management Act, S.B.C. 2003, c. 53; Environment Act, S.N.S. 1994–95, c. 1; Environment Protection Act, R.S.O. 1990, c. E-19.

[63] See, for example, Clean Air Act, S.S. 1986–87–88, c. 12.1; Environmental Protection and Enhancement Act, R.S.A. 2000, c. E-12.

[64] See, for example, Environmental Protection and Enhancement Act, R.S.A. 2000, c. E-12; Environment Act, S.N.S. 1994–95, c. 1.

[65] See, for example, Dangerous Goods Handling and Transportation Act, C.C.S.M., c. D-12; Dangerous Goods Transportation Act, R.S.O. 1990, c. D.1.

[66] See, for example, Waste Management Act, R.S.B.C. 1996, c. 482.

[67] S.C. 2012, c. 19.

[68] *Ibid.*, s. 5.

Bribery of Foreign Officials

This chapter has dealt with a number of regulations that require businesses to seek government approval. Would an ethical Canadian business ever consider bribing the Commissioner of Competition to obtain approval for a merger? Of course not; in Canada, bribery of Canadian public officials is unacceptable and government corruption is prohibited through a number of Criminal Code offences, including bribery, fraud, influence peddling, and money laundering.

Internationally, attitudes concerning the bribery of government officials vary widely. In some cultures, it is considered normal, if not acceptable, to bribe an official to get a favourable or at least more rapid response.

In 1997, the Organisation for Economic Co-operation and Development (OECD) adopted the Convention on Combating Bribery of Foreign Public Officials in International Business Transactions. This treaty called for member nations to adopt domestic legislation that criminalized bribery of foreign officials. Canada ratified the treaty and passed the Corruption of Foreign Public Officials Act (CFPOA) in 1999. This Act makes it a crime to confer any benefit, directly or indirectly, to a public official "in order to obtain or retain an advantage in the course of business." It covers any global bribery where there is a real and substantial link between the offence and Canada. The maximum penalty under the Act is 14 years in prison. Progress on the fight against corruption must be reported to Parliament on an annual basis.

In recognition of the cultural variation in bribery standards, "facilitation payments" made to expedite or secure the performance of a "routine" act by a public official are exempt for the CFPOA. Amendments introduced in 2013 anticipate the removal of the exemption.

In 2002, Hector Ramirez Garcia, a U.S. immigration officer working at the Calgary airport, was sentenced to six months in jail and deported to the United States after accepting bribes from an Alberta company, Hydro Kleen Systems Inc., in violation of the CFPOA. The company was also convicted and received a $25 000 fine. In 2013, the director of a technology company was convicted of agreeing to offer a bribe to the Indian Minister of Civil Aviation in order to obtain an Air India contract.

The United States has similar legislation known as the Foreign Corrupt Practices Act. The OECD visits participating countries to evaluate anti-corruption progress and makes recommendations about further measures. Other Canadian steps taken to reduce bribery include inserting anti–money-laundering provisions in the Income Tax Act and amending the Criminal Code to expand its applications to organizations.

Questions to Consider

1. Should Canada attempt to regulate international business conduct by extending the reach of its criminal law beyond its borders?

2. Facilitation payments are not acceptable in Canada, so why should they be exempt from the Corruption of Foreign Public Officials Act?

Sources: Corruption of Foreign Public Officials Act, S.C. 1998, c. 34; An Act to Amend the Corruption of Foreign Public Officials Act, S.C. 2013, c. 26; *R. v. Karigar* 2013 ONSC 5199; *R. v. Watts*, [2005] A.J. No. 568

Strategies to Manage the Legal Risks

This chapter provides only a general overview of the main categories of government regulation of business. Management personnel must familiarize themselves with the industry-specific rules affecting their business's activity. There must be a system in place to routinely update the regulatory information as new guidelines are adopted on an ongoing basis. Some requirements are mandatory, in the form of regulations enforced through inspection and penalties. Naturally, these must be complied with, or even directors and officers will be punished. Other standards are recommendations only, such as guidelines, codes of practice, and policies. Although these recommendations may not be mandatory, non-compliance may give rise to civil liability for those harmed—therefore, the best strategy is to conform to all recommended best practices.

Product safety is one of the major objectives of several pieces of legislation discussed in this chapter, and it is no longer a concern for just the product manufacturer. Every business involved in the manufacture, import, distribution, advertisement, or sale of a product may be liable for defects or misrepresentations. Those involved in the supply chain must inform themselves about the compliance of their distribution partners. Naturally, indemnity clauses (under which the offending party agrees to cover all costs of the defect) play a key role in managing the risk, but they may be of little help if the other businesses are foreign or insolvent. Insurance should be obtained not only for the damage caused to outside parties but also for the losses to the business itself when expensive recalls must be undertaken and funded.

Businesses need not accept all regulations imposed on them by government; sometimes the rule is beyond the power of the government, violates the Charter, or does not cover the subject conduct. Rather than waiting to complain until after their implementation, management should participate in the development of regulations. Many regulators, such as the securities commissions and the environmental protection agencies, release discussion papers seeking comments on proposed regulation. Businesses have the opportunity to respond individually or through industry-wide associations. Shaping the regulation before it is adopted is much easier and cheaper than attempting to invalidate it after enactment. This is just one of the uses of industry-wide associations. They may also be useful to supply current information about required standards of behaviour and in the development of best practices. However, caution must be exercised when developing industry-wide solutions to common challenges through an association of competitors.

QUESTIONS FOR REVIEW

1. What strategies are available to business to avoid the application of government regulation?
2. How does the Constitution divide the power to regulate business among the various levels of government in Canada?
3. Which provisions of the Charter have particular application to business activity?
4. What changes to the business environment strengthened the need for consumer protection legislation?
5. What are the principal forms of misleading advertising that are prohibited by the Competition Act, and what are the consequences?
6. What is a conspiracy? How does the Competition Act categorize conspiracies?
7. How does a court determine if competition has been unduly lessened?
8. Give examples of the principal types of abuse of dominant position.
9. Why is it thought necessary for governments to control mergers?
10. Why are horizontal mergers more likely to affect competition than other types of mergers?
11. Why is the determination of the relevant market essential to the application of competition law?
12. What is the purpose of environmental impact assessment review?

CASES AND PROBLEMS

1. Continuing Scenario

   Before opening her restaurant, Ashley contacted O'Brien's Food Service Ltd. to be her frozen poultry supplier. Because she was new to the business and her volume would be low, O'Brien's quoted her a price of $25.00 per case of frozen chicken breasts. Adam, O'Brien's salesman, told her in an email that the price was only $20 per case for restaurants that ordered more than three cases a week. Ashley could not be sure she would need this much chicken, so she proceeded on the initial quote. The following day, Adam stopped by the restaurant with the customer application form describing the price as "as quoted" and told Ashley that with every order of chicken she must also take two cases of frozen meatballs at a cost of $15.00 a case. Meatballs are not on Ashley's proposed menu—she does not want them. Adam tells her that it is both or nothing. Ashley says she needs time to think about it. Is there anything wrong with O'Brien's practice? What can Ashley do?

2. Dr. Carpenter relocated her dental practice to premises in a new shopping mall and placed an advertisement to that effect in the local newspapers. The notice conformed with the advertising standards of the dental profession in the province, but one of the newspapers decided to print a "human interest" story and did an interview with Dr. Carpenter. The story was printed without first having been shown to Dr. Carpenter, and a number of advertisements for dental supplies appeared on the same page. At the same time, Dr. Carpenter ordered a sign announcing the change of premises, which she intended to be displayed in the window of her old premises. Instead, by mistake, the sign was displayed in a public area of the shopping mall.

   The professional association considered that the sign and the advertisements that accompanied the newspaper article constituted breaches of the professional advertising code, and gave notice to Dr. Carpenter of a disciplinary hearing, which could result in the cancellation or suspension of her licence to practise.

   On what grounds, if any, can the validity of the disciplinary hearing and the professional regulations be challenged?

3. Red Square Records Inc. is a Canadian corporation holding the sole rights to import and distribute in Canada discs and tapes produced by a Russian company, Krasnayadisk. For some years, Red Square has been importing two labels that have proven very popular, partly because of their low price. It has been selling the discs to dealers at $4.99 each, and they are retailed at prices ranging from $6.99 to $8.99.

   Recently, Krasnayadisk introduced a new label, on which it is releasing previously unavailable archival recordings that are of great interest to collectors. Red Square has started to import the discs and makes them available to retailers at $18.99 each.

   Steve's Records Inc., a Canadian firm that owns a large chain of record stores across Ontario, had been selling large quantities of the cheaper Krasnayadisk recordings, and its customers had shown a lot of interest in the new label. However, many were deterred by the high price. Steve's found another source for the new label—a dealer in the United States, who was prepared to supply Steve's at a price of $11.99 per disc. This enabled Steve's to sell the new label at a much lower price than any of its competitors.

   Some months ago, Steve's received a letter from Red Square to the effect that, if Steve's did not stop purchasing the new label from the United States, Red Square would no longer be willing to supply Steve's with the two cheaper labels. Steve's ignored the warning and continued to import the new label.

   A few weeks ago, Steve's ordered some discs from Red Square and was informed that Red Square would no longer supply Steve's. The cheaper labels are also available in the United States, but at the same price of $4.99, and with higher shipping costs.

   Is there any action that Steve's can take against Red Square's refusal to supply it?

4. Truenorth Press Inc. owned both of the daily newspapers in Bayville. The papers were relatively unsuccessful compared to Truenorth's other dailies throughout Canada, and faced stiff competition for advertising revenue from a large number of small community newspapers that circulated in the same distribution area. Those community newspapers contained local news stories and advertisements from mainly local firms, appeared once or twice a week, and were distributed free of charge.

   Truenorth embarked on a campaign to acquire the community papers and, within one year, obtained control of 20 publications, including the two papers with the largest circulation.

   A group of citizens—readers, who feared that there would be fewer local stories, and small firms, who feared that their advertising rates would be increased once Truenorth gained control of the remaining papers—held a number of public meetings to express their concern.

   Is there any legal action that they could take?

Additional Resources for Chapter 3 on the Companion Website

In addition to pre- and post-tests, mini-cases, and application exercises, the Companion Website includes the following province specific resources for Chapter 3:

- **Alberta:** Dishonest Trade Practices; Fair Trading Act; Fair Trading Act
- **Atlantic Provinces:** Consumer Product and Liability Act; Public Utilities Board
- **British Columbia:** Business Practices and Consumer Protection Act; Collection Agents; Consumer Protection Legislation; Consumer Taxes; Cooling-off Period; Cost of Borrowing; Credit Cards; Credit Reporting; Direct Sales Contracts; Dishonest Trade Practices; Distance Sales Contracts; British Columbia Environmental Legislation; Sale of Goods Act
- **Manitoba/Saskatchewan:** Consumer Protection Legislation; Environmental Legislation; False or Exaggerated Claims
- **Ontario:** Agreements to Share Power; Consumer Protection Act (2002); Environmental Protection Legislation; Payday Loans; Unfair Business Practices

Chapter 4
The Law of Torts

- THE SCOPE OF TORT LAW
- DEVELOPMENT OF THE TORT CONCEPT
- THE BASIS FOR LIABILITY
- INTENTIONAL TORTS
- UNINTENTIONAL TORTS
- PRODUCT LIABILITY
- OCCUPIER'S LIABILITY
- REMEDIES
- STRATEGIES TO MANAGE THE LEGAL RISKS

tort a wrongful act causing harm to the person or property of another

The word "tort" comes from a French word meaning "wrong." A **tort** is improper behaviour by one person that causes injury to another, sometimes intentionally but more often unintentionally. The injury may be physical (to the person or property of the victim), emotional, or financial.

Tort law determines in which circumstances the person who causes an injury must compensate the victim.

In this chapter we examine such questions as:

- What is the basis for tort liability?

- What are intentional torts?

- What constitutes "negligence"?

- How does the law of negligence apply to particular situations, such as the liability of manufacturers and of the owners or occupiers of property?

- What remedies are provided for tort victims?

THE SCOPE OF TORT LAW

The purpose of tort law is to compensate victims for harm caused by the activities of others. Usually punishment is left to the criminal law, if the conduct in question happens also to amount to a crime.[1] For example, when a person punches a neighbour in the nose, the neighbour may sue the offender for the tort of battery and the government may also charge him with the criminal offence of assault causing bodily harm.

As a general statement, a tort identifies a set of circumstances that creates a right to claim compensation. When dealing with harm caused by someone else the basic question for society is who should bear the loss—the victim, the person whose act caused the harm, the group that benefits most directly from a common activity, such as all motor vehicle owners, or an even larger group such as taxpayers generally. Tort law is one way of apportioning loss, along with other approaches such as insurance and government compensation schemes.[2]

DEVELOPMENT OF THE TORT CONCEPT

Initially, societies had simple rules for imposing liability for injurious conduct: Anyone who caused direct injury to another had to pay compensation. No inquiry was made into the reasons for the injury or whether the conduct of the injurer was intentional or unintentional. This type of liability is called **strict liability**. Over time, the idea developed that a person should not be responsible for harm caused to another if he acted without fault. The courts also began to consider the way in which the harm had arisen. At first, only direct injuries were recognized by the courts—running another person down or striking a blow. Gradually the courts recognized indirect or consequential injuries. For example, A carelessly drops a log in the road and does not bother to remove it. After dark, B's horse trips over the log and is seriously injured. In early law, B would have been without a remedy. Eventually, the courts recognized that A's act was as much responsible for the injury to B's horse as if A had struck the horse by throwing the log at it.[3]

Therefore, today's tort law involves two principles: the fault of the defendant (that is, whether the behaviour was improper), and the causation of harm (that is, whether the plaintiff's injury was the result of the defendant's conduct). For more information on this topic, see the Companion Website.

strict liability liability that is imposed based upon causation regardless of fault

THE BASIS FOR LIABILITY

Fault

Fault, in the context of tort law, refers to blameworthy or culpable conduct—conduct that in the eyes of the law is unjustifiable because it intentionally or carelessly disregards the interests of others. One reason for basing liability upon fault is a belief in its deterrent effect: People will be more inclined to be careful if they must pay for the consequences of their carelessness. Highly publicized awards of damages should influence the standards and practices of manufacturers, surgeons, and similar persons affected by those awards. Even though many activities triggering tort liability—driving a car, operating a factory or store, practising medicine—are covered by insurance, a claim will still increase premiums and

fault unjustifiable injurious conduct that intentionally or carelessly disregards the interests of others

---

[1] Sometimes courts award "punitive damages" discussed later in this chapter under "Remedies."

[2] See generally *Fleming's Law of Torts*, 10th ed., C. Sappideen and P. Vines (Eds.), (Prymont, N.S.W.: Lawbook Co., 2011). See also A. M. Linden and B. Feldthusen, *Canadian Tort Law*, 9th ed. (Makham: LexisNexis, 2011).

[3] This example was first discussed in *Reynolds v. Clarke* (1726), 93 E.R. 747, and remains a classic statement of the law.

make insurance more difficult to obtain. Although carelessness is even more likely to be deterred by the likelihood of criminal penalties (for example, consider dangerous driving), not all tortious behaviour amounts to a crime.

A compensation system based on fault also has its defects. Accident victims who cannot establish fault on the part of some other person go uncompensated, and the costs and delays of litigation deter many other claims. Sometimes when fault is established, the victim may be overcompensated, especially where the defendant is a large corporation and its conduct is considered particularly bad.[4]

Strict Liability

Today, most but not all tort liability is based upon fault. Strict liability remains in only a few areas of modern tort law. For example, a person who collects potentially dangerous substances or materials on his land, which accidentally escape, is liable for any resulting damage even if he is blameless.[5]

A manufacturer stored acid in a large container on his property. The container was accidentally punctured by a visitor's truck, and the acid leaked out and damaged a neighbouring farmer's crops. The manufacturer is liable to compensate the farmer. The risk of that type of damage is a burden that the manufacturer must bear as the price for storing dangerous chemicals on his land. (The truck driver may also be liable for the damage if he is found to be at fault.)

Some activities are inherently dangerous regardless of the amount of care taken—for example, transporting high explosives. It seems logical that a person knowingly undertaking an inherently dangerous activity should be strictly liable for resulting damage, regardless of fault. Why? Because that person could charge for his services according to the degree of risk, and could carry adequate insurance to compensate for possible harm done to others. In Canada strict liability is most often imposed through legislation, although in the United States some courts have done it. In the absence of legislation, Canadian courts typically consider fault to be the primary basis of liability. However, the expected level of care rises as the danger increases. As a result, in many cases involving hazardous activities, the defendant finds that the standard of care is so high that it is virtually impossible for him to show that he has satisfied it.[6] The effect is much the same as if he were strictly liable.

Public Policy

public policy economic, social, and political considerations or objectives that are believed to be beneficial to society as a whole

Whether liability should be based on fault, on strict liability, or on some other principles is an important question of **public policy**. Policy objectives change as our social standards change. These standards force the law to adapt in many ways, ranging from direct government legislative intervention to more subtle influences on judge and jury in determining liability and the amounts of compensation awarded.

The most radical policy proposal would eliminate lawsuits for all personal injuries and compensate victims through government run compensation schemes. A step in

---

[4] This is especially so in the United States, where jury trials and awards of punitive damages are more common and has driven "tort law reform" capping damages.

[5] *Rylands v. Fletcher* (1868), L.R. 3 H.L. 330. In Canada, the *Rylands v. Fletcher* rule requires a non-natural use of the land and damage caused by accidental escape or unintended consequences. See *John Campbell Law Corporation v. Owners, Strata Plan 1350*, 2001 BCSC 1342. See also *Smith v. Inco Ltd.*, 2011 ONCA 628, 107 O.R. (3d) 321 leave to SCC denied (refinery found not to be a non-natural use and no mishap so strict liability not applicable).

[6] *Smith v. Inco Ltd.*, *supra* n. 5, para 93.

that direction has been taken in Canada with the drastic reduction of fault as the basis for defining liability in automobile accident claims through a system of compulsory **no-fault insurance**. Another example of an alternative to the tort approach is found in the scheme governing **workers' compensation** in Canada. Under this scheme, industrial accidents are seen as the inevitable price of doing business. Employers must contribute to a fund that is used to compensate workers injured in industrial accidents, even when the employer is blameless and the injury is the result of the employee's own carelessness.

Vicarious Liability

One example of strict liability in response to societal pressure relates to torts committed by employees in the course of their employment. An employer will normally be held liable when at fault for an act committed by an employee: For example, an employer may instruct an employee to perform a dangerous task for which he knows the employee is not trained. In such a case the employer is at fault, and it may be that there is no fault on the part of the employee.[7]

Employers without fault may also be liable for harm caused by the acts of an employee when those acts arose in the course of employment. An employer may even be found liable when he has given strict instructions to take proper care or not to do the particular act that causes the damage, and he may be held liable for criminal—as well as intentional and unintentional—tortious acts of an employee.[8] This principle is called **vicarious liability**, and results in an employer being liable to compensate persons for torts committed by an employee in the course of employment. (Figure 4.1.)

no-fault insurance   a system of compulsory insurance that eliminates fault as a basis for claims

workers' compensation   a scheme in which employers contribute to a fund used to compensate workers injured in industrial accidents regardless of how the accident was caused

vicarious liability   the liability of an employer to compensate for torts committed by an employee during the course of his or her employment

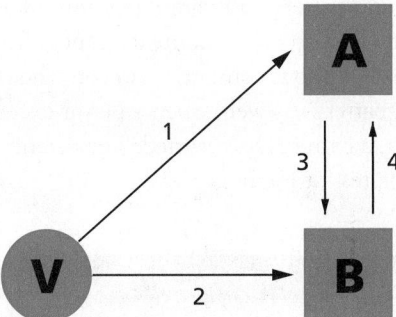

Figure 4.1   Vicarious Liability

The victim, V, is injured by A while A is acting in the course of his employment for B. V can sue A [1]. V can also sue the employer, B [2], who will normally have a greater ability to pay. (In practice, V is likely to sue both A and B.) If V does sue A, it is possible that A will have a right to be indemnified by B [3]. Or, if B has to compensate V, B may be able to sue A [4]. These rights [3 and 4] could arise under the contract of employment.

There are two public policy reasons for taking this approach. First, although an employee is personally liable for the torts he commits while acting for himself or his employer, employees often have limited assets available to pay compensation for the potential harm they can cause. Second, it seems only fair that the person who makes the profit from an activity should also be liable for any loss.

No-fault schemes and strict liability are relatively rare exceptions; the most common approach to compensation of injury remains tort liability based upon the principles of fault and causation. For more information on this topic, see the Companion Website.

---

[7] See *Edgeworth Construction Ltd. v. N.D. Lee & Associates Ltd.* (1993), 107 D.L.R. (4th) 169.

[8] *British Columbia Ferry Corp. v. Invicta Security Service Corp.* (1998), 167 D.L.R. (4th) 193.

INTENTIONAL TORTS

Torts are divided into two types: intentional and unintentional. Intentional torts are those where the activity or conduct is done deliberately, not by accident. Unintentional torts are those where the behaviour itself is accidental and not done deliberately. In both cases, the harm may be unexpected, and intention relates only to the behaviour, not the resulting damage. Consider, for example, the intentional tort of battery that arises from non-consensual physical contact. A person may intend to shake your hand, and therefore the contact is intended. However, the person does not intend to break your fingers while doing it—the harm remains unintended. Still, a battery has been committed.

trespass unlawful entering, or remaining, on the land of another without permission

Harm or damage must occur for any tort to be actionable. For example, one of the oldest intentional torts is **trespass**—entering upon another person's land without permission. Most of the time very little damage is done if someone merely steps upon another's land. There would be no point in suing unless the landowner could establish some loss—a damaged garden or fence, perhaps.

The list of torts continues to grow as courts impose liability for new behaviours causing harm. In this chapter, we will focus on the most common torts and those most applicable to the business context.

Assault and Battery

assault the threat of violence to a person

battery unlawful physical contact with a person

One of the earliest torts recognized by English law was trespass to the person. The present-day intentional torts dealing with trespass to the person are **assault** (the threat of violence) and **battery** (the actual physical contact). This behaviour may be a criminal offence, and the attacker may be fined or imprisoned. He may also be liable (in tort) to compensate his victim, though assault and battery cases are rarely fruitful against "attackers." Battery cases are common in the medical and sport contexts. Since the essence of a battery is the unlawful touching of a person without consent, a surgeon who operates on a patient without consent may commit a battery. As well, when a player exceeds the "accepted" level of contact in the specific sport, a battery has occurred. The defence most often presented to a battery is consent, either express or implied.

CASE 4.1

Steve Moore, a National Hockey League player with the Colorado Avalanche, experienced a fractured spine and a closed head injury after being hit from behind by Todd Bertuzzi of the Vancouver Canucks during their final game of the regular NHL 2004 season. The question that arises is whether the physical contact exceeded the acceptable level impliedly consented to in the sport given that many believe fighting is part of hockey.[9] This is one of those rare cases that triggered three types of liability. Bertuzzi pled guilty to criminal charges and was also disciplined (fined and suspended) by the NHL. Moore sued Bertuzzi for damages arising from battery, and sued the Vancouver Canucks for vicarious liability. The case was settled before going to trial.

Nuisance

public nuisance interference with the lawful use of public amenities

There are two nuisance torts. **Public nuisance** includes such actions as blocking public roads, interfering with the use of public amenities such as marketplaces or parks, and emitting dangerous substances in public places. Actions against the wrongdoer may ordinarily be brought by a government agency on behalf of the public as a whole. Occasionally, however, an individual who is able to show a special injury that is substantially greater than

---

[9] See *R. v. Bertuzzi*, [2004] B.C.J. No. 2692; *Moore v. Bertuzzi*, 2012 ONSC 3497 (CanLII); Patrick Thornton, "Rewriting Hockey's Unwritten Rules: *Moore v. Bertuzzi*" (2009), 61 Me. L. Rev. 2005.

that suffered by other members of the general public may bring an action for compensation against the wrongdoer.[10]

The tort of **private nuisance** protects an occupier's right to the reasonable use and enjoyment of her own land, without substantial interference from direct or indirect activity on neighbouring property. It covers things like noxious fumes, excessive noise, or contaminating liquids poured into rivers or seeping through the soil. The term "occupier" includes not only the owner of land but tenants as well.

private nuisance interference with an occupier's use and enjoyment of her land

Private nuisance can take two forms, one where the nuisance causes actual physical damage to the property or its occupiers, and a second, so called amenities nuisance, where the nuisance interferes with the use of amenities on the property. The former is established with mere proof that damage was caused. The latter requires proof that the interference is substantial and also that it is unreasonable.[11]

An occupier does not have a right to absolute freedom from trivial annoyances. The courts must weigh competing interests and balance two main issues: the degree of interference with the occupier's use and enjoyment of the land, and the economic importance of the offending activity. The level of interference that a community as a whole already tolerates and that individual members of it can be expected to tolerate also varies according to local conditions. The defence often advanced is that although interference might have taken place, it was not unreasonable. The standard of reasonable use of adjoining lands in an industrial area might be quite unreasonable and amount to tortious use in a holiday resort area. These questions are difficult to resolve in the context of private litigation. Increasingly, they have become the subject of government regulation through environmental protection legislation or noise and zoning use bylaws. For more information on this topic, see the Companion Website.

CASE 4.2

The defendant trucking company, KJS Transport, had an unpaved (sand and gravel) parking lot. The dust that was generated when trucks moved across the lot created a problem for the neighbouring lighting manufacturer, TMS Lighting. TMS sued KJS for private nuisance. The court found that the interference was substantial because it went on daily for five years—frequency, duration, and degree all pointed to substantialness. The unreasonableness was found in character of the neighbourhood, the sensitivity of the plaintiff's manufacturing business to airborne dust, and the fact that it was entirely resolved once the lot was paved.[12]

False Imprisonment and Malicious Prosecution

A tort that has significant importance to shoplifting in the retail business environment is the tort of **false imprisonment**. False imprisonment consists of intentionally restraining a person, without lawful justification, either by causing his confinement or by preventing him from leaving his location. The Criminal Code gives peace officers broader powers to arrest than private citizens.[13]

false imprisonment unlawfully restraining or confining another person

It is not necessary that there be actual physical restraint, or even the threat that it will be applied: A reasonable fear that a store detective might shout "Stop, thief!" would be enough restraint to amount to an imprisonment. There is a real risk of liability in confronting a member of the public without strong evidence that a crime has actually been committed. For example, the store manager who detained a suspected shoplifter when no

---

[10] *Ryan v. Victoria (City)*, [1999] 1 S.C.R. 201, at para 52.

[11] *Antrim Centre Ltd. v Ontario Transport*, 2011 ONCA 419 aff'd 2013 SCC 13; See also *Smith v. Inco Ltd.*, [2011] O.J. No. 4386 where the Ontario Court of Appeal held that the mere chemical alteration of the soil (increased nickel levels) did not amount to harm.

[12] *TMS Lighting Ltd. v. KJS Transport Inc.*, 2014 ONCA 1.

[13] Criminal Code, R.S.C. 1985 ss. 25, 30-35, 494-95.

shoplifting had in fact occurred might not have a defence against an action for false imprisonment, even if he believed the suspect had stolen goods. **False arrest**, a phrase often used in the same context, ordinarily includes a false imprisonment, but has the additional feature of holding the victim with the intention of turning him over to the police for prosecution. For more information on this topic, see the Companion Website.

Someone who honestly makes a complaint to the police about a suspected crime is not liable for false imprisonment if the suspected criminal is arrested by the police as a result of the complaint, but it later turns out no crime was committed. For example, if a store detective reports a suspected shoplifter to a police officer and the police officer arrests the alleged shoplifter, the store detective is not liable for false imprisonment. It is much safer to report suspicious activities to the police and let them decide whether an arrest is reasonably justified, than to attempt a citizen's arrest. False complaints can attract liability for **malicious prosecution** if there is no honest belief that a crime was committed. The elements of malicious prosecution are (1) unsuccessful charges against the plaintiff (2) initiated by the defendant (3) without reasonable and probable grounds, and (4) with malice or other improper purpose.[14]

Defamation

The torts of **defamation** are better known in their specific forms, **libel** (written defamation) and **slander** (spoken defamation). In both forms, defamation consists of a false or insulting statement that causes injury to the private, professional, or business reputation of another person. In defamation cases, the courts will not award damages unless the plaintiff can demonstrate that the defendant's remarks, taken as a whole, would discredit the plaintiff's reputation in the mind of an ordinary person. Over exaggerations, generalizations, or unbelievable remarks will be less likely to cause injury as the ordinary person would not be influenced by them.[15] Defamation torts require publication—that is, communication of the offending (written or oral) statement to someone other than the person defamed. This can be done electronically on websites or by some hyperlinking sites that repeat or endorse the linked content.[16]

One defence against defamation is that the alleged defamatory statements are true; the onus is on the defendant to prove the truth of the statements. In some circumstances, there is immunity from defamation suits. Words spoken in parliamentary debate, in proceedings in law courts and inquests, and before royal commissions are subject to **absolute privilege**. The aim is to promote candid discussion; as a result, even intentional and malicious falsehoods uttered in Parliament are immune from action in the courts.

In other cases, a **qualified privilege** applies. For example, a person may be asked to disclose information or give an opinion about another person, as in a letter of reference from a former employer or a bank manager. The person supplying the letter would be reluctant to express an honest opinion if he might later have to prove everything he had stated in a court of law. Consequently, the law gives a qualified privilege to anyone giving such information. Provided he gives it in good faith, with an honest belief in its accuracy, he is not liable for defamation even if the statements turn out to be untrue.

Provincial libel and slander legislation[17] give journalists a "fair comment" defence when they have researched and offered a reasonable opinion, honestly believing it to be true.[18] A new defence of **responsible communication on matters of public interest** was

---

false arrest causing a person to be arrested without reasonable cause

malicious prosecution causing a person to be prosecuted for a crime without an honest belief that the crime was committed

defamation making an untrue statement that causes injury to the reputation of another person

libel written defamation

slander spoken defamation

absolute privilege complete immunity from liability for defamation

qualified privilege immunity from liability for defamation provided a statement was made in good faith

responsible communication on matters of public interest a defence to defamation when the publication of the statement is in the public interest and was done responsibly

---

[14] *Miazga v. Kevello Estate*, 2009 SCC 51.

[15] *Bon Malhab v. Diffusion Métromédia CMR Inc.*, 2011 SCC 9.

[16] *Crookes v. Newton*, 2011 SCC 47.

[17] Libel and Slander Act, R.S.O. 1990 c. L-12; Libel and Slander Act, RSBC 1996, c. 263, Alberta Defamation Act, R.S.A. 2000, c. D-7.

[18] *WIC Radio Ltd. v. Simpson*, 2008 S.C.C. 40.

created by the Supreme Court in 2009 and is also most applicable to journalists.[19] This new defence is broader and applies when the matter is of substantial concern to segments of the public and when inclusion of a defamatory statement is important for the fact that it was made, not its truth. For more information on this topic, see the Companion Website.

CASE 4.3 ·

A newspaper published an article describing the opposition of local residents to a proposed private golf course development and included the suspicion of one resident that the developer was exercising political influence to obtain the necessary government approvals. The developer was invited to comment on the story before its publication but did not

do so. The developer sued in defamation and won at trial. The Supreme Court of Canada ordered a new trial, stating that the defences of fair comment and responsible communication on matters of public interest were applicable and should have been considered at trial.

Journalist behaviour could also trigger liability under a relatively new intentional tort called "intrusion on seclusion."[20] Canada's first tort protecting privacy rights imposes liability where there is intentional exposure of private affairs made without lawful justification. This tort is more fully discussed in Chapter 32.

Other Intentional Torts Related to Business

As described in Chapter 3, it is usually the government (not the courts) that sets standards for fair competition. In 2014, the Supreme Court confirmed that "Competition between businesses regularly involves each business taking steps to promote itself at the expense of the other . . . . Far from prohibiting such conduct, the common law seeks to encourage and protect it. The common law recognizes the economic advantages of competition."[21] Therefore, there are only a few economic torts targeting competitive business behaviour and they are given narrow interpretation.

Torts related to carrying on business include unlawful interference with economic relations (below), and inducing breach of contract. Usually if A convinces B to break his contract with C, C will sue B for the breach of contract.[22] However, C may also sue A for the tort of **inducing breach of contract**. As discussed below, this tort is becoming increasingly popular in the employment context, where B may have limited resources as compared to A. C must prove that C and B had a contract and A knew it. A's intentional actions caused B to breach the contract and this caused C damage.[23]

The tort of **unlawful interference with economic relations** also involves three parties. Business A commits an unlawful act against B in order to hurt C's business. B would always have the right to sue A for the unlawful act; this tort also gives C the right to sue. A simple example is if A threatens B with violence if B continues to do business with C. The elements of this tort are both an intention to interfere with C's business and

inducing breach of contract intentionally causing one party to breach his contract with another

unlawful interference with economic relations attempting by threats or other unlawful means to induce one person to discontinue business relations with another

---

[19] *Grant v. Torstar Corp.*, 2009 S.C.C. 61 (the facts are discussed in Case 4.3).

[20] *Jones v. Tsige*, 2012 ONCA 32. See http://www.canadianlawyermag.com/legalfeeds/662/Welcome-to-the-new-tort-of-intrusion-upon-seclusion.html

[21] *AI Enterprises v. Bram*, 2014 SCC 12 at paras 29-31 (citing *OBG Ltd. v. Allan*, [2007] UKHL 21 at para 142).

[22] For examples of actions brought in tort, see *Ernst & Young v. Stuart* (1997), 144 D.L.R. (4th) 328; *Gainers Inc. v. Pocklington Holdings Inc.* (2000), 194 D.L.R. (4th) 109. In certain circumstances, the conduct of the parties may be reviewable under the Competition Act, R.S.C. 1985, c. C-34; see *Harbord Insurance Services Ltd. v. Insurance Corp. of British Columbia* (1993), 9 B.L.R. (2d) 81.

[23] *Johnson v. BFI Canada Inc.*, 2010 MBCA 101 at paras 52 to 54; *Alleslev – Krofchak v. Vlacom Limited*, 2010 ONCA 557, leave to SCC denied 2011 CanLII 19613.

unlawful means used against a third party.[24] Originally, the law in this area was mainly concerned with the activities of labour unions, which now fall within the sphere of labour relations legislation. Now, acts done to influence customers, suppliers, and investors form the basis for many lawsuits.

CASE 4.4

The plaintiff corporation was one of the principal suppliers of car seat covers to Canadian Tire. A marketing company retained by one of its competitors bribed an employee of Canadian Tire to switch suppliers, with the result that the plaintiff lost future business. The Supreme Court of Canada held the marketing company liable for unlawful interference with the plaintiff's economic interests.[25]

---

product defamation making false and damaging statements about the products of another person

A second group of economic torts relates to false advertising in relation to another's products. A person commits the tort of **product defamation** when he intentionally makes false and disparaging statements about the products of another person—for example, a business competitor. A dishonest trader might also try to cash in on an established reputation by passing off his own goods as those of a competitor—for example, by using a similar label or form of packaging. Passing off is considered in Chapter 20. Breaches of copyright and of patent or trademark rights are also forms of tort; they too are dealt with in Chapter 20. Regulatory liability for unfair competition is considered in Chapter 3. For more information on this topic, see the Companion Website.

Ethical Issue   Employee Recruitment

Every employer seeks skilled and experienced employees. Ads are placed and recruitment consultants (also known as headhunters) are hired, all with a view to enticing attractive applicants. The usual result is an employee quitting her current job to join a new employer. In such a case, has the new employer committed the tort of inducing breach of contract? No—provided the employee gave the current employer proper notice, no tort has been committed. However, liability could attach if the new employer encourages the employee to ignore notice or other contractual obligations.

Recent focus has been on confidentiality obligations. It is common for employers to include confidentiality requirements in employment contracts. If an employee leaves to join a competitor, the former employer may be concerned that the employee will breach the confidentiality agreement. In addition to suing the employee, it is becoming common to sue the competitor for inducing breach of contract.[26]

An alternative strategy for employers is to agree not to poach executives from each other, invoking a no-hire policy. One such alleged agreement between Google, Apple, and other Silicon Valley giants has triggered a U.S. class action from 64 000 employees, as well as a U.S. government investigation into anti-competitive behaviour.

Question to Consider

1. How can an employer hire experienced employees without being accused of inducing breach of contract?

2. What are the competing ethical values involved in changing jobs?

Sources: Scott Deveau, "Rivals CP Rail and CN Rail Forge executive poaching accord," *Financial Post*, February 4, 2013; *In Re: High-Tech Employee Anti-Trust Litigation*, US District Court, N. Cal. Case No.: - CV-2509-LHK (Oct. 24, 2013) leave to appeal denied, U.S. Court of Appeal, 9th Cir, Jan. 14, 2014.

---

[24] *A.I. Enterprises Ltd., supra* n. 21, at para 23, 28; *1175777 Ontario Ltd. v. Magna International Inc.* (2001), 200 D.L.R. (4th) 521.

[25] *671122 Ontario Ltd. v. Sagaz Industries Canada Inc., supra*, n. 9. The competitor was held not to be vicariously liable, since the marketing company acted as an independent contractor.

[26] In 2003, BellSouth and Cingular Wireless sued Sprint for luring vice-chairman Gary Forsee to Sprint. They obtained a temporary injunction blocking Mr. Forsee's move to Sprint. Ultimately, Mr. Forsee was allowed to join Sprint subject to restrictions on the activities he could undertake.

UNINTENTIONAL TORTS

The second type of tort is an unintentional tort. Unintentional torts involve behaviour that is not done deliberately or on purpose. The incident happens unexpectedly, by mistake or accident. It follows that the resulting harm is also unintentional.

Negligence

By far the most common basis for legal actions in tort, and the one that best illustrates the fault theory of liability, is the unintentional tort of negligence. The concept of **negligence** is quite simple: Anyone who carelessly causes injury to another should compensate the victim for that injury. Negligence is a flexible tort that covers a wide variety of situations. For more information on this topic, see the Companion Website.

negligence the careless causing of injury to the person or property of another

Elements of Proof

Four requirements must be proven by the plaintiff to succeed in a negligence cause of action.[27] The first element concerns the identity of the plaintiff—should the defendant have been aware of the risk of harm to this victim? The second element relates to the behaviour of the defendant—did the defendant's conduct fall below the standard of behaviour required in the circumstances? The third and fourth elements involve what harm was suffered and whether the defendant's conduct "caused" the plaintiff's "injury."

CHECKLIST

Elements of a Negligence Action

In establishing the right to recover compensation for negligence, a plaintiff must prove four things:

1. The defendant owed the plaintiff a duty of care.
2. The defendant breached the required standard of care.
3. The plaintiff suffered injury or damage.
4. The defendant's conduct caused the plaintiff's damage.

---

1. Duty of Care In order to establish liability in negligence, a plaintiff must establish that a **duty of care** is owed to her by the defendant. Duty focuses on the relationship between the parties.

duty of care a relationship so close that one could reasonably foresee causing harm to the other

There is no finite list of situations when a duty of care exists, although courts have long recognized that a duty is owed by a doctor to a patient or a motor vehicle driver to a pedestrian. Whether a person owes a duty of care in particular circumstances is determined in two steps.

First, the closeness of the relationship between the plaintiff and defendant is examined to see if it was reasonably foreseeable that the plaintiff's conduct would cause harm to the defendant.[28] The parties must have a direct or connecting link to each other—this is known as proximity. As well, since the defendant cannot be expected to anticipate all the possible consequences of his actions, the duty will arise only where an ordinary person, sometimes called "the reasonable man," in the defendant's position would have foreseen a risk of harm

---

[27] *Mustapha v. Culligan*, 2008 SCC 27 at para 8.

[28] *Childs v. Desormeaux*, 2006 SCC 18 at para 47; *Hill v. Hamilton-Wentworth Regional Police*, 2007 SCC 47 at para 20; *Fullowka v. Pinkerton's of Canada*, 2010 SCC 5 at para 18.

to the plaintiff or to someone in the plaintiff's position. The key words are *proximity* (meaning "closeness") and *foreseeablility* (meaning "predictability").

The Province of British Columbia hired a courier to deliver an envelope to a land registry office in Prince George. Unknown to the courier company, the envelope contained a document relating to land owned by the plaintiff. If delivered on time, the document would have enabled the plaintiff to complete the sale of its land. The courier company was unreasonably slow and delivered the document too late. As a result, the plaintiff was unable to perform the contract of sale, and it suffered a loss of $77 000.

The Supreme Court of Canada held that the courier company was not liable to the plaintiff. It owed no duty of care to the plaintiff since it could not reasonably have foreseen that the delay would cause a loss to some third person outside its relationship with its client, the Province.[29]

The courts have sometimes held that a duty of care is owed to persons other than the individual who is directly injured. For example, a negligent driver was held to be liable to a parent who suffered severe nervous shock when she saw her child, who was standing nearby, run down and killed.[30] In that case, the court considered the parent's injury to be foreseeable.

The second step considers policy concerns. If both proximity and foreseeability exist, then a duty of care is owed unless there are policy reasons that justify reducing or removing it.

The Supreme Court of Canada summarized the test for duty of care in one sentence: "Whether such a relationship exists depends on foreseeability, moderated by policy concerns."[31] Policy concerns consider the effect that recognizing a duty of care will have on other legal obligations, the legal system, and society more generally.[32] Concerns include such things as the increase in lawsuits or the ability to insure against a huge new potential legal risk.

Over time, more and more duties have been imposed by statute, especially upon the operators of businesses—as discussed in Chapter 3. Breach of these duties may give rise to liability in tort to persons who are injured as a result. The courts will hold public bodies liable for the negligent performance of their statutory duties. Municipalities have been held liable to homeowners for issuing building permits for defective designs or for not carrying out proper inspections of construction works.[33] A public body may be liable even where the statute imposes no duty but merely confers a discretionary power on it—for example, to maintain a highway—if it is negligent in the exercise of that power.[34] Government often relies on the second step, relating to policy concern, to argue that a duty should not be imposed on it. The courts will normally not interfere with policy decisions taken by the appropriate body, but once a policy decision has been made (for example, to guard against rock falls onto a highway), the body will be liable if it is negligent in carrying out that policy.[35]

---

[29] *B.D.C. Ltd. v. Hofstrand Farms Ltd.* (1986), 26 D.L.R. (4th) 1. For a recent example see *Esser v. Luoma* (2004), 242 D.L.R. (4th) 112.

[30] *Hinz v. Berry*, [1970] 1 All E.R. 1074. Contrast with *Schlink v. Blackburn* (1993), 18 C.C.L.T. (2d) 173, where the plaintiff was at home, asleep in bed, when his wife was injured in a motor accident; his nervous shock occurred some time later when he was told of the accident.

[31] *Mustapha v. Culligan of Canada Ltd.*, [2008] 2 S.C.R. 114, 2008 SCC 27 at para. 4, relying on the seminal case of *Anns v. Merton London Borough Council*, [1978] A.C. 728 (H.L.).

[32] *Cooper v. Hobart*, [2001] 3 S.C.R. 537.

[33] *City of Kamloops v. Nielsen*, [1984] 2 S.C.R. 2; *Rothfield v. Manolakos* (1989), 63 D.L.R. (4th) 449.

[34] *Rausch v. Pickering (City)*, 2013 ONCA 740.

[35] *R. v. Imperial Tobacco Canada Ltd.*, 2011 SCC 42.

CASE 4.6(i)

G was injured when an electrical power line came loose and struck her car while she was driving under an overpass on a busy multi-lane controlled-access highway. The public utility company was stringing new wires across the overpass. The Ontario Court of Appeal held that the public utility owed a duty of care to G because "it was reasonably foreseeable that a careless act by the appellant in its work along the overpass above the highway could result in injury to users of the highway and there were no policy considerations to negative or limit the duty."[36]

2. Standard of Care The **standard of care** focuses on the behaviour of the defendant. The defendant's conduct is compared to the level of care that a person should take in the circumstances. If the defendant's conduct falls short of that required of the reasonable person in equivalent circumstances, he has breached the standard of care.

standard of care the level of care that a person must take in the circumstances

The law places a general duty on every person to take reasonable care to avoid causing foreseeable injury to other persons and their property. It is often said that the standard demanded is that of the ordinary reasonable person, or "the person on the Yonge Street subway."[37] However, the standard of care necessarily varies according to the activity and person in question: The standard expected of a brain surgeon when operating is that of a competent brain surgeon rather than that of the person in the subway.

The risk of harm and feasibility of eliminating it are considerations in setting the standard— a defendant need not take "all" care, only "reasonable" care. It may not be practical to take every possible precaution where the risk of serious damage or injury is small, but where there is danger of a major catastrophe, it would be unreasonable not to take every known precaution.

CASE 4.6(ii)

In Case 4.6(i), the evidence showed that the electrical wires fell because vandals visited the unattended job site during a lunch break and released the security ropes. G claimed that the public utility company fell below the standard of care by failing to take reasonable steps to secure the wires and the site. The trial judge agreed, but the Court of Appeal held that the company's conduct did not fall below the standard of care. The method of security had been used for years without incident. Vandalism occurred in broad daylight on a frequently travelled road. The workers had never encountered vandalism in their combined 60 years of work experience. Given the unlikely prospect of vandalism during a short daylight absence from the site, the method of security used was sufficient to satisfy the standard of care.[38]

Failure to strictly comply with the Electrical Utilities Safety Association Manual did not amount to a breach of the standard of care in the circumstances.

Normally, when legislation describes the appropriate standard of care for particular activities, it will almost always be considered the lowest acceptable standard of care. For example, the safety standards for the food industry are prescribed by statute, and those standards are frequently a good indication of where a court will set the negligence threshold. However in rare cases such as Case 4.6(ii), a breach of a statutory standard does not of itself make the defendant civilly liable to a person injured as a result of the breach.[39]

3. Damage to the Plaintiff Damage focuses on the type of harm or injury actually suffered by the plaintiff. Damage or loss is always a requirement of tort liability, as compensation for loss is its goal. In this way tort liability is reactive, not preventative. Harm can take the form of personal injury including physical or mental injury, property damage to the

---

[36] *Garratt et al. v. Orillia Power Distribution Corporation* (2008), 90 O.R. (3d) 161, 171 (although a duty of care was owed, the defendant's behaviour did not fall below the standard of care).

[37] Linden, *Canadian Tort Law, supra,* n. 2, at 126–7.

[38] *Garratt et al. v. Orillia Power Distribution Corporation, supra,* n. 36, at 174.

[39] *R. v. Saskatchewan Wheat Pool,* [1983] 1 S.C.R. 205; *El Dali v. Panjalingham,* 2013 ONCA 24.

land or goods of the plaintiff, and sometimes purely economic loss including loss of value or profit. It must be actually sustained, not hypothetical.

4. Causation of Damage Causation focuses on the strength of the connection between the harm suffered and the behaviour of the defendant. An extremely broad factual view of **causation** can link one act to every other act in the world. The test for legal causation is much narrower.

The basic test is known as the "but for" test—the plaintiff must show that "but for" the negligent conduct of the defendant, the injury would not have occurred.[40] No matter how blameworthy a person's conduct might be, he will not be held liable for damage that he did not cause. In a recent medical negligence case involving a baby born with brain damage, the Supreme Court of Canada found that the slow reaction times of a nurse and doctor fell below the standard of care but this was not the cause of the damage; even if the need for cesarean birth had been identified earlier, the baby would still have been born with brain damage and so the nurse and doctor were not liable.[41]

Sometime the "but for' test establishes that multiple defendants each caused or contributed to damage to the plaintiff and both will be held liable and damages apportioned between them.[42]

CASE 4.7

A bar owner allowed a customer to drink too much and then threw the customer out to walk home along a country road, where he was hit by a careless motorist. Both the bar owner and the motorist were held to have contributed to the cause of accident and therefore the customer's injury.[43]

Other times, the involvement of multiple defendants hinders the identification of the precise cause of the damage. In exceptional circumstances, when the "but for" test cannot establish causation for reasons beyond the control of the victim, the court may use a "material contribution" test. This test finds causation when the type of injury suffered is that for which the behaviour of the defendant created an unreasonable risk. Imagine that two hunters carelessly fire shots at the victim and it is unclear which shooter caused the injury. The material contribution (rather than the "but for" test) would allow liability to be assigned to both shooters.[44]

Remoteness of Damage All damage resulting directly from the negligent act will not necessarily be compensated. Even when a person is considered to have factually caused the injury, he may not be considered to have legally caused the injury if it is too **remote**. The type of damage must be reasonably foreseeable. Unusual or extreme reactions will be considered too remote.

"Reasonably foreseeable" has been defined as a real risk: "one which would occur to the mind of a reasonable man in the position of the defendant . . . which he would not brush

---

[40] *Resurfice Corp. v. Hanke*, [2007] 1 S.C.R. 333, 2007 SCC 7, paras. 18–29.

[41] *Cojocaru v. British Columbia Women's Hospital and Health Centre*, 2013 SCC 30 at paras. 110-15. See also *Ediger v. Johnston*, 2013 SCC 18.

[42] See for example Negligence Act, R.S.B.C 1996, c. 333; R.S.O. 1990, c.N-1. *Economy Foods & Hardware Ltd. v. Klassen* (2001), 196 D.L.R. (4th) 413, a fire was caused by the negligence of one defendant but spread, causing additional damage, due to the failure of the second defendant to install an adequate system of sprinklers.

[43] *Menow v. Honsberger and Jordan House Ltd.*, [1974] S.C.R. 239. See also *Murphy v. Little Memphis Cabaret Inc.* (1998), 167 D.L.R. (4th) 190; *Renaissance Leisure Group Inc. v. Frazer* (2004), 242 D.L.R. (4th) 229. By contrast, the Supreme Court of Canada held that a restaurant serving alcohol to a party of people, knowing that they had arrived by car, owed a duty to the driver and passengers, but since some members of the party were not drinking, it was entitled to assume that a non-drinker would be driving; consequently, it was not responsible for the accident: *Mayfield Investments Ltd. v. Stewart* (1995), 121 D.L.R. (4th) 222. So far, "social hosts" (for example, at a private party) have not been held liable in the same way as "commercial hosts": see *Childs v. Desormeaux, supra*, n. 28.

[44] *Resurfice Corp, supra*, n. 40, at para 27.

aside as far-fetched."[45] A court undertakes an objective assessment of what a reasonable defendant would foresee as likely injury to the average defendant. The damage is considered from the perspective of the "normal" victim—a person of "ordinary fortitude." It is not based on the actual circumstances of the particular plaintiff.

CASE 4.8

A consumer saw a dead fly in a bottle of water as he replaced a canister in his home. The observation was so upsetting that he developed serious mental disorders including anxiety and phobias. The trial judge found that the mental injuries were caused by the incident and awarded damages of approximately $340 000. The judgment was overturned by the Court of Appeal and leave to the Supreme Court of Canada was granted. The Supreme Court did not interfere with the trial judge's finding that the mental illness was caused by the incident, but found that mental illness was not a reasonably foreseeable type of damage in the circumstances. The average person would not suffer a mental disorder as a result of seeing a fly in a water bottle. This was an extreme reaction by a plaintiff with particular vulnerabilities. The same reaction would not be expected in a person of ordinary fortitude. The plaintiff could not recover because the damage was too remote.[46]

The "reasonable foreseeability test" referred to in Case 4.8 should not be confused with the legal doctrine of "thin skull" or "egg shell" plaintiff, which requires a defendant to take the victim as he or she finds him:

> The law of negligence . . . draws the line for compensability of damage, not at perfection, but at reasonable foreseeability. Once a plaintiff establishes the foreseeability that a mental injury would occur in a person of ordinary fortitude . . . the defendant must take the plaintiff as it finds him for the purpose of [quantifying] damages.[47]

The thin skull doctrine allows the injured plaintiff to recover all of his damages even though they may be much greater than an ordinary plaintiff would have suffered. If the type of damage is considered reasonably foreseeable, the court will compensate the victim for his actual damage. When a teenager negligently started his father's snowmobile, which escaped from his control, crossed a schoolyard, and collided with a gas pipe just outside the school causing gas to escape into the school and explode, he was held liable for all the resulting damage. The damage was considered to be of a general type that might reasonably have been foreseen even if the actual extent of the damage was unusually high.[48]

Defences to Negligence: The Plaintiff's Own Conduct

A defendant may dispute any of the evidence the plaintiff produces on duty of care, breach of the standard of care, damage, and causation. In addition, he or she may allege that the plaintiff's own conduct or that of another defendant provides a partial or full defence to negligence. The courts at one time took a rather narrow and mechanical approach to this issue. If the defendant could establish that the plaintiff contributed in any way to her own loss, the plaintiff would fail, even if the defendant was mainly at fault. The harshness of the **contributory negligence** rule was changed by legislation pioneered in Canada.[49] These statutes required courts to apportion damages according to the respective degree of

contributory negligence a partial defence to a negligence action when the plaintiff's or another defendant's conduct also contributed to the injury

---

[45] *Overseas Tankship (U.K.) Ltd. v. Miller Steamship Co. Pty. Ltd.* (The Wagon Mound No. 2), [1967] A.C. 617 at p. 643; *Hughes v. Lord Advocate*, [1963] A.C. 837.

[46] *Mustapha v. Culligan, supra,* n. 31.

[47] *Ibid.,* at para. 16.

[48] *Hoffer v. School Division of Assiniboine South,* [1973] W.W.R. 765 (S.C.C.). The father and the gas company that installed the pipe were also held liable.

[49] Ontario passed the first statute in the field: Negligence Act, S.O. 1924, c. 32.

responsibility of all of the parties. The statutes do not set out in detail the basis for making the apportionment, but leave it to be decided by judges and juries according to their opinion of what is fair in the circumstances.

CASE 4.9

The plaintiff, a passenger in a truck, was injured when the driver failed to negotiate a sharp curve on a rural access road. The plaintiff had been aware that the driver had been drinking when he accepted the lift. The trial judge held the plaintiff 15 percent to blame; the driver 50 percent, for driving too fast and while impaired; and the municipality 35 percent, for not having erected a sign warning of the dangerous bend.[50]

By applying an appropriate standard of care to the plaintiff as well as to the defendants, the courts have also taken account of changing social standards. For example, it is now common to find that a person injured in a motor vehicle accident has contributed to some extent to her own injuries by failure to wear a seat belt.[51]

Another partial defence arises after the injury has occurred. Every plaintiff must act quickly and reasonably to repair or heal their injury. Even when the victim is not to blame for the accident itself, her own post-injury conduct may contribute to the extent or seriousness of her original injuries—for example, where a plaintiff refuses to undergo safe and simple surgery or refuses to accept blood transfusions,[52] and worsens her condition. In some cases, the courts have decided that part of the damages were due to the plaintiff's unreasonable conduct and were therefore not recoverable.[53] This is because the plaintiff's own conduct has contributed to or increased the seriousness of the injury. It may also be regarded as an application of the principle that a plaintiff is expected to act reasonably to minimize, or **mitigate**, any damage suffered. This principle is discussed further, in the context of contract law, in Chapter 13.

mitigate duty to act reasonably and quickly to minimize the extent of damage suffered

voluntary assumption of risk a defence to a negligence action when the plaintiff was aware of the risk and continued with the activity anyway

Voluntary assumption of risk is a complete defence to a negligence action and is available to a defendant when the plaintiff was aware of the risk of harm prior to undertaking the activity and consented to it. Sometimes the defendant knows damage may occur and advises the plaintiff. We have all seen a "slippery when wet" sign after floors have been washed. If, after being fully advised of the risk or danger associated with the behaviour, the plaintiff continues the behaviour and is injured in the predicted way, the defendant will not be found liable since the plaintiff voluntarily assumed the risk. This is the legal risk management strategy underlying the use of medical consent forms advising patients of the risk of surgery prior to an operation. The challenge is that the exact risk must be described or the defence is not applicable.

The Relevance of Insurance

In many tort cases, the defendant has insurance that will cover the loss. In the case of property damage, for example, both plaintiff and defendant are normally insured. When an insured party recovers first from her insurance company, her right to claim against the wrongdoer passes to the insurance company. It "stands in the insured person's shoes"—that is, it undergoes **subrogation** to the insured party's rights and may sue the defendant and

subrogation where one person becomes entitled to the rights and claims of another

---

[50] The Supreme Court of Canada upheld the trial judge's determination: *Housen v. Nikolaisen* (2002), 211 D.L.R. (4th) 577.

[51] A driver of a vehicle may be held negligent for failure to ensure that a child passenger is wearing a seat belt: *Galaske v. O'Donnell* (1994), 112 D.L.R. (4th) 109 (S.C.C.); see also *Heller v. Martens* (2002), 213 D.L.R. (4th) 124.

[52] *Hobbs v. Robertson* (2004), 243 D.L.R. (4th) 700.

[53] See *Janiak v. Ippolito* (1985), 16 D.L.R. (4th) 1 (S.C.C.).

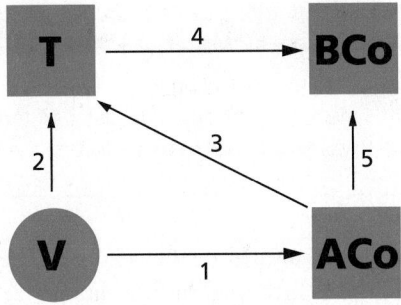

Figure 4.2 Insurance

Victim V is injured in an accident, caused by the negligence of tortfeasor T. V is insured by ACo, and T by BCo. V may claim under her policy with ACo [1], or may sue T [2]. If V claims under her policy, ACo may bring proceedings (in V's name) against T [3]. T could then claim under his policy with BCo [4]. Alternatively, ACo might settle with BCo [5].

collect (see Figure 4.2). Similarly if V recovers her loss, or part of it, by suing T, then to that extent she cannot afterward recover from her own insurance company.

In practice, it is normally simpler for V to recover under her insurance policy, leaving the company to decide whether or not to sue T. One reason is that, under the policy, V may be entitled to recover the full extent of her loss, even though she might have been partly at fault. If she sued T, the damages might be reduced on account of her own contributory negligence. Another reason is that T might have insufficient funds to pay the claim. If T also has insurance, the two insurance companies may settle the question of payment between themselves, without resorting to expensive litigation. However, just as often, the two insurance companies litigate the action in the names of their insureds. For more information on this topic, see the Companion Website.

PRODUCT LIABILITY

One of the most important business law torts involves the liability of manufacturers for injury or loss caused by defects in their products: **product liability**. This tort is a form of negligence customized to the manufacturing context. Consider who should bear the loss in each of the following four illustrations below.

product liability a negligence tort imposing liability on manufacturers for harm caused by defective products

---

ILLUSTRATION 4.2

X runs a small refreshment booth at a beach and buys his supplies from Y Bottling Co. Ltd. He sells a dark-green bottle of ginger ale to A, who gives it to her friend, B. B drinks half the contents and becomes violently ill. The balance is found to contain a decomposed snail. B is hospitalized and is unable to return to work for several weeks.

ILLUSTRATION 4.3

P buys a Q Company sports car from Dealer R. On being driven away from the showroom, the car loses a defective front wheel and collides with a parked vehicle, injuring the occupant, S.

ILLUSTRATION 4.4

M buys from the N Ski Shop a set of thermal underwear manufactured by O Company. The underwear contains a toxic acid, which when it comes in contact with perspiration causes M to have a severe skin burn.

ILLUSTRATION 4.5

J buys a bottle of cough medicine, manufactured by the K Company, from her local drugstore. To try to get rid of her cold, she drinks two stiff whiskies, takes a dose of the medicine, and goes to bed. During the night she has a heart attack. The cough medicine is extremely dangerous if taken with alcohol, but there was no warning to that effect on the bottle or package.

A buyer of defective goods may always sue the vendor for breach of contract. However, the buyer may not always be the injured user. In Illustration 4.2, X sold the soft drink to A rather than to B, the injured party: There was no contract with B. Similarly, in Illustration 4.3, the injured person, S, has no contractual relationship with Dealer R. In these circumstances, contractual remedies are not available. The tort of product liability fills this gap. (See Figure 4.3.) Product liability incorporates (with some modification) the familiar elements of negligence—duty of care, breach of the standard of care, and causation of damage.

In 1932, the British House of Lords recognized that manufacturers owe a duty of care to the ultimate consumers of their products in the famous case of *Donoghue v. Stevenson*,[54] in a situation similar to Illustration 4.2. The situation in Illustration 4.3 is drawn in part from the 1916 United States case *MacPherson v. Buick Motor Co.*,[55] also recognizing a manufacturer's duty owed to the ultimate user.

In the years since *Donoghue v. Stevenson*, its principle has been applied by the courts in a wide variety of circumstances to protect consumers and other members of the public. The complexity and sophistication of modern manufactured products makes it increasingly difficult for consumers and distributors to detect dangers in those products, and places manufacturers in a position of growing responsibility for the safety of consumers. In Case 4.8, dealing with the fly in the water bottle, the Supreme Court of Canada declared that it is well established that a manufacturer of consumable goods owes a duty of care to the ultimate consumer.[56] This duty also extends to other businesses in the chain of distribution.[57]

Holding that manufacturers owe a duty of care to consumers and others who might be injured is only a first step to imposing liability. Normally, an injured party will find it difficult to prove that the manufacturer fell below the standard of care and was negligent. However, if the product is defective, then it may be reasonable to infer that there has been negligence in some stage of its design, production, or inspection, unless there is evidence of some other

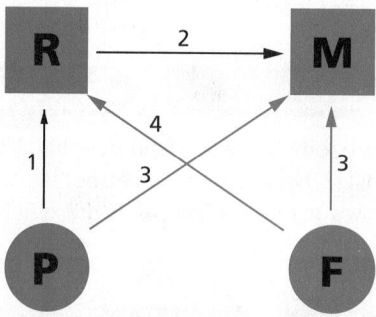

Figure 4.3 Product Liability

Manufacturer M sells a product to retailer R, which sells it to purchaser P. The product is defective and P and her friend F are injured. P can sue R in contract [1], and R can sue M for its loss, also in contract [2]. P and F can only sue M in tort [3]. F might also be able to sue R in tort, if R should have discovered the defect.

[54] [1932] A.C. 562.

[55] 111 N.E. 1050 (1916).

[56] *Mustapha v. Culligan*, *supra*, n. 31 at para. 6.

[57] New Brunswick has made this duty abundantly clear by codifying it in the Consumer Product Warranty and Liability Act, S.N.B. 1978, c. C-18.1.

reason for the defect. This **circumstantial evidence principle** (discussed below) can be applied so that the manufacturer may be found liable. It will be up to the manufacturer to show that the cause of the defect was not something for which it should be held responsible, or at least that it had taken all reasonable precautions to prevent defective goods from reaching the distribution system.[58] For more information on this topic, see the Companion Website.

circumstantial evidence principle
a prima facie case of negligence may be established by drawing reasonable inferences from the circumstances surrounding the product manufacture and failure

Proving Breach of the Standard of Care

In Canada, manufacturers are not held strictly liable for all damage caused by their products, only those defects arising from some preventable and foreseeable flaw in the product or manufacturing process. In product liability cases, the plaintiff may not have direct evidence on how the defect occurred. The product may be destroyed or the process confidential. The law takes these difficulties of proof into account. A plaintiff may initially meet his burden of proof using circumstantial evidence from which manufacturer's negligence can be inferred. Rather than identifying exactly how the manufacturer fell below the standard of care, the plaintiff need only prove that the uncharacteristic malfunction of the product is the most likely cause of his injury and that a substandard manufacturing process is the most likely reason for the malfunction. The existence of a recall notice will help with this inference. Thereafter, it will be up to the defendant to show that it was not at fault. The manufacturer will be found liable unless it produces evidence to satisfy the court that, on balance, it was not at fault and met the standard of care when producing the product.[59]

In Illustration 4.4, based on the leading case of *Grant v. Australian Knitting Mills*,[60] the manufacturing company was placed in the following dilemma: If the inspection process permitted the underwear to pass through undetected, the system was inadequate and the company was therefore negligent. If the inspection process was virtually foolproof, as the manufacturer claimed, then one of its employees must have been personally at fault, making the manufacturer vicariously liable. The court held that the plaintiff "need not lay his finger on the exact person in all the chain who was responsible or to specify what he did wrong. Negligence is found on a matter of inference form the existence of defects taken in connection with all the known circumstances."[61] Manufacturers who choose to reduce costs by omitting necessary safety features or by adopting quality control processes that are below prevailing industry standards will have difficulty rebutting the inference of negligence. In the long run, the savings in production cost may be outweighed by increased insurance premiums for product liability.

Inherently Dangerous Products

Illustration 4.5 is an example of the expansion of manufacturers' negligence to include properly produced but inherently dangerous products. Even though a product is not defective in any way, harm might be caused if the product is not used appropriately. Courts have ruled that manufacturers owe a duty to consumers to give proper warning of known dangers or dangers they ought to have known.[62] In some industries, government regulations dictate

---

[58] United States courts have gone further. They tend to favour a principle of strict liability under which the manufacturer impliedly warrants its products to be free of defects regardless of negligence. However, the end result is probably not very different.

[59] *Johansson v. General Motors of Canada Ltd.*, 2012 NSCA 120.

[60] [1936] A.C. 85.

[61] *Johansson, supra*, n. 59 at para. 81 (citing *Grant, Ibid.*, at p. 101).

[62] *Lambert v. Lastoplex Chemical Co. Ltd.*, [1972] S.C.R. 569 (inflammable lacquer); *Buchan v. Ortho Pharmaceutical (Canada) Ltd.* (1984), 28 C.C.L.T. 233 (Ont.) (side effects of contraceptive pills); *Plas-Tex Canada Ltd. v. Dow Chemical of Canada Ltd.*, 2004 ABCA 309 (defective resin). The duty to warn may be excluded by an express contractual provision; see *Bow Valley Husky (Bermuda) Ltd. v. Saint John Shipbuilding Ltd.* (1997), 153 D.L.R. (4th) 385 (S.C.C.). For an interesting analysis of the duty to warn see D.W. Boivin, "Factual Causation in the Law of Manufacturer—Failure to Warn" (1998–99) 30 Ottawa Law Rev. 47.

the type of warning that must be given, thereby establishing a standard of care that must be met. In other industries, the appropriateness of the warning will vary depending on the anticipated user group of the product. Consider children's toys as opposed to cleaning products—the appropriate placement, language, size, and symbols of the warning will be very different for these products.

The **duty to warn** is a continuing one, owed to consumers of the product. If, after a product has been placed on the market, the manufacturer becomes aware of potential dangers in its use, it must issue appropriate warnings to the public.[63] Sometimes, however, the duty may be met by issuing the warning to a "learned intermediary." In *Hollis v. Dow Corning Corp.*,[64] the Supreme Court of Canada considered that the warning of the dangers of silicone breast implants should have been given to the physicians who would perform the implant operation. Had this been done, a direct warning to the public might not have been necessary.[65] We are all familiar with the warnings associated with prescription drugs, now delivered not only to the dispensing pharmacist but also to the consumer through television advertisements.

A plaintiff whose claim is based on a breach of the duty to warn must show not only that the duty was owed and that the warning was deficient but also that, had a proper warning been given, she would not have used the product or would not have used it in the way she did—that is, the failure to warn influenced her behaviour, which caused the injury.[66] If a user continues in the behaviour after being warned of the risks, he has voluntarily assumed the risk and the manufacturer will not be liable.

duty to warn manufacturer's responsibility to make users aware of the risks associated with the use or misuse of the product

---

INTERNATIONAL ISSUE

Tobacco Litigation

Tobacco is the most infamous inherently dangerous product of our time. Huge damage awards against U.S. tobacco manufacturers have received a lot of publicity. Individual smokers who have become ill as a result of smoking have received large sums in compensation. In July 2000, in Florida, for example, a court awarded US $145 billion in punitive damages in a duty-to-warn class action on behalf of 700 000 smokers and former smokers. Two years later, a Los Angeles court awarded US $28 billion in punitive damages to a single plaintiff (though this was reduced on appeal to a mere US $28 million). State governments have also launched proceedings to recover the extra health-care costs that they have incurred in treating tobacco-related illnesses. In 1998, a settlement was reached under which the major tobacco companies

agreed to pay a group of states a total of US $246 billion over a 25-year period.

Tobacco litigation in Canada is a more recent development. Claims for compensation have been brought both by individuals[67] and in the form of class actions.[68]

Canadian governments have also joined in the action. The federal government brought an action to recover health-care costs in New York State, presumably in the expectation of obtaining much larger damages than a Canadian court was likely to award. The action was dismissed on a technicality, having cost the government about $13 million in legal fees. Meanwhile, British Columbia passed a statute specifically entitling the government to recover health-care costs.[69] The first statute was declared unconstitutional by

>

---

[63] *Nicholson v. John Deere Ltd.* (1989), 57 D.L.R. (4th) 639.

[64] (1995), 129 D.L.R. (4th) 609.

[65] The physician might then be liable if he operated without explaining the risk to the patient; this is discussed in Chapter 5.

[66] In *Hollis v. Dow Corning Corp.*, *supra*, n. 60, the Supreme Court of Canada preferred a subjective approach to causation in product liability cases; would the plaintiff have used the product if she had known of the risk? See also *Arndt v. Smith* (1997), 148 D.L.R. (4th) 48 (S.C.C.).

[67] See *McIntyre Estate v. Ontario* (2003), 218 D.L.R. (4th) 193. That case is notable in that the Ontario Court of Appeal permitted the action to be brought on a contingency-fee basis.

[68] *Caputo v. Imperial Tobacco Limited* (2004), 236 D.L.R. (4th) 348. The action was dismissed for failure to establish an identifiable class.

[69] Tobacco Damages and Health Care Costs Recovery Act, S.B.C. 1998, c. 45.

the B.C. Supreme Court.[70] A replacement statute was promptly enacted[71] and declared constitutional by the Supreme Court of Canada.[72] In the federal government's latest health cost recovery litigation, the Supreme Court of Canada had to decide if the federal government could be held liable for failure to warn consumers about the dangers of "light" cigarettes and whether it could be considered a "manufacturer" for its role in developing and promoting light cigarettes. The answer was no.[73]

Questions to Consider

1. Should individual smokers be compensated for smoking-related illnesses? How can one prove the illness was caused by smoking? Are today's smokers responsible for their own misfortunes? Should they be held contributorily negligent?

2. What is the basis for the claims to recover health-care costs? Should governments that have permitted the sale of cigarettes, knowing the health risks, and that have collected vast amounts of tax on their sale, be entitled to compensation for the costs of providing health care?

3. Is it appropriate for a government to enact a statute for the specific purpose of allowing it to bring a claim? Is that a form of retroactive legislation?

(For an interesting review of these issues relating to tobacco liability, see G. Edinger, "The Tobacco Damages and Health Care Costs Recovery Act" [2001] 35 *Canadian Business Law Journal* 95.)

OCCUPIER'S LIABILITY

Another important business law tort evolving from negligence addresses the liability of occupants for injury or loss suffered by visitors to their premises. Again this tort involves the four elements of negligence: duty of care, breach of standard of care and causation of damage to the plaintiff. However, in the context of "property" negligence, issues arise, such as: to whom is a duty of care owed? What standard must an owner or occupier of land[74] meet?

The common law first developed the tort of **occupier's liability** to address any negligence of land owners and occupants; subsequently, provincial occupier's liability legislation has refined the rules. Initially distinctions were made among three different categories or types of visitors to whom a duty could be owed—invitees, licensees, and trespassers—and the standard of care owed was different for each type of visitor. The highest duty was owed to an **invitee**—that is, a person permitted by the occupier to enter for business purposes (for example, a shopper). The duty owed by an occupier to an invitee is to take care to prevent injuries from hazards or dangers of which the occupier is aware and also those of which, as a reasonable person, he ought to be aware. By contrast, the duty owed to a **licensee**—any other visitor entering with the express or implied permission of the occupier—was simply to remove concealed dangers of which the occupier had actual knowledge.

The distinction between invitee and licensee has been abolished by statute in most Canadian provinces,[75] and the same duty of care is now owed by an occupier to all expected

occupier's liability a negligence tort imposing liability on occupants of land for harm suffered by visitors to the property

invitee a person permitted by an occupier to enter premises for business purposes

licensee a visitor (other than an invitee) who enters premises with the consent of the occupier

---

[70] *JTI-Macdonald Corp. v. British Columbia* (2000), 184 D.L.R. (4th) 335.

[71] Tobacco Damages and Health Care Costs Recovery Act, S.B.C. 2000, c. 30. The government of Newfoundland and Labrador has enacted a similar statute: Tobacco Health Care Costs Recovery Act, S.N.L. 2001, c. T-4.2.

[72] *British Columbia v. Imperial Tobacco Canada Ltd.*, [2005] 2 S.C.R. 473, 2005 SCC 49.

[73] *R. v. Imperial Tobacco Canada Ltd.*, 2011 SCC 42.

[74] An owner is not necessarily the "occupier" for the purposes of the legislation. In *Beheyt v. Chrupalo* (2004), 244 D.L.R. (4th) 688, the owners' daughter had taken full responsibility for the premises for the previous eight years, and was the landlord of the plaintiff and the person responsible under the Occupier's Liability Act.

[75] For example, R.S.A. 2000, c. O-4, s. 5; R.S.B.C. 1996, c. 337, s. 3; R.S.M. 1987, c. O-8; S.N.S. 1996, c. 27; R.S.O. 1990, c. O.2, s. 1(a). In Newfoundland and Labrador, much the same result has been achieved through the courts by "restating" the common law to the effect that an occupier now owes a duty to all lawful visitors to take reasonable care: see *Gallant v. Roman Catholic Episcopal Corp. for Labrador* (2001), 200 D.L.R. (4th) 643.

visitors lawfully on the premises. The occupier must take care to prevent harm from hazards or dangers that he is aware of or should have been aware of on his land. Not every risk of injury is a danger or hazard—some risks are ordinary demands of everyday life. They do not give rise to liability.

CASE 4.10

An escalator at a Sears store stopped working. Signs were placed at the bottom and top of the escalator saying that it was temporarily out of service and an elevator was available nearby. Initially, yellow tape blocked access to the escalator but it was removed by the next day when a shopper walked up the stopped escalator, tripped and fell near the top, breaking her elbow. It was unclear whether the signs were visible but the shopper did not see any. Sears argued that the stopped escalator was not a danger, but an ordinary risk of everyday life for which a warning is superfluous or unnecessary. The shopper knew the escalator was stopped when she climbed it. The Court disagreed; the stopped escalator was not an ordinary risk arising out of the demands of everyday life but a danger for which Sears owed a duty of care. Sears was held liable.[76]

A trespasser is someone who enters premises unlawfully. She enters without an invitation from or the permission of the occupier and is either unknown to the occupier or, if known to him, would be refused permission. A duty is still owed to a trespasser, but the level of care that must be taken is different from that for expected visitors. It is minimal—the occupier must not set out deliberately to harm the trespasser or recklessly disregard the possibility that his acts might injure a trespasser. An occupier must not set traps for a trespasser, and warning signs are required.

Occupier's liability legislation has codified the reduced standard of care for trespassers stating that such persons are deemed to assume risks. Still owners of large vacant properties, such as developers, conservation authorities, golf course owners, and municipalities, face big challenges in minimizing occupier's liability risks, despite provincial legislation intended to reduce the standard of care for rural occupiers.

CASE 4.11

S, a kinesiology professor and former Olympic athlete, went on a cross-country skiing outing in a park owned by the defendant conservation authority. The park was available to residents for recreational use even in the winter. When skiing down a berm onto the lake, she hit a concrete wall and fractured her ankle. The wall was not marked and was hidden by snow and ice. The defendant denied liability based on the provincial legislation's reduced standard of care applicable to rural properties and recreational trails where only reckless disregard for safety would trigger liability. The trial court held that the lake was not a trail within the provisions of the Occupier's Liability Act, and the defendant should have warned users about the concrete wall it had installed. The municipality had to appeal to the Court of Appeal, which overturned the judgment saying that S assumed the risk of skiing onto the lake and there was no reckless disregard.[77]

As in most negligence actions, if a visitor continues the activity after being properly warned about hazards or the risks, he will have voluntarily assumed the risk and the occupier will not be held liable for any resulting damage. For more information on this topic, see the Companion Website.

---

[76] *Sears Canada Inc. v. Bartram*, 2004 BCSC 509. See for example *Snitzer v. Becker Milk Co.* (1977), 15 O.R. (2d) 345.

[77] *Schneider v. St. Clair Region Conservation Authority* (2008), 89 O.R.(3d) 150 revs'd 2009 ONCA 640. See also *Waldick v. Malcolm*, [1991] 2 S.C.R. 456 where court held risk not willingly assumed.

Negligence Torts

Elements to prove basic negligence:

1. A duty of care is owed.

2. The applicable standard of care is breached.

3. The plaintiff suffers injury or damage.

4. The defendant's conduct caused the damage.

Other types of negligence that have been refined to adapt to common situations:

- product liability for defective products causing injury
- duty to warn for inherently dangerous products
- occupier's liability for injuries on land

Defences applicable to negligence actions include

- contributory negligence;
- voluntary assumption of risk; and
- failure to mitigate damage.

REMEDIES

Since the purpose of the law of torts is to compensate an injured party, the usual remedy for a tort (intentional or unintentional) is an award of a sum of money, known as **damages**, to compensate for physical and economic losses. Physical losses are the costs of repairing damaged property or treating injured people; economic losses are losses in monetary value such as lost profits or wages. Courts were initially reluctant to award damages for only economic loss without some corresponding physical damage, but now often do.[78] Sometimes courts award damages to cover preventive expenditures.

> **damages** a sum of money awarded as compensation for loss or injury

CASE 4.12

A land developer contracted with the defendant construction company to build an apartment building, which was later sold to the plaintiffs. About 10 years later, a section of cladding fell from the ninth floor. On examination, defects in the construction were found and the plaintiffs had the entire cladding replaced. They successfully sued the defendants for the cost of the repairs.

Although no damage had been suffered, apart from the cladding on the ninth floor, the Supreme Court of Canada held that it was foreseeable that, without the repairs, there was a strong likelihood of physical harm to persons or to property. It was right that the defendants should be liable for the cost of replacing the rest of the cladding. In reaching that conclusion, the court recognized the strong underlying policy justification of providing an incentive to prevent accidents before they happen.[79]

Generally, the purpose of damages is to restore the plaintiff, so far as is possible, to the position she would have been in if the tort had not been committed. The object of awarding damages is not to punish the wrongdoer, though **punitive or exemplary damages** may be awarded in rare cases, such as a deliberate libel or malicious prosecution.

> **punitive or exemplary damages** damages awarded with the intention of punishing a wrongdoer

---

[78] [1964] A.C. 465.

[79] *Winnipeg Condominium Corp. No. 36 v. Bird Construction Co.*, [1995] 1 S.C.R. 85.

special damages damages to compensate for quantifiable injuries

general damages damages to compensate for injuries that cannot be precisely expressed in monetary terms

restitution an order to restore property wrongfully taken

injunction a court order restraining a person from doing, or continuing to do, a particular act

mandatory injunction an order requiring a person to do a particular act

Tort damages are often classified into two categories: special damages and general damages. **Special damages** refer to monetary or pecuniary items that can be more or less accurately quantified—medical bills, the cost of repairing a car, or actual lost wages. **General damages** include less precise, more speculative items, such as future loss of earnings due to disability, and non-pecuniary losses, such as awards for the "pain and suffering" of losing a limb or one's sight. Obviously, it is impossible to put an exact money value on health and happiness, but the courts must attempt to do so.[80] They have thousands of precedents to guide them.

In some cases, remedies other than damages may be available, although they are rarely granted. Where a defendant has wrongfully converted the plaintiff's property, the court may order its specific **restitution** to the plaintiff, since to restrict the remedy to damages would in effect allow the defendant to compel a sale of the property. Courts may also grant an **injunction**—that is, order the defendant to refrain from committing further acts of a similar nature under threat of imprisonment for contempt of court if he disregards the order. For example, an injunction may restrain the defendant from committing a nuisance or from trespassing on the plaintiff's land. Less frequently, courts grant a **mandatory injunction**, ordering the defendant to take some positive action, such as removing a fence blocking the plaintiff's right-of-way to her property.

CASE 4.13

Verdun, a former newspaper editor, disagreed with a merger of two insurance companies. After the merger was complete, Verdun continued to voice criticism about Astley, the former president of one of the insurance companies. Verdun's comments turned personal and were voiced orally at shareholders meetings of major financial institutions across Ontario and written in letters of complaint. Astley won damages in a defamation (libel and slander) lawsuit. Following the judgment, Verdun continued to voice his opinion about Astley and published a book with libelous comments. The court ordered a permanent injunction against Verdun restraining further publication of remarks about Astley, because it was clear that the $650 000 damage award had not ended the defamation and without it Astley's reputation would continue to be injured. The court also ordered a mandatory injunction, requiring Verdun to remove existing blog postings. When Verdun violated the injunction, he was convicted of contempt of court and sentenced to 90 days' house arrest.[81]

INTERNATIONAL ISSUE

Strict Liability or Negligence?

Jurisdictions around the world take differing approaches to assigning liability for defective and dangerous products. As we have seen, Canadian courts apply modified principles of negligence to determine liability. However, in many states in the United States, and also in the European Union, strict liability applies to manufacturers of consumer goods, eliminating the obligation for the plaintiff to prove that the manufacturer fell below the standard of care. The impact of strict liability is different in the European Union as opposed to the U.S. because the E.U. does not allow contingency fees, applies the loser pays rule, and caps damages at 70 million euros per defect.

Questions to Consider

1. What impact do you think cost rules and damage caps have on product liability litigation?

2. What do you think will happen to the price of the goods if the manufacturer is strictly liable for all damage caused by a product?

Sources: Product Warranty Directive 1999/44/EC; Product Liability Directive 85/374/EEC; European General Product Safety Directive 2001/95/EC; Smith, "The EC Directive on Product Liability: A Comparative Study of its Implementation in the UK, France and West Germany" (1992) *Legal Issues in European Integration 101*; Roger Meiners et al., *The Legal Environment of Business* (Mason: Cengage Learning, 2009) at 169.

---

[80] The Supreme Court capped the size of damage award that can be made for pain and suffering: *Andrews v. Grand & Toy Alberta Ltd.*, [1978] 2 S.C.R. 229; *Thornton v. Prince George School District No. 57*, [1978] 2 S.C.R. 267; and, *Arnold v. Teno*, [1978] 2 S.C.R. 287.

[81] *Astley v. Verdun*, 2011 ONSC 3651; 2013 ONSC 2998; 2013 ONSC 6734.

Strategies to Manage the Legal Risks

Businesses are exposed to many legal risks which may involve being sued or suing others. Tort claims are often unpredictable; the size of the risk may be very difficult to estimate. The potential tort liability of a business affects every functional area of the business. The business may be vicariously liable for the negligent or even the intentionally wrongful acts of its employees. It may be liable for injuries caused by defects in the products it sells. It may be liable for injuries sustained by visitors to its premises, or caused by harmful substances escaping from those premises.

On the other hand, the business might suffer the harm. Its property might be damaged by the negligent act of some other person, or a competitor might unlawfully interfere with its economic interests.

Legal risks of this nature cannot be entirely eliminated, but they can be reduced by following a risk management strategy, as discussed in Chapter 1, in particular by

- increasing business awareness of potential legal problems;
- assessing the legal risks and obtaining professional legal advice before undertaking new ventures;[82]
- considering all risk management strategies, including avoiding, reducing, and transferring the risk;
- transferring the risk by insuring against damage to one's own property and against liability to others (insurance is considered in more detail in Chapter 16);
- alerting, advising, and warning potential users of identified risks so they may be considered to assume them; and
- implementing internal quality control practices within the organization consistent with prevailing industry standards.

QUESTIONS FOR REVIEW

1. What is the origin of the word "tort," and what does it mean?
2. What is the principal purpose of tort law?
3. What is meant by "strict liability"? Should liability ever be "strict"?
4. Who should bear the loss resulting from an automobile accident? What are the alternatives?
5. What is the main justification for the principle of vicarious liability?
6. What must a plaintiff prove in order to succeed in an action based on negligence?
7. In what circumstances may a public authority be held liable for damage resulting from its failure to carry out a statutory duty imposed on it?
8. How do the courts determine the appropriate standard of care to be expected of a defendant?
9. Is the "but for" test an appropriate way of determining causation?
10. What is meant by "economic loss"?
11. Should an injured party be able to recover damages despite the fact that her own conduct was negligent and contributed to the injury?
12. Is it relevant in a tort action that the injured party has taken out insurance against the loss sustained?

---

[82] Failure to obtain legal advice may even amount to contributory negligence in some circumstances: see M. *Tucci Construction Ltd. v. Lockwood*, [2000] O.J. No. 3192.

13. When is a manufacturer under a duty to warn?

14. What is the test in most Canadian provinces for establishing the liability of occupiers for injury to lawful visitors? Are trespassers treated differently?

15. What is the difference between a public and a private nuisance?

16. What constitutes false imprisonment?

17. Distinguish between libel and slander. What is meant by "privilege" in the context of defamation?

18. What are the requirements for establishing that the tort of unlawful interference with economic interests has been committed?

19. What are "punitive damages"? Should they be awarded in tort actions?

20. What is an injunction?

CASES AND PROBLEMS

1. Continuing Scenario

Ashley is preparing to open her restaurant and interviewing potential staff at her rented restaurant location. Ashley's landlord, ABC Ltd., has allowed her into the premises before the start of the lease so that she can complete some improvements prior to opening. Gerald is a tiling contractor whom Ashley has hired to put down a porcelain tile floor, and he has unpacked his tools—including a tile saw—in the centre of the dining room area. When Ashley completes her interview with Shelley, an applicant for the position of hostess, Shelley turns to leave and trips over the tile saw. She cuts her leg and it is bleeding but she does not want to let Ashley know she is hurt so she does not complain. She does not go to the hospital until three days later after she hears that she did not get the job. The cut is so deep that it requires stitches to close, and the doctor tells her she should have come to the hospital immediately. Now it will leave a permanent scar.

What are Shelley's causes of action? Against whom? Explain your reasons. Would it have made a difference if Ashley's lease had already started? Why or why not?

2. Sullivan and his friend Williams were having a quiet drink together one evening in the Tennessee Tavern when they got into an argument with four men at the next table, who had obviously had a fair amount to drink and were looking for a fight. There was a brief scuffle when one of the four men attacked Sullivan. The scuffle was broken up by two members of the tavern staff.

The tavern owner had the four men ejected by the back door of the tavern. He then told Sullivan and Williams to leave by the front door. They did so, only to be confronted by the four, who viciously attacked them, causing serious injury to Sullivan. Sullivan brought an action against the owner of the tavern, alleging that he was partly responsible for causing the injuries.

Should Sullivan succeed?

3. Smiley, a buyer for Carrefour Fashions, entered the store of a rival firm, Boulevard Boutique, in order to find out what were the latest lines they were carrying. He was recognized by Maldini, the manager of Boulevard. Maldini called the store detective, Rocco, and ordered him to "keep an eye" on Smiley while he (Maldini) called the police.

Maldini called the police, informing them that he had a "suspected shoplifter" on the premises. Smiley did not attempt to leave before the police arrived, assuming that Rocco would prevent him if he tried to do so.

Smiley accompanied the police officers to the police station, where they accepted his explanation for why he was in the store and released him.

What claim might Smiley have against Boulevard, Maldini, or Rocco? Does Boulevard have any cause of action against Smiley?

4. Prentice, an encyclopedia salesman, telephoned Hall and arranged to visit her at her apartment to show her his firm's latest volumes. When he entered the apartment building, owned by Newman, Prentice found the staircase lighting was out of order. He attempted to climb the stairs in the dark and fell on a loose step, breaking his leg. Hall knew of the faulty light and the loose step but had not thought to warn Prentice. No one had told Newman of either defect.

   What claim does Prentice have against either Hall or Newman?

5. Princess Properties Inc. is the owner of a large office building constructed in the 1930s. Renovations were carried out by Fundamental Construction Ltd. in 1975, during which fireproofing material, containing asbestos, was installed. Princess did not know that the material contained asbestos and had relied on Fundamental to select appropriate insulating material.

   In the course of further renovations in 1987, the existence of the asbestos material was discovered. Princess had it removed because it was considered a health hazard.

   Princess brought an action for the cost of removing the material and for lost rent against

   (a) Fundamental Construction Ltd;

   (b) the architects, who had specified the use of the material in 1975; and

   (c) the manufacturers of the material.

   On what basis might Princess have a valid claim against each of these defendants, and what are the principal issues that would have to be determined at trial?

6. Taylor had a student loan that was in arrears. Collection of the loan had been transferred from the original lender to Kneecap Collections Inc., a collection agency. When Kneecap demanded payment, Taylor questioned the amount that was being claimed, which was substantially larger than the amount of the original loan. Kneecap did not provide any explanation and made a further demand for immediate payment. Taylor replied that he would not pay unless he received a satisfactory explanation.

   Kneecap's goons then started a campaign of harassment. They made violent threats to Taylor, and repeatedly telephoned his employer, making various false statements about Taylor. They told his employer that Taylor had defrauded them, that he had a court order against them, and that he was secretly working part-time for a competitor firm. As a result, even though Taylor denied all of these allegations, he was fired by his employer.

   What remedies might Taylor have against Kneecap?

7. Brown is a farmer who raises chickens on a large scale. The baby chicks require a continuous supply of oxygen to survive, and the necessary equipment for that purpose is connected to the electric power supplied to the farm. Brown installed an auxiliary battery-operated power generator in the barn to be available as an emergency backup. He also had a battery-operated power failure detector installed in his bedroom so that if the power in the farmhouse failed, a warning signal would alert him to the danger of loss of power to his operation.

   Chauncey is a driver for Gardiner Transport Ltd. While driving the company's tractor-trailer, Chauncey allowed the vehicle to wander onto the shoulder of the road where it struck overhead wires. As a result, electric power service in the area was interrupted for a period of five hours. The interruption extinguished the supply of oxygen to Brown's barn and several thousand chickens died. Unfortunately, Brown had failed to replace the battery in the alarm detector in his bedroom, and so, on the one occasion he needed it, it did not work.

   Brown brought an action for damages of $30 000 against both Chauncey and Gardiner Transport Ltd. to compensate him for the loss of his chickens. At the trial, a witness estimated that about 50 percent of chicken breeders use power failure detectors.

   Discuss the merits of Brown's case. Explain with reasons what the court's decision would probably be.

Additional Resources for Chapter 4 on the Companion Website

(www.pearsoncanada.ca/smyth)

In addition to pre- and post-tests, mini-cases, and application exercises, the Companion Website includes the following province-specific resources for Chapter 4:

- **Alberta:** Auto Insurance Act; Automobile Insurance; Charitable Donation of Food Act; Contributory Negligence; Defamation; Emergency Medical Aid Act; Fatal Accidents Amendment Act (2010); Maternal Tort Liability Act; Occupiers' Liability; Social Hosts; Trespass
- **Atlantic Provinces:** Contributory Negligence; Workers' Compensation
- **British Columbia:** Apology Act; Contributory Negligence; Defamation; Good Samaritans; Insurance Corporation of British Columbia (ICBC); Motor Vehicle Insurance; Occupiers' Liability; Parental Liability; Trespass to Land; Workers' Compensation; WorkSafeBC
- **Manitoba/Saskatchewan:** Contributory Negligence; Defamation; Farming and Nuisance; No-fault Insurance; Occupiers' Liability—Trespass to Land; Vicarious Liability
- **Ontario:** Causation; Contributory Negligence; Defamation; Duty of Care; No-fault Liability Insurance; Occupiers' Liability; Parental Liability; Private Investigators and Security Guards; Reverse Onus; Strict Liability; Trespass; Vicarious Liability; Workers' Compensation

Chapter 5

Professional Liability: The Legal Challenges

This chapter describes three different ways in which the law imposes legal liability on professionals: contract, fiduciary duty, and tort. Its primary focus is the application of tort law to professionals—persons such as accountants, architects, doctors, engineers, lawyers, and pharmacists—but the principles apply to any expert giving advice.

In this chapter we examine such questions as:

■ What are the special duties owed by professionals to their clients and to others?

■ How do the obligations differ when they derive from contract? A fiduciary relationship? Tort law?

■ When are professionals in fiduciary relationships?

■ How does a plaintiff prove negligent misrepresentation?

■ How do professional organizations influence standards for professional conduct?

■ What extra legal challenges are presented when different professionals practise together in one firm?

PROFESSIONAL LIABILITY: THE LEGAL CHALLENGES

Our complex business environment makes professional services one of the fastest-growing and most important sectors of the economy. It follows that there is a significant risk of economic harm from any negligent or fraudulent conduct by professionals.

We use the term "professionals" here to apply to people who have specialized knowledge and skills that are relied upon by clients and others. Usually they belong to a professional organization and are licensed by that body to offer their services to the public. Professionals assist clients in making good and well founded business decisions. The use of professional services reduces but does not eliminate risk. When a client seeks and relies on professional advice that turns out to be wrong, a question arises: Should the professional be liable for the loss or harm suffered by the client or even by someone else who relies on and acts upon incorrect advice?

Several causes of action are available to hold professionals accountable for incorrect advice. Liability may be imposed on a professional by tort law. A professional may also be found liable for breach of contract if there is a contract to supply the advice. Finally, sometimes the professional must honour "fiduciary" responsibilities separate from any tort or contractual obligations. The causes of action discussed in this chapter are not restricted only to professionals, but they are a major legal risk for professionals.

It can be challenging to determine when liability for professional incompetence or negligence should be imposed. Some favour wide liability of professionals to encourage careful behaviour, and the professional can cover any damages by increasing fees and by purchasing insurance protection. However, if the courts go too far and award damages to compensate everyone who relies on bad advice, the increased costs will likely discourage people from entering the profession and increase the price of advice beyond reach. A proper balance must be found.

In practice, almost all professionals carry liability insurance. Recent uncertainty concerning liability and the risk of high damage awards have caused insurance premiums to rise. Professional fees, in turn, increase to cover insurance costs. As fees rise, clients expect more for their money and, when they are disappointed, are more likely to sue. The process is something of a vicious circle and striking a fair balance can be a challenge for the courts.[1]

LIABILITY OF PROFESSIONALS

Liability may arise from three relationships, generating three different causes of action:

- The contractual relationship generates a breach of contract cause of action;
- The fiduciary relationship generates a breach of fiduciary duty; and
- The tort of negligent misrepresentation is available when a tort duty of care is owed.

In most cases, the professional stands in a contractual relationship with her client. Because of the professional's position of authority, a special relationship of loyalty and trust may also exist between professional and client, giving rise to a fiduciary duty. As well, a professional, like anyone else, owes a duty of care to persons who may foreseeably be injured by her negligence.

---

[1] The dilemma is well summarized by Professor Brian Cheffins regarding the potential liability of auditors for incorrect statements in a corporation's financial statements: B.R. Cheffins, "Auditors' Liability in the House of Lords: A Signal Canadian Courts Should Follow" (1991) 18 C.B.L.J. 118 at 125–7; this passage was quoted with approval by LaForest, J. in the Supreme Court of Canada, *Hercules Managements Ltd. v. Ernst & Young* (1997), 146 D.L.R. (4th) 577 at 593.

Contractual Obligations

An agreement to provide professional services to a client contains a promise, whether stated expressly or not, to perform those services competently. A breach of that promise is a breach of the contract, and the client may then sue for damages. The next part of this book is devoted to the law of contracts, and subsequent chapters will discuss liability for breach of a contractual promise, including a promise to perform with due care. Sometimes there is no contract between the professional and the injured party; in such circumstances, fiduciary liability and tort liability are the alternatives.

Fiduciary Duty

A professional's duty may extend beyond the terms of her contract in an important way. When a person is in a "special" relationship with a professional, the law imposes a **fiduciary duty** on that professional.[2] This fiduciary duty can arise even when the professional donates services free of charge, so that no contract exists.

fiduciary duty a duty imposed on a person who stands in a special relation of trust and loyalty to another

The first step to imposing liability for breach of fiduciary duty is establishing that the relationship is a fiduciary one. In *Alberta v. Elder Advocates of Alberta Society*,[3] the Supreme Court of Canada identified three characteristics of fiduciary relationships:

- The fiduciary (often a professional) has undertaken to act in the best interests of the beneficiary (often the client)
- The beneficiary is vulnerable to or at the mercy of the fiduciary's control or discretion, and
- A legal or practical interest of the beneficiary could be harmed by the fiduciary's exercise of discretion or control.

Some statutes designate specific positions as fiduciary—trustees and corporate directors are examples. Some professional relationships are obviously fiduciary, such as lawyer–client and doctor–patient.[4] But not every professional relationship is automatically a fiduciary one, and these must be evaluated using the above criteria. For example, the broker and client relationship depends on the particular facts of the case. Vulnerability is only one factor applicable to the assessment of the fiduciary nature of a financial advisor—others are client relationship, trust, reliance, discretion, and the standards expressed in a professional code of conduct.[5]

If a fiduciary duty is found to exist, the law imposes a wider range of obligations on the professional than is expressly stated in the contract or required under tort law. The professional must act honestly, in good faith, and only in the best interests of the client. Therefore, the second step to imposing this type of liability involves determining if the professional's behaviour breaches the fiduciary obligations. For example, a lawyer who entered into a business arrangement with a long-standing client, without disclosing his own precarious financial situation, was held to be in breach of his fiduciary duty to the client.[6] Liability for breach of fiduciary duty may arise without any negligence.

---

[2] *Nocton v. Lord Ashburton*, [1914] A.C. 932 at 943–58; *Hedley, Byrne & Co. Ltd. v. Heller & Partners Ltd.*, [1964] A.C. 465 at 486.

[3] 2011 SCC 24, [2012] 2 S.C.R. 261 at para 36.

[4] *Lac Minerals Ltd. v. International Corona Resources Ltd.*, [1989] 2 S.C.R. 574 (describing these as per se fiduciary relationships).

[5] *Hodgkinson v. Simms*, [1994] 3 S.C.R. 377.

[6] *Korz v. St. Pierre* (1987), 61 O.R. (2d) 609; *Strother v. 3464920 Canada Inc.*, [2007] 2 S.C.R. 177.

CASE 5.1

Mr. and Mrs. Hunt, a retired couple in their 70s, set up an investment account with Mr. Schram of TD Evergreen. Mr. Schram considered Mr. Hunt a person of average investment knowledge. Prior to his retirement, Mr. Hunt was a vice-president and director of a large footwear manufacturer.

The account was "non-discretionary"—that is, no trade was to be completed without Mr. Hunt's express authorization. Mr. Schram sold 1349 of the Hunts' 1472 shares in BCE. By the time Mr. Hunt learned of the sale, the BCE stock price had risen and the Hunts sued for the lost profit. The Hunts claimed breach of contract and breach of fiduciary duty. The Court of Appeal found that the unauthorized sale amounted to a breach of contract but disallowed the claim for breach of fiduciary duty. The Court found that the relationship was not a fiduciary one. It lacked the necessary degree of discretion, control reliance, and trust; Schram could not exercise unilateral power over the account, and all other trades were directed by Mr. Hunt. Although there were some health and age issues, these vulnerabilities did not establish a fiduciary relationship.[7]

CASE 5.2

Hodgkinson, a stockbroker, was inexperienced in tax. He wanted an independent professional to advise him on tax planning and tax shelter needs. He retained Simms, an accountant who specialized in these areas. On Simms's advice, Hodgkinson invested in a number of multiple unit residential buildings (MURBs) as tax shelters and lost heavily when the value of the MURBs fell during a decline in the real estate market. The advice was perfectly sound at the time it was given. Unknown to Hodgkinson, Simms was also acting for the developers in structuring the MURBs and did not disclose that fact to Hodgkinson. The Supreme Court of Canada accepted the client's claim that he would not have undertaken the investment had he known of the adviser's conflict of interest. Simms was held to be in breach of his fiduciary duty to Hodgkinson and consequently liable to compensate Hodgkinson for his loss.[8]

conflict of interest a situation where a duty is owed to a client whose interests conflict with the interests of the professional, another client, or another person to whom a duty is owed

As Case 5.2 illustrates, a fiduciary should not place herself in a **conflict of interest** and has a duty not to profit, or attempt to profit, at the client's expense. A fiduciary obligation requires complete loyalty to the other party to the relationship. Consequently, a professional who acts on behalf of two or more clients who have competing interests (for example, the vendor and the purchaser of a piece of property) might well find it impossible to fulfill her duty to them both.[9] However, if no conflict of interest exists, no liability will be imposed.

CASE 5.3

A bookkeeper employed by a law firm voluntarily lent money to the financially struggling firm without being asked to do so. Separate and apart from the loan and as part of her employment contract, the bookkeeper received free legal services for the preparation of her will. When the firm was unable to repay the loan, the bookkeeper sued for breach of contract, negligence, and breach of fiduciary duty. The Supreme Court of Canada held that although solicitor–client relationships are inherently fiduciary, the loan transaction fell outside the scope of that relationship. Not all lawyers' duties toward clients are fiduciary. As well, there was no actual conflict of interest between the firm's duties to her in connection with the limited legal retainers and its interest in receiving the loan advances. The breach of fiduciary duty claim failed.[10]

---

[7] *Hunt v. TD Securities Inc.* (2003), 229 D.L.R. (4th) 609 (Ont. C.A.).

[8] *Hodgkinson v. Simms, supra,* n. 5. See also *Martin v. Goldfarb* (1998), 163 D.L.R. (4th) 639 and *Strother, supra,* n. 6. See also *Eastern Power Ltd. v. Ontario Electric Financial Corporation,* 2010 ONCA 467, 101 O.R. (3d) 81.

[9] *Chapters Inc. v. Davies, Ward & Beck LLP,* [2000] O.J. No. 4973, aff'd [2001] O.J. No. 206, 52 O.R. (3d) 566 (the Ontario Court of Appeal prohibited a law firm, one of whose lawyers had represented two book stores in an amalgamation five years earlier, from acting for a prospective purchaser of the amalgamated company because the confidential information acquired in the earlier transaction meant there would be a conflict between the firm's duty to its previous clients, which prohibited disclosure of the information, and its duty to represent the new client effectively).

[10] *Galambos v. Perez,* 2009 S.C.C. 48, [2009] 2 S.C.R. 678.

Before its demise, Enron was the seventh largest public corporation in the United States. The energy giant's collapse into bankruptcy cost investors billions of dollars and was accompanied by revelations of fraud and impropriety on a massive scale.

The Enron affair highlighted the many conflicts of interest that arise when a corporation's external auditors also act as its accountants, business advisers, or management consultants. In theory, a corporation's auditors are appointed by its shareholders; their task is to objectively review the financial management of the corporation's affairs by the directors and management and to report any irregularities to the shareholders. In reality, the auditors are usually selected by the management and their appointment is a formality. They consequently owe their position to the very people they are meant to supervise, an obvious conflict of interest.

A second conflict of interest arises when the auditors are themselves members of a firm that has lucrative contracts to supply accounting and management services to the corporation that they are required to audit. If they judge the directors too harshly, they may jeopardize those contracts and lose an important source of income for their firm.

To address these conflicts of interest and other governance problems, the United States passed the Sarbanes–Oxley Act of 2002 (SOX), which introduced a number of changes, including

- prohibiting a company from hiring the same accounting firm to provide both auditing and consulting services, and
- placing auditor selection under the control of independent directors who do not work at the company.

The application of SOX was not limited to American companies—it applied even to foreign companies trading on an American exchange. As we will discuss in Chapters 26 and 27, Canada immediately felt the impact of SOX and has now adopted many of the SOX provisions.

Questions to Consider

1. What other possible solutions would you propose to minimize conflicts of interest?

2. Is it appropriate for American legislation to apply to Canadian corporations?

3. Accountants have always been under a duty to avoid conflicts of interest. Why was this existing duty not sufficient to prevent the auditor/consultant conflict?

Sources: New York State Society of Certified Public Accountants, "The Sarbanes-Oxley Act of 2002," The website of the New York Society of CPAs, www.nysscpa.org/oxleyact2002.htm; L. McCallum and P. Puri, *Canadian Companies' Guide to Sarbanes-Oxley Act* (Markham: LexisNexis Butterworth, 2004).

Tort Liability

Tort liability occurs when a professional deliberately or carelessly causes damage to a client. Their contract may also have been breached. The client may sue in contract or in tort.[11] In a case where a solicitor was negligent in arranging a mortgage that was later found to be invalid, the Court held that the client was entitled to sue in contract or tort.[12] The negligence duty of care is not applicable only to relationships outside the contract—it coexists with and independently of the promises in the contract.[13]

CASE 5.4

A credit union was investigated by the government agency responsible for supervision. The investigation revealed that, over a number of years, the credit union had made various unauthorized and unsecured loans, and there were other irregularities. The credit union brought a negligence action against its former auditors, claiming that they ought to have discovered the irregularities if the audits had been conducted properly. The auditors were found negligent and were held liable for losses sustained by the credit union. Auditors must perform the contract services in compliance with the standards of the profession. However, the credit union was held contributorily negligent, in failing to exercise proper supervision over its loan manager, and was 30 percent to blame.[14]

---

[11] *Queen v. Cognos Inc.* [1993] 1 S.C.R. 87.

[12] *Central Trust Co. v. Rafuse* (1986), 31 D.L.R. (4th) 481.

[13] *Oz Optics Ltd., v. Timbercon, Inc.*, [2010] O.J. No. 1963 at para. 86, varied on appeal 2011 ONCA 714.

[14] *Capital Community Credit Union Ltd. v. BDO Dunwoody*, [2001] O.J. No. 4249.

Tort liability extends the range of possible plaintiffs beyond clients who have paid for the advice. Sometimes "other" people may rely on a professional opinion given to a single client or to the public at large, as, for example, when:

- an auditor expresses an opinion on the fairness and accuracy of the client firm's financial statements, which is given to lenders, potential investors, etc.

- engineers or architects recommend design specifications for structures that, if faulty, may present risks to occupiers and others

- bankers or credit analysts give assessments of creditworthiness for their customers that come to the attention of other lenders

- accountants provide a corporation with a valuation of the business or its shares, and the valuation is intended for the use of others

- one doctor gives a professional opinion to another doctor concerning the second doctor's patient

third-party liability liability to some other person who stands outside a contractual relationship

These "others" are known as third parties and any liability to them is referred to as **third-party liability**. Third-party liability is common for accountants, real estate agents, and insurance agents. The commission earned by a real estate agent is normally paid by the vendor of the property; an insurance agent usually contracts with the insurance company for which she arranges insurance.[15]

In the course of their work, however, these agents work closely with "other" persons—applicants for insurance and prospective purchasers of houses. While the commissions are paid by the insurance companies and property vendors, the "other" persons with whom these agents deal frequently rely on their advice. (See Figure 5.1.)

Later in this chapter, we will discuss the very difficult questions of where, precisely, to draw the line in deciding when a professional owes a duty of care to "other" persons, not clients, for negligent or inaccurate advice.

Choosing a Cause of Action

Sometimes a professional may be liable in tort but not in contract, or may be liable for breach of fiduciary duty without having been negligent. Other times, the professional may be liable in both contract and in tort, and also for breach of the fiduciary duty. A court will not award triple the damages; the plaintiff must choose. Does it matter whether the client sues for breach of contract, breach of fiduciary duty, or negligence?

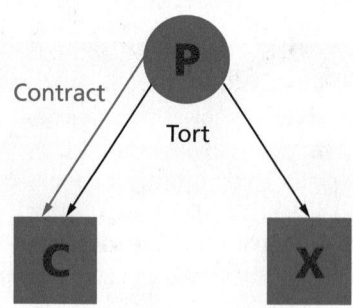

Figure 5.1 Contractual and Tort Liability

The professional P owes both a contractual duty and a duty in tort to client C. The only duty owed to a third party X is a duty in tort. (There may be occasions when a fiduciary duty is owed to C or to X.)

---

[15] By contrast, an insurance broker usually acts as agent for the insured: see the discussion in *Adams-Eden Furniture Ltd. v. Kansa General Insurance Co.* (1996), 141 D.L.R. (4th) 288, and see Chapter 16.

The choice might be important. The rules governing the time limits for bringing an action might make it advantageous to sue in one or the other.[16] As we saw in Case 5.3 above, a client's own contributory negligence may be raised as a defence in a tort action. Any term of the contract that excludes or limits liability will be raised as a defence in a contract action.[17] As Case 5.1 also demonstrates, the problem can be avoided by alleging breach of contract, negligence, and breach of fiduciary duty causes of action, in the alternative.[18]

The choice of cause of action might also affect the amount of damages awarded in some cases. The principles for determining the measure of damages are not exactly the same in contract as in tort.[19] In the case of breach of fiduciary duty, a defendant may be under a **duty to account** for any profit derived from the breach in addition to or as an alternative to damages. However, in *Hodgkinson v. Simms*,[20] the Supreme Court of Canada held that damages for breach of a fiduciary duty should place the plaintiff in the position he would have been in if the breach had not occurred. Similarly, the Ontario Court of Appeal has said that higher damage awards should not be allowed merely because a claim is characterized as breach of fiduciary duty as opposed to breach of contract or tort.[21] For more information on this topic, see the Companion Website.

duty to account the duty of a person who commits a breach of trust to hand over any profits derived from the breach

TORT LIABILITY FOR INACCURATE STATEMENTS

Misrepresentation

A misrepresentation is an untrue statement. If it is made knowing it to be untrue or without an honest belief in its truth, and with the intention to mislead some other person, the misrepresentation is fraudulent and amounts to the intentional tort of **deceit**. A victim who relies reasonably on the statement and suffers a loss may recover from the person who made it. The tort of deceit may also be committed when a person deliberately conceals or withholds information. The elements of deceit are (1) a false representation made by the defendant; (2) some level of knowledge of the falsehood of the representation on the part of the defendant (whether through knowledge or recklessness); (3) the false representation caused the plaintiff to act; and (4) the plaintiff's actions resulted in a loss.[22]

deceit an intentional tort imposing liability when damage is caused by a false statement made with the intention of misleading another person

---

CASE 5.5

A bank allowed a customer to invest in a company that owed a substantial debt to the bank. The bank's employees knew that the company was on the verge of insolvency but did not disclose this fact to the customer. The bank committed deceit and was held liable to compensate the customer.[23]

---

[16] The time limit for causes of action is normally calculated from the moment when the material facts are discovered or when a reasonable person would have discovered them, rather than when the breach occurs, as is the general rule in contract. *Ferrar v. Lorenzetti, Wolfe*, 2012 ONCA 851.

[17] *Central Trust Co. v. Rafuse, supra*, n. 12; *London Drugs Ltd. v. Kuehne & Nagel International Ltd.* (1992), 97 D.L.R. (4th) 261. See also *McDonnell v. Richter*, [2010] A.J. No. 794.

[18] Where the plaintiff sues in both contract and in tort, it seems that the defence of contributory negligence can be raised against both claims; see *Crown West Steel Fabricators v. Capri Insurance Services Ltd.* (2002), 214 D.L.R. (4th) 577, appealed [2003] B.C.J. No. 1076 (only as to costs): contrast *Caners v. Eli Lilly Canada Inc.* (1996), 134 D.L.R. (4th) 730, where the action was brought only in contract.

[19] See Chapter 4, under the heading "Remedies," and Chapter 13, under the heading "The Measurement of Damages."

[20] *Supra*, n. 5; see Case 5.1.

[21] *Martin v. Goldfarb* (1998), 163 D.L.R. (4th) 639 at 652. Clearly, some uncertainty remained: see Waddams, "Fiduciary Duties and Equitable Compensation" (1996), 27 C.B.L.J. 466; *Northwest Territories (Commissioner) v. Portz*, 27 C.C.L.T. (2d) 241, [1996] 3 W.W.R. 94.

[22] *Bruno Appliance and Furniture, Inc. v. Hryniak*, 2014 SCC 8, at para. 20.

[23] *Sugar v. Peat Marwick Ltd.* (1988), 55 D.L.R. (4th) 230.

fraudulent misrepresentation deceit

negligent misrepresentation an unintentional tort imposing liability when an incorrect statement is made without due care for its accuracy, and injury is caused

Deceit also known as **fraudulent misrepresentation** requires at least some knowledge or willful disregard for the falseness of the information. The unintentional tort of **negligent misrepresentation** does not require knowledge of the falseness of the information, only carelessness in its creation.

Negligent misrepresentation is another unintentional negligence tort that evolved over time to accommodate the very common situation where poor advice leads to financial loss. At its core are the usual negligence components of duty of care, breach of the standard of care, injury to the plaintiff, and causation of damage. However, these components were not an easy fit for the typical negligent misrepresentation scenario of inaccurate advice because information passes so quickly from one person to another and it is the listener's actions after hearing the advice that give rise to the economic loss. Over time, the courts adjusted the standard negligence elements to fit the increasingly common scenarios where flawed advice from accountants, bankers, lawyers and other experts is relied upon. For more information on this topic, see the Companion Website.

The Hedley Byrne Case

The English case of *Hedley Byrne v. Heller & Partners*[24] was the first to recognize negligent misrepresentation and still provides a good example of its reach and the importance of putting disclaimers on opinions.

CASE 5.6

Easipower asked Hedley Byrne, an advertising agency, to handle its advertising account. Since Hedley Byrne would have to extend credit to Easipower in arranging the advertising, it asked its own bank to obtain credit information on Easipower, and in particular whether Easipower would be "good for" a line of credit up to certain limits. The bank manager made inquiries from Heller & Partners (Easipower's bankers) about Easipower's creditworthiness, without revealing Hedley Byrne's identity, saying only that a customer had inquired. Heller wrote back saying that Easipower would be good for the debt. At no time did Hedley Byrne communicate directly with Heller, but its own bank did inform it of the full contents of the letter, including the disclaimer of responsibility. Hedley Byrne then accepted Easipower as an account and placed extensive advertising for it, running up a large balance. Shortly afterward, Easipower became insolvent and was unable to pay Hedley Byrne's outstanding account. Hedley Byrne sued Heller for the resulting loss, claiming it was caused by Heller's negligent misrepresentation of Easipower's creditworthiness.

disclaimer an express statement to the effect that the person making it takes no responsibility for its accuracy

When considering whether a duty of care was owed, the court found that although Heller neither dealt with nor even knew the identity of Hedley Byrne, Heller should have foreseen that its information would be used by a customer of the other bank. It therefore owed that customer a duty of care. More investigation should have been taken before expressing an opinion about the financial state of Easipower, so the standard of care was breached. However, the court held that, because the **disclaimer** of responsibility was added, Hedley Byrne could not rely on the information.

This case extended liability to a wider group than those with direct contact to the advice giver, introduced the key concept of reliance in addition to causation, and inspired the Canadian tort.

PROVING NEGLIGENT MISREPRESENTATION

When suing for negligent misrepresentation in Canada, a plaintiff must prove more than just the traditional four elements of negligence. The Supreme Court of Canada listed five requirements for proving negligent misrepresentation when it imposed liability for

---

[24] *Hedley Byrne v. Heller & Partners*, [1964] A.C. 465.

negligent misrepresentations made by an employer during a pre-employment job interview in *Queen v. Cognos Ltd.*[25]

Elements of Negligent Misrepresentation

The five requirements for proving negligent misrepresentation are

1. there must be a duty of care based on a "special relationship" between the representor and the representee;

2. the representation in question must be untrue, inaccurate, or misleading;

3. the representor must have acted negligently in making the misrepresentation—that is, he or she must have fallen below the requisite standard of care required of a professional making such a representation;

4. the representee must have relied, in a reasonable manner, on the negligent misrepresentation; and

5. the reliance must have been detrimental to the representee in the sense that damages resulted.[26]

The Duty of Care—Special Relationship

In this technological age, information is widely circulated. If the test for who was owed a duty of care turned entirely on who could foreseeably be harmed, banks, public accountants, and other financial analysts might be faced with an almost unlimited liability. For example, the auditors of a corporation whose financial statements are made public know that the statements will be relied upon by many groups of people—lenders, investors, proposed purchasers, etc. Auditors could be liable to anyone who might happen to read the financial statements.[27] The Supreme Court of Canada considered this issue in *Hercules Management Ltd. v. Ernst & Young.*[28]

CASE 5.7

Shareholders in two corporations brought an action against a firm of accountants, alleging that audits of the corporations' financial statements had been negligently prepared, and that in consequence, they had incurred investment losses and losses in the value of their shareholdings. Their claim failed.

The Supreme Court of Canada held that (a) there was no contractual relationship between the auditors of a corporation and its shareholders; (b) the purpose of the auditor's report was to oversee the management and affairs of the corporation, and (c) the auditors owed shareholders no duty of care in respect of their personal investments.

As to the existence of a duty of care, the court applied the two-part test discussed in Chapter 4.[29] The first branch of the test requires an inquiry into whether there is a sufficiently close relationship between the plaintiff and the defendant that, in the reasonable contemplation of the defendant, carelessness on its part may cause damage to the plaintiff.[30] Foreseeability and proximity are the relevant principles. The second branch of the test considers limiting the duty for public policy reasons—the extent of liability must be predictable. If the number of plaintiffs or magnitude of their losses are undeterminable, public policy concerns may cause a court to restrict the duty owed.

[25] [1993] 1 S.C.R. 87. Test applied in *R. v. Imperial Tobacco Ltd.*, 2011 SCC 42.

[26] *Ibid.*, at para. 33; see also *Sharbern Holding Inc., v. Vancouver Airport Centre Ltd.*, 2011 SCC 23 at para. 121.

[27] This fear is largely responsible for the enactment in Ontario of legislation allowing the creation of limited liability partnerships by accounting and other professional firms: see Chapter 24.

[28] *Hercules Managements Ltd. v. Ernst & Young* (1997), 146 D.L.R. (4th) 577.

[29] *Childs v. Desormeaux*, 2006 SCC 18; *Mustapha v. Culligan of Canada Ltd.*, 2008 SCC 27; *Hill v. Hamilton-Wentworth Regional Police Services Board*, 2007 S.C.C. 41.

[30] *Hercules, supra*, n. 28; Originated in *Anns v. Merton London Borough Council*, [1978] A.C. 728 at 751–2 (H.L.). Approved in *Hercules, supra*, n. 28 at 586; *Kamloops (City) v. Nielsen* (1983), 10 D.L.R. (4th) 641; *Winnipeg Condominium Corp. No. 36 v. Bird Construction Co.* (1995), 121 D.L.R. (4th) 19.

indeterminate liability inability to be determined so that the magnitude of liability cannot be reasonably predicted, anticipated, or planned for

In *Hercules*, the Court held that a duty was owed to the shareholder in the first test as the defendant knew or reasonably should have known that shareholders would receive the information. However, there was a legitimate public policy concern over **indeterminate liability**—it could be hard to anticipate the number of plaintiffs or size of the risk. This policy concern justified limiting the duty to only those plaintiffs who used the information for the purpose for which it was given. As a matter of law, the only purpose for which shareholders receive an auditor's report is to provide them with information in order to oversee the management and affairs of the corporation—not for the purpose of guiding their personal investment decisions. Therefore, no duty of care was owed to the shareholder with respect to damage to personal investments.

This approach is consistent with an earlier case where an auditor negligently prepared accounts for a corporation, knowing that they were to be shown to a potential purchaser of the corporation. The Supreme Court of Canada held that the auditor was liable for the loss suffered by the purchaser.[31]

Provincial legislation sometimes creates a statutory cause of action for damages arising from misrepresentations. Real estate agents are subject to statutory duties.[32] Securities legislation imposes duties on directors, officers, lawyers, actuaries, and other advisors of publicly traded companies for misrepresentations contained in financial documentation, as well as other documents, including press releases and prospectuses. This legislation widely defines the eligible plaintiffs as anyone completing a trade while the misrepresentation remains uncorrected.[33] The policy concern of indeterminate liability is not a component of the statutory duty of care as a cap on damages is imposed.[34]

Duty of care for negligent misrepresentation is not restricted to financial information provided by professionals such as accountants and bankers.[35] Salespeople may be held liable for representations made about the products they sell.[36] A municipality has been held liable for loss suffered by purchasers of land who relied on incorrect information given to them by the zoning department regarding permissible use of the land.[37] An engineering firm that was negligent in preparing drawings and specifications for a provincial construction project was held liable for loss suffered by the construction company that had bid successfully for the contract in reliance on the specifications.[38]

Courts remain cautious about extending the duty of care too far. For example, in a 2002 case, the British Columbia Court of Appeal held that a government department, which had negligently certified to a leasing corporation that a piece of contaminated land had been fully cleaned, was not liable to an investor who bought shares in the leasing

---

[31] *Haig v. Bamford* (1976), 72 D.L.R. (2d) 68.

[32] *Sharbern, supra,* n. 26 considering B.C. real estate legislation.

[33] Securities Act, R.S.O. 1990, c. S–5, ss. S–8.14; R.S.B.C. 1996, c. 418, ss. 131–40; R.S.A. 2000, c. S-4, ss. 203–11.095. For a discussion of the statutory liability, see *Kerr v. Danier Leather Inc.,* 2007 SCC 44.

[34] See, for example, Ontario, *ibid.,* s. 138.7. See for example certified class action brought by stockholders under the Ontario legislation: *Silver v. IMAX Corporation et al.,* 2009 CanLII 72334, [2012] ONSC 4881; 2013 ONSC 6571 (settled). Statutory and common law misrepresentation causes of action arising from estimates of earnings per share and non-compliance with GAAP standards in 2005 financial statements.

[35] A law firm was held liable for a negligent statement regarding the secured status of a loan: *347671 B.C. Ltd. v. Heenan Blaikie,* [2002] B.C.J. No. 347.

[36] *JB Printing Ltd. v. 829085 Ontario Ltd.,* [2003] O.J. No. 1230, *aff'd* (2004) 192 O.A.C. 313 (Ont. C.A.).

[37] *Bell v. City of Sarnia* (1987), 37 D.L.R. (4th) 438.

[38] *Edgeworth Constructions Ltd. v. N.D. Lea & Associates Ltd.* (1993), 107 D.L.R. (4th) 169. Company liable, individual engineers employed by the firm, who prepared the drawings, did not owe a duty to the contractor.

corporation. The relationship between the Crown and the plaintiff was not close enough to establish a duty of care and, even if a duty of care was owed, it would be negated by the policy consideration of indeterminate liability.[39] In 2011, the federal government was held not to owe a duty of care to consumers for statements made about the reduced health risks of mild cigarettes; the relationship was close enough but policy concerns negated it.[40] In another case, the Ontario Court of Appeal refused to extend liability for a defective smoke alarm system to the organization that set the safety standards and approved the product as safe. The parties did not have the necessary close and direct relationship to justify imposing a duty of care. Even if a prima facie duty of care did exist, policy considerations would negate the duty, since to do so would effectively create an insurance scheme for dissatisfied purchasers.[41]

Accuracy of the Statement

It is easy to determine the accuracy of a factual statement. If a taxpayer incurs a late payment penalty because his accountant told him the wrong due date for payment of his taxes, the mistake is easily established with proof of the correct date. However, professionals often provide expert opinions, such as "the company is financially sound" or "the stock is a good investment." These opinions or "value judgments" are considered facts when expressed by an expert but are more difficult to prove wrong. The accuracy of the statement is assessed as of the time the information was given; the fact that the statement becomes untrue later does not necessarily establish that it was untrue at the time it was made. This rule does not apply to opinions about the future such as the "good investment" opinion. This speaks to the future performance of the stock and therefore future events will establish its truthfulness. Inaccuracy alone is not enough to establish liability. The crucial question is addressed in the third element: Why was the error committed? Professionals are not required to be perfect. To trigger liability, the inaccuracy must result from the failure of the professional to meet the required standard of care.

CASE 5.8

Hodgins wished to add an indoor swimming pool to his house. Through his contractor, he sought the advice of the local hydro-electric commission on heating the addition. An employee of the the commission gave an estimate of the electric heating cost, and in reliance on the estimate, Hodgins specified electric heating for the extension. The estimate proved to be much below the actual costs. Hodgins sued the hydro-electric commission for negligent misrepresentation. Although the estimate was clearly inaccurate, the employee was found not to have been negligent in its preparation.[42]

In reaching that conclusion, the Ontario Court of Appeal explicitly rejected a hindsight approach, saying that only information and practices available in 1967 should be considered to decide if reasonable skill, competence, and diligence was used when preparing the estimate. The experts testified that the heat loss calculations were done in the same manner as anyone similarly expert in the field would have done in 1967. It is not sufficient that the plaintiff establish merely that the estimate was wrong; he must go further and establish that the incorrect estimate resulted from a lack of skill, competence, or diligence on the part of the preparer.[43]

[39] *Border Enterprises Ltd. v. Beazer East Inc.* (2002), 216 D.L.R. (4th) 107.

[40] *Imperial Tobacco, supra,* n. 25.

[41] *Hughes v. Sunbeam Corp. (Canada) Ltd.* (2003), 219 D.L.R. (4th) 467.

[42] *Hodgins v. Hydro-Electric Commission of the Township of Nepean* (1975), 60 D.L.R. (3d) 1.

[43] *Ibid.,* at 4.

The Standard of Care for Professionals

Professionals must take reasonable care before making a representation. In Chapter 4, we noted that the standard of care applied in a basic negligence action is that of "the person on the Yonge Street subway." This standard is obviously inappropriate when judging the work of an accountant, a lawyer, or a surgeon. The professional must "exercise such reasonable care as the circumstances require to ensure that the representations made are accurate and not misleading."[44] Professional behaviour should be compared to the reasonable behaviour of others in that same profession when providing the same type of advice.

The approach taken in the *Hodgins* case (Case 5.8) was to compare the quality of professional work done or advice given with the prevailing standards of the profession at the time. A professional must exercise the same degree of skill and possess the same level of knowledge as is generally expected of members of that profession.[45] The courts will normally consider multiple sources of evidence in determining what those standards are. Many professions publish a code of conduct for their members, or guidelines to be followed in particular types of work. These can usually be taken as laying down an appropriate standard. The accounting profession has created a statement of generally accepted accounting principles (GAAP), and accountants who fail to comply with GAAP are considered to have fallen below the standard of care. Sometimes legislation sets the steps that must be followed to join or practise the profession—if the expert is not properly qualified but still gives advice, this will fall below the standard of care.

Frequently, the courts also hear the testimony of practitioners who state what they consider to be a proper standard. Sometimes, of course, professional opinion is divided—for example, about the best medical treatment in a particular circumstance. In such a case it will normally be sufficient that the defendant has followed a well-recognized practice, even though some other procedure might arguably have been better.[46]

Sometimes simply complying with normal professional standards is not an adequate defence.[47] Established standards alone should not be allowed to become a means for protecting members of a profession from liability.[48] As pointed out in the Hodgins case, sometimes a professional undertakes a task that is beyond the usual skills of her profession; she cannot then rely on the normal professional standard. The degree of skill and knowledge must be commensurate with the particular task undertaken.

Omissions The standard of reasonable care includes not omitting essential information. Providing partial or incomplete information in response to an inquiry can be negligent misrepresentation where the professional has a duty to the plaintiff to make the disclosure in question.[49]

---

[44] *Cognos, supra*, n. 25, p. 121; *Sharbern, supra*, n. 26, at para 123.

[45] Inexperience is not relevant: a newly qualified professional is held to the same standard as an experienced one. However, within a profession, a higher standard may apply to a specialist than to a general practitioner.

[46] *Belknap v. Meekes* (1989), 64 D.L.R. (4th) 452; *Ter Neuzen v. Korn* (1995), 127 D.L.R. (4th) 577; *McLintock v. Alidina*, [2010] O.J. No. 49.

[47] *Hodgins v. Hydro-Electric Commission of the Township of Nepean* (1975), 60 D.L.R. (3d) 1.

[48] See, for example, the decision of the Supreme Court of Canada in *Roberge v. Bolduc*, [1991] 1 S.C.R. 374, in which a notary was held to have been negligent in conducting a title search despite having followed the common practice in the profession.

[49] *Manfacturer's Life Insurance Co., v. Pitblado & Hoskins*, 2009 MBCA 83, [2009] 2 W.W.R. 638 Man. C.A. at para. 106.

Fine's Flowers Ltd. sustained a serious loss from the freezing of flowers and plants in its greenhouse. The freezing conditions were caused by failure of a water pump, which interrupted the supply of water to boilers that heated the greenhouse. Fine's had arranged its insurance with the same agent for many years and its coverage and premium costs were extensive. It relied on the agent to recommend appropriate coverage and paid the necessary premiums without question. An inspector for the insurance company advised the agent that the insurance policy with Fine's did not cover such matters as the failure of water pumps but the agent did not report this gap in insurance coverage to Fine's.

Fine's sued the agent, claiming he owed a duty of care to notify the customer of the insufficient coverage. The agent defended on the grounds that such a duty of care was so broad and sweeping that it would make him strictly liable and that it was not part of his duty to know everything about a client's business in order to be in a position to anticipate every conceivable form of loss. The court held that, on the facts of the case, the standard required the agent to warn the policy holder, and Fine's succeeded in recovering damages from the agent. The grounds for recovery could be classified as negligent omission.[50]

As noted in Chapter 4, a surgeon who operates on a patient without the patient's consent commits the tort of battery. In this context, "consent" means informed consent: Before operating, the surgeon should explain the procedure and the possible risks to the patient. The modern tendency has been to hold a doctor liable in battery only when it can be said that there has been no genuine informed consent at all. However, the courts have recognized a patient's right to full information about the risks inherent in a treatment and the omission of relevant information is a breach of the duty to obtain informed consent, possibly also resulting in negligent misrepresentation.[51]

The court also considers a second question: Would a reasonable person in the position of the plaintiff have decided against the procedure upon a proper disclosure of the risks?[52] If the court is satisfied that the answer is "yes," then it is also saying that the failure to inform was not only a breach of the standard of care but also caused the harm—and the patient will be awarded damages in compensation. But where the court is satisfied that the patient would still have consented even if the risk had been explained, the physician will not be liable.[53] This is a question of reliance or relevance of the information to the decision of the plaintiff.

Reliance and Detriment

The essence of causation, in the context of negligent misrepresentation and the professional–client relationships, is reliance. Did the client reasonably rely and act upon the advice of the professional? Would the client have acted in that way if he had not received that advice?[54] The advice must be used by the plaintiff to make the decision that triggered the loss.

---

[50] *Fine's Flowers Ltd. v. General Accident Assurance Co. et al.* (1974), 49 D.L.R. (3d) 641 *aff'd* (1977), 81 D.L.R. (3d) 139 (could also be classified as a breach of a special fiduciary relationship between Fine's Flowers and the insurance agent). See also *Martin v. Goldfarb* (1998), 163 D.L.R. (4th) 639, *Fletcher v. Manitoba Insurance Co.*, [1990] 3 S.C.R. 191, and *CIA Inspection Inc. v. Dan Lawrie Insurance Brokers*, [2010] O.J. No. 3313 at para. 7–14.

[51] Alternatively, it may be treated as a breach of fiduciary duty: see *Seney v. Crooks* (1998), 166 D.L.R. (4th) 337.

[52] *Hopp v. Lepp* (1980), 112 D.L.R. (3d) 67; *Reibl v. Hughes* (1980), 114 D.L.R. (3d) 1. Contrast the "subjective" test applied in product liability cases, in *Hollis v. Dow Corning Corp.* (1995), 129 D.L.R. (4th) 609, considered in Chapter 4.

[53] *Kitchen v. McMullen* (1989), 62 D.L.R. (4th) 481.

[54] As noted, a surgeon will not be held liable for failure to fully inform a patient of all known risks if it is clear that the patient would have agreed to the procedure in any event.

An investment company became interested in acquiring control of an apparently prosperous family business. The company commissioned a report on the proposed acquisition from a well-known firm of investment analysts. The report estimated the family business to be worth more than $4 million and considered it to be a sound investment. Without reading the report, the directors of the investment company decided that they should move quickly—they had heard rumours that there was another prospective purchaser. They purchased all the shares in the family business for $3.5 million. Afterward, they learned that a major asset of their acquisition was almost worthless and that they had paid much more than the shares were worth.[55] Despite their negligence, the analysts were not found liable since the opinion was not relied upon and therefore did not cause the loss.

reliance   acting in a certain way because one believed the information received

A further requirement is that the plaintiff's **reliance** on the misrepresentation must be reasonable. Should the information be used in the way that it was? Were other more appropriate sources available for use? An interesting issue was raised in *Avco Financial Services Realty Ltd. v. Norman*.[56] At trial, the defendant finance company was held liable for a negligent misrepresentation for failing to point out to the plaintiff that he would need to renew a life insurance policy if he wished to renew his mortgage; the plaintiff was found contributorily negligent by not inquiring further into the terms of the mortgage. On appeal, it was argued that the two findings were mutually inconsistent. If the plaintiff's reliance on the misrepresentation was reasonable, then he could not have been negligent himself. Alternatively, if he was negligent, his reliance on the statement would not have been reasonable. The Ontario Court of Appeal rejected both arguments. The two findings could coexist: It could be reasonable to rely on a statement, but negligent to rely exclusively upon it.[57]

Finally, a loss must be caused by acting upon the information. As in all torts, there is no liability without a loss. With respect to negligent misrepresentation, **detrimental reliance** means worsening one's situation after acting upon the false information. The loss is often purely economic. For more information on this topic, see the Companion Website.

detrimental reliance   the worsening of one's situation after acting upon false information

THE ROLE OF PROFESSIONAL ORGANIZATIONS

Responsibilities and Powers

Most major professions—medicine, nursing, dentistry, accounting, law, engineering, and architecture—are governed by professional organizations established under, and to some extent regulated by, provincial statutes. A typical professional organization has a governing council composed mainly of elected representatives of the profession, but it may also have external lay representatives appointed by the government to provide an impartial voice in decision-making and to represent the public interest. Professional bodies have a number of special responsibilities:

- to set educational and entrance standards for candidates wishing to become members;
- to examine and accredit educational institutions that prepare candidates for membership;

---

[55] Case 5.10 is based in part on *Toromont Industrial Holdings v. Thorne, Gunn, Helliwell & Christenson* (1977), 14 O.R. (2d) 87 (some damages were awarded, however, on other grounds). See also *Martin v. Goldfarb* (1998), 163 D.L.R. (4th) 639.

[56] (2003), 226 D.L.R. (4th) 175.

[57] See also M. *Tucci Construction Ltd. v. Lockwood*, [2000] O.J. No. 3192 *aff'd* [2002] O.J. No. 440, where an investor was misled by his accountant as to the nature of an agreement, but was held contributorily negligent for making no effort to have the agreement explained to him and for not taking legal advice.

- to set and adjust standards of ethical conduct and professional competence;

- to hear complaints about and administer discipline to members who fail to live up to the established standards; and

- to defend the profession against attacks that it considers unfair, and to look after the general welfare of the profession.

The governing statute typically gives members of the organization the exclusive right to use a professional designation to identify themselves and often also gives members the exclusive right to practise their profession.[58] Anyone who identifies himself as a member or attempts to practise when not accredited as a member may be—and usually is—prosecuted for committing an offence under the provincial statute.

Two important consequences flow from these powers. First, the right to discipline gives the organizations great power over individual members—expulsion or suspension for an extended period might destroy a member's means of livelihood. Second, exclusivity gives these self-governing professions great power over the quality and cost of their services to the public, and there is consequently a strong public interest in the affairs of the organizations.

CASE 5.11

Schilling entrusted $600 000 to an accountant, Hofman, to invest for him. Hofman absconded with the money. Hofman was a former member of the Association of Certified General Accountants of British Columbia and, having recently been disciplined for other offences, had been forced to resign from the Association and had been deprived of the right to describe himself as a CGA. Schilling sued the Association, alleging negligence in not preventing Hofman from continuing to practise—as a result of which Hofman had been able to defraud Schilling.

The British Columbia Court of Appeal held that the Association was not liable. There was no private law duty of care that required the Association to bring a criminal prosecution against a former member or to inform potential clients of his resignation.[59]

The Supreme Court of Canada faced a similar issue in *Cooper v. Hobart*.[60] In that case, an investor entrusted funds to a mortgage broker, who dealt with those funds in an unauthorized manner. The investor brought an action claiming damages against the Registrar (appointed by a statute regulating the mortgage-brokering profession). The plaintiff claimed that the Registrar, who had been investigating the broker, should have acted more promptly and suspended his licence earlier. The court held that the Registrar owed no duty of care to individual investors. The regulatory scheme required the Registrar to balance a number of competing interests in order to protect the public as a whole. The decision to suspend a broker involved both policy and quasi-judicial elements that were inconsistent with a duty of care to investors. To impose a duty of care in such circumstances would be to create an insurance scheme for investors at the cost of the taxpaying public.[61] For more information on this topic, see the Companion Website.

---

[58] For example, the exclusive right to practise applies to medicine and law, but not to some areas of accounting.

[59] *Schilling v. Certified General Accountants Assn. of British Columbia* (1996), 135 D.L.R. (4th) 669.

[60] (2001), 206 D.L.R. (4th) 193. See also *Edwards v. Law Society of Upper Canada* (2001), 206 D.L.R. (4th) 211, holding a law society not liable for failure to issue a warning that an investigation was being conducted into the handling of a lawyer's trust account.

[61] The governing statute of the professional organization may provide for immunity in respect of acts done in good faith in the performance of a duty or exercise of a power under the statute; see, for example, Regulated Health Professions Act, 1991, S.O. 1991, c. 18, s. 38, considered in *Rogers v. Faught* (2002), 212 D.L.R. (4th) 366.

Codes of Conduct

code of conduct a common standard of behaviour that may take the form of a values statement or a prescribed set of rules often used by a professional organization setting out the duties and appropriate standards of behaviour to be observed by its members

Professional bodies require their members to observe a **code of conduct**. As noted, such codes can be important as evidence of what constitutes an appropriate standard of professional care, and can help to determine the extent of the duty owed by members to their clients. Additionally, codes of conduct can impose ethical standards on their members over and above any legal requirements. Normally responsibilities to the public, the profession, other members of the profession, and clients are addressed, sometimes in multiple codes of conduct. Examples of typical codes of conduct can be found on organization websites; for example, the Canadian Association of Management Consultants addresses all these responsibilities in one code available on its website.[62]

Discipline

One of the most important responsibilities of professional bodies is to maintain and improve standards. That may involve disciplining members of the profession. Most professions inevitably have a minority of members who act in an unprofessional, unethical, or illegal manner. The usual response of governing bodies is to punish serious cases of unethical conduct by expulsion or suspension. (There may also be provision for some form of compensation to the injured client by the governing body itself.) These actions are quite apart from any criminal prosecution of the wrongdoer or from private (civil) liability actions.

The more pervasive and difficult cases are those arising from alleged breaches of professional standards of skill and care. In what may be considered isolated cases of negligence, governing bodies ordinarily leave the matter to the regular courts, where an aggrieved client may bring an action. However, in repeated cases of violations, or where the conduct of the professional is such that her competence to remain in practice is called into question, the governing body will take disciplinary action in the same manner as it would for unethical conduct.

For the conduct of disciplinary proceedings against members, a professional organization usually has a standing discipline committee consisting of experienced members of the profession. In addition, the governing council usually designates one or more other members or a separate committee to act as "prosecutor." Both the prosecutor and the accused member may be represented by lawyers at the disciplinary hearing. Ordinarily, the finding of a discipline committee takes the form of a recommendation to the governing council of the organization, which then acts on the recommendation to expel, suspend, reprimand, or acquit. Disciplinary proceedings of this nature are subject to a general duty to act fairly[63] and are subject to review by the regular courts.

Conflict of Duty toward Clients, the Profession, and the Courts

A member of a professional body faces a dilemma when required to testify in court proceedings affecting a client or patient. On the one hand, the member is expected to reply to questions under oath when examined and cross-examined in court; on the other hand, the member's testimony may appear to be a breach of confidence in the professional relationship with the client. A member or student member of a professional organization probably has a duty to ask the court for a ruling before divulging any information obtained in a confidential capacity.

---

[62] http://www.camc.com

[63] For a discussion of this duty see *Mondesir v. Manitoba Assn. of Optometrists* (1998), 163 D.L.R. (4th) 703. Where the disciplinary body is established by statute, its procedures are also subject to the Charter: see *Costco Wholesale Canada Ltd. v. British Columbia* (1998), 157 D.L.R. (4th) 725.

A professional who learns that a client may be engaged in or is contemplating possibly illegal activities may experience a further problem of interpreting her professional duties to the client. Needless to say, the professional must not assist the client (except to advise on possible illegality) and, in dissociating herself from the client's activities, might have to terminate the relationship. It appears to be generally conceded, however, that a professional would not normally be obliged to reveal confidential knowledge to prosecuting authorities; such information is said to be covered by **privilege**. However, where keeping silent would create a serious threat to public safety, the public interest requires disclosure.[64]

privilege the right of a professional to refuse to divulge information obtained in confidence from a client

INTERNATIONAL ISSUE
Solicitor–Client Privilege

As discussed earlier, the United States' Sarbanes–Oxley Act of 2002 (SOX) was enacted in response to major corporate scandals, including that of Enron. It gave the Securities and Exchange Commission the power to regulate the conduct of attorneys. One measure adopted is known as "up the ladder" reporting.[65] This measure requires very specific conduct from lawyers acting for public corporations. If a lawyer becomes aware of improper activities within the corporation, he or she must report the activity up the chain of command, all the way to the board of directors.

The most controversial part of the reporting requirement is known as "noisy withdrawal." If a corporation refuses to discontinue the improper activity, then the lawyer must withdraw her services and report the improper activity to the Securities and Exchange Commission.

The American Bar Association (ABA) raised strong objections to the "noisy withdrawal" proposal because it undermined the solicitor–client privilege, however it was forced to address the issue in its model codes of conduct. Rule 1.13 defines the degree of knowledge needed to trigger

an obligation to report organizational illegality. Although lawyers may (but are not obligated to) report details of the violations to the SEC,[66] the SEC does require the fact of the withdrawal to be reported and requires identification of the "tainted SEC filing." This obligation applies notwithstanding any ABA rule to the contrary.

Questions to Consider

1. Why would the American Bar Association object to "noisy withdrawal"?

2. Is there a public interest argument to counter the position of the ABA?

3. How does optional reporting affect the privilege?

Sources: U.S. Securities and Exchange Commission, "Final Rule: Implementation of Standards of Professional Conduct for Attorneys," 17 CFR Part 205, September 26, 2003, www.sec.gov/rules/final/338185.htm; American Bar Association, Model Rules of Professional Conduct. Rules 1.6; 1.13; Sarbanes–Oxley Act, 17 C.F.R. §§ 205.3(d) (2010); SEC Release No. 33-8150; Theodore L. Banks and Frederick Banks, *Corporate Legal Compliance Handbook*, (Wolters Kluwer , N.Y, 2013) pp. 3-58 to 3-63.

MULTI-DISCIPLINARY PARTNERSHIPS

Traditionally, professionals have carried on their practices either alone or in partnership with fellow members of the same profession. Some professions forbid their members to incorporate. In the case of some professions—in particular, law—it has, in the past, been unlawful for a lawyer to practise in partnership with a non-lawyer. In this way, the law firm's entire activities would be subject to law society oversight and individual lawyers would remain personally liable to clients and the public. However, these rules are changing.

In the past few years, legislation has been adopted in a number of provinces to permit the creation of "professional corporations"; we discuss these further in Chapter 25. Professionals choosing to incorporate as professional corporations remain personally liable

---

[64] *Smith v. Jones* (1999), 169 D.L.R. (4th) 385 (S.C.C.). The case concerned conversations between a psychiatrist and an alleged serial rapist. See *Canada (Privacy Commissioner) v. Blood Tribe Department of Health*, 2008 S.C.C. 44 where the Supreme Court prioritized solicitor–client privilege over access rights.

[65] Title 17, Code of Federal Regulations, Part 205, s. 205.3.

[66] *Ibid.*, s. 205.3(6)(d)(2).

for their torts and fiduciary duties. The other major development is the changing attitude toward "multi-disciplinary partnerships" (MDPs). The main focus of the current debate on MDPs is on the combining of accountants and lawyers into a single firm. MDPs of this type are common in Europe, where the major international accounting firms have established their own legal departments. Advocates of MDPs claim a number of advantages—they benefit clients whose problems cannot readily be compartmentalized into legal and non-legal, and they provide a more efficient "one-stop shop" for business clients who require both accounting and legal services. By working together as a team, the quality of service provided by both professions is improved. There are, however, also concerns, including the possibility that professional duties and codes of conduct might conflict,[67] and the increased sizes of firms and diversity of services provided might more readily give rise to conflicts of interest.

Although the legal profession's licensing bodies historically opposed MDPs, the fundamental freedom of association in the Charter might well give a right to establish such partnerships.[68] In July 2010, British Columbia joined Ontario and Quebec in allowing lawyers to participate in MDPs.[69]

Strategies to Manage the Legal Risks

The rules governing most professions require members to carry public liability insurance to protect members (and their partners) from liability for unintentional wrongdoing. Anyone providing opinions to the public should have third-party liability coverage. Other preventive measures should also be taken. The risks of contractual liability are reduced when a written retainer (or contract) includes a detailed description of the scope of work and opinions to be provided to the client. Disclaimers should be used to exclude work not undertaken and limit liability for opinions expressed. A disclaimer's description of the purpose for which the information is being provided, as well as a restriction on who may use or rely on the opinions, will reduce the risk of tort and fiduciary liability.

Sometimes professionals give advice for free as part of volunteer work or marketing campaigns. Disclaimers limiting scope, use, and purpose of the work should also be applied to these services as neither tort nor fiduciary liability depends upon being paid for the advice.

Of course, reducing the number of mistakes is the most effective preventive measure. Professionals should regularly participate in continuing education and professional development programs to ensure they are practising at the standard of their profession. Indeed, most professions set annual mandatory professional development requirements; without such mandatory requirements, the profession itself might be held

---

[67] For example, an accountant may be required to report certain financial information where a lawyer has a duty of confidentiality. These concerns have increased since the Enron affair.

[68] In *Black v. Law Society of Alberta*, [1989] 1 S.C.R. 591, the Supreme Court of Canada struck down a rule that Alberta lawyers could not enter into partnership with lawyers from outside the province. The decision was based on the mobility rights provisions of the Charter, but arguably the right of association would have been equally applicable.

[69] A 2007 Competition Bureau report supported MDPs for lawyers: "Self Regulated Professions—Balancing Competition and Regulation," December 11, 2007, www.competitionbureau.gc.ca/epic/site/cbbc.nsf/en/02523e .html. See also M. Rappaport, "Competition Bureau's Study Draws Tepid Reaction from Legal Community," *The Lawyers Weekly*, January 11, 2008, www.lawyersweekly.ca/index.php?section=article&articleid=599. Rule 2-23.2, British Columbia Law Society Rules, pursuant to Legal Profession Act, S.B.C. 1998, c. 9.

liable for negligent omission—failing to monitor the competence of its members. With respect to fiduciary liability, screening for conflict of interest should be done before a new client is accepted in an effort to flag situations where the interests may conflict with existing clients. Software is available that can automatically search existing files for names, addresses, or other details that are already in the system.

Even liability arising from intentional behaviour such as fraud, deceit, or breach of fiduciary duty can be reduced if professionals practising in partnerships adopt control mechanisms requiring more than one professional to work on or be familiar with every file. The more people are involved in and familiar with a file, the more difficult it is to conceal fraudulent (or negligent) behaviour.

QUESTIONS FOR REVIEW

1. What are the arguments in favour of imposing a wide liability on professionals?
2. What is the main effect of increased use of liability insurance?
3. What is the nature of the fiduciary duty owed by a professional? In what way can that duty be wider than a contractual duty?
4. Can a client choose to sue a professional adviser in either contract or tort? What factors will influence the decision?
5. Why were the courts initially reluctant to recognize liability for negligent misstatements to persons who are not clients?
6. How did the decision in *Hedley Byrne v. Heller & Partners* address the issue in Question 5?
7. What is the test now applied in Canada to determine whether a professional owes a duty of care to a person for a negligent misstatement?
8. How does a fiduciary duty differ from the duty of care owed in negligent misrepresentation?
9. What must a plaintiff prove to establish negligent misrepresentation?
10. Why might it be difficult to establish contributory negligence as a defence in a case involving negligent misrepresentation?
11. When will a professional be liable for an omission?
12. What are the objections to a "hindsight" approach in determining the appropriate standard of professional care?
13. What is the essence of causation in most professional–client relationships?
14. What are the main responsibilities imposed or assumed by professional bodies?
15. Should professional bodies be allowed to discipline their members, or should discipline be left to the courts?
16. What are the potential advantages and possible disadvantages of multi-disciplinary partnerships?

CASES AND PROBLEMS

1. Continuing Scenario

   One of the most important pieces of equipment for a restaurant business is the stove. Ashley wanted to make sure she installed the right one in her new restaurant, so she did lots of research on the internet to identify the possible selections. After visiting several manufacturers' websites, she narrowed her choice down to two commercial ranges: the FOX 950, a gas cooktop with an electric oven for $5000, because cooking with gas was flexible; and the more expensive Hiking 760 for $7000, an electric oven with an induction cooktop, because it gave off less heat and the kitchen would remain cooler. She visited the Restaurant Association website and saw that the Association ranked the Hiking induction cooktop first in its category. Later, when discussing the cost of kitchen appliances with

Bill, her insurance agent, Bill told Ashley that she would get a reduced insurance rate for an induction range because the risk of fire was less. In the long run this could offset the higher price. Bill referred her to Smith's Appliance, where he knew she could see both floor models. Bill neglected to tell Ashley that Smith's Appliance was owned by his parents. At the appliance store, the clerk said both ranges were excellent and her choice depended on whether the flexibility of gas or the coolness of induction was most important to her; the clerk's personal preference was induction. Ashley called Bill from the store and he confirmed that induction would mean a $500 savings on her property insurance premium. Bill knew this because a previous client had saved this much; he did not think it was necessary to call the insurance company for a quote.

Ashley ordered the Hiking induction stove and paid the extra $2000. Unfortunately, once the stove was installed and working, the kitchen was not cool. The electric oven threw so much heat that it was necessary to reconfigure the air conditioning to cool down the kitchen at a cost of $4000. As well Ashley's insurance premium was not reduced because her water heater was fueled with gas and so the insurance company felt the fire risk remained the same.

Does Ashley have a claim against Bill? the Restaurant Association? Smith's Appliance? Discuss the possible causes of action and Ashley's damages.

2. Mitchell was the owner of a landscaping business. He came to know "Simpson," an apparently successful businessman who engaged in various speculative investments. In reality, "Simpson" was a former lawyer whose real name was Anderson and who had been disbarred and convicted of a number of offences involving fraud.

Mitchell and Anderson became friendly and Anderson persuaded Mitchell to join him in a number of investments, which, at first, seemed to be successful. In the course of their business dealings, Mitchell said that he thought it would be sensible for him to retain the services of a lawyer: Anderson recommended that he see a lawyer named Gordon.

Gordon quickly realized that Mitchell's business associate, "Simpson," was actually Anderson, whom he had known before Anderson's conviction. Gordon acted for Mitchell in a number of transactions, but despite his knowledge of Anderson's background, he said nothing about it to Mitchell.

A year or so later, Mitchell discovered that most of the investments that he had undertaken with Anderson (both before and after becoming a client of Gordon) turned out to be complete failures. Apparently, Anderson had siphoned off most of the value of the properties they had bought.

Mitchell brought an action against Gordon, claiming that Gordon should have told him of Anderson's history and that, if he had done so, Mitchell would have terminated the relationship.

Identify Mitchell's cause of action and what Mitchell needs to prove. Should Mitchell succeed?

3. Hedgeways Construction Inc. is a company specializing in highway construction. In response to a public invitation from the government of British Columbia to tender for an important road construction project, it submitted what turned out to be the winning bid.

The detailed description of the project in the tender invitation document contained a number of important inaccuracies. As a result, the cost of completing the project was substantially greater than Hedgeways had estimated and it ended up suffering a loss on the project.

The tender invitation document issued by the province contained a statement to the effect that any representations made therein were "general information" only and were not guaranteed by the province. The actual specifications and engineering drawings in the document had been prepared by Brown and Green, two qualified engineers employed by the firm Black and Associates Ltd., who had contracted with the province to provide the specifications.

What claim, if any, does Hedgeways have against (a) the provincial government; (b) Black and Associates; and (c) Brown and Green?

4. Hopkins Steel Ltd. was a long-established corporation operating in Ontario. A few years ago it decided to change its bank and moved its account to the Canadian Business Bank. Before accepting the account, the bank made various inquiries and, in particular, examined the audited accounts of Hopkins over the preceding three years. The accounts showed a consistent record of profitability, growing steadily over the years. With this information the bank agreed to extend a line of credit to Hopkins and, over the following year or so, made advances to it totalling more than $2 million.

Shortly thereafter, Hopkins ran into serious trouble and eventually was forced into bankruptcy with debts in excess of $2 million.

The bank brought a claim against Cross, Jones, and Sparrow, the accounting firm that had audited the annual accounts of Hopkins during the years in question. The bank claimed that the accounts for the preceding years, which it had examined before granting the loans, were inaccurate and had been negligently prepared and that Hopkins was already in serious trouble before the bank accepted it as a client.

In each case, the audited accounts contained the following statement:

> We have examined the balance sheet of Hopkins Steel Limited as at [date] and the statements of earnings, retained earnings, and changes in financial position for the year then ended. Our examination was made in accordance with generally accepted auditing standards, and accordingly included such tests and other procedures as we considered necessary in the circumstances.

According to the evidence, during the years in which Cross, Jones, and Sparrow provided services to Hopkins, it also from time to time provided further information with respect to Hopkins to third parties, such as creditors and a bonding insurer for the company, and provided Hopkins with a number of copies of its financial statements and audit reports.

Does the bank have any claim against the accounting firm?

5. Prince, a chartered accountant employed as a controller and living in Calgary, was bored with his job. He applied to an Ottawa-based software company that was advertising for a chartered accountant to help in the development of new accounting software. At the job interview, Paulson, the manager of research and development, described the new venture and told Prince that the position would involve advising on accounting standards for many new products, addressing such things as cash flow management, inventory controls, accounts receivables, and more. Prince was told that the company would commit significant funds to the project for the next 10 years. This position was the first of many accounting jobs. It was implicit that Prince (if hired) would become senior management, supervising the subsequent hires. Formal plans were still before the executive committee but would be in place before the start date of May 1. This was exactly the type of new challenge Prince was looking for, so when Paulson called to offer him the job of manager, financial standards, Prince accepted immediately. A few days later he received the employment contract by email, signed it, and returned it by courier. The job description said that Paulson would supply accounting expertise as required by the employer. Prince and his wife quit their jobs, sold their house in Calgary, bought a smaller, more expensive house in Ottawa, and moved across the country.

When the executive committee met in April to consider the development plan, they decided the plan was too aggressive and approved only the development of one aspect—cash-flow management. The project would be funded for only five months. Prince commenced work on May 1 and helped design the cash-flow software. When he asked Paulson about the next phase, he was told only that it was not firm yet. No other accountants were hired and, after five months, Prince was transferred to the accounting department to do typical controller work similar to his job in Calgary. He was unhappy with the transfer and quit.

Identify the possible causes of action and assess their chances of success. Would it make a difference to your answer if the contract of employment included a term that the employer might transfer or reassign the employee to another position within the company at any time and a term that said that all agreements between the parties were included in the written document?

6. Hansen had practised for a number of years as an investment counsellor, advising clients on how to invest their savings. He had qualified as a Member of the Association of General Investment Counsellors, which entitled him to use the letters "M.A.G.I.C." after his name.

Over the years, the association (AGIC) received numerous complaints about Hansen. Many of his suggested investment schemes turned out to be disastrous, and there were strong suspicions that not only was he wholly incompetent but he was also defrauding some of his clients.

Two years ago, after one particularly serious complaint, Hansen was called to attend a meeting of the disciplinary committee of AGIC. The committee informed him that, in view of the long history of complaints against him, it proposed to deprive him of his membership and to inform the Attorney General's department of the most recent complaint, about which there was at least a suspicion of fraud.

Hansen, who was a very persuasive talker, eventually convinced the committee not to report him, and to allow him to resign from the association rather than being dismissed. He signed an undertaking that he would not practise again as an investment counsellor and would no longer describe himself as "M.A.G.I.C."

Despite the undertaking, Hansen very soon resumed his practice, in his old office, and continued to use his title. Soon afterward, he was consulted by Thaler, who said she had heard excellent reports about him from a friend. Hansen quickly talked Thaler into entrusting her life savings to him. It appears now that Hansen has disappeared to an island in the South Pacific, taking Thaler's money with him.

Thaler has commenced proceedings against AGIC, claiming that if the association had reported Hansen to the proper authorities and had taken steps to see that he abided by his undertaking to AGIC, Hansen would not have been in a position to defraud her.

What claim does Thaler have against AGIC?

Additional Resources for Chapter 5 on the Companion Website

(www.pearsoncanada.ca/smyth)

In addition to pre- and post-tests, mini-cases, and application exercises, the Companion Website includes the following province-specific resources for Chapter 5:

- **Alberta:** Podiatrists Act; Professional Liability; Professional Liability Insurance
- **Atlantic Provinces:** Limited Liability Partnerships; Professional Corporations
- **British Columbia:** The Law Society of British Columbia; Self-Regulating Professional Bodies
- **Manitoba/Saskatchewan:** Codes of Professional Conduct; Negligent Misrepresentation
- **Ontario:** Codes of Conduct; Conflict of Interest; Disclaimers; Fiduciary Duty; Lawyers; Limited Liability Partnerships; Multi-Disciplinary Partnerships; Professional Discipline; Professional Organizations; Public Liability Insurance

Chapter 6

Formation of a Contract: Offer and Acceptance

In this chapter we describe the essential requirements of a contract, and in particular, how a contract is formed.

We examine such questions as:

- Why is a contract enforceable in law?
- How is a contract formed?
- How do we determine the terms of a contract?
- Why are standard form contracts used? What are their benefits and dangers?
- How does an offer come to an end?
- What is the difference between unilateral and bilateral contracts?

THE ROLE OF CONTRACT LAW

Contracts are a good example of voluntary legal relationships. They are not legal obligations forced upon everyone like tort or criminal liability. Parties choose to make a contract and only then become legally obligated to comply with its terms. Contract law empowers parties to create legal obligations that would otherwise not exist. Sometimes, though, inequality of bargaining power or expertise between parties results in unfair contracts. Contract law has rules to address these situations.

THE NATURE OF A CONTRACT

contract a set of promises that the law will enforce

Contracts begin with a promise, but not all promises become contracts. Although there may be a moral obligation to keep all promises, it does not follow that there is a legal obligation. Contract law sets the rules for how ordinary promises become legally binding promises. "The most popular description of a **contract** is also the most exact one, namely that it is a promise or set of promises which the law will enforce."[1] Which promises will the law enforce? There are four basic requirements to form a legally enforceable contract: offer, acceptance, consideration, and intention. This chapter addresses offer and acceptance; consideration and intention are discussed in Chapter 7.

THE NATURE OF AN OFFER

offer a description of a promise one party is willing to make, subject to the agreement of the other party

offeror the person making the offer

offeree the person to whom the offer is made

A contract does not come into existence until an offer has been made by one party and accepted by the other party. An **offer** is a description of a promise or set of promises one party, the **offeror**, is willing to make, subject to the willingness of the other party, the **offeree**, to agree to the same promises. When the offeree accepts the offer by agreeing to the description of promises or requests, the offer is transformed into a contract. The promise is no longer tentative: Both the offeror and offeree are bound to carry out their promises.

A mere invitation to do business is not an offer capable of forming a contract. The display of a coat in a store window does not amount to an offer to sell; a catalogue does not guarantee that the goods pictured or described will be delivered to all who try to order them. These are simply merchandising or advertising devices to attract customers and to start negotiations for a contract of sale. A prospective customer, acting in response to the invitation, may make an offer and the seller may in turn accept or refuse.

Advertisements to sell goods at a certain price are generally mere invitations to the public to visit the place of business. A business is not expected to sell the goods to everyone who reads its advertisement: Its supply is limited, and it cannot precisely predict the number of readers who will be seriously interested. If the advertisement were taken to be an offer and too many people accepted it, the business would be liable for breach of contract to all those who accepted and to whom it could not supply the advertised goods.

However, this does not mean that advertisements can never be offers; the courts have sometimes held them to be offers when their wording reasonably favoured this interpretation. An advertisement to sell a fixed number of items at a fixed price to those who accept first, an offer of a reward for information or for the return of a lost object, or a reward to any person using a preventive medicine who still catches an illness all may be valid offers. This group of advertisements forms a very small proportion of advertisements—the exception rather than the rule.

---

[1] P. H. Winfield, *Pollock's Principles of Contract*, 13th ed. (London: Stevens & Sons, 1950) at 1.

When self-service supermarkets and drugstores appeared, the courts had to decide whether the display of merchandise in itself amounted to an offer—and the act of the customer in taking the merchandise from the shelf amounted to an acceptance—or whether the display was merely an invitation to the customer to make an offer by taking the merchandise to the cashier. The question was important, because legislation made it unlawful to sell certain medicinal products unless the sale was supervised by a registered pharmacist.[2]

The court held that the statute was not violated because a registered pharmacist was at hand near the cashier and could refuse a customer's offer to purchase any drug. The judge said:

The mere fact that a customer picks up a bottle of medicine from the shelves in this case does not amount to an acceptance of an offer to sell. It is an offer by the customer to buy, and there is no sale effected until the buyer's offer to buy is accepted by the acceptance of the price.[3]

THE COMMUNICATION OF AN OFFER

The form of an offer is not important as long as it is heard and understood. The offeror could say, "I offer to sell you my car for $500" or "I will sell you my car for $500" or even "I'll take $500 for my car." All are equally good offers containing a tentative promise to sell the car if the buyer agrees to pay the stated price.

In most situations, an offeror communicates orally or in writing, but she can also express an offer by conduct without words. A taxi driver opening the door of her cab or a bidder raising his finger at an auction may also be offers.

An offeree cannot accept an offer until she is aware of it. Crossed offers provide an example of this rule, as shown in Illustration 6.1.

A tells B she is interested in selling her car. The next day, A writes to B offering to sell her car for $1500; B has also written a letter crossing A's letter in the mail offering to buy the car for $1500. There is no contract: B was unaware of A's offer when he wrote and so his letter could not be an acceptance; similarly, A was unaware of B's offer—A's letter, too, could not be an acceptance. Unless either A or B sends a subsequent acceptance, no contract will be formed.

Similarly, we cannot be required to pay people who do work for us without our knowledge. We are entitled first to receive an offer to do the work, which we may then accept or reject. A person for whom work has been done without his request, and without his knowledge, may well benefit from it; but as he has not accepted any offer to do the work, he has no contractual obligation to pay for it.

Suppose, however, that goods or services are provided to a person without his request but in circumstances where he has an opportunity to reject them. The general contract law rule is that if he accepts the services or uses the goods, he is presumed to have accepted the offer and to have promised to pay the price. This rule triggered unconscionable selling practices that tempt consumers to bind themselves to pay for goods they did not request. Many provinces have passed legislation to reverse the rule, at least as it relates to consumers. For example, section 12 of British Columbia's Business Practices and Consumer Protection Act[4] states the following:

(1) A consumer has no legal obligation in respect of unsolicited goods or services unless and until the consumer expressly acknowledges to the supplier in writing his or her intention to accept the goods or services.

---

[2] *Pharmaceutical Society of Great Britain v. Boots Cash Chemists (Southern) Ltd.*, [1952] 2 All E.R. 456.

[3] *Ibid.*, at p. 458.

[4] S.B.C. 2004, c. 2.

(2) Unless the consumer has given the acknowledgment referred to in subsection (1), the supplier does not have a cause of action for any loss, use, misuse, possession, damage, or misappropriation in respect of the goods or services or the value obtained by the use of the goods or services.

Section 13 of Ontario's Consumer Protection Act[5] contains a similar provision; however, consider section 68 which reads:

(1) Despite section 13, a consumer who . . . receives a credit card from a credit card issuer without applying for it shall be deemed to have entered into a credit agreement with the issuer with respect to the card on first using the card.

WRITTEN OFFERS

Standard Form Contracts: Their Risks and Benefits

Offers do not have to be in writing. However, businesses that sell to the general public often present the terms of their offers in written documents handed to their customers, or they post notices containing terms on their business websites. Sometimes both methods are used together, with the delivered document referring to the terms posted in the notice. Common examples are tickets for theatres and airlines, hotel bookings, credit card agreements, online purchases, and insurance policies.

Almost without exception, a person receiving any one of these documents is neither asked nor expected to read, approve, or change the terms. If the customer took the time to read it and suggest changes, the agent of the offeror would probably become very annoyed. She would say, "Take it or leave it." As a practical matter, an offeree cannot change any terms of a **standard form contract**, also known as a *contract of adhesion*: there is no real element of bargaining. He must accept the offer as is or not at all. Often, as when travelling by airline, there may be no other practical means of transportation between two points; an offeree does not have the choice of refusing—he must accept if he is to make his trip. In this situation, an offeror business is strongly tempted to disregard the interests of its offerees, the general public, and give itself every advantage, and it rarely resists this temptation.

Still, in fast-paced retail situations, the standard form contract is needed: Imagine waiting in line at the car rental office in an airport while each would-be passenger bargained separately for each term in his contract! Contract law recognizes the business need for standard form contracts while guarding against abuse from unequal bargaining power.

There are three means of protection from this inequality in bargaining. First, if the business falls within an area regulated by a government board, the terms of its contracts are subject to board approval. When boards operate effectively, the public is usually well protected and unreasonable terms are excluded. Second, some segments of the public, such as consumers, are offered special protection. Consumer protection legislation provides disclosure requirements and post-acceptance cancellation options. Third and finally, in the vast range of unregulated activity, the public receives only as much protection as the courts can find in the general law of contract.

Required Notice of Terms

As a general rule, without legislative intervention, the courts will normally give effect to the terms of a commercial contract freely entered into, even a contract of adhesion.[6] Suppose, however, that an offeree does not know that the offer contains a certain term

standard form contract an offer prepared in advance by the offeror, including terms favourable to the offeror that cannot be changed by the offeree, but must be accepted as is or rejected in their entirety, also known as a contract of adhesion

---

[5] S.O. 2002 c. 30, Sch. A.

[6] *Seidel v. TELUS Communications*, 2011 SCC 15, at para. 2, 36.

or the terms are not all included in one document. She purchases a ticket to attend a baseball game. A clause on the back states that the management reserves the right to remove the ticket holder at any time without giving reasons. She does not know or suspect that the ticket contains such a term. Is she bound by it? If she satisfies the court that she did not know of it, then the court will ask what steps the business took to bring the term to the attention of its customers. If the court decides that the steps were insufficient, the ticket holder is not bound by the term; and if she has been wrongfully ejected from the baseball park, she will have the same remedy as if the term had not been on the ticket.

On the other hand, if the court finds that the business did what was reasonably necessary in the circumstances to bring the term to the notice of its customers, then the ticket holder is bound by the term whether she knew of it or not. Each "ticket case" is decided on its own facts, and there is no firm list of requirements for what is or is not sufficient notice.

CASE 6.2

In *Parker v. South Eastern Railway Co.*,[7] Parker deposited his suitcase in the luggage room of a railway station, paid a fee, and received a ticket on the face of which were the words "See back." On the reverse side of the ticket, it was stated that the railway was not liable for loss in excess of £10.

The bag was lost, and Parker sued the railway for his loss, £24. On appeal, the court decided that the issue was whether the railway had done what was reasonably necessary to notify customers of the term. The court ordered a new trial because the trial judge had not asked the jury to decide this question.

The fact that the front of the ticket in Case 6.2 contained the words "See back" is important. If a ticket—or other document given to the customer at the time of purchase—contains a short and clear reference to other terms appearing either on the reverse side or posted on a sign or website, it is likely that "reasonably sufficient notice" of those terms has been given.

A sign in a parking lot disclaiming liability for loss or damage to cars or contents may not in itself be reasonably sufficient notice to bind those who park their cars there: We have to ask whether the ticket or voucher received when a customer parks her car contains a clear reference to the sign and whether, in the circumstances, a customer ought to recognize the term stated on the sign as part of the contract she is making with the operator of the lot. A printed ticket or receipt containing the words "subject to the conditions as exhibited on the premises" may be enough to tie the sign to each contract. The sign must, of course, be displayed prominently, but this in itself might not be sufficient; the fact must be brought home to the customer at the time of making the contract. The operator of the parking lot, garage, or other place of storage cannot safely assume that he may exempt himself from liability merely by putting up a sign.[8]

> The best way of proving [that a customer has knowledge of the terms] is by a written document signed by the party to be bound. Another way is by handing him, before or at the time of the contract, a written notice specifying certain terms and making it clear to him that the contract is in those terms. A prominent public notice which is plain for him to see when he makes the contract would, no doubt, have the same effect.[9]

---

[7] (1877), 2 C.P.D. 416.

[8] *Watkins v. Rymill* (1883), 10 Q.B.D. 178. It may be more difficult for the operator of a parking lot to exempt himself from liability when the customer leaves the keys in the car at the request of the parking lot operator, because a bailment for storage and safekeeping is implied. See Chapter 17, infra. See also *Brown v. Toronto Auto Parks Ltd.*, [1954] O.W.N. 869; *Samuel Smith & Sons Ltd. v. Silverman* (1961), 29 D.L.R. (2d) 98; *Hefferon v. Imperial Parking Co. Ltd.* (1973), 46 D.L.R. (3d) 642.

[9] *Olley v. Marlborough Court Ltd.*, [1949] 1 All E.R. 127, per Denning, L.J., at 134.

Unusual or Unexpected Terms

An offeree may be willing to accept terms printed on a ticket or displayed on a poster because she assumes, reasonably, that the risk relates closely to the bargain she has made—for instance, a term denying any liability for damage to her car while parked in a parking lot. She would understand that the cost of parking would be higher if the car park operator had to insure against the risk of damage to her vehicle. But she would be surprised to find that the terms also exempted the operator from liability for personal injuries suffered by her as she walked to and from her parked car. Unexpected or onerous terms need to be brought directly to the attention of the offeree; indeed, she might then decide to park elsewhere. In other words, a court may find that there was adequate notice of usual, expected terms that the offeree chose not to read, but greater effort must be made to give notice of a surprising, shocking, or unusually unfair term. Again, if the offeree signs a document, a stronger presumption arises that she has accepted all the terms it contains; avoiding the consequences becomes much more difficult.[10]

CASE 6.3

A clause on the back of a car rental contract signed by the renter said that the renter was responsible for all theft if the renter was negligent, and the renter must keep doors, windows, and ignition locked when not in the car. The renter left the car unlocked and running outside an Edmonton bar between 1:00 and 3:00 in the morning. The Alberta Court of Appeal held that the clause was not unusual, unexpected, or onerous, and therefore did not require special measures. Nor was the physical arrangement of the contract difficult to read, surprising, or tricky. Therefore, the clause applied and the renter was held liable for the damages arising from the theft of the vehicle.[11]

However, the prospects of persuading a court to disregard onerous terms imposed in a written and signed document improve somewhat[12] if there is misrepresentation or an unconscionable result, as we shall see in Chapter 9. For more information on this topic, see the Companion Website.

THE LAPSE AND REVOCATION OF AN OFFER

Lapse

lapse the termination of an offer when the offeree fails to accept it within a specified time, or if no time is specified, then within a reasonable time

When an offer has lapsed, the offeree can no longer accept it even if he is unaware that it has lapsed; it has become void and no longer exists. An offer may **lapse** in any of the following ways:

a. when the offeree fails to accept within a time specified in the offer
b. when the offeree fails to accept within a reasonable time, if the offer has not specified any time limit
c. when either of the parties dies or becomes insane prior to acceptance

Predicting what amounts to a "reasonable time" is often difficult. To say it depends upon the circumstances of each case may not seem helpful. The Supreme Court of Canada discussed how the subject matter of the contract may provide a clue for deciding whether a reasonable length of time has elapsed in an offer to buy or sell:

> Farm lands, apart from evidence to the contrary . . . are not subject to frequent or sudden changes or fluctuations in price and, therefore, in the ordinary course of business a

---

[10] See *978011 Ontario Ltd. v. Cornell Engineering Co.* (2001), 12 B.L.R. (3d) 240 (Ont. C.C.).

[11] *Budget Rent-A-Car of Edmonton Ltd. v. University of Toronto,* 1995 ABCA 52, (1995), 165 A.R. 236 (Alta. C.A.).

[12] *Tilden Rent-A-Car Co. v. Clendenning* (1978), 18 O.R. (2d) 601; *D.J.Provencher Ltd.v. Tyco Investments of Canada Ltd.* (1997), 42 B.L.R. (2nd) 45.

reasonable time for the acceptance of an offer would be longer than that with respect to such commodities as shares of stock upon an established trading market. It would also be longer than with respect to perishable goods such as food products. The fact that it was land would tend to lengthen what would be a reasonable time but other circumstances must also be considered.[13]

The "other circumstances" include the manner in which an offer is made and whether its wording indicates urgency. Often when a prospective purchaser makes an offer to buy property, she specifies that the offer must be accepted within 24 hours. The restriction is in her interest because it gives the vendor very little time to use this "firm offer" as a means of approaching other possible purchasers and bidding up the price.

Revocation

Notice of Revocation
An offeror may be able to revoke (that is, withdraw) an offer at any time before acceptance, even when it has promised to hold the offer open for a specified time. The offeror must provide notice of revocation to make it effective.

ILLUSTRATION 6.2

A Inc. sends a letter by courier on January 15 to B offering to sell its warehouse to B for $800 000, stating that the offer is open only until January 19 and that it must have heard from B by then. B receives the letter on January 16, and immediately prepares a letter of acceptance. Before B sends his reply on the morning of January 17, A changes its mind and telephones B saying that it withdraws its offer.

The revocation is valid because it has reached B before he has accepted. Accordingly, B can no longer accept A's offer.

In Illustration 6.2, the offeror clearly revoked the offer before its acceptance: Its direct communication of the revocation left no doubt about the offeree's knowledge of it. The legal position of the parties is less certain if the offeree merely hears rumours that the offeror has revoked, or hears that the offeror has made it impossible to carry out the offer because it has sold the property to someone else. The court will consider the offer revoked if it would be unreasonable for the offeree to suppose that the offeror still intended to stand by its offer.[14] Nevertheless, making an offer to sell a particular item to one party and then selling it to another without having directly withdrawn the offer to the first party is always poor business practice. Quite apart from damage to goodwill, the offeror runs the risk of the first offeree accepting and of the offeror then being in breach when unable to fulfill both contracts.

Options

An offeree may obligate an offeror to keep its offer open (that is, not to revoke it) for a specified time in a couple of ways: (1) the offer itself may specify that it is irrevocable; or (2) a subsequent contract called an **option** may be made to keep the offer open. In an option, the offeree makes a contract with the offeror in the following general terms: The offeree agrees to pay a sum of money as consideration (discussed in Chapter 7); in return the offeror agrees (1) to keep the offer open for a specified time; and (2) not to make contracts with other parties that would prevent the offeror from fulfilling its offer (that is, to give the offeree the exclusive right to accept the offer). Without consideration, an option remains a simple offer.[15] Options can be a useful tool for business decision making.

option a contract to keep an offer open for a specified time in return for a sum of money

---

[13] *Barrick v. Clark*, [1950] 4 D.L.R. 529, p. at 537.

[14] See *Dickinson v. Dodds* (1876), 2 Ch. D. 463. See also *Hughes v. Gyratron Developments Ltd.*, [1988] B.C.J. No. 1598.

[15] *Sail Labrador v. Challenge One (The)* 1999 1 S.C.R. 265, at para 42.

ILLUSTRATION 6.3

PreciseComp pays $3000 to A for the right to buy her farm within three months for $350 000 and also buys similar option agreements from other farmers in the vicinity. In this way, PreciseComp can find out at a modest cost whether all the necessary property will be available for a new plant and what the total cost will be. It need not take up or **exercise an option**—that is, accept the original offer to sell any of the farms. The relatively small sums paid for the option agreements are simply the cost of a feasibility study for the projected plant. Alternatively, PreciseComp could require each of the farmers to honour the options and sell at the agreed price—provided PreciseComp accepts the offers contained in the options within the specified time.

exercise an option accept the offer contained in an option

In Illustration 6.3, the farmers are in the position of offerors who, for an agreed period of time, are not free to withdraw their offers without being in breach of the option. The parties are really contemplating two contracts: first, the option agreement itself, and second, the actual sale that will take place only if the option is exercised.

REJECTION AND COUNTER-OFFER BY THE OFFEREE

In business negotiations the parties often make a number of offers and counter-offers, but until an offer by one side is accepted without alteration, modification, or condition by the other, there is no contract; the parties have no legal obligation to one another. When an offeree receives an offer and, though interested, chooses to change some of its terms, he has not accepted; rather, he has made a counter-offer of his own, amounting to rejection of the offer. The initiative in bargaining may shift back and forth until one party finds the last proposal of the other satisfactory and accepts it without qualification. Only then is a contract formed.

The making of a counter-offer is a rejection of the earlier offer and brings it to an end. If the offeror in turn rejects the counter-offer, the original offer does not revive. Only if the offeror agrees to re-offer it may the offeree accept the original offer. However, when an offeree merely inquires whether the terms offered are the best he can expect, it does not amount to a rejection.

ILLUSTRATION 6.4

A sent a fax to B offering to sell her car for $2000. B replied by fax, "I will give you $1900 for the car." Two days later B sent a fax again to A saying, "I have been reconsidering. I will accept your offer to sell for $2000 after all."

In Illustration 6.4, there is no contract. B's counter-offer of $1900 brought the original offer to sell for $2000 to an end. While B has phrased her final statement in the form of an acceptance, she is doing no more than making a fresh offer of her own that A may or may not wish to accept. Perhaps someone else has offered A $2100 for the car in the meantime. If, when A made the offer to sell for $2000, B had simply inquired whether this was the lowest A would go, the offer would have continued to stand. B would continue to be free to accept it within a reasonable period of time, provided A did not withdraw her offer first.

THE ELEMENTS OF ACCEPTANCE
Positive and Unconditional

Acceptance must be certain and unconditional, and must be a positive act, whether in words or in conduct. If acceptance is by conduct, the conduct must refer unequivocally to the offer made—for example, shaking hands at the conclusion of negotiations is generally regarded as an acceptance of the last offer.

On the other hand, one's conduct may happen to comply with the means of acceptance set out in an offer and yet not amount to an acceptance. Suppose A walks her dog around the park every evening. B leaves A a note saying that she will have accepted B's offer to buy her car for $2000 if she walks her dog in the park that evening. A need not abandon her normal conduct to avoid accepting the offer and having the contract forced upon her.

For the same reason, an offeror cannot insist on silence as a mode of acceptance and so require the offeree to act in order to reject the offer.

ILLUSTRATION 6.5

Sanger, a sales representative for Ion Electric Supply Inc., demonstrated a new high-speed Auto-analyzer for Glover, the owner of a car repair service. The price was $2500. Glover thought the device was useful but overpriced: "At $1500 I might consider buying it." Sanger said that he could not reduce the price and removed the machine. Two weeks later, an Auto-analyzer arrived with a letter from Sanger stating: "When I reported how impressed you were with our analyzer to the manager, he said it would be worth selling one even at a loss just to break into the market in your

city. We know what an excellent reputation you have and it would be a good move to have our product in use in your shop. Our price is reduced, only to you, to $1750. That is below cost. If we don't hear from you in 10 days we shall assume you have accepted this exceptional buy and will expect payment of our invoice."

There will be no contract even if the offeree, Glover, does not reply and simply allows the machine to sit idle; but he may well be bound if he takes the risk of using the machine, even to experiment with it.

Silence can be a sufficient mode of acceptance only if the parties have habitually used this method to communicate acceptance in previous transactions, or have agreed between themselves in advance that silence is sufficient, as where books are regularly delivered under a contract for membership in a publisher's book club. Provincial consumer protection legislation regulates business practices involving unsolicited goods and **negative option billing**. If a consumer mistakenly pays for unrequested services, he may request a refund.[16]

negative option billing   a practice of adding services and sending bills without request and relying upon the customer to cancel if they don't wish the service

Communication to the Offeror

Generally speaking, an offeree must communicate acceptance to the offeror. Some types of offers, however, can be accepted without communication because the offeror asks only that the offeree perform an act, implying that the act will amount to acceptance. The offeror may, in other words, do away with receiving notice of acceptance, and be bound to the terms of the proposal as soon as the offeree has performed whatever was required of him in the offer.

CASE 6.4

Carbolic Smoke Ball Company placed an advertisement in a newspaper promising to pay £100 to anyone who used one of its smoke balls three times daily for two weeks and still contracted influenza. Mrs. Carlill bought a smoke ball and used it following the instructions supplied and contracted influenza. She sued the Smoke Ball Company on its promise to pay £100. As a part of its defence, the company pleaded

that Mrs. Carlill had never communicated her intention to accept its offer. The court found in favour of Mrs. Carlill.[17] It held that the offer had implied that notice was not necessary because the company had asked only that readers should buy and use the smoke balls. Performance of the conditions set out was a sufficient acceptance without notifying the company.

---

[16] See, for example, Business Practices and Consumer Protection Act, S.B.C. 2004, c. 2, ss. 12–14 (B.C.) and Consumer Protection Act, 2002, S.O. 2002, c. 30, Sch. A., s. 13 (Ont.).

[17] *Carlill v. Carbolic Smoke Ball Co.*, [1892] 2 Q.B. 484. See also *Grant v. Prov. of New Brunswick* (1973), 35 D.L.R. (3d) 141, and *Dale v. Manitoba* (1997), 147 D.L.R. (4th) 605.

The *Carlill* case also established that an offer may be made to an indefinite number of people whose individual identities remain unknown to the offeror even after they have accepted. If the offer had been addressed to a particular group of persons, then only members of that group could have accepted.

The Moment of Acceptance

The moment a contract is formed by acceptance of an offer, each party is bound to its terms. Accordingly, we must be able to analyze business negotiations so that we can identify:

- who made the offer,
- when it was communicated, and
- when and by whom the offer was accepted.

Buying an automobile from a car dealer provides a good example of the importance of knowing when and how an offer is accepted.

ILLUSTRATION 6.6

Car sales agents employed by a dealer normally have no authority to enter into contracts with customers. The management of the dealership retains the final word on both price and credit terms; the agent's task is to persuade any prospective buyer to submit an offer at a specified price. When the agent takes the customer's offer to the sales manager, the manager may agree by signing the offer (the positive act), and the agent will return to the customer to tell them (communication of acceptance). This is the moment of acceptance when the contract is formed. Alternatively, the manager may strike out the proposed price and insert a higher one with a request that the prospective buyer initial the change. In so doing, the manager rejects the customer's offer by making a counter-offer. No contract is formed unless and until the customer initials the counter-offer. Communication of acceptance is effective when the agent becomes aware of the initialing of the document and does not wait until the manager is told.

---

inviting tenders seeking offers from suppliers

The common business practice of **inviting tenders** is a more complicated method of forming a contract. The purpose of inviting tenders may be either to obtain firm offers from the tenderers for a fixed quantity of goods and services over a stated period, or it may be to explore the market of available suppliers and develop the best terms for proceeding with a project. When the object is to obtain firm offers, the most satisfactory tender should become the basis for a contract between the inviter of the tenders and the successful bidder. This is normal practice when a government or business calls for tenders for the construction of a large project. In fact, the Supreme Court of Canada has described the tender process as two contracts. It held that inviting tenders amounted to an offer to enter into a construction contract if selected according to the established criteria.[18] Submission of a bid is considered acceptance and forms a contract. Any refusal to fairly consider the bid would be breach of contract. The party inviting the tenders promises—in return for the tenderer taking the trouble to prepare and submit its tender—to fairly and equally consider all tenders and to accept the most attractive tender compliant with the specifications.

If the inviting party fails to fairly and consistently consider all tenders, it will be liable since it has breached the "tender contract."[19] If all goes well, the successful

---

[18] *Ron Engineering & Construction Eastern Ltd. v. Ontario*, [1981] 1 S.C.R. 111. The Supreme Court affirmed the two-stage contract approach in *Design Services Ltd. v. Canada*, 2008 SCC 22, while rejecting a negligence duty of care.

[19] See *Martel Building Ltd. v. Canada*, [2000] 2 S.C.R. 860; *Blackpool and Fylde Aero Club Ltd.v. Blackpool Borough Council*, [1990] 1 W.L.R. 1195. For further obligations that may be implied on inviting tenders, see *M.J.B. Enterprises Ltd. v. Defence Construction (1951) Ltd. et al.*, [1999] 1 S.C.R. 619.

bidder enters into a second contract for the construction project. Bidders must carefully prepare their bids so they comply with the tender specifications or they will not be considered.

In other circumstances, there is no intention to form a contract upon the receipt of tenders and is expressly denied; the purpose of inviting tenders is to identify a supplier as the appropriate source of work to be done or goods to be supplied, if required for a future project. For example, a municipal corporation may invite tenders by private trucking firms for the removal of snow from city streets during the coming winter. The selection of the successful bidder need not be followed up by a contract to remove whatever snow may fall—no one knows how severe the winter might be. The successful bidder has made a **standing offer** and the municipality may then make specific requisitions for snow removal as needed over the winter season.[20] The terms of the invitation to tender will describe which purpose is intended. For more information on this topic, see the Companion Website.

standing offer an offer that may be accepted as needed from time to time

---

Ethical Issue	**When Is There a Duty to Negotiate in Good Faith?**

Suppose a party enters into negotiations to purchase a business only for the purpose of gaining insight on how best to launch a successful competing business. What if a television network enters negotiations over the purchase of programming not with a view to completing a contract but in order to satisfy the regulator that no purchase is possible?[21] In these situations, a party may be accused of failing to negotiate in "good faith." What should be the consequences?

Tendering is one area of contract law where obligations of good-faith negotiations exist. Bidders must be treated fairly and equally, but the law falls short of imposing a negligence duty of care.[22] Another example where good faith is required is the negotiation of options to renew an existing contractual relationship.[23]

Questions to Consider

1. Should the law recognize a duty to negotiate all contracts in good faith?

2. How could a business protect its competitive information during sale negotiations?

CHECKLIST

Ways in Which an Offer Comes to an End

Once an offer has been made, it can come to an end in a number of different ways:

- The offer may lapse when the offeree fails to accept within the time stated in the offer, or if no time limit is stated, within a reasonable time.
- The offeror revokes the offer before the offeree has accepted.
- The offeree rejects the offer or makes a counter-offer (which is, in effect, a rejection).
- The offeree accepts before any of the three above has occurred (in which case the offer ends and is replaced by a contract between the parties).

---

[20] See *Powder Mountain Resorts Ltd. v. British Columbia*, [2001] 11 W.W.R. 488 (B.C.C.A.); *Mellco Developments Ltd. v. Portage Le Prairie (City)* (2002), 222 D.L.R. (4th) 67 (Man. C.A.).

[21] *Westcom TV Group Ltd. v. CanWest Global Broadcasting Inc.*, [1997] 1 W.W.R. 761 (B.C.S.C.).

[22] *Ron Engineering & Construction Eastern Ltd. v. Ontario, supra*, n. 18; *Martel Building Ltd. v. Canada, supra*, n. 19; recently followed in *IPC Investment Corporation v. Sawaged*, 2011 ONCA 827; *Design Services Ltd. v. Canada, supra*, n. 18. *Envoy Relocation Services Inc. v. Canada* 2013 ONSC 2034.

[23] *Empress Towers Ltd. v. Bank of Nova Scotia* (1990), 73 D.L.R. (4th) 400 (B.C.C.A.). For a discussion of the duty to negotiate in good faith (if any), see J.D. McCamus, *The Law of Contracts* (Toronto: Irwin Law, 2005).

TRANSACTIONS BETWEEN PARTIES AT A DISTANCE FROM EACH OTHER

Method of Acceptance

If the offer expressly states how acceptance must be communicated, then it must be completed in exactly that way. When the offer is silent and the parties are at a distance, an offeree may communicate acceptance in any reasonable way given the circumstances and the contemplation of the parties.[24] An offer made by mail may reasonably be taken as allowing acceptance by mail. Ordinarily, any faster mode may be used: a fax, email, or telephone call in response to a letter can be valid acceptance. It may be reasonable that an offer made orally in the presence of the offeree be accepted by letter. If the offeror merely allows for acceptance by some means other than post as, for example, by telephone or in person, the offeree may still accept by post. It depends upon the pattern of negotiations between the parties and the business realities of the circumstances.

The ordinary rule is that acceptance by mail is communicated when sent—that is, when a properly addressed and stamped letter of acceptance is dropped in the mail.[25] This "postal rule" is justified in that an offeror who chooses to use the post office to send an offer is assumed to be willing to have the same means used for acceptance, and to take a chance that the post office will be efficient in delivering it.

For all other forms of acceptance, the offeror is not bound unless and until the acceptance reaches him—and it must reach him before the offer has lapsed. When his stated preference is for a mode speedier than mail, there is increased risk that his offer will have lapsed before the letter of acceptance arrives. In these circumstances, the acceptance is not valid when dropped in the mailbox (as it would be if acceptance by mail were reasonably contemplated), but only when received. Even when an offeror invites acceptance by mail, he may change the postal rule by stating that it will be effective only when received. Indeed, he may state that acceptance by letter is invalid—it must be made in person. The terms of the offer will always override the general rules.

When instantaneous means of communication such as telephone are used, the offeror must receive the acceptance before he is bound. One court considered the implications of the telephone line going dead so that the offeror did not hear the offeree's words of acceptance. The court concluded that the acceptance would be ineffective and that the offeror would have no contractual liability.[26] The common sense of this rule is that the offeree would know that the line went dead and that his acceptance might not have been heard. He must then verify that his acceptance was received.

Similarly, faxed acceptance is not effective until received, and one would expect this same rule to apply to email.[27] Ecommerce legislation establishes that acceptance may be completed by electronic mail and that email is deemed to be received when it is capable of being retrieved by the recipient—that is, arrives in the mailbox.[28] The legal issues that can arise generally in ecommerce are discussed more fully in Chapter 31.

---

[24] *Henthorn v. Fraser*, [1892] 2 Ch. 27, p. 33. The law in Canada is probably accurately represented by this case, though there is some confusion caused by a Supreme Court of Canada decision on appeal from the Quebec courts where the post office is referred to as an "agent." See *Charlebois v. Baril*, [1928] S.C.R. 88. See also *Loft v. Physicians' Services Inc.* (1966), 56 D.L.R. (2d) 481, where a letter posted in a mailbox but never received was held to be adequate notice to the defendant.

[25] S.M. Waddams, *The Law of Contracts*, 4th ed. (Toronto: Canada Law Book Company, 1999) at 76–7; also *Sibtac Corporation Ltd. v. Soo; Lienster Investments Ltd., Third Party* (1978), 18 O.R. (2d) 395 at 402. The same principle applies when correspondence is sent by courier service: *R. v. Weymouth Sea Products Ltd.* (1983), 149 D.L.R. (3d) 637.

[26] *Entores, Ltd. v. Miles Far East Corporation*, [1955] 2 Q.B. 327, per Denning, L.J., at 332.

[27] See *Eastern Power Ltd. v. Azienda Communale Energia & Ambiente* (1999), 178 D.L.R. (4th) 409 (Ont. C.A.); *Brinkibon Ltd. v. Stahag Stahl Und Stahlwarenhandelsgesellschaft mbH*, [1983] 2 A.C. 34 (H.L.).

[28] Most provinces have adopted legislation in conformity with the Uniform Electronic Commerce Act prepared by the Uniform Law Conference of Canada; see, for example, Electronic Commerce Act, 2000, S.O. 2000, c. 17, s. 22(3).

Methods of Revocation

Revocation by instantaneous means of communication is subject to the same rules as acceptance, discussed above—it must reach the offeree.

However, the rule concerning withdrawal of an offer by post differs from the usual rule concerning the time of acceptance. Revocation by post is effective only when notice is actually received by the offeree, not when it is dropped in the mailbox. As a result, the offeree may accept and a binding contract may be formed after revocation of the offer has been mailed but not yet received.

ILLUSTRATION 6.7

Chen, in a letter mailed January 15, offered to sell his business to Baker for $70 000. The letter was received by Baker on January 17. On January 19, Baker mailed her letter of acceptance, which did not reach Chen until January 21. On January 18, however, Chen had decided to withdraw his offer and mailed a letter to Baker revoking it. This letter did not reach Baker until January 20.

Chen's revocation arrived too late. There was a valid contract on January 19 when the acceptance was mailed. Chen was bound from the moment the letter was dropped into the mailbox.

What is meant by the requirement that a revocation be "actually received"? Is it "received" when delivered to the place of business or residence of the offeree, or must it reach her in person? The general rule is that, unless the offeror knows or ought to know that the revocation will not reach the offeree at her usual address, delivery at that address establishes the fact and time of revocation, and the offeree is deemed to have notice from that time. This rule applies to other means of communication; if an offeror can establish that his revocation by courier or fax arrived at the offeree's usual address, it will be effective.

Determining the Jurisdiction Where a Contract Is Made

Parties to a contract are often in different provinces or countries at the time they enter into the arrangement. If a dispute arises, knowing where the contract was formed can be important, since the law in the two places might well be different. The place—the **jurisdiction**—where the contract was formed is an important factor in deciding which law applies. The general rule is that a contract is formed at the place where the acceptance becomes effective. That place is determined by the moment in time when the contract is effective. When an offeror invites an acceptance by mail, the contract is formed at the moment when—and so at the place where—the acceptance is dropped into the mailbox. When an instantaneous means of communication such as fax, email, or telephone is used, the contract is not formed until the offeror receives the acceptance, and that is at the place where he receives it.

jurisdiction the province, state, or country whose laws apply to a particular situation

UNILATERAL AND BILATERAL CONTRACTS

The Offer of a Promise for a Promise

As described above, most offers require a promise or agreement about future performance from the offeree as the means of acceptance. For example, if A Motors offers to sell a truck to B Inc. for $32 500 and B Inc. replies accepting the offer, a contract is formed though neither party has as yet performed anything. In effect, A Motors has promised to sell the truck for $32 500, and B Inc. in return has promised to buy it for $32 500; the two parties have traded promises. If either party should refuse to perform its promise, then the other would have a right to sue:

bilateral contract a contract where offeror and offeree trade promises and both are bound to perform later

both parties are bound to perform. This type of contract is called a **bilateral contract** because it has two stages—first, promises are made to form the contract and, later, they are fulfilled.

The most common business transaction, the credit sale, is an example of a bilateral contract: It is not until well after the contract is made that the goods are delivered by the seller and paid for by the buyer. Similarly, in a contract of employment, the employer promises to pay a wage or salary and the employee promises to work for a future period.

promisor a party who is under an obligation to perform a promise according to the terms of the contract

promisee a party who has the right to performance according to the terms of the contract

In bilateral contracts, each party is both a **promisor** and a **promisee**; each has a future obligation to perform as well as a right to performance by the other. In a court action, the party who sues as the promisee alleges that she has not received the performance to which she is entitled. The promisor may offer one or more defences as reasons why his conduct should be excused and why he should not be ordered to pay damages for **breach of contract**.

breach of contract a cause of action where a party to the contract claims that the other party has not fulfilled its promises

The Offer of a Promise for an Act

Less often, an offer is accepted by performance. As in the *Carlill* case (Case 6.4), an offer may invite acceptance simply by the offeree performing its conditions without first communicating acceptance. An offer of a reward is accepted by anyone to whom the offer is made if she performs the required conditions, such as providing information or returning a lost article. As in the *Carlill* case, the offer may be accepted by multiple offerees, unless otherwise stated.

unilateral contract a contract in which the offer is accepted by performing an act or series of acts required by the terms of the offer

When offers are of a type that can be accepted by performance without prior communication, the resulting contract is called a **unilateral contract**. Once the offeree has performed, she need not do anything more—except, of course, request payment. All obligation now rests with the offeror to perform his half of the bargain. Some offers require the offeree to perform a series of acts over a long period.

Usually, offers state whether acceptance can be made by performance and specify time limits and manner of performance in order to limit the number of unilateral contracts that can be formed. Bilateral contracts are more common and courts treat offers as calling for bilateral rather than unilateral action when the language does not clearly state otherwise.[29] The advantage of treating an agreement as bilateral is that both parties are bound from the moment the offeree communicates acceptance.

subsidiary promise an implied promise that the offeror will not revoke once the offeree begins performance in good faith and continues to perform

Where the courts do not find it possible to interpret an offer as bilateral, they may still try to help the offeree by implying a **subsidiary promise** that the offeror will not revoke once the offeree begins performance in good faith and continues to perform. The offeree's effort, time, and money spent toward performance will not be wasted.[30] The obvious difficulty is that the offeror may not know when the offeree has started performance. Of course, the subsidiary promise is merely implied, and it may be excluded by an express term to the contrary in the offer.

CASE 6.5

The parties entered into a lease of a charter boat for a five-year term. At the same time, the owner and the lessee agreed that, provided the lease went well, the lessee had the option to buy the boat at the end of the lease. The Supreme Court of Canada was asked to decide whether the option to buy the boat at the end of the lease was one term of the bilateral lease contract or whether it was a unilateral contract on its own. This was important because the lessee's late rental payments were a minor breach of the lease and could impact the lessee's right to exercise the option to purchase. The Court stated:

> A bilateral contract is a contract in which both parties undertake obligations through an exchange of promises. Acceptance of a bilateral contract as a general rule, occurs when the offeree communicates its counter-promise to the offeror. In contrast a unilateral contract is one in which a party makes a promise in return for the performance

>

---

[29] *Sail Labrador v. Challenge One (The)* [1999] 1 S.C.R. 265, at para. 41.

[30] See *Brackenbury v. Hodgkin*, 102 A. 106, 116 Me. 399 (1917), and *Errington v. Errington*, [1952] 1 All E.R. 149.

or forbearance of an act. There is no counter-promise to perform or forbear. In this way, a unilateral contact is a contract in which only one party undertakes a promise. This promise takes the form of an offer which can only be accepted by performance of the required act or forbearance. Such performance provides the other party's consideration, allowing it to enforce the original promise.[31]

In this case the option was a term of the bilateral contract because it was connected to the lease in several ways: the rental payments were the consideration, it was contained in the same document and involved the same property, and it was dependent on the performance of the lease. For more information on this topic, see the Companion Website.

FORMATION OF INTERNET CONTRACTS

Internet contracts are common in the consumer context. Businesses selling online use standardized terms and conditions just as in the physical world. As will be discussed in more detail in Chapter 31, two key types of legislation govern the formation of online contracts: ecommerce and consumer protection. The ecommerce legislation has modernized contract formation rules to allow "clicking an icon" to satisfy the acceptance and communication requirements of contract formation.[32]

Consumer protection legislation deals with the problems surrounding long, detailed standard terms linked to an order webpage. Most provinces (most notably Alberta, British Columbia, and Ontario) regulate internet consumer agreements. However, these new statutory provisions may, in fact, alter the traditional rules of offer and acceptance in internet contracts.

Section 38 of the Ontario Consumer Protection Act, 2002 states that before a consumer enters into an internet agreement, the supplier shall disclose specific information about, among other things, the total price of the good or service, the terms of payment, and warranties. Subsection 38(2) states: "The supplier shall provide the consumer with an express opportunity to accept or decline the agreement . . . ."[32A] This suggests that the internet consumer is the offeree, and it seems to contradict the general rule discussed in this chapter: that a retailer advertising goods for sale is making only an invitation to consumers to make offers—and typically in retail sales the consumer is the offeror.

Since an internet consumer is considered the offeree, after seeing the terms required to be disclosed by the supplier, she will be bound by the terms of the internet contract at such time as she clicks an "I accept" icon on her computer screen. However, some etailers specifically design their websites with multiple acceptances before a "submit" icon is finally clicked. This would appear to satisfy the legislative "agreement to terms" requirement before the entire offer to purchase is submitted. The contract is not formed until the retailer communicates acceptance with a confirmation number.

INTERNATIONAL ISSUE

Jurisdiction and Internet Contracts

Online contracting has greatly increased the number of international contracts in which the offeror is in one jurisdiction while the offeree is in another. As we have already described, the laws may be different in each location, and jurisdiction is often determined by the place of acceptance. To reduce the likelihood that the rules relating to the formation of electronic contracts might be different in each jurisdiction, the United Nations has undertaken a number of initiatives:

- United Nations Convention on the Use of Electronic Communications in International Contracts (2005)
- United Nations Commission on International Trade Law (UNCITRAL) Model Law on Electronic Signatures (2001)
- UNCITRAL Model Law on Electronic Commerce (1996)

Still, international variation exists. For example, some Canadian consumer protection legislation extends protection

>

---

[31] *Sail Labrador, supra* n. 29, at para 33.

[32] See, e.g., Electronic Commerce Act, 2000, S.O. 2000, c. 17, s. 19.

[32A] Subsection 38(2), Section 38 of the Ontario Consumer Protection Act, 2002.

UNCERTAINTY IN THE WORDING OF AN OFFER

A vague offer may prove to be no offer at all, and the intended acceptance of it cannot then form a contract. If the parties enter into a loosely worded arrangement, a court may find the agreement too ambiguous and uncertain to be enforced. A court will not enforce an agreement to agree; there must be certainty about essential terms.[33]

Examples of lack of certainty in the terms of a contract are a promise to give a "fair" share in the profits of a business; a promise to "favourably consider" the renewal of the present contract "if satisfied with you";[34] and a promise made by the buyer of a race horse to pay an additional amount on the price "if the horse is lucky."[35]

Even when the wording of a contract seems uncertain, a clear enough meaning might be found in evidence of local customs or trade usage that gives a new precision to the terms. The courts have a policy of making contracts effective wherever possible; they hold that (1) anything is certain that is capable of being calculated or ascertained, and (2) where a contract may be construed as either enforceable or unenforceable, they will favour the interpretation that will see the contract enforced. Problems about meaning and certainty will be examined in greater detail in Chapters 9 and 10.

A contract for the sale of goods is different from a contract for the sale of land or shares in a proposed corporation. Where the parties have agreed on the quantity, the Sale of Goods Act provides that the price in a contract of sale of goods "may be left to be fixed in manner thereby agreed, or may be determined by the course of dealing between the parties" and that "[W]here the price is not determined in accordance with the foregoing provisions the buyer must pay a reasonable price."[36]

CASE 6.6

In *Brixham Investments Ltd. v. Hansink*,[37] both parties signed a letter providing for incorporation of the company and for entering into a further agreement. The letter did not set out the share allocation of the parties in the proposed company. When one party decided not to proceed with the project, the other sued for breach.

The Court considered whether the document was binding despite the lack of an agreement about share allocation. It held that, although a court will imply certain terms that arise by necessary inference (for instance, if the letter referred to the parties as "equal partners"), where the document did not deal in any way with this crucial question of share allocation, the court will not construct an agreement between the parties. Accordingly, the document did not constitute a binding contract.

In other words, "The law does not recognize a contract to enter into a contract."[38]

---

[33] *Olivieri v. Sherman* (2007), 86 O.R. (3d) 778 at paras. 45–51 (certainty is to be determined based upon an objective reading of the offer not on the subjective intent of a party).

[34] *Montreal Gas Co. v. Vasey*, [1900] A.C. 595.

[35] *Cuthing v. Lynn* (1831), 109 E.R. 1130.

[36] See, for example, R.S.B.C. 1996, c. 410, s. 12; R.S.O. 1990, c. S.1, s. 9; R.S.N.S. 1989, c. 408, s. 11.

[37] (1971), 18 D.L.R. (3d) 533.

[38] *Von Hatzfeldt-Wildenburg v. Alexander*, [1912] 1 Ch. 284, per Parker, J., at 289.

Strategies to Manage the Legal Risks

Disputes often arise between offeror and offeree when too little attention has been paid to the requirements of offer and acceptance or the terms of the offer. Since all terms of the contract must be in the offer prior to acceptance of it, offerors should take some simple steps to ensure a contract is properly formed:

- Advertisements should clearly state that they are not offers capable of being accepted.

- Where possible, offers should be made in writing, especially for bilateral contracts where time will elapse between the exchange of promises and their performance.

- If many similar transactions are likely, standard form contracts should be prepared in advance for use in all subsequent transactions.

- Standard form contracts should be designed so that one-sided, onerous, or unusual terms are brought to the attention of the non-drafting party.

- Standard form contracts should exclude any advertisements, representations, or pre-contract discussions as terms of the contract.

- If statements made by salespersons or in advertisements are important, they should be included in the terms of the offer.

- A specific time for acceptance should be set, after which the offer will lapse.

- The offer should set the manner for acceptance (both the act and the mode of communication).

- Essential terms should be clear or have a manner set for determination.

Offerees should also take steps to limit their legal risks:

- Ensure that acceptance is made within the designated time period and by the designated manner.

- Review standard form contracts or online terms and conditions to identify one-sided or onerous terms prior to acceptance.

- Alter an offer only when the intent is to reject it and make a counter-offer; if the intention is only to clarify its meaning, the clarification should be discussed with the offeror prior to its lapse.

QUESTIONS FOR REVIEW

1. Distinguish an offer from a promise.
2. What is a standard form contract? Describe the different ways in which it may be accepted.
3. Explain the importance of notice of terms in a standard form contract. To what extent does the law protect the interest of the public in standard form contracts?
4. Describe the ways in which an offer may come to an end.
5. What is the legal effect of a counter-offer?
6. "We cannot be obligated by people who do work for us without our knowledge." Why?
7. What elements are required for an acceptance to be effective?
8. What does it mean to "purchase an option"?
9. What does it mean to "invite tenders"? When is a contract normally created in the tendering process?

10. Can acceptance be effective from the moment a letter of acceptance is mailed even when the offer was not itself made through the mail?

11. Explain the different rules that apply to offer and acceptance when, rather than using the postal system, the parties communicate by telephone.

12. Should the same offer and acceptance rules apply to the sending of responses by fax or email? Why?

13. Explain the difference between unilateral and bilateral contracts.

14. Did the *Carlill* case concern a unilateral or a bilateral contract?

15. What is the effect of an agreement in which the parties state that certain terms will be discussed and agreed upon at a later date?

16. Give an example of circumstances in which the rule "An offer must be communicated before it can be accepted" would operate.

17. Is it true that an acceptance must be communicated before a contract can be formed?

18. May a person withdraw a bid he makes at an auction sale before the fall of the hammer?

CASES AND PROBLEMS

1. Continuing Scenario

   Very few customers came to the grand opening of Ashley's restaurant on Monday morning so she placed an ad in the following Thursday's local newspaper saying "Grand Opening Saturday Morning—Join Ashley for coffee and let her satisfy your sweet tooth." Bill and Marlene saw the ad and went to the restaurant on Saturday. They sat down at a table and waved over a waitress who was holding a coffee pot. They did not even look at the menu on the table. The waitress came over to the table and Bill pointed to his cup; she filled it up with coffee. She turned and looked at Marlene; Marlene nodded and her cup was also filled. The waitress then asked if she could get them something and Bill said, "Surprise us with something to 'satisfy our sweet tooth.'" The waitress returned with two cinnamon buns. Bill picked up the bun and took a bite. It was much too sweet; he did not like it, so Marlene did not even touch hers. They got up and left the restaurant without paying. The menu listed coffee at a price of $1.75 and cinnamon buns at $2.50. Do Bill and Marlene have a contract with the restaurant?

2. Friday evening after closing, Sackett's Appliances placed an ad in its window: "This weekend only, five Whirlwind dishwashers, reduced from $1199 to $599! Shop early!" Martens saw the ad later that evening. She appeared the next morning at 9 a.m. when Sackett's opened its doors and stated to the clerk she would take one of the Whirlwind dishwashers. The clerk replied that the ad was a mistake; the price should have been $999. Martens demanded to speak with the manager and insisted on Sackett's honouring its offer to sell at $599. The manager said, "I'm sorry, madam, but that machine cost us more than $800. We cannot sell it at $599." Martens said Sackett's was in breach of contract and she would see her lawyer about it.

   Is Martens right? Explain.

3. Garrett is the manager of Aristo Condos Inc. and is in charge of selling vacant units in the Aristo Towers. On October 4, Heilman examined several of the units with Garrett and said that he thought the prices a bit high but would think about it. Several days later, on October 7, Garrett sent Heilman an email stating, "I will sell you any one of the units we examined together (numbers 14, 236, 238, or 307) for $275 000. I am sending you all the details by courier." Garrett then sent by courier to Heilman a formal offer containing all of the necessary terms, including the required down payment and acceptable mortgage financing.

   Later that day after he had received the email message but before he had received the letter, Heilman emailed Garrett, "I accept your offer with respect to unit 307."

   Has a binding contract been formed by Garrett's email? In what circumstances might this question become the basis of a dispute between the parties?

4. Last year, Lambert bought a car on August 15 and insured it with the Reliable Insurance Company, for whom Drake was the local agent. On the following July 29, Drake telephoned Lambert about renewing her policy and learned she was on vacation at her summer cottage.

Acting on behalf of Reliable Insurance, Drake wrote to Lambert at her cottage: "As you know, your car insurance policy with us expires on August 15. We will renew this policy on the same terms unless notified to the contrary by you. You may sign the application form and pay after you return to the city."

On her way back from her holidays on August 16, Lambert struck and injured a pedestrian with her car. The pedestrian claimed $100 000 damages from Lambert and, on referring the matter to the Reliable Insurance Company, Lambert was informed that her policy of insurance had expired without renewal on August 15.

Discuss Lambert's legal position.

5. A province and its largest university created a program by which the province would give funding to disadvantaged students. Students were told by the university that they would receive funding over four years and, on that basis, they enrolled in the program. The students dealt only with the university. In the third year of the program, the province restructured it so that students had to obtain their maximum Canada Student Loan before being eligible for funding.

The students sued for a declaration requiring the province to pay them at the original funding level for the full four years on the basis of a binding contract with the province. They claimed that they reasonably believed that they had a contractual arrangement with the province not to alter the terms and conditions of the funding arrangement. The province defended by stating that there was no contract with the students because they had not communicated their acceptance to it, but dealt only with the university; if anyone was bound, it was the university.

Discuss the merits of each party's argument. Who do you think should succeed?

6. Purcell was in failing health and advertised to sell his retail computing equipment business. Quentin was familiar with Purcell's business operations; he sent Purcell a detailed offer to buy for $450 000, paying $75 000 as a cash down payment, with the balance payable in installments over two years. Purcell promptly sent an email to Quentin stating: "The price and all the other terms seem fair, except that I need substantially more cash by way of down payment—say, $125 000. Tell me how high you are willing to go." Quentin replied by email, "There is no way I can increase the cash payment."

Purcell replied the next day, "Okay. I've thought about it, and given the state of my health, I have decided to accept your offer." By then, Quentin had heard that the business had suffered because of Purcell's declining health, and he refused to go through with the purchase. He asserted that since Purcell had refused his offer, there was no deal.

Is Quentin right? Has Purcell any basis for claiming that there is a binding contract with Quentin?

7. Daly, a United States citizen, began negotiations with Stevens of Vancouver to investigate and stake mineral claims at the head of the Leduc River in British Columbia. Daly had discovered evidence of deposits there some 20 years earlier.

On January 13, Daly wrote, "A large mining company in Boise is showing an interest. To protect my interest it will be necessary for me to arrive at some definite arrangement soon." Stevens replied on January 17, "Perhaps we can make some arrangement this summer to finance you in staking claims for which I would give you an interest. I would suggest that I should pay for your time and expenses and carry you for a 10 percent interest in the claims." Daly replied on January 22, "Your proposition appeals to me as being a fair one."

Soon after, Daly was called to active duty in the United States Naval Reserve Engineering Corps and was sent to the Marshall Islands. Correspondence continued with some difficulty, but on February 28, Daly wrote, "As I informed you in a previous letter, your offer of a 10 percent interest for relocating and finding these properties is acceptable to me, provided there is a definite agreement to this effect in the near future."

On March 5, Stevens wrote, "I hereby agree that if you will take me in to the showings, and I think they warrant staking, I will stake the claims and give you a 10 percent interest. The claims would be recorded in my name and I will have full discretion in dealing with them—you are to get 10 percent of the vendor interest. I can arrange to get a pilot here."[38A]

[38A] Dawson v. Helicopter Exploration, [1955] S.C.R. 868

Daly replied on April 12, "If you will inform me when you can obtain a pilot, I will immediately take steps for a temporary release in order to be on hand."

On June 6, Stevens wrote, "I was talking to a prospector who said he had been over your showings at the head of the Leduc River, and in his opinion it would be practically impossible to operate there, as the showings were behind ice fields that, along with the extreme snowfalls, make it very doubtful if an economic operation could be carried on. I now have so much work lined up that I doubt if I would have time to visit your showings and do not think I would be warranted in making the effort to get in there due to the unfavourable conditions. I must advise you, therefore, not to depend on making this trip, and suggest if you are still determined to go in, to make some other arrangements."

Daly did not reply. On his return from the Marshall Islands the following year, he did, however, follow up his interest in the property. He discovered that in July, Stevens had sent prospectors into the area and, as a result of their investigations, had staked claims in his own name and later sold them to a mining development company. Daly brought an action against Stevens claiming damages for breach of contract.

Should Daly succeed in his action? Explain.

8. The City of Cameron had grown substantially in the past decade and needed to expand its water purification plant. For this purpose it proposed to buy two hectares of land adjacent to the purification plant from Margot Nurseries, a thriving fruit and vegetable business owning 40 hectares of prime land. As the two hectares were particularly important to Margot, she bargained for a substantial price to pay for the relocation of her business's sorting and packaging area.

The city bargained very hard, and threatened to expropriate the land—as it had power to do under the provincial Expropriation Act—if a deal could not be reached. Finally, in exasperation, Margot handed the director of the purification plant a detailed written statement of the terms upon which she would sell, the offer to be open for 10 days. She asked for a price of $200 000, with $50 000 paid on acceptance. She would permit the city to begin excavation on the nearest one-quarter hectare, but it must delay moving onto the remainder of the land for 60 days so that she could make the needed relocation. When Margot handed the director the offer, she stated that if the city began excavations on the one-quarter hectare, that would be acceptance of her offer.

Within a week, city workers began excavating about 20 metres into Margot's land, and two days later she was served with a notice of expropriation under the Expropriation Act, offering her a price of $80 000. Under the Act, if the parties do not reach a settlement, a court will hear evidence about the market value of the land and the costs caused by compulsory displacement to the owner; it then awards a sum in compensation and orders the owner to give up possession.

Margot, claiming that the city had accepted her offer before the expropriation proceedings were started, sued the city for damages for breach of the contract. Discuss the arguments of each side, and give your opinion on who should succeed. What general issue of public policy arises when a legislature grants powers of expropriation to municipalities?

Additional Resources for Chapter 6 on the Companion Website

(www.pearsoncanada.ca/smyth)

In addition to pre- and post-tests, mini-cases, and application exercises, the Companion Website includes the following province-specific resources for Chapter 6:

- **Alberta:** Cooling-Off Period; Electronic Contracts; Form of Contract
- **Atlantic Provinces:** Internet Sales Contracts; Public Tenders
- **British Columbia:** Cooling-Off Period; Electronic Transactions; Government Procurement and Tenders
- **Manitoba/Saskatchewan:** Internet Consumer Contracts and the Consumer Protection Act; Negative Marketing
- **Ontario:** Acceptance; Consumer Agreements; Consumer Protection Act 2002; Cooling-Off Periods; Electronic Contracts; Exemption Clauses; Standard Form Contracts; Terms Requiring Notice

Chapter 7

Formation of a Contract: Consideration and Intention

Before an accepted offer becomes a legally binding agreement, two other essentials requirements must be present: consideration and the intent to create a contract.

In this chapter we examine such questions as:

- What is the nature of consideration?

- How do we distinguish promises with consideration from gratuitous promises? from motive for making a promise? from an existing legal duty to perform?

- What is equitable estoppel?

- What other ways are there to make a promise binding?

- Why is it essential that parties intend their promises to be legally binding, and how is intention established?

THE MEANING OF CONSIDERATION

bargain   each party pays a price for the promise of the other

consideration   the price for which the promise of the other is bought

An accepted offer is not an enforceable contract unless it has consideration. The accepted offer must form a **bargain**—where each party pays a price or gives value for the promise obtained from the other party. In a unilateral contract, the price paid for the offeror's promise is the act done by the offeree. In a bilateral contract, the price paid for each party's promise is the promise of the other. This price is called consideration. In short, **consideration** is "the price for which the promise [or the act] of the other is bought."[1]

A promisor usually bargains for a benefit to himself, such as a promise to pay money, deliver goods, or provide services; but it need not be directly for his own benefit. So long as the promisor bargains for the other party to do something—or to promise to do something—that she otherwise would not do, the promisor will have received consideration.

ILLUSTRATION 7.1

Adams, a creditor of Brown, threatened to sue Brown for an overdue debt. Brown's friend, Cox, then promised to pay Brown's debt to Adams if Adams would refrain from suing Brown, and Adams agreed.

If Cox failed to pay Adams as agreed and Adams sued him for breach of contract, she would succeed. To establish consideration she need only show that she changed her conduct—that is, that she refrained from suing Brown—in return for Cox's promise. The "price" she agrees to pay for Cox's promise need not confer a direct benefit on him.

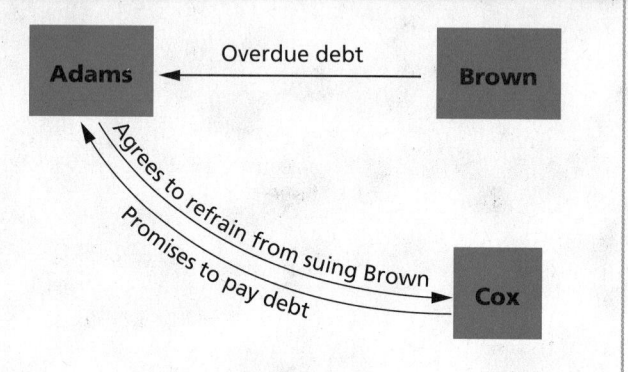

GRATUITOUS PROMISES

gratuitous promise   a promise made without bargaining for or accepting anything in return

With some exceptions discussed later, consideration is necessary to make a contract legally binding. A person may, of course, make a promise to another without bargaining for anything in return. A promise made in the absence of a bargain is called a **gratuitous promise** and, even when accepted by the offeree, the promise is not a contract enforceable in law. A promise to make a gift and a promise to perform services without remuneration are common examples of gratuitous promises. Such arrangements are not legal contracts.

The law does not prevent performance of a gratuitous promise. It simply does nothing to help if the promisor does not perform; the promisee has no legal remedy—he cannot seek compensation for loss of the benefit he was promised. Ethically, most people perform their gratuitous promises.

What about charitable donations? Charities seldom find it in their interest to sue those who have made pledges but do not perform. They rely upon their prospective donors' sense of honour; they understand that people might become reluctant to give pledges if charities were likely to sue them for non-payment.

Occasionally donors have died before honouring large pledges, and charities have sued their estates.[2] A charity claiming payment will be asked what price it paid for the pledge. A court may find consideration if the charity began a specific project, such as constructing a building, in response to the donor's promise. The court must, however, be able to find an implied request from the promisor—if not an explicit one—that the

---

[1] Winfield, *Pollock's Principles of Contract*, 13th ed., at 133.

[2] See, for example, *Governors of Dalhousie College v. Boutilier*, [1934] 3 D.L.R. 593.

charity undertake the project as the "price" of the pledge. When a pledge is for general funds, the charity can make it legally binding if it uses a seal on its pledge cards or offers something to the donor in return, such as membership rights. The use of a seal is discussed in later in this chapter.

CASE 7.1

Dr. and Mrs. Marquis met, worked, and volunteered at the Brantford General Hospital; they became regular donors. After Dr. Marquis's death, Mrs. Marquis promised to give the hospital $1 000 000 over five years. The hospital foundation requested permission to name the coronary care unit after the couple. Mrs. Marquis signed the pledge and gave the first year's installment of $200 000. Unfortunately, she died the next year. In her will, she left one-fifth of her estate to the hospital. The estate refused to pay the outstanding $800 000 on the pledge, claiming the estate gift replaced it. The foundation argued that it was entitled to both. The pledge was an enforceable contract and the consideration was the promise to name the coronary unit. The court disagreed. It was the foundation that suggested the naming; Mrs. Marquis never requested it. It was a voluntary act of gratitude. In addition, it was not a promise given by the foundation because the board had not yet approved the name.[3]

As long as a gratuitous promise remains unperformed, the promisee has no right to a remedy. If the promise is performed—a gift is made. May the donor later change her mind and demand return on grounds of lack of consideration? Generally, no: Once she has voluntarily made the gift, it is no longer her property and she does not own it, except in the rare case of undue influence, as discussed in Chapter 9. For more information on this topic, see the Companion Website.

ADEQUACY OF CONSIDERATION

While the consideration given in return for a promise must have some value, the court does not make sure the parties have made a fair bargain. If a party agreed to a grossly inadequate consideration for his promise, then that was up to him. It is not the task of the courts to assess the adequacy of the consideration; relative value is too subjective a concept.

If there is some allegation of wrongdoing by one party, a court might look at adequacy of consideration because it might point to fraud, duress, or undue influence exerted on the promisor. There would need to be other evidence of fraud before the court would hold that the promise is voidable at the promisor's option. Courts have become increasingly concerned with protecting the interests of weak parties such as consumers from unconscionable conduct.[4]

When parties agree to settle out a dispute out of court, consideration can be a question. Typically one party pays another to drop a lawsuit or to waive their right to start a lawsuit. However if the other party's case was weak and he would have lost in court, is his promise not to sue, therefore, worthless and not really consideration for the promise to pay something in settlement? The answer is no—lawsuits are expensive and unpleasant no matter who wins, and promising not to start or continue a lawsuit is sufficient consideration when the party honestly believed he had a case.[5]

If this were not the rule, no one could ever be sure that a settlement was binding; subsequent information might upset a settlement made in good faith. For more information on this topic, see the Companion Website.

---

[3] *Brantford General Hospital Foundation v. Marquis Estate* (2003), 67 O.R. (3d) 432 (S.C.J.).

[4] See Chapter 9. Unconscionable consideration is now the subject of consumer protection legislation. See, for example, Consumer Protection Act, 2002, S.O. 2002, c. 30, Sched. A., s. 15.

[5] *Haigh v. Brooks* (1839), 113 E.R. 119; *Famous Foods Ltd. v. Liddle*, [1941] 3 D.L.R. 525; *Fairgrief v. Ellis*, [1935] 2 D.L.R. 806.

MOTIVE CONTRASTED WITH CONSIDERATION: PAST CONSIDERATION

As noted, consideration is the price that makes the promisor's promise binding. However, the promisor's reason for making the promise, the motive, is irrelevant, whether it be gratitude, a sense of honour, duty, affection, or charity, or even part of an unworthy scheme. Motive cannot change a gratuitous promise into a binding contract, nor can it reduce a binding promise into a merely voluntary obligation.

CASE 7.2

In *Eastwood v. Kenyon*,[6] Eastwood, who was the guardian of Mrs. Kenyon while she was a child, personally borrowed money in order to finance her education and to maintain the estate of which she was sole heiress. On coming of age, she promised to reimburse him; after her marriage, her husband, Mr. Kenyon, promised Eastwood to pay back the sum, but he did not. Eastwood sued Mr. Kenyon, claiming that Kenyon had a moral duty to honour his promise, but his action failed. Eastwood had not given any consideration in return of Kenyon's promise to repay. Kenyon's promise happened well after the earlier loan was made and his motive, a sense of gratitude, was not consideration.

---

past consideration a gratuitous benefit previously conferred upon a promisor

If one person promises to reward another who has previously done an act gratuitously or given something of value, the promise is not binding. That promise is gratuitous—just like the benefit that the promisee had earlier conferred upon the promisor. Another approach is to say that the motive of the promisor was to return the kindness of the promisee, and, of course, motive and consideration are not the same thing. The benefit previously conferred upon the promisor is often called **past consideration**. Since there is no element of bargain—that is, of the benefit being performed in return for the promise—the expression is really contradictory, for "past consideration" is no consideration at all.

Ethical Issue   **Promises**

Ethically, it is wrong to break any promise seriously made and a promisor has a moral duty to perform. If every promise were legally enforceable simply because the promisor had a moral duty to do as he said he would, we would not need the doctrine of consideration. In civil law legal systems, where **moral cause** may be sufficient to make a promise binding, courts must probe internally into a promisor's motive in order to establish moral obligation. While the doctrine of consideration has been attacked as causing unfair decisions in some instances (and undoubtedly it sometimes does), it has the benefit of being an objective rather than a subjective test.

Questions to Consider

1. What difficulties arise when evaluating motives to establish moral obligations?

2. Is moral cause a more appropriate standard than consideration?

---

moral cause moral duty of promisor to perform his promise

RELATION BETWEEN EXISTING LEGAL DUTY AND CONSIDERATION

Where A has an existing contractual duty to B, a later promise by B to pay A something extra to perform that obligation is not binding. Performance by A is not good consideration for the later promise because A was already contractually bound to perform. Indeed, A's failure to do so would have been a breach of contract. For example, a promise to members of a crew to increase their pay if they did not desert their ship was held to be unenforceable.[7] The existing

---

[6] (1840), 113 E.R. 482.

[7] *Stilk v. Myrick* (1809), 70 E.R. 1168.

contracts of employment between the crew and the employer bound the crew to perform their duties faithfully. On the other hand, a term of such contracts is that the ship be seaworthy. If it proves unseaworthy, the crew members are released from their obligation, and then, of course, there will be consideration for the promise to increase their pay if the crew stays with the ship.[8]

The situation sometimes arises where one party threatens to default on its obligation to perform and leave the other party to sue for breach. A common example occurs in construction projects.

ILLUSTRATION 7.2

A Inc. has tendered and won the contract to build an office building for land developer B. During construction, A Inc. runs into unexpected difficulties and informs B that it is thinking of abandoning the project. However, B, relying upon completion at the agreed date, has already leased out large parts of the building. If A Inc. abandons the job, B will lose valuable time finding another builder to complete the project and will likely be in breach of leases he has made with prospective tenants.

To avoid these difficulties, B offers to pay A Inc. an extra $500 000 to pay overtime wages in order to complete construction on time. A Inc. accepts and completes on the agreed date. However, B refuses to pay the additional sum on the grounds that he received no new consideration for his promise: A Inc. was already bound by its contract to complete on time.

Canadian courts take the view that this conduct is a form of economic blackmail by the party threatening to abandon the contract, and so they hold that there is no consideration for the promise to pay an extra sum.[9] However, a supplier intent on economic blackmail can still exact a legally enforceable promise from its customer to pay an increased price by delivering a paperclip (or any other item of negligible value) to her in return for the promise, or by insisting that the customer make her promise under seal (as discussed later in this chapter).

Consideration already given will not support new promises when parties try to modify an existing contract, even though such changes are not always an unfair exploitation of the promisor. For instance, a promisor may believe it is in her best interests to pay the promisee more in order to ease the promisee's hardship and thus obtain better performance. So far, the Canadian courts have been reluctant to recognize this reality,[10] although an English case has allowed a construction company to recover a promised extra sum for completion.[11] The court was satisfied that there was no economic duress; the construction company had not exerted undue pressure and both parties benefited from performance.

A related problem arises when a stranger—a "third party" to a contract—promises to pay a sum to the promisor for his promise to perform already existing obligations to the promisee.

ILLUSTRATION 7.3

As in Illustration 7.2, A Inc. has made a contract to construct a building for B. C, who has a lease as principal tenant in the building, promises to pay A $100 000 if A completes the building on time. Is there consideration for C's promise?[12] Since A is already under a duty to B to construct the building on time, what further price does A give for C's promise?

---

[8] *Turner v. Owen* (1862), 6 E.R. 79.

[9] See *Gilbert Steel Ltd. v. University Construction Ltd.* (1976), 67 D.L.R. (3d) 606.

[10] See Stephen Waddams, "Canadian Contract Law, 1970 – 2010" (2011) 50 Can. Bus. L.J. at 416-17.

[11] *Williams v. Roffey Brothers & Nicholls (Contractors) Ltd.*, [1990] 1 All E.R. 512. See *Greater Fredericton Airport Authority Inc. v. NAV Canada*, (2008), 290 D.L.R. (4th) 405, at para 31 (holding that a threat to break the contract amounts to duress).

[12] *Shadwell v. Shadwell* (1860), 142 E.R. 62.

This problem has seldom arisen in the courts, but when it does, they seem to agree that A can enforce C's promise, and further, that if A failed to perform, A would be liable to actions by both B and C.[13] A has given new consideration by promising C to complete on time and making himself liable to C if he fails to do so. The situation where the later promise is made by the promisee in the original contract differs from that where it is made by a third party to that contract.

Suppose A's duty to perform is a public duty required by law, as where A is a police officer. If B promises to pay A for services as a police officer, the court is confronted with two problems—the question of public policy and of consideration. If police officers are asked to do something that they are already bound to do or something that will interfere with their regular duties, the court worries that the promise to pay them tends to corrupt public servants; the court will likely find the promise unenforceable on grounds of public policy. On the other hand, if the court finds that the officers have been requested to do something beyond their duties and not in conflict with them, it will likely find consideration and hold the promise binding, as in *Glasbrook Brothers v. Glamorgan County Council*,[14] where a company agreed to pay for a special police guard during a strike and was held to be bound by its promise.

GRATUITOUS REDUCTION OF A DEBT

The consideration requirement can lead to some other unsatisfactory results, especially in business transactions.

CASE 7.3

In the famous case of *Foakes v. Beer*, a debtor owed a large sum of money to his creditor and payment was overdue. The creditor agreed to accept a series of installments of the principal, and to forgo her right to interest, if the debtor paid promptly and regularly. The debtor paid the full principal as agreed, but the creditor then sued for the interest. She succeeded on the grounds that her promise to accept less than the total sum owing—that is, principal plus accrued interest—was a gratuitous promise and did not bind her.[15]

This rule is unrealistic. For a number of sensible reasons, a creditor, C, may find it beneficial to settle for a reduced amount rather than insist on full payment. First, the compromise may avoid placing a debtor in bankruptcy where, by the time all other creditors' claims have been recognized, C might end up with less money than if she had accepted a reduced sum. Second, the proposed reduction may enable the debtor to persuade friends to lend him enough money to take advantage of it and make a fresh start. Third, the debtor may simply not have the assets to enable him to pay in full, so that a court judgment against him would not realize more than the reduced amount. Finally, C may urgently need at least part of the sum owed her for other commitments: She may be happier to take the lesser amount at once, instead of later collecting the full account with all the delays inherent in a legal action.

The rule in *Foakes v. Beer* can be avoided in several ways. First, early payment before the due date is sufficient new consideration to make an agreed reduction in the debt binding on the creditor. So if the debtor pays $600 one day in advance in settlement of a $1000 debt due the next day, the agreement to accept $600 is binding. As we have seen,

---

[13] *Scotson v. Pegg* (1861), 158 E.R. 121; *Pao On v. Lau Yiu Long*, [1979] 3 W.L.R. 435.

[14] [1925] A.C. 270.

[15] (1884), 9 App. Cas. 605. *Process Automation Inc. v. Norsteam Intertec Inc. & Arroyave* 2010 ONSC 3987 (still the common law rule para 88).

the court will not inquire into the adequacy of the consideration; if the creditor chooses to reduce the debt by $400 in order to receive payment one day in advance, she may bind herself to do so.

Second, the rule in *Foakes v. Beer* applies only to payments of money. It does not apply to the transfer of goods or to the provision of services. Since an individual may make a contract for a clearly inadequate consideration if he so desires—he may agree to pay $1000 for a trinket, a cheap watch, or a package of cigarettes—similarly, he may agree to cancel a $1000 debt on receiving any one of these objects. In effect, he is trading the debt for the object, and such an agreement is valid, provided he agrees to it voluntarily. The result of this reasoning creates a paradox: If a person agrees to accept $900 in full settlement of a $1000 debt, he may later sue for the balance successfully; if a person accepts $500 and a string of beads worth 10 cents in full settlement of a $1000 debt, he will fail if he sues for the balance.

Third, the rule in *Foakes v. Beer* applies only to agreements between a creditor and debtor. A third party, who is not bound to pay anything to the creditor, may offer to pay the creditor a lesser sum if she will cancel the debt. A creditor who accepts such an offer is bound by her promise and will fail if she later sues the debtor.[16] The result is the same as if the third person had purchased the debt from the creditor.

The rule in *Foakes v. Beer* has been restricted by statute in British Columbia, Alberta, Saskatchewan, Manitoba, and Ontario.[17] Under any of these acts, when a creditor accepts part performance (that is, a lesser sum of money) in settlement of a debt and the debtor actually pays the reduced amount, the entire debt is extinguished. The payment must be acknowledged to be a full settlement of the debt. The creditor may still be able to go back on her promise to accept a lesser sum of money before the sum is actually paid.

Finally, the rule in *Foakes v. Beer* is avoided if the creditor agrees in writing and under seal to reduce the debt. The concept of a "seal" is discussed later in the chapter.

EQUITABLE ESTOPPEL

Suppose a person makes a gratuitous promise to another, fully intending to keep it, but later finds it inconvenient to perform. Meanwhile, the promisee has quite reasonably relied on the promise and has incurred expenses he would otherwise not have made. What happens if the promisor subsequently defaults? According to the strict rules of contract law, the answer is—nothing at all. The gratuitous promise remains gratuitous, the promise cannot be enforced, and the promisee suffers the burden of his expenses.

The principle of equitable estoppel may provide some relief. As noted in Chapter 2, equitable principles were developed by old English courts to soften the harshness of strict rules. The above described situation may be resolved more fairly if the equitable concept of "estoppel" is applied.

Estoppel Based on Fact

When one person asserts as true a certain statement of fact and another relies on that statement to his detriment, the maker of the statement will be **estopped** (prevented) from denying the truth of his original statement in a court of law, even if it turns out to have been untrue.

estopped prevented

---

[16] *Hirachand Punamchand v. Temple*, [1911] 2 K.B. 330.

[17] Law and Equity Act, R.S.B.C. 1996, c. 224, s. 43; Judicature Act, R.S.A. 2000, c. J-1, s. 13 (1); Queen's Bench Act, 1998, S.S. 1998, c. Q-1.01, s. 64; Mercantile Law Amendment Act, C.C.S.M., c. M-129, s. 6; and Mercantile Law Amendment Act, R.S.O. 1990, c. M.10, s. 16. See *Process Automation Inc.*, *supra* n. 15.

ILLUSTRATION 7.4

A purchased a retail shoe business from X in rented premises owned by B. After a few months, A mentions to her landlord, B, that the business does not have an adequate sales area and that she would like to turn a back room into a display and fitting salon. The room contains a number of pieces of old furniture that she believes belong to B and that she would like to get rid of. B says, "That furniture belonged to X and you acquired it when you bought the business. You can do as you like with it." A replies, "I thought it was yours. That's what X told me." "No, it's yours," B answers. The tenant next door to A is present and hears the conversation.

That evening, when B reports the incident to his wife, she becomes furious and reminds B that several antique pieces given to them by her grandmother are stored in the back room of the store. When B arrives at the shoe store the next morning, he discovers that the furniture has been taken away to the city dump and compressed by a bulldozer. He then sues A for the value of the antique furniture.

B would fail because A can prove in her defence that B said that the furniture was A's, and the court would estop B from asserting the true state of the facts.

Estoppel applies to an assertion of existing fact; but does it also apply to a promise of future conduct? This question has presented a problem for the courts. The truth of existing facts is an objective matter that can easily be determined by evidence. Future promises are a different matter.

Despite their problems with the idea of estoppel, the courts eventually found themselves unable to ignore the plea of an innocent party who had relied in good faith on a gratuitous promise only to find later that the promisor had changed his mind. On the grounds of fairness, courts exercised their equitable jurisdiction to estop the promisor from claiming that he was not bound by his gratuitous promise. This reasoning extended the idea of factual estoppel to promises. The principle has been called **promissory estoppel or equitable estoppel** because the court is acting "equitably" to override a strict common law rule. For more information on this topic, see the Companion Website.

The doctrine of equitable estoppel originated well over a century ago in the leading case of *Hughes v. Metropolitan Railway Co.*,[18] and is currently limited to use by the promisor only as a defence against a claim where a legal relationship already exists between the parties.

promissory estoppel or equitable estoppel   the court's exercise of its equitable jurisdiction to estop a promisor from claiming that she was not bound by her gratuitous promise where reliance on that promise caused injury to the promisee

CASE 7.4

Metropolitan Railway, a tenant under a 99-year lease of a large block of buildings, was required to keep the building in good repair. The penalty for failure to honour a notice to repair from the landlord, Hughes, would be forfeiture of possession—the lease would be terminated. Hughes served notice that repairs were needed and the tenant had six months to make them. The tenant then suggested that Hughes might be interested in buying back the remaining years of the tenant's 99-year lease. The lease was a valuable one as rents to subtenants had risen greatly over the long years of the master lease. When Hughes expressed interest in the proposal, the two sides began serious negotiations. With Hughes's acquiescence, all repairs were delayed, since they would have increased the tenant's investment in the property and so raised the sale price of the lease.

After several months, negotiations broke down and the tenant then proceeded with the repairs. They were not finished within six months of the original notice, but were complete within six months of the end to negotiations. Hughes sued for forfeiture of the lease, and had he succeeded he would have obtained the remaining years free.

In refusing Hughes's claim, the House of Lords stated that by entering into negotiation, Hughes had impliedly agreed to a suspension of the notice during negotiations; he could not later go back on his word and revert to his strict legal rights in the lease. The notice became effective again only on negotiations being broken off, when the tenant could no longer rely on Hughes's implied promise not to pursue his strict rights.

---

[18] (1877), 2 App. Cas. 439.

While a gratuitous promise may still be withdrawn, its withdrawal is not allowed to prejudice the promisee in respect of any past reliance on it. Notice of withdrawal (or an end to circumstances in which the promise is implied) may restore the promisor's rights to any future performance still owed by the promisee. In the *Hughes* case, the landlord was entitled, after the negotiations had broken down, to require repairs to be made within the six-month period provided in the lease.

Therefore, equitable estoppel applies in situations when

1. some form of legal relationship already exists between the parties;
2. one of the parties promises (perhaps by implication only) to release the other from some or all of the other's legal duties to him; and
3. the other party, in reliance on that promise, acts in a way that alters his position and would make it a real hardship if the promisor reneges on his promise.[19]

In these circumstances, if the promisor were to ignore his promise and sue to enforce his original rights, the promisee could successfully argue equitable estoppel to *defend* the action against him.

In *Conwest Exploration Co. v. Letain,*[20] the Supreme Court of Canada pushed the doctrine quite far, possibly suggesting that equitable estoppel might be used as a cause of action.[21] The facts were complicated, but the essential ones for our purposes can be summarized as follows in Case 7.5.

CASE 7.5

A held an option to purchase certain mining claims. Before the date of expiry of the option, B, the grantor of the option, impliedly agreed to its extension. (As in the *Hughes* case, it appeared to be in his own interest to do so.) As a result, A did not hurry to complete the required task under the option before the original expiry date, but he did try to exercise the option shortly afterward, before B had given any notice that he wished to return to his strict legal rights. In an action brought by A asking the court to permit him to exercise his option, the court did not allow B to revert to the original expiry date, and A's action succeeded.

B implicitly promised to extend the original option period, while legal relations existed between the parties. On the one hand, it can be argued that this decision amounts to no more than an application of the *Hughes* case. On the other hand, the opposing view is that once the original option had expired, without an extension having been granted for additional consideration, no existing legal relationship between A and B remained; they were as strangers. Accordingly, to permit A to succeed is to permit him to use equitable estoppel as a cause of action. So far, the Canadian courts have not embraced this second view.

Injurious Reliance

In the United States, the principle of equitable estoppel has been expanded to allow the injured party to force the promisor to perform the promise.[22] Courts in some states assert that since the promisor by his conduct induced the injured party to rely on his promise, the promisor must honour his promise to prevent an injustice. This principle, known as **injurious reliance**, is a cause of action, not just a defence.[23]

The U.S. term "injurious reliance" and the English term "equitable estoppel" are essentially two sides of the same coin: injurious reliance looks at the situation from the

injurious reliance loss or harm suffered by a promisee who, to his detriment, relied reasonably on a gratuitous promise

---

[19] See, for example: *Central London Property Trust, Ltd. v. High Trees House, Ltd.*, [1947] K.B. 130.

[20] (1964), 41 D.L.R. (2d) 198. See also *Re Tudale Exploration Ltd. and Bruce et al.* (1978), 20 O.R. (2d) 593, at pp. 597 and 599.

[21] See, for example, *Crabb v. Arun District Council*, [1976] Ch. 179; *Paul v. Lam*, 2011 BCSC 980.

[22] *Ricketts v. Scothorn*, 77 N.W. 365 (1898).

[23] American Law Institute, Restatement of Contracts, Section 90 (Washington, 1932).

point of view of enforcement, while equitable estoppel views it from the position of the defence.

INTERNATIONAL ISSUE

Will Injurious Reliance Be Adopted by the Canadian Courts?

In the American doctrine of injurious reliance, a promisee might have a cause of action against a promisor who makes and then breaks a gratuitous promise on which the promisee has relied to his detriment. The Canadian courts have been prepared to recognize some gratuitous promises as binding, but only to prevent a promisor from breaking a gratuitous promise and then suing the promisee. It is often said that Canadian courts accept the doctrine of promissory (equitable) estoppel as a "shield" (that is, a defence), but not a "sword" (that is, a cause of action). Recent decisions of Canadian appeals courts make one wonder if the Canadian common law will ever fully embrace the American notion of injurious reliance.

In *Maracle v. Travellers Indemnity Co. of Canada*,[24] the Supreme Court of Canada summarized the principles of promissory estoppel as follows:

The principles of promissory estoppel are well settled. The party relying on the doctrine must establish that the other party has, by words or conduct, made a promise or assurance which was intended to affect their legal relationship and to be acted on. Furthermore, the representee must establish that, in reliance on the representation, he acted on it or in some way changed his position.[25]

In *Maracle*, while it did not expressly adopt the doctrine of injurious reliance, the Supreme Court of Canada did not seem to limit the doctrine to its traditional place as a defence. Professor Waddams has since written: "It may therefore be suggested that the Commonwealth law is moving, though rather slowly, in the direction of [the American position in the Restatement of Contracts] towards the protection of promisees by reason of and to the extent of subsequent reliance."[26]

However, evidence in court opinions of this trend to adopt injurious reliance or promissory estoppel as a cause of action remains limited.[27] In a 2003 decision[28] of the British Columbia Court of Appeal, Madam Justice Huddart wrote:

While it may be, as Professor Waddams suggests, that the law is moving slowly toward a more generous approach to promissory estoppel than that said by Sopinka J. in *Maracle v. Travellers Indemnity Co.* to be well settled, I can see little evidence of that movement in Canadian authorities....

Some evidence of movement is apparent in the 2008 Ontario Superior Court decision of *Hepburn v. Jannock Limited*,[29] where an employee's claim for a promised wage increase was allowed on a number of grounds, including promissory estoppel.

Questions to Consider

1. Why do you think the Canadian courts seem slow to widen the scope of the doctrine of promissory estoppel to allow for injurious reliance as a cause of action?

2. Do you think the next time the Supreme Court of Canada has the opportunity to address the subject of promissory estoppel, it should endorse the American principle of injurious reliance as a cause of action?

Source: Waddams, *The Law of Contracts*, 4th ed. (1999) at pp. 141–2, 154–5.

THE EFFECT OF A REQUEST FOR GOODS OR SERVICES

When one person requests the services of another and the other performs those services, the law implies a promise to pay. Such a promise is implied between strangers or even between friends, if the services are rendered in a customary business transaction. But a promise to pay is not usually implied when the services are performed between members of a family or close friends; although the services were requested, the circumstances may show

---

[24] (1991), 2 S.C.R. 50.

[25] *Ibid.*, at p. 57.

[26] Waddams, *The Law of Contracts*, 4th ed. (Toronto: Canada Law Book Company, 1999) at 141–2, 154–5.

[27] An Ontario Court of Appeal decision, *Doef's Iron Works Ltd. v. MCCI*, [2004] O.J. No. 4358 states in paragraph 2, "It is well established that promissory estoppel can be used only as a shield and not as a sword." See *Conwest Exploration Co. v. Letain*, [1964] S.C.R. 20, 41 D.L.R (2d) 198; *Reclamation Systems Inc. v. The Honourable Bob Rae* 1996 CanLII 7950 (ON S.C.), (1996), 27 O.R. (3d) 419.

[28] N.M. v. A.T.A., 2003 BCCA 297.

[29] (2008) 63 C.C.E.L. 3d. 101, at para. 109–26.

that the parties expected them to be given gratuitously because of friendship, kindness, or family duty. For more information on this topic, see the Companion Website.

Even though neither party mentions price, the implied promise is for payment of what the services are reasonably worth—that is, for payment quantum meruit. Difficult though it may be when the services are not usual professional services with a recognized scale of fees, the court will still fix a fee that it considers to be reasonable.

After the requested services have been performed, the parties may agree on what they consider to be a reasonable price. If so, neither of them can later change his mind and ask the court to fix a reasonable price. In effect, by agreeing to a price, each party has given up his right to refer the matter to the court.

A asks computer programmer B for technical assistance. Afterward, A asks B what her fee is and B suggests a certain sum. A refuses to pay it. In an action for payment for services performed, the court may give judgment in favour of B in the amount she requested or for some other amount that it finds reasonable.

If instead, A agrees to the figure suggested by B but later changes his mind about paying, the court would not concern itself with what it considered reasonable: It would give judgment in favour of B for the amount earlier agreed upon by the parties.

The performance of requested services creates an existing obligation to pay a reasonable price for them, and by later agreeing upon a fixed price, the parties have done away with the need for an implied price. Subsequent payment of the fixed price satisfies all obligations owed by the party who requested the services.

We must be careful to distinguish this position from the situation arising when a promise is made for a past consideration.[30] If, for example, A promises to pay B $100 because B has given her and her family an excellent dinner, A is not bound, since she is under no existing legal obligation at the time she makes her promise. If, however, A promises to pay B $100 because B has catered a dinner for her at her request, A would be bound; in fact, A was already bound to pay B a reasonable price, and she and B have simply agreed later upon what this price should be.

The principle of quantum meruit applies to goods supplied on request as well as to services rendered. Generally, a court has less difficulty ascertaining the reasonable worth of goods than of services.

THE USE OF A SEAL

In medieval times, when few people could read or write, a serious promise or covenant was often recorded by a cleric. He would read the covenant to the **covenantor**, who would then show his consent by impressing his coat of arms into a pool of hot sealing wax poured at the foot of the document. Usually the coat of arms was worn on a signet ring. By impressing his seal in this way, the covenantor adopted the document as his act and deed. To this day a **document under seal** is still called a **deed** and requires *no consideration*. Methods of sealing a document evolved over time, including embossing the coat of arms directly on the paper. Today the usual method is to glue a small, red, gummed sticker to a document.

A seal must be affixed (or the word "seal" written) on the document at the time the party signs it. The word "seal" printed on the document in advance presents difficulties: It may simply indicate the place where the parties are to place a red paper wafer. In *Royal Bank of Canada v. Kiska*,[31] the bank used a printed form of guarantee that included the word "seal" and also the words "Given under seal at ..." and "Signed, sealed and delivered in the

covenantor   one who makes a covenant

document under seal   a covenant recorded in a document containing a wax seal, showing that the covenantor adopted the document as his act and deed

deed   a document under seal, which today is usually a small, red, gummed wafer

---

[30] *Lampleigh v. Braithwait* (1615), 80 E.R. 255.

[31] (1967), 63 D.L.R. (2d) 582.

presence of ...." The bank manager did not affix a red paper wafer, however, until some time after the promisor had signed and without the promisor's instructions to do so. Laskin, J. (later Chief Justice of the Supreme Court of Canada) commented:

> The respective words are merely anticipatory of a formality which must be observed and are not a substitute for it. I am not tempted by any suggestion that it would be a modern and liberal view to hold that a person who signs a document that states it is under seal should be bound accordingly although there is no seal on it. I have no regret in declining to follow this path in a case where a bank thrusts a printed form under the nose of a young man for his signature. Formality serves a purpose here and some semblance of it should be preserved ....[32]

Although some lower courts[33] have held that the words "given under seal" are sufficient without the need to affix a red paper wafer, the Supreme Court endorses the role of the seal in Canadian common law:

> To create a sealed instrument, the application of the seal must be a conscious and deliberate act. At common law, then, the relevant question is whether the party intended to create an instrument under seal ...[34]

A promise made properly under the seal of the promisor does not require consideration to make it binding. Historically, signing under seal was considered an act done with great care. It is still considered so today. The seal says, in effect, "I fully intend to be bound by this promise." Its presence means that the court will not, as it otherwise would, insist upon consideration to hold the promisor bound.

Any offer may be made under seal and so becomes irrevocable. When a business firm or public body invites tenders and requires them to be submitted under the seal of the tenderer, the legal effect is much the same as when an option is given: The tenderer cannot withdraw without being liable in damages.[35]

Certain documents, such as a deed of land and a mortgage, traditionally required a seal even if there was consideration. Electronic registration of these documents has changed some of the seal requirements. These documents will be explained as they arise in later chapters.

Although a seal is an alternative to consideration, it does not do away with any of the other requirements needed to make a promise enforceable.

INTENTION TO CREATE LEGAL RELATIONS

Even when an apparently valid offer has been accepted and consideration is present, there is no contract formed unless both sides intended to create a legally enforceable agreement. There must be agreement on all the essential terms of the deal and a mutual intention to create a legally binding contract.[36] Since parties do not ordinarily think about the legal effects of their bargains, the law presumes that the necessary intention is present in almost all instances where an agreement appears to be seriously made. A presumption in favour of an intention to contract also arises where parties have signed a commercial document.

If courts did not presume that the parties to a contract intended to be legally bound, it would be necessary to inquire into their subjective state of mind when they made their agreement and to decide whether they truly had such an intention—an impractical and time-consuming task. Instead, the law presumes an intention corresponding with the

---

[32] Laskin, J. (later Chief Justice of the Supreme Court of Canada) (1967), 63 D.L.R. (2d) 594.

[33] *Canadian Imperial Bank of Commerce v. Dene Mat Construction Ltd. and others*, [1988] 4 W.W.R. 344 (N.W.T.S.C.); *Hongkong Bank of Canada v. New Age Graphic Design Inc.*, [1996] B.C.J. No. (B.C.S.C.).

[34] *Friedmann Equity Developments Inc. v. Final Note Ltd.*, [2000] 1 S.C.R. 842 at para. 36.

[35] See *Sanitary Refuse Collectors Inc. v. City of Ottawa*, [1972] 1 O.R. 296 at 308–9.

[36] *Olivieri v. Sherman* (2007), 284 D.L.R. (4th) 516 at para. 41 (Ont. C.A.) (applying general law of contract to settlement agreements).

reasonable objective meaning of his words and actions.[37] The presumed intention is especially strong in dealings between strangers and in commerce generally.

A defendant may rebut (overcome) the presumption by using the external or objective test of the reasonable bystander: If to such a person the outward conduct of the parties lacked a serious intention to make an agreement, then no binding contract results. It is easier to rebut the presumption in arrangements between friends or members of a family, where it is often clear that there was no intention to create legal relations. For example, claiming that a failure to show up for a dinner invitation would give the host a right to sue for breach of contract appears unreasonable to us, even though the host went to considerable trouble and expense. Many domestic arrangements between spouses are on the same footing. Ultimately, each case will be determined on its own facts, objectively viewed.

CASE 7.6

Allen owned a business that his friend Wallace wanted to buy. They signed a letter of intent describing their general understanding of how the sale would proceed. The details were to be negotiated and reduced to writing in a binding share purchase agreement within 40 days. Each hired lawyers and the terms of the share purchase agreement were negotiated between them, term by term. By the time the proposed agreement was in final form, the 40 days had long passed and Allen had changed his mind. He refused to sign the purchase agreement or close the deal. Wallace sued alleging breach of contract, and demanding Allen complete the sale. Allen took the position that no legally binding agreement existed as the parties never intended that the letter of intent would be a contract. The trial judge agreed; the importance of

signing the final agreement was evident in the language of the letter of intent. However, the Court of Appeal viewed the evidence much differently. It found, first, that signing the letter of intent triggered a legal presumption that one who executes a commercial document intends to be bound by it. Second, notwithstanding the express requirement that a further agreement was to be signed, the Court of Appeal found intention to form a contract in the language of the letter of intent—words such as "it is agreed" and "upon acceptance." Finally, intent to be bound was also evident by their conduct: Allen announced his retirement after signing the letter of intent and Wallace began working at the business. Damages for breach of contract were granted.[38]

The requirement of an intention to contract has been important in interpreting the legal effect of advertisements. In *Carlill v. The Carbolic Smoke Ball Company*,[39] discussed in Chapter 6, the company pleaded that its promise to pay a £100 reward was no more than a "mere puff" and was not to be taken seriously. This defence lost any credibility because the advertisement itself stated, "£1,000 is deposited with the Alliance Bank, Regent Street, showing our sincerity in the matter." A hundred years later, Pepsi made the same legal argument about its "Pepsi Points" promotion.

CASE 7.7

PepsiCo launched a rewards program where customers earned points for each Pepsi product purchased. Points could be redeemed for merchandise from the Pepsi catalogue, and extra points could be purchased for 10 cents a point. Unfortunately, a TV commercial promoting the points program showed a teenager arriving to school in an AV-8 Harrier Jump Jet with a caption "Harrier Jet 7,000,000 Pepsi Points." Leonard collected

some points and sent Pepsi a cheque to purchase the remaining points to bring him to the necessary 7 000 000. PepsiCo successfully defended Leonard's breach of contract action to obtain the jet. The court held that, even if the commercial was an offer, intention was lacking. No reasonable person could believe that PepsiCo seriously intended to convey a jet worth approximately $23 000 000 for redemption of Pepsi points.[40]

[37] *Lindsey v. Heron & Co.* (1921) 64 D.L.R. 92, 98–9.

[38] *Wallace v. Allen* (2007), 85 O.R. (3d) 88 appeal allowed (2009), 93 O.R. (3d) 723 (Ont. C.A.).

[39] [1892] 2 Q.B. 484.

[40] *Leonard v. PepsiCo, Inc.*, 88 F. Supp. 2d 116 (S.D.N.Y. 1999), *aff'd* 210 F. 3d 88 (2d Cir. 2000); Ann C. Morales, "Pepsi's Harrier Jet Commercial Was Not a Binding Offer to Contract" (2000) 28(2) *Academy of Mark. Science J.* 318–20.

The seriousness of the intention was assessed based upon the objective standard of what a reasonable person would believe. To make its intentions clear, Pepsi modified the commercial to add the words "just kidding" beneath the caption. Other possible legal effects of advertising will be discussed under the topics of misrepresentation in Chapter 9.

Strategies to Manage the Legal Risks

Parties must be clear about their intentions to contract. Businesses offering rewards programs now commonly require participants to sign up online or create an account by visiting the company's website. As part of the enrollment process, the customer must accept the company's standard terms and conditions, which will exclude advertisements and limit entitlements. This reduces the legal risk of customers believing the advertisement is intended as the offer. As well, an advertisement should give viewers notice that it is for informational purposes only and that any described offer is subject to terms and conditions set out on the business's website.

Standard form contracts may be used to clarify uncertainty regarding the existence of consideration. Most contracts include a phrase acknowledging the existence of consideration—for example: "in consideration of the mutual promises expressed herein and one dollar, receipt of which is hereby acknowledged." Out of an abundance of caution, the signature line will have the symbol of a seal beside it and be prefaced with the phrase "signed, sealed and delivered." In this process, some consideration is present (however modest): The parties have confirmed its existence and the reference to a seal may make consideration unnecessary in any event.

Businesses sometimes include in their contracts an express term that, in the event of its breach, a party's right to sue the other is restricted. Although such an understanding may be recognized by the courts,[41] it does not mean no contract is formed. Users should be aware of the limitations of such terms. These terms come in two variations: exemption clauses, discussed previously as a means of limiting liability, and choice-of-forum clauses redirecting the dispute away from the courts, as discussed in Chapter 2. Either term may be unenforceable if it applies only to the weaker party such as a consumer or franchisee.[42] Since the franchisor often has the greater bargaining power, a franchisee may argue that the franchisor's insistence on such a clause was unconscionable and should be struck down, enabling the franchisee to sue. Unconscionability will be discussed more generally in Chapter 9.

Finally, parties to existing legal contracts should take great care when modifying or amending their arrangements. New documentation signed under seal should be completed so that changes are binding upon both parties. Settlement of lawsuit or repayment of existing indebtedness should similarly be documented under seal.

QUESTIONS FOR REVIEW

1. Describe how a promise may become binding although the promisor receives no benefit herself.
2. How might the above situation apply to a promise of a charitable donation?
3. How "valuable" does consideration have to be to make a promise binding? When might a court review the value of consideration?

---

[41] *Rose and Frank v. Crompton*, [1925] A.C. 445; *Kanitz v. Rogers* (2002), 58 O.R. (3d) 299 (S.C.J.).

[42] See, for example, Consumer Protection Act, 2002, S.O. 2002, c. 30, Sch. A, ss. 7–8 (banning pre-dispute arbitration clauses and class action waivers); Sale of Goods Act, R.S.O. 1990, c. S.1, s. 53 (allowing rights to be varied if variation applies to both parties).

4. Describe the nature of consideration in an out-of-court settlement.

5. Why is gratitude not a sufficient consideration to bind a promisor?

6. In what ways might the common law rules about the need for consideration be unsatisfactory for business purposes in altering an existing contract? How can the defect be remedied?

7. Describe how one important defect in the consideration rules has been remedied by statute in five of the provinces.

8. Describe the differing points of view taken in "equitable estoppel" and "injurious reliance."

9. Explain the requirements necessary to successfully apply equitable estoppel.

10. What question remains unresolved in the application of the concept of injurious reliance by the Canadian courts?

11. How does quantum meruit differ from doing a friend a favour?

12. Explain the nature of a seal and its legal importance in Canada.

13. What three essentials of a binding contract have we considered thus far?

14. A firm of public accountants has for years been auditing the accounts of a charitable organization without charge. It now appears that the treasurer of the organization has absconded with a sizeable amount of money and that an application of generally accepted auditing standards would have disclosed the defalcation in time to avoid the loss. Has the charitable organization any recourse against its auditors in these circumstances?

15. What factual situations give rise to a presumption that parties intended to create a legally binding contract?

16. A supplier's invoice for goods has the following common term printed on it: "Terms—Net price 30 days; 2 percent discount if paid within 10 days." If the buyer pays the price less 2 percent within 10 days, can the supplier later sue successfully for the sum deducted?

CASES AND PROBLEMS

1. Continuing Scenario

   Ashley's restaurant business is off to a slow start. Her cash flow is low and she cannot afford to pay all of her regular bills—she must pay her food suppliers so she meets with her landlord and asks if she can pay only 50% of her rent for the next six months. She expects business will improve by then and she will be able to repay the arrears with 150% rental payments beginning in the seventh month. The landlord orally agrees and Ashley thanks him in a follow up email. Two months later, Ashley's landlord is approached by the manager of a prosperous chain of restaurants who is looking for space in this complex. He is willing to pay more than double Ashley's full rent. The landlord would like to evict Ashley's restaurant and rent the space to this chain so he sends Ashley an immediate demand for payment of all the arrears of rent within two weeks or he will evict her for non-payment of rent. Evaluate Ashley's legal position. What is the status of the reduced rent conversation? Does it make a difference if Ashley paid only 25% of her rent during the first two months of the arrangement?

2. Burowski ran an office supplies business and donated one evening a week of her time helping run a bingo for charity. There, she met another donor, Adams, an investment broker. They worked well together for a few months. One evening, Burowski said to Adams that she was rather confused about her investment portfolio; she wondered where she might get advice. Adams suggested they have a coffee together after the bingo hall closed. They spent about an hour discussing Burowski's portfolio and Adams made some suggestions about how she might improve her holdings. Burowski suddenly remembered that she was late returning home to her babysitter and left quickly, thanking Adams as she got up from the table. A week later she received a bill from Adams for $150 for "professional advice."

   Discuss whether Adams has contractual grounds for making this claim.

3. The town of Broomville, along with local arts and athletic groups, decided to erect a new community centre for sports, music, and theatre. The total estimated cost was $18 000 000. In April, Jane Borkus, president and CEO of the largest local industry, Autotech, promised to

match every dollar raised through other donors, up to $9 000 000. Both she and the delighted town mayor, Geoff Johns, made the announcement over the local television station and in a joint statement in the town's newspaper. Borkus said the deadline would be 12 months.

The following January, the campaign was proceeding extremely well: other donors had pledged $5 500 000 and Borkus presented a cheque for $4 000 000 as Autotech's "down payment and pledge of goodwill."

Unfortunately, in March, Autotech lost its major contract to supply car parts to one of the big three auto manufacturers. Anticipating a large loss at year's end, Borkus withdrew the pledge and asked for the return of the down payment.

What arguments may be made on behalf of the town both to keep the money paid and to require Autotech to honour its commitment? What do you think the decision would be?

4. (a) Matsui's bank manager recommended Roberts, a business consultant, to help Matsui appraise a suitable business investment. Matsui wished to buy control of a business and was prepared to pay $200 000 or so if Roberts could find a satisfactory business.

At Matsui's request, Roberts devoted most of his time from May to February of the following year investigating three businesses in which Matsui was interested. They did not discuss Roberts's rate of remuneration for performing these services. Finally, after consultation with Matsui, Roberts managed to obtain an option for him to purchase the shares of the A.C. Electrical Co. Ltd., one of the three companies identified by Matsui. When Matsui learned of Roberts's success in obtaining the option, he promised to pay Roberts $50 000 for his services. Roberts said that would be fine.

Matsui later decided not to exercise the option and refused to pay Roberts the $50 000. Roberts brought an action against him for this sum. In defence, Matsui asserted that it was expressly agreed that if, as a result of Roberts's services or efforts, Matsui actually made a purchase, he would pay a suitable commission to Roberts, but unless Matsui made such a purchase, Roberts would be entitled to nothing. Roberts denied that Matsui's undertaking had been qualified in this manner. Faced with this conflict of evidence, the trial judge stated that he accepted the evidence of the plaintiff in preference to that of the defendant.

What is the main issue? Should Roberts succeed? Why or why not?

(b) Suppose instead that the parties had discussed $50 000 as the appropriate fee before the services were rendered and then when Matsui learned of Roberts's success in obtaining the option, he was so elated as to promise him $10 000 more. What issue would arise if Roberts found it necessary to sue Matsui for the $60 000?

5. Harris N. Dealer was sole proprietor of a profitable computer data centre, which he sold as a going concern to Alice B. Wheeler for the price of $180 000. The price was paid—$30 000 in cash and the balance in the form of a contract under Wheeler's seal, which read in part as follows:

> For value received Alice B. Wheeler promises to pay Harris N. Dealer the sum of one hundred and fifty thousand dollars ($150 000) in 10 years from April 1, 2009, together with interest at 8 percent per annum from April 1, 2009, payable monthly on the first day of May 2009 and on the first day of each and every month thereafter until payment of the principal sum on April 1, 2019.
>
> After ten (10) days' default in any interest payment due under this agreement the whole amount payable shall become immediately due.
>
> March 29, 2009. Alice B. Wheeler [SEAL]

Dealer and Wheeler remained on friendly terms throughout the balance of 2009. Wheeler was somewhat dilatory in making her monthly payments of $1000 interest, so that by the end of the year she had made six of the eight monthly payments required by then on dates more than 10 days after they were due. Dealer had acquiesced in the arrangement without complaint, though the parties had never expressly agreed on any change in the due dates and Dealer seemed merely to have been indulgent with his debtor. Unfortunately, however, the parties had a serious personal disagreement early in 2010. On February 5, 2010, the January 1 interest payment then being 35 days overdue, Dealer wrote to Wheeler as follows:

> This letter will serve to inform you that, an interest payment due under the terms of the contract dated March 29, 2009, being in default for more than 10 days, the whole amount under the contract is now due.
>
> I hereby demand immediate payment of the principal amount of $150 000 and outstanding interest.
>
> H.N. Dealer

Wheeler immediately paid the outstanding interest but refused to pay the principal sum. Dealer brought an action against her for $150 000.

Develop fully the arguments for both the plaintiff and the defendant. State with reasons, including reference to a relevant case or cases, whether the action should succeed.

6. Waymart Ltd., a full service department store, introduced a customer rewards program to encourage loyalty among shoppers and increase sales of low volume products. The program allowed customers to accumulate "W dollars" with each purchase at the store; these dollars could be redeemed toward purchases of select items. The bottom of each customer receipt states its W dollar value and customers simply bring the receipt to the store and "spend it like money."

Every Monday, the store manager designates slow-moving products eligible for purchase with W dollars. Eligible products vary weekly depending upon which items have not sold. The marketing department put together a TV advertisement showing a family enjoying a summer afternoon in their backyard. An eight-person hot tub sat beside new patio furniture while one person barbecued on an expensive grill. The family was eating hamburgers and drinking lemonade from pretty plastic glasses. The caption read "Fulfill your dreams with W dollars."

Susan was planning to buy a $5000 hot tub at another store when she saw the advertisement, so she began collecting Waymart receipts. She bought all her groceries, household, and family supplies at Waymart, as did her mother and sister. Together they collected $3000 worth of W dollars in just four weeks, but she never saw a hot tub in the store. She did see patio furniture and barbecues, but she never saw them marked as eligible W dollar products. She went to the customer service counter and asked about buying a hot tub using her points as part of the purchase price. The clerk told her that Waymart did not carry hot tubs and that the W dollar campaign applied to lower priced items such as groceries and dishware.

Can Susan sue for breach of contract? Give reasons for your opinion. What could Waymart have done differently to protect itself from this legal risk?

Additional Resources for Chapter 7 on the Companion Website

(www.pearsoncanada.ca/smyth)

In addition to pre- and post-tests, mini-cases, and application exercises, the Companion Website includes the following province-specific resources for Chapter 7:

- **Alberta:** Consumer Protection Acts; Exemption Clauses (Breach); Partial Payment of Debt; Seals
- **Atlantic Provinces:** Arbitration Clauses; Electronic Signatures
- **Manitoba/Saskatchewan:** Statutory Override of the Rule in *Foakes v. Beer*
- **Ontario:** Equitable Estoppel; Partial Payment of Debt; Seals

Chapter 8

Formation of a Contract: Capacity to Contract and Legality of Object

In this chapter, the discussion of the essential elements of a contract continues with two elements usually assumed to be present unless shown otherwise. The first is capacity to contract, and the second is the legality of the subject matter of the contract.

We examine such questions as:

■ How does capacity of a minor depend on the nature of the contract?

■ What are "necessaries"?

■ What are the effects of other types of contracts?

- What are a minor's obligations upon attaining the age of majority?

- To what extent is the contractual capacity of the following classes of persons treated differently: Aboriginal peoples? corporations? labour unions? persons of diminished mental capacity?

- What is the difference between void and illegal contracts?

- What are gaming contracts?

- How are contracts affected in different ways by statute?

- What contracts are illegal by common law and public policy?

THE BURDEN OF PROVING ESSENTIAL ELEMENTS OF A CONTRACT

As discussed in Chapter 6 and Chapter 7, once a plaintiff proves that there was offer, acceptance, and consideration for the promise, the court will ordinarily presume an intention to create legal relations. At that point, the court will also presume that two additional elements are present: (1) the defendant has the capacity to make a contract, and (2) the contract is legal. However, if the defendant shows that she did not have the capacity to enter into the contract or that the contract was not legal, she will be released from her contractual obligations.

THE MEANING OF CAPACITY TO CONTRACT

When forming a contract, we usually assume that the other party has the capacity to make a contract and is bound by it, but this is not always so. We would not expect a four-year-old child to be able to buy a $100 computer game; at that age, she would lack the competence—the **legal capacity**—to understand the meaning of a legally binding contract. Although the requirements of Chapter 6 and Chapter 7 were met, as a matter of policy the law may excuse one party, such as the four-year-old child, from her obligations. Of course, in most cases, a lack of capacity is not so obvious; one party reasonably assumes the other has capacity to enter into a contract.

legal capacity competence to bind oneself legally

In addition to age, there are other reasons that contracting parties may lack capacity and, as a result, attempt to **repudiate** their contracts. This chapter discusses the rights and remedies available to both sides in such contracts.

repudiate reject or declare an intention not to be bound by

MINORS (OR INFANTS)

Contractual Liability of Minors

A **minor or infant** is a person who has not attained the **age of majority** according to the law of her province. Historically, the age was deemed to be 21, but it now varies according to the legislation in each province.[1] The general rule is that a contract made by a minor is not binding on her but binding on the other side, whether or not the other person is aware that he is dealing with a minor. When a minor owns assets or needs to contract, her legal **guardian** or parents are ordinarily empowered to look after her affairs.

minor or infant a person who has not attained the age of majority according to the law of his or her province

age of majority the age at which a person is recognized as an adult according to the law of his or her province

guardian a person appointed to manage the affairs of a minor in the place of his or her parents

---

[1] It is usually 18 or 19 years. See, for example, Age of Majority Act, R.S.B.C. 1996, c. 7 (19 years); R.S.N.S. 1989, c. 4 (19 years); C.C.S.M. 1987, c. A-7 (18 years); Age of Majority and Accountability Act, R.S.O. 1990, c. A.7, s. 1 (18 years).

While the purpose of these rules is to protect minors, exceptions are needed so that a minor is not disadvantaged. For example, without an exception a minor in need of food or clothing—**necessaries**—might be unable to find a vendor willing to sell her these things on credit because she could not bind herself to pay for them. Therefore the first exception relates to contracts for necessaries.

Necessaries and Beneficial Contracts of Service

A minor is bound by any contract for supply of necessaries, essential goods, and services. However, she is not bound to pay the contract price as such, but rather a reasonable price on the same basis as quantum meruit, discussed in Chapter 7. In the absence of evidence that the minor has been charged a higher price than other customers, the court usually regards the contract price as evidence of what a reasonable price should be.

The courts have identified the following as necessaries: food, clothing, lodging, medical attention,[2] legal advice,[3] and also transportation—but transportation includes only the means of getting the minor to and from work, and does not include the purchase price of vehicles even if they are used by the minor in carrying on a business[4] or as a means of going to work.[5]

A minor is also bound by **beneficial contracts of service**: contracts of employment or apprenticeship when they are found to be for his benefit and not exploitative. Participating in a business venture is quite different: The courts are more hesitant to find such an arrangement to be for a minor's benefit, whether the minor is in business for himself[6] or in partnership with others.

Contracts Creating No Liability for a Minor

A minor may always repudiate (back out of) a contract for non-necessaries even where the non-necessaries are clearly beneficial to him. The purchase of a truck for use in his business may well be very useful to a minor. Even so, the truck is not a necessary.[7] A fairly large number of things have been held to be necessaries. Each case must be decided on its own facts, and judges are reluctant to enlarge the class. When a minor is living at home and supported by his parents, his purchases are less likely to be considered as necessaries than when he is on his own. The court assumes that a minor living at home is provided for.

Although there are no decisions on the point, it appears that a minor is not liable for necessaries that he has ordered but not yet received. Accordingly, he can repudiate a contract of sale before the goods are delivered.[8] The point is underlined in the Sale of Goods Act, which defines necessaries for an infant in terms of goods sold and delivered.[9]

A minor who repudiates his liability for non-necessary goods will, if the goods are still in his possession, be required to return them to the seller in whatever condition they may be at the time. In *Louden Manufacturing Co. v. Milmine*, Chief Justice Meredith said:

[2] *Miller v. Smith & Co.*, [1925] 2 W.W.R. 360 at 377 (Sask. C.A.).

[3] *Helps v. Clayton* (1864), 144 E.R. 222.

[4] *Mercantile Union Guarantee Corp. v. Ball*, [1937] 2 K.B. 498.

[5] *First Charter Financial Corp. v. Musclow* (1974), 49 D.L.R. (3d) 138 (B.C.S.C.).

[6] *Mercantile Union Guarantee Corp. v. Ball*, supra, n. 4.

[7] *Ibid.*

[8] Furmston, *Cheshire, Fifoot and Furmston's Law of Contract*, 16th ed., at 543-9.

[9] See, for example, R.S.B.C. 1996, c. 410, s. 7; R.S.O. 1990, c. S.1, s. 3 (1); R.S.N.S. 1989, c. 408, s. 5(1).

... [I]f an infant avails himself of the right he has to avoid a contract which he has entered into and upon the faith of which he has obtained goods, he is bound to restore the goods which he has in possession at the time he so repudiates. ... The authorities ... establish that the effect of repudiating the contract is to revest the property in the vendor.[10]

Similarly, when the minor is a seller rather than a buyer in a contract for the sale of goods, he cannot repudiate the contract to recover the goods delivered unless he returns the money paid.[11]

There is nothing to prevent a minor from purchasing non-necessaries if he can find a vendor who is prepared to sell to him. This most often occurs where the minor purchases goods for cash.[12]

Ordinarily a seller cannot rely on a statement by a minor that his parents will pay for the purchase.[13] Provincial family law legislation may impose liability on parents for necessaries only.[14] Authority to bind the parents may also be implied from the fact that parents have paid the account for a previous purchase by their child without complaint. Apart from these possibilities, a vendor needs express authority from the parents before being able to bind them.

Contracts Indirectly Affecting a Minor   A minor who has benefited from a contract for non-necessaries will not be able to recover money already paid, though he will be able to repudiate his remaining liability.

CASE 8.1

T, a minor, agreed to become tenant of a house and to pay L, the landlord, a certain amount for the furniture in it. T paid part of the sum, gave a promissory note for the balance, then occupied the house and had the use of the furniture for several months. Later T brought an action to have the contract rescinded and to recover from L the money he had paid. The court held that T could avoid liability on the note, but that he was not entitled to a return of what he had paid.[15]

An adult can recover money lent to a minor only if the minor used the sum to purchase necessary goods.[16] If the borrowed money was used to pay for a vacation, the lender cannot recover the debt. Minors' contracts that are not binding under the common law may be altered by statute. For example, the Canada Student Loans Act[17] states that a guaranteed bank loan to a student "is recoverable by the lender from the borrower as though the borrower had been of full age at the time the loan was made."

A minor's freedom from liability is limited to contract; she remains liable for torts such as negligence, assault, defamation, or deceit. If, however, a minor causes a loss while performing the very acts contemplated by a contract, the court will decide the case under the law of contract and not of torts, and the minor will escape liability for the consequences.

---

[10] (1908), 15 O.L.R. 53 at 54; *McGaw v. Fisk* (1908), 38 N.B.R. 354; S.A. Williston, *A Treatise on the Law of Contracts*, 4th ed. by R.A. Lord, Vol. 5 (New York: Lawyers Cooperative Publishing, 1993) at 113.

[11] Williston, *supra*, n. 10, Vol. 5, s. 9:16, at 113–33. The right to repudiate may be lost when the infant comes of age.

[12] Problems may arise for the minor if the goods have been used or damaged. This problem is discussed under the heading of "Rescission" in Chapter 13.

[13] *Hailsham, Halsbury's Laws of England*, 4th ed. rev., Vol. 5(2) 24 (London: Butterworths, 1993) at 343–51.

[14] Family Law Act, R.S.O. 1990, c. F. 3, s. 45(2).

[15] *Valenti v. Canali* (1889), 24 Q.B.D. 166.

[16] *Hailsham, supra*, n. 13, at 175.

[17] R.S.C. 1985, c. S-23, s. 19.

The other contracting party will not, in other words, be permitted to avoid the rules protecting minors in contract by suing for damages for a tort where he would otherwise fail if he sued for breach of contract.

CASE 8.2

P, a minor, hires a riding horse and promises as a term of the contract to handle the animal with care. In her exuberance, P injures the horse by riding it too hard.

Q, the owner of the horse, realizes that if he sues P for breach of contract he will fail, since the contract is not for a necessary. So instead he sues her for the tort of negligence. Q will not succeed by this tactic.[18] He will fail whichever approach he takes.

Suppose, however, that in Case 8.2 the horse is injured after P entered it in a race, something not at all contemplated in the contract. Since P's act that resulted in loss was outside the scope of the contract, Q could sue her for damages for negligence.

The Contractual Liability of Minors upon Attaining Majority A minor's liability to pay for necessaries and beneficial contracts of service continues after she attains majority, and in addition, she may become liable for obligations that could not be enforced against her while she was a minor. A non-necessary contract is a **voidable contract**, of which there are two types.

voidable contract a contract that may be rendered non-binding at the option of one of the parties

In the first type, the minor acquires "an interest of a permanent, continuous nature." This class of contracts involves ongoing obligations paid in installments, such as cell phone services, car leases, and fitness club memberships. If she wants to be released from these obligations, she must repudiate or back out of such a contract promptly upon reaching the age of majority, or she will be liable just as if she had entered into the contract after coming of age. In contracts of this type, the minor loses the right to repudiate by not doing so promptly after coming of age, or by accepting the benefits of the contract after that time.

The second and more common type of voidable contract does not create an interest of a continuous nature and is not binding upon a minor unless she expressly **ratifies** or confirms the contract after attaining majority—that is, she acknowledges the contract and promises again to perform. Some provinces require ratification to be in writing and signed by the minor.[19] This type includes a minor's promise to pay for non-necessary goods or for services performed once at her request, such as buying a television or computer. A promise to pay for necessary goods not delivered by the time she becomes of age also requires ratification.

ratifies acknowledges and promises to perform

Some provinces, such as British Columbia, have passed legislation clarifying these rules.[20]

OTHER PERSONS OF DIMINISHED CONTRACTUAL CAPACITY

The law protects a person of unsound mind or incapacitated through alcohol or drugs in the same way as a minor: He is bound to pay a reasonable price for necessaries; other contracts are voidable at his option but enforceable by him against the other contracting party.

In practice, a person who was drunk or insane at the time of making a contract often has a difficult problem of proof. A minor can more easily prove his age than can a person establish that he was so intoxicated or insane as not to know what he was doing.

---

[18] *Jennings v. Rundall* (1799), 101 E.R. 1419.

[19] The Statute of Frauds, for example, R.S.O. 1990, c. S.19, s. 7; R.S.N.S. 1989, c. 442, s. 9.

[20] Infants Act, R.S.B.C. 1996, c. 223, s. 19.

There is an additional burden of evidence on the party seeking to avoid the contract: He must show not only that he was incapable of a rational decision at the time of the agreement but also that the other party was aware of his condition. Unfortunately for the person who was so insane or drunk that he did not know what he was doing, his own observations about the other contracting party are unlikely to be reliable, and the necessary evidence must then be adduced from all the surrounding circumstances.

As with voidable contracts generally, the party seeking to avoid must act promptly upon emerging from his state of incapacity. Unless repudiation comes within a reasonable time, the privilege is lost. It is also too late to repudiate if, after regaining sanity or sobriety, the party accepts the benefits of the contract.

With an aging population, we face a growing problem of diminished contractual capacity among the elderly. In dealing with an aged person, it is often difficult to tell whether she is simply physically frail or also suffers from diminished mental capacity that might leave a contract with her open to subsequent attack.

CORPORATIONS

Since a corporation is a "legal fiction"—it is merely a creature of the law[21]—it has no physical existence: It cannot think or act or sign its name as a natural person can. Nevertheless, the law may give corporations the capacity to make any contract or enter into any obligation that a natural person possesses, and business corporations' statutes now give this capacity. However, legislatures have not extended to all corporations the widest possible contractual capacity: Public corporations, such as municipalities and Crown corporations, are restricted to the limited power conferred by the statutes creating them. Obligations that they may claim to undertake but that are outside the ambit of the statute will, if challenged, be declared by the court to be ultra vires (beyond their powers) and, therefore, **void**. The promisee cannot enforce such obligations against the corporation. The legal consequences of ultra vires contracts are often complex and difficult.

void never formed in law

The law relating to principal and agent determines whether the person or persons claiming to act on behalf of a corporation have the power to bind it in contracts (we will deal with this in Chapter 17). The matter is especially important for a corporation because, not being a natural person, it must make all its contracts through agents. Corporation officers who have the necessary authority usually issue the corporation's signature for important contracts and formal documents, such as share certificates, bonds, debentures, deeds, and mortgages, by impressing the company seal using an embossing device.[22] For ordinary day-to-day business, the signature of an authorized officer alone is used.

LABOUR UNIONS, ASSOCIATIONS, AND OTHER ORGANIZATIONS

In our legal system, the fact that a group of individuals gets together and forms an organization—be it a social club, a charity, a religious community, or a labour union—does not make that group into a legal entity (unless it incorporates). Only after the unincorporated group has applied to the appropriate government agency and been recognized as a separate

---

[21] As we shall see, our legal system recognizes—or fabricates—legal creatures with some or most of the capacity of a natural person. These creations of the law are described variously as "a legal person," "a legal entity," an entity having "separate legal status," and "corporate persons." For further discussion, see Chapter 25, "The Nature of a Corporation and Its Formation."

[22] In most provinces it is no longer necessary for a corporation to have a seal, although it is still common practice to do so.

legal person will it be capable of entering into contracts.[23] Despite their significant role in our economy, for the most part the legal status of labour unions remains limited, though the law varies significantly from province to province and the rules for recognition (certification) of a union are set out in legislation and are quite complicated.[24]

By contrast, the legal status of business corporations as employers is clearly settled. The differences between the two are evident in the processes for negotiation and enforceability of collective agreements between corporations and labour unions. The business's management has the capacity to make an offer in the course of negotiating a collective agreement. However, any acceptance of that offer by the union must be subsequently ratified by a majority of the union members before it is binding. As for enforcement, most provinces do have statutes[25] that provide for arbitration in the event of a dispute arising out of the collective agreement. If an employer does not implement the decision of the arbitrator, the union may apply to a labour relations board for permission to prosecute and for this purpose is given legal status. If a union rejects the arbitrator's decision and causes an illegal strike, damages have occasionally been awarded against the union; the enforceability of such decisions is a matter of debate. In those provinces where an employer may seek permission to prosecute a union for such a strike, the union's liability derives from a statutory provision and not from the union's contractual capacity.

representative action an action brought by one or more persons on behalf of a group having the same interest

Despite their indefinite status, labour unions may bring actions or defend against them when they so wish. By a legal technique known as a **representative action**, a union may expressly or impliedly authorize one or more persons to represent it in court simply as a group of individuals having a common interest in a particular case. As a result, union officials may bring or defend a representative action on behalf of the union's members. Chapters 18 reviews the processes involved in a unionized workplace.

ENEMY ALIENS

alien non-citizen

Ordinarily, an **alien** has the same rights as a citizen in making contracts and in all other matters of private law. In the event of a declaration of war, however, an enemy alien loses all contractual capacity, apart from any special licence granted by the Crown. For the purposes of contracts, an enemy alien is identified not by citizenship but by the fact that either his residence or business interests are located in enemy territory.

Any evidence that a contract made with an enemy alien is detrimental to the public interest will make the contract void as being against public policy, and the rights and liabilities created by the contract are wholly dissolved. In a few exceptional instances where the public interest is thought not to be affected, a contract may be regarded as being merely suspended for the duration of hostilities.

ABORIGINAL PEOPLES

aboriginal peoples Canadian Indian, Inuit, and Métis peoples

The definition of **Aboriginal peoples** in the Canadian Constitution includes Indian, Inuit, and Métis peoples of Canada.[26] The legal position and contractual capacity of Indians is governed by the Indian Act.[27] It defines Indians much more narrowly than the Constitution

---

[23] For religious communities in Ontario, for example, see Religious Organization's Lands Act, R.S.O. 1990, c. R-23.

[24] See Chapters 18 under "The Legal Status of Trade Unions."

[25] See, for example, Labour Relations Code, R.S.B.C. 1996, c. 244, s. 82(2); The Labour Relations Act, S.O. 1995, c. 1, Sch. A. s. 41; The Trade Union Act, R.S.N.S. 1989, c. 475, s. 19(1).

[26] Constitution Act, 1982, s. 35(2).

[27] R.S.C. 1985, c. I-5. Section 4 excludes Inuit people from the application of the Act Section 5 defines Status Indians.

and the complicated definition is an issue of long-standing conflict. Under the Indian Act, land is designated or reserved for use and occupation by Indians. The property comprising the reserve is held by the Crown in trust for the benefit of the Indian band. It is not owned by individual occupants, is not available as security for the claims of creditors, and any attempt to dispose of such property to an outside party is void unless the transaction has been approved by the Minister of Aboriginal Affairs and Northern Development Canada. Indians living on reserves may manufacture and sell goods to outsiders, although in the prairie provinces, sales of produce must have the approval of a superintendent under the Minister (s. 32). Other Aboriginal people and Indians not living on a reserve have the same contractual capacity as that of any other citizen.

CASE 8.3

A judgment creditor tried to collect its judgment by garnishing the bank account of the debtor, God's Lake Indian Band, an Indian band on a reserve in Northern Manitoba. The bank account was with a financial institution in Winnipeg. The Supreme Court of Canada allowed the garnishment to proceed.

It held that the bank account was not actually situated on the reserve, nor was it "deemed to be" situated on the reserve within the meaning of the Indian Act. The creditor was entitled to collect.[28]

BANKRUPT DEBTORS

During bankruptcy proceedings, a debtor is under certain contractual disabilities (except for necessaries) until after he receives a discharge from the court. We will discuss these disabilities more fully in Chapters 29.

THE ROLE OF LEGALITY IN THE FORMATION OF A CONTRACT

The object or purpose of a contract must be legal. A contract will be considered **illegal** if its purpose offends the public good (that is, it is contrary to public policy) or violates a statute. Courts presume that a transaction is legal unless a defendant produces evidence to show that it is not. It is relatively easy for judges to decide if a contract violates a statute. It is more difficult for judges to decide if a contract is contrary to public policy because there is no exhaustive list of public policies. Judges must decide for themselves whether the purpose of a particular contract offends the public good based on a general sense of what is good or bad for society as a whole.

illegal offends the public good or violates a statute

The general rule is that an illegal contract is **unenforceable**. Courts will not assist parties trying to accomplish an illegal goal. In rare circumstances, a statute will specify that contracts that conflict with its provisions are void rather than unenforceable, and this leads to different results.

unenforceable no court assistance or remedy is available to parties of the contract

THE DIFFERENCE BETWEEN VOID AND ILLEGAL CONTRACTS

In circumstances where a statute states that a contract is void, no legally binding agreement is formed. In the eyes of the court, the contract does not exist and the court will

---

[28] *McDiarmid Lumber Ltd. v. God's Lake First Nation*, [2006] 2 S.C.R. 846. The phrase "on a reserve" has been interpreted in the context of taxation in *Dube v. Canada* 2011 SCC 39. See also *Delgamuuk v. BC* [1997] 3 S.C.R. 1010 summarized in *Thomas v. Rio Tinto Alcan* 2013 BCSC 2303.

do its best to restore the parties to their pre-contract positions. The court may order the return of money paid or of property transferred. In addition, each party is released from the performance of any future obligations under the agreement. A court may find that only one term of a contract is void and that the remaining parts are valid. If it decides that the void term can be **severed** from the contract without doing injustice to the parties, it will enforce the remainder of the contract.

Most of the time, illegal contracts are considered completely unenforceable, rather than void. The court will not get involved and will refuse to help any party who knowingly agreed to an illegal arrangement. Not only may a party not sue for money promised, but the court will not help recover any property already transferred. When both parties are aware of the illegal purpose, the plaintiff is without a remedy and so the defendant may keep the ill-gotten gain. The end result is that, where both parties are equally in the wrong, the position of the defendant is the stronger. With illegal contracts, a court is less likely to sever the illegal part and enforce the rest.

It can be difficult to tell when a court will consider a contract unenforceable. Generally, the more reprehensible its purpose, the more likely the contract will be regarded as illegal and unenforceable, and a plaintiff will be denied any remedy. On rare occasions the statute will actually say whether an offending contract is void or unenforceable.

CONTRACTS AFFECTED BY STATUTE

Significance of the Wording of a Statute

Most statutes do not consider the consequences for a contract that conflicts with their purpose; they leave the matter for the courts to figure out on public policy grounds. However, on rare occasions a statute may prevent a particular type of contract from having any legal effect by stating that such agreements shall be void. Or it may go further and express disapproval by describing such agreements as "unlawful" or "illegal" or "unenforceable." A statute may even declare that performance of the agreement shall be a criminal offence, subject to prescribed penalties of a fine or imprisonment. Alternatively, legislation may be used to legalize behaviour that was previously considered to be against public policy. Examples of each type of statute are discussed below.

Examples of Contracts Void by Statute

Agreements Contrary to the Purpose of Legislation   Workers' compensation legislation provides an example of legislation that expressly declares some contracts void because they undermine the purpose of the Act. It says that any provision in an agreement between employer and employee depriving the employee of the benefits available under the Act is void.[29] The Act's purpose is to provide money to workers injured at work, and any contract that prevents that from happening undermines its purpose.

Another example is found in the Bankruptcy and Insolvency Act. Its purpose is to gather assets of a bankrupt person in order to pay his or her creditors and thereafter release the debtor from further obligation to pay. Obviously, disposing of the bankrupt person's assets before this happens conflicts with that purpose. Therefore, the statute contains a provision that if a person transfers property either by gift or for an obviously inadequate low price and becomes bankrupt within one year after, the transfer is void and the property is available to the trustee in bankruptcy.[30] The trustee may recover the property and apply

---

[29] See, for example, Workplace Safety and Insurance Act, S.O. 1997, c. 16, Sch. A., s. 16; Workers' Compensation Act, R.S.B.C. 1996, c. 492, s. 13; S.N.S. 1994–95, c. 10 s. 87.

[30] Bankruptcy and Insolvency Act, R.S.C. 1985, c. B-3, s. 95, dealt with in detail in Chapter 29.

it to the claims of the bankrupt person's creditors. The same statute provides that a transfer of property by an insolvent person to one of several creditors with a view to giving that creditor a preference over the others is "void" if it occurs within three months preceding bankruptcy.[31]

If legislation is silent about the fate of contracts affecting its purpose, a judge still has discretion to decide that a particular contract undermines the purpose of the legislation, and in this case the contract will be unenforceable on public policy grounds.

Examples of Statutes Affecting Public Policy

Promises to Pay a Betting Debt   One example involving both public policy and statutes is betting. Historically, debts resulting from bets were not considered to be against public policy, nor was there legislation against betting; accordingly, bets were not void or unenforceable. Nevertheless, the English courts did not like enforcing wagers that were based simply on speculation about an unknown result, so the courts searched for reasons to refuse them. Sometimes they looked at the subject matter of the bet and found it to be against public policy, such as "bribing voters"—a wager with voters as to the outcome of an election in their constituency.[32]

In Canada, the Criminal Code[33] makes certain betting activities illegal. It is a criminal offence to keep a gaming house (s. 201) or to operate a pool (s. 202) or a lottery (s. 206) unless they fall under specified exceptions within the Act. Major exceptions include lotteries operated by a province or by an organization licensed by a province (s. 207).

All provinces have gaming control statutes and commissions that supervise the issuing of licences for lotteries, race courses, and casinos.[34] Some statutes make specific reference to the enforcement of gambling contracts:

> No person may use civil proceedings to recover money owing to the person resulting from participating in or betting on a lottery scheme within the meaning of section 207 of the Criminal Code (Canada) conducted in Ontario unless the lottery scheme is authorized under subsection 207(1) of the Code.[35]

The Criminal Code does address the ability to pass title to an asset through an unlicensed lottery:

> Every sale, loan, gift, barter or exchange of any property, by any lottery, ticket, card or other mode of chance depending on or to be determined by chance or lot, is void, and all property so sold, lent, given, bartered or exchanged is forfeited to Her Majesty. (s. 206(5))[35A]

There is quite a large body of Canadian case law regarding betting. Most of it refuses to enforce debts, although some decisions have allowed a creditor to succeed, usually one who has lent money to the debtor but who himself did not participate in the game. For more information on this topic, see the Companion Website.

The parties to a **wager**—an agreement between two parties in which each has at the time some probability of winning or losing—must be distinguished from a **stakeholder** who manages a betting arrangement for a fee and redistributes winnings. Organizations that manage lotteries, racetracks, and casinos are stakeholders and therefore not a party to a wagering

wager   an agreement between two persons in which each has some probability of winning or losing

stakeholder   a person or organization that manages a betting arrangement for a fee and redistributes winnings

---

[31] *Ibid.* s. 95(1).

[32] *Allen v. Hearn* (1875), 1 T.R. 56; *Gilbert v. Sykes* (1812), 16 East 150 at 162.

[33] Criminal Code, R.S.C. 1985, c. C-46, ss. 201–9.

[34] See, for example, Gaming Control Act, S.B.C. 2002, c. 14; Gaming Control Act, S.N.S. 1994–95, c. 4.

[35] Gaming Control Act, S.O. 1992, c. 24, s. 47.1.

[35A] The Criminal Code of Canada (s. 206(5)).

agreement. They do, however, remain legally accountable for performing their task as stakeholders.[36] A number of contracts commonly regarded as being of a legitimate business nature have a significant element of speculation in them—insurance contracts, stock exchange transactions, and "futures" transactions in commodities. Insurance statutes, in particular, require that contracts of insurance not be regarded as wagering contracts if they are to be enforceable.

Insurance Contracts Contracts of insurance form an important class of commercial transactions. Typically, one does not hope to win the "bet" with the insurance company, but rather one hopes that, should the feared loss occur, one will receive a measure of compensation. The fear of loss is expressed in the idea of insurable interest. For a person to have an insurable interest, he must have a financial benefit from the continued existence of the property or life insured or suffer some financial detriment from its loss or destruction. Provincial insurance acts state that an insurance contract is invalid unless the party making the contract has an insurable interest in the property or life insured.

Insurance statutes define the circumstances where an insurable interest exists. With respect to life insurance, for policies on one's own life or on certain members of one's family, it is not necessary to show a financial interest—a detriment is presumed to exist in the loss of that life. But for all other persons, a policy holder must show that he has a financial interest in the person whose life is insured, such as a debtor or a business partner. The acts waive the requirement of an insurable interest only when the person whose life is insured consents in writing to placing the insurance.[37] Insurance contracts are discussed more fully in Chapters 16.

Stock Exchange Transactions Stock exchange transactions are among the more speculative business contracts. The contract itself is an actual sale of personal property. Good faith contracts for the purchase and sale of shares are therefore valid and enforceable. If, however, the subject of an agreement is a wager about what the price of a particular security will be at a specified future time, without a good faith intention of acquiring, selling, or taking delivery of the shares, such an agreement is an offence under the Criminal Code and accordingly it is illegal.[38]

Commodities trading, or "futures" as these transactions are sometimes known, involves contracts for the future delivery of goods. Whenever goods are purchased or sold for future delivery at a price agreed upon in advance, one contracting party may gain at the expense of the other because of price changes between the time of the contract and the time of delivery. Again, the speculative element in these contracts is incidental to a larger purpose of selling goods, and the contract is not illegal on the ground that it amounts to a wager.

INTERNATIONAL ISSUE

Internet Gambling

Provinces control gambling within their borders by licensing specific types of gambling for particular purposes. Naturally, this power to control gambling and issue licences has jurisdictional limits. Internet gambling makes it easy for gamblers to access sites outside a province and beyond the control of provincial gaming authorities. Therefore, private sector online gambling sites located (wholly or partially) within a province are illegal unless operated by the Province itself.[39] However, at present, foreign online gambling sites whose entire operations are outside Canada are not illegal.

>

---

[36] *Ellesmere v. Wallace*, [1929] 2 Ch. 1; *Tote Investors Ltd. v. Smoker*, [1968] 1 Q.B. 509.

[37] See, for example, Insurance Act, R.S.B.C. 2012, c. 1, s. 45(2)(b); R.S.O. 1990, c. I.8, s. 178(2)(b); R.S.N.S. 1989, c. 231, s. 180(2)(b).

[38] Criminal Code, R.S.C. 1985, c. C-46, s. 383.

[39] Those sites that are operated or sponsored by the Province itself are legal. See *R. v. Starnet Communications International Inc.* (August 17, 2001) Vancouver 125795-1 (B.C.S.C.); Criminal Code, R.S.C. 1985, c. C-46, ss. 201–9.

Calls to regulate or prohibit offshore gambling focus on the risks associated with addiction, underage access, and criminal behaviour, and, of course, lost government revenues. Prohibition may be difficult in any event. American attempts to prevent offshore gambling sites from accessing U.S. gamblers triggered an international trade dispute. The World Trade Organization (WTO) held that the U.S. prohibition violated the General Agreement on Trade in Services (1995) and authorized sanctions of (a modest) US $21 000 000 against the United States.

Questions to Consider

1. Should internet gambling be illegal?

2. Should the Criminal Code be amended to apply to offshore gambling sites that offer services to Canadian gamblers?

Sources: C.I. Kyer and D. Hough, "Is Internet Gaming Legal in Canada: A Look at Starnet," (2002) 1(1) *Canadian Journal of Law and Technology*, http://cjlt.dal.ca; T.L. Mackay, "Internet Gambling in Canada Waits in Legal Purgatory," National Policy Working Group Policy Discussion Document, July 2004, Canadian Centre on Substance Abuse, http://www.ccsa.ca/2004%20ccsa%20documents/ccsa-011128-2004.pdf; B.S. Klapper, "WTO Clears $21 Million US in Sanctions Vs. U.S.," Associated Press, December 21, 2007, www.antiguawto.com/-wto/AP_WTOClears21MSanctionsVSUS_21Dec07.pdf; *Her Majesty the Queen v. Pamajewon*, [1996] 2 S.C.R. 821.

Examples of Agreements Illegal by Statute

Some statutes describe certain types of agreements as illegal. An example is the Competition Act, discussed in a separate section below. Other statutes impose penalties for certain kinds of conduct without expressly addressing contracts. While the most important of these statutes is the Criminal Code, other examples are the Income Tax Act, which imposes penalties for false returns and evasion,[40] and the Customs Act, which exacts penalties for smuggling.[41] Any contract that involves illegal conduct is itself illegal, not because the statute refers directly to contracts, but because the common law holds that when the object of a contract is illegal by statute, then the contract itself is illegal.

CASE 8.4

A loan agreement between two parties calls for 4 percent interest per month plus other payments, such as a commitment fee and monitoring fees, which, when taken together, exceed 60 percent. Section 347 of the Criminal Code makes it an offence to enter into an agreement to receive more than 60 percent interest.

The Supreme Court held that, although the interest and fees provision violated the statute and was illegal, the illegal portion could be severed from the contract and the agreement could be allowed to proceed in its severed form. The creditor was allowed to recover a maximum of 60 percent interest.[42]

Provincial statutes and municipal bylaws require the licensing or registration of various classes of business and professional people, ranging from taxicabs and local building trades to moneylenders, trading partnerships, real estate agents, investment advisers and stockbrokers, optometrists, and public accountants.[43] When such a person sues to collect for services provided, the defendant may raise as a defence that the plaintiff has not been properly registered for his trade and is therefore not legally entitled to bill for such services.

---

[40] R.S.C. 1985, c.1, s. 239 (5th Supp.).

[41] R.S.C. 1985, c. C-1, s. 110–16, 153–61 (2nd Supp.).

[42] *Transport North American Express Inc. v. New Solutions Financial Corp.*, [2004] 1 S.C.R. 249

[43] See Ontario statutes: Business Names Act, R.S.O. 1990, c. B.17, ss. 2(6), 7(3); Real Estate and Business Brokers Act, S.O., c. 30. 2002, Sch. C, s. 3; Securities Act, R.S.O. 1990, c. S.5, s. 25; Drug and Pharmacies Regulation Act, R.S.O. 1990, c. H.4, s. 139; Public Accounting Act, 2004, S.O. 2004, c. 8, s. 3(1).

K, an electrician, sued for services rendered to A, who pleaded in defence that K was not licensed as an electrical contractor as required by the local bylaw. The court stated that the object of the bylaw was to protect the public against mistakes and loss that might arise from work done by unqualified electricians and, accordingly, held that the contract was unlawful. The court would not assist K in his attempt to collect the account.[44]

Another decision held that a person in the electrician's position in Case 8.5 would be entitled to recover for the materials supplied, though not the fee for the services provided.[45]

In contrast when an action is brought against a person who has not been licensed, the defendant cannot use his own misconduct in not complying with a statute as a defence to an action by an innocent person. This result is an application of the general principle that a person (whether as plaintiff or defendant) is not permitted to use evidence of his own wrongdoing for his advantage before the courts.

The courts are more flexible and sympathetic toward entirely innocent breaches of a statutory requirement.

S, an American citizen, was lawfully admitted to Canada and applied for permanent residence status. While waiting for her status to be granted, she accepted a position without first obtaining a work permit as required under immigration regulations; S was unaware of the requirement. She and her employer paid premiums under the Employment Insurance Act. S was laid off and applied for benefits but they were denied on the basis that her contract of employment was void for illegality.[46]

The court rejected the "classic model of illegality" and stated that the consequences of declaring a contract illegal could often be too extreme. It was preferable to adopt a general principle rather than a rigid rule, and to refuse to give relief only where it would be contrary to public policy to do so. To allow this claim would not offend the policy of making benefits available to a person innocently unemployed. Nor would it encourage illegal immigrants to come to Canada to work illegally. S was not an illegal immigrant and she acted in good faith. The Act only imposed sanctions against those who knowingly obtained work without a permit. The court gave S the right to collect employment benefits.

Examples of Agreements Made Legal by Statute

Attitudes about socially acceptable behaviour change over time, and therefore attitudes about what is in the public good also change. Legislation is sometimes passed to make previously illegal contracts legal. As discussed above, statutes have been passed to legalize otherwise illegal betting; Section 204 of the Criminal Code makes betting on horse racing legal, as well as private bets between individuals not engaged in the "business" of betting.

arbitration agreements contracts that require all disputes to be resolved in arbitration, not the courts

Arbitration agreements are another example of previously unenforceable contracts being made legal by statute. Historically, courts considered any contract that blocked access

---

[44] *Kocotis v. D'Angelo* (1957), 13 D.L.R. (2d) 69 (ONCA); but see *Sidmay Ltd. et al. v. Wehttam Investments Ltd.* (1967), 61 D.L.R. (2d) 358, aff'd (1968), 69 D.L.R. (2d) 336; *Chung v. Idan*, [2006] O.J. No. 299, paras. 52–3 (QL) aff'd 2007 ONCA 544.

[45] *Monticchio v. Torcema Construction Ltd.* (1979), 26 O.R. (2d) 305.

[46] *Re Still and Minister of National Revenue* (1997), 154 D.L.R. (4th) 229. But see *Koo v. 5220459 Manitoba Inc.*, (2010) 254 Man. R. (2d) 62.

to the courts to be against public policy and therefore unenforceable.[47] Canadian attitudes toward arbitration changed in the 1990s, and most provinces passed arbitration legislation embracing arbitration agreements and leaving only a few possible reasons for a court to find an arbitration agreement unenforceable.[48] Now attitudes toward consumer arbitration are changing again, and some provinces have passed legislation declaring consumer arbitration agreements contained in standard form purchase contracts unenforceable.[49] The illegal arbitration clause may be severed from the purchase agreement, and any disputes may be resolved in the courts.

To avoid continuously changing legislation, most decisions about the legality of a contract are left to the courts to be decided on public policy grounds with the help of precedents from past cases.

CONTRACTS ILLEGAL BY THE COMMON LAW AND PUBLIC POLICY

The Common Law

The **common law** has identified certain types of conduct that harm others, and has granted remedies, usually in the form of damages, to persons harmed by that conduct. Generally the conduct is considered a private wrong or tort, and so whenever a contract involves or requires the commission of a tort, the contract is illegal.

common law precedents developed over time from the decisions of many cases

Among the torts that typically arise in an agreement are slander and libel, trespass, deceit (fraud), and, in particular, inducement to break an existing contract with someone else.

CASE 8.7

The Wanderers Hockey Club learned that Johnson had signed a contract to play for the following season with another club managed by Patrick. The Wanderers' manager persuaded Johnson to enter into a second contract with it for the same season by offering him a higher salary. Johnson tore up his contract with Patrick, but as things turned out, he failed to perform his new contract with the Wanderers, which then sued him for breach of contract.

The action failed on the grounds that no cause of action can arise out of a wrongdoing; it had been obvious to both parties that the second contract with the Wanderers could not be performed without breaking the earlier contract with Patrick.[50]

An agreement may not have as its primary purpose the commission of a wrongful act, but what if it contains an undertaking by one party to indemnify the other against damages arising from any tort committed in the course of performing the contract?

CASE 8.8

W.H. Smith & Son's contract to print the *Vanity Fair* newspaper for Clinton included a term that Clinton would indemnify it against libel claims. Thereafter, the paper published an article containing statements libelous to Parr's Bank. W.H. Smith settled the claim against it by paying Parr's Bank a sum of money and sued Clinton to recover the money. The action failed because the court refused to assist in the recovery of money to indemnify against wrongful behaviour—publishing libelous statements.[51]

---

[47] John D. McCamus, *The Law of Contracts* (Toronto: Irwin, 2005) at 440.

[48] See, for example, Arbitration Act, R.S.A. 1991, c. A-43, ss. 6–7.

[49] Consumer Protection Act, 2002, S.O. 2002, c. 30, ss. 7–8 (exact wording is invalid). Quebec and Alberta have also limited enforcement of consumer arbitration agreements.

[50] *Wanderers Hockey Club v. Johnson* (1913), 14 D.L.R. 42. See also *Fabbi et al. v. Jones* (1972), 28 D.L.R. (3d) 224.

[51] *Smith v. Clinton* (1908), 99 L.T. 840.

There are important exceptions to this rule for contracts of insurance. For example, an insurance policy that promises to indemnify a motorist for the damages he may have to pay to third parties as a result of his negligent driving is neither void nor illegal; automobile insurance for public liability and property damage is valid. Similar policies of insurance are designed to protect professional people against the consequences of their negligence in the course of practice, and such policies are also valid. However, the insurance protects the policy holder from negligence only—that is, from unintentional wrongdoing, and not from intentional behaviour, such as fraud.

In addition, a person or a business may exempt itself from liability for negligence by the terms of a contract. A railway or other carrier may state in its standard form contract for the shipment of goods (bill of lading) that it shall not be liable for damage to goods in excess of a stated amount, whether caused by the negligence of its employees or not. The temptation to include such exemption clauses is great, and as a result these contracts are often subject to government regulation.

Public Policy

Even though a contract does not contemplate the commission of a crime or of any of the recognized torts, it may still be regarded as illegal because it is contrary to public policy. If the court decides that a particular contract is prejudicial to the interests of Canada, its relations with foreign countries, its national defence, its public service, the values of society as a whole, or the administration of justice within the country, the court will declare the contract illegal although its performance is neither a tort nor a crime in itself.

CASE 8.9

In *Symington v. Vancouver Breweries and Riefel*,[52] the plaintiff, Symington, promised the defendants (who were anxious to see a person named Ball convicted of illegal manufacture of alcohol) to give evidence that would assure Ball's conviction. The defendants promised to pay Symington $1000 for each month of imprisonment in Ball's sentence. Symington gave testimony and Ball was sentenced to 12 months' imprisonment. Symington received only part payment and sued for the balance.

Symington's suit failed on grounds of public policy that the agreement tended to pervert justice. In summarizing his reasons, Mr. Justice Martin said:

This is so direct and inevitable an incentive to perjury and other concomitant nefarious conduct that it cannot be in the public interest to countenance a transaction which is dangerous to such an exceptional degree to the administration of criminal justice.[53]

The arrangements by which a person accused of a crime may be released under bail are intended to be fair and humane.[54] However, they require that the party putting up the bail shall forfeit the bail money should the prisoner abscond. Accordingly, a promise either by the accused or by a third party to indemnify the party putting up bail is illegal.[55] For more information on this topic, see the Companion Website.

Public policy interests extend beyond the administration of justice, incorporating general values beneficial to a free society such as free speech and the right to profit from one's work.

---

[52] Court of Appeal for Ontario, [1931] 1 D.L.R. 935.

[53] *Ibid.* at 937.

[54] See M.L. Friedland, *Detention Before Trial* (Toronto: University of Toronto Press, 1965); Criminal Code, R.S.C. 1985, c. C-46, ss. 763–71.

[55] *Herman v. Jeuchner* (1885), 15 Q.B.D. 561; *Consolidated Exploration and Finance Co. v. Musgrave*, [1900] 1 Ch. 37.

Employment and research contracts often contain clauses that require the employee or the funded researcher to maintain confidentiality about sensitive information. Such information might include the company's financial affairs, its marketing plans, the products it is developing, or the progress of research it is sponsoring. There are good reasons for these clauses. Businesses do not want their competitive position undermined by having private information end up in the hands of their rivals. They do not want the price of their stock or the reputation of their products to be affected by rumours and gossip. Courts award damages and sometimes grant injunctions for breach of confidentiality clauses.

However, what if the clause prevents a person from disclosing information that shows that a company's products place consumers or patients at risk? In that case, ethical and public policy concerns arise.

Dr. Nancy Olivieri, a professor of medicine at the University of Toronto and leading researcher at the Hospital for Sick Children, received funding from Apotex, a drug manufacturer, to conduct clinical trials on a new drug.

A few years into the trial, Dr. Olivieri became concerned that the drug was not effective and that dangerously high levels of iron were building up in the livers of some of the patients in the trial. When she reported her concern to the drug company and the hospital research ethics board, the company terminated the trial at the Toronto site. When she made her findings public, Apotex accused her of violating the confidentiality agreement she had signed and threatened to sue her. The company also asserted that her methods were suspect, and her findings were unsupported by other researchers. While Dr. Olivieri published her research findings in the highly respected *New England Journal of Medicine*, Apotex did not submit its data for publication.

During the conflict, Dr. Olivieri received strong moral support from a number of her colleagues, many of whom thought the hospital had not properly supported and defended her. Eventually, Dr. Olivieri and the hospital reached a settlement of their differences.

Questions to Consider

1. Should confidentiality agreements be enforced if doing so would prevent risks from being disclosed to the public? How can the proper balance be established between a company's interest in protecting sensitive information and the public's interest in knowing about risks to health and safety?

2. What legislation, if any, do we need to protect employees and researchers who disclose information about products or activities that pose a risk to consumers or patients?

3. Should medical and physical safety risks be the only exceptions? What about risks to our privacy? Consider the situation of Edward Snowdon, the former NSA and CIA contractor who breached his confidentiality obligations when he disclosed massive government surveillance practices.

Sources: Susan Jeffrey, "Research Conflict," *The Medical Post*, January 21, 1997; Michael Valpy, "Science Friction," *Elm Street*, December 1998; University of Toronto Faculty Association Press Release, December 17, 1998; Joint Release, The Hospital for Sick Children and Dr. Nancy Olivieri, January 26, 1999; Marina Jimenez, "Olivieri, Foes Take Battle Over Drug to Ottawa," *National Post*, October 5, 1999.

Agreements in Restraint of Trade

The courts consider competition a necessary and important element of economic life, and agreements that diminish competition are undesirable and against public policy. Some **agreements in restraint** of trade—known as non-competition agreements, non-solicitation agreements and restrictive covenants—are unenforceable, while others may violate the Competition Act and trigger regulatory or criminal sanctions.

Even if a contract contains a **restrictive covenant** (a term in restraint of trade) that is found to be against public policy, the term might not invalidate the entire contract. The courts may refuse to enforce the offending term while treating the remainder of the contract as valid. The courts initially presume that any term in restraint of trade is against public policy, but the party seeking to enforce the covenant may **rebut** the presumption if it can demonstrate that it is a reasonable arrangement between the parties and does not adversely affect the public interest.

Rebutting the presumption is particularly likely for two of types of contracts in restraint of trade:

agreements in restraint agreements in restraint of trade, also known as non-competition agreements or restrictive covenants when they are included in a larger contract

restrictive covenant a term in restraint of trade, i.e., a promise not to carry on a competing business activity

rebut overcome

(a) agreements between the vendor and the purchaser of a business in which the vendor undertakes not to carry on a similar business in competition with the purchaser or solicit former customers or employees

(b) agreements between employer and employee in which the employee undertakes that after leaving her present employment, she will not compete against the employer, either by setting up her own business or by taking a position with a competing business or by soliciting the employer's customers or other employees

The courts begin by presuming that any term in restraint of trade is against public policy and is void and unenforceable, but this presumption is not absolute. It may be overcome by the party seeking to enforce the covenant if that party can prove that the agreement is a reasonable arrangement between the parties and does not adversely affect the public interest.[56] The two types of contracts discussed below are the ones most frequently considered by the courts, however, they are not treated exactly the same. Parties negotiating a sale of a business receive greater freedom to contract than do those negotiating employment contracts; therefore the court must identify the reason the contract was entered into in order to determine in which category the restrictive covenant falls.[57]

Agreements between Vendor and Purchaser of a Business

An important asset of a business is its goodwill—that is, the trade and commercial connections that it has established through years of carrying on business under its name and in a particular location. The vendor of a business can persuade the purchaser to pay for the goodwill only if he can make a binding promise that he will do nothing in the future to diminish or destroy the value of what he is selling. To do so, he must be free to promise the purchaser that he will not enter into any business that is likely to compete with the business he is selling: there will then be no danger of his attracting old customers away and so diminishing its value. After the sale, it is important that the law enforce reasonable undertakings of this kind made by the vendor, or else the purchaser, fearing she will be deprived of a valuable part of the asset she has purchased, will refuse to pay the vendor's price.

Therefore the law recognizes that both purchaser and vendor of a business may find a mutual advantage in a restrictive covenant and that such a restraint need not be against the public interest. As well, the parties usually deal with each other on a more or less equal footing in striking a bargain with respect to both the price and the protection asked for by the purchaser. The vendor's covenant not to compete with the purchaser as a term of an agreement for the sale of a business may be enforced if it can be shown that the restrictions placed on the vendor are reasonable in view of the nature of the trade or practice sold.

Whether a particular restriction is so broad that it offends the public interest is for the court to decide. On the one hand, a clause forbidding the vendor ever to enter business again anywhere would, for most types of business, be more than is needed to protect the purchaser and would be considered to deprive the public of the benefits of the vendor's abilities: accordingly, it would be void. On the other hand, a term by which the vendor undertakes for a stated period of time (or perhaps even within his lifetime) not to set up the same business again within a specified area that reasonably describes the area of competition may well be reasonable in the opinion of a court, and consequently valid. The size of the area and the period of time denied to the vendor vary with the nature of the business.

---

[56] *Shafron v. KRG Insurance Brokers*, 2009 SCC6, at para 27.

[57] *Payette v. Guay Inc.*, 2013 SCC 45

ILLUSTRATION 8.1

A dentist in Saskatoon sells his practice to a young graduate, promising that he will not practise again anywhere in Canada. The retiring dentist has a change of heart, however, and two years later sets up a practice in the same city. The other dentist brings action to obtain a court injunction restraining him from doing so.

In these circumstances a restrictive clause that denies the seller a right to practise anywhere in Canada is more than is necessary to protect the interests of the purchaser. To argue that a covenant in restraint of trade is not against public policy, it is necessary to show at least that it is reasonable between parties. The scope of this covenant, in view of the nature of a dental practice, is unreasonable, and it is therefore void. The purchaser would fail to obtain the injunction, although if the covenant had been confined to the city of Saskatoon for, say, a period of three years, it would probably have been valid.[58]

With rare exceptions, the courts have refused to take on the task of narrowing to a "reasonable scope" the area or the time within which the seller is not to set up business.[59] The basic objection to reducing a covenant is that it rewrites the contract of the parties; it gives a purchaser who has demanded an unreasonable restriction the benefit of the court's opinion about the allowable maximum area not considered detrimental to the public interest. It would also discourage the vendor from taking the risk of opening a new business. If a restrictive clause is held to be too wide or it is written describing alternatives, it is highly unlikely that courts will narrow it to a reasonable scope. The clause will be unenforceable and a vendor who might otherwise have been bound by a reasonable restriction is free of the restraint. The lesson for the purchaser is that he should demand no more than a reasonable restriction, erring on the conservative side rather than demanding too much.

The case of *Nordenfelt v. Maxim Nordenfelt Guns and Ammunition Co. Ltd.*[60] illustrates how the nature of a business may be important in determining what is a reasonable restriction on its vendor.

CASE 8.10

Nordenfelt had been a manufacturer of guns and ammunition. He transferred his patents and business to Maxim Nordenfelt Guns and Ammunition Co. Ltd. for £287 500 and covenanted that for 25 years he would not engage, except on behalf of this company, either directly or indirectly in the business of a manufacturer of guns or ammunition or in any other business competing or liable to compete in any way with the business of the company. Later, Nordenfelt entered into an agreement with other manufacturers of guns and ammunition, and the plaintiff company brought an action to enforce the covenant.

The House of Lords decided that the clause could be broken into two parts: first, the promise not to engage in the manufacture of guns or ammunition, and second, the promise not to engage in any other business competing or liable to compete with the plaintiff company. The court held that the second promise was an unreasonable restriction and declared it void. But it also held it could sever the second promise from the first and that the first promise was a reasonable restriction. Accordingly, it granted an injunction to restrain Nordenfelt from working for any other business that manufactured guns and ammunition.

Athough the courts will not save unreasonable restrictions by redrafting them or narrowing their effect, they will sever an unreasonable restriction from one that is reasonable—even if the restrictions occur in the same sentence—provided they are two distinct ideas and can be severed without changing the meaning of the reasonable

---

[58] See, for example, *Lyons v. Multari*, (2000), 50 O.R. (3d) 526 (C.A.).

[59] See *Goldsoll v. Goldman*, [1915] 1 Ch. 292, and *Attwood v. Lamont*, [1920] 3 K.B. 571. See also *Canadian American Financial Corp. v. King* (1989), 60 D.L.R. (4th) 293; *Bonazza v. Forensic Investigations Canada Inc.*, [2009] O.J. No. 2626, paras. 13–15 (QL) (specifically dealing with severance as applied to a clause drafted in the alternative).

[60] [1894] A.C. 535.

restraint. In enforcing the restraint concerning guns and ammunition, the court pointed out that improved communications and transportation facilities had enabled orders to be directed to and filled from distant sources of supply, and had greatly broadened the market in which competition might be effective in certain lines of business. The decision, though handed down in 1894, recognized that the whole world had become a market and still reflects the law today:

> All interferences with individual liberty of action in trading, and all restraints of trade of themselves, if there is nothing more, are contrary to public policy and therefore void. That is the general rule. But there are exceptions: restraints of trade . . . may be justified by the special circumstances of a particular case. It is sufficient justification, and indeed it is the only justification, if the restriction is reasonable—reasonable, that is, in reference to the interests of the public, so framed and so guarded as to afford adequate protection to the party in whose favour it is imposed, while at the same time it is in no way injurious to the public.[61]

This same passage was quoted by the Supreme Court of Canada when considering a restrictive covenant in an employment contract in *Shafron v. KRG Insurance Brokers (Western) Inc.*,[62] discussed below in Case 8.11.

Agreements between Employee and Employer

It is more difficult to convince courts that covenants between employee and employer restricting the future economic freedom of the employee are reasonable and not in restraint of trade.[63] In an employment contract, there is no payment for goodwill and bargaining power is unequal; an employer is able to impose terms on an employee that the latter must accept if he wants the position. Later he may find that the covenant, if valid, makes it virtually impossible for him to leave his employer in order to accept another position in the vicinity: He would have to sell his house and become established in another city. In protecting employees by striking down unreasonable restraints, the courts at the same time serve a second public interest—they protect the mobility of labour and so encourage more efficient allocation of human resources.

We must distinguish agreements that relate to activities undertaken after an employee leaves his present employment from those that address the employee's behaviour during employment. The law recognizes a full-time employee's primary duty of loyalty to the employer, and an absolute promise not to engage in any other business during the term of the employment is valid, whether that business competes with the employer or not. Similar agreements between partners that are operative during the life of the partnership are also binding.

An employer seeking to enforce a restrictive covenant usually asks the court for the equitable remedy of an injunction to restrain the defendant. A restrictive covenant may be enforced if it can be shown to be unambiguous, reasonable between the parties, and not injurious to the public. Again, reasonableness relates to the activity restrained, the geographic area covered, and the time period of the restriction.[64]

The courts more readily accept as reasonable certain restraints placed upon an employee who has access to valuable trade secrets or a knowledge of secret processes in his employment[65] or who has acted as the personal representative of the employer in dealings with the customers of the business.[66] In such circumstances, a promise by the

---

[61] House Of Lords, Thorsten Nordenfelt (Pauper), *Appellant; And The Maxim Nordenfelt Guns And Ammunition Company, Limited,* Respondents [1894] A.C. 565.

[62] *Supra,* n. 56, paras. 16–17, 26.

[63] *Mason v. Provident Clothing & Supply Co. Ltd.,* [1913] A.C. 724.

[64] *Ibid.* at para. 43.

[65] *Reliable Toy Co. and Reliable Plastics Co. Ltd. v. Collins,* [1950] 4 D.L.R. 499. See *Robinson (William) & Co. Ltd. v. Heuer,* [1898] 2 Ch. 451 (comparing covenants during employment and after termination).

[66] *Fitch v. Dewes,* [1921] 2 A.C. 158.

employee not to work for a competing business or to set up a business of his own after leaving his present employment is more likely to be binding upon him, particularly if the employer has evidence that its former employee is acting in a way that is depriving the employer of its proprietary interest in trade secrets or customer goodwill. Still, the clause must be reasonable as to the activity restricted, the geographic area covered, and the duration of the restriction. Courts will consider whether a less onerous form of non-solicitation clause—a restriction on marketing to a previous employer's customers—would have sufficed in the circumstances. If so, a complete ban on competition will be unenforceable.[67] However, in employment contracts the court will not sever the offending part and substitute the lesser requirement, nor will it rewrite an ambiguous or unreasonable restrictive covenant in order to make it enforceable.[68]

CASE 8.11

Shafron sold his insurance agency to KRG Western and continued as an employee of the purchaser and subsequent owners under an employment contract with a restrictive covenant. The covenant prohibited Shafron from being employed in the business of insurance brokerage within the "Metropolitan City of Vancouver" for three years after leaving KRG. Within one year of leaving KRG, Shafron began working as an insurance salesman for another agency and KRG sued. The geographic location was found to be unclear and ambiguous as there is no such place as the "Metropolitan City of Vancouver." Ambiguous clauses will naturally be unreasonable as the restriction is unclear.

However, the Court of Appeal severed the word "metropolitan" and found the remaining phrase "City of Vancouver" unambiguous and reasonable so it was enforceable. The Supreme Court of Canada overturned the Court of Appeal. First, it found the agreement to be an employment agreement subject to higher standard of scrutiny than a sale of business contract. Second, although it agreed that the geographic restriction was ambiguous, it disagreed with severing the word "metropolitan" as this amounted to rewriting the clause for the parties. Severance should not be used for restrictive covenants in employment contracts.[69]

CHECKLIST

Enforcement of Agreements in Restraint of Trade

Agreements in restraint of trade are presumed against public policy and unenforceable subject to limited exceptions:

■ They may be enforceable in two contexts: sale of business and employment.

■ The party seeking enforcement must first prove the clause is clear and unambiguous—if not, it will be unreasonable and unenforceable.

■ If the clause is unambiguous, it must also be proven to be reasonable as to restricted activity, geographic area, and time period.

■ Employment agreements will be subject to greater scrutiny than business sales.

■ Severance is not available to cure an employment contract.

A third class of agreements in restraint of trade—agreements among manufacturers or merchants to restrict output or fix the selling price of a commodity or service—is examined in Chapter 3, "Government Regulation of Business."

---

[67] *J.G. Collins Insurance Agencies Ltd. v. Elsley*, [1978] 2 S.C.R. 916 at 926; *Lyons v. Multari* (2000), 50 O.R. (3d) 526 (C.A.).

[68] *Shafron, supra*, n. 56, paras. 36–42.

[69] *Ibid*.

Strategies to Manage the Legal Risks

With respect to capacity issues and the risk that a contract may be rendered void, businesses must take steps before contracting to confirm the capacity of the other party. Government databases may be searched to determine the status of a business and its accurate name. Sole proprietors, partnerships, and corporations must register business names, and these records may be searched. Attention to this detail before the contract is formed will ensure that the named party is actually a legal entity and is bound by the obligation. Similarly, the age of an individual party may be confirmed through identification at the time of purchase. If the nature of the business involves contracting with minors, the contract should be structured to require immediate payment, so the burden will be on the minor party to nullify the agreement and not on the business to try to enforce it.

With respect to legality, business managers should familiarize themselves with industry-specific legislation that may render contracts void or unenforceable if not properly prepared in accordance with their provisions. Generally, applicable consumer protection statutes will also void non-complying contracts. Finally, non-solicitation, confidentiality, and non-competition agreements should only be employed in employment, partnership, and business sale contexts. Even in these circumstances, the terms must be reasonable in light of industry norms and the history between the parties. A severance clause should be included so that offending provisions may be removed without preventing enforcement of the balance of the contract.

QUESTIONS FOR REVIEW

1. Is a minor bound to pay the agreed contract price for necessaries? Explain.
2. What element is necessary for a contract of employment to bind a minor?
3. What obligation does a minor have when she repudiates a contract for non-necessary goods? Explain the policy reason for the rule.
4. Are minors' contracts for non-necessaries always voidable when the minors attain majority?
5. What two types of minors' contracts must be distinguished for the purpose of determining the liability of the minors after they become of age?
6. Give examples of persons of diminished contractual capacity. What special problems do such persons face when they want to deny responsibility under a contract?
7. Under what circumstances may a contract voidable at the option of one of the parties cease to be voidable?
8. What is the nature of the legal problem that adds to the uncertainty of an action against a trade union?
9. (a) When Jones was 17 years old, she took her stereo into the Mariposa Service Centre for an extensive repair job that cost $175. If she does not pay, can the Mariposa Service Centre sue her successfully?

   (b) After Jones becomes of age, she picks up the repaired stereo and does nothing to repudiate her liability to the Mariposa Service Centre. Can the Mariposa Service Centre recover the money now?

   (c) Upon becoming of age, Jones tells the manager of the Mariposa Service Centre in a telephone conversation that she will pay the $175. Can the Mariposa Service Centre recover now?
10. For what types of organization is a representative action important? Explain.
11. Why may it be important to a party to a dispute to show that a void contract is not also illegal?

12. How can we tell whether the intention of the legislature is to make a certain type of agreement illegal as well as void?

13. What are "wagering" contracts and are they legal? What government legislation should be considered when answering this question?

14. What quality must an insurance contract possess to prevent it from being a wager and therefore void?

15. What kinds of business contract may have an element of wagering incidental to the main purpose of the transaction?

16. Explain how restrictive covenants play a role in the sale of an active business.

17. What exception is there to the rule that an agreement is illegal if it purports to indemnify a person against the consequences of his own wrongdoing?

18. What factors does a court consider when determining if a restrictive covenant in an employment contract is legal and enforceable?

19. Discuss the courts' attitude toward the subsequent use of trade secrets acquired by a former employee.

CASES AND PROBLEMS

1. Continuing Scenario

   The most important hiring decisions Ashley will make are for the chef and hostess positions. The hostess will be the face of the restaurant; regular customers will build a relationship with the hostess. The chef's food will keep customers coming back and the chef's reputation will spread across the community. Ashley intends to share all her business skills with these two people. However she worries that, once trained, they could open their own restaurants and divert her customers to their businesses. How can Ashley use the employment contract to protect herself from this business risk? What are the limits of the contractual protection? Does it make a difference if she makes the chef a partner in her business? Draft the necessary clause.

2. For most of a year, Harrison acted as agent for the purpose of obtaining options on property on an island in British Columbia on behalf of the Western Development Company, which planned to develop the island industrially. These plans became known to the property owners on the island, and some of them, believing their holdings to be indispensable to the plan, sought to obtain prices much higher than the market value established there for farm or residential purposes.

   Harrison obtained, for a consideration of $1, an option to purchase within one year the property of Mrs. Foy for $200 000. Harrison had negotiated the price with a Miss Foy and a widow, Mrs. Sheridan; he had offered $1000 a hectare, which was the maximum he had been authorized to offer, but the two women had insisted upon $2000 a hectare. He had then reluctantly agreed to take an option at the price demanded, explaining that his principals would not likely take up the option at such an exorbitant price. Miss Foy had next insisted that a further $10 000 be added to the price for the barn; Harrison had agreed to that, too.

   It was only when the option agreement was prepared for signing that Harrison learned that he had not been dealing with the registered owner of the property, but with her daughters, both of whom resided there. They told him that Mrs. Foy was a very old lady and was bedridden. Harrison was taken to the bedroom where he explained, carefully and accurately, the terms and effect of the option. Mrs. Foy appeared to understand what he was saying, nodding and smiling and from time to time saying, "Yes." At that point Harrison turned to Miss Foy, who was standing at the foot of the bed, and asked her, "Do you really think your mother understands the difference between an option and an agreement to sell her land?" Miss Foy replied, "Yes, I think she understands." Then Mrs. Sheridan asked Harrison if, before getting her mother to sign, he would wait until they could get the family lawyer to be present. Harrison, exasperated with the way negotiations had been proceeding, replied testily that he was not prepared to put up with any further delay or discussion of terms. He asked Mrs. Foy to sign the option agreement. She did not sign her name but made a cross under the direction of one of her daughters who explained to Harrison that her mother used to be able to sign her name but that her hand was now too unsteady.

Harrison's principals did, in fact, elect to take up the option within the year to obtain property at the agreed price of $200 000; they had taken up the options on the adjoining properties and needed Mrs. Foy's property to complete the land they required. The two daughters said that the option agreement was "not worth the paper it was written on" because Mrs. Foy was insane at the time of her signing. The principals sued to have the option agreement enforced. It was brought out in evidence that Mrs. Foy was, indeed, insane, a fact of which Harrison denied any knowledge at the time; it was also shown that the fair market value of the property as a farm at the date of the option agreement was about $140 000.

Express an opinion about the likelihood that the action will succeed.

3. During the 1997–98 season, Harvey ("Ace") Tilson played hockey for the Medicine Hat Broncos of the Western Junior Hockey League, scoring 30 goals and assisting on another 35 goals. In recent years, many players in this league had been offered contracts to play professional hockey upon completion of their junior eligibility. They remained eligible to play in the League until the year in which they reached the age of 21.

In October 1996, Tilson signed a two-year contract with the Medicine Hat Broncos Hockey Club that was to terminate before the start of the hockey season in the early fall of 1998. However, at the beginning of training camp in September 1997, the manager of the Broncos presented Tilson and the other players with a new three-year contract. This contract contained a new set of standardized conditions of employment prescribed by the league and, by agreement among the clubs, was presented to all players in the league on a "take it or leave it" basis; the players understood that if they did not agree to waive their existing contracts and sign the new one, they would not be able to play in the league and their professional prospects would be severely harmed. The new contract included the following clauses:

1. This contract supersedes all previous contracts between the Club [Medicine Hat Broncos Hockey Club] and the Player [Harvey J. Tilson].

2. The Club employs the Player as an apprentice hockey player for the term of three years commencing 1998 and agrees, subject to the terms of this contract, to pay the Player a salary of $150.00 per week plus an allowance for room and board of $200.00 per week, these payments to terminate at the last scheduled game of the Club each year.

3. The Player acknowledges that if his hockey skills and abilities develop to the degree that he is tendered and accepts a contract of employment with a professional hockey club, then the Club shall be entitled to compensation for its contribution to his development and, in consideration for such contribution by the Club, the Player agrees to pay the Club a sum equal to 20 percent (20%) of his gross earnings attributable to his employment with such professional hockey club during a period of three (3) years beginning on the date at which he first represents and plays for that professional hockey club.

4. The Player agrees that during the term of this contract he will loyally discharge his obligations to the Club and that he will not play for or be directly or indirectly employed by or interested in any other amateur or professional hockey club. The Player agrees that the Club shall have the right, in addition to any other legal remedies that the Club may enjoy, to prevent him by appropriate injunction proceedings from committing any breach of this undertaking

5. The Player acknowledges that, if in breach of his obligations under section 4, the Player plays for any other hockey club, the Club will lose his services as a skilled hockey player and will suffer a loss of income from reduced paid attendance at

hockey games and broadcasting rights and that a genuine estimate of the amount of this loss would be the salary that the Player can earn as a hockey player for any other amateur or professional club.

The manager of the Broncos advised the players to take their copies of the contract home and discuss the contract with their parents. He added that a signed copy had to be in his hands by the beginning of the following week. Tilson's parents actively encouraged him to sign the contract, and Tilson returned a signed copy to the manager on September 5, 1997.

Tilson played for the Broncos in the 1997–98 season until March 21, 1998. On that day he became 18 years of age, the age of majority in Alberta. On March 22, 1998, in a letter to the club written by his lawyer, Tilson repudiated the contract "without in any way acknowledging the validity thereof." On the same day, in the company of his lawyer, he signed a Pan-American Hockey Conference contract with the Calgary Whippets Hockey Club Ltd. for three seasons commencing September 1 of each of 1998, 1999, and 2000, providing for annual salaries of $70 000, $80 000, and $90 000, respectively.

At the time, the 1997–98 season was almost over, and the Broncos had qualified for the playoffs and were the favourite to win the Junior Cup. Tilson offered to stay with the team at his regular weekly salary and allowance during the 1998 playoffs if the Broncos Club would sign an agreement that Tilson's three-year hockey contract with it would expire when the playoffs ended. The Broncos refused and brought an action against Tilson, seeking an injunction to restrain him from breaking his contract or, in the alternative, damages of $150 000 representing the measure of its loss for being deprived of his services for the next two years.

Explain the legal issues raised in this dispute and offer with reasons an opinion about the probable outcome of the action.

4. Assume the facts of Problem 3 above, with the exception that the Broncos Club did sign the agreement proposed by Tilson in March 1998; that Tilson had played with the team during the 1998 playoffs; and that the Broncos Club had then brought its action against Tilson. What line of reasoning might the Broncos use to support the argument that the March 1998 agreement was not binding on it? Would it be a good argument? Cite any relevant case or cases.

5. Marbett noticed that the ceiling on the upper floor of her house had become damp from water seepage. She mentioned the problem to her neighbour, who remarked that Marbett's house was 25 years old and probably needed new roofing; he recommended that she contact Riley, who had recently repaired his roof. Marbett phoned Riley and he came promptly to inspect the roof. He said he would replace it for $1800 within a few days. Marbett signed a contract to have the job done.

The day the work was being completed, Marbett was told by a friend that Riley did not have the required municipal licence for a roofing contractor. The friend said she believed Marbett did not have to pay Riley for the roofing work because the contract was illegal. Is the friend correct? Give reasons for your opinion.

6. Flanders & Co., a Montreal firm of wine importers, chartered the ship *Bacchus* from its owners, Swan Ltd., to transport a cargo of wine from Madeira to Montreal. The contract of charter party included a term to the effect that the charterer, Flanders & Co., should be liable for an additional $2500 for each additional day at the port of destination if the unloading of the ship were delayed for any reason.

Unknown to either party, the wine was a prohibited product under the federal Food and Drugs Act because of a preservative used in its production.

When the ship reached Montreal, customs officers refused permission to unload pending determination of the cargo's compliance with the federal act. The investigation and report from the government laboratory in Ottawa took 10 days; it was determined by customs officials that it would be illegal to import the wine, and the cargo was finally transferred at dockside to another ship for shipment to New York.

When Flanders & Co. refused to pay the additional $25 000 caused by the delay, Swan Ltd. sued for the amount. What defence might Flanders & Co. offer? Would Swan Ltd. succeed?

7. John Gifford and his friend, Karl Holtz, were enthusiastic followers of the commodities market, the market in which such products as wheat, cotton, tobacco, and coffee are bought and sold for future delivery. However, they did not have sufficient capital to engage in the market themselves, and so they played a game: They would "buy and sell" futures in various commodities under three-month contracts for delivery and then "settle" their fictional gains and losses on the delivery date. Karl did very well in the game and over a two-year period "earned" over $100 000 at John's expense.

One day, John finally said to Karl, "I think I have a real winner here: The price of coffee is going to rise sharply in the next three months. At what price do you want to sell to me?"

Karl disagreed with John's prediction and replied, "I'll sell you $20 000 worth of coffee at today's price. The price is going to drop and you'll lose as usual."

"For once, not only am I right, but I'm prepared to back up my words. Are you?" asked John. "Let's make this a real transaction. If the price goes up, you pay me the difference. If it goes down, I pay you."

"Okay, it's your funeral. It's a deal," Karl replied, and they shook hands on it.

Three months later, the price of $20 000 worth of coffee had risen by 30 percent, making John richer by $6000. When John demanded payment, Karl said he didn't have that much in the bank but grudgingly gave John three cheques for $2000 each, one payable immediately and the other two postdated one month and two months, respectively.

John cashed the first cheque at Karl's bank at once. A month later, he used the second cheque to buy a used car from Grace Bukowsky. She has not yet presented it to Karl's bank for payment. John still has the third cheque.

Karl has heard from a friend studying law that the whole transaction might be "illegal." Give him your opinion with reasons.

Additional Resources for Chapter 8 on the Companion Website

(www.pearsoncanada.ca/smyth)

In addition to pre- and post-tests, mini-cases, and application exercises, the Companion Website includes the following province-specific resources for Chapter 8:

- **Alberta:** Guardianship; Legality; Limited Capacity; Minor/Infants; Personal Directives; Powers of Attorney
- **Atlantic Provinces:** Adult Protection Legislation; Age of Majority
- **British Columbia:** Adult Guardianship; Business Corporations; Committee; Mentally Incompetent Persons; Minors; Parental Liability; Power of Attorney; Public Guardian and Trustee; Representation Agreement; Societies and Associations; Wills, Estates, and Succession
- **Manitoba/Saskatchewan:** Age of Majority; Majority Rules; Necessaries; Parental Responsibility Act
- **Ontario:** Age of Majority; Confidentiality Agreements; Incompetence; Insurance Legislation; Lotteries; Necessaries; Non-Competition Clauses; Powers of Attorney

Chapter 9

Grounds Upon Which a Contract May Be Set Aside: Mistake and Misrepresentation

What happens when a party realizes that the contract is not the one that was intended? A party may believe a mistake has been made.

In this chapter we examine such questions as:

■ What are common, mutual, and unilateral mistakes ?

■ What are the legal consequences of a mistake
   • about the meaning of the words?
   • about the existence or qualities of the subject matter?
   • about the identity of the parties?

■ What is misrepresentation in contract, as opposed to tort?

■ What are the legal consequences of a contractual misrepresentation?

■ What remedy is available to the victim of undue influence or duress?

■ Do consumers receive extra protection?

SETTING ASIDE A CONTRACT

Setting aside a contract is not an easy task. In the interests of commercial certainty, courts tend to hold parties to the bargains they make. However, in rare circumstances, courts recognize the need to set aside a contract. This chapter considers several equitable principles that allow a party to be released from a contract and returned to a pre-contract position. Relief may be available when there has been a mistake or a misrepresentation. As well, if one party has pressured the other into agreeing, the principles of undue influence and duress may apply. In addition, consumers are given statutory protection from some improper business behaviour. The availability of relief depends upon the factual circumstances of each case and the rules discussed below.

THE NARROW MEANING OF MISTAKE

Parties may enter into a contract only to regret it later—perhaps it turns out to be quite different from what was intended, or they decide that it was unwise. They made a "mistake" and wish to be released from it.

"Legal mistake" is not the same as "mistake" in its more general, everyday context: To say, "I made a mistake going for a walk without my umbrella" after getting wet in a storm means that I later regret acting in a particular way. Just because things do not turn out as expected does not mean a legal mistake has been made. Errors in judgment do not legally justify avoiding one's legal obligations under a contract. To excuse performance too easily would undermine certainty in contractual arrangements: Parties would be reluctant to rely on their contracts. Therefore, only certain kinds of mistakes will make a contract void or **voidable** and thereby qualify for **equitable relief**. The rules of equity require that any party asking to have a contract set aside must also be prepared to return whatever benefit he or she received under the contract.[1] If a mistaken party cannot restore the subject matter of the contract to the other party—for instance, the goods have been consumed, or have substantially deteriorated—the mistaken party loses the right to **rescind**.

To understand the law of mistake we need to look at two issues—who is mistaken and what they are mistaken about. Generally, mistakes must be about facts, not the law itself. Typically, the mistakes relate to the terms of the contract, the subject matter of the contract, or the identity of the party. When both parties to the contract are mistaken about the same facts, it is a situation known as a common or mutual mistake. In a *common mistake*, both parties believe the same erroneous fact—the car is black, when it is really navy blue. In a *mutual mistake*, both parties are mistaken but believe something different from each other—one party believes the car is black and the other believes it is charcoal grey. If only one party is mistaken, and the other knows the truth, it is a situation known as a *unilateral mistake*. In each of these types of mistake the court will decide whether to hold the parties to the bargain, however mistaken, correct the mistake for the parties, or rescind the contract completely. For more information on this topic, see the Companion Website.

VOID AND VOIDABLE CONTRACTS

If the court finds that there has been a mistake—in the legal sense of the word—the contract may be declared either void or voidable, or, in special circumstances, the mistake may be corrected (rectified). As noted in Chapter 8, if a contract is void it means that, in law, it was never formed at all. In this sense, calling an agreement a void contract is a contradiction—if a contract is void, there is no contract. It means the contract is ineffective from

voidable the contract exists until set aside by a court; rights may pass to third parties before it is set aside

equitable relief a discretionary remedy first developed by the courts of equity to undo an injustice

rescind set aside; undo or revoke a contract and return the parties as nearly as possible to their original positions

---

[1] Under "Equitable Remedies." See also Waddams, *The Law of Contracts*, 4th ed., at 444–54.

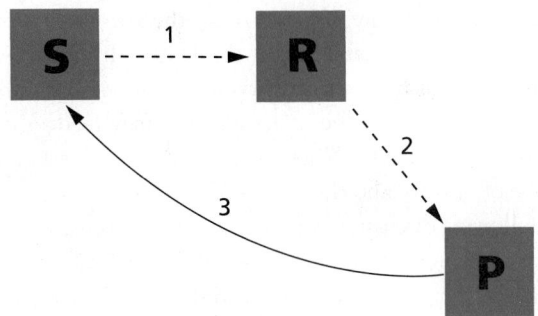

Figure 9.1 Void Contract

1. S "sells" goods to a rogue, R. R does not gain title.
2. R purports to resell the goods to P, the innocent purchaser. P does not gain title.
3. S may sue and recover the goods from P or any subsequent holder.

the very beginning. No rights, title, or ownership pass to anyone under a void contract. Consider Figure 9.1.

If the court decides the contract between S and R is void, the second contract also fails. P can have no greater rights than R, so he will have to return the goods to S and sue R for his losses. Unfortunately, R is often penniless or has disappeared, and any judgment against him will be worthless.

Unlike void contracts, voidable contracts exist until they are **set aside** by the court. Prior to that time, rights, title, and interests pass as set out in the contract. Rescission is an equitable remedy that rescinds a contract. If the contract is rescinded after R has received the goods, R will have to return both title and possession to the seller. The difference between void and voidable contracts does not matter if the goods are still in the possession of the original parties when the contract is set aside. But if the goods have been conveyed to an innocent third party prior to the contract being set aside, then the consequences of void and voidable contracts are quite different. The courts of equity thought that taking the goods away from a subsequent purchaser was too harsh in some circumstances and so created a category of mistakes that only render a contract voidable, allowing a subsequent innocent purchaser to keep the goods, even when the first contract is rescinded. Consider Figure 9.2.

In order to receive protection, a third-party purchaser must be innocent and have paid value for the goods. A seller's attempt to recover goods will not be blocked by someone who buys knowing about the fraud.

set aside   rescind; undo or revoke a contract and return the parties as nearly as possible to their original positions

Figure 9.2 Voidable Contract

1. S "sells" goods to a rogue, R. R, despite his deceit, obtains title.
2. R purports to sell the goods to P, the innocent purchaser. P obtains title to the goods.
3. S cannot recover the goods from P.

In summary, if a contract dispute concerns only the two original parties, whether the court declares it void or merely voidable might not matter. In either event, the court may order the return of property that has passed between the parties. But if the property has been transferred to an innocent purchaser, the original owner may recover it only if the original contract is declared void, not voidable. Whether any given contract is void or voidable will be determined by the type of mistake and the reasonableness of the behaviour or understanding of the parties. In the following discussion, we look at how courts use the classifications of void and voidable contracts and common, mutual, and unilateral mistake to decide what should be done in specific situations. For more information on this topic, see the Companion Website.

MISTAKES ABOUT THE TERMS

Words Used Inadvertently

unilateral mistake   a situation in which only one of the parties believes there is a mistake in the contract

In Case 9.1 below, one party inadvertently uses the wrong words in stating the terms of a contract. The result is a one sided or **unilateral mistake** by the careless party. It seems only fair that the consequences of such an error should fall on the one who caused the problem. However, when it is clear to an objective observer that the first party made a mistake in expressing the terms of the contract—the price might be absurdly low or quite unrelated to the range of prices quoted by both sides during negotiations—then the contract may be voidable for mistake.

CASE 9.1

In *Webster v. Cecil*,[2] the parties were negotiating about the sale to Webster of land owned by Cecil. Initially Cecil refused Webster's offer of £2000. Later Cecil made a counter-offer to Webster, mistakenly offering the land for £1250. Immediately after he mailed his letter, Cecil realized his error and sent a second letter stating that the price should have been £2250, but the second letter arrived after Webster posted his acceptance. Webster sued to enforce the contract and failed. The court found that he could not possibly have believed that £1250 was the intended offer price and rescinded the contract.

How does a court exercise the discretion to grant relief? It considers the behaviour of each party and whether the other party (upon receiving the mistaken document) should have realized that a mistake was made. Deciding whether a party could have relied reasonably on the words used in an offer is not always easy. Perhaps the offeree should have questioned the offeror to ask whether the offeror really meant them; on the other hand, the offeree could have believed that the offeror simply intended to make the offer so attractive that the offeree would find acceptance hard to resist. After all, a change might have occurred in the offeror's circumstances.

Errors in Recording an Agreement

common mistake   a situation in which both parties believe the same misunderstanding or mistake about the contract

Sometimes a contract contains an error but a party does not wish to be released from the obligation. Instead, he wants to have the corrected deal enforced. If the final written version of the contract does not accurately reflect the original agreement, it need not be declared voidable for mistake. The mistake may be corrected—rectified. If both parties are under a shared or **common mistake**, rectification is a simple matter. The court will order rectification of the document if, at the time the document was signed, it did not reflect their shared common intention.[3] It is necessary to show "that the parties were in complete

---

[2] (1861), 54 E.R. 812.

[3] *McLean v. McLean*, 2013 ONCA 788, at para 44; *Shanahan v. Turning Point Restaurant Ltd.* 2012 BCCA 411 at para 30.

agreement upon the terms of their contract, but by an error wrote them down wrongly."[4] Unfortunately, if one party stands to benefit from the mistake, he may insist that the final version represents the true bargain and resist any attempt to correct the document by denying a common mistake.

In this case, the party claiming that the arrangement was improperly recorded may ask the court for **rectification** of the contract based upon unilateral mistake if the following conditions are met:

(a) The court is satisfied that there was a complete oral agreement between the parties, free from ambiguity and not conditional on further adjustments.

(b) The parties did not engage in further negotiations to amend the contract.

(c) The mistake in the written document may have, but does not have to have, occurred as a result of fraud.

(d) When the written document was signed, the defendant knew or should have known of the mistake and the plaintiff did not.

(e) Any subsequent attempt to enforce the inaccurate written document would be equivalent to fraud.[5]

> **rectification** correction of a written document to reflect accurately the contract made by the parties

It is not easy to establish the conditions necessary for rectification based on unilateral mistake: If the terms were ambiguous in the original agreement or if the parties carried on subsequent negotiations, a court is very reluctant to alter the final document. Rectification will not correct an error in judgment, nor is it a substitute for due diligence.[6] For more information on this topic, see the Companion Website.

Misunderstandings about the Meanings of Words

In this type of mistake both parties to a contract agree to the words actually used—neither party put them forward accidentally, nor were any of the terms subsequently recorded incorrectly. However, the parties place different meanings on those words. In most instances, such disagreements can be treated as questions of interpretation (see Chapter 10): A court will decide which meaning is the more reasonable in light of the circumstances, including those things each party ought to have known about the subject matter of the contract and about the intentions of the other party. In some cases, the court will decide that the meaning an offeror gives to her own words was the more reasonable one. If so, the offeree will be bound by the terms as understood by the offeror. In other cases, the court will decide that the offeror was unwise to use the words as she did and that the offeree interpreted them more reasonably. In that event, the offeror will be bound by the contract as the offeree understands it.[7]

In rare cases, both parties have equally reasonable (or unreasonable) interpretations of the words, and holding one party to the other's interpretation would be unjust—a **mutual mistake** exists. Such a contract is void for mistake as to the meaning of the terms. The classic example occurred in the case of *Raffles v. Wichelhaus*.[8]

> **mutual mistake** a situation in which both parties believe a mistake exists in the contract but their understandings of the mistake are different

---

[4] *Rose v. Pim*, [1953] 2 All E.R. 739 at 747; *Brisebois v. Chamberland et al.* (1991), 77 D.L.R. (4th) 583.

[5] *Sylvan Lake Golf & Tennis Club Ltd. v. Performance Industries Ltd.* (2002), 209 D.L.R. (4th) 318 (S.C.C.) at para. 31. See also *Hepburn v. Jannock Limited* (2008), 63 C.C.E.L. (3d) 101.

[6] *Ibid.*

[7] See *Lindsey v. Heron* (1921), 50 O.L.R. 1.

[8] (1864), 159 E.R. 375. See also *Angevaare v. McKay* (1960), 25 D.L.R. (2d) 521, and *Staiman Steel Ltd. v. Commercial & Home Builders Ltd.* (1976), 71 D.L.R. (3d) 17.

The contract was for the sale of cotton that was to arrive in England from Bombay on board the ship *Peerless*. By a remarkable coincidence two ships called *Peerless* were sailing from Bombay, one in October, the other in December. Neither party was aware that there were two ships: the seller believed that he contracted to sell cotton on the later ship; the buyer believed that he contracted to buy cotton on the earlier ship.

A delay of two months in the shipment of a commodity subject to market fluctuations is a major difference in terms.

When the cotton arrived on the later ship, the buyer refused to accept it or pay for it. The seller sued for breach of contract, and the buyer pleaded mistake in defence. The defence succeeded because the court could not decide which ship *Peerless* was meant. A reasonable person would have been unable to decide that the contract was for cotton on one ship rather than the other.

MISTAKES ABOUT THE SUBJECT MATTER

Mistake about the Existence of the Subject Matter of a Contract

The most fundamental mistake is one about the very existence of the subject matter. If, at the time the contract was made, the subject matter, such as goods in the hold of a ship at sea, had been destroyed (unknown to either party), a case of shared common mistake exists. A fair way to enforce the contract is hard to imagine. Is the buyer required to pay the price for goods that cannot be delivered? Is the seller liable for breach for non-delivery? No—this is a clear example of a void contract.

This rule, as it applies to the sale of goods, has been incorporated in the Sale of Goods Act, which provides that "where there is a contract for the sale of specific goods and the goods without the knowledge of the seller have perished at the time the contract is made, the contract is void."[9] Of course, if the seller was aware that the goods had perished, his attempt to sell them would be fraudulent and the buyer could recover damages by suing in tort for deceit. For more information on this topic, see the Companion Website.

Mistake about the Value of the Subject Matter

Finding a solution that is fair to both parties is much more difficult when the subject matter of a contract is still in existence, but its qualities are radically different from those contemplated by the parties. One party may be paying far too much for what he will receive. The other party may receive a windfall. The willingness of a court to grant relief depends upon the reasonableness of the expectations of the parties.

In some types of transactions the parties are expected to know that the subject matter may quickly rise or fall in value, and any change in value is one of the risks expected in the contract. Consider, for example, real estate speculators or commodities traders.

However, when the subject matter of the contract is understood, described, or represented to have particular characteristics that give it value, then mistakes about those characteristics and the corresponding value may trigger relief. The mistake as to value may be as to its quality or quantity. In *Hyrsky et al. v. Smith*,[10] the purchased parcel of land turned out to be only half the size that was expected. The court held that:

> If the mistake as to quantity is so substantial that in essence it changes the quality of the subject-matter, then a proper case for rescission may exist.[11]

---

[9] Queen's Printer, *Sales of Goods Act*, R.S.B.C. 1996, c. 410, s. 10.

[10] (1969), 5 D.L.R. (3d) 385.

[11] *Ibid.* at 392.

In 2002, the Manitoba Court of Appeal rescinded a contract for the purchase of a BMW because the car was not the described model, and was built to American and not Canadian standards.[12] This was a substantial difference that went to value of the vehicle.

Under the principle of caveat emptor, a buyer is expected to inspect the goods and satisfy himself as to their character, quality, and value. However, when a misrepresentation has been made by the seller, or where discovery is impossible, or both parties believe the same mistaken characteristics (common mistake), rescission may be available. If the purchaser moves quickly, the contract is voidable. Delay will close the door.

CASE 9.3

A purchaser bought a painting of a cathedral from an art gallery. Both the buyer and the gallery believed the painting was painted by John Constable (1736–1837), a famous landscape painter. The purchaser took the painting home and hung it on his wall for five years before complaining that it was not painted by Constable. The court held that too much time had passed to give the purchaser any remedy for mistake or misrepresentation.[13]

MISTAKES ABOUT THE IDENTITY OF A PARTY TO A CONTRACT

Mistakes as to the identity of a party to the contract are unilateral mistakes often involving fraud, where an innocent party is deliberately tricked into believing the other party is someone that he is not. If an existing identity is assumed (rather than a fabricated identity), the contract will be void, as was the outcome in the classic English case of *Cundy v. Lindsay*.[14]

CASE 9.4

Lindsay, a manufacturer in Ireland, was persuaded to send goods on credit to a thief, Alfred Blenkarn. Blenkarn signed an order for goods with an indistinct signature that appeared to be "Blenkiron & Co.," a reputable firm with offices on the same street but at a different number from that of Blenkarn. Lindsay did not check the street number, but simply shipped the goods to Blenkarn, who then sold the goods to Cundy for cash and absconded. Cundy was unaware of the fraud. Lindsay learned the true facts when he attempted to collect payment from Blenkiron & Co.; he then sued Cundy for the goods, claiming that the sale to Blenkarn was void.

The court held that as Lindsay intended to sell to "Blenkiron & Co." and only to them, Blenkarn obtained the goods entirely without Lindsay's agreement. A mistake by the duped seller about the identity of the other party made the contract void. Since there was no contract between Lindsay and Blenkarn, ownership of the goods remained with Lindsay: Cundy was required to return them or pay damages.

The decision in *Cundy v. Lindsay* offends the general principle that between two innocent parties, both victims of a fraud, the loss should be borne by the more careless of the two. Lindsay had shipped goods on credit without a careful check of the street address of Blenkiron & Co.; as a result of Lindsay's carelessness, Blenkarn gained possession of the goods. But Cundy was blameless. Between the two, we should have expected that Lindsay would bear the loss; yet the decision that the contract was void led to a

---

[12] *Ennis v. Klassen*, [1990] 4 W.W.R. 609 (Man. C.A.).

[13] *Leaf v. International Galleries*, [1950] 1 All E.R.693 (C.A.).

[14] (1878), 3 App. Cas. 459.

hardship upon Cundy. It is not surprising that the courts attempted to limit the application of this case.

The year after Cundy, in *King's Norton Metal Co. v. Edridge*,[15] a thief once again obtained goods on credit, working more cleverly than had Blenkarn.

CASE 9.5

Using an impressive but fake letterhead with the picture of a large factory and the name of a non-existent firm—Hallam & Co.—Wallis sent an order for goods to the plaintiffs, a firm of metal manufacturers. The plaintiffs sent Wallis the goods; he resold them and absconded. The plaintiffs, claiming that their contract with Hallam & Co. was void, sought to recover the goods from the innocent purchaser.

The action failed. The court held that they must have intended to contract with someone, and since there was no "Hallam & Co.," it could only be with the writer of the letter, even though he was a very different person from the party they had in mind. Accordingly, although the contract was declared voidable, title to the goods had passed to Wallis! The plaintiff could recover the goods from Wallis so long as he still had them, but meanwhile Wallis could pass title to an innocent purchaser.

The difference between *Cundy v. Lindsay* and the *King's Norton* case is that in *King's Norton* there is only one party with whom the vendor might have contracted (Wallis, alias Hallam & Co.). In *King's Norton*, the assumed identity was fake or non-existent, but two separate entities existed in *Cundy v. Lindsay* (Blenkarn and Blenkiron & Co.). Though an innocent purchaser may be excused for failing to see the significance of this distinction, the *King's Norton* case limits the application of *Cundy v. Lindsay* to situations where the thief assumes an existing (real) identity.

In both cases, the parties dealt by mail at a distance. The same difficulty about identity can occur when the initial seller and the impersonator confront each other in person, but the law is clearer in this context—the contract will only be voidable.

CASE 9.6

In *Phillips v. Brooks*,[16] the English Court of Appeal held that the plaintiff jeweller intended to sell pearls to the man who appeared in his shop, even though the man falsely identified himself as a reputable and wealthy member of the community and whom the jeweller knew by name, but not in person.

The contract was voidable and not void. Consequently, an innocent purchaser from the impersonator was protected and able to keep the pearls, despite the jeweller's claim that he intended to deal only with the reputable named person and not the fake who had appeared in his shop.

Canadian courts have followed the English cases. In one case, the Supreme Court of Canada held that a car rental company had "consented" to the rental of a car to an impersonator who gave a false identity.[17] Subsequent purchasers are better protected when the first transaction takes place face to face than when the transaction takes place by post, phone, or internet. For more information on this topic, see the Companion Website.

---

[15] (1879), 14 T.L.R. 98.

[16] [1918–19] All E.R. 246.

[17] *Terry v. Vancouver Motors U-Drive Ltd. and Walker*, [1942] S.C.R. 391.

MISTAKES ABOUT THE NATURE OF A SIGNED DOCUMENT

Non Est Factum

Non est factum ("it is not my doing") is an ancient principle created in medieval times when most people could not read or write and usually signed documents by making a mark or imprinting with a seal. In those days, illiterate people relied on the literate party to describe the nature of the document. If the literate party materially misrepresented the nature of the document, it would be declared void. The concept was later extended and misused to allow people to carelessly sign documents without reading them. This is no longer the case today.

non est factum "it is not my doing"

In 1971, in *Saunders v. Anglia Building Society*,[18] the House of Lords declared that a careless signer could not avoid liability by pleading non est factum. Despite the fact that the plaintiff was a 78-year-old widow who had just broken her glasses, the court found her careless in signing a deed she had been unable to read, and accordingly she was bound by the document. In 1982, in *Marvco Color Research Ltd. v. Harris*,[19] the Supreme Court of Canada followed the *Saunders* case. Mr. Justice Estey said:

> This principle of law is based not only upon the principle of placing loss on the person guilty of carelessness, but also upon recognition of the need for certainty and security in commerce [of those persons who rely on signed documents] . . . the application of the principle . . . must depend on the circumstances of each case.[20]

The defence of non est factum is only available to someone who, as a result of misrepresentation, has signed a document mistaken as to its nature and character and who has not been careless in doing so.[21] In the age of internet contracting, buyers are expected to agree to terms everyone knows they did not read—no one should expect to escape liability under a contract simply because of failure to take the necessary time to familiarize oneself with its contents.

MISREPRESENTATION

Contract Versus Tort

In addition to cases of mistake, a court may also set aside a contract if a misrepresentation has occurred. As noted in Chapters 3 and 4, a misrepresentation is an untrue statement or omission that is believed and relied upon by another party. It may amount to a tort when it is made fraudulently or negligently. However, when a person makes an innocent misstatement, no tort is committed. If that person later discovers her error, she must inform the other party of the true situation as soon as she can. An innocent misrepresentation becomes fraudulent or negligent if the party responsible fails to correct it when in a position to do so.

In contract law, any **material** misrepresentations—be they innocent, negligent, or fraudulent—give rise to the right to rescind a contract. If the maker of the misrepresentation also acted fraudulently or negligently, the court may grant damages against the wrongdoer. However, if she made the misrepresentation innocently and without negligence, no damages will be awarded; the injured party's remedy is restricted to the right to rescind the contract.

material could reasonably be expected to influence or induce the decision of a party to enter into a contract

---

[18] [1971] A.C. 1004.

[19] [1982] 2 S.C.R. 744.

[20] Marvco Colour Research Ltd. v. Harris [1982] 2 S.C.R. 789–97.

[21] *Bulut v. Carter*, 2014 ONCA 424, at para 18.

A misrepresentation is not a term of the contract. It is a statement or impression usually made or formed during the pre-contract bargaining that is not included in the subsequent offer. A misrepresentation that is incorporated into the offer becomes a term of the contract, and will give rise to a breach of contract action with much broader remedies.[22] It can be difficult to distinguish between circumstances where the representation became a term of the contract and those where it did not.[23] Most standard form contracts now specifically declare that there are no representations other than those contained in the written terms of the contract.

Occasionally, courts have found statements about goods and services in advertisements and sales promotion material, read by a prospective buyer before contracting, to be terms of the contract.[24] More commonly, statements in advertisements are considered representations, not terms. A false assertion is a misrepresentation only if it is made as a statement of fact. Most statements of opinion do not amount to misrepresentations unless they are **expert opinions**—these are considered equivalent to statements of fact.

expert opinions opinions given by a person who purports to have specialized knowledge of a subject

---

ILLUSTRATION 9.1

If a car advertisement states that "this car is the best car we have ever made," the remark is just an expression of opinion. But if the ad says instead that "the car gets 100 kilometres per litre of gas in highway driving," a representation of fact has been made.

If the ad says "the Canadian Automobile Association declares this car to be the best car in its class," this is an expert opinion that will be treated as a statement of fact.

CONSEQUENCES OF MISREPRESENTATION IN CONTRACTS

When a party who relied upon a material misrepresentation learns the truth, the contract is voidable at the option of the victim. She must renounce the agreement promptly. If she allows an unreasonable length of time to pass without repudiating or she takes further benefits under the contract, she will lose her right to rescind. If she has sustained out-of-pocket expenses in performing the contract or has paid money to the other party before becoming aware of her right to rescind, she may be entitled to a money award known as an **indemnity or compensation** in addition to rescission.[25]

indemnity or compensation a money award given as a supplement to rescission for loss sustained in performing a contract

---

Ethical Issue **Employment Résumé**

In February 2006, David J. Edmondson resigned from his position as president and CEO of RadioShack Corp. after it was discovered that he had lied on his résumé. His résumé indicated that he earned a psychology degree from Pacific Coast Baptist College. After the college denied granting the degree, Mr. Edmondson acknowledged the error.

A résumé (and its corresponding covering letter) introduces an employment candidate to the employer. It describes the educational experience and work history of the candidate. An employer often decides whether to interview a candidate based on the information contained in the résumé. Most prospective employees design their résumés

>

---

[22] See Chapter 13, sections on implications of breach and damages.

[23] The closer the misrepresentation was to the time the agreement was made, the easier it is for a court to conclude that it is a term. See *Dick Bentley Productions Ltd. v. Harold Smith Motors Ltd.*, [1965] 2 All E.R. 65. See also *Esso Petroleum Co. Ltd. v. Mardon*, [1976] 2 All E.R. 5 (C.A.).

[24] *Goldthorpe v. Logan*, [1943] 2 D.L.R. 519; *Murray v. Sperry Rand Corp.* (1979), 96 D.L.R. (3d) 113.

[25] *Whittington v. Seale-Hayne* (1900), 82 L.T. 49.

Misrepresentation by Silence or Omission

Not all misrepresentations are expressed in words; conduct or even silence may amount to a misrepresentation. Particular types of contracts and relationships give rise to disclosure obligations. If the requirements are not met, a misrepresentation exists by silence or omission. Special relationships of trust between the parties, such as fiduciary relationships, give rise to a duty to disclose all pertinent information; certain types of contracts, such as insurance contracts, give rise to the duty of **utmost good faith**. The nature of the relationship or type of contract will determine if such a duty exists in the circumstances.

utmost good faith a duty of disclosure owed when a special relationship of trust exists between the parties

The requirement of utmost good faith almost always exists in a continuing business relationship. Partnership depends on mutual trust, and, accordingly, partners owe a general duty of utmost good faith to each other in all their transactions. Similarly, directors and officers owe a duty of good faith toward their corporation. Consider the following examples of specific types of contracts and relationships that have obligations to disclose. Failure to properly disclose will render the resulting contract voidable.

Contracts of Insurance   Insurance contracts have a duty of utmost good faith that requires a party seeking insurance to disclose to the insurance company all pertinent information relating to the risk the insurance company is being asked to assume. If relevant information is withheld, the insurer may refuse to pay the insurance claim. Information relevant to life insurance contracts will include health details and the refusal of coverage by another company. Fire insurance disclosure requirements are governed by legislation in most provinces,[26] and failure to disclose a previous fire has been held to be a fraudulent omission under the Insurance Act.[27] Public liability insurance—for motor vehicles, for example—presents a special difficulty because denial of coverage is likely to deny innocent third parties compensation when the negligent insured withheld previous driving information. Therefore, the courts impose a duty on insurers to investigate applicants before agreeing to insure, especially when information appears false to a reasonable insurer.[28] As well, automobile insurance legislation makes coverage of third-party losses mandatory up to the statutory minimum.[29]

---

[26] See, for example, Insurance Act, R.S.B.C. 2012, c. 1, s. 17, 29(1); R.S.O. 1990, c. I.8, s. 148; R.S.N.S. 1989, c. 231, Sch. to Part VII, s. 1.

[27] *Sherman v. American Institute Co.*, [1937] 4 D.L.R. 723.

[28] *Armstrong v. Northwest Life Insurance Co. of Canada* (1990), 72 D.L.R. (4th) 410, 414; *State Farm Mutual Automobile Insurance Co. v. General Accident Assurance Co. of Canada*, [1995] N.B.J. No. 405 (C.A.); *Coronation Insurance Co. v. Taku Air Transport* (1991), 85 D.L.R. (4th) 609; *Campanaro v. Kim* (1998), 112 O.A.C. 171.

[29] *Schoff v. Royal Insurance Company of Canada*, [2004] 10 W.W.R. 32 (Alta. C.A.); Insurance Act. R.S.A. 2000, c. I-3, s. 613, 630, 635(11); R.S.O. 1990, c. I 8, s. 258 (10)(11). The statutory minimum coverage is $200 000 in Alberta and Ontario.

Contracts Involving the Sale of Corporate Securities

Promoters or directors naturally know more about a corporation's affairs and prospects than does the investing public from whom subscriptions are being solicited. Therefore public corporations are legislatively required to give the investing public information about any new issue of shares or bonds in a statement called a prospectus, or sometimes in other documents such as circulars, letters, or notices published in newspapers.[30] Inaccurate, missing, or misleading information will attract not only the remedy of rescission but also the statutory right to claim damages from any person involved in the preparation and release of the document.

Contracts Involving the Sale of Goods

As will be discussed in Chapter 14, the Sale of Goods Act restricts the doctrine of **caveat emptor** for the sale of goods. It offers buyers the right to rescind contracts for the sale of goods if the vendor fails to disclose a problem with the ownership of the goods. Similarly, misrepresentations or omissions about the quality or characteristics of the goods give a similar right to rescind under the Sale of Goods Act. These remedies are not offered to contracts involving services or land. Land contracts have particularly narrow remedies for representation. First, no obligation exists to disclose defects in title, and second, complaints about any misrepresentation must be raised before title is transferred or any right to rescind is lost.[31]

caveat emptor let the buyer beware

Contracts with Consumers

In *Tilden Rent-A-Car Co. v. Clemdenning*, the Ontario Court of Appeal suggested that there was a special onus on suppliers dealing with consumers to point out terms in standard form contracts that differed from what a consumer might reasonably expect.[32] Current consumer protection legislation goes much further by imposing a statutory obligation on specific industries to disclose such things as cost of credit, total interest and principal repayment schedules, and business contact information.[33] Failure to meet the disclosure requirements gives the consumer the right to cancel or rescind the contract. Even after compliance, some statutes still offer consumers a **cooling-off period** during which a consumer may cancel or rescind without any reason whatsoever. Today's fast-paced online marketplace is dominated by standard form contracts prepared by business that few, if any, consumers have an opportunity to read before accepting. The legislation gives consumers time to read the document by way of a cooling-off period.

cooling-off period a time during which a consumer may cancel (rescind) a contract without any reason; length of the time period is set in provincial legislation

UNDUE INFLUENCE

Undue influence is the domination of one party over the mind of another to such a degree as to deprive the weaker party of the ability to make an independent decision. A contract formed as a result of undue influence is voidable at the option of the victim. The victim may avoid the contract only if he acts promptly after he is freed from the domination. If he acquiesces or delays, the court will refuse to assist him.

Undue influence is often an issue in disputes involving contracts, gifts, or bequests under a will. Generally speaking, the principles governing undue influence in all these circumstances are the same. Usually undue influence arises when the parties stand in a

undue influence the domination of one party over the mind of another to such a degree as to deprive the weaker party of the will to make an independent decision

---

[30] See e.g. Securities Act, R.S.O. 1990, c. S.5, s. 1(1) paras. 25, 38, 56, 122, 130, 130.1, 138.3.

[31] Over time, courts have increased protection to purchasers with regard to serious defects that would be impossible for the purchasers to discover. See e.g. *Sevidal v. Chopra* (1987), 64 O.R. (2d) 169, where the court held that the vendor had a duty to disclose that radioactive soil had been found on the property after the contract was made but before completion date.

[32] (1978), 18 O.R. (2d) 601, per Dubin, J.A. at 609 (citing Waddams, "Contracts Exemption Clauses Unconscionability Consumer Protection" [Comments; 1971)], 49 *Can. Bar Rev.* 578 at 590–1.

[33] See e.g. Consumer Protection Act, 2002, S.O. 2002, c. C, Sch. A; Business Practices and Consumer Protection Act, S.B.C. 2004, c. 2 s. 19(1), 21.

special relationship to each other: One party has a special skill, position, or knowledge, causing the other to place confidence and trust in him. Typical examples of this relationship are doctor and patient, lawyer and client, religious leader and believer, and parent and child.

Burden of Proof

A party alleging undue influence must satisfy the court that, in the circumstances, domination was probable.

It is easier to prove undue influence if a special relationship existed: The law presumes that undue influence was exerted in contracts favouring the party in the dominant position, as, for example, in relationships of doctor and patient or lawyer–client. In the absence of a special relationship, it is more difficult for a party to demonstrate undue influence, but he might still be able to show, for instance, that he was in a desperate financial state at the time of the contract. Once the alleged victim shows that circumstances existed that were likely to lead to undue influence, the burden shifts to the dominant party to prove that undue influence was not exerted by him.

Arrangements Involving Spouses

A spouse may set aside a transaction if he or she can prove actual undue influence. As well, some marital relationships will raise a presumption of undue influence. This is true when one spouse traditionally relies upon the other for major decisions. If a spouse is experienced in business and has persuaded the other, who has had little or no business experience, to pledge her separate assets as security or act as **guarantor** for his business transactions, a presumption arises, and the dominant spouse must establish that no undue influence was applied. Otherwise, the weaker spouse may rescind the contract with the lender. Two cases illustrate how undue influence may be viewed in spousal relationships.

guarantor one who agrees to pay the debts of another person if that person defaults

---

CASE 9.7

In order to obtain an increased credit limit for his company, the shareholder agreed to give the bank a mortgage on the family home. The home was jointly owned by the shareholder and his spouse. The spouse was brought to the bank and signed the mortgage documents without explanation or independent legal advice. Eventually the company failed and the bank claimed the house. The spouse successfully blocked the bank's attempt to seize the house because the bank was on notice of the special relationship and failed to inquire into undue influence.[34]

CASE 9.8

Both spouses co-signed a guarantee of the husband's business loan to fund a "tax driven real-estate investment" without independent legal advice. There was no evidence of actual undue influence and the history of the relationship was not one where the wife placed trust and confidence in the husband to make all major decisions. The wife was a real-estate agent who responded to the bank's request for income disclosure directly. The loan went into default. The marriage failed and the husband went bankrupt. The bank sued the wife, the court found no evidence of actual undue influence, and the relationship did not give rise to a presumption. Therefore, the bank won and the guarantee was enforceable.[35]

---

[34] *Barclays Bank plc v. O'Brien*, [1993] 4 All E.R. 417. See also *Gold v. Rosenberg*, [1997] 3 S.C.R. 767 (affirming reasoning).

[35] *Bank of Montreal v. Duguid* (2000), 185 D.L.R. (4th) 458.

Importance of Independent Legal Advice

The presence or absence of independent legal advice was important to the outcome of the foregoing cases. This is because independent legal advice received by the weaker party prior to signing the contract rebuts any presumption of undue influence. The legal advice must come from a lawyer not associated with the transaction or the other parties. Lenders aware of a special relationship between co-debtors are obligated to inquire into the possibility of undue influence. The standard risk management strategy is to require each party to obtain a certificate of independent legal advice from the lawyer of his or her choice, certifying that the transaction has been explained and the party is entering the agreement voluntarily, without any pressure or influence.

CONSUMER PROTECTION

unconscionable contracts
contracts where there is unequal bargaining power between the parties and the powerful party gets an extremely advantageous deal

Contracts between parties of unequal bargaining power that are unfairly advantageous to the powerful parties have long been considered **unconscionable contracts** and voidable at common law. Most provinces have also adopted legislation specifically defining unconscionable contracts and deceptive business practices that will also render a contract voidable at the option of the consumer. In British Columbia, for example, rescission is available for unconscionable practices including putting undue pressure on a consumer, and deceptive practices including claiming goods or services have sponsorship, grade, style, or quality that they do not possess. False advertising was discussed in Chapter 3, but note that such false claims amount to representations from which consumers will be given relief.

Loan transactions are among the most heavily scrutinized consumer contracts, with tight regulations about disclosure of cost of borrowing, maximum interest rates, terms of credit, and more.[36] The Criminal Code even makes charging an interest rate in excess of 60 percent an offence.[37] Consumers also have expanded remedies; courts may sever the offending interest terms entirely or lower the rate below the criminal rates.[38] Consumers receive these added protections because of their less powerful position in the purchase relationship, their relative inexperience with the type of transaction, their lack of participation in the creation of the contract, and the short time within which they must make their decisions. Unfortunately, few consumers are aware of their cancellation rights and allow them to expire without ever taking the time to examine the terms of their contracts.

INTERNATIONAL ISSUE

Regulating Payday Loans

As discussed above, unconscionable loans with excessive interest provisions have been the subject of provincial legislation for a long time. However, the North American explosion of "payday" loans has revealed vagueness in existing legislation and prompted action.

Payday loans are short-term (daily or weekly) advances of small amounts of money (usually under $1000). Lenders charge not only interest but also application fees and service charges. When calculated on an annualized basis, the total charges often exceed 300 percent of the principal borrowed, well above the criminal rate of interest.

In the United States, payday loans are governed by state legislation. Common restrictions include

■ capping the charges on a fixed basis rather than a percentage basis (for example, Iowa describes the maximum interest charge as $15 per $100 over the term of the loan),

>

---

[36] Unconscionable Transactions Act, R.S.A. 2000, c. U-2; R.S.N.B. 2011, c. 233; Unconscionable Transactions Relief Act, C.C..S.M., c. U20; c. U-2; R.S.P.E.I. 1988, c. U-2.

[37] R.S.C. 1985, c. C-46, s. 347. See *Garland v. Consumer's Gas Co.*, [1998] 3 S.C.R. 112.

[38] *Mira Design v. Seascape Holdings*, [1982] 1 W.W.R. 744 (B.C.S.C.). See Waldron (1994) 73 Can. Bar Rev. 1.

- capping the principal amount that can be borrowed (for example, Illinois describes the maximum amount that can be borrowed as $1000 or 25 percent of a borrower's monthly gross income), and

- capping the number of renewals.

In Canada, most provinces have passed legislation that regulates the payday loan industry.[39] Common restrictions include

- licence requirements for lenders,

- cost-of-borrowing (all charges) disclosure requirements,

- cooling-off periods during which a consumer can cancel the agreement, and

- capping cost of borrowing.

Lenders argue that any cap must exceed the criminal rate of interest because the default rate on payday loans is extremely high.

Questions to Consider

1. Should Canadian limits adopt the American approach of capping the cost of borrowing on a fixed rather than percentage basis?

2. What is the rationale behind the American limit on the number of renewals?

3. How should the cap relate to the criminal rate of interest?

4. Why not ban payday loans completely?

5. How will jurisdictional variation in the regulation of payday loans affect the development of the industry?

Sources: National Conference of State Legislatures, http://www.ncsl.org/research/financial-services-and-commerce/payday-lending-state-statutes.aspx; Canadian Payday Loan Association, http://cpla-acps.ca.

DURESS

Duress consists of actual or threatened violence or imprisonment as a means of coercing a party to accept a contract. The effect of duress is similar to that of undue influence: The contract is voidable at the option of the victim. The threat of violence need not be directed against the party being coerced—it may be a threat to harm the victim's spouse, parent, or child.

duress actual or threatened violence or imprisonment as a means of coercing a party to enter into a contract

Historically, duress was a concept recognized by the common law courts and was narrowly interpreted by them. Today, duress is not strictly confined by the courts to the circumstances described above. Sometimes, the concepts of duress and undue influence appear to overlap. The concept of economic duress is one example; it focuses on **coercion** as an illegitimate or inappropriate application of pressure.[40]

coercion improperly forced payment under protest

CASE 9.9

Stott was a securities salesman employed at Merit Investments Corp. A term of his contract required him to cover all bad debts of his clients. In the case of one client, Stott's boss ordered him to close out the account. Stott took the position that he should not have to cover the loss because he was ordered to close the account. Stott was called into the boss's office and asked to sign a written promise to pay the debt. When Stott argued that he was not responsible, the boss replied, "You are probably right, but if you don't sign, it won't go well with you at the firm

and it would be very difficult for you to find employment in the industry."[41] Stott signed the promise to pay. The Ontario Court of Appeal found that there was coercion and that Merit had applied illegitimate pressure. The conduct would justify rescinding the agreement based on economic duress if Stott had acted immediately to repudiate it. Unfortunately, Stott complied with the agreement and did not complain until two years later when he left Merit's employment.

---

[39] Manitoba was the first: Man. Reg. 99/2007; see also Payday Loans Act, 2008, S.O. 2008, c. 9).

[40] Coercion involves four factors: (a) protest, (b) available alternative, (c) lack of independent advice, and (d) post-contract steps to avoid it. See *Pao On v. Lau Yiu Long*, [1980] A.C. 614 (P.C.).

[41] *Stott v. Merit Investment Corp.* (1988), 63 O.R. (2d) 545 (Cont. C.A.) at para. 12.

Strategies to Manage the Legal Risks

A business can reduce the risks associated with mistake and misrepresentation by making sure that all of the information produced and relied upon by it and others is accurate. Carefully researched claims and thorough investigation before agreeing to sell or purchase will result in fewer errors. Credit checks will confirm the identity of parties, title searches will determine ownership of the product, and careful examination of proposed contracts will ensure that terms are as expected. Written rather than oral contracts are preferred. If dealing without a written document, retain all emails or pre-agreement documentation until the contract is fully performed. These may be useful to clarify meaning if a dispute arises.

Standard form contracts prepared in advance will ensure that common provisions are appropriately worded and key words are defined. In addition to exemption clauses, most standard form contracts include an **entirety clause**, a clause that specifically excludes any outside terms, conditions, or representations and confines the agreement between the parties to the single written document. This clause prevents a party from arguing that they relied on a representation when the contract they signed says that they did not. Express warranties relating to replacement and repair of the product will help to clarify expectations for the product and reduce surprises.

Extra care should be taken when dealing with certain types of parties. Each party in special relationships or power imbalances should seek independent legal advice during negotiations. Consumers should receive full copies of contracts at the time of purchase, and business should ensure the appropriate cooling off period has expired before relying upon the agreement. Any consumer contracts should comply with the requirements of the applicable consumer protection legislation, recognizing that contracts involving certain identified activities are heavily regulated. Sales staff should be trained and supervised so that no unapproved representations or inducements are made during the pre-sale process. Naturally, pressure tactics or threats are unacceptable.

entirety clause a term in a contract stating that the whole agreement is contained in the written documents and there are no other terms, conditions, representations, or warranties

QUESTIONS FOR REVIEW

1. What are common, mutual, and unilateral mistakes?

2. When will a party be granted a remedy for mistakenly using a term in a contract?

3. When parties use a term but intend it to have quite different meanings, how does the court resolve the difference?

4. What conditions must be satisfied before a court will order rectification? Under what circumstances is a court unlikely to grant such a remedy?

5. Describe the difference between void and voidable contracts. What are the consequences of each for innocent third parties?

6. Jameson appears at Klemper's Jewellery and asks to buy an expensive watch on credit. She identifies herself as Johnson, a wealthy local financier. Klemper agrees and hands over possession of the watch to Jameson. Jameson immediately pawns it at Larry's. Klemper sees the watch in Larry's window the next day. Explain whether he may reclaim it as his own without paying Larry. Are there any further facts that might influence your opinion?

7. What are the consequences of an innocent misrepresention in contract rather than tort? What if the representation later becomes a term of the contract?

8. H's business is in financial difficulties and he offers the bank a mortgage on the family home which is in his wife's name. What precautions should the bank take when having the wife sign the contract? Why?

9. Why are consumers a protected class of purchasers? Describe two forms of protection available to them.

CASES AND PROBLEMS

1. Continuing Scenario

   Ashley saw the perfect French "bistro" style chair for her restaurant when she attended a furniture expo and contacted Ben, the sales representative for the chair's Canadian distributor, Just Like Home Inc. Ben tells Ashley the price of the chosen chair, product #7733, is $150 if 15 or fewer are ordered and the price drops to $125 for orders of 16 to 50. Ashley orders 40 chairs and signs Just Like Homes' standard form contract which states that there are no representations or warranties and it is the entire agreement between the parties. Unfortunately, when the chairs arrive they are the wrong ones. Ashley checks the contract and sees that the product number has been incorrectly recorded as #3377. These chairs are not the same quality and have a price of $100 for orders of 16 to 50. Ashley wants the other chairs; Ben has left the company and her new contact, Jill, insists that the contract has been performed. The current price of the #7733 chairs is $145 for orders of 16 to 50 and Ashley will need to pay the higher price if she wants them plus the 25% restocking fee for returning the other chairs. What can Ashley do?

2. Paul, a third-year university student, was in the habit of selling his used textbooks at the conclusion of each term. He usually recouped about 50 percent of their original cost. Unfortunately, when he posted his accounting textbook for sale online, he quickly discovered that a new edition of the book had been published and there was little interest in his edition. He contacted the publisher using a fictitious name and requested a sample copy of the new edition. He told the publisher he was an accounting instructor considering adopting the book for a new course being introduced at the university. As a result, the publisher agreed to supply a copy of the new edition, provided that Paul paid the shipping cost and agreed to review the book for the publisher. Paul agreed. When Paul received the sample book, he promptly posted it for sale online. Joan, a second-year student at another university, was happy to purchase the new edition for 75 percent of the bookstore price. When Joan accessed the textbook website using the code provided with the book, the publisher became aware that the book was in the hands of a student and not an instructor. The publisher never would have agreed to release the book to a student without payment of the full list price. The publisher blocked Joan's access to the textbook website and demanded that she return the book. If the matter goes to court, will Joan have to return the book? Why or why not? What recourse will Joan have against Paul?

3. Smart was Hull's lawyer for many years and not only handled legal matters for Hull, but gave him important advice on business matters as well. At one stage, Hull owed Smart about $8500 for professional services. Smart suggested to Hull that the account could be conveniently settled in full if Hull would transfer his new 10-metre sailboat to Smart. Hull hesitated at first, but realizing how indispensable his relationship with Smart had been and how important it was that Smart should continue to respect the confidential nature of his private business affairs, he transferred the sailboat to Smart.

   A few months later Hull's daughter, who greatly enjoyed sailing, returned from graduate studies in Europe and persuaded her father to sue for recovery of the sailboat. On what grounds could Hull seek the return of the sailboat? Explain how the onus of proof will operate in the resulting legal action and indicate the probable outcome.

4. On arriving at Vancouver airport, Mr. Clemson, a frequent traveller, rented a car from Tilford Car Rentals Ltd., as he had done many times before. The clerk asked him whether he wanted additional collision insurance coverage and, as usual, Mr. Clemson said, "Yes." The clerk added a fee of $10 a day for this coverage. She then handed the contract to Clemson and he signed it in her presence. She was aware that he did not read the terms of the contract before signing it.

   Clemson's signature appeared immediately below a printed statement that read, "I, the undersigned, have read and received a copy of above and reverse side of this contract." On the back of the contract, in small type and so faint on Mr. Clemson's copy as to be hardly legible, there was a series of conditions, one of which read:

The clerk placed Clemson's copy of the contract in an envelope and gave him the envelope and car keys. He got in the car, placed the contract in the glove compartment, and drove to a nearby shopping plaza to buy a gift. While driving in the plaza parking lot, he collided with another car, causing damage of $2500 to his rented car. The car rental agency claimed that he was personally liable for repairs under the terms of their contract. Clemson refused to pay for the car repairs, and Tilford Car Rentals Ltd. sued him for breach of contract.

Outline the nature of the arguments available to Tilford Car Rentals Ltd. and of the defences available to Clemson. Express an opinion, with reasons, about whether the action is likely to succeed.

5. H. Golightly is a professional football player who has played for the Toronto Mercenaries ("Mercs") for the past three football seasons. The Toronto Mercs are a member of the Eastern Conference of the Trans-Canada Football League. Golightly lives in the southern United States during the off-season.

Golightly had an exceptionally good season last year and was in a strong bargaining position for negotiating his salary for this season when he met with Rusty Trawler, the general manager of the Mercs, last January. The parties discussed salary possibilities for the next two seasons in a tentative way but adjourned their meeting, expecting to come to final terms in early April.

In February, at the Trans-Canada Football League's annual meeting in Vancouver, it was decided to increase the number of regular games scheduled to be played in the Eastern Conference to 16, up from the usual 14 over many previous seasons, commencing with the current season. By contrast, the Western Conference already had a schedule of 16 games for several seasons; this decision brought the Eastern Conference in line with the Western Conference. It received wide publicity in the news media of the various cities with teams in the Eastern Conference.

On April 3, Golightly telephoned Trawler from Biloxi, Mississippi, and they agreed to meet on April 6 in the offices of O.J. Berman, Q.C., Golightly's solicitor in Toronto. The meeting between Golightly, Trawler, and Berman lasted about three hours. Eventually it was agreed that Golightly should be paid $150 000 for the current season and $225 000 for the following year, plus further amounts for playoffs and bonuses. Two separate contracts were signed to cover the two seasons. At the time, neither Golightly nor his lawyer, Berman, had any knowledge that the number of league games in the Eastern Football Conference had been increased to 16 from 14. In fact, the parties did not refer in any way to the number of games in their meeting in Berman's office. Trawler made no mention of the increased schedule. The contracts simply stated:

> The Player agrees that during the term of this contract he will play football and will engage in activities related to football only for the Club and will play for the Club in all its Conference's scheduled and playoff games ....

The contract also contained a clause to the effect that the player could be traded to a team in the Western Conference.

It was not until later, when Golightly reported for training, that he learned about the increase in the schedule. He then claimed that he would not have agreed to the salaries of $150 000 and $225 000, respectively, had he known about this change; he would have bargained for more. On Berman's advice, he brought an action to have these contracts set aside with a view to their renegotiation.

Express an opinion, with reasons, about whether this action should succeed.

6. Robelus Communications Inc. launched a new advertising campaign proclaiming that it was "Canada's Fastest" wireless network. It placed the statement in TV commercials, internet

ads, and store signage. Mary was shopping in the mall and saw the sign. She decided to switch her plan to Robelus. After the change, Mary did not notice any difference to her service. She began to investigate and found out that the claim was based on industry comparisons from 2007. Most competitors had put new networks in place since 2007, and there was no available data to determine whose network was fastest. Mary had had to sign up for a three-year plan when she contracted with Robelus, and the standard form contract she signed included the following term:

> This is the entire agreement between the parties. There are no representations, conditions, warranties, conditions or terms save and except for those contained in this written agreement.

Can Mary get out of her three-year commitment? Do you need to know additional facts to form an opinion?

Additional Resources for Chapter 9 on the Companion Website

(www.pearsoncanada.ca/smyth)

In addition to pre- and post-tests, mini-cases, and application exercises, the Companion Website includes the following province-specific resources for Chapter 9:

- **Alberta:** Deposits vs. Down Payments; Identity Theft
- **Atlantic Provinces:** Independent Legal Advice; Payday Loans
- **Manitoba/Saskatchewan:** Statutory Right to Cancel Contract; Unconscionable Transactions
- **Ontario:** Identity Theft; Sale of Goods Act; Consumer Protection Act (2002); Independent Legal Advice; Misrepresentation; Payday Loans; Unconscionable Transactions; Undue Influence; Unfair Business Practices

Chapter 10
Writing and Interpretation

Creating a written record of a contract makes good business sense, and failing to do so can have serious legal consequences. Every common law province has legislation requiring that some contracts be in writing to be enforceable. Even when a contract is put in writing, parties may disagree about its meaning. In this chapter, we identify which contracts must be in writing and discuss the rules for determining the meaning of the words used in a contract.

In particular, we examine such questions as:

- What legislation requires that certain contracts be in writing?

- What types of contracts are affected by the Statute of Frauds?

- How much writing is necessary to comply with the Statute?

- What is the effect of the Statute of Frauds on contracts that do not comply with the writing requirement?

- What are the writing requirements of the Sale of Goods Act?

- What writing requirements exist under general consumer protection legislation?

- What approaches are used to interpret the express terms in a contract?

- What is the parol evidence rule and how do courts apply it?

- When are terms implied into a contract?

THE DISTINCTION BETWEEN SUBSTANCE AND FORM

The Benefits of a Written Record

In previous chapters, we used the term *formation of a contract* in a legal sense, not in a physical sense. The contract is formed when there is an accepted offer, consideration, and intention. Once created, the contract may exist in the parties' recollection of the spoken words, or it may be recorded in a written document or stored electronically online, on a memory stick, or in a computer. So the substance—the terms of the contract—may have a variety of physical forms or even no form at all, other than in the minds of the parties. In this chapter, we consider the rules that apply to the physical form of the contact. Contracts may be in one the following three forms:

1. contracts whose terms are entirely oral (spoken);
2. contracts whose terms are part oral and part written; and
3. contracts whose terms are entirely in writing, whether all in one document or spread through several documents, such as a series of letters.

It is good business practice to keep some record of even the simplest transaction at the time it is made. For complicated contracts, it is best to have a complete written record signed by the parties. We forget things over time, especially when burdened with many details, and common sense tells us that relying on written records is better than on mere memory. The large majority of contractual disputes are not about the existence of contracts but about the differing recollections of the terms of the contract and the meaning of the words used. Very often, the reason a party sues over a contract is that he disagrees with its interpretation by the other party. In such cases, the court is asked to determine the meaning or interpret the contract, also known as **construing** the contract.

construing interpreting

When the court is asked to construe a contract, it tries to find the most reasonable meaning that can be attributed to the words in the circumstances. This is no easy task, and over the years courts have developed some strategies to assist them. To ensure that there is some written evidence to aid a judge in establishing the terms of "important" contracts, provincial legislation imposes specific writing requirements for some types of contracts.

Legislation Dealing with Writing

Not all contracts require writing; very often oral contracts are legally enforceable. However, over time, legislators identified some high-risk contracts and required that they be in writing. Originally, *writing* meant *recorded on paper*; as will be discussed more fully in Chapter 31, writing requirements may now be satisfied through either paper or electronic means such as PDF documents and emails.[1]

Typically the subject matter of the contract will dictate the applicable writing requirements, if any. For example, a mortgage will need to meet specific requirements in order to be registered against the land it charges. These may be set out in either the land registration or mortgage legislation. Rather than focusing on the huge number of statutes that impose precise details on specific transactions, this chapter focuses on the less specific writing requirements imposed by three common types of legislation affecting a wider range of contracts:

1. The Statute of Frauds—the first piece of legislation to impose writing requirements
2. The Sale of Goods Act—focusing on the most common type of business transaction—a purchase of goods
3. Consumer Protection Legislation—dealing with the most vulnerable type of party

---

[1] *Leoppky v. Meston*, 2008 ABQB 45; see also the Personal Information Protection and Electronic Documents Act and the Interpretation Act, including province-specific legislation such as the Electronic Transaction Act (Alberta) and Electronic Commerce Act (Ontario).

Provincial variations exist in the application of these three classes of legislation, but every province imposes writing requirements through some combination of the three statutes.

THE STATUTE OF FRAUDS

The oldest piece of legislation dealing with writing is the Statute of Frauds passed in 1677 by the English Parliament.[2] It was subsequently adopted (with some changes) by most common law jurisdictions around the world, including those of Canada and the United States. British Columbia substantially revised it,[3] and Manitoba eventually repealed it entirely.[4] In the remaining common law provinces, the Statute remains in force in one form or another.

The Statute of Frauds makes certain types of contracts unenforceable unless they are in writing. An otherwise valid oral contract that falls within the Statute is unenforceable; neither party may sue on the contract. This allows a party to avoid performing a contract solely because it is oral—the contract might be perfectly valid in every other respect. It has often been said that by defeating the reasonable expectations of parties, the Statute of Frauds promotes more frauds than it prevents. For this reason, the courts have tried to limit the application of the Statute wherever possible. As a result, the scope of the Statute has been restricted by exceptions.

The Types of Contracts Covered by the Statute of Frauds

Originally, the Statute of Frauds covered six types of contracts:

executor or administrator legal representative of the estate of a dead person

   i. A promise by an **executor or administrator** to pay estate debts out of his own money,
   ii. A promise to answer for the debt, default, or miscarriage of another (guarantee),
   iii. An agreement made in consideration of marriage,
   iv. A contract dealing with interests in land,
   v. An agreement not performed within one year of its making, and
   vi. Ratification of debts incurred while a minor.

In New Brunswick and Nova Scotia, the statute still covers five of these six categories (excepting minors).[5] In other provinces, rules about minors and marriage contracts have been moved to family law statutes and contracts lasting longer than a year are covered under consumer protection legislation.[6] Guarantees, land, and executor's promises are the categories addressed in most of the remaining provinces' Statute of Frauds. We will focus on guarantees and interests in land as the categories most relevant to business.

Guarantees   A guarantee is a promise "to answer for the debt, default, or miscarriage of another;" it is a conditional promise to pay only if the debtor defaults: "If he does not pay you, I will." Only after the debtor has defaulted may the creditor claim payment from the guarantor.

indemnity a promise by a third party to be primarily liable to pay the debt

In contrast, a person who makes a promise to indemnify a creditor makes herself primarily liable to pay the debt through her **indemnity**. When the debt falls due, the creditor

---

[2] Statute of Frauds: An Act for the prevention of frauds and perjuries, 29 Charles II, c. 3 (1677, U.K.).

[3] The Law Reform Amendment Act, S.B.C. 1985, c. 10, s. 8 repealed the Statute of Frauds, and established new writing requirements now found in the Law and Equity Act, R.S.B.C. 1996, c. 253 (dealing with land and guarantees). Alberta and Saskatchewan have adopted the original English Statute, while Ontario, P.E.I., New Brunswick and Nova Scotia have enacted their own similar statutes.

[4] R.S.M. 1987, c. F-158.

[5] Prince Edward Island retains the infant ratification category as well as guarantees R.S.P.E.I . 1988, c. S-6, ss. 1, 2.

[6] For example, Family Law Act, S.B.C. 2011 c. 25 s. 259; Family Law Act, R.S.O. 1990, c. F.3, s. 52; Matrimonial Property Act, R.S.N.S. 1989, c. 275, s. 23.

may sue either the original debtor or the person who gave the promise to indemnify, or both. "Give him the goods and I will see to it that you are paid" would usually be a promise to indemnify.[7] A promise by a purchaser of a business to its employees to pay back wages owed by the former owner would be a promise to indemnify.

This distinction is important because the courts have applied the writing requirements of the Statute of Frauds only to simple guarantees. Therefore, a guarantee must be made in writing to be enforceable, but a promise to indemnify is outside the Statute and is enforceable without being in writing. Even the class of guarantees that fall within the Statute has been narrowed; the courts have excluded those guarantees incidental to a larger contract where the element of guarantee is only one of many promises made in the contract.

CASE 10.1

Sutton & Co. were stockbrokers and members of the London Stock Exchange with access to its facilities. Grey was not a member, but he had contacts with prospective investors. The parties made an oral agreement by which Grey would receive half the commission from transactions for his clients completed through Sutton and was to pay half of any bad debts that might develop out of the transactions.

When a loss resulted from one of the transactions and Grey refused to pay his half, Sutton & Co. sued him. Grey pleaded that his promise to pay half the loss was a guarantee and was not enforceable against him because it was not in writing. The court ruled that the whole arrangement between Sutton and Grey had been a much broader one than merely guaranteeing the payment of a debt owing by a particular client, and that the Statute of Frauds should not apply. Accordingly, the agreement was enforceable, and Sutton & Co. obtained judgment against Grey.[8]

British Columbia has done away with the judge-made distinction between indemnity and guarantee by requiring that both types of promise be in writing.[9]

In contrast to the restricted meaning given to the words *debt* and *default*, the courts have given the word *miscarriage* a fairly wide meaning. They have interpreted a promise to "answer for the **miscarriage** of another" to mean "to pay damages for loss caused by the tort of another person," for example, by that person's negligence. The promise "I will pay you for the injury B caused you if B doesn't settle with you" must be in writing. On the other hand, the promise "I will pay you for the injury B caused you if you will give up absolutely any rights you have against B" is a promise of indemnity and need not be in writing to be enforceable.[10]

miscarriage an injury caused by the tort of another person

Land   Requiring that contracts concerning interests in land be in writing is necessary to protect the public record of land ownerships. The special qualities of land, in particular its virtual indestructibility and permanence, make the ability to ascertain the various outstanding interests and claims against land important. It is essential to have verified written records of transactions affecting interests in land, and these records must be available over many years for inspection by interested persons and the public. Therefore, we have systems of public records where interested parties may search and discover who owns or claims to own the interests in land.[11]

Still, some contracts concerning land are considered too remotely connected with land to be protected by the Statute. The courts have held that agreements to repair or build a

---

[7] As Furmston points out in Cheshire, Fifoot and Furmston's *Law of Contract*, 13th ed., at 212, it is the intention of the parties and not their language that determines whether the promise is a guarantee or an indemnity.

[8] *Sutton & Co. v. Grey*, [1894] 1 Q.B. 285; *Bassie v. Melnychuk* (1993), 14 Alta. L.R. (3d) 31.

[9] Law Reform (Enforcement of Contracts) Act, 1954, 2 & 3 Eliz. 2, c. 34, s. 1 (U.K.), and the Law and Equity Act R.S.B.C. 1996, c. 253 s. 59(6).

[10] *Kirkham v. Marter* (1819), 106 E.R. 490; *Read v. Nash* (1751), 95 E.R. 632.

[11] British Columbia retains the requirement of writing for contracts concerning interests in land. Law and Equity Act, R.S.B.C. 1996, c. 253, s. 59(3). Law of Property Act, 1925, 15 & 16 Geo. 5, c. 20, s. 40 (U.K.).

house, or to obtain room and board, are outside the Statute, while agreements to permit taking water from a well, to lease any land, house, or other building, or even a portion of a building, are within the Statute. Landlord and tenant statutes make oral residential leases enforceable, as we will discuss in Chapter 22.

part performance performance undertaken in reliance on an oral contract relating to an interest in land, and accepted by the courts as evidence of the contract in place of a written memorandum

Part Performance   To prevent fraud, the courts developed an exception that allows some oral land contracts to be enforced despite the Statute of Frauds. It is called the doctrine of **part performance**: If the plaintiff can show that performance of the contract has begun and he has relied on its existence, the court would accept that performance as evidence of the contract without writing.[12]

Not every act of performance under a contract qualifies as a substitute for a written document. The following conditions must be satisfied before the court will enforce the oral contract:

(a) The contract must be one concerning land.
(b) The acts of performance must suggest quite clearly the existence of a contract dealing with the land in question; they must not be ambiguous or just as possibly explained as part of a quite different transaction. The must fulfill the "very purpose" of the contract.[13]
(c) Activities of either the plaintiff or the defendant may be considered acts of performance, but the plaintiff must have relied on the existence of the contract and suffered a loss if the contract is not enforced. This is detrimental reliance.[14]

The act(s) of part performance do not need to disclose all the terms of the contract, just support the existence of the contract and then the court will enforce it according to the terms orally agreed (and proven).

CASE 10.2

The Province of Nova Scotia built a new highway through the middle of Ross Hill's farm. When it expropriated the land, it promised Mr. Hill that he would be permitted to "move people, cattle and equipment" back and forth across the highway. The Province built ramps and gates to allow for Hill's use. Twenty-seven years later, the Province tried to deny that an equitable interest in land had been created for Hill. The Supreme Court of Canada held that "the actions of the province [spoke] louder than any written document." Building and maintaining the gates and ramps were clear and unequivocal acts of part performance and Hill relied upon them to his detriment. Higher compensation for the expropriated land would have been sought if access had not been promised. Therefore, the oral contract was exempt from the Statute of Frauds and the court upheld Hill's interest in the land.[15]

Typically, mere payment of a deposit, submission of an offer, or waiver of some of the conditions in the contract will not amount to part performance, as is demonstrated in Case 10.3 below.[16] For more information on this topic, see the Companion Website.

Requirements for a Written Memorandum

The actual writing requirements of the Statute of Frauds are quite vague. It requires only a "note or memorandum" of the contract "signed by the party to be charged" or by the

---

[12] *Hill v. Nova Scotia (Attorney General)*, [1997] 1 S.C.R. 69 at para. 11–16; *Erie Sand and Gravel Ltd. v. Seres' Farms Ltd.* (2009), 97 O.R. (3d) 241 at 252–65.

[13] *Erie Sand and Gravel Ltd. v. Seres' Farms Ltd.* (2009), 97 O.R. (3d) 241 at 261–65.

[14] *B & R Development Corp.(c.o.b. Abbey Lane Homes) v. Trail South Developments Inc.* [2012] A. J. No. 1171, para 35 (ABCA); *Erie Sand and Gravel Ltd. v. Seres' Farms Ltd.* (2009), 97 O.R. (3d) 241 at 257–61.

[15] *Hill v. Nova Scotia (Attorney General)*, [1997] 1 S.C.R. 69, *supra*, n. 12.

[16] *Hunter v. Baluke* (1998), 42 O.R. (3d) 553 (Ont. S.C.J.) at paras 64–75; *Erie Sand and Gravel Ltd. v. Seres' Farms Ltd.* (2009), 97 O.R. (3d) 241 at 265.

party's authorized agent; it does not require complete detail of every term or both parties' signatures.

Electronic forms of transmitting documents satisfy the statutory requirement of being in "writing." Canadian courts have assumed that facsimile transmissions or emails are sufficient to satisfy the writing requirement of the Statute of Frauds.[17] Other legislation is being amended to specifically address writing in new ecommerce business methods. Chapter 31 specifically addresses these changes under the heading "Formal Requirements."

All Essential Terms Must Be Included   The memorandum must contain all the *essential* terms of the contract, including the identity of the parties. If the contract is for the sale of land, for example, the memorandum must name the parties, describe the subject matter (the land), and set out the consideration to be given for it.

CASE 10.3

Wayne and Janet Gretzky made a written offer to purchase a cottage property, including a main house, guesthouse, and two-storey boathouse for $1 860 000. All the terms and conditions were acceptable to the vendor except the date for vacant possession of the boathouse. The offer was rejected and a counter-offer was made. At this point, oral discussions took place between the various agents and their clients and a mutually agreeable date was established. However, the new date was not placed in the agreement and no written memorandum of the boathouse possession term was made. Subsequently, the vendors refused to complete the deal and the Gretzkys sued. The court found that vacant possession of the boathouse was obviously an important issue between the parties, and therefore it was an essential term not in writing. The contract failed to satisfy the Statute of Frauds and was unenforceable. The Gretzkys did not get the cottage.[18]

An exception exists for contracts of guarantee—the consideration for that type of promise need not appear in writing.[19]

The memorandum need not be wholly within a single document; several written notes may be taken together to satisfy the requirements of the Statute. Using more than one document to satisfy the writing requirement can be difficult if there are no cross-references within the documents. In one case, the court heard evidence that a signed letter beginning with "Dear Sir" was contained in a particular envelope that bore the name and address of the plaintiff, and in this way linked the two pieces of paper as a sufficient memorandum.[20] The court justified its decision on the grounds that, even without oral evidence, it could reasonably assume that the letter was delivered in an envelope: It admitted oral evidence merely to identify the envelope.

Signed by the Defendant   The Statute requires that the note or memorandum be signed by the party to be charged—that is, sued (the defendant)—and only that person, not the plaintiff. The plaintiff's own signature is irrelevant; if the defendant has not signed, the plaintiff's signature on the document does not help and he cannot enforce the contract against the other party.

The courts have been lenient in prescribing what amounts to a sufficient signature; it need not be in the handwriting of the defendant. A printed name will suffice as long as it is

---

[17] See *Rolling v. William Investments* (1989), 63 D.L.R. (4th) 760. The Ontario Court of Appeal decided that a facsimile transmission of acceptance of an option was a satisfactory acceptance, even though when the parties made the agreement in 1974, they "could not have anticipated delivery of a facsimile of the [accepted] offer by means of a telephone transmission. . . ." The court concluded that "Where technological advances have been made which facilitate communications and expedite transmission of documents we see no reason why they should not be utilized. Indeed, they should be encouraged and approved. . . . [The defendant] suffered no prejudice by reason of the procedure followed." See also *Leoppky v. Meston*, 2008 ABQB 45 at paras. 38–41.

[18] *Hunter v. Baluke, supra*, n 16.

[19] See, for example, R.S.O. 1990, c. S.19, s. 6; R.S.N.S. 1989, c. 442, s. 8.

[20] *Pearce v. Gardner*, [1897] 1 Q.B. 688; *Harvie and Hawryluk v. Gibbons* (1980), 12 Alta. L.R. (2d) 72.

intended to validate the whole of the document. For example, a letterhead on an invoice is designed to verify the sale of the goods described below without a signature and is sufficient. Ecommerce legislation now expands the notion of signature to include electronic signatures, as will be discussed in Chapter 31.

CASE 10.4

An unmarried couple entered into an agreement dividing the proceeds of sale of their home and its contents. One party refused to honour the deal as it violated the Statute of Frauds, and asked the court to divide the proceeds of sale of the home. The court enforced the settlement agreement, finding that, although the Statute of Frauds applied to the agreement as it related to the sale of land, the emails exchanged by the parties satisfied the written "note or memorandum" requirement. The signing requirement was met by the typed first name on the bottom of the email—even though the email was sent from someone else's email account.[21]

Consequences for Contracts within Its Scope

What do we mean when we say that the Statute of Frauds makes an oral contract unenforceable? This means the parties cannot use the courts to obtain a remedy. The courts recognize that an **unenforceable contract** still exists even though neither party is able to obtain a court remedy. Is this the same as saying it is void? The answer is a definite "No." Although no action may be brought on the contract itself, the contract may still affect the legal relations between the parties in several ways.

unenforceable contract a contract that still exists for other purposes but neither party may obtain a remedy under it through court action

1. Recovery of Money Paid under a Contract First, both parties to an unenforceable contract may, of course, choose to perform, but if they do not, recovery of any down payment made will depend upon which party repudiates the contract.

ILLUSTRATION 10.1

P orally agrees to buy V's house for $50 000 and gives a down payment of $5000, with the balance to be paid in 30 days.

Suppose that P then sees a more suitable property and refuses to pay the balance. The Statute of Frauds applies, and V cannot enforce the contract. On the other hand, P cannot by court action require V to return the payment. Although the contract is unenforceable, it still exists and may be used as a defence: V may retain the payment knowing that he will not be ordered by a court to return it.[22]

Suppose instead it is V who refuses either to complete the sale or to return the payment. P can sue successfully for the return of the payment. The court in these circumstances will not permit V to repudiate the contract and yet keep the payment received under its terms. Without an enforceable contract, no court will let him keep the deposit.

In the above illustration, we can see that the court will not permit the party who breaches an unenforceable contract to gain a further advantage. If the contract were found instead to be void, the problem of breach would not arise. A void contract cannot be "breached"; the remedy is rescission, as discussed in Chapter 9.

2. Recovery for Goods and Services Second, a party who has accepted goods and services under a contract that is unenforceable because of the Statute is not permitted to retain the benefit received without paying something for it. He would have to return the goods or pay a reasonable price for them, as was explained in Chapter 6 under the principle of quantum meruit.

---

[21] *Leoppky v. Meston*, 2008 ABQB 45 at para. 45.

[22] See e.g. *Semchyshen v. Semchyshen*, [2013] S.J.No. 342.

3. Effect of a Subsequent Written Memorandum

Third, a written document may come into existence after the contract has been formed and it will still satisfy the Statute. As long as the document comes into existence before the action is brought on the contract, it provides the necessary evidence.

ILLUSTRATION 10.2

P agrees orally to buy V's home. P then refuses to complete the contract, and V sends her a letter outlining the contract and demanding that she carry out her obligations. P replies by letter saying that she has decided not to go through with the contract referred to in V's letter and that she is not bound since the contract is not in writing. Even though the statements in P's letter were intended to deny liability, the two letters taken together would amount to a sufficient memorandum to satisfy the Statute and make the contract enforceable.

---

4. Defendant Must Expressly Plead the Statute

Fourth, a defendant who is sued upon an oral contract must expressly plead the Statute as a defence to the action. If he fails to mention it, the court will decide the case without reference to the Statute. The plaintiff will then succeed if he establishes that the contract, though oral, was validly formed.

5. Varying a Prior Written Contract

Fifth, an oral contract may effectively vary or end a prior written contract even though the oral contract could not itself be enforced. An oral contract within the Statute is effective as long as a party does not have to bring an action to have it enforced.

ILLUSTRATION 10.3

P agrees to buy Roselawn from V under a written contract containing a promise by V to give vacant possession on a certain day. V then has unexpected difficulty in removing his tenants and tells P that he will not be able to give vacant possession. P finds another property equally suitable to her and available with vacant possession. Rather than get into a dispute, the parties make a mutual oral agreement to call off the first contract: P releases V from his promise to transfer Roselawn with vacant possession in return for a release by V of P's promise to pay the purchase price. Afterward, V succeeds in removing his tenants and sues P to enforce the original written contract. P may successfully plead that the subsequent oral contract validly terminated the written contract.

However, the oral contract cannot be sued upon directly. Suppose that, in addition to terminating the prior contract, V had orally agreed to give P an option on another property. Although the oral contract effectively dissolved the prior written contract, P could not sue upon the new promise to give an option because otherwise the court would be enforcing an oral promise for an interest in land.[23]

INTERNATIONAL ISSUE

Should the Statute of Frauds Be Repealed?

The Statute of Frauds was passed over three centuries ago, and the argument has been made that the historical reasons for creating it no longer exist. In Canada, more detailed consumer protection writing requirements reduce the Statute's impact. As previously noted, the Statute has been repealed in Manitoba and amended in Ontario and British Columbia. Perhaps it is time to replace or amend it throughout Canada. When the Province of Ontario amended its Sale of Goods Act to remove the writing requirements (see footnote 25), it did so for the express purpose of facilitating electronic commerce.

On the other hand, consider this statement from Mr. Justice Côté of the Alberta Court of Appeal:

Over 20 years ago, it was fashionable to attack the Statute of Frauds, and indeed a number of jurisdictions have repealed large chunks of it. But Alberta has not touched s. 4. In my view, the trend of modern legislation is actually to call for more writing in contracts and commercial transactions. The idea that one can validly sell a valuable piece of land entirely by oral discussions runs contrary to the expectations of most lay people;

>

---

[23] See *Morris v. Baron*, [1918] A.C. 1, for a similar result.

one can almost say that absence of writing casts into doubt intention to create binding legal relations. So I feel no compulsion to undermine the Statute.[23A]

Interestingly, provincial electronic commerce legislation like the Ontario Electronic Commerce Act addresses the issues of writing and signatures in electronic documents—not by avoiding the effect of legislation such as the Statute of Frauds, but by seeking practical equivalents to those requirements in forming a contract.

Internationally, the trend may be different. Civil law jurisdictions, such as France, never had the Statute of Frauds. Even common law countries are moving away from writing requirements. England has repealed most of the Statute of Frauds. Article 11 of the United Nations Convention on Contracts for the International Sale of Goods reads:

A contract for sale need not be concluded in or evidenced by writing and is not subject to any other requirements as to form. It may be proved by any means including witnesses.[24]

Questions to Consider

1. How are business relationships and commercial activity affected by complex legal rules about the enforceability of oral contracts?

2. Are there sound policy reasons for requiring some contracts to be in writing?

3. Are amendments adequate to address the problems arising from the Statute of Frauds, or would it be better to repeal the Statute and replace it with legislation that meets contemporary needs?

4. Can the Statute of Frauds coexist with ecommerce legislation?

Sources: Austie v. Aksnowicz, [1999] 10 W.W.R. 713, 70 Alta. L.R. (3d) 154 (C.A.) at para. 55; Law Reform Commission of British Columbia, Report on the Statute of Frauds (1997), available online at www.bcli .org/pages/law-reform-resources/law-reform-database; Manitoba Law Reform Commission, Report on the Statute of Frauds (1980); University of Alberta Institute of Law Research and Reform, Background Paper No. 12: Statute of Frauds (1979); Report No. 44 (1985); S.O. 2000, c. 17.

REQUIREMENTS OF THE SALE OF GOODS ACT

Provinces other than British Columbia and Ontario[25] impose writing requirements in their Sale of Goods Acts. Although the specifics vary by province, the basic requirements are similar to those found in the Statute of Frauds—contracts for the sale of goods must be evidenced by some note or memorandum signed by the party to be charged or they are unenforceable.

What Constitutes a Sale of Goods for the Purposes of the Writing Requirement?

Goods   A sale of tangible moveable personal property is a sale of goods for the purposes of the writing provisions under this legislation. It does not apply to money or services. The challenge is that often contracts involve both the goods and services, such as a contract to provide materials and build a garage. If it is considered a contract for the sale of goods, it is subject to the writing requirements; if it is one for work and materials, it is not. The problem of defining a sale of goods is discussed in detail in Chapter 14. Typically, it will depend on the *essence* of the contract—the proportion of labour or service to goods or materials supplied under the contract.

Threshold Amounts   All provinces set a (very low) threshold value of goods supplied under the contract to trigger the writing requirement. Amounts vary from $30 to $50.[26] The contract may state a fixed price or set a formula for calculation, or the price may be determined by the past dealings between the parties.[27]

[23A] Mr. Justice Côté of the Alberta Court of Appeal, Royal Bank of Canada v Reddy, 2007 ABQB 613.

[24] (1980), www.uncitral.org/pdf/english/texts/sales/cisg/V1056997-CISG-e-book.pdf

[25] Law Reform (Enforcement of Contracts) Act, 1954, 2 & 3 Eliz. 2, c. 34, s. 1 (U.K.); Statute Law Amendment Act, 1958, S.B.C. 1958, c. 52, s. 17; Statute Law Amendment (Government Management and Services) Act 1994, S.O. 1994, c. 27, s. 54.

[26] The amount is $40 in Nova Scotia; $50 in Newfoundland and Labrador, Saskatchewan, and Alberta; and $30 in Prince Edward Island. These amounts are, of course, insignificant compared to their value over 100 years ago when the Sale of Goods Act was adopted.

[27] See, for example, Sale of Goods Act, R.S.B.C. 1996, c. 410, s. 12; R.S.O. 1990, c. S.1, s. 9; R.S.N.S. 1989, c. 408, s. 11.

Evidence That Satisfies the Act

Unlike the Statute of Frauds, the Sale of Goods Act states expressly that a party to a contract for the sale of goods who cannot produce the required written memorandum may still enforce the contract if he can show one of the following kinds of conduct:[28]

(a) "acceptance" and actual receipt of the goods (or part) by the buyer, or
(b) part payment tendered by the buyer and accepted by the seller, or
(c) something "by way of earnest" given by the buyer to the seller.

Acceptance   In the Sale of Goods Act, the word **acceptance** has a special meaning. It means any conduct by the buyer in relation to the goods that amounts to recognition of an existing contract of sale. The buyer will have "accepted" the goods when he does anything that amounts to admitting that he has a contract with respect to them.

acceptance   any conduct by the buyer in relation to the goods that amounts to recognition of an existing contract of sale

Part Payment   A **part payment** is a credit toward payment of the purchase price. Therefore, it must be made after the contract is formed and applied to reduce the debt created by the contract. It is not the same as the part performance exception for sales of land discussed under the Statute of Frauds, as a mere payment of money is usually capable of having alternative explanations.

part payment   something tendered by the buyer and accepted by the seller after formation of the contract, to be deducted from the price

Earnest   **Earnest** differs from part payment in that it is not deducted from the price to be paid. Rather it is a token sum (or article) given to seal the bargain. Although the giving of something by way of earnest was common at one time, it is now rarely, if ever, done, and the reference to this practice remains as a relic in the Act.

earnest   a token sum or article given to seal a bargain—now a rare practice

When Both Acts Apply

Both the Sale of Goods Act and the Statute of Frauds may apply to the same contract. They both apply, for example, where there is an oral agreement to sell goods that are to be delivered and paid for by installments over a period exceeding one year. The evidence may satisfy the requirements of the Sale of Goods Act if the buyer accepts some of the goods or makes part payment, but it does not comply with the Statute of Frauds because it is an oral contract that neither party can wholly perform within one year. Accordingly, it is unenforceable because of the Statute of Frauds, but not because of the Sale of Goods Act.

The requirement of a written memorandum in the Sale of Goods Act is open to the same criticism as the comparable provision in the Statute of Frauds. Its limited protection is hard to justify in today's marketplace; its arguably more important function is to imply terms into contracts for the sale of goods, as we shall discuss in Chapter 14.

CONSUMER PROTECTION LEGISLATION

A consumer is an individual who purchases goods or services for personal non-commercial use. Consumers have no power to negotiate terms of their contracts, so provincial legislation imposes some protective measures. Generally this legislation regulates the form (writing) and contents (terms) of consumer contracts, although with differing names and methods of protection.[29] The consumer protection statutes cover both goods and services and extend further than either the Sale of Goods Act or the Statute of Frauds, by dictating not only the evidence of writing but also the terms that must be included in that written document. High-risk industries and contracts formed using particular sales tactics are subject to even greater controls, including consumer cancellation options.

---

[28] Sale of Goods Act, R.S.N.S. 1989, c. 408, s. 7.

[29] See, for example, Business Practices and Consumer Protection Act, S.B.C. 2004, c. 2; Consumer Protection Act, 2002, S.O. 2002, c. C.30, Sched. A; Consumer Protection Act, R.S.N.S. 1989, c. 92.

Consumer contracts that reach the threshold value must be in writing and include the following information:

- Detailed description of goods or services.
- Itemized purchase price.
- Detailed disclosure of cost of borrowing: this includes annualized interest rates and separate disclosure of other administration fees associated with the extension of credit.
- Name, address, and contact information of the vendor.
- Notice of statutory cancellation rights.
- Complete copy provided to the consumer.

Cancellation options are attached to contracts that are formed or performed in the following ways:

- Future performance contracts—this type of contract is one where the goods are supplied or payment is made at a future time.
- Direct sales contracts—this type of contract is formed when the seller contacts a consumer outside his place of business; for example, via door-to-door sales.
- Distance or remote contracts—this type of contract is formed when the parties are separated by distance; for example, by telephone marketing or promotional mailings.
- Internet contracts—the use of online sales is now regulated by most consumer protection legislation.

Some industries are required to include special terms in their consumer contracts. Designated industries considered high risk include the following:

- Time sharing—one Alberta provision requires that time-share agreements be signed by both business and consumer, and the text of the notice provisions cannot be smaller than 12-point font.[30]
- Fitness or personal development—Saskatchewan's legislation requires these contracts to be in writing and include start and end dates, as well as a formula for reducing the amount owing if the club is not available on a specified date.[31]
- Lending (credit)—naturally, all provinces require very specific detailed descriptions of the interest calculations and the composition of the payment amounts.
- Credit card—among Manitoba's written requirements for credit card agreements are a written description of the method for determining the minimum required payments.[32]
- Leasing—many consumers do not understand how their car lease payments are calculated and the importance of the residual value of the vehicle at the end of the lease term. For this reason, Ontario's legislation requires lessors to provide a disclosure statement before the written lease is signed.[33]
- Motor vehicle repair—one Ontario provision prohibits a repairer from charging for work unless an estimate meeting the prescribed requirements has been given or waived. The estimate must be written, and must show the make, model, and odometer reading of the vehicle, as well as a detailed description of proposed work.[34]

---

[30] A. Reg.105 /10 s. 2.

[31] Consumer Protection Act, S.S. 1996, c. C-30.1, s. 76

[32] The Consumer Protection Act, C.C.S.M. c. C200, s. 35.2.

[33] Consumer Protection Act, 2002, S.O. 2002, c. 30, Sch. A, s. 89.

[34] O. Reg. 17/05 s. 51.

- Funeral services—the British Columbia legislation requires funeral services contracts to disclose in writing the address where the body will be stored pending disposition, and the name of the bank where any pre-paid funds will be held.[35]

- Arbitration—in Alberta, consumer arbitration agreements must be in writing, signed by the parties, and approved by the government before they will be enforced.[36]

Consumers are not bound by these contracts unless the business has complied with the requirements of the legislation. Provinces have set up agencies to hear consumer complaints, as well as to investigate or even negotiate on the consumer's behalf. We discuss consumer protection legislation in more detail in Chapters 3 and 14.

Ethical Issue   Do Writing Requirements Protect the Consumer or the Business?

Many of the consumer protection writing requirements involve disclosing onerous terms to the consumer as part of the written contract. As long as the consumer has received the written disclosure, he or she will be bound by the terms. In the fast-paced world of online contracting, few consumers have time to read the disclosed terms and have no power to bargain for a change in terms if they are dissatisfied. Onerous terms are presented on a take-it-or-leave-it basis. Furthermore, even when a cancellation right is available, finding a business that does not require agreement to similar one-sided terms might be impossible for the consumer. In this light, written disclosure requirements may not actually protect the consumer.

Questions to Consider:

1. Do writing requirements protect the consumer or the business? Or both?

2. Rather than being given the right to cancel an agreement, should consumers be allowed to modify the terms and conditions before agreeing to them? Would consumers take the time to do this?

3. The European Union has a directive that identifies unfair terms and declares them unenforceable against a consumer. Is this a more fair approach?

4. In *Seidel v. TELUS*, the Supreme Court of Canada said that unless the legislature intervenes, the courts will enforce contracts of adhesion that are freely entered into.[37] Should the courts ever help a consumer subject to a written contract filled with unfair terms? Consider Case 10.7 below, which shows how implied terms in the consumer contract can protect a consumer.

THE INTERPRETATION OF EXPRESS TERMS

Even when parties put their contracts in writing, disagreements about their meaning regularly occur. Words are at best an inefficient means of communicating thoughts: They can be capable of more than one meaning—ambiguous without the parties realizing it. Therefore, disagreements about express terms are a common business risk and courts are regularly asked to construe a contract's meaning.

The Goal of the Courts: To Give Validity to Contracts

Courts must make difficult interpretation decisions. Frequently, declaring an agreement void because its wording is ambiguous might seem to be the easiest thing to do, but if the courts took this attitude, they would not be performing their role of encouraging reliance on seriously made agreements. Instead, they lean toward keeping an agreement alive rather than brushing it aside as not binding. When it is possible to find one interpretation more likely in the circumstances than another, courts give ambiguous words that meaning and make the contract enforceable.

---

[35] Business Practices and Consumer Protection Act, S.B.C. 2004, c. 2, s. 34–36.

[36] Fair Trading Act, R.S.A. 1998, c. F-1.05, s. 16.

[37] 2011 S.C.C. 15 at para. 2.

ILLUSTRATION 10.4

Smith offers to build a set of cabinets for Doe for $1000, and Doe accepts. The next day, Smith appears and asks where the lumber is. Doe says, "You are supposed to supply it." Smith replies, "My price was for the work only, not for the materials."

One party may claim that the offer omitted an essential term (who should supply the lumber); such an ambiguous vague offer is not capable of acceptance, and accordingly, no contract is formed. However, if each side accepts that the agreement "to build a set of cabinets for $1000" is valid, Smith will claim that Doe should supply the lumber, and Doe will claim the contrary.

Two Approaches to Interpretation

What precisely did Smith promise when he agreed "to build a set of cabinets for $1000"? In attempting to answer such a question, there are two approaches to the interpretation of words: the **strict or plain-meaning approach** and the **liberal approach to contractual interpretation**.

strict or plain-meaning approach an approach that restricts interpretation to the ordinary or dictionary meaning of a word

liberal approach to contractual interpretation an approach that looks to the intent of the parties and surrounding circumstances, and tends to minimize, but does not ignore, the importance of the words actually used

The plain-meaning approach considers the ordinary or dictionary meaning of a word. However, few words have a "plain" or "ordinary" meaning. Browsing through a dictionary will show that many words have two or more definitions. In addition, the meanings of words change from time to time and place to place—or the context of the words in a contract may make it obvious that they have been used in a special sense.[38]

The liberal approach looks to the purposes of the particular parties in drafting their agreement: What did they intend? It stresses the circumstances surrounding the contract, the negotiations leading up to it, the knowledge of the parties, and any other relevant facts. It minimizes the importance of the words actually used. The liberal approach also has its limitations. In its extreme form, it too may lead to unsatisfactory results by inviting endless speculation about what the parties may have intended but never expressed. The particular words one chooses to use are a part of one's conduct in relation to the contract, and in law, conduct (including words) must continue to serve as the primary guide to one's intentions.

How the Courts Apply the Approaches

Rather than choosing between them, a court will apply both approaches and choose the best meaning for the circumstances. The court begins with the dictionary definitions of the words used, and then examines their meaning in the context of this contract, these parties, and the surrounding circumstances. In each case, the court decides how far it should look beyond the actual words used in search of their meanings.

In Illustration 10.4, Smith promised "to build" the cabinets. Does "to build" include "to supply materials"? Literally, "to build" means only "to construct," but in many circumstances it may include "to supply materials." As an example, when a contractor undertakes to build a house, the price usually includes the price of materials. In the illustration, the words themselves are not conclusive either way. Since the words are ambiguous, the court will look outside the contract to the surrounding circumstances as a means of clearing up this uncertainty. It will hear evidence of any past transactions between the parties to learn whether materials have been included in previous building contracts between them. It will hear evidence of the negotiations leading up to the contract: perhaps Smith had quoted different prices varying with the kind of wood to be used; perhaps Doe made it clear earlier that she wanted a price including materials. Any of these facts, if established in court, would support the claim that "to build" in this contract meant "to supply materials" as well as labour.

---

[38] See J. K. Lewison, *The Interpretation of Contracts* (London: Sweet & Maxwell, 1989); Z. Chafee, "The Disorderly Conduct of Words" (1942) 20 Can. Bar Rev. at 752. See also our discussion of the interpretation of statutes in Chapter 1 on the role of the courts as interpreters of legislation.

Special Usage of Words

Words used in a contract may have a special meaning in the particular business, trade, or geographic location. For example, a dozen typically means 12 but a baker's dozen means 13. In Illustration 10.4, Smith might produce expert witnesses who testify that, in the carpentry trade, usage of the word "build" means labour only. Or he might show that, in that part of the country, the word always has that meaning.

Evidence of special usage is not necessarily conclusive: A court may decide that the word was used in a general rather than a special way, perhaps because the user of the word was aware that the other party was not familiar with trade usage. In general, the courts construe words most strictly against the party who has suggested them because that party could have been more clear.[39]

Conflicting Testimony and Credibility

Parties to a contract may give conflicting evidence about the circumstances or conversations surrounding its formation. In order to decide which testimony to accept, the court will seek corroboration of one of their versions, if possible, from a non-party, from documentation, or from the actions of the parties in relation to the contract. When the only evidence in a case is the testimony of the disputing parties, the case becomes a "credibility contest." The judge has to assess the credibility of the witnesses and decide whose version seems more reasonable. Credibility includes both truthfulness and reliability. One person may not have seen or heard clearly, may not remember well, or may have observed only part of an event. Even though a witness is honest, his testimony might not be reliable and therefore not be credible. Judges must give reasons for why they find one witness more credible than another.

Special Types of Contracts

Some types of contracts require special approaches. In Chapter 6, we considered the standard form contract—a contract prepared in advance by one party and presented to the other on a take-it-or-leave-it basis. The law recognizes the one-sided nature of the negotiations and tries to level the playing field. When interpreting an ambiguous term in a standard form contract, the court will prefer the interpretation advanced by the non-drafting party. Of course, it must be a reasonable interpretation. This rule is known as **contra proferentem**.[40] It is also applied to the interpretation of an exemption clause and a consumer contract, as will be discussed in Chapters 13 and 14 respectively.

contra proferentem a rule of contract interpretation that prefers the interpretation of a clause that is least favourable to the party that drafted the clause

Insurance contracts are an example of a type of contract with special interpretation rules, as outlined by the Supreme Court of Canada.[41] Interpretation of insurance contracts must

1. follow the contra proferentem rule,
2. construe coverage provisions broadly, and
3. interpret exclusion clauses narrowly.[42]

We will discuss insurance contracts in Chapter 16.

---

[39] See *Manulife Bank of Canada v. Conlin*, [1996] 3 S.C.R. 415; *Philip K. Matkin Professional Corp. v. Northmont Resort Properties Ltd.*, [2013] B.C.J. No. 2492.

[40] The rule does not apply if the term is clear and unambiguous: *Hillis Oil & Sales Ltd. v. Wynnis Canada Ltd.*, [1986] 1 S.C.R. 57.

[41] *Reid Crowther & Partners Ltd. v. Simcoe & Erie General Insurance Co.*, [1993] 1 S.C.R. 252 at 259.

[42] *Non-Marine Underwriters, Lloyd's of London v. Scalera*, [2002] 1 S.C.R. 552, at 591.

THE PAROL EVIDENCE RULE

The Meaning of Parol Evidence

Before a deal is made, the parties often spend time bargaining and negotiating, making offers and counter-offers, with both sides making concessions until finally they reach a suitable compromise. The bargaining may be carried on orally or in writing. In important contracts, the parties usually put their final agreement into a formal document signed by both sides. During the negotiation process, emails, phone messages, draft documents, faxes, and letters may be created and exchanged. These documents and recordings are collectively known as parol evidence. The word *parol* means extrinsic to or outside of the written agreement.[43] If a dispute subsequently arises over the meaning of the words used in the formal signed document, this parol evidence contains valuable information about the parties' understanding of the meaning of the words used in the final contract.

CASE 10.5

When the seller asked the buyer, "What will you give me for 75 shares of Eastern Cafeterias of Canada?", the buyer said he would think about it and then make an offer. Later in the day the buyer replied, "I will give you $10.50 a share for your Eastern Cafeterias shares." The seller replied, "I accept your offer." The seller delivered the shares for Eastern Cafeterias of Canada Ltd. and received a cheque in full payment. The buyer then realized that Eastern Cafeterias Ltd. and Eastern Cafeterias of Canada Ltd. were two different companies, and that he had the former company in mind when he made his offer to buy the shares. He stopped payment on his cheque. In defending the seller's lawsuit, the buyer claimed that his offer to buy "Eastern Cafeterias" was ambiguous, as he could have meant either company. He argued that since he and the seller were talking about two different companies, there was never any agreement and no contract was formed. The court examined the pre-contractual unambiguous statement of the seller that referenced Eastern Cafeterias "of Canada" and decided that the final agreement was referring to those shares. The defendant's use of the ambiguous term in the offer was in response to the plaintiff's earlier inquiry and so the contractual language must be interpreted in the same way.[44]

Case 10.5 is an example of a court using parol evidence to establish the meaning of an ambiguous contractual term.[45]

The Meaning of the Parol Evidence Rule

parol evidence rule a rule preventing a party to a written contract from later using parol evidence to add to, subtract from, or modify the final written contract

The **parol evidence rule** puts a limit on what uses can be made of parol evidence. As we saw in Case 10.5, parol evidence can be used to help interpret ambiguous words used in a contract. It can also be used to address formation of the contract such as its legality, the capacity of the parties, mistakes, duress, undue influence, or fraud. However, it cannot be used to add a new term to a final written contract.

According to the parol evidence rule, once a final written contract has been formed, a party cannot later use parol evidence to add, subtract, contradict, or modify a term in that written contract.[46] The rule applies both to an oral agreement that has been reduced to writing and to a written agreement that has been set out in a more formal document. A party may still try to argue mistake or rectification as discussed in Chapter 9, but otherwise the contract is final.

---

[43] For a more extensive discussion of the meaning of the parol evidence rule see John D. McCamus, *The Law of Contracts* (Toronto: Irwin Law, 2005) at 193–207.

[44] *Scammell v. Ouston*, [1941] 1 All E.R. 14 at 25.

[45] See also *Campeau v. Desjardins Financial Security Life Assurance Co.*, [2005] M.J. No. 448 (Man. C.A.).

[46] *Hawrish v. Bank of Montreal*, [1969] S.C.R. 515.

Exceptions to the Parol Evidence Rule

The Document Does Not Contain the Whole Contract Once the parties have put their agreement into a document in its final form, the parol evidence rule precludes either party from adding terms not in that final agreement. However, sometimes the court may find that the written document was not intended to be the whole complete contract. Earlier in this chapter, we learned that the terms of a contract may be partly in writing and partly oral; if a party can show that the writing was not intended to contain the whole contract but was merely a part of it, then she may introduce evidence of additional oral terms using parol evidence.[47]

ILLUSTRATION 10.5

A, the owner of a fleet of dump trucks, agrees orally with B, a paving contractor, to move 3000 cubic metres of gravel within three months from Calgary to Carstairs for $18 000, and to provide any related documents that B may require for financing the project. To finance her paving operations, B applies for a bank loan, and the bank requests evidence that the paving work can be started immediately. B therefore asks A to sign a statement to the effect that he will deliver 1000 cubic metres of gravel from Calgary to Carstairs within the next month for $6000. Soon after A starts to make the deliveries, he discovers that he has quoted too low a price per cubic metre. He claims that his whole agreement with B has been reduced to writing and that he need move only the 1000 cubic metres of gravel referred to in the writing.

The parol evidence rule does not apply. The written document for the bank was not intended to be a complete statement of the contract. Rather, it was drawn up as part of A's performance of his obligation under it. Accordingly, B may sue A for damages if A refuses to perform the balance of the contract, and for this purpose B may offer evidence of the terms of the original oral agreement.

Subsequent Oral Agreement The parol evidence rule does not exclude evidence of an oral agreement that the parties may reach after they have entered into the written agreement. The subsequent oral agreement may change the terms of the written agreement,[48] or it may even discharge or rescind the prior contract altogether.[49] When such a claim is made, the court will hear evidence of a subsequent oral contract, but the contract must satisfy all the usual formation requirements: offer, acceptance, consideration, and intention.

Collateral Agreement A **collateral agreement** is an entirely separate undertaking agreed on by the parties at the same time (or prior to) the written agreement but not included in their written contract, probably because the written contract seemed unrelated or separate from it. The argument is that a collateral agreement may be enforced as a separate contract quite independent of the written document. As with oral subsequent agreements, courts will only accept such a claim when all elements of formation are separately met for the collateral agreement (especially separate consideration) and when it does not contradict the terms of the written agreement.[50]

> **collateral agreement** a separate agreement between the parties made at the same time as, but not included in, the written document

---

CASE 10.6

A lawyer signed a written personal guarantee of the indebtedness of a company. The guarantee stated that it was continuous, meaning the lawyer would be responsible not only for the existing debts of the company but also for any future indebtedness the company would create after the signing of the guarantee. It also stated that there were no

>

---

[47] *See Gallen v. Allstate Grain Co.* (1984), 9 D.L.R. (4th) 496, for a comprehensive review of the exceptions to the rule. For a contrasting view, see *Norman Estate v. Norman*, [1990] B.C.J. No. 199 (B.C.S.C.).

[48] See *Johnson Investments v. Pagritide*, [1923] 2 D.L.R. 985.

[49] *Morris v. Baron*, [1918] A.C. 1.

[50] *Hawrish, supra*, n. 46, at 524.

representations, and liability would only end upon agreement in writing. When the company went bankrupt and the bank called upon the lawyer to pay, the lawyer argued that there was a collateral agreement made at the time of signing that the lawyer would only be responsible for existing debts of the company, and he would be released from any indebtedness when guarantees from other directors were signed. The bank did obtain guarantees from other directors but argued that this in no way released the lawyer. The Supreme Court of Canada refused to allow evidence of an oral collateral agreement. The guarantee was a complete final agreement, and therefore its terms could not be modified by extrinsic parol evidence. The alleged collateral agreement discharging the lawyer directly contradicted the terms of the guarantee, and therefore they could not consistently stand together. No exception to the parol evidence rule applied, and the lawyer had to pay the debts.[51]

condition precedent any set of circumstances or events that the parties stipulate must be satisfied or must happen before their contract takes effect

Condition Precedent A **condition precedent** is any set of circumstances or events that the parties agree must be satisfied or must happen before their contract takes effect. It may be an event beyond the control of either party, such as a requirement that a licensing board approve the transfer of a business, or a student graduating before a contract of employment takes effect. Courts will admit evidence of an oral condition precedent even when the written contract expressly states that the parties' rights and duties are governed exclusively by the written terms. The courts are prepared to recognize and enforce a condition precedent agreed to orally even when the subject matter of the contract falls within the scope of the Statute of Frauds or the Sale of Goods Act. Once a court accepts a contention that the parties did indeed intend to suspend the operation of their contract subject to a condition precedent, then the whole of the contract is suspended, including any term attempting to exclude the admission of such evidence.

ILLUSTRATION 10.6

B offers to sell a car to A for $14 000. A agrees orally to buy it, provided he can persuade his bank to lend him $10 000. The parties agree orally that the contract will operate only if the bank makes the loan, and that otherwise the contract will be void. They then make a written contract in which A agrees to pay B $14 000 in 10 days, and B agrees to deliver the car to A at that time. The writing does not mention that the contract is subject to A obtaining the bank loan. The bank refuses to lend the money to A, who then informs B that the sale is off. B sues A for breach of contract and contends that their oral understanding about the bank loan is excluded by the parol evidence rule.

The parol evidence rule does not apply, and B will fail in his action. In his defence, A must show that there was an oral understanding suspending the contract of sale unless and until he could obtain the necessary bank loan. It is risky to rely on this exception because of the difficulty in proving the oral conversation. It is always better to put any conditions precedent in the written document.

CHECKLIST

Exceptions to the Parol Evidence Rule

A court will admit parol evidence about a missing term when

- the written agreement does not contain the whole agreement;
- the missing term is part of a subsequent oral agreement;
- the missing term is part of a collateral agreement for which there is separate consideration; or
- the missing term is a condition precedent to the written agreement.

---

[51] *Ibid.* See also *River Wind Ventures Ltd. v. British Columbia*, 2011 BCCA 79; but see *Corey Developments Inc. v. Eastbridge Developments (Waterloo) Ltd.* (1997), 34 O.R. (3d) 73 *aff'd* (1999) 44 O.R. (3d) 95 for an example where the court refused to follow the parol evidence rule.

IMPLIED TERMS AS A METHOD OF INTERPRETATION

It is difficult for parties to expressly address every possible scenario in a contract. Therefore, the express terms of a contract may not deal with the situation now facing the contractual parties. In such circumstances, a court may imply a term into the contract. An **implied term** is a term not expressly included by the parties in their agreement but which, in the opinion of the court, they would, as reasonable people, have included had they thought of the possibility of the subsequent difficulty arising. A term will be implied if it is obviously necessary to accomplish the purpose of the contract.

implied term   a term not expressly included by the parties in their agreement but which, as reasonable people, they would have included had they thought about it

Terms Established by Custom or Statute

Implied terms usually result from long-established customs in a particular trade or type of transaction. They exist in almost every field of commerce and were recognized among business people because they made good sense or because they led to certainty in transactions without the need to spell out every detail. In time, the courts fell into line with this business practice: when a party failed to perform in compliance with an implied term, the courts would recognize its existence and enforce the contract as though it had been an express term.

ILLUSTRATION 10.7

A asks B, a tire dealer, to supply truck tires for his five-tonne dump truck. B then shows A a set of tires and quotes a price. A purchases the tires. The sale slip merely sets out the name and the price of the tires. Later A discovers that these tires are not safe on trucks of more than three tonnes' capacity and claims that B is in breach of the contract.

On these facts, there was no express promise by B that the tires would be safe for a five-tonne truck or any other type of truck. Nevertheless, the court would hold that, under the circumstances, there was an implied term that the tires should be suitable for a five-tonne truck. It would say that, in showing A the tires after he had made his intended use of them clear, B, as a regular seller of such tires, implied that they would be suitable for A's truck.

This approach applies to all kinds of contracts, but in some fields—especially the sale of goods, insurance, partnership, and landlord and tenant relations—a large and complex body of customary terms has developed. In many jurisdictions, these customary terms have been codified in a statute that sets out in one place all the implied terms previously established by the courts for a particular field of law. For instance, court decisions in cases similar to Illustration 10.7 led to a specific provision in the Sale of Goods Act.

ILLUSTRATION 10.8

Alberta's Sale of Goods Act[52] implies the following terms into contracts for the purchases of tangible property:

- The seller is the owner of the goods with the authority to sell them.

- The goods match the description given to the buyer by the seller.

- The goods match the sample of the goods viewed by the buyer.

- The goods are not subject to any liens.

The implied terms of the Sale of Goods Act are also implied into consumer contracts for sale or lease of goods and services. Statutory terms implied into consumer contracts cannot be waived.

---

[52] Sale of Goods Act, R.S.A. 2000, c. S-2.

Szilvasy bought a new home and took over the lease of the rented hot water heater. It sprang a leak and caused $16 000 of water damage to the basement of the home. Szilvasy sued for breach of contract. She alleged that the water heater was not fit for the intended purpose. Reliance Home Comfort defended the action, saying the lease contract did not include an express term on fitness for purpose and it did include a clause exempting Reliance from liability for water damage. The Ontario Court of Appeal held that s. 9 of the Consumer Protection Act implied a term of fitness for purpose into the contract and this implied warranty could not be waived or varied by the express exemption clause. The water heater was not fit for the purpose because it leaked. Judgment was for the consumer.[53]

Reasonable Expectation of the Parties

In what other circumstances are the courts likely to find it appropriate to imply a term into a contract? As a rule, the courts will imply terms reasonably necessary to make a contract effective; if not, the fair expectations of a party would be defeated.

However, the court will not go further than is necessary and will not make a new contract for the parties. Nor will it imply a term that is contrary to the expressed intent of the agreement. A term will be implied on grounds of business efficacy. Parties should therefore consider carefully what unstated assumptions are needed for performing their contract; they need to bring as many of the important possibilities as they can think of into the terms of the written contract.

As a general rule, when parties deal expressly with a matter in their contract, a court will not insert an implied term that deals with the same matter in a different way. If the parties have been diligent in canvassing the foreseeable possibilities for future dispute, a court may conclude that they intended to deal in a comprehensive way with all future events, so that no further terms should be implied.[54]

However, even in lengthy and complex contracts, the parties might not have dealt with what later turns out to be a crucial matter. Courts will sometimes come to the conclusion that a term may be implied, so that the purpose of the contract will not be defeated.

Nickel Developments Limited (Nickel), the owner of a new shopping centre in Thompson, Manitoba, signed a long-term lease with Canada Safeway Limited containing several renewal options. Safeway was to be the "anchor" tenant and its supermarket would use more than half of the centre. The rest of the space contained 12 other non-competing retail units.

After 30 years of operation, Safeway closed its supermarket but continued to occupy the space. For some time, Safeway had been operating another supermarket in a competing shopping centre in Thompson. It decided that it could not continue operating the two in a town that had gone through a lengthy recession; it would be better to close down the premises leased from Nickel. Rather than allow its lease to expire, leaving open the prospect of unwanted competition, Safeway chose to exercise its option to renew the lease for a final term of five years and go on paying the rent in order to keep the space vacant. It already knew that one of its supermarket competitors was interested in taking over the space and was communicating with Nickel.

>

---

[53] *Szilvasy v. Reliance Home Comfort*, 2012 ONCA 821 considering Consumer Protection Act, 2002, S.O. 2002, c. C-30, Sch. A, s. 9.

[54] See *Cooke v. CKOY Ltd.* (1963), 39 D.L.R. (2d) 209; *Shaw Cablesystems (Manitoba) Ltd. v. Canadian Legion Memorial Housing Foundation (Manitoba)* (1997), 143 D.L.R. (4th) 193.

Nickel served notice on Safeway, demanding possession of the leased space, claiming that Safeway had failed to comply with the implied term to use the leased premises "only as a supermarket" and for no other purpose. It stated that "vacancy by design" was not the kind of use intended. Safeway defended by stating that there was no term in the lease expressly requiring it to keep operating its supermarket or prohibiting it from leaving the space vacant during the lease.

The Court of Appeal agreed with Nickel and held that there was an implied term in the lease that the space would be continuously used as a supermarket. It stated:

A lessee which effectively shuts down half of a shopping centre and fundamentally alters the original concept cannot, absent very unequivocal language, unilaterally alter the arrangement between the landlord and the tenant which had been followed through the entire term of the lease . . . there must be "continuous use" as a supermarket, and that promise does not include the right to intentionally maintain and renew long-term "non-use."[55]

In this case we can see how far the court would go when it found the conduct of Safeway to be clearly contrary to the intention of both parties in signing the contract.

Strategies to Manage the Legal Risks

Written documents are the best way to prove the existence of a contract, and it should be standard business practice to create written contracts. The first step toward managing the legal risks associated with oral and written contracts is to determine what legislative requirements are applicable to the particular business. This involves familiarity not only with the legislation applicable to the subject matter of the business transaction, such as land development or funeral services, but also with legislation governing the sales and marketing strategy employed to form the contract, such as internet or direct sales. Multiple statutes may apply, and the written contract must comply with all regulations in order to be enforceable.

The best way to ensure that terms advantageous to the business are enforceable against a consumer is through the use of a detailed standard form contract that meets the requirements of consumer protection legislation. Careful, consistent choice of language with clear, unambiguous meaning will avoid interpretation problems later. The consumer protection approach adopted by most provinces is to require disclosure first and allow a revocation period after the written document is signed. In this way, disclosure requirements actually help businesses bind consumers to onerous terms.

An oral agreement can be fortified with follow-up emails that confirm the terms after the fact. This subsequent behaviour can remedy defects caught by the Statute of Frauds and may be helpful to a court when determining the meaning of what was expressly agreed upon.

There are a number of strategies for reducing interpretation disputes:

- Incorporate a definition section into a contract, explaining the meaning of key words, and then be consistent with the use of those words throughout the contract.

- Begin the contract with a statement of the purpose of the agreement; this will help the court when interpreting and implying terms.

- Save pre-contract memos, emails, and the like (parol evidence) for assistance in the interpretation of the terms of the written contract.

- Include an "entirety" clause in the contract that states that the contract contains the whole agreement and no separate oral or implied terms exist. This will invoke the parol evidence rule and limit a court's power to imply terms. The clause should specifically reference subsequent oral agreements if those are to be excluded as well.[56]

---

[55] *Nickel Developments Ltd. v. Canada Safeway Ltd.* (2001), 199 D.L.R. (4th) 629.

[56] *Turner v. Visscher Holdings Inc.* (1996), 23 B.C.L.R. (3d) 303 (C.A.).

- Include a "severability" clause that allows a court to cut out an ambiguous term for which the meaning is not clear without destroying the entire contract.
- Prepare standard form contracts ahead of time for use in simple deals—these can include all of the aforesaid terms.
- Refer customers to standard terms and conditions on websites that provide detailed information.
- Request clarification of language included in an offer if it is vague prior to acceptance.
- Naturally, legal assistance in the drafting of a contract will avoid some pitfalls.

QUESTIONS FOR REVIEW

1. Distinguish among the different outcomes for contracts that are unenforceable, voidable, and void.

2. What are the consequences of failure to comply with consumer protection legislation as opposed to the Statute of Frauds or Sale of Goods Act?

3. Explain the difference between a guarantee and an indemnity. Is there any policy basis for treating the two differently?

4. What is the difference between part performance and part payment?

5. State which of the following contracts are affected by a statutory requirement that would permit the promisor to plead that the contract cannot be enforced against her because evidence of the terms is not available in the required form:

   a. A and B, having entered into a written agreement as purchaser and vendor, respectively, of a piece of land, later agree by telephone to call off the sale.

   b. C enters into an oral contract with D, a contractor, to build a house for C.

   c. E is the proprietor of a business that requires a bank loan. E's father, F, tells the bank manager that if the bank approves the loan and E does not repay it, he (F) will.

   d. G, just before she graduates from university, accepts a job at a manufacturing firm. In the exchange of letters between G and her employer, nothing is said about the duration of G's employment or the need to actually graduate.

6. Give an example of when a party to an unenforceable contract may nevertheless recover money he has paid to the other party.

7. Why does a dictionary definition of a word not always clarify its meaning in a contract? Give an example.

8. Explain and give an example of special usage of a word.

9. What are the primary goals of a court in interpreting a contract?

10. Name four ways in which a party may persuade a court that the parol evidence rule does not apply to the term or terms it asserts were part of the contract.

11. What is an implied term? Give an example from question 5 above.

12. When a contract is subject to a condition precedent, does the contract nevertheless still exist? May either party simply withdraw from the contract before the condition precedent has been met? Again, consider question 5 above.

CASES AND PROBLEMS

1. Continuing Scenario

   Before opening her restaurant, Ashley contacted O'Brien's Food Service Ltd. to be her frozen poultry supplier. Because she was new to the business and her volume would be low, O'Brien's quoted her a price of $25.00 per case of frozen chicken breasts. Adam, O'Brien's salesman, told her in an email that the price was only $20 per case for restaurants that ordered more than three cases a week. Ashley could not be sure she would need this much chicken, so she proceeded on the initial quote. The next day, Adam stopped by the restaurant with the customer application form describing the price as "as quoted" and told Ashley that because she had no history in the business, he needed a guarantor for her account. Jim, Ashley's father, was at the restaurant that day painting the dining room. Jim overheard Adam's request and volunteered to be the guarantor. He gave Adam his personal information to insert into the application form. Ashley signed the form, which stated that "upon acceptance by O'Brien's the application and corresponding terms and conditions would form the entire agreement between the parties."

At the end of Ashley's first year of business, she reviewed her chicken volume and discovered that she was ordering at least four cases or more each week. However, she was still being charged $25.00 per case. When she contacted Adam about this, he said there was no agreement to reduce her price. Ashley was angry and responded that she would not be paying this week's $320.00 bill and that would even up the amount. Adam threatened to sue her father if Ashley refused to pay. What rules of writing and interpretation are raised in this question? How will the court decide what price is a term of the contract? Will Jim be liable for this week's bill?

2. On January 15, Tonino and Logan signed a lease in which Logan agreed to rent her commercial office space to Tonino at $2000 per month for three years, commencing February 1. Tonino took possession as agreed. In March of the same year, Tonino and Logan agreed orally that Tonino would pay an additional $250 per month in rent upon the completion of some alterations and repairs to the premises within three months. Logan completed the alterations and repairs in April, but Tonino refused to pay anything but the $2000 a month specified in the lease. In August, Logan sued Tonino for the additional rent.

What points must the court settle in reaching its decision, and what should the decision be?

3. M, N, O, and P each owned 25 percent of the shares in Resort Hotel Inc. As a result of a bad season, the hotel had a cash-flow problem. M arranged to borrow $25 000 from a friend, Q, and to lend it to the hotel on condition that if the hotel did not repay the funds, his three co-owners, N, O, and P, would each pay $5000 to M. The three agreed to the arrangement. Subsequently, the hotel defaulted and M repaid the $25 000 to Q. He requested payment from N, O, and P but they refused to pay.

M sued the three for $5000 each; they defended claiming that their promises were "guarantees," and since they were not in writing they were unenforceable. M claimed that their obligations were part of a larger transaction to protect their shared interests in Resort Hotel and, therefore, were not mere guarantees. Whose argument should succeed? Give reasons.

4. The manager of Jiffy Discount Stores ordered a carload of refrigerators from Colonel Electric Company by telephone. When the refrigerators arrived at the warehouse, the transport employees and Jiffy's employees began unloading them. When about half of them were unloaded, the manager arrived and asked to examine one. An employee uncrated one refrigerator, and after looking it over, the manager stated it was not the right model and ordered the transport employees to take them back. The refrigerators were returned to Colonel Electric Company, and the company sued Jiffy Discount Stores for breach of contract. It was proven that the manager was mistaken, and the refrigerators did conform to the telephone order. What legislation applies here? Explain what the result should be.

5. Carter left a position where he was earning $48 000 a year to accept a position as general manager of Buildwell Limited at the same annual salary. All negotiations leading up to his appointment were carried on orally between Carter and Webster, the president of Buildwell Limited. Both parties assured each other in various conversations that the employment would last "for life"; they agreed that each year Carter would receive a bonus, and that if he was not satisfied with it, he could terminate his employment, but that the company could not terminate his employment unless he "did something wrong."

Over the succeeding few years, Carter's salary was increased from $4000 to $5000 per month, and he received, in addition, annual bonuses of up to $4000. A letter to Carter announcing his last bonus was signed by both the president and vice-president of the company and included the words, "And we want you to know that with all the experiences we are going through in connection with the business, your efforts are appreciated."

Shortly afterward, Webster died, and immediately the company dismissed Carter without explanation, paying him one month's salary. Carter then attempted to go into business for himself but without success. He sued Buildwell Limited for wrongful dismissal, claiming breach of his employment contract. Can Buildwell Limited successfully plead the Statute of Frauds?

6. In February, Baldwin Co. Ltd., a woollens manufacturer, contracted to sell 500 pieces of blue serge to Martin Bros., tailors, at a price of $40 000, as stated in a written memorandum signed by both parties. After 220 pieces of the cloth had been delivered, a dispute arose between the parties: Martin Bros. complained of delay in delivery, and Baldwin Co. Ltd. complained of failure to pay for the goods delivered. Baldwin Co. Ltd. sued Martin Bros. for the price of the goods delivered, and Martin Bros. counterclaimed for damages for non-delivery.

In August, before the case came to trial, the parties orally agreed to a settlement and to substitute for the original contract a new one in which Martin Bros. would have an additional three months to pay for the goods and have an option of buying the remaining 280 pieces at the prices in the earlier contract. The following November, Martin Bros. paid the amount due on the original 220 pieces of cloth and placed an order for the remaining 280 pieces under the option agreed to in the substituted contract. Baldwin Co. Ltd. refused to deliver these pieces, the agreed price being no longer profitable to them. Martin Bros. then sued Baldwin Co. Ltd. for damages for breach of contract (failure to deliver). Should this action succeed?

7. John Brown, a retired widower, said to Mrs. Adele Barber that if he could find a suitable house and if she would move into it as a housekeeper, help operate it as a rooming house, and take care of him, he would give her the house on his death. Mrs. Barber agreed. Mr. Brown purchased a house that he operated as a rooming house until his death five years later. During this period Mrs. Barber served as housekeeper; she prepared the necessary food, and made other household purchases, always turning over to Mr. Brown the balance of the board money received from the tenants. She received no remuneration for her services other than her own board and an occasional allowance for clothing.

Mr. Brown made no provision in his will for Mrs. Barber, and following his death Mrs. Barber brought an action against the executors of his estate for specific performance of his promise. In evidence, Mrs. Barber offered the testimony of her two daughters, her son, and her son-in-law, who were present at the time of the original conversation between her and Mr. Brown. The executor contested the action. What legal considerations are relevant to a decision in this case? State whether Mrs. Barber's action would succeed.

8. Provinco Grain Inc. was in the business of selling seeds and buying and reselling the crops grown from the seeds sold. Its sales manager approached Quinlan, a farmer in the Lower Fraser Valley in British Columbia, to grow an early crop of buckwheat for the Japanese market. Quinlan, an experienced farmer, was interested because it would be a valuable market. However, he had never grown the crop before and said he was worried about weeds; he understood they could be a serious problem. The sales manager replied that he need not worry—the buckwheat would smother any weeds. Quinlan bought seeds and signed a printed document stating that Provinco Grain Inc. gave no warranty as to "the productiveness or any other matter pertaining to the seed . . . and will not in any way be responsible for the crop."

Quinlan planted the seeds but weeds destroyed the crop and he suffered a substantial loss. He sued Provinco for damages on the basis that the sales manager's statement was a collateral warranty and a deliberate, material misrepresentation. With regard to the misrepresentation, the court found that the sales manager believed it to be true: he came from Saskatchewan where buckwheat did indeed suppress the weeds. Provinco further defended by claiming that the signed contract exempted it from all liability pertaining to the seeds and subsequent crop. Accordingly, any statement on this subject by the sales manager would be excluded by the parol evidence rule.

In reply, Quinlan's lawyer claimed that the sales manager's warranty was about the risk of weeds, and it did not contradict the terms of the signed contract pertaining to the seed itself. It was on the basis of that warranty that Quinlan signed the contract.

Give your view of each party's position and what the likely result would be.

9. Chénier sold the surface and minerals in her land in Alberta for $104 000 to Werner under an agreement for sale (an installment sale that reserved Chénier's ownership in the property until a specified amount of the price was paid). Werner defaulted payment, giving Chénier the right to recover possession by court action. Chénier started proceedings, but they were not yet complete when it became apparent that the land was very valuable. Werner entered into a petroleum and natural gas lease with Imperial Oil Ltd. and received a cash bonus of $110 000, which he intended to use to settle his debt to Chénier. At about the same time, Chénier, anticipating the recovery of her property by court order, entered into a similar lease of the same property with California Standard Oil Co. At the time Chénier gave her lease to California Standard Oil Co., she told the company's agent that her ability to lease the property depended upon winning her court action against Werner and that she could give the lease only if the company's agent gave her a signed statement acknowledging that she (Chénier) did not have any right to lease the mineral rights until the court action against Werner went through. The agent gave her a statement to that effect, and Chénier and California Standard Oil Co. entered into a lease of the mineral rights that made no reference to the statement signed by the company's agent and also contained a paragraph stating that the lease contained the whole of the agreement.

Werner tendered the balance of the purchase price to Chénier, but she refused it and proceeded with the court action. The court dismissed Chénier's petition for recovery of the property. She was, therefore, unable to lease the property to California Standard Oil Co. and that company sued her for breach of contract. Should the action succeed?

Additional Resources for Chapter 10 on the Companion Website

(www.pearsoncanada.ca/smyth)

In addition to pre- and post-tests, mini-cases, and application exercises, the Companion Website includes the following province-specific resources for Chapter 10:

- **Alberta:** Fair Trading Act; Consumer Protections Acts, Statute of Frauds; Implied Terms; Legislation Interpretation
- **Atlantic Provinces:** Landlord and Tenant; Statute of Frauds; International Sale of Goods Act; Interpretation Act
- **British Columbia:** Conveyance of Land; Electronic Transactions; Form of Contract; Terms Implied by Statute
- **Manitoba/Saskatchewan:** Statute of Frauds; Statutory Requirements for Written Contracts; Sale of Goods Act; Implied Terms
- **Ontario:** Consumer Protection Act (2002); Sale of Goods Act; Statute of Frauds; Credibility; Exemption Clauses; Implied Terms; Interpretation Act

Chapter 11

Privity of Contract and the Assignment of Contractual Rights

A contract creates rights and duties between the parties who enter into the agreement; the rights may have an economic value that one party wishes to transfer to an outsider—a person who was not a party to the contract. Or a party may wish to arrange for her duties under the contract to be performed by another person.

In this chapter we look at how the law of contracts accommodates these important needs, and we examine such questions as:

- Who can enforce the obligations described in a contract?

- What are the legal consequences of an outsider performing a party's obligations under a contract?

- How are trusts used to create rights for an outsider to a contract?

- In what other circumstances or special types of contracts do outsiders have the right to enforce a contract?

- How may contractual rights be transferred to an outsider, and what are the consequences?

- What are negotiable instruments, and why are they important in business?

PRIVITY OF CONTRACT

The Limited Scope of Contractual Rights and Duties

When parties make a contract, they create a small body of law for themselves. It seems reasonable that the scope of a contract—its power to affect behaviour— should be confined to the parties who agreed to it. A person outside the contract, who did not agree to its terms, should not have rights or duties under it.

This reasoning seems sound and represents the general rule of contract law. However, sometimes situations arise where justice or business convenience require that a contract affect the rights of people outside it. In the law of contract, a person who is not a party to a contract is called a **third party**, or sometimes an outsider or stranger to the contract. In this chapter, we explore the effect contracts have on third parties.

third party a person who is not one of the parties to a contract but is affected by it

The general rule is that a contract does not give any benefits to or impose any obligations on a stranger to the contract. To win a contract lawsuit, the plaintiff must prove **privity of contract** with the defendant—that is, he must show that they are both parties to the same contract.

privity of contract the relationship that exists between parties to a contract

---

ILLUSTRATION 11.1

A, a carpenter, owes $4000 to B. A offers to renovate C's kitchen if C promises to pay off A's debt to B. C accepts the offer, and A completes the renovation. A and B have a contract; A and C have a contract; but B and C have no contract with each other. As a third party to the contract for renovation, B cannot enforce C's promise to pay the debt; there is no privity of contract between them.[1] Consequently, if C fails to pay B, B cannot sue C, but may still sue A for the debt A owes her; A may then sue C for his failure to carry out his promise to pay B, and will recover damages of $4000 plus any costs he suffered as a result of B suing him. This result is an application of the privity of contract rule and is illustrated in Figure 11.1.

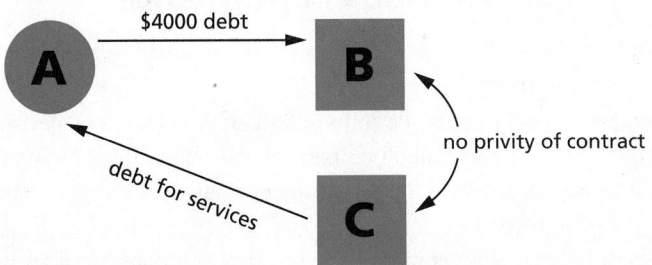

Figure 11.1 Privity and Consideration

Another reason for preventing a third person from suing on a contract is that the third party has not given consideration for the promise. Suppose in Illustration 11.1 that B also signed the contract between A and C to renovate the kitchen. There would now be privity of contract between B and C because C would have made his promise of payment to B as well as to A. However, B still could not sue C because she would not have given consideration for C's promise. Not only must consideration for a promise be given by a party to the contract, but it must be given by the party seeking to enforce the promise. As we saw in Chapter 6, signing the contract under seal could solve B's problem.

The privity of contract rule can have harsh consequences when it prevents a third person from enforcing a contract when the whole object was to benefit him. Therefore a number of exceptions have developed over time to diminish the reach of the rule. In fact, tort law developed as an exception to the privity of contract rule.

---

[1] *Price v. Easton* (1883), 110 E.R. 518.

Comparison with Rights and Duties in Tort

Liability of Sellers of Goods
We saw in Chapter 10 that a consumer who purchases goods from a retailer receives the benefit of an implied term that the goods are reasonably suited for the purpose for which they are sold. If a person buys a can of salmon that turns out to be poisonous and that seriously harms her, she may successfully sue the retailer for breach of the implied term that the fish was suitable to eat. But members of her family could not sue for breach of contract because the contract of sale was with the buyer, and only she can sue successfully for breach of contract. Other members of the family have no privity of contract with the merchant and no rights under the contract. However, they may be able to sue in tort, and New Brunswick has passed legislation that gives the user of a consumer product a right to sue the seller.[2] As well, Canada's Consumer Product Safety Act imposes some duties on sellers that could trigger tort liability.[3]

Liability of Manufacturers
As we saw in Chapter 4, although members of the family have few rights against the retailer, the manufacturer may well be liable for negligence. The tort duty of care extends well beyond the parties to the contract to include those persons that a reasonable person could foresee as likely being harmed. The buyer, too, may sue in tort since she has no contract with the manufacturer.[4] In perhaps the most famous case of the 20th century, *Donoghue v. Stevenson*,[5] the House of Lords decided that manufacturers are liable in tort to the consumer for damages caused by their defective products. As noted above, New Brunswick's Consumer Product Warranty and Liability Act and Canada's Consumer Product Safety Act extend product liability throughout the distribution chain.

Builders, engineers, architects, and designers owe a similar tort duty of care to subsequent owners and occupants of the buildings they build.[6] Their tort liability also extends beyond the parties to the original building contract. As these examples show, tort liability fills a void left by the application of the privity of contract rule.

Tort Liability and Vicarious Performance

Sometimes a business takes on more work than it can complete or a job requires more specialized skills than it has. In these circumstances, the business may hire a "subcontractor" to complete the excess or specialized work on its behalf. This is **vicarious performance**—finding a third party to perform someone else's contractual obligations. However, the original promisor cannot escape contractual liability for performance of its own contractual obligations by sending a substitute.

vicarious performance a third party performs contractual obligations on behalf of the promisor who remains responsible for proper performance

Vicarious performance is acceptable provided that the contract does not specify personal performance.[7] As in Illustration 11.2, whether a party is expected to perform personally or whether she may employ someone to perform vicariously might not always be clear.

---

[2] Consumer Product Warranty and Liability Act, S.N.B. 1978, c. C-18.1.

[3] Consumer Product Safety Act, S.C. 2010, c. 21, ss. 6, 7.

[4] Liability for "breach of implied collateral warranty" is sometimes imposed when a representation rises to the level of a warranty: see *Shanklin Pier Ltd. v. Detel Products, Ltd.*, [1952] 2 K.B. 854; See also *Cummings v. Ford Motor Co. of Canada*, [1984] O.J. No. 43; *Murray v. Sperry Rand Corp. et al.* (1979), 23 O.R. (2d) 456, 96 D.L.R. (3d) 113; for contrary, see *Olsen v. Behr Process Corporation*, [2003] B.C.J. No. 627.

[5] [1932] A.C. 562. Recently, the Supreme Court of Canada reiterated its acceptance of the manufacturer duty of care: *Mustapha v. Culligan of Canada Ltd.*, 2008 S.C.C. 27 at para. 6.

[6] *Winnipeg Condominium Corporation No. 36 v. Bird Construction Co. Ltd.*, [1995] 1 S.C.R. 85 at 121.

[7] As we shall see in Chapter 27, corporations have no physical existence—personal performance is not possible, so all contracts with them must be carried out by their agents or employees.

ILLUSTRATION 11.2

A Co. contracts with a public accountant, B, to have its accounts audited. B sends C, a senior accountant, to carry out the audit program. May A Co. object? This is a type of work that can be carried out competently by a qualified accountant and ordinarily would not require B's personal performance unless A Co. had expressly bargained for it. Consequently, the vicarious performance by C is permissible, and A Co. is not entitled to reject the tender of such performance.

Although the third party to the contract who takes over performance does not face contractual liability, he or she may face tort liability. If an employee commits a tort such as negligence while vicariously performing a contract for his employer, the injured party may sue both the employer for vicarious liability and the employee personally in tort. Since the employer ordinarily has "deeper pockets" than its employee, the injured party almost always sues the employer, but may sue the employee as well, in case the court should find that the employer is not liable because the damage did not occur in the course of employment. Therefore, an employer remains liable for defects in vicarious performance not only in contract but also in tort. For more information on this topic, see the Companion Website.

ILLUSTRATION 11.3

Suppose that in Illustration 11.2 above, C does such an inadequate job that he fails to detect a material error in the accounts, and, as a result, A Co. suffers a loss. A Co. must look to B for damages for breach of contract. However, if C's poor work amounted to negligence, C would be personally liable to A Co. in tort, and B would also be vicariously liable in tort for C's negligence.

As will be discussed later in this chapter,[8] an exemption clause contained in the contract, if properly drafted, could protect a third party facing tort liability for vicarious performance.[9] Employers often protect themselves from tort and contractual liability by placing an **exemption clause** in a contract. Such a clause restricts the application of the privity of contract rule as it prevents a party with privity from enforcing the terms of the contract and may extend protection beyond the parties to a contract.

exemption clause a clause in a contract that exempts or limits the liability of a party

ILLUSTRATION 11.4

Some exemption clauses exclude all liability while others limit a party's liability to a fixed amount. An example of an exemption clause excluding liability is as follows:

> The purchaser agrees that the company, its officers, employees, and agents shall not be liable for any claim, demand, cause of action, damage, harm, loss, or injury whatsoever, whether in contract or tort, arising from any activities carried out in furtherance of the performance of this contract.

An example of a clause limiting liability to a fixed amount is as follows:

> The liability of the airline, its agents, and employees for any claim, whether in tort or contract, arising from the loss, delay or damage of baggage is limited to $50 per bag.

---

[8] For further discussion of the effect of exemption clauses, see "The Principled Exception" in this chapter and discussion in Chapter 13.

[9] *London Drugs v. Kuehne & Nagel International* (1992), 97 D.L.R. (4th) 261. See also *Kirby v. Amalgamated Income Limited Partnership*, [2009] B.C.J. No. 1555; *M.A.N.B. & W. Diesel v. Kingsway Transports Ltd.* (1997), 33 O.R. (3d) 355.

EXCEPTIONS TO THE PRIVITY OF CONTRACT RULES

Trusts

What Is a Trust?   Suppose a mother wishes to provide financial security for her son in case she dies while he is a child. In her will, she sets aside money to be invested and directs that the income be used to care for her son. The fund will require someone to look after it—that is, to invest it and to pay money out for the child's care. The fund is called a **trust**; the person—or perhaps a trust company—who looks after the fund is called a **trustee**. A trust has been defined as "any arrangement whereby property is transferred with the intention that it be administered by a trustee for another's benefit."[10] In this definition and in the above example, the trust is created by the transfer of property to the trustee in the will for the benefit of the child.

What if, after the mother dies, the trustee refuses to pay out any income for the benefit of the child? We know that the trust fund was set up by the mother for the child's benefit and not for that of the trustee. What rights has the child as **beneficiary** of the trust? Although under common law rules the trustee becomes the legal owner of the trust, the rules of equity recognize that the son has an interest: He is the fund's true owner—the **beneficial owner**—and equity has developed procedures by which a beneficiary may compel a trustee to carry out its duties under the **trust agreement** even though the beneficiary is a third party. A trust may be created not only in a will (on death) but in any agreement that conveys property to a trustee on the understanding that it will be used for the benefit of a third-party beneficiary.

The trust concept has important applications in business. For example, income trusts are a form of business association where the business transfers its assets to a trustee for the benefit of the unit holders. Unit holders must be able to compel the trustee to comply with the terms of the trust. Income trusts will be discussed in Chapter 24.

A trust is created by operation of law when the creditors of a business convince the court that their debtor is no longer capable of paying its debts as they fall due. The court will order that the property of the bankrupt debtor be transferred to a trustee in bankruptcy who will sell the assets and distribute the proceeds to the creditors.

How Trusts Affect Third Parties: Constructive Trusts   How is the concept of a trust related to contracts and the rights of third parties? The beneficiary of a trust is a third party to the trust agreement (contract). The beneficiary is neither the person who created the trust nor the person who is appointed to administer it; yet, the rules of equity allow the beneficiary to enforce the terms of the trust.

Sometimes the contract containing the promise is not expressly described as a trust, and the promise may be only one part of a larger deal. In some circumstances, equity recognizes that a person holding property is really a trustee, and that others are entitled to a share of the property. A trust of this kind is called a **resulting trust** or a **constructive trust**.[11] When a court accepts this argument, the restrictions of the privity of contract rule do not apply.

---

trust   an arrangement that transfers property to a person who administers it for the benefit of another person

trustee   a person or company who administers a trust

beneficiary   a person who is entitled to the benefits of a trust or the person entitled to receive insurance monies

beneficial owner   a person who, although not the legal owner, may compel the trustee to provide benefits to him

trust agreement   the document that conveys property to a trustee to be used for the benefit of a third-party beneficiary

resulting trust   a trust relationship recognized when the conduct of the parties demonstrates the intention to hold property for the benefit of the other

constructive trust   a trust relationship imposed by the court to prevent a party from being unjustly enriched by keeping property that should benefit another

---

CASE 11.1

A, B, and C entered into a partnership agreement, a term of which stated that if one of the partners should die, his widow would receive a share of the future profits of the firm. When A died, the surviving partners refused to pay a share of the profits to A's widow. Would she be successful in enforcing the term?

These facts are based on *Re Flavell*,[12] where the court held that while the widow was not a party to the partnership agreement, that agreement had created a trust in her favour. It decided that her husband, as promisee of the term in the partnership agreement, had become a trustee of her interest. On his death, his executor became the trustee in his place, and the executor was successful in obtaining the share for the widow.

---

[10] *Black's Law Dictionary*, 8th ed. (St. Paul, MN: West Publishing, 2004). Reprinted with permission of Thomson Reuters.

[11] *Kerr v. Baranow* 2011 SCC 10, [2011] 1 S.C.R. 269, para. 2

[12] (1883), 25 Ch. D. 89. For an interesting later case, see *Beswick v. Beswick*, [1968] A.C. 58.

Unfortunately, parties to a contract are not likely to be aware of the subtleties of a resulting or constructive trust, nor are they likely to create a trust expressly to ensure that a third-party beneficiary will have rights enforceable in court.[13] As a result, the principles of resulting or constructive trust are not a reliable means for avoiding the privity of contract rule. For more information on this topic, see the Companion Website.

Insurance

Typically, in a contract (or policy) of life insurance, a person pays a premium in exchange for a promise from the insurance company to pay a sum of money on his or her death to a specified person—a spouse, say—who is not a party to the insurance contract. Each province has a statute that gives a beneficiary the right to force the insurance company to pay out the contract.[14] Similarly, in a contract of automobile insurance, the company may promise to indemnify not only the owner but also anyone driving with his consent. If a person driving with consent injures a pedestrian and is required to pay damages, she may in turn sue the insurance company to recover her loss, even though she was not a party to the insurance contract.[15]

The Undisclosed Principal

A further exception to the rule requiring privity of contract occurs when one of the contracting parties, unknown to the other, proves to be an agent of someone else: The person for whom the agent was acting, known as an **undisclosed principal**, may sue or be sued on the contract. The subject is discussed more fully in Chapter 17.

> **undisclosed principal** a contracting party who, unknown to the other party, is represented by an agent

Contracts Concerning Land

The rules of privity of contract do not apply in land law. People who acquire an interest in land are subject to the rights and obligations created in earlier contracts that are recorded on the public record. This is true even though the new owner is not a party to the previous contracts. For example, if the owner of land leases it to a tenant who promises to pay rent and keep the property in good repair, and the owner then sells it, the tenant must perform the promises for the new owner. The value of the land on the market would be substantially lowered if the tenant could ignore promises made to the former owner. Similarly, the new owner must respect the tenant's rights to remain on the property until the lease expires. Otherwise, tenants would always be in jeopardy of being evicted when land is sold. Land law will be discussed in Chapters 21, 22, and 23. For more information on this topic, see the Companion Website.

Express Language in the Contract: Enurement Clause

An **enurement clause** in a contract extends rights under the contract—typically it says that the contract will "bind" or "enure to the benefit" of successors, assigns, or heirs. Such a clause could be used to justify "relaxing" the privity of contract rule so that the identified third parties listed in the clause may enforce the rights under the contract.[16] As this type of clause is very common, such an interpretation significantly alters the privity rule. For more information on this topic, see the Companion Website.

> **enurement clause** a clause in a contract that extends the rights and benefits to those inheriting from a party, succeeding the party, or taking an assignment from a party

---

[13] Courts find it difficult to infer an intention to create a trust when the party to the contract has died.

[14] See, for example, Insurance Act, R.S.O. 1990 c. I.8, s. 195; R.S.B.C. 1996, c. 206, s. 53; R.S.N.S. 1989, c. 231, s. 197.

[15] See, for example, Insurance Act, R.S.O. 1990, c. I.8, s. 239; Insurance (Vehicle) Act, R.S.B.C. 2012, c. 1, s. 29, 127.

[16] *Brown v. Belleville (City)* 2013 ONCA 148

In 1953, a municipal storm drain was built on the property of a farmer and the municipality agreed to maintain and repair the drain as needed. The agreement was registered on the title to the land, but after six years the maintenance stopped. The farmer died and the property was resold many times until the Browns became owners in 2003. The municipality had also merged with the City of Belleville. The Browns could not get the City of Belleville to fix the storm drain so they sued in 2011. Belleville claimed (among other things) that the Browns lacked privity of contract and could not enforce the agreement as they were not parties to it; in fact, neither was the City of Belleville. The Ontario Court of Appeal held that the Browns could sue. There was a clause in the agreement stating that the agreement was binding on and for the benefit of the parties "and their respective heirs, administrators, successors, and assigns." The Browns were the "successor" owners of the property who, according to the term of the contract, were intended to benefit from the agreement. This clause justified "relaxing" the privity of contract rule. The City of Belleville was also a successor of the local municipality.[17]

The Principled Exception—Exemption Clauses Typical exemption clauses limit the liability of a party to the contract for damages arising in both breach of contract and tort. When the parties to the contract intend, an exemption clause may also extend that protection to third parties, including agents, employees, subcontractors, consultants, directors, officers, and others involved in the performance of the contract. In this way an exemption clause protects the business from liability for its own breach of contract or negligence, plus any vicarious liability for the torts of employees or other third parties. In 1992, the Supreme Court of Canada defined this exception and identified two criteria that will determine if a third party may rely on contractual provisions to protect it from liability.[18] Two questions are asked:

1. Did the parties to the contract intend to extend the protection to the third party claiming it?
2. Are the activities of the third party within the scope of the contract generally, and the exemption clause in particular.[19]

If the intention of the parties is to extend protection to the particular third party, and the type of work is part of the contract performance and within the scope of the clause, the exemption clause will protect the third party from liability. Application of this exception will vary depending upon the facts of each case.

London Drugs contracted with Kuehne & Nagel to store a new piece of equipment worth $7500. The standard form storage contract contained an exemption clause limiting liability to $40 per item damaged. Two employees of Kuehne & Nagel dropped the piece of equipment. London Drugs sued Kuhne & Nagel and both employees. The Supreme Court held that the employees were also protected by the contract's exemption clause. The language of the standard form contract was intended to apply to employees, and the employees were acting in the course of employment.[20]

principled exception allows third parties to rely upon a contractual exemption clause when the parties to the contract intended to include them, and their activities come within the scope of the contract and the exemption clause

This exception to the privity rule is sometimes called the **principled exception**, and it was developed because courts felt that the privity of contract rule should not stand in the way of commercial reality and justice.[21]

---

[17] *Ibid.*, at paras. 80–111.

[18] *Fraser River Pile & Dredge Ltd. v. Can-Dive Services Ltd.* (1999), 176 D.L.R. (4th) 257.

[19] *Ibid.* at para. 32.

[20] *London Drugs, supra,* n. 9.

[21] *Ibid.* at 126.

Exceptions to the privity of contract principle allow some non-parties to enforce the obligations of a contract. In most of Canada, these exceptions are limited to specific types of contracts or specific clauses with identified non-party beneficiaries. As noted earlier, insurance contracts and trust agreements are such exceptions. In Case 11.3,[22] the Supreme Court of Canada extended the protection of contractual exemption clauses to non-parties identified by the exemption clause, and the Ontario Court of Appeal allowed successors to sue to enforce a contract in *Brown v. City of Belleville*.[23]

Some jurisdictions have made sweeping changes to the privity of contract rule. New Brunswick's privity of contract rules were first changed with the passage of the Consumer Product Warranty and Liability Act in 1978.[24] Then, in 1994, the privity rule was completely abolished in favour of the identified beneficiary concept: Section 4(1) of the Law Reform Act reads:

> A person who is not a party to a contract but who is identified by or under the contract as being intended to receive some performance or forbearance under it may, unless the contract provides otherwise, enforce that performance or forbearance by a claim for damages or otherwise.[25]

In the United States, an intended beneficiary's right to sue has been recognized since 1859. In *Lawrence v. Fox*,[26] Fox promised Halley that he would pay Halley's debt. When Fox failed to make the payment, the New York Court of Appeal allowed the unpaid creditor (Lawrence) to sue Fox directly.

In 1999, England enacted the Contracts (Rights of Third Parties) Act 1999,[27] which allows non-parties to enforce any contractual obligation if the contract benefits them or specifically authorizes them to do so. Similar legislation exists in Australia and New Zealand.

Questions to Consider

1. Should all provinces abandon the privity of contract rule in favour of a third-party beneficiary rule?

2. Should the law make a distinction between an intended beneficiary and an incidental beneficiary?

3. Should the law make a distinction between defendants and plaintiffs?

Sources: R.L. Miller and G.A. Jentz, *Business Law Today*, standard ed., 7th ed. (Florence, KY: South-Western College/West, 2006) at 325–44; J. Edelman, "Taking Promises Seriously" (2007) 45(3) *Canadian Business Law Journal* 399–413; Karl Dore, New Brunswick's Consumer Products Liability Legislation, http://dspace.hil.unb.ca:8080/handle/1882/68

ASSIGNMENT OF RIGHTS

Sometimes one party is not willing to wait for the other party to perform the contract and wants to receive his or her benefit immediately. The party may need money now. In such cases, the impatient party may transfer the unperformed right or benefit of the contract to a third party who is willing to wait for performance. This is known as an *assignment* and is an important exception to the privity of contract rule.

The Nature of an Assignment

Businesses often make use of assignments to secure financing from a lender by assigning the right to collect their accounts receivable to the lender in exchange for credit now. Only rights or benefits may be assigned, not contractual obligations or liabilities. Assignments usually involve two contracts: The first contract creates the unperformed right, which is subsequently assigned to a third party in the second contract.

---

[22] *Ibid.*; *London Drugs*, *supra*, n. 9.

[23] *Brown*, *supra* n. 16.

[24] *Supra*, n. 3. This Act entitled non-parties to sue for breach of the statutory warranties implied into a contract of sale. The exception is not limited to consumers but includes any organization involved in the chain of distribution, such as retailers, wholesalers, and importers.

[25] Law Reform Act, R.S.N.B. 2011, c. 184, s. 4(1).

[26] 20 N.Y. 268 (1859).

[27] 1999, c.31 (Eng.)

A Ltd., a building contractor, has just completed a building for B. Under the terms of their building contract, B still owes A Ltd. $10 000, to be paid one month after the completion of the building. In a second contract, A Ltd. purchases $12 000 worth of materials from X Corp. In exchange for the materials, A Ltd. agrees to pay $2000 in cash and assigns to X Corp. the rights to the $10 000 still owing to A Ltd. under the building contract. As a result, X Corp. collects the $10 000 directly from B when the debt falls due.

assignor   a party that assigns its rights under a contract to a third party

assignee   a third party to whom rights under a contract have been assigned

assignment   the transfer by a party of its unperformed rights under a contract to a third party

In Illustration 11.5, the contractor A Ltd. is the **assignor** of its right to payment of $10 000 from B, the promisor in the building contract. A Ltd. assigns the right to payment to X Corp., a third party to the building contract but the **assignee** in the materials contract. The materials contract is an **assignment**. Provided B receives notice of the assignment, then B must perform for the assignee X Corp. instead of for the original party, A Ltd. X Corp. now stands in the place of A Ltd.

Contractual rights are valuable and are considered a type of personal property. The $10 000 still owing under the building contract in Illustration 11.5 is an example of this form of intangible personal property. Its value is obvious. Intangible property differs from tangible property, such as jewellery or furniture, which may be possessed physically. Tangible property has a concrete existence, whereas a right to demand performance of a contract has no concrete existence—it is valuable only because it is enforceable in the courts. The rights to intangible property—to things that have value only because they may be enforced by action in the courts—are called **choses in action**. The unpaid $10 000 in Illustration 11.5 is a chose in action. The rights to tangible property that may be possessed physically are known as **choses in possession**. There are many types of choses in action, including patents, copyrights, stocks, bonds, funds deposited in a bank account, rights to collect the proceeds of an insurance policy, rights of action against persons who have caused injury, and rights under contracts generally.

choses in action   rights to intangible property such as patents, stocks, and contracts that may be enforced in the courts

choses in possession   rights to tangible property that may be possessed physically

CHECKLIST

Third Parties Who May Play a Role in a Contract

There are many ways in which a third party to the original contract may acquire rights under it or become subject to duties to perform:

- through vicarious performance, such as an employee carrying out the obligations of one of the parties to the contract
- when an exemption clause applies to a third party
- through a trust where a trustee confers benefits on a third party
- through an insurance contract under which the insurer promises to pay a third party in the event that a particular risk occurs
- when an agent makes a contract on behalf of an undisclosed principal
- when a party acquires an interest in land and becomes subject to rights and duties owed to a third person previously registered against the land
- when contractual rights are assigned to a third party

The Importance of Assignments

Choses in action are used to accumulate wealth such as savings in bank accounts and also through the ownership of shares and bonds. These assets are put to work as capital of corporations. In other words, this device links personal saving to business investment. In some less-developed countries, where citizens have little confidence in their legal system, it has been a major problem to persuade those who own tangible property to abandon their preference for investment in gold, jewels, and real estate and to accept a portfolio of mortgages, shares, and bonds as an alternative form of property. As a result, active capital markets in these countries have been slow to develop.

In this part of the chapter, we are concerned with the assignment of contractual rights generally; a discussion of the specific features of such choses in action as mortgages, shares, bonds, and negotiable instruments is reserved for later chapters.

The Role of Equity

An assignment of rights (choses in action) and a sale of goods (choses in possession) are similar. Each involves the transfer of an asset to another party. In an assignment, the subject matter of the transfer is an intangible asset: an unperformed contractual right; in a sale, the subject matter of the transfer is the ownership in goods. The first rules about how to complete an assignment of contractual rights were developed by the courts of equity and were called "equitable" assignments.

EQUITABLE ASSIGNMENTS

Equitable assignments require only that a clear intention to **assign** all or part of a contractual benefit be shown either orally or in writing. Then the assignee may receive the benefit of the contract from the promisor. If legal action is necessary to collect from the promisor, the assignee must make the assignor a party as well. All three parties—the assignee, the assignor, and the promisor—must be part of the legal action. This is because if an assignor assigns part of her rights only, she remains vitally interested in the result of any action by the assignee against the promisor. If the court should decide that the promisor is not bound to perform any part of his obligations, its decision would adversely affect the assignor as well as the assignee.

assign transfer to another person outside the contract

ILLUSTRATION 11.6

A owes B $10 000 under a contract. At the same time, B owes $6000 to X Finance Co. B assigns $6000 of her account receivable from A to satisfy X. Subsequently, A refuses to pay X; X sues A for the $6000.

If the court were to decide that A was not bound to pay anything on the debt because, say, the contract between A and B was within the Statute of Frauds and there was an insufficient memorandum of it, B would also be affected for she could not claim her remaining $4000 of the debt either.

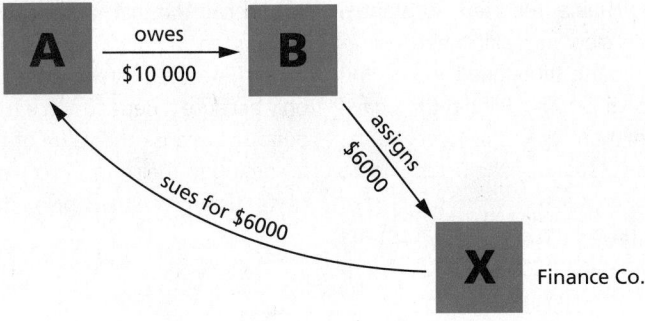

Assignment of Part of a Debt

In an assignment of part of a debt, as in Illustration 11.6, both the assignee and the assignor are equally anxious that the court find the debtor (that is, the promisor) liable. The assignor B must have her own chance to argue and to introduce evidence. For example, she might well have in her possession a memorandum sufficient to comply with the Statute of Frauds, and her evidence might be decisive in holding the debtor liable.

Similarly, in an action brought by B against A, the court would require that X Finance Co. also be made a party.

For the purposes of Illustration 11.7 below, assume that the assignor assigns only part of its rights; the promisor is willing to perform his obligation, but he does not know what part he should perform for the benefit of the assignee and what part for the benefit of the assignor.

ILLUSTRATION 11.7

A owes $100 000 to B Inc., due in 12 months. B Inc. needs short-term financing and borrows $80 000 from X Bank, repayable in 12 months. Under their loan agreement, B Inc. gives X Bank a conditional assignment of its account receivable from A as security for repayment of the loan under the following terms: As long as B Inc. pays the interest on its loan every three months, the bank will not be entitled to notify A of the assignment; but if B Inc. fails to pay the interest or fails to pay the $80 000 on the due date, the bank may advise A to pay it that sum plus unpaid interest, in reduction of his debt to B Inc. In other words, the assignment is conditional upon the default of the borrower, B Inc.

If, at the end of the year, the bank notifies A that B Inc. has assigned his account and demands that A pay the bank, A cannot afford to do so until he has verified the default and the amount owing. He must check with B Inc. Suppose B Inc. claims that it has paid the bank $60 000 of the debt. A is in a quandary: He is aware of the competing claims and fears that if he pays one party and guesses wrong, the other may sue him successfully and collect the amount in dispute a second time. In such a case, A should hand the sum claimed by the bank over to the court as custodian and let B Inc. and the bank settle their dispute before a judge.

An equitable assignment also occurs when the subject of the assignment is an aggregate of book debts (accounts receivables) whose balances fluctuate over time.

ILLUSTRATION 11.8

Fribble Corp. owes $160 000 to Tower Bank under a demand loan. Fribble is required to make regular monthly payments on the loan and to provide the bank with semi-annual financial statements. Fribble reported substantial losses six months ago and was slow in making two subsequent interest payments. The bank threatened to call the loan unless it received additional security. Fribble then gave the bank a conditional assignment of its accounts receivable, including several large accounts, some of them running to tens of thousands of dollars.

Fribble receives frequent payments on these accounts from its customers, and also ships its products to them

from time to time so that the account balances fluctuate substantially. Fribble promised to make its monthly interest payments without fail; otherwise, the bank would call the loan and notify Fribble's customers of the assignment.

In these circumstances the assignment is conditional not only because it depends on a future event (default by Fribble) but also because the value of the accounts receivable varies according to the state of accounts between Fribble and each of its customers at any given moment.

In Illustrations 11.6, 11.7, and 11.8, all the parties have a vital interest in the assignment, and must necessarily be bound by the same court decision. The requirement of equity that the assignor and the debtor(s) be made parties to the assignee's action is fair in cases where the assignor retains an interest in the contract.

STATUTORY ASSIGNMENTS

The Need for Reform

In many business transactions, an assignor does not want to retain any rights under the contract; he assigns them entirely to the assignee, and there is no need for him to remain involved in subsequent court actions. Such a requirement increases the expense of the action by bringing in a party who has no real interest.

Legislation has now removed this requirement.[28] An assignee may sue the promisor without joining the assignor in the lawsuit provided (a) the assignment was absolute (unconditional and complete), (b) it was in writing, and (c) the promisor received notice of it in writing. Most of the provinces in Canada have passed statutes setting out these requirements.[29] An assignment that complies with these requirements is known as a **statutory assignment**. Any other assignment is called an **equitable assignment**. Note that the statute did not change the effect of assignment—allowing an assignee to enforce the contract; it merely provided a streamlined procedure for hearing actions that meet the requirements laid down by statute.

> **statutory assignment** an assignment that complies with statutory provisions enabling the assignee to sue the other party without joining the assignor to the action

> **equitable assignment** an assignment other than a statutory assignment

Meeting the Requirements of the Statute

It is not always convenient in business to meet the requirements of the statute, and many assignments remain equitable rather than statutory. For instance, with regard to requirement (a), an assignment is not complete if a balance remains to be paid to the assignor after the assignee is paid—the assignor still has an interest in the contract. Nor is an assignment unconditional when the amount assigned varies according to the state of accounts between the assignor and his debtor; this situation exists when the balance of the account assigned fluctuates because the assignor continues to sell goods or services on credit to the debtor (the customer) or the debtor reduces the balance assigned by making payments on account to the assignor, in which case the balance assigned is not fixed and may need to be verified from the assignor's records. In neither of these situations is the assignment absolute.

The need for (b)—writing in support of the statutory assignment—is reasonable: If the assignment were oral, the assignee would have to call the assignor as a witness to prove that the assignment was actually made. As we noted in Chapter 2, evidence given by other persons of what the assignor said is hearsay, and for this reason the court will not allow such evidence when the assignor himself is able to testify. In most cases, a written assignment signed by the assignor is as good as his personal appearance in court. Only if there is a rare allegation of serious fraud, such as forgery, will further evidence be required to prove the assignment. Similarly, (c)—the requirement that the promisor receive the notice of assignment in writing—simplifies proving that the promisor knew of the assignment. It is good business practice and common sense to send written notice by registered letter when important rights are in question in any transaction.

NOTICE TO THE PROMISOR

The Effect of Notice on the Promisor

To be effective, all assignments require that notice be given to the promisor, but that does not mean the promisor's consent is required. A promisor ignores a notice of an assignment at his peril. Confronted with a demand for payment from one who claims to be an assignee, the

---

[28] The British Parliament remedied this defect in the 19th century when the Judicature Act amalgamated the courts of common law and equity.

[29] See, for example, Conveyancing and Law of Property Act, R.S.O. 1990, c. C.34, s. 53; Law and Equity Act, R.S.B.C. 1996, c. 253, s. 36; Judicature Act, R.S.A. 2000, c. J-2, s. 20; R.S.N.S. 1989, c. 240, s. 43(5). The statutory provisions are somewhat different in certain provinces. See, for example, Choses in Action Act, R.S.S. 1978, c. C-11, s. 2 and the Law of Property Act, C.C.S.M., c. L90, s. 31(1) and (5).

promisor should, of course, require proof of the assignment to protect himself against a possible fraud, but once he has had an opportunity to satisfy himself that there has been an assignment, he must make further payments to the assignee. If he persists in making payment to his original creditor, he can be sued by the assignee and required to pay the amount a second time.

CASE 11.4

Brian Wholesalers Ltd. buys a large quantity of goods on credit from Akron Manufacturing Inc. and defaults payment. Brian offers to pay Akron by assigning certain of its accounts receivable owed by retail merchants with excellent credit ratings. Akron agrees to this settlement and takes an absolute assignment of the debts, the largest of which is owed by Woolridge's Department Store. Akron sends to Woolridge's a notice, signed by an officer of Brian, stating that the account has been assigned to Akron, and encloses a request that Woolridge's pay Akron. Woolridge's inadvertently ignores the notice and request and pays Brian, which shortly afterward becomes bankrupt. Akron sues Woolridge's for payment of the debt again.

In these circumstances, Akron would succeed in its action: Woolridge's paid Brian at its peril after receiving valid notice of the assignment and Woolridge must pay Akron again.[30]

The Effect of Notice from Multiple Assignees

The ability to assign contractual rights is an important exception to the doctrine of privity of contract: Someone other than the original party to a contract is permitted to claim the benefit of rights under the contract. Indeed, more than one person may claim to be the assignee of the same right: An unscrupulous creditor might sell the right to collect the same debt to two different persons by assigning it to each of them. The debtor is then faced with two demands for payment. Which of the two innocent assignees is entitled to payment? And which is left only with an action for fraud against the assignor?

The law is clear: The assignee who first gave notice to the debtor is the one entitled to payment. This rule, like the rule that the debtor must receive notice of assignment before it affects him, offers the only fair treatment to the debtor. Otherwise, a debtor would be in a very insecure position, never being sure when he makes payment whether someone else to whom he should have paid the money may turn up later. An assignee who receives his assignment first might be slow in notifying the debtor, and the second assignee might notify the debtor first.

We should note that the second assignee is entitled to payment by the debtor—unless he knows of the prior assignment at the time of the assignment to him. If he knows of that prior assignment, he is a party to the fraud. He cannot take payment ahead of the first assignee without becoming liable to him. In order to determine who is entitled to the debtor's performance, the court must ascertain the validity and extent of every right claimed by contending assignees.

Mercifully, the debtor need perform his obligation only once—provided he acts prudently when it is unclear whose claim should prevail. As is suggested in Illustration 11.7, it may be necessary to pay the money into court and leave the court to decide the validity and extent of the claims by contending assignees.

THE ASSIGNEE'S TITLE

An Assignee "Takes Subject to the Equities"

A fundamental rule is that an assignee can never acquire a better right to sue the promisor than the assignor had. In legal terms, the assignee's claim is "subject to the equities": Her claim is subject to any rights the promisor had against the assignor before the promisor received notice of the assignment. Any valid defence that the promisor had against the assignor, with whom he originally contracted, will also protect him from liability to the assignee.

---

[30] See *Brandt's Sons & Co. v. Dunlop Rubber Co. Ltd.*, [1905] A.C. 454.

If a person takes an assignment of rights under a contract originally induced by the fraudulent misrepresentation of the assignor, the assignee will have no better chance to enforce her claim than if she had been the perpetrator of the fraud herself. In other words, if a debtor is the victim of fraudulent misrepresentation, the contract remains voidable at his option despite any assignment of the contractual rights. (The debtor cannot, however, sue the assignee for damages for the tort of deceit: He must sue the assignor, the person actually guilty of the fraud.) In addition to fraudulent misrepresentation, a promisor may use as any defence against an assignee mistake, undue influence, duress, and the fact that he received no consideration for his promise.

The position of an assignee is in marked contrast to the position of a person who obtains title to goods under a similarly flawed contract. For instance, we have seen in Chapter 8 that in spite of his fraud, a person may obtain title to goods so that, in turn, he may pass on valid title to a subsequent innocent purchaser, who may retain the goods against the claim of the person fraudulently persuaded to part with them.[31] But a person who obtains contractual rights by fraud does not, by assigning these rights, give an innocent assignee the right to enforce them against the defrauded promisor. Consequently, an innocent assignee is in a much more vulnerable position than is an innocent purchaser of goods.

The Right to Set Off

An important defence of a promisor is his right to **set off** any debt owed to him by the assignor at the time the assignment is made.

set off the right of a promisor to deduct an existing debt owed to him by the promisee

---

ILLUSTRATION 11.9

A is employed by B at a salary of $550 per week, payable at noon Saturdays when the business closes. On Thursday, A borrows $200 from B. On Saturday, A fails to appear at work on time. When he telephones an hour late, they argue, and B informs A that he is fired and tells him not to bother coming back. On Monday, A sues B for $550 in the small claims court. B may set off both the $200 loan and the $50 A would have earned had he come to work on Saturday morning. A obtains a court judgment for $300.

Suppose that, instead of suing B, A had assigned his claim for salary to his neighbour X for $500. X would take the claim, subject to the equities between A and B. Even though X did not know of B's loan to A and of A's failure to work on Saturday, B would be able to set off these amounts if X sued him: X would recover $300 from B, the same amount as A could recover.[32]

Until an assignee gives the promisor notice of the assignment, acts of either the assignor or the promisor or their agents may prejudice the assignee's rights. So it is important for an assignee to give notice as soon as possible. If he delays, his rights may well deteriorate.

ILLUSTRATION 11.10

Williams owes Mehta $900. Mehta assigns the debt to Young on May 1. Young neglects to notify Williams, and on May 11 Williams, unaware of the assignment, pays Mehta $300 on account. Because of her failure to notify Williams, Young, the assignee, may now recover from Williams only $600 and must look to Mehta for the $300 already paid.

---

[31] This result follows because fraud makes the contract voidable, not void. See Chapter 8 and *King's Norton Metal Co. v. Edridge* (1879), 14 T.L.R. 98; *Lewis v. Averay*, [1971] 3 All E.R. 907.

[32] Provincial legislation may provide that an assignment of wages, or any portion, to secure payment of a debt is invalid. See, for example, Wages Act, R.S.O. 1990, c. W.1, s. 7(7); Assignment of Wages Act, R.S.S. 1978, c. A-30, s. 3; Labour Standards Code, 1972, R.S.N.S. 1989, c. 246, s. 89. In the authors' opinion, the reference is to amounts of wages coming due in future and not to wages already owing at the time of assignment. The policy underlying such a rule seems to be to prevent a creditor from depriving an employee of the means of livelihood, diminishing the employee's incentive to work, and so undermining the employment relationship.

When a creditor—a building contractor, say—assigns rights to partial payment before it has completed performance, the assignee may be subject to an additional risk. Even when the assignee has given notice to the debtor (the party entitled to completion of the project), the debtor may be able to use defences based upon developments after the time of notice. The assignor's (builder's) subsequent failure to complete performance may cause the debtor damages, which he can set off against the assignee's claim. In other words, an assignee's rights under a contract that is still incomplete are imperfect and subject to proper completion of the contract.[33]

A general assignment of accounts receivable is an important business device for securing credit. The common law provinces each have statutes making such assignments void against the assignor's creditors unless the assignment is registered in a public office where its terms are available for inspection. The purpose of these statutes is to protect prospective creditors: They may inspect the registry to discover whether some assignee has a prior claim against the assets of a person who has applied to them for credit. We shall consider the reasons for providing public notice more fully in Chapters 23 and 28.

Ethical Issue **Credit Cards**

Credit cards have become one of the most common forms of payment for goods and services. There are several ways of setting up a credit card arrangement and organizing the legal relationships among the parties. Three-party credit card transactions (except when the card is issued by the merchant itself, such as a department store) are assignments of contractual rights: A business accepts a credit card and assigns to the credit card company its own right to payment for goods or services purchased on credit. The credit card issuer pays the business for goods purchased with the credit card. The customer, by entering into a contract with the credit card company, consents to the assignment and agrees to pay the credit card issuer, rather than paying the business directly.

The credit card industry is well financed by charging businesses a small percentage of credit card sales (2–10 percent, depending on volume), by charging cardholders an annual fee, and by collecting interest on unpaid balances. Retailers are subject to agreements that prevent them from surcharging credit card transactions to cover this fee. When considering the anti-competitive nature of the prohibition, one scholar wrote:

> This means that businesses that accept credit cards are forced to charge all customers the same higher prices in order to cover the costs of accepting credit card transactions. As a result, non-credit consumers (food stamps, cash, checks, debit) end up subsidizing credit card consumers and, indirectly subsidizing the entire credit card industry.[34]

Australian legislation allows businesses to charge credit card customers a higher price than customers paying cash.

Questions to Consider

1. Should cash customers be charged the same price as credit card customers when credit card customers cost the retailer more?

2. Why should credit card companies get to collect fees from both the customer and the retailer?

3. Who should bear the loss in the case of online credit card fraud: the consumer, the retailer, or the credit card issuer?

Sources: A.G. Guest and Eva Lomnicka, *An Introduction to the Law of Credit and Security* (London: Sweet & Maxwell, 1978) at para. 366; E. Warren, "Antitrust Issues in Credit Card Merchant Restraint Rules," *Discussion Paper for The Tobin Project Risk Policy Working Group*, May 6, 2007, available at http://www.docstoc.com/docs/26252409/Antitrust-Issues-in-Credit-Card-Merchant-Restraint-Rules.

---

[33] *Young v. Kitchen* (1878), 3 Ex. D. 127.

[34] E. Warren, "Antitrust Issues in Credit Card Merchant Restraint Rules," *Discussion Paper for The Tobin Project Risk Policy Working Group*, May 6, 2007, www.tobinproject.org/downloads/RP_Merchant_Restraint_Rules.pdf, at para. 2.

ASSIGNMENTS BY OPERATION OF LAW

Upon the Death of a Party

When a person dies, the law automatically assigns his or her rights and obligations under outstanding contracts to a personal representative. If the deceased person leaves a will naming a representative, the representative is called an **executor**. If the deceased failed to name an executor in the will (or the executor refuses to assume the position) or leaves no will (that is, dies **intestate**), the court will appoint a personal representative called an administrator. A representative does not have to perform a contract requiring personal services; the skill of the deceased cannot be demanded of the representative. We need only think of the executor of a deceased violinist to understand the reason for this rule.

The task of an executor or **administrator** is to pay all just claims against the deceased's estate, to complete performance of any outstanding contractual obligations of the deceased not requiring personal skill, to pursue all claims the deceased had against others, and then to distribute the assets according to the will—or, in the case of an intestate person, to distribute them to the heirs according to statutory provisions.[35]

executor the personal representative of a deceased person named in his or her will

intestate when a person dies without leaving a will

administrator the personal representative of a person who dies intestate

Bankruptcy

A person carrying on business, who becomes insolvent, may realize that his position is hopeless and may voluntarily apply for bankruptcy proceedings to avoid further loss to his creditors and injury to his name. Or it may be creditors who begin bankruptcy proceedings against a reluctant debtor by petitioning the court for an order known as a **receiving order**. If the creditors satisfy the court that their debtor is insolvent, the court will declare him bankrupt and appoint a licensed trustee to take charge of his property. Then the duty of the trustee is to liquidate the assets and to settle the creditors' claims.

receiving order a court order to commence bankruptcy proceedings

Bankruptcy is dealt with again in Chapter 29. The relationship between a bankrupt person and the trustee in bankruptcy is one of assignment. In the proceedings, the court assigns to the trustee the bankrupt person's assets, which include contractual rights and liabilities.[36]

Assignments resulting from death and from bankruptcy proceedings started by creditors differ from other assignments in that they are involuntary; they take place "by operation of law." One's affairs are seldom completely in good order when either of these events occurs, and an assignment creates an artificial extension of the assignor's legal existence until his affairs can be wound up.

NEGOTIABLE INSTRUMENTS

Their Nature and Uses

Chapter 19 in this book and on the Companion Website examines the law affecting negotiable instruments in more detail. However, since negotiable instruments are a special type of assignment, it is important to review their differences here. A **negotiable instrument**—for example, a bank draft, promissory note, or cheque—is a written document containing a promise, express or implied,[37] to pay a specific sum of money to a named person or to the "bearer" (the person in possession of the document).

negotiable instrument a written contract containing a promise, express or implied, to pay a specific sum of money to a designated person or to "bearer"

---

[35] The way in which the estate of an intestate person will be distributed to the heirs is set down in provincial statutes. See, for example, Estates Administration Act, R.S.O. 1990, c. E.22; Intestate Succession Act, R.S.N.S. 1989, c. 236, s. 153; Estate Administration Act, R.S.B.C. 1996, c. 122, Part 7.

[36] A licensed trustee may, however, with the permission of inspectors appointed by the creditors, disclaim any lease of property of the bankrupt debtor: Bankruptcy and Insolvency Act, R.S.C. 1985, c. B-3 (as amended), s. 30(1)(k).

[37] According to the wording of a cheque, the drawer does not directly promise to pay its amount, but he does promise by implication that sufficient funds will be available in his bank account for the bank (the drawee) to take and pay the cheque when it is presented.

Usually, a negotiable instrument is created to satisfy a payment obligation in a prior contract: A buyer delivers a negotiable instrument in payment for goods or services received. But delivery of the instrument does not complete the promisor's obligation. If he does not honour the instrument when it falls due and is presented to be paid, the promisee has the choice of suing under the original contract or suing for failure to honour the instrument. The negotiable instrument creates its own obligation to pay separate from the contract that triggered it. Often a promisee chooses to sue on the negotiable instrument because it is easier.

The unique aspects of the law of negotiable instruments arise when a promisee assigns an instrument to a third party.

Negotiability Compared with Assignability

The process of assigning a negotiable instrument is known as **negotiation**. A promisee or payee of an instrument may negotiate it in one of two ways: If the instrument is payable to bearer, he need only deliver it to a third party; if the instrument is payable in his name, he must **endorse** his name upon it and then deliver it. Negotiation is really a special type of assignment in which the new **holder** of the instrument acquires from the transferor (named payee) the rights and benefits of the instrument.

In a sense, negotiation is a privileged type of assignment that, for reasons of business convenience, is freed from certain of the restrictions that apply to an ordinary assignment of contractual rights. It differs from an assignment of rights generally in the following important respects.

Notice to the Promisor   As noted earlier, notice plays two important roles in assignment generally: first, written notice is necessary before an assignee may take advantage of a statutory assignment; and second, notice protects an assignee against the risk of the promisor being unaware of the assignment and paying the assignor or other assignees. However, notice is not necessary for the transfer of a negotiable instrument—indeed, it is irrelevant—because the promisor is liable to pay only one person, the holder of the instrument for the time being. Even if the promisor receives notice of the assignment, neither she nor her bank will pay the assignee unless and until the assignee presents the instrument. The promisor pays her debt only once—to the holder of the instrument at the time of the demand and in exchange for the instrument. In effect she pays for the return of her negotiable instrument: "The legal right to be paid is embedded in the document itself so that the right moves in unison with the physical document and will be paid as directed by the instructions on the document when it is presented by the holder.[38]

ILLUSTRATION 11.11

Steele receives his monthly paycheque of $3500 from Union Foundry Co. Ltd. He negotiates it to Comfy Furniture Mart for $2700 worth of furniture and $800 cash. Steele then tells his employer that he has inadvertently destroyed the cheque by throwing the envelope containing it into a fire, and he persuades Union to pay him a second time. When Comfy presents the original cheque for payment, Union must honour it even though Comfy gave no notice of the assignment.

If instead Steele had assigned to Comfy a claim against Union for arrears of wages (a contractual right not represented by any negotiable instrument) and if Comfy did not immediately notify Union of the assignment, Union could defeat the claim of Comfy, as assignee, by establishing that it had already paid Steele before receiving notice.

---

[38] Bills of Exchange Act, R.S.C. 1985, c. B-4, ss 16, 84, 86, 126; *Canada Trustco Mortgage Co.*, *v. Canada* 2011 SCC 36, [2011] 2 S.C.R. 635, at para. 21, 25, 27, 40, 51.

Defences of the Promisor   A person who writes a cheque in payment for goods may be able to deny payment of the cheque when he discovers the vendor has tricked him. If sued by that original vendor his defence will prevail, however defences available against the vendor originally named as payee on the cheque will not work against a subsequent holder of the cheque. An assignee for value of a negotiable instrument may succeed in an action against the promisor where the assignor himself would not have succeeded. Even when a promisor is induced to sign a negotiable instrument because of fraud or undue influence, he may be sued successfully by a subsequent innocent holder who has given consideration for the instrument.[39]

A defrauder may transfer enforceable rights under a negotiable instrument in much the same way that he can pass valid title to goods to an innocent purchaser. Similarly, a person who has given a negotiable instrument in payment for an illegal consideration loses the defence of illegality against an innocent holder of the instrument for value. This is a key difference from an ordinary assignment of rights discussed earlier in this chapter: The assignee never acquires a better right than the assignor had; the debtor retains her defences against all assignees.

ILLUSTRATION 11.12

Bacchus contracted with Hermes for the illegal transportation of liquor into Saskatchewan and gave Hermes his cheque for $2000 for services rendered. The police discovered and confiscated the liquor, and Bacchus then asked his bank to stop payment on the cheque to Hermes.

In the meantime, Hermes had endorsed the cheque to pay a debt to an innocent trade creditor, Argus, who knew nothing of the illegal contract for which the cheque had been issued. Argus learned that payment of the cheque had been stopped when he attempted to cash it at the bank. Argus sued Bacchus on the dishonoured instrument.

Bacchus might have used the defence of illegality successfully in an action brought against him by the party with whom he contracted—Hermes. But he must pay the holder of the cheque, Argus, if (as appears probable) Argus can prove he took the instrument unaware of its illegal origin and gave value for it.

By contrast, if Hermes's claim for $2000 against Bacchus had remained simply in the form of an account receivable, no one to whom Hermes might have assigned the account receivable would have obtained a better right to collect it than Hermes himself had.

An exception to this principle exists for consumers. Consumer negotiable instruments (except for cheques) remain subject to any defence or set off that the consumer has against the original seller.[40]

Form of Action   A holder of a negotiable instrument can sue in her own name; it is not necessary for her to join in the action of any of the other parties who have signed the instrument along the way.

Commercial Importance of Negotiability

For hundreds of years, businesses have benefited from the advantages of negotiable instruments as a special class of readily assignable promises, free from the formalities and many of the risks of an ordinary assignment of contractual rights. Business experience has

---

[39] Consumers are protected from the harshness of this rule. See The Bills of Exchange Act, R.S.C. 1985, c. B-4, s. 191, restricting the rights of finance companies to assert the status of a holder in due course. See also the Business Practices and Consumer Protection Act, S.B.C. 2004, c. 2, s. 15.

[40] Bills of Exchange Act, R.S.C. 1985, c. B-4, ss. 190–1.

shown that negotiability has a convenience far outweighing any cost of its abuse. The law reduces the possibility of abuse through fraud, undue influence, duress, and illegality by requiring a holder of a negotiable instrument to show that he was unaware of the origin of a tainted instrument, and that he or some previous holder of the instrument must have given value for it.[41]

Modern banking practice is based upon the relatively secure position of an innocent holder for value of a negotiable instrument. Banks are able to cash cheques or accept them for deposit without exhaustive inquiry into the background of the transactions out of which they arose since, as innocent holders for value, they are immune from the earlier flawed nature of the transaction. Without such a rule, banking would be much slower and less reliable for business and the public generally.

Currency

Money is a special type of negotiable instrument authorized by statute and designed to circulate with maximum ease.[42] Therefore, rules of transferability and negotiation are even more relaxed for this type of negotiable instrument to make it easy for currency to change hands.

CHECKLIST

Principles of Assignment

Equitable Assignments

■ partial or conditional in nature; promisor must receive notice of assignment before obligated to pay

■ assignor must participate in any lawsuit

■ subject to the equities

Statutory Assignments

■ provincial statutory requirements: complete (not partial), unconditional, and written

■ promisor to receive notice of transfer before being obligated to pay

■ assignor need not participate in any lawsuit

■ subject to the equities

Negotiable Instruments

■ federal statutory requirements: Bills of Exchange Act applicable to promissory notes, cheques, bills of exchange

■ promisor need not receive notice before obligated to pay

■ previous holders need not participate in any lawsuit

■ not subject to the equities (except for consumers)

■ currency special rules

---

[41] The requirements are somewhat more technical than we can conveniently describe here: the holder must be a holder in due course. See infra, Chapter 19.

[42] Currency Act, R.S.C. 1985, c. C-52; Bank of Canada Act, R.S.C. 1985, c. s. 25 (notes that are a first charge on the assets of the Bank of Canada)

Strategies to Manage the Legal Risks

Every person responsible for performance of a contract should be named as a party to it. Persons wishing to enforce the terms of a contract should sign it under seal so any lack of consideration is not a barrier to enforcement. If it is important that only the original parties complete the transaction, then the contract should include a clause that specifies personal performance, and another clause that prohibits assignment of any rights under the contract. Alternatively, assignment could be allowed with prior written consent of the other party. Exemption clauses should name all possible participants in the performance of the contract so they too benefit from its protection.

Credit arrangements should be designed to allow maximum flexibility with minimum liability. This means that, when giving a promise to pay, a debtor should preserve all possible defences for use against any subsequent assignee. This means resisting the use of negotiable instruments in favour of the standard type of contract where the promise to pay is incorporated into the original purchase agreement. As well, the contract should state that subsequent assignees are bound by the terms of the contract. By contrast, when receiving another party's promise to pay, maximum flexibility will be achieved when a separate negotiable instrument is obtained. This will be easier and more valuable to transfer.

Assignments, other than partial or conditional assignments, should be completed in writing, and immediate notice should be sent to the promisor. This reduces the likelihood of new defences arising or loss of priority to competing claims from other assignees.

QUESTIONS FOR REVIEW

1. Define the following terms: *third party*; *assignor*; *constructive trust*; *beneficiary*; *chose in action*.

2. Give an example of vicarious performance by a party other than an employee.

3. How has the privity of contract rule been modified with respect to insurance?

4. Describe the significance of exemption clauses in contracts performed by third parties.

5. P contracted with Q to move equipment from one of Q's buildings to another site. R, an employee of P, damaged some of the equipment. What facts must Q establish in order to hold P liable for R's conduct?

6. Describe the exception made for consumer negotiable instruments.

7. A debtor owed his creditor $2000. The creditor assigned her right to collect this debt to another person, X. The assignee, X, delayed in sending notice to the debtor that he was now the party entitled to payment. Before receiving any notice of assignment, the debtor paid his original creditor $750 on account. How have X's rights been affected?

8. Anderson, a skilled mechanic, agreed to do some car repair work for Bartlett. Anderson was busy when the car was delivered for repair and gave his friend Gauche the work to do, without consulting Bartlett. Gauche sent Bartlett a bill for the repair work. Bartlett refused to pay. Is he justified?

9. Give two examples of involuntary assignments.

10. What are the requirements for a statutory assignment? Describe the business advantages associated with such assignments.

11. Explain the two types of assignment by operation of law.

12. Is notice required to assign a negotiable instrument? Explain.

CASES AND PROBLEMS

1. Continuing Scenario:

Ashley asks her accountant for advice about which form or forms of payment she should allow her restaurant customers to use and how she should protect herself from the risks involved:

a.   Ashley has arranged to supply several hotels close by with muffins and pastries she bakes for her own customers. The hotels have asked to be billed at the end of each month and be given 30 days to pay. This will mean large outstanding debts for 60 days. How should she respond and why?

b.   In addition to payment by cash and debit cards, the restaurant customers surveyed asked for credit cards and cheques. Describe how the law treats these types of transactions.

2. King, a building contractor, completed the construction of a house for Harris. At completion, Harris owed King a balance of $15 000. King then borrowed $10 000 from the Brandon Bank. In consideration for this loan, King assigned to the bank as much of his account receivable from Harris as should be necessary to repay the sum borrowed plus interest and any further sums for which he might become indebted to the bank. Is the bank, as assignee, entitled to sue Harris without the assistance of King's testimony?

Suppose instead that King had borrowed $20 000 from the Brandon Bank and in partial settlement assigned the whole of the $15 000 due to him from Harris. Are these changed facts in themselves sufficient to entitle the bank to sue Harris without joining King in the action?

3. The University of Ashcroft Business School offers one-week executive courses. For its October program on marketing strategies, Ashcroft's dean managed to make a deal with Professor Bertoff, a famous specialist in the field, to give the opening lecture and remain at the business school for two full days. Less than a week before the program was to begin, Bertoff sent an email to the dean that his country's government had requested him to chair a crucial international meeting on trade policy; he would send his associate, Professor Colbert, a more junior but quite well-known person in the marketing field, to deliver the lecture prepared by Bertoff himself, and to remain on campus for the two days.

The dean is quite upset, but he has no alternative but to allow Colbert to fill in. He wishes to know whether he has a good case against Bertoff. Give your opinion with reasons.

4. Garbutt was dismissed by her employer, Carter Computers Inc., for allegedly dishonest conduct. She hired Harkin to be her lawyer and represent her in grievance arbitration for wrongful dismissal. Harkin was successful; the arbitrator found that Garbutt had been wrongfully dismissed and that she was entitled to be compensated for her losses.

During negotiations to settle the amount of compensation, Garbutt gave Harkin a signed direction to Carter Computers to pay 30 percent of the settlement proceeds to Harkin. He delivered a photocopy of the direction to Carter Computers' in-house lawyer, but she told him that Carter Computers would honour only an original signed copy.

The next day the parties reached a settlement of $20 000. Before the in-house lawyer received the original copy of the direction, she instructed the payroll department to issue a cheque to Garbutt for the full amount of the settlement proceeds. Harkin sued the defendant for failure to pay him the $6000.

Summarize the arguments of each side, and give your opinion of whether Harkin should succeed.

5. Keirson sold his taxi business to Martens, covenanting neither directly nor indirectly to carry on or be engaged in another taxi business within five kilometres of the place of business for five years from the date of sale. The agreement contained the usual clause extending the benefit of the contract to the "assigns" (assignees) of the parties. Two years later, Martens resold the taxi business to Nelman, and shortly afterward, Keirson entered into another taxi business within the five-kilometre area. Nelman brought an action against Keirson for an injunction to restrain him from operating a competing business within the five-kilometre area. Should Nelman succeed?

6. B. Flatt and F. Major made a $250 wager about the outcome of the 2014 Olympic hockey final game. Flatt lost and he gave Major a cheque for $250 drawn on his TD Canada Trust bank account. Major immediately took the cheque to Money Mart, presented it for payment, signed the back, and received the money (less Money Mart's cheque cashing fee). When Money Mart presented the cheque for payment to TD, it was discovered that Flatt had instructed his bank to stop payment on it. What are Money Mart's rights? Against whom?

7. Glashov purchased on credit from Brown a building for business purposes. In their agreement, Glashov covenanted that he would insure the property and assign the insurance to Brown, the vendor, as security for the amount that remained owing on the purchase price.

   Glashov insured the property with the Standard Insurance Company but neglected to inform the company that the proceeds in the event of a claim should be paid to Brown. The building was later destroyed in a fire.

   Immediately after the fire, three of Glashov's trade creditors sought payment of their claims and agreed to accept from him an assignment to them of the proceeds of the fire insurance. The trade creditors gave notice to Standard Insurance Company at once, before the amount of the loss had been established and before that company had admitted any liability under the policy. Brown, after learning what had happened, informed the insurance company that she wished to claim the insurance money due, and supported her claim by showing to the company the terms of the agreement for sale. The insurance company paid the money into court for settlement of the dispute.

   What is the nature of the trade creditors' argument that they should have the insurance money instead of Brown? What possible defence or defences might Brown offer against this claim? To whom would a court order the payment of the insurance money?

8. Norton responded to a campaign for funds by the National Association for the Preservation of Wildlife (NAPW) by signing the following statement, which she gave to a canvasser for NAPW:

   > $1250.00 Charlottetown, Nov. 2, 2015
   >
   > To assist in the purchase of conservation area sites and in consideration of the subscriptions of others, I promise to pay to the Treasurer of the National Association for the Preservation of Wildlife the sum of twelve hundred and fifty dollars, payable $500 on February 1, 2016, and $750 on August 1, 2016.
   >
   > Joan I. Norton

   This and other similar agreements permitted the Association to acquire property for use as conservation areas.

   In order to obtain cash immediately from some of the pledges made to it, including Norton's, NAPW sold (assigned) them to Simpson for an undisclosed cash sum. Simpson's secretary telephoned Norton to advise her of the assignment of her promise, and Norton confirmed that she had made the pledge. Norton failed, however, to pay either of the installments to Simpson. Simpson brought an action against Norton for payment of the $1250.

   Express, with reasons, an opinion about the probable outcome of this action.

Additional Resources for Chapter 11 on the Companion Website

(www.pearsoncanada.ca/smyth)

In addition to pre- and post-tests, mini-cases, and application exercises, the Companion Website includes the following province-specific resources for Chapter 11:

- **Alberta:** Credit Cards; Statutory Assignments; Trusts; Wills and Succession Amendment Act
- **Atlantic Provinces:** Probate Legislation; Public Trustee Act
- **British Columbia:** Credit Cards; Statutory Assignment
- **Ontario:** Assignment of Rents; Consumer Credit; Death Without a Will; Executors; Statutory Assignments; Trusts

Chapter 12

The Discharge of Contracts

- THE WAYS IN WHICH A CONTRACT MAY BE DISCHARGED

- DISCHARGE BY PERFORMANCE

- DISCHARGE BY AGREEMENT

- DISCHARGE BY FRUSTRATION

- DISCHARGE BY OPERATION OF LAW

- STRATEGIES TO MANAGE THE LEGAL RISKS

When a contract comes to an end—is discharged—neither party has any further obligations under it. This chapter examines the different ways of discharging a contract without breaching the contract, which is examined in Chapter 13. We also discuss the consequences of an event that makes performance impossible or pointless—a frustrating event—and its effects.

This chapter examines such questions as:

■ What is "tender of performance," and what are its requirements and consequences?

■ What are the various ways in which a contract may be discharged by agreement?

■ How might a contract provide for its own termination?

■ What are the shortcomings of common law rules in their ability to deal with frustration?

■ How have statutory reforms dealt with these problems?

■ What special problems arise from frustration as it applies to the sale of goods?

■ What is meant by "discharge by operation of law"?

THE WAYS IN WHICH A CONTRACT MAY BE DISCHARGED

To **discharge a contract** means to cancel or end the obligations of a contract; to make an agreement or contract inoperative.[1] This chapter looks at four ways to discharge a contract: by performance, agreement, frustration, and operation of law. In addition, a contract is sometimes said to be "discharged" by its breach, but this topic is reserved for separate treatment in Chapter 13.

discharge a contract cancel or end the obligations of a contract; make an agreement or contract inoperative

DISCHARGE BY PERFORMANCE

The Nature of Discharge by Performance

Parties who enter into a contract expect it to be discharged—ended—by performance. Their contract ends after they have both performed all their respective obligations satisfactorily. For a contract to be fully discharged by performance, both parties—not merely one of them—must fulfill their promises. A bilateral contract, formed by the offer of a promise for a promise, goes through three stages: first, when neither party has performed its promise; second, when one but not the other party has performed; and third, when both have performed. Only at the final stage is the contract discharged by performance.[2]

Performance may take several forms, depending on the contract. It may mean supplying the services, delivering the goods, paying the purchase price, or any combination of these.

Tender of Performance

One party may attempt to perform, but the other party might refuse to accept the performance. An attempt to perform is called a **tender of performance**, whether accepted or rejected by the other party. If a seller properly tenders delivery of goods and the buyer refuses to accept them, the seller is under no obligation to attempt delivery again and may immediately sue for breach of contract.

tender of performance an attempt by one party to perform according to the terms of the contract

A debtor who makes an unsuccessful but reasonable attempt to pay will be free from further liability for interest on the amount owing, and generally will not have to pay court costs if he is later sued for the debt.

Refusing payment does not extinguish an existing debt. There is a legal principle that the debtor must seek out her creditor. She is not excused from tendering payment because her creditor is slow or hesitant about asking for it: The onus is on the debtor to find and pay her creditor.

DISCHARGE BY AGREEMENT

Waiver

Parties may discharge their contract by agreeing between themselves not to perform it. A **waiver** is an agreement not to proceed with the performance of an existing contract. If neither party has fully performed when they agree to call off the bargain, there is automatically consideration for the waiver of each party: Each still has rights and obligations

waiver an agreement not to proceed with the performance of an existing contract

---

[1] *Black's Law Dictionary*, 6th ed., at 463.

[2] In a unilateral contract, formed by the offer of a promise for an act, the first stage is eliminated because the second takes place in the very formation of the contract through one party's performance; the last stage remains necessary for discharge by performance.

outstanding, and a promise by one party to waive its rights is sufficient consideration for it being released from its obligations to the other.

On the other hand, if one party has already fully performed its part but the other has not, the first party receives no consideration for giving a waiver of the other party's duty to perform. To be binding, its promise to release the other party should be under seal.

ILLUSTRATION 12.1

Atwater agrees to install a sound system in the Kent Theatre for $5500. Kent's right, under the contract, is to receive the benefits of the work, and Kent's obligation is to pay for the work. Atwater's right is to receive the price, and his obligation is to do the work required. If they should mutually agree to call off their contract before Atwater completes the work, there is consideration for the waiver. Atwater promises to abandon a claim for payment; in return, Kent Theatre promises to abandon a claim for services. Each party's promise is the price paid for the promise of the other.

But suppose that Kent has paid Atwater the $5500 and that to date Atwater has only partly installed the system. At this stage, any undertaking by Kent that it will "require neither completion of the work nor a return of any money" is without consideration and, therefore, not binding unless under seal.[3]

Neither party can impose a waiver on the other. A party who fails to perform without securing a waiver by the other commits a breach of the contract. As discussed in Chapter 13, the consequences of breach are quite different from discharge by agreement.

Substituted Agreement

Accord and Satisfaction   Sometimes performance becomes too difficult. One party may offer the other a monetary payment or some other substitute for performance if she discharges (releases) him from the original obligation. For example, a seller may find that he cannot obtain certain imported goods to fill an order and may offer other goods of equal quality, perhaps at a lower price, if the buyer releases him from his original promise. A promisee may be preparing to sue the promisor before a settlement is agreed on.

accord and satisfaction a compromise between contracting parties to substitute a new contractual obligation and release a party from the existing one

The distinction between a material alteration of the terms and **accord and satisfaction** is in the purpose of the arrangement. In a material alteration, the parties are primarily concerned with creating a new arrangement; the discharge of the old contract is incidental. In accord and satisfaction, the parties are seeking a way to end their existing arrangement; the new arrangement is only for that very purpose.

Accord and satisfaction is used to settle disputes out of court. Processing a lawsuit is expensive and success is not guaranteed, so settlement is encouraged. After trial, the loser must pay not only his own legal fees but the costs of the winning party too—this rule is designed to encourage settlement offers before trial. A winning party may forfeit their right to have their costs paid if they have refused a reasonable settlement offer. This rule is designed to encourage reasonable valuation of claims.[4] The consideration in such a settlement is the consent of each party to discontinue the lawsuit although usually the document is signed under seal.

novation the parties to a contract agree to terminate it and substitute a new contract

Novation   **Novation** is another method of discharge. It occurs when the parties to a contract agree to terminate it and substitute a new contract. There are two types of novation:

- a material change in terms
- a change in parties

---

[3] This statement remains subject to the discussion in Chapter 7, concerning the "Gratuitous Reduction of a Debt" and "Injurious Reliance."

[4] See e.g. Ontario Small Claims Court Rules, O. Reg. 258/98 as amended, R. 14.01

If parties agree to a material alteration of the terms, one that goes to the root of the contract, they have, in effect, agreed to discharge their original contract and replace it with a new one. One material change would be to change the subject matter of the contract. For instance, car dealer B may inform A that he cannot deliver the car A has ordered without a lengthy delay. They agree to cancel the contract and substitute a new one: For a favourable price offered by B, A buys a car that B has in stock. It is not always easy to decide whether an agreed alteration leaves the original contract intact or amounts to novation.

CASE 12.1

P, a building contractor, agreed to pay a penalty if he did not have the construction work completed by a certain date. Before completion, P and the owner, Q, agreed that P should do some additional work on the same project. The changes made it impossible for P to complete the building by the original date. Q insisted that the penalty clause allowed him to deduct the penalty from the amount he still owed to P. The court held that the new agreement had discharged the old and that the penalty clause had disappeared with it.[5]

When one of the parties to the contract "wants out" and the remaining parties agree that another party replaces the first party, they have discharged the original contract and replaced it with a new one. A common example occurs when a party purchases an existing business and assumes its outstanding liabilities as a part of the purchase price for the assets acquired. If the creditors accept the new owner as their debtor, either by an express agreement with it or by applying to the new owner for payment of claims against the former owner, the liability of the former owner is discharged and replaced by the liability of the purchaser.[6]

There must be evidence, either by words or conduct, of intention and agreement to abandon the original contract on the part of both the creditors and the new owner.[7] The burden of proof is upon the party claiming that there was novation to show that the other party has assumed all liabilities under a pre-existing contract and has acted on that contract.[8]

In good business practice, neither the vendor nor the purchaser of a business relies on implied novation with creditors. The two parties to the sale agree on what debts the new owner should assume and then call in the creditors to obtain their express consent to the substitution of a new debtor. In addition, to protect him- or herself, the purchaser of a business makes a careful examination of public records, requires the vendor to provide a declaration setting out the names of all its creditors and the amounts owing to them, and publicizes the sale. The statutory reasons for these procedures are considered more fully in Chapters 28 and 29, which discuss creditors' rights.

A Contract Provides for Its Own Dissolution

Before agreeing to a contract, one party may be worried about a possible future event affecting its ability or willingness to perform. If the other party is agreeable, the parties may include a term in the contract stating what should happen if this event occurs. Sometimes,

---

[5] *Thornhill v. Neats* (1860), 141 E.R. 1392. See also *Amirault v. M.N.R.* (1990), 90 D.T.C. 1330. See *Jedfro Investments (U.S.A.) Ltd. v. Jacyk*, 2007 S.C.C. 55: the parties must arrive at a new agreement, not merely enter into negotiations.

[6] *Re Star Flooring Co. Ltd.*, [1924] 3 D.L.R. 269 at 272.

[7] *Toronto Star v. Aiken*, [1955] O.W.N. 613.

[8] See *Pacific Wash-A-Matic Ltd. v. R.O. Booth Holdings Ltd.* (1979), 105 D.L.R. (3d) 323.

a similar term may be implied by trade usage or by the surrounding circumstances of the agreement. Such a term is known as a condition precedent, a condition subsequent, or an option to terminate, depending upon what it says.

Condition Precedent   In Chapter 10, we noted that a condition precedent is a future act or event, other than a lapse of time, that must happen before the obligation to perform a promise arises.[9] If the condition is not met and is not waived, the promisor need not perform. A condition precedent may be an oral understanding or it may be a term in a written contract.

One could argue that the contract does not come into existence until after the condition precedent is fulfilled. However, a contract subject to a condition precedent does have some legal force even before the condition is met. The condition precedent limits the parties to only one reason for not performing—the reason set out in the condition precedent. The parties are not discharged from their promises unless and until the condition precedent becomes impossible to fulfill. The arrangement is, therefore, much more than an outstanding offer that can be revoked prior to acceptance. For example, in Illustration 12.2, if immediately after B received A Co. Ltd.'s acceptance he accepted an offer for a higher-paying position with a different firm, he would be in breach of contract. The only reasons that will justify his refusal to take the job are a lack of housing or the promotion for his wife. Unless the contract says otherwise, both parties are obligated to wait and see if the condition precedent is met before their obligations to perform can be ignored.

ILLUSTRATION 12.2

A Co. Ltd., located in Moncton, writes to B in Winnipeg offering him a good employment position. B replies by letter that he will take the position if A Co. Ltd. will first find satisfactory housing in Moncton for him and his family. A Co. Ltd. accepts B's counter-offer by mail. The employer's obligation of finding the satisfactory housing is a condition precedent.

Alternatively, B might reply that he will take the position if his wife, who works for a different firm, is not offered a promotion for which she has already applied. The failure to receive the promotion is a condition precedent.

---

condition subsequent a future event that brings a promisor's liability to an end if it happens

Condition Subsequent   A **condition subsequent** is a future event that, if it happens, brings a promisor's liability to an end. Liability is established when the contract is formed, but one of the parties has reserved for itself an "out" in certain circumstances.

A buyer of a ticket for a baseball game has the benefit of a term in his contract that if the game is rained out before a stated inning, he will be given a ticket for another game.

ILLUSTRATION 12.3

Norton is the holder of a baseball season ticket that, because of some of his bad habits known to the management, was sold to him on terms that he must control his conduct at the games.

Norton attends a game and his conduct annoys not only the operators of the ballpark but also other fans and those selling tickets. He has a loud, booming voice and insists on telling other fans things they do not want to know, and by

moving about he obstructs the view of others. The management informs him that it is cancelling his season ticket and tenders him a refund for the remaining games. Norton sues the management for breach of contract.

The contract contains a term relating to a condition subsequent—Norton's objectionable conduct. It is, therefore, discharged by agreement rather than by breach, and Norton's action will fail.[10]

---

[9] *Newfoundland and Labrador (Human Rights Commission) v. Newfoundland Liquor Corp.*, [2004] N.J. No. 22 at para. 66 (NFL C.A.) (citing *Black's Law Dictionary*).

[10] See *North v. Victoria Baseball & Athletic Co.*, [1949] 1 W.W.R. 1033.

In contracts for the shipment of goods, an **act of God** (the raging of the natural elements) may be a condition subsequent if it results in the destruction of the shipment. When a railway, trucking line, airline, or marine shipping company accepts goods for shipment, it undertakes to be liable for any damage if the goods arrive at their destination in a poorer condition than they were received in by the carrier. But there is also a term discharging the carrier from this liability if the goods are destroyed by an act of God. If the goods are only partly destroyed, the contract is not discharged completely; instead, the carrier is absolved from liability to the extent that the damage was caused to the goods by an act of God, and the carrier must deliver them as they are. Such a term is implied by trade custom, but most carriers take the added precaution of expressly stating the term in their bills of lading. Therefore, when shipping goods at the owner's risk, it is wise to insure against such loss.

act of God the raging of the natural elements

For more information on this topic, see the Companion Website.

Option to Terminate   A contract may include a term that gives one party, or perhaps both, the choice to bring the contract to an end before its performance has been completed, usually by giving notice. Exercising the choice results in discharge by agreement because this way to discharge the contract was agreed upon when drawing up the contract. For example, a contract of employment often contains an option to terminate, entitling the employer to dismiss an employee by giving the required notice, as explained in Chapter 18. Many residential leases have an option clause entitling the tenant to leave before the end of the term by giving notice to the landlord. In a contract for the purchase of a business, a buyer may insist on a term allowing it to discharge the agreement if the auditor of the financial statements of the business is unable to give an unqualified opinion on their fairness. In these circumstances, an auditor's qualified opinion (or unwillingness to express any opinion) would give the purchaser an option to terminate the contract.

The distinction between an option to terminate and the previously discussed conditions is that the discharge does not happen automatically. The party decides whether to trigger the discharge of the contract.

INTERNATIONAL ISSUE

Will the NHL Come to Hamilton?

The story of Jim Balsillie's (as yet unfulfilled) dream to buy an NHL hockey team and move it to Canada is a tale of conditions precedent, conditions subsequent, and options to terminate.

A 2006 bid to buy the Pittsburgh Penguins failed because Balsillie was unwilling to promise that the team would remain in Pittsburgh. The agreement of purchase and sale contained a condition that the purchase be approved by the NHL Board of Governors before it became binding. The NHL Board would only approve the purchase if Balsillie agreed to a variety of new terms, including keeping the Pittsburgh location. As a result, Balsillie gave notice that he would not proceed with the purchase.

In 2007, negotiations with Nashville Predators again focused on league approval and on whether Balsillie would immediately move the Predators to Canada. Two contracts figured prominently in the ability to make such a move:

1. The existing lease of the Nashville arena: The lease included a term that allowed the Predators the option to end the lease early if average fan attendance at the games fell below 14 000. The City of Nashville took the position that the tenant could not take advantage of the option because it was in default under the lease.

2. A new lease (and management agreement) with the City of Hamilton for the use of Copps Coliseum: This agreement was entered into during the Predator negotiations. The deal contained a condition that it would automatically expire if Balsillie did not buy a team by December 30, 2007.

The publicity surrounding the Hamilton lease, and the acceptance of deposits on season tickets, drew the ire of the NHL Commissioner. In the end, the Board of Governors never considered the approval issue. The Predators completed a deal with a group of Nashville investors for much less than the Balsillie offer.

Questions to Consider

1. What kind of term was attached to the league approval of the Penguins sale: a condition precedent, a condition subsequent, or an option to terminate?

>

2. What kind of term was included in the City of Hamilton agreement: a condition precedent, a condition subsequent, or an option to terminate?

3. What kind of term was included in the Nashville arena lease: a condition precedent, a condition subsequent, or an option to terminate?

Sources: S. Brunt, "Balsillie Still in the Game," *Globe and Mail*, May 8, 2008, http://ctv2.theglobeandmail.com/servlet/story/RTGAM.20080508.brunt09/business/Business/Business/&id=RTGAM _20080508_brunt09; D. Schoalts, "Predators Inch Closer to Hamilton," *Globe and Mail*, June 13, 2007, http://www.theglobeandmail.com /sports/hockey/predators-inch-closer-to-hamilton/article1326638 /; Schoalts, "Tickets? Who Needs Tickets?" *Globe and Mail*, June 14, 2007, http://www.theglobeandmail.com/sports/tickets-who-needs -tickets/article1086841/; P. Waldie and S. Stewart, "RIM Boss Buys NHL's Penguins," *Globe and Mail*, October 5, 2006, http://www .theglobeandmail.com/sports/rim-boss-buys-nhls-penguins/article 1106862/; B. McKenzie, "Balsillie Pulls His Bid to Purchase Penguins," TSN, December 15, 2006, http://www.tsn.ca/story/print /?id=188556

DISCHARGE BY FRUSTRATION

It is not possible to anticipate all future events and address them in conditions to a contract. It would take too much time and money to negotiate long lists of unlikely events that would excuse performance. Therefore courts excuse or discharge parties for failure to perform their contracts, even when the contract is silent, if circumstances beyond the control of the parties make performance impossible, pointless, or radically different from that intended by the parties.[11]

Historically, courts viewed these kinds of promises as absolute, regardless of the reason for which they could not be performed.[12] Examples are covenants in commercial leases that require tenants to keep the property in good repair and to pay rent. As a result tenants found themselves liable for damages caused by fire, storms, and enemy action, and liable for rent for the duration of the lease when the property was no longer useable.[13] However, in recent cases where the whole point of the lease has disappeared or become impractical, courts applied the doctrine of frustration to leases.[14]

Several provinces have enacted legislation to expressly apply the doctrine of frustration to residential leases.[15] The application of frustration to commercial, as opposed to residential, premises continues to be decided on a case by case basis. Most commercial leases will have a clause about frustration in the lease.

Doctrine of Frustration

doctrine of frustration the law excuses a party from performance when circumstances beyond the control of the parties have made performance impossible, pointless, or radically different from that contemplated by the parties

If the courts excused a failure to perform for any flimsy excuse, there would be tremendous uncertainty in business affairs. Therefore, courts carefully consider when the **doctrine of frustration** should be applied. Sometimes the parties may include in their contract a term to deal with the particular risk that has occurred; if so, the courts will not

---

[11] John Swan, *Canadian Contract Law*, (Toronto: LexisNexis, 2006) at pp. 600-01; *Naylor Group v. Ellis-Don Construction*, 2001 SCC 58, at para 53-55.

[12] *Budgett & Co. v. Binnington & Co.*, [1891] 1 Q.B. 35; *Hills v. Sughrue* (1846), 153 E.R. 844.

[13] *Paradine v. Jane* (1647), 82 E.R. 897; *Redmond v. Dainton*, [1920] 2 K.B. 256; *Foster v. Caldwell*, [1948] 4 D.L.R. 70.

[14] *Cricklewood Property & Investment Trust, Ltd. v. Leighton's Investment Trust, Ltd.*, [1945] A.C. 221; *Capital Quality Homes Ltd. v. Colwyn Construction Ltd.* (1975), 9 O.R. (2d) 617; *Victoria Wood Development Corp. Inc. v. Ondrey* (1977), 14 O.R. (2d) 723, Aff'd (1978), 92 D.L.R. (3d) 229 (Ont. C.A.); *First Real properties Ltd. v. Biogen Idec Canada Inc.* 2013 ONSC 6281.

[15] See e.g. Residential Tenancies Act, S.O. 2006, c. 17, s. 19; The Residential Tenancies Act, 2006, S.S. 2006, c. R-22.0001, s. 11.

accept the event as frustrating the parties' contract and will honour the limited protection provided in the contract.[16]

The courts have offered a variety of definitions of the doctrine of frustration:[17]

> Frustration occurs whenever the law recognizes that without default of either party a contractual obligation has become incapable of being performed because the circumstances in which performance is called for would render it a radically different thing from that which was undertaken by contract.... It is not hardship or inconvenience or material loss itself which calls the principle of frustration into play. There must be as well such a change in the significance of the obligation that the thing undertaken would, if performed, be a different thing from that contracted for.[18]

In another case, frustration was described this way:

> If the foundation of the contract goes, either by the destruction of the subject-matter or by reason of such long interruption or delay that the performance is really in effect that of a different contract, and the parties have not provided what in that event is to happen, the performance of the contract is to be regarded as frustrated.[19]

A decision that a contract has been discharged by frustration is viewed as a practical and reasonable solution imposed by a court under circumstances that were not anticipated by the parties. The simplest cases are those where performance becomes literally impossible, and this is where the doctrine of frustration first developed.

CASE 12.2

The producer of a concert booked a music hall, but it was destroyed by fire before the scheduled date of the concert. No one was found to blame for the fire. The producer sued the owner of the hall for damages for breach of contract to compensate for losses sustained in having to cancel the concert. The court held that the contract was discharged by frustration and refused to award damages. Had the court found instead that the owner of the music hall had broken the contract, it would have ordered him to pay damages.[20]

CASE 12.3

Robinson booked Davison, a pianist, to give a concert on an agreed date. Robinson incurred expenses in preparing for the concert: advertising, selling tickets, and hiring staff for the evening. At about 9 a.m. on the morning of the concert date, he received word from Davison that a sudden illness would prevent her from performing. Robinson had further expenses in cancelling the concert. When he sued Davison for damages for his loss, the court held that the contract had been discharged by frustration, and the action failed.[21]

Today, most personal performance contracts include express options to terminate for illness and insurance to cover cancellation costs. Similar options to terminate are inserted in ticket sale contracts. Therefore, if the performer cancels her contract, the promoter may correspondingly cancel the audience contracts. As noted when the contract has a term anticipating the circumstance, the doctrine of frustration does not apply.

---

[16] *Teleflex Inc. v. I.M.P. Group Ltd.* (1996), 149 N.S.R. (2d) 355.

[17] In *Hirji Mulji v. Chong Yue Steamship Co.*, [1926] A.C. 497 at 510. Lord Sumner put it this way: "It is really a device by which the rules as to absolute contracts are reconciled with a special exception which justice demands."

[18] *Davis Contractors Ltd. v. Fareham*, [1956] A.C. 696 at 729.

[19] *Tatem Ltd. v. Gamboa*, [1939] 1 K.B. 132 at 139.

[20] *Taylor v. Caldwell* (1863), 122 E.R. 309. See also *Laurwen Investments Inc. v. 814693 N.W.T. Ltd.* (1990), 48 B.L.R. 100.

[21] *Robinson v. Davison* (1871), L.R. 6 Ex. 269.

Over time, the doctrine of frustration was adapted to cover situations when actual performance remained physically possible but would have a very different meaning from the expectations of the parties when they made their agreement.

CASE 12.4

In July 1914 in England, the contractors Dick, Kerr & Co. agreed to construct certain reservoirs for a local water board within six years at a specified price; they started work immediately. In February 1916, during the First World War, the Minister of Munitions, acting under wartime statutes, ordered the contractors to cease work. Most of their plant and materials were then sold under the minister's directions.

After the war ended, the water board insisted that the contractors resume their work under the original terms, but the contractors refused to comply. Prices and conditions of supply had changed drastically from what they had been in 1916. The court held that the contract had been discharged by frustration and the water board failed in its action.[22]

The war was an unforeseeable and unanticipated event. Usually, the fact that contractual obligations prove to be more onerous than anticipated will not, by itself, discharge a contract by frustration. A business is not excused from performance just because the most convenient or inexpensive method of performance is not available. To excuse a promisor in these circumstances would mean almost any contract could be discharged, and no one would be held to their bargains. Frustration is available only in extreme circumstances that could not have been anticipated by the parties.[23] Price increases and labour shortages are to be expected.

Where the contract involves the sale of goods which are destroyed, it will only amount to a frustrating event if the specific goods or source of goods is a term of the contract; if not, the supplier must find and the buyer must accept replacement goods from a different source.

CASE 12.5

A trucker in Parkhill contracted with a Toronto corn merchant to deliver a quantity of corn to shipping points in the Parkhill area specified by the corn merchant. The parties appeared to have understood that the trucker was to purchase the corn from certain Parkhill farmers when the crop matured. Unfortunately, the trucker was unable to obtain the required quantity of corn because of a local drought. The corn merchant sued for damages for failure to deliver according to the contract. The Court of Appeal agreed with the defendant

trucker that if the source of the goods formed a term of the contract, the failure of the crop would have amounted to a frustrating event, excusing the trucker from performance. The majority of the court found that the contract had not expressly stated that the corn should be from a particular source, and it was unwilling to find an implied term to that effect. It held that the trucker should have obtained the corn from other suppliers and that it was accordingly in breach of contract.[24]

Lastly, for a contract to be discharged by frustration, its performance must become impossible or purposeless after the agreement was made, for reasons beyond the control of the parties. This is not the same situation as one in which performance was impossible or purposeless at the very time the agreement was made. If the subject matter has ceased to exist at the time of the agreement, the agreement is void for mistake—as discussed in Chapter 9—not discharged by frustration.

---

[22] *Metropolitan Water Board v. Dick, Kerr & Co.*, [1918] A.C. 119.

[23] *Twentsche Overseas Trading Co. v. Uganda Sugar Factory Ltd.* (1945), 114 L.J.P.C. 25 at 28. See also *Graham v. Wagman* (1976), 14 O.R. (2d) 349, per Weatherston, J., at 352: "I have never heard that impecuniosity is an excuse for non-performance of a promise" varied on appeal (1978), 21 O.R. (2d) 1.

[24] *Parrish & Heimbecker Ltd. v. Gooding Lumber Ltd.*, [1968] 1 O.R. 716 at pp. 719-20.

Self-Induced Frustration

A party that deliberately makes performance impossible cannot rely on the doctrine of frustration to discharge his obligations. **Self-induced frustration** is really a breach of the contract. In most cases, the distinction between frustration and self-induced frustration is easy to see.

self-induced frustration a party willfully disables itself from performing a contract in order to claim that the contract has been frustrated

---

ILLUSTRATION 12.4

(a) A Inc. contracts to transport top soil for B. On realizing that it has made a bad bargain, A Inc. sells its only dump truck and claims that it cannot fulfill the contract because of frustration. Obviously A Inc. has broken the contract.

(b) A Inc. contracts to transport top soil for B in an isolated northern community. Shortly after the contract is made, its truck (the only available one in the area) is destroyed by a tornado. The contract is discharged by frustration, and A Inc. is freed from its obligation to perform.

(c) A Inc. contracts to transport top soil for B. Its dump truck breaks down because of an employee's negligence, and there will be a long delay in its repair as the parties are in a small northern community. Because the situation is attributable to A Inc.'s negligence, the contract is not discharged and A Inc. will be liable for breach of contract.

Not every fault or irresponsibility, however, will bar a party from claiming that the contract has been frustrated. It will depend upon how careless the owner was. Consider if the dump truck is stolen: The application of frustration may depend upon whether the truck was locked or the keys left in it.[25]

Ethical Issue **Multiple Customers**

Supposing a business has many contracts requiring the same performance, but only limited ability to perform. Which contracts should be performed and which customers should go unsatisfied? It is up to the business to choose which contract will not be performed. This is considered by the courts as a form of self-induced frustration.

A classic case involves applications for fishing licences from the Ministry of Fisheries.[26] The business had four boats that were each rented out for the season. The ministry granted the company only three licences, which could be allocated to any of the four boats. When sued by the fourth customer, the court rejected the business's defence of frustration because the business decided to breach the contract with the fourth customer.

Questions to Consider

1. Is this a fair result for the business? Would the doctrine of frustration apply if the business had not received any licences?

2. What factors should the business consider when deciding which contract(s) to perform?

3. What condition should the business place in the rental agreement to protect itself from this potential breach of contract liability?

The Effect of Frustration

Harshness of the Common Law Frustration discharges the contract at the moment of the frustrating event. In the simple situation where neither party has performed at all, frustration is a complete discharge of both parties from all obligations

---

[25] *Joseph Constantine Steamship Line Ltd. v. Imperial Smelting Corp. Ltd.*, [1942] A.C. 154 at 179. See also *Kendall v. Ivanhoe Insurance Managers Ltd.*, [1985] O.J. No. 1725; *Atcor Ltd. v. Continental Energy Marketing Ltd.*, [1996] 6 W.W.R. 274.

[26] *Maritime National Fish Ltd. v. Ocean Trawlers Ltd.*, [1935] 3 D.L.R. 12.

under the contract. But often the circumstances are not so simple. One or both parties may have partially performed before the frustrating event. When, for example, work is spread over a period of time but payment is to be made only on completion, frustration of the contract before its completion may cause serious hardship for the party doing the work. This happened in the old case of *Cutter v. Powell*.[27] A ship worker was to be paid on completion of a trip from Jamaica to Liverpool. He died en route when the voyage was nearly three-quarters complete. An action by his widow to recover a proportionate part of his wages failed; the obligation to pay never arose because he did not complete the journey.[28]

Other early decisions concerning frustration were just as harsh: The frustrating event was considered to discharge future obligations under it from the time of the frustrating event, but any obligations already due still had to be paid. See *Chandler v. Webster*[29] in Case 12.6, as an example.

CASE 12.6

In 1902, the plaintiff rented a London hotel room to view the coronation procession of Edward VII. It was the first coronation in over 60 years (since that of Queen Victoria); the demand and price for locations with a view were very high—for this room, £141, payable at once. The plaintiff was able to pay only £100 at the time and owed the remaining £41. The contract was frustrated when the king became ill and the procession was cancelled. The plaintiff not only failed to recover his £100, but the court held that since the remaining £41 was due and owing before the frustrating event occurred, he was still liable for that sum, too! The "solution" in this decision was to let the loss fall where it lies at the time of the frustrating event.

---

let the loss fall where it lies
the court will enforce the contract up to the moment of discharge—obligations due before the frustrating event remain; obligations arising after the frustrating event are discharged

The Court's Attempt to Soften the Harshness   The **let the loss fall where it lies** rule was modified or "softened" for situations where absolutely no benefit was received by a purchaser and a deposit had been paid. In *Fibrosa v. Fairborn*,[30] a purchaser who had made an advance payment on equipment was allowed to recover its money since it had received absolutely no benefit from the other party before the frustrating event, the Second World War, occurred. This solution seems reasonable from the purchaser's point of view—but what about from the seller's? While a seller might not have delivered any of the equipment, it might well have done considerable work toward the completion of the contract at its own expense. According to the *Fibrosa* decision, the buyer can still get its entire deposit back. In the *Fibrosa* case, the defendant company had partially completed expensive, custom-built machinery, and not only was it unable to require the buyer to share in its loss, but it had to return the full deposit.

Obviously, if a seller cannot retain a deposit on the grounds that it has incurred expenses, it certainly cannot recover these expenses from a buyer that has made no deposit. However, if the seller has conferred even the slightest benefit on the buyer (for example, if the seller had delivered a small advance shipment of spare parts), the seller could retain the whole deposit! The case law would not apportion the loss between the parties: It was a matter either of retaining the whole of the deposit or of returning it entirely.

---

[27] (1795), 101 E.R. 573.

[28] The harshness of this rule has since been mitigated to some extent by the doctrine of substantial performance, discussed in Chapter 13.

[29] [1904] 1 K.B. 493.

[30] *Fibrosa Spolka Akcyjna v. Fairbairn Lawson Combe Barbour, Ltd.*, [1943] A.C. 32. See also *KBK No. 138 Ventures Ltd. v. Canada Safeway Ltd.*, (2000) 185 D.L.R. (4th) 650 (B.C.C.A.); *Palachik v. Kiss*, [1983] 1 S.C.R. 623 at 631.

Statutory Reform   To fix the unfairness of the situation, legislation has been passed in most parts of Canada. Prince Edward Island, New Brunswick, Ontario, Manitoba, Alberta, and Newfoundland and Labrador passed legislation known as the Frustrated Contracts Acts.[31] British Columbia, Saskatchewan, and Yukon have also passed more comprehensive legislation.[32]

Now when a frustrating event occurs after money is already due under the contract (whether paid or not), the Frustrated Contracts Act provides for the allocation of losses between parties:

> [t]he court, if it considers it just to do so having regard to all the circumstances, may allow the party to retain or to recover, as the case may be, the whole or any part of the sums paid or payable.[33]

The recovery or retention is capped at the amount of the payment made or due. Any excess over the performing party's allowed loss will be returned to the payor. In addition, the acts authorize a court to award the performer a just proportion of any valuable benefit received by the other party, regardless of whether a deposit has been paid.

One gap remains. When a party has expended time and money in performance of a contract, but the other party, which was eventually to have received the benefit of the work, has (a) made no deposit and (b) not yet received any benefit—except in British Columbia, Yukon, and Saskatchewan—the first party is still without remedy and must bear the whole loss.[34] The British Columbia Act states, "a 'benefit' means something done in the fulfillment of contractual obligations, whether or not the person for whose benefit it was done received the benefit."[35] Therefore, in these three jurisdictions, expenditures made by the first party can be taken into account, and to the extent that the other party has received no benefit from them, the loss is divided equally.[36] This solution seems fair to both parties.

The Sale of Goods   If the contract is for the sale of goods, the Sale of Goods Act could also apply to a frustration situation. The Act states:

> Where there is an agreement to sell specific goods and subsequently the goods without any fault on the part of the seller or buyer perish before the risk has passed to the buyer, the agreement is thereby avoided.[37]

Three conditions must be present for this section to apply:

- First, the goods must be specific—that is, "they must be identified and agreed upon at the time the sale is made."

- Second, the risk must still be with the seller—that is, the seller must still be responsible for the safety of the goods.

- Third, the cause of the frustration must be the perishing or destruction of the goods.

---

[31] Frustrated Contracts Act, R.S.P.E.I. 1988, c. F-16; R.S.N.B. 2011, c. 164; R.S.O. 1990, c. F-34; C.C.S.M., c. F-190; R.S.A. 2000, c. F-27; R.S.N.L. 1990, c. F-26; R.S.N.W.T. 1988, c. F-12. These statutes were based on the original English model but with some improvements.

[32] Frustrated Contract Act, R.S.B.C. 1996, c. 166. Section 5(2) allows for restitution for performance or part performance whether or not benefit received. See also S.S. 1994, c. F-22.2; R.S.Y. 2002, c. 96.

[33] Frustrated Contracts Act, R.S.O. 1990, c. F.34, s. 3(2).

[34] See *Appleby v. Myers* (1867), L.R. 2 C.P. 651, discussed in Chapter 15 under "Quantum Meruit."

[35] Frustrated Contracts Act, R.S.B.C. 1996, c. 166, s. 5(4).

[36] *Ibid.* s. 5(3).

[37] 40 R.S.B.C. 1996, c. 410, s. 11; R.S.O. 1990, c. S.1, s. 8; R.S.N.S. 1989, c. 408, s.10.

ILLUSTRATION 12.5

A sends a fax to B offering to sell the load of flour sitting at the railroad station for $10 000, "risk to pass to you on delivery of the shipping documents in seven days' time." B accepts by return fax. Three days later a train on adjacent tracks is derailed and knocks over the freight car containing the flour. The contents are spilled out and ruined by rain, frustrating the contract.

Both parties are immediately discharged from liability under the contract: A cannot sue for the price, nor can B sue for failure to deliver. B can recover any deposit it has made. A's only remedy is against those responsible for the accident.

In Illustration 12.5, all three elements mentioned in the Sale of Goods Act are present, and the Act applies; consequently the Frustrated Contracts Act does not.[38] But if any one of these elements is missing, the Sale of Goods Act does not apply[39] and the Frustrated Contracts Act applies in those provinces having the Act; in the remaining provinces, the parties are left with the common law position up to and including the *Fibrosa* case.

For more information on this topic, see the Companion Website.

CHECKLIST

The Effect of Frustration

- Step 1: Determine if any part of performance, benefit, or expenditure was provided before the frustrating event. If not, then all obligations are discharged and no further inquiry is necessary. If the answer is yes, proceed to Step 2.
- Step 2: Identify the subject matter of the contract. If the contract deals with specific goods and they have perished, then the rules of the Sale of Goods Act decide the effect of frustration.
- Step 3: If the Sale of Goods Act does not apply, determine if the applicable province has a Frustrated Contracts Act. If so, the rules under that act determine the effect of frustration.
- Step 4: The common law rules as set out in the *Fibrosa* case will decide all remaining cases.

Let's look at some examples of the parties in each of these circumstances.

In provinces where the Frustrated Contracts Act applies, the application of the act is more easily understood if we begin with some examples.

ILLUSTRATION 12.6

(a) A sends a fax to B offering to sell "one thousand sacks of number one flour from our warehouse stock for $5000, risk to pass to you on delivery of the shipping documents in seven days' time." B accepts by return fax. Three days later, the warehouse and contents are destroyed by fire without any negligence on A's part. The goods are not specific because they have not been segregated from the larger stock and earmarked for the buyer.

(b) A sends a fax to B offering to sell "the carload of number one flour sitting at our rail siding for $10 000, risk to pass to you on delivery of the shipping documents in seven days' time." B accepts by return fax. Three days later, the government requisitions all of A's flour, including the carload sold to B, in order to help feed the victims of a flood disaster. Here the contract is frustrated by an event other than the perishing of the goods.

---

[38] Except in British Columbia, where s. 1(b) of the Frustrated Contracts Act states expressly that the Act applies even in these circumstances.

[39] See e.g., R.S.O. 1990, c. S.1, s. 2(2)(c).

In neither of the examples in Illustration 12.6 does the Sale of Goods Act apply. Under the Frustrated Contracts Act, if B had made a deposit and sued for its return, the court would consider whether A had incurred any expenses toward the completion of the contract and would take them into account in determining how much of the deposit B would recover. If B had made no deposit, A could only recover the value of any benefit already conferred upon B.[40] So, if A had delivered one sack of flour to B as a sample, it could recover the price of that sack, but no more.

The Frustrated Contracts Act also states that the courts shall give effect to any special provisions made by the parties in anticipation of a frustrating event.

ILLUSTRATION 12.7

A sends a fax to B offering to sell "the carload of number one flour sitting at our rail siding for $10 000, risk to pass to you upon acceptance of this offer. Delivery was in seven days' time." B accepts by return fax. Three days later the flour is destroyed in a derailment accident. The risk has already passed to the buyer when the frustrating event takes place.

In the above example, the parties have agreed expressly that the risk should pass to the buyer, which seems to indicate that the buyer would be liable for any loss caused by a frustrating event after the risk has passed. The buyer must then pay the price to the seller. While both the Act and the express terms of the contract indicate this result, there are no reported cases directly on point. Ordinarily, buyers arrange to insure valuable goods not in their possession when the risk passes to them.

Where the Common Law Applies   Consider Illustrations 12.6 and 12.7 again as if they had occurred in a province without the Frustrated Contracts Act. In examples (a) and (b) of Illustration 12.6, the *Fibrosa* decision applies. If B had made a deposit, it could recover it in full regardless of whether A had incurred any expenses toward the completion of the contract. If, however, B had received the slightest benefit, such as one sack of flour as a sample, it could recover none of its deposit.

The *Fibrosa* case did not consider situations where the seller had conferred a benefit on the buyer (for instance, by an advance delivery of part of the goods) and where no deposit had been made. In these circumstances, the older cases would likely govern: both parties would be immediately discharged by the frustrating event, and the seller would have no right of recovery against the buyer for the goods already delivered when, by the contract, none are to be paid for until all are delivered. This shows the value of the Frustrated Contracts Act in avoiding a harsh result.

The result in Illustration 12.7 is the same under the common law as under the statute; the common law rule as well as the statute respect the intention of the parties as contained in their contract of sale.

DISCHARGE BY OPERATION OF LAW

The Bankruptcy and Insolvency Act operates to discharge a bankrupt debtor from contractual liabilities after the processes of bankruptcy have been completed. The debtor is discharged, however, only if he qualifies for a certificate stating that the bankruptcy was caused by misfortune and without any misconduct on his part.[41]

---

[40] Except, as already noted, in British Columbia, where the court could give recovery for part or all of the expenses incurred, whether or not a benefit was conferred.

[41] R.S.C. 1985, c. B-3, s. 175.

statute barred an action that may no longer be brought before a court because the party wishing to sue has delayed beyond the limitation period in the statute

A debt or other contractual obligation that has been neglected by a creditor for a long time becomes **statute barred**—that is, the creditor loses the right to bring an action on it. Each province has a Limitations Act setting out the time at which a creditor loses its remedy. The Limitations Act "bars" (rather than completely discharges) a right of action if the promisee fails to pursue it within the time specified. The statute gives effect to the legal principle that the public interest requires a definite end to the opportunity to sue. The effect of the statute is really to banish the right of action from the courts rather than to extinguish it. The distinction is important because a claim may be rehabilitated and made enforceable by certain conduct of the promisor, as will be discussed in Chapter 29. The time period begins to run at the point when the cause of action arises or is discoverable by a reasonably diligent plaintiff.[42]

---

[42] Limitation legislation (*ibid.*) usually defines when the cause of action arises or is discoverable. See *Canada (Attorney General) v. Lamerman*, 2008 S.C.C. 14.

Strategies to Manage the Legal Risks

Thoughtfully written contracts can give parties maximum control over how and when their contracts are discharged. Businesses should identify the circumstances in which they would not want to perform and include them as conditions subsequent to the agreement. If things need to happen before the business is interested in the deal, these should be added as conditions precedent. If there is still uncertainty about whether the business should proceed with the deal, an option to terminate upon written notice should be created. Of course the most flexibility is obtained when the conditions or options depend upon the businesses' satisfaction rather than outside experts.

Where one party will have to expend considerable time, effort, or funds in preparation for performance, the contract should call for deposits or partial payments to be made. The contract should also address return or forfeiture of the deposit if performance is not completed as expected.

Frustration is only available for unanticipated or unforeseeable events, and the rules are arbitrary, so it is much better if the contract deals with all possible obstacles. Before contracting, time should be spent imagining the variables that might occur and customized frustration clauses should be included in the contract. For example, standard real estate agreements include a term setting out what will happen if the house burns down after the sale is agreed to but before the deal is completed. Businesses should maintain insurance policies until a deal closes.

Finally, if a dispute develops, any resulting settlement agreement, release, or waiver should be put in writing and under seal to avoid arguments surrounding lack of consideration.

QUESTIONS FOR REVIEW

1. What are the consequences for a creditor who refuses a tender of performance by the debtor?
2. Describe the nature of the consideration given by the parties to a waiver.
3. When a party admits liability for breach, what is his best course of action? Explain.
4. In what respect does the arrangement known as accord and satisfaction involve a discharge of a contract?

5. Describe the role of novation in the purchase of a going business.

6. Does a contract exist at all before a condition precedent has been satisfied? Explain.

7. Why may an "option to terminate" clause be described as a condition subsequent?

8. The principles of mistake and discharge by frustration may both relate to contracts in which the subject matter is non-existent. How do these principles and their remedies differ?

9. What else, apart from physical destruction of the subject matter of a contract, can result in frustration of the contract?

10. Is substantial hardship in performing sufficient to excuse a promisor from performing? Explain.

11. James had contracted to give a talk and demonstration on resolving human relations conflicts in small organizations for a management consulting firm. After dinner with his hosts the evening before his talk, he accepted a dare to slide down a lengthy banister on the main staircase of the hotel. James fell off partway down and suffered a concussion and a badly sprained ankle. He was unable to give his talk and has been sued for breach of contract. Give a brief opinion of the likely result.

12. Give two examples of the shortcomings in the *Fibrosa* case.

13. In what important respect has the British Columbia Frustrated Contracts Act provided a fairer solution when a contract is frustrated?

14. What three conditions are required for the Sale of Goods Act to apply to a frustrated contract? Does the Act apply to a case where the goods have been impounded by the government?

15. Suppose P contracts to buy 10 tonnes of corn grown in the county of Haldimand from S. Because of a local drought there is insufficient corn, but S can quite easily obtain corn of the same quality from the adjacent county of Frontenac. Has the contract been frustrated? Give reasons.

16. In what respect may bankruptcy bring about the discharge of contracts?

CASES AND PROBLEMS

1. Continuing Scenario

   In addition to serving customers in the restaurant, Ashley's restaurant does catering for weddings and corporate events. Jill books Ashley's restaurant to do part of the catering for her wedding—the hors d'oeuvres for the pre-dinner cocktail party and the wedding cake for the dessert (both the display cake and the individual pieces for guests to eat). Jill gives Ashley a $500 deposit on the quoted contract price of $3000. A month before the wedding, Jill calls to cancel because the groom has backed out. She requests return of her deposit and the contract is silent about cancellation and deposit return. Ashley has not purchased any of the food yet, however she did turn down another catering job for the same day. Can Ashley retain the deposit? Has the contract been frustrated? Would your answer change if Jill had called off the wedding rather than the groom? Is there a difference between supplying the wedding cake and the hors d'oeuvres?

2. Urban Construction Co. contracted with Mandel to build a small two-storey office building for $240 000. The contract contained a clause stating that the agreed price would be reduced by $500 for every business day the building was not completed after April 1. The price was to be paid on completion of the building.

   During construction, Mandel asked Urban Construction Co. to alter certain specifications so that a complete air-conditioning system might be installed at a later time with a minimum of inconvenience, and so that there would be an additional washroom on the second floor.

   The building was completed April 17. Urban Construction Co. refused Mandel's tender of a cheque for $243 500 (comprising $240 000 less $6500 for 13 business days, plus

$10 000, the agreed price for the extra work). Urban Construction Co. brought action for $250 000, the full price without deduction.

Examine the validity of the arguments Mandel might use in defending the action.

3. Twilight Properties agreed to purchase land on the Vancouver waterfront from the Harbour Commission, conditional upon no changes being made to the zoning bylaw that permitted high-density development for building condominium units. Twilight then began negotiations with the city for a site plan for 650 units. Its chief executive officer, Moon, was very optimistic and immediately offered 500 units for sale. (He had a fallback plan to build only that number if the zoning and site plans were restricted by municipal authority.) Moon obtained agreements to purchase 110 units from individual purchasers, who paid deposits to Twilight of $20 000 per unit. Each contract contained a clause stating

> if the development does not proceed in accordance with Twilight Properties' plans, Twilight retains the right to terminate the contract without liability on or before June 30, 2015.

This date corresponded with the closing date in the agreement with the Harbour Commission. Units were to be available, and the deals closed one year later.

On June 30, 2015, Twilight completed the purchase of the lands, but the date passed without any approval of the site plan by the city. At the end of July, the Planning and Development Department of the city approved the site plan and sent it on to the city council. However, in October the city council refused to approve the plan and stated that it intended to reduce the number of units permitted on the property. The council instructed its secretary to write to Twilight and ask whether it would be willing to provide a guarantee to the original condominium purchasers that it would perform its commitments to sell the units should the development be approved. Twilight replied that the city's request was inappropriate and an interference with its private contract rights. At its November meeting, the city passed a more restrictive rezoning bylaw that would permit only 400 units to be built.

Immediately afterward, Twilight returned the deposits of the purchasers and stated that their agreements were terminated; it was not possible to proceed with the project as planned. The unit purchasers sued for breach of contract. Twilight defended by claiming that their contracts were frustrated by the actions of the city. Summarize the arguments for each side, and give your opinion about who should succeed.

4. The Dryden Construction Co. contracted with the Ontario Hydro Electric Power Commission to build an access road seven miles long from its Manitou Falls generating station to provincial Highway No. 105. The contract contained the following clause:

> The contractor agrees that he is fully informed regarding all of the conditions affecting work to be done and labour and materials to be furnished for the completion of the contract and that his information was secured by personal investigation and research and not from the Commission or its estimates and that he will make no claim against the Commission.

In fact, the area over which the road was to be built was under heavy snow at the time, and the temperature was very low. The description of the property proved to be inaccurate, there being much more muskeg than indicated. After these facts became known, the contractor claimed to be excused from the contract, alleging that it had been frustrated and that what was required amounted to an entirely different contract.

Is there a binding contract to build the road?

5. Gilman Steel Ltd. is a large fabricator of reinforcing steel. It makes its product from steel bars purchased from steel mills in accordance with engineers' specifications for particular projects. Universal Construction Corp. is an apartment construction company.

In September 2014, Gilman and Universal signed a contract for the supply of fabricated steel at a price of $253 per tonne for use in three apartment buildings to be built consecutively by Universal at different sites.

At the first building site, deliveries were made and paid for as agreed, and construction of that building was completed. Then in July 2015, steel mill companies announced increases in the price of unfabricated steel, to take effect in two stages. The price to Gilman would increase on August 1, 2015, by $8.50 per tonne and a second increase of a then-unspecified amount would become effective as of March 1, 2016.

In the changed circumstances, Gilman suggested a new contract for the second and third apartment buildings. Universal agreed to reconsider because it found that it would not require as much fabricated steel for the remaining two buildings as it had initially contracted for. The parties signed a new contract for the supply of fabricated steel at a price of $257 per tonne, a price that only partially passed on the increase to Gilman. Universal had thus agreed to pay a higher unit price for a smaller quantity of steel. The parties did not include in the contract a clause providing for an escalation of price because Universal expected to complete the remaining buildings before the next round of price increases in March 2016.

Construction of the second apartment building began in August 2015, and Gilman made numerous deliveries of steel. Universal accepted all steel delivered and regularly paid the amount billed on each invoice at $257 per tonne. The second building was completed in January 2016, and construction of the third was started.

On March 1, while the third apartment building was still far from completion, the steel mills announced the anticipated second price increase. Officers of Gilman, hoping to agree on another new contract, met with a senior officer of Universal. They asked Universal to consider a new contract since construction had not progressed as expected. Universal agreed to accommodate Gilman on the understanding that Universal would be given favourable consideration in the supply of steel for the construction of additional apartment buildings.

Gilman then prepared an agreement dated March 1, 2016, and mailed it to Universal. It was a duplicate of the preceding contract in July except that the price of the steel was increased. Universal did not sign or return the document, but it did accept deliveries of steel invoiced at the new rates without protest. Universal adopted a new method of payment, however, after March 1, 2016. It no longer paid by cheques based on the invoice amounts but in round figures that tended at first to overpayment; however, by the end of the construction this procedure led to a net balance of some $25 000 owing by Universal.

As construction of the third apartment building neared completion, the comptroller of Gilman asked for payment in full of the account. Universal informed him that it expected some new mortgage money to become available enabling it to pay the account in full soon. At about the same time, officers of Universal met with Gilman's officers to discuss a contract for the supply of steel for a new apartment complex. Universal reminded Gilman that it had twice agreed to new contracts and asked whether Gilman could offer a good price. Gilman made an offer, and Universal said it would consider it. The meeting was conducted and concluded in an atmosphere of goodwill without complaint about the March price increase. Shortly afterward, Universal decided that the new offer was not attractive enough to accept and indicated for the first time that it would not pay the portion of the past due account that represented the increase in the March 2016 agreement.

Gilman Steel Ltd. sued Universal Construction Corp. for the balance owing according to its invoices.

a. Outline the nature of the defence or defences available to Universal.

b. Explain the nature of the argument or arguments that could be advanced for the plaintiff.

c. Indicate with reasons what the court's decision would likely be. (If you perceive any difference between what the law is and what it ought to be in a case of this kind, set out your reasoning separately from your prediction of what the decision is likely to be.)

6. Parker's Automatic Laundry Services Inc. installed coin-operated washing machines and dryers in an apartment building owned by Mountbatten Estates Ltd. under a five-year contract. The contract gave Parker's the exclusive right to install and maintain any laundry machines

in the building. No one other than the employees of the laundry service company would be permitted to repair, remove, or replace any of the machines. A clause in the contract read:

In the event the Proprietor [Mountbatten] sells or assigns its interest in the said premises, such Successor shall be fully bound by the terms of this agreement and before the Proprietor sells or assigns it shall obtain the consent in writing of the grantee or assignee to the terms of this agreement.

In return, Mountbatten was to receive 20 percent of the gross receipts collected from the use of the laundry equipment.

Six months later, Mountbatten sold the apartment building to Baldoon Holdings Ltd. for $2 500 000. The lawyer acting for Baldoon drew up the agreement of sale, one clause of which read:

The Vendor [Mountbatten] warrants to the Purchaser [Baldoon] that the 10 washing machines and 10 clothes dryers located in the apartment building have been placed there by Parker's Automatic Laundry Service Inc. pursuant to an agreement with a five-year term, a copy of which is attached hereto.

Following its purchase of the apartment building, Baldoon continued for a time to operate the building much as before and retained the same manager. Parker's made the first quarterly payment to Baldoon three months after the purchase. At that time, Baldoon approached Parker's with a view to purchasing the 10 washing machines and 10 dryers and operating them itself, as owner of the building. Parker's refused and Baldoon then instructed Parker's to remove its machines within two weeks. When Parker's failed to do so, Baldoon moved the machines to a locked storage area in the basement of the apartment building and replaced them with new washing machines and clothes dryers of its own.

Parker's Automatic Laundry Services Inc. brought an action against Baldoon Holdings Ltd. for breach of contract. Indicate with reasons what the result of this action will likely be, leaving aside the question of what the amount of damages should be, if awarded.

7. Diehl owned some land on which she planned to have a house built that would be suitable for her retirement the following year. She made a contract with Summers, a building contractor, to build a house for $80 000, the price to be paid in full on completion. The contract contained an unqualified promise by the contractor to complete the house at that price. When the house was about three-quarters finished, Diehl stored some expensive furniture in a completed part and took out a $20 000 fire insurance policy on the furniture.

Two weeks later, before the house was completed, lightning caused a serious fire that did considerable damage to both the building and the furniture. Summers learned that Diehl would receive about $16 000 in insurance money. When Diehl asked him to go ahead and complete the house, Summers said, "I believe I'm no longer bound to go on and if you do not pay me the insurance money, I will ask a court to declare that the contract has been frustrated. I'm willing to compromise if you pay me the insurance money." Diehl protested that she had lost considerably from the destruction of her furniture but finally said, "All right, go ahead and do the work."

When the house was completed Diehl paid Summers $80 000 but refused to pay anything more. Summers sued her for $16 000 on the grounds that he had been led to believe he would receive this additional sum and would not otherwise have completed the contract.

At the trial, evidence was submitted that in contracts of this kind, builders frequently require an undertaking by the owner to insure the building during its construction against loss by fire and have the insurance company include a clause agreeing that, in the event of a claim, it would pay the insurance money first to the builder "insofar as his interest may appear." A copy of the written contract between Summers and Diehl was produced and showed that the contract did not include a term of this kind. The parties testified that neither of them had insured the building itself, as distinct from the contents. It was acknowledged that the contractor, Summers, would have had an insurable interest and could have insured the house himself to the value of the contract.

Develop the arguments for the plaintiff and the defendant, and offer an opinion about whether the action should succeed.

8. M Inc. chartered a vessel from Q Corp. under a five-year agreement that gave M an option to purchase the vessel at the end of the five-year term, subject to "full performance of all its obligations under the agreement, including delivery of prompt payments in accordance with the schedule in the agreement." The agreement required seven monthly installments each year on specified dates, "in cash, by way of Bank Transfer and/or certified cheques." The parties subsequently agreed informally that M would deliver seven postdated, uncertified cheques to Q at the beginning of each operating season, and they would be deposited on the specified dates.

There were no problems with the cheques for the first four years, but the cheque for the first payment in the fifth year was returned by reason of insufficient funds. The bank's refusal to honour M's cheque was due to an error by a bank employee. Q immediately wrote to M stating that the option to purchase was void and of no further effect because of M's failure to make the payment as required. Q also gave M instructions on how to remedy its late payment. M promptly made the payment with interest in accordance with Q's instructions. All remaining payments were made on time.

As prescribed in the terms of their agreement, M gave notice to exercise the option to purchase the vessel. Q insisted that the failure to make the first payment in the fifth year on time was a precondition to exercising the option and that, accordingly, the option was void. M Inc. sued Q Corp. to enforce the option agreement. Give your opinion of which side should succeed.

Additional Resources for Chapter 12 on the Companion Website

(www.pearsoncanada.ca/smyth)

In addition to pre- and post-tests, mini-cases, and application exercises, the Companion Website includes the following province-specific resources for Chapter 12:

- **Alberta:** Limitations Period; Frustration Case
- **Atlantic Provinces:** Frustrated Contracts Act; Limitations Statutes
- **British Columbia:** Frustrated Contracts; Limitation Periods; Sale of Goods Act; Tender of Payment; Tender of Performance
- **Manitoba/Saskatchewan:** Frustrated Contracts Act; Limitations Act
- **Ontario:** Consumer Agreements; Effect of Frustration; Limitation Periods; Options to Terminate; Sale of Goods Act

Chapter 13

Breach of Contract and Its Remedies

Not all breaches are of the same importance, nor do they trigger all the same consequences or remedy. When one party commits a breach, the non-breaching party may have choices to make, and those choices depend on how the breach occurs, how serious it is, and what the losses are. The usual remedy—damages—may not always be sufficient; sometimes an equitable remedy will be more appropriate in the circumstances.

In this chapter we examine such questions as:

■ What options are available to a non-breaching party when the other party

- expressly repudiates the contract,

- simply fails to perform at the agreed time, or

- makes it impossible for itself to perform?

- How serious must the breach be to trigger various options?

- How do exemption clauses affect a non-breaching party's rights?

- What types of remedies are available to a non-breaching party?

- How are damages measured?

- When does a non-breaching party qualify for an equitable remedy?

- How is a judgment enforced?

IMPLICATIONS OF BREACH

A breach of any term in a contract entitles the non-breaching party to claim damages. However, serious breaches may also discharge a contract and release the non-breaching party from further performance of his or her contractual obligations. To discharge a contract, the breach must undermine the whole contract or a substantial part of the contract; only then is the option to discharge the contract available. The purpose of the contract must be defeated so that performance by the non-breaching party is rendered pointless.

Breach does not discharge a contract automatically (as does frustration or completed performance, for example). Even when a breach is sufficient to discharge the contract, the non-breaching party must choose to treat the contract as discharged and communicate its choice to the breaching party. Often the parties disagree over the importance of the breach and whether the non-breaching party is entitled to discharge.

Even when the non-breaching party would ordinarily have the right to treat its obligations as discharged, it loses that option in two situations. The first occurs when the innocent party decides to proceed with the contract and accept benefits under it, despite the breach. In the second, the innocent party may have received the benefit of the contract and not learned of the breach until this party's performance was already complete. Even in these circumstances, a breach of contract action claiming damages remains available.

ILLUSTRATION 13.1

(a) A agrees to sell 10 000 bags of potatoes to B Wholesale Grocers with nutritional content printed on the bag in 28-point font (twice the size required by government regulation). By mistake, the information is printed in 18-point font. B may feel annoyed and believe that its merchandise display will not be as effective. B may sue A and collect damages for its loss, but it cannot reject the potatoes without itself committing a breach that might make it also liable for damages.

(b) A agrees to sell 10 000 bags of potatoes to B Wholesale Grocers and to deliver them to B's warehouse on Wednesday in time for B to distribute them to its supermarket chain for a weekend special. A makes no delivery until late Friday afternoon. This is a breach of an essential term of the contract—delivery on Wednesday. B may reject the potatoes and discharge the contract, freeing itself from any obligation to pay for them. In addition, it may sue A for damages caused by failure to deliver on time. In the alternative, B may decide it still wants the potatoes and it may accept them. In this event, the contract is not discharged: B is liable to pay the price for the potatoes, subject to a deduction for damages caused by the failure to deliver them on time. If B should accept the potatoes and then refuse to pay for them, A could sue B for the price, and B could counter-claim for its damages.

We can see that if the breach is of a significant or essential term, the party committing the breach is still bound, but the injured party may elect to discharge the contract or to affirm the contract so that it continues to bind both parties.

We should note also that a major term may be broken in only a minor respect. Suppose in Illustration 13.1 that A delivers on time but is short by five bags. The quantity to be delivered is a major term, but delivering 9995 bags of 10 000 promised would be only a **minor breach** of that term and would not entitle B to reject the shipment. If, however, A had delivered only 5000 bags, a **major breach** would have occurred, and B could elect to reject them. Conversely, a minor term may be breached in a major way: What if the mistaken font size was smaller than government regulations required? If this rendered the product unsellable or exposed the vendor to government penalties, the wholesaler may be justified in rejecting the potatoes. It is not always easy to decide whether a term of a contract is essential or of lesser importance, or whether the breach is a serious one. In all disputes concerning a breach, the first task is to determine the importance of the term breached.

Terminology concerning essential and non-essential terms can be confusing: For a variety of reasons stemming from 19th-century developments in contract law, essential terms became known as **conditions** and non-essential terms as warranties. These names are unfortunate because "condition" may easily become confused with "condition precedent" (discussed in Chapter 12), and "warranty" may be confused with its special meaning in a sale of goods (where it means a guarantee of quality of the goods or of their ownership—usually an essential term). Despite the confusion, the use of "condition" and "warranty" to distinguish essential from non-essential terms has now become common. For more information on this topic, see the Companion Website.

minor breach   a breach of a non-essential term of a contract or of an essential term in a minor respect

major breach   a breach of the whole contract or of an essential term so that the purpose of the contract is defeated

conditions   essential terms of a contract

Ethical Issue   **Online Pharmacies**

The prices that drug manufacturers may charge for Canadian prescription drugs are controlled by the government regulatory board. This means that Canadian prescription drugs are cheaper (often significantly) than their U.S. counterparts. Online pharmacies offer Canadian pricing to American consumers. Several American states no longer block access to cheaper drugs through online Canadian pharmacies.

Not surprisingly, drug manufacturers are unhappy with the potential for reduced American profits. The contracts under which the drugs are sold to the Canadian pharmacies prohibit the export of the drugs. Beginning in 2004, several drug manufacturers, including Merck and Pfizer Inc., took the position that the online pharmacies were in substantial breach of their sale agreements. The manufacturers elected to discharge the contracts and stopped supplying further drugs to the pharmacies.

Questions to Consider

1. Do you think the prohibition against exporting is an essential term? If yes, what volume of online drug sales would amount to a major breach?

2. Is it ethical for drug manufacturers to withhold life-saving drugs? Should the consequences to the ultimate user, the patient, be relevant to the decision to discharge the contract with the pharmacy?

3. Are there public policy reasons why the Canadian government should object to the exportation of Canadian prescription drugs?

Sources: "Canadian Internet Pharmacies: Buying Drugs from Canada—Small but Growing," *Senior Magazine Online*, www.seniormag.com/canadianpharmacy/articles/growing-use.htm (accessed March 26, 2014); "Canadameds Upset With Power Struggle of Drug Companies to Stop Mail Order Pharmacy Industry in Canada," *Medical News Today*, January 18, 2005, www.medicalnewstoday.com/articles/18997.php; "Merck Cuts Off Net Pharmacies," *Canadian Press*, January 21, 2005.

HOW BREACH MAY OCCUR

A party to a contract may break it

- by expressly repudiating (rejecting) its obligations,
- by acting in a way that makes it impossible to perform its promises, or
- by either failing to perform at all or tendering an actual performance that falls short of its promise.

EXPRESS REPUDIATION

Express repudiation happens when one of the contracting parties tells the other that it does not intend to perform as it promised. If the repudiation is of the whole contract or of a substantial part of it, the promisee is entitled to treat the contract as being immediately at an end, to find another party to perform, and to sue for whatever damages it sustains. Before substituting a new party to proceed with performance, it is prudent for the promisee to inform the repudiating party that it is treating the contract as immediately terminated and is reserving its rights to sue for damages for breach. When express repudiation occurs before the time agreed for performance, it is known as **anticipatory breach** and the non-breaching party has a choice to accept it or insist on performance.[1]

Alternatively, a promisee may continue to insist on performance. If it chooses this option and does not receive performance by the time stated in the contract, it is still entitled to damages for breach of contract, but it takes a chance that intervening events may provide the promisor with an excuse for not performing—for example, a frustrating event could occur.

> **express repudiation** one of the contracting parties advises the other that it does not intend to perform as promised

> **anticipatory breach** an express repudiation that occurs before the time agreed for performance

---

ILLUSTRATION 13.2

A Co. contracts with B Ltd. for the delivery to A Co. in six months of well-drilling equipment at an agreed price. A week later, B Ltd. discovers that it has agreed to a price that is much too low and informs A Co. that it will not deliver the equipment as promised. B Ltd. has committed an anticipatory breach of its contract with A Co., and A Co. need not wait until the delivery date to sue B Ltd.

The courts have recognized that, as a promisee, A Co. is entitled not only to performance of the contract in six months' time but also to a continuous expectation of performance in the period between formation of the contract and its performance. During that period, A Co. may have entered into a drilling contract relying on delivery of the equipment. The concept is a basic one: A contract exists and has legal effect from the time of its formation, and not just from the time of its performance. Breach may occur before performance is due.

CASE 13.1

Atkinson's employment contract contained a clause that he would not work in competition with his employer in the same town for two years after the termination of his employment. The employer dismissed him without cause in breach of the contract. Atkinson recovered damages for wrongful dismissal and then began to work for a competitor within the district. His former employer sought an injunction to restrain him from competing, but failed. The court held that the company had, by its dismissal, repudiated the entire employment contract, and this entitled Atkinson to consider his own contractual obligations at an end.[2]

Major breach amounting to repudiation may also occur at the time set for performance, and it too will free the aggrieved party from further obligations.

---

[1] *Brown v. Belleville (City)* 2013 ONCA 148 at para 5; J. Cassels and E. Adjin-Tettey, *Remedies: The Law of Damages*, 3rd ed. (Toronto: Irwin Law, 2014) at 442-46.

[2] *General Billposting Co. v. Atkinson*, [1909] A.C. 118. This decision was followed in a preliminary hearing before trial in *Gerrard v. Century 21 Armour Real Estate Inc.* (1991), 4 O.R. (3d) 191, even where it was unclear whether there had been repudiation of the contract by the employer.

ILLUSTRATION 13.3

X Inc., a wholesale distributor of specialty coffee equipment, agreed to supply B Ltd., a chain of retail kitchen stores, with a large quantity of new espresso machines, along with sample coffee "pods" so that customers could sample the coffees to promote the new product. Several days before delivery, the manager of X Inc. discovers that the coffee makers are in stock but that the demonstration coffee pods have not arrived and appear to have been lost during shipment. Knowing that B Ltd. plans to feature the new product, X Inc.'s manager would be wise to notify B Ltd. at once of the expected breach of this minor term. B Ltd. might then be able to arrange in advance for an alternative supply of coffee. If X Inc. were to deliver the machines without prior notice of its inability to supply the coffee, B Ltd. might suffer a greater loss for which X Inc. would be liable.

In these examples, repudiation takes the form of words or conduct affecting performance of the whole contract. As noted above, if one party repudiates only a minor term of the contract, the other party is not entitled to treat the contract as discharged. When a business is unable to perform exactly as promised, a wise manager, as soon as she is aware of the situation, will notify the other party so that it may take immediate steps to reduce any loss that the breach may cause.

ONE PARTY RENDERS PERFORMANCE IMPOSSIBLE

A willful or negligent act by the promisor that destroys its ability to fulfill its contractual promises amounts to breach of contract—this does not include an act that is an involuntary response to forces beyond its control. A deliberate or negligent act that makes performance impossible amounts to repudiation. The promisor may not have said so in words, but has implied as much by her conduct—a form of self-induced frustration considered in Chapter 12. As with express repudiation, conduct that makes performance impossible may take place either before or during performance.

ILLUSTRATION 13.4

A agrees to sell her Ferrari sports car to B for $30 000, to be delivered in three weeks. A few days later, X, unaware of the agreement between A and B, offers A $35 000 for the car. A accepts and delivers the car to X that day. A is in breach of the contract with B the moment she makes the sale to X, and B may sue her as soon as he learns of it. A is not permitted to argue that she can still deliver the car on time by buying it back from X; B is entitled to a continuous expectation of A's performance until the day agreed for delivery arrives.

Ethical Issue   Good Faith Performance

Civil law jurisdictions, including Quebec, recognize a general duty of good-faith performance. The Civil Code of Quebec states:

> The parties shall conduct themselves in good faith both at the time the obligation is created and at the time it is performed or extinguished. (art. 1375)[2A]

The United States also recognizes a generalized duty of good faith. The United States Restatement of Contracts[3] describes it this way:

> Every contract imposes upon each party a duty of good faith and fair dealing in its performance and its enforcement. (s. 205)[3A]

>

[2A] Article 1375 C.C.Q.

[3] In the U.S., common rules of contracts and torts have been collected into one statute. The Restatement of Contracts is such a statute, as is the Restatement of Torts.

[3A] Duty of Good Faith and Fair Dealing, s. 205.

Although difficult to define, good faith is thought to include concepts of fairness, honesty, and consideration for the interests of the other party.

So far, Canadian common law jurisdictions have not recognized a generalized duty of good faith. The Ontario Court of Appeal put it this way:

> Canadian courts have not recognized a stand-alone duty of good faith that is independent from the terms expressed in a contract or from the objectives that emerge from those provisions. The implication of a duty of good faith has not gone so far as to create new, unbargained-for, rights and obligations. Nor has it been used to alter the express terms of the contract reached by the parties. Instead, courts have implied a duty of good faith with a view to securing the performance and enforcement of the contract made by the parties, or as it is sometimes put, to ensure that parties do not act in a way that eviscerates or defeats the objectives of the agreement.[4]

One particular example of this specialized, narrow approach to good faith is increased damages when employers wrongfully dismiss an employee in bad faith.[5]

Questions to Consider

1. Should Canada recognize a general duty of good faith in contractual performance and enforcement? How does a generalized duty of good faith differ from an implied duty of good faith performance of the particular terms of the contract?

2. Should a good faith duty be implied into some types of contracts?

3. How would a good faith duty be distinguished from a fiduciary duty?

Sources: J.D. McCamus, *The Law of Contracts* (Toronto: Irwin Law Inc., 2006) at 780–805; W. Tetley, "Good Faith in Contract Particularly in Contracts of Arbitration and Chartering" (2004) 35 JMLC 561–616, available online at www.mcgill.ca/files/maritimelaw/goodfaith.pdf.

FAILURE OF PERFORMANCE

Types of Failure

Unlike the other two types of breach, failure of performance usually becomes apparent only at the time set for performance. The degree of failure may vary: It may be a total failure to perform, it may be a grossly inadequate performance, or it may be very minor. There may be satisfactory performance of all but one of the terms of the contract or of only part of a main term. The extent of a failure always has an important effect on the types of remedies available to the injured party.

Inadequate performance by the first party will again trigger the decision of whether the second party is excused or must still perform, as discussed above. The question is complicated in contracts requiring the delivery of goods by installments when the first quantity delivered fails to meet the amount called for in the contract but future installments could make up the deficiency. Partial delivery may be merely inconvenient, or it may be completely unsatisfactory.

ILLUSTRATION 13.5

(a) The seller contracts to deliver 6000 tonnes of coal in 12 monthly installments of about 500 tonnes each. One of the terms is that the buyer is to provide the trucks to take the coal away. In the first month, the buyer sends sufficient trucks to take away only 400 tonnes. The buyer's default would not likely be sufficient to discharge the seller from its obligation to stand ready to provide the remaining 5600 tonnes over the following 11 months.[6]

>

---

[4] *Transamerica Life Canada Inc. v. ING Canada Inc.* (2003), 68 O.R. (3d) 457 (C.A.) at para. 53; *MHR Board Game Design Inc. v. Canadian Broadcasting Corporation* 2013 ONCA 728 at para.

[5] *Wallace v. United Grain Growers Ltd.* (1997), 152 D.L.R. (4th) 1 (S.C.C.). See also *Honda Canada Inc. v. Keays* 2008 SCC 39. For a discussion of a distributor's duty of good faith, see *1193430 Ontario Inc. v. Boa-Franc Inc.* (2005), 78 O.R. (3d) 81 (C.A.).

[6] See *Simpson v. Crippin* (1872), L.R. 8 Q.B. 14, where, in a similar situation, the buyer took delivery of only 158 tonnes in the first month, and yet the seller was held to the contract.

Often, an innocent party is left with a dilemma. If she is really concerned about the seriousness of continuing defective performance, it is wise for her to seek legal advice before claiming to be discharged of her own obligations; otherwise, she risks being held liable for wrongful repudiation should a court find that the seller's default was only a minor breach.[8]

In a contract where one party is to perform by installments, the other may consider itself freed from liability only if it can offer convincing affirmative answers to both of these questions:

(a) Is there good reason to think that future performance will be equally defective?

(b) Is either the expected deficiency or the actual deficiency to date important relative to the whole performance promised?

The Doctrine of Substantial Performance

substantial performance performance that does not comply in some minor way with the requirements of the contract

The doctrine of **substantial performance** states that a promisor is entitled to enforce a contract when it has substantially performed, even though its performance does not comply in some minor way with the requirements of the contract. The promisor's claim is, however, subject to a reduction for damages caused by its defective performance. The effect of the doctrine is that a promisee cannot use a trivial failure of performance to avoid its own obligations.[9] There can often be substantial disagreement over whether a failure in performance is serious or trivial.[10]

Mistakes in Performance

What happens when a party "overperforms" an existing obligation by paying more money than is owed? What about when it performs in a mistaken belief that an obligation existed, as when an insurance company pays a claim and then discovers that the loss arose from a risk not covered by the policy? What happens when someone simply pays the wrong person? What are the consequences for the other party to the original contract who is still waiting for performance? What are the consequences for the "lucky" recipient of mistaken or overperformance?

quasi-contract an obligation that may arise, not as a result of contractual relations, but because one party has received an unfair benefit at the expense of the other

unjust enrichment an unfair benefit

When the "lucky" recipient knows that the payment does not belong to him, the answer is straightforward: He cannot "snap up" a benefit that belongs to another person—a court will order him to restore it. The question becomes more difficult when the recipient honestly but mistakenly believes that he is entitled to the benefit. **Quasi-contract** (so called because the obligations may not arise as a direct result of contractual relations between the parties) uses the concepts of **unjust enrichment** and restitution to force the recipient of a windfall to repay it. If, in all the circumstances, a court finds that it would be an unjust enrichment to allow the recipient to keep the benefit, it will order restitution by finding a duty implied by law to pay for it.

---

[7] *Hoare v. Rennie* (1859), 157 E.R. 1083.

[8] For an example of the difficulties that a party claiming a major breach may encounter, see *Agrifoods International Corp. v. Beatrice Foods Inc.*, [1997] B.C.J. No. 393.

[9] *Dakin & Co. Ltd. v. Lee*, [1916] 1 K.B. 566.

[10] See *Miller v. Advanced Farming Systems Ltd.*, [1969] S.C.R. 845; *Sail Labrador Ltd. v. Challenge One*, [1999] 1 S.C.R. 265.

With respect to the mistaken party's obligations under the original contract, performance to the wrong person is no performance at all, and the mistaken party remains obligated to perform to the correct party. Otherwise the original contracting party has experienced a total failure of performance. The above described rules of breach (major or minor) apply. To avoid breaching the original contract, the mistaken party will have to perform again.

EXEMPTION CLAUSES

Their Purpose

Business parties must protect themselves from potential liability for breach of contract. An exemption clause included in a contract to prevent the other party from suing is popular for a number of reasons. First, exemption clauses allocate the risk so parties know who should insure against what. Next, they allow suppliers to charge lower prices, since the supplier need not increase its price to cover the costs and damages arising from customer lawsuits. Even if sued, the exemption clause will usually offer a complete defence and the business can recover its legal costs from the unsuccessful litigant. Finally, if the supplier is in the position of using a standard form contract (especially if the contract is detailed with many other terms), it will, in most circumstances, have a distinct advantage over its customer and can design the clause in its favour.

Exemption clauses usually make good sense and work reasonably well when the bargaining power and knowledge of the law are relatively equal between the parties. For example, one party may willingly assume a risk in return for a lower price; that party may already have adequate insurance coverage. Or the activity may be extremely hazardous; a charter airline may be unwilling to fly a client into northern mountain regions in winter except at the client's own risk. Generally speaking, however, the party preparing the standard form contract designs the exemption clause clearly to its own advantage, and the courts take a three-step analytical approach to deciding if a party should escape the effect of an exemption clause.[11]

Analytical Approach

Courts take a three-step approach to deciding whether or not to enforce an exemption clause: First, the court decides whether the clause covers the circumstances in question. If it does, the court moves to the second step and determines whether the clause was unconscionable at the time of contracting. If the clause is unconscionable, it will not be enforced. However, if it is not unconscionable, the court must decide a third and final question—whether there is a strong public policy reason against enforcement.[12]

Step One: Interpretation of Exemption Clauses   The court's first question is, "Does the clause apply to the facts?" The court must assess the intention of the parties by interpreting the words used in the clause to decide whether the clause applies to the given circumstances. Exemption clauses are typically written using very broad, flexible language. A supplier of machinery might exempt itself from "all liability for defects in the product supplied, for any negligence of its employees, and for any guarantees implied by custom or trade usage—except for guarantees expressly set out in the contract, such as replacing any defective parts for three months." Courts have taken the view that words must be

---

[11] *Tercon Contractors Ltd. v. British Columbia (Transportation and Highways)*, 2010 S.C.C. 4, [2010] 1 S.C.R. 59, at para 21- 23.

[12] *Ibid*; See also *Roy v. 1216393 Ontario Inc.*, 2011 BCCA 500 at para 22.

interpreted in a manner that is consistent with other terms in the contract, its commercial purpose or context, and any relevant statutory scheme.[13] If there is ambiguity, it must be interpreted against the **drawing party** because that party had every chance to make the ambiguity more clear.[14] Even so, the courts respect the theory of freedom of contract and, in the absence of special rules (such as exist for common carriers) or special statutory protection (as in consumer protection legislation), they will not make a new contract for the parties. If an exemption clause applies to the breach that has occurred, the injured party—subject to the discussion that follows—has no remedy.

drawing party the contracting party that prepared the agreement and/or the particular clause

---

CASE 13.2

Purolator undertook to deliver a tender document from Cathcart's office to the office of Ontario Hydro. The bill of lading contained a clause stating that Purolator would not be liable for "any special, consequential or other damages for any reason including delay in delivery." The tender document was never delivered to Ontario Hydro.

In an action by Cathcart to recover lost profits, Purolator admitted that had the bid been received, it would have been accepted and that the loss of profit by Cathcart was $37 000. But Purolator claimed that the clause exempted it from any liability. However, Cathcart succeeded in its action. The court construed the clause strictly against the drafter of the term, Purolator, even though the parties were of equal bargaining power: the clause, on its "true construction," covered only damages rising from delay, not from a complete failure to deliver.[15]

Step Two: Unconscionable Clauses   If the clause covers the circumstances, it may still be unenforceable. Sometimes when there is a significant imbalance in the bargaining power of the parties, the stronger party takes an unfair advantage of the weaker one by extracting unfair or **unconscionable terms**. An unfair outcome alone is not sufficient to make a clause unconscionable; similarly inequality of bargaining power alone is not sufficient. An unconscionable term has both inequality in the process of creating the clause and an unfair outcome.[16]

unconscionable terms terms agreed to by parties of unequal bargaining power that give an unfair advantage to the powerful party over the weaker party

Usually, commercial contracts are negotiated by sophisticated business parties that lack imbalance in bargaining. However, consumer contracts are one-sided in favour of the retailer and are offered on "a take it or leave it" basis, with little time to review their contents. Some web retailers simply include a link on their ordering page to the "terms and conditions" of the purchase contract (including the exemption clause); others require the purchaser to scroll through all such terms and indicate acceptance before completing an order. In a leading Ontario case, *Microsoft v. Rudder*,[17] where the consumer plaintiffs complained about the terms of Microsoft's standard form online licence, the Ontario Superior Court likened scrolling through terms of an online contract to flipping through the pages of a multi-page paper contract. The judge in *Rudder* concluded that if a consumer clicked "I agree" at the end of a series of standard-form terms, she would be bound by those terms, including, presumably, any exemption clause. Still, courts continue to examine exemption clauses very carefully, and to refuse to protect a defendant when it would appear the clause is unconscionable.[18]

---

[13] *Tercon, supra* n. 11 at para 64, 65, 72.

[14] *Tercon, supra* n. 11 at para 62, 79; *Hunter Engineering v. Syncrude*, [1989] 1 S.C.R. 426 (S.C.C.); *Hillis Oil and Sales Ltd. v. Wynn's Canada, Ltd.*, [1986] 1 S.C.R. 57 at 68–9.

[15] *Cathcart Inspection Services Ltd. v. Purolator Courier Ltd.* (1982), 34 O.R. (2d) 187.

[16] *Roy, supra* n. 12 at paras 29-30.

[17] (1999), 2 C.P.R. (4th) 474.

[18] *Monta Arbre Inc. v. Inter-Traffic (1983) Ltd.* (1989), 71 O.R. (2d) 182. See also *Hunter Engineering v. Syncrude, supra*, n. 14.

Step Three: Public Policy and Public Interest Finally, even if the wording of the clause applies to the situation and the clause was not unconscionable at the time the contract was formed, a court may still refuse to enforce an exemption clause if the injured party can "point to some paramount consideration of public policy sufficient to override the public interest in freedom of contract."[19] Is there greater harm to the public interest if the offending conduct is protected? Conduct approaching criminal or fraudulent behaviour is well recognized as being against public policy, and therefore it would not be in the public interest to allow an exemption clause to insulate the offending party from liability for such conduct. In Case 13.3, the distinction between unconscionability and violation of public policy is blurred, but the end result is the same. The court may refuse to enforce the exemption clause that would protect the offender. For more information on this topic, see the Companion Website.

CASE 13.3

Dow Chemical sold plastic resin to its customer for use in the fabrication of natural gas pipelines. At the time of the sale, Dow knew the product was defective. Instead of disclosing the known defect to the buyer, Dow chose to try to protect itself by including exemption clauses in its sales contracts. After some years, the pipelines began to deteriorate, causing considerable property damage and human health risks from leaks and explosions. The Alberta Court of Appeal refused to apply the exemption clause, concluding that "a party to a contract will not be permitted to engage in unconscionable conduct secure in the knowledge that no liability can be imposed upon it because of an exclusionary clause."[20] When the Supreme Court of Canada reviewed the case, it agreed with the result but applied public policy grounds, saying "Dow was so contemptuous of its contractual obligation and reckless as to the consequences of the breach as to forfeit the assistance of the court. The public policy that favours freedom of contract was outweighed by the public policy that seeks to curb its abuse."[21]

TYPES OF REMEDIES

In addition to the right to treat the contract as discharged as a result of breach, an injured party may have several other remedies available, depending on the type of breach and the subject matter of the contract. They are as follows:

(a) damages
(b) equitable remedies—specific performance, injunction, and rescission
(c) quantum meruit

DAMAGES

The Purpose of an Award of Damages

Damages are awarded to place the injured party in the position he would have been in if the contract had been properly completed. The award is intended to compensate an injured party for the loss caused by failure to perform, not to punish the party liable for the breach. In this respect, the purpose of an award of damages in contract is similar to that in tort law—that is, compensation and not punishment. Still, knowing that the injured party can force it to pay compensation usually deters a party from committing any breach it can avoid. There are exceptions.

---

[19] *Tercon Contractors Ltd. v. British Columbia, supra,* n. 11 at para. 82.

[20] *Plas-Tex Canada Ltd. v. Dow Chemical of Canada Ltd.,* 2004 ABCA 309, 245 D.L.R. (4th) 650 at para. 53.

[21] *Tercon Contractors Ltd. v. British Columbia, supra,* n. 11, at para. 119.

ILLUSTRATION 13.6

X Inc. contracts to supply 100 000 widgets at $2.00 each to Y Corp. It expects to earn a profit of $20 000 on the contract. Shortly afterward, X Inc. receives an offer to supply a different item to Z Ltd. at a profit of $60 000—but if it accepts the offer from Z Ltd., it will be unable to produce the 100 000 widgets for Y Corp.

X Inc. learns that a competing manufacturer can supply widgets of equal quality to Y Corp. at $2.25—that is, for

$25 000 more than its own price. In these circumstances, X Inc. would gain financially if it were to forgo its profit of $20 000 on the contract with Y Corp. and pay that company $25 000 in damages for breach while earning $60 000 on the new contract—a net gain of $15 000.

As discussed later in this chapter, less often damages are awarded to compensate for non-economic injury (such as mental distress) and to punish bad faith or malicious behaviour.[22] Additional intangible costs incurred by a breaching party include harming continuing good relations with the affected customer, as well as one's general reputation for honouring commitments.

Prerequisites for an Award of Damages

1. Loss Must Flow from the Breach. To qualify for recovery, damage must "flow naturally from the breach." This principle has been interpreted to mean that a loss resulting from breach must be within the foreseeable limits of what the parties would have expected as a likely consequence of a failure to perform, had they thought about it when they drew up their contract. Damages are not generally awarded to compensate an injured party for some unusual or unexpected consequence of breach.

A carrier failed to deliver a vital piece of machinery promptly to a sawmill as instructed by an employee of the mill. As a result, the sawmill had to suspend operations until the part arrived. The sawmill company sued the carrier for the losses suffered through the shutdown, but the court refused to award damages because the employee had not told the carrier about the vital nature of the machinery when the carrier agreed to transport it, and the carrier had no reason to foresee the loss.

If the carrier had been told of the importance of the item, it would likely have been liable for the loss—unless it exempted itself from liability and suggested that the sawmill insure the shipment against risk of delay or loss. Or it would have placed the item in a higher category of freight to ensure greater care in delivery and charged a higher rate for its services.[23]

Sometimes a party does enter into a contract with knowledge of special liability if it fails to perform.

An engineering company contracted to make a machine and deliver it by a given date. It then made a subcontract with the defendant firm to manufacture an essential part, clearly stating the date that the entire machine had to be completed

>

---

[22] Cassels and Adjin-Tettey, *supra* n. 1, at 11-12.

[23] B.C. *Saw Mill Co. v. Nettleship* (1868), L.R. 3 C.P. 499. See also *Hadley v. Baxendale* (1854), 156 E.R. 145; *Koufos v. C. Czarnikow*, The Heron II, [1969] 1 A.C. 350; *Cornwall Gravel Co. Ltd. v. Purolator Courier Ltd.* (1978), 18 O.R. (2d) 551. Cassels and Adjin-Tettey, *supra* n. 1, at 464.

The critical determination is made based upon the actual and supposed knowledge of the parties at the time the contract was formed, not at the time the breach
occurs.

2. Damages Must Be Mitigated.   A party that has suffered a loss as a result of
breach of contract is expected to do what it can to minimize its losses: the damages it can
recover at law will not include what it might reasonably have avoided. In this respect,
mitigation in contract is similar to that in tort. A business that has contracted to sell
perishable goods and had them rejected by the breaching party cannot let the goods spoil.
Instead, it should resell them at the best obtainable price as quickly as it can if it wishes
to recoup any resulting loss in an action for damages. Similarly, when a business has
agreed to buy goods and the seller fails to deliver, the buyer should move to replace the
goods from another supplier as soon as possible. The same rule applies when a contract of
employment is broken by the employer. An employee, in suing for damages for wrongful
dismissal, should be able to show that he or she made every reasonable effort to find suitable alternative employment as a means of mitigating the loss. For more information on
this topic, see the Companion Website.

In summary, an injured party can only recover for the losses resulting from the
breach that could not be reasonably avoided. Any costs associated with mitigating or
reducing the loss are recoverable as damages. It naturally follows that if a party acts in a
manner that aggravates or increases the loss, it will be denied recovery for the additional
damages.[25]

> **mitigation**   action by the injured
> party to reduce the extent of loss
> caused by the other party's breach

THE MEASUREMENT OF DAMAGES

Damages for breach of contract may arise from a number of different types of loss; depending upon the facts of the case, any one type or combination of types of damages may be
experienced by the non-breaching party and be eligible for compensation. Usually it is
the court that assesses the amount of damage and assigns a value to a particular type of
loss; however, sometimes parties set the value of possible damages in the terms of the
contract.

Liquidated Damages

When forming a contract, parties may agree on the amount of damages to be awarded for
any type of damage if a breach should occur. The actual value of any eventual loss may turn
out to be greater or less than the agreed amount, but the injured party's recovery will be
limited to the pre-set amount, provided it was a genuine attempt by the parties to estimate
a loss. The contractual terms will conclusively govern the amount of damages awarded.
Such provisions for **liquidated damages** can provide some economic certainty—each party
will know the extent of liability or recovery at the start of the contractual relationship and
may plan accordingly.

> **liquidated damages**   an amount
> agreed on to be paid in damages by a
> party to a contract if it should commit
> a breach

---

[24] *Hydraulic Engineering Co. v. McHaffie Goslett* (1878), 4 Q.B.D. 670. See also *Telecommander Corp. v. United
Parcel Service Canada Ltd.*, [1996] O.J. No. 4664.

[25] Cassels and Adjin-Tettey, *supra* n. 1 at 428-30.

ILLUSTRATION 13.7

P Inc. agrees to construct an office building for Q Properties Inc., with a completion date of May 31. Both parties agree that any delay will cause a loss in revenue to Q from prospective tenants. A term of the contract states that, for any delay in completion, Q may deduct $600 per day from its final payment of $100 000 to P, payable one month after Q obtains possession of the building. Such a term is binding upon both parties whether Q Properties Inc. suffers a larger or smaller loss because of delay.

penalty clause a term specifying an exorbitant amount for breach of contract, intended to frighten a party into performance

We must distinguish between a genuine attempt to anticipate or "liquidate" the consequences of a breach of contract and a **penalty clause**. If a term in the contract specifies an exorbitant amount, out of all relation to the probable consequences of breach, a court may find that it is intended merely to frighten a party into performance. Accordingly, the court will hold that it is a penalty clause and will disregard it and award damages based on an assessment of the actual loss suffered.

A sum paid as a deposit on the formation of a contract, to be forfeited on failure to perform, is a common type of liquidated damages provision, but it is treated somewhat differently. Partly because the money has already been paid as a guarantee of performance and partly because of a long history of deposits being forfeited, courts are reluctant to overturn such provisions even when they seem harsh. If, however, the sum is described as a part payment or a down payment, the courts are more willing to examine whether its forfeiture would be a penalty.

At the other extreme, a term limiting liquidated damages to a very small sum may be tantamount to an exemption clause. For instance, if a term states that $1 shall be payable as full compensation for breach, the court will undertake the three-step analysis discussed under "Exemption Clauses" above.

Nominal Damages

Occasionally, a court may award nominal damages to acknowledge a breach of contract where there is no real loss experienced by the non-breaching party. A court award of $1 will at least acknowledge the validity of the plaintiff's claim where a question of principle is at stake. In general, when the amount in dispute is nominal, the likelihood that a "successful" plaintiff will still have to pay or share court costs discourages such litigation.

TYPES OF DAMAGES

Expectation Damages

expectation damages an amount awarded for breach of contract, based on expected benefits or profits

Expectation damages are the usual remedy for breach of contract—the value of the expected benefit of performance. The basic calculation is as follows:

> Expectation damages = (Expected position of the plaintiff if the contract had been performed) − (The actual position the plaintiff is in after the breach of contract)

An award of expectation damages for breach of contract contrasts sharply with the measurement of tort damages where recovery is limited to actual harm or loss suffered.[26] Expectation damages in contract look to the future and value expected future profits of the aborted transaction. For example, breach of a contract to sell a limited edition baseball may include an award for the expected rise in value of the baseball—that is, the lost investment value. This would not be the case for a contract to supply baseballs for use in a little league game. In this second case, only the mitigation cost of buying replacement baseballs from another source would be recoverable.

opportunity cost the lost chance of making a similar contract with a different promisor

An award for expectation damages may also be based upon lost **opportunity cost**— this is because a party will have given up an opportunity to make a similar contract with

---

[26] Cassels and Adjin-Tettey, *supra* n. 1, at 18.

someone else in order to contract with the breaching party. Illustration 13.8 demonstrates the approach courts take in the calculation of expectation damages.

ILLUSTRATION 13.8

Suppose, first, that a buyer is in breach by refusing to accept delivery of the goods purchased. In an action for damages,[27] the first consideration is whether the seller's supply of goods exceeds the demand for them—that is, whether the seller can supply goods to all prospective customers.

If so, the buyer's breach results in the seller losing the profit on one sale, regardless of the resale of those same goods to a second buyer: The seller would have made the second sale even if the first buyer had accepted the goods, and would have made two sales instead of one. Accordingly, the seller may recover damages from the first buyer amounting to the lost profits on their contract of sale.

However, if the seller has limited supply and it could not have filled a second order if the first buyer had accepted the goods, the seller's damages will be measured, first, by its additional expenses in taking reasonable steps to find a second buyer, and second, by any loss in revenue as a result of having to accept a lower sale price to dispose of the goods. The seller may suffer no damages at all if it resells for the full contract price (or more) without additional selling expenses.[28]

Suppose, instead, a seller breaks its contract by failing to deliver on time. If the buyer can obtain the goods elsewhere, the damages will be those reasonable expenses incurred in seeking an alternative supply and any additional price the buyer has had to pay above the original contract price. Of course, if the buyer obtains an alternative supply for the same or a lower price than that in the original contract, there will be no damages without added expenses in seeking the new supply.

Consequential Damages

Consequential damages are, in a sense, secondary losses, one stage removed from the immediate effects of breach. Nevertheless, they may be both serious and reasonably foreseeable at the time of contracting, so that a defendant will be liable to compensate for them. Suppose a seller fails to deliver goods that the buyer was to use as components to build another product for resale. Damages arising from the buyer's breach of the subsequent sale contracts are consequential damages. The seller will be liable for the lost profits on any resale transactions, and damage claims may also include claims against the buyer by its own customers as a result of its unavoidable default on contracts with them.

consequential damages
secondary losses incurred by the non-breaching party that were foreseeable at the time of contracting

---

CASE 13.6

Lakelse Dairy Products purchased a new bulk-milk tank truck from General Dairy Machinery (GDM) to transport milk to its production facility. GDM specialized in building such vehicles and warranted that it was fit for the purpose. However, the truck had serious flaws—there were cracks in the tank where milk remained in sufficient quantities that when the milk deteriorated and went bad, new shipments of milk were affected. Lakelse hired experts to find the source of the problem.

It took several months to uncover the defect in the truck. Meanwhile, a substantial amount of milk had to be discarded, and some had to be taken back from customers. When the source of the problem was discovered, Lakelse had to lease another tank truck. It sued GDM successfully, not only for the direct loss in value of the defective tank truck and the cost of leasing another truck, but also for the lost profits that would have been made on the discarded milk if it had been sold by Lakelse at market value.[29]

---

[27] The Sale of Goods Act may allow the vendor to sue for the price instead of damages.

[28] In one sense, the first buyer's breach enabled the seller to make the second sale. See *Apeco of Canada Ltd. v. Windmill Place* (1978), 82 D.L.R. (3d) 1; Cassels and Adjin-Tettey, *supra* n. 1 at 28.

[29] *Lakelse Dairy Products Ltd. v. General Dairy Machinery & Supply Ltd.* (1970), 10 D.L.R. (3d) 277.

Consequential damages may arise in any contract, not only in the sale of goods. For instance, failure to repair the heating system of a concert hall as promised in time for a performance in midwinter could lead to the cancellation of the program, making the heating contractor liable for the losses due to cancellation, as well as for damage to the building by frozen pipes, since both are foreseeable harms.

General Damages

As in the tort context, the term general damages describes an estimated amount for intangible injury that a court may award, over and above specifically proven losses for harm. Damage cannot be calculated in precise monetary terms, but the court believes such an award is necessary to compensate the aggrieved party fairly. For example, if a surgeon undertook to improve the appearance of a professional entertainer by performing plastic surgery on her nose, but the result was disfigurement, a court would have to decide what general damages, over and above specific out-of-pocket medical and hospital expenses, would compensate the plaintiff for the effects of this failure on her state of mind and professional morale. A U.S. court has, in fact, awarded general damages for breach of contract in such circumstances.[30]

Reliance Damages

As an alternative to expectation damages, which place the injured party into the position it would have been in if the contract had been properly performed, an injured party may claim **reliance damages**, which compensate the injured party for wasted time, effort, and expenses preparing for performance—in essence putting the injured party back in their pre-contract position. Sometimes reliance damages yield a larger amount than expectation damages, usually when mitigation efforts have been very successful.

Suppose that a management consultant contracts to spend three months advising a manufacturing company on the reorganization of its operations. During the two months prior to commencement of the contract, the consultant spends time assembling and preparing customized material. Just prior to the start date, the client cancels the contract. Even if the management consultant replaces the lost fee with another consulting opportunity, she has still lost the time, effort, and expenditures involved in the preparation. Now it is merely wasted effort—not needed for the substituted job—that she could have used more productively for other contracts. In these circumstances, the consultant may recover as reliance damages the costs of all expenditures and wasted effort that were reasonably made in preparation for her performance of the first contract.[31]

Punitive Damages

As noted above, punishment is not the purpose of contract damages; however, in rare circumstances courts have awarded punitive damages for malicious or bad faith behaviour of the breaching party.[32] In *Whiten v. Pilot Insurance Company*, the Supreme Court of Canada confirmed the trial judge's award of $1 000 000 in punitive damages in a case concerning the defendant's refusal to pay a claim under a property insurance policy (or contract). In its decision, the Court held that, while punitive damages in contract law are exceptional, they are appropriate if there has been "high-handed, malicious, arbitrary, or highly reprehensible misconduct that departs to a marked degree from ordinary standards of decent behaviour."[33]

---

[30] *Sullivan v. O'Connor*, 296 N.E. 2d 183 (1973). Damages of $13 500 were awarded. See Cassels and Adjin-Tettey, *supra* n. 1 at 251.

[31] *PreMD Inc. v. Ogilvy Renault LLP*, 2013 ONCA 412 at paras 65-70.

[32] Cassels and Adjin-Tettey, *supra* n. 1 at 346-53. See e.g. *Ribeiro v. CIBC* (1992), 13 O.R (3d) 278; *Wallace v. United Grain Growers Ltd.* (1997), 152 D.L.R. (4th) 1 (S.C.C.).

[33] *Whiten v. Pilot Insurance Co.*, 2002 SCC 18, [2002] 1 S.C.R. 595.

This kind of "values-based" assessment of behaviour may lead to inconsistent and unpredictable results. In *Fidler v. Sun Life Assurance Co. of Canada*,[34] the British Columbia Court of Appeal's award of punitive damages arising from the five-year denial of long-term disability benefits was set aside by the Supreme Court because the conduct was not malicious or oppressive. Although rare, punitive damages are possible in extreme circumstances. Courts will exercise this discretion cautiously.

CHALLENGES IN MEASURING DAMAGES

Mental Anguish

In the context of tort law, courts recognize pain, suffering, nervous shock, and humiliation as harms for which they should grant recovery as part of general damages. In an increasing number of contract cases, mental distress resulting from breach is recognized as a form of non-economic harm entitled to compensation. The Supreme Court of Canada stated that the purpose of recognizing mental distress in an award of damages is "to substitute other amenities for those that have been lost, not to compensate for the loss of something with a money value ... [and] to provide more general physical arrangements above and beyond those directly relating to the injuries, in order to make life more endurable."[35]

Courts initially awarded this type of damage for contracts that promised some form of pleasure such as vacations or luxury items. Now, damages for mental distress may be awarded in any breach of contract action if this type of damage was reasonably foreseeable by the parties at the time the contract was created.[36] In one case, mental anguish damages were awarded against an airline for breach of contract in transporting the plaintiffs' dogs[37] as compensation for the mental suffering endured when they learned that their dogs suffocated while being carried in the baggage compartment of an airplane. The law is still evolving in this area, and it is not clear whether the plaintiff must suffer some psychological illness or whether mere mental suffering or distress is sufficient.[38] Wrongful dismissal and lost holiday cases often consider this type of general damage.

1. Wrongful Dismissal   Mental anguish often occurs when an employee is fired, especially after long years of service. Apart from direct financial loss, for which he or she is entitled to compensation, the dismissed employee may feel humiliated and suffer a serious loss of confidence. When the Supreme Court of Canada considered this type of damage it confirmed that although "normal distress and hurt feelings resulting from dismissal are not compensable . . . [mental anguish damages may be awarded] when the employer engages in conduct during the course of dismissal that is unfair or in bad faith such as [behaviour that is] untruthful, misleading or unduly insensitive."[39] Examples of behaviours that meet this test are lying about the reason for dismissal or defaming the reputation of the employee.[40]

---

[34] [2006] 2 S.C.R. 3.

[35] *Lindal v. Lindal* (1981), 129 D.L.R. (3d) 263, per Dickson, J., at 272 and 273.

[36] *Fidler, supra* n. 34 at para. 42. But see *Healey v. Lakeridge Health Corporation*, [2010] O.J. No. 417 (distinguishing *Fidler*).

[37] *Newell v. C.P. Air* (1976), 74 D.L.R. (3d) 574.

[38] See *Kotai v. Queen of the North*, [2009] B.C.J. No. 2022, where the court held that the plaintiff must suffer from a psychological illness, not just distress.

[39] *Honda Canada Inc. v. Keays*, 2008 S.C.C. 39 at paras. 56–7, referring to *Wallace v. United Grain Growers Ltd.* (1997), 152 D.L.R. (4th) 1 (S.C.C.) at para. 98, and *Vorvis v. Insurance Corporation of BC*, [1989] 1 S.C.R. 1085.

[40] *Ibid.* at para. 59.

The plaintiff must prove the psychological harm for which mental anguish damages are claimed; it will not be presumed by the court.

CASE 13.7

K worked for his employer for 11 years on the assembly line and then as a data entry clerk. After being diagnosed with chronic fatigue syndrome, he was frequently absent, which resulted in his firing. At trial, K was awarded damages for lack of notice and mental anguish, and punitive damages related to allegations of discrimination and failure to accommodate his illness. The Supreme Court of Canada overturned the punitive damage awards, saying the discretion to grant punitive damages should be exercised cautiously for only harsh, vindictive, extreme, or malicious conduct, which was not present in the subject case.[41]

We discuss this issue more fully in Chapter 18, on employment.

2. Lost Holidays   Many contracts, such as those for holiday travel and accommodation, are intended to confer an experiential rather than economic benefit. Unless courts take into account disappointment caused by the loss of an anticipated holiday, a vacationer would be without remedy apart from the return of any money paid. A return of that money would hardly be ample compensation to a vacationer who discovers at the airport that there is neither a flight nor any possibility of arranging an alternative holiday at the last minute. Therefore damages for ruined holidays include damages for mental distress, inconvenience, upset, disappointment, and frustration caused by the loss of the holiday.[42]

Cost of Performance versus Economic Loss

The following U.S. case provides a striking example of the difficulty in deciding on the appropriate standards for measuring damages in circumstances that fall outside traditional categories of economic loss.

CASE 13.8

Owners of a farm containing coal deposits leased it to a mining company for five years. The operation was strip mining, in which coal is scooped from open pits on the surface, scarring the land. The owners insisted on including a term in the lease requiring the company to restore the surface at the expiration of the lease by moving earth in order to level the pits. At the end of the lease, the company vacated without restoring the land and the owners sued for damages.

Breach was admitted by the company. However, the court was faced with the following dilemma: The cost of restoring the land as promised would be $29 000, but the market value of the farm would increase by only $300 as a result of the restoration. The owners claimed damages of $29 000, measured by the "cost of performance," and the company countered that it was liable only for damages of $300—the "depreciated [market] value"—caused by the breach. The court found that an award of $29 000 to the plaintiffs would have given them a windfall of $28 700; it awarded damages of only $300.[43]

The choice of economic value over cost of performance recognizes the basic purpose of damages—there must be a loss. If the non-breaching party is no worse off as a result of the failure to perform, it does not matter how much performance would have cost the breaching party. For more information on this topic, see the Companion Website.

---

[41] *Honda Canada Inc. v. Keays, supra*, n. 39, at para. 62–78.

[42] *Jarvis v. Swan Tours Ltd.*, [1973] Q.B. 233.; *Elder v. Koppe* (1974), 53 D.L.R. (3d) 705; *Keks v. Esquire Pleasure Tours Ltd.*, [1974] 3 W.W.R. 406; *Wolf v. Advance Fur Dressers Ltd.*, 2005 BCSC 1097.

[43] *Peevyhouse v. Garland Coal & Mining Company*, 382 P.2d 109 (Okla. 1963). See also *James v. Hutton & J. Cool & Sons Ltd.*, [1950] 1 K.B. 9, *D. Karrasch Construction Ltd. v. Telosky* 2010 BCSC 423.

EQUITABLE REMEDIES

Reasons for the Intervention of Equity

The old common law courts gave only money damages for breach of contract. But sometimes money damages alone are inadequate. For example, suppose a purchaser buys a "classic car" because it belonged to his great grandfather. If the vendor refuses to complete the deal, no amount of money will fulfill the purpose of the contract. The most sensible remedy would be to order the vendor to transfer the car to the purchaser on payment of the purchase price. The inadequacy of the common law damages led to the development of special equitable remedies, such as specific performance. Failure to comply with an equitable remedy places a defendant in "contempt of court" and can lead to a fine or imprisonment.

Prerequisites for an Equitable Remedy

Equitable remedies are discretionary—that is, the court decides whether, in view of all the circumstances, good reasons exist to go beyond the ordinary common law remedy of damages. First, the court must be satisfied that damages will not adequately compensate the loss; thereafter, an equitable remedy is granted to a plaintiff that complies with the established principles of equity. The following are among the more important requirements:

(a) A plaintiff must come to court with "clean hands"—that is, he must not himself have acted unethically; if he has, his claim will be limited to money damages.

(b) A plaintiff must not delay in bringing an action. The faster the request is made, the more likely a court will grant an equitable remedy.

(c) As we noted in Chapter 9 on "Mistake," a court will refuse to intervene on equitable principles when to do so would negatively affect an innocent purchaser.

(d) The plaintiff must have paid meaningful consideration for the defendant's promise; promises given under seal or in exchange for a nominal sum do not qualify.

(e) Finally, a plaintiff must ordinarily be a party against whom the remedy would be awarded were he the defendant instead. For example, because a court will not grant an equitable remedy against an infant defendant when a contract is voidable at his option, neither will it grant that remedy in his favour as a plaintiff. This factor is hard to justify on grounds of fairness, and is not always followed.

Specific Performance

Specific performance is an order requiring a defendant to do a specified act, most often to complete a transaction. In a real estate sale agreement, specific performance is commonly ordered, provided the purchaser can prove the piece of land is unique and no other will suffice.[44] If so, a vendor will be ordered to deliver all documents necessary to transfer of ownership, on payment of the purchase price.

specific performance an order requiring a defendant to do a contracted-for act, usually to complete a transaction

In situations where the court might be obligated to supervise a defendant, specific performance will not be granted. As a result, performance that depends on the personal skill or judgment of a defendant does not lend itself to an order for specific performance. An artist who repudiates a contract to give a concert will not be ordered to perform; to do so would be to invite a disgruntled performance. The plaintiff will be awarded of money damages.

Courts rarely grant specific performance of a contract for the sale of goods— damages are considered adequate compensation, unless the contract is for the sale of

---

[44] *Semelhago v. Paramadevan*, [1996] 2 S.C.R. 415; *Carttera Management Inc., v. Palm Holdings Canada Inc.*, 2011 ONSC 2573 (holding the subject property was not unique).

a one-of-a-kind item. Antiques, heirlooms, rare coins, and works of art are possible examples. Shares in a corporation may also be considered property for which specific performance is an appropriate remedy, especially when a plaintiff's primary purpose is to obtain a controlling or substantial interest in the business.

Injunction

An injunction is a court order restraining a party from acting in a particular manner; in relation to contract, it prohibits a party from committing a breach. For the remedy to be available, the courts require the contract to contain a **negative covenant**: a promise not to do something. However, the covenant need not be stated expressly as a prohibition but may simply be a logical consequence of an express promise. Accordingly, an express promise by a tenant to use leased premises for office space would likely be construed to contain an implied promise not to use them for a nightclub; the landlord could obtain an injunction prohibiting their use for a nightclub. The negative tone of an injunction also avoids the supervision problem discussed above. Any evidence of the prohibited activity is a violation of the injunction, and the court does not need continuous supervision.

In some circumstances, a court will grant an **interlocutory injunction**—a temporary injunction—to restrain immediate harm from being done, pending formal resolution of the dispute at trial. Courts are reluctant, however, to grant even a temporary injunction of this kind in personal service contracts, and a party must establish that irreparable harm will be done without an injunction. A typical example involves a breach of contract action claiming specific performance of a real estate transaction. The plaintiff may ask the court to prohibit the sale of the land by the vendor to anyone else until after the trial. Obviously, the purchaser could not get a specific performance remedy if the vendor had already sold the land to a third party.

Rescission

As discussed in Chapter 9, **rescission** involves returning a party as nearly as possible to the position that existed before the contract was made at all. In other words, the contract is set aside or rescinded. This is not usually the focus of a remedy for breach—those strive to place the parties, as nearly as possible, into the position that would have existed if the contract had been properly formed. However, if a breach is serious enough to discharge the plaintiff from her own obligations, she may elect rescission, provided that it is feasible to return the parties substantially to their pre-contract positions. An aggrieved party must choose between the two remedies—she cannot have both. Naturally, if it is not possible to return the parties to their pre-contract position, the court will not order it. People elect rescission whenever they decide to return defective goods to the store for a refund rather than suing for cost of repair or replacement.

Quantum Meruit

As discussed in Chapter 7, a **quantum meruit** claim arises when valuable benefit is conferred at the request of a promisee. Quantum meruit may also be claimed when a serious breach occurs and the non-breaching party has partially performed his obligations. The non-breaching party may elect to treat the contract as discharged or to rescind but still deserves payment for the value previously conveyed. Such circumstances are common in construction contracts when breach occurs after commencement of the work but prior to completion. The partially performing party may ask the court to assess the fair market value of the work already done and thereby receive compensation on a quantum meruit basis. The assessment is based upon the benefit conferred, not the cost of doing the work.

CHECKLIST

Breach of Contract Remedies

Common law damages

- expectation damages
- consequential damages
- general damages
- reliance damages
- punitive damages

Equitable remedies

- specific performance
- injunction
- rescission
- quantum meruit

METHODS OF ENFORCING JUDGMENTS

When a plaintiff obtains judgment for a sum of money, he becomes a **judgment creditor**, and the defendant a **judgment debtor**. If the judgment debtor is financially sound, the stigma of the court judgment is usually sufficient to motivate voluntary payment. If, however, the debtor resists payment or is in financial difficulty, the judgment creditor may then move to enforce payment. There are legal procedures by which a judgment creditor may seize as much of the debtor's property as is necessary to satisfy the judgment. If the assets are insufficient, he may seize more assets in the future when they become available. Judgments remain enforceable for a long time after judgment, often 20 years before they expire.

judgment creditor a party who has obtained a court judgment for a sum of money

judgment debtor a party who has been ordered by the court to pay a sum of money

The most usual collection procedure is to register the judgment with the office of the sheriff of the county or district in which the debtor resides and to request the sheriff to **levy execution** against the assets of the debtor to satisfy the judgment. An **execution order** gives the sheriff authority to seize and sell various goods and arrange for a sale of the debtor's lands after an appropriate grace period.[45] Additional procedures exist to seize money in a bank account, the contents of a safety-deposit box, or income from a trust fund. A creditor may also obtain a **garnishee order** against a debtor's wages. The order requires the employer to retain a portion of the debtor's wages each payday and forward the sum to the creditor to be applied against the judgment. If the judgment creditor does not know where the debtor works, banks, or owns land, it may summon the judgment debtor to appear for a judgment debtor examination. The debtor must attend and disclose, under oath, the details of his finances. Failure to appear at an examination or knowingly providing false information is considered **contempt of court** and may be punished by imprisonment.

levy execution to seize and sell a debtor's chattels or arrange for a sale of his lands

execution order an order that gives the sheriff authority to levy execution

garnishee order an order requiring the debtor's employer to retain a portion of the debtor's wages each payday and surrender the sum to the creditor

contempt of court a finding by a court that a person has willfully refused to obey a court order and therefore will be punished

A judgment debtor is not considered a criminal. Honest inability to pay is not punished; only willful failure to comply or fraudulent concealing of assets will trigger punishment such as imprisonment. For more information on this topic, see the Companion Website.

---

[45] See e.g. Execution Act, R.S.O. 1990, c. E.24, s. 2; Court Order Enforcement Act, R.S.B.C. 1996, c. 78, s. 71.

Sometimes the assets of a judgment debtor are located in a foreign jurisdiction. A judgment creditor must seek the foreign court's recognition of its judgment before it may seize the asset. In Canada, common law provinces recognize each other's judgments (and those of the United Kingdom) through a simple registration process. An enforcing court will recognize the judgment provided that the granting court had a real and substantial connection to the matter and followed its own jurisdictional rules. It does not matter if the defendant participated or agreed to the jurisdiction of the granting court.[46] Within Canada, there is confidence that the judicial systems offer procedural fairness, and there is no need for examination of the correctness of the decision.

The Supreme Court extended the application of this narrow procedural fairness and jurisdiction test to foreign judgments from other countries such as the United States. In *Beals v. Saldanha*,[47] the Court recognized a judgment from Florida that granted damages of $210 000 plus $50 000 of punitive damages. This was somewhat controversial because circumstances of the case stemmed from an $8000 real estate transaction and there was no evidence to support punitive damages. The dissent felt that the excessive damages and the lack of notice associated with this potential outcome was a barrier to the recognition of the judgment. However, the majority disagreed and the judgment was recognized.

Questions to Consider

1. Should foreign judgments containing excessive damage awards be recognized by Canadian courts if the same damages would not be recoverable here?

2. Is it relevant to consider whether the foreign court easily recognizes Canadian judgments?

Sources: H.S. Fairley, "Open Season: Recognition and Enforcement of Foreign Judgments in Canada After *Beals v. Saldanha*" (2005), 11(2) ILSA Journal of International and Comparative Law 305–18; J.S. Ziegel, "Enforcement of Foreign Judgments in Canada, Unlevel Playing Fields and *Beals v. Saldanha*: A Consumer Perspective" (2003) 38 *Canadian Business Law Journal* 294–308.

Strategies to Manage the Legal Risks

There are a number of proactive steps a business can take that will reduce the costs and losses associated with breach of contract, should one occur. The first step is to determine the risks that are likely to make performance difficult for the business or the customer and quantify the value of those risks. The business should adopt some or all of the following strategies to manage the risks:

- A party may obtain insurance against the risk and raise its price accordingly.

- It may "self-insure"—that is, charge a higher fee and build up a reserve fund to pay any claim that arises later from harm to a customer.

- For reoccurring transactions, the business should develop a standard form contract that specifically addresses the risks from the business's perspective.

- It may include an exemption clause in the contract to exclude any liability for the risk, and transferring the risk of harm to its customer.

- Parties may include liquidated damage clauses to quantify the risk ahead of time and provide incentive for parties to perform.

- Contracts may require the payment of a deposit, installments, or the posting of a performance bond, to be released only after full performance. In this way, an injured party will have some funds available to them in the event of a breach, avoiding collection problems.

---

[46] *Morguard Investments v. De Savoye*, [1990] 3 S.C.R. 1077; *Club Resorts Ltd., v. Van Breda*, 2012 SCC 17

[47] [2003] 3 S.C.R. 416

- Parties should identify essential terms of the contract, breach of which would trigger their discharge from the contract. This will avoid arguments about the seriousness of the risk.

- Businesses should keep detailed records of expenses incurred in preparation for or reliance upon a contract. Expenses associated with mitigation should also be documented.

Whenever a business is unable to perform exactly as promised, a wise manager will notify the other party as soon as she is aware of the inability to perform. In this way, the non-breaching party may take immediate steps to mitigate any loss that the breach may cause, minimizing unnecessary reliance and consequential damages.

QUESTIONS FOR REVIEW

1. Why does a major breach not automatically discharge a contract? Give an example.
2. Describe two ways in which anticipatory breach may occur.
3. In what types of contracts does it become particularly difficult to ascertain whether a breach is sufficient to allow the injured party to be freed from its part of the bargain? Explain.
4. Describe why the doctrine of substantial performance is of practical importance.
5. What is the reasoning behind the requirement that an injured party mitigate its losses?
6. When a buyer refuses to accept delivery of goods, explain the significance of supply and demand when determining the value of damages suffered.
7. Explain the attitude of the courts toward exemption clauses.
8. Give an example of strict interpretation of an exemption clause.
9. In what circumstances might a court grant an interlocutory injunction?
10. When a judgment debtor refuses to pay the judgment, what recourse does the judgment creditor have?
11. Describe the nature and purpose of liquidated damage clauses and how they are distinguished from penalty clauses.
12. Define expectation damages, consequential damages, and specific performance. Give an example of each.

CASES AND PROBLEMS

1. Continuing Scenario

   In the coat room at Ashley's restaurant there is a posted sign that says "Not responsible for loss or damage." Joan arrives for lunch, hangs her coat in the coat room, and is seated in the dining area. After lunch, Joan begins feeling ill and goes to the hospital, where it is determined that Joan got food poisoning from the chili she ordered and ate at Ashley's restaurant. When Joan contacts Ashley for compensation, she is told that Ashley is "not responsible for loss or damage" because the sign is an exemption clause. Will the alleged exemption clause protect Ashley from liability? How will the court approach the analysis?

2. Stellar Construction Inc. agreed to build a new Olympic swimming pool for the Thomson Aquatic Centre for $450 000. The completion date was May 1. Thomson visited the pool on April 23, and was very disappointed with the quality of the tiles and caulking on the edges of the pool. She complained at once to Urqhart, Stellar's on-site manager.

   Urqhart said that the tiles and caulking complied with the specifications, but if Thomson wanted them replaced there would be a delay of two weeks for completing the project. Thomson insisted that the quality was inadequate but that she needed to have the pool ready by May 3 when she had scheduled the grand opening celebration of the renovated centre. Urqhart replied that she would have to choose between a delayed opening and accepting the tiles as is. Thomson then said, "Leave it. We'll settle it later."

Stellar continued its work and completed the project on May 2, in time for the grand opening. The final payment of $100 000 to Stellar was due May 15, but Thomson refused to pay it. She claimed that she had an independent appraisal of the tile work, that it would cost at least $50 000 to have the work done, and that the pool would have to be closed for two weeks, causing substantial losses in revenue to the Aquatic Centre.

Stellar sued Thomson for the $100 000, denying that Thomson's complaint was valid. It was established that the tiles failed to meet the specifications in the contract between the parties, and that replacing them would indeed cost $50 000 plus the cost of business disruption. However, the diminished appearance of the pool caused by the tiles reduced the value of the pool by no more than $15 000.

Give your opinion about whether it was Thomson's choice to replace or leave the tiles. In either case, would Stellar's failure to perform amount to a minor or major breach?

3. In December, Carvel Estates Ltd., a real estate developer, contracted to buy 24 large suburban lots from Dalquith Enterprises Inc., with the transaction to close May 15. Carvel had hired an architect and intended to build expensive "up-market" homes. The plans for each house were at an advanced stage by late March, when, without any prior notice, Dalquith sent Carvel a cheque refunding Carvel's down payment. Dalquith informed Carvel that it could not go through with the deal because Dalquith's parent corporation had applied for a zoning change and wished to construct luxury condominiums on the site. Dalquith also stated it had discussed the situation with the owner of land adjacent to the site Carvel had purchased, and the owner was willing to discuss selling an equivalent number of lots to Carvel.

Carvel's manager was very upset because the firm would have been ready to begin work immediately after the May 15 closing date. Carvel refused to consider the alternative lots offered by Dalquith. Carvel commenced an action, requesting transfer of the property and damages for any additional costs as a result of delay in the project. Name the remedy Carvel is requesting, explain whether it is likely that Carvel will succeed, and if not, what other remedies might be available to Carvel.

4. Complicated Machinery Co. Ltd. manufactures and assembles heavy equipment for industry. It accepted an order from Northern Paper Co. for a large machine that would automate certain processes; one of the terms of the order was that the machine was to be completed by October 31. The contract further stated that if the machine was not completed by October 31, Complicated Machinery Co. Ltd. would pay Northern Paper Co. $1000 for each week of delay. The manager of Northern Paper Co. had written in a letter accompanying the offer: "Until the machine is in full operation it is hard to say what our savings will be. A thousand dollars a week is a rough guess."

Complicated Machinery Co. Ltd. failed to deliver until December 26, eight weeks late. It billed the paper company for the full price less $8000 (eight weeks at $1000). The paper company discovered that the machine actually saved $2400 weekly in production costs. It therefore tendered as payment the full price less $19 200 (eight weeks at $2400). Which party is correct and why?

5. Brown, a painting contractor, made an oral contract with Hilton to paint the interior of Hilton's house for $1600, to be paid on completion of the work. Brown ran into difficulty when he painted the walls of the living room because the paint was pulled into the wall by the porous plaster. He had the same problem when he applied a second coat. He then realized what was causing the trouble and applied what is known as a "sealer," so that the next coat would adhere properly. Leaving the living room until the sealer was dry, he began painting the dining room.

At that point, Hilton inspected the work and complained to Brown that the colour of the paint was not the colour she had selected. Brown became very annoyed and emphatically announced he would quit the job. Hilton urged him not to abandon the work without first seeing her husband, but in a huff he removed his materials and equipment. When he abandoned the work, Brown still had to finish painting the living room and had not begun to paint several other rooms in the house. It also appeared that the woodwork had been painted without having been sanded, and would have to be stripped and repainted. Brown brought an action against Hilton for $890, claiming $230 for materials and $660 for 33 hours' work. Should he succeed?

Additional Resources for Chapter 13 on the Companion Website

(www.pearsoncanada.ca/smyth)

In addition to pre- and post-tests, mini-cases, and application exercises, the Companion Website includes the following resources for Chapter 13:

- **Alberta:** Disclosure Requirements; Fundamental Breach Case; Substantial Performance; Enforcement of Judgments; Garnishment Case; Limitation of Actions
- **Atlantic Provinces:** Garnishment; Seizure and Sale
- **British Columbia:** Enforcement of Judgments; Garnishment; Injunction; Seizure and Sale; Specific Performance; Writ of Execution
- **Manitoba/Saskatchewan:** Conditions and Warrantees; Consumer Protection Legislation—Disclosure of Restrictions; Collection of Judgments
- **Ontario:** Debt Collection Processes; Debtor Examination; Equitable Remedies; Executions; Exemption Clauses; Foreign Judgments; Fundamental Breach; Garnishment; Judgment Debtor Examination Substantial Performance

Chapter 14

Sale of Goods and Consumer Contracts

- THE SALE OF GOODS ACT
- TERMS IN A CONTRACT OF SALE
- TITLE TO GOODS
- REMEDIES OF THE SELLER
- THE SELLER'S LIABILITY
- REMEDIES OF THE BUYER
- CONSUMER CONTRACTS
- BUSINESS SALES TACTICS TARGETING CONSUMERS
- TERMS ADDED TO CONSUMER CONTRACTS
- SPECIFIC TYPES OF TERMS
- STRATEGIES TO MANAGE THE LEGAL RISKS

Contracts for the sale of goods are the most common type of contract and are identified by the subject matter of the contract—goods. Over time, they generated a vast amount of case law, which was eventually collected into one statute—the Sale of Goods Act.

Consumer contracts are identified by the types of contracting parties involved—consumers and business. A severe imbalance of bargaining power exists between these types of parties, allowing business to impose its will on consumers without negotiation. A variety of statutes attempt to level the playing field for consumers; these are collectively known as consumer protection legislation.

Unlike the chapters in Part 3, this chapter concentrates on the substantive rules contained in the legislation. In it, we examine such questions as:

- What is the scope of the Sale of Goods Act?
- What are the terms that it implies into a contract of sale?
- How is the ownership of goods transferred?
- To what extent is the seller liable for defective or unsatisfactory goods?
- What are the remedies available to buyers and sellers?
- What is a consumer contract?
- What pressure sales tactics are regulated?
- What additional terms are implied into a consumer contract?
- What additional remedies are available to a consumer?

THE SALE OF GOODS ACT

History of the Sale of Goods Act

When the term *contract* is used, the type of contract that usually comes to mind is a contract for the sale of goods. Goods have been sold for centuries, and the body of case law that developed was so immense that the British Parliament simplified the rules by putting them all in a comprehensive statute called the Sale of Goods Act. All the common law provinces in Canada subsequently passed similar acts.[1]

The Sale of Goods Act did not change the law. Its purpose was to organize the existing law, with clarification where necessary to resolve conflicts between competing principles. Importantly, the cases decided before the Act recognized several implied terms that were added to every contract for the sale of goods, unless they were inconsistent with the purposes of the contract or were expressly excluded by the parties. Those terms were **codified**, or collected in the act—they are now implied into every contract covered by the Sale of Goods Act. We discuss these implied terms in the next section of this chapter.

codified existing common law rules collected and put in statute form

---

CHECKLIST

Application of the Sale of Goods Act

The Sale of Goods Act applies to

- sales (and agreements to sell)
- goods (not services, unless other legislation extends the protection)
- all parties to the sale contract, including businesses, consumers, individuals, and corporations

The Sale of Goods Act does not apply to

- exchanges of goods (barter)
- bailments or leases (see Chapter 15)
- consignments (see below)
- non-contractual transfers of property or goods
- sales of land or of intangible property
- supply of services (see consumer protection exception)

Contracts of Sale

In the Sale of Goods Act, a contract of sale "is a contract whereby the seller transfers or agrees to transfer the property in the goods to the buyer for a money consideration, called the price." Money must form a part of the transaction. A straight barter of goods where no money changes hands does not come within the statute.

The Act distinguishes between a sale and an **agreement to sell**. In a sale, the seller transfers ownership or title in goods to the buyer at the moment the contract is made. In an agreement to sell, the transfer is deferred until a future time; that time is either a specified date or an indefinite date that depends on the fulfillment of a particular requirement.

agreement to sell a contract of sale in which the transfer of ownership in the goods is deferred to some future time

---

[1] The wording of the various provincial Sale of Goods Acts is fairly similar, but the numbering of sections differs from one province to another. In this chapter, we quote from the Ontario act and give the corresponding section numbers in Alberta, British Columbia, Newfoundland and Labrador, and Manitoba as well as other provinces where applicable.

The Act applies to both sales and agreements to sell. An agreement to sell may be formed even when the goods are non-existent. A contract to sell goods to be manufactured in three months' time or to sell a crop at a stated price per bushel once it has grown are examples of agreements to sell. An agreement to sell is a binding contract, as are other contracts containing promises of future conduct.

consignment the transfer of only possession of goods from one business to another for the purpose of offering for sale

We should also distinguish a contract of sale from a transaction known as a **consignment**. This is not always easy, since the word *consignment* is used in two different senses. In common usage, a consignment is simply a shipment of goods from one person or business to another in performance of a contract of sale. Here, the consignor is a seller and the consignee a buyer. But in a more technical sense, a consignor may send goods to an agent (consignee) who will offer them for sale at their new location on behalf of the consignor. In this instance, ownership in the goods does not pass between the consignor and consignee: If the consignee sells the goods, the title passes directly from the consignor to the purchaser. Expensive items displayed in a jeweller's shop, for example, may not be part of the jeweller's own stock-in-trade but simply may be held on consignment from a manufacturer or wholesaler. The distinction between sale and consignment may be important, since it will determine if the Sale of Goods Act applies.

CASE 14.1

Win Sun Produce, a small family business engaged in importing fruit and vegetables, entered into an agreement with Pacific Produce, a large wholesale fruit and vegetable business, to supply Pacific with a container shipment of 950 boxes of pomelos imported from Thailand. The pomelos were delivered to Pacific, together with a "purchase order" invoicing the pomelos at $47 per box. A "load sheet," signed by the person at Pacific who took delivery, referred to the "consignment" as having been received. Pacific had not previously stocked pomelos and found that they did not sell well. Pacific asked Win Sun to take back 140 boxes, which Win Sun did, crediting Pacific with the sum of $6580.

Pacific was still unable to sell all the remaining pomelos and eventually many of them rotted. Win Sun claimed the balance of the price. Pacific contested this, claiming that the pomelos had been supplied on consignment and still belonged to Win Sun.

The trial judge held that the contract was one of consignment. On appeal, the British Columbia Court of Appeal ruled that the contract was one of sale. The word *consignment* in the load sheet had been used in the sense of "shipment." If the contract had been one of consignment, there would have been no need for Pacific to ask Win Sun to take some back or for Pacific to have been credited with part of the price.[2]

Goods

goods personal property, excluding both money and choses in action

For the Sale of Goods Act to apply, the subject matter of the contract must be **goods**, which the Act (section 1(1)) defines as meaning "all chattels personal, other than things in action and money. . . ."[2A] Property is divided into two main classes: real property and personal property. Real property is confined to interests in land. All other property is called personal property. Personal property is also divided into two categories: intangible property, known as choses ("things") in action; and tangible property, known as goods or chattels. In Chapter 11, we discussed the nature of choses in action in relation to the assignment of contractual rights. In contrast to choses in action, which have a value because they represent binding obligations, goods derive their value intrinsically from the utility or satisfaction they provide.

When discussing the requirement of writing in Chapter 10, we noted that a distinction is made between contracts for the sale of goods and contracts for services, for instance, those

---

[2] *Win Sun Produce Co. v. Albert Fisher Canada Ltd.* (1998), 111 B.C.A.C. 295 (B.C.C.A.), varying cost order [1999] B.C.J. No. 294, *leave denied* [1998] S.C.C.A. No. 522 (QL).

[2A] Sale of Goods Act, R.S.O. 1990 (section 1(1)).

for work and materials. The distinction is not always an easy one to make. For example, in contracting to have a house constructed, a boat built, or a central heating system installed, the buyer agrees to pay for a finished product as well as for the labour that produced it. A court may have to decide whether it was the work or the materials that constituted the essence of the contract. If the final value is mainly the result of the skill and labour that have gone into its preparation, the contract will be one for work and materials and not for "goods" as defined by the Act.[3] In practice, the distinction is not always important, since many of the legal principles that apply to contracts for work and materials are much the same as provisions in the Sale of Goods Act. For example, the Supreme Court held that a contract for work and materials is also subject, as a matter of common law, to an implied condition of fitness, analogous to the condition of fitness implied in contracts for the sale of goods.[4] This is not true in every case.

CASE 14.2

The plaintiff was infected with HIV as a result of artificial insemination performed by her physician in 1985. The physician screened the donors and took the usual precautions according to the standard practice in Canada at that time (when no test was available to detect the virus in blood or semen). The trial jury found the physician negligent and awarded damages of $883 800, but the finding of negligence was overturned on appeal.

The plaintiff also based her claim on another ground. The physician had supplied "goods," namely, the semen. The semen was not fit for the purpose for which it was supplied, the plaintiff claimed, and therefore there was a breach of the "seller's" duty under the Sale of Goods Act.

The Supreme Court of Canada ruled

1. that the contract was one for the supply of services, not of goods,

2. that the courts should be wary of implying terms in contracts for the supply of services, especially when the contract involved the supply of products that carry inherent risks.

The physician had not been negligent and should not face a stricter liability for goods that are incidental to the service supplied than that imposed by the normal duty of care.[5]

Ownership and Possession

The words *ownership* (legal title) and *possession* (physical control) involve difficult legal problems. We understand the distinction in everyday activity, as when we lend possession of an object to someone yet retain ownership of it. We correctly assume that if that person refused to return the object, we would have a remedy in the courts to protect our ownership or title.

The separation of ownership and possession occurs frequently in contracts for the sale of goods: when the contract is a sale that passes title to the buyer immediately, possession often remains with the seller or with a carrier for some time afterward. By contrast, under installment sales contracts, a vendor often keeps title to goods until the last payment is made while possession passes to the buyer immediately.

---

[3] The examples mentioned—a house, a boat, and a central heating system—have all been held to be contracts for "work and materials"; see *Hodgkinson v. Hitch House Ltd.* (1985), 60 O.R. (2d) 793. By contrast, a restaurant meal has been held to be "goods." *Gee v. White Spot Ltd.* (1986), 32 D.L.R. (4th) 238.

[4] *A.G. of Canada v. Laminated Structures & Holdings Ltd.* (1961), 28 D.L.R. (2d) 92, per Macdonald, J., at 100–1, aff'd *Laminated Structures & Holdings Ltd. v. Easter Woodworkers Ltd.*, [1962] S.C.R. 160. Also see *Spanos v. Dufferin Tile & Marble Inc.*, 2007 Carswell Ont 8625.

[5] *Ter Neuzen v. Korn*, [1995] 3. S.C.R. 674. See also *Pittman Estate v. Bain* (1994), 19 C.C.L.T. (2d) 1 (Ont. Gen. Div.), a case involving HIV-tainted blood.

TERMS IN A CONTRACT OF SALE

The Caveat Emptor Principle

The legal saying **caveat emptor** is one of the few Latin phrases that most people know. *Caveat emptor* means "let the buyer beware"—that is, the risk is with the buyer. He must investigate the purchase or suffer the consequences. However, it is not a rigid rule but a flexible general principle, subject to the limits put on it by customary business practice and the Sale of Goods Act.

The caveat emptor principle applies where the goods in existence are specific items that may be inspected by the buyer, and when the seller has made no misrepresentations about them. See the Companion Website for more on this topic. In these circumstances, it is a sensible rule. The buyer has the opportunity to exercise her judgment by examining the goods, and if she distrusts her own judgment or has doubts, she may bargain for an express term stating that the goods have the particular quality she requires.

Caveat emptor encourages buyers to determine if the goods are what they want before they contract to buy. However, in certain circumstances, the principle, if not qualified, would invite abuse by fraudulent sellers. For example, a buyer sometimes relies upon the knowledge or expert judgment of the seller, or a buyer may place special confidence or trust in the seller. Consequently, various implied terms that protect buyers are found in the Sale of Goods Act.

Statutory Protection for the Buyer: Implied Terms

Conditions and Warranties   The Sale of Goods Act uses **condition** to mean a major or essential term of a contract, the breach of which relieves the injured party from further duty to perform the contract. The Act uses **warranty** to mean a lesser or non-essential term, the breach of which does not relieve the injured party from the bargain—she must perform her side, but she may sue for damages. In this chapter, we use the two words with the meanings given them by the Act. Some terms implied by the Act are conditions and others are warranties.

In the majority of provinces, the terms are only implied if there is no express provision to the contrary in the contract. In some provinces, however, the most important implied terms cannot be excluded in the case of **retail sales**—that is, sales of consumer goods by retail businesses to private individuals in the ordinary course of business. In New Brunswick, the warranties are set out in a separate statute—the Consumer Product Warranty and Liability Act.[6] Saskatchewan originally followed the same approach, but has since incorporated the warranties into its Consumer Protection Act.[7] British Columbia, by contrast, simply provides in its Sale of Goods Act that the implied warranties and conditions cannot be excluded in the case of retail sales or leases.[8]

Seller's Title   Caveat emptor applies to the qualities of goods, not their ownership. Inspection by the buyer normally does nothing to indicate who owns the goods. In offering

---

[6] S.N.B. 1978, c. C-18.1, ss. 7, 24.

[7] S.S. 1996, c. C-30.1, s. 48, replacing the Consumer Products Warranties Act. In Manitoba, the statutory warranties are also contained in the Consumer Protection Act, C.C.S.M., c. C200, s. 58. Consumer protection is discussed further in Chapter 31.

[8] R.S.B.C. 1996, c. 410, s. 20.

to sell goods, the seller impliedly represents that he has the right to do so. The (Ontario) Sale of Goods Act states:

In a contract of sale, unless the circumstances of the contract are such as to show a different intention, there is

(a) An implied condition on the part of the seller that in the case of a sale the seller has a right to sell the goods, and that in the case of an agreement to sell the seller will have a right to sell the goods at the time when the property is to pass;

(b) An implied warranty that the buyer will have and enjoy quiet possession of the goods; and

(c) An implied warranty that the goods will be free from any charge or encumbrance in favour of any third party, not declared or known to the buyer before or at the time when the contract is made.[9]

An example of the **implied term as to title** is provided in Illustration 14.1.

implied term as to title it is implied that the seller has a right to sell the goods

---

ILLUSTRATION 14.1

Alberti purchases a second-hand refrigerator from Blake. It later turns out that Cowan, not Blake, was the owner of the refrigerator. Cowan retakes possession of the refrigerator from Alberti.

In the contract of sale between Alberti and Blake, there is an implied promise by Blake that he had a right to sell the refrigerator, that Alberti should have quiet possession of it (that is, not have physical possession of it interrupted), and that it would be free from any encumbrance in favour of a third person (that is, no third person would have a right to the property). None of these requirements was satisfied. Alberti is therefore entitled to sue Blake for breach of contract based upon an implied condition of title to the refrigerator.

Description   Where the actual goods are not available for prior inspection, the buyer often makes his decision to buy based upon a description of the goods contained in a catalogue, included on a website, or written on a sealed package. The resulting contract is a contract for the sale of goods by description. The Act sets out the circumstances in which there is an **implied term as to description**—that is, that the goods will match the description given by the seller.[10]

implied term as to description it is implied that goods sold by description will conform to the description

This means that the goods will meet the specifications in the description and have the characteristics described. The word *description* applies to a generic characteristic of the goods (for example, that blouses offered for sale are cotton blouses instead of polyester blouses) and not to words of praise about the blouses (for example, "It is classic and elegant").

ILLUSTRATION 14.2

ProMotors sold Bridges an electric motor for use in his workshop. The motor was described in ProMotors' catalogue as "heavy-duty, double bearing." After only three months' use, the motor burned out. It turned out that the motor supplied had only a single bearing, although that was not apparent until the motor was taken apart following the burnout.

Bridges may sue ProMotors based on the breach of an implied term to the effect that the goods will correspond with the description. While the expression "heavy-duty" may be a matter of opinion, "double bearing" is clearly a factual description within the meaning of the Act.

---

[9] (Ontario) Sale of Goods Act R.S.O. 1990, c. S-1, s. 13. The corresponding provisions in the Alberta, British Columbia, and Newfoundland and Labrador acts are R.S.A. 2000, c. S-2, s. 14; R.S.B.C. 1996, c. 410, s. 16; R.S.N.L. 1990, c. S-6, s. 14.

[10] Ont., s. 14; see also Alta., s. 15; B.C., s. 17; Nfld., s. 15.

Providing a sample good for inspection does not remove the implied term about description; the goods must still match any description given. In fact, it may expand the description as the characteristics of the sample can be considered to form part of the description.

CASE 14.3

A hotel chain ordered tableware, after having inspected samples. The tableware was delivered over a period of three years. The purchasers had no complaint regarding the earlier deliveries but discovered that the sets delivered later did not have the same manufacturer's embossed stamp on the back.

They rejected the goods and sued for damages. The court held that the stamp, which had been on the sample, formed part of the description of the goods and the vendor was in breach of the implied warranty.[11]

Sale by Sample   Sometimes sample goods are displayed for prior inspection by the buyer without any corresponding description. In such cases, the Act inserts into the contract an **implied term that goods correspond with sample**. The Act provides the following:

> In the case of a contract for sale by sample, there is an implied condition
>
> (a) that the bulk will correspond with the sample in quality;
> (b) that the buyer will have a reasonable opportunity of comparing the bulk with the sample; and
> (c) that the goods will be free from any defect rendering them unmerchantable that would not be apparent on reasonable examination of the sample.[12]

implied term that goods correspond with sample   it is implied that, when a sample of the goods to be sold has been provided, the actual goods supplied will correspond to that sample in type and quality

ILLUSTRATION 14.3

The plant supervisor at High Grade Printing Company examined a sample of choice quality paper supplied by Universal Paper Co. Ltd. and approved its purchase. When the paper was used in one of the books printed by High Grade, it turned yellow and the entire run had to be done again. High Grade sued Universal Paper for damages for its loss. In defence, Universal Paper pleaded that the paper supplied was

exactly the same as the sample on which the purchase was based, and that a chemical test of the sample would have revealed the defect.

The printing company should succeed in its action if it can show that the defect would not have been apparent on an ordinary examination, and that an ordinary examination would not include a chemical test.

Suitability and Quality   The Sale of Goods Act makes two exceptions to the general rule that the buyer must satisfy himself as to the suitability and quality of the goods:

> Subject to this Act and any statute in that behalf, there is no implied warranty or condition as to the quality or fitness for any particular purpose of goods supplied under a contract of sale, except as follows:
>
> 1. Where the buyer, expressly or by implication, makes known to the seller the particular purpose for which the goods are required so as to show that the buyer relies on the seller's skill or judgment, and the goods are of a description that it is in the course of the seller's business to supply (whether he is the manufacturer or not), there is an implied condition that the goods will be reasonably fit for such purpose, but in the case of a contract for the sale of a specified article under its patent or other trade name, there is no implied condition as to its fitness for any particular purpose.

---

[11] *Coast Hotels Ltd. v. Royal Doulton Canada Ltd.*, [2000] B.C.J. 2115, 2000 BCSC 1545.

[12] Sale of Goods Act [RSBC 1996], Ont., s. 16; see also Alta., s. 17; B.C., s. 19; Nfld., s. 17.

2. Where the goods are bought by description from a seller who deals in goods of that description (whether he is the manufacturer or not), there is an implied condition that the goods shall be of merchantable quality, but if the buyer has examined the goods, there is no implied condition as regards defects that such examination ought to have revealed.[13]

The **implied term of fitness** offers protection to a buyer who has a particular purpose in mind for the goods and relies on the seller's expertise in selling this type of goods. The buyer should declare this purpose specifically if it is not one of the general uses for such goods but the court can find purpose and reliance were inferred by actions.

implied term of fitness it is implied that the goods are of a type that is suitable for the purpose for which they are bought

---

ILLUSTRATION 14.4

Slack buys 30 metres of clothesline wire from a hardware store and uses it as a cable for a homemade elevator in his barn. The wire breaks with him in the elevator, causing him injury. He sues the hardware dealer for breach of contract damages.

Slack will not succeed because (1) he did not expressly state the particular purpose for which he intended to use the wire and so did not rely on the seller's skill and judgment, and (2) the use to which he put the wire was not a normal use for clothesline wire so could not be inferred.

A purpose need not be stated in so many words if it is obvious. When buying cakes in a bakery, one need not state, "I propose to eat these." The essential requirement for Part 1 of section 15 noted above is that the buyer relied upon the seller's skill and judgment.[14]

CASE 14.4

Lavalin ordered 57 000 kilograms of welding electrodes from Carbonic for use in a project involving the fabrication of a cross-country gas transmission line. The electrodes turned out to be incapable of producing a satisfactory weld in a vertical position. Lavalin had made known to Carbonic the fact that the electrodes were to be used in a gas transmission line, apparently assuming that Carbonic's engineers would know that the

electrodes would have to be capable of functioning in a vertical position. In fact, Carbonic had no experience of pipeline work.

The court held that Carbonic had implied that it was familiar with pipeline work and that Lavalin had relied on Carbonic's skill and judgment. Lavalin was entitled to damages for the costs incurred with respect to the acquisition and handling of the useless electrodes.[15]

The implied condition of fitness does not apply when an article is sold under its trade name:

> The mere fact that an article sold is described in the contract by its trade name does not necessarily make the sale a sale under a trade name. Whether it is so or not depends upon the circumstances. . . . In my opinion the test of an article having been sold under its trade name within the meaning of the proviso is: did the buyer specify it under its trade name in such a way as to indicate that he is satisfied, rightly or wrongly, that it will answer his purpose, and that he is not relying on the skill or judgment of the seller, however great that skill or judgment may be?[16]

---

[13] Sale of Goods Act [RSBC 1996], Ont., s. 15: see also Alta., s. 16; B.C., s. 18; Nfld., s. 16. See *Borgo Upholstery Ltd. v. Canada*, [2004] N.S.J. No. 7 (N.S.C.A.).

[14] *Chaproniere v. Mason* (1905), 21 T.L.R. 633; *McCready Products Ltd. v. Sherwin Williams Co. of Canada Ltd.* (1985), 61 A.R. 234. The seller's failure to provide adequate instructions as to use of the product and to warn of possible dangers may constitute a breach of the warranty: see *Caners v. Eli Lilly Canada Inc.* (1996), 134 D.L.R. (4th) 730.

[15] *SNC-Lavalin International Inc. v. Liquid Carbonic Inc.* (1996), 28 B.L.R. (2d) 1.

[16] *Baldry v. Marshall*, [1925] 1 K.B. 260, at 266-7.

CASE 14.5

Nikka Trader, a Vancouver-based exporter of Canadian goods, hired Gizella Pastrys to create a mouse cake for export to Japan, after confirming Gizella's extensive experience with the Japanese market in a meeting with Gizella's export sales manager. Over the next several years, Gizella created several custom products for Nikka, specifically designed to pass easily through Japanese customs. In 2007, Gizella advised that the price of the Kona Pie cookies, one of the custom Japan products, would need to increase unless margarine was substituted for butter in the recipe. Nikka agreed to the substitution. After the substitution, the Kona Pie cookies were detained and quarantined at Japanese customs because the margarine contained a banned substance. Nikka sued Gizella for damages arising from breach of the implied term of fitness for purpose—the cookies were not fit for export to Japan. The Court held that when Nikka was asked to agree to the butter substitution, Gizella knew that the cookies would still be exported to Japan, Gizella was an expert on exporting products to Japan, and Nikka relied on Gizella's expertise. This was all that was necessary to prove breach of the implied warranty as to fitness for purpose under British Columbia's Sale of Goods Act. Fitness for sale in Canada did not satisfy the implied warranty of fitness for sale in Japan. The use of the trade name Kona Pie on the order form did not preclude the implied warranty when the other factors of knowledge, expertise, and reliance were present. Nikka was entitled to its damages.[17]

Part 2 of the section deals with quality of goods rather than their particular purpose. To establish a breach of condition under this part, the buyer need not show that she relied on the seller's skill and judgment, but only that the buyer could not have discovered the defect.[18]

implied term of merchantable quality   it is implied that the goods are in reasonable condition and free from defects that would make them unsuitable for use

The **implied term of merchantable quality** needs explanation. Goods of merchantable quality should be in such a condition that a reasonable buyer, fully acquainted with the facts and condition of the product, would buy them without reduction below the current market price and without special guarantees.[19] The word *reasonable* needs to be emphasized; especially in the case of the sale of used goods, there is no warranty that the goods are entirely free from defect.

One problem is that the implied condition relates to the quality of the goods at the time of the contract, yet it may be some time later that the defect is discovered. Or it may be that the defect did not exist at the time of the sale but developed later, perhaps due to misuse by the buyer. It is, consequently, a question of fact whether an article that ceases to function properly was defective at the time of sale. A new car that develops transmission problems within a few months is likely to have been defective all along; one that runs well for several years before developing a fault may well have been in satisfactory condition at the time of sale.

CASE 14.6

McCann bought an electric blanket from Sears. More than 10 years later it caught fire, causing damage to McCann's bedroom. McCann brought an action for breach of contract on the grounds that there was an implied condition that the electric blanket was reasonably free from defect. The court held that, in view of the time that had elapsed (during which the blanket had functioned without any problems), the buyer had failed to satisfy the burden of proving that the defect existed when the blanket was bought.[20]

---

[17] *Nikka Traders, Inc. v. Gizella Pastry Ltd.*, 2012 BCSC 1412.

[18] *Wren v. Holt*, [1903] 1 K.B. 610.

[19] *Australian Knitting Mills Ltd. v. Grant* (1933), 50 C.L.R. 387, per Dixon, J., at 418; also *Bristol Tramways v. Fiat Motors*, [1910] 2 K.B. 831, per Farwell, L.J., at 841.

[20] *McCann v. Sears Canada Ltd.* (1998), 43 B.L.R. (2d) 217, Aff'd. (1999) 122 O.C.C. 91.

In practice, it is often difficult to tell which part of the section is the more relevant to a buyer's complaint, as the two parts tend to overlap.[21]

Subject to certain exceptions and qualifications, the Sale of Goods Act implies the following contractual terms into contracts for the sale of goods:

- an implied condition that the seller has (or will have) a right to sell the goods
- an implied warranty that the buyer will have and enjoy quiet possession of the goods
- an implied warranty that the goods will be free from any undisclosed charge or encumbrance
- an implied condition that the goods will correspond with the description under which they are sold
- an implied condition that the goods will be reasonably fit for the purpose for which they are required if that purpose was made known to the seller
- an implied condition that the goods will be of merchantable quality
- in the case of a sale by sample, an implied condition that the bulk will correspond with the sample

Exemption Clauses

The Sale of Goods Act contains the following provision:

> Where any right, duty or liability would arise under a contract of sale by implication of law, it may be negatived or varied by express agreement or by the course of dealing between the parties, or by usage, if the usage is such as to bind both parties to the contract.[22]

Therefore, a seller may include in a standard form contract of sale an express term exempting it from the liability normally imposed by the implied terms.

The courts have restricted the circumstances in which a seller may excuse himself from liability under the Act. Clear and direct language must be used to contract out of the statutory protections.

CASE 14.7

Syncrude ordered 32 gearboxes from Hunter, a manufacturer, to drive its conveyor belts in the Alberta tar sands project. Syncrude provided specifications of what the gearboxes were required to do, and Hunter designed them to meet those specifications.

The contract contained an express term guaranteeing the gearboxes for two years. When the period had expired, the gearboxes developed faults that were found to be due to faulty design. Syncrude could not succeed in an action on the express term because the two-year period had elapsed, but the Supreme Court of Canada held that the implied term of fitness under the Act could still be relied on. The existence of an express warranty was not inconsistent with the statutory warranties.[23]

---

[21] Nevertheless, the two warranties are not identical. In *Wharton v. Tom Harris Chevrolet Oldsmobile Cadillac Ltd.*, [2002] B.C.J. No. 233, the B.C.C.A. held that a defective stereo system in a luxury car was a breach of the fitness warranty, although it did not render the car unmerchantable.

[22] Sale of Goods Act, R.S.O. 1990, c. S.1, s. 53.; see also Alta., s. 54; B.C., s. 69; Nfld., s. 56.

[23] *Hunter Engineering Co. v. Syncrude Canada Ltd.* (1989), 57 D.L.R. (4th) 321 (S.C.C.). See also *Fording Coal Ltd. v. Harnischfeger Corp. of Canada* (1991), 6 B.L.R. (2d) 157.

If the words used in an exemption clause do not precisely describe the type of liability disclaimed, the courts will normally find that the implied liability is still part of the contract. If a seller includes an express term that "all warranties implied by statute are hereby excluded," the seller will avoid liability under all those implied terms that are warranties but not under those that are conditions.[24] If the seller expressly promised that the goods would be of a certain quality or type, an exemption clause that refers only to implied terms will not free him from obligations under this express term.

The courts have also held that a seller cannot so completely exempt himself from liability that he may default on his bargain entirely. They will not give effect to an exemption clause that gives a seller immunity from action if he delivers goods that are totally different from those contracted for by the buyer or if he delivers goods to which he does not have good title.[26] In effect, the courts have held that a contract for the sale of goods would be deprived of all meaning if a seller's obligation were merely to deliver the goods "if he felt like it."

Payment

Many contracts of sale set out the time of payment expressly—in others it may be implied from the terms of the contract and the particular circumstances. When the contract itself gives no guidance about when the buyer is to pay, the courts assume that delivery and

---

[24] *Gregorio v. Intrans-Corp.* (1994), 115 D.L.R. (4th) 200 (Ont. C.A.).

[25] *Andrews Bros. Ltd. v. Singer & Co. Ltd.,* [1934] 1 K.B. 17.

[26] *Pinnock Brothers v. Lewis and Peat Ltd.,* [1923] 1 K.B. 690; *Karsales (Harrow) Ltd. v. Wallis,* [1956] 2 All E.R. 866; *Canadian-Dominion Leasing Corp. Ltd. v. Suburban Superdrug Ltd.* (1966), 56 D.L.R. (2d) 43.

[26A] Sale of Goods Act, the Ontario Consumer Protection Act S.O. 2002 (s. 9(3)).

payment are to happen together; the transaction is presumed to be a cash sale. But this presumption may be rebutted by the circumstances in which the contract is made. For example, when payment from a customer is accepted by credit card, the buyer is normally entitled to delivery of the goods immediately, before payment by the credit card company.

The courts interpret the time set for payment as a warranty unless the parties have expressed themselves otherwise. Therefore, a seller is not entitled to rescind the contract of sale and have the goods back simply because payment is not made on time. He must be content with a breach of contract action for the price of the goods. But the parties may agree on other terms. A seller may insist on a term entitling him to retake possession in the event of non-payment. This provision is characteristic of the installment sale, to be considered separately in Chapter 28.

Delivery

Delivery terms should specify the date and time, the location, and the quantity to be delivered.

A term specifying the quantity of goods to be delivered is a condition. If the term is broken—that is, if the seller delivers a substantially different quantity—the buyer is free to reject the goods. Her right to do so exists whether a greater or lesser quantity than promised is delivered. The buyer may, of course, choose to take all or part of what is delivered. If she does so, she must pay for what she takes at the contract rate.

The time specified for delivery is also usually a condition, so that if the goods are not delivered on time the buyer may rescind the contract. She is free to look elsewhere for the goods she needs as soon as she learns they will not be available on time. If the parties agree that the goods are to be delivered as soon as they are available, without specifying a time, then delivery must occur within a reasonable time, taking into account all the circumstances.

The place of delivery is normally either the seller's place of business or wherever the goods happen to be located at the time of the contract. The parties may, however, express a different intention—for example, that the goods should be delivered to the buyer's home—or their intention may be implied from trade custom.

An offer for sale sometimes states, along with the asking price, the terms of delivery. It may, for example, quote wheat at so much per bushel FOB Winnipeg, or steel at so much per tonne CIF Hamilton. *FOB* means that the seller will place the goods at that location "free on board" the type of transportation specified. When a *CIF* (cost, insurance, freight) price is quoted, the seller undertakes to arrange insurance and to ship the goods to the buyer. (These and other standard terms are widely used in international trade and are discussed further in Chapter 30.) Another common type of contract is the *COD* (cash on delivery) contract in which the seller undertakes to deliver the goods at the buyer's place of business or residence.

Risk of Loss before Delivery

The contract should also describe who is required to insure the goods throughout the delivery process. If the goods are damaged or lost during delivery, ideally the contract will indicate who—the buyer or seller—must compensate for the loss. If the contract does not expressly state when the risk of loss (responsibility for damage to or destruction of the goods) moves from the seller to the buyer, the courts typically imply a term that reflects the ownership of the goods. Whoever owns the goods at the time of loss is the one who is at risk. The risk of loss follows the title to the goods unless the parties have agreed otherwise: the party that has title ordinarily suffers the loss.[27] For this reason, we must identify the moment in time when ownership passes from seller to buyer—when does title pass?

---

[27] For an example of this rule, see A.M.S. *Equipment Inc. v. Case*, [1999] B.C.J. No. 124.

TITLE TO GOODS
Who May Pass Title?

Subject to this Act, where goods are sold by a person who is not their owner and who does not sell them under the authority or with the consent of the owner, the buyer acquires no better title to the goods than the seller had, unless the owner of the goods is by conduct precluded from denying the seller's authority to sell.[28]

That is, only the owner, or a person authorized by the owner, can pass a good title to goods. To this principle, the Act allows two main exceptions: certain sales made by an agent (considered below) and sales made under any special common law or statutory power of sale or under a court order.

The Effect of Agency When a business ships goods to its agent for the agent to sell, the effect of the consignment is to give the agent (the consignee) the appearance of ownership in the eyes of the public. Statutes in the various provinces give the agent the same authority to deal with the goods as their owner has.[29] The agent may, therefore, validly pass title to anyone who purchases the goods in good faith, even though the sale may not be authorized or is on terms forbidden by the owner (the consignor).

Seller or Buyer in Possession A seller could mistakenly sell the same goods twice, or a buyer could re-sell goods before she actually owns them. The Act protects an innocent purchaser who "buys" the goods in the normal course of business without notice of any defect in the seller's title.[30]

CASE 14.9

Western Environmental acquired the assets of a Canadian oil refinery that was being closed down. It proceeded to sell off various assets of the refinery, including a quantity of pipe, which it sold to the plaintiff, Epscan, for $260 000. It was agreed that Epscan would cut and remove the pipe over the following three months. Before it could do so, Western sold the same pipe to another Canadian corporation, Bartin, and was paid $162 000. Epscan learned that Bartin was removing the pipe and sued Bartin for conversion. Meanwhile, Western and its employees had disappeared.

At trial, Epscan was awarded damages for the conversion. On appeal, the Alberta Court of Appeal held that Bartin was protected under the Sale of Goods Act.[31] The vendor, Western, remained in possession, there were no suspicious circumstances, and Bartin had no knowledge of Epscan's interest.[32]

A buyer who does not take immediate possession of goods when title passes runs the risk that a fraudulent seller may resell them to an innocent third party who will obtain a good title. A similar risk exists where a seller allows the buyer to take possession of goods before title has passed.[33]

---

[28] Ont., s. 22; Alta., s. 23; B.C., s. 26; Nfld., s. 23.

[29] See, for example, Factors Act, R.S.O. 1990, c. F.1, s. 2; R.S.A. 2000, c. F-1, s. 2; Sale of Goods Act, R.S.B.C. 1996, c. 410, s. 59.

[30] Ont., s. 25; Alta., s. 26; B.C., s. 30; Nfld., s. 27. An exception may apply where the situation is governed by the Personal Property Security Act (discussed in Chapter 29).

[31] Alta., s. 27(1), now s. 26(1).

[32] *Bartin Pipe & Piling Supply Ltd. v. Epscan Industries Ltd.* (2004), 236 D.L.R. (4th) 75.

[33] Usually fraud is involved, but that is not necessarily so; see *Sun Toyota Ltd. v. Granville Toyota Ltd.*, [2002] B.C.J. No. 847 (QL).

When Does Title Pass?

As we have already noted, the risk—of loss or damage—generally passes with the title (ownership) to goods. It is therefore essential to know when title passes; usually the contract expressly says. If not, the Sale of Goods Act has five rules that determine when title passes[34]

The Sale of Goods Act Rules for Passing of Title Unless otherwise agreed, the Sale of Goods Act provides that title to goods passes from the seller to the buyer

- Rule 1: where there is an unconditional contract for the sale of **specific goods** in a deliverable state, when the contract is made;

- Rule 2: where there is a contract for the sale of specific goods and the seller is bound to do something to the goods to put them into a deliverable state, when the buyer has received notice that it has been done;

- Rule 3: where there is a contract for the sale of specific goods in a deliverable state but the seller is bound to do something to ascertain their price, when the buyer has received notice that it has been done;

- Rule 4: where goods are delivered to the buyer on approval or on "sale or return," when the buyer signifies his approval, or does some other act adopting the transaction, or when the buyer retains the goods beyond a reasonable time;

- Rule 5: where there is a contract for the sale of **unascertained goods** or **future goods** by description, when goods of that description and in a deliverable state are **appropriated** to the contract by one party with the assent of the other.[34A]

For more information on this topic, see the Companion Website.

> **specific goods** goods in existence, identified and agreed upon as the subject matter of the sale

> **unascertained goods** goods that have not been set aside and agreed upon as the subject of a sale

> **future goods** goods that have not yet been produced

> **appropriated** designated as the subject matter of the contract

Bills of Lading

Historically a paper **bill of lading** was the essential document of all commercial sales transactions and it travelled with the goods and was signed by each new custodian. The purpose was to transfer title and to record changes in possession. Today a broadly similar result is now achieved through an electronic exchange of data and documents. See the Companion Website for more information on this topic.

> **bill of lading** a document signed by a carrier acknowledging that specified goods have been received by it for shipment

REMEDIES OF THE SELLER

Lien

The purpose of selling goods is to get paid. One way of ensure payment is to withhold delivery until payment is made. While the goods remain in an unpaid seller's possession, the seller has a **lien** on the goods regardless of whether title has passed to the buyer. The seller has a claim or charge on them for their agreed price, and can refuse to release them until full payment is made. Once the seller delivers the goods to the buyer, however, he normally loses this special lien. The right of lien is based upon possession and is gone if possession passes in good faith to the buyer.[35]

The lien remedy arises in the following situations:

(a) where the contract does not state that the buyer is to have credit, so that payment may be required upon delivery

> **lien** a right of a person in possession of property to retain that property until payment

---

[34] Ont., s. 19: see also Alta., s. 20; B.C., s. 23; Nfld., s. 20.

[34A] Rules of Sale of Goods Act.

[35] An exception to this rule applies when an unpaid seller repossesses goods under the provisions of the Bankruptcy and Insolvency Act; this exception is discussed below under the heading "Repossession."

(b) where the goods have been sold on credit, the term of credit has expired without payment being made, and the seller still has possession of the goods

(c) where the buyer becomes insolvent before delivery[36]

In (c), a seller who refuses to deliver is excused only if the buyer is insolvent. A seller should be sure of the facts before exercising the right of lien; otherwise, he takes the risk that the buyer may subsequently sue for breach of the promise to deliver. It is not enough simply to hear that the buyer's financial position is questionable. See the Companion Website for more information on this topic.

A seller may waive his right of lien—and rely on the buyer's credit—in two ways. He may waive the right by implication, as in the usual credit sale, simply by agreeing to deliver before payment is due. Second, he may voluntarily deliver the goods before he needs to do so.

Repossession

Once possession passes in good faith to a buyer, the seller loses the right to repossess the goods even if the buyer fails to pay for them. Bankruptcy law creates an important exception to the rule.[37] Where a seller has delivered goods to a buyer and the buyer, before having paid in full for the goods, becomes bankrupt or insolvent within 30 days, the seller may make a written demand for the return of the goods. The demand must be presented within 15 days after the buyer goes bankrupt to the trustee in bankruptcy or receiver appointed to manage the debtor's affairs. The right to repossess applies only to goods that were delivered in relation to the buyer's business, not to consumer goods. The goods must still be in the possession of the buyer, must be identifiable, and must be in the same condition as they were when sold. If the price has been partly paid, the seller has a choice between repossessing a portion of the goods in proportion to the amount still owing and repossessing all of the goods and refunding the amount already paid. The right of repossession ranks above any other claim to the goods, except those of a subsequent purchaser who has bought the goods for value and in good faith, without notice of the unpaid seller's claim.

Resale

After exercising a right of lien under the Sale of Goods Act, an unpaid seller may give notice to the buyer and resell the goods to a third party. The new purchaser obtains good title to them. Although not expressly authorized under the Bankruptcy and Insolvency Act, it seems that an unpaid seller who repossesses goods under that Act also has the right to resell them. The right of resale is especially helpful when the goods are perishable, but is not confined to such emergencies.

This right also arises whenever a buyer commits a breach by refusing to accept goods. Resale is the way a seller mitigates his loss. If the seller makes a reasonable effort to get a good price on resale but obtains a lower price than that promised in the original contract, he may sue the original buyer for the deficiency.

Damages for Non-Acceptance

A critical factor in determining the seller's damages when a buyer refuses the goods is whether the seller is in a position to supply more goods than prospective customers might order. If so, the seller's damages are measured by the profits lost due to the buyer's breach;

---

[36] Section 39 (B.C.) insolvent is not a defined term under the Sale of Goods Act.

[37] Bankruptcy and Insolvency Act, R.S.C. 1985, c. B-3, s. 81.1.

if not, damages are generally measured by any deficiency in the resale price of the rejected goods compared with the original contract price.

ILLUSTRATION 14.5

Read examined a used accordion for sale in Crescendo Music Stores Ltd. She agreed in writing to buy it for $600 provided the bellows were repaired and gold monogram initials were affixed to it. Before the repairs were made, Read informed Crescendo that she had decided to take up the saxophone instead and refused to accept the accordion. Crescendo sued Read.

The appropriate action would be for damages for non-acceptance because the title had not passed to Read at the time of her repudiation. If the music store had more used accordions in stock than it had customers wanting to buy them, it would have sustained damages equal to the profit it would have made had Read purchased the instrument as she promised.

If the store had no other used accordions and was able to resell the accordion, but for less than $600, it would have sustained damages equal to the difference between the two prices. If the repairs and changes had been made but Read had not been notified before she repudiated the contract, title would still not have passed to her, and the seller might have a claim for additional damages equal to its expenses. That would depend on whether the required changes had enhanced the value of the instrument: Crescendo should be able to recover the cost of affixing the gold monogram, but not that of repairing the bellows.

Action for the Price

When title has passed to the buyer, a seller is entitled to the full price regardless of whether the buyer has taken delivery. If the buyer rejects goods after title has passed to her, she is rejecting what she already owns.

ILLUSTRATION 14.6

Anderson bought a sound system on display at Burton's Appliance Store for installation at her dental office. The system was tagged "sold" with Anderson's name on it, and Anderson signed a form identifying the purchase and stating its price. On her way back to the office, Anderson saw another model in the window of Modern Electronics Ltd., and decided that she would prefer it. She refused to take delivery of the sound system from Burton, and Burton sued her for the full price of the machine.

The action would succeed. At the time Anderson attempted to repudiate the contract of sale, title had already passed to her. If Burton sues for the price, however, he must be willing and able to deliver the sound system.

The conclusion in Illustration 14.6 is based on a strict application of the Sale of Goods Act. When the seller still has the goods, courts may want to see mitigation efforts. If the buyer is a consumer, special cancellation options are available as discussed later in this chapter. Most retail businesses make it a practice to include return options in their consumer sales contracts.

Retention of Deposit

In a contract of sale, as in any contract, the parties may provide that, in the event of breach, the party in default shall pay the other a specified sum of money by way of liquidated damages. As discussed in Chapter 13, the court will enforce such a term if the amount specified is a genuine estimate by the parties of the probable loss. Depending upon the circumstances, an amount paid by a buyer as a deposit may be treated as liquidated damages in the event of her default. In many contracts of sale, the reason the seller demands a deposit is to protect himself at least to that extent in the event of the buyer's non-acceptance. The intention is clear that the deposit will be forfeited upon breach by the buyer.[38]

Legally speaking, there is a difference between a **deposit**, which is intended primarily to provide a sanction to induce performance of the contract by the buyer, and a **down payment**, which constitutes a part payment of the purchase price and is unrelated to the seller's loss in the event of breach by the buyer. If the title to the goods has already passed to the buyer at the time the buyer repudiates, the seller is entitled not only to retain the down payment, but also to sue for the balance of the price. If title has not yet passed, the seller is entitled to retain out of the down payment any damages for non-acceptance that he can prove, and is accountable to the buyer for any remaining surplus.[39] If the seller has no damages, he must return the down payment in full.

THE SELLER'S LIABILITY
Breach of a Term

Generally, breach of a warranty gives rise to only an action for damages, but a breach of a condition entitles the injured party to discharge the contract as well as to sue for damages for any loss suffered. The Sale of Goods Act, however, sets down circumstances where a buyer will not be entitled to terminate the contract and return the goods, even though the seller has breached a condition.[40]

First, that the buyer must keep the goods and be content with damages when the broken contract of sale does not contemplate delivery by installments (is not severable) and the buyer has indicated an intention to keep the goods or treated them in a way inconsistent with the seller's ownership of them.

A second situation arises where the right to repudiate would be lost when the contract is for specific goods, the title in which has passed to the buyer even though the goods are still in the seller's possession. However, when the seller has committed a breach of condition by allocating unsatisfactory goods to fill the contract, such a result would seem surprising. Courts avoid applying this part of the section and sometimes even seem to ignore it as inappropriate to modern selling practices.

ILLUSTRATION 14.7

A sales agent for Agrarian Implements Ltd. showed to Macdonald, a farmer, a catalogue containing pictures of agricultural equipment that his firm had for sale. The agent told Macdonald that the company had just taken into stock "one brand new" combine of a type pictured in the catalogue. Macdonald agreed to buy it and signed the necessary papers.

When the combine was delivered, a neighbour of Macdonald recognized it as the one with which the same sales agent had earlier given him an extensive demonstration, and which the sales agent had referred to as "a demonstrator model that we could let you have at a bargain."

Macdonald at once shipped the combine back to Agrarian Implements, and the firm then sued him for the price.

The combine was a specific article at the time Macdonald agreed to buy it. Nevertheless, he would be entitled to treat the contract as discharged and to refuse to accept the combine. Agrarian Implements breached the condition as to description (that the combine was new), and title did not pass to Macdonald.[41] If, however, Macdonald took delivery of the combine and used it for farm work, he could not subsequently, upon learning that it was not new when he bought it, insist he had a right to return it. He must be content with damages.

---

[38] See *Stockloser v. Johnson*, [1954] 1 Q.B. 476. If the contract provides for a non-refundable deposit but the deposit has not been paid, for example, when the purchaser has stopped payment on the cheque, the vendor is entitled to recover the agreed sum: *Vanvic Enterprises Ltd. v. Mark*, [1985] 3 W.W.R. 644.

[39] *Stevenson v. Colonial Homes Ltd.* (1961), 27 D.L.R. (2d) 698.

[40] Ont., s. 12(3); see also Alta., s. 13(4); B.C., s. 15(4); Nfld., s. 13(4).

[41] See *Varley v. Whipp*, [1900] 1 Q.B. 513.

In Case 14.10, we see the consequences for the buyer when the seller breaches a condition but the buyer has accepted the goods.

CASE 14.10

Leaf purchased a painting of Salisbury Cathedral that the seller, International Galleries, represented to him as the work of the famous artist Constable. When Leaf attempted to resell the picture five years later, it was discovered that it had not been painted by Constable but by a much less-famous artist. Its value was consequently only a small fraction of what both the seller and buyer had thought.

Leaf tried to return the picture to International Galleries and recover the purchase price. The court held that the Sale of Goods Act applied, so that Leaf did not have the right to treat the contract as being at an end. Since he did not sue for damages, as he might have done, his action failed.[42]

Wrongful Withholding or Disposition by the Seller

When the title to goods has already passed to the buyer, a seller who refuses to deliver them according to the terms of the contract commits a tort: the buyer may sue the seller for damages for **wrongful detention**. Moreover, the buyer may occasionally obtain a court order for the delivery of the goods. If, in addition to a failure to deliver, the seller transfers the goods to a third party, he will have disposed of goods that do not belong to him; the buyer may sue for damages for the tort of conversion—that is, for converting the buyer's goods to his own use or purposes.

wrongful detention the refusal by the seller to deliver goods whose title has passed to the buyer

REMEDIES OF THE BUYER

A buyer has a range of possible remedies in contract, in tort, and under consumer protection legislation, which have been discussed in earlier chapters.

In tort and in contract, a buyer's usual remedy will be to claim damages. In Chapter 13, under the heading "Expectation Damages," we discussed the measure of damages available to a buyer when the seller fails to deliver. If delivery is merely delayed and the buyer still accepts the goods, the measure of damages is the value the goods would have had for the buyer if they had been delivered on time, less their actual value when delivered.

As an alternative to damages, a buyer may be able to claim the equitable remedy of specific performance or of rescission; both of these remedies were discussed in Chapter 13. The Sale of Goods Act gives the court discretion to order specific performance of a contract for the sale of goods—that is, to order the seller to deliver the goods to the buyer. Generally, the court does not grant this remedy when a seller refuses to deliver, because money damages are nearly always an adequate remedy. Where the goods have a unique value for the buyer, however, the court may exercise its discretion in her favour and order specific performance.

INTERNATIONAL ISSUE

International Sale of Goods

In 1980, the United Nations Commission on International Trade Law (UNCITRAL) developed a set of uniform rules for international sale of goods. The Convention on Contracts for the International Sale of Goods (CISG) establishes substantive rules relating to the formation of a contract, buyers' and sellers' obligations, and remedies. Its goals are to overcome the problems associated with conflicting principles of law between buyer and seller jurisdictions and provide certainty and consistency in the resolution of international trade disputes. It applies to sales of commercial

>

---

[42] *Leaf v. International Galleries*, [1950] 2 K.B. 86.43.

goods between businesses in different countries (providing the countries subscribe to the convention). It does not apply to sales for personal or household use (consumer transactions).

In 1992, the convention became law in Canada,[43] and federal and provincial legislation has been adopted to implement its terms.[44] This means that when a dispute arises in a contract covered by the convention, a Canadian court should apply the rules of the convention rather than the domestic laws relating to sale of goods. Parties may specifically opt out of the application of CISG by inserting a term in their contract (article 6). The United States has implemented the convention but the United Kingdom has not.

CONSUMER CONTRACTS

We discussed regulation of consumer contracts and consumer protection in Chapters 3 and 10. In this chapter, we focus on how the contractual relationship between the parties—the business and the individual consumer—is controlled by legislation. As noted in Chapter 6, the unequal bargaining positions in consumer transactions leave the consumer at the mercy of business, ultimately resulting in one-sided contracts presented to the consumer on a take-it-or-leave-it basis. A standard form contract is prepared in advance by the business party with the goals of reducing potential liability for the business and eliminating consumer rights. The legislation described below does not ban these one-sided contracts entirely; instead it controls the use of pressure sales tactics, inserts terms into the contract, requires notice and disclosure of onerous terms, and gives the consumer a chance to back out once they have time to consider these terms.

consumer an individual (not an organization) purchasing a product or service for personal, family, household, non-business purposes

A **consumer** is an individual (not an organization) purchasing a product or service for personal, family, household, non-business purposes. (See the Companion Website for more on this topic.) In Chapter 6, *standard form contract* was defined as an offer prepared in advance by the offeror, including terms favourable to the offeror that cannot be changed by the offeree, but must be accepted as is or rejected. Businesses typically use standard form contracts in their dealings with consumers. These agreements, also known as contracts of adhesion, typically favour the business party and so consumer protection legislation tries to level the playing field.[45]

Consumer Protection

In addition to the Sale of Goods Act, most provinces have developed separate legislation addressing the specific needs of the consumer. Consumer protection legislation applies to the sale of goods, as well as to the supply of services, and extends the warranties described in the Sale of Goods Acts to goods that are leased, traded, or otherwise supplied.[46] Unlike the Sale of Goods Act, consumer protection legislation does not apply to business-to-business

---

[43] International Sale of Goods Contracts Convention Act, S.C. 1991, c. 13.

[44] International Conventions Implementation Act, R.S.A. 2000, c. I-6; International Sale of Goods Act, R.S.B.C. 1996, c. 236; International Sale of Goods Act, R.S.N.L. 1990, c. I-16; International Sale of Goods Act, R.S.O. 1990, c. I.10.

[45] See e.g. Business Practices and Consumer Protection Act, S.B.C. 2004, c. 2; Fair Trading Act, R.S.A. 2000, c. F-2; Consumer Protection Act 2002, S.O. 2002, c. 30, Sch. A; Consumer Protection Act, R.S.M. 1987, c. 200, s. 58.

[46] *Ibid*, s. 9 (Ont.). See also Consumer Product Warranty and Liability Act, S.N.B. 1978, c. C-18.1.

commercial transactions. As discussed in Chapter 10, it targets the practices of particularly "high risk" business sectors such as timeshares, travel, and fitness industries.

BUSINESS SALES TACTICS TARGETING CONSUMERS

Problematic business sales tactics often result in unwanted consumer contracts; consumer protection legislation regulates these tactics by ensuring the necessary detailed information is supplied to the customer, by adding cancellation options to the contract or by blocking the contract's enforcement.

Pressure Selling

As a response to high-pressure door-to-door selling methods, most provinces enacted legislation making the **direct sales contract** non-binding on consumers.[47] Consumers are given a cooling-off period after contracting, during which they may terminate the contract by giving written notice to the seller. Upon doing so, the consumer has no further obligation under the contract and may recover any money already paid. This marks an important departure from the common law rule that the rights and liabilities of the parties are established at the time the contract is formed.

direct sales contract a contract formed at a place other than the business's place of business

The statutory cooling-off periods vary in length from two to ten days. In some provinces, it is based on the time when the contract is entered into; in others, from the date on which a copy of the contract is received by the buyer. The legislation applies to both goods and services, but in some provinces it does not apply to sales under $50. Cooling-off periods are also used to address the inequities of other distance contracts such as those entered into using the internet or by telephone, or anytime the contracting parties are separated by distance.

Unsolicited Goods

Pressure selling can also take the form of sending goods not ordered by the consumer, hoping the recipient will pay for them. Consumer protection statutes expressly state that use of unrequested goods by the recipient does not amount to an acceptance of the seller's offer. Accordingly, a recipient of unsolicited goods may use them without becoming liable for their price.[48] The purpose of the provision is to discourage sellers from sending unsolicited goods to consumers, and it seems to have been quite effective. Some provinces have taken a similar approach to unsolicited credit cards.[49]

Telemarketing

The Federal Competition Act[50] defines **telemarketing** as "the practice of using interactive telephone communications for the purpose of promoting, directly or indirectly, the supply or use of a product or for the purpose of promoting, directly or indirectly, any business interest."[51] It can be a pressure sales tactic because it targets people in their homes who are not considering any purchases. Sometimes callers mislead purchasers about their intentions

telemarketing the use of telephone communications for promoting the supply of a product or for promoting a business interest

---

[47] See, for example, Business Practices and Consumer Protection Act, S.B.C. 2004, c. 2, ss. 17, 20, 21.

[48] See Business Practices and Consumer Protection Act, S.B.C. 2004, c. 2, ss. 12, 13, 14; Consumer Protection Act, S.O. 2002, c. C.30, Sch. A, s. 13.

[49] See Business Practices and Consumer Protection Act, S.B.C. 2004, c. 2, s. 96; Consumer Protection Act, R.S.N.S. 1989, c. 92, s. 23; S.O. 2002, c. C.30, Sch. A, s. 13 (although use of the card triggers an agreement, s. 68).

[50] Federal Competition Act.

[51] Internet communications, automated pre-recorded messages, and consumer-instigated calls to a customer relations line are not covered.

and leave out important information. Therefore the above described cooling-off period and disclosure requirements apply to these contracts.

In addition, under the Competition Act, deceptive telemarketing is a criminal offence, punishable by a maximum of 14 years in prison and a fine within the discretion of the court; or a fine of up to $200 000 may be imposed on summary conviction. The provisions also extend criminal responsibility to directors and officers of a corporation when its employees are found guilty of deceptive telemarketing. In 1999, a Quebec court imposed a record $1 million fine for deceptive telemarketing and imposed the first-ever jail sentences. The firm's president and several of the firm's sales agents were sentenced to six months in jail.[52]

Callers must disclose the name of the company they represent, the purpose of the call, the kind and value of the product or service being promoted, the terms or restrictions relating to delivery of the product to customers, and other specified information. Additionally, the provisions prohibit telemarketers from conducting contests where the participant can receive prizes only after she makes some kind of prior payment, or from offering gifts or prizes for buying a product unless the value of the gift is disclosed. It is also illegal for telemarketers to offer a product for sale at a price grossly in excess of its fair market value, where delivery of the product is conditional on prior payment by the customer.

In 2008, a National Do Not Call List was established by the Canadian Radio-television and Telecommunications Commission.[53] Once a consumer registers his or her number, telemarketers must not call to solicit unless the telemarketer is a registered charity, is a political party, or has an existing business relationship with the consumer. Registration is effective for a period of three years. Corporations face a possible $15 000 fine for each violation. Canadian anti-spam legislation, discussed in Chapters 31 and 32, regulates bulk emailing and online solicitations.

TERMS ADDED TO CONSUMER CONTRACTS
Legislated Terms

Provincial statutes provide protection for consumers by implying terms into the contract or requiring businesses to expressly state certain terms in the contract. First, the above described implied terms under the Sale of Goods Act with respect to seller's right to sell, merchantability, and fitness, etc., are made binding on sellers in contracts—goods and services—with consumers; sellers cannot escape liability by requiring buyers to sign exemption clauses.[54]

CASE 14.11

Szilvasy bought a new home and took over the lease of the rented hot water heater. It sprang a leak and caused $16 000 of water damage to the basement of the home. Szilvasy sued for breach of contract. She alleged that the water heater was not fit for the intended purpose. Reliance Home Comfort defended the action, saying the lease contract did not include an express term on fitness for purpose and it did include a clause exempting Reliance from liability for water damage. The Ontario Court of Appeal held that s. 9 of the Consumer Protection Act implied a Sale of Goods Act term of fitness for purpose into this leasing contract and this implied warranty could not be waived or varied by the express exemption clause. The water heater was not fit for the purpose because it leaked. The consumer contract was breached by the business.[55]

---

[52] American Family Publishers et al., Competition Bureau Annual Report 98/99.

[53] Telecommunications Act, S.C. 1993, c. 38, s. 41; Telecom Decision CRTC 2008-6.

[54] See, for example, Consumer Protection Act, R.S.N.S. 1989, c. 92, s. 26(3); S.O. 2002, c. C.30, Sch. A, s. 9(2)(3). BPCPA s.3.

[55] Szilvasy v. Reliance Home Comfort, 2012 ONCA 821 considering the combined impact of the Consumer Protection Act, 2002, S.O. 2002, c. C-30, Sch. A, s. 9 and the Sale of Goods Act, R.S.O. 1990 c. S-1.

This approach, of imposing contractual liability on sellers by inserting compulsory terms in consumer contracts, has been taken further in the Saskatchewan and New Brunswick statutes, which imply additional warranties and extend protection to third persons who were not parties to the contract, such as members of the buyer's family.[56]

Second, consumer protection legislation requires businesses to give consumers subject to pressure sales tactics or involved in high risk industries specific detailed information about their transaction. This includes obvious information about the names, addresses, and phone numbers, as well as notice of how to cancel their contracts. The above described cooling-off periods and cancellation rights created for high pressure sales tactics must be expressly described in the contract, along with instructions about how to exercise the option to cancel. Failure to include the statutory information results in the contract being void or unenforceable.[57]

Finally, all terms in the consumer contract (whether implied or express) that are capable of more than one reasonable interpretation must be given the interpretation most favourable to the consumer.[58] This is an application of the contra proferentem rule because business will have drafted the contract.

SPECIFIC TYPES OF TERMS

Exemption Clauses

As repeatedly discussed, exemption clauses (also known as exculpatory clauses or limitation of liability terms) are regularly used by business to restrict their liability—arising from breach of contract, tort, or statute. As noted above, some provinces contain their scope in the consumer context.[59] Most importantly, they are not capable of excluding liability for breach of either the implied Sale of Goods Act warranties or any of the obligations imposed on business under the consumer protection legislation. Business cannot "contract out" of the duties imposed upon it by the statutes discussed in this part.

Repossession

A standard form consumer contract involving goods typically contains a term giving the lender or seller a repossession remedy should the consumer default. For example, the contract may authorize the seller to take back the goods from the consumer if installment payments are not kept up, or to sue for the entire balance due under the contract if the consumer defaults in a single installment payment. Consumer protection statutes in some provinces state that the seller's remedy of repossession is lost once the buyer has paid a specified proportion (for example, two-thirds) of the purchase price, and other statutes limit the circumstances in which a seller or creditor can enforce an acceleration clause, which is a provision in the contract that stipulates that the entire unpaid balance of the price is immediately payable should the buyer default.[60] A further example occurs in

---

[56] Consumer Protection Act, S.S. 1996, c. C-30.1; Consumer Product Warranty and Liability Act, S.N.B. 1978, c. C-18.1.

[57] Alta. Reg. 191/99.

[58] Ontario Consumer Protection Act, 2002, S.O. 2002, c. C30, Sch. A, s. 11; Business Practices and Consumer Protection Act S.B.C. 2004, c. 2, s. 18(2); *Seidel v. TELUS Communications*, 2011 SCC 15 para 2.

[59] As noted earlier, in British Columbia, New Brunswick, Ontario, and Saskatchewan, the warranties cannot be contracted out of in the case of retail sales.

[60] See, for example, Personal Property Security Act, R.S.O. 1990, c. P.10, s. 66(2), stating that a consumer may redeem seized property without paying full purchase price by merely paying arrears in installments.

the law of landlord and tenant, where some provinces have abolished a landlord's self-help remedy of seizing a residential tenant's goods for arrears of rent.[61]

Arbitration

Some businesses prevent consumers from using the courts to enforce their rights, particularly class actions and small claims court. This is done by placing a term in the contract that designates individual arbitration as the only process that may be used to resolve any disputes with the business arising from the contract. Consumers waive their right to participate in class actions. This discourages most consumer claims because such claims are usually worth so little money that it does not make sense to pursue them individually. It only makes monetary sense to collect all consumers with the same complaints into one class action. This works in every province except Ontario, Alberta, and Quebec—the consumer protection legislation in these provinces makes arbitration clauses in consumer contracts void and unenforceable.[62] Consumers in other provinces will have the arbitration term in their contracts enforced.

Severance

Businesses that operate in multiple provinces often use the same standard form contract across the entire country. They manage the differences between provincial consumer protection laws by including whatever terms they want plus a term that states that any term deemed to be illegal, void, or unenforceable may be severed or cut out of the contract, leaving the balance of the contract to be enforced. This is known as a severance clause and it prevents the entire contract from being struck down when one of its clauses is illegal.

Financing Arrangements and Disclosure of the True Cost of Credit

Consumer protection statutes require that detailed description of all financial arrangements between business and consumer be included in the written contract, a copy of which must be given to the consumer. These disclosure requirements apply to all contracts where a buyer of goods or services or a borrower of money repays the debt by installments. They require sellers and lenders to give their customers a detailed statement of the terms of credit in dollars and cents and in percentage terms as an effective annual rate of interest, as well as any charges for insurance and registration fees. Payments must be broken down separately and aggregated to show a total cost of borrowing. A customer is not bound by the contract if the seller fails to comply with the requirements.[63]

The Criminal Code sets a maximum "legal" interest rate and the federal Interest Act requires that interest rates in written contracts be expressed in annual percentages.[64] Non-compliance makes interest agreements void and unenforceable.

Many vendors who sell goods to consumers on the installment plan assign their consumer credit contracts to finance companies. Typically, a vendor assigns the contract to a finance company and receives immediate payment of a sum that is less than the full amount to be paid by the buyer. The buyer then receives notice of assignment and makes the installment payments to the finance company. The general rule about assignment of contractual rights, as discussed in Chapter 11, is that an assignee "takes subject to the

---

[61] See, for example, Residential Tenancy Act, S.B.C. 2002, c. 78, s. 26(3)(a).

[62] Consumer Protection Act, 2002, S.O. 2002, c. C30, Sch. A, ss. 7,8; Fair Trading Act, R.S.A. 2000, c. F-2, s. 16; Consumer Protection Act, R.S.Q., c. P-40.1, s. 11; *Seidel V. TELUS Communications Inc.* 2011 SCC 15, para 2.

[63] See, for example, Business Practices and Consumer Protection Act, S.B.C. 2004, c. 2, Part V; Consumer Protection Act, S.O. 2002, c. C.30, Part VII.

[64] R.S.C. 1985, c. I-15, s. 4.

equities" and acquires no more enforceable claim than the assignor had. There is little doubt that a vendor can more readily find an assignee to buy its installment receivables if the assignee acquires rights against the buyer that are not subject to any complaints the buyer (consumer) may have about the goods.

Therefore, vendors and finance companies looked for a way around the general rule about assignments by using a negotiable instrument: a buyer was required to sign a promissory note for the balance of the purchase price plus finance charges, and this note, along with the conditional sale contract, was endorsed by the vendor to the finance company. As a result, the finance company became a holder in due course of the note, theoretically immuned to any "personal defences" the buyer might have against the vendor. Until the matter was corrected by legislation, a consumer might be liable to a finance company with no opportunity to refuse to pay for the goods if they proved defective or if the dealer refused to perform its warranties. An amendment to the Bills of Exchange Act made finance companies subject to consumers' defences against sellers.[65]

Another way around the rule was to use the contract of sale itself to waive the consumer's rights by a rather special kind of exempting clause: the consumer was asked to sign a standard form contract of sale containing a clause (sometimes referred to as a "cut-out clause") agreeing that any assignee of the contract (for example, a finance company), when seeking to enforce the debt, would not be subject to the defences that the debtor (consumer) might have against the assignor (dealer). As noted in Chapters 11 and 28, most consumer protection acts now state that an assignee of a consumer credit contract shall have no greater rights than the assignor and is subject to the same obligations.[66]

The purpose of these statutes is to make the costs of obtaining credit clearer to the prospective debtor, who is then able to compare offers of credit and to shop around for the lowest effective rate of interest.

Some provincial consumer legislation imposes higher standards of financial disclosure on particular industries. Under the Ontario Consumer Protection Act, time share, personal development, leasing, and motor vehicle repair contracts are required to contain special terms including detailed financial disclosure and cost-of-borrowing calculations. Several provinces regulate the payday lending industry, imposing relatively high caps on lending rates, under an exception to the general Criminal Code limit.[67]

CHECKLIST

Relevant Legislation

Business sales tactics targeting consumers
- Provincial consumer protection statutes
- Competition Act

Terms added to a consumer contract
- Provincial consumer protection statutes
- Sale of Goods Act(s)
- Interest Act
- Bills of Exchange Act

---

[65] R.S.C. 1985, c. B-4, s. 191.

[66] See, for example, Business Practices and Consumer Protection Act, S.B.C. 2004, c. 2, ss. 15–16; Consumer Protection Act, R.S.N.S. 1989, c. 92, s. 25; S.O. 2002, c. C.30, Sch. A, s. 83.

[67] See e.g. Payday Loans Act, 2008, S.O. 2008, c. 9; O. Reg. 98/09; B.C. Reg. 57/2009; Alta. Reg. 157/2009.

Strategies to Manage the Legal Risks

The Sale of Goods Act is a statute designed to address the legal risks associated with the sale of goods. However, for sellers, it adds risk to a contract silent on such things as quality and ownership. The key to managing these risks lies in the ability to contractually vary, limit, or exclude some of the implied protections. This is most important for business-to-business transactions, as most provincial consumer protection legislation prohibits any variation or limitation in consumer transactions. Where possible, vendors should design standard form contracts to

- limit, vary, or exclude the implied protections of the Sale of Goods Act;
- use clear and unambiguous language when excluding liability;
- cover all forms of protection by referring to all warranties, conditions, or terms, whether implied by statute or common law;
- specify their own return policy and warranty for repair or replacement of goods;
- state when title passes and which party has the obligation to insure the goods in the interim and during transit;
- confirm the purchaser's inspection and acceptance of the goods while excluding reliance on any representations, skill, or expertise of the vendor; and
- adopt language for installment payments (deposit or down payment) that reflects the desired result.

Businesses must respect the legislative limitations imposed on the use of consumer standard form contracts. Therefore, in the consumer context, standard form contracts should include all required detail and notices together with a severance clause to save the contract if offending clauses are struck down. Sales strategies should be cross referenced against required disclosure and cooling-off provisions. Telemarketers must be trained to comply with restrictions on their practices. Finally, businesses should be aware of industry-specific requirements and consider variation across the provinces in which they do business.

QUESTIONS FOR REVIEW

1. What was the principal purpose of the original Sale of Goods Act?
2. Distinguish between ownership and possession.
3. How are "goods" defined in the Sale of Goods Act? What types of personal property are not within the definition?
4. Is a contract for the installation of a central heating system a contract for the sale of goods?
5. What is the distinction between a sale and an agreement to sell?
6. What is meant by a "consignment"?
7. When does the caveat emptor principle apply to the sale of goods?
8. Distinguish between the implied term as to fitness and the implied term of merchantable quality.
9. What is the significance of an article being sold under its trade name?
10. What terms are implied in the case of a sale by sample?
11. What does it mean to say that the courts interpret the time set for payment as a warranty unless the parties have expressed otherwise?

12. What determines who bears the risk of loss when goods that are the subject matter of a contract of sale are destroyed?

13. When does title pass in the case of specific goods that are in a deliverable state?

14. In what circumstances can a person who is not the owner of goods pass a good title to them?

15. What is the distinction between unascertained goods and future goods?

16. What is a "bill of lading"?

17. When does an unpaid seller have a lien on the goods sold? When is there a right of repossession?

18. Who is a consumer?

19. What is the purpose of a cooling-off period?

20. How does the Competition Act attempt to prevent fraudulent telemarketing?

CASES AND PROBLEMS

1. Continuing Scenario

   Ashley wants to put fresh flowers on the tables in her restaurant. She wants the flowers to last longer than seven days without losing petals or wilting and she wants them to match her décor—white, blue, and yellow. Finally they must have a very mild scent so as not to interfere with the pleasant food smells. She goes online and locates a flower shop within a few blocks of her restaurant. She goes to the shop and speaks to Gladys, who suggests the Generosia blue hydrangea—it is the only blue flower they carry although they have many yellow ones. Gladys shows her a sample she has in the cooler—the flower is a round ball approximately the size of a baseball—Ashley loves it. Gladys describes the blue hydrangea as long lasting, low fragrance, and blue. In particular, the ones grown by Generosia are very intense blue and large. Ashley places an order for 50 Generosia blue hydrangeas to be delivered every Friday morning so they will be fresh for the weekend diners.

   The first week, the order arrives on time; the flowers are big and blue but by Tuesday they are drooping and beginning to look wilted. The next week, the flowers are not quite as big and they also wilt by Tuesday. Ashley calls Gladys and is told to call Generosia, the grower. When Ashley speaks to the customer service agent from Generosia, she is told that hydrangeas are not long lasting flowers—they need lots of water and will wilt within five days. He also says the Generosia blue are especially likely to droop because of the weight of the extra big flower.

   Ashley wants Gladys's flower shop to refund all her money plus some compensation for the inconvenience of having to replace the flowers. What are her rights? Would your answer be different if these flowers were ordered for Ashley's home?

2. On a Friday afternoon, Harris went into a store owned by Kabul Karpets Inc. and saw a large Uzbek carpet, which she immediately decided would be perfect on the wall of her sitting room. She promptly bought the carpet for $2000, paying by credit card.

   Because of the large size of the carpet—and the smallness of her car—she asked the store to deliver it and was told that they would do so on the following Monday. The sales assistant attached a "sold" notice to the carpet with a small piece of adhesive tape, leaving the carpet prominently displayed on the wall of the store.

   The following Monday morning, Lewis saw the carpet through the store window and at once realized it was just what he was looking for to hang on his study wall. He entered the store, paid $2000 by credit card, and had the carpet loaded into his large van. The shop assistant who served Lewis was not the same one who had been on duty on the Friday, and the "sold" notice had somehow become detached from the carpet and presumably had been swept up by the cleaners. On the Tuesday, Harris phoned the store to inquire why her carpet had not been delivered.

   Who owns the carpet? Is there a remedy if the carpet is not perfect for the study wall?

3. Dorothy receives a phone call during the dinner hour from a company selling magazine subscriptions; at first, she tries to get off the phone and tells the caller she is not interested. However, she recalls that her son's birthday is coming up so she asks the caller if they have *Golf Magazine*; they do. The caller tells her that she will get a better price if she orders two magazine subscriptions rather than just one; he tells her that it is no problem to have the magazines sent to different addresses. Therefore, she orders *Golf Magazine* to be delivered to her son's home and *Better Homes & Gardens* for herself. The caller tells her she is getting 24 months at 50% off of the in-store price. She agrees to pay by monthly installments and gives her credit card information. The first month, *Golf Magazine* is delivered to her home and not her son's; when she looks at the back of the magazine in search of a phone number to call, she sees the in-store price and realizes it is the same as the price she is paying.

Discuss Dorothy's remedies. Does it make a difference if she never received a full copy of the magazine subscription contract?

4. Gabrieli bought a truck from a dealer, Transit Inc. Gabrieli signed a "purchase order" on May 12, at which time Transit ordered the truck from the manufacturer. It was agreed that the sale was subject to Gabrieli's being able to arrange suitable financing.

Three weeks later, Gabrieli informed Transit that she had been able to obtain a loan from her bank and was in a position to give Transit a bank draft for the full price. Transit confirmed that the arrangement was satisfactory. On August 2, the truck was delivered to Transit from the manufacturer. Transit called Gabrieli, telling her, "Your truck is here and ready for you to collect." Gabrieli went straight to the Transit premises, handed over the bank draft, and received the keys, papers, and the truck. At that time, Transit's sales manager also handed her a number of other documents, including one that the manager described as "your warranty," which he asked Gabrieli to sign. Gabrieli did so. The document gave a limited one-year warranty for defects but excluded implied warranties and excluded liability for consequential damages.

The truck proved to be defective and soon developed a number of faults. Gabrieli took the truck back to Transit on numerous occasions for various repairs, but these were mostly unsuccessful. Finally, after more than two years of unsatisfactory operation, Gabrieli returned the truck to Transit and demanded her money back.

Transit denied liability, pointing to the one-year warranty that excluded the statutory implied warranties.

Is Gabrieli entitled to any remedy? Why or why not?

5. Benner's Sawmill Inc. entered into a contract with Chen to purchase a quantity of timber growing on land leased by Chen. A price of $150 per cubic metre was agreed, and the quantity set at approximately 600 cubic metres. Chen was to cut and trim the timber ready for collection by Benner's, who paid an initial deposit of $15 000. Benner's asked its insurance company about insuring the timber and was told that the timber could not be insured until it had been felled, trimmed, and "timbermarked" (that is, marked with a provincially registered mark applied by swinging a timber hammer and striking the wood surface at both ends).

Some weeks later, Chen phoned Benner's and informed them that the timber had been cut, trimmed, and stacked. The total price was $94 000 (the quantity being a little more than 600 cubic metres). When asked if the timber had been timbermarked, Chen replied that it had not. He was going away on a short vacation but would see to it as soon as he returned. In accordance with the contract, Benner's sent Chen a cheque for the full price, less the deposit already paid.

Before Chen returned from vacation, his sheds were destroyed by fire. When Benner's demanded the timber or their money back, Chen replied: "Sorry, but it was your timber that burned."

Advise Benner's.

6. The Granite County School Board placed an order with Borough Furniture Ltd, a furniture manufacturer, for 2500 folding chairs. Before placing the order, an officer of the board had examined a number of chairs produced by Borough (as well as chairs of other manufacturers). Eventually, they settled upon one particular model, but required a number of modifications to be made. Borough produced a prototype of the chair, which was examined by the officer, who expressed satisfaction.

Borough delivered a first batch of 500 chairs and continued with the manufacture of the remaining 2000. A few days after the first delivery, it was found that the chairs tipped rather easily and were unsuitable for use in classrooms. The board refused to take delivery of any more chairs and demanded that Borough take back the 500 that they had delivered. Borough claimed that they had made the chairs according to the board's specifications and demanded payment for the full 2500.

Which party has the better claim?

7. In December, Winnipeg Seafoods Ltd. orally agreed to purchase from Lakehead Fish Wholesale Co. 1000 five-kilogram boxes of frozen Lake Superior herring at $1.40 per kilogram. The fish were being stored in the cold storage warehouse of a third party, the Bailey Co. of Thunder Bay. The Bailey Co. operated as a storage company that processed and stored fresh fish. At the time, it held some 1500 boxes of this type of fish in storage.

Because Winnipeg Seafoods was short of storage space, it did not want the fish shipped to it but preferred to have it remain in the warehouse at Thunder Bay. Lakehead Fish then arranged with Bailey to transfer the storage account to the name of Winnipeg Seafoods in respect of the 1000 boxes, and Lakehead Fish sent an invoice for $7000 to Winnipeg Seafoods. The invoice indicated that the merchandise was in storage at Bailey's in Thunder Bay. Immediately afterward, Bailey sent its invoice to Winnipeg Seafoods for one month's storage charges, payable in advance. Winnipeg Seafoods did not pay either of these accounts. The price of frozen herring started to fall in the middle of January. The fish were held in storage until the end of January and then processed to prevent spoilage. On February 2, Winnipeg Seafoods returned the invoice of Lakehead Fish with an accompanying letter to the effect that it had decided to "cancel the order." Lakehead Fish then sued Winnipeg Seafoods Ltd. for the price of the fish, $7000, or in the alternative, for damages for non-acceptance.

Should it succeed?

8. Ebrahim bought a used car from Cival Autos Inc. for $8000. The car was described by Cival as follows: "one careful owner only, low mileage, excellent condition." In fact, Cival's manager was aware that the car had had three previous owners, the most recent of whom had been convicted of dangerous driving following a collision in which the car had sustained serious damage. He also knew that the odometer had been altered and that the car was generally in very poor condition.

Very soon after Ebrahim took delivery, the car started to develop problems. At first he took the car back to Cival, where he was told that the problems were minor and that they had "fixed" them. After three such visits to Cival, Ebrahim took the car to an independent garage, and the true facts about the car became known.

Apart from the normal remedies in contract and tort, is there any other legal action that Ebrahim can take against Cival?

Chapter 15

Bailment and Leasing

Ownership and possession of goods do not always go together. Bailment and leasing are two common types of contract in which ownership and possession are separated. Leasing of personal property is a form of bailment, although from a business point of view, leasing has a very different function from other forms of bailment. A lease of personal property—a chattel lease—is frequently regarded as a form of financing or an alternative to sale. By contrast, most other types of bailment involve parting with possession of an item only temporarily—for storage, repair, or transportation. Legally, however, they share the same essential features.

In this chapter we examine such questions as:

- What is the legal nature of bailment?
- What are the principal types of bailment contract?
- What are the rights and duties of the parties to a contract of bailment?
- What are the principal types of chattel lease?
- Why are leasing contracts used, and why have they become so important?
- What are the terms that are commonly found in leasing contracts?
- What are the respective rights of the lessor and the lessee?

BAILMENT

Definition

A **bailment** is a transfer of possession of personal property without a transfer of ownership; the receiving party agrees to return the property at a later time. The transferor of the property, usually its owner, is called the **bailor**, and the party that receives custody of it, the **bailee**. During a bailment, the bailee must take care of the bailor's goods

Nature of Bailment

The nature of bailment can be illustrated by comparing it to other common transactions or relationships—in particular, sale, trust, debt, and licence:

- sale: A sale transfers ownership, with or without a change in possession. By contrast, a bailment does not alter ownership but requires a change in possession.

- trust: The creation of a trust gives legal ownership to the trustee, and the beneficiary acquires an equitable interest in the subject of the trust. Possession is not relevant; the property could be in the possession of the trustee, the beneficiary, or the creator of the trust.

- debt: A deposit of money in a bank or trust company creates a creditor–debtor rather than a bailor–bailee relationship. It is not bailment because only property of equal value is returned, not the exact asset given. By contrast, a deposit of specific items of personal property for safekeeping with a bank or trust company does create a bailment.[1]

- licence: A bailment requires a transfer of possession and a voluntary acceptance of the common law duty of safekeeping. A licence amounts to no more than a grant of permission to make use of the licensor's land on the understanding that possession of any chattel is not transferred, and responsibility for guarding the chattel is not accepted.[2] For example, the owner of a parking lot normally does not accept responsibility for storage of the vehicle and grants only a licence to use the spot.[3] Alternatively, when a vehicle is left at a garage for servicing, the garage owner does assume responsibility for its safekeeping.[4]

Most bailments are contractual and involve payment, but a bailment can also occur without a contract between a bailor and bailee. The essential elements of bailment are delivery of possession without the intention to transfer title and with the intention that the property will be returned to the bailor. These elements may exist without a contract, as when the owner of a car lends it gratuitously to a friend. A bailment may also be involuntary; if a customer leaves a coat behind in a restaurant, the restaurateur becomes a bailee of the coat and cannot refuse to return it at the customer's request.

Bailments may benefit the bailor or the bailee, or both parties. By their nature, contractual bailments are intended to be of benefit to both parties: One party obtains the service desired and the other receives payment. A non-contractual or **gratuitous bailment** may be for the benefit of either party. In the examples given above, the bailment of the coat benefits the bailor, whereas the loan of a car benefits the bailee.

For more information on this topic, see the Companion Website.

bailment possession of personal property without ownership

bailor owner or transferor of the goods

bailee party accepting possession of goods from a bailor

gratuitous bailment a bailment where one party provides no consideration, or where there is no intention to create a contractual relationship

---

[1] *Royal Bank of Canada v. Reynolds* (1976), 66 D.L.R. (3d) 88; *Cuvelier v. Bank of Montreal* (2002), 212 N.S.R. (2d) 17.

[2] *Heffron v. Imperial Parking Co. et al.* (1974), 3 O.R. (2d) 722 at 727.

[3] *Bata v. City Parking Canada Ltd.* (1973), 2 O.R. (2d) 446. *Heffron v. Imperial Parking Co. et al.*, *supra*, n. 2.

[4] *Hertz Canada Ltd. v. Suburban Motors Ltd.*, [2000] B.C.J. No. 830.

Sub-Bailment

sub-bailee a person who receives a bailment of property from a bailee

In a sub-bailment, after receiving the property from the bailor, the bailee transfers possession to someone else, a **sub-bailee**.

CASE 15.1

After Mason's mother died he contracted with Thompson Funeral Home to have her body cremated and her ashes stored in an urn. The urn was to be held until after Mason's father died, when Mason would then make a decision about what was to be done. When Mason's father died four years later, Thompson cremated the remains and placed them in another urn. Thompson sought Mason's instructions about what to do with the two urns, but Mason was still not sure where he wanted to bury them. Mason instructed Thompson to send the urns to Westside Cemetery for burial in common ground. Common ground involves one storage vault without

marker, which allows easy retrieval, so Mason would be able to move them later. Thompson sent the urns to Westside and instructed them to place them in common ground. When Mason requested retrieval of the urns from Westside 10 years later, the urns could not be found. Mason sued Thompson and Westside in bailment. The court held that the urns and ashes were Mason's property. A bailment contract was formed with Thompson, and Mason had authorized a sub-bailment to Westside. Both the bailee and sub-bailee owed Mason a duty to take care of the urns as instructed. The urns were lost by Westside and only Westside was held liable.[5]

To avoid liability when creating a bailment relationship between the bailor and the sub-bailee, the bailee must obtain permission or consent from the bailor for the sub-bailment, and the sub-bailee must be aware of the bailor's interest. For usual or expected sub-bailments, permission may be implied. Obvious examples of sub-bailment include postal or courier services used to transport the bailed goods. For more information on this topic, see the Companion Website.

CASE 15.2

Punch took her diamond ring, worth $11 000, to Savoy Jewellers in Sault Ste. Marie for repair. Savoy was unable to make the repair, so they sent it to Walker Jewellers in Toronto. Savoy sent the ring by registered mail and stated the value for insurance purposes as $100. Apparently, this was normal trade practice.

After Walker repaired the ring, it returned the ring to Savoy using a delivery service operated by Canadian National (CN).

Again, the value was declared as $100. The contract between Walker and CN limited CN's liability for loss or damage to the declared value of $100. The ring was never delivered to Savoy.

Punch sued Savoy, Walker, and CN. The court found that Savoy was a bailee, and both Walker and CN were sub-bailees. All three owed a duty of care directly to Punch, and the burden on each of them was to show it was not responsible for the loss or for inadequately insuring the ring.[6]

In *Punch v. Savoy Jewellers* (Case 15.2) the court held that the clause in the contract between CN and Walker, which limited CN's liability, could not be relied on by CN against either Savoy or Punch, since they were not parties to the contract and lacked privity. All three parties were found liable. Is this fair?[7] Suppose, for example, that Punch agreed that Savoy's liability should be limited to $100 when it sent the ring by registered mail; why should CN and Walker not be entitled to rely on a similar limitation in their contracts? This question was considered in *The Pioneer Container* (Case 15.3 below).

---

[5] *Mason v. Westside Cemeteries Ltd.*, 1996 CanLII 9113, 135 D.L.R. (4th) 361 (Ont. S.C.).

[6] *Punch v. Savoy Jewellers Ltd.* (1986), 26 D.L.R. (4th) 546.

[7] Contrast *London Drugs Ltd. v. Kuehne and Nagel International Ltd.* (1992), 97 D.L.R. (4th) 261.

CASE 15.3

The plaintiffs hired Hanjin Container Lines to ship goods from the United States to Hong Kong. The contract with Hanjin contained a term that "the carrier shall be entitled to sub-contract *on any terms* the whole or any part of the handling of the goods" (italics added). Hanjin contracted with Pioneer Container to ship the goods on the last leg of their journey, from Taiwan to Hong Kong. The goods were lost in a collision off the coast of Taiwan. The bill of lading contract between Hanjin and Pioneer contained a term that the contract should be governed by Chinese law, and any dispute should be determined in Taiwan.

The plaintiffs sued the defendants in Hong Kong. The defendants objected that, under the terms of the bill of lading, they could be sued only in Taiwan. The court ruled that, although there was no contract between the plaintiffs and the defendants, the plaintiffs had authorized the sub-bailment and effectively consented to the terms of the sub-bailment.[8]

RIGHTS AND DUTIES OF A BAILEE

Liability under Contract and Tort

Sometimes bailed goods are lost, damaged, or destroyed while in the possession of a bailee. Who is liable for the loss suffered? When the bailment is the result of a contract, its terms, either express or implied by trade custom, establish the duties, level of care and liabilities of the bailee for the goods in its possession. All bailees are, however, under a duty to take care of property bailed to them. The duty of care required by the law of torts applies to circumstances not covered expressly or impliedly by the bailment contract, and applies also to gratuitous bailments involving no contract at all. The required standard of care varies according to the type of bailment.

Sometimes, a contract of bailment includes a term that the bailee is not liable for damage to the goods while in her custody, even when the damage is caused by negligence in the course of performing the contract. The courts construe this type of exemption clause very strictly against the bailee. If the goods are damaged for any reason not related to the actual performance contemplated by the contract, the bailee is not protected by the exemption clause.[9]

CASE 15.4

An army officer took his uniform to the dry cleaners to be cleaned. The cleaners gave him a receipt in which they disclaimed all liability for damage arising in the course of "necessary handling." The uniform was never returned, and when the officer sued for its value, the cleaners pleaded the exemption clause. It was established that the loss arose when the cleaning firm sent the uniform to someone else for cleaning. The court found that the wording of the contract required personal performance by the bailee. The damage had not taken place during "necessary handling." The exemption clause did not apply, and the cleaners were held liable for the loss.[10]

Although the law of bailment is derived from principles of both tort and contract law, bailment is a distinct relationship governed by its own rules. When goods are damaged or lost while in the possession of a bailee, it is often difficult for the bailor to ascertain exactly how the harm occurred. Since a bailee is better able to establish the facts, the law of bailment places the burden of showing that she was not negligent on the bailee. She must offer some reasonable alternative explanation for the loss and show she met the standard of care. This burden of proof makes it easier for a bailor to sue under the rules of bailment than under the ordinary rules of tort.

---

[8] *The Pioneer Container*, [1994] 2 A.C. 324 (P.C.).

[9] *Solway v. Davis Moving & Storage Inc.* (2002), 62 O.R. (3d) 522, leave dismissed [2003] S.C.C.A. No. 57.

[10] *Davies v. Collins*, [1945] 1 All E.R. 247.

The Standard of Care

The required level or standard of care varies according to the type of bailment. The standard is lowest when the bailment is both gratuitous and for the benefit of the bailor, as when A permits B to leave her car in A's garage without charge. After all, the bailee is doing the bailor a favour; but even a gratuitous bailee is liable for gross negligence.

The standard of care is highest on a bailee when the bailment is gratuitous and for the benefit of the bailee, as when one borrows a friend's car for personal use. The bailor receives no valuable consideration, so it is fair that, in such circumstances, the bailee should compensate the bailor when damage to the goods results from even slight carelessness on the bailee's part. In **bailments for value**, the standard of care falls between that of gratuitous bailments for the benefit of the bailee and those for the benefit of the bailor. (A bailee who allows a friend to leave her car in the bailee's garage is not under as high a duty of care as would a warehousing firm being paid to store the car.) Generally, a bailee for value is expected to take the same care of goods as a prudent and diligent person should take of goods belonging to those with whom she transacts business—a standard of care that is at least as high and probably higher than she might choose to apply to her own goods.

bailments for value contractual bailment

CASE 15.5

A car rental firm left one of its cars at a garage for routine servicing. The car was locked and left overnight in an unsecured parking lot adjacent to the garage. During the night, a thief broke into the locked office where the car keys were kept (with tags on them in order to identify the car), stole the key to the rental car, and drove it away.

The rental firm claimed damages for the loss of the car. The court held that there had been no breach on the part of the garage of its duty of care. It had taken reasonable precautions to prevent loss. The loss was a result of the efforts of a "truly determined thief."[11]

CASE 15.6

Duckworth owned a classic sports car that was damaged in an accident. He took the car to Superior Autobody to have repairs done, and left a deposit of $500. The shop did not have an alarm system and did not have padlocks on the latches of the overhead doors. Keys were left in the ignition to allow easy removal. Thieves broke in and stole the car, which was never recovered. The court held that the repairers were bailees for value and were liable for the loss since they had failed to take appropriate care of the car while it was in their charge.[12]

The standard also varies according to the type of goods bailed and the extent of the promise to look after the goods. In interpreting both express and implied promises of the bailee, the courts consider all the circumstances. If the property is very valuable and easily damaged, the standard of care required will be higher: One must take greater care with expensive jewellery than with a bicycle stored in one's shed. In the words of one judge, "The substantial question must always be, whether that care has been exhibited which the special circumstances reasonably demand."[13]

Some special classes of bailee are subject to higher standards of care because they deal with the public generally. These include common carriers and hoteliers or innkeepers, discussed later in this chapter.

---

[11] *Hertz Canada Ltd. v. Suburban Motors Ltd., supra*, n. 4.

[12] *Duckworth v. Armstrong* (1996), 29 C.C.L.T. (2d) 239.

[13] *Fitzgerald v. Grand Trunk Railway* (1880), 4 O.A.R. 601, per Moss, C.J.A., at 624. For a recent example, see *Solway v. Davis Moving & Storage Inc., supra*, n. 9.

Rights and Remedies

Damages and Quantum Meruit
In a contractual bailment, the bailee has the usual contractual remedies for breach by the bailor. Because of the character of bailment, the main concern of a bailee is collecting compensation for services rendered.

When a bailee has performed her part of a contract, as when a warehouse returns goods that have been stored with it, the usual remedy is an action for the contract price. Occasionally a bailee may not be able to complete performance, as when a carrier has contracted to transport goods in several installments but the bailor delivers only part of the goods for shipment. The carrier may then sue quantum meruit for the value of the services it has performed and for damages compensating it for its loss of profits.

Lien

An important additional remedy available to a bailee is a lien on the bailed goods in its possession. This gives the bailee a right to retain possession of the goods until the bailor pays what is due for the services. The bailor cannot normally repossess the goods until he has paid the sum due. Generally, a right of lien arises only when the services have been performed and payment is already due.

ILLUSTRATION 15.1

Pliable Plastics Ltd. has very little storage space for its manufactured products. It enters into an arrangement with Stately Storage Limited whereby Pliable Plastics delivers its products for storage on a daily charge basis, and when the products are sold, picks them up again for delivery to the buyer. Storage charges are billed and become payable every three months.

Stately Storage has no lien upon the goods stored with it until the end of the three-month period and until it has billed Pliable Plastics. If, after two-and-one-half months have passed, Pliable Plastics sells a portion of the stored goods, Stately Storage must surrender the goods on demand to Pliable Plastics or to a buyer who presents proper documents. When three months have expired and Stately Storage bills Pliable Plastics, Stately Storage has a lien for all the accrued storage charges upon the goods remaining in the warehouse at that time.

As noted in Chapter 14, the lien of an unpaid seller is a possessory remedy; an unpaid bailee loses her lien on the bailed goods as soon as the bailor obtains possession of them without deceit or fraud.

A right of lien under common law rules is available to any bailees who perform services such as repairs or improvements to goods bailed with them, to innkeepers, to common carriers (who are under a duty to accept goods from anyone so long as they have space for them), and also to professional people like lawyers and bankers (who have a common law right of lien over documents in their possession when they have performed services related to the documents). Various statutes give liens in other types of bailment and, even though they may have a common law or statutory right of lien, many businesses acting as bailees make the lien right a term in their contracts with customers. For more information on this topic, see the Companion Website.

The Right of Sale

The right of lien is valuable to a bailee because the bailor usually needs to recover his goods, and to do so he must first pay off overdue charges. If, however, the bailor is unable to pay off the charges—say, he becomes insolvent—the bailee is left with goods she cannot use because she has no title to them, and yet she has the burden of storing them. The bailment contract may contain a right of sale, and various statutes give bailees who have a lien upon goods stored with them an additional right to sell the goods.

The exact provisions of the statutes vary in detail, but generally they require (1) that a certain time elapse after payment falls due; (2) that advance notice be given to the bailor of the bailee's intention to sell; (3) that the sale be advertised; and (4) that it be held by public auction. Until the time of sale, the owner of the goods (or other person entitled to possession) is usually entitled to recover them on payment in full of the bailee's charges.[14] The proceeds of the sale are used, first, to reimburse the bailee for her costs of holding the sale and, second, to pay the overdue charges for her services. Any surplus belongs to the bailor.

SPECIAL TYPES OF BAILMENT

There are various types of bailment, and both the common law and the statutory rules vary to some extent according to the type of bailment.

Storage and Safekeeping

A warehousing firm that accepts goods for storage and a bank that rents a safety deposit box are bailees for storage or safekeeping and are under a duty to take care of the goods stored with them.

The terms of a contract may reduce liability; for example, if the bailor specifically directs where the goods are to be placed, the liability of the warehouse keeper will be restricted to complying with those instructions.

fungible goods goods that may be replaced with different but identical goods

A warehouse firm is not customarily obliged to insure goods stored with it against loss by fire unless it has expressly contracted to do so.[15] Ordinarily, a bailee must return to the bailor the exact goods stored. When, however, the goods stored are **fungible goods** (that is, replaceable with identical goods also in storage), the bailee's liability is discharged when she returns to the bailor goods of the exact description in the warehouse receipt. For example, when a quantity of grain of a specific grade is stored in a grain elevator in bins containing other grain of the same grade, the elevator company is bound to deliver not the exact grain that was bailed with it, but an equivalent quantity of the same grade.

At common law, a warehousing firm did not obtain a right of lien on goods stored with it unless it had specifically bargained for the lien. Now all common law provinces have legislation giving a warehouse a right of lien on goods stored with it for the amount of its charges.

The statutes contain words such as "every warehouser has a lien on goods deposited with the warehouser for storage whether deposited by the owner of the goods, or by the owner's authority or by any person entrusted with the possession of the goods by the owner or by the owner's authority."[16] The statutes further provide that "a warehouser may sell by public auction, in the manner provided in this section, any goods on which the warehouser has a lien for charges which have become due."[17] The statutes set out the details of the notice that must be given and the way in which the sale is to be advertised and held. The aim is to give adequate protection to the bailor or owner while giving the bailee a reasonably prompt method of obtaining payment.

---

[14] For example, Warehouse Lien Act, R.S.B.C. 1996, c. 480, s. 7; Repair and Storage Liens Act, R.S.O. 1990, c. R-25, s. 22.

[15] See *Neff v. St. Catharines Marina Ltd.* (1998), 155 D.L.R. (4th) 647. But the warehouse firms must exercise due care to prevent fire: *Hogarth v. Archibald Moving & Storage Ltd.* (1991), 57 B.C.L.R. (2d) 319.

[16] Warehouse Lien Act, R.S.B.C. 1996, c. 480, s. 2; Warehousemen's Lien Act, R.S.N.S. 1989, c. 499, s. 3. In Ontario, warehousing is covered in the Repair and Storage Liens Act, R.S.O. 1990, c. R-25. Section 4(1) gives a similar lien to a "storer" of goods.

[17] R.S.B.C. 1996, c. 480, s. 4; R.S.N.S. 1989, c. 499, s. 5. In Ontario, a storer has a similar right: Repair and Storage Liens Act, R.S.O. 1990, c. R-25, s. 4(7)

Repairs and Work on a Chattel

Bailment is often a normal consequence of contracts made for the maintenance of, or repairs to, various articles, as when a truck is delivered to a garage for repair, or when an electronics firm receives business machines for servicing. A repairer who works on these articles on her own premises is a bailee for value. In accepting the work, the repairer undertakes to do it in a competent manner, employing the skill she professes to have and to have the work done by the promised time. The bailee is also under a duty to take care of the article while it is in her possession, just as a warehousing company.[18] Failure to do so is a breach of contract on the bailee's part, and a breach may entitle the bailor to deny payment for work already done or to sue for damages. The bailor is also entitled to the return of the chattel.

As noted earlier, the common law gives a repairer a lien on the goods for the value of the work done. The common law right does not extend to the right to sell the goods, but some of the provinces give an additional statutory right to the repairer to sell the goods once the repair charges are three months overdue.[19]

Transportation

The law identifies three types of carriers.

1. A gratuitous carrier is anyone who agrees to move goods from one place to another without reward.
2. A private carrier is a business that undertakes on occasion to carry goods for reward, but reserves the right to select its customers and restrict the type of goods it is willing to carry.
3. A **common carrier** is a business that holds itself out to the public as a transporter of goods (or passengers) for reward.

common carrier a business that holds itself out to the public as a transporter of goods for reward

The public nature of a common carrier is that it does not discriminate among those who request its services, nor does it reserve the right to refuse an offer of goods for shipment when it has the means of shipping them. A common carrier may restrict its services to a certain area and to certain goods that are suitable for carriage by its equipment. Most railway and steamship companies are common carriers, as are some trucking companies and even gas and oil pipeline companies. Airlines may repudiate the status of a common carrier by reserving the right to refuse goods. The Canada Transportation Act regulates air and rail carriers.[20] A proprietor of an amusement ride is not a common carrier because the ride's purpose is not to transport but rather to thrill.[21] Alternatively, the operator of an escalator may be a common carrier when it moves passengers between destinations.[22]

A carrier's liability for damage to goods in the course of transit depends upon the type of carrier. All carriers are bailees and always have some responsibility for the goods under their control. Even a gratuitous bailee must exercise at least the diligence and care to be expected of a reasonable person in handling his or her own property.

The duty of care required of a private carrier is greater. It owes a degree of care commensurate with the skill reasonably expected of a competent firm in its line of business. The liability of a common carrier is still greater, although it may take advantage of certain recognized defences.

---

[18] *Letourneau v. Otto Mobiles Edmonton (1984) Ltd.*, [2002] A.J. No. 825.

[19] See e.g. Repairers' Lien Act, R.S.B.C. 1996, c. 404, s. 2; Repair and Storage Liens Act, R.S.O. 1990, c. R-25, s. 3(3) (60 days overdue).

[20] S.C. 1996, c. 10.

[21] *Mallais v. D.A. Campbell Amusements Ltd.* (2007), 84 O.R. (3d) 687 (C.A.).

[22] *Kauffman v. Toronto Transit Commission*, [1960] S.C.R. 251.

A common carrier undertakes to indemnify the shipper (the bailor) against loss whether the loss occurs through the carrier's fault or not. The carrier is, therefore, an insurer as well as a bailee.[23] This rule makes sense: Its practical effect is to relieve the shipper of the burden of producing evidence that it was the common carrier's lack of care that caused the loss or damage. In most circumstances, it would be impossible for the carrier to gather this evidence. The shipper need only prove (1) that the carrier received the goods in good condition, and (2) that the carrier delivered them in bad condition or failed to deliver them at all. The burden is then on the carrier to establish that the cause of the loss was within one of the recognized defences available to common carriers. These defences are

- an act of God;
- inherent vice in the goods; and
- default by the shipper.

It is not enough for a common carrier to show that it was not negligent—it has only those three defences. An "act of God," refers to a natural catastrophe; fire is not an act of God unless caused by lightning. Even when the cause of the loss is a natural catastrophe, the carrier may still be liable if it has negligently contributed to the loss, for example, by failing to install a sprinkler system. A common carrier may also avoid liability if it can show that the goods had an **inherent vice** at the time of shipment; for example, the goods may have been in a combustible condition or may have had latent defects that made them more susceptible to breakage than is typical of goods of their category.

inherent vice a latent defect or dangerous condition of goods

A common carrier can offer a third defence: that the shipper has been guilty of a breach of duty or is in some way at fault. A contract for the transportation of goods includes an implied promise on the part of the shipper that the goods are safe to carry. The shipper's breach of this duty releases the carrier from its part of the bargain, and if the goods cause damage to the carrier's equipment, for instance by exploding, the carrier may successfully sue for damages.

Unless otherwise agreed,[24] a common carrier is liable for the full value of goods lost or destroyed. However, the carrier may, and frequently does, limit the amount of its liability when the shipper does not declare the value of the goods. Where the shipper declares less than the full value of the goods to the carrier, in order to pay a lower freight charge than it would have paid had it declared their true value, the carrier is not released from its duty, but its liability is limited to the declared value. For more information on this topic, see the Companion Website.

INTERNATIONAL ISSUE

International Transport of Goods

The global marketplace has created an explosion in international transportation of goods. Often, multiple carriers move the goods across borders and over roads, rail, and water. Sometimes a "multimodal transport operator" coordinates the movement of the goods from one carrier to the next. Goods may be in sealed containers, unavailable for inspection by any of the carriers.

If the goods arrive damaged, it is very difficult to determine when (or in which carrier's possession) the damage occurred and what jurisdiction's rules or laws should be applied in the circumstances.

The global community has been trying to unify the liability rules for international carriage but has had little success. The 1980 United Nations Convention on International Multimodal Transport of Goods failed to attract support and never came into force. The United Nations Conference on Trade and Development (UNCTAD) produced rules in 1992, but their effectiveness depends on the private sector incorporating the terms into their agreements. Although a review of the 1992 rules was commenced over 10 years ago, adoption of new multimodal rules has not occurred despite the prevailing

>

[23] *Canadian National Railway Co. v. Harris* [1946] S.C.R. 352 at 369-370.

[24] *Supra* n. 20, s. 137; *Mitsubishi Heavy Industries Ltd. v. Canadian National Railway Co.* 2012 BCSC 1415 para 23.

view that existing liability framework does not take into account modern changes in transport patterns, technology and markets. New rules for transportation by sea were adopted by the UN in 2008.

Question to Consider

1. How should liability be assigned when the point of damage cannot be established and multiple carriers are involved?

Sources: Based on United Nations Commission on International Trade Law (UNCITRAL) website, www.uncitral.org; UNCTAD website, www.unctad.org; M. Faghfouri, "The International Regulation of Liability for Multimodal Transport—In Search of Uniformity" (2006) 5(1) *WMU Journal of Maritime Affairs* 95–114; Report by the UNCTAD secretariat for United Nations Conference on Trade and Development Jan. 2003, "Multimodal Transport: The Feasibility of an International Legal Instrument" (available at www.unctad website); The United Nations Convention on International Carriage of Goods Wholly or Partly by Sea, also known as the "Rotterdam Rules," December 2008.

Innkeepers

Under common law, the word **innkeeper** refers to a person or establishment offering lodging to any member of the public. An inn, or a hotel, differs from a boardinghouse, whose owner may pick and choose whom he or she is willing to accommodate, and also from a restaurant, which offers only food to guests. Most provincial statutes, however, have broadened the definition considerably.

All businesses offering accommodation to the public are under a duty to take reasonable care of the belongings of their guests and patrons. Like warehousing firms, they are liable for damage or loss caused by their negligence or the negligence of their employees. Under the common law, however, innkeepers are also liable for the loss or theft of their guests' goods. There is, however, an important difference between goods bailed to a common carrier and goods left in the room of a hotel guest: The bailor of goods to a common carrier gives them over completely to the care of the carrier, whereas the hotel guest shares the responsibility with the hotel, since he or she has control over the goods when occupying the room. Accordingly, a hotel may avoid liability if it can show that the disappearance was due to the carelessness of the guest. A hotel is liable for damage to the goods of its guests—as distinct from its liability for their disappearance through loss or theft—only if the damage was caused by the negligence of the hotel's employees.

The strict liability of an innkeeper at common law has been modified by legislation in most provinces. Usually, the innkeeper is liable only where the goods have been stolen, lost, or damaged through the willful act, default, or neglect of the innkeeper or an employee, or where the goods have been deposited expressly for safe custody with the innkeeper.[25] The Innkeepers Acts of the various provinces usually also give the right to sell the goods of guests by public auction if their bills remain unpaid for a specified period.[26]

innkeeper a person or firm that maintains an establishment offering lodging to any member of the public

Pledge or Pawn

While the two terms "pledge" and "pawn" have the same legal significance, a "pawn" refers only to transactions with a pawnbroker. A **pledge or pawn** is a bailment of personal property as security for repayment of a loan. The borrower is the pledgor and the creditor the pledgee. The subject matter of a pledge may be goods left with a **pawnbroker**, for example, or share certificates left with a bank.

A pledgee is a bailee for value and must exercise such care as is reasonable in the ordinary and proper course of its business. A pledgee obtains a lien on the personal property pledged with it, and the pledgor cannot recover possession of the goods until it repays

pledge or pawn a bailment of personal property as security for repayment of a loan where possession passes to the bailee

pawnbroker a business that loans money on the security of pawned goods

---

[25] See e.g. Hotel Keepers Act, R.S.B.C. 1996, c. 206, s. 3; Tourist Accommodation Act, S.N.S. 1994–5, c. 9, s. 11; Tourism Industry Act, R.S.P.E.I. 1988, c. T-3.3, s. 9. In some provinces, strict liability is retained but only up to a fixed amount: Innkeepers Act, R.S.N.L. 1990, c. I-7, s. 3 ($200); Innkeepers Act, R.S.O. 1990, c. I-7, s. 4 ($40).

[26] R.S.B.C. 1996, c. 206, s. 2; R.S.O. 1990, c. I-7, s. 2; S.N.S. 1994–5, c. 9, s. 10; R.S.P.E.I. 1988, c. T-3.3, s. 8.

the debt for which they are security. In addition, by pledging the goods, the pledgor gives authority to the pledgee to sell the pledged goods upon default and to reimburse itself out of the proceeds of the sale for any costs incurred as a result of the default and for the amount of the unpaid loan. The surplus, if any, belongs to the borrower.[27]

CHECKLIST

Types of Bailment

- gratuitous bailment for the benefit of bailee
- bailment for value (contractual bailment)
- gratuitous bailment for the benefit of the bailor
- sub-bailment

Special types of bailment

- storage and safekeeping
- repairing
- transportation
- innkeeping
- pledge or pawn

LEASING

Leasing is a major growth industry and has become a multibillion-dollar business in both Canada and the United States. At the consumer level, automobile leasing is a common alternative to purchasing on credit. In business, it is common to lease capital equipment, such as heavy machinery and aircraft. Leasing is a bailment for value usually governed by the terms of a detailed standard form contract.

The essence of a **lease** is that the owner of an item of property, referred to as the **lessor**, rents the property to the **lessee**—that is, allows the lessee to have possession and use of the property for a specific period, in return for the payment of rent. Leasing traditionally has been associated with real estate—leasing, or renting, a house, an apartment, or office space for a business has always been an alternative to purchase. We consider leases of land in Chapter 22.

Although renting personal property, or chattels, has always been recognized by the law, such contracts were comparatively rare until recently. A major reason was the risk that an owner ran when he parted with possession of personal property. A person who obtains a lease of land cannot remove it, and if she fails to pay the rent, the owner can repossess it. But chattels are transportable, and a lessee might simply disappear with the leased property and stop paying rent for it. Modern systems of registration of property rights have reduced this risk.

The other factor that led to the great increase in the leasing of personal property was the realization that a lease could be used as a security device. This was first recognized in England more than 100 years ago, in the leading House of Lords decision of *Helby v. Matthews*,[28] which recognized a hiring agreement with an option to purchase at the end of the hiring term as an effective method of selling goods on credit. It opened the way for the

lease (1) an agreement where the owner of property allows another person to have possession and use of the property for a specific period in return for the payment of rent and (2) the agreement between landlord and tenant creating the leasehold interest

lessor the owner of the leased property; when applied to land, known as a landlord being a grantor

lessee the person who takes possession of the leased property; when applied to land the lessee is a tenant, the person to whom an interest in a leasehold estate is granted

---

[27] In some provinces ownership passes to a pawnbroker after a specified period; see e.g., Pawnbrokers Act, R.S.O. 1990, c. P. 6, ss. 20–2.

[28] [1895] A.C. 471.

popular type of transaction known in Britain as **hire-purchase**. In a typical hire-purchase agreement, the lessee/purchaser agrees to lease an item of property for a specified number of years, paying a monthly rental, with an option to purchase it at the end of the term—provided the rent has been paid in full—for a nominal amount, such as $1.

This type of transaction is well known in Canada, principally as a means of marketing automobiles. In reality, it is a method of purchasing on credit, and, as such, is an alternative to the conditional sale and to the chattel mortgage. However, not all chattel leases are intended as security devices.

hire-purchase an agreement to lease an item of property with an option for the lessee to purchase it at the end of the stipulated term

TYPES OF CHATTEL LEASE

Two main types of **chattel** lease exist: operating leases, or "true" leases, where the intention is that possession will revert to the owner at the end of the term; and purchase leases, where it is anticipated that the lessee will eventually become the owner. Purchase leases can be further subdivided into security leases, where the credit is provided by the lessor/vendor, and finance leases, where a third party finances the transaction on credit.

chattel moveable personal property or goods; not land

Operating Leases

In an **operating lease**, since there is no intention to transfer ownership, the term tends to be relatively short—substantially less than the expected working life of the property leased. Examples include a car rental for a weekend or a month and the renting of specialized machinery for the duration of a construction contract or of farm machinery for the harvest season.

operating lease a lease under which there is no intention to transfer ownership

Purchase Leases

Long-term leases in which payments add up to the value of the property are more likely to be purchase leases. When determining the true nature of a lease, courts consider the position of the parties, their intention, and the true effect of the transaction.[29] In practice, however, this test has been difficult to apply and has led to contradictory results. The accounting profession has developed a more objective approach to determine whether to classify a lease as an operating lease or a purchase lease. A lease is treated as a **purchase lease**, or "capital lease,"[30] if one of three conditions exists:

purchase lease a lease whereby ownership is intended to change hands at the end of the lease term

- Title passes automatically to the lessee at the end of the lease or on the exercise of a "bargain purchase option."
- There is a non-cancellable term for at least 75 percent of the economic life of the asset.
- The present value of the minimum lease payments exceeds 90 percent of the market value of the asset at the time the lease commences.[31]

The distinction between an operating lease and a purchase lease is important for accounting purposes. If a lease is a purchase, or "capital," lease, the asset and the accompanying liability must be recorded in the balance sheet of the lessee/purchaser. From a taxation perspective, the distinction determines whether the lease payments are rental payments—and thus deductible by the lessee in determining the profits of the business—or are installments of the purchase price and not deductible (apart from any interest element). It also determines which party is regarded as the true owner and entitled to claim capital

---

[29] *Re Speedrack Ltd.* (1980), 1 P.P.S.A.C. 109. In *Adelaide Capital Corp. v. Integrated Transportation Finance Inc.* (1994), 111 D.L.R. (4th) 493 (Ont. Gen. Div.).

[30] Also known as "lease-to-own."

[31] *CICA Handbook*, section 3065. See also Canada Revenue Agency Interpretation Bulletin IT-233R.

Figure 15.1   Comparing Purchase Lease and Finance Lease

In (A), a conventional purchase lease, the supplier, S, leases the property to the user, U, who pays rent in return. In (B), a finance lease, the supplier, S, sells the property to the financer, F, who in turn leases it to the user, U. U pays rent to F.

cost allowances in respect of depreciation of the asset. From a legal perspective, all lessors' interests should be registered under Personal Property Security legislation.[32]

Security and Finance Leases

In the typical purchase lease arrangement, it is the lessor who effectively provides the credit. The lessee pays what is, in reality, the purchase price by installments—in the form of "rent." Until the price is paid in full, the lessor has a security interest by virtue of his continued ownership of the leased property—hence the expression **security lease**.

security lease   a purchase lease in which the lessor provides the credit

An alternative that is becoming increasingly common is for a third person, such as a financial institution, to provide the credit financing. In this type of transaction, commonly known as a **finance lease**, the supplier of the goods sells them to the financer, who in turn leases them to the lessee. The financer is technically the owner of the goods, even though it probably has never had possession of them and will ultimately pass title to the lessee.

finance lease   an arrangement where a third person provides credit financing, becomes the owner of the property, and leases it to the lessee

The major auto manufacturing companies commonly establish their own leasing companies to provide consumer financing in this manner. Figure 15.1 gives a comparison of purchase and finance leases.

Sale-and-Leaseback

sale-and-leaseback   a transaction in which the owner of property sells it and immediately leases it back from the new owner

A business with cash-flow problems may enter into a **sale-and-leaseback** transaction to raise working capital. The business sells assets for cash, and leases them back in return for future rental payments. The leaseback may take the form of an operating lease or of a purchase lease. In the latter case, the effect is similar to raising cash by mortgaging the asset.

REASONS FOR CHATTEL LEASING

A person may be reluctant to purchase an item that may be used only for a limited period, even though it may be possible to resell that item when it is no longer needed. An operating lease will normally be a more convenient, and frequently less expensive, alternative to purchase.

The advantages of purchase leases and finance leases are less obvious. The lessor's perception may be that continued ownership of the asset, until payment has been made in full, provides more security in the case of default or insolvency of the lessee than would a conditional sale or chattel mortgage, though that view is questionable under modern personal property security legislation.[33] The lessee may find it preferable to lease assets as a form of off-balance-sheet financing—that is, since the asset is not owned by the business, it

---

[32] *Mitsui & Co. (Canada) Ltd. v. Royal Bank of Canada* (1995), 123 D.L.R. (4th) 449; *Adelaide Capital Corp. v. Integrated Transportation Finance Inc.*, *supra*, n. 29. See Chapter 28.

[33] See *Re Giffen*, [1998] 1 S.C.R. 91. See Chapter 28.

does not appear on the balance sheet, but neither does the future rental obligation appear as a liability. The net result is to record a lower debt-to-assets ratio than would be the case if the asset had been purchased with borrowed funds. Whether that is in fact the case depends upon the proper classification of the lease for accounting purposes.

Initially, the main reason for preferring leasing lay in the way the transaction was treated for tax purposes. Some of these tax advantages have been countered by legislation, but the rapid growth of leasing, and especially of international leasing, owes much to ingenious tax planning.

COMMON TERMS IN CHATTEL LEASES

The following terms are commonly found in chattel leases.

Duration

The lease normally sets out the time period during which it is intended to continue in force. In purchase lease arrangements, this is usually a fixed number of years. Operating leases may not contain a fixed term, but rather provide for termination by one party or the other on giving notice. If the term of the lease is shorter than the period for which the lessee is likely to want to use the asset, it is common to include an option for renewal.

Rent

Most leases provide for equal monthly or quarterly payments of rent, usually payable in advance. In a lease-to-own contract, the rent is calculated with reference to the normal selling price of the asset, with an additional "interest" element to take account of the period over which it is payable. Operating lease rentals take more account of the probable depreciation of the asset over the period of the lease and of the cost to the lessor of the asset, with an appropriate profit margin.

Insurance and Other Costs Payable by the Lessee

In short-term operating leases, the lessor normally insures the leased asset and bears the costs of maintenance and repairs. In longer leases, and especially in purchase leases, the lessee is usually required to covenant to keep the asset insured, to maintain it properly, and to pay the costs of maintenance and repairs. Sometimes the lessee is required to provide a "residual guarantee"—that is, a guarantee that the lessor will receive a minimum resale value at the end of the lease or, if not, the lessee will be responsible for the difference. This is a means to ensure the lessee takes good care of the asset.

Purchase Option

A purchase lease always contains an option for the lessee to purchase the asset at the end of the term, usually for a relatively small amount. In practice, a distinction is made between fair-market-value (FMV) leases and lease-to-buy (LTB) leases. In FMV leases, the purchase option corresponds to an estimate of the value of the asset at the end of the lease term; in LTB leases, the price is nominal (for example, $1). This difference is reflected in the rental payments—an FMV lease will have lower monthly payments than an LTB lease. Operating leases sometimes also include a purchase option, at a price to be agreed upon, with the price reducing over the lease term to offset depreciation.

Consent to Assignment (Sub-Bailment)

Purchase leases will prohibit the assignment of the lease without the prior written consent of the lessor. This is really a sub-bailment and likely to arise in purchase leases involving motor vehicles. Lessees cannot simply find someone to take over the payments of the purchase lease and give them the vehicle. As discussed in Chapter 11, the right to assign may be contractually limited. Sub-bailment also requires express or implied permission of the bailor.

Early Termination—Minimum Payment

Where the leased asset is new, or relatively new, the decrease in its value due to depreciation will often be greater than the amount of rent payable in the early part of the lease term. Consequently, it is usual for the lessor to insist on a minimum rental payment, to act as a deterrent against default or early termination. In some provinces, consumers receive protection from such clauses, as consumer protection legislation caps the amount of compensation a lessor can receive for early termination.[35]

Implied Terms

Remarkably, very little case law exists in Canada relating expressly to chattel leasing, and there is no Canadian legislation specifically dealing with chattel leases. There is little authority for additional implied terms.

Nevertheless, the law implies on the part of the lessor a warranty of **quiet possession**—that is, there will be no interference with the lessee's possession or use of the asset so long as the rent is paid and other terms are complied with.[36] Implied warranties, such as the

quiet possession a warranty that there will be no interference with the lessee's possession or use of the asset

---

[34] *Wallace Sign Crafters West Ltd. v. Delta Hotels Ltd.*, 1994 CanLII 1510 (B.C.S.C.).

[35] See Consumer Protection Act, 2002, S.O. 2002, c. 30 Sch. A, s. 90; O. Reg. 17/05 s. 76 (formula for calculating maximum); see also Alberta, British Columbia, and Saskatchewan. Cost of credit disclosure provisions are also requirements in Alberta, British Columbia, Manitoba, and Ontario.

[36] See e.g. Sale of Goods Act, s. 16.

warranty of fitness, are equally applicable to purchase lease contracts as they are to sales.[37] It has been held that the lessor impliedly warrants that leased equipment is reasonably fit for the purpose for which it was leased.[38] Some doubt exists as to whether this warranty is limited to defects of which the lessor ought to have been aware. A number of provinces have resolved these doubts by extending to consumer leases the implied warranties that apply in the case of sale of goods. For example, in British Columbia the warranties implied under the Sale of Goods Act apply equally to retail leases,[39] and in Manitoba and Saskatchewan, the implied warranties under the Consumer Protection Act are expressly made applicable to consumer leases.[40]

As with all bailments for value, the contractual terms set the standard of care. If silent, the standard of care required of a lessee who rents equipment is to take such care as is prudent and usual in the industry for those who own the equipment.

CASE 15.8

Roxburgh rented a portable steam engine from Reynolds to power a wood-cutting saw. The engine exploded immediately after it was put into use, killing one worker and injuring another. Reynolds sued Roxburgh for the value of the destroyed engine and boiler. He alleged that Roxburgh had not tested the steam gauge and safety valve before running the machine. The court applied the rule that "the hirer of a chattel is required to use . . . the degree of diligence which prudent men use . . . in keeping their own goods of the same kind."

However, the court held that this standard of care did not require the lessee to test the safety gauge and valve. Accordingly, the defendant was not in breach of his duty as a lessee and was not liable to pay for the destroyed steam engine.[41]

The question of who was liable for the injuries to the workers—the lessor or the lessee—was not raised in the case.

RIGHTS OF THE PARTIES

The Lessor

The rights of the parties under a lease contract are, of course, governed by the terms, express and implied, of the contract. The principal remedies available to the lessor are the right to sue for rent that is due and unpaid, and the right to retake possession of the leased property at the end of the lease or in the event of earlier default by the lessee. When a lessee contracts to hire a chattel for a given period, she remains liable for the whole rental, even if she finds that she has overestimated the time needed to use the equipment. (In the same way, a tenant of a building is liable for rent for the full period of the lease whether she occupies or uses the premises or not.) A lessor may agree to take equipment back ahead of time and to reduce the rental charges; when he does so, he is consenting to a discharge of the original lease contract and to replacing it with a substituted agreement.

The lessor is entitled both to retake possession of the chattel and to sue for damages for loss of bargain in respect of the rent that would have been payable if there had been no default, or for any minimum rent stipulated in the contract.[42] Additionally, if the lessee is in

---

[37] Ibid, s. 18; see Astley Industrial Trust Ltd. v. Grimley, [1963] 1 W.L.R. 584.

[38] Griffith S.S. Co. v. Western Plywood Co., [1953] 3 D.L.R. 29.

[39] R.S.B.C. 1996, c. 410, s. 20.

[40] C.C.S.M. c. 200, s. 58; S.S. 1996, c. 30.1., s. 48.

[41] Reynolds v. Roxburgh (1886), 10 O.R. 649, at 655.

[42] Keneric Tractor Sales Ltd. v. Langille (1987), 43 D.L.R. (4th) 171 (S.C.C.).

breach of her duty to take proper care of the leased property, the lessor will have an action for damages for the loss. Damages should be calculated in accordance with the general principles applied to a breach of contract action.

The Lessee

As noted above, the lessor impliedly warrants that the lessee shall have quiet possession and, probably, that the goods are fit for the purpose for which they are hired. Consequently, the lessee is entitled to sue for damages if she is wrongfully dispossessed during the term of the lease, or if she suffers loss because of some defect in the goods.

The law is less clear in the case of finance leases where the supplier sells an article to the financer, who in turn leases it to the actual user, the lessee. The lessee's contract is with the financer, although most of her dealings will have been with the supplier, with whom she has no contract. Where the supplier has made express representations to the lessee to induce her to enter into the contract, a collateral contract may be implied between supplier and lessee—that is, in return for the supplier's warranty that the goods conform to a particular quality or have a particular characteristic, the lessee agrees to enter into the contract with the financer, a contract which is of benefit to the supplier.[43]

The lessee would have the usual contractual remedies against the financer, although in practice finance leases routinely exclude all implied warranties on the part of the lessor.

A common complaint about leasing contracts is that the consumer lessee rarely understands the terms of the contract—how much is she really paying, and what happens if she wishes to terminate the lease? According to one recent report,

> People sometimes confuse leasing with renting—when they don't want the car anymore, they think they can just walk away from their monthly payments. . . . In fact, they cannot, without incurring adjustment costs.[44]

During the term of the lease, circumstances may change. The lessee may lose her job and be unable to keep up the payments, or may move and find that the leased article is no longer suited to her needs. It is then that she discovers that she cannot just stop payments and return the article. In the majority of cases, the lease terms are quite fair—it is simply that the terms were never properly explained to the lessee. But in some cases, the terms that apply on early termination can be quite harsh.

Some provincial consumer protection legislation (including that of Ontario, British Columbia, Alberta, and Manitoba) specifically addresses the harshness of consumer leasing contracts through the following requirements and limitations:

- a written disclosure statement showing the itemized costs of the lease, including the financed amount, interest rates and calculations, and implicit financing charges

- caps on termination penalties equal to three months of average payments (British Columbia and Alberta cap this amount if the goods have been returned)

- disclosure and restrictions on form and content of advertising (not in the B.C. statute)

Questions to Consider

1. Does a disclosure requirement provide sufficient protection? Should there be a set of statutory implied terms to protect consumers, as in some provincial Sale of Goods Acts?

2. Does capping the termination penalties unfairly penalize lessors?

3. Why is leasing less popular with the auto industry since the 2008 economic crisis?

---

[43] See *Hallmark Pool Corp. v. Storey* (1983), 144 D.L.R. (3d) 56. This is consistent with the principle established in *Shanklin Pier Ltd. v. Detel Products Ltd.*, [1951] 2 K.B. 854, discussed in Chapter 11, "Exceptions to the Privity of Contract Rule."

[44] Ken Shaw, "Lease Penalties Offset Costs," *Toronto Star*, July 24, 2004, at G10.

Strategies to Manage the Legal Risks

Bailments and leases benefit from written contracts that describe and limit the expectations and obligations of both parties. The type of bailment will determine the terms of the contract and how effective any exemption clause will be. Businesses must be familiar with industry-specific and province-specific legislation that will influence the form and contents of any contract. For example, Ontario carriers cannot be bound by any requirement to deliver to a particular address or by a particular time unless the requirement is in writing and signed by both shipper and carrier.

Best practices should be developed with the onus of proof in mind. Bailors should document the pre-transfer condition of the goods. Signed acknowledgments of the condition of the goods at the commencement and conclusion of the bailment protect both bailor and bailee. Pictures should be taken. Record keeping during the bailment is fundamental for a bailee who must prove it met the standard of care. Bailees must keep pace with the best practices of their competitors and ensure that measures to protect goods in their care meet or exceed these standards. Bailees should obtain consent to any sub-bailment or include a standard authorization in the contract. To preserve the availability of the bailee's lien rights, goods should not be released to the bailor until full payment is received. Finally, insurance coverage for the bailed goods remains a vital component of any bailment risk management strategy.

QUESTIONS FOR REVIEW

1. What is the principal difference between an operating lease and a purchase lease?
2. Distinguish between a security lease and a finance lease.
3. What warranties will normally be implied in a chattel lease?
4. What are the main perceived advantages of leasing capital assets as opposed to borrowing in order to purchase them?
5. Why would a business enter into a sale-and-leaseback transaction?
6. If a lessee defaults in paying the rent, is the lessor entitled to retake possession of the leased property as well as to sue for the rent owing?
7. Give an example of (a) a non-contractual bailment and (b) an involuntary bailment.
8. Distinguish between a bailment and a licence. In what circumstances is the distinction especially important?
9. What factors determine the standard of care to be expected of a bailee?
10. What is a "sub-bailment"?
11. In what circumstances may a bailee claim a lien on bailed goods?
12. What does it mean that goods are "fungible"? How does that affect a bailee's liability?
13. Who normally bears the loss if goods left in a warehouse are stolen or destroyed?
14. Distinguish between a common carrier and a private carrier.
15. What does it mean to say that a common carrier "is an insurer as well as a bailee"?
16. What are the principal defences available to a common carrier when goods in its possession are damaged or lost?
17. Is a hotel keeper liable if a guest's property is stolen from his or her room?
18. What is meant by a "pledge"?

CASES AND PROBLEMS

1. Continuing Scenario

   At Ashley's restaurant, there is an open coat room with hooks on the wall. There is a posted sign that says "For the use and convenience of our customers only—not responsible for loss or damage." Joan and Gloria arrive for lunch and Joan hangs her coat in the coat room; Gloria wears her coat to the table. Part way through lunch Gloria removes her coat and places it on the chair beside her. The waiter asks Gloria if she would like him to take her coat. She says yes and he takes it to the coat room. After lunch, Joan and Gloria go to the coat room and discover that both coats are missing; Gloria's coat had her car keys in the pocket and unfortunately Gloria's car was parked in one of the free parking spaces reserved for Ashley's customers. It is gone too. Is Ashley liable for the lost coats? How will the court approach the analysis for Joan's missing coat? Will Gloria's coat be treated differently? How about Gloria's car? Explain your reasons.

2. Intrepid Exploration Inc. is a comparatively small corporation engaged in exploring and drilling for oil in shallow coastal waters, usually as a subcontractor for major companies. Intrepid's owners recently entered into a contract with Globres Inc., one of those major companies, to provide specialized drilling services in a project off the New Brunswick coast. Intrepid anticipated making a substantial profit on the contract.

   Intrepid found that, to perform the contract, it would need a high-pressure drilling unit of a particular type that it did not own. Normally such units are custom-made, cost about $500 000, and take about six months to construct. Fortunately, Intrepid was able to locate such a unit, which was owned by Banditoil, a rather larger corporation in the same line of business as Intrepid. The unit was not in use at the time and was unlikely to be needed by Banditoil for at least 18 months.

   Intrepid negotiated a contract with Banditoil, under which it would lease the drilling unit for 12 months, with an option to extend the lease for a further six months, at a monthly rental of $15 000. Shortly thereafter, and before Intrepid took delivery of the drilling unit, Globres informed Intrepid that it was unwilling to have Intrepid do the work contracted for and that it was awarding the contract to another corporation, Cutprice Inc. Globres claimed to be entitled to do so under a clause in the contract, a claim that Intrepid contested. Intrepid immediately informed Banditoil that it no longer needed the drilling unit. Banditoil acknowledged receiving the information and replied that it was considering what action, if any, to take.

   Intrepid has now received a demand from Banditoil for payment in full of the sum of $180 000 under the lease contract. Intrepid has also learned that Cutprice has agreed to rent the same drilling unit.

   What is the extent of Intrepid's liability toward Banditoil?

3. Firth contracted with Dave the Mover Inc. to have her furniture and household effects moved from her house, stored for a week (until she moved into her new home), and then delivered to the new home. Firth told Dave's manager that she was particularly concerned about security, since the effects included some rare and valuable antiques and artifacts. She was told there was nothing to worry about. The articles would remain in the trailer until delivery at her new home, and the trailer would be locked at all times and parked in their yard, which was securely fenced, locked at night, and kept under regular supervision.

   The trailer was kept in the yard as promised for several days, but one night, after a heavy snowfall, it was moved and parked, unattended, on a public street while the yard was being plowed. While it was parked on the street, the trailer was stolen.

   Firth claimed damages for the full value of the goods lost. Dave's admitted liability, but pointed out that the bill of lading limited damages to $0.60 per pound weight of the goods, which came to just over $7000, a small fraction of their true value.

   Firth admitted she was aware of the limitation when she entered into the contract, but claimed she only agreed to it because of the assurance that the trailer would be properly supervised at all times.

   Should Dave's be allowed to rely on the limitation clause?

4. Nerdley is a skilled interior designer who decided to go freelance after years of being employed by a large construction company. Although accustomed to using a computer in her work, she understands very little about their characteristics and specifications, having always relied in the past on other specialist employees of the company for advice and assistance.

Nerdley realized that she would need to acquire her own computer equipment. She was told by a friend that Millennium Electronics had "the best prices in town" and a competent sales staff. She visited their local store, briefly explained to Boffin, a salesperson, what she perceived her needs to be, and eventually decided to acquire two computers, a printer, and various other items of equipment. Boffin assured her that they were "state of the art" and should be able to do everything she needed them to do.

The total price came to around $11 000. Nerdley then asked about credit and was told that Millennium recommended a leasing agreement with a finance company that it normally used in such cases. Under the agreement, Millennium sold the equipment to the finance company for $10 500, and Nerdley entered into a lease agreement with the finance company under which she agreed to make 36 monthly payments of $400, with an option at the end of the three-year period to buy the equipment for a further $400. The lease was on a standard printed form, and included the following clause:

> The lessee acknowledges that the equipment hereby leased was personally selected by the lessee for business purposes and purchased by the lessor at the lessee's request from a supplier designated by the lessee. The lessee takes full responsibility for such selection and waives all defences predicated on the failure of the said equipment to perform the function for which it was designed or selected and further acknowledges that such failure shall not be deemed to be in breach of this lease.

Nerdley very soon discovered that the computer did not have sufficient memory to operate some of the sophisticated design programs that she used, and that the printer did not have sufficiently high definition to reproduce her designs adequately.

When she attempted to take the equipment back to Millennium, she was told that the problems had nothing to do with them and that she should take it up with the finance company. Advise her.

5. 4D Enterprises Ltd. hired Jung to design and develop a website for its business. According to the agreement, Jung was to install the servers and all necessary software and to test the system fully. To enable him to do so, 4D delivered to him the two computers that would be used.

During the following three weeks, 4D phoned Jung several times to ask how the work was going. Each time, Jung assured them that it was "coming along fine" and would be ready soon. 4D started to become anxious, as they had expected the work to be done within two or three days. They made some enquiries and heard a few rather negative reports about Jung's work. As a result, they decided to find someone else to do the work and asked Jung to return their computers. Jung refused, claiming that he had done a substantial amount of work on the project, and demanded payment in full of the agreed amount.

Is Jung entitled to keep the computers until he has been paid?

Additional Resources for Chapter 15 on the Companion Website

(www.pearsoncanada.ca/smyth)

In addition to pre- and post-tests, mini-cases, and application exercises, the Companion Website includes the following province-specific resources for Chapter 15:

- **Alberta:** Common Carriers; Innkeepers' Liability; Mechanics' Liens; Possessory Liens; Warehouseman's Liens
- **Atlantic Provinces:** Innkeepers' Act; Mechanics' Lien Act
- **British Columbia:** Hotel Keepers; Lien; Repairers' Lien; Warehouse Lien
- **Manitoba/Saskatchewan:** Common Carriers; Innkeeper = Hotel Keeper; Warehouse Storage
- **Ontario:** Common Carriers; Consumer Leases; Consumer Protection Act 2002; Innkeepers' Liability; Pawnbrokers; Repair and Storage Liens; Warehousing

Chapter 16

Insurance and Guarantee

- INSURANCE AND THE MANAGEMENT OF LEGAL RISK

- INSURANCE TERMINOLOGY

- REGULATION OF INSURANCE BUSINESS

- TYPES OF INSURANCE

- SPECIAL ASPECTS OF THE CONTRACT OF INSURANCE

- GUARANTEE

- STRATEGIES TO MANAGE THE LEGAL RISKS

The two types of contracts dealt with in this chapter redistribute risk. They often form part of a business's legal risk management strategy. Insurance enables a business to shift the risk of loss—from damage to its own property or liability for damage to someone else's person or property—to an insurance company. In return, the business pays for that protection. A contract of guarantee allows a lender or creditor to reduce the risk of non-payment by obtaining a promise from a third person to pay the debt if the debtor defaults.

In this chapter we examine such questions as:

- What is the nature of the contract of insurance?

- What role does insurance play in risk management?

- What types of insurance protect against liability or loss in the operation of a business?

- What are the special characteristics of insurance contracts?

- What is the legal nature of a guarantee?

- How may a guarantee be discharged?

- What are the rights and liabilities of a guarantor?

INSURANCE AND THE MANAGEMENT OF LEGAL RISK

Insurance is a method of purchasing protection against a possible loss. The insured agrees with an insurance company that, in return for the payment of a premium or regular premiums, the company will compensate the insured if a specified loss occurs. The insurance company calculates the amount of payment required based on experience with the type of risk in question. A business faces two main types of "legal" risk:

- the risk that its own property or assets might be destroyed or damaged as a result of an accident or due to the fault of some other person
- the risk that it may be held liable for some loss or injury caused to another person and/or their property

In the first type of risk, no one may be held responsible, as in the case of storm damage, for example. Or, where the loss was caused by another person, tracing that person might be impossible, or he might have insufficient funds to pay compensation. Even when recovery is possible, legal proceedings are likely to be time-consuming and expensive. With this type of risk, it is possible to estimate the extent of the possible loss—one cannot lose more than the total value of all one's assets.

The second type of risk, known as third-party liability, is more open-ended. A very large business may be able to make an estimate of its potential liability: If one sells 100 000 cars of a particular model, it may be possible to calculate, based on experience, that a given number of defects will pass the inspection system and, of those, a certain percentage will cause serious injury. For a small business, however, such a calculation will be impossible—a shopper may trip on an uneven floor tile and suffer a crippling injury, resulting in a damage award of hundreds of thousands of dollars. (By contrast, an insurance company can make the calculation, based on the experience of thousands of similar businesses.)

What steps can a business take to guard against these risks, apart from the obvious one of taking all possible care to minimize the chances of their occurring? One possibility is to set aside a reserve or contingency fund to meet future expenses—in effect, to act as one's own insurer. That strategy is not possible for most businesses. The unfortunate event may occur before it has been possible to build up a sufficient reserve and, in any case, the business cannot afford to tie up so much capital to cover a risk that might never materialize. The more realistic alternative is to purchase insurance coverage.

INSURANCE TERMINOLOGY

An **insurance policy** is a document that provides written evidence of the terms of an insurance contract. The insurance company providing the protection is called the insurer; the party contracting for the insurance protection is the insured.[1] The **premium** is the price paid by the insured for the insurance coverage specified in the policy. The premium may be paid in a single sum, but more often it is paid yearly or at some other shorter interval throughout the term of the insurance.

> **insurance policy** the written evidence of the terms of a contract of insurance
>
> **premium** the price paid by the insured to purchase insurance coverage

The four key issues for an insurance contract are

- the nature of the risk covered (cause of the loss),
- the amount for which it is insured (extent of damage),
- the duration of the protection, and
- the amount of the premium.

---

[1] In life insurance, we distinguish between the insured and the life-insured when the subject of the insurance is the life of someone other than the party contracting for insurance.

The terms of a policy may require the insurer to pay the insurance money, in the event of a claim, to the insured, to the insured's estate, or to some other person designated as **beneficiary**. When an insured requires additional coverage—that is, wider protection than is available under the insurer's standard form policy—additional clauses are incorporated in the contract by attaching them to the policy in a **rider**. When the parties agree to a change in the terms of an existing insurance contract, they may do so without rewriting the entire policy, but rather by attaching a separate **endorsement** to the policy.

beneficiary a person who is entitled to the benefits of a trust or the person entitled to receive insurance monies

rider additional provisions attached to a standard policy of insurance

endorsement written evidence of a change in the terms of a policy

insurance agent an agent or employee of an insurance company

insurance broker an independent business that arranges insurance coverage for its clients

An **insurance agent** is an employee or agent of the insurance company whose function is to arrange contracts with persons seeking insurance protection for themselves. By contrast, an **insurance broker** conducts an independent business and generally acts for the insured rather than for the insurer.[2] A broker is a specialist in insurance problems who advises on the coverage required and arranges insurance with the companies best suited to provide it. However, the distinction between an agent and a broker is not always a clear one. In practice, an insurance agent often gives advice to the insured about the appropriate coverage, and it is possible in some cases for an agent, or a broker, to be considered to be acting as agent for both the insurer and the insured and to owe a duty to both.[3]

CASE 16.1

Miller was injured in a motor vehicle accident caused by the negligence of a person who was underinsured. Miller had purchased an insurance policy from an agent of the Guardian company. He had requested full coverage, but the agent did not suggest that the policy should contain an "underinsured motorist endorsement," which was available at a modest premium. As a result, Miller was not fully covered for the accident that occurred.

The court held that the agent had a duty to advise the insured on suitable coverage, and since the agent was acting as the agent of the insurance company, the company was also liable.[4]

insurance adjuster a person who appraises property losses

An **insurance adjuster** is an expert in the appraisal of property losses and provides these services to insurance companies for a fee. When a claim has been made, the adjuster gives an opinion to the insurer about whether the loss is covered by the insurance contract and, if so, what the amount of the loss is.

personal insurance insurance against death, injury, or ill health of an individual

property insurance insurance against damage to property

term insurance personal insurance that provides coverage for a limited period only

Insurance falls into two main classes: **personal insurance** and **property insurance**. Personal insurance, as the name implies, covers risk to life and health, and includes life insurance, medical insurance, accident and disability insurance, and workers' compensation. All other types of insurance are property insurance. Life insurance is unique in that the risk insured against is certain to materialize eventually, though in the case of **term insurance**, it may not occur during the period covered by the policy.

REGULATION OF INSURANCE BUSINESS

Each province has one or more statutes regulating the practice of insurance business within its borders. The main purpose of these statutes is to protect the public by requiring responsible behaviour on the part of insurance companies and others in the business. Among other matters, the statutes authorize the appointment of a superintendent of insurance to oversee the operations and financial responsibility of licensed insurers within the province,

[2] See *Adams Eden Furniture Ltd. v. Kansa General Insurance Co.* (1996), 141 D.L.R. (4th) 288, leave denied [1997] S.C.C.A. No. 42.

[3] See the discussion of an agent's duty in Chapter 17.

[4] *Miller v. Guardian Insurance Co. of Canada* (1997), 149 D.L.R. (4th) 375, leave denied [1997] S.C.C.A. No. 480. Contrast *Planidin v. Insurance Corporation of British Columbia* (2004), 245 D.L.R. (4th) 511, where it was held that the insurer owes no duty to provide advice on the extent of the coverage of a policy. Motor vehicle insurance coverage is subject to legislative minimums, the details of which are beyond the scope of this chapter.

describe the terms that must be included in insurance policies, and define the extent to which an insurer may limit its liability. In addition to these provincial statutes, the federal Insurance Companies Act[5] provides for compulsory registration of federal and foreign insurance companies wishing to carry on insurance business in Canada, and for voluntary registration of provincial insurance companies. Its aim is to ensure financial stability in the insurance industry by providing a system of inspection and by requiring statements and returns from these companies.

TYPES OF INSURANCE

Insurance against Loss or Damage

Just as risk can be divided into two categories, so can business insurance: One can insure against loss or damage to one's own property or assets, and one can insure against liability to others. Until recently, it was usual to insure against different risks in separate insurance policies: Some types of insurance—for example, fire insurance and marine insurance—go back several centuries. Typically, a business will insure against

- damage to buildings and contents (inventory, fixtures, and equipment) due to fire or storm,
- loss due to theft, and
- loss of or damage to vehicles used in the business.

In addition, it might take out insurance against

- loss of profit due to interruption of business activities,
- bad debt losses (credit insurance),
- losses caused by theft or fraud of employees (fidelity insurance), and
- loss due to injury to or death of important personnel (key-person insurance).

The precise extent of the coverage will vary from policy to policy and from one insurance company to another. Determining precisely what types of losses are covered is of crucial importance. One should always read the "small print." For example, does fire insurance also cover relocation expenses or loss of profit while the business is unable to operate? Does it include damage to a client's property that happens to be on the premises at the time of the fire? One recent case held that insurance against accidental damage to the insured's photocopying machines did not cover damage due to faulty manufacture because this was not an accident.[6]

In most instances, the insurer is liable either for the cost of repairing damaged property or for the value of the destroyed property. Value takes into account the condition of the property immediately before destruction. One may purchase insurance for full replacement value, but this higher protection is more expensive.

An insurance contract frequently contains a **deductible clause**, under which the insured is required to pay the first $500 (or some higher amount) in respect of each claim. A deductible feature gives the insured a greater incentive to take care of the insured property and, by eliminating small claims, makes the insurance cheaper.

deductible clause a clause requiring the insured to bear the loss up to a stated amount

---

[5] S.C. 1991, c. 47.

[6] *Celestica Inc. v. ACE INA Insurance* (2003), 229 D.L.R. (4th) 392. This case was distinguished in *Chanore Property Inc. v. ING Insurance Co. of Canada* (2010), 94 C.L.R. (3d) 223, because *Celestica* dealt with a comprehensive policy and was seeking compensation for its faulty manufacture of its product. In *Chanore*, damages for faulty work carried out by a tenant could be covered under the landlord's property insurance, provided the faulty workmanship exclusion did not apply.

Insurance against Liability

As noted in Chapters 4 and 5, businesses may be held liable to others in various ways, including liability for their own acts, or the acts of their employees, that cause damage to their customers, distributors, suppliers, and the general public. The type of insurance that covers this risk, known as **public liability insurance**, obligates the insurer to defend the insured against lawsuits and pay the amount of any judgment, up to the policy limit. As long as the claim alleges damage that might be covered, the insurer must defend.[7] For more information on this topic, see the Companion Website.

Businesses will normally insure against

- liability for negligent acts and omissions,
- liability for defective products,
- liability for the dangerous state of their premises, and
- liability for breach of their professional duty of care.

Public liability insurance is compulsory for most professions and provincial legislation requires that owners of motor vehicles carry third-party liability insurance.

Comprehensive Insurance

Rather than issue multiple policies, each providing protection against specific risks, comprehensive general insurance policies are available to cover most types of damage to the insured's property as well as liability to others. Such insurance tends to be expensive, however, the great advantage lies in the completeness of the coverage—unexpected risks do not fall into the cracks between two or more separate policies.

CASE 16.2

Goderich insured grain stored in its elevator under an "all risks" insurance policy that covered "all risk of direct physical loss or damage . . . except as excluded." The policy excluded "loss or damage caused directly or indirectly by . . . dryness of atmosphere, changes of temperature, heating, shrinkage, evaporation. . . ." Some of the stored grain was devalued due to a condition known as "heated grain." The cause of the heated grain could not be established, but there was no evidence of external causes. Goderich's claim under the insurance policy was contested by the insurance company. The court held that the loss was covered by an "all risk" policy, and the insurance company had not shown that the cause was within the exclusion.[8]

INTERNATIONAL ISSUE

Medical Malpractice Insurance

Many professions require their members to insure against liability for malpractice or breach of their duty of care. Those professionals who are not so required usually find it advisable to do so. Unfortunately, the cost of malpractice insurance, or public liability insurance, has been escalating rapidly—and that cost must be passed on to the client.

In the United States, it is not uncommon for doctors to pay $100 000 a year or more in premiums. Premiums are assessed

>

---

[7] *Monenco Ltd. v. Commonwealth Insurance Co* [2001] 2 S.C.R. 699.

[8] *Goderich Elevators Ltd. v. Royal Insurance Co.* (1999), 169 D.L.R. (4th) 763. The court applied one of the "general principles of interpretation of insurance policies" set out by McLachlin, J. in *Reid Crowther & Partners Ltd. v. Simcoe & Erie General Insurance Co.* (1993), 99 D.L.R. (4th) 741 (S.C.C.), namely, that "coverage provisions should be construed broadly and exclusion provisions narrowly."

based on the physician's specialty and location. In Florida, rates increased by 60 percent between 2000 and 2004, and an obstetrician's premium in Dade County (Florida) was $201 376 in 2003.[9] By contrast, an obstetrician's premium in Minnesota was only $17 431. This difference in rates could have an impact on the availability of care and specialist expertise in certain states. Some states have introduced tort reform including damage award caps and limits on plaintiffs' lawyer fees.

Things are not quite as bad in Canada—an Ontario obstetrician's premium was $78 120 in 2005.[10] In 2004, the Canadian Health Research Foundation reported that the number of medical malpractice lawsuits was steadily declining: Such lawsuits peaked in 1996 but declined by 23 percent by 2004. As in the United States, however, the size of the average settlement is increasing.[11] Other professions face similar problems: Accountants, in particular, have been hit with huge damage awards that increase their insurance costs.

Questions to Consider

1. Which of the following do you consider to be most responsible for the differences between the Canadian and American malpractice insurance premiums? Explain your choice.

   (a) high legal fees
   (b) excessive damages awards
   (c) lack of competition in the insurance industry

2. Can you suggest other ways of tackling the problem of skyrocketing malpractice insurance premiums?

SPECIAL ASPECTS OF THE CONTRACT OF INSURANCE

Legality of Objects—Wrongful Act of the Insured

A general principle of insurance law is that the courts will not enforce a contract of insurance when the claim arises out of a criminal or deliberate wrongful act by the insured.[12] Two reasons are commonly given for this rule: (1) It would be contrary to public policy to allow the insured to profit from his own crime, and (2) it would be contrary to the purpose of insurance to allow the insured to recover compensation for a loss that he had deliberately caused himself. Therefore, a beneficiary under a life insurance policy who murders the insured is not entitled to claim,[13] and an arsonist is not entitled to recover under a policy of fire insurance.[14] However, the courts have been careful to restrict the scope of the public policy exception, and the fact that the loss occurred as a consequence of the insured's deliberate wrongful act will not prevent recovery if that consequence was not intended.[15]

CASE 16.3

A dentist died as a result of substance abuse, the dangers of which were obvious and were presumably known by him. The insurance company refused to pay under a policy of insurance that he had taken out on his life, claiming that his death resulted from his own intentional act. The court held that, although the act of administering the substance was deliberate, the deceased had no intention of committing suicide. His estate was entitled to claim under the policy.[16]

[9] U.S. General Accounting Office, "Medical Malpractice, Excerpts from Medical Malpractice and Access to Health Care (GAO-03-836)," *Almanac of Policy Issues*, August 2003, http://www.policyalmanac.org/health /archive/medical_malpractice.shtml.

[10] Canadian Medical Protection Association, 2005 Fee Schedule, www.cmpaacpm.ca.

[11] "Myth: Medical Malpractice Lawsuits Plague Canada," MythBusters, Canadian Health Service Research Foundation, March 2006, www.chsrf.ca.

[12] *Beresford v. Royal Insurance Co.*, [1938] A.C. 586.

[13] *Demeter v. Dominion Life Assurance Co.* (1982), 132 D.L.R. (3d) 248, where the husband who was convicted of the murder of his wife was the owner and beneficiary under personal policies issued on the life of his wife. See also *Brisette Estate v. Westbury Life Insurance Co.*, [1992] 3 S.C.R. 87; *Lachman Estate v. Norwich Union Life Insurance Co.* (1998), 40 O.R. (3d) 393.

[14] See *Scott v. Wawanesa Mutual Insurance Co.* (1989), 59 D.L.R. (4th) 660.

[15] *Oldfield v. Transamerica Life Insurance Co. of Canada* (1998), 43 O.R. (3d) 114 aff'd (2002), 210 D.L.R. (4th) 1.

[16] *Bertalan Estate v. American Home Assurance Co.* (2001), 196 D.L.R. (4th) 445; *American International Assurance Life Company Ltd. v. Martin* (2003), 223 D.L.R. (4th) 1.

Insurance companies tend not to rely upon the common law principle and frequently insert an express provision that coverage does not extend to damage or injury resulting from an intentional or criminal act of the insured.[17]

Insurable Interest

insurable interest   genuine risk of loss that may be suffered from damage to the thing insured

An insurance contract is distinguished from a wager by the fact that the insured has an insurable interest; the contract shifts a genuine risk of loss from the insured to the insurer. An **insurable interest** is the genuine loss that would be suffered by the insured from damage to or destruction of the thing insured, or from the death of or injury to the person insured. Insurable interest is not confined to ownership of property. A person who owns all the shares in a corporation does have an insurable interest in the corporation's property; the Supreme Court of Canada held that an insurable interest exists where an insured benefits from the property's existence and is prejudiced by the property's destruction.[18] Obviously, damage to the property of the corporation would necessarily reduce the value of his shares. Similarly, a tenant might have an insurable interest in leased premises that he uses for his business, since he may suffer financial and other loss if the premises are destroyed or damaged.[19] Although the insured need not be the owner of the insured property, he must have some form of interest in that property.[20]

When must the insurable interest exist? When the contract is for life insurance, the person buying the insurance must either obtain the written consent of the person whose life is to be insured or have an insurable interest at the time the contract is formed, though not necessarily at the time of death of the person whose life is insured. When the contract is for property insurance, the insured must have an insurable interest at the time the contract was formed; otherwise the contract is void. And, since the purpose of insurance is to indemnify for loss suffered, the insured must still have an interest at the time the claim arises; otherwise there will be no loss to be recovered by the insured.

CASE 16.4

The owner of mortgaged premises insured them against damage by fire. Subsequently, the owner failed to keep up the mortgage payments and the mortgagee foreclosed. While the mortgagor was still in possession, the premises were destroyed by fire. On a claim by the mortgagor under the insurance policy, the Court held that the foreclosure had extinguished all rights and interest of the mortgagor in the property and had vested the title in the mortgagee. Therefore, the mortgagor no longer had an insurable interest in the premises.[21]

Formation of the Contract

A proposal drafted by an insurance agent is usually a mere invitation to treat, not an offer. The offer to purchase insurance coverage is made by the party seeking the insurance protection—the prospective insured—by signing an application form. What constitutes acceptance by the insurer? We need to know so that we can tell when the insurance is in force. These questions are usually answered by provincial legislation or the offer itself.

---

[17] See e.g. *British Columbia Insurance Corp. v. Kraiger* (2002), 219 D.L.R. (4th) 49 (arson); *Hodgkinson v. Economic Mutual Insurance Co.* (2003), 235 D.L.R. (4th) 1 (defamation). Where coverage is for accidental damage, it is not sufficient that the event is unexpected: see *Co-operators Life Insurance Co. v. Gibbens*, [2009] 3 S.C.R. 605.

[18] *Kosmopoulos v. Constitution Insurance Co.* (1987), 34 D.L.R. (4th) 208. It is unclear whether a holder of only a small proportion would be found to have an interest.

[19] *Evergreen Manufacturing Corp. v. Dominion of Canada General Insurance Co.* (1999), 170 D.L.R. (4th) 240.

[20] See *Assaad v. Economic Mutual Insurance Group* (2002), 214 D.L.R. (4th) 655.

[21] *Walton v. General Accident Assurance Co. of Canada* (2000), 194 D.L.R. (4th) 315.

With life insurance, the applicant's offer is not accepted until the insurance company delivers the policy. It is a condition precedent to delivery of the policy that the first premium be paid.[22]

Making contracts for property insurance is typically less formal than for life insurance. An agent dealing in property insurance may have agency contracts with a number of insurance companies. Each contract gives the agent authority to sign and deliver policies and renewal certificates and generally to bind the company concerned; a business seeking property insurance can obtain the desired protection immediately, before paying the premium or receiving a policy. The agent need only prepare a memorandum or binder for the agency's records as evidence of the time and nature of the request for insurance. When immediate protection is required, an insured should be satisfied that the agent has an agency contract with the proposed insurer.

Renewal

Property insurance is written for a specified period of time (usually for one year). Frequently, the intention is that the insurance should be renewed at the end of the period, and it is not uncommon for the insured to fail to renew it in time. What is the situation in the meantime? A common practice is for an insurance company, or its agent, to prepare a renewal policy or memorandum and send it to the insured shortly before the current policy expires. This acts as a reminder that the insurance protection is about to cease if not renewed. But unless there is evidence of an agreement between the company and the insured that they intend the delivery of a renewal policy or memorandum to create a new contract of insurance, or such an agreement can be inferred from their past dealings with one another, the act of delivering the renewal policy amounts to no more than making an offer to the insured. No contract is formed until the insured communicates acceptance, and because the offer is open, at most, for a reasonable time, the insured cannot wait indefinitely.

CASE 16.5

The insured's auto insurance policy expired on February 5, 1989. About a month before, the insurance company sent him an offer to renew if the premium was paid before February 5, and a "pink slip" certifying that the insurance was in effect until August 5, 1989. The insured did not pay the renewal premium and was injured in an accident on February 20.

The Supreme Court of Canada held that the pink slip did not amount to a renewal of the contract. It was sent to the insured for convenience only and did not bind the company.[23]

Absent legislation to the contrary (such as exists for mandatory motor vehicle coverage in some provinces), a policy that expires for non-payment of renewal does not need any formal termination process.

CASE 16.6

Under a life insurance policy, a premium payment became due on July 26, 1984. The grace period expired and the company sent a "late payment offer," offering to receive late payment under certain conditions. Four months later, the company sent a letter to the insured saying that the policy was "technically out of force" and that immediate payment of the premium was required. In February 1985 the company sent a further letter, stating that the insurance had lapsed. The letters did not come to the insured's attention until April 1985, and in July, he sent a cheque. By then, his life had become uninsurable and he died a month later.

The Supreme Court of Canada held that the July payment was too late. The company had offered to renew the policy, but that offer was open only for a reasonable time.[24]

---

[22] See e.g. Insurance Act, R.S.B.C. 2012, c.1, s. 48.

[23] *Patterson v. Gallant* (1994), 120 D.L.R. (4th) 1 at para. 35.

[24] *Saskatchewan River Bungalows Ltd. v. Maritime Life Assurance Co.* (1994), 115 D.L.R. (4th) 478.

Terms of the Contract

An insurance policy is an example of a standard form contract—it is prepared unilaterally in advance by the insurer. To offset this advantage for insurers, the courts subject such contracts to a strict interpretation: They construe any ambiguous words in favour of the insured. They take the view that clauses exempting an insurer from liability in specific circumstances must be stated in clear and unambiguous terms if they are to be binding.[25]

CASE 16.7

A group of tenants brought a class action against the owner of an apartment complex, claiming that they became ill after breathing carbon monoxide leaking from the apartment furnace. The apartment owner had a commercial liability insurance policy, but the policy contained an exclusion clause for "pollution liability." The insurance company claimed that the clause exempted them from liability.

The court held that, although carbon monoxide could be considered a pollutant, the clause was intended to exclude coverage for damages from environmental pollution. The clause should be strictly and narrowly interpreted against the insurer: It was not intended to apply to circumstances such as a leak from a faulty furnace.[26]

Good Faith, Fairness, and Disclosure

Insurance contracts are contracts of the utmost good faith. This means parties to the contract must act fairly and with integrity in their dealings with each other. In our discussion of misrepresentation in Chapter 9, we noted that an insurer may avoid paying a claim if it can show that the insured did not exercise the utmost good faith in the application for insurance. In particular, full disclosure must be made of all material facts and circumstances that are known, or should have been known, to the insured.

CASE 16.8

A corporation took out a fidelity insurance policy to protect itself against losses caused by dishonest employees. The corporation's accountant stole over $20 million over a 10-year period. The fraud should have been easily detected from the

corporation's financial statements. The Court held that the insured corporation had constructive knowledge of the fraud and had a duty to disclose it. Therefore, it was not entitled to recover under the policy.[27]

The disclosure requirement has traditionally been applied strictly. For example, it has been held that an insured may be unable to collect for a claim even when the loss arose from causes unrelated to the facts that the insured should have disclosed.[28] However, some Canadian decisions have adopted a more flexible approach. For example, a statement by the insured that a night watchman would be present on the premises every night was held not to be material when the actual loss occurred in the afternoon.[29] As well, the insured need not disclose information of a general nature that should be well known to the insurer: An asbestos manufacturer was not required to inform its insurer that there were health risks related to working with asbestos, so long as the likelihood of exposure to asbestos was disclosed.[30]

---

[25] *Somersall v. Friedman* (2002), 215 D.L.R. (4th) 577 (S.C.C.) at para 46-48.See, e.g., *British Columbia Ferry Corp. v. Commonwealth Insurance Co.* (1985), 40 D.L.R. (4th) 766.

[26] *Zurich Insurance Co. v. 686234 Ontario Ltd.* (2002), 222 D.L.R. (4th) 655, leave denied [2003] S.C.C.A. No. 33.

[27] *J. J. Barnicke Ltd. v. Commercial Union Assurance Co. of Canada* (2000), 5 B.L.R. (3d) 199.

[28] See *Lachman Estate v. Norwich Union Life Insurance Co.* (1998), 40 O.R. (3d) 393.

[29] Case *Existological Laboratories Ltd. v. Century Insurance Co.* (1982), 133 D.L.R. (3d) 727, aff'd [1983] S.C.J. No. 61.

[30] *Canadian Indemnity Co. v. Canadian Johns Mansville Co.*, [1990] 2 S.C.R. 549.

In *Coronation Insurance Company v. Taku Air Transport Ltd.*,[31] the Supreme Court of Canada went even further, holding that the utmost good faith principle should not apply at all in the highly regulated field of aviation insurance. The requirement that air carriers have insurance for their passengers was primarily intended for the benefit of the public, whose protection should not depend entirely on the good faith of the carrier. Consequently, the failure of a carrier to fully disclose its past safety record did not invalidate the policy. The insurance company had a duty at least to check its own files and the public records.[32]

An insurer may insert terms in an insurance contract to extend the obligation of the insured even beyond that imposed by the requirement of utmost good faith. The application form signed by the party seeking insurance may contain a provision that the applicant warrants the accuracy—not merely the truthfulness—of any declarations made. If in these circumstances an applicant for life insurance replies in the negative to the question "Have you any disease?" and proves later to have had a disease of which he or she was unaware, the insurer may avoid its liability. The courts dislike this type of provision and insist on strict proof by the insurer that the question was answered inaccurately.

Insurance contracts other than for life insurance contain a statutory term that the insured shall notify the insurer promptly of any change that is material to the risk and within the control or knowledge of the insured. Such a term then gives the insurer some options. It may either cancel the insurance and return the unexpired portion of the premium, or inform the insured that the insurance will continue only on payment of an increased premium. Prompt notice by the insured in these circumstances is a condition precedent. An insurer is absolved from liability under the policy if it does not receive such notice. Insurance contracts normally also contain a term requiring the insured to notify the insurer promptly of any loss that occurs. Failure to give notice promptly may free the insurer from liability to pay the claim.

Ethical Issue Bad Faith

Frequently an insurance company disagrees with the insured over the entitlement to compensation or the amount of compensation. The manner in which an insurance company proceeds in cases of disagreement was dramatically changed in 2002. In that year, the Supreme Court of Canada released its decision in *Whiten v. Pilot Insurance*.[33] It held that Pilot acted in bad faith during the management of the claim and this entitled the insured to $1 000 000 in punitive damages. Pilot alleged arson with little or no evidence to support such an allegation. Pilot rejected independent advice that the claim should be paid and even influenced an independent investigator to change his opinion. In the circumstances, the Court held that Pilot breached its duty of good faith. This duty requires prompt and fair treatment of the insured.

In 2006, the Supreme Court awarded punitive damages again when an insurer unreasonably denied disability benefits in *Fidler v. Sun Life Assurance Co*. Mental anguish damages that stemmed from the long delay in receiving benefits were also allowed.[34] Since *Whiten*, insurers are required to balance their right to investigate with the responsibility not to unduly delay the processing of claims, not to pursue unfounded defences, and to treat the insured fairly.

Question to Consider

1. What strategies should an insurance company employ to avoid allegations of bad faith?

---

[31] [1991] 3 S.C.R. 622. See also *MacNeil (Litigation Guardian of) v. Bryan*, (2009) C.C.L.I. (4th) 96 (Ont. S.C.)

[32] Unfortunately, the crash victims still did not recover compensation. The aircraft was carrying more passengers than provided for in the policy, and the policy was consequently void.

[33] [2002] 1 S.C.R. 595.

[34] *Fidler v. Sun Life Assurance Co.*, [2006] 2 S.C.R. 3.

The duty of good faith is owed by both insured and insurer, and applies to the making of the contract, as well as its performance.[35] An insurer must deal with claims fairly both in the manner in which it investigates and values a claim and in the way it defends any lawsuit. It must not take advantage of its position of power over a vulnerable insured.

CASE 16.9

Wilson was injured in two motor vehicle accidents one year apart. He underwent surgery and rehabilitation for the next decade; the cost of each was covered by his insurance. When a new claims adjuster took over the case, benefits were terminated despite reports recommending continued treatment from those involved with Wilson's care. Only the consultant hired by the insurer suggested that treatment was unnecessary, and he did so without meeting Wilson or any of those treating Wilson. The Saskatchewan Court of Queens Bench held that the insurer was "looking for an excuse to terminate benefits" and that it had breached its duty of good faith. The Court also held that the insurer manipulated the rules relating to witnesses and settlement offers in order to disadvantage Wilson. Damages and solicitor client costs were awarded.[36]

Subrogation

If a storeowner has obtained fire insurance for her premises and suffers a loss because of a fire negligently caused by her neighbour, she can recover from her own insurance company without having to sue the neighbour. However, she cannot recover twice. If she were subsequently to sue the neighbour and recover damages that, when added to her insurance compensation, would give her a sum in excess of her loss, she would hold that excess in trust for her insurer. As a result, as long as she is fully insured, she will have no incentive to sue her neighbour. If that ended the matter, many people would escape liability for their careless acts. However, under general principles of insurance law, when an insurer has *fully* compensated an insured for all losses, it is entitled to "step into the shoes of the insured" and sue the person liable for the loss.[37] But the right of subrogation cannot place the insurer in a better position than the insured. For more information on this topic, see the Companion Website.

CASE 16.10

A fire broke out in leased premises, apparently due to the negligence of the tenant. The landlord was fully indemnified by its insurer who brought an action for damages against the tenant by way of subrogation. In the lease, the landlord had covenanted to insure against damage by fire, and the tenant had agreed to pay a proportionate share of the landlord's cost of insuring. The tenant covenanted to repair the premises, except for insured fire damage.

The court held that the terms of the lease indicated that the tenant had bargained for the right to be free of liability for fire arising from its negligence. Regardless of the terms of the policy between the insurer and the landlord, the insurer could have no better claim against the tenant than the lease gave to the landlord.[38]

Recovery

In many types of insurance, property is insured for a stipulated amount (usually the estimated value of the property), and the insurer's liability is limited to that amount. However,

---

[35] *Zurich Insurance Co. v. Ison T.H. Auto Sales Inc.*, [2011] O.J. No. 1487 at para. 29 (Ont. S.C.) (citing *Whiten*, *supra*, n. 33).

[36] *Wilson v. Saskatchewan Government Insurance*, [2011] 2 W.W.R. 154 (Sask. Q.B.) punitive damages varied on appeal 2012 SKCA 106.

[37] *Zurich Insurance*, *supra*, n. 35, at paras. 32–41.

[38] *Amexon Realty Inc. v. Comcheq Services Ltd.* (1998), 155 D.L.R. (4th) 661. But an agreement between the insured plaintiff and the defendant (for example, not to sue for more than the amount of the defendant's own insurance cover) does not bind the plaintiff's insurer and cannot restrict its right of subrogation: *Somersall*, *supra* n. 25.

it is a basic principle of insurance law that the insured may not recover more than the amount of the actual loss. For example, if a business insures its warehouse against damage by fire for $300 000, but the warehouse is actually worth only $275 000, that lower amount is the maximum that may be recovered. A person or business might think of saving premium costs by insuring property for less than its total value, since fires and accidents rarely result in total loss. Insurance companies often insert a clause in the contract stating that an insured that does not purchase coverage of at least a stated percentage of the value of the property (usually 80 percent) will become a "co-insurer" proportional to the lower coverage, along with the insurance company, for any loss that results. The insured would not recover the total loss, even though the loss itself was less than the face value of fire insurance policy.

Sometimes the same loss is covered by two or more separate insurance policies (especially where different risks are insured separately rather than under a single comprehensive policy): That does not permit the insured to recover twice for the same loss, and where the policies are issued by different insurance companies, they will have to determine which one must bear the loss or how it must be shared.[39]

The fact that the insured received insurance proceeds does not mean the defendant or tortfeasor is not liable—the insurance proceeds are not deducted from the damages payable by the defendant. This is known as the private insurance exception and is justified on the basis that the plaintiff has paid premiums in consideration of the insurance coverage.[40] For more information on this topic, see the Companion Website.

Assignment

A life insurance policy of the type that accumulates a cash surrender value is an item of property—a chose in action—which the insured may assign for value, for example, by giving a conditional assignment of the policy to a bank as security for a loan. If the insured defaults on the loan, the bank is entitled to the cash surrender value up to the amount due on the loan. The insurer's consent to an assignment of life insurance is not necessary, although the insurer is entitled to notice. The risk of the insurer is not affected by an assignment of the benefits of a life insurance contract.

In contrast, property insurance is not assignable without the consent of the insurer. The reason for this rule is that an assignment substitutes a new person as the insured, and the personal qualities of the insured may be relevant to the risk assumed by the insurer. When a person sells a house or an automobile, there is usually unexpired insurance on the property; the purchaser must therefore renegotiate the insurance with the insurer, possibly at different premium rates. On the other hand, after a risk materializes and an insurance claim is established, an insured may assign the claim (say, to creditors) without the consent of the insurer.

GUARANTEE

The Nature of a Guarantee

A **guarantee** usually arises in one of three common business situations:

guarantee a promise to perform the obligation of another person if that person defaults

- A prospective creditor may refuse to advance money, goods, or services solely on the prospective debtor's promise to pay for them.

- A creditor may state that it intends to start an action against its debtor for an overdue debt unless the debtor can offer additional security to support a further delay in repayment.

---

[39] *Family Insurance Corp. v. Lombard Canada Ltd.* (2002), 212 D.L.R. (4th) 193; *Unger v. Unger* (2003), 234 D.L.R. (4th) 119.

[40] *Krawchuk v. Scherbak*, 2011 ONCA 352 at para 98-101 (citing *Cunningham v. Wheeler* [1994] 1 S.C.R.359)

■ A prospective assignee of rights under a contract may be unwilling to do so if he or she only receives the promise of payment in the original contract.

In each of these circumstances, the creditor or assignee may be reassured if he also receives a third party's promise to perform the obligation of the debtor if the debtor defaults. The debtor is then called the principal debtor, and his obligation is known as the principal or primary debt. The person who promises to answer for the default of the principal debtor is called the guarantor or surety, and her promise is a guarantee or contract of suretyship.

ILLUSTRATION 16.1

(a) Crown Autos Ltd. agrees to sell a sports car to Tomins, provided that her uncle, Gilmour, guarantees payment. Gilmour agrees to assist his niece, and both join in signing an installment purchase agreement whereby Tomins promises (as principal debtor) to make all payments promptly, and Gilmour promises (as guarantor) to pay off the debt if Tomins defaults.

(b) Arthur purchases a delivery truck from Bigtown Trucks Ltd. under an installment agreement. After Arthur has made more than half his payments, he defaults because of business difficulties. Bigtown threatens to retake possession of the truck. Arthur asks Bigtown to give him an extra six months to pay if he can obtain a satisfactory guarantor. Bigtown agrees, and Arthur's friend Campbell signs a contract of guarantee, promising to pay the balance in six months if Arthur fails to do so.

(c) Perez buys a freezer from Quincy and gives a promissory note payable in 60 days for the full purchase price. Quincy is in need of cash and takes the note to her banker who agrees to give her cash for it, less a 5 percent charge. Quincy endorses the note in favour of the bank—that is, she signs it when assigning it to the bank, and thereby guarantees payment if Perez defaults.

There are three important characteristics of a guarantee. First, a guarantor makes a promise to the creditor, not to the principal debtor. A promise made to a debtor to assist in the event of default is not a guarantee, and since the promise is not made to the creditor, the creditor cannot recover on it. Second, a guarantee is a secondary obligation arising only on default of the primary debt. For this reason it is a contingent liability in contrast to the absolute liability of the principal debtor. A creditor has no rights against the guarantor until default by the principal debtor. Third, a guarantor's duty to pay arises immediately on default by the principal debtor. The creditor need not first sue the debtor. Strictly speaking, the creditor need not even notify the guarantor of the default before starting an action to enforce the guarantee. As a practical matter, however, the creditor always makes a demand on the guarantor before suing. Of course, when giving a guarantee, a guarantor may stipulate that the creditor must first have sued the debtor. It is more common that the guarantee specifically releases the creditor from any obligation to proceed against the debtor first. Figure 16.1 illustrates the relationships involved in a guarantee.

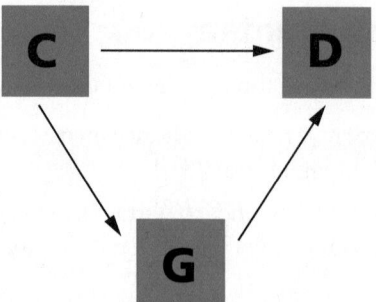

Figure 16.1 Liability on a Guarantee

The creditor, C, may sue either the principal debtor, D, or the guarantor, G, once D has defaulted. Normally, G will be entitled to sue D to recover what she has paid on D's account.

ILLUSTRATION 16.2

William tries to rent a launch from Boat Rentals Ltd. but is refused because of his youth. William's father, a reputable businessman, informs the manager of Boat Rentals that if the company rents the launch to his son, he will be responsible for any damage caused by his negligent acts if his son does not reimburse the company for any such damage. Boat Rentals accepts his offer.

In Illustration 16.2, the guarantee is rather like a contract of insurance in which the father is the counterpart of an insurer, and the boat rental firm is the counterpart of the insured. If William's father had undertaken absolutely (without reference to a failure by his son to make good the loss himself) to assume any costs of his son's possible negligence, his promise would have been an indemnity and even more like a contract of insurance.

The distinction between guarantee and indemnity is important in that the liability of a guarantor depends on the continuing existence of the liability of the principal debtor, whereas the liability under a promise of indemnity stands alone. If a person guarantees the debt of a consumer debtor and the obligation is not binding under consumer legislation (for example, for failure to deliver a written statement of the terms of credit), the guarantor is not bound to pay either. On the other hand, a promise of indemnity is independent of any obligation of the person who benefits from that promise.

Continuing Guarantee

A continuing guarantee covers a series of transactions between a creditor and its principal debtor. A guarantor may, for example, agree to guarantee X Co.'s account with supplier Y up to an amount of $5000. In a series of purchases by X Co. and payments by it, X Co.'s indebtedness to Y will fluctuate considerably. At any given date during the currency of the guarantee, the guarantor is contingently liable for the debt, to a maximum of $5000. A continuing guarantee is often given for a specific length of time, and debts contracted afterward are not the liability of the guarantor. In any event, the death of a guarantor ends liability with respect to further transactions, although the guarantor's estate remains contingently liable for the debt existing at death.

A guarantor may limit liability under a continuing guarantee until a specified date: If the principal debtor has not defaulted or been sued by that date, then the guarantor's liability terminates. The variety of terms of a guarantee is virtually limitless, and they depend only upon the ability of the parties to reach agreement.

Consideration

To be a legally enforceable promise, the guarantee must be given either under seal or for consideration. Usually a guarantor makes the promise in writing and under seal. If not, what is the consideration for a guarantee?

Consideration is clearest when the guarantor receives an economic benefit—when she obtains a higher price as an assignor of an account receivable because she is willing to guarantee payment by the debtor. More frequently, the guarantor does not receive any economic benefit for her promise; but as noted, consideration need not confer an economic benefit on the promisor. The essential element of consideration is simply that the promisee pays a price for the promise of the other party. The creditor gives sufficient consideration for the promise of the guarantor by performing some act or forbearing to do some act at the request of the guarantor. The guarantor's request need not even be express; it may be implied from the circumstances.

Creely threatens to sue Dobbs for his past-due debt. Dobbs asks for 60 days more to raise the money, but Creely refuses to give the extra time unless Dobbs obtains a guarantee from his cousin Guara. Guara signs a guarantee, and Creely allows Dobbs a further 60 days. When Dobbs defaults payment again, Creely sues Guara.

Creely is entitled to recover. Guara impliedly requested Creely to give Dobbs extra time to pay, and Creely gave consideration by doing so.

Discharge of Guarantee

The liability of a guarantor may be discharged by subsequent acts by the creditor. In an important decision of the Supreme Court of Canada the following principles were stated:[41]

1. The guarantor will be discharged if the creditor breaches the terms of the contract of guarantee. For example, where a creditor commenced proceedings against the principal debtor without giving notice to the guarantor and making it a party to the proceedings, as required by the contract of guarantee, the guarantor was discharged.[42]

2. The guarantor will be discharged if the principal contract between the creditor and the debtor is varied without the guarantor's consent and in a manner that is not obviously to the benefit of the guarantor. The rationale for this rule is that the guarantor has undertaken to underwrite a particular risk and is entitled not to have that risk materially altered to his detriment. For example, where an individual guaranteed a mortgage to a bank for a three-year term and, prior to the end of the term, the mortgagor and the bank renewed the mortgage for a further term at a higher rate of interest, the guarantor was held not liable when the mortgagor subsequently defaulted. The guarantor had not been given notice of the renewal and did not sign as guarantor on the renewal form. The contract had been materially altered without his consent, and he was relieved from liability on his original guarantee.[43]

3. If the creditor acts in breach of its contract with the principal debtor, and that breach materially affects the risk assumed by the guarantor, the guarantor will be discharged. When a bank, having agreed to give a family company more time to pay off its debt, in return for a personal guarantee from its principal shareholders, made a demand for immediate payment and put the company into receivership, the guarantors were held to be discharged.[44] But in another case, where a bank appointed a receiver without first demanding repayment from the debtor, the guarantor was held not to be discharged since, on the evidence, there was nothing the debtor could have done even if it had been given proper notice. There was consequently no prejudice to the guarantor.[45]

4. Finally, when the creditor does something that impairs the value of any security given by the principal debtor, but without materially affecting the guarantor's risk under the original contract of guarantee, the guarantor is entitled to be partially discharged from her obligation, but only to the extent that the value of the security is reduced.[46]

For more information on this topic, see the Companion Website.

---

[41] *Pax Management Ltd. v. Canadian Imperial Bank of Commerce*, [1992] 2 S.C.R. 998.

[42] *Bank of British Columbia v. Turbo Resources Ltd.* (1983), 23 B.L.R. 152.

[43] *Manulife Bank of Canada v. Conlin* (1996), 139 D.L.R. (4th) 426 (S.C.C.). See also *Royal Bank of Canada v. Bruce Industrial Sales Ltd.* (1998), 40 O.R. (3d) 307.

[44] *Bank of Montreal v. Wilder* (1986), 32 D.L.R. (4th) 9 (S.C.C.).

[45] *Royal Bank of Canada v. Nobes* (1982), 49 N.S.R. (2d) 634.

[46] *Rose v. Aftenberger* (1969), 9 D.L.R. (3d) 42. See also *Bank of Montreal v. Korico Enterprises Limited* (2000), 50 O.R. (3d) 520.

Rights of the Guarantor on Default

Defences   A guarantor may generally defend an action by the creditor on any grounds that would be open to the principal debtor. If a debtor has a good defence because of the misrepresentation of the creditor in selling the goods, the guarantor may take advantage of this defence. A guarantor may reduce the outstanding amount by any claim the debtor has against the creditor, as when the debtor has performed services for the creditor which also remain unpaid.

If the principal contract is void—as, for example, in the case of a prohibited loan to a company—then any guarantee will also be a nullity.[47] It is uncertain whether a guarantor can plead the principal debtor's infancy as a defence on the grounds that if, as guarantor, she were to pay the debt to the creditor, she could not herself succeed in an action to recover it from the principal debtor. However, the general rule is that a contract made with an infant is not void but merely unenforceable against the infant and might not necessarily prevent the enforcement of a guarantee.

Subrogation   Subrogation, as described in the insurance section of this chapter, also applies to a guarantee. A guarantor who pays off the creditor becomes subrogated to the rights of the creditor against the debtor and the debtor's assets. She may sue the debtor for the amount she has paid the creditor and for any expenses she has incurred because of the debtor's default. She is also entitled to an assignment of any security the creditor holds.

A guarantor may choose to pay off the creditor and become subrogated to its rights as soon as the debt falls due: She need not wait for the creditor to make a demand or to sue. The guarantor may wish to act even when the creditor is content to wait. The guarantor may have ascertained that the debtor is failing and may wish to take action before the debtor becomes insolvent—if she waits until the creditor demands payment, it may no longer be worthwhile to sue the debtor.

Requirement of Writing

Chapter 10 discussed that a contract of guarantee must be in writing and signed by the guarantor to be enforceable against him. This requirement has been retained even in those jurisdictions where the Statute of Frauds has largely been repealed.[48] Most guarantees, such as those given to a bank, are in writing, regardless of whether writing is required by law. For more information on this topic, see the Companion Website.

Strategies to Manage the Legal Risks

Insurance and guarantee contracts are valuable risk management tools that virtually every business uses. Their effectiveness depends upon their form and content, as well as compliance with the legislation that governs their use. Scope of coverage is the most important term of an insurance contract. Typical insurance contracts contain many exclusions, and

---

[47] *Communities Economic Development Fund v. Maxwell*, [1991] 3 S.C.R. 388; *Jer-Mar Foods Ltd. v. Arrand Refrigeration Inc.*, [2010] O.J. No. 1119 (Ont. S.C.) (QL). In *William E. Thompson Associates Inc. v. Carpenter* (1989), 61 D.L.R. (4th) 1, the principal debtor's obligation was held to be unenforceable because the interest rate exceeded the maximum permitted under the Criminal Code. Nevertheless, the guarantee of repayment of the principal sum only was held to be severable and enforceable.

[48] Only Manitoba does not require a guarantee to be in writing: Act to Repeal the Statute of Frauds, R.S.M. 1987, c. F-158. In Alberta, the requirement is more stringent. A guarantee by an individual must also be acknowledged before a notary public: Guarantees Acknowledgement Act, R.S.A. 2000, c. G-11.

coverage may be denied if full disclosure has not been made at the time of contracting. Therefore, careful attention must be paid to exclusions and riders attached to policy, and a comprehensive insurance policy is less likely to create gaps in coverage. Renewal dates should be monitored and any material change in circumstances (that is, risk) should be reported to the insurer immediately.

Businesses using guarantees to reduce the chances of bad debts among their accounts receivable should prepare written documents under seal. A guarantor's right to subrogation means any dealings with the primary debtor or security should be completed with the full knowledge and agreement of the guarantor.

QUESTIONS FOR REVIEW

1. What are the two principal types of "legal risk" that a business may insure against?
2. Distinguish between an insurance agent and an insurance broker.
3. What are the principal types of insurance that a business is likely to need?
4. What are the advantages and disadvantages of "comprehensive" insurance?
5. What is meant by an "insurable interest"?
6. Does a shareholder have an insurable interest in the property of his or her corporation?
7. What is the legal position where an insured fails to renew an insurance policy by the due date?
8. Is it necessary for an insured to notify the insurer of changes of circumstance that occur after the policy enters into force?
9. Can an insurance policy be assigned to a third person?
10. What is "subrogation"?
11. In what business circumstances are guarantees commonly required and given?
12. To whom does a guarantor give his or her promise?
13. What normally constitutes the consideration for a guarantee?
14. How may a guarantee be discharged?
15. Does a contract of guarantee have to be in writing?

CASES AND PROBLEMS

1. Continuing Scenario

Ashley's parents, Jim and Shelley, want to assist her in building the business, so in 2009 they signed limited guarantees for the principal sum of $128 000, with interest, at bank prime rate plus 1.5 percent in favour of the Monarch Bank. The guarantees were given to secure a line of credit for Ashley and were provided for (1) a $100 000 term loan with interest at bank prime plus 2.25 percent, and (2) a revolving demand loan for general operating purposes. The revolving loan was not to exceed the principal sum of $125 000, and the lending was subject to an accounts receivable margin requirement. Interest under the revolving loan was at prime plus 1.5 percent per annum. The revolving loan contained a provision under which the bank agreed to apply specified credit balances to repay the loan.

In 2012, Ashley's business seemed to be doing fine so she told her parents she no longer needed their help. Jim and Shelley gave the bank notice in writing that they were ending their liability in accordance with the guarantee. (Their understanding was that this fixed their maximum liability at the amount then outstanding under the loan.) At the time of the notice, their liability under the revolving loan was $95 000.

After receiving the notice, the bank converted the revolving loan into a fixed loan without the knowledge or consent of Jim and Shelley. In 2013, Ashley renegotiated the loan arrangements to comprise (1) a $100 000 term loan with interest at prime plus 2.5

percent, and (2) a fixed operating loan with interest at prime plus 2 percent and with more flexible margin requirements. If Ashley defaults on the loan, will the bank be able to sue Jim and Shelley to enforce the guarantees?

2. Whitehorse Furniture Ltd. took out a fire insurance policy on its premises with Kansafe Insurance Co., with the coverage being arranged through an insurance broker, J&H Ltd. Whitehorse did not inform J&H that it had made a previous substantial claim against another insurance company (for a fire in which arson was suspected) and that there had also been two previous fires at its premises that had caused little or no damage. Consequently, Kansafe was also unaware of those facts.

   A further fire occurred at the Whitehorse premises. When Kansafe learned of the previous fires, it initially denied liability because of the non-disclosure. Whitehorse claimed that it had not thought the earlier fires were relevant. Since J&H had not asked any questions about previous fires or claims, Whitehorse had not mentioned them. Kansafe eventually agreed to settle the Whitehorse claim and made a payment of $550 000, without admitting liability.

   Subsequently, Kansafe brought an action against J&H, alleging that it had been negligent in not making proper inquiries of Whitehorse and in failing to disclose important information when it applied for the insurance coverage on behalf of Whitehorse.

   Should Kansafe succeed against J&H?

3. Perennial Manufacturing Inc. carried on a foundry business in premises leased from Sharbo Investments Ltd. Perennial arranged a contract of fire insurance with the Commonwealth Insurance Co. The insurance covered equipment, business interruption, and the value of the building. At the time when the insurance was arranged, Vandervelde was the controlling shareholder of both Perennial and Sharbo. He subsequently sold his shares in Perennial and no longer had an interest in that corporation.

   The building burned down. Perennial claimed on the insurance policy, and Commonwealth paid out $700 000 for the loss of stock and equipment, business interruption, and extra expenses. It refused to make any payments for the loss of the building on the ground that the building was not owned by Perennial. (It was not insured by Sharbo.)

   Is that a valid defence to the claim?

4. Two years before her death, Desai took out a term life insurance policy for $400 000 on her own life. Her friend, Trumble, was named as beneficiary.

   In her application for the insurance, Desai described her occupation as "business administrator," Trumble was described as her "business associate," and she stated that her net financial worth was $100 000. None of those statements was entirely accurate. Although she had studied business administration, she was then working as an office cleaner. She did not have a business relationship with Trumble, and her net worth was considerably less than $100 000.

   Desai was subsequently murdered by Trumble. Desai's sister claimed on the policy as executrix. The insurance company refused to pay.

   What defences are available to the insurance company?

5. Blackgold Investments Limited required additional financing in order to exploit some apparently attractive opportunities. Its directors decided to assist the company by raising the sum of $500 000 on their own credit. The corporation then applied for a loan with Merchants' Bank, on the terms that a guarantee would be signed jointly by all the directors. The guarantee was on a standard form provided by the bank and included the clause:

   This guarantee shall be binding upon every person signing the same, notwithstanding the non-execution thereof by any other proposed guarantor.

   Four directors signed the guarantee in the office of the bank manager in Calgary. Then it was sent to Edmonton, where four other directors signed it together. They noted the absence at the time of the signature of Fowler, the corporation's president (also a director), and agreed among themselves that they were signing only on the condition that the guarantee would not be delivered to the bank until Fowler had signed as well.

When the guarantee was returned to one of the directors in Calgary, she gave it to the bank manager with instructions that it was not to be treated as having been delivered to the bank as an operative instrument until Fowler had signed. In the end, Fowler refused to do so because he did not want to reduce his own line of credit at the bank. Nevertheless, the bank manager advanced the corporation $500 000, and the corporation gave the bank its promissory note for that amount.

Blackgold subsequently defaulted on the note, and the bank claimed the sum owing from those directors who had signed the guarantee. They refused to pay on the grounds that the guarantee would not operate unless and until all directors had signed. The bank sued them to enforce the guarantee.

Explain whether this action should succeed.

6. Maria owned a policy that insured the life of her husband, Paul, and named her as the beneficiary. Paul also owned two policies, each of which insured his life and named Maria the beneficiary. The couple subsequently separated.

About a year after the separation, Paul died while on a trip to Bolivia. An autopsy revealed a number of condoms filled with cocaine in his digestive tract. One of the bags had burst, causing his death. The circumstances indicated the death was accidental. It was agreed that the husband's ingestion of the cocaine amounted to possession of a narcotic and was a crime under the laws of Bolivia and of Canada.

When Maria wrote to the insurance company, claiming payment under the policies, the company refused to pay on the ground that the claims resulted from a criminal act of the life insured.

Should Maria be entitled to recover?

Additional Resources for Chapter 16 on the Companion Website

(www.pearsoncanada.ca/smyth)

In addition to pre- and post-tests, mini-cases, and application exercises, the Companion Website includes the following province-specific resources for Chapter 16:

- **Alberta:** Crown's Right to Recover Health-Care Costs; Good Faith; Guarantees; Insurance; Alberta Insurance Act; Subrogation
- **Atlantic Provinces:** Insurance Legislation; Subrogation
- **British Columbia:** Health Insurance; Insurance Corporation of British Columbia (ICBC); Motor Vehicle Insurance
- **Manitoba/Saskatchewan:** Insurable Interest in a Life; No-fault Insurance
- **Ontario:** Duty to Disclose; Good Faith; Insurance Legislation; Subrogation

Chapter 17

Agency and Franchising

Two types of contract that allow a business to expand its operations are agency and franchising. The contract of agency has ancient origins, while franchising, by contrast, is a relatively recent phenomenon.

In this chapter we examine the following issues:

- What is agency?

- How is an agency relationship created?

- What are the duties of the agent and the principal?

- What is the extent of the liability of the principal and of the agent to third parties?

- How is an agency relationship terminated?

- What is the legal nature of franchising?

- What are the usual contents of a franchising agreement?

- What are the rights and duties of the parties to a franchising agreement?

DEFINING AGENCY

agent a person acting for another person in contractual relations with third parties

principal the person on whose behalf the agent acts

Agency is a relationship in which one person, known as an **agent**, is authorized by another person for whom she acts, known as a **principal**, to form contracts with third parties on the principal's behalf. The relationship between agent and principal is usually a contractual one, with the agent being paid by the principal. Employment is the obvious example. A person may also act gratuitously as an agent, in which case she is bound by all the duties imposed by agency law.

dependent agent an agent who acts exclusively, or mostly, for a single principal

A distinction is sometimes made between a **dependent agent** and an independent agent. A dependent agent is one who acts exclusively, or mostly, for a single principal. Insurance agents, for example, are usually dependent agents, representing only one insurance company.[1] Agency may be created by the terms of an employment contract in which an employer (as principal) delegates to an employee (as agent) the authority to make contracts. However, the functions of agency and employment may be entirely separate: an agent need not be an employee, just as not all employees are agents. Sometimes it is difficult to determine whether an agent is an employee; usually, a self-employed agent is compensated solely by commissions and does not receive any salary, but that is not always conclusive. The distinction is important in employment law and is discussed further in Chapter 18; it is also important for income tax purposes.

independent agent an agent who carries on an independent business and acts for a number of principals

commission agent one who sells on behalf of a principal to third parties and receives compensation through commissions

An **independent agent** is not an employee and usually acts on behalf of several principals or clients. Lawyers frequently act as agents for their clients in the settlement of lawsuits. Stockbrokers are agents for clients who place orders with them to buy or sell shares. Auctioneers have authority to sell goods for their principals. A person may be a **commission agent**—that is, one who sells on behalf of a principal to third parties and receives compensation through commissions on those sales.

In the words of the Supreme Court of Canada, "Society today simply could not function without the services of agents."[2] A corporation, as an entirely artificial "person," can enter into contractual relations only when its officers and employees act as agents on its behalf. In partnerships too, agency plays an important role. Each partner is presumed by law to be an agent of the other partners, with very wide authority to act on behalf of the firm. Sometimes the term "agent" is used in a general sense to mean "representative." The so-called real estate agent does not have authority to sell the property of a client—instead her role is to introduce prospective purchasers, and the client contracts directly with the purchaser. Without the power to contract, a representative is not an agent in the legal sense.

CREATION OF AN AGENCY RELATIONSHIP

Any person who has the capacity to contract may appoint an agent to contract on his behalf. An agent's power to contract on behalf of her principal is limited to the capacity that the principal possesses. If a minor appoints an agent, the contracts made for him by the agent are as voidable as if he had made them personally. However, a minor may act as an agent and bind her principal in contracts with third parties, even where she would not bind herself.

agency agreement the agreement between principal and agent whereby the agent undertakes to act on behalf of the principal

In the law of principal and agent, there are two contractual relationships: first, the relationship between principal and agent, usually expressed in the form of an **agency agreement**, and second, the relationship between the principal and third parties with whom the agent makes contracts on the principal's behalf (see Figure 17.1).

---

[1] See Chapter 16 on insurance.

[2] *R. v. Kelly*, [1992] S.C.J. No. 53 at para. 26, (1992), 92 D.L.R. (4th) 643 (S.C.C.).

Figure 17.1   Agency Relationships

By Agreement

The easiest way to create an agency relationship is by agreement. An agency agreement may be express or implied, oral, written, or in writing under seal. If an agency agreement is to extend beyond one year, it must be in writing to be enforceable in those provinces where the relevant section of the Statute of Frauds continues to apply.[3]

The agreement should clearly define the limits of the agent's authority: how far she can go in making a contract with a third party without obtaining further instructions from the principal. An agency agreement may confer on an agent a very wide and general authority to make contracts, or her authority may be narrowly restricted to making a specific contract.

An agent should always have authorization in writing if she wishes to issue promissory notes or draw cheques in the name of her principal, and she should sign them in a way that makes it clear that she is acting in a representative capacity; otherwise she may be personally liable for the promise.[4]

A **power of attorney** is a special type of express agency agreement.[5] Normally, a power of attorney is issued under seal, since an agent who does not receive authority under seal cannot be authorized to sign documents under seal on behalf of the principal.

power of attorney   a type of agency agreement authorizing the agent to sign documents on behalf of the principal

Other Ways to Create an Agency Relationship

An agency relationship may be implied through the conduct of the principal and the agent. Consent to act as an agent is not usually hard to find if the agent has negotiated a contract with the third party. The more difficult question is whether the conduct of the principal was sufficient to create the agency relationship. If the principal has allowed the agent to act like his agent in dealings with third parties, agency will be implied. This is an application of the estoppel principle—when someone allows another to believe something, he cannot later deny it. In these circumstances, agency is created by estoppel.

Agency may also be created retroactively. If an unauthorized agent negotiates a contract with a third party on another's behalf, that person may subsequently approve the agent's

---

[3] The absence of a written agreement does not prevent a third party from asserting the existence of an agency relationship.

[4] See Bills of Exchange Act, R.S.C. 1985, c. B-4, s. 51(1).

[5] See The Power of Attorney Act, R.S.B.C. 1996, c. 370; The Powers of Attorney Act, 2002, S.S. 2002, c. P20.3; The Power of Attorney and Mental Health Amendment Act, C.C.S.M. 1996, c. P97; The Substitute Decisions Act, 1992, S.O. 1992, c. 30.

behaviour and adopt or ratify the contract as his own. In this case, agency is created by ratification. These concepts (ratification and estoppel) are considered again later in this chapter under "The Authority of the Agent." Often, a principal admits that an agency relationship exists, but still disputes his liability to a third party because the agent exceeded the power or authority he was given. Again, the behaviour of the principal may be used to imply authority in the agent.

DUTIES OWED BY AN AGENT TO THE PRINCIPAL

Duty to Comply with the Agency Agreement

The duties of an agent are determined by the terms—express and implied—of the agreement with the principal. A number of rights and duties, for both agent and principal, are implied by custom as terms of the agency agreement. Any of these implied terms may, of course, be incorporated expressly in the agency agreement or may be excluded by an express term. The breach of any term, whether express or implied, gives the aggrieved party the usual remedies against the other for breach of contract. For example, an agent may have private instructions restricting her authority; if she exceeds that authority and the principal suffers damage, the principal will be able to recover from the agent any loss that results from her breach of duty.

Duty of Care

An agent owes a duty of care to her principal, even when she acts without payment. The degree of skill that the principal can expect depends upon the nature of the agent's task and her apparent competence for the purpose.

The courts generally regard notice to an agent as being the equivalent of notice to her principal. An agent therefore has a duty to be diligent in keeping her principal informed about all important developments affecting their relationship.

Personal Performance

Because of the high degree of confidence and trust implicit in an agency relationship, the general rule is that an agent cannot delegate her duties without the principal's agreement. An agent's usual responsibilities include the exercise of her judgment, skill, and discretion on the principal's behalf.

However, there are some circumstances where the nature of the agency relationship or trade usage will give the agent an implied authority to delegate all or part of her duties. For example, when a bank acts as agent for its customers, it may sometimes require the services of other banks to represent it in countries where it has no branches itself. When a corporation is appointed as an agent, it can only perform through sub-agents, namely, its directors or employees.

When an agent has implied authority to perform through a sub-agent, there is generally privity of contract between only the principal and the agent. The principal has no claim for breach of contract against the sub-agent. The agent must in turn recover from the sub-agent.

Good Faith

An agent owes a fiduciary duty to the principal.[6] This duty of good faith requires that an agent be loyal, act in the best interests of the principal, and keep the principal fully

---

[6] *R. v. Kelly, supra,* n. 2, at para 33. See Gerald Fridman, *Canadian Agency Law* (Markham: LexisNexis, 2009) at 106–21. Fridman notes that there are exceptions to this rule: see, for example, *Knoch Estate v. Jon Picken Ltd.,* [1991] O.J. No. 1394 (Ont. C.A.). The duty may be varied by the terms of the agency contract: *Kelly v. Cooper,* [1993] A.C. 205.

informed. If she has been authorized to buy property at a certain price and learns that it can be obtained more cheaply, she is bound to inform the principal. If she buys at the lower price, she must pass on the savings to the principal, rather than make a secret profit for herself.[7]

Money that comes into an agent's possession in respect of contracts made for the principal belongs to the principal, although the agent may be entitled to withhold amounts due to her as commission. She should keep separate records so that she can account to the principal for money received. An agent who fails to keep proper accounts may be liable to her principal for any unexplained shortfalls.[8]

In most circumstances, an agent will not be acting in good faith when she serves two principals in the same transaction without their knowledge and consent. This is allowed only if they are both aware of the arrangement and have consented to it. However, the practice is still discouraged. The two principals will normally have conflicting interests, as each will want to get the best possible bargain. By considering both their interests, the agent places herself in a conflict of interest.

In *Andrews v. Ramsay*,[9] a real estate agent agreed to assist in selling property on a commission basis. Subsequently, the agent accepted a commission from the purchaser. The court held that he was liable to his principal not only for the return of his regular selling commission but also for the commission he received from the third party. In *Salomons v. Pender*,[10] a real estate agent arranged a sale of land for the owner to a corporation of which the agent was a director and shareholder. The court held that he was not entitled to a commission because he also had an interest in the business of the other contracting party.

An agent also has a conflict of interest if she enters into a contract on her own behalf with the principal, without his knowledge and approval—for example, buying property from or selling property to the principal.

CASE 17.1

A solicitor agreed to sell property for a client and then decided that he would like to own it himself. He bought it ostensibly in the name of someone else. The court held that the solicitor could not enforce the purchase.[11]

Under the Criminal Code, it is a criminal offence for an agent to corruptly demand or accept any remuneration from a third party in the conduct of her principal's business affairs.[12] The third party that offers such a bribe or kickback is also criminally liable.

DUTIES OWED BY THE PRINCIPAL TO THE AGENT

A principal does not owe a fiduciary duty to the agent. (For more information on this topic, see the Companion Website.) Where the agency is created by contract, the principal's duties will be set out in the contract. For other agencies, the law imposes only two duties on a principal:

- the duty to compensate the agent for his or her effort (by commission or otherwise)
- the duty to pay the agent's expenses and compensate for losses

---

[7] *McCullough v. Teniglia* (1999), 40 B.L.R. (2d) 222, aff'd [1999] O.J. No. 4401 (QL).

[8] See *Killoran v. RMO Site Management Inc.* (1997), 33 B.L.R. (2d) 240.

[9] [1903] 2 K.B. 635.

[10] (1865), 195 E.R. 682.

[11] *McPherson v. Watt* (1877), 3 App. Cas. 254. See also *Aaron Acceptance Corp. v. Adam* (1987), 37 D.L.R. (4th) 133.

[12] R.S.C. 1985, c. C-46, s. 426 (1). See also *R. v. Kelly, supra*, n. 2.

Usually an agency agreement sets out how an agent's fee or commission is to be determined. In the absence of an express term, an agent is entitled to a reasonable fee—another example of quantum meruit. A term may be implied into the contract prohibiting the principal from acting in a way that interferes with the agent's ability to earn commission.[13]

A listing agreement between a prospective seller and a real estate agent frequently states that the agent is entitled to commission when she introduces to the seller a prospective purchaser who is "ready, willing, and able to purchase." The fact that the sale is not completed by reason of the purchaser's refusal to perform will not deprive the agent of this right.[14] Some listing agreements require commission to be paid if the vendor accepts an offer during the term of the listing. Again, completion of the sale is not necessary. A prospective seller should insist that the listing agreement contain a term that the agent is not entitled to commission unless and until a sale is completed.

Some provinces have statutes rendering a contract to pay commission to a real estate agent unenforceable unless it is in writing and signed by the prospective seller of the property. In these provinces, when an agreement for an agent's services is entirely oral, the agent does not acquire an enforceable right, even though she may have introduced a willing and able purchaser to the client.[15]

Even if an agency agreement does not say so directly, there is an implied term that the principal will reimburse the agent for all reasonable expenses incurred when acting within the scope of her authority. An agent should consequently keep proper accounts and records to substantiate her claim. The principal is under no obligation to reimburse an agent for unauthorized acts unless he ratifies them.

Ethical Issue   Insurance Broker Compensation

Independent insurance brokers offer insurance products from a number of different insurance companies. They are often considered agents of the insured and owe the insured a duty of good faith. However, they are paid by the insurance companies. A potential conflict of interest arises for two reasons:

- not all insurance companies pay the same percentage of commission
- some companies pay an additional amount of "contingent commission" based on the overall business placed with the company

It is possible that an unethical insurance broker may recommend a particular product in order to maximize his own commission, rather than considering the best interests of the consumer. The Code of Conduct governing Ontario insurance brokers requires a broker to disclose any real or potential conflict of interest associated with the transaction and not to charge or accept a commission that is not fully disclosed to the consumer. The Insurance Brokers Association established a protocol for disclosure of commission. The disclosure sheet shows the range of commission paid by every insurance company carried by the broker and identifies whether contingent commission is paid.

Questions to Consider

1. Is disclosure a satisfactory solution for this conflict of interest?

2. What other measures would you recommend?

Sources: Insurance Broker Commission Disclosure, Insurance Brokers Association of Ontario, http://public.ibao.vaultso lutions.com/sf-docs/default-document-library/point_or_sale _protociol.pdf?sfvrsn=0; Registered Insurance Brokers Act, R.S.O. 1990, Reg. 991, s. 14 (7.1), (8).

---

[13] *Pure Energy Marketing Ltd. v. Ramarro Resources Inc.*, [2003] A.J. No. 1105.

[14] *Columbia Caterers & Sherlock Co. v. Famous Restaurants Ltd.* (1956), 4 D.L.R. (2d) 601.

[15] See, for example, Real Estate Act, R.S.A. 2000, c. R-5, s. 22; Real Estate Trading Act, S.N.S. 1996, c. 28, s. 26. But see Real Estate and Business Brokers Act 2002, S.O. 2002, c. 30, Sch. C 3, ss. 33 (3), 36 and O. Reg 567/05, s. 1, suggesting that representation agreements may be oral and may not even specify the commission charged.

THE AUTHORITY OF THE AGENT

The whole purpose of the agency relationship is to allow one person (the agent) to form, on behalf of a second person (the principal), a contract with a third person (the third party). Whether, in fact, a contract comes into existence depends not only upon the existence of an agency relationship but also upon the authority that the agent possesses. As with the agency relationship itself, an agent's authority may be either actual or apparent.

Actual Authority

Actual authority may, in turn, be either express or implied. Express authority is the authority given orally or in writing by the principal. It may be set out in the agency agreement or might be given subsequently in separate instructions.

actual authority the authority given expressly or impliedly to the agent by the principal

A contract of agency, like any other contract, frequently contains implied terms; these terms may supplement the express authority in the contract. When a principal expressly authorizes an agent to make a purchase of, say, Italian wine from Tuscany, the agent would also have implied authority to make a contract for shipment of the goods to Canada.

Authority may be implied by commercial usage or by conduct. For example, if a person is appointed as an insurance agent, it is implied that she possesses the usual authority for such an agent, except to the extent that the usual authority is expressly restricted. In the same way, a person appointed as company secretary will have all the usual authority of a company secretary, in the absence of express limitations.[16] Actual authority may also be inferred from the conduct of the parties. If an agent purchases goods for the principal without having express authority to do so, the question of whether she had an implied authority to do so might arise. But if the principal pays for the goods without complaining, that act may amount to an implied authority to act in the same way in the future.

Apparent Authority

In most cases, a third party will not have any knowledge of the contents of the agency agreement, or of any special restrictions upon an agent's authority. The third party can only rely upon the **apparent authority** of the agent—that is, the authority that the third party is entitled to assume the agent possesses. Consequently, agency law provides that a contract is valid and enforceable, even when the agent had no actual authority to enter into it—if she had the apparent authority to do so. However, as we have already noted, by acting beyond the limits of her authority, the agent has breached her duty to the principal and is liable to compensate him for any loss suffered as a result.

apparent authority the authority that a third party is entitled to assume that the agent possesses

Like actual authority, apparent authority can arise in two ways: by commercial usage and by conduct (holding out).

Usual Authority An agent has the apparent authority to act in the manner that is usual for that type of agent in that type of business, unless the third party knows, or ought to know, of any restriction upon that authority. As far as the third party is concerned, apparent authority is frequently the same as actual, implied authority; but if there is a restriction on the agent's usual authority, of which the third party is unaware, the agent will possess apparent authority but not actual authority.

---

[16] *Panorama Developments (Guildford) Ltd. v. Fidelis Furnishing Fabrics Ltd.*, [1971] 2 Q.B. 711.

Garrod and Parkin entered into a partnership to run a car repair business. Parkin was to be the active partner; Garrod provided most of the financing. When the partnership agreement was drawn up, Garrod insisted that an express provision be included that the business of the firm should not include the buying or selling of cars. Parkin later sold a car belonging to a customer who had left it with the firm for repairs, without the knowledge of the owner, and disappeared with the proceeds. The car was later recovered by the owner, and the purchaser, who had innocently bought the car from Parkin, brought an action against Garrod (for breach of the implied condition in the contract of sale that the seller has title). The court ruled that, in selling the car, Parkin was acting as agent for Garrod since, in partnership law, each partner is an agent for the other partners. Parkin had no actual authority to sell the car because of the express provision in the partnership agreement, but he did have apparent authority. Selling used cars is a common part of the car repair business.[17]

Of course, if the third party is aware of a restriction on the usual authority of such an agent, or ought to be aware because there are suspicious circumstances, then the third party cannot claim that there is an apparent authority.[18] If the proposed contract is not within an area ordinarily entrusted to such agents, or if its consequences are of unusual importance for the principal and the third party, the third party should first check with the principal about the agent's authority. For example, an agent does not usually have authority to borrow money in the principal's name or to commit the principal to new lines of activity. An agent who is authorized to sell goods is not necessarily authorized to accept the purchase money, particularly where payment to the agent is not customary trade practice or where the principal has sent an invoice to the third party requesting payment. If the third party pays the money to the agent and the agent absconds, the third party may have to pay the money again to the principal.[19]

Holding Out   Even when an act or contract falls outside the usual authority of a particular agent, the agent may still possess apparent authority because she has been represented by the principal as having that authority. The principal may be estopped (prevented) from denying liability on a contract with a third party because of conduct known as **holding out**: when a principal acts in a way that suggests agency. The behaviour may be by words or conduct, and includes such things as honouring similar contracts made for it by that person in the past. If the behaviour may be reasonably interpreted by the third party as consistent with the agent having authority, the principal cannot deny the authority of the agent.[20]

holding out   representing by words or conduct that a person is one's agent or has a particular authority

A has a contract with P, a retailer of women's fashion accessories, to act as P's purchasing agent in western Canada. The agency contract expressly provides that A may not enter into contracts in excess of $25 000 without first obtaining P's approval. On a number of previous occasions, A negotiated the purchase of quantities of costume jewellery from X, for prices varying between $10 000 and $20 000. Recently, A placed an order with X for goods at a price of $40 000, without consulting P. X did not question the order, and two weeks later received payment from P, as usual. P reprimanded A, reminded her of the $25 000 limit, and told her not to exceed that limit again without approval. Despite that warning A placed another order with X, this time for $30 000. P refused to pay and demanded that X take the goods back.

>

---

[17] *Mercantile Credit Co. Ltd. v. Garrod*, [1962] 3 All E.R. 1103. See also *Financial Management Inc. v. Associated Financial Planners Ltd.* (2006), 56 Alta. L.R. (4th) 207 (Alta. C.A.).

[18] *32262 B.C. Ltd. v. 411676 Alberta Ltd.* (1995), 29 Alta. L.R. (3d) 415 (Alta. Q.B.).

[19] *Butwick v. Grant*, [1924] 2 K.B. 483.

[20] *Doiron v. Devon Capital Corp.* (2003), 232 D.L.R. (4th) 732 (Alta C.A.). But see *McRae Management Ltd. v. Breezy Properties Ltd.* (2008), 74 R.P.R. (4th) 50 (B.C.S.C.).

A clearly did not have actual authority to enter into either contract. In the case of the first ($40 000) contract, P might have been able to argue successfully that, because of the unusually large amount, A did not have apparent authority either. But in the case of the second ($30 000) contract, A almost certainly did have apparent authority. By paying X on the first occasion, without mentioning the fact that A had exceeded her limit, P had held A out as having authority, at least up to $40 000.

Holding out may also occur when an agency agreement ends. If an agent continues to enter into contracts for the principal after the agency has ended, and third parties have had no notice of the termination, the principal is bound by the contracts. This is of practical importance when a partner retires from a partnership firm, since partners customarily act as agents for the partnership in contracts with outside parties such as suppliers.

For more information on this topic, see the Companion Website.

CHECKLIST

An Agent's Authority

An agent's authority may be

- actual, or
- apparent.

Actual authority may be

- express, or
- implied from (1) commercial usage or (2) conduct.

Even when an agent does not have actual authority, she may have apparent authority, derived from

- commercial usage (usual authority), or
- holding out.

Ratification

Sometimes a person purports to act as an agent, knowing she has no authority but hoping that the proposed principal will later adopt the contract. Subsequent adoption by the principal is called **ratification**. The need for ratification may arise either because the person purporting to act as agent is not one or because she has only a limited authority and has exceeded it.

ratification subsequent adoption by the proposed principal of a contract made by an agent acting without authority

When a principal ratifies, the effect is to establish the contract with the third party retroactively, as if the agent had possessed actual authority at the time she made the contract. The principal, agent, and third party are then in the same position regarding the contract as if the agency relationship had existed from the beginning.

A named principal need not state his ratification expressly. It may be implied from the fact of his assuming the benefits of the contract, or perhaps even from failing to notify the third party of the absence of authority when it is discovered.[21] Ratification cannot be partial: A principal cannot accept the benefits without also reimbursing the agent for her costs. He cannot ratify only those aspects of the transaction that prove to be to his advantage but refuse to ratify the balance of the contract. A principal must also ratify within a reasonable time to be able to claim the benefit of a contract.[22]

---

[21] *Community Savings Credit Union v. United Assn. of Journeymen and Apprentices of the Plumbing and Pipefitting Industry*, [2002] B.C.J. No. 654.

[22] *Metropolitan Asylums Board Managers v. Kingham & Sons* (1890), 6 T.L.R. 217.

Not all contracts made by an agent without authority may be ratified by the principal; a principal may not be able to ratify a contract made for him if, at the time the contract was made, he would have been unable to enter into the contract himself.

ILLUSTRATION 17.2

A arranges on behalf of P, but without P's authority, to insure P's buildings against fire damage. The buildings burn down, and P then purports to ratify the contract of insurance. The ratification is not effective because at the time P attempts to ratify, the buildings are already destroyed, and it is too late for P to insure them.[23]

ILLUSTRATION 17.3

A, without authority from P, purports to accept T's offer to sell a large quantity of canned goods to P. Before the delivery date, T learns that A had no authority. Because the market is uncertain, T is unwilling to wait for P's ratification and makes a contract to sell the same goods to X. Ratification by P will now be ineffective because X has acquired rights to the goods.

Again, a principal cannot ratify when the rights of an outsider are affected, and must ratify within a reasonable time.

Finally, a principal cannot ratify if, at the time the agent made the contract, the agent failed to name the intended principal or at least mention the existence of a principal whose identity could then be ascertained. An undisclosed principal cannot afterward ratify a contract made without his authority.

When an agent purports to accept an offer "subject to the ratification of my principal," the later ratification will not be retroactive. This exception is simply an application of the rules of offer and acceptance: A conditional acceptance by an agent is not acceptance at all. The offeror may revoke the offer at any time before acceptance. In these circumstances, the eventual "ratification" of the principal is really only an acceptance of the original offer.

CHECKLIST

Ratification

An agent's contract with a third party may be ratified

- expressly or impliedly;
- within a reasonable time;
- by a named principal;
- if the rights of an outsider are not affected; and
- if, at the time of creation and ratification, the principal was capable of making the contract.

RIGHTS AND LIABILITY OF PRINCIPAL AND AGENT

When an agent makes a contract with a third party on behalf of her principal, who is liable on the contract—the agent or the principal? The answer should be "the principal," but it depends upon a number of factors: Was the agent acting within the scope of her authority

---

[23] See *Portavon Cinema Co. Ltd. v. Price and Century Insurance Co. Ltd.*, [1939] 4 All E.R. 601 at 607.

in making the contract? Was the identity or existence of the principal disclosed to the other party? There are three possible outcomes:

- The principal alone is liable on the contract.
- The agent alone is liable.
- Either the principal or the agent may be held liable.

The Principal Alone Is Liable on the Contract

An agent is not liable on contracts made for her principal when the agency relationship is functioning properly. After creating the contract, the principal is liable for performance and is the one able to enforce it against the third party. Further, an agent has no liability to the third party even when she acts outside her real authority, so long as she acts within her apparent authority. She may be liable to the principal for breach of the agency agreement.

To ensure that she has no liability in contracts made for her principal, an agent should indicate that she acts as agent and should identify the principal. The following are examples of signatures that accomplish this purpose:

"The Smith Corporation Limited, per W.A. Jones"

"W.A. Jones, for The Smith Corporation Limited"

Sometimes, an agent may persuade a third party to enter into a contract with her principal, without disclosing the exact identity of the principal. She may describe herself as agent for a party that does not want to reveal his name. For example, an agent may negotiate in this way in order to obtain options for the purchase of individual pieces of land intended for assembly into a large block. The reasoning is that if the prospective purchaser is a large developer, the disclosure of his identity and purpose might induce some owners to hold out for much higher prices. In this situation, although the principal was not named in the contract, it was nevertheless made on his behalf and with his authority, and he alone is liable on, and entitled to enforce, the contract. The third party has no rights against the agent.[24]

The Agent Alone Is Liable on the Contract

When an agent contracts on terms that she is the real contracting party, though she is in reality acting or intending to act for an undisclosed principal, the agent alone has rights and liabilities relative to the third party. The principal can neither sue nor be sued on the contract. In the next section we look at what happens if the existence of a principal is discovered by the third party after contracting with the agent personally.[25]

Either the Principal or the Agent May Be Held Liable on the Contract

Sometimes a person who is an agent does not mention her status and deals with a third party without making it apparent that she is acting as an agent. In that case, the third party is entitled to sue the agent on the contract. That is fair, since the third party may have been influenced by the personal credit and character of the agent. What are the third party's rights if and when it discovers the existence and identity of the principal? If the contract was one that the agent had authority to make, the third party has the option of holding either principal or agent liable for performance of the contract, but not both. If the third

---

[24] See *QNS Paper Co. v. Chartwell Shipping Ltd.* (1989), 62 D.L.R. (4th) 36; *Lang Transport Ltd. v. Plus Factor International Trucking Ltd.* (1997), 143 D.L.R. (4th) 672.

[25] *Jade West Holdings Ltd. v. Canada Zau Fu Trade Ltd.*, 2002 BCSC 420.

party sues and obtains judgment against the agent before it learns of the real principal, it has no rights against the principal.[26] If, however, the fact of agency becomes known before judgment, the action may be discontinued and fresh proceedings taken against the principal.

Rights of the Undisclosed Principal Can an undisclosed principal enforce a contract made on his behalf and with his authority? Generally, the answer is yes; he may normally intervene and enforce the contract against the other party.[27]

To succeed, an undisclosed principal must show that the contract was made with his authority. If the agent had no real authority, the undisclosed principal cannot ratify the contract and enforce it. If he were allowed to do so, he would be in a position to choose whether to be bound by the contract. Nor can the third party hold the principal liable in such a case. See Figure 17.2 to compare contractual liability in various agency situations.

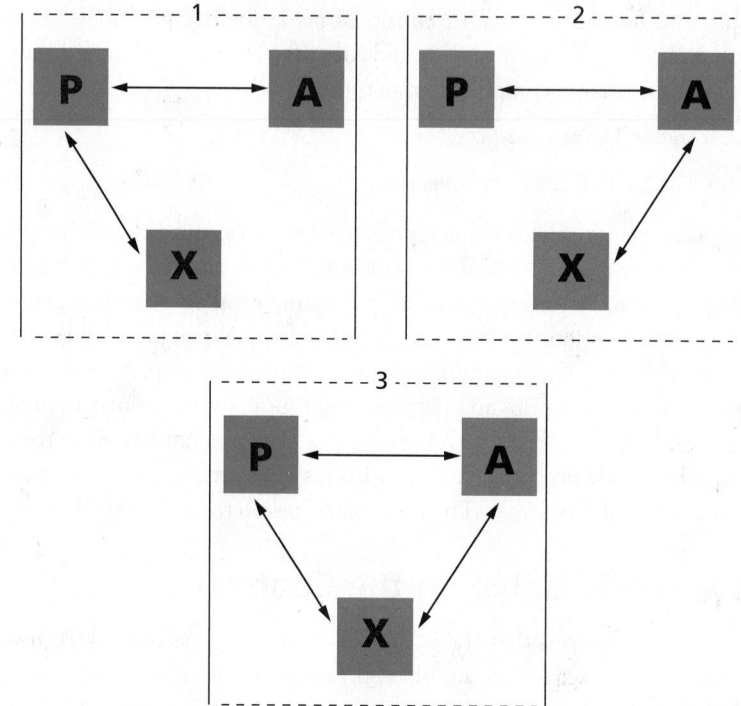

Figure 17.2   Liability on Agency Contract

In the most common situation (1), an agency contract exists between the principal (P) and the agent (A). A, acting within her authority, actual or apparent, negotiates a contract with a third person (X). That contract is legally formed between P and X. In case (2), A describes herself as principal and does not disclose the existence of P. The result is that the contract is between A and X. In case (3), A says nothing about her status as agent. X is entitled to assume that A was acting on her own account and can sue A. But if A was in fact acting on behalf of P, X can choose to sue P instead.

CASE 17.3

A Co. was a management company controlled by the owner of a shopping mall. It entered into a contract to rent an electronic sign from T for use in the shopping mall. Later, P Co. bought the mall; A Co. continued to manage the mall

>

---

[26] *Kendall v. Hamilton* (1879), 4 App. Cas. 504.

[27] A major exception to this rule are contracts that are essentially personal in nature: *Collins v. Associated Greyhound Racecourses*, [1930] 1 Ch. 1.

as its agent. T was unaware of the change of ownership. No mention of P Co.'s ownership was made when T and A Co. renewed the sign rental contract. P Co. refused to honour the contract and was sued by T. The British Columbia Court of Appeal held that P Co., the undisclosed principal, was not liable on the contract. The agent had no authority, and the plaintiff had no knowledge of the principal's existence. The plaintiff's right of recovery was limited to A Co.[28]

Liability for Torts

When an agent commits fraudulent misrepresentation in making a contract, even though the principal did not authorize the misrepresentation or had forbidden it, the third party may rescind the contract, just as if the principal had made the misrepresentation himself. If the agent was acting within her apparent authority, the third party may sue the principal as well as the agent for the tort of deceit.[29] An agent may be similarly liable to a third party for negligent misrepresentation. For example, Canadian courts have held that a real estate agent, though engaged and paid by the vendor, also owes a duty of care in the statements she makes to the purchaser.[30]

More generally, a principal is vicariously liable for torts committed by his agent while acting within the scope of her actual or apparent authority. This is so whether the agent is an employee or an independent contractor.[31] As we saw in Chapter 3, the actual tortfeasor (in this case, the agent) remains liable for her torts, even though the principal is liable as well. For more information on this topic, see the Companion Website.

CASE 17.4

D was an agent for an insurance company, contracted to sell annuities. He persuaded W to buy an annuity, and W paid the purchase money by cheque, made out to D. D did not purchase the annuity and instead ran off with the money. W sued the insurance company for return of the money he had paid.

The court held that the insurance company was liable because (1) D received the money as their agent, acting within the scope of his authority to sell annuities; (2) D committed the tort of deceit, and although he was a self-employed contractor, the company was vicariously liable since D was acting within the scope of his contract; and (3) the company was directly liable for its own negligence in hiring D and putting him in a position of trust, because it was known that D had a history of improper dealings.[32]

Breach of Warranty of Authority

There is no contract when a person holds herself out to be an agent but has no authority, actual or apparent, and the named principal does not ratify. The situation may arise because the alleged agent has acted fraudulently; for example, she may give the name of a reputable party as principal in order to obtain goods on credit. The seller will have an action in tort for deceit against the fraudulent agent, though the action may not be worth pursuing. An action in tort will also lie where an agent makes a negligent misrepresentation that she has authority that she does not possess.[33]

---

[28] *Sign-O-Lite Plastics Ltd. v. Metropolitan Life Insurance Co.* (1990), 49 B.C.L.R. (2d) 183.

[29] *Lloyd v. Grace, Smith & Co. Ltd.*, [1912] A.C. 716. If the principal was innocent of the fraud, he may in turn sue the agent for damages to compensate for the loss.

[30] See *Avery v. Salie* (1972), 25 D.L.R. (3d) 495; *Krawchuk v. Scherbak* 2011 ONCA 352

[31] *Thiessen v. Mutual Life Assurance Co. of Canada* (2002), 219 D.L.R. (4th) 98. See also *Straus Estate v. Decaire*, [2011] O.J. No. 737 at paras. 48–56 (Ont. S.C.) (QL) aff'd 2012 ONCA 918.

[32] *Wilson v. Clarica Life Insurance Co.*, [2002] B.C.J. No. 292.

[33] *Attis v. Ontario*, 2011 ONCA 675 at para 18.

Breach of warranty of authority occurs when an agent creates the impression of agency when none exists.[34] An agent may innocently act without authority when she mistakenly believes she has the necessary authority, or, unknown to her, her principal has become bankrupt or insane or has died. No contract between a third party and the principal can be formed after the principal has lost contractual capacity or has ceased to exist. And no contract is formed between the agent and the third party either, because there was no intention that the agent should be a party to the contract. In such a case, however, the third party may bring an action against the agent for breach of **warranty of authority**.

warranty of authority a person who purports to act as agent represents that she has authority to contract on behalf of the principal

An agent may be liable if she acts expecting ratification by the principal that never occurs or if she contracts on behalf of a non-existent principal. These are examples of breach of warranty of authority. The damages will be the amount necessary to put the other party in the position in which he would have been had the representation been true.[35]

CASE 17.5

The plaintiff owned shares in a corporation of which he was the treasurer. He was dismissed from that position and, in the course of negotiations, the defendant, a solicitor, purportedly acting on behalf of the majority shareholders, made an offer to buy out the plaintiff's shares. The solicitor did not have authority to make the offer, and the majority shareholders refused to go through with the purchase. In the meantime, the shares were de-listed and became worthless.

The solicitor was held to be in breach of warranty of authority, and the plaintiff was entitled to damages representing his loss of bargain—namely, the difference between the price offered and their new value, which was zero.[36]

For more information on this topic, see the Companion Website.

TERMINATING AN AGENCY RELATIONSHIP

An agent's authority may be terminated on any of the following occasions:

- at the end of a time specified in the agency agreement
- at the completion of the particular project for which the agency was formed
- on notice by either the principal or the agent that he or she wishes to end the agency
- on the death or insanity of either the principal or the agent
- on the bankruptcy of the principal
- on an event that makes performance of the agency agreement impossible

Where no specific time is fixed for an agency relationship, it is implied that either party may end the relationship by giving reasonable notice to the other. If, however, the agreement is for a specified time, early withdrawal by either principal or agent without the consent of the other constitutes a breach of contract.

When an agency ends for any reason other than the bankruptcy, death, or insanity of the principal, the principal should bring the termination to the attention of all third parties likely to be affected. This precaution is especially important when a partnership is dissolved and will be discussed in Chapter 24.

---

[34] *Alvin's Auto Service Ltd. v. Clew Holdings Ltd.*, [1997] S.J. No. 387.

[35] *Attis, supra* n. 33, at para 19-20; *Delta Construction Co. Ltd. v. Lidstone* (1979), 96 D.L.R. (3d) 457.

[36] *Salter v. Cormie* (1993), 108 D.L.R. (4th) 372 (Alta. C.A.).

FRANCHISING

At first glance, agency and franchising appear to have much in common. Both are methods that permit a business to expand rapidly. In both, the proprietor of the original business—the principal or the franchisor—employs the assistance of other persons or business entities to reach out to a wider public. Independent agents market the principal's products, just as franchisees market the franchisor's products. In law, however, there are important differences between the two relationships. Franchisees are not in an agency relationship with the franchisor.

The Nature of Franchising

Canada has the second largest franchise industry in the world, behind the United States.[37] Franchises account for close to 50 percent of all retail sales in Canada. When people are asked about franchising, most think of fast food, yet franchising has become common in many sectors—from hotels and restaurants to office supplies, real estate agencies, and video stores.

Despite its economic importance, there is remarkably little "law" on the subject in Canada. In many provinces, the law applicable to franchising must be found in the general principles of contract and tort law and more specific areas of law, such as consumer protection and intellectual property law.[38]

In a franchising relationship, one party, the franchisor, grants a licence to the other party, the franchisee, to sell its product and use its name and trademark in return for payment of a franchise fee. However, a franchise normally amounts to considerably more than the mere granting of a licence. It involves a substantial degree of control by the franchisor over the franchisee's business. The franchisee, nevertheless, operates as an independent business and is not simply an employee or agent of the franchisor. It does not sell or contract "on behalf" of the franchisor. As described by one judge:

> [F]ranchising promises to provide the independent merchant with the means to become an efficient and effective competitor of large integrated firms. Through various forms of franchising, the manufacturer is assured qualified and effective outlets for his products, and the franchisee enjoys backing in the form of know-how and financial assistance.[39]

When it operates well, franchising provides benefits to both the franchisor and the franchisee. However, to quote from a 2001 judgment:

> To say that franchising is a risky business is, if anything, an understatement.[40]

In theory, franchises offer the investor an opportunity to reduce the risk of business failure by providing a proven business concept, and it is true that franchises tend to fail less frequently than independent businesses that are started from scratch. But franchising is not a guarantee of success, and potential investors need to do their homework carefully.

Contents of a Franchising Agreement

A franchise is created when the franchisor and franchisee enter into a contract, referred to as the **franchise agreement**. Since the franchisor normally makes a substantial number of such agreements—Subway has more than 20 000 franchises worldwide, including more than 2000

franchise agreement an agreement under which a franchisor grants to the franchisee a right to market the franchisor's products

---

[37] For statistics on franchising, see http://www.franchiselink.ca/canadian-franchise-faqs/canadian-franchise-statistics-info/

[38] Legislation governing franchising has been adopted in Alberta, Ontario, Prince Edward Island, and New Brunswick, and is discussed in the last part of this chapter.

[39] Stewart, J., of the U.S. Supreme Court, in *United States v. Arnold, Schwinn & Co.*, 388 U.S. 365 at 386 (dissenting opinion) (1967).

[40] *Country Style Food Services Inc. v. Hotoyan*, [2001] O.J. No. 2889, per Dilks, J.

in Canada alone—whereas the franchisee normally enters into only one such agreement, the agreement is usually the franchisor's standard form contract, often accompanied by an operating manual for the franchisee. Typically, the agreement will deal with the following subjects.

Consideration Provided by the Franchisor

The essential feature of the agreement is the grant to the franchisee of a right, or licence, to market goods or services supplied by or made to specifications provided by the franchisor. The agreement further allows the franchisee to use trademarks, trade names, logos, secret processes, and so on that belong to the franchisor.

While the above features are also found in simple licensing agreements, a franchise agreement goes further. It normally provides for training the franchisee in the operation of the business, and for ongoing supervision, assistance, and management services. The franchisor frequently assists in the design of the business premises—usually to a standard design—and in establishing accounting, inventory control, and purchasing systems. It is also common for the franchisor to provide financial assistance to the franchisor through loans or guarantees.

Franchising lets independent entrepreneurs take advantage of well-known and widely recognized trade names and reputations. The franchisor usually undertakes to provide advertising and promotion on a national or regional scale.

Consideration Provided by the Franchisee

For its part, the franchisee is required to provide an initial contribution of capital. The size of the contribution varies widely, according to whether premises and equipment are purchased (and perhaps custom built) or leased from the franchisor or from some other person. Additionally, the franchisee agrees to pay for the services and assistance provided by the franchisor. Normally, there is an initial franchise fee, and there are ongoing payments, which may take the form of a percentage of the revenues of the franchise, rentals for premises or equipment, payments for management services, or contributions to the cost of advertising campaigns.

A further source of profit to the franchisor is often derived from exclusive supply arrangements. In some types of franchise, the franchisee acts as a retailer for products manufactured or supplied by the franchisor; the franchisee normally undertakes to sell only the franchisor's products. In other types of franchise, the franchisor is primarily selling an idea or a process; the actual goods sold to the public may be manufactured locally according to a set formula, and usually the franchisee may purchase the components only from suppliers approved by the franchisor.

Conduct of the Business

As noted above, a franchise agreement commonly provides for a substantial degree of supervision by the franchisor. The franchisee must agree to give the franchisor right of access to carry out inspections as well as to provide proper accounts and regular information. Usually, the franchisee is required to promise that the business will be carried on only in accordance with the franchisor's regular operating instructions and that no other competing business will be carried on by the franchisee. Since it is the franchisor's reputation that is the basis of the arrangement, the franchisee also promises to protect the goodwill, trademarks, and trade secrets of the franchisor. A franchise agreement may also include expensive obligations to renovate or redecorate premises in accordance with the franchisor's specifications. Participation in the franchisor's online program will require the franchisor to coordinate websites, share data, and maintain security.

CASE 17.6

Robin's Foods was a franchisor of doughnut stores. A numbered Ontario corporation owned one of the franchises. The numbered corporation, in addition to operating the franchise, supplied wholesale doughnuts to other shops for resale. The packaging did not identify the doughnuts as Robin's doughnuts, and the doughnut mix used was

>

Termination of the Franchise   It is common for serious breaches of the franchising agreement to constitute a repudiation of the agreement, allowing the other party to treat it as terminated. Additionally, the agreement normally contains detailed provisions regarding the duration and termination of the relationship. Franchising usually involves a substantial investment by both parties and an expectation that the relationship will continue for a number of years. Consequently, the agreement typically provides for a long fixed term, followed with an option to renew, and requires a substantial period of notice to terminate, with penalties for premature termination.

To protect the franchisor against assignment of the franchise to an unsuitable operator, the franchise agreement normally stipulates that any assignment of the franchisee's interest may only be made with the consent of the franchisor.[42]

Restrictive Covenants   Franchises are usually territorial in nature: A franchisee is assigned a particular area—a county, city, or part of a city—in which to operate, and the franchisor often undertakes not to grant any other franchise within the same territory. In return, the franchisee agrees not to carry on business outside that territory.

An obvious risk taken by franchisors is that their franchisees, having operated a franchise successfully, will gain valuable experience and information, and establish relationships with customers and suppliers that they will take to an independent business of their own. To guard against this danger, the franchisee is normally required to covenant that it will not, for a given number of years after termination of the agreement, carry on a similar or competing business within a stipulated radius from the franchise location. As noted in Chapter 8, such covenants may be unenforceable if they constitute an unreasonable restraint on trade.

Intellectual Property Rights   Intellectual property involves things such as trademarks, copyright, patents, and industrial designs discussed in Chapter 20. Protection of these rights is at the heart of a franchisor's business and the value of the franchise. Agreements will describe these intangible assets and reserve ownership to the franchisor, restrict use by the franchisee to activities within the franchise business, and prohibit copying, variation, or misuse of these assets. The computer operating system will be among these assets. Franchisees will not be allowed to install unapproved software into the system for fear it will be incompatible with or corrupt the system. The agreement will specify requirements for software, hardware, and security. These costs are most often at the expense of the franchisee, at times designated by the franchisor.

CASE 17.7

Hohnjec had been the holder of a franchise granted by Yesac Foods to operate a restaurant in Barrie, Ontario. Subsequently, after termination of the franchise, Hohnjec opened a restaurant in Toronto. The new restaurant was not similar in concept to the Yesac franchise.

Yesac sought to enforce a provision in the franchise agreement, which purported to prevent the franchisee from engaging "in any other business . . . related to the food, beverage or restaurant business." The court held that the clause, which had no time or geographical limitations, was invalid and unenforceable.[43]

---

[41] *1017933 Ontario Ltd. v. Robin's Foods Inc.*, [1998] O.J. No. 1110.

[42] See *Kentucky Fried Chicken Canada v. Scott's Food Services Inc.* (1998), 41 B.L.R. (2d) 42.

[43] *Yesac Creative Foods Inc. v. Hohnjec* (1985), 6 C.P.R. (3d) 398. See also *Kardish Food Franchising Corp. v. 874073 Ontario Inc.*, [1995] O.J. No. 2849; *Cash Converters Pty. Ltd. v. Armstrong*, [1997] O.J. No. 2659; *Nutrilawn International Inc. v. Stewart*, [1999] O.J. No. 643.

Dispute Resolution Franchising agreements are intended to run for a number of years and contain a substantial number of provisions, each of which could become the subject of dispute. To avoid the expense and the possible ill will involved in litigation, it is not uncommon for franchise agreements to contain a provision establishing a procedure for resolving disputes that may arise during the operation of the franchise. Such a provision may, for example, oblige the parties to submit to mediation before the contract may be terminated for alleged breach by one of the parties.[44] Franchisees often resort to class actions to resolve common disputes.

CHECKLIST

Contents of a Typical Franchise Agreement

Franchise agreements usually cover the following:

- activity and geographic limits of the franchise
- services to be provided by franchisor (training, management services, advertising, etc.)
- licensing of trademarks, know-how, etc.
- provision of financial assistance
- capital to be provided by franchisee
- franchise fee
- ongoing payments by franchisee (percentage of receipts, payments for services, etc.)
- arrangements for supply of materials and inventory
- provisions governing conduct of business (supervision, accounting, renovations, etc.)
- duration of relationship
- termination of relationship (notice, restrictions on assignment, penalties, etc.)
- restrictive covenants—confidentiality, and non-competition and non-solicitation agreements
- covenants relating to intellectual property and system operation
- procedures for resolving disputes

Legal Relationships Created by Franchising

The relationship between franchisor and franchisee is a contractual one between independent entrepreneurs. The Supreme Court of Canada has held that the relationship between the parties is not a fiduciary relationship.[45] Nevertheless, the ongoing nature of the relationship imposes upon them a duty of the utmost good faith.[46] As explained in a recent case:

> Franchisors are not required to act selflessly in placing the interests of the franchisee ahead of their own. However, it appears clear from the case law that a franchisor is subject to the duty to act in the utmost good faith toward a franchisee.[46A]

---

[44] See, for example, *Toronto Truck Centre Ltd. v. Volvo Trucks Canada Inc.* (1998), 163 D.L.R. (4th) 740; *Ellis v. Subway Franchise Systems of Canada Ltd.*, [2000] O.J. No. 3849 (where the contract provided for arbitration in the state of Connecticut).

[45] *Jirna Ltd. v. Mister Donut of Canada Ltd.* (1973), 40 D.L.R. (3d) 303.

[46] The Ontario Court of Appeal held that the franchisor owes a duty of good faith in the sense of an obligation to have regard to the franchisee's legitimate interests and to deal promptly, honestly, fairly, and reasonably with the franchisee: *Shelanu Inc. v. Print Three Franchising Corp.* (2003), 226 D.L.R. (4th) 577.

[46A] *Machias v. Mr. Submarine Ltd.*, Ontario Superior Court of Justice Wilson J., Ontario Supreme Court.

In particular:

> Part of the obligations in this special relationship with the franchisee includes a positive obligation to disclose accurate financial information to a prospective franchisee at the time of entering into a franchise agreement. Misrepresentations may result from silence or omissions.[47]

CASE 17.8

Neish entered into a franchise agreement with Melenchuk. He received financial statements that purported to be historical records for the franchise. In fact, the records did not relate to the particular outlet but rather were reconstructed records of other outlets. The records significantly misrepresented the profit and loss situation of the outlet. Neish's bank provided financing based upon the financial records provided.

Subsequently, Neish had to borrow more money to keep the business alive. When he could not borrow any further,

he abandoned the business. He brought an action seeking compensation for his losses.

The court found that there was no evidence that Melenchuk knew that the records were actually misleading so as to constitute fraud. However, he had been negligent in putting the records together and was liable for negligent misrepresentation and breach of contract. Neish was entitled to damages for his lost investment.[48]

With respect to customers, it is important to remember that franchising is entirely different from agency. The franchisee contracts with members of the public on its own behalf, not as agent for the franchisor. There is thus no contract between the customer and the franchisor, though the franchisor might be considered, in some cases, as having held the franchisee out as having authority to act on its behalf and consequently be estopped from denying an agency relationship. When defective goods have been manufactured or supplied by the franchisor, it may, of course, be liable in tort.

Franchise Legislation

At least five provinces—Alberta, Manitoba, Ontario, Prince Edward Island, and New Brunswick—have legislation regulating franchising.[49] The most important features of these laws, which are broadly similar, are as follows.

Disclosure Franchisors are required to give every prospective franchisee a copy of the franchisor's disclosure document at least 14 days before the signing of any agreement or the payment of any consideration. The disclosure document must comply with the requirements of regulations and contain detailed information about the business and the franchise system, including financial statements and reports (s. 4 [Alta.]; s. 5 [Man., Ont., P.E.I., N.B.]).[50] Failure to provide a disclosure document as required gives the franchisee the right to rescind the agreement within two years, and misrepresentation in the document entitles the franchisee to compensation. Inadequate disclosure does not render the agreement invalid or void.[51] The disclosure requirements generally do not apply in the case of a sale of a franchise by a franchisee.

---

[47] *Machias v. Mr. Submarine Ltd.*, [2002] O.J. No. 1261. The Alberta, Manitoba and Ontario legislation require the parties to a franchise agreement to deal fairly with each other; see "Fair Dealing" in the next section.

[48] *Neish v. Melenchuk* (1993), 120 N.S.R. (2d) 239. See also *Nutrilawn International Inc. v. Stewart, supra,* n. 43

[49] *Franchises Act*, R.S.A. 2000, c. F-23; *The Franchise Act*, C.C.S.M. c. F156; *Arthur Wishart Act (Franchise Disclosure)*, S.O. 2000, c. 3; *Franchises Act*, R.S.P.E.I. 1998, c. F-14.1; *Franchises Act*, S.N.B. 2007, c. F-23.5. Quebec has some provisions in its Civil Code.

[50] It is not possible to contract out of the disclosure requirement; *MAA Diners Inc. v. 3 for 1 Pizza & Wings (Canada) Inc.*, [2003] O.J. No. 430, aff'd [2004] O.J. No. 297 (QL).

[51] *MDG Kingston Inc. et al. v. MDG Computers Canada Inc. et al.* (2008), 92 O.R. (3d) 4 (Ont. C.A.) (considering the effect of inadequate disclosure on the franchise agreements arbitration clause). The Arthur Wishart Act, *supra* n. 49, s. 5, sets disclosure requirements with respect to alternative dispute resolution processes.

Fair Dealing   All acts provide that a franchise agreement imposes on each party a duty of fair dealing in its performance and enforcement (s. 7 [Alta.]; s. 3 [Man., Ont., P.E.I., N.B.]). This probably does no more than codify the position at common law.[52]

Right to Associate   In the past, some franchisors have tried by various means to prevent their franchisees from getting together to "compare notes" and, perhaps, to take class action against what are perceived to be unfair practices. The Acts (s. 8 [Alta.]; s. 4 [Man., Ont., P.E.I., N.B.]) expressly recognize a "right of association" among franchisees; a franchisor may not prohibit or restrict its franchisees from forming an organization and may not penalize them in any way for doing so.

INTERNATIONAL ISSUE

Resolving Franchise Disputes

Despite the fact that most franchising agreements are carefully drafted, franchising seems to give rise to an excessive number of disputes. The termination of a franchise, in particular, is often a very contentious matter. Frequently it is not until a franchise is terminated that the franchisee really understands the nature of the agreement that he has signed. There is an obvious inequality in bargaining power between the franchisor, often a very large international corporation, and the franchisee, usually a small local business.

This inequality sometimes results in the insertion of unfair terms in the franchising contract.[53] Franchise agreements commonly contain a choice of law clause designating the foreign franchisor's jurisdiction as the choice of law. As well, a dispute resolution clause may require mandatory arbitration with a foreign arbitrator. It also means that, when there is a dispute, the franchisor is far more able to finance the costs than is the franchisee.

In 2009, the U.S. Congress held hearings to consider a bill that would have prevented a franchisor from forcing a franchisee into arbitration. The proposed Arbitration Fairness Act 2009 would have rendered all pre-dispute arbitration clauses in franchise agreements void and unenforceable but it failed.[54] Current Canadian provincial legislation contemplates the use of alternative dispute resolution and imposes disclosure or notice obligations on the franchisor. It does not render such terms invalid.

Questions to Consider

1. Should franchise agreements be required to contain certain standard terms that protect franchisees against unfair termination and other harsh conditions?

2. Should a mandatory requirement to submit all franchising disputes to arbitration be enforceable?

Strategies to Manage the Legal Risks

It is best for both principal and agent to have a written, signed copy of an agency agreement in order to minimize future misunderstandings about the terms of the arrangement. Neither should rely on principles of implied or apparent authority. Where the actual authority of an agent varies from that expected or usual in the industry, a principal should publicize the restrictions to those dealing with his agent. This will reduce the likelihood of liability for unwanted contracts based upon apparent authority.

Agents should protect themselves from unwanted liability by ensuring that their agency contract includes indemnification by the principal and that any exclusion clause

---

[52] See *Machias v. Mr. Submarine Ltd.*, *supra*, n. 47.

[53] See, for example, *B.B.J. Enterprises Ltd. v. Wendy's Restaurants of Canada Inc.*, [2004] N.S.J. No. 81.

[54] A bill to amend chapter 1 of title 9 of United States Code with respect to arbitration, S. 931; H.R. 1020, 111th Congress (died with the end of the 111th Congress in 2010). See *MDG Kingston Inc. et al. v. MDG Computers Canada Inc. et al.*, *supra*, n. 51 for current Ontario position on the enforcement of arbitration clauses contained in franchise agreements that do not meet the ADR disclosure requirement—they are not considered void or unenforceable but merely subject to a right to rescind.

in the third party's contract expressly refers to agents. Care should be taken when signing documents to ensure that the agent's representative status is disclosed to third parties, even where the name of the principal is not. Finally, as an agent is a fiduciary, conflicts of interest must be avoided. Agents should not act for both parties, even if both consent. If conflicts arise with the agent's own interests or those with whom he is connected, immediate disclosure to all persons affected is necessary.

Franchising agreements are typically standard form contracts prepared by the franchisor and presented to the franchisee on a take it or leave it basis. Therefore, franchisees must examine the terms carefully before agreeing. Often there are onerous fees for advertising. Regular capital expenditures will be required to keep physical and electronic systems in conformity with the franchisor standards. Disclosure requirements in those provinces with legislation may give an uninformed franchisor an option to rescind. This will not be the case in other provinces.

Franchisors must treat the protection of their intellectual property as a priority. This property is at the heart of the value of each franchise. Chapter 20 describes the steps necessary to establish ownership in copyrights, trademarks, and patents. Agreements must preserve ownership and restrict use to only that authorized. Proprietary interests in software systems for the operation of the franchise are no less important than the logos. Agreements should ensure that electronic data generated by the franchisee is shared with the franchisor. Such data provides valuable strategic planning information.

QUESTIONS FOR REVIEW

1. Distinguish between dependent agents and independent agents.
2. Is a "real estate agent" a true agent?
3. What is a power of attorney?
4. What is the effect when a principal ratifies a contract made on its behalf by an agent who lacked the authority to enter into the contract?
5. What are the limits of ratification by a principal?
6. How does an agent acquire actual authority?
7. How does an agent acquire apparent authority?
8. What is meant by "holding out"?
9. Is an agent entitled to delegate his or her duties to some other person?
10. Why should an agent not act for both parties to a transaction? What are the probable legal consequences of doing so?
11. In what circumstances may an agent be held liable on a contract that he or she has negotiated?
12. Can an undisclosed principal enforce a contract made on his or her behalf?
13. What is meant by "breach of warranty of authority"?
14. Distinguish between a franchise and a licence.
15. What restrictions are usually placed on a franchisee carrying on other business activities?
16. What is the relationship between a franchisor and the eventual customer of the franchisee?
17. Is the relationship between franchisor and franchisee a fiduciary relationship?
18. What are the principal additional protections given to franchisees by the Alberta, Ontario, P.E.I., and New Brunswick legislation?

CASES AND PROBLEMS

1. Continuing Scenario

   Gail and Kevin are frequent guests at Ashley's Restaurant. Karen is their favourite server because she allows them to substitute different menu items without charge and sometimes even arranges custom take-out menus. Therefore, when they became engaged, they went to talk to Karen about catering the wedding. They knew Ashley's Restaurant did catering because it was advertised on the menus. Karen agreed to sit down with them and plan the menu even though this was not her job—Ashley negotiated all the catering contracts herself. Karen was very knowledgeable because she had packed and served many catered menus and knew what the restaurant could do. She let Gail and Kevin look at a catering menu the restaurant was putting together for another client that weekend. They loved everything on it and Karen told them the same price as the existing order. Gail and Kevin agreed to the price so Karen took a $200 deposit and wrote the date in the restaurant's calendar. When Ashley returned, Karen told her about the order. Ashley was not happy with Karen's behaviour and told her not to do it again. Two days later Ashley looked at the calendar and realized that the restaurant had too many orders to fill for that weekend and told Karen they could not cater Gail and Kevin's wedding. Has a contract been formed? With whom? Explain your answer.

2. Halloran entered into a contract with Scallop Petroleum Ltd. to manage one of Scallop's gas stations. The contract set out detailed arrangements for the operation of the station. It provided that all inventory should be the property of Scallop until sold, and that all proceeds of sale belonged to Scallop, out of which Halloran was to receive a fixed percentage as commission. Halloran was required to maintain two bank accounts, to pay all sales receipts into one of those accounts, and to provide Scallop with regular records of all transactions.

   At first, the relationship seemed to be working well. Then Halloran became less diligent in furnishing accounts, and Scallop began to notice various other irregularities. Halloran's records were inadequate, and an investigation revealed a shortfall in the sales account of about $80 000, which appeared to have accrued over more than a year. Scallop suspected Halloran of theft and the police were called in. Their investigation was inconclusive; it seemed probable that the money had been stolen by a former employee of Halloran, who could not be traced.

   Halloran was cleared of all involvement in the theft. However, it became clear that he had not been operating the station in accordance with the instructions set out in the contract. For example, he had been keeping cash and credit card receipts in a freezer and in a locked tin box, instead of paying them into the bank as required.

   Scallop gave Halloran notice that it was terminating their relationship; it refused to pay Halloran commission on the previous month's sales, and brought an action against him for the balance of the $80 000.

   Is Scallop entitled to succeed?

3. Da Silva entered into a franchising agreement with Snacks Unlimited Ltd. to operate a fast-food outlet in Regina. Under the contract, the store was to make and sell hot dogs and hamburgers, the ingredients were to be of a specified quality, and the products were to be made to uniform standards. The premises were to be equipped and maintained according to a prescribed format and would have the decor and distinctive sign of "Snacks." Large sales were anticipated since Snacks was already a well-known operation and had carried on extensive advertising.

   The franchising agreement signed by Da Silva required him to do five things:

   - pay a franchise fee of $40 000
   - pay a royalty of 2 percent on gross sales
   - pay an annual fee of $10 000 for advertising services provided by Snacks
   - buy his store equipment from Snacks
   - buy his ingredients from sources indicated by Snacks

The agreement set out detailed provisions about how the business was to be conducted and concluded with the words, "The relationship between the parties is only that of independent contractors. No partnership, joint venture, or relationship of principal and agent is intended."

Da Silva operated the business successfully for two years and showed a reasonable profit. Last year, he discovered that the firms from whom he was required to purchase his supplies were paying substantial rebates to Snacks. On the question of whether he had paid prices higher than the prevailing market prices for comparable supplies, it was difficult to generalize. For some materials, this was true; for others, he paid much the same price, and in some instances even a somewhat lower price. In any event, Snacks had instructed all the suppliers to have no dealings or negotiations with its franchisees that might indicate the true nature of the arrangements made with them for rebates.

Da Silva sued Snacks for an accounting of these undisclosed profits and rebates and an order requiring them to be paid over to him.

Discuss the merits of his case, and indicate with reasons whether his action should succeed.

4. On a number of occasions over the past two years, Longhaul Transport Ltd. had carried goods belonging to Factorplus Products Inc. The shipments were arranged by a broker, Transshipments Inc. Longhaul invoiced Transshipments, which in turn invoiced Factorplus. The normal procedure was for Transshipments to pay Longhaul out of funds received by it from Factorplus. Longhaul was aware that the goods belonged to Factorplus and was under the mistaken impression that Transshipments was simply a division or subsidiary of Factorplus, rather than an independent broker.

Following one major shipment, Longhaul invoiced Transshipments but was not paid; Transshipments had received no payment from Factorplus in respect of the shipment and refused to pay the shipping charges.

Advise Longhaul whether it should sue (a) Transshipments, (b) Factorplus, or (c) both.

5. Strauss, an experienced business administrator, became unemployed six years ago when his firm "downsized." He was unable to find suitable similar employment and decided to set up his own business. He was especially attracted to the lawn care business, which he considered to have excellent growth potential. He also thought that a franchised operation provided the best chance of establishing a successful business quickly.

After examining a number of lawn care franchises, Strauss concluded that a firm called Sodmaster Inc. was the franchisor best suited to his requirements. Strauss contacted Sodmaster and had several discussions with the area manager for Eastern Ontario. Strauss was provided with a vast amount of information about Sodmaster's operations, including various projections of costs and profits based on the operation of other Sodmaster franchises. Strauss also visited other franchisees and talked with them about their experiences.

According to the financial projections in the booklet given to him by Sodmaster, a franchise with a gross annual revenue of $200 000 would normally make a small loss (after allowing for a modest management fee); one with revenue of $400 000 would show a reasonable profit, and one with revenue of $800 000 or more would show an excellent profit. Potential franchisees were warned that it was unusual to break even in the first year of operation. The projections were essentially accurate, based on the actual experience of Sodmaster franchises, though the booklet omitted to point out that only one of the franchises actually grossed more than $800 000 per year.

Strauss also made his own projections of his probable revenues and decided to go ahead and purchase a franchise for Frontenac County, Ontario. He agreed to pay a franchise fee of $40 000 ($25 000 payable immediately and the balance after two years) and to pay royalties of 6 percent on gross revenues. He also entered into the usual restrictive covenants not to carry on a competing business within 30 km of the franchise area for a period of five years after termination of the franchise. In order to get started, Strauss borrowed money on the security of his home and, in all, invested about $100 000 of his own money.

The business did not work out nearly as well as Strauss had expected. In his first year, he had sales of only $60 000 (when he had anticipated twice that figure), and he made a loss of $75 000. The second year's sales reached $100 000 (with a loss of $12 000); by the third year, sales had risen to $180 000, still with a small loss; in the fourth and fifth years, Strauss's sales levelled out at a little more than $200 000, and he was still making a loss.

Because of his financial problems, Strauss never paid the remaining $15 000 owing on the franchise fee, and he also fell behind early on in the payment of the royalties. Relations between Strauss and Sodmaster became strained, and eventually Sodmaster informed Strauss that they would not be prepared to renew the franchise at the end of its five-year term. Strauss then abandoned the franchise and set up his own lawn care business in the same area.

Sodmaster brought an action against Strauss, claiming payment of the balance of the franchise fee, the unpaid royalties, and an injunction to restrain the breach of the restrictive covenant. Strauss counterclaimed for damages, alleging that he had been misled into entering into the franchise agreement in the first place.

Who should succeed?

Additional Resources for Chapter 17 on the Companion Website

(www.pearsoncanada.ca/smyth)

In addition to pre- and post-tests, mini-cases, and application exercises, the Companion Website includes the following province-specific resources for Chapter 17:

- **Alberta:** Agency by Necessity; Enduring Power of Attorney; Franchises; Liability for Agent's Tortious Conduct; Personal Directives; Real Estate Agents
- **Atlantic Provinces:** Franchise Legislation; Real Estate Agents
- **British Columbia:** Collection Agents; Power of Attorney; Real Estate Agents; Travel Agents
- **Manitoba/Saskatchewan:** Real Estate Agency Rules
- **Ontario:** Agency by Necessity; Fiduciary Duty; Franchising Legislation; Parental Liability; Power of Attorney; Real Estate Agents

Chapter 18

The Contract of Employment

Employers contract with employees either individually, or collectively for unionized workplaces. Modern legislation provides protection for workers, as do trade unions, with the collective bargaining process and the system of regulation in place to facilitate resolving disputes.

In this chapter we examine the following issues:

- What is the difference between an employer's liability in contract and in tort?

- What are the grounds for dismissal "with cause"?

- What is "wrongful dismissal," and what are its consequences?

- What are the effects of human rights requirements, and pay and employment equity statutes?

- What are the consequences of regulation on general working conditions?

- How is mandatory retirement affected by the Canadian Charter of Rights and Freedoms?

- How are employment conditions affected by workers' compensation and occupational health regulations?

- What are the implications of a collective agreement for the individual employee?

- What is the legal status of trade unions?

DEVELOPMENT OF THE LAW GOVERNING EMPLOYMENT

relationship of master and servant the contractual relationship between an employer and an employee

The principles of modern employment law are derived from the common law rules defining the **relationship of master and servant**. This law developed in an early business environment where the employer (master) had a separate contract with each employee (servant); welfare legislation and trade unions were unknown. Today, the individual contract of employment remains the most common form of employment relationship, and the law of master and servant continues to be important. Nevertheless, the economic and social changes of the past century have changed the employment relationship in two respects:

- First, statutes have been passed to establish minimum standards for safe and fair working conditions; this branch of the law as is known as employee welfare legislation.

- Second, the organization of labour into trade unions has led to the evolution of the collective agreement; a separate body of law known as labour law or the law of collective bargaining governs the relationship between employers, trade unions, and their members.

This chapter deals with the individual employment relationship, employee welfare legislation, and collective bargaining.

First a note of caution: We cannot cite all the relevant statutes in the space available, and in any event it might be dangerous to do so, as this part of the law frequently changes. The purpose of the chapter is to give only a general overview of the law. More detail can be found in the resources cited in the footnotes.[1]

RELATIONSHIP OF EMPLOYER AND EMPLOYEE

Compared with Agency

The relationship of employer and employee is established by a contract that gives one party, the employer, authority to direct and control the work of the other party, the employee. The services that are contracted for may or may not include making contracts with third parties as agent for the employer.

The same person is often both an employee and an agent. For example, a purchasing agent for a company has the responsibility to order goods on the company's credit and has authority to do so within the limits of her agency. She is also a company employee and subject to the direction of management. Other employees may have very limited duties as agents of their employer: The driver of a delivery truck is an employee who may act as an agent when taking the truck into a garage for servicing and binding the

---

[1] See J.R. Sproat, *Wrongful Dismissal Handbook*, 3rd ed. (Toronto: Thomson Canada, 2004); W. Rayner, *Canadian Collective Bargaining Law*, 2nd ed. (Toronto: Carswell, 2007).

employer to pay the charges. In many types of employment, an employee—a lathe operator, for instance—has no reason to enter into contracts on behalf of the employer and no authority, express or implied, to do so.

An agent may have no recourse against a principal that terminates the agreement without notice. By contrast, an employee, as we shall see, often has a right of action for damages for wrongful dismissal in comparable circumstances.

Both principals and employers may be liable in tort for the acts of their agents and employees, respectively. For various reasons—some historical and some related to the different functions of agents and employees—the liability of an employer may be wider than that of a principal; the basis for vicarious liability is not the same for principals and employers. Accordingly, when a third party is injured, it may be important to establish whether the wrongdoer was acting as an employee, an agent of a firm, or an independent contractor.

Compared with an Independent Contractor

An independent contractor undertakes to do a specified task such as building a house. The contract between the parties does not create an employer–employee relationship because the contractor is not subject to the supervision and control of the person engaging him. His job is to produce a specified result, but the means he employs are his own affair.

It is not always easy to distinguish between an independent contractor and an employee. Occasionally the two functions are combined in a single person: The owner of a building may hire a building contractor to do certain repairs for a fixed price, but the agreement may also require the repairs to be made under the supervision of the owner. It may be difficult to decide whether the person doing the work is primarily an independent contractor or an employee.

When a firm undertakes work as an independent contractor, any liabilities it incurs in carrying out its task are almost entirely its own. A business engaging a building contractor may have to follow certain procedures in paying the contractor in order to avoid having its land and buildings subject to liens filed by employees of the contractor or by subcontractors such as suppliers of materials. Apart from this complication, a person engaging an independent contractor is not generally responsible for the contractor's obligations.[2]

CHECKLIST

Characteristics of an Independent Contractor

- hired to complete a task or deliver a result for a fee
- owns the tools necessary to do the work
- controls his own hours and time of work
- controls how the work is done
- no tax, pension, benefit, or government deductions withheld from payment
- invoices for work done and charges GST/HST
- pays his own expenses
- assumes the risk of profit or loss[3]

---

[2] See *Vic Priestly Landscaping Contracting Ltd. v. Elder* (1978), 19 O.R. (2d) 591 at 601–5.

[3] *671122 Ontario Ltd. v Sagaz Industries Canada Inc.* 2001 SCC 59 at para 34–48; For discussion of control and dependence see *McCormick v. Fasken, Martineau, DuMoulin, LLP*, 2014 SCC 39.

ILLUSTRATION 18.1

Imperial Builders contracted with Parkinson Corp. to erect an administration building. During the construction work, Miss Chance, walking on the sidewalk far below, is injured by a falling brick. The accident is the result of inadequate protection for pedestrians provided by Imperial. Imperial—not Parkinson Corp.—would very likely be liable for the injury so caused.

On the other hand, Parkinson does have a duty to take reasonable care to hire a competent contractor. Also, if, by the nature of the work undertaken, the possibility of damage to adjoining property is apparent—for example, through blasting with dynamite[4]—or if the work is inherently dangerous to third parties, Parkinson has an obligation to see to it that the contractor takes reasonable precautions to avoid such damage.

For more information on this topic, see the Companion Website.

EMPLOYMENT RELATIONSHIP AT COMMON LAW

At common law, the relationship of employer and employee carried with it responsibilities about

- the employer's liability to third persons,
- the notice required to terminate the relationship,
- the limited reasons an employer could terminate the relationship without notice, and
- assessment of damages for wrongful dismissal.

These rules are part of the common law as it continues to apply to individual employment contracts.

THE EMPLOYER'S LIABILITY TO THIRD PERSONS

Liability in Contract

Often, parties to a contract do not intend to perform personally—corporations cannot do so—and they expect employees or an independent contractor will perform. The promisor remains liable for satisfactory performance, as when a construction firm undertakes to build a building according to specifications and hires a subcontractor to put up the structural steel, but the subcontractor does defective work. So, too, will the promisor be liable for breach of contract should its own employees do improper work.

Liability in Tort

A business is liable for damages to a third party for the consequences of any tort an employee may commit in the course of employment. The employer may not have authorized the wrongful act; it is liable even though it has forbidden such conduct. All the injured party need establish is that the employee caused the damage while engaged at work. If, however, the harm results while the employee is not engaged in the employer's work, as when he takes time off from his duties to attend to some personal matter, the employer is not liable: the employee alone is liable. Nor is the employer liable if the employee delegates the work to someone else without the employer's consent.

---

[4] *Savage v. Wilby*, [1954] S.C.R. 376; *Chappell's Ltd. v. Municipality of County of Cape Breton*, [1963] S.C.R. 340; *Sickel v. Gordy* 2008 SKCA 100 at para 48–49.

Adair is employed by Magnum Computers as a sales agent. While doing a sales demonstration at a client's office, he negligently breaks the client's existing projector. He has committed a tort in the course of his employment; the owner of the damaged projector may sue both Magnum Computers and Adair.

Adair injures a neighbour's projector equipment as a result of negligently using the company equipment to host an in-home theatre event for the neighbourhood, without permission or knowledge of his employer. In the words of a Nova Scotia judgment in a similar case, Adair has "departed from the course of his employment and . . . embarked upon an independent enterprise—'a frolic of his own'—for purposes wholly unconnected with his master's business."[5] He alone is liable; Magnum Computers is not.

While delivering a computer, Adair becomes embroiled in an argument with a customer about the quality of the product. He pushes the customer, who falls and injures himself. Is Magnum Computers vicariously liable to the customer for the assault?

Of the three examples in Illustrations 18.2, 18.3, and 18.4, the last is the most difficult to resolve. As one judge put it, "Before the employer can be held liable, the blow complained of must be closely connected with a duty being carried out in the authorized course of employment and not delivered at a time when the servant has divested himself of his character as a servant."[6] We must ask whether the unauthorized and wrongful act of the employee is "so connected with the authorized act as to be a mode of doing it" or whether it is "an independent act."[7]

If having conversations about his employer's product at the time of delivery is an authorized incident of Adair's employment so as to be a way of carrying out his duties, his employer is also liable for the assault; but if his conversation is an independent act, Adair alone is liable. The court will hear evidence of trade practice in this matter before reaching its decision.

Sometimes when an employer has been held liable for the negligence of an employee, there is a right to be indemnified by the employee.[8] Each case is decided on its own facts.[9]

NOTICE OF TERMINATION OF INDIVIDUAL EMPLOYMENT CONTRACTS

Express Term of the Contract

When an employer hires an employee for a **fixed term**, no notice of termination is necessary on the part of either party. The relationship naturally comes to an end when the fixed time period expires. Neither one has a right to expect anything more from the other at the

fixed term a contract of employment with defined start and end dates

---

[5] *Hall v. Halifax Transfer Co. Ltd.* (1959), 18 D.L.R. (2d) 115, per MacDonald, J., at 120.

[6] *Wenz v. Royal Trust Co.*, [1953] O.W.N. 798, per Aylen, J., at 800.

[7] R.F.V. Heuston and R.A. Buckley, eds., *Salmond and Heuston on The Law of Torts*, 20th ed. (London: Sweet & Maxwell, 1992) at 457.

[8] *Finnegan v. Riley*, [1939] 4 D.L.R. 434.

[9] *Douglas v. Kinger*, 2008 ONCA 452 at para 21–24.

end of the specified time: Each has been aware of the end date from the beginning, as, for example, where a student expects summer employment to terminate on the Friday before Labour Day.[10]

Alternatively, the employment contract may contain an option to terminate. Such a clause will describe the process to be followed for either party to bring the contract to an end. It will usually specify a required amount of advance notice. In most provinces and at the federal level as well, the minimum length of required notice is specifically set down by statute, and any attempt by an employer to impose a term shorter than the minimum is void.[11]

Implied Term of Reasonable Notice

notice advance warning that the employment relationship will end

Most employment contracts do not say how or when they will come to an end. Therefore, the common law implies a term requiring reasonable **notice** of termination into employment contracts. Notice of termination involves telling an employee in advance that the employment relationship will end.

Often, employers and employees do not discuss when the employment relationship is to end, nor do they expressly agree on the length of notice required to terminate employment. They may intend the hiring to be by the week, the month, or some other length of time, renewable for successive periods, and possibly lasting for many years. Or, as more often happens, they may simply regard the employment as a general or **indefinite hiring**.

indefinite hiring a contract of employment for an undetermined length of time, with no expectation of termination or described end date

When no evidence about the intention of the parties is given to the court, it may infer a weekly or a monthly hiring from the mere fact that the employee receives pay by the week or the month. Usually a hiring is indefinite, even though the employee is paid by the week.

Length of Reasonable Notice

reasonable notice the acceptable length of notice of termination considering the nature of the contract, intentions of the parties, circumstance of the employment, and characteristics of the employee

Without an express term about termination in a contract of employment, **reasonable notice** must be given—but exactly how much notice is *reasonable*? The answer is: it depends. Each case is decided on its own facts and length of notice varies depending on the circumstances. Sometimes a court can determine the length of reasonable notice from evidence of an established customary practice followed by the particular employer for the type of employee in question. In other circumstances, the court will ask what type of hiring the parties intended when they made the employment contract. The usual minimum reasonable notice for a weekly hiring is one work week, and for a monthly hiring, one work month. If the hiring is general or indefinite, reasonable notice depends upon a variety of factors and the circumstances of the employment; it usually varies between three and six months, and occasionally is as long as one year or more.[12] Key considerations or "factors" in determining the length of reasonable notice are the length and character of employment, the age of the employee, and the availability of similar employment, given the education, training, and experience of the employee.[13] Executive compensation settlements are often

[10] See, for example, Employment Standards Act, S.O. 2000, c. 41.

[11] See, e.g., Labour Standards Act, R.S.S. 1978, c. L-1, s. 44.2; Labour Standards Code, R.S.N.S. 1989, c. 246, s. 72; Employment Standards Act, S.O. 2000, c. 41, s. 54 as applied in *Machtinger v. HOJ Industries Ltd.* (1992), 91 D.L.R. (4th) 491 (S.C.C.) and *Rizzo & Rizzo Shoes Ltd.* (Re), [1998] 1 S.C.R. 26. For contrary finding see *A.A. Waters & Brookes v. Lachini*, [2001] O.L.R.B. Rep. 1119.

[12] See *Bardal v. The Globe and Mail Ltd.* (1960), 24 D.L.R. (2d) 140; *Stevens v. Globe and Mail et al.* (1992), 86 D.L.R. (4th) 204; *Minott v. O'Shanter Development Company Ltd.* (1999), 42 O.R. (3d) 321.

[13] The relative importance of each factor is not uniformly accepted. See *Bramble v. Medis Health & Pharmaceutical Services Inc.* (1999), 175 D.L.R. (4th) 385 (N.B.C.A.) and B. Fisher, "Is Occupation Still a Relevant Factor in Determining Notice Periods in Wrongful Dismissal Cases?" (1995), 6 C.C.E.L. (2d) 29. The managerial and non-managerial character of the employment is not relevant to the length of notice except as it relates to the availability of similar employment: *Cronk v. Canadian General Insurance Co.* (1995), 128 D.L.R. (4th) 147 (Ont. C.A.). See also *Honda v. Keays*, [2008] 2 S.C.R. 362 at 379–80; *Bardal, supra* n. 12.

for as much as several years' salary.[14] Since the legislative provisions referred to above are minimum requirements only, reasonable notice periods and contractual notice terms are usually substantially longer. For more information on this topic, see the Companion Website.

If an employer wants to dismiss an employee immediately, it may satisfy its obligation to give reasonable notice if it pays the employee for a period equal to the time required for reasonable notice. This is known as **payment in lieu of notice**. Employers commonly terminate this way to avoid friction with the now-terminated employee. If, for example, a court finds that reasonable notice in the circumstances is three months and the employee had been given only one week's salary in lieu of notice, it will order payment of the balance of three months' salary.

CHECKLIST
Factors Relevant to Length of Reasonable Notice

- length of employment
- character of employment
- age of employee
- education or training of employee
- experience of employee
- availability of similar employment in the industry (market conditions)

This is not an exhaustive list of relevant factors, and the importance of individual factors will vary with the circumstances of the particular case.

An employee who decides to leave voluntarily must give the employer the same amount of notice as he himself would be entitled to receive for dismissal. If he does not do so, the employer may, if it considers it worthwhile, sue the employee for damages equal to the loss caused by this breach of contract.[15] Most employers do not insist on anything more than two weeks' notice for the same reasons they would rather pay an employee in lieu of giving notice.

An employee is justified in leaving without giving the usual notice if he can show that he was "forced to quit." For example, he is not required to work under dangerous conditions that the employer refuses to correct. An employee also has grounds for leaving immediately if he is ordered to perform an illegal act. The employer has broken the contract, freeing the employee from his obligations, for it is an implied term that the employer will maintain a safe place to work. If an employer substantially changes an employee's job, for example, by a **demotion** or a geographic transfer, the employee is not obliged to accept the change. Under such circumstances, the unilateral change amounts to **constructive dismissal** and the employee is entitled to receive reasonable notice.[16] For more information on this topic, see the Companion Website.

demotion transferring an employee to a job with less responsibility and/or income potential

constructive dismissal a substantial change to an employee's job that amounts to termination of the existing employment

DISMISSAL WITHOUT NOTICE

An employer need not give notice of termination when it can show that the employee was dismissed for good reason or "cause." **Dismissal for cause** is allowed when an employee's conduct amounts to a breach of the employment contract. The employer

dismissal for cause dismissal without notice or further obligation by the employer when the employee's conduct amounts to breach of contract

---

[14] Eric Dash, "Executive Pay: Has the Exit Sign Ever Looked So Good?" *New York Times*, April 8, 2007, www.cslproductions.com/scrapbook/NYTimes-Executive-Pay-4-8-07/.

[15] *RBC Dominion Securities Inc. v. Merrill Lynch Canada Inc.*, 2008 S.C.C. 54.

[16] *Farber v. Royal Trust Co.*, [1997] 1 S.C.R. 845 but see *Brown v. Pronghorn Controls Ltd.*, 2011 ABCA 328.

is entitled to consider itself discharged from any further obligations and to terminate the contract at once. As we know, in contract law, generally not every petty breach would have this result. The common law has classified the kinds of breach that are sufficient grounds for dismissal without notice, although there are always questions of degree.

The collective bargaining process has developed the idea further. In some jurisdictions, employees have gained additional protection by statute.[17]

Misconduct

Misconduct may be a crime associated with employment, such as embezzlement, or it can be dismissal for cause related to conduct outside of employment. An employee guilty of grossly immoral conduct that might bring the employer's business into public disrepute, disturb the morale of other employees, or cause the employer direct financial loss may be dismissed at once. Conviction for a crime is grounds for immediate dismissal, especially when it involves immoral conduct such as stealing or fraud.[18]

A business is entitled to place confidence in its employees, and, depending on the nature of the employment, evidence of a lack of integrity is often grounds for instant dismissal. An employee's deception need cause no financial loss to his employer: It is enough that the employer can no longer trust him.[19]

Employers also set their own standards of conduct or misconduct. Codes of conduct addressing activities such as harassment, discrimination, privacy, and use of technology are used to set standards of appropriate behaviour for employees. Provided the employee is made aware of the code, he or she may be dismissed for code violations.

Disobedience

job description a description of the responsibilities of a position, including objectives, qualifications, and supervisor

Willful disobedience of a reasonable and lawful order from an employer is grounds for immediate dismissal without notice. An accurate **job description** and identified chain of command help an employer avoid employee confusion about expected behaviour and disobedience. The concept of disobedience is broad enough to include situations where the employee does not directly disobey but acts in a manner inconsistent with the usual loyalty expected of that kind of employee. In the old case of *Ridgway v. Hungerford Market Co.*,[20] a clerk wrote in a company minute book a protest against a resolution of the directors calling a meeting to appoint his successor. He was dismissed at once and forfeited the right to any reasonable notice that would normally have been implied in the directors' resolution.

Incompetence

The degree of skill an employer may demand depends partly on the representations made by the employee when seeking the position and partly on the degree of skill ordinarily to be expected of an employee of that category and rate of pay. Again, accurate job descriptions and recruitment activities reduce the likeliness of hiring an incompetent applicant. If an employee accepts a position on the understanding that he is capable of doing a particular kind of work and it becomes apparent that he cannot, in fact, do this work satisfactorily, the employer may then dismiss him without notice. On the other

---

[17] See, for example, Employment Standards Act, S.O. 2000, c. 41.

[18] *Pliniussen v. University of Western Ontario* (1983), 2 C.C.E.L. 1.

[19] *Werle v. Saskenergy Inc.* (1992), 103 Sask. R. 241.

[20] (1835), 111 E.R. 378. See also *Hodgkin v. Aylmer (Town)* (1996), 23 C.C.E.L. (2d) 297.

hand, incompetence as a cause for dismissal becomes more difficult to justify the longer an employee has been employed.[21] An employer must make an effort to remedy incompetence with training and education. If these efforts fail then the employer may dismiss without notice.

Illness

Permanent disability or constantly recurring illness entitles an employer to consider the contract at an end, regardless of any terms in the contract requiring notice. An employer cannot, however, recover damages from an employee for breach of contract in these circumstances: the contract is discharged by frustration and not by breach. Human rights legislation imposes a duty on employers to accommodate an employee's disability. A disabled person's employment may only be terminated after all reasonable efforts to accommodate the disability have been exhausted. Many employers offer disability benefits to employees as part of the compensation package.

EFFECT OF DISMISSAL

Any of the four grounds for dismissal set out above justifies an employer treating the contract of employment as discharged. Misconduct, disobedience, or incompetence amounts to discharge by the employee's breach, but illness discharges the contract by frustration. Discharge for any one of these personal failures of performance by an employee relieves the employer of the duty to give notice, but it must still pay the dismissed employee any wages earned until the time of dismissal.

Sometimes an employer has such a general dissatisfaction with or mistrust of an employee that it dismisses him apparently without cause. If the employer should later discover that there was in fact cause for dismissing the employee without notice, it could use these grounds to defeat an action by the employee for wrongful dismissal.[22]

Failure to Warn

Only the most serious events of cause entitle an employer to immediately (summarily) terminate an employee after the first incident. The conduct must be considered in context and be so serious as to amount to a total breakdown in the employment relationship.[23] This means

- violating an essential term of the employment contract,
- breaching the faith inherent in the relationship, or
- fundamentally or directly conflicting with the employee's obligations to the employer.

The employer bears the burden of proof. Most circumstances require an employer to warn the employee that the offending conduct is unacceptable and further occurrences will result in termination.[24] Even a series of events may not justify dismissal if the employer has failed to warn the employee in the past. Ignoring the initial events may be seen as

---

[21] See *Duncan v. Cockshutt Farm Equipment Ltd.* (1956), 19 W.W.R. 554; *Bardal v. The Globe and Mail Ltd.*, *supra*, n. 12.

[22] The courts admit such evidence even if it becomes known after the action has been started. See, for example: *Lake Ontario Portland Cement v. Groner* (1961), 28 D.L.R. (2d) 589; *Bannister v. General Motors of Canada Limited* (1998), 40 O.R. (3d) 577.

[23] *McKinley v. BC Tel*, [2001] 2 S.C.R. 161.

[24] *Rajakaruna v. Peel (Regional Municipality)* (1981), 10 A.C.W.S. (2d) 522 (Ont. Co. Ct.).

condoning or accepting the behaviour, and the employer may forfeit the right to complain later.[25] As noted by the British Columbia Supreme Court:

> In order to dismiss an employee summarily . . . the employer must provide the employee with a clear warning which specifically informs the employee that his or her job is in jeopardy. The employer cannot employ oblique language when warning the employee that his or her employment may be terminated. It is not sufficient for the employer to merely criticize the employee's performance or simply urge improvement.[26]

progressive employee discipline imposing increasingly serious consequences for each event of improper employee behaviour beginning with a warning and ending with dismissal

Therefore, courts expect a structured approach to dismissal for cause including **progressive employee discipline**, noting all infractions and warnings on an employment record, and exhausting all less severe consequences before resorting to dismissal. As noted above, an employer must be able to establish that training or education was attempted when relying on incompetence. If the employer allows unacceptable behaviour to continue without comment or correction, it may be taken as accepting or condoning the behaviour and release the right to consider it cause.

Some view an employee's interest in a job as being more than just contractual. In particular, the growing remedy of reinstatement, discussed in the next section, suggests a kind of ownership. With this in mind, before an employee is dismissed—and deprived of an "interest" in his job—he is entitled to a fair hearing. The employer should confront him with the allegation and provide an opportunity to explain his acts and minimize their significance.[27]

Adverse Economic Conditions

Adverse economic conditions do not excuse an employer from its implied obligation to give employees reasonable notice of termination. An employer might overcome this implied obligation by getting his employee to agree expressly that in adverse economic conditions he may be dismissed without notice. However, when a right to notice is required by statute, even an express agreement to give it up is ineffective; the statute prevails, and the employer must still give notice or wages in lieu of notice.

Some statutes now permit an employer to temporarily lay off employees without notice for periods as long as three months under certain economic conditions prescribed by regulation.[28]

WRONGFUL DISMISSAL

If the employer does not follow the rules for cause or reasonable notice, the employee has a cause of action against her employer for breach of the employment contract. This cause of action is known as wrongful dismissal and entitles the employee to damages and/or reinstatement.

Damages

An employee in a wrongful dismissal action must show that she was an employee who was fired without reasonable notice. An employer often defends its actions by claiming either that the employee was dismissed for cause or that reasonable notice was given. If the employer's defence fails, the court is left with the task of assessing damages.

---

[25] *Varsity Plymouth Chrysler (1994) Ltd. v. Pomerleau* (2002), 23 C.C.E.L. (3d) 148 (Alta. Q.B.).

[26] *Bomford v. Wayden Transportation Systems Inc.*, [2010] B.C.J. No. 2080 (B.C.S.C.) at para. 5.

[27] See *Reilly v. Steelcase Canada Ltd.* (1979), 26 O.R. (2d) 725; *Pulsifer v. GTE Sylvania Canada Ltd.* (1983), 56 N.S.R. (2d) 424; *Pilato v. Hamilton Place Convention Centre* (1984), 45 O.R. (2d) 652.

[28] *Canada Labour Code*, R.S.C. 1985, c. L-2; *Canada Labour Standards Regulation*, C.R.C. 1978, c. 986, s. 30; *Employment Standards Act*, 2000, S.O. 2000, c. 41, s. 56.

The measure of damages for wrongful dismissal is a particular application of the rules for assessing damages in contracts generally. In Chapter 13, we saw that the purpose of an award of damages is to place an injured party in the position it would have been in if the contract had been completed; for an employment contract, proper completion means terminating the employment with the appropriate reasonable notice To calculate the damages, the length of reasonable notice is multiplied by the employee's rate of pay and the value of fringe benefits by the length of reasonable notice. As noted earlier, the court has considerable discretion when the contract is for a general or indefinite hiring, and each case must be decided on its own facts after consideration of the following factors:

> There can be no catalogue laid down as to what is reasonable notice in particular classes of cases. The reasonableness of the notice must be decided with reference to each particular case, having regard to the character of the employment, the length of service of the servant, the age of the servant and the availability of similar employment, having regard to the experience, training and qualifications of the servant.[29]

In addition to damages for the lack of notice, employers may be liable for other aggravated or "moral" damages[30] when they act in bad faith, use hardball tactics, or humiliate an employee causing harm. Employers are under an obligation to behave fairly, honestly, candidly, and reasonably when dismissing an employee. When the bad faith or malicious behaviour of the employer adds to the harm caused—as where the employer falsely makes it appear that the employee was dismissed for serious misconduct or where the employee is terminated in a public or humiliating way—damages may be assessed against the employer for mental anguish, pain and suffering or, in extreme circumstances, punitive damages.[31]

Finally, the court will consider any other damage that flows naturally from the employer's breach. For example, the employee may have incurred travelling expenses in seeking other employment.

Mitigation

A party injured by breach of contract is expected to act reasonably in order to mitigate her loss. Mitigation in the wrongful dismissal context means finding another job. Accordingly, the employer may be able to defeat or reduce the employee's claim for damages by proving that she has not made a serious attempt to obtain reasonably comparable work elsewhere. If the employer shows that the employee had an opportunity to work elsewhere but declined it, the court will reduce the award of damages by the amount the employee might have earned during the required term of notice. However, a dismissed employee is not required to take any work simply to mitigate her loss; if the only work available is substantially below what she might reasonably expect based on her qualifications and experience, she may refuse it without fear that the court will reduce an award of damages. Nor need she move to a distant location, requiring her to give up her current residence and find another. If she does accept a

---

[29] *Bardal v. The Globe and Mail Ltd.*, per McRuer, C.J.H.C., *supra*, n. 12, at 145. *Machtinger v. HOJ Industries Ltd.*, [1992] 1 S.C.R. 986.

[30] *Capital Pontiac Buick Cadillac GMC Ltd., v. Coppolla* 2013 SKCA 80 at para 26 (upholding an award of $20 000 of moral damages).

[31] For a detailed discussion by the Supreme Court of Canada of additional factors affecting damage awards for wrongful dismissal, see *Honda Canada Inc. v. Keays*, 2008 S.C.C. 39 (where damages can include mental anguish, punitive, or moral damages). In one case, $15 000 was added to damages for the malicious, high-handed, and cavalier behaviour of the employer: *Brito v. Canac Kitchens*, [2011] O.J. No. 1117 at paras. 18–9 (Ont. S.C.). See also *Fidler v. Sun Life Assurance Co. of Canada*, [2006] 2 S.C.R. 3, and *Wallace v. United Grain Growers Ltd.*, [1997] 3 S.C.R. 701.

lower-paying job, she will be entitled to the lost difference in remuneration during the term of notice.

In rare circumstances, the employee may be expected to mitigate by accepting alternative employment with the dismissing employer.[32] This is most common in constructive dismissal situations. Employees are not expected to work in hostile or humiliating environments, and, in most situations, this precludes returning to the same.[33]

Reinstatement

In addition to damages for wrongful dismissal, employees may seek other remedies such as reinstatement—a form of specific performance by which the court orders the employer to continue to employ the aggrieved employee. We noted in Chapter 13 the great reluctance of courts to order specific performance of contracts of service against an employee. Based on common law principles alone,[34] they are as unlikely to award reinstatement. However, the impersonal nature of most employment in large business enterprises has diminished the strength of argument against reinstatement based on the personal aspect of services. Unions have long bargained for arbitration procedures in cases of dismissal and for reinstatement in appropriate cases. Indeed, reinstatement has become the norm as the remedy for wrongful dismissal under collective agreements. Another example of the use of reinstatement occurs at universities; professors who have been wrongfully dismissed are ordinarily entitled to reinstatement.

Non-union employees in industries within the federal jurisdiction have a statutory right to reinstatement. The Canada Labour Code provides that

240 any [dismissed] person

(a) who has completed twelve consecutive months of continuous employment by an employer, and
(b) who is not a member of a group of employees subject to a collective agreement may make a complaint.[35]

If an adjudicator decides that the person has been "unjustly dismissed," she may order the employer to reinstate the employee. The Quebec Labour Standards Act and the Nova

---

CHECKLIST

Remedies Available in a Wrongful Dismissal Action

A. Damages:
- payment in lieu of notice
- damages for mental anguish or pain and suffering
- special damages associated with the cost of mitigation
- punitive damages from an employer acting in bad faith
- reduction for failure to mitigate their damages

B. Reinstatement

---

[32] *Evans v. Teamsters Local Union No. 31*, 2008 S.C.C. 20, [2008] 1 S.C.R. 661. The test is whether a reasonable person would accept the offer to return to work: *Turner v. Indirect Enterprises Inc.*, [2009] O.J. No. 6345 at paras. 9–10, aff'd [2011] O.J. No. 621.

[33] See e.g. *Renard v. Facet Decision Systems Inc.*, [2010] B.C.J. No. 2694, but see *Chevalier v. Active Tire & Auto Centre Inc.*, 2013 ONCA 548 (employee was expected to accept offer of re-employment).

[34] See e.g. *Hill v. Parsons*, [1971] 3 All E.R. 1345.

[35] Canada Labour Code, R.S.C. 1985, c. L-2, s. 240.

Scotia Act create a similar right for employees, but in Quebec, only after two years of uninterrupted service with one employer, and in Nova Scotia, only after 10 years.[36]

Ethical Issue — Protection of Employee Privacy

Employers provide their employees with telephone, facsimile, internet, and email capabilities in order to communicate with colleagues and customers, but employers are increasingly concerned about employee misuse of this technology. To justify surveillance, employers argue that telephones and computers are company property. Therefore, the employer has the right to ensure they are used only for work rather than for personal purposes, and that employees are not jeopardizing the security of confidential information. Employers also cite their duty to maintain a safe workplace—including the protection of employees against sexual harassment—as justification for monitoring employees.

Common forms of technological monitoring include

- data shadowing,
- video surveillance, and
- GPS tracking,

One of the most controversial forms of monitoring involves biometrics. Biometrics use digital scans of personal features such as fingerprints and retinas to control access to computers, work premises, and so on.

Monitoring of employees is becoming commonplace. The American Management Association, in conjunction with the ePolicy Institute, has been surveying the use of employee monitoring for over 15 years. In 1993, only 33 percent of employers reported using some form of monitoring. However, by 2001 usage had risen to 79 percent.[37]

The federal Personal Information Protection and Electronic Documents Act (PIPEDA) provides that "organizations" must obtain consent of "individuals" to the collection, use, and disclosure of personal information, except where it would be "inappropriate" to do so. Section 4 extends the application of PIPEDA to personal information collected in some employment relationships (except an employee's name, title, business address, or telephone number). Surveillance of employees is not expressly forbidden by PIPEDA, but employers must use the least invasive form of surveillance and should give the employee advance notice.

The Office of the Privacy Commissioner of Canada has had several opportunities to consider the appropriateness of workplace surveillance under PIPEDA. In PIPEDA Case #279 (issued July 26, 2004), the assistant privacy commissioner found that an internet service provider's use of web cameras to monitor its employees was inappropriate. The employer's stated purposes for use of the cameras included security of the workplace, especially from theft, and monitoring of employee productivity. The assistant commissioner commented that there were less intrusive ways for the employer to have achieved these purposes. She further noted that

> Continuous, indiscriminate surveillance of employees . . . was based on a lack of trust and treats all employees with suspicion when the underlying problems may rest with a few individuals or with a management plan that may not be entirely sound.[37A]

In other words, the position of the assistant commissioner was that the "cost to human dignity," in the form of the right to privacy, must also be a factor in the assessment of the appropriateness of surveillance.

Questions to Consider

1. Should employees have the right to know they are being monitored and how? Should an employee have the right to object to surveillance?

2. Is it appropriate to "reduce privacy to a contractual right," as one commentator has put it? If a prospective employee is asked in a job application if she would consent to the electronic monitoring of her work by the employer, and she declines to give her consent, is the employer entitled to dismiss her application?

3. Is personal privacy a "fundamental human right"?

Sources: Privacy Commission of Canada, Commissioner's Findings, August 14, 2002, and Case Summary #279 (July 26, 2004) www.privcom.gc.ca; Anik Morrow, "Privacy and Data Protection," Paper for Ontario Bar Association Institute, January 24, 2002; B. McIsaac, R. Shields, and K. Klien, *Privacy Law in Canada*, student ed. (Toronto: Thomson Canada, 2007); *Eastmond v. Canadian Pacific Railway*, [2004] F.C.J. No 1043; M.A. Geist, "Computer and E-mail Workplace Surveillance in Canada: The Shift From Reasonable Expectation of Privacy to Reasonable Surveillance" (2003) 82(2) *Canadian Bar Review* 152–89; Shelley McGill and Mark Baetz, "Technology Use Codes of Conduct: Is It a Choice Between Shaping the Organizational Culture and Effective Legal Enforcement?" (2012) 15(2) *Employee Rights and Employment Policy Journal* 101.

---

[36] An Act Respecting Labour Standards Act, R.S.Q. 1991, c. N-1.1, ss. 124–8; Labour Standards Code, R.S.N.S. 1989, c. 246, ss. 71(1) and 26(2)(a).

[37] American Management Association, Electronic Monitoring & Surveillance Survey, Executive Summary 2001, 2005, 2007, http://press.amanet.org/category/press-releases/.

[37A] PIPEDA Case Summary #2004-279, ARCHIVED - Surveillance of employees at work (issued July 26, 2004) (Section 3; subsection 5(3)).

EMPLOYEE WELFARE LEGISLATION

Background

Employee welfare legislation was a reaction to unfair and harmful working conditions present in the early 19th century. These statutes marked a new role for the state—actively intervening on the side of the employees.

Initially, reform statutes dealt with the minimum age of workers, maximum hours of work, the presence of safety devices for machinery, the maintenance of safe premises in which to work, and the definition of the liability of employers when an employee was injured in the course of employment. These measures were only a beginning. Modern statutes attempt to level the playing field among employees with equal pay and anti-discrimination measures.

For those employees represented by trade unions, the disparity in bargaining power between employer and employees has been reduced. However, there remain many categories of work in which employees typically are not unionized: They still negotiate contracts of employment on an individual basis with their employers. Accordingly, legislation enacted for the welfare and protection of employees continues to provide a minimum standard of fair working conditions for many people.

Legislative Jurisdiction

In Canada, the activities of a comparatively small but very important group of businesses bring them under federal jurisdiction, and, for them, the rights and duties of employers and employees are governed by federal legislation. These industries include shipping, air transport, interprovincial transportation and telephone systems, radio, banking, and the operations of federal Crown corporations.[38] The remainder of our economic activity—the bulk of what we think of as industrial and commercial enterprise—is subject to provincial rather than federal legislation.

Employee Rights

Human Rights Protecting the rights of employees through human rights legislation began in the 1970s, before the Canadian Charter of Rights and Freedoms was enacted in 1982. However, the process was accelerated by the words in section 15 of the Charter:

> Every individual . . . has the right to the equal protection and equal benefit of the law without discrimination and, in particular without discrimination based on race, national or ethnic origin, colour, religion, sex, age or mental or physical disability.[38A]

Section 28 emphasizes that Charter rights "are guaranteed equally to male and female persons."[38B]

As noted in Chapter 1, the Charter applies to government, not to the private sector, but similar human rights legislation passed by each province and the federal Parliament applies to the private sector.[39] Most complaints under the provincial legislation relate to employment. The wording varies considerably but, generally speaking, the acts make it an offence to engage in

> a discriminatory practice . . . to refuse to employ or continue to employ an individual, or . . . to differentiate adversely . . . on a prohibited ground,[40] that is, on the basis of race, national

---

[38] Constitution Act, 1867, s. 91.

[38A] Section 15 of the Charter, Canadian Charter of Rights and Freedoms.

[38B] Section 28 of the Charter, Canadian Charter of Rights and Freedoms.

[39] See, for example, The Human Rights Code, R.S.B.C. 1996, c. 210; R.S.O. 1990, c. H-19; S.S. 1979, c. S-24.1; C.C.S.M. c. H-175.

[40] Canadian Human Rights Act, R.S.C. 1985, c. H-6, s. 7(a) and (b).

or ethnic origin, colour, religion, age, sex, sexual orientation, marital status, family status, disability and conviction for which a pardon has been granted.[41]

Complaints are typically adjudicated by an administrative tribunal set up under the legislation but damages for human rights violations may be added to a common law claim for wrongful dismissal filed in the courts.[42] Employers must not only comply with the human rights legislation themselves but also ensure others in the workplace do the same. For more information on this topic, see the Companion Website.

Pay Equity   Pay equity legislation is directed toward eliminating gender discrimination in remuneration. There are two ways of assessing the wage gap between men and women. The more traditional is through the principle of "equal pay for equal work." The law prohibits different levels of pay for substantially the same kind of work performed in the same establishment, requiring substantially the same skill, effort, and responsibility, and performed under similar working conditions.[43]

The second approach requires a focus not on the similarity of the jobs done by women and men, but on their **comparative value** to the employer—the concept of "equal pay for work of equal value" or "comparable worth."[44] The legislation requires employers to pay employees performing jobs traditionally done by women the same as those performing jobs done by men if the jobs are of equal or comparable value. The main task is to give a meaning to the word "value." It is not the same as current market value of work, but rather involves evaluating based upon criteria such as effort, training necessary, skills required, and contribution of the work. Assessing the relative value of different kinds of work can be the subject of much debate.

> **comparative value**   equal pay for work of equal value

Once a job evaluation results in a finding that one group of employees is paid too little in comparison with another, the employer must increase the wages of the lower-paid group. This may substantially raise the labour costs of an employer, making it likely that the employer will contest the job evaluation.

Usually, someone must file a complaint in order to trigger enforcement of the legislation. However, for **systemic discrimination**, the complaint system is less effective than of a regulatory model that not only prohibits wage discrimination but also places positive obligations on employers to scrutinize their pay practices and ensure that these practices comply with the legislation.

> **systemic discrimination**   discrimination that is pervasive throughout an employer's work force

At present, the regulatory model applies to the public sectors in Manitoba, New Brunswick, Newfoundland and Labrador, Nova Scotia, and Prince Edward Island; and in Ontario to both the public sector and to private sector employers who employ 10 or more persons. Throughout the rest of Canada, the complaints system alone remains in force.[45]

Employment Equity   Employment equity requires employers to treat individual applicants for jobs equally, regardless of personal characteristics. It strives to make the work force reflect the various underrepresented classes of disadvantaged persons in the general population.

The Federal Employment Equity Act[46] applies to all employers with 100 or more employees, "in connection with federal work, undertaking or business as defined in section 2 of the

---

[41] *Ibid.*, s. 3(1), amended to include "sexual orientation," by S.C. 1996, c. 1. Human rights legislation applies to employees not partners in a partnership: *McCormick v. Fasken Martineau DuMoulin LLP*, 2014 SCC 39.

[42] See e.g. Ontario Human Rights Code, *supra* n. 39, ss. 27–31.7 (Ontario Human Rights Commission), s. 46.1 (Civil Remedy).

[43] *Ibid.*, s. 5.

[44] This standard applies to both public and private sectors in areas of federal jurisdiction and in Quebec and Ontario. See Canadian Pay Equity Compliance Guide (North York, ON: CCH Canadian Ltd., 1990). Manitoba, New Brunswick, P.E.I., and Nova Scotia have pay equity legislation applicable to public sector only.

[45] The Pay Equity Act, R.S.O. 1990, c. P-7, s. 3.

[46] Federal Employment Equity Act, S.C. 1995, c. 44.

Canada Labour Code . . . ." Employers are required to conduct a "workforce analysis"—that is, to obtain relevant information about the personal characteristics of their current employees, in order to determine underrepresentation of designated groups—women, visible minorities, Aboriginals, and persons with disabilities—in the work force generally. In addition to information from their current employees, employers must seek the same information from job applicants before determining whether certain applicants should be given preference. Employers are required to review their formal and informal hiring policies in order to remove all systemic discrimination against the designated groups, and to set goals and timetables for achieving representation based on the working-age population within each employer's community. Finally, they must prepare a plan to carry out their goals, including monitoring systems to assess their progress. Critics claimed this was nothing more than a quota system.

Despite strong criticism about intrusiveness in obtaining information about the personal characteristics of both employees and job applicants, and also about the weighting of designated characteristics in hiring decisions, the federal legislation has remained in force. In December 1993, the Ontario legislature passed a bill similar to the federal Act,[47] which applied to all public sector employment and to private sector employers with more than 50 employees. It became a major issue in the 1995 provincial election; the Progressive Conservative Party vowed to repeal the legislation, and did so after it was elected to power.[48] No other province has passed similar legislation.

Mandatory Retirement and the Charter of Rights and Freedoms

Mandatory retirement schemes expect workers to leave their jobs, usually at age 65, and enjoy retirement, thereby making room for younger workers seeking employment. However, as people live longer and save less, courts and governments have been forced to reevaluate the legality of mandatory retirement.

Section 15 of the Charter of Rights and Freedoms, which guarantees "equal protection and benefit of the law without discrimination . . . based on . . . age," was first used by public sector employees wishing to remain in their jobs to challenge mandatory retirement provisions. Next, the Charter was used to challenge provincial human rights legislation that exempt mandatory retirement from age discrimination provisions. Challengers claimed that mandatory retirement based solely on age, without regard to the health or competence of an employee, is arbitrary and discriminatory and therefore offends the Charter. A similar argument was made successfully under the Manitoba Human Rights Code in 1981; the court held that a mandatory retirement provision at the University of Manitoba offended the provincial Code and was void.[49] The province of Quebec abolished compulsory retirement in 1982.[50] In 1985, the federal government abolished mandatory retirement in its civil service. Since 2005, all of the remaining common law provinces and territories have eliminated mandatory retirement and extended protection against age discrimination to workers over 65.

Defenders of mandatory retirement schemes claim that, because the schemes are socially desirable, under section 1 of the Charter they are valid because they are a "reasonable limit prescribed by law" and "can be demonstrably justified in a free and democratic society."[50A] The British Columbia and New Brunswick human rights statutes prohibit discrimination based on age but not if it is part of a "bona fide" retirement plan.[51] This is because many pension plans

---

[47] Employment Equity Act, S.O. 1993, c. 35.

[48] Job Quotas Repeal Act, S.O. 1995, c. 4.

[49] *McIntire v. University of Manitoba* (1981), 119 D.L.R. (3d) 352, followed by *Newport v. Government of Manitoba* (1982), 131 D.L.R. (3d) 564. Both cases held that section 6(1) of the Human Rights Code, S.M. 1974, c. 65, made mandatory retirement provisions void.

[50] Abolition of Compulsory Retirement Act, S.Q. 1982, c. 12.

[50A] Section 1 of the Charter, Canadian Charter of Rights and Freedoms.

[51] See, for example, *Air Canada Pilots Assn. v. Kelly*, infra n. 53. See B.C. Human Rights Code, R.S.B.C. 1996, c. 210, s. 13(b); see also N.B. Human Rights Act, R.S.N.B. 2011, c. 171, s. 4(6). A similar section in the Canada Human Rights Code was repealed in 2012.

and collective agreements depend upon a fixed retirement age to value contributions and benefits. In the past, the Supreme Court of Canada allowed such schemes in a group of four decisions dealing with complaints made by employees of hospitals, community colleges, and universities.[52] However, more recent cases suggest that societal attitudes have changed, and bona fide retirement plan exceptions may violate the Charter.[53] In all provinces, mandatory retirement schemes may be upheld when they are a genuine occupational requirement.[54]

Regulation of Working Conditions

Each province has enacted a variety of statutes prohibiting child labour, regulating the hours of work of young persons, and providing for the health and safety of employees while at work. Provinces may appoint inspectors to see that these requirements are complied with. Other statutes specify a minimum age at which children may leave school and accept full-time employment.

All provinces and the federal government set statutory minimum wage rates and grant discretionary power to certain government agencies to fix a minimum wage that varies with the industry. The legislation sets limited working hours of, with some exceptions, eight hours a day and a maximum of 40 or 48 hours a week. These statutes also require overtime rates if the number of hours worked exceeds the specified maximum.[55]

All provinces provide for annual vacations with pay. The most frequent requirement is for employers to grant their employees one week's paid vacation after one year of work. Some provinces also require public holidays with pay and minimum notice of termination.

Employment Insurance

The Employment Insurance Act[56] manages a federal employment insurance fund to which both employers and employees must contribute through payroll deductions according to a published schedule of rates. Coverage is not extended to persons who are receiving retirement pensions, self-employed, employed by a spouse, or employed by provincial governments, foreign governments, and international organizations.[57] The employer must account for all employee contributions and, along with its own contributions, regularly send them to the government. Benefits are payable out of the fund to workers who have contributed in the past and are currently unemployed. These benefits are not available in some circumstances, one of which is loss of work caused by a labour dispute in which the employee is on strike. Other employees, not on strike but "locked out" because a plant or business is shut down by a strike, remain eligible for benefits.

---

[52] *McKinney v. University of Guelph*, [1990] 3 S.C.R. 229; *Harrison v. University of British Columbia*, [1990] 3 S.C.R. 451; *Stoffman v. Vancouver General Hospital*, [1990]3 S.C.R. 483; *Douglas/Kwantlen Faculty Association v. Douglas College*, [1990] 3 S.C.R. 570. Provincial human rights codes and the federal Human Rights Act apply to all employment contracts within their jurisdiction, both in the public and private sectors. In contrast, section 15 of the Charter applies to all employment contracts made in the public sector—contracts made by governments at all levels, by Crown corporations, school boards, community colleges, etc. It does not bind the private sector, including universities (see the *McKinney* case), even though they may receive a high proportion of their funding from governments.

[53] *Air Canada Pilots Assn. v. Kelly*, [2011] F.C.J. No. 152, paras. 98–156, reversed 2012 FCA 209, leave denied; *Greater Vancouver Regional District Employees' Union v. Greater Vancouver Regional District*, 2001 BCCA 435, 206 D.L.R. (4th) 220; *Assn. of Justices of the Peace of Ontario v. Ontario (Attorney General)* (2008), 92 O.R. (3d) 16, [2008] O.J. No. 2131. *New Brunswick (Human Rights Commission) v. Potash Corporation of Saskatchewan Inc.* 2008 SCC 45.

[54] *Air Canada Pilots Assn. v. Kelly*, [2011] F.C.J. No. 152, paras. 98–156, 353–85. *British Columbia (Public Service Employee Relations Commission) v. British Columbia Government and Service Employees' Union*, 1999 3 S.C.R. 3.

[55] See e.g. Employment Standards Act 2000, S.O. 2000, c. 41.

[56] Employment Insurance Act, S.C. 1996, c. 23 E-5.6.

[57] *Ibid.*, s. 5(2).

Most important, if an employee voluntarily leaves employment without just cause—or is justifiably dismissed for misconduct—he or she will not be eligible for benefits.

Workers' Compensation

Harshness of the Common Law
While the common law recognized that an employer could be liable to an employee for injury sustained in the course of employment, it was notoriously difficult for the employee to recover damages. The employer might defend the action successfully if it could show that the injury

(a) resulted from the contributory negligence of the employee;

(b) was caused by the negligence of a fellow employee, provided the employer took reasonable care to hire competent workers;

(c) was an **assumed risk**, accepted by the employee as a normal incident of the type of work he had agreed to do.

assumed risk risk assumed by an employee in accepting a particular employment

It would also be difficult for dependants of an employee who had been killed at work to obtain the necessary proof to meet the burden of proof.

Statutory Reform
Each of the provinces has replaced the common law action with a statutory no-fault compensation scheme.[58]

The statutes create Workers' Compensation Boards to hear employees' claims and also establish funds to which employers subject to the Act must contribute regularly and which are used to pay claims. Such payment replaces any personal action against an employer. To succeed, an employee need only show that the injury was caused by an accident in the course of employment. The principles of contributory negligence, negligence of a fellow employee, and assumed risk no longer apply. An employee's claim will fail only if it is shown that the accident was caused substantially by his willful misconduct. Even then, the employee or the dependants will recover if the accident has caused death or serious disablement. There is no requirement of proving negligence by the employer. There is also a major advantage in avoiding the costs and hazards of litigation. As well, since an employee claims recovery from a compensation board and not from his employer, he need not fear prejudicing his future with the employer.

Variations in Provincial Reforms
Coverage varies somewhat among the provinces. Generally included are workers in the following industries: construction, mining, manufacturing, lumbering, fishing, transportation, communications, and public utilities. Industries are classified according to the degree of hazard. Exemptions may include casual employees and employees of small businesses employing fewer than a stated number of workers. For employees excluded from the usual workers' compensation benefits, several provinces have added a second part to their legislation, defining the employer's liability for injuries caused by defective plant or equipment or by the negligence of other employees, and granting employees a right to damages in spite of contributory negligence on their part. In other jurisdictions, the common law rules still apply to casual employees and to those in small businesses.

Occupational Health
Occupational health focuses on the prevention of harm and on occupational safety. There are several reasons for the increasing awareness of health standards in the workplace. First, the general concern over environmental hazards to health has made the public much more sensitive to the special problems of the work environment: If a chemical dispersed in the atmosphere can harm people at a great distance, how much more dangerous is it for the workers who handle it and are directly exposed?

---

[58] See, for example, Workers' Compensation Act, R.S.B.C. 1996, c. 492; S.N.S. 1994–5, c. 10; Workplace Safety and Insurance Act, 1997, S.O. 1997, c. 16, Sch. A.

Second, improvement in the general level of public health has drawn attention to the fact that persons in particular occupations suffer from certain illnesses to a greater degree than does the general public. Third, improvement in the quality of medical records and the sophistication of medical diagnosis have made connecting certain diseases with some occupations easier. This last aspect has received great prominence in industries where large numbers of workers have been found to have very high rates of some illnesses 20 or 30 years after starting work.

Provincial occupational health and safety legislation takes a proactive approach to preventing injury in the workplace.[59] It requires a business to establish an in-house committee to identify, investigate, and correct dangers in the workplace. Government inspections are randomly carried out, and companies may be fined for failing to remedy a dangerous situation. Injuries in the workplace automatically trigger an investigation. Employees have the right to refuse to perform unsafe work without breaching their employment contract.[60] In Ontario, harassment in the workplace is considered an occupational health and safety issue.[61]

INTERNATIONAL ISSUE

Global Employment Standards

On April 24, 2013, more than 1100 workers were killed when a garment factory building collapsed in Bangladesh. This was another tragic reminder of the wide variation in wages and employment conditions that exist around the world. Two prominent initiatives aimed at harmonizing and improving employment standards in developing nations are

- the United Nations (UN) Global Compact, and
- the Organisation for Economic Co-operation and Development (OECD) Guidelines for Multinational Enterprises.

Both initiatives take a corporate social responsibility approach. The UN Global Compact is a set of 10 principles addressing human rights, labour, the environment, and corruption. A business voluntarily undertakes to participate in the compact and, in so doing, agrees to adopt policies and operations furthering the compact's objectives and to publicize the results of their progress. The four principles dealing with labour are

- freedom of association and the right to collective bargaining,
- elimination of all forms of forced and compulsory labour,
- effective abolition of child labour, and
- elimination of discrimination in respect of employment and occupation.

Many of Canada's largest companies participate in the Global Compact, including Rio Tinto Alcan, Bombardier, Enbridge, Hydro-Québec, and Petro-Canada.

The OECD guidelines are also voluntary standards but they are the recommendations of the participating governments to the multinationals within their respective jurisdictions. Canada is a participating country. The guidelines include eight standards addressing employment and industrial relations that are more detailed than those in the Global Compact.

Questions to Consider

1. Do you think voluntary compliance with these international codes of conduct is more likely to be achieved through the business network approach of the Global Compact or the government backed approach of the OECD? Why?

2. Discuss the pros and cons of the broad general principles of the Global Compact as distinct from the more detailed set of standards of the OECD.

Sources: "The Ten Principles," The United Nations Global Compact, www.unglobalcompact.org/AbouttheGC /TheTENPrinciples/index.html; Organisation for Economic Co-operation and Development, The OECD Guidelines for Multinational Enterprises (Paris: OECD Publications, 2000), www.oecd.org/dataoecd/-56/-36/-1922428.pdf; The UN Global Compact Office and OECD Secretariat, The UN Global Compact and the OECD Guidelines for Multinational Enterprises: Complementarities and Distinctive Contributions, Investment Division, Organisation for Economic Co-operation and Development, April 26, 2005, www.oecd.org/dataoecd/23/2/34873731.pdf.

---

[59] Some provinces, such as British Columbia, cover this issue in the workers' compensation legislation while others have separate legislation: Occupational Health and Safety Act, R.S.O. 1990, c. O.1.

[60] See e.g. Occupational Health and Safety Act, R.S.O. 1990, c. O.1. s. 43(3); see also *Dionne v. Commission scolaire des Patriotes*, 2014 SCC 33, [2014] 1 S.C.R. 765, at para. 20.

[61] *Ibid*, ss. 32.0.1–32.0.7; it is also a human rights issue.

COLLECTIVE BARGAINING

The Process

collective bargaining establishing conditions of employment by negotiation between an employer and the bargaining agent for its employees

The process of negotiating terms of employment with a group of employees rather than individuals is known as **collective bargaining**. For those industries within federal jurisdiction, a federal statute regulates how collective bargaining is done.[62] Statutes passed by each of the provinces regulate all other industries.[63] These acts state that all employees are free to belong to trade unions and that membership in a trade union does not provide the employer with grounds for dismissing an employee. The acts also require employers to recognize the representative union as the bargaining agent for employees for reaching an agreement on the general terms of their employment.

certification an acknowledgment by an administrative tribunal that a particular union commands sufficient membership to justify its role as exclusive bargaining agent for the employees

If an employer is unwilling to recognize a trade union voluntarily, as often happens, the union may have to apply to be certified before it can proceed to bargain for the employees. **Certification** is an acknowledgment by an administrative tribunal (called in some provinces a **labour relations board**) that a particular union has won sufficient membership to justify its role as exclusive bargaining agent for the employees. This arrangement has the practical advantage of confining the negotiations to a single representative of the employees, and it avoids the confusion of rival unions claiming the right to act as bargaining agents for a group of employees. We must distinguish between a bargaining agent and a bargaining unit: A **bargaining agent** is a union that has the exclusive right to bargain with the employer on behalf of the bargaining unit. The **bargaining unit** includes a specific group of employees eligible to join the union, whether they join or not. For more information on this topic, see the Companion Website.

labour relations board an administrative tribunal regulating labour relations

bargaining agent a union that has the exclusive right to bargain with the employer on behalf of the bargaining unit

bargaining unit a specified group of employees eligible to join the union

Content of a Collective Agreement

When an employer and union reach an agreement, the members vote to approve or ratify the agreement and the terms are placed in a contract called a collective agreement. The terms usually include a definition of the employees covered, an acknowledgment by the employer that the contracting union is their recognized bargaining agent, an outline of the steps that both parties must take in settling **grievances**, seniority provisions in the promotion and laying off of employees, wage rates, hours, vacation periods and other fringe benefits, the duration of the collective agreement, and the means by which it may be amended or renewed. Often there is a clause acknowledging that maintaining discipline and efficiency of employees is the exclusive task of the management of the company, subject to the right of an employee to lodge a grievance. The agreement almost invariably forbids strikes or lockouts as long as the agreement continues to operate; indeed, most provinces require that such a term be included. The employees covered do not generally include those employed in a confidential capacity, those who have managerial responsibilities such as the authority to hire or discharge others, or those employed as guards or security police in the protection of business property. Some provinces have also excluded certain professional groups such as engineers, although the recent tendency has been to include more of the professions.

grievances disputes arising under the collective agreement

The terms of a collective agreement set the procedure for dismissing employees, replacing the common law rules for reasonable notice of dismissal, grounds for dismissal, progressive discipline, and reinstatement. To the extent that the collective agreement prescribes working conditions above the level required by existing legislation, it replaces employee welfare legislation in protecting the interests of workers. Human rights legislation continues to apply. For more information on this topic, see the Companion Website.

---

[62] Canada Labour Code, R.S.C. 1985, c. L-2.

[63] See, for example: Labour Relations Code, R.S.B.C. 1996, c. 244; Labour Relations Act, 1995, S.O. 1995, c. 1, Sch. A; Trade Union Act, R.S.N.S. 1989, c. 475.

First Collective Agreement

Frequently the most difficult collective agreement to reach is the first one after certification: The union is new and its local members are inexperienced (even if they have advice from other union officials); management is unaccustomed to working with a union; and often there has been some hostility and bitterness between employer and employees during the certification campaign. In response to the problem, most provinces and the federal government have legislation providing for "first contract arbitration."[64] If the parties cannot reach agreement on a contract within the time stated in the Act, then the applicable provincial or federal labour board may impose a first contract on them after hearing the parties in an arbitration.

LABOUR DISPUTES

Types of Disputes

There are four major types of disputes affecting trade unions: jurisdictional disputes, recognition disputes, interest disputes, and rights disputes.

1. A **jurisdictional dispute** is a disagreement between unions competing for the right to represent a group of employees. For instance, the type of work the employees do might seem to bring them within the terms of reference of two different trade unions. A single operation of drilling a hole through both metal and wood might raise a question of whether the worker should belong to the metalworkers' or the woodworkers' union.

2. A **recognition dispute** arises between an employer and a union when the employer insists on negotiating employment contracts directly with its employees and resists a union demand that it be recognized as the employees' bargaining agent.

3. An **interest dispute** arises when an employer and a union cannot reach agreement about the terms to be included in a collective agreement.

4. A **rights dispute**, commonly known as a grievance, is a difference of opinion between employer and union on the interpretation of terms in a collective agreement already in existence.

For more information on this topic, see the Companion Website.

jurisdictional dispute two or more unions compete for the right to represent a particular group of employees

recognition dispute an employer refuses to recognize the union as the employees' bargaining agent

interest dispute an employer and the union disagree about the particular terms to be included in the collective agreement

rights dispute an employer and the union differ in their interpretation of terms in an existing collective agreement

Legislative Regulation of Dispute Resolution

The regulation of labour disputes is a field of study in its own right, and we cannot do more than indicate a few of the basic methods used. For an adequate treatment of the law, it is necessary to consult recognized works in the field; a few are listed in the bibliography at the end of this book.

Statutes now provide machinery that either eliminates or minimizes the need to resort to strike action in each of the four main types of dispute mentioned above. Certification procedure, briefly considered in the preceding section, has done much to resolve jurisdictional disputes and is the only legal means of settling recognition disputes.

Provincial statutes require both employer and employees to follow a series of procedures designed to aid in the settlement of interest disputes:

■ First, they require a genuine attempt over a specified period to bargain to reach agreement.[65]

---

[64] R.S.B.C. 1996, c. 244, s. 55; R.S.Q. 1991, c. C-27, s. 93.1; R.S.M. 1987, c. L-10, s. 75; S.O. 1995, c. 1, Sch. A, s. 43.

[65] In Canada, an employer need not bargain with a union that has not been certified and with which it has not previously made a collective agreement. In the United States, an employer must bargain with a union representing the majority of its employees, whether it is certified or not.

■ Second, if the parties fail to agree, they must submit to **conciliation procedure**—that is, continue to bargain with the help of a conciliation officer or board.

■ Third, if the parties still fail to agree, the conciliator will file a "no board report"; the employer cannot declare a lockout, nor can the union begin strike action, until a further specified **cooling-off period** has elapsed.

For a rights dispute, the law imposes **arbitration procedure**: the parties are bound by the interpretation placed on the collective agreement by an arbitrator. In conciliation procedure, the parties are not bound to accept the solution proposed by the conciliation officer, but in arbitration procedure, the decision of the arbitrator is binding.

Only in interest disputes is there the possibility of lawful strike action, and then only after the prescribed conciliation procedure and cooling-off period. A strike is illegal if the preliminary grievance procedures set down by statute have not been followed or, even when they have been followed, if the strike is not conducted according to carefully defined rules. The conduct of a strike by the union must be free of compulsion, intimidation, and threat. Furthermore, a strike may become unlawful if it is undertaken with an intent to injure another party and not with the intent of improving the employment interests of the strikers.

Although strikers are entitled to picket at or near the place of the employer's business, they must do so peaceably and only for the purpose of obtaining or communicating information. Statements made on placards or in literature distributed at the scene of the picketing must be correct and factual. Mr. Chief Justice McRuer of the Ontario Supreme Court outlined the scope of these rights as follows:

> It is one thing to exercise all the lawful rights to strike and the lawful rights to picket; that is a freedom that should be preserved and its preservation has advanced the interests of the labouring man and the community as a whole to an untold degree over the last half-century. But it is another thing to recognize a conspiracy to injure so that benefits to any particular person or class may be realized. Further, if what any person or group of persons does amounts to a common law nuisance to another what is being done may be restrained by injunction.[66]

For more information on this topic, see the Companion Website.

IMPLICATIONS OF THE COLLECTIVE AGREEMENT FOR THE INDIVIDUAL EMPLOYEE

The parties to a collective agreement are the employer and the representative union; generally, each party is a large organization or institution, and the individual employee does not actively participate in negotiating the terms of employment. The union may also be a large organization with smaller segments known as locals representing specific workplaces. The union bargaining team is elected by the members of the local. Since nearly all the bargaining is done by the union, comparatively little ground is left for an employee to negotiate with the employer at the time of making an individual contract of employment.

The province of Quebec has a unique piece of legislation that takes this process a stage further: The terms of a collective agreement may apply even to workers who are not members of the bargaining unit for which the union was entitled to negotiate.[67] Under the legislation, when a union has bargained for a certain rate of pay with one or more large employers within the industry, the parties may apply to the Minister of Labour for a decree extending the provisions of the collective agreement to all other employers and

---

[66] *General Dry Batteries of Canada Ltd. v. Brigenshaw*, [1951] O.R. 522, per McRuer, C.J.H.C., at 528.

[67] Collective Agreement Decrees Act, R.S.Q. 1991, c. D-2.

employees within the industry or trade in the province or within a region of the province. To succeed, the application must show that the collective agreements already written have acquired a dominance and importance for establishing conditions of labour within the industry or region. The effect is to establish a minimum wage law within the area covered by the decree, and to extend the terms of the collective agreement to workers within the industry not represented when the contract was made.

Unions have more than the dominant role in bargaining on behalf of individual workers; often workers do not have the freedom to choose whether to belong to the union. In *Bonsor v. Musicians' Union*,[68] the plaintiff, who had been wrongfully expelled from the union and found it impossible to earn a livelihood as a musician without being a member, testified as follows:

> I would like to tell his lordship that if I could earn my living forthwith without being a member of this so-called Musicians' Union I would not want to join it, but I have got to join it in order to work because it is a closed shop. I will always pay my subscriptions, but I will not take any active part in union matters. I will be a member by force because I am forced to be a member.[69]

After quoting the above statement of the plaintiff, Lord Denning commented:

> When one remembers that the rules are applied to a man in that state of mind, it will be appreciated that they are not so much a contract as we used to understand a contract, but they are much more a legislative code laid down by some members of the union to be imposed on all members of the union. They are more like by-laws than a contract.[70]

THE LEGAL STATUS OF TRADE UNIONS

We touched briefly on the legal status of trade unions when discussing capacity to contract in Chapter 7. We noted that trade unions are recognized as legal entities before labour relations boards in order to bind them to the board's rulings; but this recognition is for a limited purpose, and we must not infer from the fact that unions have a separate existence before an administrative tribunal that they necessarily have comparable standing before the courts. We noted also that using a representative action provides a possible means by which unions may sue or be sued in the courts.

For various reasons, our legislatures have avoided the otherwise obvious path of requiring trade unions to come within existing legislation for corporations, and so conferring on them a corporate existence comparable with that of other business organizations. Nevertheless, the legislatures seem to be moving in that direction, and when there is no decisive statutory authority, the courts are able to cite the reasoning in the famous *Taff Vale* case, a decision handed down by the House of Lords in 1901.[71]

CASE 18.1

During a strike, two agents of a union "put themselves in charge . . . and . . . illegally watched and beset men to prevent them from working for the company, and illegally ordered men to break their contracts." The court interpreted the strike as a conspiracy in restraint of trade under the then-existing law of England. As a result, the company suffered business losses and sued the union. But even though there was an admitted wrong, could the union as such be sued for damages? The House of Lords found the trade union to be a "quasi-corporate" body that could be sued. It held the union liable in damages for the company's losses.

---

[68] [1954] Ch. 479. (The dissenting judgment of Denning, L.J., was approved on appeal to the House of Lords: [1956] A.C. 105.)

[69] *Bonsor v. Musicians' Union* [1954] Ch. 479. (The dissenting judgment of Denning, L.J., was approved on appeal to the House of Lords: [1956] A.C. 105.) at 485.

[70] *Ibid.*

[71] *Taff Vale Railway Co. v. Amalgamated Society of Railway Servants*, [1901] A.C. 426.

Although the result of the *Taff Vale* case was nullified shortly afterward by an exempt that exempted the union for restraint of trade accusations,[72] and although this act was adopted by provinces in Canada, the principle that trade unions could be sued survived.

The Supreme Court of Canada in 1960 made extensive use of the *Taff Vale* decision in the case of *International Brotherhood of Teamsters v. Thérien.*[73]

closed-shop agreement a collective agreement requiring all employees to be union members

---

CASE 18.2

Thérien was the owner of a Vancouver trucking business and had been doing business with City Construction Company for some years when the company entered into a collective agreement with the Teamsters' Union requiring, as one of its terms, that all employees be union members (a **closed-shop agreement**). Thérien agreed then to hire only union members for the operation of his trucks. However, he declined to join the union personally because he wished to maintain his relationship as an independent contractor in dealings with City Construction. He further claimed that, in the capacity of an employer in his own right, he was forbidden by the Labour Relations Code of British Columbia from participating in union activities.

The union opposed that view, and because of its threats to picket City Construction, the general manager of the company informed Thérien that the company must terminate his services. Thérien suffered a significant loss of business, and he sued the union, claiming damages for its wrongful conduct. The union defended on the grounds that, first, it was not a legal entity and so could not be sued and, second, in any case it had not been guilty of conduct that might constitute a tort.

On the first argument of the union, the court noted that the union had been certified as a bargaining agent under the terms of the Labour Relations Act, and stated:

> It is necessary for the exercise of the [statutory] powers given that such unions should have officers or other agents to act in their names and on their behalf. The Legislature, by giving the right to act as agent for others and to contract on their behalf, has given them two of the essential qualities of a corporation in respect of liability for tort since a corporation can only act by its agents.[74]

The court quoted the *Taff Vale* case:

> If the Legislature has created a thing which can own property, which can employ servants, and which can inflict injury, it must be taken, I think, to have impliedly given the power to make it suable in a Court of Law for injuries purposely done by its authority and procurement.[75]

Having identified the union as a suable legal entity, the court found, first, that the union had threatened to resort to picketing instead of following the grievance procedure set out in the collective agreement, and second, that the consequence of its conduct was the injurious termination of Thérien's arrangement with City Construction Company. The court awarded damages to Thérien and ordered an injunction restraining the union from interfering with him in the operation of his business.

The *Thérien* decision is one of a succession of Canadian cases developing the common law on the subject of the legal status of trade unions.[76] It does not apply, of course, in

---

[72] See Trade Disputes Act, 1906, 6 Ed. VII, c. 47, s. 1, declaring that actions of a trade union in furtherance of its interests would not thenceforth be interpreted as a restraint of trade.

[73] (1960), 22 D.L.R. (2d) 1. This decision has been followed in a Manitoba case: *Dusessoy's Supermarket St. James Ltd. v. Retail Clerks Union Local No. 832* (1961), 34 W.W.R. 577.

[74] *International Brotherhood of Teamsters v. Thérien, ibid*, per Locke, J., at 11.

[75] *Taff Vale Railway Co. v. Amalgamated Society of Railway Servants, supra*, n. 71, per Halsbury, L.C., at 436.

[76] See e.g. *U.N.A. v. Alberta (Attorney-General)* (1990), 89 D.L.R. (4th) 609.

provinces whose statutes specifically define the circumstances in which trade unions may be sued. In particular, Ontario has a statutory provision that restricts the possibility of an action against a trade union for torts.[77]

For more information on this topic, see the Companion Website.

Strategies to Manage the Legal Risks

When dealing with individual employment relationships:

- Establish job related criteria for job applicants—this will avoid consideration of the personal characteristics of prospective employees in violation of human rights legislation.

- Initially hire employees on short fixed-term contracts that naturally come to an end.

- Replace implied terms for reasonable notice of termination in employment of indefinite length with express contractual terms designating the amount of notice that will serve to terminate the agreement.

- Create detailed job descriptions and codes of conduct describing employee responsibilities and share them with prospective employees as part of the employment contract.

- Create, publish, and follow a protocol for progressive employee discipline.

- Document infractions and responses.

- Follow consistent warning and discipline processes that allow employees to respond to allegations.

- Offer incompetent employees training or education opportunities.

- Dismiss employees privately, at the end of the day, and in the most sensitive, fair, and respectful manner possible.

When dealing with independent contractors:

- Respect the characteristics of an independent contractorship to avoid confusing the relationship for one of employment.

- Require independent contractors to carry their own liability insurance and obtain a promise to indemnify the business if it is held liable for substandard work or negligence of the independent contractor.

- Ensure that exemption clauses in contracts with customers extend protection to independent contractors completing work under it.

When dealing with a unionized workforce, specialized legal advice should be obtained to guide management through the processes, especially when interest- or jurisdictional-based disputes arise. For rights-based disputes, the grievance process of arbitration should be followed. Parties should commence negotiations well in advance of the expiration of the existing collective agreement so that a new contract may be in place before the former's end.

---

[77] Rights of Labour Act, R.S.O. 1990, c. R.33, s. 3. For legislation expressly making unions suable entities, see Labour Relations Code, R.S.B.C. 1996, c. 144, s. 154; Industrial Relations Act, R.S.N.B. 1973, c. I-4, s. 114(2); Trade Union Act, R.S.S. 1978, c. T-17, s. 29, as amended by S.S. 1983, c. 81, s. 9.

QUESTIONS FOR REVIEW

1. Briefly describe two employees, each of whom has varying degrees of responsibility as agent.

2. How does an independent contractor differ from an employee?

3. Give an example of circumstances where an employee commits a tort but his employer is not liable. What element is necessary to make the employer liable?

4. After earning his B. Comm. degree, Bruce was hired as a junior accountant by Cargo Wholesale Inc. He received favourable assessment letters and salary increases after year one and year two. At the end of his third year, he received his final paycheque with a letter stating that he was dismissed for incompetence. What points might Bruce argue to show that he was wrongfully dismissed?

5. Norman is hired as a waiter in a restaurant at a summer resort without any discussion about the length of his employment contract. He receives a weekly paycheque. He is let go without notice at the end of the summer. Explain whether he has been wrongfully dismissed.

6. On what grounds is a business justified in dismissing its employees without notice?

7. What are the main factors to be taken into account when assessing damages for wrongful dismissal?

8. When is reinstatement an unlikely remedy for wrongful dismissal?

9. Why is it not effective to define pay equity solely in terms of the market value of comparable jobs?

10. Describe briefly the benefits of and problems with compulsory retirement.

11. Why was it difficult before the passing of the Workers' Compensation Act for an employee injured at work to obtain a remedy against her employer?

12. Under workers' compensation legislation, who pays compensation to an injured employee? How are the funds raised?

13. Describe some of the main elements in a collective agreement.

14. In certain provinces and in federal jurisdiction, what happens when the parties do not succeed in making a deal for their first collective agreement?

15. What is the difference between a jurisdictional dispute and an interest dispute?

16. Collective agreements have been described by some commentators as being more like legislation for individual workers. Explain.

17. Quality Meat Packers Ltd. has major factories and warehouses from coast to coast. How does this fact complicate the company's collective bargaining with its employees?

CASES AND PROBLEMS

1. Continuing Scenario

   Benson was hired as a waiter at Ashley's restaurant; he had 15 years of table service experience even though he was just 30 years old. Six months after he began work, Ashley learned that Benson had behaved inappropriately at the restaurant, insulting several customers after he had too much to drink. Ashley called Benson on the telephone and told him that he would be fired if he ever drank alcohol at work again. Two months later, there was another incident at work when Benson was rude to customers. Benson was not working at the time and had only stopped by the restaurant to pick up his jacket. Ashley was furious: She dismissed Benson and gave him two weeks' payment in lieu of notice.

   Benson sued for damages for wrongful dismissal, claiming 12 months' salary.

   Ashley did not claim that she dismissed Benson for drinking while on duty; in fact, Ashley was not aware of such conduct. She argued that two weeks' notice was all that

Benson should receive. However, at the trial, evidence of other employees and patrons of the restaurant established that Benson had been drinking at work on many occasions after Ashley's warning.

Should Benson's action succeed? Why? Would your answer be different if Ashley had simply demoted Benson to kitchen dishwasher (where he wouldn't see customers) with a reduction in pay?

2. Taxi drivers owned their own taxis and worked for Welcome Taxis Ltd. The taxi company called them "independent contractors" and distinguished them from employees in that they were not covered by the Employment Insurance Act. Although the company neither owned nor leased the vehicles, the drivers were required to comply with the company's directions about the dispatch services and how the vehicles were operated. They were also obligated to use the company's bookkeeping and fuel provision services—and the company could suspend or discharge the drivers for any breach of its rules.

The Ministry of National Revenue decided to assess Welcome and require it to pay premiums for each of its drivers as an employee. Welcome appealed to the court, and the trial judge concluded that such a degree of control was exercised by the taxi company over the drivers that all the drivers were in insurable employment, pursuant to section 6(e) of the Act. The taxi company brought an application for judicial review to the Federal Court of Appeal. The following arguments were made:

- *By Welcome Taxis Ltd.*—The drivers were owners or operators of their own businesses within the meaning of section 6(e) of the Regulations. The trial judge erred in considering only the factor of control to the exclusion of other relevant factors. Another consideration was who owned the tools of the trade. Not only did the drivers own the vehicles, but they were in a position to gain a profit or suffer a loss from the operation of the business. The degree of financial risk taken by the drivers was considerably more than that taken by the company. The drivers were in a position to delegate their driving duties, which indicated independent status. Given the chance of profit, the relative degree of financial risk, and the ability of the drivers to "operate their own business," they were not employees of the company.

- *By the Ministry of National Revenue*—Under a traditional employee/independent contractor analysis, the drivers appeared to be in business for their own account, as independent contractors. However, the breadth of section 6(e) was broad enough to extend the conventional meaning of "employment." The company exercised a great deal of control over the drivers. Although it did not own or lease the vehicles, it retained the right to cancel the lease agreement or exercise its option to purchase the vehicle if the drivers should fail to observe its rules. The trial judge had not erred in applying a liberal interpretation of section 6(e) and finding that the drivers were included in insurable employment.

Which argument do you think should succeed in the Court of Appeal? Give reasons for your opinion.

3. C.W. Jonas was a conductor employed by the East-West Railway Company. While the passenger train on which he was working was standing in a railway station, it was struck by another train. Because of the negligent operation of the train, Jonas was severely injured. He sued the East-West Railway Company for damages for negligence.

In defence, the railway company produced its copy of an employment contract signed by Jonas. The contract included the following clause:

The employee, C.W. Jonas, agrees that in consideration of employment and wages by the Great East-West Railway Company, he will assume all risks of accident or casualty incident to such employment and service whether caused by the negligence of the Company or of its employees or otherwise, and will forever release, acquit, and discharge the said Company from all liability. The employee waives all rights to worker's compensation that might otherwise arise under this contract.

Without rendering a decision, discuss the public policy considerations inherent in a dispute of this kind.

4. Devellano operated a retail food supermarket that bought 60 percent of its merchandise from Prairie Wholesale Grocers Limited. Because of a wage dispute, the employees of Prairie Wholesale Grocers, who were members of the Office and Shop Clerks Union, went on strike. An official of that union then telephoned Devellano to enlist her support and apply economic pressure on Prairie Wholesale Grocers by reducing purchases from it. When Devellano refused, members of the union picketed her supermarket. They stopped cars on their way into the parking lot of the supermarket and distributed leaflets, intimating, inaccurately, that Devellano's store was controlled by Prairie Wholesale Grocers. The placards used while picketing contained the words "Devellano's Supermarket" and "Strike" in large letters, although none of Devellano's own employees were on strike. As a result, Devellano lost customers and sued the union for damages and an injunction to restrain the picketing of her premises.

Discuss the defences available to the union, and state whether they would succeed.

5. Lucy Anang was hired as a chemist by the Plastic Toy Co. Her employment contract stated that, following termination of her employment with the company, she would not work for any competitor in the province for five years or at any time in the future disclose to anyone any information about secret processes used by Plastic Toy Co. Anang had worked in the laboratory of the company for a period of about three years when she was given two months' notice of dismissal.

After her dismissal, Anang tried to earn a living as a consulting chemist. The plant supervisor at Plastic Toy then learned that she was disclosing certain information about manufacturing processes to one of the company's chief competitors. Specifically, it appeared that she had disclosed secret processes related to the production of equipment used in the colouring of toys, processes of value to the company.

Plastic Toy Co. sued Anang for damages and for an injunction restraining her from disclosing further information. One of Anang's defences was that no injunction could be granted to deprive her of the right to practise her profession as a chemist. What is the likelihood that the action will succeed?

Suppose instead that Anang had left Plastic Toy Co. because she had received an offer of a higher salary from a competitor of Plastic Toy. The management of Plastic Toy had no evidence that she disclosed any of its secret processes to her new employer, but was concerned that she might do so. Is it likely that Plastic Toy could obtain an injunction restraining Anang from working for its competitor? What conflicting policy issues must the court resolve?

6. In May 1986, the directors of Universal Printing Co., publishers of a newspaper with a large circulation, approached Bell to persuade him to become their assistant advertising manager. They suggested that, if he accepted, he would probably succeed the present advertising manager upon that manager's retirement. At the time, Bell held a responsible position with an advertising agency and was 42. During the discussions, Bell emphasized that his present position was a very satisfactory one, that it was important at his age that his employment be permanent, and that he would not consider a change that did not offer the prospect of a position lasting for the balance of his working life.

After careful consideration, Bell accepted the position offered at a salary of $65 000 a year. He was promoted to advertising manager in 1994, and in the period from May 1986 to July 2002, his salary was increased regularly until it reached an annual sum of $160 000. In addition, every year he received a discretionary Christmas bonus approved by the directors and a special distribution pursuant to a profit-sharing plan confined to selected employees and made under the sole direction of the principal shareholder of Universal Printing Co. Ltd. Bell's receipts under the profit-sharing plan were $23 600 in 1999, $20 400 in 2000, and $17 000 in 2001.

In August 2002, the president of Universal Printing Co. Ltd., T.G. Dodds, called Bell into his office and, after some opening pleasantries about Bell's prowess in golf, told Bell that he thought another advertising manager he had in mind could produce better results for the company. Dodds told Bell that if he could see his way clear to resigning forthwith, he might have three months' salary in lieu of notice. Bell replied that he could not afford at this stage in his career to admit to the incompetence implied in a resignation and refused. Later in the afternoon, his secretary brought him the following letter:

August 8, 2002

Dear Mr. Bell:

This is to confirm the notice given to you today of the termination of your employment with Universal Printing Co. Ltd. as of this date. Enclosed is a cheque for your salary to date. Your pension plan has been commuted to a paid-up basis that will pay you $3500 a month commencing at age 65.

T.G. Dodds

Bell at once made efforts to secure other employment, and by December 8, 2002, found a position with an advertising agency at a salary of $42 000 a year. If he had remained a further year with Universal Printing Co. Ltd., the paid-up value of his pension would have increased to $6500 per month.

Bell brought an action against Universal Printing Co. Ltd. for damages for wrongful dismissal. What amount of damages, if any, should he recover? Are there any additional facts you would like to know?

7. In September, Knowles, the owner of a professional hockey club, began negotiations with Meyer, a professional hockey player, for Meyer's services for the following two years. The two agreed orally to a salary of $3000 a week for Meyer during the training and playing seasons. At the time, Meyer asked whether players would be covered by workers' compensation insurance if injured. Knowles replied that the club's lawyer had advised that players were not covered, but that in any event he was having written contracts drawn up by the lawyer in which a clause would provide that every player would be insured against injury and that if a player were disabled he would be looked after.

Written contracts were then prepared and presented to all the players (including Meyer) for signing. The contracts in their written form stated the agreed salary for each individual player, and outlined the usual conditions regarding the player's obligations to the club, but there was no reference to insurance protection against injury or to the employer's obligation in the event of a player being disabled.

Meyer played for the team for six weeks and then received a serious injury to his eye during a hockey game. He was immediately taken to the hospital. At the end of the game, Knowles announced to Meyer's teammates in the dressing room that he would pay Meyer's salary to the end of the season.

Knowles paid Meyer's salary to the date of his injury and refused to pay any additional sum. Meyer brought an action for damages claiming $45 000 representing his salary for the remaining 15 weeks of the playing season; $500 for the cost of an artificial eye; and $100 000 general damages as compensation for the loss of his eye.

Discuss the issues raised by these facts, and explain whether Meyer's action is likely to succeed.

(www.pearsoncanada.ca/smyth)

In addition to pre- and post-tests, mini-cases, and application exercises, the Companion Website includes the following province-specific resources for Chapter 18:

- **Alberta:** Conditions of Employment; Constructive Dismissal; Worker Cooling-off Period; Duty to Accommodate; Employment Standards; Employment Standards (Reservist Leave) Amendment Act; Labour Relations Code; Summary Dismissal; Termination and Layoffs; Workers' Compensation; Workers' Compensation Amendment Act; Wrongful Dismissal
- **Atlantic Provinces:** Employment Standards Act; Labour Relations Legislation; Occupational Health and Safety
- **British Columbia:** Child Employment; Collective Bargaining; Discrimination in the Workplace; Employment Standards Act; Essential Services; Leave of Absence; Mediation and Arbitration; Minimum Wage; Occupational Health and Safety; Privacy Rights; Strikes, Lockouts and Picketing; Termination of Temporary Employees; Termination and Layoff; Termination of Probationary Employees; Unfair Labour Practices; Union Certification and Decertification; Worker Pay; Workers' Compensation
- **Manitoba/Saskatchewan:** Employment Standards—Minimum Standards in Legislation; Human Rights; Labour Relations Boards; Reasonable Notice—Statutory Minimums; Vicarious Liability and Motor Vehicles; Vicarious Liability of Employers; Workers' Compensation
- **Ontario:** Bad Faith; Discrimination; Duty to Accommodate; Employment Equity; Employment Standards; Human Rights; Labour Relations; Mandatory Retirement; Occupational Health; Pay Equity; Public Sector and Essential Services; Workers' Compensation

Chapter 19

Negotiable Instruments

For centuries, negotiable instruments were the main method of paying debts, moving money, and financing transactions in both domestic and international business. This has changed: The electronic transfer of funds has transformed the traditional payment system and the law is struggling to keep up. The legal risks of the emerging payment systems and the longstanding regulation of paper documents under the Bills of Exchange Act are discussed here.

We examine such questions as:

■ What types of negotiable instrument are governed by the Act, and how are they utilized?

■ What is meant by negotiability?

■ What are the methods, purposes, and consequences of endorsement?

■ What is the liability of various parties to a negotiable instrument?

- What is a "holder in due course"?

- What are the three defences available to the parties?

- How do these defences differ?

- How are consumer bills and notes treated differently?

WHAT IS A NEGOTIABLE INSTRUMENT?—ORIGIN

A negotiable instrument is a document directing the payment of money and it may be transferred from one person to another. It is an alternative to carrying cash; examples are cheques and bank drafts. Negotiable instruments fall under federal jurisdiction so the legal rules about creating and transferring negotiable instruments are standard across the country. They are found in the Bills of Exchange Act.[1] The last section of Chapter 11 introduced the special rules about negotiable instruments; rereading that section will be helpful before proceeding with the balance of this chapter.

bill of exchange a written order by one party to another party to pay a specified sum of money to a named party or to the bearer of the document

Negotiable instruments are a form of **bill of exchange**, a document made by a purchaser or banker in one location instructing a colleague elsewhere to make a payment to a certain person or to the bearer of the document. Bills of exchange helped early exporters and importers do business across borders. A buyer in England who bought goods from a vendor located in Germany could arrange for payment for the goods by a banker in Germany, making it unnecessary to transport cash. For a small fee, the English buyer could arrange for an English firm dealing in bills of exchange to draw a bill on its agent in Germany, instructing him to pay the German vendor on a certain date. The vendor would accept the bill of exchange as payment for his product. At regular intervals, all the firms dealing in bills of exchange would get together and tally the "bills" they had honoured and pay each other any difference owing. This form of setting off credits eventually grew into more sophisticated government regulated "clearing houses."

Today's payment system for clearing and settlement of payments is overseen by the Canadian Payments Association under authority of the Canadian Payments Act. Its members are the national banks, loan and trust companies, and credit unions.[2]

MODERN ALTERNATIVES TO CASH

Initially, bank drafts and cheques, forms of negotiable instrument, were the primary substitutes for cash. Next, telegraph, cable, and telex "transmission of funds" took over a significant portion of business-to-business transactions. In the 1950s and 1960s, credit cards surpassed both cash and cheques as the preferred method of payment. Credit cards assured retailers that funds were available, and reduced the risk of bad debts experienced with payment by cheque. Early in the new millennium, direct debit cards displaced credit cards in an increasing proportion of transactions; the current decade is trending toward virtual wallets and even digital currency. These modern alternatives are reducing the reliance on paper negotiable instruments and cash.

Canadians are among the world's top users of debit cards, completing over 3 billion debit transactions in 2012,[3] and 87 percent of Canadians want to abandon physical

---

[1] The Bills of Exchange Act, R.S.C. 1985, c. B-4. When a footnote mentions a section only, the reference will be to this Act. Canada's statute follows the English version.

[2] R.S.C. 1985, c. C-21, ss. 3, 4, 5.

[3] Canadian Bankers Association - Select Delivery Channel Statistics (2013), http://www.cba.ca/contents/files/statistics/stat_abmstat_db219_en.pdf

wallets entirely.[4] While internet banking is on the rise, telephone banking and the use of cheques have steadily declined since 2004.[5] Less than 7 percent of Canadians currently use cheques as their primary bill payment method.[6]

In 2011, the federal government's Task Force for Payment System Review recommended that the Government of Canada take the lead in moving Canada's payment system into the digital age by passing legislation that regulates digital payment service providers and creates a public oversight body for the digital payment industry.[7] The federal government retains the power to recognize new payment systems under the Canadian Payments Act.[8] Payment card (credit, debit, and gift) providers are regulated under the Payment Card Networks Act.[9]

Does this mean that electronic transfers of funds will soon completely replace the traditional paper methods and make cash, paper bills of exchange, and cheques obsolete? Answering this question involves both international and ethical considerations.

INTERNATIONAL ISSUE

Electronic Transfers of Funds: Are Negotiable Instruments Becoming Obsolete?

A 2002 report of the Organisation for Economic Co-operation and Development entitled "The Future of Money" concluded that the disappearance of physical money is inevitable; it is just a question of time. It suggested that a coordinated transition to digital payments would be good for the world economy for a number of reasons, including

- the elimination of the high costs associated with the transfer and protection of physical forms of money including cash, cheques, bills of exchange, etc., and

- the decrease in underground, illegal, and even terrorist activities as a result of the ability to track the movement of money.

If countries proceed at their own pace without a coordinated timetable or approach, international transactions will be cumbersome and less secure. A uniform international approach and commitment to digitization could make the inevitable transition much easier.

So far, no common digitalization strategy is in place. The use of cheques remains relatively high in some countries (United States) while they have been abolished for decades in others (Finland). Unregulated digital or cryptocurrencies such as Bitcoin are emerging that lack a centralized monetary authority, which actually increases rather than decreases the risk of illegal activities.

Questions to Consider

1. How will a move to digital transactions affect developing or emerging economies?

2. Do you think digital transactions increase the likelihood of fraud or affect the evidence available to prove fraud?

3. Should the marketplace rather than government dictate when money disappears? What are the risks?

Source: Organisation for Economic Co-operation and Development, The Future of Money (Paris: OECD Publications Service, 2002), www.oecd.org/dataoecd/40/31/35391062.pdf; The Economist explains: How does Bitcoin work? April 11, 2013, http://www.economist.com/blogs/economist-explains/2013/04/economist-explains-how-does-bitcoin-work.

---

[4] *PayPal Study Reveals Majority of Canadians Feel trapped by Their Wallet*, (May 23, 2013) http://www.paypal-media.com/ca/press-releases# .

[5] The number of cheques cleared in Canada fell from 1.11 billion in 2004, to 1.05 billion in 2007, and to 930 million in 2009. See *infra*, n. 7.

[6] Statistics obtained from the Canadian Bankers Association website, www.cba.ca/en/section.asp?fl=3&sl=251&tl=252&docid= (accessed October 18, 2008) and http://www.cba.ca/contents/files/statistics/stat_faststat_2009_en.pdf (accessed May 17, 2011).

[7] It was thought that the Canadian Payments Association was not proceeding quickly enough. The Task Force for the Payments System Review, Moving Canada into the Digital Age, December 2011, http://paymentsystemreview.ca/wp-content/themes/psr-esp-hub/reports/rf_eng/files/assets/downloads/publication.pdf

[8] Canadian Payments Act, R.S.C. 1985, c. C-21, s. 37.

[9] S.C. 2010, c. 12, s. 1834.

Despite the speed and efficiency of electronic payment methods, it does not appear that the world is ready to eliminate negotiable instruments. After severe public backlash, the United Kingdom abandoned its plan to end the use of cheques by 2018. Rather than abolishing cheques entirely, the Canadian government is leading by example and phasing out its own use of cheques by 2016.[10] In contrast, Canadian banks are expanding the number of physical branches, which are used by 82 percent of Canadians.[11] Banks also continue to process about 930 million cheques each year.[12] The certainty in using paper negotiable instruments continues to make them attractive in particular transactions.[13] While the law governing negotiable instruments developed in the paper world, it is slowly being adapted to function in the electronic world as well.

We introduced the law of negotiable instruments in Chapter 11; this chapter contains a more in-depth description. For more information on this topic, see the Companion Website.

NATURE AND USES OF NEGOTIABLE INSTRUMENTS

As Personal Property

In Chapter 11, we discussed the rights to intangible property—choses in action—and noted that negotiable instruments are a special kind of chose in action. This chapter considers the distinctive characteristics of negotiable instruments that have made them a useful business tool.

Every negotiable instrument contains an express or implied promise made by one or more parties to pay the amount stated in the instrument. In the absence of evidence to the contrary, the promisee is presumed to have given good consideration for the promise.

---

[10] Public and Government Service Canada, News Release, April 11, 2012. It costs 82 cents to produce a cheque and only 13 cents to complete a direct deposit.

[11] The number of physical bank branches grew from 5902 in 2006 to 6205 in 2012: Canadian Bankers Association—Bank Branch Statistics, http://www.cba.ca/contents/files/statistics/stat_bankbranches_en.pdf

[12] Canadian Bankers Association, *supra*, n. 6 and n. 7.

[13] *Canada Trustco Mortgage Company v. Canada* 2011 SCC 36, [2011] 2 S.C.R. 635 at para. 1.

A negotiable instrument is normally a self-contained contract with all the necessary written evidence of its terms stated on its face. In practice, a negotiable instrument is given as part of performance of a contract in which one side satisfies its promise to pay for goods or services by giving the other side the instrument. Delivery of the instrument is only a **conditional discharge** because if the debtor dishonours it, the promisee's right to payment continues. Promisees generally choose to sue on the negotiable instrument rather than on the original contract because it is simpler to do so.

conditional discharge   the debtor is discharged under the original contract only if the negotiable instrument given in payment is honoured when presented

Types of Instruments

The three common types of negotiable instruments covered by the Bills of Exchange Act are bills of exchange (or drafts), promissory notes, and cheques. There are other kinds of instruments with the special quality of negotiability, but disputes concerning them are resolved by common law and not by the Bills of Exchange Act.

Share certificates could be negotiable instruments. The Canada Business Corporations Act states expressly that a share certificate whose transfer is not restricted by words printed on its face is a negotiable instrument.[14] Of course, it is very common for the articles of incorporation or unanimous shareholder agreement to restrict the transfer of shares so most shares are not negotiable instruments.

Bills of Exchange (Drafts)

A bill of exchange (see Figure 19.1) is a written order by one party, the **drawer**, addressed to another party, the **drawee**, to pay a specified sum of money to a named party, the **payee**, or to the bearer, at a fixed or determinable future time or on demand. A bill of exchange originates with a drawer (creditor) and requires a drawee (debtor) to acknowledge indebtedness and to agree to pay according to the terms stated in the document. A drawer sometimes designates itself as a payee. At other times, it may direct that some other person or business to whom it owes money shall be the payee instead. The drawer expects the debtor (drawee) to consent by signing the instrument together with the word "accepted" and the date; the drawee then becomes an **acceptor**. A bill of exchange may circulate among a number of holders as an item of valuable personal property even before it has been accepted. It has value for a holder because the drawer, by drawing and delivering it, has made an implied promise guaranteeing its payment.[15] Its subsequent acceptance adds the express promise of the acceptor.

drawer   the party who draws up the bill of exchange

drawee   the party who is required to make payment on the bill of exchange

payee   the party named to receive payment on the bill of exchange

acceptor   the drawee who consents to the bill of exchange by signing it together with the word "accepted" and the date

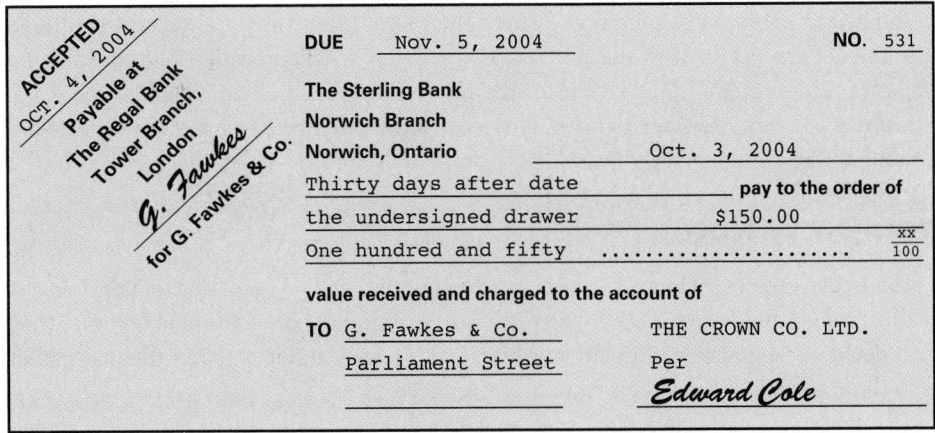

Figure 19.1   A Bill of Exchange (Accepted Time Draft)

---

[14] Canada Business Corporations Act, R.S.C. 1985, c. C-44, s. 48(3), 49, National Instrument 56-106.

[15] *Ibid.*, s. 129.

An acceptor may indicate that the bill is to be paid out of its bank account. The drawer (or a subsequent holder) may then leave the instrument with its own bank for collection and have it deposited in its account. That bank will present the bill to the acceptor's bank for payment out of the acceptor's account. After the amount is deducted from the acceptor's account, the cancelled bill of exchange is returned to the acceptor as evidence of payment, just as cancelled cheques are returned.

There are three types of bills of exchange, depending upon the time at which they are to be paid:

<table>
<tr><td>

demand draft a bill of exchange payable immediately upon presentation without any days of grace

</td><td>

- **Demand draft**, payable immediately upon presentation without any days of grace before payment. The cheque is the leading example of a demand draft and we treat it separately below.

</td></tr>
<tr><td>

sight draft a bill of exchange payable "at sight"—three days of grace are allowed after presentation

time draft a bill of exchange payable within a stipulated period after the date stated on the instrument or after presentation

</td><td>

- **Sight draft**, which the drawee is ordered to pay "at sight." In Canada, three days of grace for making payment are allowed after presentation for acceptance.

- **Time draft**, payable a stipulated number of days, months, or other period "after date" (after the date stated on the instrument) or "after sight" (after presentation for acceptance). Three days of grace should be added in fixing the maturity of a time draft. A bill payable at a given time after sight is a time draft, not a sight draft. Presentation for acceptance is necessary whenever a bill is payable at sight or after sight, so that the time at which payment is due may be determined.[16]

</td></tr>
</table>

Sight drafts can be used as a collection device. Instead of employing a collection agency to recover its slow accounts, a business may draw sight drafts on difficult customers and have the drafts presented for acceptance and payment through the bank. The drawees will have a new incentive to accept and pay, not wanting to become known to the bank as poor credit risks.

Time drafts can be used as a means of finance for the business drawing them. By discounting them at a bank or by pledging them as security for a bank loan, the drawer can obtain cash in advance of the time when payment is due from the customer. Instead of waiting to be paid until the credit term granted to a customer expires, a business may draw a time draft on the customer immediately following the sale, and discount or pledge the draft. As we will see in Chapter 28, however, there are other means of achieving this result. For example, a business may borrow from a bank by conditionally assigning its accounts receivable, it may sell its accounts to a factor, or it may assign them to a finance company.

Drafts and bills of lading often complement one another when goods sold on credit are shipped to the buyer by common carrier. Their joint use permits the seller to withhold possession of the goods from the purchaser when they reach their destination until the purchaser accepts a draft drawn on it for the price. The purchaser can examine the goods but cannot obtain possession from the carrier until the seller or its agent transfers the bill of lading to the purchaser.

Promissory Notes

<table>
<tr><td>

promissory note a written promise to pay a specified sum of money to another party at a fixed or determinable future time or on demand

maker the party who signs and delivers a promissory note

</td><td>

A **promissory note** (see Figure 19.2) is a written promise by one party, the **maker**, to pay a specified sum of money to another party, the payee, at a fixed or determinable future time or on demand. The maker is usually a debtor of the payee, and it prepares the instrument itself, though it may do so at the request of the payee.

A maker of a note may word it so that it will be payable out of the maker's bank account at maturity; it is then paid through its bank and returned cancelled to the maker.

</td></tr>
</table>

---

[16] *Ibid.*, s. 74.

Figure 19.2 A Promissory Note

Unlike a bill of exchange, a promissory note is not presented for acceptance. It contains an express promise to pay that is triggered by a due date or demand. To a subsequent holder, a promissory note that has been endorsed by the payee has the same effect as an accepted bill of exchange. The Bills of Exchange Act applies both to accepted bills and to notes, but the provisions relating to the acceptance of bills of exchange do not apply to promissory notes.

Cheques

A **cheque** (see Figure 19.3) is a bill of exchange drawn against a bank and payable on demand. From the point of view of the holder, a cheque contains the implied promise of its drawer that the drawer has funds on deposit at the bank sufficient to meet the cheque's amount, or that the amount is within the terms of a line of credit granted by the bank. For this reason, it is sometimes convenient to think of the drawer of a cheque as a "promisor."

cheque a bill of exchange drawn against a bank and payable on demand

Figure 19.3 A Cheque

holder in due course a party who is not the original payee that aquires the cheque from that payee or a subsequent holder

The bank on which the cheque is drawn is called the drawee bank. If the holder of the cheque takes it to his own bank for deposit in an account, once an equal amount is credited to the account, the bank becomes the **holder in due course** of the cheque and will present it to the drawee bank through the payment settlement system described above.

Certification

certification an undertaking by the bank to pay the amount of the cheque to its holder when later presented for payment

Since a cheque is payable on demand, the payee does not ordinarily present it to a bank for acceptance, but cashes it or deposits it to the credit of its own account. The Bills of Exchange Act does not expressly deal with the acceptance of cheques by the bank, nor does it refer specifically to the current banking practice of certifying cheques.[17] **Certification** amounts to an undertaking by the drawee bank to pay the amount of the cheque to its holder when later presented for payment, and to ensure this result, the bank immediately deducts the amount of the cheque from the drawer's account. Certification takes the form of the bank's stamped acknowledgment, with date, on the face of the cheque.

Occasionally, a supplier will refuse to release goods until paid by certified cheque. The buyer prepares a cheque payable to the supplier, has the drawee bank certify it, and then delivers it to the supplier. Or a payee may receive the cheque uncertified and, before releasing the goods, will have the bank certify it. Such a cheque is safer to hold than cash—a thief would have to forge an endorsement before being able to cash it. In addition, certification at the request of the holder also prevents any attempt by the drawer to stop payment on the cheque: Since the payee could have cashed it instead of having it certified, the act of certifying makes the drawee bank liable directly to the payee.[18]

Certification of a cheque is comparable to the acceptance of other types of bills of exchange.[19] The bank concerned is the drawee to whom the instrument is addressed. Once having undertaken certification, it assumes a liability to the holder for the amount of the cheque.

Postdated Cheques

postdate give a cheque a date later than the time when it is delivered to the payee

The drawer may **postdate** a cheque by giving it a date later than the time when it is delivered to the payee. A cheque is an order addressed to a bank, and the bank must follow the instructions given to it on the face of the cheque—the bank is not entitled to pay the instrument before its date. While a cheque is by definition payable "on demand," a holder's right to demand payment is not effective until the date on the cheque. In the meantime, the instrument operates like a time draft, though without the benefit for the drawer of three days of grace. Postdating is convenient for a drawer who expects to be unavailable at the time a debt is due and who does not wish to pay in advance. It is common for a drawer to give a series of postdated cheques to meet installment payments.

Stop Payment

stop payment an instruction from the drawer of a cheque to the bank not to pay the cheque

After delivering a cheque, the drawer may learn that the payee is in serious breach of the contract between them. Before the cheque has been charged against its account, the drawer may countermand or **stop payment** by instructing its bank not to pay the cheque. The bank may require the drawer to agree that it will not be held responsible if, through its inadvertence, the cheque is paid out of the drawer's account in spite of the countermand.

Even a cheque certified at the request of its drawer and not yet delivered to the payee may be countermanded and the amount returned to the drawer's account at the bank. Since the bank has a liability on the certified cheque, it will reject the countermand unless the cheque is surrendered by the drawer for cancellation or the drawer agrees to indemnify the bank should the bank be sued for refusing to honour the cheque.

---

[17] See J.D. Falconbridge, *The Law of Negotiable Instruments in Canada* (Toronto: Ryerson, 1955) at 43.

[18] When a cheque is certified at the request of the holder, the drawer is entirely discharged by its implied promise that the bank will honour the cheque. See B. Crawford and J.D. Falconbridge, *Banking and Bills of Exchange*, 8th ed. (Toronto: Canada Law Book, 1986) at 1791.

[19] The difference between certification and acceptance is confined to the circumstance where the drawee bank fails, and even then relates only to certification at the request of the holder (rather than of the drawer).

Electronic Cheques Just as paper cheques replaced sight drafts, time drafts, and promissory notes as the preferred manner of payment, electronic transfers of funds through electronic cheques, payment cards, and ecash are replacing paper cheques. This development is due in part to the speed and efficiency of electronic transfers. Many of the physical steps involved in processing a paper cheque may be completed much more quickly electronically. Electronic processing is known as **cheque truncation**.[20] The Bills of Exchange Act allows an "official image" of a cheque to be created by a bank and used for all purposes as though it were the original.[21] To facilitate the conversion from paper, the Canadian Payments Association, created under the Canadian Payments Act,[22] regulates the size, form, and information contained on a paper cheque. The original paper cheque may be destroyed and the official digital image saved electronically. For more on the electronic transfer of cheques see the Companion Website.

A cheque, whether transferred electronically or physically—even one certified by a bank—is not legal tender. Strictly speaking, a creditor is entitled to payment in Bank of Canada notes and in coins up to the designated amounts for each denomination. He cannot be forced to accept payment by cheque physically or electronically. However, to insist upon payment in cash would be inconvenient to both parties, and if a creditor refused a reasonable tender of payment by cheque and sued for payment in cash, court costs would likely be awarded against the creditor.

Finally we should mention the use of cheques as a source of information to initiate a separate electronic transfer of funds. Who has not been asked to provide a "void" cheque, sometimes as a form of payment to facilitate regular automatic debits? Such a payment is sometimes referred to as an electronic cheque. Alternatively, a void cheque may be provided as a source of information so an electronic payment may be made to the provider of the cheque, such as direct deposit of employee paycheques.

CHECKLIST

Classes of Negotiable Instruments

Three classes of negotiable instruments are governed by the federal Bills of Exchange Act. They include:

- bills of exchange (or drafts)
  - demand drafts
  - sight drafts
  - time drafts
- promissory notes
- cheques
  - postdated
  - certified
  - electronic

---

[20] Benjamin Geva, "Recent International Developments in the Law of Negotiable Instruments and Payment and Settlement Systems" (2007) 42 Texas Int'l L.J. 685 at 688.

[21] Bills of Exchange Act, s. 163.2.

[22] R.S.C. 1985, c. C-21, ss. 3, 38, 39; see Canadian Payments Association Manual, available at www.cpa.ca/ (under Acts and Rules).

PREREQUISITES FOR LIABILITY

Until an instrument is delivered, a drawer, acceptor, or maker has no liability, and even after signing, he may reconsider and tear it up before delivering it. A drawee has no liability in respect of a bill of exchange until after acceptance and delivery.

Delivery may be "actual"—the instrument being issued directly by the promisor to the payee; or it may be "constructive"—simply by notice to the payee that the instrument is complete and ready for delivery.[23] Once an instrument has been delivered, the term "negotiation" is used to describe any subsequent transfer of it by the payee to a new holder, as well as any later transfers to other holders. The term "presentment" refers to the time when the instrument is finally submitted for payment to the named promisor or drawee bank. This final payment discharges the instrument or "cancels" the cheque.

NEGOTIABILITY

Meaning of Negotiability

negotiability the special quality possessed by negotiable instruments as a distinct class of assignable contract

Negotiability is the special characteristic of negotiable instruments that does not come from assigning contracts. As noted in Chapter 11, their transfer is different from ordinary assignments of contracts by three legal features:

■ A negotiable instrument may be transferred (or assigned) from one holder to another without notice to the promisor; the promisor becomes liable to each successive holder in turn but only pays the holder who presents the instrument for payment.

subject to the equities subject to any rights or defences the promisor had against the original assignor

■ An assignee may sometimes acquire a better right to sue on the instrument than its predecessor (assignor) had. Negotiable instruments are not **subject to the equities**.

■ A holder may sue in its own name any other party liable on the instrument without joining any of the remaining parties.

The above legal features make it much easier to transfer negotiable instruments from one person to another than regular assignments. As a practical matter, ease of transfer enables negotiable instruments to meet business needs, because on their face they are sufficiently reliable for transferees to accept them without hesitation.

For negotiable instruments to acquire these desirable qualities, they must meet the following criteria:

(a) The promise or order must be set out in writing—otherwise the transferee would hold no evidence of the promise.

(b) The obligation must be for a money payment only, requiring no further inquiry into its value. Other types of obligation—to perform services or transfer ownership of a chattel—would require a prospective assignee to investigate the value of what is being promised.

(c) The money promised must be an exact sum. It may be repayable in installments or with interest and still be a "sum certain."[24] But a promise to pay "the balance owing to you for services rendered" is not a sum certain because it is not possible from the face of the instrument to quantify the value of the promise.

---

[23] Bills of Exchange Act, s. 38.

[24] Ibid., ss. 27 and 186. Problems arise where the instrument provides for payment of a fixed sum plus a variable or "floating" rate of interest, for example, "prime rate plus 2 percent." The Supreme Court of Canada has held that the sum must be capable of being ascertained by numerical calculation from the information contained in the instrument itself: *MacLeod Savings & Credit Union Ltd. v. Perrett*, [1981] 1 S.C.R. 78. The courts have difficulty in applying this test with consistency. See also *Canadian Imperial Bank of Commerce (CIBC) v. Morgan* (1993), 143 A.R. 36.

(d) The promise or order must be unconditional so that the holder need not look outside the instrument to learn the implications of some qualifying phrase, such as "if the goods are delivered in good condition" or "subject to an allowance for poor material." A contract subject to a condition, though it may be valid between the immediate parties, lacks the certainty needed for a negotiable instrument: Any attempt to transfer rights under it would be a mere assignment.

(e) The negotiable instrument must be payable at a fixed or determinable future time or on demand.[25] The value of a contractual right can be appraised only when it indicates the time at which it is to be performed.

(f) Negotiation must be of the whole instrument, not for part of the amount.

(g) The negotiable instrument must be signed by the drawer (or authorized signing officers of a drawer business)[26] if it is a draft or cheque, or by the maker if a promissory note.

CHECKLIST

Formal Requirements of Negotiable Instruments

Negotiable instruments must:

- be in writing and signed by creator or drawer,
- be an unconditional obligation to pay a fixed amount of money,
- indicate a specific time when payment is due, and
- be a transfer of the whole obligation.

Consequences When a Document Is Not Negotiable

Although a document may not amount to a negotiable instrument (where, for example, the order or promise is conditional), it may still be enforceable between the original parties and be capable of assignment as an ordinary contractual right. In these circumstances, the Bills of Exchange Act does not apply, and the parties' rights are subject to the general rules governing contractual assignments as discussed in Chapter 11. Accordingly, a holder of the instrument cannot enforce the promise until the condition is met.

METHODS OF NEGOTIATION

By Endorsement and Delivery

An order instrument is one expressed to be payable "to A," "to A or order," or "to the order of A." To negotiate it (transfer it), A must endorse as well as deliver it to a new holder. Endorsement may take a number of forms, which we shall examine below, but essentially it is the signature (traditionally on the reverse side of the instrument) of the payee transferring its right to the new holder.

---

[25] It is difficult to justify the uncertainty introduced by the definition of "determinable future time" in section 23(b), viz., "on or at a fixed period after the occurrence of a specified event which is certain to happen though the time of happening is uncertain."

[26] The signer is personally liable unless he states that he signs in a representative capacity: section 51. The usual practice for a corporation is for its name to be printed on the instrument and for the officer to sign "per X" or "X, director." For an interesting case, see *Allprint Co. Ltd. v. Erwin* (1982), 136 D.L.R. (3d) 587.

A party that purchases an order instrument without the proper endorsement on it acquires a very limited legal right, probably confined to recourse against the transferor, and has no rights against any prior parties.[27] In any event, a new holder cannot acquire a better legal right than the transferor had until it has obtained the transferor's endorsement on the instrument. A new holder has a right to require the transferor to make the needed endorsement.[28]

By Delivery Only

Endorsement is not necessary for an instrument in "bearer" form. It is in bearer form when initially it is made payable "to bearer," or "to A Co. or bearer," or when no payee has been named and a space is left blank for the insertion of a name. It is also in bearer form when it is payable to an abstraction (for example, "Pay to Petty Cash") or to a fictitious or non-existent person.[29] In addition, an order instrument becomes a bearer instrument when the named payee endorses it (signs his name) without any redirecting words such as "pay to the order of Jane Doe." Unless and until a subsequent payee endorses it payable to order, it may be negotiated by delivery alone.

An order instrument is safer because any attempt to negotiate it dishonestly amounts to the criminal offence of forgery.[30] The Bills of Exchange Act makes forgery one of the exceptions to the rule that a holder may acquire a better right than the transferor had. Forgery is a defence to the parties liable on an order instrument. By contrast, because a bearer instrument may be negotiated by delivery only, a thief may successfully negotiate it without resorting to forgery. As a result, even if a bearer instrument was lost or stolen at some previous time, its holder can require the party liable to pay—but only if he can show that he acquired the instrument without knowledge of the loss or theft.[31]

Businesses rarely prepare negotiable instruments in bearer form, although, as we have noted, order instruments may be converted into bearer form by their holders. An employee, for example, may endorse her paycheque before taking it to the bank. If her endorsement is simply her signature, she has converted the cheque into a bearer instrument and it becomes subject to the risks discussed above.

At one time, bank notes were promissory notes in bearer form; we still refer to paper money as "dollar bills." Now bank notes or dollar bills simply state that they are legal tender and are freely negotiable by virtue of the Bank of Canada Act.[32]

ENDORSEMENT

Types of Endorsement

Endorsement in Blank   The payee on an order instrument signs his name—and nothing else—by way of endorsement, thus making it payable to bearer.

[27] See Crawford and Falconbridge, *supra*, n. 18, at 1503.

[28] S. 60.

[29] S. 20(5). See *Westboro Flooring & Decor Inc.* v. *Bank of Nova Scotia* (2004), 241 D.L.R. (4th) 257 (Ont. C.A.); *Rouge Valley Health System* v. *TD Canada Trust*, [2010] O.J. No. 5302 (Ont. S.C.).

[30] The Criminal Code, R.S.C. 1985, c. C-46, s. 374.

[31] N. Elliott, J. Odgers, and J.M. Phillips, eds., *Byles on Bills of Exchange*, 27th ed. (London: Sweet & Maxwell, 2001) at 231, 445.

[32] Bank of Canada Act, R.S.C. 1985, c. B-2, s. 25; Currency Act, R.S.C. 1985, c. C-52.

Special Endorsement The payee specifies the next person to whom payment is to be made. For example:

Pay to Jane Doe

(signed) *John Brown*

Restrictive Endorsement By endorsing an instrument "for deposit only," the payee makes it non-negotiable. There is a risk that, if an instrument is stolen from a payee, the thief may forge the payee's endorsement and sell the instrument to a new holder—for example, by cashing it at a bank. When endorsed "for deposit only," an instrument can then only be deposited to the credit of the payee's account at the bank. It is no longer possible to transfer it to other holders.

Conditional Endorsement The payee specifies a party to whom payment is next to be made, provided he has lived up to the terms of a contract between them as, for example, "pay to the order of Bacchus if sober." Such a condition differs from a condition written into the instrument by a drawer, an acceptor, or a maker because it does not make the original promise in the instrument conditional. The party primarily liable may disregard a conditional endorsement in making payment, but the endorser may recover from the endorsee (Bacchus) if the condition was not satisfied.

Qualified Endorsement The payee transfers rights in a way that denies liability as an endorser—for example, "Jane Bond, without recourse." Anyone giving value for the instrument is on notice that no remedy is available against Ms. Bond should the party primarily liable default. (As we shall see, in the absence of a qualified endorsement, an endorser normally is liable to subsequent endorsees.) Manufacturers or wholesalers that "factor" their accounts receivable sometimes use a qualified endorsement. A **factor** may be willing to purchase drafts drawn on customers and endorsed over to it **without recourse**; the factor bears the risk of collection, without recourse to its client (the manufacturer or wholesaler).

> **factor** a party who purchases drafts drawn on customers at a discount and then collects directly from the customer
>
> **without recourse** no ability to claim against the endorser

Anomalous Endorsement Suppose a party to a negotiable instrument is not sufficiently creditworthy to persuade a prospective holder to buy it. For instance, a purchaser starting up a new business wishes to pay for goods by draft but the seller is unwilling to accept the purchaser's signature alone. The purchaser then obtains the signature of his sister. As a person with a recognized credit standing, she signs the instrument solely to add her liability, as endorser (guarantor), to that of her brother who is primarily liable. It is an **anomalous endorsement**, or exceptional endorsement, because it is not added for the purpose of negotiating the instrument; the endorser was not a holder in her own right.

A bill endorsed in this manner is called an **accommodation bill**. The acceptor or endorser usually signs to accommodate the drawer—that is, to make it easier for the drawer to obtain credit on the bill. An anomalous endorser contributes to negotiability because of her good credit standing.

> **anomalous endorsement** an endorsement that is not added for the purpose of negotiating the instrument but as a guarantee to make it easier for the drawer to obtain credit on the bill
>
> **accommodation bill** bill of exchange that contains an anomalous endorsement

Purposes of Endorsement

An endorsement may be the means of carrying out one of the following purposes.

Transferring Rights to an Instrument Payable to Order We examined this purpose above when we looked at the methods of negotiation and the types of endorsement. Most endorsements serve simply as the method of transferring right in the instrument.

Giving Increased Security to the Payee (or Subsequent Holder) We have also seen that an anomalous endorsement can make a negotiable instrument more marketable because the endorsement makes the endorser liable if the party with primary liability defaults. This is so, even though the endorser has never owned the instrument and has not negotiated it to someone else.[33] An anomalous endorsement is a means of guaranteeing a debt, with the endorser in the role of guarantor.[34]

Identifying the Party Entitled to Payment   A holder of a negotiable instrument has no claim against the drawer if an intermediate holder has forged a signature. When a bank has cashed a cheque containing an endorsement forged by the person cashing it, the bank becomes a holder with no right to claim the amount from the drawee customer's account. To protect itself, a bank may (rarely) require an endorsement from someone known to it for the purpose of identifying the person seeking to cash a cheque. For instance, it may require an endorsement in the following form:

T. Smith is hereby identified

(signed) *R. Jones*

As endorser, Jones is not liable for payment, as are other endorsers, should the party primarily liable default. Her liability is limited to the loss that would follow from having identified someone as T. Smith who later proved not to be that person.

Acknowledging a Partial Payment   If the maker of a note is to pay her debt by installments, it is up to her to see that every time she makes a partial payment she obtains an endorsement on the instrument by its holder for the amount paid. Otherwise she remains liable for the full, face amount of the instrument if it is subsequently negotiated to a holder who is unaware of the partial payments. An example of this type of endorsement is the following:

May 12, 2015

Received in part payment, $175.00

(signed) *B. Brown*

As an alternative arrangement, the debtor may make a series of separate notes bearing the dates of the various installments and require the surrender of the related note each time she pays an installment.

LIABILITY OF PARTIES

An Endorser

dishonour   the failure by the party primarily liable to pay the instrument according to its terms

Dishonour is the failure by the party who is primarily liable to pay the instrument according to its terms. If the instrument is a draft, dishonour may take the form of either the drawee's refusal to accept or, if he accepts, of his later refusal to pay.[35] As noted above, an endorser is liable to any holder for the amount of the instrument should the party primarily liable dishonour it, but this statement needs to be qualified. If an endorser does not receive prompt notice of the dishonour from the holder, the endorser will be freed from liability.

If an order instrument is negotiated several times, a particular endorser's liability extends to any subsequent endorser as well as the current holder. He has no liability to prior endorsers—indeed, they are liable to him. The holder has a choice of endorsers to require payment from when the instrument is dishonoured, provided each of them has received the

---

[33] S. 130. The endorser is liable to the payee even though the payee has not himself endorsed. *Robinson v. Mann* (1901), 331 S.C.R. 484. Also see Byles on Bills of Exchange, *supra*, n. 31, at 203.

[34] The same effect may be had without endorsement if both the guarantor and debtor sign in the first instance as joint makers of a promissory note.

[35] S. 132(a).

necessary notice of dishonour.[36] In turn, an endorser who is held liable has recourse against any prior endorser but not against any subsequent one.[37] Assuming he cannot recover from the party primarily liable, the ultimate loser will be the first endorser (or the drawer if the instrument is a draft).

When an endorsement is forged, the drawer and any endorser prior to the forgery are not liable. The only holder who can recover from an endorser in these circumstances is one who has satisfied the conditions for qualifying as a "holder in due course," as explained later. When such a holder suffers a loss arising from a forged endorsement or the forged signature of the drawer, unless the forger can be caught and made to pay, the loss will ultimately be borne by the person who acquires the instrument immediately following the forgery.[38]

ILLUSTRATION 19.1

A knew that C maintained an account at the B Bank. She drew a cheque on the B Bank payable to herself, forging C's signature as drawer. She then endorsed the cheque with her own signature and cashed it at a hotel operated by D.

D endorsed the cheque and deposited it in the hotel account at the X Bank. The X Bank presented the cheque for payment to the B Bank through the bank clearing system. The B Bank recognized the forgery and refused to pay the cheque out of C's account. The cheque was then returned to the X Bank.

The X Bank is entitled to recover the amount that it had previously credited to D's account in respect of the cheque. The X Bank is the holder (in fact, a holder in due course), and D, as the endorser immediately after the forgery, is liable.[39] In this illustration, there is no other endorser between D and A, the perpetrator of the fraud. The loss must fall upon D unless A can be apprehended and the funds recovered from her.

An endorser also warrants to any later party that she had a good title to the instrument.[40]

Finally, unless a holder duly **presents** the instrument for payment, endorsers will not have any liability to him. Accordingly, an instrument payable on demand must be presented for payment within a reasonable time after its endorsement, and an instrument that is not payable on demand must be presented on the day it falls due.[41]

presents produces the instrument to the drawee bank, promisor, or maker

A Drawer

The drawer of a draft undertakes that on duly presenting the draft, it will be accepted and paid according to its terms, and that if it is dishonoured, the drawer will compensate the holder or any endorser who is compelled to pay it.[42] The drawer of a cheque undertakes that the cheque will be paid from his account on demand. If there are insufficient funds in his account, he is liable to the holder or to any endorser from whom the holder may recover. Because the parties to a cheque do not ordinarily expect a formal acceptance of it by the drawee bank, the drawer of the cheque becomes, for practical purposes, "the party primarily liable," comparable to the acceptor of a draft or the maker of a note.

---

[36] Alternatively, the holder may sue all the endorsers as codefendants in a single action and leave them to work out their individual liability among themselves.

[37] S. 100. Each endorser has, after receiving notice of dishonour, the same period for giving notice to earlier endorsers that the holder had after dishonour.

[38] S. 132(b).

[39] S. 49(1) and (2).

[40] S. 132(c).

[41] S. 85.

[42] S. 129.

A bank follows instructions from its customer in disposing of the funds on deposit with it. Its authority to pay a cheque ends when its customer stops payment or when it receives notice of the customer's death.[43] While a holder cannot then hold the bank liable, his rights against the drawer remain unaffected by the countermand. By stopping payment, a drawer dishonours the instrument and may be sued by the holder. The death of the drawer makes the amount of the cheque a charge against the drawer's estate, and it becomes one of the debts the personal representative (executor or administrator) must settle.

Notice of Dishonour

Neither an endorser nor a drawer will be liable in the absence of prompt, express notice of dishonour from the holder—it is not enough for the holder to show that the endorser or drawer heard about the dishonour from some other source.[44] Notice must be given not later than the business day next following the dishonour.[45] If notice is mailed, the time limit applies to the time of depositing it in the post office and not to the time it is received.[46]

No special form of notice is required as long as the essential message is conveyed. In two instances, however, a special form of notice of dishonour, known as protest, is required. Protest is required if the instrument is drawn, payable, or accepted outside Canada.[47] The services of a notary public—or justice of the peace where no notary public is available—are required to confirm the dishonour, prepare a notice of the protest in prescribed form,[48] and deliver it to the endorsers and drawer within the same time as for a notice of dishonour generally.[49] The holder is responsible for contacting a notary public and is entitled to be reimbursed for the notary's fee by the endorser or drawer to whom the notice of protest is delivered.[50] An endorser may waive the right to any notice of dishonour, and avoid the expense of the fee, by including the words "No Protest" in his endorsement.[51]

A Transferor by Delivery

The term "transferor by delivery" describes anyone who negotiates an instrument in bearer form. Since no endorsement is required, a transferor by delivery is not liable on the instrument as an endorser if the party primarily liable simply proves financially incapable of paying it.[52] However, he may be liable to the one person to whom he has negotiated the instrument, his immediate transferee, but only for such loss as that transferee would sustain if the instrument were not genuine—that is, if the instrument is not what the transferor represented it to be, or he was aware that it was valueless, or if he had no right to transfer it.[53]

---

[43] S. 167.

[44] S. 98. See also Crawford and Falconbridge, *supra*, n. 18, at 1576.

[45] S. 96. Under some circumstances, a delay in giving notice may be excused (s. 104).

[46] S. 102(2).

[47] S. 111.

[48] The prescribed forms are set out in the Schedule at the end of the Act.

[49] S. 125.

[50] S. 123.

[51] S. 105(1)(b).

[52] S. 136(2).

[53] S. 137.

A Drawee, Acceptor, or Maker

By accepting a bill, a drawee undertakes to pay it according to the terms of his acceptance.[54]

M was a lawyer who owed tax to the federal government. His law firm issued three cheques payable to M from its trust account. M endorsed each cheque "to be deposited" to the joint bank account M held with a third party at Canada Trustco Mortgage Co. The cheques were then delivered to Canada Trustco, the joint account was credited, and the cheques were sent for clearing. Minister of National Revenue sued Canada Trustco because at the time the cheques were deposited, the bank was subject to a "requirement to pay" notice. Any payments owed to M were to be redirected to the government. Canada Trustco denied owing any payments to M. The Supreme Court of Canada agreed. Just because M was the original payee on the face of the cheque did not mean that payment was to be made to M. A drawee is answerable to the drawer (law firm) and to whom the drawee must make payment is determined by the endorsements on the back of the cheque. When the cheques were presented, the instructions were to credit the joint bank account. At no time was Canada Trustco instructed to pay M alone.[55]

Similarly, the maker of a promissory note undertakes to pay it according to its terms.[56] On the death of either the maker or the acceptor, their liability passes to their personal representatives.

Limitation Periods

The holder of a negotiable instrument must duly present the instrument for payment and, when necessary, give the required notice of dishonour in order to establish his legal rights against all prior parties to the instrument. He must then also advance his legal rights, by court action if necessary, within the time prescribed by the relevant provincial legislation.[57] The limitation period begins to run from the maturity of the instrument, the time of the most recent payment made in respect of it, or any written acknowledgment from which a promise to pay may be implied—whichever is the latest date.

HOLDER IN DUE COURSE

Negotiation Compared with Assignment of a Chose in Action

In Chapter 9, we learned that an innocent purchaser of goods can often retain them even when the transferor, who had obtained them fraudulently, would have had to surrender them to the original vendor. We have also noted that an innocent transferee of a negotiable instrument may be able to enforce payment when the transferor himself could not do so. In this sense, a transfer of a negotiable instrument more closely resembles a transfer of title to goods than an assignment of a chose in action—negotiation is an exception to the general principle that an assignee of a chose in action takes no greater rights than the assignor had. Accordingly, a negotiable instrument may become more valuable when it is transferred. The greater rights available to innocent third-party holders of negotiable instruments make them useful tools of commerce.

---

[54] S. 127; *Canada Trustco Mortgage Co., v. Canada*, 2011 SCC 36, [2011] 2 S.C.R. 635 at para 51.

[55] *Canada Trustco Mortgage Co. v. Canada*, 2011 SCC 36, [2011] 2 S.C.R. 635 at para 51.

[56] S. 185. If the party seeking payment is a "holder in due course" as defined below, the maker of a note cannot refuse to pay on the grounds that the payee who he has named in his note either does not exist or lacks capacity to endorse.

[57] In most provinces the relevant period is six years, but in some it has been reduced to two years; see the discussion of limitation periods in Chapter 29.

Requirements to Become a Holder in Due Course

For the holder of a negotiable instrument to acquire something more than the transferor himself had, the holder must satisfy four conditions:[58]

(a) The holder must have taken the instrument complete and regular on its face.
(b) She must have acquired it before it was overdue and without notice of any prior dishonour.
(c) She, or someone through whom she claims, must have given consideration ("value") for the instrument.[59]
(d) She must have taken the instrument in good faith and without notice of any defect in the title of the person who negotiated it.

A holder who satisfies these conditions becomes a holder in due course.[60] Business experience has shown that the concept of negotiability has a convenience far outweighing the cost of its occasional abuse. In any event, the possibility of abuse is greatly reduced by confining the legal advantage to a holder in due course. When a cheque is delivered to a bank for deposit to an account and the bank credits the account for the amount, the bank also gets the protection of a holder in due course (s. 165(3)).

Purpose of the Requirements

Notice   The rule that a person cannot be a holder in due course if she has taken the instrument with knowledge of its previous dishonour, or in bad faith, or with notice of a defect of title, has one purpose—to deprive a holder of any advantage in conspiring with a transferee to take the instrument from him with a view to evading the defences of the party liable. Such a transferee does not qualify as a holder in due course and can be defeated by any of the defences that the party liable might have used against the transferor. The transferee gains nothing by the maneuver.

When the instrument is a time draft or note, a prospective holder of it can tell at a glance whether it is overdue or not. If it is already due, an obvious question to ask is why the present holder is trying to negotiate it instead of presenting it for payment. A prospective holder will have more difficulty deciding whether a demand draft is overdue. If it has been outstanding for an "unreasonable" length of time (the meaning of "unreasonable" varies with the circumstances), it is deemed to be overdue,[61] and a new holder does not then become a holder in due course.

An outstanding demand note may have a different significance from a demand draft. A demand note is sometimes given as evidence of long-term indebtedness and may remain outstanding a long time without necessarily raising doubts about its collectability. Consequently, the criterion of an unreasonable length of time used in other areas of the law may be unsuitable in determining whether a demand note is overdue.[62]

Advantages   An important benefit of the concept of a holder in due course is that banks are willing to discount drafts and cash cheques drawn on other banks with relatively little delay and at much reduced risk to themselves, since they acquire the instruments in the capacity of a holder in due course. If the law did not recognize the concept, banks would

---

[58] S. 55.

[59] S. 55 requires that she shall have taken the instrument "for value," but section 53 states that where value has been given at any time for a bill, the holder is deemed to be a holder for value.

[60] A subsequent holder will succeed to the rights of a holder in due course whether or not he himself satisfies all the essential conditions, unless he was a party to fraud or illegality affecting the instrument: section 56.

[61] S. 69(2).

[62] S. 182. See also Crawford and Falconbridge, *supra*, n. 18, at 1510–11.

be reluctant to purchase negotiable instruments and hold them as assets. They would first have to make exhaustive inquiries to be sure that valuable consideration was given for an instrument and that it was free of fraud, illegality, duress, or undue influence. Banks would not risk acquiring instruments that might be subject to such defences when the time came to collect from the party primarily liable.[63]

DEFENCES

Meaning of Defence

The term "defence" is a legal description for the various arguments that a party liable on an instrument may put up against a holder who demands payment. In determining whether a defence will succeed, there are two aspects to consider: (a) the status of the holder relative to the party liable and (b) the type of defence of the party liable. The following is an overview of legal actions in which the plaintiff is the holder of the instrument and the defendant an acceptor, maker, drawer, or endorser.

Types of Holders

First, it is important to examine the relationship between the holder and the party alleged to be liable on the instrument. When a holder has had direct dealings with that party, the two of them are **immediate parties**. If they have not had direct dealings with one another and yet are parties to the same instrument, they are **remote parties**. Since a holder in due course is, by definition, a party who acquires the instrument by negotiation from the payee or from a subsequent endorser, he is always a party remote from the acceptor of a draft, maker of a note, or drawer of a cheque.

immediate parties the holder of an instrument and the party alleged to be liable on it who have had direct dealings with each other

remote parties parties to an instrument who have not had direct dealings with one another

---

ILLUSTRATION 19.2

A draws a cheque in favour of B. B endorses it to the order of C. C endorses it to the order of D. D is the present holder of the cheque.

A and B, B and C, and C and D are immediate parties of each other. The remote party relationships are between A and C, A and D, and B and D. Whether the present holder, D, is a holder in due course will depend upon whether he satisfies the four essential conditions.

Types of Defences

A holder's chance of success in collecting from an immediate party is no better than his contractual rights under the agreement between them. The negotiable instrument does not increase the holder's rights. Against an immediate party, the party liable can use a line of *mere personal defences*, usually not available against remote parties.

By contrast, a remote party who is a holder in due course has the best chance of success in collecting payment. The party liable has a greatly reduced list of possible defences, termed *real defences*, with which to resist the demands of a holder in due course.

If a remote party fails to meet the standards of a holder in due course, his position lies between an immediate party and a holder in due course. He is subject not only to

---

[63] As an additional protection, a bank will require the endorsement of the person from whom it acquires the instrument; but recourse against endorsers is at best a second resort, which banks naturally wish to avoid.

real defences but also to *defect of title defences*. He is not, however, subject to *mere personal defences*. This area is quite detailed and technical, so we shall simply list the defences.[64]

Mere Personal Defences

All the defences—real, defect of title, and mere personal—are available to the defendant when the contestants are immediate parties, but the mere personal defences are available only when they are immediate parties. Defences that are good only against an immediate party are (a) lack of consideration and (b) the right of set off, as discussed in Chapter 11.

Defect of Title Defences

We have seen that a holder in due course must have taken the instrument without knowledge of any defect in title and, when he has done so, defences based on such defects will fail. Generally speaking, when an instrument is **regular on its face**, there is no defence against a holder in due course. But if a holder takes the instrument with knowledge of one or more defects, or when there is an irregularity on the face of the instrument, he is not a holder in due course, and a defence based on a defect will be successful.[65] Such defects are

(a) incapacity to contract as a result of drunkenness or insanity;[66]
(b) discharge of the instrument by payment, or renunciation of a holder's rights in it;
(c) absence of delivery when the instrument was complete at the time;
(d) fraud, duress, undue influence, illegality; and
(e) want of authority in an agent to complete the instrument on behalf of the party primarily liable.

Real Defences

The following defences are good against any holder, even a holder in due course:

(a) incapacity to contract because of infancy
(b) cancellation of the instrument
(c) absence of delivery where the instrument is incomplete when taken
(d) fraud as to the nature of the instrument when the promisor is blind or illiterate
(e) a forged signature on the instrument
(f) want of authority, in someone who has represented himself as an agent, to sign on behalf of the party liable
(g) alteration of the instrument

CHECKLIST

Key Terms Relating to Negotiable Instruments

Parties	Actions
■ Maker	■ Delivery
■ Drawer	■ Acceptance
■ Promisor	■ Endorsement
■ Drawee	■ Negotiation
■ Holder in due course	■ Presentment
	■ Dishonour

---

[64] For a full discussion see Crawford and Falconbridge, *supra*, n. 18.

[65] Ss. 55 and 57(2).

[66] Depending upon the circumstances, insanity might instead be interpreted as a real defence. See Crawford and Falconbridge, *supra*, n. 18, at 1348–51.

CONSUMER BILLS AND NOTES

The modern concept of negotiability is a highly refined one, developed over the centuries and adapted to the convenience of business. Its advantages have had to be restricted, however, because of certain abuses. One abuse, in particular, related to consumer sales where the price was to be paid by installments. The seller might assign the contract to a finance company and receive immediate payment; the buyer would receive notice of assignment and make the installment payments to the finance company. The general rule about assignment of contractual rights, as we have seen in Chapter 11, is that an assignee acquires no better claim than the assignor had. Therefore, if the buyer had some claim against the seller, for breach of warranty or because the contract was induced by some misrepresentation, that claim can normally be asserted against the assignee. However, merchants and finance companies found a way around the general rule about assignments by using a negotiable instrument. The buyer was required to sign a promissory note for the balance of the purchase price plus finance charges, and this note, along with the conditional sale contract, was endorsed by the merchant to the finance company. The finance company became a holder in due course of the note, immune to any personal defences the buyer might have against the original merchant.

This loophole was closed by an amendment to the Bills of Exchange Act,[67] which removed the protection otherwise accorded to a holder in due course in consumer credit arrangements where a finance company acts with a seller of goods on the installment plan. The Act requires that every consumer bill or consumer note be prominently and legibly marked on its face with the words "consumer purchase" before or at the time the instrument is signed by the purchaser or by anyone signing to accommodate the purchaser (that is, a guarantor).[68] It also provided that the right of the holder of a consumer bill or consumer note to have the whole or any part thereof paid by the purchaser or a guarantor is subject to any defence or right of set-off, other than counterclaim, that the purchaser would have had in an action by the seller on the bill or note.[69]

Therefore, a consumer buying on credit may now use all the personal defences (formerly available only against the seller) to defend against a finance company that sues him as holder of his promissory note.

Strategies to Manage the Legal Risks

Many retail businesses have already acted to minimize the risks associated with negotiable instruments. They do not accept cheques or bills of exchange as payment for goods. The wide availability of credit cards has reduced the need to accept these forms of payment, although there are costs for such services. If offering financing for the purchases of customers, businesses involve a separate finance company to lend directly to the customer, rather than accepting a promissory note and transferring it to a factoring company. This provides

---

[67] See also the discussion of this issue in Chapter 3, under the heading "Consumer Protection."

[68] S. 190(1). If not so marked, the instrument is void in the hands of either the seller or the finance company [s. 190(2)].

[69] S. 191.

immediate cash flow and reduces the defences that may be available to the customer against the lender. As noted above, this is less effective when the finance company is connected to the vendor or if the customer is a consumer.

For those businesses that extend credit and cash cheques, including banks and payday loan companies, forgery and false identity are major legal risks. Strict policies involving proof of identity, inspection of the physical cheque for any sign of irregularity, and implementation of high fees for dishonouring help to minimize the risks.

QUESTIONS FOR REVIEW

1. Describe the changing way in which banks are processing cheques.

2. What types of negotiable instruments are governed by the Bills of Exchange Act? What is money?

3. Describe briefly the respective uses of demand drafts, sight drafts, and time drafts in commercial practice.

4. What is the difference in legal effect between a drawer having her cheque certified and a payee later having the cheque certified?

5. Describe the three qualities of negotiable instruments that distinguish such instruments from ordinary assignments. How do these qualities make them commercially useful?

6. Donna draws a cheque payable to Edgar for "a maximum of $1000 for carpentry work." Edgar completes the work while Donna is out of town and takes the cheque to his bank to cash it. The bank refuses on the grounds that it is not a valid cheque. Is the bank correct? Explain.

7. Describe the difference between a "bearer" instrument and an "order" instrument.

8. Explain the significance of a party transferring a negotiable instrument endorsed "without recourse." When is this type of endorsement used?

9. J delivers a cheque for $500 in payment for a second-hand computer purchased from K. K inadvertently leaves the cheque on a restaurant table. Q picks it up from the table, forges K's name, and cashes the cheque at the L Bank. K reports the loss of the cheque to J, who immediately informs her bank to stop payment. What rights does the L Bank have?

10. W delivers a cheque for $1000 in payment of a debt owed to X. X endorses the cheque to Y's Second Hand Shop to purchase a television set. Y endorses the cheque to her landlord, Z, in part payment of her monthly rent. When Z takes the cheque to his bank, the teller recognizes W's signature and has heard that he is in financial difficulty. She contacts W's bank and learns that there are not sufficient funds in W's account. What should Z do to protect his claim?

11. Describe the requirements for a party to be considered a holder in due course.

12. You are the maker of a note in which you undertake to pay $500 to a moneylender on demand. Subsequently you pay an installment of $200 to the moneylender on this liability. What steps should you take to ensure that you will not have to pay a further $500 at some later time?

13. Gower has drawn a time draft on Cohen payable three months after sight to Jenkins. The draft is complete and regular, with the possible exception of a clause that Cohen, the drawee, is "to pay the amount of this draft out of money due me on December 31 for professional services rendered." If Cohen refuses to accept the draft, does he owe its amount in future to Gower or to Jenkins?

14. The endorsements appearing on the back of each of three negotiable instruments are reproduced below. An asterisk following a name indicates an actual signature. Identify each of the endorsements by type, and explain its effect for the parties concerned:

(a) Pay to John Factor, Without Recourse

The Synthetic Textile Co. Ltd.

per Terry Lean,*/Manager.

John Factor*

(b) Pay to James Hawkins,

S. Trelawney*

For deposit only,

James Hawkins*

(c) Pay to Archibald Grosvenor only

No Protest Reginald Bunthorne*

Archibald Grosvenor*

Archibald Grosvenor is hereby identified,

Ralph Rackstraw*

15. Wilma purchased a used minivan, including a three-month warranty on parts and labour, from Xenon Used Cars Inc. for $10 000. She paid $1500 down and signed a promissory note for $8500, payable in monthly installments of $285 for three years. If any payment is missed by Wilma, the entire sum will fall due at once because of her default. Xenon immediately transferred the note to Yarrow Finance Corp. and received payment of $7750. Wilma received notice of the transfer with a request to make her monthly payments directly to Yarrow Finance. The van broke down repeatedly within the first month, and Wilma was unable to obtain proper repairs from Xenon. She refused to make the payments to Yarrow Finance, and it sued her for the full sum due. Describe the nature of Wilma's defence against Yarrow Finance and whether she will succeed.

CASES AND PROBLEMS

1. Continuing Scenario

Ashley arranged a credit line at her bank; only Ashley or her father, Jim, were authorized to sign the credit line cheques. The cheques were kept in her office at the restaurant. Miranda was Ashley's assistant manager responsible for making the daily bank deposit and had regular access to Ashley's office. Over time, she became familiar with Ashley's signature and started preparing credit line cheques payable to herself. She would take them to the bank with the regular bank deposit and endorse the cheques for deposit to her account. On the one occasion when a bank teller questioned her, she said the cheque was for overtime she had worked. Only after Miranda quit did Ashley discover that over $2000 had been taken in the last two years. Ashley is now arguing with her bank over whether she should have to pay the outstanding $2000 withdrawn on the credit line. Identify the roles of the bank, Ashley, and Miranda. What negotiable instrument legal principles and defences are involved in this dispute?

2. On April 28, the University of Penticton made a note payable to the Baroque Construction Co. Ltd., three months after date. The amount of the note was expressed simply as "the balance due to you for construction of our Arts Building." On May 2 following, the Baroque Construction Co. Ltd. sold the note to a private financier, R. Jay, for $47 500, having shown him accounts and vouchers indicating a balance of $50 000 due from the university. On July 31, R. Jay presented the note to the treasurer of the university for payment and was advised by him that the construction contract with the Baroque Construction Co. Ltd. contained a guarantee clause and that serious defects had developed in the foundation of the Arts Building. The treasurer stated that the university was not prepared to pay the note for this reason. R. Jay countered with the argument that the defective work was not the slightest concern of his, and that the proper officer of the university had signed the note. He then sued the University of Penticton on its note. Should he succeed? Give reasons.

3. On the afternoon of October 27, Connor supplied office furniture valued at $48 000 to Osmond. When the furniture was delivered, Connor received a certified cheque for $48 000 from Osmond. The cheque, drawn on Osmond's account at the Kelsey Bank, had been certified earlier that afternoon by the bank at Osmond's request. That morning, Osmond had deposited a cheque from a customer for $76 000; the cheque had not yet been cleared, but the bank took the risk that it would be honoured by the Portage Bank, where Osmond's customer had his account.

On October 28, after having been informed by Portage that it would not honour the $76 000 cheque, the Kelsey Bank called Connor to say that certification had been revoked and that she should not attempt to negotiate the cheque. The next day, Connor presented the certified cheque for payment. The Kelsey Bank refused payment, and Connor sued the bank.

Is the Kelsey Bank legally bound to honour the cheque? Explain.

4. Elston owned all the issued common shares of Ham Ltd. He lent Ham Ltd. $160 000 of his personal funds and obtained in return a promissory note from the company payable to his order.

For personal reasons, Elston subsequently had to borrow money on his own account from the Atlas Bank. To secure this loan he delivered the Ham Ltd. promissory note to the bank, but without endorsing it. The bank gave no notice to Ham Ltd. that it was the transferee.

Two months later, Elston sold his shares in Ham Ltd. to new owners who had no knowledge of the existence of the note. At the same time, Elston gave Ham Ltd. a general release of all claims he had against it in terms wide enough to include the company's obligation to him on the $160 000 note.

Elston defaulted on his personal loan from the Atlas Bank, and it then demanded payment of the note from Ham Ltd. Ham Ltd. refused to pay, and the bank brought an action against it for $160 000.

Give reasons whether or not this action should succeed.

5. Allison opened a chequing account with the Picton Bank and signed an "Operation of Account" agreement; she agreed to notify the bank of any discrepancies and errors in her bank balance within 30 days of receiving her monthly statement and to notify the bank of any forgeries or frauds within her organization as soon as she became aware of them. Soon after, she hired Ralph, a new bookkeeper. Just two weeks later Ralph forged four cheques, worth $24 000, on Allison's chequing account. Ralph was very shrewd; he had done this while Allison's general manager, who was in charge of dealings with the bank, was on vacation. Each of the four cheques was made out to a fictitious payee named Quigley, and each was marked "for deposit only." Ralph had set up an account for Quigley in another bank, deposited the cheques, and within a few days withdrew all the money.

The general manager discovered Ralph's fraud on the day he returned; he immediately told Allison about it and she phoned the bank at once—but it was too late. Ralph had absconded. The Picton Bank refused to return the funds to Allison's account, claiming that she had been negligent. In reply, Allison claimed she had complied with the Operation of Account agreement.

Outline the legal argument that Allison would use and the defence of the Picton Bank. Give your opinion on whether she should succeed.

6. As accountant at a branch of the Crown Bank, Cole misappropriated rent of $3000 due to the bank. When the bank inspector discovered these facts, the bank notified the Flin Flon Fidelity and Guarantee Co., which had previously bonded Cole for the bank, and claimed the $3000. The bonding company told Cole that it preferred not to prosecute if it could avoid it, and a possible way out would be for Cole to get his friends to come to his assistance. Cole then prevailed on his friend Smith to sign a promissory note payable 12 months after date in favour of the bonding company. When Smith dishonoured his note at maturity, the bonding company sued him. Should it succeed? Would the result be different if the bonding company had discounted Smith's note at its bank and Smith had refused to pay the bank at the note's maturity?

7. VanWyck drew a cheque payable to Lockhart but decided not to send it until he had examined the goods purchased from Lockhart to see whether they were satisfactory. VanWyck's

clerk, Anderson, inadvertently gave the cheque to Lockhart without first getting permission from VanWyck. (Anderson normally had nothing to do with the preparation or delivery of VanWyck's negotiable instruments.) Lockhart endorsed the cheque for value to Snider, who took it without notice of the circumstances. When Snider attempted to cash the cheque, she discovered that VanWyck had requested his bank to stop payment on it. Snider sued both VanWyck and Lockhart for the amount.

State with reasons the rights of the respective parties and the probable result of the action.

8. Originals Inc. held an auction of antique furniture and received a winning bid of $18 000 from Parker. Parker gave his cheque, drawn on the Regal Bank, to Originals Inc. and asked that the furniture be delivered to his warehouse the next day. Originals' clerk deposited the cheque at its bank the afternoon of the auction.

When the furniture arrived the following morning, Parker examined the items on the delivery truck and realized that most of them did not meet the description provided by the auctioneer. He rejected them and the deliverer returned them to Originals Inc. Parker immediately telephoned his bank to stop payment on the cheque and then telephoned Originals to inform them of what he had done. Originals protested but accepted the furniture and said it would sue Parker.

Regal Bank's employee erroneously overlooked Parker's stop payment order and paid the cheque to Originals. When the error came to light, the Regal Bank credited the amount of the cheque to Parker and brought an action against Originals Inc. to recover the amount of the payment. Originals claimed it was entitled to hold onto the funds because of breach of contract.

Summarize the arguments of both sides. Who should succeed?

Additional Resources for Chapter 19 on the Companion Website

(www.pearsoncanada.ca/smyth)

In addition to pre- and post-tests, mini-cases, and application exercises, the Companion Website includes the following province-specific resources for Chapter 19:
- **Alberta:** Consumer Credit
- **Atlantic:** Provinces: Consumer Credit
- **Ontario:** Consumer Credit; Limitation Periods

Chapter 20
Intellectual Property

- THE NATURE OF INTELLECTUAL PROPERTY

- TRADEMARKS

- COPYRIGHT

- PATENTS

- INDUSTRIAL DESIGNS

- CONFIDENTIAL INFORMATION, TRADE SECRETS, AND KNOW-HOW

- TECHNOLOGICAL CHANGE AND INTELLECTUAL PROPERTY LAW

- STRATEGIES TO MANAGE THE LEGAL RISKS

In this chapter, we review the various forms of intellectual property—trademarks, copyright, patents, and industrial designs.

We examine the following issues:

- What is "intellectual property"?

- How is intellectual property acquired?

- What types of intellectual property are protected by law?

- What constitutes an infringement of intellectual property?

- What are the remedies for infringement?

- How does intellectual property law adapt to new technologies?

- How should the rights of inventors and innovators be balanced against the general public interest?

THE NATURE OF INTELLECTUAL PROPERTY

Forms of Intellectual Property

Intellectual property is intangible property that is the product of mental activity. The four most recognized forms of intellectual property are trademarks, copyright, patents, and industrial designs. Each type of intellectual property deals with ideas or inventions; originality is an essential feature. Each particular type of property is protected by its own rules and statutes which are administered through the Canadian Intellectual Property Office (CIPO), an agency of Industry Canada.

Intellectual property law is complicated and technical. Some property rights are protected solely by statute, while others are also protected by common law rules. For some interests, registration is essential, while other rights arise upon creation. Some types of intellectual property may fall within two different categories, while others may fall into gaps between the categories so that no protection is provided. In addition, since intellectual property is essentially concerned with knowledge, information, and, above all, innovation, it is linked to technological progress. New methods of storing, presenting, and transmitting information and ideas are constantly being devised, and some of these techniques do not fit neatly into the traditional categories of intellectual property. Rules are constantly being revised to address the new challenges. This chapter is designed to present a general overview of intellectual property rights and protections and some guidance on how to avoid infringing the rights of others. Specific rules may have changed since this edition's publication date. Legislative jurisdiction over intellectual property is assigned to the federal government and the legislation discussed below applies across the country.[1]

Not all ideas, information, or knowledge qualify as intellectual property: confidential information, trade secrets, and what is commonly referred to as "know-how," though they may be protected by law, are not regarded as forms of property.

CHECKLIST

Forms of Intellectual Property

Canadian law recognizes the following basic forms of intellectual property:

- trademarks
- copyright
- patents
- industrial designs

Should Intellectual Property Be Protected?

As already discussed, tort law protects ideas with causes of action such as passing off and product defamation. The increasing value of intellectual property motivated the government to create additional legislative protection. The proposition that ideas should receive statutory protection as a form of property has not always been universally accepted.

Those supporting protection claim that creators such as writers, inventors, and designers deserve compensation for their efforts and that without protection, creativity is discouraged. By contrast, opponents of protection claim that ideas and inventions—especially those concerning matters such as health, medicine, food production, and

---

[1] Constitution Act, 1867, s. 91(22–23). Disputes over intellectual property are heard in the Federal Court of Canada.

education—properly belong to the whole world. They point to the heavy social costs of protection—higher prices due to the payment of royalties and licence fees, and inefficiency resulting from restrictions on the use of new techniques and from the abuse of monopoly power. Overprotection, as much as lack of protection, may hinder economic and social progress.

The problem, especially for a country such as Canada, which is both an exporter and importer of cultural and technological innovation, is to find the right balance. The United States seems to be moving toward greater protection of "ownership rights," for example, by lengthening the period of copyright protection and criminalizing infringement (mostly for the benefit of large corporations).[2] Canadian courts and legislators show more concern for what may be termed "user rights."[3] For more information on this topic, see the Companion Website.

TRADEMARKS

Nature of Trademarks

trademark an identifiable feature that is used by a person for the purpose of distinguishing his goods or services from those of others

Section 2 of the federal Trade-marks Act[4] defines a **trademark** as

(a) a mark that is used by a person for the purpose of distinguishing or so as to distinguish wares or services manufactured, sold, leased, hired, or performed by him from those manufactured, sold, leased, hired, or performed by others
(b) a certification mark
(c) a distinguishing guise
(d) a proposed trademark[4A]

Although the Act does not define the word "mark," any visual characteristic of goods or their presentation that serves to distinguish them from goods and services that do not have the same trade connection can be considered a "mark." CIPO is now accepting applications for non-traditional marks such as sounds.[5]

certification mark a special type of trademark used to identify goods or services that conform to a particular standard

distinguishing guise the shaping of goods or their containers, or a distinctive mode of wrapping or packaging

A **certification mark** is a special type of trademark used to identify goods or services that conform to a particular standard, a typical example being the "TRUSTe" mark for internet security.[6] The owner of the certification mark may register it and license its use to other persons whose goods or services meet the defined standards. A **distinguishing guise** usually refers to the shaping of goods or their containers, or to a mode of wrapping or packaging that is distinctive—a Coca-Cola bottle, for example.[7] For more information on this topic, see the Companion Website.

---

[2] The Sonny Bono Copyright Extension Act of 1998, which extends U.S. copyright protection by 20 years, to 70 years after the creator's death, is commonly known as the "Mickey Mouse Act," because of the benefit it conferred on the Walt Disney Company.

[3] See the Supreme Court of Canada decisions in *Theberge v. Galerie d'Art du Petit Champlain*, [2002] 2 S.C.R. 336; *CCH Canadian Ltd. v. Law Society of Upper Canada*, [2004] 1 S.C.R. 339; *Bell Canada v. SOCAN* [2012] 2 S.C.R. 326; *Alberta (Minister of Education) v. Canadian Copyright Licensing Agency*, [2012] 2 S.C.R. 345 .

[4] Trade-marks Act, R.S.C. 1985, c. T-13. (Unless otherwise stated, statutory references in this part of the chapter are to this Act.)

[4A] Section 2 of the Trade-marks Act, R.S.C. 1985, c. T-13. (Unless otherwise stated, statutory references in this part of the chapter are to this Act.)

[5] CIPO Practice Notice: Trade-mark consisting of a sound (Publication Date: 2012-03-28); CIPO Practice Notice: Three-dimensional Marks (Publication Date: 2000-12-06).

[6] U.S. Trademark No. 3695190 registered October 2009 to True Ultimate Standards Everywhere Inc. Description of the mark: "The colors green, white, and black are claimed as features of the mark. The mark consists of a stylized 'e' in black with a white half circle arc above the 'e' and green background above the arc. The word 'TRUSTe:' appears in black letters above the green."

[7] In order to qualify as a trademark, a distinguishing guise must be more than purely functional: see *Kirkbi AG v. Ritvik Holdings Inc.* (2003), 228 D.L.R. (4th) 297, aff'd [2005] 3 S.C.R. 302 (Lego Block case).

Business Names

Businesses operate using a variety of business names, domain names, brands, and trade names. Each of these names involves trademark. The name of an established business is a valuable asset that forms part of the goodwill of the business. A trademark may be and frequently is part of a business name, but the entire name may not be a trademark. For example, the word "Ford" is a trademark of the Ford Motor Company, but the full name is not a trademark. Common words such as "company" or "limited" are not trademarkable. Similarly, only portions of a domain name are eligible for trademark protection. Although a domain name is technically only an address, that portion of the name that is uniquely linked to goods or services may be registered as a trademark.[8] Businesses often register separate trade names to market different product lines or represent different divisions of a business (sometimes referred to as brands). For example, Cara Operations Limited owns the trademark "Harvey's" for its fast-food restaurant brand, as well as the advertising slogan "Harvey's Makes Your Hamburger a Beautiful Thing."[8A] A business should investigate trademark protection and availability for its name, domain name, and any trade names before investing in them.[9] Free online trademark searches are available through Industry Canada's Canadian Intellectual Property Office (CIPO) website.[10]

The names of all corporations, and those of some unincorporated businesses, must be registered with the government under which the business operates. Registration of a business name does not give a business the right to carry on business under that name if to do so would infringe the trademark of some other business. The government specifically excludes any suggestion that granting incorporation or registering a particular name guarantees the use of that name, and it specifically warns applicants of this limitation.[11] Therefore, a separate trademark search and registration should be completed. Since section 40(2) of the Trade-marks Act allows a proposed trademark to be registered, a business can gain trademark protection before it spends too much promoting its names.

Protection of Trademarks

Common Law: The Tort of Passing-Off
The common law protects a trademark owner through the tort of passing-off. A person commits the tort of passing-off when he misrepresents goods, services, or a business in such a way as to deceive the public into believing that those things are the goods, services, or business of some other person, thereby causing damage to the latter. The main purpose of a passing-off action is to protect the trademark owner from the sale of counterfeit goods, which is actually theft of goodwill.

The legal definition of **goodwill** is "the benefit and advantage of the good name, reputation, and connection of a business."[12] Consider goodwill as the difference between the market value of a business as a going concern and its break-up value—that is, the sum that could be obtained by selling off all of its fixed tangible assets and inventory piece by piece. The name of the business and any mark associated with it forms part of a business's intangible reputation and goodwill.

goodwill the benefit and advantage of the good name, reputation, and connections of a business

---

[8] For a historic perspective of this topic, see L.K. Jones, "Trademark.com: Trademark Law in Cyberspace" (1999) 37 Alta. L. Rev. 991. This issue is discussed further in Chapter 31.

[8A] ® Registered trademark of *Cara Operations Limited*.

[9] Canadian Trademark Registration Number TMA147423 (registered in 1966), TMA315056 (registered in 1986).

[10] See http://www.ic.gc.ca/app/opic-cipo/trdmrks/srch/tmSrch.do?lang=eng

[11] When applying for federal incorporation with a specific name, the applicant is required by the federal government to perform a NUANS (Newly Upgraded Automated Name Search) search. Names likely to cause confusion are rejected. The federal government limits its investigation to the contents of this search, and applicants are warned to complete a trademark registration and monitor ongoing applications. See the Industry Canada website: www.ic.gc.ca.

[12] *Inland Revenue Commissioners v. Muller*, [1901] A.C. 217 at 223.

CASE 20.1

Ray Plastics Ltd. manufactured a successful tool—a combined snow brush, ice scraper, and squeegee—called "Snow Trooper." It supplied the tool to a number of large retailers, including Canadian Tire. Canadian Tire suggested to another of its suppliers, Dustbane Products Ltd., that it consider producing a similar type of tool. Dustbane did so, producing a tool that was virtually identical and at a lower price; it took over all of Canadian Tire's snow-brush business.

The court found that the design of the "Snow Trooper" was very distinctive, that it had been intentionally copied, and that this constituted the tort of "passing-off." It awarded an injunction and damages to Ray Plastics.[13]

Elements of the tort of passing-off are:

- The plaintiff's goods, services, or business must enjoy a reputation that is of some value worth protecting.
- The defendant must have misrepresented its goods, service, or business as those of the plaintiff.
- There must either be actual confusion or a likelihood of confusion in the public's mind between the goods, services, or business of the plaintiff and those produced or licensed by the defendant.[14]
- The plaintiff must suffer or be likely to suffer damage in consequence of the passing-off.[15]

CASE 20.2

The plaintiff, Greystone Capital Management, was a firm of real estate and investment managers conducting business in British Columbia. The firm was well regarded and enjoyed an excellent reputation in the B.C. real estate industry. The defendant company also operated as property developers and managers in British Columbia. It changed its name to Greystone Real Estate Corporation, even though its principals were aware of the plaintiff's existence.

The court ordered the defendant to change its name and to refrain from using the word "Greystone" in any future name. It also awarded damages to the plaintiff. The plaintiff established the existence of goodwill associated with its name. The defendant's use of the name "Greystone" was likely to mislead the public and to cause injury to the plaintiff.[16]

Some plaintiffs argue that the definition of passing-off should be expanded to include situations where one person makes use of a well-known trade name or mark in order to obtain a benefit, even though the owner cannot show any damage and there is no likelihood of confusion in the minds of the public.[17] This view has only limited success in the courts, and the argument is more effective under the statutory causes of action discussed next.

---

[13] *Ray Plastics Ltd. v. Dustbane Products Ltd.* (1994), 57 C.P.R. (3d) 474. See also *Eli Lilly and Co. v. Novopharm Ltd.* (2000), 195 D.L.R. (4th) 547 leave to appeal denied [2001] S.C.C.A. No. 100, in which the shape and colouring of a drug capsule were held to be distinctive packaging. However, the combination of shape and colour must be unique or sufficiently unusual to clearly distinguish the product from other products: *Novopharm Ltd. v. AstraZeneca AB* (2003), 233 D.L.R. (4th) 150, supp'l reasons [2006] F.C.J. No. 854.

[14] This may simply be a mistaken belief that the defendant has a licence to produce associated goods—see *Paramount Pictures Corp. v. Howley*, [1992] O.J. No. 1921.

[15] See *Ciba-Geigy Canada Ltd. v. Apotex Inc.* (1992), 44 C.P.R. (3d) 289 (S.C.C.), per Gonthier, J. See also *Kirkbi*, *supra*, n. 7; *Paramount Pictures*, *supra*, n. 14.

[16] *Greystone Capital Management Inc. v. Greystone Properties Ltd.*, [1999] B.C.J. No. 514.

[17] In rare circumstances, when the passing-off deliberately suggests an association with another's product, it may not be necessary to show damage. For example, an advertising campaign that incorrectly associates a product with another's product may actually benefit that other product, but might still amount to passing-off: see *National Hockey League v. Pepsi-Cola Canada Ltd.* (1995), 122 D.L.R. (4th) 412.

The defendant named its new hotel in Edmonton the "Fantasyland Hotel." An injunction was sought by Walt Disney Productions, which had used the name "Fantasyland" in connection with its amusement parks. The Alberta Court of Appeal refused the injunction. According to the court:

> Passing-off cases fall into two broad categories. In the first are those where competitors are engaged in a common field of activity and the plaintiff has alleged that the defendant has named, packaged or described its product or business in a manner likely to lead the public to believe the defendant's product or business is that of the plaintiff. The second, and nowadays perhaps more common type of passing-off, is where it is alleged that a defendant has promoted his product or business in such a way as to create the false impression that his product or business is in some way approved, authorized or endorsed by the plaintiff or that there is some business connection between the defendant and the plaintiff. By these means a defendant may hope to cash in on the goodwill of the plaintiff. The appellant argued the second type saying that using the name "Fantasyland" for its hotel created the false impression that the hotel was connected to Disney. Disney lost because the belief that the respondent is benefiting from the use of the name "Fantasyland" is not enough to found the tort of passing-off without proof of confusion.[18]

Section 7 of the Trade-marks Act

The Trade-marks Act provides additional statutory causes of action that are closely related to the common law action of passing-off. Section 7 prohibits[18A]

- making a false or misleading statement tending to discredit the business, wares, or services of a competitor

- directing public attention to one's wares, services, or business in such a way as to cause or be likely to cause confusion in Canada between those wares, services, or business and the wares, services, or business of another

- passing-off other wares or services as and for those ordered or requested

- making, in association with wares or services, any description that is false in a material respect and likely to mislead the public as to their character, quality, geographic origin, or mode of production

- doing any other act or adopting any other business practice contrary to honest industrial or commercial use in Canada

Although section 7 appears to restate the common law, it gives wider protection in some cases, since it applies to the whole of Canada and appears to be broader in scope than the common law action.

Registered Trademarks

Unregistered trademarks are protected by the passing-off tort and under section 7 of the Trade-marks Act. However, additional advantages are available if a business registers its trademarks under the Trade-marks Act.

When a registered mark is used, there is no need to indicate that it is registered in order to obtain the benefits of registration, but it has become common practice, on labels and in advertisements, to use the symbol ® or ™, frequently accompanied by words such as "... is the registered trademark of XYZ Inc."

---

[18] *Walt Disney Productions v. Fantasyland Hotel Inc.* (1998), 85 C.P.R. (3d) 36, aff'd (2000), 4 C.P.R. (4th) 370; [1994] A.J. No. 484, aff'd [1996] A.J. No. 415. Disney won an earlier case over the use of the name "Fantasyland" for a theme park in West Edmonton Mall: Use within the same genre or business activity is relevant. See *Walt Disney Productions v. Triple Five Corp.*, [1992] A.J. No. 571, aff'd [1994] A.J. No. 196. The use of the trademark "Playboy" in connection with magazines and hotels was held not to be confusing with the same name for hair stylists: *Playboy Enterprises Inc. v. Germain* (1978), 39 C.P.R. (2d) 32, aff'd. (1979), 43 C.P.R. (2d) 271 (Fed. C.A.). See also *Toyota Jidosha Kabushiki Kaisha v. Lexus Foods Inc.* (2000), 194 D.L.R. (4th) 491.

[18A] Section 7 of the Trade-marks Act.

Rights Obtained by Registration   Section 19 of the Act gives the owner of a valid registered trademark the exclusive right to its use throughout Canada in respect of the goods and services for which it was registered. No unauthorized person may then sell, distribute, or advertise any goods or services in association with a confusing trademark or trade name (section 20), or otherwise use the mark in a manner that is likely to have the effect of depreciating the value of the goodwill attached to it (section 22). Registration provides a complete defence to a passing-off action. If another person claims that he had already been using the mark, or a deceptively similar mark, before the registration, his only recourse is to attack the validity of the registration.[19] If, after a trademark has been registered, it is discovered that some other person had been using a similar trademark before the registered owner first used it, the first user may bring proceedings to have the registration "expunged"—that is, removed (section 17).[20]

Registration gives the owner other advantages; normally it applies to the whole of Canada so that the right of exclusive use is not restricted to the area in which the owner actually does business and has established a reputation. A trademark that has been registered in Canada may also be registered in other countries that adhere to the International Convention for the Protection of Industrial Property.[21] Although a separate foreign application must be filed, the Canadian registration creates a presumption in favour of validity, distinctiveness, and ownership.

Duration   A trademark registration is valid for a period of 15 years and may be renewed indefinitely. The Registrar may from time to time request evidence that the trademark is still being used, and if it has been abandoned or is not renewed at the end of the 15-year period, it may be expunged from the register (sections 44, 45, 46).

Requirements for Registration

The Mark   In order for a trademark to be registered, it must satisfy a number of conditions (section 12). In particular, the mark must <u>not</u> be

(a)   a word that is primarily merely the name or surname of an individual who is living or died within the preceding 30 years; a person may continue to use her own name despite the existence of a registered trademark (section 19)

(b)   clearly descriptive or deceptively misdescriptive of the character or quality of the wares or services, or of their place of origin

(c)   the name of any of the wares or services in connection with which it is used

(d)   likely to be confused with another registered trademark (for more information on this topic, see the Companion Website)

(e–f)   a mark that is prohibited by sections 9, 10, or 10.1 of the Trade-marks Act

(g–i)   a protected geographic, Olympic, or Paralympic mark.

Prohibitions (a), (b), and (c) ensure that the names of people and places, and descriptive words that are in common usage, are not taken out of circulation through registration by giving a monopoly to the registered owner. The intention of prohibition (d) is to carry out the main purpose of the Act: Trademarks are designed to be distinctive, and such distinctiveness would be lost if two or more persons were allowed to register "confusingly similar" marks. Although each case of confusion must be determined on its own facts with

---

[19] *Molson Canada v. Oland Brewery Ltd.* (2002), 214 D.L.R. (4th) 473; *Philip Morris Products S.A. v. Marlboro Canada Ltd.*, [2010] F.C.J. No. 1385.

[20] *Masterpiece Inc. v. Alavida Lifestyles Inc.*, 2011 SCC 27, [2011] 2 S.C.R. 387

[21] This was an early treaty dealing with the protection of intellectual property rights arising out of the Paris Convention of 1883 and it remains in force today (obviously in an amended form). Participating states guarantee the protection of intellectual property rights to each other's regimes. It is administered by the World Intellectual Property Organization, which facilitates international cooperation in intellectual property regulation. See http://www.wipo.int

regard to all the surrounding circumstances, section 6 provides a list of relevant considerations, including the nature of the wares, the degree of resemblance, and the nature of the trade. Finally, sections 9 and 10 prohibit registration of marks that suggest an association with royalty, the government, or certain international organizations or professional groups, or that are scandalous or obscene.

Selecting and designing a suitable trademark is difficult. The mark should be distinctive and eye-catching and should quickly become associated in the public mind with the goods or services of its owner. It must be original so that it is not confusingly similar to some other registered mark. The normal practice is to search the Trade-marks databank on the CIPO website for other marks that are visually or phonetically similar to the mark being proposed for registration;[22] U.S. searches might also be advisable. In practice, the application to register is normally prepared and filed by a specialist trademark agent, who will give advice on the likelihood of an application being accepted.

ILLUSTRATION 20.1

(a) A mark consisting of the name of a historical figure, such as "William Shakespeare" or "John A. Macdonald," would probably be acceptable; even though it is very likely that there are living persons with those names—they are not "primarily merely" surnames. Similarly, fictitious names, such as "Captain Kirk" or "Darth Vader," are registrable because the public would not identify the names with living individuals. In one instance, an invented name, "Marco Pecci," was held to be registrable in the absence of evidence that such an individual actually existed, despite the possibility that there might somewhere be a person of that name.[23]

(b) Words, especially adjectives, that are merely descriptive (or misdescriptive) of the quality of the goods are not acceptable. "Instant" or "Super" would be rejected, though "Kold One" has been accepted when applied to beer.[24] The word "Golden" was held to be descriptive of a beer and therefore not registrable.[25]

(c) The use of a place name as descriptive of the quality or origin of goods is normally not permitted. The mark "Toscano," applied to wine, was disallowed since that is the Italian name for wine from a famous region.[26] In another case, however, a producer was permitted to register the mark "Oberhaus" in relation to wine, despite the fact that there is in Germany a small village called Oberhausen where wine is produced. It was considered unlikely that the Canadian wine-buying public would know of the place.[27]

(d) A proposed trademark is confusing if a casual consumer somewhat in a hurry is likely to draw a mistaken inference. An applicant was allowed to register the trademark "Barbie's" for restaurant, take-out, catering, and banquet services despite the objections of Mattel Inc., owners of the famous "BARBIE" mark in association with dolls and doll accessories. The Supreme Court of Canada held that the doll and restaurant business appealed to different consumers and confusion was unlikely. The average consumer is not so easily confused.[28]

---

[22] A computerized search system is operated by Industry Canada for all federally (and some provincially) registered companies and trademarks. The Canadian Intellectual Property Office Canadian Trade-marks Database website also has database search capabilities: http://www.cipo.ic.gc.ca/eic/site/cipointernet-internetopic.nsf/eng/h_wr03082.html

[23] *Gerhard Horn Investments Ltd. v. Registrar of Trade Marks*, [1983] 2 F.C. 878. See also *Jurak Holdings Ltd. v. Matol Biotech Laboratories Ltd.*, [2006] T.M.O.B. No. 36 at paras. 23–7, aff'd [2008] F.C.J. No. 1367.

[24] *Registrar of Trade Marks v. Provenzano* (1978), 40 C.P.R. (2d) 288.

[25] *John Labatt Ltd. v. Molson Cos.* (1987), 19 C.P.R. (3d) 88 (Fed. C.A.), leave to appeal to the Supreme Court denied [1988] S.C.C.A. No. 109.

[26] *Jordan & Ste Michelle Cellars Ltd. v. Gillespies & Co.* (1985), 6 C.P.R. (3d) 377. In that case, the words were also deceptively misdescriptive, since the wine was Canadian.

[27] *Stabilisierungsfonds fur Wein v. T.G. Bright & Co. Ltd.* (1985), 4 C.P.R. (3d) 526. Sections 11.11 to 11.19 of the Trade-marks Act now contain detailed provisions regarding the names and geographical descriptions of origin approved by the government that may be used in connection with wines and spirits. Those provisions are intended to comply with Canada's obligations under the World Trade Organization rules. See *Sociedad Agricola Santa Teresa Ltda. v. VinaLeyda Limitada*, [2007] F.C.J. No. 1681.

[28] *Mattel, Inc. v. 3894207 Canada Inc.*, [2006] 1 S.C.R. 772. For an expanded discussion about the determination of confusion see *Veuve Clicquot Ponsardin v. Boutiques Cliquot Ltee*, [2006] 1 S.C.R. 824 and *Masterpiece Inc. v. Alvida Lifestyles Inc.*, [2011] S.C.J. No. 27.

Ownership and Use   Registration creates a presumption of ownership. It does not make a person the owner of a trademark; that person must already be the owner at the time of registration. Even in the case of an approved application based upon proposed use, the mark will be registered only after the applicant has filed a declaration that it has started to use the mark in Canada.

The application to register may be based upon any one of the following grounds (section 16):[28A]

- the mark has been previously used or made known in Canada,

- the mark has been registered and used abroad, in a country that is a party to the international convention, or

- the use of the mark is proposed in Canada

Generally, the advertising of a trademark is not sufficient to constitute "use"; the goods to which the mark relates must have been sold or the services performed. However, advertising alone may be sufficient to amount to "making known" the mark in Canada.

Opposition Proceedings

The initial obstacle in registering a trademark is to satisfy the Registrar that the chosen mark is eligible for registration. If the Registrar refuses registration, the owner may appeal that decision to the courts. If there is no objection by the Registrar, or an objection has been overcome, the Trade-marks Office issues a notice that the application has been approved for advertisement in the Trade-marks Journal, and, subsequently, the application must be advertised. Any person may file a notice of opposition within two months of the advertisement. Registration may be opposed on any of the following grounds:

- the application did not comply with the various formal requirements for filing,

- the mark is not registrable,

- the applicant is not the person entitled to registration, or

- the mark is not "distinctive" (sections 37, 38)

The opponent must describe the reason for the opposition in sufficient detail to allow the applicant to reply to the objection. However, the onus of satisfying the Registrar that the trademark should be registered still rests on the applicant. This is so, even though the Registrar has in effect already reached a preliminary decision in favour of the application by permitting it to be advertised. Opposition proceedings are determined in the first place by hearing officers, with appeal to the Federal Court.

An objection that the mark is not registrable may be based on any of the elements set out in section 12 of the Act. The motivation behind a challenge is usually to prevent a business competitor from gaining an advantage by being granted the exclusive right to use the mark. The other common reason is that the objector claims pre-existing rights to an identical or confusingly similar mark, whether or not it is registered. Determining what is "confusing" depends on all the surrounding circumstances, including the nature of the business concerned and the goods or services supplied.[29]

[28A] Section 16 of the Trade-marks Act.

[29] Section 6(5) contains a non-exhaustive list; whether confusion is likely is determined on a balance of probabilities: *Masterpiece Inc. v. Alavida Lifestyles Inc.*, 2011 SCC 27, [2011] 2 S.C.R. 387; *Veuve Clicquot Ponsardin v. Boutiques Cliquot Ltee*, 2006 SCC 23, [2006] 1 S.C.R. 824 .

CASE 20.4

A small Ontario corporation, Pink Panther Beauty Corp., applied to register the name "Pink Panther" as a trademark for hair-care and beauty supplies that it proposed to market. The application was opposed by United Artists, the well-known movie studio that owns the Pink Panther movies, the Pink Panther cartoon character, and the accompanying music. United Artists has its own "Pink Panther" registrations for movie-related services. It argued that the application by the Ontario corporation should not be granted because of the risk of confusion with its existing marks. Further, it claimed that the applicants were simply trying to cash in on the famous name.

The court allowed the Ontario corporation's application to register the mark. There was no likelihood of confusion and the average consumer is not so devoid of intelligence as to confuse the applicant's beauty products with the complainant's movies.[30]

Actions for Infringement

Unauthorized Use　One major advantage of registration is that, unlike passing-off, a registered trademark may be infringed by any unauthorized use of that mark or a confusingly similar mark by some other person.

Any use of another's name or mark, even without any intent to deceive, is to infringe another's mark.[31] It is not necessary for the defendant to have attempted to pass off its products as those of the owner of the mark. Comparative advertising, where one firm attempts to demonstrate that its product is superior to a rival's, may constitute a "use" of the rival's mark if the advertisement refers to the name or mark of the rival product.[32] An infringement may be accidental or deliberate; it is not necessary to show intent to damage the goodwill of the owner of the mark,[33] though such an intention may persuade a court to award punitive damages.

CASE 20.5

In *Coca-Cola Ltd. v. Pardhan*[34] the well-known soft-drink company brought an action alleging infringement of its trademark on the ground that the defendant bought quantities of the beverage in Canada and then exported it for resale without the consent of the manufacturer. Coca-Cola argued that the defendant's export amounted to infringement because exporting is deemed to be use under the Trademarks Act.[35] The Federal Court of Appeal rejected the argument, and found that improperly distributing authentic goods did not amount to infringement.[36] The court held that "goods which originate in the stream of commerce with the owner of a trademark are not counterfeit."[37]

---

[30] *Pink Panther Beauty Corp. v. United Artists Corp.* (1998), 80 C.P.R. (3d) 247 (F.C.A.) (The dissenting judge would have disallowed the application: the applicant was simply attempting to cash in on the goodwill associated with the name.) The Supreme Court of Canada has held that this case should not be interpreted to suggest that some resemblance of linkage to the wares in question is necessary for confusion to exist. The wares or services in question do not have to be of the same general class; this is but one factor to consider: *Mattel, supra*, n. 28, at paras. 57–71.

[31] *Walt Disney Productions v. Triple Five Corp., supra*, n. 18. In *Pro-C Ltd. v. Computer City Inc.* (2001), 205 D.L.R. (4th) 568, the Ontario Court of Appeal held that a trademark was not "used" simply because it appeared on a passive website. This case is considered further in Chapter 31.

[32] *Eye Masters Ltd. v. Ross King Holdings Ltd.* (1992), 44 C.P.R. (3d) 459. *Contrast Future Shop Ltd. v. A & B Sound Ltd.* (1994), 55 C.P.R. (3d) 182.

[33] Even a "spoof" upon a trademark may be actionable: see *Source Perrier S.A. v. Fira-Less Marketing Co. Ltd.* (1983), 70 C.P.R. (2d) 61.

[34] (1999), 85 C.P.R. (3d) 489.

[35] Section 4(3).

[36] The purpose of section 4(3) is not to equate exporting with "use," but rather to enable Canadian producers who do not make local sales but simply ship their goods abroad to establish "use" in Canada for the purposes of obtaining Canadian trademark registration. See also *Molson Cos. v. Moosehead Breweries Ltd. et al.* (1990), 32 C.P.R. (3d) 363.

[37] Stayer, J., relied on the Federal Court of Appeal decision in *Smith & Nephew Inc. v. Glen Oak Inc. et al.* (1996), 68 C.P.R. (3d) 153.

Jurisdiction and Remedies   Both the civil provincial courts and the Federal Court of Canada have jurisdiction to hear an action for infringement. The appropriate provincial court may deal with both passing-off and Trade-marks Act claims, but the resulting judgment will be enforceable in the specific province only. On the other hand, if an action is brought in the Federal Court, the judgment is enforceable anywhere in Canada. However, the Federal Court has jurisdiction to deal only with statutory actions brought under the Trade-marks Act. Normally, that should not cause any difficulty since, as we have seen, section 7 of the Act seems to provide greater protection to even unregistered trademark owners than does the common law tort of passing-off.

The remedies that either court may grant are almost the same. If there is injury to the goodwill of the owner, then damages may be awarded; if the defendant has profited from the infringement, an account of profits may be ordered. The defendant may be restrained from further infringement by an injunction and may be required to deliver up or dispose of infringing materials. The court may also order the defendant to allow the plaintiff to search for and seize offending wares and relevant books and records,[38] and, in a statutory action, may impose a ban upon further imports of offending products.[39]

Assignment, Licensing, and Franchising

Section 48 of the Trade-marks Act allows an owner to transfer a trademark (a) whether or not it is registered, (b) either as part of or separately from the goodwill of the business, and (c) in respect of either all or some of the goods and services with which it is associated. An owner may also license the use of a registered trademark under specific conditions set out in the licence (section 50).

When a business is sold, the rights in a trademark with which it is associated pass to the purchaser—a transfer of the business operates to assign the trademark. If the mark is registered, the fact of the assignment may be entered on the register, but an assignment may be valid even if unregistered. If a mark is unregistered, the new owner may seek to register it after having commenced to use it. A more difficult situation occurs when an owner keeps the business but assigns the trademark, perhaps because the business is to discontinue production of the particular line of goods with which the mark is associated. An example occurs when a foreign company that has previously marketed its goods in Canada and has established rights to a trademark here forms a subsidiary company in Canada to take over the manufacture or distribution of its goods. The difficulty arises because, in the eyes of the public, the trademark may remain distinctive of the goods of the previous owner rather than those of the new owner, who consequently will not immediately have an established right to it.[40]

When licensing a trademark, the owner may want to continue to use the mark and also to allow use by one or more other businesses, usually in return for payment of a fee or royalty. This may be done by giving notice to the public that the use is under licence. In that case, use by the licensee is deemed to be use by the registered owner itself so as to preserve the distinctiveness of the mark (section 50). A licensed user cannot transfer the right to use a mark, and a breach of any of the terms of the licence will normally constitute an infringement of the trademark.

Although a franchise agreement, as discussed in Chapter 17, usually involves much more than the licensing of a trademark, the franchiser will, in most cases, require that the

---

[38] This is the so-called Anton Piller relief: see *Anton Piller KG. v. Manufacturing Processing Ltd.*, [1976] Ch. 55; *Coca-Cola Ltd. v. Pardhan*, [2003] F.C.J. No. 22.

[39] The power to ban imports has been restricted by the North American Free Trade Agreement Implementation Act, S.C. 1993, c. 44.

[40] See *Wilkinson Sword (Canada) Ltd. v. Juda*, [1968] 2 Ex. C.R. 137.

franchisee market goods or services under the franchiser's trademark. Franchisers normally insist on strict conditions in the franchise agreement, relating to such matters as quality control, purchasing of supplies and equipment, advertising, and the use of trademarks, trade names, designs, and the like. Breach of the agreement by a franchisee normally terminates its right to use the trademark so that continued use would amount to infringement.

COPYRIGHT

Statutory Origin

Copyright law balances public access to creations of art and intellect with fair compensation for creators.[41] Unlike trademarks, copyright is entirely the creation of statute. There is no common law action for infringement of copyright. Copyright law first developed to protect the written word after the invention of the printing press; over time its scope grew to cover drawings, paintings, movies, and musical scores. Current rules address radio and television broadcasting, computer software, digital copying, and the internet.

Canadian copyright law is governed by the Copyright Act,[42] originally adopted in 1924 and substantially amended in 1988, 1993, 1997, and 2012.

International Treaties

International treaties try to standardize copyright protection across international borders. The Berne Convention is an agreement among more than 150 countries including Canada. An author who is a citizen of a Convention country has copyright protection in Canada, and Canadian authors enjoy protection in other Convention countries. Canada also signed the Universal Copyright Convention, which gives a citizen of a contracting state the same copyright protection in another contracting state as it gives its own citizens. Therefore, a Canadian can obtain protection in the United States simply by following the American practice of marking the work with the symbol "©" or the word "copyright," followed by the name of the copyright owner and the year of first publication. In 1997, Canada signed two treaties developed by the **World Intellectual Property Organization** that are especially concerned with the impact of new technologies and the internet on creators' rights: the WIPO Copyright Treaty (1996) and the WIPO Performances and Phonograms Treaty (1996). These treaties came into force in 2002, and require participating countries to adopt domestic legislation creating copyright enforcement remedies with significant infringement deterrence effect. In 2014, the Canadian Parliament finally ratified both treaties.[43]

World Intellectual Property Organization a specialized agency of the United Nations dedicated to harmonizing intellectual property laws and regimes worldwide

Reform—2012

As will be discussed in Chapter 31, computer technology and the internet have created unparalleled access to copyrighted material. They have also created the ability to instantaneously copy, distribute, and alter that material, and this has led to tension between owners and users. Even ordinary good faith computer use involves copying that could technically violate traditional copyright law.

---

[41] *Galerie d'Art du Petit Champlain Inc. v. Theberge* [2002] SCC 34 at para. 30.

[42] R.S.C. 1985, c. C-42. Unless otherwise stated, references in this part of the chapter are to this Act, as amended.

[43] Bill C-11, Copyright Modernization Act, S.C. 2012, c. 20 began the process of bringing Canadian copyright law into conformity with international treaties. Canada is not the only signatory country that has been slow to implement the corresponding domestic legislation. France, Germany, the European Community, and the United Kingdom have also failed to implement the treaty provisions. The United States has adopted the 1996 treaty provisions in the Digital Millennium Copyright Act (DMCA). Treaty compliance will improve with passage of Bill C-8, 2d Sess., 41st Parl., 2013. This Bill substantially increases the penalties for importing, exporting, or possessing goods that infringe trademark or copyright; its short title is the Combating Counterfeit Products Act.

Since the signing of the 1996 WIPO treaties, the Canadian government has talked of copyright reform to address such activities as downloading, uploading, sharing, updating, burning, copying, and storing electronic material.[44] The 1996 WIPO treaties prioritize owners' rights by calling for criminalization of these activities, strong enforcement procedures and remedies, and support for security technology in the form of **digital rights management technology** (DRMT) and technological protection measures (TPM). Users argue that DRMT violates privacy rights and does not distinguish between acceptable and unacceptable copying. The pivotal year for Canadian copyright reform came in 2012, when the Supreme Court decided five copyright cases[45] and Parliament passed the Copyright Modernization Act. Together, these initiatives clarified the law with respect to fair dealing, technical copying, and the role of DRMT. For more information on this topic, see the Companion Website.

As a result Canada has become the international standard for balancing both creator and user rights.[46]

digital rights management technology a system collecting data about the licensing, payment, use, and authenticity of a work

INTERNATIONAL ISSUE

Canada–U.S. Tension

Arguably, the Canada–United States border is the easiest border to cross in the world, and in the internet age, information flows invisibly across the boundary. This is cause for concern for copyright owners and users as each country has different rules for the protection and use of copyrighted material. The United States' copyright regime is dominated by the Digital Millennium Copyright Act, which puts the rights of creators first. Unauthorized downloading of copyrighted material is illegal, including peer-to-peer software and music transfers.[47] The use of DRMT is supported, and ISPs are required to block access to infringing material and turn over the names of their subscribers that download and share material illegally. In addition, the Sonny Bono Copyright Extension Act provides copyright owners 70 years of posthumous protection compared to Canada's 50 years.

The current Canadian copyright regime supports user rights, sometimes in contrast to the U.S. approach. The private-use exceptions for uploading, downloading, and copying have been expanded, especially in the education category.[48] In an apparent recognition of everyday activities, time shifting (i.e., PVR recording) and **format shifting** (moving works between digital formats) are permitted.[49] Canadian privacy laws forbid the arbitrary release of subscribers' names by ISPs,[50] which has protected Canadians from the types of infringement lawsuits music producers have launched in the United States, and Canadian law does not require ISPs to block access to infringing material as American law does. Still, the 2012 reforms move Canada closer to the American position on DRMT, thereby reducing some of the tension between the two regimes. Despite the Canadian Privacy Commissioner's opposition to the

>

format shifting transferring purchased material, such as music, from one of the owner's devices to another

[44] For a review of Canadian copyright reform issues, see Michael Geist (ed.), *In the Public Interest: The Future of Canadian Copyright Law* (Toronto: Irwin Law Inc., 2005). See also Nathan Irving, "Copyright Law for the Digital World: An Evaluation of Reform Proposals" (2010) *Asper Rev. Int'l Bus. Trade L.* 141–62; Michael Geist, *The Copyright Pentalogy – How the Supreme Court of Canada Shook the Foundations of Canadian Copyright Law*, (University of Ottawa Press, 2013).

[45] *Rogers Communications Inc. v Society of Composers, Authors and Music Publishers of Canada*, 2012 SCC 35, [2012] 2 SCR 283; *Society of Composers, Authors and Music Publishers of Canada v Bell Canada*, 2012 SCC 36, [2012] 2 SCR 326; *Entertainment Software Association v Society of Composers, Authors and Music Publishers of Canada*, 2012 SCC 34, [2012] 2 SCR 231; *Alberta (Education) v Canadian Copyright Licensing Agency (Access Copyright)*, 2012 SCC 37, [2012] 2 SCR 345; *Re: Sound v Motion Picture Theatre Associations of Canada*, 2012 SCC 38, [2012] 2 SCR 376.

[46] Michael Geist, *The Copyright Pentalogy—How the Supreme Court of Canada Shook the Foundations of Canadian Copyright Law*, (University of Ottawa Press, 2013) at p. iv.

[47] See, for example, *Robertson v. Thomson Corp.*, [2006] 2 S.C.R. 363.

[48] Section 80 specifically exempts private-use copying of music from infringement provisions, Section 29 fair dealing includes exceptions for research, private study, education, parody and satire; s. 29.21 exempts user generated non-commercial content; s. 29.22 deals with private use; s. 29.4 deals with instruction.

[49] Sections 29.22 and 29.23.

[50] In *BMG Canada Inc. v. John Doe* (2004), 239 D.L.R. (4th) 7f26, partially aff'd (2005) 252 D.L.R. (4th) 332 (F.C.A.), the Federal Court rejected a request from a music producer that five major ISPs disclose the identity of customers who traded music downloaded from the internet. In May 2005, the Federal Court of Appeal dismissed an appeal from that decision, but without prejudice to the plaintiffs' right to commence a further action for disclosure based on clearer evidence.

use of DRMT,[51] the Copyright Modernization Act makes it illegal to use or sell technology to circumvent digital locks or TPMs.[52] As a result, in 2013 the Office of the United States Trade Representative moved Canada off the "Priority Watch List" where it was listed from 2009 until 2012, returning Canada to the less serious "Watch List" of countries needing to improve their intellectual property policies.[53]

Questions to Consider
1. Should Canada synchronize its copyright regime with that of the United States in order to reduce all tension between the countries?
2. Did Canada lose the ability to independently determine its own copyright direction when it signed the 1996 WIPO treaties?

Nature of Copyright

Rights of Owner   What is commonly referred to as "copyright" is really a collection of distinct rights conferred by statute. The basic rights of the owner of copyright are

- the right to produce or reproduce the work in question, or any substantial part of it, in any material form;
- the right to perform or deliver the work in public;
- the right to publish an unpublished work.

The Act is "technologically neutral"—reproduction in any form (print, telecommunication, internet) is covered and **royalty payments** should not differ according to the medium used to deliver the work to the end user.[54]

royalty payments   fees paid for permission to use another person's copyrighted material

---

CASE 20.6

The Society of Composers, Authors and Music Publishers of Canada (SOCAN), a collective association that charges royalties for performance and communication of copyrighted musical works, wanted payment for music included in downloaded video games. The Supreme Court denied the request, saying downloading was no different from buying a physical copy in a store and additional payments applying to only downloaded copies would violate the principle of technological neutrality. The Copyright Act does not impose additional layers of protections and fees based solely on the method of delivery of the work.[55]

The Act lists examples of specific rights protected:

- the right to translate the work
- the right to convert the work from one form into another (for example, to convert a novel into a play, or vice versa)
- the right to make a recording or film of the work
- the right to communicate the work to the public by telecommunication
- the right to exhibit the work in public
- the right to authorize any of the above (section 3)

The nature of copyright is best understood as the power of the owner of the copyright to prevent others from doing any of those things that only the owner has the right to do.

---

[51] Letter from Jennifer Stoddart, Privacy Commissioner of Canada, to the Industry Minister, dated January 18, 2008.

[52] Section 41.1.

[53] Office of the United States Trade Representative, 2007, 2008, 2009, 2010, 2011, 2012, 2013 Special 301 Reports, http://www.ustr.-gov/-about-us/press-office/-reports-and-publications

[54] Section 3; *Robertson, supra*, n. 47, para. 49; *Entertainment Software Association v. SOCAN* 2012 SCC 34 at para 9.

[55] *Entertainment Software Association v. SOCAN* 2012 SCC 34 at para 9.

Copyright arises automatically, without any registration or publication. The private act of creating a work gives rise to copyright protection without the need to publish the work to a wider audience. The author or creator of the work is the original owner and may assign the copyright. Copyright may be owned by the author of a book or by the firm that publishes it, by the composer of a piece of music or by the recording company, or it may be transferred to some person not connected in any way with the creation or production process, such as an heir or creditor of the author. However, there are other rights known as **moral rights**, which are personal to the author or creator and cannot be assigned to others.

moral rights   the non-transferable rights of an author or creator to prevent a work from being distorted or misused

Moral Rights   These include

- the right to integrity of the work;
- the right to prevent distortion or mutilation of the work;
- the right to prevent it from being used in association with some product, service, cause, or institution; and
- where the work is copied, published, or performed, the right to be associated with the work as author or to remain anonymous (Section 14.1).

The author of a play is entitled to have the authorship properly attributed to her when it is performed or, if she wishes to remain anonymous or use an alias, the right not to have her true identity revealed. The integrity of the work is infringed if the creator's honour or reputation is damaged (Section 28.2). An artist who paints a picture is entitled not to have it defaced. For more information on this topic, see the Companion Website.

CASE 20.7

A sculptor who created a flock of flying geese, to be displayed in a shopping centre, is entitled not to have them decorated with red ribbons at Christmas time.[56] This is the case whether or not he still owns the copyright.

Limits to Copyright

There is no copyright in a mere idea or thought. Copyright attaches to the expression of an idea in a material form. As was stated in one leading case:

> An author has no copyright in ideas but only in his expression of them. The law of copyright does not give him any monopoly in the use of the ideas with which he deals ..., even if they are original. His copyright is confined to the literary work in which he has expressed them.[57]

A playwright could "borrow" the plot from another person's novel, provided the play is expressed entirely in her own words. Such conduct might be considered to be unprofessional and to amount to plagiarism, but it would not by itself constitute an infringement of copyright.

Works in Which Copyright Exists

Copyright exists in every *original* literary, dramatic, musical, and artistic work (section 5). "Originality" means that the work must have originated from its creator; there is no requirement that it must be particularly imaginative, novel, or skillful. Nevertheless, for a

---

[56] *Snow v. Eaton Centre Ltd.* (1982), 70 C.P.R. (2d) 105. In *Theberge v. Galerie d'Art du Petit Champlain Inc.* (2002), 210 D.L.R. (4th) 385, the Supreme Court of Canada ruled that moral rights are infringed only if the work is modified in a manner that is prejudicial to the honour or integrity of its creator.

[57] *Moreau v. St. Vincent*, [1950] Ex. C.R. 198, per Thorson, P., at 202.

work to be "original," it must be work independently created by its author and must display at least a minimal degree of skill and judgment. The fact that it may have involved substantial effort does not by itself mean the work has originality.

Tele-Direct Publications Inc. sued American Business Information Inc., claiming copyright on its "Yellow Pages" directories because of the extra work done to arrange phone number information and add other data, such as fax numbers. The Federal Court of Appeal ruled that compilations of this nature, which simply rearrange existing data, are not typically copyrightable.

However, the Yellow Pages, taken as a whole and given the visual aspects of the pages and manner of their arrangement, are protected by copyright. The information that they contain is not. The court concluded that Tele-Direct had exercised only a minimal degree of skill, judgment, or labour in its overall arrangement, which was insufficient to support a claim of originality so as to be entitled to copyright protection.[58] This analysis conforms with the 1996 WIPO Copyright Treaty, which includes databases if the data selection or arrangement amounts to an "intellectual creation."

Literary Works   The Copyright Act gives a non-exhaustive definition of "literary work." The expression "includes tables, computer programs and compilations of literary works" (section 2). There must, however, be some reduction into a lasting or retrievable form, such as writing, film, digital form, or sound recording. There is no copyright in spoken words as such.

A book was published about the late classical pianist Glenn Gould. The book was largely based on private interviews between Gould and the author, Jock Carroll. Gould's estate sued, claiming, among other things, that copyright in the interviews belonged to Gould. The court held that Carroll was the sole author and owner of the copyright in the notes and recordings of his interviews of Gould, and that Gould (and his estate) had no copyright in the spoken words.[59]

As well as the obvious items such as books and magazine and newspaper articles, the term "literary works" has been held to include income tax tables, street directories, examination papers, insurance forms, parts catalogues, and the like. From this list, it is apparent that literary merit is not an essential element of a "literary work."

Computer Software   Computer programs are protected as literary works. Section 2 defines "computer program" to mean instruction or statements expressed, fixed, embodied, or stored in any manner, for use directly or indirectly in a computer in order to bring about a specific result. However, not every part of a software program is necessarily protected by copyright; some parts of the program may be purely functional or minor modifications, and to copy those parts would not constitute an infringement.[60] The statutory provisions also contain certain exemptions, permitting the making of single copies for a specific purpose, such as a backup copy or reproducing the program in another form in order to render it compatible with a particular computer.

---

[58] *Tele-Direct (Publications) Inc. v. American Business Information, Inc.*, [1998] 2 F.C. 22. See also *Edutile Inc. v. Automobile Protection Association* (2000), 188 D.L.R. (4th) 132. Prior to the 1993 amendments to the Copyright Act (introduced to implement NAFTA, Art. 1705), compilations were protected only insofar as they could be characterized as literary works. Compilations may now also be related to artistic, dramatic, and musical works.

[59] *Gould Estate v. Stoddard Publishing* (1998), 161 D.L.R. (4th) 321. Contrast *Hager v. ECW Press Ltd.*, [1999] 2 F.C. 287.

[60] *Delrina Corp. v. Triolet Systems Inc.*, [2002] O.J. No. 3729; *Harmony Consulting Ltd. v. G.A. Foss Transport Ltd.*, [2011] F.C.J. No. 451.

Dramatic Works

A "dramatic work" is defined to include "any piece for recitation, choreographic work, or mime, the scenic arrangement or acting form of which is fixed in writing or otherwise," as well as "any cinematographic work, and any compilation of dramatic works" (section 2).[60A] The category is sufficiently wide to include not only the older forms of drama, such as plays, operas, and ballets, but also most new forms of entertainment. The key words in the definition are "fixed in writing or otherwise." The text of a play and score of a musical comedy are protected since they are fixed in written form. But so are films, video recordings of dramatic works, and sound recordings of an interview.

Although an event such as a street riot or a plane crash, or perhaps even a football game, occurs independently of a person making a video of it, and is not itself a "dramatic work," videoing such an event can constitute the dramatic work of the videographer. Copyright can subsist in video, and to copy the video would constitute an infringement of copyright.

Communication Signals and Telecommunications

A "live" broadcast of an event is a communication signal—radio waves transmitted through space (without wires or cables) for reception by the public—and a broadcaster has copyright in the communication signals it broadcasts. These signals are protected by copyright despite the fact that they are not **fixed**.[61] A "live" broadcast is considered to be "fixed" even if it becomes fixed simultaneously with its transmission. In addition, communicating a work to the public by any form of telecommunication is an infringement of copyright unless the retransmission complies with the Broadcasting Act.[62] The definition of a telecommunication is much wider than a communication signal as it includes radio as well as wire, cable, visual, optical, or electromagnetic systems. This definition is how the internet transmissions are caught.

fixed stored in a permanent or lasting form

Musical Works

A "musical work" refers to a musical composition with or without words. A performance of a musical work is not within the definition, but is separately protected. Separate protection is also given to sound recordings. The recording is itself regarded as a work in which copyright subsists, whether or not the work being performed also has its own copyright (section 18). A recording of a live performance by a jazz musician, in which a new work is improvised, is protected by copyright even though the music itself was never written down. A recording of a performance of a symphony by Beethoven is similarly protected, even though any copyright in the symphony itself would long ago have expired.

Artistic Works

An "artistic work" is defined by section 2 to include "paintings, drawings, maps, charts, plans, photographs, engravings, sculptures, works of artistic craftsmanship, architectural works, and compilations of artistic works."[62A] Architectural work means "any building or structure, or model of a building or structure." For architectural works, copyright is restricted to the artistic character and design and does not extend to the processes or methods of construction. A trademark of distinctive design may also qualify as an artistic work and may be protected by copyright. In addition, plans and drawings of machinery or other devices may be protected by copyright as artistic works, and at the same time may depict or describe an invention that is protected by patent. It is also frequently difficult to determine whether a particular piece of work is an artistic work, protected by copyright, or an industrial design, which may receive a different form of protection.

Performers' Performances

A performance of an artistic, dramatic or musical work qualifies for copyright protection separate and apart from the copyright given to the

---

[60A] Section 2 of the Copyright Act, Government of Canada.

[61] Section 21.

[62] Section 31, Copyright Act. Regulation of broadcasting by the Canadian Radio-television and Telecommunications Commission (CRTC) sometimes conflicts with copyright law. For a discussion of the interaction of the two, see Reference *re Broadcasting Act (Can.)* [2011] F.C.J. No. 197.

[62A] Section 2 of the Copyright Act, Government of Canada.

work itself. Unlike other works, performers receive copyright even if the performance is not converted to a fixed format. One of the rights section 15 gives a performer is the right to transform the performance into a material form. A live broadcast of a performance will be protected as telecommunication.

The Protection of Copyright

Registration   Copyright comes into existence automatically on the creation of a work. Registration of copyright is not necessary, but the Act gives the option of registration (section 54), and it does confer certain advantages on the registered owner. In particular, the certificate of registration creates a presumption that copyright subsists in the work and that the person registered is the owner of the copyright. Still, the advantages to be gained from registration are relatively small, and the practice is not widely used except by performing rights societies.

Duration of Copyright   In Canada, a work is usually protected by copyright during the life of its author and for a further period of 50 years after the author's death (section 6). The deceased author's estate or an assignee of the copyright—for example, a publisher—may use the protection. The Act prescribes different terms for the following:

- Photographs are protected for 50 years from the making of the original negative or plate.
- Cinematographic works are protected for 50 years after first publication.
- Posthumous works—works not published before the death of the author—are protected for 50 years from the date of first publication.
- Jointly authored works are protected for 50 years after the death of the last surviving author.
- Crown copyright persists for 50 years from the date of first publication.

Ownership of Copyright   Copyright belongs initially to the author or creator of a work. Copyright in a work may be jointly owned by two or more authors, such as the joint authors of a book. It is also possible for separate copyrights to exist in different parts of the same complete work; for example, the writer of the lyrics of a song may hold copyright in the words (as a literary work), and the composer may hold copyright in the music.

There are a number of exceptions to the general rule. Works that have been prepared or published by or under the direction of the government belong to the Crown, subject to contrary agreement. Most important is the rule that where the author of a work was employed by some other person and the work was made in the course of employment, copyright belongs to the employer—again, unless otherwise agreed.[63] This does not change the length of protection which remains tied to the human author.

As discussed in the next section, copyright may be assigned by the original owner to some other person. Section 14 provides that, when an author has assigned a work, copyright in it reverts automatically to the author's estate 25 years after the death of the author. However, the rule applies only in cases of sole authorship where the original copyright belonged to the author and nothing to the contrary is said in the will.

Assignment and Licensing   An owner of copyright may assign it, for payment of a royalty or by way of gift, or it may pass to heirs upon the death of the owner. An owner may also assign only part of a copyright in a work or divide it territorially. For example, one

---

[63] Section 13(3). *Hanis v. Teevan* (1998), 162 D.L.R. (4th) 414, copyright in computer software developed by an employee was held to belong to the employer university. A special rule (art. 13) applies to employees of newspapers: see *Robertson v. Thomson Corp.* (2004), 243 D.L.R. (4th) 257.

person might own the copyright of a book in Canada and another in the United States. Authors often assign the copyright in a book to their publishing company in return for the payment of a royalty—for example, 10 percent of total sales revenue. The parties may attach a variety of conditions to an assignment, dealing with such matters as publication in other countries, translations, and reproduction in other forms.

Alternatively, an author may retain the copyright in a work but give the publisher a licence to print or reproduce and sell it, again normally in return for a royalty. An author may grant a licence for the single performance of a play or musical work, on a specified date at a particular theatre, or for the reproduction of an extract from a work in some other work—for example a collection of essays, or a set of teaching materials.

A special arrangement is available for management of rights in literary, musical, and dramatic works, recordings, and performances. An author may assign his or her rights in the work to a **collective rights society** (Section 2, 19, 81). In turn, the society grants licences for a fee, pays part of the fee to the author, and retains the remainder to cover the society's costs. The Copyright Board has authority to approve and to regulate the rates (tariffs) set by the collectives. A collective society can only impose a fee for what would otherwise amount to an infringement of copyright. Collectively managed tariffs have been imposed on many internet business activities, as is discussed more fully in Chapter 31. The Society for Composers and Music Publishers (SOCAN) has attempted to impose fees on a number of activities that the Supreme Court decided do not infringe copyright.

collective rights society a society to which authors of musical and dramatic works assign performing and communication rights and which grants licences and collects fees

---

CASE 20.10

SOCAN applied to the Copyright Board for approval of a special tariff on Canadian internet service providers (ISPs) applicable to internet transmissions of copyrighted music (known as Tariff 22). SOCAN's application was opposed by the Canadian Association of Internet Providers, which argued that ISPs did not commit any breach of copyright by transmitting or caching copyrighted music often from international sources.

The Supreme Court of Canada ruled that the ISPs committed no breach of copyright. They were merely intermediaries who provided the means of telecommunication. They were not communicators and could not be required to pay the tariff.[64]

Infringement of Copyright

What Constitutes Infringement?
Copyright consists of a number of exclusive rights vested in the owner. An infringement occurs when another person, without the consent of the owner, does an act that only the owner has the right to do. An unauthorized public performance, communication, publication, or reproduction of a copyrighted work constitutes an infringement, as does the translation of a work, or recording, broadcasting, or exhibiting it in public. A person who purports to authorize some other person to do any of those acts, without the copyright owner's consent, also infringes copyright.

CASE 20.11

SOCAN alleged that online music service providers that allow consumers to download or stream music are "communicating a musical work to the public by telecommunication" and thereby infringe copyright. SOCAN requested separate tariff for the downloading or streaming. The music service providers argued that each transaction was a private communication by the individual user and therefore should not be considered communication to the public. The Supreme Court distinguished between downloading and streaming; downloading is not communication by telecommunication but rather reproduction already covered by the existing royalty. Streaming, on the other hand, was held to be a communication "to the public" regardless of whether the members of the public receive their communications at the same place or time or at their own request.[65]

---

64 *Canadian Association of Internet Providers v. SOCAN*, (2004), 240 D.L.R. (4th) 193.

65 *Rogers Communications Inc. v. SOCAN*, 2012 SCC 35 [2012] 2 S.C.R. 283.

It is not necessary for the entire work to be copied to constitute an infringement of copyright; the unauthorized copying of a substantial part is sufficient. What amounts to a "substantial" part is a question of fact and degree and should be determined on a holistic not piecemeal basis.[66] A quotation of a few lines from a written work, especially if attributed to its author, does not constitute an infringement, but the quotation of several pages might. The offending copy need not be identical to the original work, and one cannot avoid liability simply by arranging the copied work in a different format or by making minor changes.

CASE 20.12

Hager was the author of a book about famous Canadians of Aboriginal heritage, which included a nine-page chapter about country music star Shania Twain. The chapter was based on Hager's interviews with Twain and included many quotations from those interviews. Subsequently, Holmes was commissioned by ECW Press to write a book about Twain. The ECW book was found to contain substantial portions of Hager's work, including most of the direct quotations from the interviews with Twain. Hager sued ECW for breach of copyright. ECW argued that the quoted words of Twain were not protected by copyright because they were not the original work of Hager. They also claimed that the copying was not substantial (it amounted to about one-third of the Hager chapter) and that it constituted fair dealing for research purposes.

These defences were rejected, and Hager was awarded damages, plus an accounting equal to 10 percent of ECW's profits from the sale of their book. The court held that Hager's work was protected by copyright because it was a product of her skill, judgment, and labour. Twain's quoted words were in response to Hager's questions, and had been selected by Hager for inclusion in her book. The copying was substantial and could not be said to have been done for research purposes.[67]

The person who actually makes the copy is not the only one who may be liable for infringement of copyright. A theatre owner who permits the theatre to be used by a group of actors or musicians for a performance that infringes the author's copyright is as guilty of infringement as the performers are. Also, a bookseller who imports and sells a "pirated" edition of a copyrighted book is as guilty as the illegal publisher. It is an infringement of copyright to authorize a person to do something that the owner of the copyright has the sole right to do. A person who buys a book and lends it to a friend for the purpose of photocopying it infringes the copyright in the book as much as the friend does. However, the manufacturing and selling of equipment that can be used for creating copies has been held not to constitute authorizing an infringement.[68]

Internet service providers (ISPs) are currently considered more like manufacturers than theatre owners, not liable because they are only intermediaries for communication (Section 2.4(1)(b)). However, reform measures will impose liability on internet service providers that have notice of infringement and do nothing to stop it. A "notice to notice" scheme is contained in the new legislation requiring an ISP to give notice to a subscriber when it is aware of or receives notice of an alleged infringement. Canada rejected the more drastic U.S. "notice and takedown" scheme, which would obligate an ISP to withdraw service from an alleged infringer.[69] The specific application of copyright law to the internet context will be discussed again in Chapter 31.

Fair Dealing and Other Permitted Uses   Certain acts that would otherwise amount to infringements of copyright are expressly permitted by the Copyright Act. The

---

[66] *Cinar Corporation v. Robinson* 2013 SCC 73, at paras 26-29, 36.

[67] *Hager v. ECW Press Ltd.*, *supra*, n. 59.

[68] *CBS Songs Ltd. v. Amstrad Consumer Electronics*, [1988] 2 All E.R. 484. The Act imposes a levy on the sale of blank cassette tapes and compact discs (sections 82, 83).

[69] Sections 41.25, 41.26, 41.27(3) not yet proclaimed in force at time of writing. See Irving, *supra*, n. 44.

most important exemption allows the fair use of copyright works for research, private study, education, parody, or satire (section 29), for criticism and review (section 29.1), or for news reporting (section 29.2). A user may use copyrighted work to generate his or her own content for non-commercial purposes (section 29.21). Subject to a number of conditions, educational institutions are permitted to copy and reproduce works for purposes of instruction (section 29.4).[70]

CASE 20.13

Access Copyright is a collective society representing authors and publishers of literary and artistic works. Access Copyright sought to renew its tariff agreement with school boards covering photocopying of sections of textbooks for distribution to students. The Supreme Court determined that photocopies made by teachers for distribution to students were part of class instruction and qualified as fair dealing. Photocopying part of textbooks qualified as research or private study and the extent of the copying was fair given the purpose of education and instruction, the small amount copied, the limited alternatives, and the low effect on textbook sales.[71]

Copying a musical work or performance of a musical work for the private use of the copier is also not infringement (section 80). Instead, a levy is imposed on blank CDs, and the money collected is distributed to musical work copyright owners (section 82).

CASE 20.14

A provincial law society provided various services to its members. These included providing photocopying machines in the library so that members could make copies of law reports and other documents and, for an additional fee, have library staff make copies of documents on request and fax or courier those copies to members. A publisher of law reports claimed that these practices constituted infringements of its copyright in the reports.

The Supreme Court of Canada agreed that the publishers owned the copyright in the reports. Although the actual judgments of the courts are in the public domain, the reports contained headnotes and annotations that met the requirement of originality.

However, the Court held that there was no infringement of that copyright by the law society. In particular, (1) the mere provision of photocopiers, which might be used to infringe copyright, did not constitute authorization to infringe; (2) the fax transmission of a single copy of a work to a single individual does not constitute "communication to the public" under the Act; and (3) under the fair dealing provisions of the Act, a person is permitted to use and copy copyrighted works for purposes of research. Research is not limited to non-commercial use, and lawyers carrying on their profession conduct research within the meaning of the Act.[72]

Courts apply a two-step process to the determination of fair dealing. First the court determines if the activity is done for one of the allowable purposes described above (i.e., research, private study ...). Second, the court decides if the activity is "fair" in light of its purpose, character, amount, or alternatives, and the nature of the work and effect the activity has on the work.[73] For more information on this topic, see the Companion Website.

---

[70] It does not permit the reproduction of an entire work or a substantial portion thereof: *Alberta (Education) vs. Canadian Copyright Licensing Agency (Access Copyright)* 2012 SCC 37

[71] *Alberta (Education) vs. Canadian Copyright Licensing Agency (Access Copyright)* 2012 SCC 37. Access Copyright continued the fight with new lawsuits in the post-secondary market commenced in 2013 against York University. This was a stark contrast to the wind-up application of Education Rights Collective: Copyright Board Decision: File Education Rights 2012-2016, http://cb-cda.gc.ca/decisions/2013ercc-19122013.pdf

[72] *Law Society of Upper Canada v. CCH Canadian Ltd.* (2004), 236 D.L.R. (4th) 395. Section 30.2(1) of the Act provides that a library or person acting under its authority does not infringe copyright to do anything on behalf of a patron that the patron could personally have done under the fair dealing exception. The library must not be established or operated for profit.

[73] *Alberta (Education) vs. Canadian Copyright Licensing Agency (Access Copyright)* 2012 SCC 37 at para 12.

SOCAN collects a royalty tariff from online music service providers that sell downloads of digital music. It wanted to apply a tariff to the 30 to 90 second free preview of the music that could be streamed by prospective purchasers. The Supreme Court held that previews were not copyright infringement because they fell under the fair dealing exception for research—consumers were doing research before their purchases. It was fair because there were no alternatives to hearing the music, the amount of dealing was modest, and its effect on the work was to increase sales. No royalties or tariff were applicable.[74]

Remedies for Infringement   The usual civil remedies are available in cases of infringement of copyright including:

- damages for profit or income lost by the owner, or for conversion of the owner's property

- accounting for profits made by the defendant as a result of the infringement (normally an alternative to damages)[75]

- injunction to restrain the defendant from further infringement and to require the surrender of any offending copies

Some criminal offences trigger fines up to $1 million and/or imprisonment for up to five years to deter bootlegging and pirating copyrighted materials (section 42). **Statutory damages** for non-commercial infringement are capped at $5000 (section 38.1). However in the commercial context, the Supreme Court has given punitive damages.[76] For more information on this topic, see the Companion Website.

> **statutory damages**   damages a plaintiff may request instead of proving actual loss

PATENTS

At common law, an inventor had no inherent right to profit from his or her creation, and no law was broken by making use of another's invention. Like copyright, the law of patents is entirely based upon statute. However, a patent differs fundamentally from copyright: While copyright comes into existence automatically upon creation of the work, a patent exists only after a grant from the appropriate government body.

The first federal Patent Act was adopted in 1869, largely based upon the existing American legislation rather than British or European models.[77] Canada's current Patent Act[78] was substantially amended in 1987, in part to bring Canada's law into partial conformity with international practice under the Patent Cooperation Treaty. The 1987 amendments changed a number of the specifically American features of our law. These amendments came into effect on October 1, 1989; patents granted or applied for prior to that date remain subject to the earlier law. Further substantial amendments, notably in respect of pharmaceutical products, were introduced in 1992 and 1993. The result is that there are distinct differences between Canadian patent law and U.S., British, and European rules, for example on the patentability of business methods, which is discussed below.

---

[74] *Society of Composers, Authors and Music Publishers of Canada v. Bell Canada*, 2012 SCC 36. Intellectual property rights in relation to the internet are also discussed in Chapter 31.

[75] *Cinar v. Robinson Corporation* 2013 SCC 73 (discussing proof of profit and entitlement to non-pecuniary and punitive damages).

[76] *Ibid.*

[77] British and European patent laws are based in large part on the European Patent Convention (Convention on the Grant of European Patents, 1973, now in its 14th edition), which defines inventions (art. 52) based upon exclusions rather than an inclusive definition: *Amazon.com, Inc. v. Canada (Attorney General)*, [2010] F.C.J. No. 1209 revs'd [2012] 2 F.C.R. 459 (FCA).

[78] R.S.C. 1985, c. P-4. (Unless otherwise stated, references in this part of the chapter are to that Act, as amended.)

International Treaties

The concept of a patent is now almost universally recognized, although in differing forms. Over 120 countries now adhere to the Patent Cooperation Treaty administrated by the World Intellectual Property Organization. It provides for the filing of a single international patent application, which then gives patent protection in all the signatory countries.[79] More than 160 countries belong to the Paris Union and comply with the Paris Convention for the Protection of Industrial Property, which gives an applicant one year from the date of filing in Canada to file in a member country. Canada belongs to both treaties.

The Nature of Patents

An inventor or the legal representative of an inventor may obtain a patent that gives the applicant a monopoly over the invention for a period of 20 years (section 44).[80] This secures the "exclusive right, privilege and liberty of making, constructing and using the invention and selling it to others to be used" (section 42).[80A]

In exchange for this monopoly, the inventor must make the invention public, by filing an adequate description of the invention, so that others will be able to duplicate the invention freely when the statutory 20 year period expires.[81]

CASE 20.16

Pfizer opposed a request by Teva Canada to sell a generic version of Viagra, a drug already patented by Pfizer. Teva claimed that Pfizer's patent was invalid because the application did not meet the Patent Act's disclosure requirements: It failed to specify which of the many compounds was effective for treating erectile dysfunction. The Supreme Court of Canada agreed with Teva—the application did not make proper disclosure. Since the patent system is a bargain—the inventor gets exclusive rights in exchange for disclosure of the invention—the logical consequence of insufficient disclosure is patent invalidity. Pfizer's Viagra patent was declared invalid.[82]

An inventor has a choice: (1) keep the invention entirely secret and continue to exploit it indefinitely but run the risk that some other person will sooner or later stumble upon the same invention or unravel the secret; or (2) reveal it and enjoy exclusive rights for a limited period only. Given the speed at which technological advances are now being made, and the perhaps over-generous period of protection, applying for a patent would seem advisable for inventions that have lasting appeal. However, obtaining a patent is a complex and fairly expensive business, and if an invention is likely to have only a short productive life, secrecy may be the better option. The alternatives of registering the invention as an industrial design or relying upon copyright protection of the plans or specifications and requiring confidentiality agreements should also be considered. But while copyright provides protection for a much longer period, that protection is more limited, since it extends only to the method of expression and not to the idea itself.

---

[79] In 2008, Canada and the United States started the Patent Prosecution Highway Pilot Program, designed to accelerate patent application processing in one country if the application had already been favourably examined in the other country.

[80] For patents issuing from applications filed before October 1989, the period is 17 years. The new 20-year period runs from the date of filing the application; the previous period ran from the date of the grant.

[80A] Section 42 of the Patent Act, Patent infringement and the Patent Act in Canada.

[81] Some aspects of the patented invention may continue to be protected after the expiry of the patent, for example, under trademark law. Thus, others may be free to use the invention, but not to copy a distinctive shape or format. See *Eli Lilly and Co. v. Novopharm Ltd.* (*supra*, n. 13); *Thomas & Betts Ltd. v. Panduit Corp.* (2000), 185 D.L.R. (4th) 150. Contrast *Kirkbi AG v. Ritvik Holdings Inc.*, *supra*, n. 7.

[82] *Teva Canada Ltd. v. Pfizer Canada Inc.*, 2012 SCC 60, [2012] 3 S.C.R. 625.

Patentable Inventions

Only "inventions" qualify for patent protection. The Patent Act defines an invention as "any new and useful art, process, machine, manufacture or composition of matter, or any new and useful improvement in any art, process, machine, manufacture or composition of matter" (section 2).[82A] Three elements in the definition must be present for an invention to be patentable. It must be

- an art, process, machine, manufacture, or composition of matter, or an improvement to such;
- new;
- useful.

As well, inherent in the notion of an invention is the requirement that it is something that possesses the quality of ingenuity and is not simply an obvious step that any person with ordinary skill in the field might have taken.

Art, Process, Machine, Manufacture, or Composition of Matter For an invention to be patentable, it must fall within one of these categories. The word "art" refers to the manual or productive arts, as distinct from the fine arts. A "process" means a method of manufacture or operation designed to produce a particular result—for example, a new process for the chemical cleaning of fabrics. "Machine" and "manufacture" are given their usual meanings, and a "composition of matter" refers to such things as chemical formulae that produce new compounds and substances.

A patent will not be issued solely for a scientific principle or abstract theorem, such as a mathematical formula (section 27(8)). For these purposes, a computer program is equated to an abstract theorem and is not by itself patentable.[83] Computer-implemented inventions may be patented as a business method, a machine, or a product, but not as computer programs, data structures, or computer generated signals.

CASE 20.17

Researchers at Harvard College developed a method of genetically altering mice to make them more likely to develop cancer following exposure to chemicals. This made the mice valuable for experimentation purposes. The invention was registered as a patent in the United States (and in a number of European countries) by the college. The college applied to register a patent for the "Harvard mouse" (or "oncomouse," to give it its technical name) in Canada.

Registration was refused by the Patent Appeal Board, and by the Federal Court. The process lacked the element of reproducibility required of a patent.

The Supreme Court of Canada, (by a 5–4 majority) held that the oncomouse could not be patented.[84] Although some "lower" forms of life have been held to be patentable,[85] the majority considered that patenting higher life forms would involve a radical departure from the traditional patent regime and must only be done under the clear and unequivocal direction of Parliament. No clear direction existed.

Business Methods Whether a business method is a patentable invention depends upon its novel, useful, and ingenious contribution. Both in Canada and in the United

---

[82A] Section 2 of the Patent Act, R.S.C., 1985, c. P-4.

[83] *Schlumberger Canada Ltd. v. Commissioner of Patents*, [1982] 1 F.C. 845.

[84] *Harvard College v. Canada (Commissioner of Patents)* (2002), 219 D.L.R. (4th) 577.

[85] Genetically modified yeast has been patented; see *Re Application of Abitibi Co.* (1982), 62 C.P.R. (2d) 81. However, in *Pioneer Hi-Bred Ltd. v. Canada (Commissioner of Patents)* (1987), 14 C.P.R. (3d) 491 (F.C.A.), aff'd (1989), 25 C.P.R. (3d) 257 (S.C.C.), it was held that a soybean variety developed by traditional plant cross-breeding was not patentable subject matter. The rights of plant breeders may now be protected under the Plant Breeders' Rights Act, S.C. 1990, c. 20; see below, under the heading "Technological Change and Intellectual Property Law."

States, business methods are processes eligible to be patented if they meet the regular requirements of the legislation. This is not so in countries covered by the European Patent Convention, which contains an express exclusion of "methods of doing business."[86]

Amazon.com applied for a patent of a "single click" online purchasing method whereby cookies stored in customer and server computer systems would recognize each other and exchange purchasing information without the purchaser having to check out or enter purchasing data. Initially, the patent examiner rejected the patent. The Patent Appeal Board upheld the rejection finding that a business method was not patentable. In 2010, Amazon.com won its appeal before the Federal Court. The Court held that the patent examiner wrongly applied the European definition of patentable inventions. Canadian law is different—business methods are patentable as an "art" or a "process" if they are new and useful with practical applications. They should be assessed like any other invention.[87] It was sent back for assessment by the Patent Commissioner who issued a patent in December 2011.

Novelty An essential element of an invention is that it be "new." A patent will not be granted for a machine or process that is already known or in use, even if it has not been patented by some other person.[88]

Until 1989, Canada had a "first-to-invent" system; that is, if two or more persons applied for a patent for the same invention, only the first inventor was considered the true inventor and entitled to the patent. The present law adopts the more common "first-to-file" system; in cases of conflicting applications, the application with the earlier filing date prevails (section 28.4).

An invention for which a patent is claimed must be one that has not been disclosed to the public anywhere in the world before the filing date. The exception to this rule occurs when the inventor himself makes the disclosure, but even then he must file the application within one year of making the disclosure.

Utility For an invention to qualify as "useful" it must possess industrial value—for example, by making a process easier, cheaper, or faster. Also implied is that it be usable—that is, it should be reproducible and operable, so that a skilled worker, by following the specifications published in the patent, should be able to reproduce the invention and obtain the desired result.

Ingenuity An invention requires an element of ingenuity. As we have noted, it must be more than an obvious step. As has been said:

> The question to be answered is whether at the date of invention ... an unimaginative skilled technician, in light of his general knowledge and the literature and information on the subject available to him on that date, would have been led directly and without difficulty to [the] invention.[89]

In reaching such a conclusion, the patent office or court must be careful not to be influenced by hindsight. Great inventions often seem deceptively simple and obvious in retrospect.

---

[86] *Amazon.com, supra,* n. 77; *Bilski v. Kappos* 561 U.S.__ (2010).

[87] *Amazon.com, supra,* n. 77. The Federal Court of Appeal agreed that business methods are patentable and reversed the lower court's holding that the Amazon method was patentable—this was for the commissioner to assess. Australia also recognizes the patentability of business methods: *Grant v. Commissioner of Patents,* [2006] FCAFC 120.

[88] The discovery of a new use for a known compound is patentable: see *Apotex Inc. v. Wellcome Foundation Ltd.* (2002), 219 D.L.R. (4th) 660.

[89] *Beecham Canada Ltd. v. Proctor & Gamble Co.* (1982), 61 C.P.R. (2d) 1 at 27, per Urie, J.A.

Obtaining a Patent

Only the inventor or the legal representatives of the inventor may apply for the grant of a patent. "Legal representatives" include not only heirs and executors, but also persons claiming through the inventor. If an inventor has assigned the rights to an invention to another person or to a corporation, the assignee may apply. An employer usually owns inventions made by its employees, and is the rightful applicant for a patent.[90]

Applications for patents are made to the Commissioner of Patents and are processed by the Patent Office, a branch of the Canadian Intellectual Property Office. Individual inventors may pursue their own applications, but any other applicants must use the services of a registered **patent agent**. In practice, making an application is a highly complex and specialized matter, and is almost invariably handled by a patent agent.

The agent first makes a search of the online register of patents, and frequently also a search at the U.S. Patent Office, to ensure that no patent has already been granted in respect of the invention. The next major task is to draft the application, in a form prescribed by the Patent Rules. The most important part of the application has two elements: (a) the **specification**, providing a full description of the invention, its use, operation, or manufacture, and (b) the **claim**, setting out the features claimed to be new and in respect of which the applicant claims an exclusive right. Particular care must be taken to ensure that the claim is sufficiently broad to obtain the maximum benefit from the invention. At the same time, it must not be excessively wide so as to include matters that are obvious or already known, and thus render the claim invalid.

When an application has been filed, a further application must be made for the claim to be examined. The Patent Office then appoints an examiner to consider the application. The examiner makes searches of patents, and frequently of technical publications, to ensure that the claimed invention is indeed novel and otherwise complies with the requirements of the Patent Act. The examiner scrutinizes the specification and claim to ensure that complete disclosure has been made and that the invention is described in a way that would enable other persons to utilize it once the period of protection has elapsed. During this stage, the applicant may make amendments to the application in order to satisfy objections raised by the examiner. When the process is complete, the examiner determines whether or not a patent should be granted. An appeal from a rejection of the application may be made to the Patent Appeal Board and then to the courts. For more information on this topic, see the Companion Website.

When the application is successful, the Patent Office issues a "Notice of Allowance," and on payment of a fee (which is additional to the application fee), it issues the patent. Since 1989, the Act has required that a further yearly fee be paid in order to maintain the patent. The fees, however, are relatively modest and vary according to the nature of the applicant entity: for an applicant that qualifies as a "small entity,"[91] the government fees to obtain a patent and to maintain it for the full 20-year period could be less than $2500. The cost of protection for a five-year period could be as little as $500. However, the services of a skilled patent agent will cost considerably more than the fees paid to the Patent Office.

Protection of Patent Rights

Patent rights last for 20 years, so long as the yearly maintenance fee is paid. A patent confers on its owner the exclusive right of constructing and using the invention, and selling it

patent agent a registered agent who pursues applications for patents on behalf of individual inventors

specification the description of the invention, its use, operation, or manufacture

claim a statement of the features claimed to be new and in respect of which the applicant claims an exclusive right

---

[90] *Techform v. Wolda* (2001), 206 D.L.R. (4th) 171.

[91] A "small entity" means an individual inventor or a business concern that employs 50 or fewer persons, or is a university, and that meets a number of other conditions. The fees payable by other applicants are twice as high.

to others to be used. An owner may assign patent rights to others or grant a licence for their limited or exclusive use. An assignment must be in writing and registered with the Patent Office, as must a grant of an exclusive licence.

Any unauthorized act that interferes with the full enjoyment of the exclusive rights conferred by the patent is an infringement. The usual remedies of damages, injunction, and accounting for profit are available to the patentee and to anyone (for example, an assignee or licensee) claiming under him. An action to protect or enforce a patent right may be brought in the Federal Court or in the appropriate provincial court.

Patents and the Public Interest

The granting of a patent is a serious matter, since giving an exclusive right to use and exploit an invention for a period of up to 20 years in effect creates a monopoly. The result is to confer a considerable advantage over business competitors and sometimes, if the patentee chooses not to exploit the invention, to deprive the public of the use of the invention. There are many stories—most of them probably fabrications—of large corporations buying up inventions (such as everlasting light bulbs) that threaten their business in order to suppress the invention.

Patent legislation attempts to protect the public in a number of ways, which are discussed below.

Scope of the Claim   Only genuine inventions qualify for the grant of a patent; claims that are too broad in scope fail. One of the most important functions of the patent examiner is to enforce these policies using a purpose-based evaluation. Third parties, such as business competitors or rival researchers, may challenge the validity of a patent by bringing an **action for impeachment** in the Federal Court. The Attorney General of Canada may also bring such an action.

For patent applications filed after October 1, 1989, an alternative form of challenge is available. Any person may apply to the Commissioner of Patents for re-examination of any claim of a patent. Upon receiving such a request, the commissioner establishes a re-examination board to examine the request.

action for impeachment   an action challenging the validity of a patent

---

CASE 20.19

Research in Motion (now known as BlackBerry) found itself embroiled in a patent dispute in the United States that highlights the complications associated with multiple dispute resolution venues. NTP Inc. claimed that RIM's BlackBerry infringed NTP's patent rights, and NTP started an infringement action in the U.S. federal court in Virginia. In addition to defending the court action, RIM challenged the validity of the NTP patents through the patent re-examination process of the U.S. Patent and Trademark Office. RIM found itself in the confusing position of losing the court action[92] while achieving preliminary success in the patent challenges. RIM eventually settled both actions with a payment of over US $600 million for a licence of the NTP patents.

Abuse of Patent Rights   Another form of protection allows the Attorney General or any interested person to apply to the Commissioner of Patents when it is alleged that patent rights are being abused. An abuse occurs, for example,

- if demand for the patented article in Canada is not being met to a reasonable extent and on reasonable terms;
- if the patentee is hindering the creation of new industries or damaging the public interest by refusing to grant licences;

---

[92] *NTP, Inc. v. Research in Motion Ltd.*, (2005) 418 F. 3d. 1282 (U.S. App.); (2006) 546 U.S. 1157.

- if any trade, industry, or person engaged therein is unfairly prejudiced by the conditions attached to a patent;

- if the existence of a patent has been used so as to unfairly prejudice in Canada the manufacture, use, or sale of any materials.

Compulsory Licensing

The aim of patent law is not only to encourage new inventions by protecting them, but also to encourage the working of those inventions in Canada without undue delay. A patentee cannot simply hold a patent for the purpose of blocking trade. If it does not exploit the invention itself in a reasonable manner, it must sell it or grant a licence on reasonable terms. Where there is abuse, another person who wishes to make use of the invention may apply for the grant of a **compulsory licence**, which may be ordered on terms that allow the applicant to work the patent while giving the patentee a fair return.

compulsory licence a licence granted to a person to work a patent without the consent of the owner of the patent

For pharmaceutical products protected by patent in other countries, a system of compulsory licensing existed, prior to 1987, that allowed Canadian firms to manufacture or import drugs upon payment of a low royalty to the patentee. This system led to the development of a thriving generic drug industry in Canada, to the economic benefit of the Canadian consumer but to the detriment of foreign pharmaceutical companies. It also arguably acted as a deterrent to research and development of pharmaceutical products within Canada. It became a controversial issue that featured prominently in the debates on the Free Trade Agreement between Canada and the United States and in the subsequent NAFTA negotiations; American pressure led to changes in the law.

The 1987 and 1993 amendments to the Act reformed the compulsory licensing scheme for patented medicines with special regulations that established a framework for allowing generic drug companies to obtain the right to produce patented drugs on payment of a royalty to the patent owner. The regulations are extremely complex and have produced one of the most hotly contested areas of litigation.[93] In part due to the problems highlighted by this litigation, the regulations were amended in 1999.

Competition Law

The Competition Act[94] provides a further form of protection of the public interest. It prohibits the exploitation of a patent in such a way as to unduly restrain trade or prevent or lessen competition, and authorizes the Federal Court to grant appropriate relief.

Ethical Issue   Drugs for AIDS

Almost 5 million people are infected with AIDS in Africa; fewer than 100 000 are receiving treatment. The key reason is cost: The patented drugs necessary to treat AIDS cost between $8000 and $15 000 per person, per year. Generic drugs could reduce that cost to a few hundred dollars.

The World Health Organization has urged that countries be allowed to produce generic drugs to counter the AIDS epidemic, and the World Trade Organization has now agreed to allow its members to do so in times of health crises.

Canada's Access to Medicines Regime (CAMR), enacted in May 2004, is an example of compulsory licensing. It amends the Patent Act (section 21.1) and the Food and Drugs Act to approve the production of generic drugs in Canada, for

>

---

[93] See, for, example the decisions of the Supreme Court of Canada in *Eli Lilly and Co. v. Novopharm Ltd.* (1998), 161 D.L.R. (4th) 1; *Merck Frosst Canada Inc. v. Canada* (1998), 161 D.L.R. (4th) 47; also, at lower levels, see *Sanofi-Aventis Canada Inc. v. Hospira Healthcare Corp.*, [2009] F.C.J. No. 1380.

[94] R.S.C. 1985, c. C-34. See further in Chapter 30. The assignment of a patent could as a matter of law unduly lessen competition: see *Apotex Inc. v. Eli Lilly and Co.* (2005), 260 D.L.R. (4th) 202 (FCA).

export to countries that could not otherwise afford drugs to fight AIDS, malaria, tuberculosis, and other diseases. In September 2007, the first authorization was granted to a generic drug company to produce a patented HIV/AIDS drug for export to Rwanda. Critics complain that the system is too complicated and have urged reform.[95]

Questions to Consider

1. Why should Canadians not also be entitled to benefit from cheaper drugs?

2. Should there be any restrictions on the production of generic drugs for fighting potentially fatal illnesses and diseases?

INDUSTRIAL DESIGNS

Industrial designs comprise the fourth type of intellectual property registerable under the Industrial Design Act.[96] Originally enacted in 1868, the Act has been amended on a number of occasions. Despite the amendments, the Act remains a somewhat archaic and rather unsatisfactory piece of legislation.

Meaning of "Industrial Design"

The Act (section 2) defines "industrial design" as:

> features of shape, configuration, pattern or ornament and any combination of those features that, in a finished article, appeal to and are judged solely by the eye.[96A]

Features that are solely utilitarian or functional are not protected, nor is any method or principle of manufacture or construction. For many years it was thought that the Act referred only to designs placed on an article, such as a decorative design on a dinner service, a crest or emblem on a sports shirt, or a design on a roll of wallpaper. More recently, however, it has been held to also apply to the design of the shape of the article itself, insofar as the design is ornamental and not dictated by the function of the article. The shape of a stacking chair or a knife handle may be registered. In order to secure registration, some degree of originality is required.

Protection by Registration

The Act permits the proprietor of an industrial design to register it and obtain exclusive rights to its use in Canada for a term of five years, with the possibility of renewing the registration for one further term of five years. At common law, there is no property in an industrial design, except insofar as it may qualify for protection as a trademark. Protection is consequently dependent upon registration. A proprietor may apply to register a design with the Commissioner of Patents. Application must be made within one year of the first publication of the design. "Publication" in this sense means making the design available to the public—for example, by selling an article to which the design has been applied.

The only person entitled to apply for registration is the "proprietor," who is usually the designer, but if a client or customer commissioned and paid for the design, that person is considered to be the proprietor. If the design was produced by an employee in the normal course of employment, the employer will normally be the proprietor.

---

[95] George Tsai, "Canada's Access to Medicines Regime: Lessons for Compulsory Licensing Schemes Under the WTO Doha Declaration" (2009) 49(2) *Virginia J. of Int'l L.* 1064; Bill C-393, 3rd Sess., 40th Parl., 2011 passed second reading but died when Parliament dissolved in May 2011; Bill C-398, 1st, Sess., 41st Parl., 2012, defeated at second reading on Nov. 28, 2012 (by seven votes).

[96] R.S.C. 1985, c. I-9. (Unless otherwise stated, references in this part are to this Act, as amended.)

[96A] Act (section 2) defines "industrial design," Government of Canada.

Registration gives the proprietor the exclusive right to apply the design to any article for the purpose of sale. However, in order to protect the design, each article to which the design is applied must be marked with the name of the proprietor, the word "Registered" or its abbreviation, "Rd," and the year of registration. A proprietor may assign or grant a licence for the use of a registered design, but the assignment or licence must be recorded on the register in order to preserve the exclusive right.

During the existence of the exclusive right, no other person may apply the design, or any imitation of it, to any article for the purpose of sale without the written consent of the proprietor. The usual remedies of damages, injunction, and account for profits are available to the proprietor; in addition, the Act prescribes a number of summary offences, punishable by fine, for infringement of industrial design rights.

As we have seen, both industrial designs and patents may be protected only by prompt registration. Normally, it will not be difficult to decide whether a design qualifies for patent protection or should be registered as an industrial design. Industrial designs are essentially ornamental, whereas a patentable invention must be useful. In cases of doubt, the advice of a qualified patent agent should be sought.

Industrial Designs, Trademarks, and Copyright

The same design or logo that may be applied to an article as an industrial design may also be considered a trademark. Similarly, the ornamental shape of a container or wrapper may be registered as an industrial design as well as protected under trademark law as a "distinguishing guise." Protection as a trademark is clearly superior, since property rights in a trademark are not dependent upon registration and are not limited to a maximum period of 10 years. However, the two forms of protection do not conflict: A proprietor may register an industrial design and still claim protection for the design as a trademark.

The situation with respect to copyright is more complex. The Copyright Act originally refused copyright protection for designs capable of being registered under the Industrial Design Act. An exception was made for designs that were not used or intended to be used as models or patterns to be multiplied by any industrial process. This provision was revised in 1988, though the intent of the new provision remains essentially similar. Now, if the design is applied to a useful article and the article is reproduced in a quantity of more than 50, some other person does not infringe copyright in the design simply by reproducing the article (section 64). Thus, protection for the design can only be secured by registering it under the Industrial Design Act.[97]

CONFIDENTIAL INFORMATION, TRADE SECRETS, AND KNOW-HOW

Mere ideas or knowledge, however valuable, are not regarded as intellectual property in the strict sense of the term. The Supreme Court of Canada has ruled that confidential information is not property that can be the subject of theft under the Criminal Code.[98]

Confidential information may nevertheless have commercial value. A secret manufacturing process—if it can be kept secret—may be more valuable not patented than patented. And a uniquely efficient way of operating a business, though not capable of being patented at all, may be worth millions in extra profits to its owner. Similarly, a list of customers or clients may constitute an important part of the goodwill of a business. Information can also be valuable to people other than its owner. Although not property in the strict sense,

---

[97] Copyright Act, s. 64(4). See *Bayliner Marine Corp. v. Doral Boats Ltd.* (1986), 10 C.P.R. (3d) 289.

[98] *R. v. Stewart,* [1988] 1 S.C.R. 963; *R. v. Benson,* [2009] O.J. No. 239 (O.S.C.).

information can still be sold to others as, for example, where data is made available to subscribers to a computerized data retrieval service.

The possessor of confidential information, trade secrets, or know-how is not entirely without legal protection, though such protection normally arises out of a contractual or fiduciary relationship. A seller may supply machinery or equipment to a buyer and at the same time license the buyer to use the seller's know-how or some secret process. It is usual to stipulate in the contract that the licensee will not divulge the secret to anyone else.[99] Similarly, as discussed in Chapter 18, some employment contracts include a restrictive covenant restraining the employee, if she leaves the employment, from making use of the employer's confidential information or divulging it to someone else. The employer may claim breach of contract and seek an injunction to prevent the employee from joining a competitor. As well, the employer may sue the competitor for the tort of inducing breach of contract. In other circumstances, a claim for breach of confidence arises if

- confidential information is communicated to someone in confidence, and
- the information is subsequently misused by the person to whom it was communicated.[100]

As will be discussed in Chapter 26, officers, company directors, and partners stand in a fiduciary relationship to their employers, corporations, or co-partners. To misuse or divulge confidential information acquired in the course of such a relationship may constitute a breach of fiduciary duty, which can be restrained by injunction or punished by an award of damages or an accounting for profits made as a result of the breach.[101]

CASE 20.20

A former employee of Apotex took up a new position with a competing firm, Novopharm. He brought with him confidential information about a process for making the drug Lovastatin. Apotex brought an action for an injunction restraining Novopharm from carrying out further research on the drug and for damages against the employee and against Novopharm.

The court held both the employee and the new employer liable. Novopharm knew, or ought to have known, that the information was confidential and had been obtained from Apotex. They were consequently liable for the breach of trust of their new employee.[102]

For more information on this topic, see the Companion Website.

TECHNOLOGICAL CHANGE AND INTELLECTUAL PROPERTY LAW

The problems created by new technology are not easily solved by analogy to old situations. The Harvard mouse case illustrates the ongoing debate about the legitimacy of, and possible limitations that should be imposed upon, genetic engineering, especially of human life forms. A related issue concerns the genetic modification of foods: Are genetically modified foods a great benefit to humankind that should be protected by patent law, or are they a

---

[99] In *Cadbury Schweppes Inc. v. FBI Foods Ltd.* (1999), 167 D.L.R. (4th) 577, the Supreme Court of Canada held that a manufacturer under licence who produced a competing product after the termination of the licence, using confidential information, was liable in damages for the loss suffered by the licensor.

[100] See *Free Trade Medical Network Inc. v. RBC Travel Insurance Co.* (2006), 215 O.A.C. 230 (O.C.A.); *Lysko v. Braley* (2006), 79 O.R. (3d) 721 (O.C.A.); *Sabre Inc. v. International Air Transport Assn.*, [2011] O.J. No. 95, aff'd 2011 ONCA 747.

[101] See *LAC Minerals Ltd. v. International Corona Resources Ltd.* (1989), 61 D.L.R. (4th) 14. Misuse of confidential information by corporate directors or officers is discussed further in Chapter 26.

[102] *Apotex Fermentation Inc. v. Novopharm Ltd.* (1998), 162 D.L.R. (4th) 111.

potential cause of uncontrollable catastrophe? This debate was given a new focus in the recent case of the Saskatchewan farmer accused of infringing a patent for genetically modified canola.[103]

Technological change has also led to two relatively recent statutes, enacted to protect the rights of plant breeders and the designers of integrated circuits. The Plant Breeders' Rights Act[104] provides exclusive rights, similar to patent rights in respect of new varieties of plants, including genetically modified plants. To qualify, a plant variety must be clearly distinguishable from all other commonly known varieties of the species, be both stable and homogeneous, and be of a variety not yet sold in Canada. Application is made to a Commissioner of Plant Breeders' Rights, who may require or conduct such tests as are necessary to establish the novelty of the variety. A grant is for a term of 18 years, subject to payment of an annual fee, and confers the exclusive right to sell, produce, and use the variety.

The Integrated Circuit Topography Act[105] also provides exclusive rights similar to patent rights in the "topography" or design of integrated circuits (semiconductor chips) and in the circuits that incorporate such designs themselves. Registration is required, and protection is for a period of 10 years.

New technologies have not only given rise to the creation of new types of intellectual property and new rights—the ways in which existing rights may be exercised and infringed are also changing. To quote the Economic Council of Canada:

> [N]ew technology and the movement towards an increasingly knowledge-based economy and society are throwing up issues of such scale and significance that no part of the existing policy structure can remain unaffected.[106]

Strategies to Manage the Legal Risks

Intellectual property (IP) is an increasingly important area not only for product development but also for marketing, business systems, communications, and technology services. Every business needs an all-encompassing IP strategy. Determining whether a concept, activity, or system is protected as a trademark, copyright, patent, or industrial design can be difficult. Sometimes a concept is entitled to protection in multiple categories: A copyrighted drawing may also be a trademark for a product (Mickey Mouse, for example). All available forms of protection should be sought.

A trademark is relatively easy to register and may be renewed indefinitely, so registration should be completed before a business invests heavily in naming a company or promoting a brand. Searches of trademark databases should be undertaken, as well as of corporate and business name registries. When licensing others, use should be confined to specific duration, activities, products, and geographic locations. To preserve the exclusivity of the mark, the business should defend or oppose all applications that might be even slightly similar.

Copyright protection arises automatically without registration, so this protection should be part of a business's IP strategy. Even though the legislation does not require notice of copyright, creators are recommended to give notice of ownership through the universal symbol "©"; this may have a deterrent effect on would-be thieves. Only important

---

[103] *Schmeiser v. Monsanto Canada Inc.* (2004), 239 D.L.R. (4th) 271. The farmer had claimed that the genetically modified seed had blown onto his land. The Supreme Court of Canada upheld the grant of a patent for the seed, but held that the farmer had obtained no benefit from its use and was not liable to compensate the patent owner.

[104] S.C. 1990, c. 20.

[105] S.C. 1990, c. 37.

[106] Report on Intellectual and Industrial Property (Ottawa: Economic Council of Canada, 1971) at 5–6.

comprehensive works need be registered. Computer technology producers should consider the use of DRMT to discourage the casual copier, and also recognize that, although computer programs may be the subject of copyright, business methods or inventions involving computer programs are patentable.

Managing protection decisions is more difficult when dealing with patents. A business cannot delay funding for projects involving inventions—that is, patent or industrial design—until after protection is in place, as such projects require prior research and development. Patent applications are complicated, requiring the assistance of lawyers and engineers, and can take a long time. Products that will have a short window of marketability may not be worth the process. As well, the monopoly lasts only 20 years, so if the formula is complicated, longer protection may be available if the product is just kept secret.

Everyone involved in the business's IP or with the development of a new concept should be subject to a confidentiality agreement and an agreement establishing ownership of the property in the business. Employees, consultants, or independent contractors seeking to retain ownership of their work products should preserve this right in their engagement contracts. Similarly, employees must honour the confidentiality obligations owed to past employers. A breach of confidence cause of action is not confined to contractual relationships but may arise from fiduciary relations or any communication of confidential information. Businesses may be liable for any infringing behaviour carried on by their employees. An IP code of conduct should be developed to protect the integrity of the business's IP, and to limit liability for the infringing behaviour of others. The code should set standards for use and misuse, and control use of technology by prohibiting downloading, uploading, sharing, and format shifting, except in accordance with defined rules.

Finally, IP risks must be assessed when international business strategies are formed. Although some international coordination has been undertaken, this is largely in the areas of application, processing, and recognition. Other laws may still vary. In many countries, IP rights are routinely violated with little consequence. Ukraine is identified by the Office of the United States Trade Representative as presenting the greatest IP risk.[107] The specific grounds for this designation are the unfair, non-transparent system for collecting and distributing royalties to rights holders; the widespread (and admitted) use of illegal software by Ukrainian government agencies; and failure to combat the widespread online infringement of copyright. China is a major source of counterfeit goods, violating trademarks, patents, copyrights, and industrial rights in the process. Most troubling are China's limited legal structure, enforcement, and political desire to stop this abuse. A business entering the Ukrainian or Chinese markets can take little comfort in Canadian IP protection. A good source of information on the IP habits of countries around the world is the Office of the United States Trade Representative. As noted, Canada is also on the USTR Watch List.

QUESTIONS FOR REVIEW

1. What types of intellectual property are protected by law?
2. What are the principal costs and benefits of protecting intellectual property?
3. What is a "trademark"?
4. What are the essential elements of the tort of passing-off?
5. Are there any advantages to be gained in registering a trademark?
6. What is a "certification mark"?

---

[107] Office of the United States Trade Representative, 2013 Special 301 Report, *supra*, n. 53.

7. On what grounds may the registration of a trademark be opposed?

8. What are the principal rights possessed by an owner of copyright?

9. In relation to copyright, what are "moral rights"?

10. Does copyright exist in computer software?

11. For how long does copyright usually last?

12. In what ways may a person become an owner of copyright?

13. What constitutes "fair dealing" in relation to copyright?

14. What qualities must an invention have in order to be patented?

15. Why might an inventor choose not to register a patent?

16. What is meant by an "industrial design"?

17. In what circumstances should a business owner require a confidentiality agreement?

CASES AND PROBLEMS

1. Continuing Scenario

Ashley hired Jordan, a co-op culinary student from her alma mater, George Brown College, to work as a sous chef in her restaurant for the summer. Although Jordan's passion was food, he also had superior computer skills and, after examining the restaurant's website, volunteered to make some improvements. He made two visual and style changes—(1) he standardized the website colours to match the décor of the restaurant (white, blue, and yellow), and (2) he stylized the initials in the name into a visual symbol and repeated the use of this symbol throughout the website wherever the name formerly appeared. Ashley liked this symbol so much that she changed the front of the menu to include it, she had it etched into the glass on the restaurant windows, and she planned to put it on the sign outside when the current one was replaced. On the technical side, Jordan designed an online reservation system where customers could not only view and book available time slots but also designate the table they wanted from a colour coded map of the restaurant. The map shaded tables that were already booked and colour coded tables based on three levels of noise (secluded, active, high activity). Again, Ashley was thrilled; no other restaurant that she knew of had such a user friendly process.

Jordan was a wonderful employee but Ashley did not promise to hire him upon his graduation. Jordan was disappointed but he easily obtained a job at Kate's Kitchen, another restaurant in Toronto. Soon after starting at Kate's, Jordan redesigned that restaurant's website using the same colour scheme as Ashley's, the same stylized font for the symbol (although the letters in the name were different), and—most upsetting to Ashley—the same reservation booking process complete with colour coded table map.

Can Ashley do anything about this? Are there intellectual property rights in any of the website components, and if so, who owns them? What preventative steps should Ashley have taken?

2. In 1955, a successful novel entitled *Lolita*, authored by Vladimir Nabokov, was published. The novel recounts the story of a middle-aged man, Humbert Humbert, who becomes infatuated with his 12-year-old stepdaughter, Lolita, eventually descending to rape, murder, and madness.

In 1995, the Italian author Pia Pera wrote a book entitled *Lo's Diary*, which was subsequently translated into English. The book purports to tell the story of the affair as experienced by Lolita herself. The principal events of the earlier parts of the story are the same as described in the Nabokov book, though described from the very different perspective of the young girl. (Ms. Pera's book goes on to describe events that occurred after the two parted.)

The late Mr. Nabokov's son and executor threatened action for infringement of copyright. Should the action succeed? Why or why not?

3. A small Canadian corporation, Lexus Foods Inc., applied to register the name Lexus as a trademark for its range of canned fruit products.

The application was opposed by the Japanese manufacturer of the well-known Lexus model of automobiles. It argued that the application by the Canadian corporation should not be granted because of the risk of confusion with its existing marks. Further, it claimed that the applicants were simply trying to cash in on its famous name.

Is the objection a valid one? Why or why not?

4. Shamrock Homes Inc. is a major construction company that specializes in the construction of large residential developments. Brendan, their chief engineer, has worked out an entirely new method of planning a development, requiring the construction of a factory in which prefabricated components for houses are manufactured and assembled to speed up the construction of houses. The factory is specially designed to be converted into a shopping mall when all the houses are completed. Shamrock estimates that the new method reduces construction costs by as much as 15 percent.

Shamrock wishes to patent this new method, fearing that competitors will easily be able to copy it otherwise. Give your opinion as to whether the method is patentable.

5. Dolphin Marine Ltd. is a well-established firm with an excellent reputation for building racing sailboats. It has recently produced a new 12-metre model, the DM35X, with a fibreglass hull of novel design, which has been highly successful in a number of important races.

Kopikat Inc. is a small firm that has been building sailboats for a number of years with little success, either sporting or financial. Kenny, the controlling shareholder and president of Kopikat, buys one of the new Dolphin models, constructs a mould of the hull, and commences to produce a racer with a hull identical to the DM35X and with other features that are very similar. Kopikat is planning to market it at a price $8000 lower than the DM35X.

Has Kopikat infringed any right of Dolphin? Why or why not?

6. Richards, a freelance writer, wrote a long article on the devastating effects of a tsunami in Asia, and submitted it to the *Global Post*, a leading newspaper that had published other articles by her. The newspaper agreed to publish her article in its December 2015 print edition.

In early 2016, the *Global Post* published a number of extracts from what it described as "the best GP articles of 2015" on its website. Included was Richards's tsunami article. Richards complains that (1) she had never agreed to the publication on the internet, and (2) in editing the article for the website, the newspaper had omitted important details so that the edited version did not properly represent the original work.

Does Richards have an action against the newspaper? Why or why not?

For more cases and problems, see the Companion Website.

Additional Resources for Chapter 20 on the Companion Website

(www.pearsoncanada.ca/smyth)

In addition to pre- and post-tests, mini-cases, and application exercises, the Companion Website includes the following province-specific resources for Chapter 20:

- **Alberta:** Copyright Act; Trade Name/Trademark
- **Atlantic Provinces:** Business Names
- **British Columbia:** Business Names
- **Manitoba/Saskatchewan:** Business Names
- **Ontario:** Business Names

Chapter 21

Interests in Land and Their Transfer

Since land is the most long-lasting business asset and the "ultimate platform of human activity," the ownership of land is a primary concern both in private life and in carrying on business.

In this chapter, we examine land ownership through such questions as:

- What is land or real property?

- How is land owned?

- What are the various levels of ownership in land?

- How is ownership shared?

- What are the legal characteristics of "estates" and "interests less than estates"?

- How is condominium ownership structured?

- How are interests in land transferred and protected?

THE NATURE OF INTERESTS IN LAND

The Definition of Land

land comprises the surface, all that is under the surface, including the minerals and oil, and everything above the surface, including buildings

When we think of land, we usually think of its surface. In law, **land** includes not only the surface but all that is under the surface, including the natural resources such as minerals or oil, and much of what is above the surface, including the buildings on the land. A landowner's entitlement to the air above the surface is restricted. Various statutes, international treaties concerning air travel, and municipal bylaws limiting the use of land have reduced ownership of the air.[1] Aircraft may pass freely over the land at a safe altitude, and buildings must not exceed a certain height.

fixtures all things permanently attached to land are deemed part of the land

The legal concept of land also includes all things permanently attached to it—trees, buildings, and fences—known as **fixtures**. When A transfers her house and lot to B, the document describes the land only, according to its location and dimensions, but everything attached to the land goes with it. Lawyers do not draw a distinction between land and buildings as do businesses and accountants. For business purposes, the depreciation of buildings is reported, not of land; in law, the two are considered one when determining or transferring ownership.

Real Property or Real Estate

property (1) everything that is the subject of ownership or (2) the legal interest in a thing

The Meaning of "Property"   Land is often referred to as real property or real estate, two terms that need some explanation. The term **property** means "everything which is the subject of ownership . . . everything that has exchangeable value or which goes to make up wealth. . . ."[2] By this definition, "property" refers to the thing itself, whether it is a piece of land or a piece of cheese or share certificates or the tangible things documents represent.[3]

title holding ownership of a thing

The person or entity that holds the ownership to the property is said to have **title** to the property: "ownership of a thing," or "title to a thing." For more information on this topic, see the Companion Website.

The Meaning of "Real"   The word "real" originated from an ancient remedy. Certain interests in land gave the owner the right to repossess it—this was referred to as a

real action an action to repossess an interest in land that had been interfered with

real action—rather than a personal action, an action for money damages without a right to recover the interest. Eventually the term "real" property came to refer to interests in land generally.

The Meaning of "Estate"   Land is permanent, except on the rare occasions when a piece of it slides into the sea. Its value may drop but it exists forever. Each owner of land is a temporary owner because eventually the land will pass to another owner. As a result, the law defines ownership of land based on the length of time that the owner is entitled to exclusive possession of the land, and calls such ownership arrangements **estates in time**.

estates in time the right to exclusive possession of the land for a period of time

Any interest in land that gives someone exclusive possession for some period of time is known as an estate.

Crown Grant and Aboriginal Land Claims

All land originally vested in the government (referred to as the "Crown"). The first transfer of title from the government to a person is known as the Crown grant. It conveys an estate

---

[1] See e.g. Aeronautics Act, R.S.C. 1985, c. A-2, s. 5.4. In *Didow v. Alberta Power Ltd.*, [1988] A.J. No. 620: overhead power lines constituted a trespass into his airspace. A subsequent amendment to the Hydro and Electric Energy Act, R.S.A. 2000, c. H-16, permitted this type of intrusion without compensation.

[2] *Black's Law Dictionary*, 6th ed. (St. Paul: West Publishing, 1990) at 1216. Reprinted with permission of Thomson Reuters.

[3] The lesser-known meaning of "property" is not the thing itself but the legal interest in the thing. *Ibid.*

in time to the first owner. Sometimes Crown grants imposed restrictions on use or excluded some rights such as mineral rights or timber rights which meant that ownership of these rights stayed with the government.[4] The first owner can transfer his estate to a subsequent owner but he cannot create a greater interest than he received in the Crown grant.[5]

During an owner's exclusive possession of the land, he may reduce the estate for those that come after him. For instance, if the owner of land grants to a city the right to lay watermains across the land, that right could affect a subsequent owner who would like to tear up the pipes and erect a building. Each subsequent holder of an estate in time would own the land minus the rights granted away. Rights dealing with the use of the land and not exclusive possession to it are referred to as **interests less than estates**. Land use is regulated by all three levels of government, as discussed below.

> **interests less than estates** interests in land that do not give the right to exclusive possession

A challenge to the Crown grant will undermine the title to all those receiving grants after or through it. Aboriginal land claims are the most common challenges and come in two forms. Specific land claims allege that the crown has improperly dealt with the land in violation of a historic treaty; comprehensive claims deal with lands that have not been subject to a treaty but in which an Aboriginal interest or title is claimed.[6] For more information on this topic, see the Companion Website.

ESTATES IN TIME

Freehold Estates

The first category of estates in time is freehold estates. A **freehold estate** is indeterminate in time; it cannot be predicted how long the interest of the owner will last.

> **freehold estate** an interest in land that is indeterminate in time

Fee Simple Estate   This estate, referred to as the **fee simple**, is the longest interest a person can own in land and is as close to complete ownership as the law allows. Everyday reference to land ownership means fee simple. The holder of the fee simple holds it for all time present and future. The holder of the fee simple may designate the next owner by selling it, transferring it, or leaving the property to someone in a will. Even if there is not a will, the relatives of a deceased fee simple owner are entitled to inherit it. He may grant the whole of the fee simple away; he may grant away a lesser interest, keeping the rest for himself; or he may sever off smaller portions of the whole parcel and convey them to different persons.

> **fee simple** the interest in land closest to complete ownership

---

ILLUSTRATION 21.1

(a) A, the holder of the fee simple in Blackacre, may grant it to an older brother B for the rest of B's life. At B's death it returns to A, or to A's heirs if A dies before B. A retains the fee simple subject to a life estate to B.

(b) A may grant Blackacre to a brother for life with the rest of the fee simple going to a niece, C, at the brother's death.

Illustration 21.1 serves merely to provide examples of some of the ways a fee simple owner may carve out lesser estates. If the owner dies without relatives or a will, then it is transferred to the government.

---

[4] *Wardle v. Manitoba Farm Loan Association*, [1956] SCR 3.

[5] *Herbison v. Canada (Attorney General)*, 2013 BCSC 2020, para 26.

[6] See Constitution Act, 1982, Schedule B to the Canada Act 1982 (UK), 1982, c 11 s. 35; Aboriginal Affairs and Northern Development Canada website, http://www.aadnc-aandc.gc.ca/eng/1100100030285/1100100030289. See *Tsilhqot'in Nation v. British Columbia*, 2014 SCC 44.

life estate an estate in land that lasts for the life of one person

Life Estate

A **life estate** is an estate in land that lasts for the life of one person—usually for the life of the person who holds the estate, but not necessarily: A person may hold an estate, measured by the life of another person. A may convey his cottage to B for the rest of A's own life—if A dies within a few months, the life estate ends. B retains no interest in the cottage. This type of life estate is, however, quite rare. The more usual life estate is for the life of the person to whom the interest is given and often arises under the terms of a will. For example, the owner of a fee simple may, by the terms of her will, give a life estate in the family home to her spouse, who becomes the **life tenant**. She then directs that the rest of the fee simple pass to the children after the death of the spouse.

life tenant a holder of a life estate

The balance of the fee simple, after a life estate has been carved out, is called either a reversion or a remainder. It is called a **reversion** when the grantor of the life estate reserves the balance of the fee simple for herself and her heirs (that is, it reverts back to the grantor or her heirs after the life estate ends). It is called a **remainder** when it goes to some third person. The balance of the estate in example (a) in Illustration 21.1 above is a reversion, and in example (b) is a remainder. Unfortunately, life estates create many problems.

reversion the balance of a fee simple reserved to the grantor and her heirs at the end of a life estate

remainder the balance of a fee simple that goes to a third person at the end of a life estate

- First, it is difficult to sell land subject to a life estate. Very few people will buy only the remaining years of a life tenant's interest, an uncertain period of time. Only if both the life tenant and the **remainderman** join in the sale and together grant the whole of the fee simple will it likely be possible to sell the land.

remainderman a person who holds the reversion or remainder in a fee simple

- Second, a life tenant is limited in the changes she can make on the land without the consent of the remainderman. She cannot tear down buildings or cut down trees without the permission of the remainderman, even if it would increase the land's value; she must leave the land to the remainderman substantially as she received it. On the other hand, she is under no duty to make repairs and may let buildings decay.

- Third, she cannot compel the remainderman to contribute anything to the cost of substantial repairs and maintenance needed on the land, though they will ultimately be of benefit to the remainderman in preserving its value.

Life estates are not typically used in business. However, they are used for personal tax planning purposes and family situations. For example, parents may wish to transfer the fee simple in the family cottage to the children but retain a life estate to enjoy until their deaths. Capital gain is the children's and tax will not be triggered on the death of the parents.

A spouse may wish to create a life estate in the family home for her second spouse and leave the fee simple to the children of her first marriage. This will allow the current spouse to continue to live in the home for life without disinheriting the children of the first marriage.

Leasehold Estates

leasehold an interest in land for a definite period of time

The other major category of estates is leasehold estates. A **leasehold** estate is an exclusive interest in land for a definite period of time—a week, a month, a year, a hundred years, or any other specific period. This is the big difference between a freehold and a leasehold estate: A freehold estate is either for an infinite time (the fee simple) or an indefinite time (the life estate), but the leasehold is for a definite time. In a leasehold estate, the person to whom the interest is granted is called the lessee or tenant, and the grantor of the interest is called the lessor or landlord.

Historically, leaseholds have always been considered lesser estates than freeholds, even though leases for 100 years would almost invariably last longer than a freehold life estate. However, a leasehold interest must be created from a freehold estate and cannot last longer than the freehold from which it is created.

ILLUSTRATION 21.2

In her will, T gives A a life estate in the cottage with the remainder after A's death to X in fee simple. A leases the cottage to B Inc. for 100 years. Several months later, A dies. X, the remainderman, can take possession of the cottage and evict B Inc. X is not bound by the lease because A could not create a leasehold interest in the cottage to last longer than his own life estate.

The result in Illustration 21.2 is an application of the rule that a person cannot grant to another a greater interest than he himself holds.[7]

Leasehold interests share an important characteristic with freehold interests—a lease gives a lessee the right to exclusive possession of the land described in the lease. A lessee has the right to keep all persons off the leased land, including the lessor himself, unless the lessor has reserved the right to enter the property for inspection and repairs. The law concerning leasehold interests combines the strict concepts of real property, the flexible concepts of contract, and the changing policies of government regulation. The legislative rules vary depending upon whether the purpose of the lease is residential or commercial.[8] The provincial regulations dealing with leasehold interests in land are discussed in more detail in Chapter 22, "Landlord and Tenant."

Sharing Title: Co-Ownership

Tenancy in Common   Two or more persons may share ownership of the same estate in land at the same time. They are concurrent holders of the estate, whether it is a fee simple, a life estate, or a leasehold estate. In the absence of any special agreement between them or of special terms set out in the initial grant, co-owners are deemed to be tenants in common. **Tenants in common** hold equal shares in the estate; that is, each is entitled to the same rights over the property and an equal share of the income. Each interest is an undivided interest. One tenant cannot fence off a portion of the property for her exclusive use—each is entitled to the use of the whole property. However, tenants in common may agree to hold unequal shares, transfer the share of one to another, or divide and fence the property into exclusive lots. In addition, a tenant in common may transfer her interest to any third party without the consent of the others: The transferee becomes a tenant in common with them. When a tenant in common dies, her interest goes to her heirs, who continue to hold the interest with the other tenants in common. Business partners usually hold title to real property as tenants in common.

tenants in common   concurrent holders of equal undivided shares in an estate

Joint Tenancy   Another form of co-ownership is joint tenancy. Two or more persons become **joint tenants** only when expressly stated at the time the estate is granted to them or afterward by an express agreement among them. The feature that distinguishes a joint tenancy from a tenancy in common is the **right of survivorship**. Under the right of survivorship, the interest of a deceased joint tenant passes on his death to the surviving tenant instead of to the heirs of the deceased. If A, B, and C own a building in joint tenancy, upon C's death his interest will pass to A and B, who will continue to own the building in joint tenancy between them. C's interest does not go to his heirs.

joint tenants   concurrent holders, each of whom has a right of survivorship

right of survivorship   the right of a surviving tenant to the interest of a deceased joint tenant

---

[7] An important exception to the rule exists in some provinces. Under the Settled Estates Act in Ontario and British Columbia, a life tenant may lease his estate for a term not exceeding 21 years, and the lease will be valid against the remainderman. If the life tenant dies, the lessee pays the rent to the remainderman for the balance of the lease and may stay in possession.

[8] See e.g. Commercial Tenancies Act, R.S.O. 1990, c. L-7; The Residential Tenancies Act, S.O. 2006, c. 17.

Husband and wife often take title to their family home in joint tenancy. On the death of either spouse, the survivor automatically receives full title to the property. Joint tenancy is an advantage to the survivor because the house does not form part of the deceased partner's estate and become entangled in problems of **probate** (administration and settling of the deceased person's estate). Legal fees and probate costs are significantly reduced.

probate the process of administering and settling the estate of a deceased person

Severance A joint tenant may end the right of survivorship at any time before his death without the consent of the other joint tenants. By a procedure called **severance**, he may turn his joint tenancy into a tenancy in common. If there are two or more other tenants remaining, they continue as joint tenants with each other, but are tenants in common with the one who has severed his joint tenancy. The most common method of severance is by a joint tenant granting his interest to a third party. The grant automatically turns the interest transferred into a tenancy in common with the remaining interests. A joint tenancy is also severed by giving a mortgage on one's share. However, a joint tenant cannot sever his share by disposing of it in his will: The courts have held that a will speaks only at the moment a testator has died, and at that moment his share has already passed to the surviving joint tenant or tenants.

severance a procedure that turns a joint tenancy into a tenancy in common

INTERESTS LESS THAN ESTATES

Easements

In addition to estates in land that are divided according to time, there are other interests distinguished by the use or benefit they confer upon the land of the holder. None of these interests gives the right to exclusive possession.

An **easement** is a right enjoyed by one landowner over the land of another, for a special purpose rather than for the general use and occupation of land. The most common type of easement is a **right-of-way**: The holder of a right-of-way may pass back and forth over the land of another in order to get to and from her own land. She does not have the right to remain on the other's land or bring things on the land and leave them there or to obstruct others from using the land, but she can maintain an action against anyone who interferes with her right to pass. Other examples of easements are the right to hang eaves of a building over another's land and to drain water or waste materials from one piece of land over a watercourse on another's land. Adjoining landowners frequently have mutual easements over each other's land, such as a shared driveway or a narrow strip between houses to provide access for maintenance and repairs.[9] Once granted, an easement attaches to the land and binds subsequent owners—they cannot interfere with the exercise of the easement. Similarly, purchasers of the land benefiting from the easement acquire the former owner's easement rights.

easement a right enjoyed by one landowner over the land of another for a special purpose but not for occupation of the land

right-of-way an easement that gives the holder a right to pass back and forth over the land of another in order to get to and from her own land

Essential requirements of an easement, at common law, are that there must be a **dominant tenement** (a piece of land that benefits from the easement) and a **servient tenement** (the land subject to the easement) owned by a different person. The dominant tenement must be close to the servient tenement; how close is a subjective determination based on the facts of each situation. If the right to enjoy another's land benefits a person, not another piece of land, then the right is only a personal right, known as a **licence**.[10]

dominant tenement the piece of land that benefits from an easement

servient tenement the land subject to the easement

Statutory Easements The term "easement" is sometimes used to describe certain statutory rights, such as the right granted to a telephone company to run wires and

licence a right to use another's land for the benefit of a person

---

[9] See e.g. *Rose v. Krieser* (2002), 212 D.L.R. (4th) 123; *Fallowfield v. Bourgault* (2003), 235 D.L.R. (4th) 263. Alternatively, it could be a licence—a personal contractual right to use another's land—*394 Lakeshore Oakville Holdings Inc. v. Misek*, [2010] O.J. No. 4659 at paras. 61, 69–70 aff'd. *Mechanical Services Inc. v. Flesch* 2011 ONCA 764.

[10] *Mechanical Services Inc. v. Flesch* 2011 ONCA 764 at para 203.

cables either underground or overhead on poles. The telephone company has the right to leave wires where they have been installed and to inspect and repair them when necessary—rights very similar to easements. But often the telephone company owns no land in the area. The nearest land that could be considered a dominant tenement may be many kilometres away. Therefore, strictly speaking, the right is not an easement—it is a right created by statute.[11]

Easements by Prescription   In some parts of Canada, simply using another person's land may give an adjoining landowner an easement over his neighbour's land without a written grant. The method is called **prescription**, and an easement is created if a person

- continuously exercises a right for a period of at least 20 years,
- openly,
- without fraud, deceit, force, or threats against the owner of the land, and
- without consent or permission of the owner or payment to the owner.

prescription the creation of an easement over adjoining land through exercising a right continuously and openly

An easement by prescription is recognized in some parts of Atlantic Canada and in parts of Manitoba and Ontario where land ownership is recorded in a registry system. Easements by prescription are not recognized in the three western provinces or in those parts of Manitoba, Ontario, and Atlantic Canada covered by land titles registration.[12] Both of these systems of recording interests in land are discussed later in this chapter. In areas where easements by prescription may arise, a landowner must guard against them. For more information on this topic, see the Companion Website.

CONTEMPORARY ISSUE

Conservation Easements

Past decades have seen the creation of legislation in several Canadian provinces concerning conservation easements. These statutes reflect a compromise between the legal rights of landowners (protected under statute and at common law) and the concerns of those who would like to protect environmentally sensitive land.

The easements created by this legislation, such as the Alberta Land Stewardship Act, the Conservation Land Act in Ontario, and the Conservation Easements Act in Saskatchewan,[13] more closely resemble restrictive covenants than easements in their traditional sense—although the Ontario legislation states that such an easement shall not be deemed a restrictive covenant. Pursuant to these statutes, landowners may enter agreements with conservation organizations or bodies whereby the landowner retains ownership to the land, but the conservation body gains the right to access the land for purposes of "conservation, maintenance, restoration or enhancement" of the land. The easements can also include positive or negative covenants that bind the landowner in his use of the land—presumably to safeguard environmental sensitivities inherent in the land. The easement is to be registered against the property and, once registered, shall run with the land.

The Alberta government, in its January 3, 2005, issue of "Agri-News," heralded the use of conservation easements. It quoted Andy Murphy, of the Alberta Conservation Association: "Conservation easements are a great concept that farmers and ranchers would likely be interested in as an easy way they can preserve precious tracts of land they have for future generations."[13A] At the beginning of 2003,

>

---

[11] The example given at the beginning of this chapter of a municipality being given a right to lay watermains over a landowner's property might be an easement proper or merely a statutory right, depending upon whether the municipality owned land nearby.

[12] See, e.g., Ontario Land Titles Act, R.S.O. 1990, c. L.5 s. 51(1) (some preservation of prescriptive easements created before transfer to land titles). *Millstone Consulting Services Inc. v. Cleary*, [2008] O.J. No. 3106, aff'd [2009] O.J. No. 4510 (Ont. C.A.).

[13] S.A. 2009, c. A-26.8, ss. 28–35; R.S.O. 1990, c. C.28; S.S. 1996, c. C-27.01.

[13A] Andy Murphy, of the Alberta Conservation Association, January 3, 2005, issue of "Agri-News."

over 35 000 acres in Alberta had been brought under the protection of 52 different conservation easements. Of these easements, 15 had been purchased, while the land under the remaining 37 had been donated. In 2009, the largest single conservation easement donation was made by Daryl "Doc" Seaman (late) and family to Ducks Unlimited Canada, covering 45.5 square kilometres of their Alberta ranch.[14]

Questions to Consider

1. Do you think conservation easements are an effective method of protecting environmentally sensitive land?
2. Are conservation easements more effective than restrictive covenants? Why or why not?
3. Do you foresee any legal difficulties with conservation easements—for instance, will they be popular with mortgagees?

Covenants

An owner of land may wish to restrict or control the use of land after she sells it. This is especially true when she is retaining abutting property. She may wish to see the property kept in good repair so that the area does not deteriorate, to prevent the carrying on of a noisy business that would interfere with neighbours' privacy, or to have the purchaser improve the land by planting trees and shrubs to enhance the beauty of the area. She may, of course, require the purchaser to do any or all of these things as part of the consideration for the contract of sale of the land. However, this would not bind any subsequent buyer. The solution is to create an interest in land that is binding upon all subsequent owners.

The courts have held that it is too onerous to bind subsequent owners to positive duties (such as the obligation to plant trees), and that as a matter of public policy it would be dangerous to permit the creation of interests in land requiring all subsequent owners to personally perform promises indefinitely. Lands might eventually be tied up by multiple promises or covenants for the benefit of surrounding lands.[15]

restrictive covenant a covenant requiring the holder of the land to refrain from certain conduct or certain use of the land

Restrictive Covenants   Courts have taken a more favourable view of covenants that require the owner to refrain from doing something. These negative covenants are known as "covenants running with the land," or **restrictive covenants**. Restrictive covenants are subject to a rule similar to that concerning easements—there must be a piece of land subject to the covenant and another piece that receives the be nefit of the covenant. A covenant recognized by the courts as running with the land is enforceable by any subsequent holder of the land benefiting from it against any subsequent holder of the land subject to it.

A number of rules govern the types of conduct that may be regulated by restrictive covenants, how the benefits of the covenants may be transferred, and how they may be enforced.[16] Covenants found to be highly unreasonable, against public policy, or not properly registered against the land will not be enforced by the courts against subsequent owners.

Remedies for Breach of a Covenant   If a landowner ignores a restrictive covenant and, for example builds a fence or clothesline, the court may grant a mandatory injunction requiring the wrongdoer to tear down the prohibited fence or clothesline. If it is

---

[14] Alberta NAWMP Partnership, Partners Celebrate Alberta's Largest Conservation Easement Donation, October 4, 2009, available at http://www.abnawmp.ca/news/2009/oct/04/partners-celebrate-albertas-largest-conservation-e/

[15] Although the refusal to enforce positive covenants may occasionally cause inconvenience and unfairness, the rule is well established and ought not to be changed: *Amberwood Investments Ltd. v. Durham Condominium Corp. No. 123* (2002), 211 D.L.R. (4th) 1; *Innisfil 400 Group Ltd. v. Ontario*, [2007] O.J. No. 2863.

[16] Not only must the party seeking to enforce it (the covenantee) own land to be benefited by the covenant, but the land must be identified in the instrument creating the covenant. *Re Sekretov and City of Toronto* (1973), 33 D.L.R. (3d) 257; *Canada Safeway v. Thompson (City)*, [1997] 7 W.W.R. 565. For statutory authority to modify or discharge a restrictive covenant see, for example, Conveyancing and Law of Property Act, R.S.O. 1990, c. C-34, s. 61(1).

too late to repair the damage, as when the wrongdoer has cut down a row of 100-year-old oak trees, the court may award damages in lieu of an injunction.

Building-Scheme Covenants   A restrictive covenant that regulates land use over an entire neighbourhood or a shopping centre is referred to as a **building-scheme covenant**; these are widely used by residential housing developers to control the uses and look of the subdivision. Covenants are included in the deed to each builder or homeowner. Typical residential covenants prohibit commercial use, limit building on the land to one-family dwellings, require minimum frontage or square footage per house, specify maximum fence heights, and ban outdoor clotheslines.

building-scheme covenant   a restrictive covenant that regulates land use over an entire neighbourhood or a shopping centre

If a once-reasonable covenant has become unduly restrictive, an affected landowner may apply to the court to have the covenant terminated. The court will require that the owner of the land for whose benefit the covenant was made be served with notice and given an opportunity to defend the covenant.

Covenants are gradually being replaced by municipal regulations in the form of zoning and building bylaws, and development agreements (between developer and municipality), especially in newly developed areas. Nevertheless, covenants still play an important role in older settled parts of our cities and towns; sometimes they unduly restrict the development of an area.

Ethical Issue   Airing Laundry in Ontario

On April 18, 2008, then Ontario Premier Dalton McGuinty announced that his government would pass legislation to render unenforceable all restrictive covenants that prevent homeowners from installing outdoor clotheslines. In his opinion, these covenants encourage the use of clothes dryers, and a return to outdoor clotheslines will help conserve energy, save money, and cut greenhouse emissions. Florida, Utah, and Hawaii have taken similar steps in the United States. Regulations under The Green Energy Act, 2009, now permit the installation of clotheslines on the ground or deck of the rear or side yards of residential properties.[17]

This may sound like a wonderful idea, but there is another position to consider. Many homeowners have purchased small residential lots in dense subdivisions in reliance upon the restrictive covenant that was supposed to prevent their neighbours from hanging their wash outside.

Questions to Consider

1. Do height, location, and size limitations effectively balance these competing interests?

Source: Ontario Office of the Premier, "Ontarians Get to Air Their Laundry," news release, April 18, 2008, http://news.ontario.ca/opo /en/2008/04/0ntarians-get-to-air-their-laundry.html

---

Other Interests

Oil, Gas, and Mineral Leases   It is beyond the scope of this chapter to review the many other interests less than estates.[18] One interest deserves special mention, however—the right to take minerals, oil, and gas from under the surface of land occupied by others. The right to remove materials is usually found in an agreement commonly called a lease. An oil, gas, or mineral lease bears little similarity to a true leasehold interest. Rather, it combines several contractual rights and interests in land into one agreement.

■ First, to the extent that the agreement permits the lessee to occupy a portion of the surface area of the land (often only a very small proportion of the area from which the oil, gas, or mineral is taken), it has elements of a true lease.

---

[17] O. Reg. 97/08.

[18] See, e.g., A.H. Oosterhoff and W.B. Rayner, *Anger & Honsberger's Law of Real Property*, 3rd ed. (Aurora, Ont.: Canada Law Book Co., 2006); B. Ziff, *Principles of Property Law*, 5th ed. (Toronto: Carswell, 2010).

- Second, to the extent that it grants the lessee the right to travel back and forth over the owner's land, lay pipes, and move equipment, it is similar to an easement.

- Third, to the extent that it permits the lessee to permanently remove materials extracted from the ground (previously the real property of the owner and now the personal property of the lessee), it is similar to a contract or sale.[19]

Obviously gas, oil, gold, or other minerals significantly increase the value of land, and owners tend to keep these rights for themselves when they sell the rest of the land. As a result, these rights are often withheld by a former owner or even the government in the original Crown grant. Extraction may still require the grant of a right of way or easement from the current landowner to gain access.[20] The law concerning mineral, oil, and gas leases has become highly specialized in recent years and heavily regulated by government. Such agreements are more than mere leases in that they form their own highly developed field of study. For more information on this topic, see the Companion Website.

Licences A licence given to another person by an owner to use his land is personal and not an interest in land at all. If B gives his friend, A, permission to hold a garage sale on his front lawn, A becomes a "licensee" on B's land during the garage sale; she is not a trespasser. However, she has no "right" to remain on B's land, and if he should revoke permission, something he may do at any time, A would have only a reasonable minimum time to remove her goods and herself from B's lawn. Suppose, however, that parties enter into a contractual licence.

Contractual licences between enterprises that have entered into long-term and stable relations can have substantial business value, and they do create rights binding between the original parties. They do not need to benefit any nearby land. Their relative simplicity, when contrasted with the formalities of creating an interest in land, has made licences a useful business tool.

In summary, Figure 21.1 illustrates the various types of interests in real property that we have just discussed.

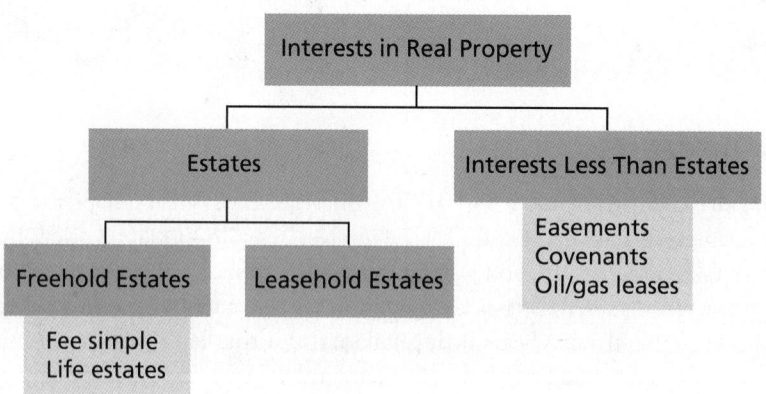

Figure 21.1   Interests in Real Property

---

[19] An ancient interest in land known as a profit à prendre that permitted the lessee to remove material extracted from the ground. See *Bank of Montreal v. Dynex Petroleum* [2002] 1 S.C.R. 146.

[20] For a discussion of historic relationship between mineral and surface rights, see *Forty Ninth Ventures Ltd. v. British Columbia*, 2005 BCCA 213.

The city of Brockville charges the Jazz Theatre Company a fee to use its municipal auditorium and grants it a licence to perform a play for one week. The city also provides box-office facilities and janitorial services. Revocation of permission to use the auditorium for that week would be a breach of contract. If the breach were sufficiently serious, Jazz Theatre might get an injunction preventing the city from removing its stage settings and players until the end of the week. An injunction—or any other remedy—would be a contractual right enforceable only against the city. If the city sold the auditorium before the week scheduled for the performances, Jazz Theatre would have no rights against the purchaser. Its only remedy would be for damages against the city as the breaching contractual party.

GOVERNMENT REGULATION OF LAND

Use and Development

Landowners are not free to do whatever they want with their land. All three levels of government (federal, provincial, and municipal) regulate land use or development. Originally, fire and health hazards were the focus of regulation; now, municipal zoning bylaws prescribe the use and type of buildings that may be erected in various districts of a municipality. Building regulations prescribe minimum standards of quality for materials and the size of all parts of structures erected within an area. Planning bylaws set out requirements for roadways and for water and sewage services, and often prescribe the amounts of land a land developer must give to the municipality for use as school and park areas.

Provincial legislation regulates land development. Land development historically involved reconfiguring large blocks of land into new smaller parcels. The most common example is farm property that is converted into a residential subdivision of separate building lots. Two key components are involved: changing the allowed use—for example, from agricultural to residential; and changing the size of the parcel—for example, subdividing a farm into city-sized lots. Provincial planning legislation limits the right of an owner to subdivide his property into smaller parcels without prior permission of the municipality. This allows a municipality to control the density of an urban centre.

Increasingly, land development is focusing on repurposing previously developed sites, such as taking existing commercially developed sites and adapting them to residential use (converting a factory into lofts, for example). Municipal approval is also required for change of use. When regulating use, government power is also not without limits.

The City of Kitchener's core neighbourhood had a variety of housing types ranging from heritage houses, high-rise condominiums, and apartment buildings to group homes, duplexes, seniors' residences, and public housing. The City estimated that 20 percent of neighbourhood residents were persons with disabilities or in receipt of social assistance. Residents regularly complained about unmaintained properties and criminal activity such as drug dealing and prostitution. The City believed that the "over-concentration" of "low income households" was an "unhealthy social environment" and passed a bylaw that required landlords to live in their buildings and banned all new facilities for the "targeted (low-income) population." In 2010, a tenants' advocacy group challenged the bylaw before the Ontario Municipal Board (OMB). The OMB found that the bylaw failed to consider the needs of persons with disabilities as required by the provincial Planning Act and the Charter of Rights and Freedoms. It appeared to be "people zoning" rather than "use zoning." The City was given 15 months to redraft the bylaw. Instead, the bylaw was withdrawn completely in 2011.[21]

---

[21] [2010] O.M.B.D. No. PL050611; Terry Pender, "City Kills Cedar Hill Bylaw," *Waterloo Region Record*, June 22, 2011, B1.

Another area of concern for redevelopment projects has been the protection of historical, architectural, and archeological buildings and sites, a concern reflected in provincial heritage statutes. This provincial legislation allows municipalities to designate sites for preservation and monitor any proposed changes to them.

Growing public concern about long-term environmental hazards has led to provincial and federal environmental assessment and protection legislation, discussed in Chapter 3. A proposed development requires an environmental impact assessment before development can proceed.

Federal legislation regulates land use in areas of federal jurisdiction such as airports, national parks, natural resources, military sites, and Indian lands. These matters often have interprovincial or international dimensions, and involve considerations beyond those of the local community. Some land development projects involve all three levels of government regulation, as the following recent conflict over an Aboriginal land claim illustrates.

CASE 21.2

The municipal government for Haldimand County gave all necessary approvals for a residential subdivision, known as Douglas Creek Estates, in Caledonia, Ontario. In July 1995, the developer registered a plan of subdivision and began selling lots. Also in 1995, Six Nations (an organization of 13 Indian Bands) sued the federal and provincial governments, claiming interest in and entitlement to Douglas Creek Estates (among other things), and warned the developer of the "dangers" associated with development. In February of 2006, Six Nations protesters took possession of the site. Occupation, protests, road blockages, and sometimes violent disruptions occurred. In March 2006, the protesters ignored a court-ordered injunction to leave the site. Negotiations between Six Nations, the Ontario government, and the federal government proceeded on an irregular basis. In June 2006, the Ontario government agreed to pay $15 million to purchase the land from the developer plus additional compensation for lost profit. As the new title holder of the land, the Ontario government withdrew objections to the Six Nations occupation, despite the disapproval of surrounding neighbours. To date, the land ownership dispute remains unresolved.[22] The province, the police, and the municipality faced a class action lawsuit filed by residents, businesses, and contractors displaced by the occupation. The class action was settled in July 2011 with the creation of a $20 million compensation fund.

Rights in the Matrimonial Home

dower a widow's right to a life interest in one-third of the real property held by her husband in fee simple before his death

For many centuries, a widow's principal security on the death of her husband was a common law right to **dower**—that is, a right to a life interest in one-third of the real property held by her husband in fee simple during their married life.

Dower has been abolished in most provinces[23] and replaced by family law legislation that still recognizes the special interest that a spouse has in the family home. The

<hr>

[22] *Henco Industries Limited v. Haudenosaunee Six Nations Confederacy Council*, (2006) O.R. (3d) 721; *CBC News In Depth*, "Caledonia Land Claim," CBC News, November 1, 2006, http://www.cbc.ca/news2/background/caledonia-landclaim/. See http://www.caledoniaclassaction.com; Province of Ontario, http://www.ontario.ca/government/six-nations-grand-river

[23] It was replaced by "homesteads" legislation, giving a surviving spouse a life interest in the entire family home. Manitoba and Saskatchewan retain Homesteads Acts: C.C.S.M., c. H80; S.S. 1989–90, c. H-5.1. Alberta retains a Dower Act (R.S.A. 2000, c. D-15), which grants a life interest in the matrimonial home to a surviving spouse, but the common law right to one-third of the deceased husband's property is abolished: Law of Property Act, R.S.A. 2000, c. L-7, s. 3.

legislation varies greatly from province to province, so attempting a summary is not useful.[24] Generally, statutory rights go much farther than the ancient right to dower and—most importantly—include the right to refuse consent to any change in the title to the family home or to its sale (a sale without consent is void).[25]

No transaction involving residential property should be entered into without taking into account the relevant matrimonial property legislation. This legislation complicates the use of the matrimonial home as collateral security for business loans or lines of credit.

Leasehold Estates

Provincial legislation exists in all provinces regulating the rules for landlords and tenants. Tenancies are regulated based on the nature of the use of the property: commercial or residential. Residential tenancy statutes often take the form of consumer protection legislation where rent increases are regulated, landlord remedies curtailed, and writing requirements softened. Commercial tenancy legislation is less protective and preserves many of the common law remedies available to landlords. This topic will be discussed in more detail in Chapter 22.

Condominiums

The condominium is a provincial legislative solution to a shortage of housing and recreational areas in large urban centres. The provinces passed legislation recognizing fee simple ownership of a **condominium unit** within a multiple-unit development, such as a high-rise apartment or row housing block, without an interest in the surface land or ground.[26] The legislation is not restricted to residential housing and also applies to commercial and industrial developments.

condominium unit a unit in a multiple-unit development that may be owned in fee simple

The Nature of Ownership in a Condominium
An owner of a unit owns a fee simple estate in that unit and also obtains an undivided part ownership, shared with other unit owners, of the shared areas of the development known as **common elements**. These include structures and areas external to the unit such as entrances, hallways, stairs, and elevators, and communal facilities such as laundries, recreation rooms, garages, swimming pools, and tennis courts. Each unit can be bought and sold, mortgaged, and passed to successors on death. It is separately assessed and taxed. Transfers do not affect the ownership of other units. A purchaser acquires a unit subject to several important conditions. In a multiple-unit building he must, like a tenant, allow entry to make necessary repairs to services; contribute to the cost of operation, upkeep, and, in some degree, to the restoration of the common property; and insure his own unit. In addition, he becomes a member of the **condominium corporation** responsible for management of the property as a whole, and he is subject to the rules and regulations governing the development.

common elements structures and areas external to a condominium unit, including communal facilities

condominium corporation a corporation—whose members are the condominium owners—that is responsible for managing the property as a whole

Responsibility for Maintaining Units
The unit owner is responsible for maintaining his unit. Therefore, the definition of the boundaries of a unit is very importance:

---

[24] For example, the definition of "spouse" is restricted to married couples in most provinces, but extends to cohabiting partners in British Columbia, Manitoba, and Saskatchewan. The Supreme Court of Canada held that a restriction to married couples does not offend against the Charter: Nova Scotia (*Attorney General v. Walsh* 2002, SCC 83; *Kerr v. Baranow* 2011 SCC 10.

[25] See e.g. Homesteads Act, C.C.S.M. s. H80, s. 4; Matrimonial Property Act, R.S.N.S. 1989, c. 275, s. 8; Family Law Act, R.S.O. 1990, c. F.34, s. 21.

[26] See, e.g., Strata Property Act, S.B.C. 1998, c. 43; Condominium Act, S.O. 1998, c. 19; R.S.N.S. 1989, c. 85.

does a unit owner's property extend beyond the surface of the walls of the rooms? If the drywall is knocked out of the wall, is the damage to the property in the unit or in the common elements? Is the unit owner responsible for repairs to plumbing behind the drywall, even if the plumbing served an adjoining unit and not his own? It may be a serious disadvantage to own much of the area beyond the surface of the inner walls. The definition of the unit is established by the developer during the initial stages of condominium development.

Maintenance and Management of a Condominium In a rental apartment building, a competent landlord manages the property and has necessary repairs and maintenance completed. In a condominium, after the last unit is sold, the developer turns over the management of the condominium corporation to the owners of the condominium units. Collectively they become responsible for managing and maintaining the condominium common elements in a good state of repair, and paying its bills. Usually, the individual owners do not want to run a large development, and they authorize the corporation to hire an expert such as a property management company to oversee the operation. Each unit owner pays a proportionate monthly amount toward the costs of maintenance and management known as common area expense; unpaid expenses may be registered as a lien against the owner's unit. Unit owners must remain concerned about the sound management of the condominium corporation on a continuing long-term basis. Most legislative schemes require a condominium to undertake periodic property reviews, schedule routine maintenance, and maintain a reserve fund to cover the cost of major projects and emergencies. Prospective buyers are entitled to receive a status certificate before buying that describes outstanding repair issues and the adequacy of the reserve fund, among other things.

Financing and Insurance A buyer must maintain fire and liability insurance on his unit in order to comply with mortgage requirements and the condominium rules. If something happens to the unit and/or the complex, the mortgage holders and insurers must consider the interests of the development as a whole, not just the specific unit owner. The most common method of dealing with the problem is through an "insurance trust." A trustee insures the entire building for the benefit of both the condominium corporation and every individual unit owner; each pays part of the premium proportionate to its interest.

There are both advantages and disadvantages to condominium ownership. For more information on this topic, see the Companion Website.

Cooperative Housing

An alternative to condominiums is cooperative housing. In a cooperative housing development, a member merely buys a share in the cooperative corporation, which entitles the shareholder to occupy one of the units in the development. A risk of this type of home ownership is that the whole cooperative venture may flounder because of bad management and insolvency. All members are affected equally by the failure and may lose their equity investment, even though they may personally have been honouring their obligations and paying the required contributions for taxes and upkeep. Financing a share in cooperative housing presents difficulties of its own. A member buys an equity share and has rights, similar to a leasehold interest, to occupy a unit. The method of borrowing money on the value of a share in a cooperative, combined with the right to occupy a unit, is more complicated than a straight loan by way of mortgage on a private residence.

A cooperative venture usually requires a high degree of commitment to a community project and more direct involvement in management than is typical of condominium ownership. A high level of involvement in the management of the cooperative is probably the best assurance of sound management and survival.

THE TRANSFER OF INTERESTS IN LAND

By a Sale or Gift

An interest in land may be transferred in any one of several ways. The most common way is by a voluntary transfer between living persons, in performance of a contract for the sale of land or, less commonly, as a gift. A grant of land contains a description of the grantor, the grantee, and the interest being transferred, and was originally signed and sealed by the grantor before a witness. Since the document was under seal, it is often called a **deed of conveyance**—frequently shortened to *deed*. A grant under the land titles system, used in an ever expanding number of jurisdictions across the country, is called a **transfer** and is effective without being made under seal. As we shall discuss later in this chapter, modern title conveyancing is handled electronically without seals or even signatures.

When the owner grants only part of his interest, the balance remains his. As noted earlier in this chapter under "Government Regulation of Land," some grants of only part of the land require prior approval of the municipality under planning control legislation. A transfer of an interest in land can have two results. First, if it is a transfer of the whole interest, then the interest passes unaltered to another person. Second, if it is a transfer of only part of an interest, then the interest is divided into two parts and there are two holders—the grantee with the interest he has obtained under the grant, and the grantor with the interest he has retained after splitting his initial interest.

On Death of the Owner   Interests in land are also transferred on the death of the owner, either by will or according to the rules of **intestate succession**. The owner may dispose of her property by will according to her wishes and the claims she feels she should satisfy.[27] If she dies intestate (without leaving a will), the interest passes according to statutory rules of inheritance to the holder's heir or heirs—that is, the interest passes automatically to the closest relatives. If, for example, a widow with two adult children holds a fee simple ownership in a condominium unit and dies without a will, the children will become

deed of conveyance   a document under seal that transfers an interest in land from the owner to another party

transfer   under the land titles system, the equivalent of a grant; not required to be made under seal

intestate succession   government rules that determine who gets the property of someone who dies without a will

---

[27] Subject to any rights of a surviving spouse, discussed above.

the co-owners of the fee simple. As noted earlier, if title is held in joint tenancy, the land will pass automatically to the surviving joint tenant.

By Compulsory Sale The holder of an interest in land may be compelled to transfer it against her will. A creditor may hold a mortgage or obtain judgment against her in court and eventually have the land sold in order to satisfy the debt, discussed under mortgage remedies in Chapter 23. A second type of compulsory transfer of land is expropriation. When a public body such as the federal government or a local school board requires land for its activities, it may proceed under statute to force the transfer of land to itself. It must, of course, pay compensation for taking the land, and if the parties cannot agree upon a price, the statute provides for arbitration or judicial proceedings to determine the price to be paid.

Adverse Possession

Just as we saw with easements of prescription, at common law the continuous exclusive use of land could create an interest in it. An unauthorized occupant of land could **extinguish the title** of an owner and gain the title for himself. This is known as **adverse possession** and it requires the following conditions:

- open, notorious, exclusive possession of the land[28]
- possession without the permission or consent of the owner[29]
- possession for the legislated **limitation period** for real property claims (for example, 10 years; longer against the Crown)[30]

Most Canadian jurisdictions using the land titles system of registration no longer allow a transfer of title by adverse possession.[31]

REGISTRATION OF INTERESTS IN LAND

First in Time

Establishing who owns the property and what other claims or interests non-owners may have is done through provincially regulated public registration systems that record all interests in land.[32] Owners must register their interests or the interests are not valid. The priority of each interest is determined based on the order of registration, with earlier registrations having priority over subsequent registrations. Therefore, a purchaser should not rely on a properly executed grant of title unless it is registered in the public system. The date on the grant does not establish ownership; the date and time of registration does. A public record of registrations on each parcel of land is available for review by anyone.

As already noted throughout this chapter, two different types of registration systems are employed throughout Canada: the registry system and the land titles system. Both systems

extinguish the title end the title of the owner and the owner's right to regain possession

adverse possession the exclusive possession of land by someone who openly uses it like an owner and ignores the claims of other persons including the owner

limitation period the time period within which a right of action must be pursued or it is lost forever

---

[28] See for example, *Shennan v. Szewczyk* 2010 ONCA 679 at para 18; *Teis v. Ancaster (Town)* (1997), 35 O.R. (3d) 216; *Leichner v. Canada Attorney General* (1996), 31 O.R. (3d) 700.

[29] *Nadherny v. 880474 Ontario Inc.*, [2010] O.J. No. 2263.

[30] See e.g. Real Property Limitations Act, R.S.O. 1990, c. L.15, s. 4 (10 years); Limitations of Actions Act, R.S.N.S. 1989, c. 258, s. 10 (20 years).

[31] See e.g. Limitation Act, R.S.B.C. 1996 c. 266, s. 12; Real Property Act, C.C.S.M. c. R-30, s. 61(2); Land Titles Act, R.S.O. 1990, c. L-5, s. 51. In Alberta, a claim based on adverse possession may be registered; Land Titles Act, R.S.A. 2000, c. L-4, s. 39. Unless it is registered, it is not binding upon a transferee of the land. In Nova Scotia, adverse possession claims are allowed provided they do not affect more than 20 percent of the area of the parcel: Land Registration Act, S.N.S. 2001, c. 6, s. 75.

[32] Subject to very few exceptions that will be noted later, such as adverse possession.

subscribe to the "first in time" concept, also known as the **priority of registration** rule.[33] This rule encourages a purchaser to register her grant immediately.

priority of registration priority of interests in real property is determined based on the order of registration in the public system

Registry System

The registry system is the older of the two systems and is being phased out in favour of the land titles system. This is because it is a labour-intensive system that places the responsibility for establishing good title on the users of the system or their real estate lawyers. Each transaction involving land requires an examination of the registered interests in order to establish the proper chain of ownership, identify any defects or other interests, and take corrective action. Each document must be examined to confirm that it meets the requirements to effectively deal with the interest. In the registry system, one cannot simply rely on the printed record or the fact of registration to confirm title; an evaluation of all documents registered in the title search period must be undertaken. Ownership may only be relied upon if a **chain of title** can be established throughout the search period. The specific length of the search period is usually set out in the legislation. Some registry systems limit the required search period to the proceeding 40 years, which can mean hundreds of registrations.[34]

chain of title the series of grants over the title search period that can be traced to the current owner (vendor)

ILLUSTRATION 21.4

In 2008, X is considering the purchase of Red Oaks from Y. The registry system registration record for Red Oaks shows the following:

Registration Number	Date of Registration	Type of Document	Amount	Parties (from)	Parties (to)
112345	Jan. 1, 1945	Grant/Transfer	$100	A	B
276654	Feb. 2, 1960	Grant/Transfer	$9000	M	N
325671	May 1, 1982	Grant/Transfer	$50 000	N	P
399871	May 1, 1992	Easement (South 2 metres)	$1	P	Hydro Commission
423567	June 1, 1999	Grant/Transfer	$150 000	P	Y

(a) There is a continuous chain of title to the present holder, Y. X need not worry about the transfer from A to B or any subsequent transfer by B. The fact that M conveyed the land to N more than 40 years ago and there was no subsequent difficulty with the title establishes a chain of title upon which X can rely.

(b) X should be concerned about the easement granted in 1992. It is inside the 40-year search period, and, therefore, the subsequent grant to Y is subject to this easement. X should examine the document to determine how it affects Red Oaks. Given that the grantee is a utility company, the easement is likely for the supply of electrical power. X must decide if he is willing to accept the title subject to the Hydro Commission's easement.

Searching the title to a real property under the registry system can be a laborious and sometimes hazardous task. An error in one of the documents that has gone undetected may later be discovered and disclose an outstanding interest, defeating the title of the current owner. If harm results through the negligence of a lawyer, he or she must compensate the client. Lawyers carry liability insurance to compensate clients in case such an error occurs. The registry system is being phased out in the last remaining jurisdictions of the Atlantic provinces, Manitoba, and Ontario.

searching the title to examine the title to a piece of land

---

[33] There are other variations between the systems that are discussed below.

[34] Registry Act, R.S.O. 1990, c. R-20, s. 112(1); Limitations of Actions Act, R.S.N.S. 1989, c. 258, s. 23.

Land Titles System

land titles system a system of land registration where the land titles office brings all outstanding interests in the land up-to-date and certifies them as being correct

certificate of title summary of registered interests in a property, showing the owner and any mortgages, easements, or other interests held by others, which may be relied upon by the public

The risks inherent in the registry system led to creation of the **land titles system**.[35] It began in the western provinces, and is now moving across the rest of Canada.[36] The distinctive feature of the system is that every document submitted for registration must be approved by the land titles office before it is recorded against title. Lawyers need not review individual documents to detect errors; the record of registration may be relied upon as a **certificate of title**. Section 23(2) of the British Columbia Land Titles Act specifically states that the certificate of title is conclusive evidence in any court that the person named in the certificate is the holder in fee simple of the property.[37] In effect, the government guarantees the accuracy of the title as shown on the record. There are variations from jurisdiction to jurisdiction in the methods of recording and in the type of guarantee given by the government. The great advantage of the system is that a purchaser need not search through 40 or more years of records to discover the state of the title. The land titles office produces a complete statement, valid to the moment the statement is issued. If errors occur, land titles systems have assurance funds available to compensate injured parties. A land titles system does not completely eliminate the need to search title—exceptions to the certificate must be separately searched—but it drastically reduces the work involved.

The reason the land titles system does away with adverse possession and prescriptive easements is to ensure that only registered documents can affect the state of the title.[38] The older registry system makes no attempt to do this: Its purpose is simply to provide an inventory of title documents and let the searcher assess their validity. Of course, "off title" searches must still be completed for such things as zoning compliance, utility arrears, and environmental regulation.

Electronic Registration

The shift from registry to land titles systems has been expedited by the automation of land registration. Historically, paper documents were created in duplicate and one original copy was maintained in the system. In the registry system (unlike the land titles system), access to original documents is essential since users must assess the validity of the documents themselves. Storage issues led to standardization of forms for both registry and land titles, microfilming of documents, and less use of formalities such as seals and witnesses.[39] Now all provinces are moving to electronic systems with three key components:

- electronic record keeping—a computerized data bank of registered interests in land
- electronic search capabilities—the ability to electronically search existing registrations using assigned "property identifier numbers" (called PINs or PIDs)
- electronic registration of documents—paperless registration of interests completed online[40]

As part of the automation process, most registry lands are being converted to the land titles system. Properties are mapped and issued an identification number. In New

---

[35] The system was also adopted in some states of the United States and is now in use in most of England.

[36] British Columbia, Alberta, and Saskatchewan; conversion is underway in Ontario, New Brunswick, Nova Scotia, and Manitoba. As well, the old paper system is rapidly being converted to an electronic title registry.

[37] In British Columbia, the Land Titles Act, R.S.B.C. (1996) c. 250, s. 23(2).

[38] See e.g. the British Columbia Land Titles Act, *ibid.*, s. 24, or the Ontario Land Titles Act, R.S.O. 1990, c. L.5, s. 51.

[39] The Ontario Land Registration Reform Act abolished the need for seals or witnesses in the registry system so that the same form of transfer could be used in both registry and land titles and so that documents would be shorter to microfilm.

[40] See British Columbia Land Titles Act, *supra*, n. 38; Ontario Land Registration Reform Act, R.S.O. 1990, c. L.4 (applies to both registry and land titles systems); Land Registration Act, S.N.S. 2001, c. 6.

Brunswick, any sale or new mortgaging of a property requires that it first be converted into the land titles system. Subdivision of lots triggers immediate conversion in Nova Scotia.

There are advantages and disadvantages to electronic registration systems. The electronic system is far more accessible. Searches may be completed online and there is no longer a need to physically travel to the local registry or land titles office in order to complete a title search. Similarly, electronic systems can handle a much higher volume of searches and registrations with virtually no physical storage requirements. However, the electronic system faces new problems such as capacity, viruses, and crashes. One of the most serious threats is fraud. The elimination of signatures, witnesses, and paper, together with the wide access to the electronic system, has led to increased **title fraud**—the fraudulent transfer or mortgaging of land by a non-owner. This has led some provinces to restrict access to electronic registration.

title fraud fraudulent transfer or mortgaging of land by a non-owner

---

Ethical Issue **Real Estate Fraud Prevention**

Part of the Ontario Real Estate Fraud Prevention Plan involves restricting access to electronic registration. In order to register any document, one must be an account holder. Account applications are screened on the following criteria:

- identity of applicant—is the applicant entitled to access?
- financial resources—does the applicant have resources to compensate victims of fraud?
- good character/accountability—does the applicant have integrity?

Registrations for the transfer (grant) of title are further restricted to lawyers only, and each lawyer (one acting for the vendor and one for the purchaser) must confirm completeness of the transfer registration. The rationale for these restrictions is that lawyers are governed by a self-regulating profession with discipline and investigatory powers. Requiring the consent of two lawyers on opposing sides of the transaction will further reduce the likelihood that fraud will go undetected. Lawyers are subject to "know your client" directives that require verification of client identity prior to registrations. The search-only accounts remain widely available to the public.

Questions to Consider

1. Consider the role of self-regulating law societies in inspiring integrity in the legal profession.

2. Does restricting access to electronic registration undermine the goals of the automated system generally?

Source: Ontario Ministry of Government and Consumer Services, "New Access Requirements for ELRS; Registration Requirements for Transfers and Powers of Attorney," Bulletin No. 2009-01, ServiceOntario, January 8, 2009, http://files.ontariogovernment.ca/bulletin_2009-01_-_access_requirements_for_electronic_land_registration.pdf

---

Claims That Are Not Registered on Title

It is possible for some unregistered claims or interests to affect a landowner's title in both the registry and land titles systems. Therefore, in addition to a title search, potential purchasers often undertake "off title" searches or investigations.

Adverse Possession In jurisdictions where the registry system is still in use, a purchaser cannot rely solely on the records because the vendor's title may have been extinguished by adverse possession. Adverse possession is also still possible in some land titles systems: for example, adverse possession claims of less than 20 percent of the parcel of land are allowed in the Nova Scotia land titles system.[41]

Small encroachments may not be detectable by a purchaser. A **survey** of the real property is one way to uncover problems. It is a detailed drawing or map of the real property showing all the boundaries of the land and the location of all buildings, fixtures, encroachments, or overhangs. A survey can be used to

survey detailed drawing or map of the real property showing all the boundaries of the land and the location of all fixtures, encroachments, or overhangs

- confirm that the buildings are actually on the land being purchased (something the registration system does not confirm),
- confirm that the location of all buildings complies with the municipal zoning bylaws,

---

[41] Land Registration Act, S.N.S. 2001, c. 6, s. 75.

- identify any possible claims for adverse possession, and
- locate fences, driveways, etc., in relation to the boundaries of the property.

Arrears of Taxes   Two other claims against lands not ordinarily registered under either the registry or the land titles system are arrears of municipal tax on the land and, in some provinces, arrears of tax against corporations accruing while they hold the land. Tax arrears attach to the real property as if they had been registered. If any of these claims appear after a purchaser has paid the vendor, the purchaser must pay them in order to protect her interest in the land. A prospective purchaser should request a tax certificate from the municipality showing any taxes outstanding, and evidence from the provincial government of any arrears of corporation taxes. This information cannot be obtained from the registry or land titles office, but only from the government concerned.

Creditors' Claims   A claim against land may arise when the vendor is a judgment debtor at the time of the sale—that is, he has been sued successfully by a creditor who has filed its judgment with the sheriff for the county or district. If a claim of this kind is outstanding (unpaid) at the time the land is sold, the judgment creditor may still require the sheriff to levy execution against the land—that is, seize and hold a sale of the land in order to recover the amount due under the judgment. The purchaser will then have to pay the debt to save the land. Accordingly, a purchaser should also make a search for executions in the sheriff's office to ensure that there are none before completing the sale. Various other claims against a vendor, such as debts owed to public bodies for fines or taxes, may be registered with the sheriff's office, according to each province's own rules. In order to facilitate a search for these claims, the sheriff's office and the land registry office are often in the same building, or special facilities are provided in the registry office to search the execution records. These records may also be searched electronically.

Tenant in Possession   Another hazard to a purchaser may be created by a tenant in possession of the land. In most jurisdictions, short-term leases—usually for three years or less—need not be registered or even be in writing and are valid against purchasers who buy the interest of the landlord. A purchaser must inspect the property to see whether there are any tenants, and if there are, she should obtain an acknowledgment from them of the type of tenancy they claim to hold.

Title Insurance

The transfer of an interest in land is a complex transaction requiring careful examination of the registry or land titles records, the municipal and provincial bylaws and regulations, the local sheriff's office records, and an inspection of the land itself. These complicated search requirements, as well as the risk of title fraud in electronic registration, have increased the popularity of **title insurance**. Title insurance allows a potential purchaser or lender to buy insurance covering defects in the title to the real property. Though many variations exist, basic title insurance usually covers

- title (fee simple estate) in the subject land;
- a defect, charge, lien, or other interest (discoverable in the public record);
- lack of access to the property;
- costs of defending the title to the property.

Additional coverage is available for such things as off-title risks, known defects in title, and survey-related issues. Title insurance takes away the need to prove negligence against a real estate lawyer for a subsequently discovered defect in title. However, it does not eliminate the need for a lawyer during a real estate deal; lawyers play a pivotal role in negotiating coverage, exclusions, and premiums associated with title insurance. In some

title insurance   a policy of insurance that compensates the policy holder for defects in a title provinces, lawyers are specifically required to explain and offer title insurance to prospective purchasers.[42]

Title Insurance

Although it is a relatively recent phenomenon in Canada, title insurance has been considered almost essential in the United States for decades. One reason for this is the fact that U.S. lawyers are not required to carry mandatory public liability insurance. Therefore, even proven claims of negligence may go unsatisfied. In addition, state-run land registration systems vary widely across the United States. Most are registry-style systems lacking any certification of title from the government, and some even record interests by name of grantor and grantee rather than property description. Recording by name rather than property description makes it difficult to detect a fraudulent conveyance. The very active U.S. secondary mortgage market has also contributed to the popularity of title insurance. A lender's title insurance policy makes the mortgage more saleable, and, in fact, many lenders make title insurance a condition of granting the mortgage.

Criticism of the American $15 billion secondary mortgage industry focuses on the high profit margin and questionable sales tactics of the title insurance industry. In 2003, only 4 percent of the total premiums collected were paid out as compensation.[43] Usually, real estate agents or mortgage brokers, rather than the purchaser, select the title insurance company, and the industry markets to these groups using incentives such as free vacations.[44] Iowa prohibits private-sector title insurance and offers a cheaper state-run program.

Question to Consider

1. What lessons should Canada learn from the American experience?

Sources: Joyce Dickey Palomar, "Title Insurance Companies' Liability for Failure to Search Title and Disclose Record Title" (1987) 20 *Creighton L. Re.* 455; Deborah J. Cook, "Iowa's Prohibition of Title Insurance—Leadership or Folly" (1983–84) 33 *Drake L. Rev.* 883.

Strategies to Manage the Legal Risks

The value of land is affected by the marketability of its title. Therefore, agreements to purchase land should allow a sufficient amount of time prior to completion to obtain a survey, investigate the state of the title, and confirm that the intended use of the land is legal. Potential purchasers should take advantage of four key sources of information (even before offering to buy the property) to reduce the risks of receiving defective title or paying too much for the property:

- Title Registry—both registry and land titles systems offer publicly searchable databases that will reveal the number of mortgages currently on the property and the price paid by the current owner.

- Municipal Zoning Files—municipalities maintain zoning information on the subject property and can confirm allowed uses, issuance of building permits, and completion of inspections. The file may even contain a copy of an existing survey. Zoning may change at any time, so checking the official plan will give an idea of the municipality's long-term goals for the neighbourhood and may give early warning of a potential zone change.

- Survey—this drawing is the only way to confirm the exact physical location of buildings and fences on the property, and since most of us value the building more than the land, it is important to confirm that the house is actually on the lot. A survey is expensive to obtain so the agreement of purchase and sale should address the obligation to supply a survey.

---

[42] Law Society of Upper Canada, Rules of Professional Conduct, Rules 2.02(10), 5.01.

[43] Les Christie, "Title Insurance: Getting Ripped Off?" CNNMoney.com, January 11, 2006, http://money.cnn.com/2006/01/11/real_estate/title_insurance_exposed/index.htm.

[44] *Ibid.*

- Title Insurance—the existence of an insurance policy that will pay out if title defects are later discovered is a valuable safety net, particularly for land in older neighbourhoods with complicated title histories. Lenders often require it in any event. However, title insurance does not eliminate the need for a lawyer on the transaction.

When sharing land ownership for business purposes, tenancy in common is the usual arrangement. Most often, joint tenancy is reserved for personal relationships where the intention is to gift the property to the co-owner on death. Most businesses would incorporate a company to own the land and then divide the shares in the company to reflect the percentage ownership. Death is not an issue for corporations. Finally, if considering a condominium, review the creating documentation carefully to determine the parameters of the unit and the formula for calculation of the common expenses. These expenses vary depending upon the condominium and may have a significant impact on the cost of maintaining the unit.

QUESTIONS FOR REVIEW

1. Define the terms "title," "real," "land," "property," and "estate."
2. What factors have encouraged the growth of public regulation of land use?
3. Describe the two main classifications of interests in land. Distinguish between freehold and leasehold estates.
4. How does the existence of a life estate make selling land difficult?
5. Describe the nature of the interest that a spouse has in the family home. How did this interest evolve?
6. In what ways may title to land be acquired?
7. What are the principal differences between joint tenancy and tenancy in common?
8. Describe the two elements of ownership in a condominium and how they affect responsibility for maintenance.
9. What is the special nature of insurance for a high-rise condominium building?
10. In cooperative housing, who owns the property?
11. What are the reasons for limitation periods generally? How do they apply to land?
12. Distinguish between the circumstances under which an easement may be obtained by prescription and a title may be extinguished by adverse possession.
13. Describe the three typical characteristics of oil, gas, and mineral leases.
14. Distinguish between a restrictive covenant in a grant, a building-scheme covenant, and a zoning bylaw.
15. For decades, each winter Timson has openly entered the fields of an uninhabited farm adjoining his home and cross-country skied several times a week. He knows the Abel family that used to farm there, but they have moved to a town 25 kilometres away. The Abels have just sold the farm to Belsen, and he has erected a sign at the gate, "No Trespassing." Does Timson have a right to continue his cross-country skiing?
16. What is expropriation and how does it take place?
17. What is the main difference between the registry system of registration and the land titles system?
18. How is electronic registration connected to the expansion of the land titles system?
19. What must a prospective purchaser of land do to ensure that the vendor has the right to transfer the property clear of any claims? Does the purchase of title insurance change this answer?
20. What is the purpose of a survey?

CASES AND PROBLEMS

1. Continuing Scenario

   Ashley's Restaurant has been in leased premises since it opened and there are things she wants to change the next time she renegotiates her leasehold interest with the landlord. Her issues are as follows:

   (i) The lease prohibits any lit or neon sign that shows in the dark. Ashley would like this term removed. The landlord says that he cannot change this as this was a covenant included in his grant from the developer in order to fit in with the very residential surroundings of the neighbourhood.

   (ii) Ashley would like an outdoor patio area for the summer months on the sidewalk in front of the restaurant. The landlord will not agree to this because he thinks the City won't like it.

   (iii) In the current lease, Ashley pays the landlord for tax bills associated with her unit. She would rather pay these directly to the City. The landlord does not want to let her do this.

   What are the legal reasons why the landlord is resisting each of Ashley's requests? The landlord is considering selling the complex; should Ashley be worried about a new owner evicting her business?

2. Rumford College was established in the centre of the city in the late 19th century when the city was still small. It was granted 20 acres at the time—about nine hectares—and occupied two hectares with its buildings and lawns, expanding to about four hectares over the years. As the city grew, the remaining five hectares became extremely valuable, and Rumford ultimately agreed to sell certain portions for commercial development. It sold one hectare to each of three developers, including a restrictive covenant with each grant limiting the height of any buildings to 20 metres so as to protect the view of Rumford's college towers. Two of the three developers erected buildings complying with the restriction. The third, Townhouse Inc., kept the land vacant.

   Savvy Developers Inc. wished to erect a 25-storey luxury apartment building in the area to a height about five times more than the 20-metre limit. In addition to paying market value to Rumford for one-half hectare of land, it offered to donate $500 000 to the college's endowment fund if it would forgo the restrictive covenant to allow the construction of the apartment building. Rumford agreed and sold the land. When Townhouse learned about the deal with Savvy, it resold its hectare to Upper Developments Ltd., deliberately omitting the restrictive covenant from the grant.

   Upper Developments then sought a declaration from the court that the restrictive covenant no longer applied because of the concession made to Savvy. How do you think this dispute should be resolved by the court?

3. Peter Green owned and operated Green's General Hardware as well as the lands and buildings where he carried on business. His younger brother John worked for him as manager, as did his daughter, Susan. Peter died, leaving a will in which he gave the business and real property to John for life, with the remainder to Susan at John's death. John and Susan could not agree on how to run the business. John wanted to push sales and expansion as quickly as possible; Susan feared that such action would make the business unstable—she preferred to build more slowly, consolidating the gains of the business. The dispute became heated, and John fired Susan. Within a few years the business was in serious financial difficulty. John had allowed several buildings, including a warehouse, to fall into disrepair. Susan sought by court action to force John to keep the buildings in good repair. Should she succeed? Why?

   John died and left a will giving his whole estate including the business and buildings to his wife. Who is entitled to the business and why?

4. Ferrand owned a summer cottage near Fredericton, New Brunswick. He sold it and delivered a grant to Simpson in exchange for $35 000 cash on June 10. On June 11, Simpson received a telephone call to return home to Newfoundland where her mother was seriously ill. She left without registering her grant to the cottage. When Ferrand learned that Simpson had left the area, he called an acquaintance, Entwistle, and asked him whether he was interested in buying the cottage at a bargain price of $26 000. Entwistle had offered Ferrand that amount several months before and Ferrand had refused. Entwistle eagerly accepted the offer on June 20 and paid Ferrand. On the same day, Entwistle received a

grant to the cottage and registered it without knowledge of its prior sale to Simpson. Ferrand then absconded with the money from both sales.

Several weeks later, Simpson returned to find Entwistle occupying the cottage. When Entwistle refused to move, Simpson brought an action to have Entwistle put out and herself declared the owner.

The Registry Act, R.S.N.B. 1973, c. R-6, contains the following provision:

> 19. All instruments may be registered in the registry office for the county where the lands lie, and if not so registered, shall . . . be deemed fraudulent and void against subsequent purchasers for valuable consideration whose conveyances are previously registered.

Will Simpson succeed in her action? Would the result be different if Entwistle had heard that Simpson had purchased the cottage before he paid Ferrand the $26 000? Give reasons.

5. Don Wellman owned his own home, subject to a mortgage, when he married Victoria Selva. The two lived in the house for 20 years. Since Victoria earned a higher salary than Don, she made most of the payments on the house mortgage and also financed various improvements as well as an addition to the house. They had two children. Don suffered from severe depression, and as he aged he became violent during arguments with Victoria. One day, during a fit of rage, he killed her and was convicted of manslaughter and sentenced to prison.

Her estate sued Don, claiming a transfer of one-half the value of the house for the benefit of her heirs, including the two children. Give your opinion of the arguments that might be made for both sides and whether the action would succeed.

6. For over 30 years Montgomery owned two farms—Green Gables, on which he lived, and Wildwood. The two were separated by a farm owned by Cavendish. Montgomery continually used a road across the Cavendish farm to go to and from Green Gables and Wildwood. The access to the road was through a gate on the boundary of the Cavendish property. During most of these years Montgomery gave Cavendish a large turkey for New Year's, presumably as a gesture of goodwill and appreciation for the use of the road.

Three years ago, Montgomery sold Wildwood to Radoja. Radoja made relatively little use of the road over the Cavendish property (going across twice yearly to visit Montgomery with mortgage payments) until last year, when she also bought Green Gables. The old road then became valuable to Radoja as the most convenient access between her two properties. In the meantime, however, the Cavendish family had extended their lawn across the roadway and Radoja's suddenly increased use of the road led to a dispute about her rights.

Cavendish sought a court injunction to restrain Radoja's use of the alleged right-of-way. Indicate, with reasons, whether the court will grant the injunction.

Additional Resources for Chapter 21 on the Companion Website

(www.pearsoncanada.ca/smyth)

In addition to pre- and post-tests, mini-cases, and application exercises, the Companion Website includes the following province-specific resources for Chapter 21:

- **Alberta:** Builders' Liens; Land Assembly Project Area Act; Alberta Land Stewardship Act; Land Titles System; Spousal Interests in Land (Dower Rights); Surface Rights Amendment Act; Title Insurance
- **Atlantic Provinces:** Condominium Legislation; Expropriation; Title Insurance
- **British Columbia:** Adverse Possession and Prescriptive Easements; Builders' Liens; Condominium; Conveyance of Land; Expropriation; Fixtures; Fraudulent Transfer of Property; Land Title and Survey Authority; Partition of Property; Power of Attorney; Property Taxes; Riparian Rights; Strata Title; Trespass to Land
- **Manitoba/Saskatchewan:** Condominiums; Conservation Easements; Registry System (in Manitoba) and the Land Titles System
- **Ontario:** Adverse Possession; Condominiums; Dower—Family Law Legislation; Electronic Registration; Land Registration Reform; Land Titles; Matrimonial Homes; Real Estate Fraud; Registry Systems; Reserve Funds; Restrictive Covenants; Title Insurance

Chapter 22

Landlord and Tenant

There are many reasons why someone leases real property, whether in the form of vacant land, buildings and surrounding land, or just space within a building. The premises may be used for residential, recreational, and social or business purposes.

In this chapter we examine such questions as:

■ What is the nature of the landlord-and-tenant relationship?

■ What classes of tenancies may be created?

■ What are the typical covenants put into leases?

■ How are tenancies terminated and renewed?

■ What are "fixtures," and why are they important?

■ What are the consequences of a landlord transferring his or her interest?

■ What are "leasebacks," and how are they used?

■ Why are residential tenancies treated in a special way?

THE NATURE OF THE RELATIONSHIP

Definition of a Tenancy

term an interest in land for a definite period of time

A leasehold interest is created when a landlord (lessor) grants, to a tenant (lessee), exclusive possession of land for a fixed term. A **term** is the definite period of time for which the interest lasts. The landlord divides his interest in the land between himself and the tenant by giving an interest to the tenant for a limited time and retaining the reversion. At the end of the term, the tenant must give up the land. The right to possession reverts to the landlord. The word lease is a short form for the creation of the leasehold interest and also refers to the agreement or contract between landlord and tenant creating the leasehold.

A leasehold interest is an estate in land.[1] When parties create a leasehold, certain rights and duties are automatically given to both the landlord and the tenant. The requirements of land law are strict and, if they are not met, no estate in the land is created—the usual rights and duties between landlord and tenant do not arise. The consequences of failing to create a lease may be serious for either party but especially for a would-be tenant:

- He may be evicted by the owner at once.
- He has no right himself to evict strangers.
- In the case of residential tenants, he is not covered by protective legislation.

The essential requirements for the creation of a leasehold are, first, that the tenant must obtain the right to exclusive possession, and second, that the tenancy must be for a definite or ascertainable period of time. Depending upon the length of the term of the lease (and the jurisdiction), the lease may have to be in writing.

The rules applicable to leasehold interests are found in the common law on real property interests, statutes passed by government, and the specific contractual covenants in the lease. Rules vary depending upon the proposed use of the property. All provinces designate **residential tenancies** as a separate class of tenancy and offer tenants special protection in residential landlord and tenant legislation.[2] They do so in order to recognize the special importance of basic shelter. The special statutory provisions applicable to residential tenancies are discussed in the final section of this chapter. Most of this chapter applies to **commercial tenancies** only, and separate legislation is applicable to this type of leasehold interest.[3] Do not assume the rules are the same for residential and commercial tenancies.

residential tenancies a lease of premises used as living accommodation

commercial tenancies a lease of premises used for a business or non-residential purpose

Exclusive Possession

Exclusive possession is the difference between estates in land and lesser interests in land. It gives control over the land rather than a right merely to use the land in common with others. A person who has a right to use land in common with others may be merely a licensee. A licensee enters upon land with the consent of the owner, as, for example, when he is allowed to go fishing in a farmer's stream. He is on the land lawfully, not as a trespasser, but he has no interest in the land. He does not have the right to exclude others from the land or to object to the activities of others.

A tenant's right to exclusive possession gives him far greater power than a licensee. He may keep anyone off the land, and his landlord has no right to evict him from the land until the term ends. A tenant may prevent even the landlord from entering the land unless the lease gives the landlord a right to enter for a specific purpose, such as to view the state of repair

---

[1] Estates in time were considered in Chapter 21.

[2] See e.g. Residential Tenancy Act, S.B.C. 2002, c. 78; Residential Tenancies Act, 2006, S.O. 2006, c. 17.

[3] See e.g. Commercial Tenancies Act, R.S.O. 1990, c. L.7; Commercial Tenancy Act, R.S.B.C. 1996, c. 57.

of the property and to make repairs. The right to exclusive possession of land gives a tenant the ability to acquire other lesser rights—a tenant may acquire an easement over adjoining land for the duration of his tenancy in the same manner as the holder of a fee simple.

There have been numerous cases about the meaning of exclusive possession. The main issue is whether a person is considered to have exclusive possession if, under the terms of the lease, others are given limited rights to use or have access over the land. Generally, it is not wise for a business to enter into a lease that grants a right of use to a third person or to the landlord, except (as already noted) for the limited purpose of inspecting the premises and making repairs.

Definite or Ascertainable Period

A lease must begin on a fixed date, and it must end on a fixed or ascertainable date. The final date need not be stated if the period itself is definite: A lease that begins in March of a certain year to run for a week, a month, a year, five years, or 500 years is a valid leasehold interest because the date of expiry can always be worked out accurately. Long leases—for 99 years, or even for 999 years—were fairly common in England but are rarely found in Canada, although terms of 25 to 50 years are not uncommon in the case of large commercial developments (see the discussion of leasebacks later in this chapter).

If the parties attempt to create a term for an uncertain period, the term is void and no leasehold interest is created. A lease "for as long as the tenant holds a Tim Hortons franchise" or "until the tenant becomes insolvent" is void. However, parties who wish to have such a lease can accomplish their purpose through conditions subsequent or options to terminate. The requirement of certainty is satisfied if a lease ends at the latest upon a certain date, but may be brought to an end at an earlier date upon the happening of a particular event. A lease from A to B for 10 years that may be terminated earlier "should B lose its Tim Hortons franchise" is a valid lease condition.[4]

CLASSES OF TENANCIES

Term Certain

A **term certain** is a tenancy that expires on a specific day; the term ends without any further act by either the landlord or the tenant. A lease of a restaurant at a summer resort "from May 24 to September 15" of a particular year and a long-term lease of a cold storage plant "from March 1, 2015, to February 28, 2025" are examples of typical commercial leases for a term certain. The tenant is expected to vacate before the end of the last day of the tenancy unless he has made new arrangements with the landlord. If he stays on without making any arrangements, he becomes an **overholding tenant**, liable for the payment of rent, but he may be evicted by the landlord. If, however, the landlord accepts further rent without protesting, a new tenancy may be created, as explained below.

term certain a tenancy that expires on a specific day

overholding tenant a tenant who remains on the premises without a new agreement with the landlord after the term of the lease expires

Periodic Tenancy

A **periodic tenancy** is a leasehold interest that renews itself automatically on the last day of the term for a further term of the same duration, unless either the landlord or the tenant serves notice to bring the tenancy to an end. A periodic tenancy may be created by a formal agreement, but in Canada it arises more often in an informal way when a tenant moves into possession and pays an agreed rent to the landlord at regular

periodic tenancy a leasehold interest that renews itself automatically on the last day of the term for a further term of the same duration

---

[4] Bankruptcy law would void a termination clause triggered by bankruptcy; see s. 84.2(2)(5) of the Bankruptcy and Insolvency Act R.S.C. 1985, c. B-3, and the discussion in Chapter 29. It is a trustee's right to assume the tenancy is preserved by provincial law; see e.g. Landlord's Rights on Bankruptcy Act, R.S.A. 2000, c. L-5, ss. 1, 5.

intervals as agreed between them, either in writing or orally. If, for example, a business pays rent on the first day of each month, the tenancy renews itself for another month without further agreement between the parties. A periodic tenancy also comes into existence when a tenant remains in possession after the tenancy for a term certain has expired, and pays further rent to the landlord. The most common periodic tenancies are weekly, monthly, and yearly. The yearly tenancy is often called a **tenancy from year to year**.

The difference between a term certain and a periodic tenancy is this: a term certain ends automatically unless the parties make an arrangement to continue it; a periodic tenancy renews automatically unless either of the parties serves notice to end it. The requirements of notice are below, under "Termination and Renewal of a Tenancy."

tenancy from year to year a periodic tenancy that renews itself yearly

Tenancy at Will

A tenancy at will is not a true leasehold interest because it does not last for a definite period, nor does the tenant have any right to exclude the landlord and remain on the premises. The tenant is there merely at the landlord's will, and the landlord may demand possession at any time without notice. The tenant does, however, have a reasonable time to gather up possessions and leave.

On the other hand, a tenant at will is under no obligation to remain in possession and pay rent—he may vacate possession at any time without notice. Such a tenancy may exist when the owner of real property allows a prospective purchaser to occupy the premises pending the conveyance of the title to the purchaser, or when a landlord permits a tenant to remain on a day-to-day basis pending the wrecking of the building to make way for new construction. A tenancy at will may be gratuitous, or the landlord may exact a payment without turning the arrangement into a leasehold.

Tenancy at Sufferance

A tenancy at sufferance is not a true tenancy either. The typical example is that of an overholding tenant who entered into possession rightfully under a lease but now stays in possession wrongfully after the term has expired. Since he came into possession lawfully, he is not treated as a trespasser unless the landlord orders him to leave and he refuses. (Ordinarily, a **trespasser** is one who enters without consent or lawful right on the lands of another or who, having entered lawfully, refuses to leave when ordered to do so by the owner.) We should contrast the position of a tenant at sufferance with that of a tenant at will. Although a tenant at will has no estate in the land and can be put out by the landlord, he is nonetheless there lawfully, by agreement. A tenant at sufferance also initially entered the premises lawfully, but has no agreement with the landlord: his occupation of the land is merely tolerated by the landlord until the landlord acts to put the occupier out.[5]

trespasser one who enters without consent or lawful right on the lands of another or who, having entered lawfully, refuses to leave when ordered to do so by the owner

COVENANTS

To Pay Rent

The **covenant** to pay rent is the consideration given for receiving the leasehold interest. Often leases describe the total rent to be paid during the whole term of the lease, and then set out how this sum is to be paid. For example, the tenant may promise to pay the sum of $120 000 to lease a suite of offices for five years, to be paid in 60 monthly installments of $2000 due on the first day of each month.

covenant a term, clause, or promise contained in a contract or lease

---

[5] *Gari Holdings Ltd. v. Lanham Credit Union* (2005), D.L.R. (4th) 74 at para. 37 (Sask. C.A.).

The promise to pay rent is unconditional and must be performed despite misconduct by the landlord. Only an act of the landlord that amounts to an eviction of the tenant discharges the obligation of the tenant to pay rent.[6] If the leased premises are destroyed, in the absence of a specific term in the lease dealing with the problem, the tenant is still liable for the rent. He has purchased a leasehold interest consisting of a certain geographically defined area, and must pay for it whether or not the building and amenities continue to exist for the full term. Sometimes, the doctrine of frustration applies to commercial lease-holds.[7] One example involves leasehold interests above the ground floor in a multi-storey building. If a 10-storey building burns down, the landlord cannot insist that a tenant on the ninth floor continue to be liable for rent.[8] For more information on this topic, see the Companion Website.

When a tenant leases only a portion of the landlord's building, the landlord usually retains control over heating, repairs, and maintenance. In these circumstances, it is common to state in the lease that liability to pay rent shall be suspended if the leased premises are substantially destroyed by fire or other cause, and not by the tenant's own negligence. Unless it is expressly stated in the lease, the tenant remains liable for the rent—subject to our discussion above concerning leases of premises above the ground floor.

A tenant's covenant to pay rent is independent of any express promise by the landlord to make repairs to the property, and the tenant is not excused from paying rent on the grounds that the landlord has not performed her part of the bargain. A tenant is not, however, liable for further rent when the acts of the landlord amount to an eviction.

The terms of the covenant to pay rent are binding on both parties. During the term, the landlord cannot increase the rent unless express provision has been made, as in the case where the parties agree that the landlord may increase the rent by an amount equal to any increase in property taxes. If the landlord wishes to increase the rent, she cannot do so until the term expires. She may, of course, bargain for an increase in any subsequent lease.

Assignment and Subletting

Freedom to Assign   A tenant may wish to assign the balance of the term of a tenancy before it expires. For example, the tenant's business may have become so successful that he requires larger premises, or he may have received an offer to sell the business as a going concern provided he assigns the balance of the lease to the purchaser so that the business may continue at the same location. A tenant, as owner of a leasehold interest, has (subject to the terms of the lease) the right to assign it. A tenant does not, however, terminate his contractual obligations to the landlord by assigning: the landlord may still hold him accountable for performance of those obligations if, after the assignment, the assignee does not perform them or goes bankrupt.[9] For this reason, a tenant should make it a term of the assignment of the tenancy that the assignee shall carry out all the tenant's covenants in the lease and indemnify him against any loss caused by the assignee's default.

---

[6] *Cross v. Piggott*, [1922] 2 W.W.R. 662; *Northern Cartage Ltd.v. Motorway (1980) Ltd.*, [1999] M.J. No. 323 at para. 64.

[7] *National Carriers v. Panalpina (Northern) Ltd.*, [1981] A.C. 675. *Canadian Western Bank v. 702348 Alberta Ltd.*, [2009] A.J. No. 481 at para. 55 (citing *Great Lakes Bick and Stone Ltd. v. Vanderlinder*, [1993] O.J. No. 2763 at para 18), aff'd [2010] A.J. No. 784 (Alta C.A.); Commercial Tenancy Act, R.S.B.C. 1996, c. 57, s. 30.

[8] C. Bentley, J. McNair, and M. Butkus, eds., *Williams and Rhodes: Canadian Law of Landlord and Tenant*, 6th ed. (Toronto: Carswell, 1988) at 6–41.

[9] *Crystalline Investments Ltd. v. Domgroup Ltd.*, [2004] S.C.J. No. 3.

The Landlord's Consent to Assignment

When leasing premises, a landlord is often concerned with the reputation of the tenant as well as with his ability to pay the rent. Having, for instance, the head office of a large corporation as a tenant in a new building might be a matter of prestige. A landlord may also be concerned about the type of business to be carried on for any of several reasons. Here are a few examples:

- the risk of unprofitable competition with the business of other tenants or with that of the landlord herself—a problem often arising in large business blocks and shopping centres
- noise, fumes, or traffic interfering with other tenants
- the wear and tear that certain businesses may inflict upon the premises

For these reasons, a landlord almost invariably requires a tenant to agree that he will not assign the lease without first obtaining consent (permission) from the landlord.

On the other hand, if a landlord were free to withhold consent for any reason, the tenant might be placed in a difficult position. A landlord could arbitrarily refuse to give consent to an assignment that would in no way be harmful to her. Accordingly, tenants often require that the words "but such consent shall not be unreasonably withheld" be added to the covenant. In most provinces, these words are implied by statute as part of the covenant unless they are expressly excluded, and a tenant may apply to the court for an assessment of the reasonableness of any refusal.[10] For more information on this topic, see the Companion Website.

Subletting

A sublease is different from an assignment. An assignment is a transfer of the whole of the remainder of the tenant's term to the assignee; so long as the assignee performs all its covenants, the tenant retains no further right or interest in the lease. A sublease is a transfer of part only of the tenant's term to the subtenant. If the term given to the subtenant expires just one day before the expiration of the main lease (leaving the tenant with a reversion of one day), the tenancy of the subtenant is created not by an assignment but by a sublease. The tenant becomes the landlord of the subtenant. The sublease may differ materially from the main lease in the rent payable, in any of the covenants given by either party, and in the extent of the premises sublet (the subtenant may hold only a portion of the premises leased to the tenant). In both sublease and assignment, the tenant remains liable to the landlord to perform all the covenants under the main lease. The discussion concerning the requirement of consent of the landlord for assignment applies equally to subleases.[11]

Restrictions on Use of Premises

A landlord is usually concerned with the proposed use of the premises. This is controlled by requiring a covenant in the lease that restricts the use of the premises to particular activities. Such covenants are also enforceable against the tenant's assignees and subtenants.

A tenant may, in turn, insist that the landlord give a covenant not to rent adjoining premises to a competing business; this is known as an **exclusive use clause**. If, however, the landlord should commit a breach by renting adjoining premises to an innocent third party unaware of the covenant, the tenant would have no rights against the other tenant. His remedy would be limited to an action for damages against the landlord.

exclusive use clause a landlord's promise not to rent adjoining premises to any other entity in the same or competing business as the tenant

---

[10] See e.g. Commercial Tenancies Act, R.S.O. 1990, c. L-7, s. 23

[11] See *Zurich Canadian Holdings v. Questar Exploration Inc.* (1999), 171 D.L.R. (4th) 457 (Alta. C.A.).

Even in the absence of an express covenant, there is an implied covenant by the tenant to treat the premises in a "tenant-like manner"—that is, use them only for those purposes for which they are reasonably intended. A tenant could not turn a cold storage plant into a glue factory, or a restaurant into a hotel. In other words, a tenant may be prevented from carrying on activities for which the premises were not intended or zoned, or that would cause excessive wear and tear.

Fitness for Occupancy

At common law, there is generally no covenant of fitness implied by a lessor in granting a commercial lease. The lessee takes the premises as he finds them and at his own risk. Unless a tenant obtained an express covenant in the lease concerning the fitness of the premises for a particular use, or unless the landlord made a misrepresentation, the tenant is responsible for his own investigation of the premises.[12] However, courts have suggested that the course of dealing between the parties may create an implied covenant that the premises will be fit for the lessee's purposes, if they are disclosed to the lessor, much as the implied condition of fitness arises in a sale of goods.[13]

A landlord is not liable to a tenant or the tenant's customers, family, or guests for injuries caused by the unsafe condition of the premises, unless the landlord actually created the danger. However, where the landlord covenants to maintain and repair the premises, and fails to carry out that responsibility, occupiers' liability legislation generally equates her duty to visitors to the duty of an occupier.[14] In all other circumstances, the tenant, as the party in exclusive possession of the property, bears the responsibility that arises from injuries caused to persons in the leased premises.

Repairs

As a general rule, a landlord is not liable to make repairs to the property unless she expressly covenants to do so. Of course, a landlord has an economic incentive to maintain her property in good condition.

A landlord may, however, be liable to repair structural defects that develop, particularly if failure to repair would amount to an indirect eviction of the tenant and consequently a breach of the covenant for quiet enjoyment, as we shall see. For example, if a landlord fails to repair a leak in the roof of an office building and it results in the soaking and eventual crumbling of the ceiling and walls in an office suite, the tenant has an action against the landlord even where no covenant to repair has been given. In addition, when rented premises are in a large building, the landlord is responsible to the tenants for the maintenance of corridors, stairways, and elevators.

The general rule is that a tenant is not liable to make repairs to the premises unless he has expressly covenanted to do so. The rule is subject to two exceptions. First, as we have already noted, the tenant must not make such use of the premises that will cause excessive wear. Second, he is liable for committing **waste**. Waste may be voluntary—as when a tenant pulls down part of a building or otherwise damages it, or makes alterations that reduce its value. Alternatively, it may be permissive—that is, negligent—as when a tenant fails to repair a leak in the roof even though he is aware that more serious harm will result if he does not correct the problem.

waste damage to the premises that reduces its value

---

[12] Covenant relating to fitness for habitation is incorporated into residential tenancy legislation.

[13] *Telex (Austral/Asia) Proprietary Ltd. v. Thomas Cook & Sons (Austral/Asia) Proprietary Ltd.*, [1970] 2 N.S.W.R. 257 (C.A.).

[14] Occupiers' Liability Act, R.S.B.C. 1996, c. 337, s. 6; C.C.S.M., c. O8, s. 6; S.N.S. 1996, c. 27, s. 9; R.S.O. 1990, c. O-2, s. 8. See the discussion of occupiers' liability in Chapter 4.

Usual Covenants in the Lease of a Building

When a tenant leases an entire building or property, the landlord frequently obtains a covenant from him to keep the property in good repair, reasonable wear and tear excepted. Accordingly, the tenant agrees to make such repairs as are necessary to keep the property in the same condition as when the lease began, except for normal depreciation. The tenant is not liable for damage caused by faulty construction or for deterioration in the property due to the normal forces of nature. Unless the lease exempts the tenant, however, the tenant's covenant to repair includes liability to make good any loss by fire or storm. Often a tenant exempts himself from liability in this respect by qualifying the covenant to repair with the words "loss by fire, lightning, and tempest excepted."

When a tenant leases only part of a building, the landlord usually undertakes to provide various services such as heat, water, and elevator service, and also to keep the premises in good repair. There is an important difference between a covenant to repair given by the tenant and one given by the landlord. A tenant is in possession of his premises and should be aware of their falling into disrepair—it is not up to the landlord to remind the tenant or give notice.

In contrast, the landlord, not being in possession of the tenant's premises, is not presumed to be aware of any disrepair in them, and her duty to repair does not arise until the tenant gives her notice. A landlord who undertakes to repair the premises often reserves the right to go on the premises at reasonable hours and inspect and view the state of repair. Reserving this right, however, does not place any duty upon her to make inspections or to repair until she has received notice from the tenant.

Quiet Enjoyment

covenant of quiet enjoyment a landlord's promise to do nothing to interfere with the tenant's possession and use of the premises

The whole purpose of a lease is to give the tenant possession and the right to "enjoy" the premises during the term of the lease. Accordingly, the landlord gives a **covenant of quiet enjoyment** either impliedly, simply by granting the lease, or expressly, in a specific covenant for that purpose. The covenant has two aspects. First, it is an assurance that the landlord has good title to the property at the time she gives the lease; second, it is a covenant that, subsequent to the making of the lease, the landlord will not herself interfere or permit anyone obtaining an interest in land from her to interfere with the tenant's enjoyment of the premises.

ILLUSTRATION 22.1

(a) Greer owns a piece of land including some warehouses. A mining company survey shows valuable ore deposits. She grants the company a long-term mining lease, and the company begins extensive mining excavations. Subsequently, she leases the warehouses to Atkins Inc., which intends to use them to store heavy machinery. Atkins discovers that the mining operations have undermined the foundations of the warehouses, making them unsafe for use. Since the mining company is conducting its activities properly, and Greer cannot prevent its operations because she validly granted it a mining lease before granting Atkins Inc. its lease, Greer's interest was defective. Therefore, she committed a breach of her covenant to Atkins Inc. for quiet enjoyment.

(b) Mendoza leases a suite of offices to McAdam and McCollum, a firm of practising accountants. Subsequently, he leases the area on the floor directly above to a machine shop. The machine shop operations create noise and heavy vibrations, making it impossible for the accountants to carry on their practice. Mendoza is in breach of his covenant.

Breach of the covenant of quiet enjoyment no longer requires physical interference with the enjoyment of the premises. Substantial noise or vibration that interferes with the comfort or convenience of a lessee will be recognized as a breach of the covenant of quiet enjoyment. Accordingly, a court may reduce the rent of the tenant during the period of interference.[15]

---

[15] For a full review of the law in this area, see *Caldwell v. Valiant Property Management* (1997), 145 D.L.R. (4th) 559. A tenant's right to quiet enjoyment extends to non-interference with the guests whom she might invite to visit her: *Cunningham v. Whitby Christian Non-Profit Housing Corp.* (1997), 33 O.R. (3d) 171.

Insurance

In the absence of a covenant in the lease, neither landlord nor tenant is under a duty to insure the premises for the benefit of the other. In most cases, of course, the landlord insures the premises to protect her own investment. If the leased property consists of an entire building or a group of buildings under the complete control of one tenant, especially if the lease is for a long term, the lease may impose on the tenant full responsibility for the premises, including obtaining insurance.

The complexity of liability and insurance problems increases when there is a large number of business tenants, each with its own employees, as in a large office building or a shopping mall. Who is liable for the loss if an employee should negligently cause a fire that substantially destroys a mall? Providing insurance protection and allocating risk through the use of exemption clauses requires great expertise.[16]

The question of insurance is closely tied to the problem of what should happen to the tenancy in case of severe damage to the premises by fire, flood, or storm. Failure to make proper provision can lead to great hardship, particularly for the tenant. A tenant may not get much benefit from a lease stating that, if the premises are substantially destroyed, the liability to pay rent is suspended until the building is repaired; such a clause may place the tenant at the mercy of the landlord. While the landlord decides what to do, the tenant, although not paying rent, is temporarily out of business. If he leases premises elsewhere, he may find that when the building is repaired he is liable to pay rent for both locations.

A lease should state that the repairs must be made within a certain time and that, if they are not made within that time, the tenant then has the option of terminating the lease rather than waiting until the premises are restored. Another possibility is to give the tenant the right to make the repairs himself and to deduct the costs from future rent.

Provision of Services and Payment of Taxes

When a tenancy is for a portion of a building only and the landlord retains control over the building as a whole, it is usual for the landlord to covenant to provide heat, water, electricity, and occasionally even telephone service. When the tenancy is for the whole of the building, it is usual for the tenant to provide all these things himself.

Generally, property taxes are paid by the landlord when the tenant leases only a portion of the building. If the lease is of the whole of the building, the taxes may be paid by either party. As long as the agreement is clear, who pays is not important. If the landlord pays, the rent will be that much higher; if the tenant pays, then the rent is that much lower. In the absence of an agreement on the matter, it is the landlord's duty to pay the taxes. Often, the cost of these items is passed on to the tenant in the form of **additional rent**. Some leases include a term that each tenant must pay his proportionate share of maintenance expenses, utilities, and taxes. Tenants should carefully review the formula used to determine proportionate share, as it is often based upon the area of the leased premises as a percentage of the total area of the building. The definition of "total area of the building" could include all hallways and common areas, or it could be restricted to rentable areas. The most expensive scenario is if the area of the building only includes actually rented areas, resulting in the tenants, not the landlord, assuming the cost of unrented space.

additional rent a tenant's proportionate share of maintenance costs, utilities, and taxes

---

[16] See *Greenwood Shopping Plaza Ltd. v. Beattie*, [1980] 2 S.C.R. 228, where employees were held personally liable and could not take advantage of an exemption clause as third parties, but see more recent cases where the rule of privity was relaxed to give employees protection under their employer's exemption clause: *London Drugs v. Kuehne & Nagel International Ltd.* (1992), 97 D.L.R. (4th) 261. See also *Laing Property Corp. v. All Seasons Display Inc.* (1998), 53 B.C.L.R. (3d) 142, aff'd (2000) 6 B.L.R. (3d) 206 (B.C.C.A.).

REMEDIES OF THE LANDLORD

Damages and Recovery of Rent

A landlord may sue for damages caused by a tenant's breach of any covenant. However, the right to recover rent requires further discussion and often presents a dilemma. If a tenant abandons the premises and pays no further rent, the old rules concerning interests in land placed the landlord in a predicament. On the one hand, by leaving the premises vacant and insisting on her rights under the lease, she could claim the entire rent due under it. In land law, apart from any statutory provisions to the contrary, there is no duty to mitigate damages as there is in contract law. Still, the tenant might never be able to pay, so doing nothing could be expensive. On the other hand, the landlord could terminate the lease and re-let the property to a new tenant, but she lost all right to future rent and could only collect arrears at termination from the former tenant. If the landlord tried to sublet the premises "on behalf of the defaulting tenant" in order to reduce her loss but keep the right to collect rent for the entire term, she risked being seen as accepting the **surrender** by the tenant, thereby terminating the lease and freeing the tenant from future obligations to pay rent.

surrender abandonment of the premises by the tenant during the term of the lease

Courts now recognize that a lease creates both an interest in land and a contract, and so the principles of contract law are applied to resolve the landlord's dilemma. If a landlord wishes to terminate the lease and to continue to hold the tenant liable for future losses of rent, she may do so by informing the tenant at the time of termination that she will hold him responsible for all future losses arising from his breach. A landlord may mitigate her losses without losing her rights against the defaulting tenant.[17] The Supreme Court of Canada accepted the rule that a landlord has no duty to mitigate if she chooses not to assume control of the premises.[18] However, if the landlord does terminate the lease and gives notice to seek future damages, she must mitigate her damage.[19] The law is complicated in this area, and a commercial landlord should obtain a legal opinion before acting to terminate the tenancy.[20] For more information on this topic, see the Companion Website.

With respect *only* to residential tenancies, the duty to mitigate is clearer. Several provinces have amended their landlord and tenant laws as follows:

> A landlord or tenant who claims compensation for damage or loss that results from the other's non-compliance with this Act, the regulations or their tenancy agreement must do whatever is reasonable to minimize the damage or loss.[21]

Eviction

This remedy is sometimes called the landlord's **right of re-entry**. The right of re-entry for failure to pay rent is a term implied by statute, if not expressly included in the lease. The period for which rent must be in arrears before a landlord is entitled to re-enter and evict the tenant varies considerably from province to province and is longer in the case of residential tenancies. Before evicting a tenant in default, the landlord must follow the procedure laid down in the legislation of the province.

Leases often provide that the landlord may re-enter and evict the tenant for breach of any of the other covenants in the lease. Since eviction amounts to a **forfeiture**— that is, forfeiting (losing) the remainder of the term to the landlord, the court is very reluctant to permit eviction for breach of any covenant other than one relating to payment of rent, use of the property, or assignment of the lease. A court may grant a tenant relief against forfeitures either under the general principles of equity or under various statutory reliefs found in provincial legislation.[22] Generally speaking, so long as the tenant corrects the breach and proves it will not reoccur, the court will restrain the landlord from evicting him and will declare the lease to be valid under its original terms.

right of re-entry a landlord's remedy of evicting the tenant for failure to pay rent or breach of another major covenant

forfeiture to lose or give back to the landlord the balance of the term of a lease

Distress

The landlord has a power of **distress**, or the right to distrain for rent—that is, she may seize assets of the tenant found on the premises and sell them to recover arrears of rent. Usually, the landlord authorizes a bailiff to distrain on the property of the tenant. The right to distrain does not arise until the day after the rent is due and a demand for

distress the right of the landlord to seize assets of the tenant found on the premises and sell them to realize arrears of rent

---

[17] *Highway Properties Ltd. v. Kelly, Douglas & Co. Ltd.* (1971), 17 D.L.R. (3d) 710; *Manufacturers Life Insurance Co. v. Executive Centre at Manulife Place Inc.*, [2011] A.J. No. 320; *Langley Crossing Shopping Centre v. North-West Produce Ltd.*, 2000 BCCA 107 at para 44; *Learmonth v. Letroy Holdings Ltd.*, 2011 BCSC 143 at para 40-50 aff'd 2012 BCCA 262

[18] *Ibid.*

[19] *B.G. Preeco 3 Ltd. v. Universal Exploration*, [1987] 6 W.W.R. 127 (as long as the claim is for rent due and not damages, there is not duty to mitigate). *AGC Flat Glass North America Ltd. v. CCP Atlantic Specialty Products Inc.*, [2010] N.S.J. No. 140.

[20] See e.g. *Smith v. Busler*, [1988] B.C.J. No. 2739 (S.C.); *Globe Convestra Ltd. v. Vucetic* (1990), 15 R.P.R. (2d) 220 (Ont. Gen. Div.). See also *Transco Mills Ltd. v. Percan Enterprises Ltd.* (1993), 83 B.C.L.R. (2d) 254 (C.A.); *Jade Agencies Ltd. v. Meadow's Management Ltd.*, [1999] B.C.J. No. 214.

[21] Residential Tenancy Act, S.B.C. 2002, c. 78, s. 7(2); C.C.S.M. c. R119, s. 55(2); S.O. 2006, c. 17, s. 16.

[22] See e.g. Commercial Tenancies Act, R.S.O. 1990, c. L-7, s. 20; Courts of Justice Act, R.S.O. 1990, c. C.43, s. 98; Law and Equity Act, R.S.B.C. 1996, c. 253, s. 24.

payment has been made. A landlord cannot prevent the tenant from removing goods from the premises even as late as the day the rent is due. She may, however, object if the tenant is clearly removing all the goods in order to avoid the landlord's power of distress. If the tenant removes the goods in spite of the landlord's objection, or later removes them fraudulently to prevent the landlord from asserting her rights after the right has arisen, the landlord may follow the goods and have them seized in another location, provided they have not been sold in the meantime to an innocent purchaser.[23] The time limit within which a landlord may seize goods in this fashion varies from province to province.

A landlord is not permitted to exercise the right of eviction and simultaneously or subsequently exercise a right of distress. The right to distrain is limited to situations where the relationship of landlord and tenant still exists.[24]

Certain personal property is exempt from seizure—necessary household furniture, a limited supply of food and fuel, and mechanic's tools. A commercial lease may contain a term by which the tenant "contracts out" of its right to exemptions should the landlord distrain for rent.[25] If the landlord by mistake seizes the goods of third parties such as customers or consignors, they must be released on proof of ownership. The landlord may also seize equipment or appliances purchased on the installment plan and not fully paid for, but before selling them she must first pay the balance owing to the seller. For more information on this topic, see the Companion Website.

CASE 22.1

A bakery bought an oven, dough mixer, and other bakery equipment on an installment payment plan and placed them in the leased premises in which it carried on business. The credit agreement stated that the equipment remained the property of the manufacturer until the purchase price was paid in full. The bakery ran into financial difficulties and stopped paying the installments and its rent. The landlord attempted to distrain the bakery equipment and the manufacturer wanted to repossess the equipment. The Court held that the landlord could distrain the equipment only after it paid the balance owing to the manufacturer.[26]

Injunction

If a tenant proposes or has begun to use the premises in a manner that would be in breach of a covenant restricting use, the landlord may obtain an injunction ordering the tenant to cease the prohibited use. An injunction may be obtained against certain types of use, even when they are not expressly prohibited under the terms of the lease, if they are inconsistent with the general design and ordinary use to which the property would be put. For example, a landlord could obtain an injunction to prevent a house ordinarily used as residential property from being turned into a medical clinic.[27]

Generally speaking, whenever a landlord is entitled to obtain an injunction, she also has the right to re-enter the property and evict the tenant. She will make her choice based on the circumstances and, in particular, on whether the lease is an otherwise desirable one from her point of view.

---

[23] See *Albo v. Concorde Group Corp.* (2004), 235 D.L.R. (4th) 465, where the purchaser was a party to the fraud.

[24] *Mundell v. 796586 Ontario Ltd.* (1996), 3 R.P.R. (3d) 277. *Delane Industry Co. Ltd. v. PCI Properties Corp.*, 2014 BCCA 285.

[25] Distress for residential tenancies has been abolished in some provinces.

[26] *Emcan Bakey Equipment & Supply Ltd. v. DMI Property Management Inc.*, [2010] O.J. No. 2315.

[27] *McCuaig v. Lalonde* (1911), 23 O.L.R. 312.

Bankruptcy of the Tenant

Under the Bankruptcy and Insolvency Act, a landlord has priority over the proven claims of general unsecured creditors in the event of the tenant's bankruptcy for the amount of three months of rent arrears.[28] For any additional arrears, she ranks among the general creditors. Any term that automatically terminates a lease upon the bankruptcy of the tenant is void.[29] This preserves the asset for use by the trustee in bankruptcy. The purpose of the three months' preference is to encourage landlords to be a little more patient with a defaulting commercial tenant. Inability to pay rent may be only temporary, but eviction will close the business down, probably causing greater hardship to both the tenant and other creditors of the tenant. Provincial landlord and tenant acts recognize the right of a trustee in bankruptcy to repudiate an outstanding lease without further liability[30] or, with proper notice, to continue to use the premises for so long as may serve the purpose of liquidating the tenant's assets and to pay rent at the rate specified in the lease.[31] Recognizing that in some circumstances the unexpired term of the lease may have value, a trustee may also assign the lease to a new tenant in circumstances that are acceptable to the court.[32] A landlord's right to distrain also ends when a tenant goes bankrupt.

REMEDIES OF THE TENANT

Damages

A tenant may recover damages from the landlord arising from breach by the landlord of any of her covenants. For instance, a landlord, believing the tenant has committed a breach, may wrongfully infringe the tenant's rights; she may evict the tenant, mistakenly believing that the tenant was in arrears of rent and had been served with notice. The wrongful eviction by the landlord is a breach of the covenant for quiet enjoyment. Similarly, if a landlord distrains upon more goods than were reasonably necessary to satisfy a claim for arrears of rent, the tenant may recover damages. If the landlord or her bailiff, in attempting to distrain upon the goods of the tenant, enters the premises illegally—that is, by use of force—she will be liable for damages for trespass. A tenant is entitled to prevent an exercise of the power of distress by keeping the premises continually locked, but in these circumstances the threat of distress can be an ongoing harassment to the tenant.

If a landlord has expressly covenanted to keep the premises in good repair or to rebuild them if they are destroyed, her failure to do so will be a breach not only of the covenant to repair but also of the covenant for quiet enjoyment.

Injunction

A tenant may also obtain an injunction to restrain a landlord from a continuing breach of the covenant of quiet enjoyment. A court will grant an injunction against a landlord for

---

[28] R.S.C. 1985, c. B-3, s. 136(1)(f), as amended by S.C. 1992, c. 27 (and an additional amount of three months of accelerated rent after bankruptcy). In the absence of bankruptcy proceedings, a landlord's priority under provincial legislation is usually greater than three months.

[29] Ibid., s. 84.2.

[30] Repudiation does not terminate the lease. It terminates the liability of the lessee, but not of any guarantor: *KKBL No. 297 Ventures Ltd. v. IKON Office Solutions Inc.* (2004), 243 D.L.R. (4th) 602. Where a lease has been assigned, repudiation by the assignee's trustee does not terminate the liability of the original lessee: *Crystalline Investments Ltd. v. Domgroup Ltd.* (2004), 234 D.L.R. (4th) 513.

[31] See e.g. Commercial Tenancy Act, R.S.B.C. 1996, c. 57, s. 29; Commercial Tenancies Act, R.S.O. 1990, c. L.7, ss. 38(2) and 39(1); Landlord and Tenant Act, C.C.S.M., c. L-70, ss. 46(2) and 47(1).

[32] See e.g. Landlord's Rights on Bankruptcy Act, R.S.A. 2000, c. L-5, s. 8.

interfering with quiet enjoyment caused by a continuing nuisance such as vibrations, noise, or fumes escaping from the landlord's premises. The court will not grant an injunction, however, where it would be futile to do so—for example, where vibration caused by the landlord has so damaged the structure that it has been condemned as unsafe for occupation, destroying its usefulness to the tenant. The tenant's remedy is to vacate the premises and seek damages. An important covenant often given by a landlord to a retail tenant is a promise not to lease premises in the same building or shopping centre to a competing business. When a breach occurs, an injunction restraining the second tenant from carrying on the competing business will be granted only if the second tenant was aware of the covenant.

Termination of the Lease

When a landlord's breach of the covenant of quiet enjoyment has made the premises unfit for the tenant's normal use and occupation, the tenant, in addition to any other remedy, may terminate the lease and vacate the premises. Upon vacating, the tenant ends any further liability to the landlord. The landlord's breach must make the entire premises unfit for the tenant's use—amounting to a total eviction—before the tenant has this option.

If the landlord's interference is only with part of the premises, or is only a nuisance or inconvenience rather than amounting to a total eviction, the tenant remains bound to pay the rent and cannot terminate the lease. His remedies are then an action for damages for the injury suffered and an injunction to restrain further breach.

TERMINATION AND RENEWAL OF A TENANCY

Surrender

A term certain expires automatically without notice. Although not required by law, a landlord often delivers a reminder to the tenant that the lease is about to expire and that he must vacate on the date of expiry. Upon vacating the premises, the tenant surrenders them to the landlord.

A surrender may also take place during the term of a tenancy by express agreement between landlord and tenant, as when a tenant no longer desires to keep the premises and pays the landlord a sum of money to release him from obligations for the balance of the term. A landlord may also bargain for the tenant's surrender of the remainder of the term when she needs vacant possession in order to sell the property or wishes to make substantial alterations or to demolish the building.

Suppose a tenant abandons the premises without making an agreement to surrender to the landlord. As discussed above, a landlord may be presumed to have treated an abandonment as a surrender of the premises when she re-lets to another tenant or takes possession of the premises herself to make use of them for her own purposes. Often it may be difficult to decide from the circumstances whether the landlord has accepted an abandonment and so released the tenant from further obligation to pay rent. Since abandonment is usually committed by an insolvent tenant, the landlord's rights against the tenant may have little practical value.

Forfeiture

In our discussion of a landlord's remedies, we noted that breach of certain covenants by a tenant (such as failure to pay rent) entitles the landlord to evict the tenant and impose a forfeiture of the lease. Once the forfeiture takes place, the relationship of landlord and tenant is terminated. The tenant has no further obligations under the lease, although he may be liable because of his breach before forfeiture for damages suffered by the landlord. Similarly, if a landlord has attempted to impose forfeiture by improperly evicting her tenant—entitling the tenant to consider his obligations under the lease at an end—the relationship of landlord and tenant is terminated, but the tenant may still recover damages for the landlord's breach of covenants.

Termination by Notice to Quit

Periodic Tenancies   A periodic tenancy renews itself automatically unless either the landlord or the tenant serves **notice to quit** on the other party—that is, serves notice of an intention to bring the tenancy to an end. Notice to quit served by a tenant is sometimes called notice of intention to vacate. In weekly, monthly, or quarterly tenancies, the length of notice required to bring the tenancy to an end is one clear period of tenancy. In other words, one party must give the other notice on or before the last day of one tenancy period for the tenancy to come to an end on the last day of the next period.

notice to quit   notice of an intention to bring the tenancy to an end

The common law rule that six clear months' notice is necessary to terminate a yearly tenancy at the end of the first year or any succeeding year of the tenancy applies to commercial leases in all provinces except New Brunswick, Nova Scotia, Quebec, and Prince Edward Island. In these provinces, only three clear months' notice is required. Common law and statutory notice periods are of little importance because virtually all commercial leases specify their own notice of termination requirements for fixed term leases.

ILLUSTRATION 22.2

West Side Corp. rents a small warehouse from Bernstein on a monthly basis, commencing March 1, at a rent of $1250 per month. The following September, West Side buys a warehouse building with possession available on November 1. West Side must serve Bernstein with notice to quit on or before September 30 if it wishes to terminate the tenancy on October 31. October is then a clear month. If, however, it does not serve notice until after September 30—say, on October 3—October is no longer a clear month, and West Side Corp. is not able to terminate the tenancy until November 30. In these circumstances, November will be the clear month.

ILLUSTRATION 22.3

Bok leases the Greenbrier summer hotel in Alberta from O'Brien at a yearly rental of $30 000, commencing April 1, 2012. The yearly tenancy will renew itself automatically each April 1 unless either party gives six clear months' notice before April 1—that is, on or before September 30 of the preceding year. If Bok wishes to vacate the property by March 31, 2017, he must serve notice on or before September 30, 2016. If he serves notice on October 1, 2016, it is too late; the tenancy will automatically renew itself on April 1, 2017, and continue to March 31, 2018. Therefore, the maximum time that may elapse between giving notice and terminating the tenancy may be 18 months less a day, that is, from October 1, 2016, to March 31, 2018.

Tenant Remaining in Possession after the Expiration of a Fixed Term   If a tenant remains in possession after the expiration of a fixed term, he becomes a tenant at sufferance and may be evicted by the landlord at any time on demand. What happens, however, if the landlord accepts further rent from the tenant? A periodic tenancy then arises on all the terms of the original lease except those that are inconsistent with a periodic tenancy. An example of an inconsistent term would be a covenant by the landlord to redecorate the premises every three years during a 12-year term. This covenant would not become part of a subsequent periodic tenancy.

Generally speaking, if a periodic tenancy arises after the expiry of a fixed term expressed in years (for example, a lease for five years at an annual rental of $8400 payable in installments of $700 per month), then the periodic tenancy created will be a yearly tenancy. If instead the term certain is stated as a term of months (say, a lease for eight months at a monthly rent of $700), then the periodic tenancy created will be a monthly one; similarly, if the term certain is expressed in terms of weeks or quarter-years, a succeeding periodic tenancy will be weekly or quarterly, respectively.

Parties May Set Their Own Terms for Notice

The requirements for a valid notice to quit discussed above are those that apply in the absence of express agreement; the parties to a lease usually agree to vary them to suit their own needs. Landlord and tenant may agree that some period less than six months is sufficient notice for either party to terminate a yearly tenancy. Remaining in possession after giving notice to quit can attract contractual penalties in addition to damages and eviction. For example, in British Columbia, a tenant who remains in possession after the date mentioned in his notice is liable for double the rent.[33]

Renewal

A lease for a fixed term, particularly a lease of premises for a retail store, often provides for a renewal at the option of the tenant. Asking for such an option makes good business sense: An option permits the tenant to terminate the tenancy at the end of the original lease if the business is unsuccessful or so successful that larger premises are needed, yet he has the security of exercising the option if the business proves successful.

Landlords usually require some increase in rent for the renewal term and sufficient notice to obtain a new tenant if the option is not exercised. Rent increases may be tied to the consumer price index or some other measure of the rate of inflation. At least three months' notice from the tenant that he intends to exercise the option is typical.

FIXTURES

As noted in Chapter 21, land includes everything fixed to it. Trees, fences, and buildings form part of the land, but they are distinguished from the land itself in that they are called fixtures. Technically, a grain elevator, a stand of timber, and a large office building are all fixtures, although in the everyday language of business they are not usually called fixtures. An object that is affixed to a fixture (such as a furnace installed in a building) is also a fixture. It is in this more restricted sense that the word is often used.

General Rules for Ownership of Fixtures

Whether an object is held to be a fixture may decide its ownership. Generally, an object permanently affixed to a building becomes a part of the building and of the real property itself. In a sale of land, the vendor cannot remove fixtures that were attached at the time of the contract of sale; they belong to the purchaser. Similarly, since fixtures belong to the landlord, a tenant cannot remove them.

In a sale of land, the purchaser and vendor usually agree between them what fixtures remain with the land. If the vendor wishes to take certain fixtures away, he expressly reserves that right in the agreement of sale, and the sale price may be adjusted accordingly. In tenancy, however, a problem may arise after the lease begins. The tenant may attach objects to the premises for his own benefit without any agreement with the landlord. A creditor may see the secured chattels transformed into fixtures when the tenant installs them into leased premises. Questions arise whether he may

---

[33] Commercial Tenancy Act, R.S.B.C. 1996, c. 57, s. 16.

take them away when he vacates the premises or whether the landlord or creditor is entitled to them.

The result would be very harsh if a tenant temporarily attached valuable objects to the building, unaware of the consequences of so doing, and later discovered he could not remove them under any circumstances. In such a case the landlord would reap an unjust benefit. Understandably, the law has developed more flexible rules in these circumstances than in a sale of land. To apply the rules we must decide, first, whether the object has become a fixture and, second, if it has become a fixture, whether it belongs to those classes of fixtures that may be removed by a tenant. Obviously the safest course of action is to negotiate the fate of tenant leasehold improvements as part of the lease.

Determining Whether an Object Is a Fixture

To determine whether an object has become a fixture, we may ask a number of questions:

- Has the object been fastened to the building with the intention that it become a fixture?
- What use is to be made of it?
- How securely and permanently is it attached?
- How much damage, if any, will be caused to the building by its removal?

A picture hanging on a hook in the wall is not a fixture. A partition nailed and bolted to the walls of the building is a fixture. But what would we conclude about the following—a table that has been bolted to the floor to prevent delicate machinery on it from being jarred; machinery bolted to the floor to prevent vibration; a display stand tacked to a wall so that it will not topple over; or a neon sign held in place by guy wires bolted to the roof of the building?

Ordinarily, objects not bolted or anchored in any way but merely resting on their own weight are presumed not to be fixtures. Objects affixed in any way create a presumption that they are fixtures, although this presumption may be rebutted by asking what a reasonable person would intend when attaching the object (for instance, the display stand mentioned above). When objects are held not to be fixtures, they may be removed by the tenant at any time. If the tenant should inadvertently forget to remove them from the premises when the lease expires, they still remain the property of the tenant and may be claimed afterward.

There is no precise test to determine whether an object attached to the premises by a tenant remains his property or becomes a part of the building. The problem can often be avoided in advance by making an agreement concerning specific fixtures. If the parties expressly agree that a particular object—one that would otherwise undoubtedly be a fixture—is to remain the property of the tenant, the agreement is conclusive.

Tenant's Fixtures

Even when it is decided that an object has become a fixture, the tenant may still have the right to remove it if he can show that either (a) it was attached for the convenience of the tenant or for the better enjoyment of the object, as when it is purely ornamental, or (b) it was a **trade fixture**—that is, an article brought onto the premises for the purpose of carrying on some trade or business, including manufacturing. Both these classes of fixtures are commonly called **tenant's fixtures**. A tenant may remove them before the end of his tenancy, provided that in doing so he does not cause permanent damage to the structure of the building and he repairs what damage is done. If, however, a tenant leaves without removing his fixtures and the term expires, they are presumed to become part of the premises and the property of the

trade fixture an object attached to the premises for the purpose of carrying on a trade or business

tenant's fixtures trade fixtures or any other fixtures attached for the convenience of the tenant or for the better enjoyment of the object landlord. Tenant's fixtures include only those fixtures brought onto the premises by the tenant himself. Fixtures installed by the landlord or left by preceding tenants are the landlord's property from the time of installation or from the beginning of the tenancy and may not be removed.

ORAL LEASES

In most jurisdictions, when a tenant is in possession under a short-term lease of three years or less, the lease need not be in writing in order to satisfy the Statute of Frauds, although, of course, a written lease is advisable in any event.[34] Leases of longer than three years are usually unenforceable if they are not in writing. If, for example, a tenant enters into an oral lease for five years and the landlord later changes her mind and refuses to let the tenant into possession, the tenant is without remedy. If, however, the tenant is already in possession and has paid rent, the doctrine of part performance, as discussed in Chapter 10 under the Statute of Frauds, will apply. Under the rules of equity, the court will order the landlord to give the tenant his lease in the terms originally agreed between them. A landlord too may obtain specific performance and hold the tenant bound to a long-term lease if, after taking possession, the tenant wishes to avoid the lease and vacate the premises.

SALE OF THE LANDLORD'S INTEREST

Relationship between a Tenant and a Purchaser of the Landlord's Interest

In a lease, a landlord grants away a right to possession of her land for a term and reserves to herself the right to possession at the end of the term—that is, the reversion. She also receives the benefit of the tenant's covenants, including the promise to pay rent. When a landlord sells land subject to a lease, she parts with both the reversion and the benefits of the covenants given by the tenant. A purchaser acquires the whole interest in the land subject to the outstanding lease, and is bound to both the rights and duties of the former landlord. We may ask, "How can a purchaser receive both the rights and duties of the landlord when the tenant was not a party to the sale and there is no privity of contract between purchaser and tenant?" The answer is that the lease is more than just a contract: It also creates an interest or estate in the land, resulting in **privity of estate**. Neither landlord nor tenant can destroy the privity of estate by claiming that the original contract of lease does not bind them. Their respective interests in the land create the relationship between them.

privity of estate the relationship between tenant and landlord created by their respective interests in the land that passes to a transferee of the interest

Privity of Contract with the Former Landlord

The creation of privity of estate with a new landlord does not bring to an end privity of contract with the former landlord. Although a landlord may sell her reversion, she still remains personally liable on her covenants to her tenant, in particular, the covenant for quiet enjoyment. If the new landlord should interfere with the covenant for quiet enjoyment in an irreparable manner, the tenant, if he chooses, may sue the original landlord in contract. He might well have to do so if the new landlord has subsequently become insolvent or has little in the way of assets. The doctrine of privity of estate is a concept of real property and does not apply to personal property.

---

[34] See e.g. Statute of Frauds, R.S.O. 1990, c. S. 19, s. 3, and R.S.N.S. 1989, c. 442, s. 3; *Carter v. Irving Oil Co.*, [1952] 4 D.L.R. 128, per MacDonald, J., at 131; Bentley, McNair, and Butkus, *Williams and Rhodes: Canadian Law of Landlord and Tenant, supra*, n. 8, at 2:1–2.

Relationship between a Tenant and the Landlord's Mortgagee

The leasehold estate acquired by a tenant, like other interests in real property, is valid against parties that subsequently acquire an interest in the land provided land registration requirements are met. If, after leasing her land, the landlord borrows against it under a mortgage, the mortgagee's (that is, the lender's) interest will be subject to the rights of the tenant. If the mortgagor (the landlord–borrower) defaults, the mortgagee may claim the reversion but is not entitled to evict the tenant. So long as the tenant observes the terms of the lease, the mortgagee is bound by it and cannot obtain possession, except as provided under the lease.

On the other hand, when the landlord mortgages her land before leasing it, the tenant is, in theory at least, at the mercy of the mortgagee if the landlord defaults, unless the mortgagee concurred in the lease at the time it was given. However, it is almost always in the best interest of the mortgagee to collect the rent rather than put the tenant out and try to obtain a new tenant. The risk to a tenant is greater if the lease is a long-term one and if, at the time of default, the value of the premises for leasing purposes has increased substantially beyond the current rent. For this reason, it is wise for a tenant to obtain the agreement of the mortgagee before entering into a long-term lease.

The Need to Register a Long-Term Lease

To preserve priority of his leasehold interest over subsequently acquired interests, a tenant should always register notice of a long-term lease in the land registry office. Otherwise, the interest may be destroyed if the landlord fraudulently sells to a bona fide purchaser who has no notice of the tenancy. The need for registration varies from province to province. In some provinces, leases as short as three years must be registered, while in others, only leases over seven years need be. Leases under three years need not be registered in any province.[35] The safest course of action is to register notice of any lease on the title to the land.

CONTEMPORARY ISSUE

Commercial Condominium Ownership: An Alternative to Leasing?

Leasing premises is not the only option when a business does not wish to purchase or construct an entire building. Non-residential condominiums are increasingly being used for professional, office, retail, commercial, and even industrial purposes. Mixed-use condominiums might have retail stores and services at ground level, perhaps offices above them, and residential units on the higher levels.

There are several advantages to buying a commercial condominium unit rather than leasing. Among them are stability and security of tenure (no need to worry about changes in ownership/management or being refused renewal when the lease expires), the opportunity to own a specific location, the benefits of a sound capital investment, tax advantages of ownership, the opportunity to have a say in the operation of the building without being solely responsible for its management, and ownership of improvements. In a mixed-use condominium, the residents on the upper floors are a potential "captive audience" for the businesses below.

Nevertheless, the disadvantages of owning a non-residential condominium should also be considered. The initial capital investment and the carrying costs might be expensive; high maintenance costs are charged back to unit owners through common expenses. If the business grows and requires more space, adjacent units might not be available. Resale potential might not be good. A wise choice of location is very important. In a mixed-use development, the developer may not have structured voting rights and cost allocations equitably. Conflict and bad feeling between residential and non-residential owners and poor management of the development might result.

>

---

[35] See, for example, Land Titles Act, S.N.B. 1981, c. L-1.1, s. 27(1); R.S.B.C. 1996. c. 250 s. 20(3).

LEASEBACKS

An established company with a good record of earnings is often able to arrange financing of the acquisition of a new building by a long-term leasing device known as a **leaseback**. First, the business obtains a short-term loan, usually from a bank, to finance construction of the building. As soon as the building is completed, the business sells it to the finance company and pays off its bank loan. The finance company then leases the building back to the business. The lease is usually for a period of 20 or 25 years, with the lessee business receiving an option to renew for additional periods. The lessee business acts very much as the owner of the property rather than as a tenant, paying for all repairs, maintenance, insurance, and property taxes during the currency of the lease.

leaseback a financial arrangement enabling a business to buy a building and sell it to a financial institution that, in turn, gives a long-term lease of the property back to the business

The leaseback device has several advantages for the lessee business. First, the business has a relatively easy means of financing its expansion once a willing financial institution is found to undertake the project. Second, in terms of financing, a leaseback may be more advantageous than buying the property and mortgaging it because a mortgagee will not generally provide the full value of the project (as the leaseback does), leaving the company to raise the balance. Third, there may be tax advantages for the lessee business.

From the point of view of a lessor financial institution, rented property represents an investment of funds that not only provides regular rental revenue that includes the amortization of the cost of the property, but also gives the lessor ownership of the entire property at the expiration of the lease. Any improvements in the building added by the tenant and any inflation in land values accrue to the benefit of the landlord. In addition, if the lessee business gets into financial difficulty, the legal formalities in evicting it are simpler and quicker than those required for a mortgagee to foreclose on a mortgage.

The leaseback, as compared with other leases, is a relatively long, detailed, and complex document, often carefully setting out the rights a tenant has in making alterations and adding fixtures to the building, as well as in the types of trade it may carry on. Sometimes the lessor may impose restrictions on the future borrowing of the lessee business, as a means of ensuring that it will not enter into obligations so great as to impair its ability to pay the rent.

Sometimes a leaseback includes an option for the lessee business to purchase the premises at the end of the term. The price at which the option may be exercised by the lessee may be determined in a variety of ways. It may be simply a specified sum of money, or it may be calculated by a formula taking into account, for example, whether the option is exercised at the end of the original term or the end of a renewal.

RESIDENTIAL TENANCIES

The Changing Needs of Residential Tenants

The demand for rental accommodation has spawned large developments of high-rise apartment buildings in most urban Canadian cities. The typical city tenant now lives in a large apartment complex and may not have even met his landlord. He has come to regard himself as a consumer of housing and to think of his relation with his landlord as based on a contract for services rather than an acquisition of an estate in land. Provincial legislation addresses the unique needs of the residential tenant with specific legislation applicable only to residential tenancies.

Ethical Issue **Discrimination**

Provincial human rights legislation protects tenants and prospective tenants against discrimination based on such things as race, colour, gender, ancestry, sexual orientation, lawful source of income, and age. However, exceptions exist; for example, British Columbia allows seniors' buildings, reserved for persons over the age of 55. Ontario allows same-gender buildings, occupied by either all men or all women. Landlords are also allowed to select tenants based on income information and credit checks.

Questions to Consider

1. Do you think these protections and exceptions are enough to prevent discrimination against students?

2. Are the poor protected? Consider the role of publicly subsidized housing.

Source: Human Rights Code, R.S.B.C. 1996, c. 210, s. 10; R.S.O. 1990, c. H-19, ss. 4, 21.

Legislative Protection for Tenants

Residential tenancy legislation varies considerably from province to province, but certain basic features are commonly found in most of the laws:

- Restrictions are imposed on the landlord's right to demand security deposits.
- Landlords are required to maintain the premises in a reasonable state of repair.
- Tenants are relieved from paying rent in the event of certain breaches of covenant by the landlord or if the lease contract is frustrated.
- The landlord's remedy of distress is abolished.
- The landlord has a duty to mitigate any loss caused by the tenant's breach.
- The landlord may not arbitrarily or unreasonably withhold consent to an assignment or subletting.
- It is more difficult to evict a tenant, even for non-payment of rent.
- Restrictions are imposed on the amount of rents and rent increases.
- Special tribunals and procedures have been established to deal with disputes.

As a general rule, the landlord in a residential tenancy is prohibited from requiring any security deposit in excess of one month's rent, and even that sum may only be applied to the payment of rent for the last rent period under the tenancy agreement. The landlord must also pay interest on the amount of the deposit at a specified rate.[36]

The legislation makes the landlord liable for maintaining residential premises in a good state of repair fit for habitation and further states that the tenant's knowledge of the lack of repair before the lease is irrelevant.[37]

In commercial tenancies, the failure of a landlord to perform her own covenants, even if they were major terms, does not release the tenant from the obligation to pay rent unless the landlord's breach amounted to an eviction of the tenant. The legislation makes some promises or covenants in a residential lease interdependent, so that breach by one party of

---

[36] Residential Tenancies Act, 2006, S.O. 2006, c. 17, ss. 105, 106. The rules about security deposits vary considerably from province to province. See, for example, Residential Tenancy Act, S.B.C. 2002, c. 78, ss. 17–22; Residential Tenancies Act, C.C.S.M. c. R. 119, ss. 29–36.1.

[37] Ibid., S.B.C. 2002, c. 78, s. 32; C.S.S.M. c. R. 119, s. 59; S.O. 2006, c. 17, s. 20.

a condition frees the other from his or her obligations.[38] Before withholding rent, a tenant should review the rules; some provinces require the rent to be deposited with the tribunal pending resolution of a dispute.

The doctrine of frustration is expressly declared to apply to residential tenancies,[39] so that a tenant is no longer liable to pay rent for the balance of the term when the premises became uninhabitable through no fault of his own, or to restore the property if it was destroyed during the tenancy.

The landlord's remedy of distress has also been abolished.[40] It eases the requirements when a tenant wishes to move from the premises—a landlord may not arbitrarily or unreasonably withhold consent to an assignment or subletting.[41]

Nor can a tenant be evicted as easily. Termination by notice to quit has been changed to require notice even for a term certain tenancy that would otherwise end without any act by either landlord or tenant.[42] In the absence of notice to quit, a tenancy is deemed to continue as a periodic tenancy. In addition, the notice period has been lengthened in some provinces. In Ontario, for example, all tenancies other than weekly tenancies require at least 60 clear days' notice prior to the termination date, and weekly (or daily) tenancies require 28 days, on the part of both landlord and tenant.[43] Landlords are precluded from terminating tenancies and evicting tenants except for a serious breach of the lease by a tenant; or because at the end of the current lease the landlord wishes to repossess the premises for occupation by herself or her immediate family; or because the premises are going to be torn down or substantially altered in order to be used for different purposes such as conversion to commercial premises.[44]

Finally, the legislation imposes restrictions in many cases on the amount of rent that may be charged and on increasing existing rents.[45]

INTERNATIONAL ISSUE

Rent Control

Affordable housing is a necessity in a healthy community, and ensuring its supply involves balancing the interests of tenants and landlords. When housing prices or unemployment rates rise, the demand for rental units increases. In a purely supply-and-demand scenario, low vacancy rates would lead to escalating rents. Tenants might be required to move out at the end of their term unless they were willing to pay large (unaffordable) rent increases. As a result, it is common for provinces to fix the amount of rent that can be charged or limit the amount of any rent increase. The distinction between these two controls is made clear by reviewing the history of rent controls in Ontario. Prior to 1998, the Ontario rent control system established a baseline legal rent for each existing or new rental unit.[46] Thereafter, only annual rent increases were allowed at the prescribed percentage (tied to the consumer price index). This cap on rent increases applied regardless of any change in tenant. Since 1998, the system provides protection from unreasonable rent increases only to existing or continuing

>

---

[38] S.B.C. 2002, c. 78, ss. 45, 47; S.O. 2006, c. 24, ss. 12(4).

[39] S.B.C. 2002, c. 78, s. 92; C.S.S.M., c. R. 119, s. 105; S.O. 2006, c. 17, s. 19.

[40] S.B.C. 2002, c. 78, s. 26; C.S.S.M. c. R. 119, s. 192; S.O. 2006, c. 17, s. 40.

[41] S.B.C. 2002, c. 78, s. 34; C.S.S.M. c. R. 119, s. 43; S.O. 2006, c. 17, s. 95.

[42] For example: S.B.C. 2002, c. 78, s. 57; S.O. 2006, c. 17, s. 47.

[43] S.O. 2006, c. 17, s. 44(1), (2), and (3).

[44] S.O. 2006, c. 17, ss. 48, 49, 50.

[45] S.B.C. 2002, c. 78, s. 41; C.S.S.M. c. R. 119, ss. 117, 118; S.O. 2006, c. 17, ss. 110–36.

[46] Rent Controls Act 1992, S.O. c. 11, replaced by the Tenant Protection Act, S.O. 1997, c. 24. Landlords could apply for permission to increase rents above guidelines in prescribed circumstances and some building built after 1991 are not covered by rent control.

tenants (subject to some exceptions). When a new tenant rents the unit, the landlord may set a new rent based upon market conditions, without regard to past rental rates or increases.[47]

In the United States, rent control is implemented at the municipal level in accordance with governing state legislation. As of 2003, only 125 cities had some form of rent control, including New York, San Francisco, Washington D.C., and Los Angeles. Several states have banned rent control entirely, including Florida and Illinois. In 1995, California restricted rent control protection to existing and continuing tenants. In 2008, California voters defeated a proposition that would have abolished rent control entirely.

The worldwide trend is mixed: Both China and Japan have eliminated rent control, while countries in the Middle East seem to be embracing it. Dubai and Qatar implemented new rent control programs in 2005 and 2007, respectively.

Questions to Consider

1. What are the arguments for and against rent control?

2. Why is Ontario's current stabilization system hailed by some as a fair compromise?

Sources: Prince Christian Cruz, "The Pros and Cons of Rent Control," Global Property Guide, January 19, 2009, www.globalpropertyguide .com/investment-analysis/The-pros-and-cons-of-rent-control (accessed May 22, 2014); Peter Dreier, "Californians Defend Rent Control," *Rooflines*, June 5, 2008 www.rooflines.org/941 /californians_defend_rent_control/ (accessed October 22, 2008).

Strategies to Manage the Legal Risks

In commercial tenancies, the interests of landlords and tenants and their respective creditors often conflict. Priority is usually determined by the wording of the covenants in the lease, the contents of the credit agreement, and the timing of notice and registration under land titles and personal property systems. Therefore, careful attention needs to be paid to all of these steps.

From the tenant's perspective, ownership of goods, trade fixtures, and leasehold improvements should be spelled out in the lease. Options to renew or terminate should also be established, as well as the right to assign any unexpired term. This gives the tenant the maximum amount of flexibility for the expansion, stability, or relocation of their business. However, tenants should remember when assigning a lease that they remain liable to the landlord if the assignee defaults or goes bankrupt. Since a tenant does not have a common law right to withhold rent for breaches by the landlord, the lease should designate specific incidents that suspend the obligation to pay rent, including destruction or damage to the premises.

When considering multi-unit locations, the tenant should focus on two key concerns. First, the additional rent charged for the share of maintenance and operation of the entire development is often more complicated than traditional rent. Careful attention to the formula for its calculation can save money. The second issue relates to the presence of competing businesses; an exclusivity clause restricting the landlord from renting to competitors is fundamentally important to the success of the location. The exclusion should be as broad as possible to give the tenant the greatest flexibility in his business model. Finally, with respect to all leases, multi- or single unit, notice of lease should be registered within the provincial land titles system so that all prospective purchasers and mortgagees have prior notice of the tenant's leasehold interest.

From the landlord's perspective, the two greatest concerns are payment of rent and care of the premises. If the tenant should go bankrupt, the rights of the landlord to deal with the unexpired term or to distrain goods are supplanted to those of the trustee. Any clause purporting to end the lease due solely to the bankruptcy of the tenant is void. However, other triggers for options to terminate, such as the tenant ceasing to carry on business at the premises, are enforceable and may give the landlord the opportunity to end the lease

---

[47] Residential Tenancies Act 2006, S.O. 2006, c. 17, ss. 110–36 (maximum 2.5% increase).

prior to the trustee assuming control. When faced with an absconding tenant, the landlord should proceed cautiously, depending upon the desire to terminate the tenancy or not. Legal advice should be sought. Obligations to mitigate vary. With respect to care of the premises, precise notice obligations should be imposed on the tenant to advise of deterioration at its earliest indication.

Creditors of both landlords and tenants must be aware that the right to seize and sell the financed asset, whether it is the landlord's land or the tenant's goods, may be displaced by rights under the lease. Goods of the tenant may become attached to the landlord's land as fixtures. A landlord's right to distrain may take precedence over the creditor. Reserving title to the goods in the creditor's name until the full purchase price is paid will help to give the creditor priority. Registration of the credit agreement under the provincial personal property system (discussed in Chapter 28) is vitally important.

Mortgagees of the landlord may also be subordinate to the interests of a commercial tenancy shorter than three years, even if it is not registered on title. Taking an assignment of rents for the mortgaged premises in all cases of mortgaging commercial property will ensure that rents can be applied to delinquent mortgage payments of the landlord. Notice of assignment of rents should be registered on the land title so new tenants have notice.

QUESTIONS FOR REVIEW

1. Define *tenancy at will, term certain, overholding tenant, subletting, eviction, forfeiture, surrender,* and *quiet enjoyment.*

2. What are the risks for a tenant if he limits his right to exclusive possession of the premises? Explain.

3. Should a leasehold interest be shown as an asset (with an equal and offsetting liability) on the balance sheet of a business? If so, at what amount?

4. Describe the difficulty caused by the strict covenant to pay rent as it relates to frustration in contract law.

5. What are the concerns of a landlord with respect to a tenant's right to assign the remainder of a leasehold interest?

6. Lewis owns a five-bedroom house next to his own home in Niagara-on-the-Lake, and rents it to Tessa for three years. Tessa then applies for a licence to operate a bed and breakfast on the premises. Lewis objects to such use of the house. Would he have any legal recourse against Tessa?

7. Describe the usual responsibilities of a landlord for repairs when a tenant leases only part of a building. How does this situation differ from a lease of an entire building?

8. Turner rented a store from Lauren on the ground floor of a multi-storey building as an art gallery to sell paintings and small statues. Turner's hours of business were normal retail business hours. A few months later, Lauren leased the adjoining store to Rockbar Inc. It played very loud music from noon until Turner's closing time. The music, especially the thumping sounds, could be heard clearly in Turner's store and interfered with normal conversation. Does Turner have any remedies?

9. How would you suggest that responsibility for insuring the premises be allocated in a large shopping mall? Describe the most difficult aspects of the problem.

10. What is the dilemma for the landlord when a tenant abandons the premises during the term of the lease?

11. Describe the landlord's duty to mitigate after a tenant abandons the premises.

12. In what way may a tenant be in a difficult position when the premises burn down, even if the lease states that the rent is suspended until the premises are rebuilt?

13. What property is exempt from a landlord's right to distrain?

14. Under the common law, how long a period of notice must be given to terminate a yearly tenancy? What is the meaning of "clear" as it relates to notice?

15. Oscar leased Blackacre from Brenda for five years at a monthly rent of $1200. Neither of them seemed to notice when the lease had expired. For several months, Oscar continued to pay his rent on the first day of each month. Brenda now needs to take possession of Blackacre for a large construction project. How much notice must she give to Oscar?

16. Explain the importance of renewal clauses in business leases.

17. How is the relationship of a tenant affected by his landlord's sale of her interest to a purchaser? What is the nature of the new relationship?

18. Stroll leases a warehouse for a term certain of five years. During the second year of the lease, the landlord, Vernon, mortgages the land. At the end of the fifth year of the lease, Stroll and Vernon enter into another lease for a further five years. Explain the difference, if any, in Stroll's position in the first term and in the second term insofar as the mortgage is concerned.

19. (a) What are three characteristics that make leaseback arrangements attractive to lessee businesses?

    (b) What are the characteristics that make them attractive to lessor financial institutions?

20. Describe briefly the reasons for treating residential tenancies differently from commercial tenancies.

CASES AND PROBLEMS

1. Continuing Scenario

   Ashley is approached by a land developer about opening a third location in the new strip mall being constructed in a subdivision on the edge of Ottawa. The developer is offering her a great deal on reduced rent for two years and customized premises, because he is having trouble attracting tenants as the surrounding area is still under construction with few residents in occupancy. Ashley has the draft lease documents to review—what additional terms should be inserted into the lease to address the following concerns?

   ■ The area may not have the population base to sustain enough business for the restaurant to be profitable; a restaurant should have a significant following once it has been open for six months.

   ■ If she is able to attract a clientele, she does not want to face large rent increases or be forced to move at the end of one term just as she is building a reputation.

   ■ The developer may be so desperate for tenants that he will rent to anyone—undesirable tenants would be veterinary clinics, walk-in medical clinics, and hair salons as well as other competing restaurants.

   ■ The developer is offering to customize the space with all the improvements Ashley usually does for herself—upholstered benches, walk-in refrigerator, and custom signage. These are items she would want to re-use in another location if this spot does not work out.

2. Ms. Bone, the owner of a downtown block of stores, rented one of them to Mr. Bull, who opened a retail china shop on the premises. Bull's tenancy was from year to year. He had a number of display cases built with glass doors to keep their fragile contents out of the reach of curious customers. The cases were secured to the wall by three-centimetre nails. Bull also purchased and installed heavy-duty air-conditioning equipment, which was connected to the water supply and anchored to the floor.

   Several years later, Bull was adjudged bankrupt on a petition of his creditors. At the time, he owed Bone $3600 for three months' rent. The trustee in bankruptcy remained in possession of the store pending liquidation of the business assets. The trustee claimed the display cases and air conditioner for the benefit of Bull's general creditors, but Bone claimed them as lessor of the store.

   Discuss the respective rights of Bone and of the trustee in bankruptcy.

3. Kruger leased a warehouse to Pool Corp. for a fixed term of eight months at a rent of $3000 per month, commencing January 1 and expiring August 31. Pool did not move out on August 31 and tendered its cheque for $3000 to pay the rent for September. It was accepted by Kruger. On October 1, Pool's manager appeared at Kruger's office with another cheque for $3000. Kruger said he had inspected the warehouse and was disappointed by the rough treatment the building was receiving from Pool's employees. When the manager replied that he could hardly expect otherwise in a busy operation, Kruger stated it was not worth his while to rent it under those conditions unless he received at least $4000 per month. The manager refused to pay that much and tendered the company's cheque for $3000. Kruger refused the cheque and ordered Pool to "clear out of the warehouse at once." The manager left and mailed the cheque to Kruger, who simply held it and did not cash it.

On November 1, Kruger called Pool by telephone and asked if the company would pay $4000. The manager replied, "No." Kruger said that he was at the end of his patience and had given Pool a full month to reconsider. He sent a bailiff to evict Pool that very day, cashed its cheque for the previous month, and sent it a demand for "the $1000 still owing."

Pool was forced to move its stock to a more expensive warehouse at once and suffered some damage to its goods when they were moved into the street by the bailiff. It sued Kruger for losses of $8000 caused by the eviction. Should it succeed? Give reasons for your opinion.

4. Rogers, a dance teacher, was looking for space to operate a dance studio. She visited premises on the second floor of Hart's building four times with other people who concluded that the premises were suitable for the purposes intended. Rogers signed a lease and, with Hart's approval, she installed a special dance floor, cabinets, dance bars, and mirrors and did painting and electrical work, including installation of light fixtures. She then began her classes.

Hart immediately noticed that the building began to vibrate. Within 24 hours, he had a special beam installed but the vibrating continued. Hart hired a structural engineer at once to examine the building. The engineer concluded that the vibration was caused by harmonic pressure created by the coordinated movement of the dancers. He stated that the vibration could not be avoided by structural changes and it could ultimately cause the building or parts of it to collapse. Hart worried about the safety of the patrons of the restaurant situated under the dance studio, as well as of Rogers herself and her students. Three days after classes had begun, he told Rogers that the classes had to stop.

Rogers immediately began to look for new premises and took the position that, by preventing her from continuing dance classes, Hart terminated the lease without notice. She sued Hart for damages for the cost of all the improvements she had made, the cost of moving, and general damages for loss of business. She argued that, because the defect in the premises was latent and did not become apparent until after she had begun the dance lessons, it was unreasonable to ask her to ensure the soundness and safety of the premises. It was Hart's problem as landlord to deal with.

Give your opinion of Rogers's claims and whether they should succeed.

5. Allgate Realties Ltd. constructed a new building suitable for a restaurant in a suburb of Calgary. Streeter, the manager, invited Kratinsky to examine it. Kratinsky already owned and operated a restaurant in the city and was hesitant. Streeter assured him that the suburb was growing rapidly, with new businesses about to open as well as new housing developments being built. He offered Kratinsky a five-year lease including a sale to him of the building at the end of the lease. Kratinsky finally accepted; he opened the restaurant three months later.

Almost no new construction took place in the area; the restaurant was isolated and business was very poor. Within six months, Kratinsky closed the restaurant and refused to pay further rent, claiming that Allgate had made serious misrepresentations and was in breach of the contract. Allgate responded that there were no covenants in the lease referring to future development in the area and that Kratinsky remained bound by the lease and sale of the property.

Whose argument do you think will prevail?

6. Ivan Drugs Inc., a drugstore chain, leased premises from Hay Investments Ltd. in its shopping mall. The lease was for 10 years, at a "base" rent of $46 200 per year in monthly installments of $3850, plus Ivan's share of the taxes, insurance, and common expenses of the mall. Ivan also agreed to pay an additional 6 percent of gross annual sales as rent, to the extent that its gross sales exceeded $770 000 for the year ($46 200 represents 6 percent of $770 000). The lease also contained a usual covenant allowing Ivan to assign the lease with consent of Hay.

   In the first three years, Ivan's sales exceeded $1 500 000, and it duly paid the additional sums to Hay. However, during the third year a much larger shopping mall was opened across the street from Hay's mall. Ivan, fearing its sales at the current location would suffer, leased larger premises at the new mall and moved from its old premises, leaving them vacant. Ivan continued to pay the "base" rent and its share of the taxes, insurance, and common expenses, but paid no additional rent based on its sales in the new mall.

   Partly as a result of receiving diminished rent, Hay was unable to obtain extensions of its mortgages or new financing for the mall and was in financial difficulty. Hay served notice on Ivan to enforce the original agreement according to its terms and to pay rent based on sales that could be attributed to Ivan's business if it had remained in Hay's mall. Hay Investments Ltd. asserted that Ivan Drugs Inc. had impliedly promised to carry on business for the full term of the lease.

   Give your opinion of the validity of Hay's claim and what you think the result should be.

7. Frost Investments Limited owned three adjoining buildings downtown that it rented to various tenants as office space. All three buildings were heated centrally from a single heating plant in Building No. 1. The Generous Loan Company occupied offices in Building No. 3 under a lease in which the lessor, Frost, covenanted to maintain the heat continuously above 15 degrees Celsius from October 1 to May 24, except for weekends. In January, a serious fire occurred in Building No. 2, breaking the heating connections between Buildings No. 1 and No. 3. The damage was so serious that Frost decided to demolish Building No. 2 and rebuild.

   In the meantime, Generous Loan Company suffered a significant drop in business because of very low temperatures in its offices. It eventually vacated the premises and leased other quarters at a higher rent. It then sued Frost, claiming damages of $1750 for the additional amount of rent it had to pay the new landlord for what otherwise would have been the balance of the term of its lease with Frost, and $6000 for its estimated loss of profits. Frost counterclaimed for rent for the balance of the term of the lease, seven months at $2150 per month. What do you think the decision should be?

8. Tagom rented a service station from Oil Can Limited for a term of 12 months, commencing July 1, at a rent of $975 per month payable on the first day of each month. The lease contained the following clause:

   > If the lessee shall hold over after the term . . . the resulting tenancy shall be a tenancy from month to month and not a tenancy from year to year, subject to all the terms, conditions, and agreements herein contained insofar as same may be applicable to a tenancy from month to month.

   On May 28 of the following year, Oil Can sent Tagom a notice stating that he must give vacant possession on the expiry of the lease. On June 30, Oil Can representatives visited Tagom and asked him what he intended to do. He replied that he would not leave the premises "peacefully." Tagom remained in possession on July 1, and sent a cheque by registered mail to Oil Can as rent for that month. Although the area superintendent had given instructions to the accounting department not to accept any rent from Tagom, a junior clerk deposited it in the company bank account. Soon afterward, a senior officer discovered the error, informed Tagom that the act of the clerk in accepting the cheque had been inadvertent and against instructions, and delivered a refund cheque from the company to Tagom for $975. Tagom returned the cheque.

   Was a new tenancy created, or could Oil Can obtain a court order for immediate possession?

Chapter 23
Mortgages of Land and Real Estate Transactions

A purchaser of land rarely has the resources to pay the full price at the time of completing the purchase. A mortgage plays a central role in financing the transaction. In this chapter we discuss the nature of mortgages, the rights and obligations of both lenders and borrowers, and the various stages of a typical real estate transaction.

We examine such questions as:

■ What is a mortgage, and what are the important mortgage terms?

■ What are the rights of the mortgagor and mortgagee?

■ What remedies are available to the mortgagee?

■ What is a "second mortgage," and how is it used?

■ In what ways are a mortgagee's rights different from those of other creditors?

- What is an "offer to purchase"?
- What are the usual steps in a real estate transaction?
- What is the process of "closing" the transaction?

THE ESSENCE OF MORTGAGE LAW

The Mortgage as a Contract

mortgage a loan contract that gives the lender an interest in the borrower's land as security for a debt

mortgagor a borrower who gives his lender an interest in his land as security for repayment of a debt

mortgagee a lender who accepts an interest in land as security for a loan

maturity date the end of the term when debt must be repaid

calculation period stages at which accrued interest is added to principal

amortization period length of time it should take to repay an entire debt with the specified payment schedule

term the time period during which an interest rate is fixed and principal lent

mortgage commitment document in which parties to a mortgage initially agree to borrow and lend

A **mortgage** document creates both an interest in land and a loan contract containing a number of important terms. The most important terms are the **mortgagor's** (borrower's) personal promise to pay off the debt and the **mortgagee's** (lender's) promise to discharge its interest in the land upon repayment. The most important promises of the mortgagor are:

(a) to pay the principal debt and accrued interest, either at the **maturity date** or in installments as agreed by the parties,[1]

(b) to keep the property adequately insured in the name of the mortgagee,

(c) to pay taxes on the land and buildings, and

(d) to keep the premises in a reasonable state of repair.

Interest charged on the principal sum is expressed as an annual percentage rate, and the mortgage specifies the **calculation period**—stages when interest is added to the principal. Periodic payments are usually required, and they are commonly a blend of interest and principal. The amount of each payment is determined by the **amortization period**—the maximum length of time it should take to repay the entire debt (interest and principal). Spreading the debt over a longer amortization period reduces the size of each periodic payment but increases the total amount of the debt. The interest rate is set for a specific time period—typically much shorter than the amortization period—that is known as the **term** of the mortgage. At the expiration of the term, the mortgage must be paid off, renewed at a new agreed-upon interest rate, or refinanced with a new mortgagee. Together, these provisions establish the financial arrangement for the mortgage loan. They are first described in the **mortgage commitment** letter, in which the parties initially agree to borrow and lend. For more information on this topic, see the Companion Website.

Mortgages almost always contain an acceleration clause, which states that upon default of any installment, the whole of the principal sum of the mortgage and accrued interest immediately falls due. Default accelerates the maturity date, and the mortgagee may pursue all its remedies.

The most important promises of the mortgagee are:

(a) to execute the necessary discharge of the mortgage upon repayment in full, and

(b) to leave the mortgagor in possession and not interfere with his use and enjoyment of the mortgaged premises so long as the mortgagor observes all his covenants.

The mortgagor signs the mortgage and the mortgagee merely accepts the document without signing it. Since the mortgagee's promises are set out as provisos or standard charge terms—some are simply implied by the common law and statutory principles of mortgage law—its acceptance of the document binds it to the mortgage terms.

Although some mortgages are private transactions between two individuals, most real estate mortgage lending to individual borrowers is done by financial institutions—insurance companies, trust companies, and banks.

---

[1] Except in Alberta and Saskatchewan, where a mortgagor cannot be sued personally for the mortgage debt. See provincial variations, below.

The Mortgage as an Interest in Land

The concept of the mortgage as an interest in land developed through case law and is now summarized in provincial legislation. Originally, a mortgage was an actual conveyance of the **legal title** to a fee simple interest in land by the mortgagor to the mortgagee as security for a debt. The transfer of title had two conditions: first, that the mortgagor could remain in possession of land as long as payments were up to date, and second, that the mortgagor was entitled to have the legal title returned to him upon full payment of the debt. However, if the appointed day passed without the debt being repaid, the conditions then expired, and the mortgagee owned the interest absolutely.

legal title an interest in land recognized by the common law

The Mortgagor's Right to Redeem

It seemed unfair to allow a mortgagee to keep title to land in situations where only a small amount of the debt remained unpaid. The courts of equity created a remedy for these cases of hardship. If the mortgagor pleaded hardship and tendered payment of the debt in full, the court would acknowledge his interest in the land and permit him to **redeem** it. It would order the mortgagee to reconvey the land to the mortgagor. This right to redeem obtained by the mortgagor from a court of equity is known as the **equity of redemption**, and it is often called simply "the equity." This is the source of the modern business term "equity," meaning the interest of the proprietors of a business in its total assets after allowing for mortgagees' claims.

redeem have the land reconveyed to the mortgagor

equity of redemption the right of the mortgagor to redeem mortgaged land on payment of the debt in full

The Mortgagee's Right to Foreclose

The courts of equity also recognized that limits needed to be placed on a mortgagor's equity of redemption. A mortgagor should not be entitled to redeem his property years later, after the mortgagee had significantly improved the land. The courts agreed that after a reasonable period of time had passed, the right to redeem the property should expire and the mortgagee could then safely treat the land as his own. The foreclosure period became generally accepted as six months from the date of the hearing in the case. Provincial mortgage legislation now establishes minimum time periods within which a defaulting mortgagor may redeem, after which his interest is foreclosed.

Why Mortgagees Rarely Take Possession Although a mortgagee may take possession upon default of the mortgagor, in practice, a mortgagee rarely does so until after it has obtained **foreclosure**. There are exceptions, such as when it believes that the mortgagor has no intention of trying to redeem, when the property is vacant, or when the premises become dilapidated. There are three main reasons for not going into possession:

foreclosure an order by a court ending the mortgagor's right to redeem within a fixed time

- First, a mortgagee generally wants its money rather than the mortgagor's property, and it would prefer to encourage the mortgagor to pay off the debt.
- Second, its possession would be uncertain, since the mortgagor might at any moment tender payment, redeem his interest, and demand possession.
- Third, it must account for any benefit it receives from occupation of the land and deduct it from the amount owing if the mortgagor tenders payment, losing any material advantage gained from taking possession.

Land Titles System

The land titles system, created through provincial legislation, has changed the legal nature of a mortgagee's interest in land. Under the land titles system (which is being used in most areas across Canada, as discussed in Chapter 21), a mortgage is called a **charge**, a mortgagor is a

charge a lien or encumbrance on land

chargor, and a mortgagee is a **chargee**.[2] Charges are no longer, strictly speaking, conveyances of the legal title. Rather, they are liens or encumbrances recorded on the title to the land, for which the ordinary remedy is to force a sale of the land and then apply the proceeds toward repayment of the debt.[3] Despite this significant legal distinction, basic mortgage procedure and remedies remain mostly unchanged. Chargors execute a charge document containing the terms of the loan and a personal promise to pay, remain in possession of the land, and, upon payment in full, are entitled to a discharge of the charge. If there is default, the chargee is given the right to dispossess the charger, foreclose his interest, and sell the property. The chargor still has a "redemption period" during which he may tender full payment of the debt and stop the foreclosure or sale of the property.[4] The mortgagee's remedies are discussed more fully below.

Registration

A mortgage or charge must be registered in the appropriate registry or land titles system as discussed in Chapter 21. It must be in the proper written form and identify the parties and the land involved. The priority of the mortgage interest is determined by the order of registration.[5] Consequently, if a mortgagee fails to register its mortgage, a subsequent purchaser will be unaware of the mortgage and will acquire title free from it. Similarly, a subsequent mortgagee has priority over an earlier mortgage if it registered first. Failure to register may result in the complete loss of the land as security, although the mortgagor's personal covenant to pay would still survive. Registration of the mortgage is public notice of its existence.

RIGHTS OF THE MORTGAGEE AND MORTGAGOR

The Mortgagee

Although the courts of common law and equity are merged and most registry systems have been converted to land titles, the interests of the mortgagee and mortgagor are still interpreted according to the remedies and principles developed before the merger.[6] If the mortgagor defaults on any of the terms of the mortgage, the mortgagee has the following remedies:

(a) It may sue the mortgagor on his personal covenant to repay, just as any creditor may sue any debtor who is in default, and obtain a personal judgment against him.

(b) It may dispossess the mortgagor and occupy the land itself (or put in a tenant). As noted above, this is not an attractive remedy until after foreclosure.

(c) It may sell the land under its contractual or statutory power of sale and apply the proceeds to pay the debt, as explained below.

(d) It may proceed with a court action for foreclosure and eventually destroy the mortgagor's right to redeem and, usually, the mortgagee's right to sue on the personal covenant as well.[7]

---

[2] Mortgages throughout Ontario, including those regions under the registry system, have been converted to charges and no longer represent legal title to the land: Land Registration Reform Act, R.S.O. 1990, c. L-4, ss. 1, 6.

[3] Land Titles Act, R.S.A. 2000, c. L-4, ss. 1(e), 1(o), 103.

[4] Land Registration Reform Act, *supra*, n. 2, s. 6(3).

[5] See, e.g., Land Titles Act, R.S.A. 2000, c. L-4, s. 14.

[6] Despite these reforms, the old terminology concerning legal and equitable title, rights, and remedies remains in common use.

[7] See e.g. British Columbia, Alberta, Manitoba, and Saskatchewan, where a final order of foreclosure extinguishes the right to sue on the personal covenant of the mortgagor: The Property Law Act, R.S.B.C. 1996, c. 377, s. 32; Law of Property Act, R.S.A. 2000, c. L-7, s. 40; The Mortgage Act, C.C.S.M. 2000, c. M200, s. 16; Limitation of Civil Rights Act, R.S.S. 1978, c. L-16, ss. 2(1–2), 6. In Ontario, a mortgagee may only sue on the covenant after foreclosure if it is in a position to reconvey the property to the debtor: *Price v. Letros*, [1973] O.J. No. 2260 at paras. 7–9 (Ont. C.A.); *L-Jalco Holdings Inc. v. Marino*, [2011] O.J. No. 419 at paras. 67–73 aff'd 2011 ONCA 639.

A mortgagee frequently chooses a combination of these remedies.[8]

The Mortgagor

The rights of a mortgagor after default are as follows:

(a) He may repay the mortgage loan together with interest and all expenses incurred by the mortgagee at any time, up to and including the date of the order of foreclosure, and obtain a release of his land.

(b) He may obtain an accounting for any benefits obtained from the land by the mortgagee and deduct them from the amount owing on redemption.

(c) If sued on his covenant to repay after foreclosure, he may require the mortgagee to prove that it is ready and able to reconvey the land upon repayment.

(d) If sued on his covenant to repay after sale of the property under power of sale, he may attack the sale price or sale expenses as unreasonable and have the amount outstanding reduced.

(e) He may also obtain relief against the consequences of an acceleration clause. If he pays all prior accrued payments, performs all other terms of which he may have been in default, and pays all costs incurred by the mortgagee, a court will permit him to continue to make regular payments under the original terms of the mortgage.[9]

(f) He may ask a court to stop the foreclosure proceedings and hold a sale instead (as discussed below).

THE MORTGAGEE'S REMEDIES UPON DEFAULT

There are advantages and disadvantages to each of the various remedies listed above. In this section, we examine the basic procedures, benefits, and drawbacks of the primary remedies.

Foreclosure

The process of obtaining foreclosure consists of three stages:

- Upon default, the mortgagee goes to court and asks for an order setting a time limit within which the mortgagor can redeem.

- Once the redemption period has expired, the court issues a final order of foreclosure that ends any further claim of the mortgagor and the claims of any other subsequent registered interests.

- Upon registration of the final order of foreclosure, the mortgagee is recognized as the owner of the property.

As the owner of the property, the mortgagee is deemed to accept the land in full satisfaction of the debt; it no longer has any right to demand payment.[10] Most mortgagees do not want to be landowners. Therefore, foreclosure is an attractive remedy only when the value of the property is high and the amount of the debt is low. However, in these circumstances, the mortgagor is likely to redeem.

---

[8] There are rules about how or in what order the remedies may be enforced. For example, a judge may stop a foreclosure and turn it into a sale: Law and Equity Act, R.S.B.C. 1996, c. 253, s. 15; Real Property Act, R.S.P.E.I. 1988, c. R-3, s. 72.

[9] Mortgages Act, R.S.O. 1990, c. M.40, ss. 22(1), 23(1); The Law of Property Act, R.S.A. 2000, c. L-7, s. 38.

[10] Some provinces allow an action on the personal covenant if the mortgagee still has the property: *supra*, n. 7. Proceeding on separate security such as a chattel mortgage or security agreement may still be possible: *Aros Investments Ltd. v. Picchi*, 2003 BCSC 78 (CanLII).

In some provinces (discussed below), if a mortgagee starts a foreclosure action and the mortgagor believes that the land is worth more than his mortgage debt, the mortgagor or any other subsequent secured creditor may ask the court to hold a sale instead.[11]

Sale by the Court

A mortgagee may request that the land be sold under the supervision of the court (or in some of the western provinces, under the supervision of the registrar of titles), with the sale to be either by tender or by auction.[12] Some jurisdictions permit the mortgagee or its agent to bid; others prohibit such bidding. The sale must be advertised for a specified period and carried out according to provincial statutes and regulations. In some jurisdictions, the court or registrar sets a reserve price below which no tenders will be accepted. The reserve price is not disclosed. When the tenders are opened, the highest one is accepted if it is over the reserve price. If no bid is above the reserve price, then the land remains unsold and the mortgagee may resort to its other remedies.

When a sale produces a successful bid, the mortgagee is entitled to recover the principal sum owing, accrued interest, and expenses of the court action and the sale. If the sale produces a smaller sum, the mortgagee may obtain judgment against the mortgagor for the deficiency. If the sale is for a larger sum, the surplus is returned to the mortgagor or his other secured creditors of the land.

Sale by the Mortgagee

power of sale a right upon default to sell mortgaged land

Most mortgages—and, in some jurisdictions, the statutes governing mortgages—give the mortgagee a contractual and statutory **power of sale** that may be exercised privately without court action or supervision, although advance notice to the mortgagor is generally required. A mortgagee may exercise its power of sale at any time after default, subject to any statutory period of grace. By executing a proper conveyance and declaring that it is made in pursuance of a power of sale, the mortgagee may validly transfer the title to the land to any third party. The sale must, however, be a genuine sale and not a fraud upon the mortgagor. A mortgagee may not sell to itself either directly or through an agent. Whenever a mortgagee exercises a power of sale, it is under a duty to take reasonable steps to obtain a fair price for the land. If the mortgagor can show that the mortgagee sold for an unreasonably low price, the court will reduce the deficiency accordingly or give the mortgagor judgment for any surplus he should have received.

The same rules concerning the proceeds of a sale apply here as in a sale by the court. If there is a deficiency, the mortgagee may still sue the mortgagor for the sum; if there is a surplus, it must be returned to the mortgagor or to the remaining secured creditors.

INTERNATIONAL ISSUE

Mortgage Crisis

Over the last two decades, the United States experienced a major crisis in its mortgage industry. Homeowners defaulted on residential mortgages in record numbers, and the resulting explosion in power-of-sale and foreclosure proceedings created a glut in the real estate market and a decline in housing prices.

The National Consumer Law Center reports that between 1980 and 2005, American foreclosures increased almost 300 percent, while home ownership increased by only 5 percent. The *Los Angeles Times* reported a record 47 171 foreclosures in California during the first quarter of 2008, more than four

>

---

[11] Law and Equity Act, R.S.B.C. 1996, c. 253, s. 15; Real Property Act, R.S.P.E.I. 1988, c. R-3, s. 72.

[12] Law of Property Act, R.S.A. 2000, c. L-7, s. 40.

times as many as in the first quarter of 2007. By May 2011, one in every 103 housing units in Nevada was in foreclosure.

Some factors contributing to the high number of defaults were

- loans given to borrowers with poor credit,
- misleading lending terms that included low interest-only payments to start (teaser rates) with large balloon payments of principal required at the end of the term, and
- mortgages with no down payments, or fully financed housing purchases.

As a result, homeowners found themselves with mortgages they could not afford to maintain after the initial low-interest term. They could not refinance due to falling real estate values and they could not sell because too many other homes were already for sale at low prices.

Suggested legislative initiatives to ease the crisis and prevent future instability in the mortgage market include

- regulating lending criteria,
- restricting predatory lending practices,
- extending low "teaser" rates, and
- altering foreclosure and power-of-sale procedures to provide greater protection for mortgagors.

Possible changes to foreclosure and power-of-sale procedures include

- longer redemption periods,
- restrictions on possession rights, and
- expanded defences available to mortgagors.

In 2011, the foreclosure rates were still paralyzing economic recovery and attorneys general in several states were investigating the foreclosure practices of lenders after documentation discrepancies and inaccurate calculation of indebtedness were reported.

Questions to Consider

1. What measures do you think best protect both mortgagors and mortgagees?

2. In this market, which remedy best protects a mortgagee?

3. Is it possible that the U.S. income tax rule that allows homeowners to deduct mortgage interest from taxable income contributed to the foreclosure crisis? Why?

Sources: Peter Y. Hong, "California Home Entering Foreclosure Hit Record," *Los Angeles Times*, April 23, 2008, http://articles.latimes .com/2008/apr/-23/business/fi-foreclose23; the National Consumer Law Center and the National Association of Consumer Advocates, "Comments to the Board of Governors to the Federal Reserve System Regarding the Board's Authority Under HOEPA to Prohibit Unfair Acts or Practices in Connection With Mortgage Lending," Docket No. OP-1288, August 15, 2007, www.consumerlaw.org/issues /predatory_mortgage/content/HOEPA_CommentsAug07.pdf; Ruth Simon and Nick Timiraos, "California and Illinois Expand Foreclosure Probe," *Wall Street Journal*, May 26, 2011, available at http://online .wsj.com/article/SB100014240527023040665045763454224532 84118.html; Pam Bennett, "The Aftermath of the Great Recession: Financially Fragile Families and How Professionals Can Help," The Forum for Family and Consumer Issues NC State University, http://ncsu .edu/ffci/publications/2012/v17-n1-2012-spring/bennett.php.

SALE BY A MORTGAGOR OF HIS INTEREST

Financial Arrangements

A mortgagor struggling to keep up with mortgage payments may need or want to sell his property before the maturity date. A mortgagor may transfer the property to a new purchaser, but the existing mortgage must be dealt with as part of the financial arrangements between the two.

assumption of the mortgage a subsequent purchaser takes over the responsibility of paying off the vendor's existing mortgage

---

ILLUSTRATION 23.1

Adam, the owner of Blackacre farm, mortgages it to BCD Trust Co. for $100 000. Subsequently, he sells Blackacre to Rona for $160 000. How is the price to be paid by Rona? There are three possibilities:

- First, Rona may pay Adam the full $160 000 and obtain an undertaking from Adam that he will pay off the mortgage to BCD Trust Co.

- Second, Rona may pay $60 000 to Adam for Adam's equity of redemption and a further $100 000 to BCD Trust Co. in full payment of the mortgage.

- Third, Rona may pay Adam $60 000, as above, and accept Blackacre subject to the mortgage; that is, Rona will herself assume responsibility for paying off the mortgage. We can see that the third possibility is really a variation of the second: Instead of paying the mortgage off at once, Rona simply pays it off as it falls due. This is known as an **assumption of the mortgage**.

In circumstances like those in Illustration 23.1, the first possibility rarely occurs because Rona takes the risk that Adam's other creditors might obtain the purchase money through court action, or Adam might abscond so that the funds never reach BCD Trust Co., leaving Rona to pay BCD in order to redeem the mortgage. She might end up paying $260 000 for Blackacre instead of $160 000. The second option can be very expensive for two reasons. First, by the terms of the mortgage, the mortgagor may not have the right to pay off the mortgage before the due date without a substantial penalty; this is a **closed mortgage**. Also, purchasers rarely pay the full purchase price up front for land. Land transactions are almost invariably financed by a credit arrangement, usually in the form of a mortgage. If interest rates have risen, the purchaser will wind up replacing a low interest mortgage with a new higher interest mortgage. Therefore, the third option is most attractive for Rona; however, as we shall discuss below, Adam may not agree.

Sometimes, the purchaser may not have the cash to pay fully for the vendor's equity and needs more financing than the vendor's existing mortgage provides. She will arrange through a financial institution for a new mortgage for a larger sum of money and then use the proceeds of the new mortgage to pay off the existing mortgage, with the balance going toward the cash portion of the purchase price.

Effect of Default by the Purchaser
What happens if the purchaser, Rona, defaults on payment of the original mortgage?

- The fact that Adam has sold his land to Rona does not affect BCD's rights as mortgagee of Blackacre; BCD retains all its rights against the land. It may obtain possession and sell the land. It may also recover from Adam, the original mortgagor, on his personal covenant—his contractual obligation—to repay the debt. This continuing liability discourages many vendors from agreeing to an assumption by the purchaser. Some provinces limit the right to sue an original mortgagor on a personal covenant in a residential mortgage if the mortgagee has approved the new purchaser.[13] Once the new purchaser renews the mortgage for a subsequent term, his own personal covenant (given upon renewal) replaces that of the original mortgagor.

If BCD sues Adam, what rights does Adam have upon paying off the mortgage?

- Adam may successfully sue Rona for the full sum of money he was required to pay to BCD. One reason for this result is that, as part of her purchase price for Blackacre, Rona assumed the mortgage and agreed to pay it off. The law implies that the promise to pay off the mortgage includes a promise to indemnify Adam—that is, to protect Adam from any liability under it. A second reason is that by paying off the mortgage Adam has, in effect, purchased the mortgagee's rights. He becomes subrogated to the mortgagee's rights and is, in effect, the mortgagee to whom Rona is now a mortgagor. At this point, Adam may use all the remedies against Rona that BCD Trust Co. might itself have utilized against the land and the mortgagor.

Instead of suing Adam, may the mortgagee BCD sue the purchaser Rona directly?

- At common law, BDC could not sue Rona because the mortgage (alone) does not create privity of contract (or estate) between BCD and Rona. However, most lenders will not allow their mortgage to be assumed unless the purchaser signs a contract with them, agreeing to make all the remaining payments. This contract is known as an **assumption agreement** and gives BCD privity of contract (and a breach of contract cause of action) with Rona. In addition, some provincial mortgage legislation gives the mortgagee a statutory right to sue the purchaser, Rona, directly, while Rona holds the land.[14]

closed mortgage a mortgage that does not permit early repayment of the debt without a substantial penalty

assumption agreement a contract between the mortgagee and the new purchaser in which the new purchaser agrees to comply with all the requirements in the original mortgage

---

[13] Property Law Act, R.S.B.C. c. 377, ss. 23, 24; Real Property Act, C.C.S.M. c. R.30, s. 77.2; R.S.P.E.I. 1988, c. R-3, s. 79.

[14] Mortgages Act (Ont.), *supra*, n. 9, ss. 20(2), (3).

If she sells it to yet another purchaser, Bill, then Bill becomes liable to pay the mortgage, and Rona is released from her statutory obligation to the mortgagee. As a last resort, BCD may obtain an assignment of Adam's right to indemnity discussed in the preceding paragraph. As a practical matter, Adam will often agree to assign his right in order to avoid having the mortgagee sue him on his covenant in the mortgage.

SECOND MORTGAGES

Uses of a Second Mortgage

A prospective purchaser often finds she does not have sufficient money to buy land that is already subject to a mortgage. An existing landowner may wish to use some of its existing equity in land to renovate the property. Second mortgages (that is, mortgages registered after one prior mortgage) are commonly used for both reasons. Less common are third and fourth mortgages. The subsequent mortgages rank behind prior registered mortgages and their interests may be wiped out by the remedies of the first mortgagee.

Rights of a Second Mortgagee

A second mortgagee has rights similar to those of a first mortgagee except that he ranks behind the first mortgagee in priority of payment out of the proceeds of the land. If the mortgagor defaults on payment of both mortgages, the first mortgagee may start an action for foreclosure. The second mortgagee may decide to stand by and do nothing. If the first mortgagee completes the foreclosure, the interest of both mortgagor and the second mortgagee is destroyed. The second mortgagee loses his security in the land and is left with only a right of action for debt against the mortgagor, who may be insolvent.

If the first mortgagee proceeds with a sale under power of sale, or sale by the court, the proceeds will be paid, first, to satisfy the first mortgage debt and expenses of the sale, and second, to satisfy the second mortgage debt. The second mortgagee will be paid only to the extent that there is any surplus after paying off the first mortgagee. Of course, the sale may bring in more money than the total amount owed on both mortgages, and in that case the excess will go to the mortgagor.

If the first mortgagee begins a foreclosure action, the second mortgagee has the same opportunity to redeem as the mortgagor—that is, to pay off the first mortgage himself and receive an assignment of it. Thereafter he may commence his own foreclosure action, or he may proceed with either of the two remedies of sale, taking the risk that a sale may not bring in enough to pay off the two sums he has invested.

Risks for a Second Mortgagee When the Mortgagor Defaults

A second mortgage always provides that default on the first mortgage is also immediate default on the second mortgage—that is, a breach of the mortgagor's obligation to protect the second mortgagee's interest in the land—and the second mortgagee may immediately act upon the usual remedies. In the absence of such protection, a second mortgagee might find himself in the following position:

(a) Payment of the second mortgage is not yet due, so there is no default on it.
(b) The first mortgage, having an earlier due date, is in default and the first mortgagee promptly pursues one of its remedies against the land—foreclosure, sale by court, or exercise of the power of sale.
(c) The result of either of these remedies would be to destroy the second mortgagee's interest in the land.

In a sale either by the court or by the first mortgagee, to the extent that the sale brought in more than the debt due on the first mortgage, the second mortgagee would receive compensation, but he might well recover only a part of the debt. To avoid these risks, a second mortgagee may himself act promptly to pursue his remedies.

Sometimes a mortgagor defaults on only the second mortgage, or, if he has defaulted on the first as well, the first mortgagee might be quite satisfied with the adequacy of its security and be willing to "sit tight" and see what the subsequent mortgagees and creditors intend to do. The first mortgagee need not worry since it has priority in the land and no one can affect its position. If the second mortgagee forecloses, he becomes the owner of the property, subject to the prior interest of the first mortgagee. He must now make the payments and assume the responsibilities of the original mortgagor. A second mortgagee rarely proceeds by sale, but in such circumstances, the purchaser would obtain title clear of the mortgagor's interest and the second mortgage, but, of course, still subject to the first mortgage. In either case the new owner must make satisfactory arrangements with the first mortgagee.

Subsequent Mortgages after a Second Mortgage

Each successive mortgage ranks in priority according to its registration. Each subsequent mortgage gives all the usual remedies to the mortgagee, subject to the prior rights of any earlier mortgagee. Each subsequent mortgagee takes a greater risk as creditor for several reasons:

- First, the land is subject to a larger financial debt, and any drop in price will injure the security of the latest mortgagee first.

- Second, a succession of mortgages on one piece of land usually indicates financial instability and poor management on the part of the borrower.

- Third, failure by a subsequent mortgagee to act promptly in case of default may result in the destruction of its secured interest in the land, if a prior mortgagee exercises its power of sale or right to redeem first.

- Fourth, the cost of redeeming prior mortgages may be too high—in order to prevent foreclosure of its interest, a subsequent mortgagee may have to lay out more money than it can afford.

This is why interest rates are higher on subsequent mortgages and lenders frequently demand additional security, such as mortgages on other lands or personal property, before advancing a mortgage loan.

MORTGAGEE'S RIGHTS COMPARED WITH RIGHTS OF OTHER CREDITORS

general creditor a creditor that has no security other than the debtor's promise to pay

secured creditor a creditor that has collateral security in the form of a recognized claim against specified assets of the debtor

A creditor that has no security other than its debtor's promise is a **general creditor**, and its claim ranks as a general claim. A creditor that has collateral security—that is, a recognized prior claim against one or more specified assets of the debtor, is a **secured creditor**. If the debtor becomes insolvent, the general creditors must wait until the claims of the secured creditors have been satisfied out of the assets against which they have their claims. When the sale of an asset brings in more than the amount owing to the secured creditor, the excess becomes available for the settlement of general claims. A mortgagee is a secured creditor in the land. As noted earlier, after a sale of the mortgaged land by the mortgagee, the sale proceeds first go to satisfy the mortgage debt and sale expenses. Any surplus is returned to the mortgagor; if the mortgagor is insolvent, the surplus goes to his creditors. However, if there is a deficiency—that is, the particular security realizes less than the amount of the secured creditor's claim—to the extent of that deficiency, the secured creditor then ranks as a general creditor along with all the general creditors.

ILLUSTRATION 23.2

(a) Harper is the proprietor of a successful, small retail business with some land worth about $320 000. He has mortgaged the land for $250 000 to Commerce Trust Co. Unfortunately, his area suffers a serious recession when a large local industry closes; he has little working capital and cannot weather the indefinite loss in sales. He becomes insolvent and is declared bankrupt. A trustee is appointed, and, in due course, the land is sold. The rest of Harper's assets are also sold. The following is a statement of Harper's financial position after all the assets are liquidated:

Assets		Liabilities	
Bank balance from:		Commerce	
sale of land	$270 000	Trust Co.	$247 000
sale of other		General	
assets	38 000	creditors	85 000
TOTAL	$308 000	TOTAL	$332 000

The assets would be distributed as follows:

Commerce Trust Co.	$247 000
General Creditors	61 000
	$308 000

We see that the mortgagee receives 100 cents on each dollar of debt owed to it from the sale of the building. In addition, the sale produces a surplus of $23 000. This sum is added to the $38 000 realized from all other assets, and is paid out rateably to the general creditors. Here, they receive 61 000 ÷ 85 000 of each dollar of indebtedness—about 72 cents on each dollar.

(b) Suppose, however, that the sale of the building brings a much smaller sum because of the depressed market—say, $200 000. The assets and liabilities are now as follows:

Assets		Liabilities	
Bank balance from:		Commerce	
sale of land	$200 000	Trust Co.	$247 000
sale of other		General	
assets	38 000	creditors	85 000
TOTAL	$238 000	TOTAL	$332 000

The assets would now be distributed as follows:

Creditors	Secured	General	Total
Commerce Trust Co.	$200 000		
plus $\frac{47\,000}{132\,000} \times 38\,000$		$13 530	$213 530
General Creditors			
$\frac{85\,000}{132\,000} \times 38\,000$		24 470	24 470
	$200 000	$38 000	$238 000

Note: We obtain the figure of $132 000 by adding the deficiency of $47 000 on the mortgage debt to the total unsecured debt of $85 000. In these circumstances the mortgagee receives a total of over $213 000 from a debt of $247 000—about 86 cents on each dollar of debt. On the other hand, the general creditors suffer much more severely: They receive about 24 500 ÷ 85 000 of each dollar of indebtedness—about 29 cents on each dollar. We may note that their position is worsened by the fact that the mortgagee joined them to rank as a general creditor for that portion of the debt unsatisfied by the sale of the land, thus dividing the assets among a larger group of claims.

TRANSFERRING A MORTGAGEE'S INTEREST IN LAND

Assignment

A mortgagee may wish to obtain cash by selling the mortgage rather than waiting for the mortgage debt to fall due in order to collect. The mortgage may be a sound investment, having good security and a reliable debtor, or it may be a risky investment as when the value of the land falls below the outstanding mortgage debt. In either case, the mortgagee may sell its mortgage at the best price it can get. The sale of a mortgage is a transaction involving both contractual and real property aspects. The mortgagee assigns its rights to the covenants made by the mortgagor, and grants or transfers its interest in the land to the purchaser (assignee) of the mortgage. Sometimes, in order to obtain a higher price, an assignor–mortgagee guarantees payment—that is, if the mortgagor defaults in payment, the assignor, on the assignee's demand, will pay off the mortgage and take back an assignment of it. In most sales, however, a mortgagee sells the mortgage outright, and the purchaser takes the risk of default together with all the usual remedies of a mortgagee.

A purchaser of a mortgage, as an assignee of contractual rights, is bound by the usual rules of assignment in contract. As we saw in Chapter 11, the debtor—in this case, the mortgagor—is not bound by the assignment until receiving notice of it, and the assignee takes the mortgage subject to the equities and the state of the mortgage account between mortgagor and mortgagee. Assignments are registered on the title to the land.

Discharge of Mortgages

Effects of a Discharge
When a mortgagor or a subsequent purchaser pays off the whole of the mortgage debt at maturity of the loan, he is entitled to a discharge from the mortgagee. A discharge operates both as an acknowledgment that the debt has been paid in full and as a cancellation of the lien or encumbrance on the land. To clear his title to the property, the mortgagor promptly registers the discharge in the land titles office. A fraudulent mortgagee cannot then successfully exercise a power of sale and grant the legal title to an innocent purchaser on the pretence that the mortgage is unpaid and in arrears.[15] In areas where the registry system still exists, a discharge from the mortgagee operates to reconvey the legal title of the land to the mortgagor.

Arrangements for Prepayment of Mortgage Debt
A mortgage sometimes contains a contractual provision permitting the mortgagor to repay the mortgage and to obtain a discharge even before the end of the term. Such repayment options have conditions attached to them. Often a mortgagee requires a period of notice, usually three months, before it need accept the money. Such a requirement gives it time to find a new borrower so that the money received does not lie idle until it finds a new investment. A mortgagee usually requires payment of a bonus—for example, three months' interest in lieu of notice—or it may require both notice and a bonus. Flexible mortgage-prepayment clauses often contain various other prepayment possibilities. A mortgagor may be permitted to prepay part of the debt rather than all of it, in order to make good use of extra earnings and to reduce the interest payable on the mortgage loan. Certain types of mortgages, particularly second mortgages and short-term mortgages, permit repayment "at any time without notice or bonus." A mortgage containing such a provision is usually called an **open mortgage**.

open mortgage a mortgage permitting repayment of the debt at any time without notice or bonus

Partial Discharges
A mortgage may also permit the mortgagor to prepay a specified portion of the mortgage debt and to obtain a **partial discharge**—that is, a discharge of a definite portion of the mortgaged lands. Partial discharges are common when the mortgagor is a land developer. The developer may own a large piece of undeveloped land and wish to sell off a part free from any encumbrance; or he may wish to build a large building on a particular part of the land and may require financing in the form of a large, new mortgage—which he cannot obtain except as a first mortgage. These various methods of prepaying part or all of a mortgage debt play an important role in the credit financing of land development.

partial discharge a discharge of a definite portion of the mortgaged lands

PROVINCIAL VARIATIONS

The remedies available to mortgagees and mortgagors developed over a long period time. The various provinces of Canada adopted existing English law at different times. Accordingly, the variations in the mortgage law among the provinces are considerable. Although the basic provisions are similar, the specifics differ according to the economy

---

[15] A fraudulent mortgagee may deprive a mortgagor of the land when the mortgagor has neglected to obtain a discharge and register it: *Dicker v. Angerstein* (1876), 3 Ch. D. 395.

of the province and the character of business within it. Examples of variations in rights of mortgagees and mortgagors are discussed below.

The Mortgagee's Rights

In Alberta, British Columbia, Manitoba, and Saskatchewan, a mortgagee's right to sue on the covenant to repay has been restricted by statute.[16]

In British Columbia, in that portion of Manitoba under the registry system, and in Ontario, New Brunswick, Prince Edward Island, and Newfoundland and Labrador, a mortgagee may foreclose the equity of redemption in the manner already discussed. In Alberta, Saskatchewan, and Manitoba, the usual remedy is sale by the court.[17] If the sale does not produce any satisfactory bids, then the mortgagee may proceed to foreclose, but foreclosure appears to be a rare remedy in practice. In all provinces, a mortgagee may request the court or registrar to hold a sale of mortgaged land and, except in Nova Scotia, may sell under a power of sale if it is provided for either by statute or under the terms of the mortgage.[18] In Nova Scotia, although the court issues an order of "foreclosure and sale," foreclosure is not really permitted: The court must hold a sale.

The Mortgagor's Rights

Except for New Brunswick, those provinces permitting a mortgagee to start an action for foreclosure also allow the mortgagor to request the court to hold a sale, provided he deposits a sum of money as security for the costs of the sale if it produces no acceptable bids. Accordingly, a mortgagor may prevent the mortgagee from acquiring the mortgagor's interest in the land. This right of the mortgagor can be an important protection when the land is worth substantially more than the mortgage debt. However, if the market value of the land does exceed the mortgage debt by a significant amount, the mortgagor, unless he is considered a bad personal credit risk, should be able to refinance the land by obtaining an extension of his mortgage or arranging for a new mortgage and paying off his old mortgage. In any event, he should be able to sell the equity of redemption at its market value. In all jurisdictions, a mortgagor has the right to redeem the land by paying off the entire debt before foreclosure or sale.

REVERSE MORTGAGES

A recent development in Canadian law has been the recognition of the European concept of the **reverse mortgage**. It can be a benefit, especially to senior citizens who are retired and are "house rich and cash poor." Typically, a homeowner purchased a house many years earlier and has paid off the mortgage debt on the property; she owns it without debt. Suppose that her retirement income is very small while her house has increased substantially in market value.

Using the reverse mortgage concept, she may give a mortgage on her house and receive a lump sum or a periodic payment based on the market value of the property, prevailing interest rates, and actuarial calculations of her life expectancy. She remains in possession of the house while the principal and interest on the reverse mortgage accrue; no repayment is due until she sells the house or dies. When one of these two events occurs, and if the market value of the house is greater than the accrued debt, the lender pays the excess to

reverse mortgage a form of mortgage under which no repayment is due until the mortgagor sells or dies

---

[16] *Supra*, n. 7. See also *National Trust Co. v. Mead*, [1990] 2 S.C.R. 410.

[17] See e.g. Real Property Act, C.C.S.M. c. R30, s. 138; *supra*, n. 14, s. 40(2).

[18] See e.g. Manitoba, *ibid.*, s. 135.

the owner or her estate. If the value of the house is less than the accrued debt, then the lender absorbs the deficiency.[19]

The aging population and the increasing number of persons in financial difficulty has made the reverse mortgage more common.[20] Some financial institutions have begun to promote this new area. There are wide variations in the design of reverse mortgages. Provinces regulate the reverse mortgage contract with mandatory disclosure and cooling-off periods.[21]

MORTGAGE FRAUD

In the summer of 2004, it was reported that Canada was experiencing a rise in "mortgage fraud."[22] This increased incidence of fraud was said to be linked to the "hot" real estate market in many Canadian cities, automation of the land registration systems, and the rise in the incidence of identity theft.

This mortgage fraud—which takes as its primary victim mortgage lenders but also creates costs for homeowners and society generally—can take two forms.

The first is essentially a form of identity theft, whereby one fraudster assumes the identity of a registered land title holder, while a second "conspirator" assumes the identity of a purchaser. An agreement of purchase and sale is drawn up and used to obtain mortgage financing, which is never repaid. When the mortgage goes into default, the true owner of the property is surprised to learn of power of sale proceeding by an unknown lender.

The second form of mortgage fraud involves the artificial inflation of the value of a property, through "flips" of properties (a property is purchased and then immediately resold at an inflated price, so as to increase the purported value of the property, and increase the amount of mortgage financing) or through misrepresentations of the purchase price using falsified purchase agreements or phony appraisers.

While the mortgagees are defrauded of the mortgage amount, homeowners are also affected. In the case of identity fraud, not only will the real homeowner have to convince the mortgagee that he is not the debtor, but he will likely have to spend additional money on land registry and legal fees to restore his title on the register. Additionally, the costs of mortgage fraud borne by the mortgage lenders will inevitably be passed on to mortgagors in the form of higher lending costs. The initial response by the courts was not favourable to the homeowner. In *Household Realty Corp. v. Liu*,[23] the Ontario Court of Appeal upheld a fraudulent mortgage against an innocent homeowner. The lender was entitled to enforce its remedies. In 2007, the court took the rare step of overruling itself. In *Lawrence v. Maple Trust Co.*, it held that only a true owner could give a valid charge, so this mortgage was held invalid and the innocent homeowner's title was cleared.[24] The Ontario land titles legislation has since been amended to invalidate fraudulent documents.[25] The losing party, either the duped lender or the innocent homeowner, is entitled to make a claim against the

---

[19] See, for example, The Mortgage Act, C.C.S.M. s. 31(2).

[20] For a useful discussion of the reverse mortgage, see the Canadian Centre for Elder Law Studies, Consultation Paper on Reverse Mortgages (B.C. Law Institute, February 2005).

[21] Manitoba was the first to adopt legislation directed specifically at reverse mortgages. See Part III of the Mortgages Act, C.C.S.M., c. M200.

[22] In a *Toronto Sun* business column, it was reported that real estate fraud cost an estimated $300 million in Canada in the year 2001 alone: Linda Leatherdale, "Homes Fall Prey to Identity Thieves," *Toronto Sun*, August 15, 2004.

[23] (2005), 261 D.L.R. (4th) 679 (On. C.A.).

[24] [2007] 84 O.R. (3d) 94 (On. C.A.); but see *Reviczky v. Meleknia* (2008), 88 O.R. (3d) 699, where the court felt the victim had an opportunity to avoid the fraud.

[25] The Ontario Land Titles Act, s. 78(4.1), invalidates fraudulent documents registered after October 19, 2006. However, the amendment does not invalidate the chain of documents stemming from the document—only the initial fraud.

Land Titles Assurance Fund. Alberta legislation strengthens the proof of identity require-ments for the registrar of land titles and imposes a duty on the real estate industry to protect against mortgage fraud.[26]

Fraudulent registration of any document in a real property transaction is a criminal offence with a maximum penalty of five years in prison.

Ethical Issue Money Laundering and Solicitor–Client Privilege

As part of a federal anti-terrorism initiative, the federal gov-ernment enacted the Proceeds of Crime (Money Laundering) and Terrorist Financing Act. Under the federal legislation, professionals and financial institutions are required to report suspicious transactions or large cash payments of $10 000 or more. An independent government agency (FINTRAC) investigates and analyzes reports and tracks cross-border movements of currency.

Lawyers were among the professionals covered by the Act, and real estate lawyers were particularly affected since their work involves receiving large sums of money from their clients.

The Federation of Law Societies of Canada launched a successful court challenge of the law. It argued that requiring lawyers to report on their clients was a violation of solicitor–client privilege and a breach of the constitu-tional right to independent counsel. The courts agreed with the Federation's position and restricted the application of the new law. As a result, the Minister of Finance introduced amendments to the Act exempting lawyers from its reporting requirements.

In recognition of the fact that preventing money laun-dering is a worthy goal, the Federation developed model rules for lawyers' codes of professional conduct. The model "know your client" rule requires lawyers to confirm their clients' identities with independent documents and collect information such as addresses and occupations. The model "no cash" rule prohibits lawyers from accepting cash payments of $7500 or more.

Questions to Consider

1. Do you think law societies are in a better position to deal with money laundering than FINTRAC?

2. This is another example of a conflict between two worthy goals. What are the arguments that justify the priority of solicitor–client privilege?

Sources: Proceeds of Crime (Money Laundering) and Terrorist Fi-nancing Act, S.C. 2000, c. 17; Committee on Anti-Money Laun-dering, Federation of Law Societies of Canada, "The Federation of Law Societies of Canada Submission in Response to Finance Canada's Enhancing Canada's Anti-Money Laundering and Anti-Terrorist Financing Regime Consultation," Department of Finance Canada, September 30, 2005, http://www.fin.gc.-ca/-consultresp /regime_14-eng.asp; *Law Society of British Columbia v. Attorney General of Canada* (2002), 207 D.L.R. (4th) 736 (B.C.C.A.); Federa-tion of Law Societies of Canada, "Model Rule on Client Identification and Verification Requirements," March 20, 2008, http://www .flsc.ca/_documents/Client-Identification-Dec-2008.pdf.

A TYPICAL REAL ESTATE TRANSACTION

The Circumstances

A real estate transaction can best be understood by following a typical sale from start to finish. We examine the sale of a fictional piece of land in Oshawa, Ontario, governed by the registry system (as it is the more onerous type of transaction). Land covered by the land titles system will not require the title search described below.

Vincent owns the land and office building at 99 Main Street, legally described as Lot 27, Plan 7654, in the City of Oshawa (Property Identification Number (PIN) R234). In addition to Vincent's office, the building holds three other offices. One is rented to a den-tist, the second to an auto insurance company, and the third to a chartered accountant. Business has been poor; Vincent wishes to retire and decides to sell the building.

---

[26] A. Reg. 174/08; Land Titles Act, R.S.A. 2000, c. L-4, s. 43.1; The Real Estate Amendment Act, 2006, S.A. 2006, c. 29, s. 2.

Listing the Property for Sale

Vincent hires a real estate agent to help him find a buyer for the property. Vincent signs a standard form **listing agreement** that appoints the agent and

- designates a list price (selling price) and term (length of the agent's appointment);
- gives the agent the exclusive right to advertise the property on MLS (Multiple Listing Service) and via the internet and television during the term of the listing;
- allows the agent to show the property to prospective buyers, either individually or collectively at "open houses";
- requires Vincent to pay the agent a commission (usually a percentage of the sale price) if the agent "procures an offer" at the list price or Vincent accepts an offer at any price;[27] and
- directs Vincent's lawyer to pay the commission directly to the agent out of the sale proceeds.

The duties and responsibilities of an agent are discussed in Chapter 17. For more information on this topic, see the Companion Website.

The Offer to Purchase

Hi-Style Centres Ltd., a firm selling women's wear, operates a chain of stores and is anxious to have an outlet in Oshawa. Hi-Style's first offer to purchase the building for $600 000 is rejected and Vincent counter-offers $675 000. This is rejected, and Hi-Style makes a counter-offer. These are the essential terms:[28]

(a) Hi-Style offers to buy the premises for $645 000, payable as follows:
   (i) $25 000 as a deposit by certified cheque attached to the offer;
   (ii) assume the first mortgage of about $375 000 held by the Grimm Mortgage Company; the offer is conditional on Grimm approving Hi-Style's assumption;
   (iii) give back to Vincent a second mortgage of $125 000 (interest and other terms set out in detail);
   (iv) pay the balance on closing date (completion date).
(b) The sale is to be closed 90 days after the date of the offer.

(c) Hi-Style may search the title and submit **requisitions** (questions concerning claims against Vincent's title) within 60 days of acceptance of the offer. Vincent promises to deliver a copy of any survey of the lot, which he has in his possession, for examination by Hi-Style. If serious claims against Vincent's title are raised and Vincent cannot answer them satisfactorily, the contract will be terminated and the deposit returned to Hi-Style. If requisitions are answered satisfactorily or no requisitions are submitted within 60 days, it is presumed that Hi-Style accepts Vincent's title as satisfactory.
(d) Vincent is to remain in possession, and the building is to remain at his risk until closing. He promises to keep the building insured to its full insurable value.

---

[27] If the vendor accepts an offer after the expiration of the term of the listing from a purchaser introduced to the property by the agent.

[28] An offer to purchase may also include other terms, the importance of which varies according to the circumstances, and, in particular, the nature of the property. For example, the vendor might be required to give a warranty that the heating plant conforms to regulations, to warrant that the premises do not violate existing zoning bylaws.

He also undertakes to give possession of the building in substantially the same condition as it was at the time of making the contract.[29]

(e) Vincent is to pay all taxes and insurance until closing and deduct from the amount due at closing all outstanding current expenses, such as accrued water and electric bills, and unpaid taxes. Hi-Style will arrange its own insurance to commence on the day of closing.

(f) Vincent warrants that his three suites of offices are leased to tenants as stated at rents of $1250 monthly per suite under leases expiring two years after date of closing for Suite No. 1; two years and four months after closing for Suite No. 2; and Suite No. 3 as a monthly tenancy only. He will deliver the original of the two leases and assignments of the leases on closing, an acknowledgment from the third tenant that she is only a monthly tenant, and signed notices to the tenants that Hi-Style is the new landlord to whom they are to pay their rent.

(g) The offer is conditional on Hi-Style obtaining a satisfactory property inspection report within 10 days of acceptance, failing which the offer is null and void. The condition may be waived by Hi-Style.

(h) The offer is open for two days, and acceptance must be communicated to the office of the lawyer for Hi-Style in Oshawa before 5:00 p.m. on the second day.

The rules of offer and acceptance are discussed in Chapters 6 and 7.

Accepting the Offer and Waiver of Conditions

Vincent decides to accept Hi-Style's counter-offer and signs four copies. The agent sends two signed copies back to Hi-Style (one for Hi-Style's lawyer, Harmon) prior to 5:00 P.M., retaining the other copies for Vincent and his lawyer, Vale.

Ideally, Harmon would have reviewed the offer prior to submission, and already be familiar with the dates to submit requisitions concerning title to the land and to close the transaction. The agent and Hi-Style, with Harmon's assistance (if necessary), immediately request Grimm's approval of Hi-Style's assumption of the first mortgage; credit checks and financial disclosure will be necessary. When the approval is obtained, Hi-Style signs a waiver of condition, copies of which are sent to Vincent and both lawyers.

The condition on satisfactory property inspection report may be in the form of an option to terminate, condition precedent, or condition subsequent (as defined in Chapter 12). It gives Hi-Style the right to have a professional of its choice visit the property and report on its physical soundness. If Hi-Style is not happy with the condition of the property as revealed in the report, it may terminate the contract. This is important because the general rule of **caveat emptor** applies to land purchases. There are some exceptions; for example, under fraudulent misrepresentation (i.e., where the vendor conceals defects of which he is aware), the vendor remains liable. Another exception exists for a **latent defect** not discoverable by a purchaser when doing ordinary inspection. If a vendor is aware of such a defect, he must disclose it. However, a **patent defect**, one apparent by ordinary inspection, need not be disclosed by the vendor.

caveat emptor let the buyer beware

latent defect defect not readily apparent to an ordinary purchaser during an ordinary inspection

patent defect a defect discoverable by a purchaser during an ordinary inspection

Preparations for Completing the Transaction

Verifying Title and Possession   As the purchaser's lawyer, Harmon takes the following steps:

1. First, she discusses the purpose and availability of title insurance with the purchaser. Title insurance is usually a mandatory requirement if new mortgage

---

[29] Standard form purchase agreements usually include a frustration clause. For example, if the building is destroyed or seriously damaged, Hi-Style may elect to take over the premises and to receive the proceeds of all insurance, or it may elect to terminate the contract, with Vincent to suffer the loss, if any.

financing is being arranged. In our scenario, Hi-Style may choose title insurance (as most purchasers do), and, if so, obtaining a survey and completing title and off-title searches will be unnecessary. The insurance company will compensate for any title defects, zoning non-compliance, or tax arrears that are discovered after closing. The lawyer can proceed to preparation of the documentation. However, if Hi-Style decides against title insurance, Harmon will complete the following steps.

2. Harmon orders an electronic search of the title to the lot (referencing the PIN) and also compares the survey received from Vincent with the plan of the whole area as filed in the registry office, to make sure there are no discrepancies in the boundaries of the lot and to learn whether there are any outstanding claims registered. In the registry system, it will be necessary to hire a title searcher to review actual documents (a step not necessary in land titles).

3. Harmon conducts "off title searches" by sending letters to various agencies with the necessary fee. For example, she writes to the city tax department asking for a certificate showing the state of real property taxes, both arrears and current, and to Oshawa's zoning and building department requesting confirmation that the property complies with current zoning and there are no outstanding work orders and deficiency notices under municipal bylaws. Most of these searches (and fees) are unnecessary if title insurance is purchased.

4. Harmon writes to the Grimm Mortgage Company asking for a mortgage statement showing what the exact amount outstanding on the mortgage will be, including accrued interest, on the date of closing and for the assumption agreement for Hi-Style to sign.

5. She asks her client to arrange insurance for April 15 and to examine the premises carefully to confirm that the building is occupied by the tenants and by Vincent, as stated in the contract, and that no other persons appear to be exercising an adverse claim over any part of the premises. Harmon may advise Hi-Style to hire a surveyor to make a new survey and compare it with the old, although not if title insurance is being purchased.

6. Harmon completes an electronic search of execution claims (judgments) that may be filed against the vendor.

7. After collecting all the aforesaid information, Harmon writes a requisition letter to Vale identifying all discrepancies she has found in the title and off-title searches and requesting that Vale correct any problems. Harmon must make sure that Vale receives this letter by the requisition date. In the letter Harmon asks for copies of all leases. She asks Vale to obtain tenant acknowledgments—standard form questionnaires describing the terms of the tenancy, the state of premises, and the status of rent and security deposits. Harmon also confirms who will be preparing the electronic documents.

Preparing the Documents for Closing Within a few days, Vincent's lawyer, Vale, prepares a transfer and second mortgage (charge), the documents both lawyers will authorize for electronic registration. Harmon examines them and approves their contents. Most real estate lawyers have a software package that generates all necessary documents in registrable form. Still, both lawyers check the details against identification supplied by their clients to confirm accuracy. A few days before closing, each lawyer meets with his or her respective client and reviews the draft documents and **statement of adjustments** (discussed below). The electronic registration system no longer requires the vendor to sign the transfer. However, both vendor and purchaser are asked to sign an authorization and direction allowing their lawyers to electronically register the documents in the form presented. Other tangible documents are signed and delivered on closing. Vale has prepared a charge document for the second mortgage and Hi-Style will sign this. Both clients sign

statement of adjustments a document setting out all the items—both credits and debits—that must be adjusted between the parties to arrive at the correct amount to be paid on closing undertakings to readjust the accounts after closing if there is a mistake on the statement of adjustments (as discussed below).

Re: Lot 27, Plan 7654, in the City of Oshawa
Hi-Style Centres Ltd. purchase from Vincent

STATEMENT OF ADJUSTMENTS

as at April 15

	Vendor	Purchaser
1. SALE PRICE		$645 000.00
2. Deposit paid by purchaser	$ 25 000.00	
3. (a) Principal amount first mortgage to Grimm Mortgage Co. to be assumed by purchaser	373 580.60	
(b) Plus interest, April 1 to 15 at 10.5%	1 612.03	
4. Second mortgage back to vendor	125 000.00	
5. Total taxes for current year, $8695.00, vendor paid first two installments totaling $4000. Vendor share is 105 days ($23.82/day = $2501.30) overpayment charged to purchaser.		1 498.70
6. Rent received in advance (deposits):		
(a) Suite #1: 1.5 months	1 875.00	
(b) Suite #2: 1.5 months	1 875.00	
(c) Suite #3: 0.5 months	450.00	
7. BALANCE DUE ON CLOSING	117 106.07	
	$646 498.70	$646 498.70

Preparing for Closing Harmon finds that Vincent's title to the land is in good order, and she is satisfied with Vale's response to her requisition letter. She receives a mortgage statement (consistent with Vincent's representation) and an assumption agreement from Grimm. A few weeks before the date of closing, Vale prepares a document called a statement of adjustments (see above) reconciling the financial items, both credits and debits, that must be adjusted between the parties to arrive at the correct amount to be paid by Hi-Style to Vincent on the date of closing. The closing date is to be April 15.

The Closing

Exchanging Documents Since all registrations can be completed online, the lawyers agree to close the deal without a face-to-face meeting. Each lawyer sends a package of documents to the other's office to be held in escrow (an agreement that the documents and keys will not be released, used, or registered without the prior authorization of the other). Vale's package includes

- (a) the undertaking to readjust,
- (b) the original copies of the leases to Suites No. 1 and No. 2,
- (c) the properly executed assignments of each lease,
- (d) the acknowledgment of the tenant in Suite No. 3 that she is a monthly tenant at a rent of $900 payable in advance,
- (e) the notice signed by Vincent to each tenant of Suites No. 1, No. 2, and No. 3 informing tenants of the change of ownership and requesting them to pay all future rent to Hi-Style, and
- (f) keys to the building.

On the morning of April 15, Harmon updates all her searches and electronically transfers $117 106.07 to Vale's trust account. Both lawyers access the electronic registration system and authorize the registration of the transfer and the charge (second mortgage). The assumption agreement has been provided to Grimm and the corresponding first mortgage is already on title. The new second mortgage will rank behind it.

Delivering Possession   Vale agrees not to release the funds he has received until registration is complete. On rare occasions, the vendor's lawyer may agree not to release the funds until the purchaser confirms possession. The mechanics of delivering possession to a purchaser sometimes cause great friction and even court action. To avoid such friction, the vendor should arrange to be completely out of the premises by the time the deal is closed and to deliver the keys to the purchaser. If this is not done, the purchaser may understandably be very upset and demand that the money not be released. Once anger replaces common sense, both vendor and purchaser may become obstinate, and the vendor's lawyer holding the funds is caught between them. In the present case, Vincent has vacated the premises the day before and the Hi-Style manager picks up the keys, goes to the building, and finds the store vacant. The transaction is complete.

After the Closing   Each lawyer still has several things to do besides submitting a bill. Vale will write to the city tax office to inform them of the change of ownership. Vale will pay the commission owed to the real estate agent from the proceeds of sale in accordance with the direction in the listing agreement.

Harmon will communicate with Vale to see that all these things have been completed. She will write to each of the tenants to inform them of the change of ownership, enclosing Vincent's notice and giving them the address at which Hi-Style would like the rent to be paid.

Only after all these things have been done, when the lawyers are able to return all the documents to their respective clients and to make a full written report of all details, will the transaction be complete.

The Distinctiveness of Each Transaction   The terms of each sale of land should be tailored to meet the specific requirements of the parties in the circumstances. Even with standardization in contracts for the sale of similar houses in a subdivision, significant variations occur in credit arrangements, extra features installed by the builder, or arrangements for completion of the house after possession. In the sale of commercial property, the variations are far greater: Often, possession does not pass to the purchaser on closing, as where the whole premises are already rented to tenants and are purchased for their investment value, or where the vendor stays on as a tenant. Sometimes when the sale of a business is involved, the purchaser covenants to buy other assets from the vendor, or the vendor covenants to refrain from opening a competing business in the same neighbourhood. Our fictional illustration set out above does not deal with every detail that might arise in the circumstances. Rather it is intended to illustrate the steps in a real estate transaction.

Strategies to Manage the Legal Risks

The typical real estate transaction is far less complicated if the land is registered in the land titles system or if title insurance is purchased. Expecting real estate purchasers and mortgagees to restrict their endeavours to only land titles property is illogical; however, buying title insurance for every real estate transaction, whether in registry or land titles systems, is sound strategy. This does not eliminate the need for legal representation in real estate transactions, as lawyers generally control access to the electronic registration system, and immediate registration is the key to protecting priority of any interest in land. Lawyers should be involved early in the transaction, ideally prior to submitting the offer to purchase. Conditions and warranties are more likely to be effective if they are drafted by a lawyer and included in the offer to purchase.

Mortgages remain the most common way to finance the purchase of land, and the amortization and calculation periods, term, prepayment options, and fixed or floating interest rates will have a dramatic impact on the financial feasibility of the financing and its long-term cost. Mortgagees are required to disclose the full cost of borrowing as part of consumer protection measures, and these should be reviewed carefully before accepting a commitment. If the arrangement proves to be too expensive, the property may be sold with an existing mortgage on it—however, the mortgagee will require full payment (plus penalty if inside the term) or will allow the new purchaser to assume the payments. In the latter case, the financial soundness of the new purchaser is just as important to the vendor as to the mortgagee since the vendor remains liable for the payments.

If a mortgagor goes into default and the mortgagee commences foreclosure, the value of the property relative to the outstanding mortgage indebtedness will dictate whether the mortgagor should request a sale instead of foreclosure. Generally, where the value of the property greatly exceeds the indebtedness, a sale is more advantageous to the debtor. This will give the debtor his equity in the property. Mortgagees should proceed with sale rather than foreclosure when the debt is close to or exceeds the value of the property. This will preserve the right to proceed on the personal covenant.

QUESTIONS FOR REVIEW

1. Describe the contractual aspects of a mortgage.

2. How does a mortgagee's interest in land under the land titles system differ from the type of interest a mortgagee receives under a registry system?

3. Describe the two harshest of the common law rules for mortgagors. How did equity remedy this?

4. Why does a mortgagee rarely take possession immediately on default by the mortgagor?

5. Define *foreclosure, acceleration clause, redemption, charge,* and *power of sale.*

6. In a sale of mortgaged land by the court, what are the consequences for the mortgagor if there is a deficiency? If there is a surplus?

7. When a purchaser acquires land from the mortgagor and defaults, whom may the mortgagee sue? Why? Are there any exceptions to this rule?

8. What are the main options open to a second mortgagee when the mortgagor defaults?

9. In addition to timely repayment of the loan, what other duties does a mortgagor assume?

10. M, a mortgagee, wishes to sell you a $20 000 mortgage on Blackacre. M states that Q, the mortgagor, is already in default, but M needs money quickly to proceed with another transaction. M offers to assign the mortgage to you for $16 000. Name the two most important things you would need to verify before accepting the offer.

11. Distinguish between a general creditor and a secured creditor.

12. Greenacre, a five-hectare field in a new subdivision, is available for sale. You would like to divide it into 20 lots, develop eight of them yourself, and eventually sell off the remaining 12 lots. Describe an important term you would want in the mortgage you need to finance the purchase.

13. Why would a mortgagor who has defaulted request the court to hold a sale of his property rather than allow the mortgagee to foreclose?

14. What is the appeal of a reverse mortgage on their home to a retired elderly couple?

15. In our "typical real estate transaction," explain why Vincent would agree to take back a second mortgage.

16. How does title insurance change the tasks that the purchaser's lawyer must complete? Discuss the consequences of title insurance.

CASES AND PROBLEMS

1. Continuing Scenario

   Ashley needs an increase in the credit line for the restaurant business. The existing out-standing balance of the business's unsecured credit line is $23 450 and she wants it raised to $50 000. The bank will not agree to the increased limit without getting security in the form of a mortgage on land. Since all the restaurant's locations are leased, the only available property is Ashley's home, where she lives with her husband and co-owner, Michael. It has a market value of $450 000 and a first mortgage in favour of another bank with $300 000 outstanding. Michael is willing to give the mortgage but wants the payments as low as possible (in case he and Ashley need to cover them) and does not care if that increases the amount of the debt. Ashley thinks current interest rates are going to fall so she wants the opportunity to lower her rate at the earliest possible time. Explain how Ashley and Michael should negotiate term, interest rate, calculation period, and amortization period in order to address both of their concerns. What conditions should the bank demand in order to address the first mortgage and Michael's interest in the home?

2. Four years ago, Azoic Wholesalers Ltd. purchased a warehouse building for $550 000. To finance the purchase, the company paid $75 000 in cash, and gave a 7.5 percent first mortgage to the Reliable Insurance Company for $315 000 and an 11 percent second mortgage of $160 000 to the vendor. The vendor subsequently sold the second mortgage to Sharpe Realties Ltd. for $145 000. All documents were duly registered. For the next few years, Azoic Wholesalers Ltd. managed to pay interest on both mortgages and somewhat reduce the principal.

   Azoic Wholesalers Ltd.

   STATEMENT OF CONDITION AT DATE OF DISTRIBUTION

Assets		**Liabilities**	
Bank balance from:		**Reliable Insurance Co.**	
sale of building	$425 000	(first mortgage)	$296 000
sale of all other assets	78 000	Sharpe Realties Ltd.	
		(second mortgage)	151 000
Total available cash	503 000		
Deficiency of assets	83 000	General creditors	139 000
	$586 000		$586 000

   Azoic Wholesalers Ltd. subsequently became insolvent and was declared bankrupt. A trustee in bankruptcy was appointed, and all the assets of the company sold. The statement above shows its financial condition after all assets were liquidated.

   Calculate how the available cash will be distributed to the various creditors.

3. Fedorkow purchased a 100-hectare farm on the St. John River in New Brunswick for $90 000. He paid $12 000 cash and gave back a mortgage of $78 000 to the vendor, Bowes. The mortgage was payable over a 15-year period, with interest at 8.5 percent in installments of about $630 per month. Within a year, Bowes fell ill and decided to retire to a warm climate. She sold the mortgage to Manor Mortgage Co. with only a slight discount on the amount then outstanding because she personally guaranteed payment by Fedorkow.

   A year later Fedorkow received an offer to purchase his frontage on the St. John River, an area of about five hectares, for $32 000. He visited the offices of Manor Mortgage Co. and asked if they would be interested in giving a discharge of the mortgage over the five hectares. Manor Mortgage Co. agreed to do so provided Fedorkow gave a $1000 bonus and a further $12 000 in reduction of the mortgage debt. The parties carried out the arrangement, and the five hectares were discharged from the mortgage, leaving the mortgage on the remainder of the farm. Subsequently, Fedorkow defaulted on the mortgage, having also let the farm fall into disrepair. Manor Mortgage Co. sued Bowes as guarantor of the mortgage debt for the balance of $31 560 then outstanding.

Should Manor Mortgage Co. succeed? Explain.

4. Expecting to make a quick profit, Pender purchased two hectares of land in a suburban community outside Fredericton for $85 000. He paid $20 000 in cash and obtained a loan for $65 000 by mortgaging the property to Quincy for two years with interest at 11 percent. Under the terms of the mortgage, Pender was to make quarterly payments of $5000 plus interest, with the balance of the principal sum and interest due at the end of two years. Pender's attempts to sell the land failed because the suburb did not develop as he had hoped. He paid the first quarterly installment but missed the second.

Quincy took possession shortly after the default in payment and applied for foreclosure. The market for land in the area continued to weaken, and shortly after he obtained a final order of foreclosure, Quincy advertised the property for sale "under the mortgagee's power of sale." He accepted the highest offer of $50 000 and sued Pender for the deficiency of $10 000 plus accrued interest and the costs of obtaining foreclosure and conducting the sale, for a total of $15 600.

Pender defended by claiming that Quincy had given up all rights against him when he foreclosed Pender's equity of redemption, unless he could return the land. Quincy argued that he retained the choice to exercise his power of sale with a claim for any deficiency.

Which argument do you believe is more sound? Explain.

5. Keller owned and operated the Serene Bed & Breakfast near Sarnia for many years. It was a small business, and her health was not good. She decided to sell but found the market very limited. Jepson agreed to purchase Serene Bed & Breakfast from her for $195 000 if she agreed to take back a second mortgage. On March 31, Jepson paid Keller $30 000 on closing, assumed the first mortgage of $150 000 held by Huron Co-op Inc., and gave Keller a second mortgage for the balance of $15 000.

The spring and summer tourist seasons were very poor, and Jepson lost money during the first six months. He defaulted on payments to both mortgagees and informed them that he could not carry on. Huron replied that it intended to commence foreclosure proceedings immediately. Both Jepson and Keller then met several times with the manager of Huron at his office to try to work out the most convenient arrangement and keep expenses to a minimum, avoiding court costs. They agreed to avoid court proceedings by Jepson's conveying the property to Huron—and Keller would also transfer her interest as second mortgagee to Huron in return for the nominal sum of $100.

Several months later Keller learned that Jepson owned a substantial interest in a large retail hardware store; Jepson earned a good salary there as manager. She requested that he pay the unpaid debt on the second mortgage, but he refused on the basis that Keller could no longer reconvey the interest she held, having already transferred it to Huron. Keller believed that she was entitled to repayment and sued Jepson.

Give your opinion of the defence raised by Jepson and whether Keller should succeed.

6. Lawlor purchased a small house from Cloutier at a price of $80 000. She paid $15 000 in cash and gave Cloutier a first mortgage for the balance. A year later, when Lawlor had reduced the principal amount of the mortgage to $52 000, she suffered financial reverses that made it impossible for her to continue to repay mortgage principal as required. Cloutier brought an action against Lawlor and on May 15 obtained an order for foreclosure, with the deadline for payment by Lawlor specified as November 15.

On July 10, the insurance of $50 000 on the house expired and Lawlor renewed it while she was seeking to refinance with a new mortgagee. A few weeks later, the house was seriously damaged by fire; the insurance adjuster appraised the loss at $35 000.

Both Cloutier and Lawlor immediately claimed the insurance money. The insurance company refused to pay Cloutier on the grounds that the insurance policy contained no mortgage clause that would have assigned to him rights in any claim "in so far as his interest may appear." The insurance company also refused to pay any part of the loss to Lawlor on the grounds that she had no insurable interest in the property.

Discuss the validity of the claims of Cloutier and Lawlor. Assume that there is no evidence to show that the fire was other than accidental in its origin.

7. Three years ago, the Lister Co. Ltd. borrowed $200 000 from the Hi-Rise Bank. Lister Co. was in the textile business and gave a real estate mortgage on one of its buildings as collateral security for the bank loan: The mortgage provided security in the land, building, and fixtures in the building.

The company was later adjudged bankrupt on a petition of its creditors. A question arose about whether a certain piece of expensive machinery in the mortgaged building was in fact a fixture against which the bank would retain priority in liquidation. The trustee in bankruptcy, representing the general creditors, claimed it was not a fixture, so that the proceeds from its sale would be applied to all creditors' claims and not solely to that of the bank as mortgagee.

An officer of the bank and the trustee in bankruptcy went personally to inspect the machine, but were unable to agree whether it could be described as being "permanently" affixed. The bank then started legal action to have its claim as mortgagee of the machine confirmed. At this point, the trustee offered as a compromise to recognize the bank's priority to the extent of $20 000, a sum much less than the probable resale value of the machine. The bank accepted the offer and withdrew its action.

A few days later the bank learned that, at the time it took the mortgage on the building, the machine in question had been affixed to a cement floor in the plant in a permanent way, but that the building had since been renovated and the machine had been reattached much less securely to the new floor. Neither the bank nor the trustee had this information when they contracted to substitute $20 000 in cash for the mortgage claim. The trustee refused to waive the agreement, however, and the Hi-Rise Bank brought an action asking the court for rescission of that contract and an order acknowledging its claim as a secured creditor with respect to the machine.

Discuss the nature of the argument on which the bank would base its claim and indicate whether its action should succeed.

Give an opinion on the probable outcome of this litigation with reasons.

8. Victor Contractors Ltd. financed the construction of a high-rise apartment tower in Hamilton by receiving "draws" on first mortgage financing as work progressed. Rail Canada Pension Fund held the first mortgage for $10 700 000. The mortgage contained the following clause:

> The Mortgagor [Victor Contractors Ltd.] covenants and agrees with the Mortgagee [Rail Canada Pension Fund] that, except with the prior consent of the Mortgagee (which consent shall not be unreasonably withheld), it will not enter into any agreement for the sale, transfer or other disposition of the mortgaged premises.

On May 31, Victor Contractors agreed to sell the apartment building to Steel City Developers Corp. for $16 000 000. Steel City Developers paid a deposit of $75 000 and agreed to assume the existing first mortgage. The closing date was December 1, with the balance due on closing. The contract included the following clause:

> This Agreement is conditional upon the Vendor [Victor Contractors Ltd.] being able to obtain within thirty days following this date the consent of the first mortgagee [Rail Canada Pension Fund] to this sale and to the assumption of the first mortgage obligations by the Purchaser [Steel City Developers Corp.].

When Victor Contractors requested consent from Rail Canada Pension Fund, its manager stated that he would have to be satisfied with the financial capability of Steel City Developers and wished to see its audited financial statements. The secretary–treasurer of Steel City Developers refused to produce the statements on the grounds that her company had a firm policy of never disclosing its financial affairs to anyone except its bank because this policy gave it an advantage over its competitors.

With matters at an impasse, the solicitors for Steel City Developers finally wrote on June 28, informing Victor Contractors that since, as vendor, it had been unable to obtain the consent of the first mortgagee as required, "This Agreement is now null and void." In reply, Victor Contractors wrote, "It is clear that your letter of June 28 written on behalf of your client constituted a wrongful renunciation of the contract of sale and purchase."

Victor Contractors then sued Steel City Developers for specific performance or, alternatively, for damages for breach of contract. Steel City Developers counter-claimed for the return of the deposit of $75 000.

Outline what you consider to be the main issue that the court will have to resolve in this case, and offer with reasons an opinion about the probable outcome. Why would Rail Canada Pension Fund have insisted upon a right to satisfy itself of the financial capability of any purchaser of the apartment building?

Additional Resources for Chapter 23 on the Companion Website

(www.pearsoncanada.ca/smyth)

In addition to pre- and post-tests, mini-cases, and application exercises, the Companion Website includes the following province-specific resources for Chapter 23:

- **Alberta:** Foreclosure; Personal Covenants; Real Estate Agents; Restrictive Covenants
- **Atlantic Provinces:** Mortgage Brokers; Power of and Court-ordered Sales
- **British Columbia:** Conveyance of Land; Cost of Borrowing; Credit Reporting; Real Estate Agents
- **Manitoba/Saskatchewan:** Mortgage Legislation
- **Ontario:** Charge; Discharge; Electronic Registration; Foreclosure; Judicial Sale; Land Registration Reform Act; Mortgages Act; Personal Covenant; Power of Sale; Ontario Real Estate Association; Real Estate Agent

Chapter 24

Sole Proprietorships and Partnerships

This chapter examines unincorporated business entities—sole proprietorships, partnerships, joint ventures, and income trusts, with the main emphasis on partnerships.

In this chapter we examine such questions as:

- Why are partnerships formed?

- What is the legal nature of a partnership?

- Why is it important to establish whether a partnership exists between persons carrying on a business?

- How are partnerships created?

- What are the usual contents of a partnership agreement?

- To what extent are partners liable for the acts of their co-partners and for the debts of the firm?

- What are the duties owed by partners to one another?

- How are partnerships terminated, and what happens when they are?

- What are limited partnerships?

- What are limited liability partnerships?

- What are joint ventures?

- What are income trusts?

CHOOSING THE APPROPRIATE FORM OF BUSINESS ORGANIZATION

Almost all businesses in Canada are carried on in at least one of the following forms:[1]

- sole proprietorship,
- partnership, or
- corporation.

Sole proprietorships and partnerships come into existence without government involvement—the actions of the individuals involved establish the business. However, a corporation may only be formed by following the steps outlined in the legislation and registering with the designated government department. The procedure for incorporation was originally expensive and cumbersome, but now a corporation can be formed quickly and for a few hundred dollars. In addition, almost all provinces currently permit a corporation to be created with a single shareholder and director, so that corporations are a viable alternative not only to partnerships but also to sole proprietorships. When an individual or a group of persons contemplate establishing a business, an initial decision must be made whether or not to incorporate. At this point, professional legal, accounting, and management advice should be sought. Many small businesses decide to incorporate at the outset, while others make the decision to do so later, or they remain unincorporated. One factor that must be considered is that a number of professions do not permit their members to carry on their practice in the form of a corporation: In those cases, sole proprietorship or partnership is the only option. This chapter addresses the legal environment surrounding unincorporated businesses. Chapter 25 considers the legal issues surrounding incorporation of a business.

SOLE PROPRIETORSHIPS

As soon as an individual starts doing business, a **sole proprietorship** is created. No formalities are necessary. The business activity is still subject to the same regulations that apply to all forms of business. Laws regarding public health, zoning, and, of course, taxation apply to all businesses, whether sole proprietorships, partnerships, or corporations. A sole proprietor may have to obtain a licence to carry on a particular type of business. For example, a municipal licence is normally required before one may start business as an electrician, plumber, restaurateur, or taxi driver. Provincial licensing and registration may be required for a car dealer, insurance broker, or employment agency. The proprietor must keep proper accounts

sole proprietorship an unincorporated business owned by a single individual

---

[1] Few businesses operate as cooperatives, trusts, and other types of unincorporated associations. Sometimes multiple business forms are used, such as when two corporations form a joint venture or partnership.

for income tax purposes but sole proprietor income is reported on the personal income tax form. No separate filing is done. The proprietor must make payroll deductions for employee income tax, employment insurance, and Canada Pension Plan. In hiring staff, she must observe human rights legislation and must comply with health and safety regulations.

In most provinces, if a business operates under a name other than the actual name of the owner, the name must be registered.[2]

PARTNERSHIPS

Advantages and Disadvantages

partnership the relationship between two or more persons carrying on a business with a view to profit

A **partnership** may be formed by two or more persons, who may be natural persons (individuals) or legal persons (corporations). There are obvious advantages in carrying on a business venture with others. Working together, members of a group can pool their knowledge and skills, and their physical and financial resources. There are also obvious disadvantages. Disagreements may lead to stalemate; the dishonesty or incompetence of one member may lead to losses suffered by other members; when a group wishes to make important decisions, it may lose valuable time in reaching agreement. None of these problems exists when a person acts solely on his or her own behalf.

The Partnership Act

Although partnerships may be established without government approval, their affairs are governed by a well developed body of laws. This is because, until the 20th century, partnership was the usual way for two or more persons to carry on business. Problems concerning almost every aspect of partnership were litigated through the courts and a complete set of common law rules was created. There were so many cases that it was difficult to keep track of the broader principles. To remedy this situation, the case law was collected into one statute called the Partnership Act,[3] which organized the numerous cases under general principles. Each Canadian common law province has a Partnership Act containing the general rules of operation.[4] With one important exception,[5] the legislation has remained virtually unchanged from its original form, and there have been comparatively few cases on its interpretation, so it reflects the legal rules applicable to today's partnerships.

THE NATURE OF PARTNERSHIP

The Definition of Partnership

"Partnership is the relation which subsists between persons carrying on a business in common with a view of profit."[6] Originally there was just one type of partnership, now known as a general partnership. Two additional specialized forms of partnership—limited partnerships and limited liability partnerships—developed over time and are discussed later in this chapter.

---

[2] See e.g. Business Names Act, R.S.O. 1990, c. B.17, s. 2(2), and the discussion in Chapter 20. Saskatchewan requires registration even when an owner operates under her own name: The Business Names Registration Act, R.S.S. 1978, B-11, s. 2(c).

[3] 1890, 53 and 54 Vict., c. 39 (U.K.).

[4] See e.g. The Partnerships Act, R.S.O. 1990, c. P.5; The Partnership Act R.S.B.C. 1996, c. 348; R.S.N.S. 1989, c. 334; Partnerships Act, R.S.O. 1990, c. P.5.

[5] The introduction of the limited liability partnership, considered later in this chapter.

[6] See: Partnership Act, R.S.B.C. 1996, c. 348, s. 2; R.S.N.S. 1989, c. 334, s. 4; Partnerships Act, R.S.O. 1990, c. P.5, s. 2. Subsequent references within this chapter to British Columbia, Ontario, and Nova Scotia are to these statutes.

There are four basic elements in the definition of "partnership." A partnership is

- a relationship,
- between persons,
- carrying on business in common,
- with a view to profit.

This definition of partnership is extremely important because of the consequences that flow from a finding that a person is a partner. Whether two or more persons are partners depends upon all the circumstances of a case.

The Partnership Relationship   Partnership is a consensual and contractual relationship. Normally, a written partnership agreement is drawn up and signed by all the partners. However, persons may be found to be partners although no written or even oral agreement exists.[7] In the absence of an express agreement, they may still be held to be partners if they have acted as such.[8] The courts look at the substance of the relationship no matter what the parties may call it.[9]

The Business Nature of Partnership   The Partnership Act defines partnership as a relationship between persons carrying on a business for profit. It does not apply to other associations, such as charitable enterprises, joint trustees of an estate, public boards, or corporations.

The term "business" is an imprecise one. It includes "every trade, occupation, or profession," but it does not include every activity carried on for a profit. For instance, owning property and collecting rent from tenants does not necessarily amount to carrying on a business. The joint ownership of property does not of itself make the owners partners. Similarly, if a group of investors forms a syndicate to hold a portfolio of securities, that arrangement does not amount to carrying on a business unless the investors engage in the trading of shares, rather than merely retaining them for investment income.

CASE 24.1

A group of persons, including a corporation (Kamex), purchased a piece of development property with a view to reselling it at a profit. One of the co-owners, March, entered into an exclusive listing agreement with a real estate agent (Le Page) without the agreement of his co-owners.

The group sold the property, and Le Page sued all the owners for its commission. It claimed that they had formed a partnership and that they were consequently jointly liable on the contract made by March.

The court held that there was no partnership. The members of the group were not carrying on a business, but were merely co-owners of the property. Consequently, March alone was liable for the commission.[10]

---

[7] Conversely, a written "partnership agreement" will not create a partnership if it is found that no such intention existed: M. *Tucci Construction Ltd. v. Lockwood*, [2000] O.J. No. 3192, aff'd [2002] O.J. No. 440 (Ont. C.A.).

[8] See e.g. *Pinteric v. People's Bar and Eatery Ltd.*, [2001] O.J. No. 499, where the plaintiff alleged the existence of an oral partnership agreement; the Ontario Court of Appeal held that the receipt of "advances" rather than a salary pointed to a partnership relationship.

[9] In *Lansing Building Supply (Ontario) Ltd. v. Ierullo* (1990), 71 O.R. (2d) 173, co-developers of land entered into a joint venture agreement that specifically provided that they were not to be considered partners. Nevertheless, the court held that the true nature of their relationship was one of partnership.

[10] *A.E. Le Page Ltd. v. Kamex Developments Ltd.* (1977), 78 D.L.R. (3d) 223, aff'd [1979] 2 S.C.R. 155.

Although a partnership must be a business relationship, not every business relationship makes the parties to the relationship partners with each other. The Act speaks of "carrying on" a business. Isolated transactions undertaken jointly do not by themselves make the parties partners. For example, if two merchants in the Atlantic Provinces pool an order of goods purchased in Montreal so that they can fill one freight car and obtain a lower freight rate, that arrangement does not by itself make them partners. However, a partnership may exist for even a single venture, depending upon the circumstances.

CASE 24.2

A group of Canadian investors purchased the interests of the members of a Texas partnership that owned a large apartment building. The value of the building had declined drastically, and the whole purpose of the transaction was to realize the loss, which the Canadian investors hoped to set off against their income tax liability. After the transfer of the partnership interests, the building was immediately sold.

The Supreme Court of Canada held that a tax motivation and a short duration do not by themselves negate the existence of a partnership. However, in this case there was never any intention to carry on a "business" as a continuing activity and therefore the relationship was not a partnership.[11]

The Profit Motive   The words "with a view to profit" have generally been taken to mean that a sharing of profits is an essential element of partnership.

Normally, the sharing of gross receipts does not create a partnership. For example, if an owner of a theatre were to rent it to a drama group and one of the terms of the contract was that she would receive 10 percent of the gross receipts, such an arrangement would not make the owner a partner of the group. Similarly, in our example of the two merchants pooling an order to reduce shipping charges, there is a sharing of costs, but not of profits.

The receipt of a share of the profits of the business is strong evidence of a partnership, though it is not by itself conclusive. In particular, it does not by itself amount to a partnership if the sharing of profits is part of an arrangement to

- repay a debt owed;
- pay an employee or agent of the business as part of his remuneration;
- pay an annuity to a widow, widower, or child of a deceased partner;
- repay a loan under which the lender is to receive a rate of interest varying with the profits;
- pay the seller of a business an amount for goodwill that varies according to the profits (B.C., s. 4; Ont. s. 3.; N.S., s. 5).

Apart from the above situations, it is difficult to imagine circumstances in which the only evidence of a partnership would be the fact that a person is sharing in the profits of a business. A person receiving a share of profits has usually contributed property or money to the business. Even though partners often share profits according to a ratio that is not based solely on capital contribution, the courts consider profit-sharing that coincides with the ratio of capital contribution to be strong evidence of partnership.

---

[11] *Backman v. Canada* (2001), 196 D.L.R. (4th) 193 (S.C.C.). Since there was no business, there was no business loss for which tax relief could be claimed. See also *Hayter v. Canada*, [2010] T.C.J. No 175, in which the business was found not to be a partnership because it lacked a continuing nature, but it qualified as a joint venture (an adventure in the nature of a trade covered by the Income Tax Act). Contrast *Backman* with *Spire Freezers Ltd. v. Canada* (2001), 196 D.L.R. (4th) 211 (S.C.C.) (a case with a similar tax motive, decided at the same time as the *Backman* case), where the Canadian investors retained some of the assets of a California partnership and were held to be carrying on a business. See also *Stow v. Canada*, [2010] T.C.J. No. 322.

Another important factor is whether the person receiving the profits has taken part in the management of the business. Evidence showing that she has taken some active role in the business, particularly in making decisions on important matters, when added to the fact that she has shared in the profits, will usually suffice to establish her as a partner.

The Legal Nature of Partnership

Legal Personality   As a matter of law, a corporation has a separate legal identity of its own. The law of partnerships is not the same. The Act defines a partnership as a "relation" between persons. Strictly, a partnership has no independent existence and merely represents the collective rights and duties of all the partners. Logically, this means that whenever a partner dies or retires or a new partner is admitted, the partnership comes to an end and is replaced by a new relationship. In actual practice, however, and in some of its legal implications, a partnership may be treated as separate from its partners. Certainly, as an accounting matter, a partnership is treated as a separate entity with its own assets, the ability to create liabilities, and financial statements. However, in the end, all assets and liabilities are the responsibility of the partners.

The Continuing Relationship between Partners   The Partnership Act itself recognizes, in a number of places, the concept of a **firm**,[12] which members join or leave. It speaks of a person being admitted as a partner into an existing firm, or retiring from a firm, or being expelled from a firm, and of the composition of a firm being changed. And while it provides that the death (or insolvency) of a partner dissolves the partnership, the Act accepts that the partners may agree that the partnership should continue between the survivors (B.C., s. 36(1); Ont., s. 33(1); N.S., s. 36(1)). It is consequently possible, and normally advisable, for partners to agree expressly that on the death, bankruptcy, or retirement of one of them, the partnership relation among the others will continue.

firm   collective reference to the partners in a partnership

Partnership Property   Again, it is clear from the Act that a partnership may have property that is distinct from the property of the individual partners. In particular, real property held by a partnership is treated according to the usual rules governing real property as far as the partnership is concerned, but insofar as the individual partners are concerned, their interest in the real property is considered personal property; that is, they do not own the property itself, but rather an interest in that property.

Creditors of the Firm   Partnership creditors have first call against partnership assets before the personal creditors of an individual partner. This is so because, until the creditors of the partnership have been paid, it is impossible to identify and distribute the share of an individual partner. If, after these creditors are paid, no assets remain, then the partner has no share for personal creditors to seize.

Another example of the separate existence of the firm occurs in the rule that a deceased partner's personal creditors have first call against the personal assets of her estate (B.C., s. 11; Ont., s. 10; N.S., s. 11). If the partnership assets are insufficient to pay off the partnership creditors, they must wait for the personal creditors to be paid out of the personal estate of the deceased partner before they can take what is left in order to satisfy their debt. Under the Bankruptcy and Insolvency Act, this rule also applies to the estate of a living partner who becomes bankrupt.[13]

Legal Proceedings   For the purposes of processing a court action, a partnership may be treated as if it were a separate entity. The partnership may bring an action in the name

---

[12] See e.g. B.C., s. 1; Ont., s. 5; N.S., s. 7.

[13] R.S.C. 1985, c. B-3, s. 142.

of the firm without naming all the partners as plaintiffs, and an outside party may sue a partnership in its firm name without naming all the partners as defendants. It is, in fact, wise to sue a partnership in the firm name rather than in the names of the individual partners, as we shall see when we consider the question of the liability of partners.

THE CREATION OF A PARTNERSHIP
The Partnership Agreement

partnership agreement an agreement between persons to create a partnership and (usually) to set out the terms of the relationship

A partnership comes into existence through agreement, express or implied, of the partners. Generally speaking, partners may agree to whatever terms they wish, provided the terms are not illegal and do not offend public policy. A **partnership agreement** may be wholly oral and yet be valid and enforceable.[14] As we know an oral agreement is subject to the lapses of memory of the parties to the agreement, and, if only for certainty, it is important to have a written record of the agreement.

Dissolving a partnership is relatively easy, and a high proportion of them break up after a short time. There are many reasons for dissolution; the business may have proven unprofitable or may have been so profitable that the partners have gone on to form a corporation. Still others dissolve because of a conflict of personalities between the partners. A substantial number of profitable partnerships are destroyed by misunderstanding or mistrust. The failure to decide important issues in advance often leads to the kind of misunderstanding and mistrust that, in turn, creates an irreparable breach between the parties.

The main purpose of a partnership agreement is to set out, as carefully and as clearly as possible, the entire terms of the relationship.

CHECKLIST
Contents of a Partnership Agreement

Normally, a partnership agreement will deal with the following matters. Depending upon the circumstances, there are likely other matters that should also be covered:

- identity of the partners
- name of the firm
- nature of the business to be carried on
- duration of the relationship
- method of terminating the partnership
- rules for introducing new partners
- what is to happen on the retirement or death of an existing partner
- participation in management and in making major decisions
- contribution of each partner in terms of work and responsibilities
- capital contribution of each partner
- ownership of property used in the business
- sharing of profits and losses
- procedure for resolving disputes

---

[14] In some provinces the Statute of Frauds applies (see Chapter 10). However, once the partnership exists, the statute no longer applies.

Gaps in the agreement may be filled by the Partnership Act, which sets out a number of implied terms that apply in the absence of any provision in the agreement to the contrary. It is normally preferable, however, for the parties to make their own express terms rather than rely on implied terms from the Act.

Partners should not draft their own agreement. The usual problems of ambiguous words can create the same misunderstandings that generally arise in the law of contracts. In addition, novice partners may be unaware of many of the pitfalls that accumulated experience in business and knowledge of partnership law may avoid. It is also recommended that each partner have his or her own legal counsel to help protect their investment and provide independent legal advice. For more information on this topic, see the Companion Website.

Registration

No specific formal requirements are necessary to form a general partnership; by contrast, as discussed later in this chapter, limited partnerships and limited liability partnerships require registration. However, almost all provinces require even general partnerships to file a declaration giving essential information about the partnership, such as the names and addresses of each partner and the name under which they intend to carry on business. Declarations must also be filed when there is any change in membership or when a firm is dissolved. The registration requirements do not necessarily apply to all partnerships. For example, in British Columbia only partnerships engaged in trading, manufacturing, or mining are required to register, and in Ontario a partnership is not required to register if it carries on business under a name that is composed solely of the names of all of the partners.[15]

There are penalties for failure to carry out the requirements of the statute, and they vary from province to province, but non-registration in no way affects the existence of the partnership as such. The purposes of this registration system are obvious. The register is open to the public and makes information about a partnership and particularly about the partners in the firm available to those doing business with it. A plaintiff can find out where to serve each partner with notice of an action if she wishes to do so. It is also helpful to prospective creditors or other suppliers in checking the accuracy of information given by a member of the partnership concerning the membership of the firm. For more information on this topic, see the Companion Website.

THE LIABILITY OF A PARTNER

The most important characteristic of a general partnership is that partners are personally liable for the debts of the partnership. A person who is a partner in a general partnership becomes personally responsible for the debts and liabilities of the partnership.[16]

Contractual Liability

Agency Principles Probably the greatest risk of liability to a partner comes from the contractual obligations of the partnership: "Every partner is an agent of the firm and his other partners for the purpose of the business of the partnership, and the acts of every partner who does any act for carrying on in the usual way business of the kind carried on by the firm of which he is a member, bind the firm and its partners".[16A] That is so unless the authority of the partner has been restricted by an agreement with the other partners and the third party knows of this restriction. Any acts done by a partner within the scope of his apparent authority and relied upon by an outsider bind the firm and all the partners.

---

[15] Partnership Act, R.S.B.C., 1996, c. 342, s. 81; Business Names Act, R.S.O. 1990, c. B.17, s. 2(4).

[16] Limited liability partnership and limited partnership are different.

[16A] Partnerships Act, R.S.O. 1990, B.C., s. 7; Ont., s. 6; N.S., s. 8.

A restriction placed upon the authority of a partner has the same effect as a restriction placed upon the authority of an agent by his principal: It affects only those outsiders who have knowledge of it (B.C., s. 10; Ont., s. 9; N.S., s. 11). Apparent authority was discussed in Chapter 17, in the context of the law of agency.[17]

Joint Liability   "Every partner in a firm is liable jointly with the other partners for all debts and obligations of the firm incurred while he is a partner. . . ."[17A] The effect of the **joint liability** rule is that each partner is personally liable for the full amount of the firm's debts. When the liabilities of a partnership exceed its assets, a creditor or injured party, having obtained judgment against the partnership and exhausted its assets in trying to satisfy judgment, may look to the personal assets of any partner or partners for payment of the judgment. Accordingly, it is important for a person advancing credit to a firm to determine whether it is a partnership and, if so, who are the partners.

Another consequence of this rule is that only one cause of action arises from the obligation. If, by carelessness or ignorance of the facts, a plaintiff brings action against only some of the partners and obtains judgment against them, her rights will be exhausted. If their assets are insufficient to satisfy the judgment and she later discovers that there are other partners, she will not be able to sue those others for the deficiency. This risk is eliminated if she sues the defendants in the firm name since that has the effect of suing all the persons who were partners at the relevant time.

If a partner pays the firm's debts in full, he is entitled to be reimbursed by his co-partners for their shares of the debt (B.C., s. 27(b); Ont., s. 24(2); N.S., s. 27(b)). See Figure 24.1 for an illustration. But if the other partners are insolvent, one partner may be left with payment of the full debt. It is consequently most important to choose one's partners carefully.

joint liability the situation where each of a number of persons is personally liable for the full amount of a debt

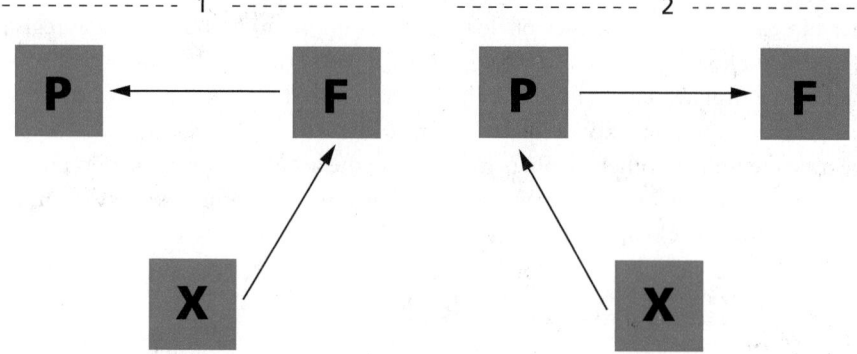

Figure 24.1   Joint Liability

(1) If the outsider (X) sues the firm (F), then any partner (P) is liable to contribute his share to the firm and may be sued by the firm for that share.
(2) If X instead sues P, P is fully liable but is entitled to be indemnified by the firm; that is, P can sue F or his co-partners personally.

Apparent Partners   A person is liable only for the obligations of a partnership incurred while he is a member of the firm. "A person who is admitted as a partner into an existing firm does not thereby become liable to the creditors of the firm for anything done before he became a partner," and "a partner who retires from a firm does not thereby cease to be liable for partnership debts or obligations incurred before his retirement".[17B] The only way he may free himself from his obligations is by novation—that is, by agreement with the partners remaining in the firm and with the firm's creditors.[18]

[17] *See Mercantile Credit Co. Ltd. v. Garrod*, [1962] 3 All E.R. 1103.

[17A] Partnerships Act, R.S.O. 1990, B.C., s. 11; Ont., s. 10; N.S., s. 12.

[17B] Partnerships Act, R.S.O. 1990, B.C., s. 19; Ont., s. 18; N.S., s. 20.

[18] See Chapter 12 under "Discharge by Agreement" (Substituted Agreement).

A person who, not being a partner, represents himself to be, or allows himself to be represented as a partner in a firm, is liable to any person who has given credit to the firm on the faith of that representation (B.C., s. 16; Ont., s. 15; N.S., s. 17).

Although a partner who retires is not supposed to be liable for debts of the firm contracted after he ceased to be a partner, he may be liable if third parties reasonably believe he is still a member of the firm and advance credit to the firm in reliance on his membership. A retiring partner may free himself from this liability by carrying out the requirements of the Partnership Act (B.C., s. 39; Ont., s. 36; N.S., s. 39). An advertisement in the official gazette of the province is adequate notice to persons generally who had not dealt with the firm before the retiring partner left the firm, but all persons who have dealt with the firm before the partner's retirement should receive actual notice of the retirement if the retiring partner is to be fully protected. It is customary, therefore, to send notices to all those persons who have dealt with the firm recently. As well, the retiring partner's name should be removed from the list of partners on all registration.

CHECKLIST

Steps to Be Taken on Retirement from a Partnership

To protect himself against possible liability for future acts of his partners, a retiring partner should

- ensure that all existing clients of the firm are notified
- place a notice in the official gazette of the province (and perhaps also in the local newspaper)
- ensure that his name is removed from the register
- ensure to the best of his ability that any letterheads are destroyed or altered to remove his name

Tort and Breach of Trust

The liability of a firm and of its partners is not restricted to contracts. The Act makes the firm liable for "any wrongful act or omission of any partner acting in the ordinary course of the business of the firm".[19A] Therefore the firm, including all the partners, is liable for injuries or damage caused by a partner doing the firm's business, such as a defamatory

---

[19] *Bet-Mur Investments Ltd. v. Spring* (1994), 17 B.L.R. (2d) 55, aff'd [1999] O.J. No. 342 (Ont. C.A.). See also *Brown Economic Assessments Inc. v. Stevenson*, [2003] S.J. No. 295, aff'd [2004] S.J. No. 377 (Sask. C.A.).

[19A] Partnerships Act, R.S.O. 1990, B.C., s. 12; Ont., s. 11; N.S., s. 13.

statement made by him in business correspondence, or for negligence in dealing with a client's affairs.[20] The principle is similar to that of vicarious liability, discussed in Chapter 4. The firm is also liable for some breaches of fiduciary duty and breaches of trust committed by a partner; for example, for any misapplication by a partner of funds that have been placed in the care of the partner while acting within the scope of his apparent authority, or that have been entrusted to the firm.[21] The Act (B.C., s. 12, 13; Ont., s. 12; N.S., s. 14) specifically describes two situations: see Figure 24.2.

Figure 24.2   Misapplication of Funds

In situation 1, X entrusts P with money or property to be handed over to the firm (F); instead, P keeps the money or property for himself. In situation 2, X entrusts money or property to the firm, and it is subsequently misappropriated by P.

CASE 24.4

A partner in a law firm undertook (privately) the administration of his aunt's estate. The firm's letterhead was used, and funds belonging to the estate passed through the firm's bank accounts.

The partner defrauded the estate and transferred funds to his own account.

In an action against the firm, it was held that the firm was liable, even though the other partners were not aware of the activities in relation to the estate. The partner had been acting within the scope of his apparent authority, since the administration of estates is a matter normally undertaken by lawyers.[22]

THE RELATIONSHIP BETWEEN PARTNERS

Partnership is a contractual relationship, and the relations between partners are governed by the terms of their contract. These terms may be found in the partnership agreement, they may be inferred from the conduct of the parties, or they may be implied from the Partnership Act. A partner who acts in a manner that is contrary to the partnership agreement commits a breach of contract and may be liable to compensate the other partners for any damage resulting from the breach.[23]

---

[20] *McDonic v. Hetherington* (1997), 142 D.L.R. (4th) 648.

[21] See *McDonic Estate (Re)* (1997) 31 O.R. (3d) 577 (O.C.A.); see also *Strother v. 3464920 Canada Inc.*, [2007] 2 S.C.R. 177 at paras. 113–4.

[22] *Public Trustee v. Mortimer* (1985), 16 D.L.R. (4th) 404; see also *Korz v. St. Pierre* (1988), 43 D.L.R. (4th) 528.

[23] See e.g. *Ernst & Young v. Stuart* (1997), 144 D.L.R. (4th) 328 (partner leaving firm without giving proper notice and joining competitor).

Implied Terms

The Act sets out a number of terms that are implied if those matters are not expressly covered in a partnership agreement. The key implied terms are summarized below.[24] A partnership agreement may, and frequently does, vary these terms either at the time of the original agreement or later by unanimous consent of the partners.[25]

Partnership Property   "All property and rights and interests in property originally brought into the partnership stock or acquired, whether by purchase or otherwise, on account of the firm or for the purposes and in the course of the partnership's business are called . . . 'partnership property' and must be held and applied by the partners exclusively for the purposes of the partnership and in accordance with the partnership agreement".[25A] Additionally, the Act provides that, unless the contrary intention appears, all property bought with money belonging to the firm is deemed to have been bought on account of the firm and is available only for the use of the firm (B.C., s. 24; Ont., s. 22; N.S., s. 24).

It is not always clear whether a particular item of property is "brought into the partnership stock." Property that is used in the business is not necessarily partnership property, but may remain the property of the individual partners. Consequently, the partnership agreement should make clear precisely what property is to be considered to have been contributed as "capital."

ILLUSTRATION 24.1

A and B decide to go into partnership in a local delivery business. A owns a warehouse, valued at $50 000. B owns two vans, also valued at $50 000. Two years later, the partnership is dissolved. The warehouse is now worth $70 000, and the vans are worth $20 000. How much is each entitled to?

(a) If the warehouse and vans were brought in as partnership property, then the total value of the assets—$90 000—would be divided equally between them and each would receive $45 000.

(b) If the assets brought into the business remained the individual property of A and B, then A would recover the warehouse ($70 000) and B only the depreciated vans ($20 000).

Either result might be fair, depending upon the original intentions of the parties, but in the absence of a clear agreement, one party might receive a windfall of $25 000 at the expense of the other.

Financial Arrangements   The Act sets out a number of basic presumptions with respect to capital and profits, which apply "subject to any agreement express or implied between the partners." It should be emphasized that these rules are more often than not varied by agreement.

1. "All the partners are entitled to share equally in the capital and profits of the business and must contribute equally towards the losses, whether of capital or otherwise, sustained by the firm" (B.C., s. 27(a); Ont., s. 24(1); N.S., s. 27(a)). Partners commonly vary this term: They contribute different proportions of capital and share profits based on other criteria, such as time spent on partnership business.

2. If a partner incurs expenses or personal liabilities "in the ordinary and proper conduct of the business of the firm," or in doing anything to preserve the business or property of the firm, the firm must indemnify him for these expenses or liabilities (B.C., s. 27(b); Ont., s. 24(2); N.S., s. 27(b)). If one partner is sued for the firm's debts, he is entitled to a contribution from his fellow partners.[26]

---

[24] Quotations are from the Ontario statute; the British Columbia and Nova Scotia versions differ slightly in a few cases.

[25] See B.C., s. 21; Ont., s. 20; N.S., s. 22.

[25A] Partnerships Act, R.S.O. 1990, B.C., s. 23(1); Ont., s. 21(1); N.S., s. 23(1).

[26] There is an exception for limited liability partnerships, discussed at the end of this chapter.

3. A partner is not entitled, before the determination of profits, to interest on the capital subscribed by him (B.C., s. 27(d); Ont., s. 24(4); N.S., s. 27(d)). In other words, if the agreement provides for the payment of "interest" on a partner's capital, the payment is not regarded as an expense of the firm, but rather as an appropriation of profits. But if a partner makes a loan to the firm in addition to what he has agreed to subscribe as capital under the partnership agreement, he is entitled to interest at the rate of 5 percent on the value of the excess contribution while it remains with the firm. The rate of interest may be varied by agreement.

4. "No partner is entitled to remuneration for acting in the partnership business".[26A] Partnership agreements frequently do provide for periodic payments to partners. Normally, partners are not willing and able to wait until sometime after the end of the firm's accounting year, when the year's profits have been ascertained, before receiving income. It is common, therefore, to provide that a partner may "draw" up to a specified amount each month out of his prospective share of profits. Such an amount will be considered merely an advance on his share of the projected profits, repayable to the firm to the extent that it exceeds his share of the actual profits when they are determined.

CASE 24.5

M was described as a "salaried partner" in a law firm. He was to be paid a fixed salary of £1200 per year out of profits, plus one-third of the profits of the branch office that he ran.

The firm suffered a substantial loss. M claimed he was still entitled to his salary of £1200, which should be paid by the other partners.

It was held that M was entitled to nothing. He was a partner, not an employee. His "salary" was a first charge on the profits of the firm. Since there were no profits, his share was nothing.[27]

Conduct of the Business   The Act provides the following, unless there is agreement to the contrary:

1. "Every partner may take part in the management of the partnership business".[27A] This implied term is often varied. Very large partnerships, such as large law or accounting firms, often have two or more classes of partners, and it may be that only the senior partners take part in the management of the firm or partners elect a management committee.

2. "Any difference arising as to ordinary matters connected with the partnership business may be decided by a majority of the partners, but no change may be made in the nature of the partnership business without the consent of all existing partners".[27B] In cases of a serious disagreement, this provision can be troublesome. The minority may insist that the particular decision did not concern an ordinary matter but affected the nature of the partnership business. It is advisable to clearly identify which matters must be decided unanimously.

3. "The partnership books are to be kept at the place of business of the partnership or the principal place if there is more than one and every partner may, when he thinks fit, have access to and inspect and copy any of them".[27C]

[26A] Partnerships Act, R.S.O. 1990, B.C., s. 27(f); Ont., s. 24(6); N.S., s. 27(f).

[27] *Marsh v. Stacey* (1963), 103 Sol. J. 512 (U.K.).

[27A] Partnerships Act, R.S.O. 1990, B.C., s. 27(e); Ont., s. 24(5); N.S., s. 27(e).

[27B] Partnerships Act, R.S.O. 1990, B.C., s. 27(h); Ont., s. 24(8); N.S., s. 27(h).

[27C] Partnerships Act, R.S.O. 1990, B.C., s. 27(i); Ont., s. 24(9); N.S., s. 27(i).

Membership   Partnership is a personal relationship, a fact that is underlined by two further provisions of the Act:

1. "No person may be introduced as a partner without the consent of all existing partners".[27D] Two common variations occur—where there are senior and junior partners and the consent of only the senior partners is required, and where a partner has reserved the right to have a son or daughter join the firm at a later date.

2. No partner may assign his share in the partnership, either absolutely or by way of mortgage, so as to permit the assignees to take over his duties or "to interfere in the management or administration of the partnership business or affairs, or to require any accounts of the partnership transactions, or to inspect the partnership books." An assignee may, however, "receive the share of profits to which the assigning partner would otherwise be entitled and the assignee must accept the account of profits agreed to by the partners".[27E]

An assignee becomes entitled to receive a share of the profits, but does not become a partner.[28]

Fiduciary Duties

The Act contains three provisions that, together, set out the fiduciary duties owed by partners to one another.[29] Partners may not contract out of these duties, meaning the partnership agreement may not alter them.

Information   "Partners are bound to render true accounts and full information of all things affecting the partnership to any partner or his legal representatives".[29A]

Information regarding the firm's business that is provided to any of the partners must be made available to all of them.[30] The only circumstances under which this term might be varied would be in a partnership having several classes of partners. It is possible that, by express agreement, the most junior group of partners might not have access to all the books and records of the partnership. Even such a reservation, however, would be restricted to a narrow class of information.

Secret Benefits   "Every partner must account to the firm for any benefit derived by him without the consent of the other partners from any transaction concerning the partnership or from any use by him of the partnership property, name or business connection".[30A] A partner may be given permission by his co-partners to use partnership property for his own purposes, or to take advantage of an opportunity offered to the firm. But without full disclosure and authorization, any benefit belongs to the firm. A partner in a law firm who teaches a university course part-time would need to seek permission from his firm and assign the compensation to the firm.

[27D] Partnerships Act, R.S.O. 1990, B.C., section 27(g); Ont., section 24(7); N.S., section 27(g).

[27E] Partnerships Act, R.S.O. 1990, B.C., section 34; Ont., section 31; N.S., section 34.

[28] The assignee owes no fiduciary duty to the partnership: *Zawadzki v. Matthews Group Ltd.*, [1999] O.J. No. 2012 at paras. 218–25, aff'd [2001] O.J. No. 3808 (Ont. C.A.).

[29] The B.C. Act (s. 22(1)) also contains a general rule that "a partner shall act with the utmost fairness and good faith towards the other members of the firm in the business of the firm."

[29A] Partnerships Act, R.S.O. 1990, B.C., s. 31; Ont., s. 28; N.S., s. 31.

[30] See *Dockrill v. Coopers & Lybrand* (1994), 111 D.L.R. (4th) 62.

[30A] Partnerships Act, R.S.O. 1990, B.C., s. 32; Ont., s. 29; N.S., s. 32.

CASE 24.6

A partner in a firm of chartered accountants had responsibility for a major corporate client. After some time, he was offered a directorship in the corporation. He disclosed this to the firm and paid his director's fees to the firm. However, he failed to disclose that he was also entitled to shares and stock options. When this was discovered, on the dissolution of the partnership, he was held liable to account to the firm for the value of the shares and options.[31]

Duty Not to Compete "Where a partner without the consent of the other partners carries on any business of the same nature as and competing with that of the firm, he must account for and pay over to the firm all profits made by him in that business".[31A] These terms are varied occasionally according to the circumstances of the partnership. For example, an individual might be carrying on a retail business in the downtown area and subsequently enter into a partnership to carry on a similar business in a suburban shopping centre. Since the two businesses might well be considered "of the same nature and competing with" each other, the partner owning the downtown business would require, as a term of the partnership agreement, that the partners in the suburban business consent to his continuing the downtown business.

The duty to account for secret profits and the duty not to compete sometimes overlap.

CASE 24.7

Davis and Ouellette formed a partnership to secure certain mining claims. The scheme fell through, but the partnership was never formally dissolved. Ouellette subsequently acquired the opportunity to buy the shares of a corporation that owned some of the claims. He notified Davis that he was terminating the partnership and then purchased the shares on his own behalf.

It was held that when Ouellette acquired the opportunity to buy the shares, he was still a partner. The opportunity belonged to the firm, and he had derived a benefit without the consent of his partner. He was liable to account for the profit that he made.[32]

CASE 24.8

Olson and Gullo were partners involved in property development and speculation. Gullo acted fraudulently. He bought a piece of land and resold it at a profit of $2.5 million. (Apparently, he also attempted to have Olson killed—which was presumably a breach of his fiduciary duty!) The trial judge awarded the whole profit to Olson. On appeal by Gullo's estate, it was held that he was accountable for only half of the profit. It was incorrect to say that this would allow him to profit from his own wrong. As a partner, half of the profit should have belonged to him anyway. It was the other half that should go to the plaintiff.[33]

For more information on this topic, see the Companion Website.

TERMINATION OF PARTNERSHIP

Express Provision

It is advisable for the partnership agreement to make express provision for what is to happen on termination—in particular, on the retirement or death of a partner. What events justify termination? How much notice must a partner give to terminate the arrangement?

---

[31] *Rochwerg v. Truster* (2002), 212 D.L.R. (4th) 498 (Ont. C.A.). See also *McKnight v. Hutchison* (2002), 28 B.L.R. (3d) 269.

[31A] Partnerships Act, R.S.O. 1990, B.C., s. 33; Ont., s. 30; N.S., s. 33.

[32] *Davis v. Ouellette* (1981), 27 B.C.L.R. 162.

[33] *Olson v. Gullo* (1994), 113 D.L.R. (4th) 42, leave to appeal refused (1994), 20 B.L.R. (2d) 47 (S.C.C.).

Will the partnership among the remaining members continue? How is the retiring partner's share to be valued? What are the arrangements for the continuing partners to buy out the share of a deceased or retired partner? These are among the most important matters that should be settled in advance.

Implied Statutory Rules

In the absence of express agreement, the Partnership Act sets out a number of rules to govern termination.

Termination by Notice or Expiry "Where no fixed term is agreed upon for the duration of the partnership, any partner may determine the partnership at any time on giving notice of his intention so to do to all other partners".[33A] The notice so given may be oral or in writing, unless the partnership was originally formed by deed, in which case notice in writing is necessary.

A partnership may be for a fixed term, or may simply be a partnership at will—that is, so long as the partners wish to continue. Where a partnership was entered into for a fixed term, but is continued after the term has expired and without any express new agreement, the rights and duties of the partners remain the same as they were at the expiration of the term (B.C., s. 30; Ont., s. 27; N.S., s. 30). Without continuing conduct, however, the partnership is dissolved by the expiration of the fixed term. Similarly, if the partnership was entered into for a single venture or undertaking, it expires with the termination of that venture or undertaking.

Termination on Death or Insolvency Since partnership is a personal relationship, it automatically terminates on the death of a partner, at least so far as the relationship between the deceased and the other partners is concerned. The Act, however, provides that, subject to any contrary agreement, "every partnership is dissolved as regards all the partners by the death or bankruptcy or insolvency of any partner".[33B]

This term, perhaps more than any other, is usually varied by the partnership agreement. In a partnership having substantial assets and many members, the operation of this implied term dissolving the partnership could be disastrous. Accordingly, the partnership agreement usually provides that the partnership will continue in existence upon the death or insolvency of any partner. The partnership agreement usually provides that the surviving partners will buy out the share of a deceased partner, often using life insurance purchased on the life of each partner for that purpose.

Even in a simple partnership between two persons, their agreement should provide for some means of ascertaining the value of the partnership on the death of either of them. Although the partnership will be terminated, the survivor may wish to continue the business as a sole proprietor—or find a new partner—and to buy out the share of the deceased partner.

The problem is primarily financial rather than legal. The arrangements must take into account the ability of the remaining partners to pay for the share of the deceased or insolvent partner, methods for ascertaining the value of that share, and the tax consequences of a particular method.

The Act further provides that, if a partner causes his share of the partnership property to be charged as security for his personal debts, the other partners are entitled to terminate the relationship (B.C., s. 36(2); Ont., s. 33(2); N.S., s. 36(2)).[34]

[33A] Partnerships Act, R.S.O. 1990, B.C., s. 29; Ont., s. 26; N.S., s. 29.

[33B] Partnerships Act, R.S.O. 1990, B.C., s. 36(1); Ont., s. 33(1); N.S., s. 36(1).

[34] Under the B.C. Act, where there are three or more partners, this terminates the relationship only as between the partner whose share is charged and the other partners. The relationship between the other partners remains intact (s. 36(2)).

Dissolution by Law

A partnership is dissolved by any event that makes it unlawful for the business of the firm to be carried on or for members of the firm to carry it on in partnership (B.C., s. 37; Ont., s. 34; N.S., s. 37). The results here are in keeping with the general law of contract concerning illegality.

Even when there is disagreement among the partners concerning dissolution, or where dissolution at a specific time would be contrary to the terms of the partnership agreement, the court may (on an application by one or more partners) order the partnership dissolved under the following circumstances:

- where a partner is found to be mentally incompetent
- where a partner becomes permanently incapable of performing his part of the agreement
- where a partner has been guilty of conduct likely to prejudicially affect the business
- where a partner commits a breach of the agreement or otherwise conducts himself in such a manner that it is not reasonably practicable for the other partners to carry on the business in partnership with him
- where it is just and equitable that the partnership be dissolved (B.C., s. 38; Ont., s. 35; N.S., s. 38)

Effects of Dissolution

When a partnership dissolves, the property of the partnership is applied in payment of the debts and liabilities of the firm, and the surplus assets are applied in payment of what is due to the partners, according to their interests (B.C., s. 42; Ont., s. 39; N.S., s. 42). The Act further provides that, subject to any contrary agreement, in settling accounts between the partners after a dissolution of the partnership, losses (including losses and deficiencies of capital) are to be paid first out of profits, next out of capital, and last, if necessary, by the partners individually in the proportion in which they were entitled to share in the profits. The Act (B.C., s. 47; Ont., s. 44; N.S., s. 47) also prescribes the sequence in which the liabilities of the firm must be met.

CHECKLIST

Sequence of Payments on Dissolution

The assets of the firm must be applied in the following sequence:

1. payment of the debts of the firm owed to non-partners
2. repayment of loans made to the firm by partners
3. repayment of the capital contributed by partners
4. sharing any surplus among the partners according to their entitlement to share in profits

---

The above provisions may be varied, though not so as to affect the rights of non-partners. It could, for example, be agreed that any loss be borne by the wealthier partner, even though he was not entitled to all the profits. What is important to note is that deficiencies of capital are treated as a loss of the firm; this is in contrast to the situation of shareholders in a corporation.[35]

---

[35] See *Garner v. Murray*, [1904] 1 Ch. 57, for an interpretation of this section when partners make unequal capital contributions or share losses unequally.

LIMITED PARTNERSHIPS

All provinces have created a specialized form of partnership through either a Limited Partnership Act or a set of provisions in their Partnership Act. A limited partnership allows a partnership to raise capital from general partners, without borrowing, just as a corporation does with shareholders.

A limited partnership may carry on business, under certain very restricted conditions, without exposing some of its partners to personal liability.[36] Limited partnerships came into existence about the same time that the private limited company (discussed in Chapter 25) came into being. Since, for most business ventures, incorporating a company is a more effective way of raising capital, very little use has been made of limited partnerships.[37]

The major requirement for the formation of a **limited partnership** is that there must be one or more general partners. A **general partner** has unlimited liability, while a **limited partner** has a liability limited to the amount paid by her to the limited partnership as capital contribution. That is, she stands to lose only what she has invested in the business but is not liable to contribute anything further toward the debts or liabilities of the business.

All the Acts prohibit a limited partner from taking an active part in the management of the partnership. If she does so, she becomes liable as a general partner. The words of prohibition vary considerably in each of the statutes.[38] A limited partner would be "taking an active part" if she were personally to transact any business for the firm or be employed for that purpose as an agent or as a lawyer. She can examine the records of the firm, inquire into its progress, and advise on its management without incurring the liability of a general partner. The result is that a limited partner who attempts to take part in the management of the firm does so at a considerable personal risk. She may find herself in the dilemma that if she does not interfere, the business may fail completely; yet if she chooses to exercise some control in order to save the business, she will incur unlimited liability. For this reason more than any other, limited partnerships have rarely been used, except for tax-planning purposes.

There are more stringent regulations for registration for this type than for ordinary partnerships. Failure to comply with requirements of detailed essential information also results in the loss of limited liability.

> **limited partnership** a partnership in which some of the partners limit their liability to the amount of their capital contributions

> **general partner** a partner in a limited partnership whose liability is not limited

> **limited partner** a partner in a limited partnership whose liability is limited to the amount of his or her capital contribution

INTERNATIONAL ISSUE

Enron and Limited Partnerships

One of the most high-profile financial scandals in recent U.S. history involved the use of limited partnerships. As with Canadian limited partnerships, the United States requires that at least one general partner be liable for all the debts and liabilities of the operations, and no more than 35 limited partners can belong to the firm.

Enron Corp. set up many limited partnerships, parking debt in each one. Lenders became limited partners instead of creditors. Andrew Fastow, Enron's CFO and architect of the limited partnership strategy, moved the company away from the use of corporate subsidiaries. In an interview with *CFO Magazine* in 1999, Fastow described the benefits of the limited partnership: "You can get together with one or two investors and craft a particular structure to meet your and their objectives, which is very difficult if you have a public entity [where] you might have to go with shareholder votes and amendments of charters and the like."[39]

>

---

[36] Alberta, British Columbia, Manitoba, and Saskatchewan include the limited partnership provisions in the Partnership Act; the other provinces have separate Limited Partnership(s) Acts.

[37] Limited partnerships do have tax advantages in some circumstances.

[38] See e.g. Partnership Act, R.S.B.C. 1996, c. 348, s. 64; Limited Partnerships Act, R.S.O. 1990, c. L.16, s. 13; R.S.N.S. 1989, c. 259, s. 17.

[39] Ronald Fink, "Beyond Enron," *CFO Magazine*, February 1, 2002, http://ww2.cfo.com/banking-capital-markets/2002/02/beyond-enron/.

Amid much scandal, Enron filed for bankruptcy in late 2001. Of course, the ultimate downfall of Enron did not lie in the use of limited partnerships, but in the way those relationships were accounted for and disclosed to the public. Fastow pleaded guilty to several counts of fraud and was sent to jail. The Enron fiasco triggered a massive overhaul in accounting and corporate governance rules.

One interesting American variety of limited partnership is the public limited partnership. An unlimited number of public investors may become limited partners if the partnership is registered with the Securities and Exchange Commission. Shares in these partnerships are sold through brokerage houses rather than on the exchange.

Questions to Consider

1. How did the layering of limited partnerships on top of a corporation nullify the effect of the general partner's liability?

2. What are the pros and cons of public limited partnerships?

Sources: Ronald Fink, "Beyond Enron," *CFO Magazine*, February 1, 2002, http://ww2.cfo.com/banking-capital-markets/2002/02/beyond-enron/; Richard DeGeorge, Chapter 9, "Business Ethics," in *Corporate Governance, Accounting Disclosure and Insider Trading* (Upper Saddle River, NJ: Prentice Hall, 2004); "10 Enron Players: Where They Landed After the Fall," *New York Times*, January 29, 2006, http://www.nytimes.com/2006/01/29/business/businessspecial3/29profiles.html?pagewanted=all&_r=0.

LIMITED LIABILITY PARTNERSHIPS

limited liability partnership a partnership in which non-negligent partners are not personally liable for losses caused by the negligence of a partner

After remaining virtually unchanged for more than 100 years, Canadian partnership law saw a radical change in 1998 with the introduction in Ontario of another specialized form of partnership: the **limited liability partnership** (LLP).[40] Alberta followed in 1999, and Saskatchewan in 2001.[41] Since then, the LLP has also been introduced in Manitoba, New Brunswick, Nova Scotia, and British Columbia.[42] LLPs are principally used by large accounting and law firms.

As noted, a major disadvantage of a general partnership is the firm's liability for torts committed by a partner in the ordinary course of the business (section 11), and corresponding joint liability of each partner for the debts and obligations of the firm (section 1). An LLP protects a partner from some of this personal liability:

> [A] partner in a limited liability partnership is not liable . . . for debts, liabilities or obligations of the partnership or any partner arising from the negligent acts or omissions that another partner or an employee, agent or representative of the partnership commits in the course of the partnership business while the partnership is a limited liability partnership.[43]

A partner remains liable for his own negligent acts or omissions, and for those of a person who is under the partner's direct supervision or control.[44] It also appears that the firm itself remains liable, so that a non-negligent partner still stands to lose the entire value of his partnership share. However, an injured party may not look beyond the assets of the firm to the personal assets of the non-negligent partners.[45]

Under the Ontario law, the protection of non-negligent partners appears to extend only to the negligent acts or omissions of a partner—it does not apply to other torts or to breaches of trust, nor does it affect the contractual liability of partners. The Alberta legislation provides broader protection. A member of an LLP is not liable for the "negligence, wrongful acts or omissions, malpractice or misconduct" of a partner, or of an employee or

[40] Partnerships Statute Law Amendment Act, 1998, S.O. 1998, c. 2.

[41] Partnership Act, R.S.A. 2000, c. P-3, ss. 81–104: R.S.S. 1978, c. P-3 (as amended), ss. 78–110.

[42] Partnership Act, C.C.S.M., c. P30, ss. 51–88; R.S.N.B. 1973, c. P-4, ss. 46–54; R.S.N.S. 1989, c. 334, ss. 48–71; R.S.B.C. 1996, c. 348 ss. 94–125. The Ontario legislation is far less comprehensive than that of the other provinces. Only the Yukon and Prince Edward Island lack LLPs.

[43] Partnerships Act, R.S.O. 1990, c. P.5 (as amended), s. 10(2).

[44] *Ibid.*, s. 10(3).

[45] *Ibid.*, s. 10(4).

agent of the firm, unless he knew of the act in question and failed to take reasonable steps to prevent its commission, or the act was committed by someone for whom he was directly responsible and he had failed to provide adequate supervision.[46]

The Saskatchewan legislation adopts an entirely different approach: partners in an LLP are personally liable for any partnership obligation for which they would be liable if the partnership were a corporation of which they were directors.[47] The Manitoba provisions on liability (s. 75) follow those of Alberta quite closely, while New Brunswick (ss. 48, 49) and Nova Scotia adopt both approaches (ss. 57, 58).

Although there are substantial differences in detail, all the provinces require a written agreement that designates the partnership as an LLP. An existing partnership may convert itself into an LLP if all the partners agree. An LLP must register its firm name, and the name must contain the words "limited liability partnership" or the abbreviation "LLP" or "L.L.P." Those provinces that have adopted the LLP form all permit LLPs from other jurisdictions to register as extra-provincial LLPs.

The most important restriction is that an LLP may carry on business only for the purpose of practising an "eligible profession."[48] In addition, that statute must expressly permit an LLP to practise the profession, and the governing body of the profession must require the partnership to maintain a minimum amount of liability insurance.

The LLP should not be confused with the limited partnership, discussed in the preceding section. In particular,

- in a limited partnership there must be at least one general partner who has unlimited liability;
- limited partners, unlike partners in an LLP, lose their limited liability if they participate in management;
- limited partnerships are not restricted to the professions.

Ethical Issue   To Limit or Not to Limit?

Limited liability partnerships have been allowed in Canada since 1998, though they have been permitted in many states of the United States for even longer. Their use has spread to a number of other countries, especially since the Enron case. Nevertheless, there is still disagreement as to whether becoming "limited," where it is permitted, is necessarily a good move. It involves questions of trust and privacy.

In favour of LLPs, it is argued that

- it obviously makes sense to limit one's personal liability when claims in the millions of dollars are being made against accounting and law firms,
- without LLP status it may be difficult to attract new partners, and
- all the big firms are going limited, so LLP status is a mark of success.

Arguments against LLP status suggest that

- it is a signal to clients that even the partners do not trust each other,
- the conversion from unlimited to limited status poses some difficult problems and requires unanimity among existing partners,
- disclosure requirements result in a loss of privacy and, perhaps, confidentiality, and
- it is not yet clear just how much legal protection the LLP status provides.

Questions to Consider

1. Which of the above arguments do you find convincing?

2. In what circumstances, if any, would you recommend that an existing partnership "go limited"?

---

[46] R.S.A. 2000, c. P-3, s. 12.

[47] R.S.S. 1978, c. P-3 (as amended), ss. 80, 81.

[48] Most provinces define it as a profession governed by statute. Alberta permits LLPs for any profession that allows the formation of professional corporations.

JOINT VENTURES

A joint venture is an agreement between two or more parties (often corporations) to collaborate on the management of a specific project, to each contribute a part of their respective resources (particular assets and expertise), and to share the profits.[49] Sometimes a project requires a greater capital outlay than any one corporation may be prepared to put at risk. A joint venture spreads the risk among the participants. In the oil and gas industry, for example, corporations have found it practical to undertake exploration expenditures jointly to discover and develop oil and gas reserves, as in the Arctic and Atlantic continental shelf explorations.

contractual joint venture a joint venture effected by agreement without the creation of any separate legal entity

Legally, a joint venture is contractual. It is just a contractual relationship between the parties for a specific undertaking, and is sometimes referred to as a **contractual joint venture**. However, an alternative method of accomplishing the same end is for the parties to incorporate a separate corporation (a joint subsidiary) for the venture with each participant holding shares in it. This type of arrangement has become known as an **equity joint venture** but is subject to the general rules of corporation law, not contract.

equity joint venture a corporation formed, and jointly owned, by the parties to a joint venture for the purpose of carrying on the venture

Participants typically regard a contractual joint venture as an extension of their own operations and a collaboration with other parties, rather than as a separate business. While they may look like a partnership, joint ventures are quite different. The venture is for a specific project or series of explorations, and of limited duration, not a continuing activity like a partnership. Nor are they inherently fiduciary relationships as are partnerships.[50] Normally, profits are not retained jointly for investment in other projects, but are distributed to each of the participants in proportions set down in the joint venture agreement. The parties may also try to limit their liability by providing that their only contribution will be those things specifically set out in the agreement, that the agreement shall not be construed as a partnership, and that their liability will not be joint and several. They may also try to limit the authority of members to act as agents for one another in the operation of a joint venture and may identify one of themselves (or an independent party) as the "operator" of the joint venture. Whether such an arrangement will be effective to limit the agency of each participating member remains a question of fact to be determined by the court if a dispute arises with an outside third party. Such restrictions may not be effective if it is determined that the venture was, as a matter of fact, a partnership.[51]

INCOME TRUSTS

Trusts are a complicated area of the law, as noted in Chapter 11, and this section will attempt only a basic explanation of their latest business application. Over the past decade, income trusts emerged as a popular Canadian business entity. This was largely due to favourable tax treatment and their unique liability structure. The tax advantage was removed in 2008.[52]

---

[49] *Canlan Investment Corp. v. Gettling* (1997), 37 B.C.L.R. (3d) 140 (B.C.C.A.); *Blue Line Hockey Acquisition Co. v. Orca Bay Hockey Limited Partnership*, [2008] B.C.J. No. 24 at paras. 57–77 (B.C.S.C.) affirmed 2009 BCCA 34.

[50] A majority of the Supreme Court of Canada held, in *LAC Minerals Ltd. v. International Corona Resources Ltd.* (1989), 61 D.L.R. (4th) 14, that there was no fiduciary duty between parties to a joint venture (though there was a duty not to misuse confidential information). See also *Chitel v. Bank of Montreal*, [2002] O.J. No. 2170; *CadburySchweppes Inc. v. FBI Foods Ltd.*, [1999] 1 S.C.R. 142 at para. 30.

[51] *Central Mortgage and Housing Corp. v. Graham* (1973), 43 D.L.R. (3d) 686; *Lansing Building Supply (Ontario) Ltd. v. Ierullo, supra*, n. 9. *LAC Minerals Ltd. v. International Corona Resources Ltd.* (1989), 61 D.L.R. (4th) 14, (each case will turn on its own facts). See also *Chitel v. Bank of Montreal*, [2002] O.J. No. 2170.

[52] Department of Finance, Canada, "Canada's New Government Announces Tax Fairness Plan," press release, October 31, 2008, http://www.fin.gc.ca/n06/06-061-eng.asp.

The income trust structure involves the transfer of income-producing assets from the operating company to a trust. The trust is created by an agreement known as a **declaration of trust** and this document (in conjunction with trust law) governs the trust. The operating company continues to manage the assets under the supervision of the trustees, but all income (less expenses) is the property of the trust. The income is then distributed by the trust to **unitholders** (rather than shareholders) and taxed only once in the hands of the unitholders. When units are offered to the public, the trust is also governed by securities legislation. New tax rules phased in between 2008 and 2011 impose a second layer of taxation and thereby eliminate a trust's major tax advantage over corporations.

As for the liability and governance issues, income trusts are operated by trustees, and their liability has historically been determined under the rules of trust law, not corporate governance law. The Uniform Law Commission of Canada has proposed a model law addressing the structure and governance issues, which recommends that income trusts be treated more like corporations; for example,

- unitholders should have limited liability;
- unitholders should be entitled to elect trustees;
- unitholders should have the same remedies as shareholders; and
- trustees should have the same powers, duties, and liability as directors of a corporation.[53]

So far, only the tax changes have been adopted.

declaration of trust an agreement that establishes a trust and designates the trustees

unitholders beneficiaries of an income trust

Strategies to Manage the Legal Risks

One of the most important legal risk management decisions a business owner and operator will make is to choose the appropriate entity within which to operate the business. This should be done after seeking financial, accounting, and legal advice. Incorporating is a natural choice where the type of business allows it, but it may not be appropriate for short-term, low-risk, and modestly financed ventures. One entity may be converted into another once the business is operating profitably.

For all forms of business, complying with registration requirements is vital. Business names must be registered in all provinces, but this does not give a business ownership of the name. Prior to registering the business name, steps as outlined in Chapter 20 should be followed to protect ownership in the intellectual property and trademarks of the business. There may be liability for registering a name that infringes the intellectual property rights of others. Make the appropriate searches before registering.

Written partnership agreements are essential; partners should not rely on the "one size fits all" model set out in the Partnership Act. Non-competition agreements and partner buy-out mechanisms are just two examples of things not covered in the legislation. Each partner should seek independent legal advice prior to signing the agreement.

If a need for regular capital infusion is expected, consider the use of a limited partnership so that investors may be sought in the form of limited partners without having to include them in the operation of the business. Accounting and legal partnerships should consider the use of limited liability partnerships to reduce personal liability for torts of other

---

[53] Uniform Law Commission of Canada, The Uniform Income Trusts Act, http://www.ulcc.ca/en /uniform-acts-new-order/current-uniform-acts/672-trusts/income-trusts/1444-income-trusts-act.

partners. Partners should consider arranging their personal affairs so that family assets are not owned by them and thereby available to satisfy partnership debts.

For specific projects, consider the use of several entities. For example, two corporations may form a partnership for a specific business neither carries on alone. Although the partners will have personal liability, the shareholders of the corporation will be immune from liability. Alternatively, where two limited partnerships form a joint venture, only the general partners in each partnership will face possible liability. It is very common for businesses to layer one entity on top of another.

QUESTIONS FOR REVIEW

1. To what laws are sole proprietorships subject?
2. Is it necessary to have a written agreement in order to create a partnership?
3. What are the advantages and disadvantages of partnerships as opposed to sole proprietorships?
4. What are the basic elements of the partnership relationship?
5. What is the difference between sharing profits and sharing gross receipts?
6. In what circumstances may a person receive a share of the profits of a partnership business without herself being a partner?
7. Why is it important to distinguish between partnership property and the personal property of the individual partners?
8. When is it necessary for a partnership to be registered?
9. What does it mean to say "every partner is an agent of the firm"?
10. What is meant by "apparent authority"?
11. What is "joint liability"?
12. What steps should a partner take to protect herself against ongoing liability when she retires?
13. Can a partner receive a "salary" from the firm? What is the real nature of a partner's salary?
14. What are the three principal fiduciary duties imposed on partners?
15. How is partnership property distributed on the dissolution of a partnership?
16. Is there any difference between a partnership and a joint venture?
17. What are the principal forms that a joint venture may take?
18. What are the principal advantages and disadvantages of being a limited partner?
19. What is a limited liability partnership? How does it differ from a limited partnership?
20. In what ways is the liability of a partner in an LLP limited?
21. What was the motivation for the creation of income trusts?

CASES AND PROBLEMS

1. Continuing Scenario

At the end of the first year in business, it appears that Ashley's Restaurant has made a profit. She won't know the exact amount until her accountant finishes the financial statements, but he is asking questions about what "type" of business entity she is operating. She knows it is not a corporation because she has not filed *any* government forms or registrations. But she has promised to share some of the profits with others. To her father, Jim—who guaranteed the poultry supplier account, co-signed her lease, and painted the whole restaurant before opening—Ashley promised she would "pay him back" for all his hard work when the restaurant started making money. Ashley told her mother, who advanced her $50 000 at the start of the business, that there would be a good "return on her investment" and Ashley has already paid her $3000 for use of the money. Ashley asks her lawyer, Brendan, the following questions: Is she in a partnership with her parents? Why or why not? If so what kind of partnership is it, and how will they share the profits? Ashley's parents are old; what would be the consequences to the business if one of them died? What registrations should she have made?

2. Giovanni and Leporello were in partnership together under the registered name "Adventures Unlimited." The partnership was formed for the purpose of providing guided adventure vacations for rich clients. Under a clause in the partnership agreement, it was provided that neither partner may incur expenditures on behalf of the firm in excess of $500 without the approval of the other partner.

   Giovanni purported to enter into a contract—in the name of Adventures Unlimited—with Elvira Sails Ltd. (a corporation engaged in selling and leasing boats) to rent a large cabin cruiser for a period of three months, at a rent of $10 000 per month. He signed the rental agreement in his own name, paid a deposit for $1000 by a cheque drawn on the partnership's bank account, took delivery of the cruiser, and has not been seen since. The cruiser was reportedly last seen in the Virgin Islands.

   What rights (if any) does Elvira Sails have against Leporello?

3. Crawford and McDougall were sisters of relatively advanced years. For some years they had entrusted their financial affairs to Watson, a lawyer, who was a partner in the firm of Heather & Co. Due to some disastrous investments that they made on Watson's advice, they lost almost $250 000.

   The loss was discovered when they learned that Watson had been disbarred for misconduct. It was evident that their loss had been caused either by fraud or by negligence on the part of Watson, though it was less clear which.

   The sisters brought an action against Heather & Co, claiming damages for their loss.

   Should they succeed? What particular circumstances might be relevant?

4. Adders LLP is a limited liability partnership, registered in Ontario, practising as chartered accountants. It has 15 partners and over 200 employees. One of its major clients, Norne Inc., is a small but dynamic resource company, incorporated in Ontario.

   Until about two years ago, the Norne account was supervised by Counter, a senior partner. More recently, the corporation's account has been handled by Turner, a young accountant who is considered to be in line for a partnership. Counter has continued to exercise nominal supervision, discussing the account with Turner from time to time, but increasingly Turner has been left to work by herself.

   Shortly after taking over the account, Turner was approached by Plotter, Norne's chief financial officer, who outlined to her a scheme to extract large sums of money from Norne through unauthorized borrowings. Turner would be able to use her position to falsify the accounts and to conceal the transactions. Turner agreed, and over the next 18 months they were able to divert over $5 million from Norne before their scheme was discovered. Turner, Plotter, and the money have all disappeared.

   Adders LLP is now being sued by Norne Inc. and also by Driller, an investor resident in British Columbia, who recently purchased a 20 percent share in Norne after examining the accounts prepared by Adders.

   Consider the liability of (a) Adders LLP, (b) Counter, and (c) the other partners in the firm.

5. Albinoni, Bonporti, and Corelli were partners. According to the partnership agreement, the following provisions applied:

   (a) **Capital:**
   Albinoni and Bonporti each contributed $20 000; Corelli contributed no capital.

   (b) **Advances:**
   Albinoni advanced $10 000 to the firm by way of a loan, repayable on six months' notice or on dissolution.

(c) **Profits:**

Profits were to be shared in the following proportions: Albinoni, 40 percent; Bonporti, 40 percent; Corelli, 20 percent. They were to contribute in the same proportions (40/40/20) to make up any loss or deficiency.

(d) **Drawings:**

The partners were entitled to draw, by way of an advance on their prospective shares of profits, up to $60 000 in any year. Since the end of the last accounting period, the following drawings were made: Albinoni, $8000; Bonporti, $7000; Corelli, $15 000.

The partnership has now been dissolved. At the time of dissolution, the total value of the firm's assets, including undrawn profits, was $100 000. (This does not include the $30 000 already drawn by the partners.)

Calculate how the surplus, or deficiency, should be shared, if the total liabilities to the firm's external creditors (that is, not including debts owed to partners) are as follows:

(1) $10 000

(2) $90 000

(3) $150 000

For more cases and problems, see the Companion Website.

Additional Resources for Chapter 24 on the Companion Website

(www.pearsoncanada.ca/smyth)

In addition to pre- and post-tests, mini-cases, and application exercises, the Companion Website includes the following province-specific resources for Chapter 24:

- **Alberta:** International Partnerships; Limited Liability Partnerships; Limited Partnerships; Partnership in Alberta
- **Atlantic Provinces:** Partnership Legislation; Public–Private Partnerships
- **British Columbia:** Business Names; Limited Liability Partnerships; Limited Partnerships; Partnerships; Sole Proprietorships
- **Manitoba/Saskatchewan:** Partnerships
- **Ontario:** Business Names; Fiduciary Duty; Limited Liability Partnerships; Limited Partnerships; Multi-Disciplinary Partnerships; Partnership Agreements; Registration of Partnerships

Chapter 25

The Nature of a Corporation and Its Formation

This is the first of three chapters dealing with corporations. In it, we discuss some of the most fundamental issues concerning the nature of a corporation and examine such questions as:

- What is a corporation?

- What are the consequences that flow from incorporation?

- What is meant by "limited liability"?

- How is a corporation formed?

- What are the usual provisions of the corporate charter?

- What is corporate capital?

- What are shares?

- What are the main distinctions between shares and bonds?

THE NATURE OF A CORPORATION

The corporation, or limited company, is the dominant business entity in the world. Not only is it the main instrument of big business, but it also exceeds sole proprietorship and partnership as a means of carrying on smaller businesses.

The Corporation as a Legal Person

corporation a legal person formed by incorporation according to a prescribed legal procedure

legal person an entity recognized at law as having its own legal rights, duties, and responsibilities

A **corporation** is a person in the eyes of the law; it is a **legal person** (an entity recognized by law as having rights and duties of its own). A distinction is commonly drawn between legal persons and natural persons. Natural persons are human beings—they automatically have rights and obligations. Their rights and obligations may vary according to age, mental capacity, and other factors,[1] but they are all "persons." By contrast, a legal person is entirely a creation of the state. A legal person has rights and duties under the law, distinct from its owner or creator, but it cannot insist on those rights or carry out its duties except through human agents.

It is a well established legal principle that once a corporation is created, it is a separate and distinct legal person apart from its members.[2]

There are numerous types of corporations: publicly owned corporations created by governments to carry on special activities (for example, the Bank of Canada, the Canadian Broadcasting Corporation, Central Mortgage and Housing Corporation, and Canadian National Railway); municipal corporations to run local government; charitable corporations (for example, the Red Cross, the Heart and Stroke Foundation, the Ford Foundation); educational institutions; and business corporations—the most numerous type of all. We are concerned with business corporations.[3]

Characteristics of Corporations vs. Partnerships

The significance of the separate legal personality of a business corporation is obvious when compared with partnership.

Liability As noted in Chapter 24, each partner in a partnership is normally liable for payment of the debts of the firm, including payment from his or her personal assets.[4] A corporation is liable for its own debts. A shareholder in a corporation is not required to pay the corporation's debts; shareholders can lose no more than the price paid for the shares in the event that creditors seize the corporation's assets. This **limited liability** of shareholders is why business corporations are called "limited" companies, although this is really a misnomer since the corporation itself is liable to the full extent of its assets.[5]

limited liability the liability of shareholders is limited to the amount of their capital contributions

Limited liability is widely regarded as the main advantage of incorporation. However, the benefits of limited liability are sometimes overestimated since, for a small corporation to obtain credit, its directors or shareholders are often required to give personal guarantees or mortgage their own property as collateral security. In addition, when shareholders become directors—as they usually do in smaller enterprises—they are subject to a wide and increasing range of personal liability from which their limited liability as shareholders does not protect them.

---

[1] See Chapter 8.

[2] See D.H. Bonham and D.A. Soberman, "The Nature of Corporate Personality," in *Studies in Canadian Company Law*, J.S. Ziegel, ed., Vol. 1, Chapter 1 (Toronto: Butterworths, 1967).

[3] Business corporations can be divided into a number of sub-categories.

[4] Exceptions are the limited liability partnership and limited partnership.

[5] In British Columbia, Alberta, and Nova Scotia, it is possible to form an unlimited company in which the shareholders are liable for the company's debts. The main attraction of this form has been to create tax-planning opportunities for U.S. businesses.

Transfer of Ownership A partner cannot release herself unilaterally from her liabilities—to her partners, to the firm, and to its clients—simply by retiring. She must negotiate her release with both her partners and her creditors. She may even be liable for debts contracted after her retirement, unless she has given notice to persons who regularly deal with the firm and has fulfilled the requirements of the Partnership Act. Since a shareholder has no liability for corporate debts even while he retains his shares, creditors of the corporation have no interest in his shares or personal assets. The shareholder may sever all connections with the corporation simply by transferring his shares to another person. However, sometimes restrictions are imposed on the transfer of shares by the corporation.

Management A partnership is not suitable for a venture involving a large number of investors. Each partner, as an agent of the firm, may enter into contracts on behalf of the firm. By contrast, shareholders have no authority to bind their corporation to contractual obligations—only officers of the corporation may do so.

A partnership usually requires unanimity on major business decisions, a requirement that could stalemate a firm with a large number of partners. In a corporation, management is delegated to an elected board of directors that normally reaches decisions by simple majority votes. Major decisions that are referred back to the shareholders do not require unanimity, but at most a two-thirds or three-quarters majority, depending upon the issue and the requirements of the corporation law statutes in the jurisdiction.

Separation of ownership and management and limited liability are the primary advantages of the business corporation. These two features enable an investor to invest a specific sum of money and receive a return on it, without either taking any additional risk beyond the sum invested or having to take an active part in the management of business affairs.

Although at one time the major shareholders in a corporation were usually its managers as well, there has been an increasing separation between those who invest and those who manage.[6] The separation is, however, less pronounced in Canada than in the United States because many large Canadian corporations are controlled by a single individual or by members of a family, or are wholly owned subsidiaries of foreign parent corporations.[7]

Duty of Good Faith As noted in Chapter 24, partners owe each other a duty of good faith or fiduciary duty. It would normally be a breach of duty for a partner to carry on another business independently without the consent of her other partners (especially if it were a competing business), or to enter into contracts with the firm on her own behalf. A shareholder owes no such duty to the corporation:[8] He may carry on any independent business himself and may deal freely with the corporation as if he were a stranger.

Continuity In the absence of special provisions in the partnership agreement, the death or bankruptcy of a partner dissolves a partnership. Even when provisions are made in advance to continue the partnership and to buy out the share of the deceased or bankrupt partner, the procedure is often cumbersome and expensive. A corporation exists independently of any of its shareholders.[9] A person's shares may be transferred by gift or by sale, by will or by statute transmitting them to the personal representative on death, or by creditors seizing them— none of these events affects the existence of the corporation. A corporation

---

[6] The classic study of this subject is that by A.A. Berle and G.C. Means, *The Modern Corporation and Private Property* (New York: Macmillan, 1932). It is still worth reading.

[7] Randall K. Morck, David A. Stangeland, and Bernard Yeung, "Inherited Wealth, Corporate Control, and Economic Growth: The Canadian Disease?" in *Concentrated Corporate Ownership*, Randall K. Morck, ed. (Chicago: National Bureau of Economic Research and University of Chicago Press, 2000).

[8] See *Blacklaws v. 470433 Alberta Ltd.* (2000), 187 D.L.R. (4th) 614. Directors owe a duty of good faith to their corporation.

[9] It survives even the death of all its shareholders: *Re Noel Tedman Holdings Pty. Ltd.*, [1967] Qd. R. 561 (Queensland S.C.).

continues in existence indefinitely unless it is dissolved by order of a court or by a voluntary resolution of its shareholders, or it is struck off the register for failure to comply with statutory regulations.

Taxation   Unlike a partnership, a corporation is a taxable entity. Income of a corporation is taxed first in the corporation and again in the hands of a shareholder when a dividend is declared. To offset this double taxation, small corporations are taxed at an especially low rate and dividends from Canadian corporations receive preferential tax treatment.[10]

CHECKLIST

Partnerships and Corporate Ownership Contrasted

Characteristic	Partnership	Corporation
Separate legal entity	no	yes
Personal liability of owners	yes*	no
Duty of good faith	yes	no
Agency	yes	no
Transferability of ownership	no	yes
Participation of owners in management	yes*	no
Continuity of business	no	yes
Taxable entity	no	yes

*There are exceptions; see Chapter 24.

Consequences of Separate Corporate Personality

Capacity   A corporation is created by statute law and has the characteristics that the legislators give it. Originally, corporations were formed for specific purposes and could act only for those purposes expressly stated in their constitution. Any act outside the scope of those objects was ultra vires—beyond the powers—of the corporation. Contracts made for an unauthorized purpose were invalid.

The ultra vires doctrine, as it applied to corporations, was abolished throughout Canada. Under the federal Canada Business Corporations Act,[11] and most of the provincial statutes under which business corporations are formed, a corporation has the capacity and all the rights, powers, and privileges of a natural person (section 15).

However, as an artificial person, a corporation can act only through its human agents—its directors and officers. When a corporation purports to make a contract, it is necessary to determine whether its agent has authority.

Separate Existence: *Salomon*   As noted, a corporation is a legal entity distinct from its shareholders. The classic case on the existence of the corporation as a separate entity came in 1897 in *Salomon v. Salomon & Co. Ltd.*[12] It is probably the most widely quoted decision in the whole of corporate law.

---

[10] The small business combined (federal and provincial) tax rate in Ontario was approximately 15.5 percent in 2013 (available on up to $500 000 of business income).

[11] R.S.C. 1985, c. C-44, referred to hereafter as the CBCA.

[12] [1897] A.C. 22.

Salomon carried on a successful shoe manufacturing business. In 1892, he formed a corporation in which he held almost all the shares (20 001 out of 20 007, the remaining six shares being held by members of his family, in order to meet what was then the statutory requirement of seven shareholders). He then sold his business to the corporation but continued to operate it as a director and employee. Soon afterward, a downturn in the shoe industry, caused by loss of government contracts and a series of strikes, drove the corporation into insolvency, and a trustee was appointed to wind it up. The trustee claimed that the corporation was merely a sham, that Salomon was the true owner of the business and the real debtor, and, as such, that he should pay off all debts owed by the corporation. The lower courts supported the trustee's position, but the Court decided in favour of Salomon. Either the corporation was a true legal entity or it was not. Since there was no fraud or any intention to deceive, all transactions having been fully disclosed to the parties and the statutory regulations complied with, the corporation was properly created and was solely responsible for its own debts.

The decision in the *Salomon* case was important because it recognized the separate legal personality of the so-called one-man company at the time when it was becoming a common form of doing business.[13] As a leading writer on the subject has said, "Since the *Salomon* case, the complete separation of the company and its members has never been doubted."[14]

For the most part, the principle of separate legal personality prevails, but in some circumstances, the shareholders' interests may be recognized. In the 1987 *Kosmopoulos* case, the Supreme Court of Canada held that a shareholder, even one who owns all the shares of a corporation, does not own its assets, but still has an insurable interest in those assets. If they are destroyed, his shares will lose value, and, consequently, he should be entitled to insure against their destruction.[15]

It remains unclear how far the principle in the *Kosmopoulos* case can be taken and whether it is restricted to insurance claims. Certainly, it does not seem to follow that, where an injury is done to a corporation, a shareholder will always have a claim for the consequent reduction in the value of his or her shares. As the Ontario Court of Appeal has since ruled, the fact that the plaintiff is the principal shareholder and directing mind of the corporation that was defrauded does not entitle him to personal compensation for the losses suffered by the corporation.[16] To hold otherwise would enable him to jump to the front of the payment line to the prejudice of other corporate creditors. Where a wrong is done to a corporation, a shareholder has no claim for damages in respect of that wrong.

An oil exploration company formed two subsidiaries, apparently to take advantage of government financing. One subsidiary owned a drilling rig; the other contracted to provide drilling services. The rig was damaged due to the alleged negligence of the defendant. The defendant was prima facie liable to the corporation that owned the rig, but not for the economic loss sustained by the service corporation. The two corporations were separate entities, and the loss to the service corporation was too remote.[17]

---

[13] The CBCA, s. 5, allows a corporation to be formed with only one shareholder, as do the laws of almost all provinces.

[14] *Gower's Principles of Modern Company Law*, 6th ed., (London: Sweet & Maxwell, 1997) at 79–80.

[15] *Kosmopoulos v. Constitution Insurance Co. of Canada* (1987), 34 D.L.R. (4th) 208. The concept of insurable interest is discussed in Chapter 16.

[16] *Martin v. Goldfarb* (1998), 163 D.L.R. (4th) 639; *Meditrust Healthcare Inc. v. Shoppers Drug Mart* (2002), 220 D.L.R. (4th) 611; *R.L.T.V. Investments Inc. v. Saskatchewan Telecommunications*, [2009] 9 W.W.R. 15 (Sask. C.A.).

[17] *Bow Valley Husky (Bermuda) Ltd. v. Saint John Shipbuilding Ltd.* (1997), 153 D.L.R. (4th) 385. The question of recovery for economic loss was considered in Chapter 4.

The same reasoning applies in cases where the hardship is suffered not by the owners of the corporation but by the persons who deal with it. As stated in section 45 of the Canada Business Corporations Act, shareholders are not liable for any act or default of debt of the corporation.

CASE 25.3

K, a Toronto lawyer, incorporated a real estate company, Rockwell, of which he effectively owned almost all the shares. Rockwell became involved in a contractual dispute with another corporation, Newtonbrook, and eventually brought an action against Newtonbrook for specific performance of the contract. Rockwell lost the action, and Newtonbrook was awarded costs of $4800. When Newtonbrook sought to recover the costs, it found that Rockwell's entire assets consisted of $31.85 in its bank account. Newtonbrook's attempt to recover from K personally failed.[18]

Limitations on the Principle of Separate Corporate Existence

When application of the *Salomon* decision leads to unfair results, should the courts refuse to follow it? When should legislation disregard the principle of separate legal identity?

Exceptions to Limited Liability The limited liability of shareholders is not absolute. In practice, shareholders of small private companies are often required to provide security or personal guarantees for loans made to their corporations. The Canada Business Corporations Act (CBCA) provides a further exception to the principle: Where shareholders have received an improper distribution of corporate assets—for example, where a dividend has been paid although the corporation had made no profits—they are liable for the corporation's debts to that extent (section 118(4)).[19] Other statutes, such as the federal Bankruptcy and Insolvency Act,[20] require shareholders who have received property from a corporation before it became insolvent to repay the amounts received in certain circumstances.

It is also important to note that the principle of limited liability does not protect persons who happen to be shareholders of corporations from personal liability. For example, a director who behaves negligently while doing company business is not absolved from liability in tort, even though the corporation may also be vicariously liable.[21] And directors who make negligent misrepresentations regarding the affairs of their corporation may be personally liable for any resulting loss.[22] In Chapter 26, we will discuss the other circumstances in which officers and directors are exposed to personal liability.

Other Statutory Provisions There are numerous examples, especially in taxation and labour law, where statutes require the separate personality of corporations to be disregarded. For example, Canadian-controlled private corporations are taxed at a lower rate on the first $500 000 of their annual income; but it is not possible to multiply this concession by forming several distinct corporations, because **associated corporations** are only entitled to a single concession between them.[23] Again, employers are not allowed to avoid statutory

associated corporations corporations that are related either (a) vertically, as where one corporation controls the other (parent–subsidiary), or (b) horizontally, as where both corporations are controlled by the same person (affiliates)

---

[18] *Rockwell Developments Ltd. v. Newtonbrook Plaza Ltd.* (1972), 27 D.L.R. (3d) 651.

[19] There are also several provisions that make directors liable for the debts of their corporation; these are considered in Chapter 27.

[20] R.S.C. 1985, c. B-3. See Chapter 29.

[21] See *Berger v. Willowdale* (1983), 41 O.R. (2d) 89, leave to appeal denied [1983] S.C.C.A. No. 353.

[22] *NBD Bank of Canada v. Dofasco Inc.* (1999), 181 D.L.R. (4th) 37, leave to appeal denied [2000] S.C.C.A. No. 96; contrast *Scotia McLeod Inc v. Peoples Jewellers Limited et al.* (1995), 26 O.R. (3d) 481, leave to appeal denied [1996] S.C.C.A. No. 40. See also discussion of secondary market liability in Chapters 5, 26, 27.

[23] Income Tax Act, R.S.C. 1985, c. 1 (5th Supp.), s. 125. Corporations are associated where one corporation controls the other (parent–subsidiary relationship), or where both corporations are controlled by the same person or group of persons (affiliates) s. 256.

employment standards by transferring their assets to an associated corporation, thereby leaving the employer unable to meet employee claims for unpaid wages, vacation pay, and other benefits.[24] Nevertheless, the courts and legislature have stopped short of imposing any form of group liability. It is only in exceptional circumstances that a parent company will be held liable for the debts of its subsidiary or vice versa.

ILLUSTRATION 25.1

Holdco is the parent company of a major marketing group. It has a number of divisions, each operated by a wholly owned subsidiary corporation. Retailco, its retailing subsidiary, recently became bankrupt, owing $100 million. At the same time, Creditco, the corporation that operates its credit financing division, has profits of $20 million. The assets of Creditco are not available to pay the creditors of Retailco.

Lifting the Corporate Veil

There have also been cases—although in Canada they are quite rare—where the courts have been prepared to disregard the separate existence of corporations and "lift the veil" of incorporation to impose liability on those that control it. It seems that, in order to find an individual within a corporation liable, three conditions must be met:

- The individual must control the corporation.

- That control must have been exercised to commit a fraud, a wrong, or a breach of duty.

- The misconduct must be the cause of the plaintiff's injury.[25]

Rather than equate a controlling shareholder with the corporation that he controls, Canadian courts have generally preferred to seek other routes to secure a just result. As we saw in the *Kosmopoulos* case,[26] the Supreme Court of Canada refused to lift the veil and to hold that the corporation and the individual who owned all of its shares were one and the same person, but reached the same result by finding that he had an insurable interest in the corporation's property.

INTERNATIONAL ISSUE

Foreign Investment in Canadian Corporations

As will be discussed in Chapters 30 and 31, foreign investment in Canadian corporations is monitored and controlled by Industry Canada, pursuant to the Investment Canada Act.[27] In addition, the Canada Business Corporations Act (s. 105(3)) requires that 25 percent of a Canadian corporation's directors be resident Canadians (as does[28] the Ontario, Alberta, Saskatchewan, and Manitoba legislation). However, there are variations among the provinces in the related legislation. To encourage foreign investment, British Columbia and Nova Scotia have dropped directors' residency requirements.

>

---

[24] See e.g. Employment Standards Act, S.O. 2000, c. 41, s. 4, regarding associated businesses being treated as one employer but excluding shareholders from this principle.

[25] *W.D. Latimer Co. Ltd. v. Dijon Investments Ltd.* (1992), 12 O.R. (3d) 415. Courts are more likely to pierce the corporate veil when a shareholder engages in conduct amounting to fraud. See *Gilford Motor Company v. Horne,* [1933] Ch. 935 (C.A.).

[26] *Supra*, n. 15.

[27] R.S.C. 1985, c. 28 (1st Supp.).

[28] See Business Corporations Act, R.S.O. 1990, c. B-16, s. 118(3); R.S.A. 2000, c. B-9, s. 105(3); R.S.S. 1978, c. B-10, s. 100(3); Corporations Act C.C.S.M., c. C225, s. 100(3).

Another strategy to increase foreign investment (particularly by Americans) is a different type of corporation: the unlimited liability corporation (ULC). As the name suggests, these corporations do not benefit from the protection of limited liability. On windup or dissolution, shareholders in a ULC are personally liable to the ULC's creditors for any unsatisfied debts.[29] So far, Nova Scotia, Alberta, and British Columbia have introduced foreign ULCs in their provincial incorporation legislation.[30] Ontario did not authorize ULCs when it amended its incorporation legislation in 2007. The attraction of ULCs for investors lies in the different tax treatment they receive in the United States. Although ULCs are taxed like any other corporation in Canada, in the United States they are viewed as "flow through" vehicles and no federal income tax is collected from them. When considering investing in this type of corporation, potential shareholders must weigh the tax benefits against the potential liability involved.

Question to Consider

1. What impact will provincial variation in the availability of ULCs have on foreign investment decisions?

Sources: Geoff Kirbyson, "Alberta's Unlimited Liability Corporations Will Draw Them In," *The Lawyers Weekly*, April 7, 2006, http://www.carters.ca/news/2006/lawyerwkly/tsckjc0407.pdf; Maria Severino, "Canadian Unlimited Liability Companies (ULC)—A Viable Vehicle for US Investors Expanding into Canada?" Collins Barrow Chartered Accountants, *Tax Flash*, June 2012, http://www.collinsbarrow.com/uploads/docs/newsletter/national/archive/TaxFlash_May2012.pdf.

METHODS OF INCORPORATION

Early Methods of Incorporation

royal charter a special licence given by the Crown to form a corporation for the purpose of carrying on a particular activity

The oldest method of incorporation in the common law system—dating back to the 16th century—is by **royal charter** granted by the sovereign. Until the 19th century, all corporations were created by charter. Some of these are still in existence—the best known to Canadians being the Hudson's Bay Company, founded in 1670. A few royal charters are still issued today to universities and charitable institutions, but none to business corporations.

special Acts of Parliament legislative acts creating a specific corporation

At the end of the 18th century, the government began creating corporations by **special Acts of Parliament**, especially for large projects of public interest—railroads, canals, waterworks, and other public utilities. Today, special acts are still used to create such corporations as Bell Canada and Canadian Pacific, and also to create special government corporations such as the Central Mortgage and Housing Corporation, the Canadian Broadcasting Corporation, and Air Canada. Parliament and the provincial legislatures have also passed statutes setting out procedures for the incorporation of particular types of businesses, such as banks and trust and loan companies. Such businesses may be incorporated only under those acts.

General Incorporation Statutes

Today, almost all business (for profit) corporations are incorporated under general incorporation statutes. Under a statute of this type, any group of persons that complies with its requirements may form a corporation. In Canada, there is both federal and provincial incorporation legislation. The provincial systems vary from one province to another.

Incorporation Roots: The Memorandum and Letters Patent Systems   In 1862, a system was introduced in England that depended upon Parliament rather than the royal prerogative, and that system was adopted by five provinces. It now remains in force in only one—Nova Scotia.[31] The system requires applicants to register a document that

---

[29] There is some provincial variation in the extent of shareholder liability. Alberta extends shareholder liability beyond liquidation and windup situations. Liability also applies to former shareholders.

[30] See, for example, Business Corporations Act, S.B.C. 2002, c. 57, s. 51.1.

[31] Companies Act, R.S.N.S. 1989, c. 81.

sets out the fundamental terms of their agreement, called a **memorandum of association**. If the memorandum and certain other prescribed documents comply with the statute and the registration fee is paid, the authorized government office issues a **certificate of incorporation** and the corporation comes into existence. We shall call corporations incorporated in this manner "memorandum corporations."

The other five provinces and the federal government employed a different system that survives today only in Quebec and Prince Edward Island.[32] There, the incorporating document is called the **letters patent**, an offspring of the royal charter, but issued under the authority of the Crown's representative in each jurisdiction. Under the letters patent system, a general statute regulates the conditions under which the letters patent may be issued. Although in theory the granting of letters patent is discretionary, in practice, the steps taken by applicants do not differ greatly from those for registering a memorandum under the English system. For more information on this topic, see the Companion Website.

The Articles of Incorporation System In 1970, Ontario passed a substantially different Business Corporations Act, creating a new method of incorporation adapted from a system in use in the United States. In 1975, the federal Parliament adopted the same system in its new statute, although many of the provisions of the federal act were quite different from those of the Ontario version. The CBCA became the model for the rest of the provinces. Alberta, Manitoba, New Brunswick, Newfoundland and Labrador, Ontario, Saskatchewan, and, most recently, British Columbia[33] have followed with acts based on the federal scheme, although with local variations. Under the articles of incorporation system, persons who wish to create a corporation sign and deliver the articles of incorporation forms to a government office and are issued a certificate of incorporation as a purely administrative process.

As the articles of incorporation system is now the most widely used one in Canada, our discussion will focus on it.

The Choice of Jurisdiction

The first decision to be made in forming a corporation is whether to incorporate federally or provincially. The CBCA is especially suitable for large businesses that carry on their activities nationwide; but even a small, local, one-person business may incorporate under it.

The activities of a business incorporated under provincial jurisdiction are not restricted to that province. It may carry on business anywhere inside or outside Canada. However, corporations not incorporated within a province—and this includes federally incorporated corporations as well as those incorporated in other provinces—must comply with certain registration requirements in order to carry on business there.[34] Nevertheless, the act under which it was incorporated governs its internal operating rules for holding shareholder meetings, electing directors, declaring dividends, and other matters that are examined in Chapter 26. The checklist below outlines some of the considerations involved in choosing whether to incorporate under federal or provincial jurisdiction.

memorandum of association a document setting out the essential terms of an agreement to form a corporation

certificate of incorporation a certificate that a corporation has come into existence

letters patent a document incorporating a corporation, issued by the appropriate authority, and constituting the "charter" of the corporation

---

[32] See Companies Act, R.S.P.E.I. 1988, c. C-14.

[33] Canada Business Corporations Act, R.S.C. 1985, c. C-44; Ontario Business Corporations Act, R.S.O. 1990, c. B-16; Alberta Business Corporations Act, R.S.A. 2000, c. B-9; New Brunswick Corporations Act, S.N.B. 1981, c. B-9.1; Saskatchewan Corporations Act, R.S.S. 1977, c. B-10; and Newfoundland Corporations Act, R.S.N.L. 1990, c. C-36.

[34] See e.g. the Ontario Extra-Provincial Corporations Act, R.S.O. 1990, c. E.27. The formalities that must be complied with vary to some extent according to whether the corporation is incorporated federally, elsewhere in Canada, or abroad; for example, only non-Canadian corporations require a licence to do business in Ontario. The Corporations Information Act, R.S.O. 1990, c. C.39, requires registration of certain information—for example, place of registered office, names of directors, and place within the province where notice may be served.

Federal or Provincial Incorporation?

Considerations	Federal	Provincial
Type of business activity	Mandatory for federally regulated activities (s. 91) such as banking	
Location of business activity	All across the country	One province
Registered office	In Canada	In the province
Name selections	Pre-screened	Variation (many leave burden on business)
Name use	Throughout Canada	Within province
Prestige value	Increased prestige	
Initial government fees	Approx. $200	Approx. $300
Directors' Canadian residency	25%	0%–25%*
Annual filings	Multiple separate	Combined

*Saskatchewan, Ontario, Alberta, Manitoba, and Newfoundland and Labrador require 25 percent, and British Columbia, Nova Scotia, P.E.I., New Brunswick, and Quebec have eliminated the residency requirement.

THE CONSTITUTION OF A CORPORATION

Articles of Incorporation

articles of incorporation founding corporate document, often referred to as the charter or constitution of the corporation

Under the articles of incorporation system, a corporation is formed by filing **articles of incorporation** in the prescribed form and paying the required registration fee.[35] The articles of incorporation are often referred to as the "charter" or "constitution" of the corporation and set out essential information about the corporation. In those provinces that have not adopted the articles of incorporation system, the corresponding "charter" document is the letters patent or the memorandum of association.

Contents of the Articles of Incorporation

- name of the corporation
- place where the registered office is situated
- classes and any maximum number of shares that the corporation is authorized to issue
- if there are two or more classes of shares, the rights and restrictions attached to each class
- any restriction on the transfer of shares
- number of directors
- any restrictions on the business that may be carried on other provisions that the incorporators choose to include

---

[35] The incorporation fee under the CBCA is $250 (reduced to $200 for electronic filing). The corresponding Ontario fee is $360 ($300 for electronic filing).

Occasionally, matters not usually found in a charter will also be included. This may be done in order to give certain "entrenched" rights to minority shareholders. Normally, the charter can be altered only by a special resolution, requiring the approval of a two-thirds majority of the shareholders, and the filing of the amended charter. In most circumstances, however, the charter is not the appropriate place for special arrangements among the shareholders. Instead, shareholders enter into a separate shareholders' agreement outside the corporate constitution, setting out how they will exercise their powers. This topic will be discussed further in Chapter 26.

The Corporate Name

As noted above, the articles must include the name of the proposed corporation. The registration of corporate names is closely regulated. The appropriate government office must approve the name and will refuse to register the corporation if it falls within certain prohibited categories (in particular, those that falsely suggest an association with the government or with certain professional bodies, or that are scandalous or obscene), or if it is likely to be confused with the name of some other existing corporation. In order to avoid the inconvenience and delay caused by the rejection of a chosen name, intending incorporators normally first make a "name search" to check that no existing corporation is registered with a similar name, and undertake trademark searches. Records of corporations are now computerized,[36] which facilitates such checks. Incorporating under a name does not protect the intellectual property rights to the name; see Chapter 20 for the appropriate steps to be followed.

If the name is not important to the incorporators, the problem can be avoided by using a "number name," where the registry simply assigns a number to the new corporation.[37]

When the business chooses a name after incorporation, it must register the name under the business names legislation discussed in Chapter 24. One of the words "Limited," "Incorporated," or "Corporation" (or their respective short forms) must form part of the name of every corporation (CBCA, section 10). For more information on this topic, see the Companion Website.

Bylaws

Nature of Bylaws   Incorporators generally keep the incorporating documents as short as possible to gain flexibility in the operation of the corporation, but detailed operating rules are needed for its day-to-day affairs. Under both the articles of incorporation and letters patent systems, these operating rules are called **bylaws**.[38] Bylaws are flexible, requiring confirmation by only a simple majority of shareholders, although corporation acts do specify some matters that must be dealt with by special resolution requiring a two-thirds majority.

bylaws   the internal working rules of a corporation

It is not strictly necessary to have bylaws at all. However, it is normal and convenient to have them, and they may be amended or new bylaws may be adopted, as and when required, with a minimum of formality. Usually, the directors amend bylaws or adopt new ones, assigning each a sequential number, but the new or amended bylaws need confirmation at the next general meeting of shareholders in order to remain valid. Bylaws fall into two main categories: general operating rules and specific director authorizations.

---

[36] The name search system is known as NUANS (Newly Upgraded Automated Name Search) system.

[37] CBCA, s. 11(2). A number name may be subsequently changed to a "normal" name without the usual formality that is required to amend the articles: CBCA, s. 173(3).

[38] For a memorandum corporation they are called articles of association, which causes confusion. In the memorandum system, articles of association can only be altered by a special resolution of the shareholders, requiring a three-quarters majority.

General Operating Rules Usually, the general operating rules for the business are passed at the first meeting of the shareholders. The first bylaws are often quite long and elaborate, dealing with such matters as the election of directors, their term of office, the place and required notice for meetings of directors, the quorum necessary (that is, the minimum number who must be present) before a meeting of directors can act on behalf of the corporation, the categories of executive officers, provisions for the allotment of shares and for the declaration of dividends, and procedures for holding the annual general meeting and other meetings of shareholders.

CHECKLIST

Provisions Often Included in Typical Bylaws*

- The qualification of a director shall be the holding of at least one share in the capital stock of the corporation.
- A director shall hold office until the third annual general meeting following his appointment.
- Notice of a meeting of directors shall be given in writing to each director not less than seven days before the meeting.
- Three directors shall constitute a quorum for the transaction of any business, except as otherwise provided in these bylaws.
- Questions arising at any meeting of directors shall, except as herein provided, be decided by a majority of votes: In the event of an equality of votes, the Chair of the meeting shall have a second or casting vote.
- Any contract entered into by the corporation that involves the expenditure or the incurring of a liability in excess of $10 000 must be approved by a majority of all the directors.
- Written notice of not less than 28 days, in the case of an annual general meeting, and 21 days, in the case of other shareholder meetings, shall be given to all shareholders entitled to vote at the meeting.
- A quorum is present at a general meeting of shareholders if no fewer than 10 shareholders, together holding a majority of the shares entitled to vote at the meeting, are present in person or by proxy.
- Shares in the corporation shall be allotted by resolution of the board of directors, approved by not less than two-thirds of all directors, on such terms, for such consideration, and to such persons as the directors determine.
- The directors may, at any time, by resolution approved by not less than two-thirds of all directors, declare a dividend or an interim dividend, and pay the same out of the funds of the corporation available for that purpose.

* These are not mandatory requirements.

Authorization to Directors Most statutes no longer require a bylaw to be passed in order to confer any particular power on the directors (unless the corporation's own constitution does).[39] Certain matters, such as the sale of substantially all of a corporation's property or the amalgamation with another corporation, are required to be approved by special resolution of the shareholders, and although directors now normally have the power to borrow money on the security of the corporation's assets without special authorization, it is common for them to ask the shareholders to confirm a major loan transaction, because

---

[39] See CBCA, s. 16(1).

creditors may insist upon such confirmation. Shareholder resolutions of this type are still often referred to as "bylaws."

TYPES OF BUSINESS CORPORATIONS

Public and Private Corporations

Initially, legislators believed that limited companies would be used primarily for large undertakings having many shareholders (that is, public corporations). Consequently, the regulations focused on protection of the general public through disclosure and publication obligations. By the end of the 19th century, it became evident that incorporation was also a useful and fully effective tool for small ventures and family businesses. Since these small corporations did not seek investment from the general public, the disclosure and publication requirements were unnecessary.

In 1908, the British Parliament changed the provisions to permit the formation of **private companies**, which were not permitted to offer shares to the public and in which the right to transfer shares had to be restricted in some manner. Those provisions found their way into Canadian incorporation statutes, but now remain only in Prince Edward Island and Nova Scotia. The CBCA and most other provincial statutes now permit even a single shareholder to form a corporation and do not maintain a formal distinction between public and private corporations. Instead, a more realistic distinction is made between those corporations that issue their shares to the general public[40] and those that do not.

private companies corporations with a restricted number of shareholders prohibited from issuing their shares to the general public

Public Corporations Incorporation statutes, such as the CBCA, apply to both public and private corporations but draw a number of distinctions between them. The CBCA, for example, imposes various obligations upon what it calls a **distributing corporation** with respect to such matters as proxy solicitation, the number of directors, and the need for an audit committee. These requirements are considered further in Chapter 26. But the most important difference is that distributing corporations are also subject to regulation under the relevant provincial securities acts in those provinces in which their securities are issued or traded. As provincial securities regulators control access to the public market through stock exchanges, securities legislation and the policies of securities regulators play an important role in the way in which Canada's larger corporations are structured and conduct their business and affairs. Securities legislation also describes the steps that must be followed to change a private corporation into a publicly traded or distributing corporation. Those topics are considered in Chapters 26 and 27.

distributing corporation a corporation that issues its securities to the public; also referred to as an issuing corporation, reporting issuer, and publicly traded corporation

Private Corporations The main use of the private corporation is to incorporate small- and medium-sized business enterprises where the number of participants and owners is small. A private corporation is a true limited company with the same legal significance and corporate independence as the public corporation. In fact, when a public corporation creates a subsidiary, it usually does so by incorporating a private corporation. Many large U.S. and other foreign corporations operate wholly owned subsidiaries in Canada that are private. All the shares are held by the parent corporation, except for a few that may be held here by corporate officers. A number of these subsidiaries rival our own large public corporations in size. For example, General Motors of Canada Limited is a private corporation owned by its public U.S. parent, General Motors Company.[41]

---

[40] The CBCA describes these as "distributing" corporations. Securities legislation refers to these as issuing corporations or reporting issuers.

[41] For a list of the 350 biggest private corporations in Canada and their major shareholders, see *The Globe and Mail*, "Rankings of Canada's 350 Biggest Companies", June 18, 2010, http://www.theglobeandmail.com/report-on-business/-rob-magazine/-top-1000/rankings-of-canadas-350-biggest-private-companies/article1608845/.

The vast majority of corporations are private—over 90 percent in Canada. It is, therefore, rather surprising that they are largely neglected as a subject of study in business administration. The literature of economics, finance, accounting, and management directs its attention to public corporations. Private corporations have been permitted the luxury of operating in an atmosphere of relative privacy, as disclosure and transparency obligations are relatively light. In a private corporation, the owners are usually the managers as well, focusing questions of management and ultimate decision making within a small group. The legal implications of this characteristic of private corporations are examined in Chapter 26.

Corporate Groups

The largest businesses, in Canada and internationally, frequently comprise a group of corporations, one or more of which is public, with shares held by the public and listed on one or more stock exchanges, together with a number of subsidiaries that are private, in the sense that they are often wholly owned by their parent company. For example, the corporate structure of the Hollinger companies and related entities (formerly controlled by Conrad Black) involved over 60 companies—some public, some private—and were subject to a number of different jurisdictions.[42] Groups of this nature can give rise to extremely complex relationships and to possible conflicts.

Professional Corporations

As noted in Chapter 24, members of many of the leading professions have been prohibited from incorporating their practices, either by the rules of the professional body to which they belong or under the statute governing the profession. They have consequently been restricted to practising as sole proprietors or in partnership, with the disadvantage, in the latter case, of being liable for obligations incurred by their co-partners. One response to that problem, which has already been discussed, is the creation of limited liability partnerships (LLPs).

professional corporation (PC)
a special type of business corporation that may be formed by members of a profession

Most provinces now allow the incorporation of a **professional corporation (PC)**. Under the legislation, members of listed professions may form a PC, provided it is permitted by the rules of the profession itself and the professional controls the voting shares. The Saskatchewan act provides:

> One or more members of an association may incorporate a corporation pursuant to the Business Corporations Act for the purpose of carrying on, in the name of the corporation, the business of providing professional services that may lawfully be performed by members of the association.[43]

The words "Professional Corporation" or the abbreviation "PC" must appear in the name of the corporation,[44] and all members of the corporation must be members of the profession.[45] Regarding liability, the act provides:

> The liability of a member of an association to a person who receives services from the member is not affected by the fact that the services were provided by the member as an employee of, or on behalf of, a professional corporation.[46]

In effect, a member of a profession who incorporates (either alone or together with other members) remains responsible for her own negligence or misconduct toward clients,

---

[42] See *Catalyst Fund General Partner I Inc. v. Hollinger Inc.*, [2004] O.J. No. 4722, aff'd [2006] O.J. No. 944 (Ont. C.A.).

[43] Professional Corporations Act, S.S. 2001, c. P-27.1, s. 4(1).

[44] *Ibid.*, s. 4(2).

[45] *Ibid.*, ss. 5(2), 6(1). Thus, multidisciplinary PCs are not (yet) permitted.

[46] *Ibid.*, s. 15.

although the principle of limited liability does seem to provide protection against the claims of other creditors—for example, landlords of premises or suppliers of equipment. The principal advantage of professional incorporation is not to obtain limited liability, but rather to enjoy a number of tax advantages that are not available to sole proprietorships and partnerships. Many professionals will benefit from the small business tax rate if they practise as a professional corporation, in contrast to the much higher personal income tax rate applied to sole proprietors or partners.

Only members of listed professions may form a PC, but not all professions are prohibited from incorporating. For example, engineers and geophysicists are not "listed" and consequently cannot form a PC; however, that is no disadvantage since they are able to establish a "normal" business corporation. For more information on this topic, see the Companion Website.

Ethical Issue   Undermining Professional Standards?

Recent legislative changes have introduced the LLP and the professional corporation as alternative vehicles for conducting professional activities, and the concept of multidisciplinary partnerships is also gaining ground. This has led to fears, in some quarters, that professional standards are being undermined. In particular, it is argued that such developments may lead to the destruction of the professional–client relationship. Do you really want to have your teeth pulled by a corporation?

Others would argue that there are adequate safeguards to ensure that professional standards are maintained and that there is no valid reason for denying to professionals the benefits of incorporation that are enjoyed by other business-persons (and by some professions).

Questions to Consider

1. Are the recent changes discarding the traditions of a century, or are they simply keeping up with the times?

2. Is there any reason why professionals, such as accountants, doctors, and lawyers, should not be allowed to incorporate in the normal way?

3. Do professionals comply with professional standards only to avoid personal liability?

CORPORATE CAPITAL

Equity and Debt

There are two principal ways in which a corporation can raise funds: by issuing shares (equity) and by borrowing (debt). A third method—financing the corporation's activities out of retained profits—is really the same as the first, since the shareholders are effectively reinvesting part of their profit. Although borrowing increases the funds that are at the disposal of the corporation's management, it is really misleading to speak of debt capital, since borrowing increases both assets and liabilities. A corporation's true capital is its equity capital or share capital—the investment in the company by its owners.

Share Capital

Every business corporation must have a share capital.[47] The word "capital" has different meanings in different contexts. In letters patent and memorandum jurisdictions, when a corporation is incorporated, its charter places an upper limit on the number or money value of shares it may issue. This limit is called the **authorized capital**. A corporation need not issue all its authorized share capital. The **issued capital** and **paid-up capital** of a corporation are, as their names indicate, the parts of the authorized capital that have been issued and paid for.

authorized capital   the maximum number (or value) of shares that a corporation is permitted by its charter to issue

issued capital   the shares that have been issued by a corporation

paid-up capital   the shares that have been issued and fully paid for

---

[47] Charitable and non-profit corporations need not have a share capital.

In articles of incorporation jurisdictions, a corporation may state the maximum number of shares that can be issued if it so wishes, but does not have to do so. A corporation must still keep a **stated capital account** disclosing the consideration received for each **share** issued. Shares must be fully paid for at the time of issue.[48] Consequently, there is no difference between issued capital and paid-up capital.

There are several ways of becoming a shareholder:

- by being one of the original applicants for incorporation
- by buying shares issued by a corporation subsequent to its incorporation
- by acquiring (by purchase or gift) previously issued shares from another shareholder

The first two ways result from contracts between the shareholder and the corporation, and the transactions increase the issued capital as shown in the accounts of the corporation. The third way is the result of a transfer to which the corporation is not a party at all, and does not affect its accounts.

Par Values

Until the early part of the 20th century, all shares had a nominal or **par value**—a fixed value established in the charter like a bank note or a bond. Shares were issued by the corporation at their par value. However, par value provided little indication of a share's real value; once issued, a share rarely had a market price identical with its par value.

A corporation was prohibited from issuing its shares for less than their par value (that is, at a discount). If a corporation's shares were selling on the market below their par value and the corporation required additional capital, investors would not purchase a new issue at par. In order to make an issue of shares, the corporation would be compelled to reduce the par value of the shares to a more realistic figure and to reduce its capital accordingly by obtaining an amendment to its charter, causing delay and expense.

The United States introduced **no par value shares**—that is, shares that represent a specific proportion of the issued capital of the corporation, rather than a fixed sum of money. The advantages of no par value shares, and in particular the fact that they may be issued from time to time at prices that correspond to their current market value, resulted in their adoption by all the jurisdictions in the United States; soon afterward, they were permitted in Canada. The articles of incorporation system has abolished par value shares entirely.

ILLUSTRATION 25.2

Pliable Plastics Inc. is incorporated under the articles of incorporation system. Its articles contain no restriction on the total number of shares that may be issued, and its shares have no par value. Initially, it issued 50 000 shares at $100 each, giving it a stated capital of $5 000 000. The directors wish to raise a further $3 000 000.

If the current market price of the shares has fallen to $60, they can raise $3 000 000 by issuing 50 000 new shares at that price. On the other hand, if the market price has risen to $120, they will need to issue only 25 000.

Until the introduction of the articles of incorporation system, **preferred shares** were almost always issued with a par value. They paid a preferred dividend expressed as a percentage of the par value, and the corporation could redeem them at par value. For example, a share might have a par value of $100 (and be redeemable at that price) and pay a dividend of 8 percent (that is, $8 per share). With the abolition of par values, preferred shares are now stated to have a redemption price ($100), with a preferred dividend expressed simply as a sum of money ($8).

---

[48] CBCA, s. 25(3). Previously, shares could be issued partly paid, with the corporation being able to make a subsequent call for the remainder of the price.

CORPORATE SECURITIES

The Distinction between Shares and Bonds

A corporation may borrow money in a number of ways, but when it borrows substantial sums on a long-term basis, it normally does so by issuing a **bond**. The classic distinction between shares and bonds (or "debentures," as they are sometimes called) is that the holder of a share is a member of and owner of an interest in the corporation. The holder of a bond is a creditor. In the business world, there is no such clear-cut distinction. In the language of modern business, the true equity owner of a corporation, and the person who takes the greatest risk, is the **common share** holder. From this end of the scale, we proceed by degrees to the person who is a mortgagee or bondholder, who takes the least risk. In between, we may have the holders of preferred shares. Today, most large corporations have, in addition to an issue of common shares, one or more classes of bonds or debentures and probably also a class of preferred shares.

bond a document evidencing a debt owed by a corporation

common share a share carrying no preferential right

When deciding whether to invest in the shares or the bonds of a corporation, an individual usually does not make a conscious choice between becoming a member (that is, an equity owner) and becoming a creditor. She regards herself in both instances as an investor. Her investment decisions are determined primarily by economic considerations. Bonds provide a fixed and guaranteed return (provided the corporation remains solvent), in the form of regular interest payments and the right to be redeemed in full at their maturity date. Common shares carry no guarantee that their holders will receive anything, either in the form of dividends or on dissolution, but their holders participate in any "growth" of the corporation. Preferred shareholders come somewhere in between. They are entitled to receive dividends and to have their shares redeemed on the dissolution of the corporation, before payments are made to the holders of the common shares, but those rights are often restricted to a fixed dividend and a fixed amount payable on redemption.

The line between shareholder and bondholder is nonetheless a distinct and important one in its legal consequences for a corporation. First of all, since bondholders are creditors, interest paid to them is a debt of the corporation. It must be paid whether or not the corporation has earned profits for the year. Shareholders are not creditors and receive dividends only when the directors declare them. One consequence, especially important for taxation, is that interest payments are normally an expense of doing business and are deducted before taxable income is calculated; dividends, on the other hand, are payable out of after-tax profits. Second, bonds are usually secured by a mortgage or charge on the property of the corporation (see the discussion in Chapter 28 under "Floating Charges"). If a corporation becomes insolvent, its secured bondholders are entitled to be repaid not only before the shareholders but also before the general creditors. They are secured creditors, and the trustee acting for them can sell the corporation's assets to satisfy the debt owed to them.

Rights of Security Holders

Bondholders   Bondholders do not normally have a direct voice in the management of the corporation unless it is in breach of the terms of the trust deed or indenture under which the securities were created. Only when a corporation gets into financial difficulty or is in breach of the trust deed may the trustee step in and take part in management on behalf of the bondholders. It is true, however, that bondholders do exert an indirect form of control over management in the restrictive clauses commonly written into bond indentures, which may place a ceiling on the further long-term borrowing of the corporation, on the amount of dividends it may pay, and even, in smaller corporations, on the salaries it pays to its officers.

Common Shareholders   By contrast, common shareholders have, in theory at least, a strong voice in the management of the corporation. As we shall see in Chapter 26, it is they who elect the board of directors and who must approve major changes in the corporation's activities. Otherwise, however, their rights are limited. They have no entitlement to a dividend and can receive one only after bondholders and preferred shareholders have been paid. On the liquidation of the corporation, their entitlement is to share what is left after the claims of creditors and preferred shareholders have been satisfied.

Preferred Shareholders Preferred shareholders are in an intermediate category. Usually, they are entitled to be paid a fixed dividend before any dividend is paid to the common shareholders, and they are entitled to be paid the fixed redemption price of their shares on liquidation of the corporation before any surplus is distributed to the common shareholders. Frequently, they have no right to vote unless the payment of dividends to them is in arrears. In this respect they are more like creditors than investors. However, payment of preferred dividends is not a contractual commitment of a corporation as bond interest is; a preferred shareholder must enforce her rights as an individual and is not dependent upon a trustee taking action, as a bondholder normally is.

Class Rights Where a corporation issues more than one class of shares—for example, common shares and preferred shares—the precise rights of each class must be set out in its constitution.[49] The various combinations of rights and privileges that may attach to a class of shares are extensive and may relate not only to dividend rights and rights of redemption but also to voting rights, to rights to appoint directors, and sometimes to the right to convert a security of one class into a security of another class. A **pre-emptive right**, that is, the right to buy the same percentage ownership in any new issue of shares, is discussed in Chapter 26.

Problems of interpretation arise in the drafting of rights for various classes of shareholders. Two questions with respect to preferred shareholders' rights to dividends are particularly important. The first is whether it is a **cumulative right**: if the full preferred dividend is not paid in one year, do the arrears accumulate so that they must be paid in a subsequent year or on winding up the corporation, before the common shareholders are entitled to anything? The second is whether on winding up, it is a **participating right**: if, after the preferred shareholders have been fully paid, do they still participate in any remaining surplus along with the common shareholders? This uncertainty makes it all the more important to draft class rights with the greatest care.

pre-emptive right the right of a holder of shares to protect his percentage ownership in the company by buying the same percentage in any new issue of shares

cumulative right the right of the holder of a preferred share to be paid arrears from previous years before any dividend is paid on the common shares

participating right the right of a holder of a preferred share to participate in surplus profits or assets of the corporation in addition to the amount of the preferred dividend or redemption price

---

CHECKLIST

Priority of Payment on Liquidation of a Corporation

On liquidation of a corporation, its assets must be distributed in the following sequence. (Note that bondholders are creditors—and usually they are secured creditors.)

1. secured creditors
2. unsecured creditors
3. preferred shareholders
4. common shareholders

The Transfer of Corporate Securities

Share and bond certificates are a type of personal property known as negotiable instruments subject to different rules of transfer and ownership from those that apply to sales of goods. Articles of incorporation statutes may expressly designate share

---

[49] See CBCA, s. 6(1)(c).

certificates as a type of negotiable instrument.[50] When bonds and shares are treated as negotiable instruments, an innocent holder for value may acquire a better title than his predecessor had, as, for example, when he purchases valid bonds or share certificates that have been stolen. Only those with notice of a defect are subject to it. The innocent holder of a forged (fake) negotiable instrument, as we have seen, obtains no title.

CASE 25.4

One of the largest fraud schemes in Canadian history involved the creation of fake share certificates of a small trust company, Vanguard Trust. As a former member of the board of directors, lawyer Julius Melnitzer had access to the company's corporate seal and he created five certificates totalling 900 000 shares. He used the fake shares as security to borrow $5.6 million from five major Canadian banks. When the banks got suspicious, he tricked a printing company into helping him forge shares of other companies by saying they were for use as evidence in a case he was defending. Eventually the National Bank obtained an expert opinion, and the fraud was discovered. Melnitzer pleaded guilty and was fined $20 000 000, sentenced to nine years in prison, and disbarred.[51]

Few shareholders of public corporations receive physical share certificates. Investors trade shares using securities accounts held with intermediaries such as brokers, dealers, and banks. Share purchases are credited to the account as financial assets; rather than holding the security itself, the investor holds a "security entitlement" which gives him the right to the benefits of the share and to direct its transfer. Most provinces have securities transfer legislation defining the rights and obligations of securities intermediaries and securities entitlement holders, establishing the rules for transfer of securities and security entitlements, and protecting innocent purchasers of security entitlements from unknown adverse claims.[52]

Restrictions on Share Transfer   In public corporations, shares are almost always freely transferable; if not, the shares will not be accepted for listing on a stock exchange; in fact, when securities intermediaries transfer security entitlements, they warrant that there are no restrictions on share transfer. In contrast, private corporations almost always restrict the transfer of shares; otherwise, it would be difficult for them to remain private.

Restrictions on share transfer must be listed in the corporation's constitution[53] and can take almost any form. Such restrictions must also be noted on the share certificate; otherwise, they are not binding on a purchaser who has no notice of the restriction.[54] The most common restriction is to require the consent of the board of directors to any transfer, but there are other varieties, such as giving the right of first refusal to existing shareholders or directors before a shareholder can sell to an outsider, or giving a major shareholder the right of veto. Requiring the consent of directors gives them the discretion to approve or reject a proposed member of the corporation, much as partners determine whether they will admit a new partner.

---

[50] Unless there are restrictions on transfer noted on the certificate: CBCA, s. 48(3).

[51] *R. v. Melnitzer*, [1992] O.J. No. 1363; *Canadian Imperial Bank of Commerce v. Melnitzer (Trustee)*, [1993] O.J. No. 3021, aff'd [1997] O.J. No. 3021; see also Department of Justice website, "A Typology of Profit Driven Crimes—Bank Fraud," http://www.justice.gc.ca/eng/rp-pr/csj-sjc/crime/rr02_3/p3.html.

[52] See e.g. Securities Transfer Act, S.O. 2006, c.8.

[53] See, for example, CBCA, s. 6(1)(d).

[54] CBCA, s. 49(8). See *Bank Leu AG v. Gaming Lottery Corp.* (2003), 231 D.L.R. (4th) 251.

Strategies to Manage the Legal Risks

Planning before incorporating can save time and money in the long run. The first decision is whether to incorporate under the federal or provincial jurisdiction. Provincial incorporation may seem easier and cheaper initially, but if the future plans for the business involve operating in multiple provinces and possibly internationally, federal incorporation may be a better fit.

Careful consideration should also be given to the share structure of the corporation. This should anticipate the short-term and long-term needs of the company. Ownership can be divided among classes of shares so that preferred shares are available to raise capital and common shares may hold the power to vote. Class rights can vary to differentiate between financing and control. Odd numbers are necessary so that majority votes can be obtained.

The company's name also needs attention before incorporating. Ensure that the name is an available trademark, not in use by another business. Search not only corporation registries and business name registrations, but registered trademark data banks as well. All are publicly available. It is often easier to incorporate a numbered company and then register the business names separately, once the intellectual property rights have been secured. One corporation may operate several businesses under different business names as long as all are properly registered.

All corporations start as private corporations that may subsequently be taken public through the steps outlined in the securities legislation. If "going public" is expected, incorporating documents—that is, articles of incorporation and bylaws—should comply with the higher standards of corporate governance discussed in Chapter 26.

Finally, corporations are legal persons and may own shares in other corporations. This permits a business to use multiple corporations, in both private and public forms, in order to operate high-risk activities in separate corporations and protect the existence of the entire business. Subject to some exceptions, assets of one corporation are not available to satisfy the debts of others. Try not to think of business entities such as partnerships, joint ventures, or private and public corporations only as alternatives to each other. They can be employed together to meet the specific needs of the business.

QUESTIONS FOR REVIEW

1. What is meant by a "legal person"?

2. What is meant by "limited liability"? Whose liability is limited?

3. What are the main differences between partnerships and corporations?

4. What were the principal arguments made by the creditors in the *Salomon* case in attempting to make Salomon personally liable?

5. In what ways may two or more corporations be said to be "associated"?

6. What is meant by "lifting the corporate veil"?

7. How does the articles of incorporation system of forming a corporation differ from (a) the letters patent system and (b) the memorandum and articles system?

8. What information must be set out in articles of incorporation?

9. Why must care be taken in selecting a corporate name? What is a "number name"?

10. What is the main function of a corporation's bylaws?

11. What are the principal characteristics of closely held corporations?

12. What are the main advantages of forming a professional corporation?

13. What is the function of a corporation's stated capital account?

14. What special rights are normally carried by preferred shares?

15. What are the usual rights of bondholders?

16. What factors influence an investor's choice between shares and bonds?

17. In what sequence should a corporation's assets be distributed on liquidation of the corporation?

18. In what circumstances are restrictions on the transfer of shares binding on purchasers of the shares?

CASES AND PROBLEMS

1. Continuing Scenario

   Ashley decided to incorporate her restaurant business. Her lawyer, Brendan, is advising her about the steps involved and the structure her corporation should take. So far, Ashley has two restaurants located within 25 kilometres of each other—the first was called "Ashley's Restaurant" and the second she named "Ashley's Too." Ashley's mother invested $50 000 in the business at the start but Ashley does not want her mother to be involved in business decisions. Ashley promised her mother a good return on her investment, but Ashley wants to stay in complete control of the business. Ashley also promised each of her chefs that there will be profit sharing opportunities after five years with the restaurants. State how Brendan should respond to the following questions, and give reasons for your answers. How many corporations should she incorporate? Should incorporation occur under federal or provincial legislation? Does Ashley have to decide on a name now? What classes of shares should be issued with what rights and restrictions?

2. Oakdale Motors Inc. is a corporation, incorporated under the Canada Business Corporations Act, engaged in the selling, repairing, and servicing of automobiles. All of its shares are owned by Faulkner, who is also the sole director. Faulkner acts as the general manager of the corporation and supervises its day-to-day operations.

   Last winter, Hill visited the premises of Oakdale Motors to look at a used car that she saw advertised. The area outside the sales office was extremely slippery, being covered by ice that was, in turn, covered by a thin layer of snow that had fallen overnight. Faulkner was working at the Oakdale premises that day and knew of the dangerous state of the premises, but had made no effort to have the danger removed.

   Hill slipped on the ice, fell, and broke her leg. The injury was a serious one and has left her with a permanent disability.

   She has learned that Oakdale Motors Inc. is in severe financial difficulties and is likely to be made bankrupt. However, Faulkner appears to be quite wealthy.

   Would Hill have any claim against Faulkner?

3. Macbeth, the owner of 20 hectares located on the outskirts of Niagara Falls, decided to sell, and on January 2 signed an exclusive listing agreement with Ross, a real estate broker. Macbeth agreed to pay Ross a commission of 5 percent on the sale of the property, which he listed at $350 000.

   On January 19, Ross filed articles of incorporation for a new corporation, Burnam Woods Properties Ltd., of which he was the sole shareholder. He appointed his friend Lennox as general manager.

   Several weeks later, Ross introduced Macbeth to Lennox as general manager of Burnam Woods but said nothing to suggest that he, Ross, had any interest in the corporation. Within a few days, Lennox submitted an offer on behalf of the corporation to purchase Macbeth's property for $240 000. Macbeth rejected the offer but made a counter-offer to sell at $290 000. Burnam Woods accepted the counter-offer, and the deal was closed on March 15, when Macbeth paid Ross his commission of $14 500.

   Shortly afterward, Burnam Woods entered into negotiations with another corporation, Castle Hall Developments Ltd., and sold the 20 hectares to it for $450 000, realizing a quick profit of $160 000.

On April 24 following, Macbeth learned of the resale by Burnam Woods and also learned about Ross's share ownership in the Burnam Woods company. Macbeth immediately sued Ross and Burnam Woods jointly for recovery of the real estate commission of $14 500 and for the $160 000 profit realized on the second sale by Burnam Woods Properties Ltd. to Castle Hall Developments Ltd.

Examine the validity of Macbeth's claim, and offer an opinion about its chances for success.

4. Stick and Twist are lawyers who have practised in partnership for a number of years. With the introduction of legislation permitting the formation of professional corporations in their province, they decided to convert their partnership into a PC.

The new corporation, "Stick and Twist Lawyers PC," was formed with a share capital of $1000, with Stick and Twist each holding one share. They are the sole directors. The corporation has very few tangible assets, since its office is rented, as is much of its office equipment.

Twist "disappeared" a few months ago, and Stick has discovered that

(a) a client is claiming $200 000 from the corporation in respect of money that she had entrusted to Twist for the purchase of a condominium; and

(b) the landlord is claiming $12 000 in respect of rent owing on the premises. Twist had assured Stick that the rent had been paid.

To what extent are (1) the corporation and (2) Stick liable?

5. Pliable Plastics Inc. issued 50 000 common shares at $100 each. Some years later, in order to raise additional capital, it issued 20 000 Class "A" preferred shares, also at $100 each. The preferred shares were stated to have a redemption price of $100, and were entitled to receive a first dividend of $8 per share. The following year, to raise further funds, the corporation made an issue of bonds, in the sum of $2 000 000, secured by a floating charge on all of its assets.

Soon afterward, Pliable Plastics found itself in serious financial difficulties. Although it had substantial assets, these were not readily realizable, and it was unable to pay its debts as they fell due. The directors resolved to sell off the corporation's assets and to wind up the corporation.

The sale of the assets realized $7 000 000, and, after paying off its creditors (other than the bondholders), the corporation was left with $5 500 000. How much will each common share receive?

For more cases and problems, see the Companion Website.

Additional Resources for Chapter 25 on the Companion Website

(www.pearsoncanada.ca/smyth)

In addition to pre- and post-tests, mini-cases, and application exercises, the Companion Website includes the following province-specific resources for Chapter 25:

- **Alberta:** Business Corporations Act; Income Trusts; Incorporation; NUANS Reports; Other Incorporated Bodies; Pre-incorporation Contracts; Professional Corporations; Taxation of Corporations; Unlimited Liability Corporations
- **Atlantic Provinces:** Business Corporation Legislation; Co-operative Associations Act; Extra-Provincial Registration; Non-Profit Corporations; Unlimited Liability Corporations
- **British Columbia:** Business Corporations; Corporate Name Registration; Incorporation
- **Manitoba/Saskatchewan:** Directors; Non-Share Capital Corporations; Process of Incorporation; Separate Legal Entity; Shareholders
- **Ontario:** Annual Filing; Articles of Incorporation; Not-for-Profit Corporations; Ontario Corporations; Professional Corporations; Promoters; Reporting Issues; Securities Legislation

Chapter 26

Corporate Governance: The Internal Affairs of Corporations

This chapter and Chapter 27 address corporate governance. They discuss the internal and external affairs and the business of a corporation.

In this chapter, we examine such questions as:

- How is a corporation organized and managed?

- What is the function of the board of directors?

- How are the directors appointed and removed?

- Who is an officer?

- What are the duties of directors and officers?

- What are the consequences of a breach of duty by a director or an officer?

- What defences are available to directors and officers?

- What are the rights and duties of shareholders?

- How are the rights of minority shareholders protected?

WHAT IS CORPORATE GOVERNANCE?

corporate governance the rules governing the organization and management of the business and affairs of a corporation in order to meet its internal objectives and external responsibilities

Corporate governance refers to the organization and management of the business and affairs of a corporation in order to meet its internal objectives and external responsibilities. Where do we find the rules of corporate governance? As discussed in Chapter 25, the incorporating documents—the articles of incorporation and the bylaws—create the management structure within the corporation and establish the corporation's own set of corporate governance standards. In addition each incorporating jurisdiction—Canada and each province—has corporation legislation that must be followed. This legislation establishes the legal standards of corporate governance.

The Canada Business Corporations Act (CBCA)[1] and the corresponding provincial statutes draw a broad distinction between two aspects of a corporation's activities. Section 102 states that "the directors shall manage, or supervise the management of, the *business* and *affairs* of a corporation" (italics added). The difference between these two terms is explained in section 2(1), where "affairs" are defined as "the relationships among a corporation . . . and the shareholders, directors and officers . . . but *does not include the business carried on* [by the corporation] . . ."[1A] (italics added). The distinction, which is helpful in understanding the complex activities of corporations, is between

(a) the *affairs*: the internal arrangements among those responsible for running a corporation—the directors and officers—and its main beneficiaries, the shareholders, which we discuss in this chapter; and

(b) the *business*: the external relations between a corporation and those who deal with it as a business enterprise—its customers, suppliers, creditors, and employees—as well as government regulators and society as a whole (discussed in Chapter 27).

The distinction is blurred for at least one group: the shareholders in a publicly traded corporation. An invitation to the public to invest in a corporation is directed toward those who may not yet be part of its internal relations, but if the members of the public accept an offer to buy shares, they become involved in its "affairs." These potential public shareholders are protected by special provincial securities regulations imposed on only those companies issuing shares to the public, and so securities regulation is discussed in both Chapters 26 and 27. This chapter covers the basic legal rules of corporate governance and the liability arising from their breach. The rules discussed in this chapter apply to both privately and publicly held corporations and are codified in federal and provincial legislation. Breach of the rules may trigger civil, regulatory, or even criminal liability or a combination of all three.

CORPORATE GOVERNANCE OF PUBLICLY TRADED CORPORATIONS

publicly traded corporations corporations that issue shares to the public, also known as public corporations, widely held corporations, reporting issuers, and issuing corporations

Public corporate scandals such as those involving Enron and WorldCom led securities regulators to tighten the rules of corporate governance for **publicly traded corporations** (this chapter will also use the CBCA term, *distributing corporation*). First, the United States passed the Sarbanes-Oxley Act of 2002 (SOX), and next, the Securities and Exchange Commission introduced new rules, policies, and recommendations for the internal

---

[1] R.S.C. 1985, c. C-44 (CBCA). The Act was substantially amended by Bill S-11, S.C. 2001, c. 14. Unless otherwise stated, statutory references in this chapter are to the CBCA as amended. Corresponding provincial legislation: Business Corporations Act, S.B.C. 2002, c. 57; Business Corporations Act, R.S.A. 2000, c. B-9; Business Corporations Act, R.S.S. 1978, c. B-10; Corporations Act, C.C.S.M. c. C225; Business Corporations Act (OBCA) R.S.O. 1990, c. B-16; Companies Act, R.S.N.S. 1989, c. 81; Companies Act, R.S.N.B. 1973, c. C-13; Companies Act, R.S.P.E.I. 1988, c. C-14; Corporations Act, R.S.N.L. 1990, c. C-36. Most provincial legislation is similar to the federal legislation. Relevant major departures will be noted.

[1A] Canada Business Corporations Act, Section 2(1).

operations of public companies.[2] Canadian securities regulators adopted some of the SOX standards.[3] This means that publicly traded companies are required to meet the standards in both the CBCA (or the relevant provincial incorporating legislation) and the provincial securities legislation. These rules and recommendations increase the protection available to the public stakeholders—public shareholders, creditors, employees, and lenders. The general themes and principles underlying the legislation are independence of decision makers, transparency, disclosure, accountability, and organizational checks and balances.[4] Following are some of the recommendations:

- A majority of directors should be independent.
- The CEO should not also hold the position of chair of the board.
- The corporation should establish separate, independent committees of the board to address executive compensation and nomination of board members.
- The corporation should adopt and publish a "code of ethics."
- The board should perform regular self-assessments.

Many privately held corporations choose to comply with the higher standard of corporate governance in order to meet their ethical responsibilities and in preparation for any future **public offering**. Where relevant, this chapter will identify the heightened requirements for public companies. For more information on this topic, see the Companion Website.

public offering selling shares to the public, which must be done in compliance with provincial securities regulations

THE STRUCTURE OF THE MODERN BUSINESS CORPORATION

Business corporations differ greatly from one another in their size and composition. Modern legislation tries to accommodate these differences. However, there are certain essential elements that are the same for all corporations.

Three basic groups are common to all corporations: the shareholders, the **board of directors** (generally referred to as "the board"), and the **officers**. In small private corporations, such as family companies, it often happens that most or even all of the shareholders are also directors and officers. Even if the distinction between shareholders and directors may sometimes become blurred in practice—for example, if they get together to discuss business and do not specify whether the meeting is a directors' meeting or a shareholders' meeting—the distinction remains important legally.

In a large corporation, by contrast, the board of directors may have as many as 15 or 20 members who are elected by shareholders. Generally in such cases, the board will appoint or hire a chief executive officer (CEO, also often called the president or managing director) or a smaller committee of directors (the management committee or executive committee) to direct the affairs and business of the corporation and to supervise its other officers and employees. CEOs are most often full-time employees of the company who, together with other officers, manage the corporation. It is this team, not the board, that is known collectively as "the management." The management refers only the important policy matters to the full board of directors. In turn, the board of directors usually calls no more than the

board of directors the governing body of a corporation, responsible for the management of its business and affairs

officers high-ranking members of a corporation's management team as defined in the bylaws or appointed by the directors, such as the president, vice-president, controller, chief executive officer, chief financial officer, general counsel, and general manager

---

[2] 15 U.S.C. s. 7201 *et. seq.*

[3] National Policy Instrument 58-201. Although securities regulation is a matter of provincial jurisdiction and each province has its own legislation and Securities Commission, the 13 provincial and territorial regulators cooperate on most regulation through the Canadian Securities Administrators (CSA). The result is nationally consistent instruments, guidelines, and policies that are adopted under the same numbering system. Instruments are mandatory requirements, and policies and guidelines are only recommendations.

[4] Richard DeGeorge, Chapter 9, "Corporate Governance, Accounting Disclosure and Insider Trading," in *Business Ethics*, 6th ed. (Upper Saddle River, NJ: Prentice Hall, 2006).

Figure 26.1 Corporate Structure

Power originates with the general meeting of shareholders. The shareholders elect a board of directors to manage the corporation. The directors, in turn, appoint or hire a chief executive officer, who is the highest-ranking employee in charge of the day-to-day running of the corporation. Various committees are given tasks by and report to the board.

audit committee a group of directors responsible for overseeing the corporate audit and the preparation of financial statements; the committee has wider responsibilities in a distributing corporation

compensation committee committee responsible for setting director and officer pay

nominating committee committee responsible for proposing and recruiting new directors

required annual meeting of shareholders, at which time it reports to them on the state of the corporation's business and affairs and holds elections to determine the board of directors for the coming year.

Public or distributing corporations are required to have an **audit committee**, whose members include at least three directors. Originally, the audit committee's task was only to review the financial statements of the corporation before they were submitted to the full board for approval.[5] Recent provincial securities regulations expand the responsibilities of the committee and require all audit committee members to be independent directors; the auditor must be retained by and report to the audit committee rather than the board or corporate management.[6] A **compensation committee**, responsible for setting director and officer compensation, and a **nominating committee**, responsible for finding new directors, are also recommended but not mandatory.[7] For more information on this topic, see the Companion Website. Figure 26.1 (above) illustrates the general structure of a corporation.

INTERNATIONAL ISSUE

Sarbanes-Oxley Act of 2002

The U.S. Sarbanes-Oxley Act of 2002 (SOX) set higher standards for the internal organization of publicly traded companies. These standards exceed the Canadian regulations and include mandatory codes of ethics and compensation committees, expanded disclosure requirements, and CEO and CFO compensation clawbacks. Compliance does not come cheaply: American businesses are complaining about the high cost of implementing SOX standards.

SOX also influenced the Canadian standards for corporate governance because its reach extends beyond American geographic borders and applies to many Canadian corporations. Canadian corporations trading on an American stock

>

---

[5] CBCA, s. 171. Any other corporation (that is not public or distributing) may have an audit committee, but it is not required.

[6] National Instrument No. 52-110, ss. 2.3, 3.1. This instrument also creates an expanded definition of "independent" that means free of "any direct or indirect material relationship." Previously, only the majority of the directors on this committee had to be independent, and this remains the requirement of the CBCA.

[7] National Policy No. 58-201; Multilateral Instrument 58-101.

exchange must comply with SOX, as must Canadian subsidiaries of U.S. parent corporations. The difficulty in complying with multiple different corporate governance regimes was one of the reasons a proposed overhaul of Canadian corporate governance rules was abandoned in 2009. The abandoned proposal would have moved Canada to a more principle-based regime and away from the rules-based systems currently operating in both Canada and the United States.

Question to Consider

1. Should public corporate governance rules be those of the incorporating jurisdiction or those of the jurisdiction where the shares are sold? Or both?

Sources: L. McCallum and P. Puri, *Canadian Companies' Guide to the Sarbanes-Oxley Act* (Toronto: Butterworths, 2004); Kevin Drawback, "Reform Backlash Gathers Momentum: Restriction on Class-action Suits Part of a Trend," *National Post*, February 21, 2005; Canadian Securities Administrators' Staff Notice 58-3-5—Status Report on the Proposed Changes to the Corporate Governance Regime, November 13, 2009.

DIRECTORS

The Role of the Directors

Section 102 of the CBCA provides that the directors shall manage or supervise the management of the business and affairs of the corporation. In addition to the general power of management, the Act confers a number of specific powers on the directors. Following are the most important powers:

(a) to issue shares—Subject to the corporation's constitution, the directors may issue shares at such times, to such persons, and for such consideration as they may determine (section 25).

(b) to declare dividends—The directors determine whether or to what extent profits should be distributed to the shareholders or retained in the corporation.

(c) to adopt bylaws governing the day-to-day affairs of the corporation—The directors may adopt new bylaws or amend existing ones. Although they must be submitted for approval at the next meeting of shareholders, the bylaws remain effective until then (section 103).

(d) to call meetings of shareholders (section 133)—The directors must call an annual general meeting each year, but they may call additional meetings whenever they wish.

(e) to delegate responsibilities (except those outlined in (a) to (d)) and appoint officers (sections 115 and 121)—Officers do not have to be directors.

CHECKLIST

Powers of Directors

In relation to the internal affairs of the corporation, these are the most important powers given to the directors:

■ to issue shares,

■ to declare dividends,

■ to adopt bylaws,

■ to call meetings of shareholders, and

■ to delegate responsibilities and appoint officers.

A corporation is required to have one or more directors.[8] A distributing public corporation must have a minimum of three directors, at least two of whom must be independent; that is, they must not be officers or employees of the corporation (section 102(2)). Provincial securities regulations define "independent" more broadly as "no direct or indirect material relationship with the corporation."

Where a corporation has more than one director, decisions of the board of directors are normally made by majority vote, unless the corporate constitution requires a higher special majority or unanimity. Usually, the bylaws make provision for the holding of meetings of the board, the election of a chairperson, rules on voting, quorums, and like matters. When making decisions, directors are not obligated to follow the instructions of shareholders.

CASE 26.1

The majority shareholder of a corporation wanted the corporation to sell its main asset. At his request the directors called a general meeting of shareholders, which passed a resolution (over the opposition of some of the minority shareholders) instructing the board of directors to go ahead with the sale.

The board refused to do so, believing that the sale was not in the best interests of the corporation. The majority shareholder sued, claiming that the board was bound to carry out the instructions of the general meeting of shareholders.

The court disagreed, ruling that it is the directors who manage the business of a corporation and, until such time as they are replaced, they must act as they think best for the corporation and are not bound to follow instructions from the shareholders.[9]

One very important effect of this rule is that the shareholders cannot compel the directors to declare a dividend unless there is an express requirement in the corporation's constitution that a dividend be paid in particular circumstances.

Appointment and Removal of Directors

A director of a corporation must be a minimum of 18 years of age, be of sound mind, and not have declared bankruptcy (section 105). In addition, at least 25 percent of the directors of a corporation must be resident Canadians.[10] Unless required by the articles of incorporation, a director need not hold shares in the corporation.

A corporation's first directors are appointed at the time of incorporation and hold office until the first meeting of shareholders, which must be held not less than 18 months after the corporation comes into existence (section 133). Subsequently, directors are elected, re-elected, or replaced on a regular basis. Normally this occurs at the annual general meeting of the corporation, but elections may be held at any time at a special meeting called for that purpose. Casual vacancies on the board—for example, where a director dies or becomes seriously ill—may normally be filled by the remaining directors.

Directors are elected by ordinary resolution of the shareholders (section 106(3)); that is, a simple majority vote is sufficient and usually each share entitles a shareholder to one vote per director position.[11] The result is that one shareholder holding anything more than 50 percent of the total shares is able to elect the entire board of directors.

---

[8] Even a corporation with only a single shareholder must have one or more directors, though there is no reason why the shareholder should not also be the sole director. The articles of incorporation are required to state the number (or the minimum and maximum number) of directors that the corporation is to have (section 6(1)(e)).

[9] *Automatic Self-Cleansing Filter Syndicate Co. Ltd. v. Cuninghame*, [1906] 2 Ch. 34 (U.K.C.A.).

[10] S. 105(3), as amended.

[11] The Alberta and Saskatchewan statutes allow directors to be appointed by a class of shareholders, or by creditors or employees, if the articles so provide: Business Corporations Act, R.S.A. 2000, c. B-9, s. 106(9); R.S.S. c. B-10, s. 101(8).

The articles of incorporation may specify an alternative voting structure,[12] that directors be elected by a system of **cumulative voting**—a form of proportional representation designed to ensure that any substantial minority of shareholders will be represented on the board. The system would allow a shareholder to cast all his votes for one director position.[13]

cumulative voting   a method of electing directors by a form of proportional representation

If shareholders are dissatisfied with current directors, a special meeting may be called to vote on the removal of a director before the expiration of the term.[14] Except where cumulative voting is provided for, an ordinary resolution (simple majority) is sufficient for the removal of any director, and the articles may not prescribe a greater majority (section 6(4)). For more information on this topic, see the Companion Website.

OFFICERS

As noted, officers are responsible for the day-to-day "hands on" management of the corporation. Officers derive their power from the directors. The CBCA defines an officer as "someone appointed by the directors" with functions similar to "a president, vice-president, secretary, treasurer etc. . . ." (section 2(1)).[14A] It is for the directors to define and designate responsibilities of each officer (section 121), and this is usually done in the bylaws. The only statutory requirement is that the officer be of "full capacity." Officers may be removed by the directors. In most corporations, officers exercise tremendous power and, as will be discussed in the next section, they are subject to the same duties as directors. The responsibilities of officers of public (distributing) corporations are attracting more attention from provincial regulators, which now require CEOs and CFOs to certify contents of a corporation's audited financial statements and annual reports.

CHECKLIST

Corporate Governance Legislative Overview

Requirements	Private Corporations	Public Corporations	
	CBCA	CBCA	Provincial Securities Regulation*
Minimum directors	1 (s. 102(2))	3 (s. 102(2))	3
Independent directors	Not required	2 (minimum) (s. 102(2))	*Majority* (*Recommended*)
Chair of board			*Independent* (*Recommended*)
Financial statements	Unaudited (optional) (s. 163(1))	Audited (s. 162)	Audited by public accountant, and certified by CEO/CFO
Annual general meeting of shareholders	Yes (s. 133(1))	Yes (s. 133(1))	Yes

(continued)

---

[12] S. 140(1).

[13] In New Brunswick, where cumulative voting is mandatory: Business Corporations Act, R.S.N.B. c. 9.1, s. 65.

[14] Section 109; to call such a meeting, shareholders must have at least 5 percent of the outstanding shares of the corporation.

[14A] Canada Business Corporations Act, Section 2(1).

Requirements	Private Corporations	Public Corporations	
Audit committee	Optional (s. 171)	Required: 3 director minimum, majority independent (s. 171)	Required: All members to be financially literate independent directors
Compensation committee	No	No	*Recommended:* Disclose alternative method
Nominating committee	No (s. 137 (4))	No (s. 137 (4))	*Recommended*
Disclosure of corporate governance practices	No	No	Required
Code of ethics	No	No	*Recommended*

* "Securities regulation" refers to the provincial securities regulators rules, recommendations, and guidelines as set out in the National Instruments and Policies created by the Canadian Securities Administrators and adopted by each province's Securities Commission. See, for example, Securities Act, R.S.O. 1990, c. S-5, s. 121.3. Information drawn from NI-52-110, ss. 2.1, 3.1; NI-58-101F1; NP-58-201, ss. 3.1, 3.2, 3.10, 3.15.

Ethical Issue   Who Is "Independent"?

When Bill Gates was appointed to Berkshire Hathaway Inc.'s board of directors in 2004, he was designated by the board as an independent director. His only preexisting relationship with the corporation was as a shareholder. Still, critics complained about the designation, citing his long friendship with chair Warren Buffett.[15]

What does "independent" mean? The commonly understood meaning of the word is that an independent party is free of any conflicting interests or ties. The CBCA definition designates only employees and officers of the corporation as being non-independent (s. 102(2)). The provincial securities regulation definition excludes anyone with a "direct or indirect material relationship with the corporation," and it leaves the determination of what amounts to a "material relationship" for the directors themselves to decide with some minor direction.[16]

The regulation suggests that a material relationship is one that could "reasonably interfere with the exercise of

independent judgment." It goes on to suggest that examples include employees, officers, and their immediate family members. But what about friends, distant relatives, or competitors?

Questions to Consider

1. Should a director be free of any potential conflict of interest to be considered independent?

2. Is it appropriate to let the board of directors determine its own members' independence?

3. How can a nominating committee or a code of ethics help with this issue?

Sources: National Instrument 52-110, s. 1.4; Belle Kaura, "The Corporate Governance Conundrum: Re-inventing the Board of Directors and Board Committees" in P. Puri and J. Larson, eds., *Corporate Governance and Securities Regulation in the 21st Century* (Toronto: Butterworths, 2004).

DUTIES OF DIRECTORS AND OFFICERS

Section 122 of the CBCA describes the statutory duties of directors and officers:[16A]

1. Every director and officer of a corporation in exercising their powers and discharging their duties shall
    (a) act honestly and in good faith with a view to the best interests of the corporation; and

---

[15] David Pauly, "Just How 'Independent' Is Berkshire's Board?" *National Post*, January 26, 2005.

[16] NI 58-101, s. 1.2, citing NI 52-110, s. 1.4.

[16A] Section 122 of the Canada Business Corporations Act.

(b) exercise the care, diligence and skill that a reasonably prudent person would exercise in comparable circumstances.

2. Every director and officer of a corporation shall comply with this Act, the regulations, articles, bylaws and any unanimous shareholder agreement.

To fully understand these responsibilities we must consider what duties are owed and also to whom the duties are owed.

What Duties Are Owed?

Section 122(1)(a): Fiduciary Duties The CBCA requires that directors and officers "act *honestly* and in *good faith* with a view to the best interests of the corporation" (section 122(1) (a)) (italics added).[16B] This is a fiduciary duty, a duty with which we are already familiar. It imposes on directors and officers a high standard of conduct involving loyalty, integrity, and trust.[17] This duty addresses the motives, considerations, and factors that influence decision making separately from the decisions themselves. We will discuss particular examples of common conflicts of interest in the section called "Specific Conduct." All of the examples involve, in one way or another, situations where there is a conflict (at least potentially) between a director's personal interest and that of the corporation. However, it is important to understand that Section 122(1)(a) imposes a general duty on directors and officers to avoid any conflict of interest with their corporation and to act in the corporation's best interests.

Section 122(1)(b): Duty of Care, Diligence, and Skill Section 122(1)(b) of the CBCA requires directors and officers to exercise the care, diligence, and skill that a reasonably prudent person would exercise in comparable circumstances. A director or officer owes a duty not to be negligent in carrying out his or her duties. This is an objective standard; behaviour must be comparable to the average director in the same circumstances. There are no precise standards for a professional class of directors.[18] Standards are higher for directors of public corporations; they must be financially literate if they sit on the audit committee, and public directors are recommended to participate in continuing education to enhance their skills as directors and their understanding of the corporation's business.[19] For more information on this topic, see the Companion Website. Many corporations have codes of ethics and conduct that set standards of behaviour for directors and employees.

Directors are not expected to give continuous attention to the affairs of the corporation and, unless there are suspicious circumstances, directors are entitled to rely on information received from the officers of the corporation.[20] However, they should read and challenge material provided to them and may not willfully close their eyes to mistakes and misconduct. If they acquiesce in such matters, they may be liable in damages to the corporation for any losses that result.

To Whom Are Directors' and Officers' Duties Owed?

To the Corporation Section 122 has been interpreted by the courts to mean that the duties of directors and officers are owed, first and foremost, to the corporation. The interests of "the corporation" are normally taken to mean the interests of the corporate legal entity, present and future. Directors and officers may—and should—consider the short-term and long-term interests of the corporation and not merely the present interests

---

[16B] Section 122(1)(a) of the Canada Business Corporations Act.

[17] It may also extend to senior employees. See *MacMillan-Bloedel Ltd. v. Binstead* (1983), 22 B.L.R. 255.

[18] National Instrument 52-110: Financial literacy means that the individual "has the ability to read and understand a set of financial statements. . . ." (s. 1.6).

[19] *Ibid.*; see also NP 58-201, ss. 3.6, 3.7.

[20] *Dovey v. Corey*, [1901] A.C. 477.

or wishes of the shareholders or other stakeholders. But do directors and officers owe duties to anyone other than the corporation? How should they balance competing interests?

To the Shareholders and Other Stakeholders   Although directors are elected and can be removed by a majority of the shareholders, it would be **wrong** to conclude that their first duty is to those shareholders who have elected them—as was demonstrated in Case 26.1. The fiduciary duty of a director is owed to the corporation as a whole.

However, this does not answer the question whether, in addition to the duties owed to the corporation as a whole, any duty is owed to individual shareholders or other stakeholders. Modern corporate governance theory recognizes that the conduct of a corporation's business affects not only shareholders but many other sectors of the public as well. If a large corporation is badly managed, the well-being of many people and even the national interest may be seriously affected. Creditors of a bankrupt corporation go unpaid. Employees may lose their jobs, as may other members of the community where the corporation carries on business. A corporation that produces defective products may injure consumers, and one that does not take effective measures to prevent pollution may cause severe damage to the environment. Consequently, creditors, employees, and the public in general have a stake in good corporate management.

Therefore, corporate governance law recognizes that directors and officers must act in the best interests of the corporation viewed as a good corporate citizen,[21] meaning that there is an obligation to consider the interests of other stakeholders. The corporation's interests remain paramount. Directors must fulfill these duties as they manage the affairs of the corporation or they will be personally liable. The courts have drawn a distinction between duties owed to the corporation only and those owed to stakeholders. For more information on this topic, see the Companion Website.

The *Peoples v. Wise* Distinction   In *Peoples v. Wise*, the Supreme Court of Canada considered the directors' and officers' duties in section 122 and drew a clear distinction between the fiduciary duty in (a) and the duty of skill and care in (b).[22]

CASE 26.2

Wise Stores Inc. (Wise) bought Peoples Department Stores Inc. (Peoples). The three sons of the Wise founder (Wise brothers) were the majority shareholders, officers, and directors of Wise. After the purchase they also became the sole directors of Peoples. The integration of the two operations did not go smoothly, especially in the area of inventory control and bookkeeping. The Wise brothers reviewed the inventory problems and accepted the recommendation of the vice-president of administration and finance. They implemented a joint inventory procurement policy that divided purchasing responsibilities between the two operations. Peoples would make purchases from North America and Wise would make all other international purchases. Within a year of implementation, the inventory system was in total chaos; suppliers went unpaid. Eventually both Wise and Peoples declared bankruptcy and Peoples' bankruptcy trustee sued the Wise brothers personally, claiming they breached the duties owed to Peoples' creditors.

The Supreme Court of Canada held that there was no fiduciary duty owing to the creditors or other stakeholders, stating "At all times directors and officers owe their fiduciary obligation to only the corporation. The interests of the corporation are not to be confused with the interests of the creditors or those of any other stakeholders."[23] However,

>

---

[21] *BCE Inc., Re*, 2008 S.C.C. 69 at para. 66.

[22] *Peoples Department Stores Inc. v. Wise* (2004), 244 D.L.R. (4th) 564 at 582. In Alberta, a director who is appointed by a particular class of shareholders (or by creditors of employees) may give special (but not exclusive) consideration to the interests of that class: R.S.A. 2000, c. B-9, s. 122(4). There may be special circumstances in which directors owe a fiduciary duty to others—for example, to clients of the firm; see *Air Canada v. M & L Travel Ltd.* (1993), 108 D.L.R. (4th) 592., *BCE Inc., supra*, n. 21. It is clear, then, that the fiduciary duty is owed only to the corporation and not the shareholders (except in rare circumstances; see also *Vlastiak v. Valastiak*, [2010] B.C.J. No. 233 (B.C.A.A.) (an example of a rare case where a fiduciary duty was owed to the only other shareholder).

[23] *Peoples, ibid.*, at paras. 43–4.

In *Peoples v. Wise*, the Supreme Court extended the director's duty of skill and care (s. 122(1)(b)) to other stakeholders including shareholders, creditors, and employees. In refusing to extend the fiduciary duty (s. 122(1)(a)) the same way, the Court acknowledged the broad protection afforded to these groups under other statutory provisions. Some of that legislation is discussed later in this chapter, in Chapter 27, and in Chapter 3. Corporate directors must manage their corporations in conformity with these duties, failing which they may incur personal liability.

In *Peoples v. Wise*, the Court also noted that it is often in the best interests of the corporation to consider the interests of others.[25] A corporation that promotes good labour relations by considering the welfare of its employees, enjoys good customer and community relations, and is perceived as socially responsible and responsive to environmental concerns is likely to prosper better in the longer term than one that does not. A corporation's management rightly devotes considerable attention to its public image and relations. The argument may even be made that directors owe a duty to the corporation to do so.[26]

The situation is different in Ontario. In 2007, possibly in response to the *Peoples* decision, the Ontario Business Corporations Act was amended to make it clear that both the fiduciary duty and the duty of skill and care are owed only to the corporation.[27]

Defences to Breach of Duty

Directors and officers are personally liable for a breach of duty. If the corporation goes bankrupt, disgruntled shareholders, employees, and creditors often accuse officers and directors of breach of duty or "mismanagement." How can directors and officers protect themselves? What defences are available? What risk-management strategies should be in place? Both legislation and the common law provide some guidance.

The CBCA includes the following defences and risk-management strategies:[28]

(a) Reasonable diligence, also known as the **due diligence defence**: By establishing that the required degree of care was taken, directors and officers can defend themselves against claims of breach of the articles, bylaws, and the Act (section 123(4)).

due diligence defence establishing that an acceptable standard of care and skill was exercised by a director or officer

(b) Good faith reliance: Good faith reliance on audited financial statements or expert reports is a defence to breach of fiduciary duty or duty of skill and care (section 123(5)). Therefore, obtaining expert reports prior to key decisions is a good risk-management strategy.

(c) Corporate indemnity: An agreement with the corporation to reimburse a director or officer for any costs associated with liability for breach of duty is enforceable provided that the director acted honestly, reasonably, and in good faith (section 124). Naturally, the effectiveness of this risk-management strategy depends on the financial health of the corporation.

---

[24] *Peoples Department Stores Inc. v. Wise* (2004), 244 D.L.R. (4th) 564 at para 57.

[25] *Ibid.*, at para. 42.

[26] *Re Olympia & York Enterprises Ltd. and Hiram Walker Resources Ltd.* (1986), 59 O.R. (2d) 254 at 271 (On. Div. Ct.).

[27] Section 134 (1) (OBCA).

[28] There is some provincial variation: Ontario's reasonable diligence and good faith defence extends to interim financial reports and reports or advice of an officer or employee (section 135(4)).

(d) Directors' and officers' liability insurance: A corporation may purchase directors' liability insurance on behalf of its board (section 124(6)). These policies have many exclusions, including bad faith and fraud, and are very expensive.

business judgment rule courts will defer to the business decisions of directors and officers provided they are arrived at using an appropriate degree of prudence and diligence

The key common law defence available to directors and officers is known as the **business judgment rule**. Under this rule, courts will grant business experts the benefit of the doubt and not easily criticize a business decision.[29] Judges recognize that they are not business experts and that even sound decisions may ultimately be unsuccessful. Therefore, courts focus on the process used to arrive at the decision; as long as directors and officers exercise an appropriate degree of prudence and diligence while making the decision, the court will hold that the duty of skill and care is met. As was noted in *Peoples*, establishing and following good corporate governance rules can protect directors and officers from allegations that they have breached their duty of care.[30]

The business judgment rule has its limits. It will not protect a director from liability for a failure to comply with specific legal obligations such as mandatory disclosure under securities legislation.[31]

Strict Liability

Directors may also be subject to strict liability, where no breach of duty need be established. The CBCA and corresponding provincial statutes make directors liable to their corporation when they vote at meetings of the board on specified matters that cause financial losses to the corporation, such as the improper redemption of shares or the payment of a dividend in circumstances that leave the corporation unable to meet its liabilities (section 118(2)). In addition, if the corporation becomes insolvent, the directors are personally liable to all employees of the corporation for unpaid wages while they were directors, up to the amount of six months' wages (section 119).[32] Directors may also be liable for failure to comply with other statutes. For example, if the corporation is insolvent, the federal government may collect from the directors the income tax that the corporation was required to withhold from the wages and salaries of employees.[33] Even volunteer directors of a non-profit corporation have been held liable under this provision.[34]

Specific Conduct Involving Conflicts of Interest

Contracts with the Corporation

Perhaps the most important fiduciary obligation is the duty to disclose any interest that the director may have in contracts made with the corporation. This duty arises where a director negotiates the sale of her own property to the corporation, or the purchase of property from the corporation. It may arise indirectly; for example, a director may be a shareholder in another corporation that is selling to or buying from her corporation. The problem occurs frequently among related corporations, where a director of one corporation is a shareholder and perhaps a director of a second corporation.

---

[29] *BCE Inc.*, *supra*, n. 21, at paras. 96–100.

[30] *Peoples*, *supra*, n. 22, at para. 64.

[31] *Kerr v. Danier Leather Inc.*, 2007 S.C.C. 44 at para. 55.

[32] Section 119 uses the word "debts," though it limits the amount to six months' wages. It is, however, not necessary to establish that the debt claimed is for "wages," provided it was incurred for services performed. The section 123(4) defence of reasonable diligence applies to both section 118 and section 119. In *Proulx v. Sahelian Goldfields Inc.* (2001), 204 D.L.R. (4th) 670, the Ontario Court of Appeal (considering s. 131 of the Ontario act) held that vacation pay owing constituted a debt, whether or not it should be regarded as "wages," and was within the section.

[33] Income Tax Act, R.S.C. 1985, c. 1 (5th Supp.), s. 227.1.

[34] *MNR. v. Corsano* (1999), [1999] F.C.J. No. 401 (F.C.C.A.).

ILLUSTRATION 26.1

Brown holds a large number of shares in each of World Electric and Universal Shipbuilding, and is a director of each of these corporations. Universal Shipbuilding requires expensive turbo-generator sets for two large ships under construction. World Electric is one of several manufacturers of turbo-generators.

Brown is faced with an obvious conflict of interest: Can she encourage or even support a contract between the two corporations? On one side, it is in Brown's interest to see Universal Shipbuilding obtain the equipment at the lowest possible price. On the other side, it is in her interest to see World Electric get the contract and obtain the highest possible price.

Under section 120 of the CBCA, a director who has an interest in a contract must disclose this fact at a meeting of the board of directors that considers the contract, and must not vote on the matter. If, after learning of the interest, the remaining members of the board still wish to go through with the contract, they may enter into a binding contract. If the remaining directors are not enough to form a quorum, the contract should be ratified at a general meeting of the shareholders. Failure by a director to disclose an interest gives that director's corporation the right to rescind the contract upon learning of the interest.

One type of contract in which a director clearly has a personal interest is the contract providing for her own remuneration, so it is perhaps surprising that the CBCA simply provides that directors may fix the remuneration of the directors, officers, and employees of the corporation (section 125). There is an obvious risk that the directors will be excessively generous to each other or to their CEO.[35] Securities regulations require public (distributing) corporations to disclose executive compensation and to develop independent methods of establishing executive compensation, and the creation of compensation committees is recommended.

Interception of Corporate Opportunity A different situation arises when it is a director's duty to acquire a particular item of property for the corporation or to give the corporation the chance of first refusal, and instead she acquires the property for herself. In that case, she has intercepted an opportunity belonging to the corporation and has committed a breach of duty. If a director has received a mandate to act as agent for the corporation to purchase a specific piece of property or a particular type of property, she is under the same duty as that placed upon any agent to acquire property for her principal. If she buys the property for herself, she has breached her duty. The property is deemed to be held in trust for the corporation, as is any profit made.

Corporate Information A rather different situation arises when a director receives information about a profitable venture or an opportunity to buy property at an advantageous price. She may be under no duty to acquire the property for the corporation, but if the information is received in her capacity as a director of the corporation, then it is her duty to give the corporation first chance of acquiring an interest in the venture or property. If the corporation decides not to acquire the property, the director is probably free to do so. But she makes a dangerous decision if she assumes that the corporation would not want the property anyway, and then acquires it for herself without consulting the corporation. In practice, it is sometimes difficult for a court to decide whether, in the circumstances, the information came to the director personally or in her role as a director of the corporation. But once the court decides that the opportunity belonged to the corporation, the result is quite clear: Purchasing on her own behalf is a breach of duty.

---

[35] See *UPM-Kymmene Corp. v. UPM-Kymmene Miramichi Inc.* (2002), 214 D.L.R. (4th) 496, where the board approved a "compensation agreement" for the chairman that included a "signing bonus" of 25 million shares. The court held that there had been inadequate disclosure and set aside the agreement.

CASE 26.3

R was a director of a large corporation that was in the process of expanding its chain of retail grocery stores. A major part of his duties was to travel around the country looking for suitable independent stores for the corporation to purchase. R entered into an arrangement with a friend to buy those stores that seemed especially good bargains and to resell them to the corporation, concealing the fact of his ownership. When this was later discovered, the corporation brought proceedings against him.

The court held that R was under a duty to acquire the stores for the corporation, and therefore was held to have done so as its agent.[36]

CASE 26.4

C was a director of a corporation involved in exploration and natural resource development. C was approached by a prospector, who asked if the corporation would be interested in acquiring certain claims. He reported this at a meeting of the board of directors. A majority of the board considered that the corporation was already overcommitted financially and decided against taking up the offer.

When the prospector approached C again, C decided to take up the claims for himself. He later left the corporation, after a disagreement. The corporation learned of his acquisition of the claims and brought proceedings against him.

The court held that, once the corporation had rejected the opportunity, it no longer belonged to the corporation and C was free to take advantage of it.[37]

Competing with the Corporation Another aspect of the conflict of interest principle is the rule that a director may not carry on a business competing with that of her corporation, except with the permission of the corporation. The corporation is entitled to claim all the profit made by the director and to obtain an injunction prohibiting the director from any future competition.

CASE 26.5

O'Malley was a director of Canaero, a corporation specializing in aerial surveying. He was hired to work on a project for the corporation in Guyana, during which he learned a lot about the terrain and made some useful contacts. He subsequently resigned from Canaero, formed his own corporation, and successfully tendered for a surveying contract with the government of Guyana.

O'Malley was held to be in breach of his fiduciary duty to Canaero and accountable to them for his profit on the contract.[38]

Related Party Transactions Large businesses often operate through a group of related corporations. Those corporations deal with each other on a regular basis. Frequently, they share some of the same directors. The potential for conflicts of interest is obvious. Almost inevitably, some intergroup contracts or arrangements will be more beneficial to one party than to the other. The situation becomes especially perilous where the two or more corporations concerned do not have the same shareholders or creditors.

The likelihood of impropriety (or at least of perceptions of impropriety) is further increased where the corporate group is effectively controlled by a single individual or family—a situation that is quite common in Canada.

---

[36] *Canada Safeway Ltd. v. Thompson*, [1951] 3 D.L.R. 295. Note that in reselling the stores to the corporation, the director was also in breach of his duty to disclose his interest. The corporation could have chosen instead to rescind the contracts. See also *Slate Ventures Inc. v. Hurley* (1998), 37 B.L.R. (2d) 138.

[37] *Peso Silver Mines Ltd. v. Cropper* (1966), 56 D.L.R. (2d) 117 (S.C.C.). In contrast, where a majority of the directors (and shareholders) of a corporation purported to pass a resolution rejecting a contractual opportunity offered to the corporation and then took it for themselves, that was held to be a breach of their duties. The resolution was not adopted in good faith: *Cook v. Deeks*, [1916] A.C. 554.

[38] *Canadian Aero Service Ltd. v. O'Malley* (1973), 40 D.L.R. (3d) 371 (S.C.C.).

Hollinger Inc., a corporation in which 12 percent of its voting shares were held by the public and the remaining shares were owned by Conrad Black and his associates, made a loan of $1.1 million to Ravelston Corp., all of whose shares were owned or controlled by Black. Minority shareholders in Hollinger alleged that the loan had not been properly approved.[39] In related proceedings it was alleged that improper payments totalling $32 million were made from one Hollinger corporation to another corporation and its directors. The court appointed an inspector to investigate.[40]

Insider Trading

Insider trading is one type of conduct for which English and Canadian courts were reluctant to impose liability, so the legislatures intervened to impose liability. Insider trading attracts all three types of liability: civil liability, regulatory liability, and criminal liability.

Insider trading occurs when a director or officer of a corporation, or some other person (for example, a shareholder or employee of the corporation), buys or sells the corporation's shares or other securities, making use of confidential inside information in order to make a profit or avoid a loss.

insider trading the use of confidential information relating to a corporation in dealing in its securities

(a) The directors of a small family company are approached by a large public corporation that offers to buy all the shares of the family company at a price considerably above that at which the shares had previously been valued. The next day, one of the directors is approached by her uncle, who is a shareholder and who offers to sell some of his shares to her. Without disclosing the proposed takeover, she buys the shares at a price well below that of the offer.

(b) The directors of a mining corporation receive a confidential report from their surveyor that very valuable mineral deposits have just been discovered. One of the directors immediately instructs her broker to buy as many of the corporation's shares as possible on the stock exchange, before the good news is released and forces up the price.

(c) The directors of a corporation learn that their major customer has just declared bankruptcy, owing the corporation a large sum of money. Default on the account by their customer is likely to result in the corporation showing a substantial loss in the forthcoming half-yearly accounts. One of the directors promptly sells her shares just before the news becomes public and the shares drop in value.

In each of the hypothetical cases in Illustration 26.2, a director has used information that came to her in her capacity as a director for her own benefit.

Legislation imposes liability for this type of behaviour and sets strict disclosure requirements whenever a director or other insider trades in the securities of her own corporation, and has made insider trading a criminal offence, punishable by fines or imprisonment or both. Under the Ontario Securities Act, for example, fines of up to $5 million and prison terms of up to five years may be imposed.[41] There is a possible penalty of 10 years' imprisonment under the Criminal Code.[42] Despite the heavy penalties, however, the number of prosecutions for insider trading seems to be increasing, both in Canada and in the United States.

---

[39] *Catalyst Fund General Partner I Inc. v. Hollinger Inc.*, [2004] O.J. No. 4722, aff'd [2006] O.J. No. 944 (On. C.A.).

[40] *Ibid.*, In U.S. criminal proceedings initiated by the American Securities and Exchange Commission, Black was convicted of fraud and obstruction of justice arising from redirection of sale proceeds from Hollinger corporations to directors through artificial non-competition agreements (some convictions were reversed on appeal).

[41] Securities Act, R.S.O. 1990, c. S. 5, s. 122(4). An offender may also be required to pay back three times the amount of any profit made. In *R. v. Harper* (2003), 232 D.L.R. (4th) 738, a fine of almost $4 million was imposed, though it was reduced to $2 million on appeal.

[42] Criminal Code, R.S.C. 1985, c. C-46, s. 382.1, as amended by S.C. 2004, c. 3. In Canada, most inside traders receive fines and are banned from the securities industry and public boards.

The above provisions apply principally to corporations whose securities are publicly traded as a way of promoting public confidence in the markets. However, section 131 of the CBCA provides that, even in the case of a private corporation, an insider who purchases or sells a security of the corporation with knowledge of specific, confidential, price-sensitive information is liable

(a) to compensate the seller or purchaser (as the case may be) for any loss suffered as a result of the transaction, and

(b) to account to the corporation for any benefit or advantage obtained.[42A]

For the purposes of the legislation, "insider" includes a director or officer, an employee, any shareholder who holds more than a prescribed percentage of the corporation's securities, and a "tippee"—that is, a person who knowingly receives confidential information from an insider.

CHECKLIST

Directors' Personal Liability

A director faces the following types of personal liability for breach of her duties:

Type of Personal Liability	Available Remedy
(a) Civil liability	
(i) to the corporation	
■ breach of fiduciary duty, s. 122(1)(a)	■ damages for losses arising from breach
■ specific conduct involving conflicts of interest, s. 120	■ accounting of amounts paid for improper dividends or share redemption
■ breach of duty of skill, diligence, and care, s. 122(1)(b)	■ rescission of contract involving conflict of interest
	■ constructive trust of property
	■ accounting of profits
	■ injunction to restrain breach of duty
(ii) to others	
■ breach of duty of skill, diligence, and care, s. 122(1)(b)	■ damages for losses arising from the liability
■ strict liability for six months' unpaid wages	
■ strict liability for unpaid taxes	
■ liability for insider trading damages	
(b) Regulatory and criminal liability	
■ insider trading	■ fines and imprisonment (Criminal Code)
■ other statutory offences discussed in Chapter 27	■ fines and imprisonment (Securities Act)

SHAREHOLDERS

The Role of Shareholders

Shareholders play little or no part in management. They have some rights, the most important being the right to vote at meetings, but generally, once the shareholders have elected a board of directors, they have no further power to participate in management. If they do not like the way the directors are running the corporation's business and affairs, they cannot

---

[42A] Section 131 of the Canada Business Corporations Act.

interfere. Legally, their main course of action is to dismiss the directors and elect new ones in their place.[43]

Publicly Traded Corporations   In large, publicly traded corporations, shareholdings may be widely distributed, with no single shareholder or group holding more than 5 percent of the voting stock. Less frequently, one entity may control a majority of shares. Both situations make changing management difficult. Management may respond to calls for change with a piece of practical advice to investors: "If you don't like the management, sell!" In other words, "Do not get into costly corporate struggles. Cut your losses by getting out and reinvesting in a corporation more to your liking." All that may be changing with the recent attempts to strengthen corporate governance through independent directors and the wide use of the oppression remedy (discussed below). However, shareholders do not have direct power over the management of the corporation.

Private Corporations   In private corporations, shareholders' problems are radically different. There is no easily accessible way to sell shares in a private company if a shareholder wants to sell. The usual problem is a serious disagreement among the principal shareholders, who are frequently also directors and senior employees of the corporation. In the absence of careful contractual arrangements providing safeguards, a minority shareholder may find himself "locked in" and "frozen out" at the same time.

The minority shareholder is "locked in" in the sense that he probably cannot sell his shares except at a fraction of what he believes they should be worth. There are two reasons for this. First, in most private corporations the transfer of shares is restricted, usually requiring the consent of the board of directors. They may be unwilling to agree to the transfer of his shares except to someone of their own choosing. Second, even if the minority shareholder is free to sell the shares, he will have great difficulty in finding a buyer who would consider acquiring a minority position in a private corporation.

The minority shareholder may be "frozen out" in the following manner. First, the majority directors may fire him from his job with the corporation or, at the very least, refuse to renew his employment contract when it expires. Second, they may remove him from the board of directors or elect someone else in his place at the next election. Third, they may increase salaries to themselves, so that the corporation itself earns no apparent profit. Even if a profit is shown, it may be retained by the corporation, since dividends are payable only at the discretion of the board of directors. Therefore, a minority shareholder may find himself deprived of his salary-earning position, his directorship, and his prospect of any dividends on his investment.

In these circumstances the majority shareholders may not have broken any law, and no remedy existed at common law. However, a number of statutory provisions provide relief for minority shareholders. We will discuss these, as well as strategies to avoid the problem, under "The Protection of Minority Shareholders" later in this chapter.

Rights Attached to Shares

Shareholder rights come from two principal sources—the rights attached to their shares by the articles of the corporation and the rights conferred on them by the relevant corporate legislation.

The corporate constitution sets out the rights attached to each class of shares. For example, the CBCA requires that the articles state the classes of shares that may be issued and, if there are to be two or more classes of shares, the rights, privileges, restrictions, and

---

[43] If dissatisfied shareholders hold a sufficient proportion of the shares, they need not wait until the next meeting called by the directors; they may requisition a meeting (s. 143) to elect a new board. As will be discussed under the section called "The Protection of Minority Shareholders," in some situations there may be other court remedies available.

conditions attaching to each class (section 6(1)(c) and section 24(4)). If there is only one class of shares, the rights of the shareholders include the rights

- to vote at any meeting of shareholders,
- to receive any dividend that is declared, and
- to receive the remaining property of the corporation (after payment of its debts) on dissolution (section 24(3)).

Additional rights may be attached to shares, and, if there are different classes of shares, rights may be granted to some shares and not others; but the three basic rights must exist and be exercisable by one or other class of shares.

Meetings and Voting

Notice and Attendance at Meetings If shareholders wish to voice their objections about the management, they need a forum to do so. The forum provided under all statutes is the **general meeting of shareholders**. The corporation may hold other meetings of shareholders in the course of the year, but it is required by statute to hold at least one **annual general meeting**.[44] Shareholders are entitled to advance notice of all general meetings and are entitled to receive copies of the financial statements before the annual general meeting. They may attend the meetings, question the directors, and criticize the management of the corporation.[45]

The Right to Requisition Meetings All the provinces provide in their statutes that the shareholders themselves may call a meeting. However, these provisions require a relatively large proportion of the shareholders to petition for the meeting, a requirement that is virtually impossible to meet in big corporations where even a large number of shareholders may hold only a small percentage of the total shares.[46] The right to requisition a **special meeting** is therefore of limited use in large corporations, but is especially valuable in the smaller, private companies.

The Right to Vote The right to attend meetings and to criticize management is reinforced with the right to vote. The shareholders pass (or defeat) resolutions—an **ordinary resolution**, which is passed by a simple majority of votes cast, and a **special resolution**, which requires a two-thirds majority.[47] The CBCA sets out a number of matters that must be approved by the shareholders in either an ordinary or a special resolution, the most important being

(a) the approval of alterations to the articles of incorporation—special resolution (section 173),

(b) the approval of certain other fundamental changes, such as amalgamation with another corporation (section 183) or the sale of all, or substantially all, of the corporation's property—special resolution (section 189),

(c) the approval of any amendments made by the directors to the bylaws—ordinary resolution (section 103),

(d) the election of the auditor—ordinary resolution (section 162), and

(e) the election or removal of directors—ordinary resolution (sections 106, 109).

Except for the items described in (a) and (b), the most important matter voted upon by the shareholders is the election of directors.

general meeting of shareholders a formal meeting of shareholders at which they are able to vote on matters concerning the corporation

annual general meeting the general meeting of shareholders that is required by law to be held each year to transact certain specified business

special meeting any general meeting of shareholders other than the annual general meeting

ordinary resolution a resolution adopted by the general meeting and passed by a simple majority

special resolution a resolution of the general meeting required to be passed by a special (usually two-thirds) majority

---

[44] CBCA, s. 133.

[45] CBCA (ss. 132(4) (5))

[46] CBCA, s. 143.

[47] S. 2. In Nova Scotia, a special resolution requires a three-quarters majority.

Class Voting Rights   Not all shareholders necessarily have the right to vote. A corporation's shares may be divided into different classes, with different voting rights. Common shares almost always carry the right to vote; preferred shares often carry a right to vote only in specified circumstances, such as when preferred dividends are in arrears. The founders of a corporation may create several classes of shares and weigh the voting heavily in favour of a small group of shares held by themselves. For example, they could give Class "A" shares 100 votes per share and Class "B," issued to a broader group of shareholders, only one vote per share. This is most popular for private corporations because it would be virtually impossible for a publicly traded corporation to have such a share structure today. Securities commissions, stock exchanges, and underwriters would probably refuse such an issue, and without their concurrence a public offering is impossible. Virtually all common stock offered on the public market today carries one vote per share. Within a particular class, however, all shares must enjoy the same rights (section 24).

Class rights, which may relate not only to voting but also to other matters such as rights to have priority in payment of dividends or to receive the surplus on liquidation of the corporation, must be set out in the articles of incorporation. Consequently, they may only be varied by special resolution of the shareholders. In addition, altering the rights of a particular class requires approval by the votes of two-thirds of that class and of any other class that may be adversely affected (section 176).

> **class rights**   special rights attached to a particular class of shares

Proxies   In most publicly traded corporations, only a small proportion of shareholders actually attend general meetings. All corporation statutes permit a shareholder to nominate a **proxy** to attend a general meeting and to cast that shareholder's votes at the meeting as instructed. This is done by signing a form naming the proxy, and sending it to the corporation before the meeting. Most jurisdictions now go further and require all corporations, except the smallest private ones, to send a **proxy form**, the contents of which are prescribed in detail, to all shareholders at the same time as notice of a meeting is given.

In the event of a proxy fight between two groups of shareholders—usually the board of directors and a dissenting group—each group solicits all the shareholders by mail in order to persuade them to give their proxy forms to the group making the solicitation. The dissenting group may go to the corporation's head office to obtain lists of all the shareholders from the share register in order to make their solicitations. Here the board of directors has a great advantage. As a matter of practice, they include proxy forms, naming an existing director as the proposed proxy, with the mailed notice of the annual general meeting.[48]

> **proxy**   a person appointed to attend a general meeting of shareholders and to cast the votes of the shareholder appointing him or her

> **proxy form**   a form required to be circulated to shareholders before a general meeting, inviting them to appoint a proxy if they so wish

Financial Rights

Shareholders expect to receive a return on their investment in one or both of two forms—earnings distributed regularly in the form of dividends, and growth that can be realized by selling the shares or on dissolution of the corporation. Holders of common shares may be satisfied with smaller dividends if there is capital appreciation in the corporation's assets or if a significant part of the profits is retained within the business and has the effect of increasing the value of the shares. Preferred shares often do not participate in growth, and their holders are primarily concerned with receiving dividends.

Dividends   A fundamental right attached to shares is the right to receive any **dividend** that is declared by the corporation. The declaration of dividends is entirely within the discretion of the board of directors. Shareholders normally have no right to be paid a dividend, even when the corporation makes large profits.

There can be no discrimination, however, in the payment of dividends among shareholders of the same class. Each shareholder is entitled to such dividends as are declared in

> **dividend**   a distribution to shareholders of a share of the profits of the corporation

---

[48] This advantage is only partly offset by disclosure requirements and by compelling management to provide shareholders with a means to nominate a different proxy.

proportion to the number of shares of that class held. In addition, directors are bound to pay dividends in the order of preference assigned to the classes of shareholders. They may not pay the common shareholders a dividend without first paying the whole of any preferred dividends owing to preference shareholders.

Distribution of Surplus   On the dissolution of a corporation, provided it has assets remaining after paying off all its creditors, shareholders are entitled to a proportionate share of the remaining net assets. The distribution of these net assets among the various classes of shareholders must also be made in accordance with the respective priorities of each class.

Preemptive Rights   One of the more important powers given to the board of directors is the power to issue shares. The issue of new shares involves two possible risks for existing shareholders. First, the issue of shares to some other person will necessarily reduce the proportion of the total number of shares that a shareholder holds. Second, there is the risk of "stock watering"; if new shares are issued for a price that is less than the value of the existing shares, the value of the existing shares will be diluted.

ILLUSTRATION 26.3

A owns 34 of the total of 100 shares issued by XYZ Inc. The assets of XYZ Inc. are worth approximately $1 million. The directors wish to raise additional capital and resolve to issue 20 new shares to T, at a price of $5000 per share. As a result, A will now own only 28.3 percent of the total shares and can no longer block the adoption of a special resolution. A's shares, previously worth $10 000 each, will be worth only $9167.

Canadian courts do not recognize a general principle giving all shareholders a preemptive right. This right must be expressly attached to a share when the corporation creates the class of shares in the articles of incorporation (s. 28). Without a preemptive right, directors have the right to issue authorized share capital of the corporation at their discretion, but they must issue shares only for the purpose of raising capital or for purposes that are in the best interest of the corporation. If they have a good faith intention of raising capital, they may distribute the shares to whomever they wish, upon payment of a fair price. But if directors issue shares not for the benefit of the corporation but instead to affect voting control, the issue may be declared void. For example, if directors were to issue shares to themselves for the purpose of outvoting shareholders who, up to that point, had a majority of the issued shares, the extra share issue could be set aside by the court.

CASE 26.7

Bonisteel was a director of Collis Leather Co. and the owner of 458 of a total of 1208 issued shares. He entered into an agreement with another shareholder to buy that shareholder's 150 shares. The purchase would have given him control of the corporation. Collis, the general manager and the person most responsible for the corporation's success, threatened to leave if Bonisteel took control. In order to forestall Bonisteel, the directors resolved to issue 292 new shares, and each director was asked how many shares he wished to subscribe for. Most of the new shares were taken up by directors other than Bonisteel, with the result that he would be left with less than 50 percent of the total shares. Bonisteel brought an action to restrain the directors from making the allotment.

The court held that such an allotment would be invalid. The corporation was not in need of additional funds, and it was improper to issue new shares solely for the purpose of altering the balance of control.[49]

---

[49] *Bonisteel v. Collis Leather Co. Ltd.* (1919), 45 O.R. 195.

Afton was a "junior" mining company, incorporated in British Columbia. As was common in the industry, it was looking for a "major" company to help finance a large drilling program. Teck, a large resource corporation, made an offer to buy a controlling block of Afton's shares. The directors of Afton, led by its chief engineer, Millar, rejected the offer and preferred to enter into an arrangement with Canex, the subsidiary of another Canadian corporation, even though Canex was not prepared to match the Teck offer. Following the rejection, Teck started buying Afton shares on the stock exchange, and soon announced that it had acquired more than 50 percent of the issued shares. The Afton directors then entered into a long-term contract with Canex, which involved issuing a large block of new shares to Canex. This arrangement reduced the Teck holding to less than 50 percent.

The share issue was challenged by Teck but upheld by the court. The Afton directors had entered into the arrangement with Canex and had issued the new shares because they genuinely believed that the interests of Afton would be better served as a "partner" of Canex than as a subsidiary of Teck.[50]

While not required to do so, most corporations give shareholders a preemptive right. When a corporation proposes to issue further shares, it may first issue subscription rights or share rights to all existing shareholders, giving each shareholder one right for each share held. The shareholder then has an option to purchase a new share at a specified price for a specified number of subscription rights. For example, a shareholder owning 50 shares may receive 50 rights entitling him to buy 10 shares (one share for every five rights) at a specified price per share. Subscription rights are normally made transferable, and if the market value of the existing shares significantly exceeds the specified price for the new shares, the rights themselves will have a market value; they may be sold to anyone who wishes to purchase them and exercise the option.

The Right to Information

Disclosure is one of the fundamental principles of modern corporate governance. Prompt disclosure of relevant information enables investors to evaluate the effectiveness of management, and publicity may be an effective deterrent to high-handed behaviour or misconduct in management.

The Financial Statements   Annual **financial statements** must be presented to the shareholders prior to the annual general meeting. All corporation acts require that basic information be part of the financial statements, though the detailed requirements vary. Generally, the basic items required are

financial statements   annual accounts that are required to be presented to the shareholders at the annual general meeting

- the income statement, showing the results of operations for the financial year;
- the balance sheet, showing the corporation's assets as of the financial year-end (including details of changes in share capital during the year);
- a statement of changes in financial position, analyzing changes in working capital;
- a statement of retained earnings showing changes during the year, including the declaration of dividends; and
- a statement of contributed surplus.

The annual financial statements should be in comparative form, showing corresponding data for the preceding financial year. In addition, some statutes require that shareholders be sent comparative interim quarterly financial statements. Public companies must produce audited financial statements and securities regulations require that CEOs and CFOs of public (distributing) companies also certify that the statements fairly reflect the financial condition of the corporation.[51]

---

[50] *Teck Corp. v. Millar* (1973), 33 D.L.R. (3d) 288. See also *Icahn Partners LP v. Lionsgate Entertainment Corp.*, [2010] B.C.J. No. 2130, at paras. 128–54 (B.C.S.C.) aff'd 2011 BCCA 228.

[51] NI 52-109.

Documents of Record

A corporation must maintain certain documents of record at its head office, which may be inspected by any shareholder during usual business hours. These **documents of record** include

- minutes of shareholders' meetings;
- a register of all transfers of shares, including the date and other particulars of each transfer;
- a copy of the corporation's charter, a copy of all bylaws (or articles) and special resolutions, and a register of shareholders; and
- a register of the directors.

These documents are useful to a minority group of shareholders attempting to collect evidence to support a claim of misconduct or ineffectiveness on the part of the directors. Access to the share register permits a dissentient group to obtain the names and addresses of all other shareholders so that they may communicate with them, explain their complaints, and attempt to enlist shareholders' support.

Another document of record is the collection of minutes from directors' meetings. Unlike the other documents of record, however, directors alone, not the shareholders, have a right of access to it.[52]

The Auditor

To assist in the analysis and evaluation of the financial statements, and to ensure their accuracy so far as possible, the acts provide for the appointment of an independent auditor by the shareholders. Private companies may dispense with this requirement, but only if the shareholders unanimously agree to do so. The auditor must be an independent person who is not employed by the corporation.[53] In order to confirm the accuracy of the financial statements, the auditor examines all the records and books of accounts of the corporation. The auditor provides an opinion on whether the statements fairly present the financial position of the corporation in accordance with generally accepted accounting principles.[54] Both the auditor's report and the financial statements must be sent to all shareholders before the corporation's annual general meeting; the period usually specified is at least 21 days before the meeting. These items are included in the corporation's **annual report** to shareholders.

Only the auditor and the directors have the right to examine the books of account; shareholders as such do not have access to them. If a shareholder suspects that something is wrong, he may communicate his information to the auditor, but the auditor has no duty to undertake a special examination at the request of a shareholder; the auditor's duty is owed to the corporation itself rather than the shareholders.[55] As a last resort, a shareholder may apply to a court for the appointment of an inspector.

In a public (distributing) corporation, the audit must be completed by an auditor registered with the Canadian Public Accountability Board. The audit committee, made up of independent directors, supervises the auditor and must create a process to receive anonymous complaints and reports of irregularities in the financial affairs of the corporation, often referred to as whistleblower protection.[56]

Appointment of Inspector

Case 26.6 provides an example of the typical situation where an inspector is appointed. All the jurisdictions, with the exception of Prince

---

[52] CBCA, ss. 20, 21.

[53] The auditor's contract is with the corporation, not with the shareholders: see *Roman Corp. v. Peat Marwick Thorne* (1992), 8 B.L.R. (2d) 43; see *Hercules Managements Ltd. v. Ernst & Young* (1997), 146 D.L.R. (4th) 577 (S.C.C.) (as to auditors duty).

[54] See *CPA Canada Public Sector Accounting Handbook* (Chartered Professional Accountants), for a complete statement of the form and content of the auditor's report.

[55] *Hercules, supra*, n. 53.

[56] National Instruments 52–108 (amendments proposed in 2013) and 52–110.

Edward Island, have statutory provisions enabling shareholders to apply to the courts to appoint an **inspector** to investigate the affairs of the corporation and to audit its books. The statutes give inspectors sweeping powers of inquiry, and the remedy can be a very effective one. The CBCA and most of the provincial acts based on it permit a single shareholder to apply, and they expressly state that the applicant is not required to give security for costs (section 229). A concerned shareholder may choose either of two options: He may request the director—a government official appointed to supervise the affairs of corporations—to apply to the court to order an investigation, or he may apply directly to the court himself. In either event, it is necessary to make out a prima facie case—that is, produce sufficient evidence of the probability of serious mismanagement to warrant further investigation.

inspector a person appointed by the court to investigate the affairs of a corporation

Duties of Shareholders

Directors of corporations are under strict duties of good faith. They use their own assessment of what is in the best interests of the corporation, and they are not bound to follow the instructions of the shareholders. However, when there is a controlling shareholder (or group of shareholders)—with the power to call a general meeting, dismiss directors, and appoint new ones in their place—it is usually the controlling shareholder who determines corporate policy, and the directors often act as a "rubber stamp." In such circumstances do shareholders—and especially controlling shareholders—owe any duty to their corporation?

Unlike some U.S. courts, Canadian courts have consistently held that a majority shareholder owes no positive duty to act for either the welfare of the corporation itself or the welfare of his fellow shareholders.[57] His obligation ends when he has paid the full purchase price for his shares. He has no obligation to attend meetings or to return proxy forms, and he is free to exercise his vote in whatever way he pleases and for whatever purposes he desires. His share is an item of property that he is free to use as he pleases, even if that is against the interests of the corporation or of his fellow shareholders. However, if the shareholder is also a director of the corporation, he must comply with all his director's duties to act honestly and in good faith with a view to the best interests of the corporation (section 122), but when he votes as a shareholder, he is entitled to consider his own personal interests.[58]

For more information on this topic, see the Companion Website.

THE PROTECTION OF MINORITY SHAREHOLDERS

Majority Rule

At the very least, a shareholder's freedom to use his vote as he chooses means that the courts will not substitute their judgment for his when his actions are based upon business considerations. As a consequence, a controlling group of shareholders—through its ability to determine the composition of the board of directors, to approve their actions or decline to do anything about their misdeeds, and even (if they have a two-thirds majority) to amend the corporation's constitution—could ensure that the affairs of the corporation were managed entirely for their own benefit and to the detriment of the minority. As in the dilemma of the "frozen-out" shareholder, these things can happen without any law being broken.

---

[57] See *Brant Investments Ltd. v. Keeprite Inc.* (1991), 3 O.R. (3d) 289.

[58] *North-West Transportation v. Beatty* (1887), 12 App. Cas. 589.

ILLUSTRATION 26.4

A, B, C, and D are the equal shareholders and directors of a corporation, Trattoria Ltd. The articles of incorporation restrict the business of the corporation to the operation of one or more restaurants. Contrary to D's wishes, A, B, and C decide to sell the restaurant to a property developer and to invest the proceeds in a casino business. They use their votes to pass two special resolutions: (1) approving the sale of the restaurant (substantially the only asset of the corporation) and (2) amending the articles to remove the restriction on the business that may be carried on by the corporation.

In this example, the majority has acted within its rights. Nevertheless, D may be upset because the reason he became a shareholder in the corporation has changed.

ILLUSTRATION 26.5

Figaro Ltd.'s shares are divided between two entities: 60 percent are held by Almaviva Inc., a large public corporation, and 40 percent are held by its original founder, Susanna. Following a disagreement over company policy, Almaviva uses its majority voting power to appoint three of its own directors to be directors of Figaro. The new directors subsequently sell an important piece of Figaro's property to Bartolo Ltd., a corporation wholly owned by Almaviva. The sale is at a gross undervalue.

Here, the directors of Figaro have probably breached either their duty of care and skill, or their duty to act in good faith and in the interests of their corporation. The corporation, Figaro, has been injured, since the value of its assets has been reduced, but the loss falls entirely on its minority shareholder, Susanna, since the majority shareholder, Almaviva, gains more as shareholder of the purchaser, Bartolo (100 percent of the undervalue), than it loses as shareholder of the vendor, Figaro (60 percent of the undervalue). Consequently, Almaviva, as controlling shareholder of Figaro, will not complain about any breach of duty by its directors.

ILLUSTRATION 26.6

The shares in Jenufa Ltd. are held in equal proportions by A, her husband B, and his two sons by a previous marriage, C and D, all of whom had until recently been directors. After A and B's acrimonious divorce, B, C, and D use their majority voting power to remove A from the board. Subsequently, instead of distributing the profits as dividends, they decide to reinvest them in a fund to provide for the long-term capital needs of the corporation. They also refuse to consent to A transferring her shares to any third party.

In this example, A is locked in and frozen out. But the corporation has not been injured, and, unless it can be shown that B, C, and D acted in bad faith, there may have been nothing improper in their actions.

Under traditional principles of corporation law, the aggrieved minority shareholders in the above illustrations received little or no help from the courts. However, special statutory remedies have greatly improved the situation of the minority. The following are the most important minority shareholder remedies.

The Appraisal Remedy

In some situations, where the majority shareholders make fundamental changes to the corporation, section 190 offers a procedure whereby a dissenting shareholder need not go along with the change. He may elect instead to have his shares bought out by the corporation. If a price cannot be agreed, the court will fix a fair price. However, this **appraisal remedy** is limited to specific actions by the majority, the most important of which are:

appraisal remedy the right to have one's shares bought by the corporation at a fair price

- changing any restriction on the issue, transfer, or ownership of shares;
- changing any restriction on the business that the corporation may carry on;
- amalgamating or merging with another corporation;

- selling, leasing, or exchanging substantially all the assets of the corporation; and
- "going private" or "squeezing out" transactions.

The remedy is of most use in private corporations, where no ready public market exists for minority shareholdings, since a dissenter in a public corporation would normally just sell his shares on the stock exchange. However, the procedure is a complicated one, and the dissenter must comply with every step prescribed by the Act in order to take advantage of it. If, instead, the shareholder can show that his interests have been "unfairly disregarded," he is more likely to resort to the oppression remedy discussed below.

The Derivative Action

When a corporation has suffered an injury, as in Illustration 26.5 or, for example, where directors have made a secret profit for themselves by exploiting a "corporate opportunity," the corporation may sue the wrongdoer to recover its losses.

Ordinarily, an action on behalf of the corporation must be started by its directors—it is part of the management function. However, if the directors are the wrongdoers, they are not likely to commence an action against themselves. The common law recognized the right of a minority shareholder to start an action on behalf of the corporation, frequently called a **derivative action**—but it was procedurally difficult.

derivative action proceedings brought by one or more shareholders in the name of the corporation in respect of a wrong done to the corporation

The modern statutory derivative action (section 239) overcomes most of the procedural barriers. It permits a shareholder to obtain leave from the court to bring an action in the name and on behalf of the corporation. To do so he need only establish that the directors refuse to bring the action themselves, that he is acting in good faith, and that it appears to be in the interests of the corporation or its shareholders that the action be commenced. If he establishes these things, then the court may make an order to commence the action. The acts prohibit the court from requiring the shareholder to give security for costs. At any time, a court may order the corporation to pay to the complainant costs, including legal fees and disbursements (sections 242(4) and 240(d)). The court may also direct "that any amount payable by a defendant in the action shall be paid, in whole or in part, directly to former and present shareholders of the corporation . . . instead of to the corporation . . ." (section 240(c)).[58A] In Illustration 26.5 above, Susanna could receive direct compensation for her loss, rather than being compensated only indirectly through an increase in the assets of the corporation.

Although the statutory derivative action has substantially improved the position of minority shareholders, the remedy has been somewhat overshadowed by the oppression remedy, discussed below.

Winding Up

Minority partners have better protection than most minority shareholders. They are entitled to an accounting of profits and to receive their share of them regularly. In the event of a total breakdown in relations, they can normally insist on a dissolution and sale of the assets and receipt of a proportionate part of the proceeds. Since the other partners cannot continue to use the partnership assets for their sole benefit, they must either face dissolution or come to a reasonable settlement. Not so in a private corporation. In the absence of a separate agreement among the shareholders, a minority shareholder has none of the rights of a partner.

Corporation statutes have, however, followed partnership law in one important respect. They give the courts discretion to make an order **winding up** a corporation where it is "just and equitable" to do so.[59] It is a drastic remedy, and the courts have been reluctant to

winding up the dissolution (or liquidation) of a corporation

[58A] [Section 240(c)] of the Business Corporations Act, R.S.O. 1990, Chapter B.16.

[59] CBCA, s. 214(1)(b)(ii).

use it if the corporation is successful or large. Typically, the remedy is used when the corporation is a small family business or an "incorporated partnership," where there is deadlock, where relations between the participants have broken down, or where a "partner" has been frozen out. In these cases, the remedy is quite effective, since the mere threat of its use may persuade the majority to reach a compromise.

CASE 26.9

G Corp. was a joint venture corporation with two shareholders—J, who owned 52 percent of the shares, and P, who owned the remaining 48 percent. The relationship between J and P broke down, largely as a result of different expectations about the operation of the venture. P applied for an order directing the winding up of the corporation and its sale as a going concern. J responded by offering to purchase P's shares, but P rejected the offer, and instead made a counteroffer. No agreement was reached.

The court found that the circumstances justified winding up the corporation, since the parties had lost confidence in each other, but since each party would prefer to continue the business alone, it ordered a "buy/sell shotgun" solution.[60]

Oppression Remedy

oppression remedy a statutory procedure allowing individual shareholders to seek a personal remedy if they have been unfairly treated

The **oppression remedy** is by far the broadest and most flexible remedy available to shareholders. In fact, it is available to more than just shareholders; section 238 of the CBCA describes a "complainant" as any person the court approves. Courts will approve persons with a legitimate interest, including creditors. It is not necessary to establish wrongdoing; complainants need only show that their interests or reasonable expectations have been treated unfairly or oppressively disregarded by the behaviour of the corporation or its directors. Courts are empowered to make any order they consider just and appropriate to remedy the situation.

The oppression remedy is typically sought where a minority shareholder is frozen out, as in Illustration 26.6,[61] but it has also been applied in cases of deadlock or breakdown in the relations between shareholders or directors;[62] in a few cases, the oppression remedy has been used where a wrong has been done to the corporation and a minority shareholder has suffered in consequence, even though a derivative action would seem to be more appropriate in such circumstances. It is possible that Susanna, in Illustration 26.5, might seek an oppression remedy rather than bring a derivative action.[63] It is also commonly used by creditors as in Case 26.10.

To justify the making of an order under section 241, a complainant[64] must prove two things:

1. First, that the complainant's expectations about how their interests would be managed are reasonable. A court will decide on reasonableness by looking at factors such as
   - general commercial behaviour,
   - the nature of the corporation,
   - the relationship between the complainant and the defendant,

---

[60] *Patheon Inc. v. Global Pharm Inc.*, [2000] O.J. No. 2532. For more information about the buy/sell shotgun solution, see the Companion Website.

[61] *Re Ferguson and Imax Systems Corp.* (1983), 150 D.L.R. (3d) 718; *Daniels v. Fielder* (1989), 52 D.L.R. (4th) 424.

[62] *Eiserman v. Ara Farms* (1989), 52 D.L.R. (4th) 498; *Tilley v. Hailes* (1992), 7 O.R. (3d) 257.

[63] See e.g. *Journet v. Superchef Food Industries Ltd.* (1984), 29 B.L.R. 206. However, it seems that the plaintiff must still show that he has been affected in a way different from that of other shareholders: *NPV Management Ltd. v. Anthony* (2003), 231 D.L.R. (4th) 681; *Pasnak v. Chura*, [2004] B.C.J. No. 790.

[64] In some circumstances a creditor has been held to be a proper "complainant" for the purposes of the section: *Piller Sausages & Delicatessen Ltd. v. Cobb International Corp.*, [2003] O.J. No. 2647; *Dylex Ltd. v. Anderson* (2003), 63 O.R. (3d) 659.

- past practice,
- representations and agreements,
- conflicting interests of other stakeholders, and
- evasive steps the complainant could have taken.

2. If the complainant's expectations were reasonable, the complainant must then show that the conduct in question "oppressively or unfairly disregards or prejudices the interests." The focus here is on unfair conduct and prejudicial consequences.[65]

However, the courts have emphasized that the conduct need not be wrongful or in bad faith, though this will be a factor to take into account.[66] Obviously, stakeholder interests and expectations may conflict and cannot all be met. Directors do not owe a duty to satisfy individual stakeholders. As already stated, the paramount consideration must be the best interests of the corporation as a whole.

CASE 26.10

The board of directors of BCE Inc. approved a plan of arrangement involving the sale of all of its shares to a group of purchasers by way of a leveraged buyout with a share price 40 percent above existing market value The buyout would convert the public company back to a private one. The board believed that the sale was in the best interests of the company and shareholders. The shareholders agreed, voting 97.93 percent in favour of the plan. However, a major group of creditors (debenture holders) opposed the idea and applied to the court for an oppression remedy to block the sale. Their complaint was that the trading value of their debentures would drop by approximately 20 percent. The

Supreme Court of Canada refused the oppression remedy, saying that the reasonableness of expectations must be evaluated in the context of the particular situation. Here, the debenture holders did not prove that they had a reasonable expectation that BCE would protect the investment grade or trading value of their debentures. A plan may be in the best interests of a corporation and benefit some stakeholders at the expense of others. The Court held that the directors fulfilled their duty by considering the interests of debenture holders and thereafter deciding that fulfillment of contractual obligations was the only promise that could be made.[67]

Section 241(3) allows the court to make any order it thinks fit. One remedy granted has been to require the majority to buy out the minority interest at a fair price, but a wide range of other orders may be made.[68] Judges may customize a solution that suits the particular needs of the corporation. Because of its great flexibility and the absence of technical obstacles, the oppression remedy is quickly becoming the most widely used shareholder remedy in Canada.

CASE 26.11

In proceedings related to the improper loan described in Case 26.6, Catalyst, a Hollinger non-voting minority shareholder, sought an oppression remedy removing eight of the 10 Hollinger directors. Conrad Black resigned prior to the hearing. The trial judge ordered the removal of every

Hollinger director who was also associated with Ravelston, except Peter White. Although White's conduct was found to be oppressive, he was allowed to remain on the board "at the pleasure" of the remaining independent Hollinger directors. The trial judge felt that White's continued service

>

---

[65] *BCE Inc.*, *supra*, n. 21, paras. 68, 72, 89, 95.

[66] *Brant Investments Ltd. v. Keeprite Inc.*, *supra*, n. 57; *Westfair Food Ltd. v. Watt* (1991), 79 D.L.R. (4th) 48 (leave to appeal refused).

[67] *BCE Inc.*, *supra*, n. 21. For another example of a protracted family dispute under the oppression procedure, see *Waxman v. Waxman*, [2004] O.J. No. 1765 (leave to appeal refused).

[68] In some cases the court has allowed the minority petitioner to buy out the majority oppressor: see *Tilley v. Hailes*, *supra*, n. 62.

SHAREHOLDER AGREEMENTS

Advantages

Although the oppression remedy has greatly increased the protection given to minority
shareholders, it still depends on the court exercising its discretion in their favour. A shareholder is still in a less secure position than is a partner.

This uncertainty is a factor to be considered if a small group of equal partners propose to
transform their business into a corporation. It may make good business sense to incorporate
because of the nature of the business, its growth, and its tax position. Yet each of the partners, if aware of the dangers of being a minority shareholder at odds with the others, might
well hesitate to give up the protection of partnership law.

Fortunately, it is possible to approximate the protection available to partners with two
agreements. The solution is an agreement among the shareholders that is outside the constitution of the corporation. This process is not simple because, as we have seen, directors
owe their primary duty to the corporation. They must not compromise their duty to act
in the best interests of the corporation. Subject to an important exception to be discussed
below, any agreement among shareholders must be restricted to their role as shareholders
and must not infringe on their role as directors.[70] This danger can be avoided in a well
drafted **shareholder agreement**. Each agreement must be tailored to the needs of the individual business. Two key elements are normally included in a shareholder agreement.

shareholder agreement an
agreement between two or more
shareholders that is distinct from the
corporation's charter and bylaws

Right to Participate in Management   The shareholders promise to elect each other
to the board of directors at each annual meeting and not to nominate or vote for any
other person. They may also promise not to vote for any major change in the corporation's
capital structure or in the nature of its business except by unanimous agreement.

Right to a Fair Price for a Share Interest   The shareholders may agree to a regular
method of valuation of their shares. They may agree not to sell their shares to an outsider
without giving the right of first refusal proportionately to the remaining shareholders. If one of
them commits a major breach of the shareholder agreement and remains unwilling to remedy
it, he can be required to sell his interest to the others at the appraised value. In addition, if any
shareholder is wrongfully expelled or dismissed by the others, he may require them to buy out his
interest at the appraised value. This provision may also state that in the event of a dispute about
appraisal, a named person, usually the auditor, will arbitrate and assess the value of the interest.

Unanimous Shareholder Agreements

**unanimous shareholder agree-
ment** a shareholder agreement to
which all shareholders are parties

The CBCA and most provincial statutes formally recognize the **unanimous shareholder
agreement** and permit these to govern relationships among shareholders in a private corporation in much the same manner as in a partnership. The CBCA states that "an agreement

---

[69] *Catalyst Fund General Partner 1 Inc. v. Hollinger Inc.* (2006), 79 O.R. (3d) 288 (On. C.A.) at para. 50.

[70] *Motherwell v. Schoof,* [1949] 4 D.L.R. 812.

among all the shareholders . . . that restricts in whole or in part the powers of the directors to manage the business and affairs of the corporation is valid" (section 146(2)),[70A] and that the shareholders who are given the power to manage "have all the rights, powers, duties and liabilities of a director . . . and the directors are thereby relieved of their rights, powers, duties and liabilities to the same extent" (section 146(5)).[70B]

The Act also states that "a purchaser or transferee of shares subject to a unanimous shareholder agreement is deemed to be a party to the agreement" (section 146(3)).[70C] Thus, on the sale of a share interest in a private corporation that is subject to such an agreement, the transferee not only receives an assignment of rights as a shareholder, but is also bound to carry out the duties of the transferor. A unanimous shareholder agreement must be "noted conspicuously" on the face of a share certificate in order to bind subsequent transferees (section 49(8)).

These provisions modify the common law rule that no agreement may fetter the discretion of directors. However, only unanimous agreements have special status under the acts. The CBCA makes frequent reference to unanimous shareholder agreements and treats them almost as if they were part of the corporate constitution, rather like bylaws. In doing so, it has provided the opportunity to develop a new, flexible device for business planning in private corporations.

Strategies to Manage the Legal Risks

As discussed above, shareholders of private corporations can protect themselves from the abuse of the majority shareholder and unfair behaviour of the corporation and its management through the use of a unanimous shareholder agreement. These agreements will preserve the shareholders' percentage interest in the company, maintain the decision-making power as part of management, and create liquidity through a prearranged sale formula. Unfortunately, this is not a viable option for public shareholders and they will be left with only the statutory remedies created for minority interests. Shares should be issued with preemptive rights that allow the shareholder the first opportunity to buy up new issues.

The legal risks for directors and officers of a company are different from those of private and public shareholders. Directors and officers of a corporation risk personal liability if they fail to comply with the statutory and corporation specific governance rules. Therefore, when acting in these positions, certain steps should be followed:

- ensure the corporation maintains directors' liability insurance
- familiarize oneself with the duties of a director and the operation of the business
- participate in continuing education
- develop a code of conduct relating to ethics and conflicts of interests
- design corporate governance structures that ensure independence and transparency, including independent directors, audit committees, nominating committees, and compensation committees—especially if the private corporation intends to go public
- follow the processes in place for proper decision making by reading materials in advance, attending and participating in meetings, and investigating; this will allow the use of the business judgment rule defence if complaints are made
- seek out and rely upon expert opinions when high value changes are proposed
- make prompt public disclosure of key changes to reduce the possibility of insider trading

---

[70A] Section 146(2) of the Canada Business Corporations Act.

[70B] Section 146(5) of the Canada Business Corporations Act.

[70C] Section 146(3) of the Canada Business Corporations Act.

- declare even possible conflicts of interests and seek shareholder approval in border-line circumstance
- arrange personal affairs to reduce the exposure of personal assets

It goes without saying that there are many legal and financial issues about which directors and officers will need to consult lawyers and accountants. Form these relationships early so that ongoing advice may be obtained easily and quickly.

QUESTIONS FOR REVIEW

1. What is the distinction between the business and the affairs of a corporation?
2. Where are the rules of corporate governance found?
3. What are the principal powers given to the board of directors of a corporation incorporated under the CBCA?
4. How are directors appointed? How may they be removed?
5. To whom are directors' and officers' duties owed?
6. What defences are available to a director accused of breach of duty?
7. When a director enters into a contract with his or her own corporation, what precautions should be taken to ensure the validity of the contract?
8. What is meant by intercepting a corporate opportunity?
9. In what circumstances might a director have a conflict of interest?
10. What is insider trading?
11. Who is an "insider"?
12. What is meant when one says that a minority shareholder is (a) "locked in" and (b) "frozen out"?
13. What are the principal rights attached to shares in a corporation?
14. What is the difference between an ordinary resolution and a special resolution?
15. What are class rights?
16. What is a proxy? How are proxies appointed?
17. Do shareholders have any right to receive a dividend if the corporation is profitable?
18. What are "preemptive rights" in relation to a corporation's shares?
19. Are there any restrictions on the directors' powers to issue new shares?
20. What information must be provided in a corporation's annual financial statements?
21. What is the role of a corporation's auditor? To whom is the auditor's duty owed?
22. What are a corporation's "documents of record"?
23. Do shareholders owe any duty to their corporation?
24. Explain the "appraisal remedy" and the "derivative action"?
25. What are the principal differences between the "just and equitable" winding-up procedure and the oppression remedy?
26. What matters are commonly dealt with in shareholder agreements? Why?

CASES AND PROBLEMS

1. Continuing Scenario

Ashley incorporated her restaurant business under the Canada Business Corporations Act and the articles of incorporation named three directors to the board. Ashley was one, her father Jim was another, and her accountant Kristen was the third. During the last directors' meeting, Ashley suggested it was time for a third restaurant location. Currently, she has one location in downtown Toronto, and another in the west end near a congested shopping area. She would like to place a new one in the busy tourist area of Niagara Falls. Kristen volunteers to investigate possible restaurant sites, as she was raised in Niagara Falls. At the next meeting, Kristen presents a report on the Niagara Falls tourist district, identifying three possible sites available for lease. Two are in view of the falls, but Kristen recommends the more expensive location without a view because it is better for parking. Ashley and Jim defer to Kristen's expertise without making any independent investigation; Jim arrived late to the meeting without even reading the report. They instruct her to make the deal. When the lease is signed Kristen sends a copy to Ashley's lawyer, Brendan. It shows the landlord as 123456 Ontario Limited. Brendan completes a corporate search of the company and is surprised to discover that Kristen is also a director of the landlord company. Further investigation reveals that the rent being charged is well above the typical rent for equivalent premises. What advice should Brendan give Ashley about Kristen and the Niagara Falls lease? Explain the legal principles involved.

2. Ten years ago, Davidson and Farmer formed a corporation to develop a fishing lodge that they had bought (in the name of the corporation). They each owned 50 shares in the corporation. There were no other shareholders, and Davidson and Farmer were the only directors.

   They worked hard to develop the business, which became quite successful. No dividends were ever paid by the corporation, but Davidson and Farmer had paid themselves generous salaries for their work as directors.

   Last year, Davidson died. In his will he left his entire estate to his sister, Eriksen. Before her marriage, Eriksen had occasionally worked at the lodge (for a salary), but recently had not been involved in the business.

   Shortly after Davidson's death, Farmer (as the sole surviving director) appointed his niece, Greenberg, as a director to fill the vacancy on the board. Next, Farmer and Greenberg passed a resolution issuing one share in the corporation to Greenberg for a consideration of $10 000 (which was estimated to be approximately 1 percent of the value of the business).

   In response to requests from Eriksen, Farmer has agreed to register the transfer of Davidson's shares to her, but has made it clear that he will not agree to her becoming a director and that he intends to continue running the business together with Greenberg.

   Does Eriksen have any remedy?

3. Until three years ago, Slater was the sole shareholder and director of Lockley Quarries Ltd., a small corporation that owned a quarry and produced trimmed limestone blocks. Then an opportunity arose to purchase a second quarry at a very good price. Slater did not have sufficient funds and persuaded Mason to come into business with him and to help finance the purchase of the new quarry. As a result, Mason became a 40 percent shareholder and a director of Lockley Quarries. Slater and Mason got on well together and the business prospered.

   A few months ago, Slater was approached by an old friend, Chalker, who proposed that they—Chalker and Slater—purchase and operate a gravel pit that had come on the market. Slater agreed and a new corporation was formed to acquire the gravel pit, with Chalker and Slater as equal shareholders and directors.

   Mason has learned of the dealings between Slater and Chalker. He considers that he should have been given the opportunity to participate in the new gravel pit venture. Do you agree? Does Mason have any remedy against Slater?

4. Normin Inc. is a large mining corporation, incorporated under the CBCA, the shares of which are publicly traded and are listed on the Toronto Stock Exchange. It has recently been conducting extensive exploration on land acquired in the Canadian Arctic.

   Late in the afternoon of March 31, Normin's chief executive officer, Baffin, received a fax from the mineralogist in charge of the explorations. The fax, headed "Highly Confidential," informed Baffin that a giant deposit of tin had been discovered. It appeared that it would be fairly easy to extract and would be extremely profitable.

Baffin at once informed as many of the directors and senior officers as he could contact. After some discussion they agreed to prepare a press release the next morning. However, the following occurred on the evening of March 31:

(a) One of the directors, Banks, telephoned his broker, Charles, and, without giving any reason, instructed Charles to buy as many Normin shares on his account as he could, provided the price did not exceed $30 per share. The following morning, Normin shares opened on the exchange at $28.75. Charles bought 10 000 shares for Banks, at prices between $28.75 and $29.50.

(b) Another director, Melville, contacted her brother, Parry, and offered to buy his shares in Normin. Parry had acquired the shares some years before, but had since lost interest in the investment and had several times asked Melville if she would like to buy them. Melville offered to pay $29 per share, and Parry accepted and transferred his 15 000 shares to his sister.

(c) Hudson, a senior executive of Normin, told his bridge partner, Frobisher, that she should tell no one and buy Normin shares as soon as possible. Frobisher bought 2000 shares on the exchange the following morning, at $29.25 per share.

At midday on April 1, the press release was published, giving details of the find. Trading on the exchange became brisk, and by the end of the day the price of Normin shares had reached $47.50.

Discuss the possible liability of any of the individuals mentioned, and the remedies, if any, that Parry and other shareholders who sold their shares before midday on April 1 might have.

5. For many years Sergei (a widower) owned and ran a large farm, initially by himself and later with the help of his four children. Eight years ago, on the advice of his accountant and his lawyer, he decided to transfer the farm to a corporation and, with a view to keeping the farm in the family (and to saving taxes), to make his children shareholders in the corporation.

A corporation, Eisenstein Farms Inc., was formed with two classes of shares. As consideration for the transfer of the farm to the corporation, Sergei received 1000 Class "A" preferred shares, with each share carrying one vote. The four children—Galina, Ivan, Oleg, and Tanya—each received 100 Class "B" common shares, also carrying one vote per share, for which they paid $10 per share. Two of the children—Galina and Ivan—had left home and no longer took an active part in running the farm. The other two—Oleg and Tanya—continued to live with their father and work on the farm, and were made directors and employees of the corporation along with Sergei. No dividends were paid by the corporation in respect of the common shares (Sergei received dividends on his preferred shares), but Sergei, Oleg, and Tanya all received salaries.

A year ago things started to turn sour. Oleg married, and neither Sergei nor Tanya got on with his wife. They complained that he was neglecting the farm and spending most of his time helping his wife with her business. (Oleg denied this.) After a series of heated arguments, Oleg threatened to resign from the board of directors and to quit his employment with the corporation. Sergei and Tanya immediately accepted his "resignation." Since then, relations between them have deteriorated further. Oleg is no longer receiving any remuneration from the corporation, either as a director or employee, has been excluded from directors' meetings, and has been given no information about the corporation's business or affairs.

Oleg considers that he has been treated unfairly. Does he have any remedy?

6. Aldeburgh Inc. is a corporation incorporated under the CBCA. It has never issued shares to the public. It owns a large piece of land and a number of vacation cottages fronting on a lake some distance north of Queensville, Ontario. The property has produced relatively little income in the past.

Until recently, Aldeburgh had four shareholders—Balstrode, Crabbe, Orford, and Swallow—who each owned 25 percent of the issued shares. Balstrode, Crabbe, and Orford are the directors of the corporation. Swallow is retired and has taken little interest in the business.

A few months ago, the three directors received a tip from Grimes (a friend of theirs and a prominent local politician) that a large corporation, Maltings Developments Inc., was proposing to establish a major recreational complex along the lake and was almost certain to get permission for the development. When the news became public, he suggested, the price of land in the area would soar.

Balstrode, Crabbe, and Orford held a directors' meeting and resolved that Aldeburgh should try to buy up as much property in the area as possible. They did not tell Swallow the good news. Aldeburgh borrowed as much money as it was able to and bought a number of lots.

During the same period, the following events occurred:

(a) Balstrode approached Swallow and persuaded Swallow to sell her his shares. She said nothing about the proposed development.

(b) Crabbe personally bought one lot for herself (without disclosing the fact to anyone), which she was later able to resell to Maltings at a large profit.

(c) Orford bought one lot (in the name of a numbered company) that she resold to Aldeburgh at a quick profit, without disclosing that she was the beneficial owner.

(d) Grimes bought several lots himself, which he later sold to Maltings at a large profit.

Soon afterward, Maltings offered to buy all the land owned by Aldeburgh or, alternatively, to buy all its shares. An agreement was reached to sell the shares, with the result that all the Aldeburgh shares are now owned by Maltings, and the shareholders of Aldeburgh all made large profits on the sale of their shares.

Maltings has now discovered the secret activities of Balstrode, Crabbe, Orford, and Grimes. Swallow has learned about the profit that Balstrode made on the resale of his shares.

Who is liable for what? To whom? On what grounds? How can liability be enforced?

Additional Resources for Chapter 26 on the Companion Website

(www.pearsoncanada.ca/smyth)

In addition to pre- and post-tests, mini-cases, and application exercises, the Companion Website includes the following province-specific resources for Chapter 26:

- **Alberta:** Corporate Management; Directors' Liability; Alberta Investment Management Corporation; Oppression Remedy; Shareholders' Remedies
- **Atlantic Provinces:** Derivative Actions and the Oppression Remedy; Directors' Liability
- **British Columbia:** Corporate Dissolution; Derivative Actions; Due Diligence and Limited Liability; Liability of Management; Liability of Shareholders; Oppression Remedy; Shareholder Remedies
- **Manitoba/Saskatchewan:** Corporate Internal Liability
- **Ontario:** Business Judgment Rule; Codes of Conduct; Conflict of Interest; Corporate Governance; Directors' and Officers' Duties; Directors' and Officers' Liability; Disclosure; Fiduciary Duty; Insider Trading; Oppression Remedy; Sarbanes-Oxley Act

Chapter 27

Corporate Governance: External Responsibilities

This chapter examines the relationship between the corporation and the outside world—its customers, creditors, employees, competitors, potential investors, and the general public. The corporation is an artificial person that is responsible for its own actions. Still, it acts only through its directors, officers, and agents, and so requires multiple layers of accountability.

In this chapter we examine such questions as:

- How does legislation protect creditors, investors, and other persons who deal with, or are affected by, corporations?

- To what extent is a corporation liable for the acts of its directors, officers, and agents?

- How do corporations enter into contracts?

- Can a corporation be negligent?

- Can a corporation commit a crime?

- To what extent may directors, officers, or agents be held personally liable for acts done, or not done, in the name of a corporation?

- What liability is imposed on corporate officers under environmental legislation?

LIABILITY ARISING FROM BUSINESS RESPONSIBILITIES

The business activities of a corporation affect many external groups or **stakeholders**. These stakeholders include the corporation's creditors, employees, consumers, competitors, potential public investors, and the public at large. In this chapter we discuss some of the legislative measures that protect these stakeholders by setting standards and imposing liability on the corporation itself, as well as on its directors and senior officers. The circle of liability includes outside experts working on behalf of the corporation, such as accountants, underwriters, and lawyers.

stakeholders groups affected by the business activities of a corporation

Types of Liability

Some of the protective requirements are proactive, such as requiring disclosure of information or licensing of professionals; these are designed to prevent problems before they occur. Other legislative measures are punitive, such as imprisoning for insider trading; these are designed to punish bad behaviour and deter others.

Breach of a legislative requirement may attract civil, regulatory, and even criminal liability. Stakeholders are empowered to enforce some of these standards through civil causes of action. Chapter 26 focused primarily on breaches of duty that create civil causes of action. This chapter expands on the civil causes of action available to stakeholder groups and considers the criminal and regulatory offences created to punish corporations, directors and officers, and others when wrongdoing occurs.

Criminal offences address the most serious types of misconduct and result in the most serious form of punishment: imprisonment. These offences are most often (but not always) found in the Criminal Code.[1]

As discussed first in Chapter 1, subordinate legislation may give a specialized government agency or tribunal, such as the securities commission, the task of implementing programs, monitoring conduct, or investigating misconduct. As part of this responsibility, it implements rules known as regulations to establish the standard of acceptable conduct. These regulations often assign a penalty for failure to comply. The rules and penalties are known as **regulatory offences**. Regulatory offences resemble traditional criminal law because, in order to protect the public interest, they punish those who ignore the rules; however, the penalties are usually less serious. Therefore, the approaches to proving regulatory and criminal offences are similar but not identical.[2]

regulatory offences less serious offences created by government regulation through specialized legislation, agencies, and tribunals

The Requirement of Mens Rea

For most offences, the prosecution must prove beyond a reasonable doubt not only that the accused actually did commit the act described in the offence but also that he had the intention to do it—that is, the "intent." The prosecution must establish that the accused had mens rea (a guilty mind)—that is, a guilty intention or guilty knowledge. For example, a person who possesses stolen goods has not committed an offence if he did not know that they were stolen.

The Presumption of Intent
For regulatory offences, we find that the courts and statutes tend to reduce the need for mens rea. It may be enough to show that if any ordinary person would or should have realized that his conduct was an offence, the wrongdoer

---

[1] The federal government is given legislative jurisdiction over criminal law, and the Criminal Code, R.S.C. 1985, c. C-46, this comprehensive act contains most criminal offences. Other statutes may create offences dealing with the specific topic of that legislation.

[2] Some statutory regulations also create civil liability so that a wrongdoer may have to compensate a party harmed by its breach.

will be convicted. For instance, if a person drove his car at 80 km/h through a crowded shopping area, he would very likely be convicted of the regulatory offence of careless driving, even if he did not intend to harm anyone.

For these strict liability offences, the courts hold that there is a presumption that the accused, in committing the wrongful act, had the requisite mens rea. However, the accused can overcome the presumption by persuading the court that he acted with reasonable care in the circumstances.

Absolute Liability   No mens rea at all is required for a conviction of an absolute liability offence. It is enough for the prosecution simply to prove that the accused committed the wrongful act—for example, a driver in a vehicle with a faulty speedometer who is unaware that he is exceeding the speed limit. Absolute liability offences are typically confined to statutes dealing with public health and safety.

This third class remains a very limited one. The Supreme Court of Canada has held that an absolute liability offence may be unconstitutional when conviction could lead to an accused being imprisoned.[4] For more information on this topic, see the Companion Website.

CHECKLIST

Classification of Offences

The Supreme Court of Canada has classified offences into three categories, depending upon the importance of the penalty and the language of the statute. They are summarized as follows:[3]

- **Mens rea offences**, where the prosecution must demonstrate the existence of some positive state of mind such as intent, knowledge, or recklessness.

- **Offences of strict liability**, where the commission of the prohibited act raises a presumption that an offence has been committed, leaving it open to the accused to avoid liability by proving that he took all reasonable care (due diligence).

- **Offences of absolute liability**, where it is not open to the accused to excuse himself by showing that he was free of fault. Simply doing the act makes one guilty of the offence.

---

mens rea offences   offences where the prosecution must establish a "guilty mind" on the part of the defendant

offences of strict liability   offences where there is a presumption of guilt unless the defendant can show that he or she took reasonable care

offences of absolute liability   offences where the absence of fault is no defence

This chapter examines situations where each type of liability (civil, regulatory, and criminal) and various types of offences (mens rea, strict liability, and absolute liability) are used to protect stakeholders.

PROTECTION OF CREDITORS

Implications of Limited Liability

When an unincorporated business becomes insolvent, the creditors are entitled to whatever assets are available. If a deficiency remains, they may look to the personal assets of the owner: the sole proprietor or partners. In a corporation, however, a creditor's rights are limited to only the assets owned by the corporation itself. If those assets are inadequate,

---

[3] See *R. v. City of Sault Ste. Marie* (1978), 85 D.L.R. (3d) 161 (S.C.C.); *R. v. Kanda* (2008) 88 O.R. (3d) 732, ONCA 22(CanLII).

[4] *Re B.C. Motor Vehicle Act*, [1985] 2 S.C.R. 486; *R. v. Transport Robert (1973) Ltee* (2003), 234 D.L.R. (4th) 546. *R. v. Wilson* 2014 ONCA 212 (holding the adult seatbelt offence is only strict liability not absolute).

the creditor normally has no further remedy against the owners: the shareholders.[5] For this reason, legislatures and courts have established rules to assure creditors that the corporation's assets will not be wasted. As noted in Chapter 26, if the assets are wasted, a creditor may have a claim against the directors and officers personally for breach of their duty of skill and care.

Preservation of Capital

Except for financial institutions such as banks and insurance companies, there are no minimum issued capital requirements for corporations.[6] Legally, a corporation may carry on business with a share capital of $1. Of course, it would be difficult to obtain credit with only a nominal equity investment. Therefore, corporations raise capital by selling shares to shareholders, and this value helps a lender assess the creditworthiness of the corporation.

It is difficult to devise legal rules that will protect creditors from the risk of extending credit to a corporation that becomes unable to pay. The primary concern of the law has therefore been to ensure that a corporation's stated capital (money raised from the sale of shares) is not improperly reduced by preferring the rights of shareholders over those of creditors.

On the winding up of a corporation, its creditors are entitled to have the assets applied in satisfaction of their claims before any capital is returned to the shareholders. Sometimes there is not enough money to pay all creditors and return capital to the shareholders. The CBCA (and those provincial statutes modelled on it) set out rules to protect creditors. The rules are divided into two types: rules that prohibit any payment by the corporation to its shareholders that renders the corporation's liquid assets insufficient to pay the existing claims of creditors; and rules that restrict the return of capital to shareholders even when the corporation might still be left with sufficient liquid assets to pay its creditors. Any improper payment of dividends or return of capital will trigger personal liability of the directors.

The Solvency Test

Shareholders usually receive money from the corporation by way of dividends or, in certain circumstances, through redemption or repurchase by the corporation of its own shares. If payments by the corporation in either of these instances are made when the corporation is insolvent, or would have the effect of making the corporation insolvent, the directors may be held personally liable to the corporation for the deficiency.[7]

The effectiveness of this rule depends upon the definition of **insolvency** that is used. Two factors must be considered: a corporation is deemed insolvent if the realizable value of its assets has become less than its total liabilities, or if it is unable to pay its debts as they become due.[8]

insolvency having liabilities in excess of the realizable value of one's assets or being unable to pay one's debts as they fall due

---

[5] There are a few limited exceptions to this principle: see the discussion under "Exceptions to Limited Liability" in Chapter 25. As discussed in Chapter 26, creditors may claim against directors and officers personally if the insolvency arises from breach of their duty of skill (except in Ontario): See *Peoples v. Wise*, [2004] 3 S.C.R. 461; Ontario Business Corporations Act, R.S.O. 1990, c. B.16, s. 134.

[6] As to banks, see Bank Act, S.C. 1991, c. 46, ss. 59–35. Rules regulate three forms of capital: type one includes common and preferred shares, and these must be subordinate to depositors and general creditors and have fully discretionary non-cumulative dividends without maturity dates or incentives to redeem. Common shares must have preemptive rights. See Christopher C. Nicholls, "The Regulation of Financial Institutions: A Reflective but Selective Retrospective" (2011), 50 Can. Bus. L.J. 129–55.

[7] See e.g. CBCA, ss. 42, 118(2)(c).

[8] The federal Bankruptcy and Insolvency Act provides, additionally, an "after the fact" test that permits a trustee in bankruptcy to apply for a court inquiry in respect of dividends paid within 12 months preceding bankruptcy to determine whether the dividend rendered the corporation insolvent and that authorizes the court to give judgment to the trustee against the directors, jointly and severally, in the amount of such dividend: Bankruptcy and Insolvency Act, R.S.C. 1985, c. B-3, s. 101.

The Maintenance of Capital Test In theory, the money paid into the corporation by shareholders should be preserved as far as possible within the corporation as a capital fund, available for absorbing business losses so that creditors (and in some cases, preferred shareholders) may be paid in full. The maintenance of capital test therefore goes beyond the solvency test. It applies in the following cases.

(i) Dividends The CBCA, in section 42, provides that a corporation may not pay a dividend if there are reasonable grounds for believing that (a) the corporation is, or would be after the payment, unable to pay its liabilities as they become due (the solvency test), and (b) the realizable value of the corporation's assets would thereby be less than the aggregate of its liabilities and its stated capital of all classes (maintenance of capital test). In other words, after the dividend has been paid, the corporation's net assets must not be less than the amount of its stated capital. The effect of this rule is that dividends may only be paid out of profits. A corporation's net assets will only exceed its stated capital if either it has undistributed profits or its assets have increased in value.

ILLUSTRATION 27.1

A corporation originally issued shares for a total of $5 million. For several years it made a profit, in the sense that its revenues exceeded its expenditures. However, its capital assets have depreciated in value. It now has net assets of exactly $5 million. Despite having a trading profit, it cannot pay a dividend. Payment of a dividend in these circumstances will expose the directors to personal civil liability.

(ii) Return of Capital A corporation may return a part of its capital to its shareholders either by making a pro rata payment to each shareholder—in which case the effect is essentially the same as the payment of a dividend—or by buying back the shares of some of its shareholders. A return of capital, like the payment of a dividend when there are no profits or capital gain out of which to pay it, reduces the funds available to meet the claims of creditors and, if the corporation should subsequently become insolvent, would give a preferred repayment to shareholders before the creditors' claims are met.

The CBCA provides that a corporation may repay capital to its shareholders provided that it will be able to satisfy the solvency and maintenance of capital tests.[9] This rule is reasonable since shareholders may have contributed substantially more capital than the corporation really needs. So long as creditors are protected, there is no reason to insist that excess capital remain in the corporation.

Corporations may also redeem or purchase their own shares for a number of specified reasons, subject to solvency requirements to protect creditors.[10]

Loans to Shareholders, Directors, and Employees Although the CBCA does not prohibit the corporation from lending money to shareholders, directors, or officers, there are income rules that include the loan as income to the borrower.[11] The concern behind considering restricting such loans, especially those that are interest-free, is that they might amount to an indirect return of capital and might deprive the corporation of liquidity. Recent focus on ethics in corporate governance has revived this concern.

---

[9] CBCA, s. 38. To do so requires a special resolution.

[10] CBCA, ss. 30–7. Reducing the stated capital recognizes that the corporation's net assets have decreased in value. As such, it is not objectionable (s. 38(1)(c) and (3)).

[11] There are exceptions for corporations in the business of lending money, for loans repaid within one year, and for employee home or share purchases. See Canada Revenue Agency Bulletin IT421R2; Income Tax Act, R.S.C. 1985, c. 1, 5th Supp. s. 15, 246.

PROTECTION OF EMPLOYEES

Chapter 18 dealt with employee/employer relationships in detail and so here we make only brief mention of some employee protections. In Chapter 26, we discussed the personal liability of directors for up to six months' wages of employees. Employee safety is protected through occupation health and safety legislation, which requires ongoing monitoring and creates regulatory offences for unsafe workplaces. Injured employees are covered by no-fault insurance through workplace safety legislation. Human rights legislation and tribunals create civil liability and regulatory offences to promote non-discriminatory work environments.

PROTECTION OF CONSUMERS AND COMPETITORS

Businesses compete with each other for customers so the protection of these two stakeholder groups naturally fits together. Their protection involves multiple provincial and federal statutes. Consumer protection is a matter of provincial jurisdiction, and all provinces have legislation limiting unfair business practices and creating regulatory offences and civil causes of action. The federal Competition Act addresses unfair conduct among competitors and improper marketing and advertising strategies. The Competition Act creates both regulatory and criminal offences. Chapter 3, "Government Regulation of Business," deals with the competitive business environment in detail.

PROTECTION OF INVESTORS

Securities Legislation

Canadian securities regulation is a matter within provincial jurisdiction. Each Canadian province has a Securities Act, under which a government board is created, known in most of the provinces as the **securities commission**. The securities commission operates as the regulating, licensing, and enforcing agency charged with ensuring that the requirements of the Act are complied with. All 13 provincial and territorial securities commissions cooperate on creating standardized regulation, policy, and administration through a single organization known as the Canadian Securities Administrators and the creation and adoption of "National Policies" and "National Instruments".[12]

securities commission the statutory authority appointed to supervise the issue of securities to the general public, the operation of the securities industry, and the stock exchange

---

CONTEMPORARY ISSUE

One Federal Securities Regulator

Over the past decade, there has been a push to change Canadian securities regulation. Proposed reforms would see the 13 provincial securities commissions replaced by a single federal regulator. Advantages include consistency, efficiency, lack of duplication, and cost effectiveness.

The 2008 chaos in world financial markets led then federal Finance Minister Jim Flaherty to announce that "it was time to move toward a single securities regulator . . . [that] reflects regional interests, yet can quickly respond with a single voice to market developments."[13] Not all provinces supported the consolidation. Alberta and Quebec oppose a national securities regulator, and both the Alberta and Quebec Courts of Appeal held that the proposed federal legislation would be an unconstitutional intrusion into an area long recognized

>

---

[12] Many of the National Rules and Policies have a common number identification system.

[13] Eoin Callan and Barbara Shecter, "Crisis Used to Push for Single Regulator," *National Post*, October 30, 2009, at 1, reporting speech by Jim Flaherty on October 29, 2008.

as within provincial jurisdiction.[14] The constitutional question was argued before the Supreme Court of Canada, and the Supreme Court held that the federal government lacked the constitutional authority to impose a single regulator; provincial agreement and cooperation was required.[15]

Questions to Consider

1. Should a single securities regulator be a legal issue, a financial issue, or a national security issue?

2. Which federal and provincial constitutional powers are relevant to this reform?

3. How could this reform improve Canada's position when dealing with international financial issues?

Sources: Eoin Callan and Barbara Shecter, "Crisis Used to Push for Single Regulator," *National Post*, October 30, 2009, at 1, reporting speech by Jim Flaherty on October 29, 2008; Wise Persons' Committee (Committee to Review the Structure of Securities Regulation in Canada), It's Time—WPC Final Report, December 17, 2003, www.wiseaverties.ca/main_en.html; Ian B. Lee, "Balancing and Its Alternatives: Jurisprudential Choice, Federal Securities Legislation and the Trade and Commerce Power" (2011) 50 Can. Bus. L.J. 95–128.

Objectives of Securities Legislation   Provincial securities legislation assigns governmental control over the public offering of shares to provincial securities commissions.[16] The goals of the legislation are to ensure the integrity, fairness, and efficiency of the market and promote investor confidence in it.[17] To accomplish these goals, securities commissions have three key areas of responsibility:

- the securities industry
- the corporations offering their shares to the public
- the stock exchanges within the provinces (for example, the Toronto Stock Exchange in Ontario)[18]

Canadian securities legislation employs several devices to achieve the objectives described above. They include

1. registering or licensing those engaged in various aspects of the securities business,
2. requiring the issuer of securities to the public to file a prospectus with the securities commission,
3. regulating continuous disclosure by public corporations, and
4. as discussed in Chapter 26, setting standards of corporate governance for public corporations.

The Securities Industry

Licensing   Registering people engaged in the securities industry is an important device for ensuring ethical conduct. Licensing is done on an annual basis, and each securities commission has authority under its provincial statute to revoke, suspend, or refuse to renew the licence of anyone when, in its opinion, such action is in the public interest. Operating without a licence is a criminal offence. Depending upon the jurisdiction, a licence may be required of persons engaged in a wide variety of activities. Those affected include brokers (who buy and sell securities as agents), investment dealers (who buy and sell securities as principals), broker dealers (who may act as either principal or agent in the promotion

---

[14] *Reference Re Securities Act (Canada), Quebec (Procureure generale) v. Canada (Procureure general)*, 2011 ABCA 77; 2011 QCCA 591.

[15] *Reference Re Securities Act*, 2011 SCC 66.

[16] See e.g. Securities Act, R.S.O. 1990, c. S-5; R.S.B.C. 1996, c. 418; R.S.A. 2000, c. S-4; R.S.Q. c. V-1.1.

[17] Securities Act, R.S.O. 1990, c. S-5, s. 1.1.

[18] *Ibid.*, ss. 21–21.11. It is beyond the scope of this chapter to review the detailed regulations governing stock exchanges.

of companies), securities issuers (companies issuing their securities directly to the public without the intermediate services of investment dealers), salespeople employed by any of these businesses, and investment counsel and securities advisers. Self-regulating organizations such as the Investment Industry Regulatory Organization of Canada (IIROC) and the Mutual Fund Dealers Association of Canada (MFDA) work with their members to meet requirements of the securities commission.

The Public Corporation: Public Offering

Corporate Governance   Before any company may make a public offering, the internal structure of the company must meet the high standards of corporate governance required by the securities regulations. As discussed in Chapter 26, the internal structure requirements include a larger board of directors than private companies, audit committees, mandatory independent compensation-setting, and audited financial statements, among other things. The specific requirements are based on the following fundamental principles:

- Independence: Decision-makers should be free of conflicts.
- Transparency: Decisions should be made through an open process.
- Disclosure: Information should be available to the public.
- Accountability: Decision-makers should be responsible for their conduct.
- Checks and balances: Internal structures should bring irregularities to light.

Prospectus   No corporation, partnership, or other form of business organization may issue securities to the public unless a **prospectus** has been filed with and approved by the securities commission of the province or territory in which the securities are to be sold. Prospectus requirements are an attempt to ensure that prospective investors have the relevant facts about a corporation before deciding to invest in it. In most instances, an investor is entitled to a copy of the prospectus before buying securities and may rescind the purchase contract if he or she does not receive the prospectus.

prospectus   the document that a corporation is required to publish when inviting the public to subscribe for its securities

The contents of a prospectus are prescribed by statute or in regulations and are too detailed to describe here. It is sufficient to note that the prospectus must include the following items (among others):

- a full description of the securities to be offered (either shares or bonds), with a statement of their voting rights, preference, conversion privileges, and rights on liquidation
- the nature of the business carried on
- the names, addresses, and occupations of the directors
- the proposed use of the proceeds from the issue of securities
- details of any share options to be given by the corporation[19]
- the remuneration of the underwriter
- the dividend record of the corporation
- the particulars of property and services to be paid for out of the proceeds of the issue
- recent audited financial statements
- a certificate of accuracy signed by the CEO, CFO, the promoter, and two directors

The prospectus must contain full, true, and plain disclosure of all material facts. Failure to do this is a strict liability regulatory offence, punishable by a fine of up to $5 million

---

[19] A share (or stock) option is a right to subscribe for shares in the corporation at a fixed price within a specified time, given by a corporation as consideration for the payment of money, the rendering of services (often the services of directors), or any other valuable consideration. The option becomes valuable at any time before expiry that the market price exceeds the option price.

and/or five years in prison. Knowingly falsifying a prospectus is a criminal offence.[20] It also attracts civil liability on behalf of the corporation and personal liability for the directors, officers, underwriters, and any person that signed the prospectus.[21] There are some exceptions to the requirement of a prospectus for sales to **non-public purchasers**.

non-public purchasers purchasers that are not members of the general public, such as banks, insurance companies, and municipal corporations

Continuing Disclosure
Control by the securities commission extends not only to issues of new securities but also to trading in already outstanding securities. Public corporations must make annual and quarterly filings[22] with the securities commissions, disclosing financial and other material information, including

■ audited financial information with management's discussion and analysis;[23]

■ notice of any change in auditor;

■ notice of any change in corporate structure and intercorporate relationships;

■ descriptions of internal corporate governance practices, including details of directors' identities and independence, compensation setting and nomination processes, existence of a code of ethics, and ongoing assessment of governance effectiveness;[24]

■ notice of material changes relating to the business, operations, or capital of an issuer that would reasonably be expected to affect the share price; and[25]

■ acquisitions of other businesses.

CEOs and CFOs must certify the accuracy of all information contained in the annual filing. The Canadian Securities Administrators operate the System of Electronic Disclosure for Analysis and Retrieval (SEDAR) that gives the public electronic access to the filings of public companies.

Other provisions contained in the legislation

■ make the proxy a more effective means of registering shareholders' opinions,[26]

■ require publication of insiders' transactions involving their corporation's shares[27] (as noted in Chapter 26),

■ authorize civil actions against insiders, and

■ make insider trading a regulatory and criminal offence.[28]

The Canadian Securities Administrators operate the SEDI, the System of Electronic Disclosure by Insiders, where insiders may submit their reports online and the public may view the reports.

The Public Accounting Industry
Reliable financial information is at the heart of investor protection. In 2004, the Canadian Securities Administrators imposed requirements for accountants engaged in public accounting or auditing. National Instrument 52-108 created the Canadian Public Accountability Board (CPAB), responsible for setting new standards for public accountants, overseeing their work, and promoting quality independent

---

[20] Securities Act, R.S.O. 1990, c. S-5, s. 122(1)(b); Criminal Code, R.S.C. 1985, c. C-46, s. 400.

[21] Securities Act, R.S.O. 1990, s. 130. In 2007, the Supreme Court of Canada declined to impose civil liability under the Ontario Securities Act with respect to a forecast contained in a prospectus: *Kerr v. Danier Leather Inc.*, 2007 S.C.C. 44.

[22] This filing is called the Annual Information Filing (AIF), and its contents are prescribed by National Instrument 51-102.

[23] Securities Act, R.S.O. 1990, c. S-5, ss. 75–83.

[24] National Instrument 58-101, Disclosure of Corporate Governance Practices.

[25] The Supreme Court of Canada considered the distinction between material change and material fact in a 2007 decision: *Kerr, supra*, n. 21.

[26] Securities Act, R.S.O. 1990, c. S-5, ss. 84–8(1).

[27] *Ibid.*, ss. 106–9.

[28] *Ibid.*, ss. 76, 122(1)(c), 134.

auditing. The CPAB carries out regular inspections of audit firms as a means of quality control and has disciplinary power. Only those public accountants recognized by and in good standing with the CPAB may provide an auditor's report for the purposes of the securities commission.

Secondary Market Liability   Civil liability for inaccurate information extends beyond the information relating to the initial public offering to ongoing release of information during secondary trades in securities. The word *secondary* refers to the "resale" of existing shares between investors as distinct from initial purchases from the corporation. Securities legislation[29] creates a civil cause of action for any person who trades in a corporation's shares while inaccurate public information remains uncorrected. The corporation, its directors, officers, and influential insiders may all be held liable for damages suffered by a shareholder or former shareholder. Independent experts such as lawyers, accountants, or financial analysts may also be liable if their reports contain misrepresentations. The plaintiff need not prove that he or she relied on the misrepresentation, just that it remained uncorrected at the time of the transaction. A due diligence defence is available and damage awards are capped. For more information on this topic, see the Companion Website.

Takeovers and Reorganizations   Another important objective of securities legislation is to give shareholders who have received a **takeover bid** for their shares sufficient information and time to assess the merits of the bid.[30] Takeover provisions include a requirement for disclosure of the number of shares in the offeree corporation held by the offeror corporation and its officers, and details of recent trading in those shares. In addition, the directors of an offeree corporation are required to issue a **directors' circular** to the shareholders setting out, among other things, their own intentions with respect to the takeover offer, and details of any arrangements made with the offeror corporation concerning their continuance in office or compensation for loss of office. However, this legislation does not apply to all corporations; in particular, takeovers of small private corporations are not regulated.

Both corporate and securities legislation contain detailed and complex rules dealing with mergers, with various types of corporate reorganization, and with winding up. Needless to say, no one should make a decision in one of the above areas without expert assistance. The problems involved usually concern creditors' rights, the effects of taxation, the relevance of competition legislation, and the rights of various classes of shareholders, in addition to the general economic consequences for the corporations involved.

> **takeover bid**   an offer by one corporation to acquire all or a substantial part of the shares of another corporation
>
> **directors' circular**   a document required to be issued to the shareholders by the board of directors when a takeover of a widely held corporation is proposed

PROTECTION OF THE PUBLIC INTEREST

Protecting the public interest is a difficult challenge that involves balancing the interests of multiple stakeholders. Usually government is responsible for protecting the public, and the interests of the public are diverse. For example, it is in the public interest that people are employed, that employees earn a competitive wage, that business has access to foreign markets, that domestic products are competitive with imports, and that the environment is preserved. It is impossible to establish standards that protect all of the interests of the public, and difficult choices must be made. Government uses regulation to balance the interests of business, stakeholders, and the public at large. The remaining part of this chapter will examine civil, regulatory, and criminal liability in place to protect the public interest without designating a particular stakeholder. By way of example, this chapter will look at the environmental regulatory scheme. The legal requirements should be viewed as a minimum standard of behaviour that management is encouraged to exceed.

---

[29] Securities Act, R.S.O. 1990, c. S-5, s. 138.1; Ontario was the first province to create secondary market liability in its securities act. Others have followed: B.C. (s. 140.1) Nov. 22/07; Alta. (s. 211.03) Dec. 31/06; Sask. (s. 147) Feb. 15/08; Man. (s. 174) Nov. 11/06; Que. (s. 225.3) Nov. 9/07; N.S. (s. 146) Nov. 15/07; N.B. (s. 161.1) May 30/07; Nfld. (s. 138.1) Jun. 1/07; P.E.I. Nov. 2/07.

[30] *Ibid.*, ss. 89–105.

As discussed in Chapter 1, corporate social responsibility is a principle that suggests that corporate management should consider not only what is profitable and legal but also what is ethical when making strategic decisions. Corporations should consider the interests of the communities in which they operate and the public as a whole. Corporate social responsibility is gaining support within the business community. According to one commentator, "hard-edged capitalism is falling out of favour in the nation's executive suites."[31]

One explanation for this change is, again, the Enron debacle, which demonstrated the dangers of corporate greed. Another lies in the collapse of the market in hi-tech stocks, which suggests that the "bottom line" is not necessarily an accurate measure of corporate success and viability. Hopefully, the lesson will finally be learned from the worldwide collapse of the credit and asset-backed paper markets in 2008.

The Canadian Democracy and Corporate Accountability Commission's 2002 report made a series of recommendations, including the following:

- The law should make it clear that social responsibility considerations may be taken into account by corporate management.
- The structure of corporate governance should be modified to include a corporate social responsibility committee of the board of directors.
- Large corporations should be required to publish a "social audit."
- The law should protect employees against adverse action taken against them for "whistle-blowing."
- Canadian corporations should be required to adhere to a core set of human rights standards in their operations overseas.

- Business schools should develop mandatory courses focusing on corporate social responsibility.

Unfortunately, few of the above described recommendations were implemented. Many blame the continued primacy of the profit motive on the structure of executive compensation. Traditionally, executive compensation schemes link performance bonuses to the profitability of the company rather than long-term stability or corporate social responsibility. Bonuses are often in the form of stock options, whose values rise with the price of corporate shares. This structure reinforces "bottom-line" decision-making with a view to short-term profit and may even encourage inflated financial reporting.

The US $700 billion Wall Street bailout, approved by Congress in October 2008, may change executive compensation. Some of the conditions attached to the bailout were limits on executive severance packages and clawbacks of bonuses. Critics argued that no bailout at all would have been the best way to teach a lesson about greed.

Questions to Consider

1. Are these recommendations realistic? Can ethics be legislated?

2. Is there really a conflict between the long-term interests of a corporation and a requirement of social responsibility?

3. How should executive compensation be restructured to encourage socially responsible behaviour?

Sources: Canadian Democracy and Corporate Accountability Report, The New Balance Sheet: Corporate Profits and Responsibility in the 21st Century, January 2002; Stephen Gandel, "How Washington's Bailout Will Boost Wall Street Bonuses," *Time*, October 27, 2008, www.time.com/time/business/article/0,8599,1853846,00.html?imw=Y.

CIVIL LIABILITY OF CORPORATIONS

As already noted, corporations are exposed to civil liability—liability toward a plaintiff, typically to pay damages for harm done through committing a tort, breaking a contract, or breaching a statutory duty. In the early parts of this chapter and in Chapter 26, we focused on civil liability triggered by statute. We complete this discussion by commenting on key issues in tort and contract.

Liability in Tort

A corporation acts through its human agents. Where a corporation is held liable in tort, it is almost invariably on account of a negligent or wrongful act committed by an employee, agent, or officer, and its liability is vicarious.[32] As with any defendant, liability depends

---

[31] *Toronto Star*, May 18, 2002, at H6.

[32] Vicarious liability is discussed in Chapter 4. It is possible for a corporate employer to have primary liability in tort, without the employee being personally liable: see *Edgeworth Construction Ltd. v. N.D. Lee & Associates* (1993), 107 D.L.R. (4th) 169.

on the plaintiff's proving each element of the tort. The corporation might be the only defendant liable if the elements of the tort are committed by separate employees. As noted in Chapter 2, class actions have levelled the playing field between business and the small stakeholder. Business can no longer ignore minor consequences of its actions.

Contractual Liability

Generally speaking, a corporation is liable for the contracts made by its agents in the ordinary course of business under the rules of agency (discussed in Chapter 17). Agents of a corporation acting within their actual or apparent authority[33] bind the corporation to contracts made with third parties.

The bylaws and other internal corporate documents will define agency powers and the proper process for contract ratification. Still, the courts have held contracts to be enforceable even when the proper rules were not followed. In the absence of notice of an irregularity or of suspicious circumstances, everything that appears normal may be relied upon by an outsider, and the contract will bind the corporation.[34] This principle is known as the **indoor management rule**,[35] and is really just an application of the apparent authority principle in agency law. An innocent third party may rely upon the regularity of a corporate act, just as he may rely upon the apparent authority of an agent, if it is reasonable for him to do so in the circumstances.

indoor management rule the principle that a person dealing with a corporation is entitled to assume that its internal procedural rules have been complied with unless it is apparent that such is not the case

---

ILLUSTRATION 27.2

W, the chief executive officer of A Ltd., negotiates a contract to buy equipment from B Inc. for $1 million. The bylaws of A Ltd. provide that any contract involving expenditure of more than $50 000 must be approved by the board of its Japanese parent company. That approval has not been obtained.

Consequently, W is acting outside the scope of her actual authority. Can B Inc. enforce the contract?

The answer is "yes" unless B Inc. knew of the restriction in the bylaws and that the approval of the parent board had not been obtained.

As noted in Chapter 26, certain corporate documents must be filed in a government office and are available to the public for examination. Even so, the public is not deemed to have notice of the contents of those documents. Section 17 of the Canada Business Corporations Act (CBCA) provides:

> No person is affected by or is deemed to have notice or knowledge of the content of a document concerning a corporation by reason only that the document has been filed by the Director or is available for inspection at an office of the corporation.[35A]

A contracting third party who actually has read or knows the contents of a restriction will be bound by it, but in saying this we are merely restating the common law rule of agency—a third party who knows of an express restriction between the principal and agent cannot claim to rely upon an apparent authority that ignores the restriction. For large or important contracts, one should not take the indoor management rule for granted. Third parties usually hire corporate lawyers to review the corporation's documents of record and ensure that all necessary authorizations have been obtained.

---

[33] Where a director or officer acts within the scope of her usual, or apparent, authority, even though she has no actual authority to do so, the corporation will be bound unless the third party knew (or ought to have known) of the lack of authority.

[34] *Royal British Bank v. Turquand* (1856), 119 E.R. 886.

[35] This rule receives statutory recognition in the Canada Business Corporations Act (CBCA), R.S.C. 1985, c. C-44, s. 18. Subsequent references in this chapter are to the CBCA unless otherwise stated.

[35A] *Section 17 of the Canada Business Corporations Act (CBCA).*

Pre-Incorporation Contracts

pre-incorporation contract a purported contract made in the name of a corporation before it comes into existence

As noted in Chapter 17, at common law, a corporation could not ratify a **pre-incorporation contract**—that is, a contract made on its behalf before it came into existence. If a "contract" was made in the name of a corporation even one day before it came into existence, the purported contract is of no effect and a new contract would have to be negotiated once the corporation was formed. Further, the individual who purported to contract on behalf of the corporation normally could not be held to the contract either, since the intention was to contract with the corporation.[36]

The CBCA and the provincial statutes based on it have changed this, by providing that a person who enters into, or purports to enter into, a written contract in the name of or on behalf of a corporation before it comes into existence is personally bound by the contract and is entitled to its benefits.[37] In addition, a corporation may, within a reasonable time after it comes into existence, adopt a written pre-incorporation contract. In that event, the corporation is bound by the contract and is entitled to its benefits, and the person who purported to act in the name of the corporation ceases to be liable.[38]

The clear intention is that, whether or not the contract is adopted, it will be enforceable by the other party. To prevent unfair manipulation by a corporation and a contractor, the Act (section 14(3)) gives the court power to apportion liability between the corporation and the contractor in any manner it thinks fit.

A promoter acting on behalf of a corporation before it comes into existence may avoid personal liability and waive any benefits under the contract when the contract includes an express term that the promoter will not be bound by the agreement.[39] Figure 27.1 illustrates some of the possible relationships involved in pre-incorporation contracts.

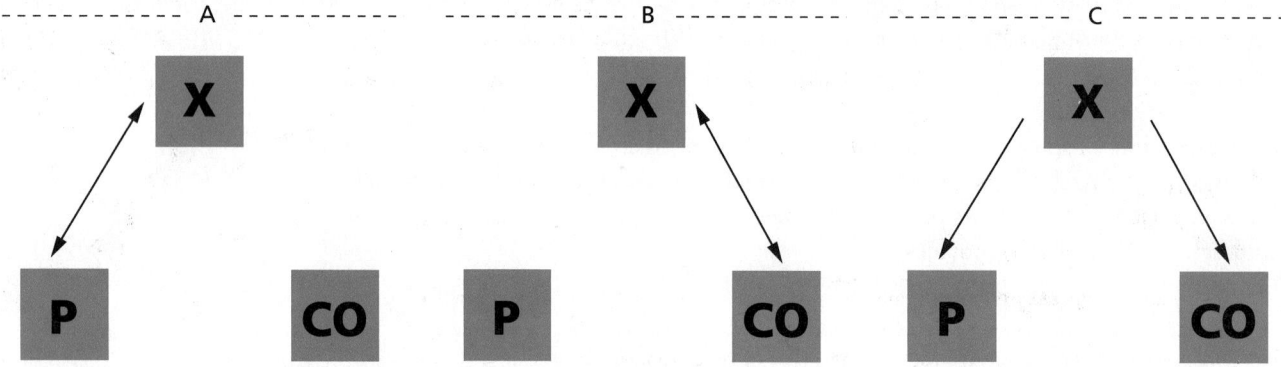

Figure 27.1 Pre-incorporation Contracts

In situation A, the promoter, P, has entered into a contract with a third party, X, in the name of corporation CO, before it has come into existence. The effect is to create a contract between P and X. In situation B, the corporation has since been formed and has adopted the contract. There is now a contract between CO and X, and P is no longer a party to it. In situation C, the court has, on an application by X, apportioned liability, and both P and CO are liable.

---

[36] See *Delta Construction Co. Ltd. v. Lidstone* (1979), 96 D.L.R. (3d) 457. The individual may be liable for breach of warranty of authority: this is discussed in Chapter 17. Contrast *Kelner v. Baxter* (1866), L.R.2 C.P. 174, where the court found that there was an intention that the individual contractor be bound.

[37] S. 14(1).

[38] S. 14(2). There are some variations from province to province. For example, Ontario does not restrict the rule to written contracts. In the case of a corporation incorporated under the CBCA, it would seem that the effect of an oral pre-incorporation contract would be decided under the common law rules: see *Kettle v. Borris* (2000), 10 B.L.R. (3d) 122.

[39] S. 14(4). To be effective, there must be an express exclusion of liability: see *Szecket v. Huang* (1998), 168 D.L.R. (4th) 402; *1394918 Ontario Ltd. v. 1310210 Ontario Inc.* (2002), 57 O.R. (3d) 607.

CRIMINAL LIABILITY OF CORPORATIONS

A corporation can be charged with, and convicted of, an offence under the Criminal Code in the same way as a natural person.[40] For example, in one of the leading Canadian cases on corporate criminal liability, a number of corporations were convicted of conspiracy in rigging bids for a construction contract.[41]

The Nature of Corporate Criminal Liability

How Can Corporations Commit Crimes?   The characteristics of corporations present special problems for criminal liability:

(a) Most criminal offences require the Crown to prove both that the accused actually committed the act and that there was some level of intent—but a corporation has neither a physical body with which to carry out the act nor a "mind" of its own capable of forming an intent.

(b) If convicted, a guilty person's punishment is often imprisonment—but a corporation cannot be imprisoned.

The consequences of (b) are that, if convicted, a corporation will be fined or ordered to refrain from certain conduct or, in rare cases, dissolved—all relatively painless forms of punishment. Charges may also be laid personally against directors and senior officers of a corporation, a topic considered later.

With regard to (a), it may be impossible to convict at all if the offence requires intent. Regulatory offences, which are most often strict or absolute liability, are much more popular vehicles to address corporate conduct. However, the public interest demands that serious corporate misconduct attract criminal consequences, and so the courts and legislature (through the Criminal Code) have created rules that attribute individual acts and intent to the corporation.

The "Directing Mind" Principle   The earliest test used to establish corporate criminal liability was the "directing mind" principle. It held that corporate mens rea existed if a guilty mind could be found in an "active director" or the "directing mind or will" at the "the centre of the personality of the corporation."[42] This meant a person with policy making authority rather than just supervisory or implementation responsibilities.

What if the wrongful act is committed not by a senior officer or director but by a person lower down in the hierarchy? Canadian courts tended to find an act committed by an employee who has significant responsibilities, such as the head of an important department or a branch, to be an act of the corporation itself. But the courts would not hold the act of a low-level employee, for example, a clerk who cheated a customer, to be the act of the corporation. However, drawing the line between those employees and officers whose acts will be identified as acts of the corporate employer and those whose acts will not be so identified is not an easy task.

CASE 27.1

A corporation was charged with fraud, contrary to section 338 of the Criminal Code, as a result of the activities of the manager of its used-car sales division in turning back odometers. Although the corporation had issued written instructions that such practices should not occur, the corporation was convicted. The manager had sole responsibility for managing the division and, in that respect, was "the directing will" of the corporation: His acts were those of the corporation.[43]

---

[40] There are some crimes that it would seem to be impossible for a corporation to commit—for example, bigamy. Corporations have been convicted of manslaughter in some common law jurisdictions.

[41] *R. v. Canadian Dredge & Dock Co. Ltd.* (1985), 19 D.L.R. (4th) 314 (S.C.C.).

[42] *Lennard's Carrying Co. Ltd. v. Asiatic Petroleum Co. Ltd.*, [1915] A.C. 705.

[43] *R. v. Waterloo Mercury Sales Ltd.* (1974), 49 D.L.R. (3d) 131.

By contrast, it has been held that a truck driver employee of a waste disposal corporation was not a "directing mind" of the corporation, and his conduct did not make the corporation liable for an offence that required mens rea.[44]

The Criminal Code's New Test   Recent amendments to the Criminal Code have clarified the situation and increased corporate exposure to criminal liability,[45] with these important changes:

- First, the physical act and mental intent of any offence are no longer required to be found in the same person. Now, corporate criminal liability can be established in multiple employees with different responsibilities.

- Second, the physical act may be committed by virtually any employee or contractor or an aggregate of them.

- Third, corporate mens rea may be found not only in those with policy making authority but also in a **senior officer** or employee with operational responsibilities.[46]

The type of intent required by the offence will determine the rule:

1. In the case of an offence that requires the prosecution to prove negligence (for example, criminal negligence causing death), an organization is a party to the offence if (a) one of its representatives, acting within the scope of his authority, is a party to the offence, and (b) the senior officer responsible for that aspect of the organization's activities departs markedly from the standard of care that could reasonably be expected to prevent the representative from being a party to the offence.

2. In the case of an offence that requires the prosecution to prove intent (other than negligence), an organization is a party to the offence if one of its senior officers (a) acting within the scope of her authority and with the intent, at least in part, to benefit the organization, is a party to the offence, or (b) with the required intent directs the work of other representatives of the organization so that they commit the specified act or omission, or (c) knowing that a representative of the organization is about to be a party to the offence, does not take all reasonable measures to stop them.

For more information on this topic, see the Companion Website.

Criminal Code Offences

As already noted, an organization may be charged with any offence, but the Criminal Code contains some offences that are particularly applicable to corporate conduct:

- Fraud (section 380) and fraud affecting the public markets (section 380(2)).

- Market manipulation—false market activity or manipulating share prices (section 382).

- Distributing false prospectuses, statements, or accounts (section 400).

- Criminal negligence causing bodily harm—any duty imposed by common law or statute may form the basis of this offence (section 219). Section 217.1 specifically imposes a duty on those who direct (or supervise) work to protect workers and the public.

---

senior officer   a representative who plays an important role in establishing an organization's policies or is responsible for managing an important aspect of its activities, including the directors, the CEO, and the CFO of a corporation

---

[44] *R. v. Safety-Kleen Canada Inc.* (1997), 145 D.L.R. (4th) 276. The corporation was found guilty of another strict liability, regulatory offence.

[45] Criminal Code, R.S.C. 1985, c. C-46, ss. 22.1, 22.2. A broader range of organizations are now exposed to criminal liability, including partnerships, trade unions, and municipalities (s. 2).

[46] *Ibid.*, s. 2 (as amended).

- Whistle-blower retaliation—includes threatening, disciplining, demoting, or firing a whistle-blower or potential whistle-blower (section 425.1).

Sentencing

Criminal sentences should denounce the conduct, protect the public, deter the offender and others, repair the harm done, rehabilitate the offender, encourage assumption of responsibility by the offender, and promote public confidence (section 718). Sentencing a corporation is a challenge: it cannot be imprisoned, and a fine is a punishment ultimately borne by the shareholders. The Criminal Code addresses corporate penalties in the following ways:

- Criminal fines cannot be deducted as a cost of doing business.
- Specific aggravating and mitigating factors for organizations include degree of planning, public costs, depletion of corporate assets, other regulatory offences, and convictions of corporate representatives (section 718.21).
- Probation for corporations may involve the development of policies and procedures and supervision of management by a court-appointed compliance officer (section 732.1).

CRIMINAL LIABILITY OF DIRECTORS AND OFFICERS

As we noted in Chapter 25, the principle of limited liability does not protect directors from liability for torts or breaches of fiduciary duty that they personally commit. In principle, directors, like employees, are liable for their own torts that are committed in the course of performing their duties, even though the corporation may also be vicariously liable.[47]

The question we address here is whether directors (and officers) should be held criminally liable for offences committed by their corporation while under their supervision.

One view is that simply holding corporations liable is not in itself a strong enough deterrent to ensure effective enforcement of regulatory schemes. A large corporation with sufficient assets might consider the penalty merely a "licence"; it pays the fine and carries on with its activities. The corporation's manager may pass the costs on to the consumer through higher prices or to the corporation's shareholders through lower dividends. At the other extreme, a corporation may be merely a "shell" with virtually no assets to pay its fine; those who control the enterprise walk away from it and start up a similar activity using a new corporation.

A strong argument can be made that effective deterrence requires that the individuals responsible for the offence, as well as the corporation, be punished directly. Directors and senior officers should be criminally liable for offences committed by their corporation. As has been said, ". . . the threat of jail sends a clear message to corporate executives that they are not immune to criminal sanctions. . . . Incarceration is one cost of business that you can't pass to the consumer."[48]

---

[47] The fact that they are acting in the corporation's interest does not by itself protect them from personal liability; see *ADGA Systems International Ltd. v. Valcom Ltd.* (1999), 43 O.R. (3d) 101; *Lana International Ltd. v. Menasco Aerospace Ltd.* (2000), 181 D.L.R. (4th) 534. For a comprehensive analysis, see Flannigan, "The Personal Tort Liability of Directors" (2002) 81 Can. Bar Rev. 247.

[48] See Nelson Smith, "No Longer Just a Cost of Doing Business . . ." (1992) 53 La. L. Rev. 119 at 126.

However, there are problems in attempting to prosecute individuals. In complex organizations, where responsibility is shared among a number of persons, identifying with any certainty who is responsible and who can—and should—be convicted of committing an offence is often difficult. These two factors—a belief that directors and officers and not just corporations should be made liable and that it may be difficult to obtain convictions—have led legislatures to

- enact express provisions making senior officers and directors liable,
- require CEOs and CFOs to certify annual filings, and
- make the grounds for individual liability much broader.

LIABILITY FOR ENVIRONMENTAL OFFENCES

Liability for environmental offences provides a good illustration of the wider general issue of corporate and director liability, as well as being a question of major practical concern to corporations and their officers. Environmental protection involves air, water, and land pollution; preservation of natural resources; acceptable use, transportation, and disposal of waste, toxins, and dangerous goods; and assessment of the environmental impact of any activity. These topics are regulated by municipal, provincial, and federal governments. The Canadian Environmental Protection Act, 1999, and most of the corresponding provincial statutes create strict liability offences for corporations and their directors and officers when the Act or its regulations are breached. For these offences, establishing due diligence is the only defence.[49] It is beyond the scope of this chapter to review the voluminous federal and provincial legislation[50] on this topic; instead, we will discuss basic principles common to many environmental offences.

What Standard of Skill and Care Must Be Met?

The challenge for the accused is to meet what is generally acknowledged to be a steadily rising standard of care. The enterprise must demonstrate that it has an effective system to prevent offences, must monitor the results of the system, and must improve the system if problems occur. A corporation cannot escape liability simply by delegating responsibility to an employee. Any employee's actions may be treated as those of the corporation itself. If not, the corporation will have failed to put in place an effective system of control.

Each enterprise whose activities may pose a risk must show that it reviews its current monitoring system frequently and makes reasonable efforts to remain current on technological change in the field.

The Expertise Required of Directors and Senior Officers   Should a higher standard of care and skill be imposed if directors or senior officers have expertise in the area where a hazardous activity is carried on? Suppose a senior officer is an engineer with long experience in the field. Would she be expected to take precautions against a risk that an accountant would unlikely be aware of? A common-sense view would say "Yes." There

---

[49] See, for example, *R. v. MacMillan Bloedel Ltd.* (2002), 220 D.L.R. (4th) 173.

[50] Examples: Federal Legislation: Canadian Environmental Protection Act, 1999 (CEPA 1999) and the Canadian Environmental Assessment Act, 2012 (CEAA); British Columbia: Environmental Management Act, 2003, Environmental Assessment Act, 2002, Waste Management Act, 1996, Water Act, 1996; Alberta: Environmental Protection and Enhancement Act, 2000, Natural Resources Conservation Board Act, 2000, Climate Change and Emissions Management Act, 2003, Water Act, 2000; Ontario: The Environmental Protection Act, 1990, The Environmental Bill of Rights, 1993, The Environmental Assessment Act, 1990, The Waste Diversion Act, 2002, The Ontario Water Resources Act, 1990.

is some support for this view in a 1983 case, *R. v. Placer Developments Ltd.*,[51] where the accused corporation allowed diesel fuel to escape into fishing waters. The court seemed to expect greater diligence from the corporation's experienced senior officers:

> The accused was required to possess, and did possess sufficient expertise to be aware of the potential risk to the environment posed by a fuel system in northern mining camps. . . . [T]he accused had the opportunity and knowledge in the field, through their employees Mr. Morganti with thirty two months' field experience and Mr. Goddard with twenty five years' experience, to influence the offending conduct on the site.[52]

On the other hand, the court suggested that even if the accused firm did not possess that expertise, it would still be liable for the offence:

> The greater the likelihood of harm, the higher the duty of care. . . . Anyone choosing to become involved in activities posing danger to the public or to the environment assumes an obligation to take whatever measures may be necessary to prevent harm. . . . Unless equipped with appropriate professional skills, no one ought to undertake any activity involving a danger to the public. . . . Mining in the north requires not only an expert knowledge of mining, but equally important, an expert appreciation of the special problems caused by remote operations in northern environments.[53]

These observations suggest that the accused corporation was caught in one of two ways. Either it failed to employ the expertise it ought to have known that it needed in order to manage the hazardous activity, or if it did employ the necessary expertise, then the person with that expertise failed to use the professional care and skill attributed to him. Perhaps an unskilled employee who had been sent to the site would not be found personally liable because he could not have been expected to anticipate the risk, but the employer enterprise would then be caught by its failure to send an employee with the necessary skills to carry out the task.

Who Should Be Found Liable?

Those in Charge of an Activity   Apart from the liability of an enterprise itself, any person who actually commits an offence is personally liable, even when he was acting within the scope of his authorized activities. The issues become more difficult when legislatures enact regulations to make senior officers and directors liable because they are considered to be in charge of an activity, even though they have not participated directly in the offence. The task is to find appropriate language, sufficient to capture those who should bear the blame and yet absolve those who were innocent. With this purpose in mind, our legislatures have tended to use two phrases: the first makes liable those who "cause or permit" a hazardous substance to be discharged;[54] the second makes liable "any officer, director or agent . . . who directed, authorized, assented to, acquiesced in, or participated in the commission of an offence."[55]

So, who are these persons? In order to "permit" or "acquiesce in" an activity such as disposing of hazardous materials, one must have a significant role in controlling those who actually carry it out. Permitting or acquiescing has no meaning if the person charged is merely one who learned about the activity but could do nothing to affect it. Accordingly, the prosecution must first persuade a court that a person charged had effective powers and

---

[51] *R. v. Placer Developments Ltd* (1983), 13 C.E.L.R. 42 (Y.T. Terr. Ct.).

[52] *Ibid.*, at 49.

[53] *Ibid.*, at 52.

[54] See e.g. Fisheries Act, R.S.C. 1985, c. F-14, s. 36(3).

[55] Canadian Environmental Protection Act, S.C. 1999, c. 33, s. 280.

responsibility. A senior officer and director who is personally in charge of a hazardous procedure (that is, she is the person to whom those performing the activity report on a regular basis) presents a clear case of effective control and responsibility for the activity. For more information on this topic, see the Companion Website.

The Difficulty of Determining Responsibility   What about an independent or "outside" director—a person who was elected to the board because of his experience in financial services and who faithfully attends board meetings twice a year? He reads all the material sent to him and asks probing and useful questions at meetings. However, when it comes to environmental concerns, he relies on the reports and assurances given by the senior officer, the "inside" director, who is in charge. Should the independent director also be considered to share in control? Did he "permit" or "acquiesce in" an offence that occurred under the supervision of the inside director?

Since the law is not intended to punish innocent and reasonably diligent people, it would seem that ordinarily an independent director in those circumstances ought not to be held personally liable for the offence. This view seems to be confirmed by the current case law: Virtually all the charges brought under Canadian legislation have been against inside directors. However, in many situations there is not a clear-cut division between insider and outsider: For instance, did the outsider receive any reports that disclosed questionable practices to a reasonable person in his position? Were answers to his questions evasive? What should an outsider do when he feels uneasy with the information provided?

We should also note that not all insiders are in control of an operation, or directly involved in it, simply because they are directors and senior officers within the enterprise. Should an inside director who learns second-hand about a potential problem in another branch of the enterprise be expected to undertake a personal investigation, outside her normal responsibilities? These questions remain very difficult and depend upon the degree of involvement of the specific director in the particular circumstances of each case.

CASE 27.2

A corporation's premises contained a large, toxic, chemical waste storage site with many decaying, rusting, and uncovered containers; soil samples revealed concentrations of various dangerous chemicals. The prosecution charged the corporation with permitting the discharge of liquid industrial waste that could impair the quality of the groundwater and contaminate the environment. Charges were also laid against three directors.

All the defendants argued that they had shown due diligence in carrying out their duties. Ormston, J., found that the corporation—Bata Industries—did not establish a proper system to prevent the escape of toxic substances and did not take reasonable steps to ensure the effective operation of even their faulty system. The corporation was found guilty.[56]

With respect to the directors, the court provided a useful summary of the questions that should be asked in assessing a director's defence of having shown "due diligence" in his particular circumstances:

(a) Did the board of directors establish a pollution-prevention "system"—that is, was there supervision or inspection?

(b) Did each director ensure that the corporate officers had been instructed to set up a system sufficient within the terms and practices of the industry of ensuring compliance with environmental laws, to ensure that the officers report back periodically to the board?

(c) The directors are responsible for reviewing the environmental compliance reports provided by the officers, but are justified in placing reasonable reliance on reports.

(d) The directors should substantiate that the officers are promptly addressing environmental concerns brought to their attention by government agencies or other concerned parties including shareholders.

(e) The directors should be aware of the standards of their industry and other industries that deal with similar environmental pollutants or risks.

>

---

[56] *R. v. Bata Industries Ltd.* (1992), 9 O.R. (3d) 329 at 362. Sentences were appealed and fines were reduced [1993] O.J. No. 1679.

(f) The directors should immediately and personally react when they have notice that the system has failed.

Of the directors, Mr. Bata was found to be "the director with the least personal contact with the plant" where the offence occurred. His responsibilities were at other plants and "he attended on-site . . . once or twice a year to review the operation and performance goals. . . ." Although Mr. Bata did not personally review the operation when he was on site,

> He responded to the matters brought to his attention promptly and appropriately. He had placed an experienced director on site and was entitled in the circumstances to assume that . . . [the on-site director] was addressing the environmental concerns. . . . He was entitled to rely upon his system . . . unless he became aware the system was defective.[57]

Accordingly, Mr. Bata was acquitted.

In contrast, another director, Mr. Marchant, was found to have more responsibility than Mr. Bata but less than a third director who was held to be "on site." Mr. Marchant came to the facility once a month and toured the plant. The court found that the problem was brought to his "personal attention" and that

> [H]e had personal knowledge. There is no evidence that he took any steps after having knowledge to view the site and assess the problem. . . . [D]ue diligence requires him to exercise a degree of supervision and control that demonstrate that he was exhorting those whom he may be normally expected to influence or control to an accepted standard of behaviour.

Mr. Marchant was found guilty and ordered to pay a fine. At trial, Bata was ordered not to pay the fine on behalf of the convicted director. The Court of Appeal set aside the prohibition on indemnification by the company. It agreed that the court had the power to make such an order but disagreed that the circumstances justified it here.[58]

What Should the Punishment Be?

A further question is, what punishment should a court impose? Generally, corporations are fined according to the seriousness of the breach and the harm caused. Directors and officers receive somewhat smaller fines, but in extreme cases, they may be sentenced to prison terms.[59]

CASE 27.3

A corporation, Varnicolor Chemical Ltd., reprocessed and disposed of industrial wastes. Waste materials escaped from its toxic disposal site into the groundwater, and moved toward a river that was used as a source of drinking water for downriver communities. The corporation took no action to clean up the spill; rather, it was the Ministry of the Environment that did so at an estimated cost of $2.5 million. Both the corporation and one of its directors, Mr. Argenton, were charged with offences.[60]

Mr. Argenton was "the only officer and director to take an active part in the operations and actual management of . . . [Varnicolor]. He was clearly, at all relevant times, the sole directing mind of the company. . . ." Accordingly, his actions were the actions of the corporation. Mr. Argenton pleaded guilty. Charges against the corporation were stayed. The court discussed in detail the criteria for sentencing Mr. Argenton. It described the purposes of sentencing as protecting the public, deterring and rehabilitating offenders,

promoting compliance with the law, and expressing public disapproval.

It summarized the factors that should affect the severity of a sentence as follows:

- *The nature of the environment affected:* The concern is both with the sensitivity of the environment affected and the gravity of the risk. In this case, the drinking water of residents in the area would be contaminated.
- *The extent of the damage actually inflicted:* Here, there was a high cost of cleanup.
- *The deliberateness of the offence:* In considering this factor, the court stated:

> Not only was Mr. Argenton involved on site in the operations of the company, but he was as well involved in the negotiations which preceded the issuance of the certificate of approval by the Ministry . . . for the Varnicolor site. . . . Therefore, as a result of this

>

---

[57] *Ibid.*, at 364.

[58] *R. v. Bata Industries Ltd.*, [1995] O.J. No. 2691 at para. 30 (Ont. C.A.).

[59] For a case in which both a fine ($76 000) and a jail sentence (30 days) were imposed, see *R. v. Romaniuk* (1993), 112 Sask. R. 129 (Q.B.).

[60] *R. v. Varnicolor Chemical Ltd.*, [1992] O.J. No. 1978.

active involvement and in depth knowledge of the business operations, it is clear that Mr. Argenton was uniquely in a position to be aware . . . of . . . the requirements of the Ministry. Mr. Argenton has indicated that he found these requirements to be unclear and ambiguous; however, it was at all times open to . . . [him] to seek clarification. . . . There is no indication . . . that he made any attempts to do so. In a number of respects, Mr. Argenton acted in defiance of the requirements. . . . Such violations are in effect a breach of trust on the part of the person to whom such a certificate has been granted and, as such, jail terms are an appropriate penalty to ensure compliance with the law by both the person being sentenced and society in general.

■ *The attitude of the defendant:* In this case, Mr. Argenton did not voluntarily report the escape of toxic waste, nor did he show a cooperative attitude.

■ *Attempts to comply with the regulations:* There was no evidence of a cleanup at the site by Varnicolor or by Mr. Argenton, and indeed, the corporation had become inactive.

The maximum sentence under the Environmental Protection Act was 12 months. The court found that the conduct of the defendant amounted to a serious breach of the Act and sentenced him to eight months in jail.

The Business Consequences

What conclusions can we draw from these developments, and how will they affect the conduct of business? Clearly, there is a public consensus that protecting the environment is a high priority, in response to which legislatures have created extensive regulatory schemes. Meeting the standards under these schemes imposes substantial costs on many businesses, especially on resource industries and manufacturing and transportation enterprises. The most important challenge is to meet the requirements effectively and efficiently.

INTERNATIONAL ISSUE

International Environmental Regulation

Environmental protection is a global problem because we share the environment with the rest of the world, and pollutants move invisibly across national boundaries. Unfortunately, standards vary by jurisdiction, but a number of strategies are being employed to establish universal standards of environmental protection. The Canadian Environmental Protection Act, 1999, attempts to extend its reach beyond Canadian borders by addressing international air and water pollution (Part 7, Division 6). The Minister is empowered to regulate polluters and collect clean-up costs. Section 166(4) recognizes the jurisdictional limits of this power:

If the air pollution referred to in paragraph (1)(a) is in a country where Canada does not have substantially the same rights with respect to the prevention, control or correction of air pollution as that country has under this Division, the Minister shall decide whether to act under subsections (2) and (3) or to take no action at all.

Governments try to create uniform standards around the world by entering into conventions and treaties, such as the Kyoto Protocol. The Kyoto Protocol (an amendment to the United Nations Framework Convention on Climate Change, ratified by Canada in 2002) requires greenhouse gas emissions to be reduced by 6 percent (from 1990 levels) by 2012.

After failing to reach past targets, Canada announced that it would not accept new targets beyond 2012. The United States is a signatory of Kyoto but never ratified it.

The International Organization for Standardization, a non-governmental organization, has also created an environmental standards program. It established a voluntary certification standard for environmental management systems (ISO 14000). Participating organizations complete environmental audits of their business processes and design customized systems for effective environmental management.

The United Nations Global Compact designates 10 guiding principles of corporate social responsibility, three of which relate to environmental issues:

■ to encourage the development of environmentally friendly technologies

■ to support the precautionary principle (prove activity does no harm)

■ to promote greater environmental responsibility

Organizations voluntarily agree to comply with the principles and publicly report their progress. Canadian participants in the Global Compact include Bell Canada Enterprises, Enbridge, Hydro-Québec, Talisman Energy Inc., and Petro-Canada.

>

Question to Consider

1. What measures are most likely to achieve uniform global environmental protection?

Sources: Doug Struck, "Canada Altars Course on Kyoto," Washington Post, May 3, 2006; "ISO 14000—Environmental Management Standards," International Organization for Standardization, http:// www.iso.org/iso/home/standards/management-standards/iso14000 .htm; "Essential Background," United Nations Framework Convention on Climate Change, http://unfccc.int/essential_background /items/2877.php; United Nations Global Compact website, www .unglobalcompact.org; Mike De Souza, "Canada wants new climate deal by 2015: Environment Minister" Ottawa Citizen, December 8, 2011.

Strategies to Manage the Legal Risks

For many businesses, regulatory compliance is a full-time job. Meeting securities reporting and disclosure obligations requires knowledge of and familiarity with the many layers of regulations that apply to public companies generally and to specific industries. The best approach is to hire a compliance officer who will put a system in place, meet day-to-day obligations, monitor compliance, confirm accuracy of filings, and respond early to irregularities.

Disclosure requirements exist so that outside stakeholders can protect themselves by making informed decisions. Creditors, shareholders, and potential investors should use the information available to them.

Environmental accidents can result in insurmountable financial obstacles for a business. Steps should be taken to avoid a catastrophe. First, businesses need to review their practices to learn whether any of their activities create a concern about health, safety, or the breach of environmental regulations. They must seek the best advice available and keep up-to-date with current technology and best practices adopted across their industry. They are expected to take every reasonable precaution to meet the latest standards.

Second, once they are informed about the risks, they should review their insurance coverage with a view to obtaining the maximum risk protection that is available and affordable. The cost of insurance coverage leads to the third stage. If, after obtaining the best advice for implementing safety systems and obtaining insurance, a particular business activity ceases to be competitive, then it becomes necessary to decide whether to continue that branch of operations.

Third, directors and officers cannot turn a blind eye to operational details or suspicious behaviour. Concerns should be expressed and investigated. Directors should educate themselves about the business's activities and risks so that informed decisions are made and personal liability is avoided.

QUESTIONS FOR REVIEW

1. What is meant by the "indoor management rule"?
2. Is a person dealing with a corporation expected to know the contents of the corporation's articles of incorporation or its bylaws?
3. Can a corporation adopt a pre-incorporation contract? What is the effect of its purporting to do so?
4. What are the possible legal consequences when a false statement is made in a prospectus?
5. Are there any restrictions on a corporation paying dividends to its shareholders?
6. Why are there restrictions against a corporation returning capital to its shareholders?
7. What are the principal objectives of securities legislation?
8. What is a prospectus?

9. What liability is triggered by a false or misleading prospectus?

10. What is the difference between strict liability and absolute liability?

11. Can a corporation be convicted of a criminal offence? How?

12. Does the principle of limited liability protect a director from criminal liability in the course of performing her duties?

13. What standard of care and skill is expected of corporate directors in relation to environmental offences?

14. Who may perform an audit for a public corporation?

CASES AND PROBLEMS

1. Continuing Scenario

Adam is the new chef at Ashley's Restaurant and his specialty is mozza sticks, deep fried in vats of peanut oil. At the end of each week, Adam dumps the vats of old oil in the back parking lot and fills the pots again. Erin, the dishwasher, has watched Adam dump the oil for months and is sure this is not the proper way to dispose of used oil so she calls the Ministry of Environment (MOE) hotline and asks some questions about disposal of cooking oil. After the call, the MOE arrives to investigate and issues a "stop order" prohibiting any further dumping of oil and orders Ashley, personally, as director of the company, to "clean up" the soil under the parking lot. The estimated cost of cleanup is $25 000. Ashley is upset and fires Erin for "going behind her back" to the MOE. What advice will Ashley's lawyer, Brendan, give about her personal liability for the cleanup and firing Erin?

2. About a year ago, MacIntosh, a qualified accountant with substantial business experience, met Kellerman, the owner of a number of business ventures. Kellerman persuaded MacIntosh that her experience would be valuable to him in his own business activities, which he was seeking to expand. He persuaded MacIntosh to invest a substantial proportion of her savings in his ventures, in return for which it was agreed that she would become a shareholder and director of Kellerman's corporation, "AJP Enterprises Inc." In the course of their discussions, MacIntosh was shown books of accounts and other records that appeared to relate to AJP Enterprises.

MacIntosh transferred $50 000 into a bank account in the name of AJP Enterprises Inc. In return, Kellerman gave her a document assigning to her one-half of his shares in that corporation.

Soon afterward, MacIntosh negotiated an arrangement with an advertising agency, Occidental Broadcasts Ltd., to provide radio and television advertising for the AJP business in return for monthly payments of $2000. Occidental was paid (out of the AJP Enterprises bank account) for the first three months, but has not been paid since then, although the company continued to provide advertising services for a further five months.

When Occidental eventually demanded payment of a further $10 000, MacIntosh discovered that

(a) the AJP Enterprises bank account contained only $1.73,

(b) Kellerman had disappeared, and

(c) there was no record of any corporation by the name of "AJP Enterprises Inc.," or any similar name, having been incorporated in any jurisdiction in Canada.

Can MacIntosh be held personally liable for the $10 000 claimed by Occidental?

3. Rainbow Sails Ltd. is a corporation incorporated under the CBCA. It has three shareholders, Brown, Green, and White, who are also the directors of the corporation. White acts as CEO, though he has never been formally appointed to that position.

The articles of the corporation included the following provisions (among others):

■ The business of the corporation is restricted to the manufacture, buying, and selling of sailboats, and under no circumstances is the corporation to engage in the manufacture, buying, or selling of mechanically powered boats or other craft.

- Any contract or proposed contract involving an expenditure in excess of $5000 must be approved unanimously by the board of directors.

Some months ago, White sold, on behalf of Rainbow, a new sailboat that they had manufactured to a customer, Mermaid Marinas Inc. White agreed to accept from Mermaid a small motorboat in part exchange. Although White had no difficulty reselling the motorboat, Brown and Green were angry when they learned of the transaction since they both had an aversion to power boats. They warned White not to enter into any other similar transactions; otherwise, they would deprive him of his powers as CEO.

Some weeks later, Mermaid's sales manager asked White if Rainbow would be interested in buying a floatplane that Mermaid no longer had much use for. White thought the plane was an excellent bargain and agreed to pay $15 000 for it. White took delivery of the plane, and the next day he crashed it.

Brown and Green refuse to countersign any cheque to Mermaid, and Mermaid is now threatening to sue for the price of the plane.

Is Rainbow liable to pay for the plane? If so, does Rainbow have any right of action against White personally?

4. Queensville Quality Cars Ltd. is a large automobile dealership specializing in the sale of both new and used cars and light trucks. Until recently its used-car division was managed by Murphy, who was in charge of a dozen salespersons and mechanics. Murphy was not a director of the corporation.

Following several complaints from customers, alleging, among other things, that the odometers on used cars appeared to have been altered, the managing director of the corporation, Patel, sent written instructions to all division heads (including Murphy) warning them that tampering with odometers is a serious offence and that any officer or employee of the corporation found doing so would face instant dismissal.

Notwithstanding the warning, Murphy instructed one of his mechanics, Ferreira, to change the odometer on a car that the corporation had recently obtained as a trade-in. Ferreira did so, the car was resold, and the purchaser subsequently complained about the condition of the car.

When questioned, Ferreira admitted to having changed the odometer and was dismissed. At about the same time, Murphy disappeared, taking with him a substantial amount of cash belonging to the corporation. Patel reported both the theft and the tampering with odometers to the police.

Queensville Quality Cars Ltd. has now been charged with an offence under the Criminal Code in respect of altering an odometer. Should the company be convicted?

5. Gigantic Forestry Inc. has multiple pulp and paper mills in various locations across the country, including one in Grizzly River in British Columbia. It has a government permit to discharge up to 18 200 kg of suspended solids per day into the river. The main suspended solids consist of a lime mud, ash, wood bark, clay, sand, and pulp fibre. Gigantic was charged with exceeding the permitted levels of discharge and pleaded guilty. There had been a previous conviction 18 months earlier, with a fine of $50 000 against the corporation. Two directors, described below, were also charged.

On February 27, Gigantic discharged suspended solids at a level significantly in excess of its permit. The spill resulted from a mechanical failure causing an overflow of lime mud from the storage tank into an emergency spill pond. The pond, being near to capacity when the emergency occurred, overflowed to the river. The suspended solid emission was 35 483 kg per day, almost double the permitted level.

Aggravating factors are as follows: (1) Gigantic had a "response manual" to deal with spills but with no specific guidelines in place to deal with this type of event. The general approach followed was a complete shutdown of production until machinery was repaired. (2) The emergency spill pond had not been cleaned for five or six days. (3) The high-level alarm in the storage tank was not working that evening.

Even with the shutdown of the mud system, mud continued to flow from the mud washer to the storage tank. The shift supervisor instituted procedures to minimize the flow of mud from the mud washer. Unfortunately, unknown to the shift supervisor, mud continued to escape from the pond into the sewer. According to the plant people interviewed following this incident, this was the first time the pond had overflowed to the sewer.

Blinkov is a director and president of Gigantic. He resides in Vancouver where the corporation has its head office and visits the Grizzly River site several times a year, but spends most of his workdays in Vancouver or visiting the other 11 mills. His assistant, Crowe, is in charge of environmental control systems at all 12 mills and regularly prepares detailed reports on each plant for Blinkov to review. Charbonneau is a director and manager of the Grizzly River mill. She spends most of each day at the mill. The supervisors report to her at least once each month and are instructed to report any problems immediately. She had not personally examined the storage tank or emergency spill pond for several months before the spill. When the night shift supervisor telephoned Charbonneau about the spill, she said she would examine the situation the following morning.

The court fined Gigantic $200 000. Should either or both directors, Blinkov and Charbonneau, be found guilty?

Additional Resources for Chapter 27 on the Companion Website

(www.pearsoncanada.ca/smyth)

In addition to pre- and post-tests, mini-cases, and application exercises, the Companion Website includes the following province-specific resources for Chapter 27:

- **Alberta:** Alberta Corporate Tax; Environmental Legislation; Fisheries Alberta; Securities Commission
- **Atlantic Provinces:** Environmental Legislation; Securities Commissions
- **British Columbia:** British Columbia Environmental Legislation; Liability of Management
- **Manitoba/Saskatchewan:** Business Practices Act; Environmental Liability; Personal Liabilities of Directors and Officers; Securities Commission
- **Ontario:** Directors' Liability; Environmental Protection Legislation; Legislation Imposing Directors' Liability; Prospectus; Secondary Market Liability; Toronto Stock Exchange

Chapter 28

Secured Transactions

- THE MEANING OF "SECURITY"

- CREATING A SECURITY INTEREST IN PERSONAL PROPERTY

- PERSONAL PROPERTY SECURITY LEGISLATION

- EFFECT OF SECURITY INTERESTS ON PURCHASERS

- SECURITY INTERESTS IN INTANGIBLE PROPERTY

- EFFECT OF SECURITY INTERESTS ON OTHER CREDITORS

- SECURITY FOR BANK LOANS

- STRATEGIES TO MANAGE THE LEGAL RISKS

Almost all businesses operate on credit to some extent. Most businesses owe debts, and most have accounts receivable (debts owed to them by others). An important distinction is drawn—in law and in business practice—between secured and unsecured credit.

In this chapter, we describe the various legal devices for securing credit and examine such questions as:

- What is meant by "security"?

- What is the nature of a conditional sale as compared to a lease?

- How are security interests created?

- What is a floating charge?

- How do the Personal Property Security Acts operate to protect secured creditors?

- How are secured creditors' rights enforced?

- How do secured interests affect the rights of third parties?

- What additional protection is given to banks as secured creditors?

THE MEANING OF "SECURITY"

Types of Security Interest

In daily life, we associate the word "security" with safety and reduced risk. The same is true of secured debts—they are considered safer than unsecured debts because they have additional ways to collect the debt beyond the debtor's willingness or promise to pay. Various legal devices give a secured creditor additional assurance that debts owing will be repaid. Most of these devices are agreed to in the contract that creates the debt. They are often called consensual security interests and typically give a creditor **collateral security**—that is, a right to take possession of and to sell specified assets of the debtor in satisfaction of the debt. Security agreements can be very broad, and it is theoretically possible to cover virtually all existing and future property owned by a debtor.

There are also security interests that arise automatically as a consequence of a transaction, not because the parties to a credit transaction have bargained for them, but because of rules of the common law or in statutes. They may be described as non-consensual security interests. We examined examples of such interests as rights of lien and resale available to unpaid sellers of goods and repair services in earlier chapters[1] and will examine other interests in Chapter 29. In this chapter, our main concern is with consensual security interests.

collateral security an interest in property of a debtor that gives a creditor the right to seize and sell it in the event of non-payment of the debt

Security Practices

Suppliers often do not require collateral security when extending credit to regular customers. Unsecured transactions are simpler and cheaper to record, their risk is relatively small because trade credit is usually short-term, and competition may make it unwise for a supplier to offend customers by demanding security. If a supplier loses only a small proportion of its sales revenue by defaults in payment, it may be better to accept the loss than incur additional administrative costs and perhaps lose sales by requiring security for each sale and then seizing secured assets if default occurs.

Collateral security is not a good substitute for a "quality" debtor. However, security reduces risk of non-payment and makes sense in large transactions and in consumer sales. In addition, it gives a creditor priority relative to other creditors in the event of a debtor's bankruptcy.

In consumer transactions, security devices operate primarily as a form of incentive to pay the money owing and avoid repossession of the article purchased. The right of repossession is most likely to be used for only expensive durable goods. Even then, the resale value will often be less than the amount owing. It is common for goods in the hands of a defaulting debtor to deteriorate considerably before repossession.

Rights of a Secured Creditor

An **unsecured creditor**—that is, a general creditor with no security interest in any of the debtor's assets—may ultimately acquire an interest like a security interest through a court action to collect an overdue debt. When a creditor obtains judgment for the amount of the debt and the debtor fails to pay, the creditor can then obtain an execution order or writ authorizing the seizure and sale of certain of the debtor's assets.[2] By contrast, a secured creditor does not need a judgment or an execution order, but can proceed on its own to enforce its rights over the secured asset. In this sense, a security interest provides a creditor with a quick self-help remedy. An unsecured judgment creditor generally has no right to

unsecured creditor a creditor who has no security interest in any of the debtor's property

---

[1] See Chapter 14 for an explanation of an unpaid seller's rights of lien and resale and Chapter 15 for similar rights available to warehousing and repair service businesses and common carriers.

[2] See the discussion of "Methods of Enforcing Judgment" in Chapter 13.

seize any assets already subject to a security interest of another creditor. The secured creditor has **priority**.

priority a first, or prior, right to be repaid out of the debtor's assets

However, even when a debt is stated to be payable "on demand," the debtor must normally be given time to raise the funds to repay the debt before an asset is seized. If the creditor seizes property without giving reasonable notice, it may be liable in damages.[3]

CASE 28.1

Murano operated a video store financed in part by a loan from the Bank of Montreal. The bank became concerned about the financial affairs of the store and wrote to Murano, indicating their intention to liquidate if adequate arrangements were not made within the next six weeks. In fact, the bank took no further steps for three months, at which time the parties met to discuss a request by Murano for a new financing arrangement. The bank agreed to consider the request, but one week later, without giving notice, it

appointed a receiver and took possession of the store. It also informed other creditors of Murano of its actions.

Murano lost his entire business, including another store that was not included in the bank's financing arrangement. The court held that the bank had failed to give reasonable notice, and that the bank was in breach of duty to its client in disclosing information to other creditors. The bank was liable for Murano's damages.[4]

Unfortunately for the creditor, when a debtor's financial position has deteriorated to the point that the creditor decides it must act, the secured assets in the possession of the debtor may already be in a deteriorating condition or may even have disappeared, and other creditors may also have interest in them. Consequently, security agreements frequently require a debtor to waive any right to notice. After a creditor takes possession, however, statutes generally require the creditor to give notice to the debtor of the time and place at which the goods are to be sold.[5]

CREATING A SECURITY INTEREST IN PERSONAL PROPERTY

A **security interest** is created by an agreement between a lender and borrower that secures a debt against personal property controlled by the debtor. Such an agreement may take any number of forms, but the result is the same: a security interest is created. Historically, the law affecting security agreements was drawn from a combination of real estate mortgage law and the law of the sale of goods. Now it is largely governed by provincial personal property security legislation discussed in the next section.[6] It is still important for us to individually consider the specific types of **security agreements**, as the terms of these agreements will also affect the creditor's rights and remedies.[7]

security interest an interest in goods, intangible property, or personal property that secures payment of a debt or performance of an obligation

security agreements agreements that create a security interest, including chattel mortgages, conditional sales contracts, pledges, etc.

---

[3] *Ronald Elwyn Lister Ltd. v. Dunlop Canada Ltd.* (1982), 135 D.L.R. (3d) 1. At least 10 days' notice must be given before enforcing security in the property of an insolvent debtor; see Chapter 29.

[4] *Murano v. Bank of Montreal* (1998), 163 D.L.R. (4th) 21. In *Royal Bank of Canada v. W. Got & Associates Electric Ltd.* (1999), 178 D.L.R. (4th) 385; where the bank failed to give notice before foreclosing on a loan, the bank was held to be in breach of contract and to have committed the tort of conversion. The Supreme Court of Canada upheld an award of punitive damages.

[5] See e.g. Personal Property Security Act (hereafter PPSA), R.S.O. 1990, c. P.10, s. 63(4); C.C.S.M., c. P35, s. 59(6); S.S. 1993, c. P-6.2, s. 59(6).

[6] All types of security agreements are dealt with under one comprehensive statute known as the Personal Property Security Act. See, for example, PPSA, s. 75 (1) (B.C.).

[7] *Bank of Montreal v. Innovation Credit Union*, [2010] 3 S.C.R. 3. The Supreme Court went behind the label of security agreement to assess the characteristics of a fixed charge as a matter of property law in order to determine a priority question with the Bank Act.

Security Agreements Previously Considered

Several types of security agreements have already been considered in previous chapters, particularly the following.

Mortgages   Although this chapter deals with collateral security in the form of personal property rather than real property, the concept of priority in relation to land mortgages and to other creditors' claims explained in Chapter 23 remains relevant.

Leases   Leases of equipment were examined as an example of bailment in Chapter 15, and leases of land as an interest in real property in Chapter 22. As discussed in Chapter 15, leases may also serve as a type of security device, where items of personal property are acquired on credit.

Consignments   The distinction between a consignment of goods and a sale of goods was discussed in Chapter 14. A consignment may also amount to an indirect type of secured credit. Retailers may not have sufficient capital to carry all the inventory they need and may bring in a stock of goods shipped on consignment by a manufacturer or wholesaler. The merchandise remains the property of the manufacturer or wholesaler, who effectively provides financing in the form of goods rather than money.

Other Credit Devices   Earlier chapters also dealt with assignments of book debts (Chapter 11) and with pledges (Chapter 15), both of which can be considered methods of securing credit. A third-party guarantee (considered in Chapter 16) is slightly different because the "security" consists of a promise by an additional person, rather than a legal interest in an item of property.

Additional Security Agreements

The other important forms of security agreements are conditional sale contracts, chattel mortgages, and floating charges.[8]

Conditional Sales   A conditional sale is similar to a purchase lease. In a lease, the lessee pays to use the item for a specified period and at the end of that period can elect to buy it, applying rent already paid toward the purchase price. In a conditional sale, the sale is agreed to but the transfer of title to the buyer is delayed until the buyer completes the scheduled installment payments. In the meantime, the buyer has possession of the goods, and the seller retains the title to them as security for the full payment of the purchase price. Both a lessee and a conditional buyer are bailees of the goods.[9]

A conditional sale contract serves two main security functions: It gives the secured party (vendor) a right to take the goods if the debtor defaults, and it gives the secured party priority in the goods over the interests of third parties, especially other creditors.

As a creditor, the conditional seller has the ordinary contractual remedy of suing the debtor for the unpaid balance of the debt. In addition, a conditional seller invariably makes it a term of the agreement that he may retake possession of the goods on default by the buyer. **Repossession** does not affect the ownership of the goods since the seller has retained title from the outset.

repossession the act of taking back possession of property that is in the possession of a defaulting debtor

A conditional seller is not entitled to use force in recovering the goods. In some provinces a seller is not entitled to repossess goods except by court process. However, in most provinces a conditional seller may repossess the goods upon default and later sue the buyer for any deficiency arising because the amount still owed by the buyer exceeds the amount

---

[8] Chattel mortgages, conditional sales contracts, floating charges, pledges, and assignments of book debts are all security agreements covered under the PPSA. See, for example, s. 75(2) (B.C.).

[9] A conditional sale contract often places the conditional buyer under a higher duty by making her responsible for damage to the article whether caused by her or not.

realized on resale of the goods.[10] Consumer protection legislation in some provinces provides that a term in the conditional sale contract allowing the conditional seller to repossess and resell the goods on default is unenforceable once the conditional buyer has paid a certain proportion (for example, two-thirds) of the purchase price.[11]

The rights of a conditional buyer also vary considerably from one province to another. Some provinces permit a conditional buyer to **redeem** within specified periods upon payment of the installments in arrears plus interest, and any costs incurred by the seller in repossessing.[12] Other provinces require a conditional buyer who has defaulted to pay the whole unpaid balance of the price—not merely the amounts in arrears—when an **acceleration clause** is included in the conditional sale contract.[13] In most jurisdictions a conditional buyer has a statutory right to receive any surplus realized by a conditional seller that repossesses and resells the goods for more than the amount owed by the buyer plus costs of reselling.[14]

Many vendors who sell goods on the installment plan do not finance the credit transactions themselves. Instead, they sell or assign their conditional sale agreements to finance companies that collect the installments and administer the contracts. Conditional sale contracts also play an important role in financing wholesale purchasers. A retailer or dealer may finance its purchases of stock-in-trade from a manufacturer by buying them from the manufacturer under a conditional sale contract. As a conditional seller, the manufacturer acquires an asset in the form of an account receivable, which it almost invariably assigns to a finance company. As an assignee, the finance company stands in the position of the manufacturing company, with title in the goods withheld from the dealer or merchant (the conditional buyer) until the account is paid in full.

Chattel Mortgages

A **chattel mortgage** is a transfer of an interest in personal property by the mortgagor (borrower) to the mortgagee (lender) as security for a debt, with a condition that if the debt is repaid by a specified date, the interest in the property reverts to the mortgagor.

There are two basic ways a chattel mortgage is created. In the first, the vendor of an article of property "takes back" a mortgage on the property sold. Title is transferred to the buyer with possession and immediately charged with the debt to the vendor. In the second case, the owner of an article mortgages it to the lender—usually a bank or financial institution—as security for a loan. That loan may be used either to pay for the article that is being mortgaged or to purchase an entirely different article. A chattel mortgage is often used in the sale of a business as a going concern where all of the office equipment, machinery, or vehicles are included in the sale transaction.

Another common use of the chattel mortgage occurs in the sale of a building with equipment, such as a furnished office building or apartment building. Frequently the price includes both real property and equipment in the building. Not only may the vendor take back a real estate mortgage for the unpaid balance of the purchase price, but he may also take back a concurrent chattel mortgage on all moveable equipment. The chattel mortgage (so long as it is duly registered) avoids any question about whether certain equipment is a fixture; a real estate mortgage would cover only fixtures, but with a concurrent chattel mortgage covering furniture and equipment, the question becomes irrelevant.

---

[10] See e.g. PPSA, S.N.S. 1995–6, c. 13, s. 61(6); s. 63(5)(f) (Ont.); s. 60(5) (B.C.).

[11] See e.g. Consumer Protection Act 2002, S.O. 2002, c. 30, Sch. A, s. 25; PPSA, s. 58(3) (B.C.). However, a court may still grant the right to repossess and resell on special application by the conditional seller.

[12] See e.g. PPSA, s. 62(1) (Man. and Sask.).

[13] See e.g. PPSA, s. 66(2)(a) (Ont.).

[14] See e.g. PPSA, s. 64 (Ont.).

redeem reclaim the goods and continue with the conditional sale

acceleration clause a provision whereby the full outstanding amount of a debt becomes immediately payable if the debtor defaults in making any installment payment

chattel mortgage a mortgage of personal property

More commonly, chattel mortgages are used as security for loans made by financial institutions. In particular, banks use chattel mortgages as a device for securing credit in the field of consumer financing.

When a borrower finances the purchase of goods with a chattel mortgage, the effect may not seem much different from buying the goods under a conditional sale contract. However, in a conditional sale, the actual goods purchased comprise the collateral. In a chattel mortgage, the debtor may give security in the form of other personal property and even in property acquired after the chattel mortgage has been executed.

after-acquired property property acquired by the debtor after the debt has been incurred

A chattel mortgage that includes **after-acquired property** is a very flexible device. It may cover inventories that fluctuate during its term, as some goods are bought and added to inventory while others are sold and subtracted from inventory. The mortgage does not transfer title to specific goods to the creditor, and buyers acquire good title to goods sold by the debtor in the ordinary course of business. The creditor's security interest remains as a suspended priority against general creditors. If the debtor defaults, the secured creditor may then seize whatever property is covered by the chattel mortgage and sell it to satisfy the debt. A chattel mortgage may also cover goods not yet in a deliverable state, such as goods in production and growing crops.

Contractual remedies for a chattel mortgagee are the same as those of a conditional seller; they are determined by the language of the "contract" and the provisions of the security legislation discussed in the next section. As a creditor, he may sue on the mortgagor's promise to pay the debt, and he may take possession of the mortgaged goods upon default by the mortgagor. A chattel mortgagee invariably reserves the right upon default to resell the goods to a third party. In exercising this right of sale, he must act reasonably and fairly to obtain a good price for them. If not, he may be liable to the mortgagor for the deficiency below the goods' fair market price. If on selling at a fair price the mortgagee obtains less than the debt outstanding, he may sue the mortgagor for the deficiency, but if there is any surplus he must return that surplus to the mortgagor.

Floating Charges It is common for a corporation to borrow money by issuing bonds to the public, using its assets as security. Each certificate issued to a bondholder is evidence of an interest in a **trust deed**—an elaborate form of mortgage on the lands and buildings of the company. The parties to a trust deed are the borrowing corporation (as mortgagor) and a trustee for the bondholders (as mortgagee). Generally, a trust company acts as trustee for the bondholders.

trust deed a document evidencing a mortgage on the property of a corporation

Bonds issued by Canadian corporations frequently provide additional security over and above the mortgage of real property through the creation of a **floating charge**. A floating charge adds those remaining corporate assets not already mortgaged or pledged to the security. When a trust deed includes a provision for a floating charge, the trustee also has access to business assets, including chattels and choses in action, ahead of the unsecured creditors of the corporation.

floating charge a form of mortgage on all the assets of a corporation other than those already specifically charged

A floating charge nicely complements a mortgage of real property because it provides security over the whole of the assets as a working unit. If the corporation defaults in the payment of its bond obligations, the trustee may then more easily place the corporation in the hands of a receiver and manager who can operate it in the interest of the bondholders.

debenture an alternative term to describe a corporate bond

Corporations sometimes issue bonds secured by a floating charge alone and without a mortgage of specific assets. Such a bond is commonly called a **debenture**. The interests that are secured by floating charges also fall within the general scope of personal property security legislation (discussed in the next section), as do other security devices.

PERSONAL PROPERTY SECURITY LEGISLATION

Jurisdiction and Application

Every province and territory has a Personal Property Security Act (PPSA) in substantially the same form.[15] This single legislation applies "to every transaction . . . that in substance creates a security interest";[16] it governs not only conditional sale contracts, chattel mortgages, and assignments of book debts, but also floating charges, pledges, leases and consignments intended as security, and other less common forms. These forms of security are collectively referred to as security agreements.

The PPSA consolidates all the rules into one statute and supports electronic public registry for recording interests.[17] A few concerns remain. Although the provinces are working to reduce the minor variations among the Acts, some inconsistencies still exist.[18] Additionally, conflicts can arise between the relevant provincial legislation and federal laws, such as the Bank Act. Finally, the Act does not apply to non-consensual security interests, nor does it apply to interests in real property.

The very nature of personal property means that it is moveable and may cross jurisdictional boundaries. Each Act contains conflict-of-law provisions that determine which province's law applies in various circumstances.

CASE 28.2

Xtra, a corporation with its head office in Ontario, leased 75 truck trailers to TCT, a corporation located in Alberta. The truck trailers were used throughout the country. TCT became bankrupt. Xtra claimed its truck trailers back. The claim was

>

---

[15] See e.g. Personal Property Security Act, R.S.O. 1990 c. P-10.

[16] Security interest is a defined term under each of the Acts: PPSA, s. 1 (B.C., Ont., Alta., Man.). *Bank of Montreal v. Innovation Credit Union*, 2010 SCC 47, [2010] 3 S.C.R. 3, at para 18.

[17] Ronald C.C. Cuming et al., "Secured Transactions Law in Canada—Significant Achievements, Unfinished Business and Ongoing Challenges" (2011) 50 Can. Bus. L.J. 156 at 158.

[18] One inconsistency relates to which motor vehicles require serial numbers to be included in the registration. Ontario's requirement only applies to consumer vehicles while Saskatchewan's requirements apply to many more vehicles and beyond consumer goods; see s. 2(1)(o) (Sask.).

opposed by GMAC, which had a security interest over all the assets of TCT. The security interest was registered in Alberta. Xtra's lease was not registered.

At the time, Ontario law did not require the registration of a "true lease," whereas the Alberta PPSA did. However, the Ontario PPSA (section 7(1)) provides that "the validity, perfection and effect of perfection . . . of a security interest in an intangible, or goods that are normally used in more than one jurisdiction . . . shall be governed by the law of the jurisdiction where the debtor is located at the time the security interest attaches.[18A]" As the debtor's main place of business was in Alberta, the law of Alberta applied, and GMAC's claim prevailed.[19]

Purpose of PPSA Legislation

When parties create a security interest, they create a relationship that may take priority over the interests of others. The PPSA legislation works to instill confidence in lenders, borrowers, buyers, and owners by establishing a uniform public system that deals with all types of security interests and priority questions. The Acts are complex and technical. We will provide only a general description of how the legislation works.

The Acts recognize that all security devices have the same purpose—to secure repayment by the debtor. They establish a single unified system with common rules for all security agreements, and the following purposes:

- to define and standardize a secured party's remedies against a defaulting debtor
- to create one system of registration to record and give notice of all secured interests
- to define priorities between a secured party on the one hand, and third party purchasers, subsequent secured parties, and general creditors on the other

The legislation does not prohibit businesses from using their standard contract forms to create security interests or from continuing to refer to them by such traditional labels as "conditional sale contracts" or "chattel mortgages." The legislation does not distinguish between the particular forms of security interest—all are considered security agreements. Interests are entered in the registry through the registration of a common form of **financing statement**. Just as in land registry systems, anyone may search the public system and discover the interests recorded there.

financing statement the document summarizing the details of a security interest that is filed in order to protect that interest

The Acts recognize that both leases and consignments of goods can be used as forms of security. However, as we saw in Chapters 14 and 15, these arrangements are frequently used quite apart from any intention to create a security interest. Most provinces have adopted an approach that effectively avoids the difficulty of distinguishing between the two purposes. A consignment or a lease that secures payment or performance of an obligation is within the scope of the Act.[20] Additionally, the Act applies to commercial consignments and to leases for a term in excess of one year, whether or not they are intended to create a security interest.[21]

CASE 28.3

Telecom Leasing leased a car to the B.C. Telephone Company, which in turn leased the car to one of its employees, Giffen, who subsequently became bankrupt. The lease was for a term of more than one year and gave the lessee the option of purchasing the vehicle. Telecom failed to register a financing statement under the (B.C.) PPSA.

It was accepted that the lease was a genuine lease, rather than a security arrangement. Nevertheless, the lessor's interest was required to be registered (perfected under the PPSA), and since it had not been, Telecom had no right to retake possession of the vehicle. Giffen's trustee in bankruptcy had priority.[22]

[18A] Section 7(1) of the Personal Property Security Act, R.S.O. 1990.

[19] *GMAC Commercial Credit Corp. v. TCT Logistics Inc.* (2004), 238 D.L.R. (4th) 487. See also *Gimli Auto Ltd. v. BDO Dunwoody Ltd.* (1998), 160 D.L.R. (4th) 373.

[20] See e.g. s. 1(1) (B.C.); s. 4(1)(b) (N.S.); s. 2 (Ont.).

[21] *Ibid.*, s. 3(c) (B.C.); s. 3(2) (N.B.); s. 4(2) (N.S.).

[22] *Re Giffen*, [1998] 1 S.C.R. 91.

PPSA legislation also recognizes that assets subsequently acquired by a debtor can be added to a security interest already in existence, and it permits the use of chattel mortgages to cover after-acquired property such as inventories. This is practical in the business setting because goods in inventory are always changing. However, in consumer transactions, the security interest of sellers or creditors is confined to the exact goods financed and does not extend to any other after-acquired assets of the consumer.

Where the property charged as collateral is disposed of by the debtor, the Acts provide that the security interest attaches to the proceeds.[23]

CASE 28.4

Cardinali bought a boat from a marina under a conditional sale agreement. The marina assigned the contract to a financing company. The boat was defective, and the marina gave Cardinali a new boat in its place. When Cardinali subsequently defaulted in his payments, the finance company repossessed the boat, sold it, and sued Cardinali for the deficiency.

The trial judge found that the new boat represented proceeds of the disposal of the first boat and that the finance company had a security interest in it. On appeal, the Ontario Court of Appeal held that the new boat had not been exchanged for the first boat and consequently did not represent proceeds of disposal.[24]

Key Components of the Personal Property Security Act

The Act is organized around three key components:

- creation of a security interest
- attachment of the security interest
- perfection of the security interest

As noted, a security interest is created when the creditor and debtor enter into some form of security agreement that gives the creditor an interest in the debtor's personal property to secure repayment of a debt or satisfaction of an obligation.

Attachment occurs upon performance of the security agreement by both debtor and creditor. A security interest cannot attach to an asset until the debtor has acquired a right to it. Nor does a security interest attach until the creditor has performed his part of the bargain by giving the value promised to the debtor.

attachment the moment in time when a debtor's property becomes subject to a security interest

Perfection protects and establishes priority of the security interest, and it may occur in one of two ways:

perfection the moment in time when a creditor's security interest becomes protected

- when the secured party takes possession of the asset(s)—as in a pledge—ending any false impression of ownership given by the debtor's possession, or
- most often, when a secured party registers a financing statement in the PPSA system. The financing statement gives details of the security interest and provides notice of the creditor's interest. Registration is done online.[25]

---

[23] See e.g. R.S.A. 2000, c. P-7, s. 28(1); s. 28(1) (N.B.); s. 25(1)(b) (Ont.). Consequently, a secured creditor will be able to trace the proceeds into the debtor's bank account: *Massey-Ferguson Industries Ltd. v. Bank of Montreal* (1983), 4 D.L.R. (4th) 96, varied (1985) 21 D.L.R. (4th) 640 (Ont. C.A.).

[24] *General Motors Acceptance Corp. of Canada v. Cardinali* (2000), 185 D.L.R. (4th) 141. However, the court found in favour of the finance company on the grounds that the purchaser had agreed to an alteration of the original contract.

[25] See e.g. s. 1(1) defining financing statement and s. 43 as to registration (B.C.). The two alternatives are not available for every form of security interest. Perfection of an interest in a share with a certificate may be done by delivery of the certificate s. 22(2) (Ont.).

PPSA System

Perfection:
- Possession
- Registration

Creation:
- Security agreement (collateral mortgage, etc.)

Attachment:
- Performance of agreement

Perfected Security Interest:
Creation, attachment, and an act of perfection have all taken place

Figure 28.1 The PPSA System

A perfected security interest is one that has all three components: creation, attachment, and perfection, as illustrated in Figure 28.1 (above).

Registration

If security interests are to be protected by the law, an effective system of alerting third parties to those interests, whatever their form, needs to be in place. As described above, the PPSA establishes a centralized registration system within each province for recording security interests. By using computer facilities to record and revise security information and by enlarging the geographic area over which a search can be made, a large database is established and maintained. However, there is at present no comprehensive nationwide system of registration comparable to the system of corporate name registration discussed in earlier chapters. PPSA searches are completed on a province-by-province basis.

The registration system operates rather like the land titles system except that the search is usually made against the name of a particular debtor, whereas under the land titles system it is made against a described parcel of land.[26] Where goods have a serial number, this number may be searched as well. The provincial government maintains a compensation fund to reimburse losses caused by incorrectly processed information, and the system provides a guaranteed certificate of search.

Priority and Competing Interests

unperfected security interest a security interest that is not attached or perfected

The three stages of creation, attachment, and perfection are necessary to protect the security against competing an **unperfected security interest** of another.

---

[26] A search may also be made against the property charged. In particular, it is advisable to search against the V.I.N. of any vehicle that may be subject to a security interest; see *Re Lambert* (1994), 119 D.L.R. (4th) 93. This provides additional protection in cases where the debtor's name is incorrectly spelled.

X Co. borrows money from Y Bank to buy a truck. X Co. gives Y Bank a chattel mortgage on the truck and takes delivery of it. The security interest is created by the loan contract and chattel mortgage. The interest attaches when

Y Bank hands over the money to X Co. and X Co. uses it to obtain delivery of the truck from the dealer. Two of the three PPSA requirements are met. The interest will be perfected as soon as Y Bank registers a financing statement.

Pinpointing the exact moment of perfection is important in order to determine priority between two perfected security interests in the same asset. Generally, the legislation assigns priority to the creditor that first perfects his interest. In practice, this generally means that priority goes to the first to register. A creditor who first creates and attaches his interest might nevertheless lose his priority if he delays perfecting that interest and a subsequent creditor perfects first. The subsequent creditor might be aware of the unperfected security interest of the first creditor; even so, by registering first, that interest is perfected and obtains priority.

CASE 28.5

BMP Corp. sold the assets of its doughnut business to a numbered corporation and took back a chattel mortgage. The mortgage was guaranteed by a Mr. Trafford, whose wife was the sole shareholder of the numbered corporation. Due to an oversight, the financing statement was not registered. Subsequently, Mrs. Trafford registered a financing statement regarding loans she made to the numbered company. She

had actual notice of the guarantee given by her husband and of BMP's security interest. When BMP discovered the oversight, it registered its financing statement and brought an application for an order setting aside Mrs. Trafford's financing statement or postponing her interest.

The court held that, notwithstanding her knowledge of the chattel mortgage, Mrs. Trafford's interest had priority.[27]

Perfection or attachment need not occur in any particular order. For example, some lenders register the financing statement (the act of perfection) before the loan money is advanced to the debtor (the act of attachment). Once the loan attaches, perfection dates back to the time of registration.

There are some exceptions to the general priority rule. Consider a situation where one creditor takes security in after-acquired property and a subsequent creditor supplies new assets to the same debtor, taking back a security interest in them. Although the new assets become after-acquired property of the debtor, a good case can be made for giving the one who supplies later credit a priority over the existing perfected security interests. Otherwise, a business in financial straits will find it difficult to obtain additional credit needed to rehabilitate itself and survive. The debtor's assets have been increased by the value of the new assets financed by credit, so that the first creditor has not had the value of his security diminished.

In recognition of this problem, the Acts give special priority to a **purchase-money security interest (PMSI)**. This interest arises when a seller (for example, a conditional seller) reserves a security interest in the actual goods sold to the debtor, or when a lender (for example, a chattel mortgagee) finances a debtor's acquisition of the same assets that are used as collateral. The rule is a necessary qualification to a system that makes it easy to include after-acquired assets and their proceeds in a security interest.

Rules for determining priorities among competing perfected security interests can be very complex, especially for the financing of business inventories. Fortunately, in

purchase-money security interest (PMSI) the interest that arises when goods purchased by a debtor are charged as security for a loan made to enable those actual goods being acquired

---

[27] *BMP & Daughters Investment Corp. v. 941242 Ontario Ltd.* (1993), 7 B.L.R. (2d) 270.

practice, a business often has only a single source of financing for its inventories, in which case the need to establish priorities does not arise. In financing other business assets, however, competition is more likely between one secured creditor claiming a charge on after-acquired assets and another claiming a purchase-money security interest, as when a company gives a floating charge over all its assets and then acquires new equipment under a conditional sale contract. In these circumstances, the legislation gives priority to the PMSI of the conditional seller.[28] For more information on this topic, see the Companion Website.

EFFECT OF SECURITY INTERESTS ON PURCHASERS

Separation of Possession and Ownership

Security interests typically allow the debtor to have possession of property even when he does not have formal legal ownership of it. Since possession of goods usually creates an appearance of ownership to a third party, the effect may be to mislead an innocent third person. A debtor left in possession of goods may appear to own assets that she, in fact, does not own. The principal safeguard for purchasers now lies in the PPSA requirement that a security interest in goods left in the possession of a debtor must be perfected by registration. Innocent third parties may now search the PPSA databank and discover outstanding registered interests.

Effect of Registration

A properly registered security interest is generally effective to give priority against third parties, except for specified classes of good-faith transferees.[29]

Registration is effective indefinitely or for the time period specified in the financing statement, in which case it must be renewed before its expiration in order to maintain its priority.

ILLUSTRATION 28.2

Peng Ltd. purchases a truck from Federchuk's Ltd. under a conditional sale agreement. Peng makes a down payment and agrees to pay the balance plus finance charges in 18 equal monthly installments. Two months later Peng sells the truck to Tse Ltd. without disclosing the existence of the conditional sale contract. Can Federchuk's gain possession of the truck from Tse despite the fact that it is an innocent purchaser?

In Illustration 28.2, Federchuk's would be able to recover the truck from Tse if it had properly registered its security interest before Peng resold the machine to Tse, since it could have discovered the security interest before making the purchase by making the appropriate search. Tse is not in a stronger position because of her ignorance. Federchuk's claim takes priority because it was perfected before the purported sale to Tse. The same effect would be achieved if, instead of buying on credit by means of a conditional sale, Peng had borrowed the money from a bank, given a chattel mortgage as security, and used the proceeds of the loan to buy the truck. The bank would then have been in a position analogous to Federchuk's for the purposes of registration and of maintaining its rights of repossession against third parties.

---

[28] Provided, of course, that that interest has been perfected; see *Canadian Imperial Bank of Commerce v. Otto Timm Enterprises Ltd.* (1995), 130 D.L.R. (4th) 91.

[29] See e.g. s. 9(1) (Ont.).

Exceptions for Good Faith Buyers

Exceptions to the rights of secured creditors are made for two types of good faith buyers. First, some provinces exempt good faith purchases of small value goods (under $1000) from the PPSA priority rules.[30] This is done because these goods rarely have serial numbers and would be difficult to search effectively. As well, purchase decisions are usually made quickly without the time to do a PPSA search.

The second exception is made for goods sold or leased in the ordinary course of business. When retail purchasers enter a retail outlet, they are entitled to presume that the retailer has ownership of the goods and can sell them free from any security interest. Imagine having to complete a PPSA search before buying a sofa from a furniture store. Still, in the reality of today's business financing, the furniture store has probably financed its entire inventory, which means that the sofa is subject to a registered security interest in favour of the finance company. The PPSA provides that when a business secures its inventory either to the original supplier or a finance company, and then sells the products in the ordinary course of business, a retail buyer acquires a good title to the goods.[31] If the dealer fails to meet its obligations, the manufacturer or a finance company holding a registered security interest cannot seize the goods from the retail buyer.

The above rule does not protect buyers of goods from someone who is not a regular seller of those goods. A secured party or his assignee can lawfully seize the goods purchased in a private sale. The buyer's only remedy is to sue the seller for breach of an implied promise to convey good title. Unfortunately, a seller's warranty in a private sale is likely to be of little value.

Registration Practice

PPSA legislation does not require registration in the sense that failure to register is an offence; nor does it invalidate the creditor's interest. If a secured creditor (or his assignee) chooses not to register, his interest continues as an unperfected security interest and he simply takes a risk that a third party may acquire interests that prevail over his own. Why might a creditor choose not to register? The answer turns on the nature of the creditor's business. Suppose that a creditor's business is primarily one of selling relatively low-value goods to many different customers. He may not find it worthwhile to trace goods wrongfully disposed of by a debtor and then to sue in order to recover them from an innocent purchaser. Instead, he may decide to save the trouble and expense of registering the security interest in the first place. In practice, disputes do not often arise between a secured creditor and a subsequent transferee of goods, and, except for more expensive durable goods, retail conditional sellers (or finance companies as their assignees) may decide not to register conditional sale contracts.

On the other hand, sales by a manufacturer or wholesaler often involve taking a security interest in assets of a business that has other creditors as well. For instance, a truck manufacturer may sell a fleet of vehicles under a conditional sale agreement to a large retail business. The retail business purchases stock-in-trade from suppliers who also provide credit. If the business becomes insolvent, a dispute may arise over the truck manufacturer's claim to repossess the vehicles and thus to deprive the other creditors of an important asset from which to realize their own claims. Risk of this kind of dispute provides the main incentive for registration, since registration of a security interest is essential for a creditor to maintain priority against other creditors.[32]

---

[30] See e.g. s. 30 (B.C.), ss. 3, 4 (Sask.); Ontario does not have this exception.

[31] See e.g. s. 28(1) (Ont.).

[32] See e.g. s. 20 (Alta., B.C., Ont., and Sask.).

SECURITY INTERESTS IN INTANGIBLE PROPERTY

Assignment of Book Debts

assignment of book debts security interest in the debtor's accounts receivable

Businesses often give a conditional **assignment of book debts** or accounts receivable to a bank or other creditor to secure continuing indebtedness such as a line of credit. As noted in Chapter 11, an assignment of this kind is conditional in two respects. First, the amount of the accounts receivable used as security fluctuates with the state of accounts between the borrowing business (assignor) and its customers. Second, the assignment is only triggered by default. As long as the borrowing business keeps its loan in good standing, the security arrangement does not materialize in an actual assignment, with notice to the borrowing business's customers.

Under the PPSA, an assignment is ineffective against creditors of an assignor and against subsequent assignees of the book debts unless it is properly registered.[33] The object is to assure prospective creditors of a business that, unless there is registered public notice to the contrary, the assets of the business in the form of accounts receivable will be available to meet their claims. Registration provides public notice that those accounts are not available to satisfy debts. Defences available to the account debtor against the business will be equally effective against the secured creditor.[34]

Investment Property

Financial assets and investment property receive special treatment under the PPSA. Investment property includes shares or bonds (with or without physical certificates), securities accounts (where a dealer, broker or bank holds financial assets in an investment account on behalf of the investor), futures contracts, and futures accounts. Typically these assets are held by an intermediary (bank, broker, or dealer) and not the investor himself, so customized rules for attaching and perfecting a PPSA security interest are required. In addition to possession and registration, a creditor's security interest in investment property may be perfected by "control."[35] The creditor may establish control by changing the name on the intermediary's account to the creditor's or, more often, by entering into a control agreement with the investor and the securities account intermediary under which the investor transfers his power to instruct the intermediary to the creditor. Control is the best way to perfect interests in this type of intangible property because interests perfected by control get priority over registration when there are competing claims.[36] More than one creditor may have control over financial assets and, if so, priority goes to the one who first obtained control.[37]

EFFECT OF SECURITY INTERESTS ON OTHER CREDITORS

Conflicting Priorities

Debtors often have multiple creditors who may compete with each other for priority over the debtor's assets, especially when a liquidation of all the assets of a debtor is insufficient to pay the full claims of all creditors. Information about the existence of other security interests is essential in making decisions about granting credit. The PPSAs' single registration

---

[33] Registration is the only way to perfect an interest in accounts receivable. See, for example, ss. 22, 23 (Ont.).

[34] See s. 40 (Ont.).

[35] PPSA, s. 22.1 (Ont), s. 24.1(B.C.); Securities Transfer Act, S.O. 2006, c. 8, ss. 26-28.

[36] See e.g. PPSA, s. 30.1 (Ont).

[37] *Ibid.*

system covering most forms of security interest makes the necessary information available and sorts out priority problems among them.

However, there may still be problems in interprovincial situations and there are some personal property security interests remaining outside the scope of the PPSA.[38] Therefore conflicts may arise, for example, where a landlord of premises distrains for arrears of rent and claims fixtures that are subject to a security interest that has been registered under the PPSA.[39] Or the conditional seller of a vehicle may have an interest, protected by the PPSA, that conflicts with the lien of a repairer.[40] Some acts include priority provisions; for example British Columbia's PPSA states that it has priority over other statutes but not the consumer protection legislation.[41] Conflicting claims to priority frequently arise in bankruptcy proceedings,[42] and, conflicts exist between provincial PPSA laws and the federal Bank Act.

CHECKLIST

Priority Rules under the PPSA

(a) First to perfect has priority.

(b) When all competing interests have been perfected by registration, first to register has priority.

(c) The first security interest perfected by registration may lose priority to

   (i) a security interest perfected by possession prior to the other interest's registration,

   (ii) a security interest in investment property perfected by control,

   (iii) a purchase-money security interest,

   (iv) a statutory lien (landlord/tenant, repairer's lien, bankruptcy),

   (v) a good faith purchaser of small valued goods or goods in the ordinary course of business, or

   (vi) a subsequent registered interest if the first registration expires (in some provinces registrations expire and must be renewed to maintain priority).

INTERNATIONAL ISSUE

Mobile Equipment

Large mobile equipment presents a financing challenge. Lenders involved in financing the purchase of things like aircraft equipment often take an interest in the equipment as security for the loan, knowing that the equipment will often be in foreign jurisdictions. Creditors need reassurance that their security will be protected and have priority over other interests even when the equipment is far from home.

>

---

[38] See e.g. *GMS Securities & Appraisals Ltd. v. Rich-Wood Kitchens Ltd.* (1995), 121 D.L.R. (4th) 278, in which a conflict existed between the (Ontario) Mortgages Act, the Registry Act, and the Personal Property Security Act.

[39] *859587 Ontario Ltd. v. Starmark Property Management Ltd.* (1999), 42 B.L.R. (2d) 16.

[40] See *Canadian Imperial Bank of Commerce v. Kawartha Feed Mills Inc.* (1998), 41 O.R. (3d) 124; *General Electric Capital Canada Inc. v. Interlink Freight Systems Inc.* (1998), 42 O.R. (3d) 348; not followed in *Riordan Leasing Inc. v. Veer Transportation Services Inc.* (2002), 61 O.R. (3d) 536.

[41] Ss. 73, 74 (B.C.).

[42] See e.g. *Royal Bank of Canada v. Sparrow Electric Corp.* (1997), 143 D.L.R. (4th) 385, in which the trustee in bankruptcy was faced with claims under the Alberta PPSA, the federal Bank Act, and the Income Tax Act.

In 2001, 53 member states of the United Nations International Institute for the Unification of Private Law (UNIDROIT) adopted the Convention on International Interests in Mobile Equipment (the Cape Town Convention), which addressed the creation, perfection, and priority of security in large mobile equipment.[43] The convention proposes a system similar to the domestic PPSA system with the creation of an "international interest" and a searchable electronic registration system. Priority is determined on a "first in time" registration basis. Creditors with priority in the international system are entitled to repossess the secured equipment even when it is in a foreign (member) jurisdiction. The convention came into force on March 1, 2006, after ratification by eight countries. Canada, the United States, the United Kingdom, France, and Germany have ratified the convention and are introducing domestic legislation to implement its terms with respect to aircraft equipment.[44] The international priority regime would override PPSA rules, so provinces across Canada are also in the process of adopting corresponding legislation.[45] The international registry is supervised by the International Civil Aviation Organization.

Questions to Consider

1. An international interest would override the domestic rules of priority for PPSA and bankruptcy. What is the rationale for this position?

2. How do you think this convention will affect lending decisions and terms?

3. What is the incentive for a developing nation to adopt the convention?

Sources: Sean D. Murphy, United States Practice in International Law, Vol. 2, (Cambridge: Cambridge University Press, 2005) at 383–90; "Cape Town Convention on Financing of High-Value, Mobile Equipment" (2004) 94(4) *American Journal of International Law* 852–4; www.unidroit.org/english/conventions /mobile-equipment/mobile-equipment.pdf.

SECURITY FOR BANK LOANS

Loans under the Bank Act

The right to lend to primary producers against the security of their products is a distinctive feature of Canadian banking practice. The production of raw materials dominated the early Canadian economy. Typically the producers—usually small-scale farmers—required short-term financial assistance to help defray costs through the growing season. Appropriate financing is a short-term loan that must be repaid from the proceeds of sale of the goods whose production the loan is financing. The Bank Act creates a completely separate system for the types of assets that may serve as security and the types of borrowers who may qualify for this type of bank loan.

Section 427 of the current federal Bank Act[46] empowers Canadian chartered banks to lend to the following types of borrower:

- wholesale or retail purchasers or shippers of, or dealers in (i) products of agriculture, the forest, the quarry and mine, the sea, lakes, and rivers; and (ii) wares and merchandise whether manufactured or not
- manufacturers
- aquaculturalists
- farmers
- fishermen

The types of security that banks are authorized to take vary with the type of borrower and have become quite diverse. At the retail and wholesale level, a bank may take primary

[43] UNIDROIT, Convention on International Interests in Mobile Equipment, November 16, 2001, http://www .unidroit.org/instruments/security-interests/cape-town-convention.

[44] International Interests in Mobile Equipment (Aircraft Equipment) Act, S.C. 2005, c. 3 (proclaimed in force). The Convention was extended beyond aircraft equipment to include railway and space assets.

[45] See e.g. International Interests in Mobile Aircraft Equipment Act, S.A. 2006, c. I-6.5 (proclaimed in force April 1, 2013).

[46] Bank Act, S.C. 1991, c. 46.

produce or manufactured items of inventory held in stock pending resale. Manufacturers may borrow under the section on the security of inventories of raw materials, work-in-process, and finished goods. When lending to farmers, a bank may accept as security crops growing or produced on the farm, livestock, or agricultural equipment. The section permits advances to a farmer for the purchase of seed, fertilizer, or pesticides with future crops serving as security for the loan; the purchase of feed with the livestock as security; the purchase of agricultural equipment, with the equipment itself as security; and repairs, improvements, and additions to farm buildings on the security of agricultural equipment. Fishermen may obtain loans on the security of fishing vessels, equipment, supplies, or products of the sea.

Rights of a Lending Bank

The security taken by a bank is neither a pledge nor a chattel mortgage. The borrower does not physically transfer the assets to the bank as security, and the bank does not acquire title to the property as security as the debtor must be free to sell them.

A borrower under section 427 signs an agreement containing the following promises:[46A]

- to keep the property insured and free from claims
- to account to the bank for the proceeds of sales
- to give the bank a right to take possession in the event of default or neglect
- to grant a power of attorney to the bank
- to consent to the sale of the security without notice or advertisement if the borrower defaults

While the loan is in good standing, the borrower must apply the money realized from the sale of the goods toward a reduction of the loan. As a further assurance that the proceeds from sales are applied against the loan, a bank frequently takes a conditional assignment of the borrower's accounts receivable. If the borrower defaults and the bank takes possession of the goods in the borrower's hands and sells them, the bank is entitled to retain out of the proceeds whatever amount will repay the balance owing on the loan plus costs.[47] Any surplus belongs to the borrower, and any deficiency represents a debt still due.

To protect its security against a borrower's unsecured creditors and subsequent purchasers or mortgagees in good faith, notice of Bank Act security is filed with the Bank of Canada.[48] Filing a notice gives the bank priority over other persons dealing with the borrower.[49] In order to protect the value of the security itself, a bank may also require borrowers other than farmers or fishermen to submit at frequent intervals a statement showing the current value and location of the goods comprising the security.

Other Forms of Collateral Security for Bank Loans

In addition to or instead of security under section 427, a bank may require any of the following types of security as a condition for granting credit:

- an assignment of a warehouse receipt, representing title to goods while held in storage, or of an order bill of lading representing title to goods while in the course of transit
- a pledge of shares or bonds, accompanied by a power of attorney signed by the borrower, authorizing the bank to sell them as the borrower's agent if need be

---

[46A] Section 427 of the Bank Act.

[47] Employees of the borrower take priority over the bank to the extent of three months' arrears of wages. Bank Act, S.C. 1991, c. 46, s. 427(7).

[48] Bank Act, s. 427(4), (5).

[49] See *Royal Bank of Canada v. Lions Gate Fisheries Ltd.* (1991), 76 D.L.R. (4th) 289.

- a pledge of drafts drawn by the borrower against his customers
- an assignment of book debts
- an assignment of the cash surrender value of a life insurance policy
- a chattel mortgage
- a real estate mortgage[50]
- a guarantee by a third party

In addition to holding collateral security provided by the borrower, the bank may exercise a right of lien on other personal property belonging to the borrower in the bank's possession.[51] A bank may apply against a loan any draft that the borrowing business has left with it for collection.[52] It may apply in settlement of the loan any bank deposit balances kept with it by the borrowing business if it has not previously earmarked these balances for some particular purpose.[53] A bank lien does not extend to property left with the bank for safekeeping.[54] When a bank is acting as a securities administrator (administering an investor's securities account), it is entitled to a security interest in the financial assets of the account for unpaid balances; these rights are governed not by the Bank Act but by special PPSA rules of attachment and perfection in conjunction with Securities Transfer Acts.[55] For more information on this topic, see the Companion Website.

Conflicts between the Bank Act and Personal Property Security Acts

As described above, banks may utilize a wide range of security devices. They can take advantage of the provisions of section 427 of the Bank Act or they can use the more common forms of security governed by the PPSA. The range of options available, however, can lead to conflicting claims between them and other creditors.

One problem is that a degree of overlap exists between section 427 of the Bank Act and the PPSA security interests. For example, while section 427 does not extend to all forms of property that can be the subject of a security interest under personal property security acts, it is unclear to what extent security interests under section 427 fall within the scope of the provincial acts and are protected by registering under those acts.[56]

Second, the Bank Act and the provincial acts have separate systems of registration and priority, which can result in conflict between creditors, each claiming priority under a different scheme.[57]

Third, since the Bank Act is federal legislation but other personal property security legislation is within provincial jurisdiction, neither level of government can

---

[50] Normally, a mortgage loan is limited to 80 percent of the value of the property; further restrictions apply to loans made on the security of residential (as opposed to commercial) property: Bank Act, s. 418(1).

[51] *Re Williams* (1903), 7 O.L.R. 156.

[52] *Merchants Bank v. Thompson* (1912), 26 O.L.R. 183.

[53] *Riddell v. Bank of Upper Canada* (1859), 18 U.C.Q.B. 139.

[54] *Leese v. Martin* (1873), L.R. 17 Eq. 224. Rights may vary depending upon terms of the securities administrator contract.

[55] See e.g. PPSA s. 12.1, 19.1, 24.1 (B.C.).

[56] See *Rogerson Lumber Co. Ltd. v. Four Seasons Chalet Ltd. and Bank of Montreal* (1980), 113 D.L.R. (3d) 671; *Re Bank of Nova Scotia and International Harvester Credit Corp. of Canada Ltd.* (1990), 73 D.L.R. (4th) 385. For a full discussion of this issue, see Ronald C.C. Cuming, "The Position Paper on Revised Bank Act Security: Rehabilitation of Canadian Personal Property Security Law or Curing the Illness by Killing the Patient" (1992) 20 Can. Bus. L.J. 336.

[57] See e.g. *Bank of Montreal v. Pulsar Ventures Inc. and City of Moose Jaw*, [1988] 1 W.W.R. 250; *Royal Bank of Canada v. Sparrow Electric Corp.* (1997), 143 D.L.R. (4th) 385. Cuming et al., (2011), *supra*, n. 17, at 172–4.

resolve the problems alone. Although the operation of section 427 cannot be made subject to provincial legislation, the respective spheres of operation of the different laws remain a difficult challenge.[58] For more information on this topic, see the Companion Website.

| Ethical Issue | **Is the Law Too Favourable toward Secured Creditors?** |

What about the interests of other stakeholders? According to one commentator, "Nowhere in the world is there a system for the regulation of secured financing that is more accommodating to secured creditors than the Canadian PPSAs."[59] It has been estimated that, in most insolvencies, at least 90 percent of the debtor's assets go to satisfy the claims of secured creditors—mainly the banks—leaving little or nothing for unsecured creditors such as suppliers, contractors, and employees.

Recent high-profile bankruptcies highlighted the problem. Often, employees have been left with unpaid wages and have lost their accrued pension benefits while the banks walk away with all the assets.[60] What is perhaps even worse are those cases where the secured creditors are the owners of the business themselves. In 2004, a pulp plant closed down in a small New Brunswick mill town. About 400 people lost their jobs when the owners of the pulp mill decided to close the plant and declare bankruptcy. Most employees also lost their pensions. Many of them had worked at the plant for over 20 years. The primary secured creditor, with claims exceeding $34 million, was the New York corporation that owned all the company's shares.

Questions to Consider

1. Are secured creditors given too much protection?

2. Should the owners of a business be allowed to be its secured creditors?

Strategies to Manage the Legal Risks

Businesses may become creditors as suppliers of goods and services or as financiers of large scale projects. Obviously the strategy to manage the risks will be different depending upon the amount of money involved. Small amounts owed by many debtors for individually small valued goods may not be worth the time and expense associated with repossession. If this is the case, there is little point in spending the time and money on complying with the PPSA. The creditor may always still sue the debtor on his promise to pay. However, for durable goods of high value, businesses will want to preserve their rights against other creditors and third party purchasers, and this can only be done if they perfect their interests under the PPSA. Searches of PPSA and Bank Act databanks should be completed prior to extending credit. Search not only by debtor name but by serial number whenever possible. Searches should be completed even by consumers whenever they are completing a private sale, such as a used motor vehicle purchase.

Since PPSA priority goes to the first to register and registration need not wait until attachment, creditors should register immediately upon completion of the agreement. Subsequent attachment will retroactively set the priority date as of registration. Since registration is done by the user online, careful attention to spelling, birth dates, and serial numbers will reduce the possibility of errors that could invalidate the security interest.

---

[58] *Bank of Montreal v. Hall*, [1990] 1 S.C.R. 121.

[59] *Bank of Montreal v. Innovation Credit Union*, [2010] 3 S.C.R. 3.

[60] See e.g. Nortel Retirees and former employees Protection Canada (NRPC), http://www.nortelpensioners.ca

QUESTIONS FOR REVIEW

1. What is meant by "collateral security"?
2. Why might a creditor choose not to take security for a debt?
3. In what way do security devices act as an incentive to repay one's debts?
4. What are the principal types of security interest?
5. Why is a lease of personal property commonly treated as a security interest?
6. What is an "acceleration clause"?
7. Distinguish between a chattel mortgage and a pledge.
8. What is the principal difference between a conditional sale agreement and a chattel mortgage?
9. How can a creditor obtain a security interest in property that the debtor does not yet possess?
10. What is a "floating charge"?
11. How is priority determined in the PPSA system?
12. What is the function of a "financing statement"?
13. What does it mean that a security interest must be "perfected"?
14. What is a "purchase-money security interest," and why is it given special priority?
15. What allowance is made for a consumer buying goods from a seller in the business of selling those goods?
16. What types of loan receive special protection under the Bank Act?
17. How is a security interest protected under the Bank Act?

CASES AND PROBLEMS

1. Continuing Scenario

   Ashley renovated the "Ashley's Too" kitchen including a new built in refrigeration system. She financed the improvements as follows:

   ■ The restaurant entered into a conditional sales contract with the manufacturer of the refrigerator.

   ■ Ashley paid for the remaining renovation out of the existing "Ashley's Too" credit line at the bank. When the credit line was opened four years ago, it was secured by a chattel mortgage over all existing and future restaurant equipment.

   Explain how each creditor would obtain maximum protection for its security under the PPSA. Give your opinion on who would have priority if all creditors properly completed all requirements. How would your answer change if Ashley financed the remaining renovation with a separate bank loan secured against her personal investment account held at the same bank?

2. In May 1994, SIS Ltd. leased two large, portable, tent-like structures to Cansaw Services Inc. for a term of 24 months, at a monthly rental of $11 000. In December of the same year, Cansaw negotiated a loan from the Regal Bank and executed a general security agreement, which gave the Bank a security interest in

   > the undertaking of Cansaw and all of Cansaw's present and after-acquired personal property including, without limitation, in all goods, intangibles, money, and securities now owned or hereafter owned or acquired by or on behalf of Cansaw . . . and in all proceeds and renewals thereof, accretions thereto and substitutions therefor..., and including, without limitation, all of the following now owned or hereafter owned or acquired by or on behalf of Cansaw: all equipment (other than inventory) of whatever kind and wherever situated, including, without limitation, all machinery, tools, apparatus, plant, furniture, fixtures, and vehicles of whatsoever nature or kind.

   The bank registered its security interest under the (Alberta) Personal Property Security Act on the same day.

By May 1996, Cansaw's business was in severe financial difficulties. It had not paid rent to SIS for almost six months and owed them $65 000 in arrears. Its debts to the bank now totalled almost $1 million.

On May 3, 1996, the bank delivered a written notice to Cansaw that it was in breach of the financing agreement and gave it one week to remedy its breach. On May 16, 1996, the bank demanded payment of the outstanding debt and delivered a notice of intention to enforce its security (under section 244 of the Bankruptcy and Insolvency Act). A few days later, the directors of SIS learned of Cansaw's problems with the bank and gave instructions to a civil enforcement company to enter Cansaw's premises and to dismantle and repossess the structures. At the same time, acting on the advice of its lawyer, SIS registered a security interest in the structures.

The bank demanded that SIS return the structures, claiming that their general security agreement covered the structures and had priority over the claim of SIS. SIS replied that they were the owners of the structures and were entitled to repossess them since Cansaw had defaulted on payment of the rent. Who has the better claim?

3. Clarkson purchased an automobile from Easyprice Autos for $17 000, under a conditional sale agreement. Easyprice assigned the conditional sale contract to CVF Inc., which advanced Clarkson the bulk of the purchase price. CVF immediately registered its security interest under the (Ontario) Personal Property Security Act.

Six months later, Clarkson entered into a second conditional sales contract with Sonmax Corp. for the purchase and installation of stereo equipment in the vehicle at a cost of $3500, including financing charges. CVF was not informed of this second contract. Sonmax promptly registered a lien against the vehicle under the Repairs and Storage Liens Act.

A few months later, when Clarkson fell into arrears with his repayments, Sonmax repossessed the vehicle, and gave Clarkson notice of its intention to sell the vehicle to secure repayment of what was owed it. At that point, CVF learned of the action by Sonmax and also claimed the vehicle.

Which firm has the prior claim?

4. Avila purchased a secondhand Cadillac from Better Buy Motors Ltd. under a conditional sale agreement. She used the car for several months in her work as a sales representative and paid her installments regularly. When she had only two installments left to pay, the car was towed out of her driveway and delivered to Fancy Finance Corp., on instructions of that company. Avila had never heard of Fancy Finance before. It informed her that it had "repossessed" the car under a prior, properly registered chattel mortgage that it held, and that the chattel mortgagor had fraudulently sold the car to Better Buy Motors.

Examine the nature of Avila's rights and indicate against whom they are available. What factors should be taken into account in assessing her loss?

5. Holmes purchased a refrigerator and stove from Watts Electric Ltd. under a conditional sale agreement. Watts Electric Ltd. discounted the contract with Domestic Finance Co. Neither Watts Electric nor Domestic Finance registered the agreement.

Several months later, Holmes sold the appliances to Fischer for cash, without disclosing that there was still an unpaid balance owing to Domestic Finance, and left the province. After Holmes defaulted payment, Domestic Finance discovered that Fischer had possession of the appliances and repossessed them. Fischer then sued Domestic Finance for wrongful seizure of the appliances.

State the arguments for the plaintiff and the defendant. What should the decision be?

6. Oliver purchased a used car from Hardy Motors Ltd. for $5500 and paid $3800 in cash as a down payment on the understanding that he would have 30 days to pay the balance. The manager of Hardy Motors Ltd. stated that 30-day credit was unusual for this type of purchase and that he would still have to get Oliver's signature on a conditional sale agreement "as a matter of form." Oliver signed the agreement, which included a term that Oliver would pay the balance of the purchase price over 24 months in monthly installments of

$89.50 each. The manager told Oliver that he would hold the conditional sale agreement for 30 days so that Oliver would have that time to raise the balance of the purchase price.

Hardy Motors Ltd. was in financial trouble. In breach of its understanding with Oliver, the company at once discounted (assigned) the conditional sale contract with Vanguard Finance Co. The finance company informed Oliver of the assignment and requested payment to it of the monthly installments specified in the conditional sale agreement. Oliver ignored the notice, and before the expiration of the 30 days, paid the balance of $1700 directly to Hardy Motors Ltd. Soon after, Hardy Motors Ltd. was adjudged bankrupt, and the manager absconded with the cash assets of the business. Vanguard Finance seized the car from Oliver, who then sued the finance company for wrongful seizure, asking for a court order for return of the car to him.

Should Oliver's action succeed?

Additional Resources for Chapter 28 on the Companion Website

(www.pearsoncanada.ca/smyth)

In addition to pre- and post-tests, mini-cases, and application exercises, the Companion Website includes the following province-specific resources for Chapter 28:

- **Alberta:** Builders' Liens; Debt Collections; Garnishment; Liens; Loan Transactions; Personal Money Security Interest; Personal Property Registry; Personal Property Security Act
- **Atlantic Provinces:** Chattel Mortgages; Conditional Sales; Personal Property Security Legislation
- **British Columbia:** Enforcement of Security Interests; Perfection and Priority of Security Interests; Personal Property Registry; Personal Property Security Act
- **Manitoba/Saskatchewan:** Personal Property Security Acts; Seizing Goods
- **Ontario:** Assignment of Rents; Attachment; Bulk Sales; Financing Statement; Personal Property; Personal Property Security Act; Purchase Money Security Interest; Registration; Sale of Collateral; Security Interest

Chapter 29

Creditors' Rights

In this chapter, we examine the ways in which the rights of creditors are protected and enforced. The main focus is on the Bankruptcy and Insolvency Act, but consideration is also given to other statutes and, in particular, to the provincial laws regarding builders' liens, also known as mechanics' liens or construction liens in some provinces.

We consider such questions as:

- What are the principal objectives of bankruptcy law?
- How does bankruptcy law distinguish between different types of debtors—and why?
- What constitutes an "act of bankruptcy"?
- What principles govern the administration of a bankrupt's assets?
- What is a builders' lien?
- How are the interests of contractors and subcontractors protected?
- What is the effect of limitation periods on creditors' rights?

STATUTORY ARRANGEMENTS FOR THE PROTECTION OF CREDITORS

Most debt debtors are honest and pay their debts promptly if they are able to do so. Consequently, resorting to legal procedures to collect money owed by solvent debtors is comparatively unusual. But, in some cases, a debtor's financial position may become so hopeless that it is unwise or impossible for him to continue to carry on business. A debtor becomes **insolvent** when he is unable to pay his debts as they fall due or when his liabilities exceed his realizable assets. When a debtor finds himself in that condition, at least some of his creditors will go unpaid.

> **insolvent** unable to pay one's debts as they fall due or liabilities exceed realizable assets

A business is usually both a creditor and a debtor. It uses credit to grow the business and extends credit to customers in the ordinary course of doing business. Therefore, it is important to understand the rules of debt collection. A number of statutes have as their main purpose the protection of creditors' claims. These acts set out the rights of creditors both against their debtors and against other creditors. In this chapter, we will review the ways in which the Bankruptcy and Insolvency Act (BIA), the Companies' Creditors Arrangement Act, and the Builders' Lien Acts assist in this purpose.

THE BANKRUPTCY AND INSOLVENCY ACT

Under the Constitution Act, 1867, the federal Parliament has jurisdiction over bankruptcy.[1] It passed the Bankruptcy and Insolvency Act[2] to provide a formal way of releasing an honest debtor from his obligations once all his assets had been distributed to his creditors. For more information about the background of the Bankruptcy and Insolvency Act, see the Companion Website.

The Bankruptcy and Insolvency Act performs a number of functions:

- It establishes a uniform practice in bankruptcy proceedings throughout the country as inexpensively as possible.

- It provides for an equitable distribution of the debtor's assets among his various creditors.

- It provides a framework for preserving and reorganizing the debtor's business or affairs by working out an arrangement with the agreement of his creditors to avoid a total liquidation of a debtor's estate, if possible.

- It provides for the release of an honest but unfortunate debtor from his obligations and offers him a fresh start free of debts.

INTERNATIONAL ISSUE

Cross-Border Insolvency

In 1997, the United Nations Commission on International Trade Law adopted a Model Law on Cross-Border Insolvency.[3]

It addresses the jurisdictional issues associated with multinational corporations and foreign bankruptcy proceedings.

>

---

[1] Other federal insolvency statutes include the Companies' Creditors Arrangement Act, R.S.C. 1985, c. C-36 and the Winding-Up and Restructuring Act, R.S.C. 1985, c. W-11. Some provincial legislation also deals with debtor behaviour; see, e.g., the Assignments and Preferences Act, R.S.O. 1990, c. A.33. When provincial and federal legislation dealing with insolvency conflicts, the federal statute prevails: *British Columbia v. Henfrey Samson Belair Ltd.* (1989), 59 D.L.R. (4th) 726 (S.C.C.).

[2] Bankruptcy and Insolvency Act, R.S.C. 1985, c. B-3, as significantly amended by S.C. 1992, c. 27; S.C. 2005, c. 47; and S.C. 2007, c. 36 (in force 2009). Unless otherwise stated, statutory references in this part of the chapter are to this Act.

[3] www.uncitral.org/uncitral/en/uncitral_texts/insolvency/1997Model.html.

The model law proposes that international cooperation in trans-border insolvency be achieved using three strategies:

- authorizing courts to coordinate and cooperate with each other
- restricting the scope of local (domestic) bankruptcy proceedings
- granting local relief to representatives of foreign proceedings.[4]

Canada's 2009 reform of insolvency law incorporates the general concepts advanced by the model law with some modification in form. One interesting variation is the inclusion of a provision that allows a court to refuse to make an order that is not in compliance with Canadian law or if doing so would be contrary to public policy. Also, Canadian courts are not obligated to enforce an order made by a foreign court.[5]

Questions to Consider

1. Why is international cooperation important?
2. What circumstances might be considered contrary to public policy?
3. How do these limitations respect domestic sovereignty?

Competing Policy Issues

Insolvency involves the consideration and balancing of many stakeholder interests: creditors, debtors, consumers, business, government, and the public as a whole. Business confidence and respect for the law are reinforced if creditors are able to recover what is lawfully owing to them. But their interests may diverge from that of society generally in a number of ways. The chief concern of most creditors is to quickly collect as much as possible of what is owed to them. They will normally have little interest in whether a debtor's business can be saved and turned around. Bankruptcy law, however, contains provisions whereby creditors may be encouraged, and sometimes compelled, to accept an arrangement designed to save a business and therefore the jobs it provides. Again, a creditor normally wishes to preserve the possibility of recovering in full what she is owed, even if this is not possible in the debtor's present financial circumstances. However, it is in the public interest to allow an honest but unfortunate debtor to be discharged from his debts once he has paid as much as possible and to give him a fresh start.

One of the aims of bankruptcy legislation is to promote an atmosphere of confidence in business relations, and confidence would be undermined if bankruptcy fraud went unpunished. Therefore, the Act contains provisions to punish dishonest debtors and to prevent them from re-engaging in business activities.

There are, of course, limits to what even well-drafted legislation can achieve. In many situations, the damage done to creditors' claims by the time bankruptcy occurs is largely irreparable. The best protection for creditors is to be careful in granting credit. To assist prospective creditors by making more information available to them, the Act requires certain information to be filed concerning bankrupt debtors and the directors and officers of bankrupt corporations.

Government Supervision

The Act (section 5) creates the position of superintendent of bankruptcy, who keeps a record of all bankruptcy proceedings in Canada and has a general supervisory function over all bankrupt estates. The superintendent is responsible for investigating the character and qualifications of persons applying for licences to act as trustees and has the power to suspend or cancel a trustee's licence. He or she may issue directives to trustees or receivers regarding

---

[4] Industry Canada, Office of the Superintendent of Bankruptcy, http://strategis.ic.gc.ca/eic/site/bsf-osb.nsf/eng/br02261.html.

[5] S. 284(2); Macia Jones, Bill C-12: An Act to amend the Bankruptcy and Insolvency Act, the Companies' Creditors Arrangement Act, the Wage Earner Protection Program Act, and chapter 47 of the Statutes of Canada 2005, LS-584E, Legislative Summaries, Library of Parliament, December 14, 2007, (clauses 60, 81), www.parl.gc.ca/common/bills_ls.asp?lang=E&ls=c12&source=library_prb&Parl=39&Ses=2 (last visited May 30, 2014).

the administration of a bankrupt estate, intervene in any court proceeding, and investigate situations where a bankruptcy offence may have been committed (section 10(1)).

For the purposes of administration, the Act makes each province and territory a bankruptcy district. Each district may be divided into two or more divisions, according to the size of the province or territory. For each division, an **official receiver** is appointed (or more than one). Official receivers are officers of the court and are required to report to the superintendent all bankruptcies originating in their divisions (section 12). The superintendent must maintain a public record of all licences issued to trustees and all debtor proposals and bankruptcies (section 11.1).

The Act designates the highest trial court in each province or territory as the court to hear bankruptcy proceedings (section 183). Usually a particular judge or judges of the provincial court are designated to deal with bankruptcy matters, and their courts are commonly referred to as the Bankruptcy Court, though strictly speaking no separate bankruptcy court exists. The courts hear creditors' **petitions** for the bankruptcy of their debtors and determine whether or on what terms certain debtors should be discharged after their affairs have been wound up.

The actual administration of a debtor's estate is placed in the hands of a licensed **trustee in bankruptcy**, who is normally an accountant and is appointed by the court or, in the case of a voluntary assignment in bankruptcy, by the official receiver. In either case, in appointing the trustee, regard must be paid to the wishes of the creditors, who retain the power to appoint a substitute trustee (section 14). The creditors also appoint one or more (but not exceeding five) inspectors to instruct and supervise the trustee (section 116).

Persons to Whom the Act Applies

Bankrupts and Insolvent Persons

The Act applies, in general, to debtors who are individuals, partnerships, and corporations—apart from banks, insurance companies, and trust, loan, and railway companies. A **bankrupt** is defined as a person who has made an assignment or against whom a bankruptcy order has been made—that is, a formal legal step must be taken in order to declare a person bankrupt. A distinction is made between debtors who voluntarily declare bankruptcy and those who are petitioned into bankruptcy by their creditors.

The Act, as its title indicates, applies to insolvent persons as well as to bankrupts. An **insolvent person** is defined, for the purposes of the Act, as a person who is not bankrupt, whose liabilities to creditors amount to at least $1000, and who either

- is unable to meet his obligations as they generally become due,
- has ceased paying his current obligations in the ordinary course of business as they generally become due, or
- has debts due and accruing due, the aggregate of which exceeds the realizable value of his assets (section 2).

The Act distinguishes between two basic types of person: those who are potential candidates for bankruptcy (insolvents), and those who have been declared bankrupt (bankrupts). A person may be insolvent without having been declared bankrupt, and a bankrupt may turn out not to be insolvent.

Consumer Debtors

An important distinction is drawn in the Act between consumer debtors and other debtors. The Act defines a **consumer debtor** as an insolvent natural person (that is, an individual) whose aggregate debts, excluding any debt secured by the person's principal residence, do not exceed $250 000 (section 66.11). Consumer bankruptcies represent the vast majority of all bankruptcies (69 224 out of a total of 72 411 in 2013); business bankruptcies fell by 65.1 percent over the 15 years between 1990 and 2010 (4072 in 2010).[6] Consumer bankruptcies rose by 116 percent over the same time period.

official receiver a public official responsible for the supervision of bankruptcy proceedings

petitions requests to commence bankruptcy proceedings against a defaulting debtor

trustee in bankruptcy the person appointed to administer the property of a bankrupt

bankrupt a person who has made a voluntary assignment in bankruptcy or against whom a bankruptcy order has been made

insolvent person a person who is unable to meet (or has ceased to pay) his or her debts as they become due, or whose debts exceed the value of his or her realizable assets

consumer debtor an individual who is insolvent but whose aggregate debts do not exceed $75 000 (soon to be changed to $250 000)

---

[6] Statistics are available at the Office of the Superintendant of Bankruptcy, https://www.ic.gc.ca/eic/site/bsf-osb.nsf/eng/h_br01011.html and "Canadian Bankruptcy Statistics (1980–2013)," BankruptcyCanada.com, www.bankruptcycanada.com/bankstats1.htm (last visited May 24, 2014).

The relevance of the distinctions—between insolvent persons and bankrupts, and between commercial and consumer debtors—will be considered when we discuss the various procedures provided for under the Act.

Corporations   The principle of limited liability means that the shareholders of a corporation are not liable for its debts. The corporation is liable for its own debts to the full extent of its assets, and it may go bankrupt. Notions of punishment and rehabilitation have little meaning for a bankrupt corporation. A group of individuals may form a corporation with very little capital and, if the corporation becomes bankrupt, they lose very little (unless they have personally guaranteed its debts). To make a fresh start in business, they may simply form a new corporation. However, the worst abuses—for example, where the assets of a corporation are drained by the payment of excessive dividends or by redeeming shares—are governed by provisions that allow such transactions to be reviewed and set aside. Further, where a corporation commits a bankruptcy offence, any director or officer who authorized, participated in, or acquiesced in the offence is liable to punishment for the offence (section 204).[7] The Court may order the removal of a director if the director is acting inappropriately or impairing the corporation's ability to comply with a proposal. Conversely, a court may protect a director or officer from liability arising from a proposal by granting a charge on the property of the corporation in favour of indemnification of director liability (sections 64, 64.1). Such indemnification does not cover willful misconduct.

Procedures under the Act

The Act makes provision for three distinct types of procedure, available in different circumstances and each with its own special consequences:

1. a **proposal**—a procedure to avoid formal liquidation of the debtor's estate, at least temporarily, by allowing the debtor time to attempt to reorganize and save a viable business or, in the case of a consumer debtor, to reorganize his affairs
2. an **assignment**—a voluntary application by a debtor to institute bankruptcy proceedings
3. a **bankruptcy order**—initiated by creditors' petition to have their debtor declared bankrupt by the court.

proposal   a procedure whereby a debtor, by agreement with the creditors, reorganizes his or her affairs without being made bankrupt

assignment into bankruptcy   a voluntary declaration of bankruptcy by the debtor

bankruptcy order   a court order made in proceedings instituted by creditors, whereby a debtor is declared bankrupt

Proposals   The Act makes provision for two types of proposal, commonly referred to as commercial proposals (Division I) and consumer proposals (Division II), the latter being a simplified procedure available to individual consumer debtors. For corporations, an alternative method of avoiding liquidation of the business is provided under the Companies' Creditors Arrangement Act. That Act is considered later in this chapter, under the heading "Other Methods of Liquidation and Reorganization."

Commercial Proposals   A Division I proposal may be made by an insolvent person, a liquidator of an insolvent person's property, or a receiver in relation to an insolvent person. A proposal may also be made by a bankrupt or by the trustee of a bankrupt's estate, provided the estate has not yet been wound up (section 50(1)).

A proposal is an offer made by the debtor to his creditors, providing for the orderly repayment of his debts or of some part of his debts,[8] over a period of time. If the proposal is accepted by a sufficient proportion of the creditors, the court will declare it binding upon all the creditors (except the government) and no other collection efforts may be taken.

---

[7] An individual who is a bankrupt is not permitted to be a director of a corporation; see, for example, Canada Business Corporations Act, R.S.C. 1985, c. C-44, s. 105(1)(d).

[8] Certain debts, notably those to the Crown (government) and to employees, must be paid in full; s. 60(1.1), (1.3).

Where a proposal is made before bankruptcy, the debtor files a copy of the proposal with the official receiver in the debtor's district. The proposal must be accompanied by a statement showing the debtor's financial position, verified by affidavit of a licensed trustee. An insolvent person can gain additional time by filing a notice of intention with the official receiver, stating his intention to make a proposal (section 50.4). If the debtor has already been made bankrupt, the proposal and statement of financial position are delivered to the existing trustee. The proposal must be approved by the inspectors (appointed by the creditors to supervise the trustee) before any further action is taken.

The next stage is to obtain approval for the proposal at a meeting of the creditors. The proposal may be made to secured creditors or to one or more classes of secured creditors, as well as to unsecured creditors. Acceptance of a proposal requires the approval of a majority in number, and two-thirds in value, of the unsecured creditors, and a similar proportion of each class of secured creditors. Secured creditors not included in the proposal, or whose class has rejected the proposal, keep the protection provided by their security.

If the proposal is accepted by a sufficient proportion of creditors, the next step is for the trustee to apply to the court for approval. Although the court will be reluctant to refuse approval to a proposal that is acceptable to the majority of creditors, it must be satisfied that the terms of the proposal are reasonable and for the benefit of the general body of creditors (section 59(2)). In particular, it may withhold approval if the proposal fails to provide reasonable security for repayment of at least 50 cents on the dollar to unsecured creditors, or if the debtor has committed a bankruptcy offence. If a proposal is rejected by the majority of creditors or by the court, the insolvent debtor is deemed to have made an assignment into bankruptcy (section 57, 61(2)).

Once approved by the court, the proposal is binding on all unsecured creditors and on all secured creditors of a class that has given its approval. Unless the proposal provides to the contrary, the debtor retains control of his property. However, monies payable under the proposal must be paid to the trustee for distribution to the creditors. If the debtor defaults in the performance of any provision of the proposal, the trustee is required to notify all creditors and the official receiver. Application may then be made, by any creditor or by the trustee, to have the proposal annulled (section 63(3)). The effect of annulment is that the debtor is deemed to have made an assignment (see below).

Consumer Proposals An insolvent individual who owes no more than $250 000, not including any debt secured by mortgage on a principal residence, may make a proposal to his creditors for the reduction of, or extension of time for the payment of, his debts (section 66.12). A Division II proposal must be prepared with the assistance of an "administrator," a licensed trustee or other person appointed by the superintendent to administer consumer proposals. The administrator is responsible for investigating the debtor's financial affairs and for providing counselling. Procedures are simplified, and a formal meeting of creditors is not required unless requested by creditors representing 25 percent in value of the proven debts. Where no meeting is requested, the proposal is deemed to be accepted by the creditors. A proposal that has been accepted or is deemed to be accepted does not require approval of the court.

An important consequence of filing a consumer proposal is that the debtor also obtains protection against lease terminations, acceleration of installment payments, or having utilities shut off (section 66.34). Consumers making a proposal must undergo mandatory debt counselling, and there are only limited rights to revive a proposal once a consumer debtor defaults.

Assignments By making an assignment, an insolvent person voluntarily declares himself bankrupt. A debtor who is no longer able to meet his debts as they fall due may prefer to initiate bankruptcy proceedings himself, rather than wait for his creditors to do so. By making an assignment, he puts an end to an unsatisfactory situation and makes an earlier rehabilitation possible. Also, to continue to carry on a business once he knows he is insolvent might well involve him in the commission of a bankruptcy offence and jeopardize his eventual discharge (section 173(1)(c)).

A debtor makes an assignment by filing a petition with the official receiver, accompanied by a sworn statement listing his property and his debts and creditors (section 49).[9] When the official receiver files the petition, she appoints a trustee, who becomes responsible for the administration of the debtor's estate and to whom the debtor's property is assigned. From that point on, the debtor ceases to have any right to dispose of or deal with his property.

The estate of a bankrupt who has made an assignment is administered in the same manner as one administered under a receiving order (the procedure will be dealt with in the next section). However, a special simplified form of administration is provided in the case of an individual bankrupt who has made an assignment and whose realizable assets, after deducting the claims of secured creditors, do not exceed $5000 in value (section 49(6)).

Bankruptcy Orders   A creditor or group of creditors may file a petition with the court in the judicial district where the debtor is located in order to have the debtor declared bankrupt, provided the creditor (or group) is owed not less than $1000 and the debtor has committed an **act of bankruptcy** within the previous six months (section 43). A secured creditor may initiate a petition, but must elect to either give up her security or participate in the bankruptcy only to the extent of any deficiency after deduction of the security's value.

act of bankruptcy   a prescribed act of a debtor that must be proved before the debtor may be declared bankrupt

Unlike the rules for making proposals and assignments, there is no requirement that the debtor be insolvent; it is sufficient that he has committed an act of bankruptcy. An act of bankruptcy, discussed below, may be committed by a person who is not insolvent. However, in most cases where a bankruptcy order is made, the debtor is insolvent.

Subject to a few exceptions, a petition may be filed in respect of any debtor, whether an individual, partnership, or corporation. No petition may be made against an individual who is engaged solely in fishing or farming, or against a wage earner who does not earn more than $2500 a year and does not carry on any business on his own account (section 48).[10]

The burden of proving the facts alleged is on the petitioning creditors, who must comply with all the formalities required by the Act. The petition may be opposed by the debtor, who may dispute the existence of the debt or of an alleged act of bankruptcy. Even where the petitioning creditors succeed in establishing facts that would justify the making of a receiving order, the court has a general discretion to refuse to make the order or to grant a stay of proceedings. For example, it may decline to make an order if it considers that, given a fair chance, the debtor will be able to meet his obligations within a reasonable period. It may also decline to make an order where the debtor has no assets to divide among the creditors and there is no likelihood that he will have assets in the future.

Where a bankruptcy order is made, its effect is to vest the bankrupt's property in the trustee appointed by the court to administer the estate.

Acts of Bankruptcy

Before creditors can obtain a bankruptcy order, they must prove that the debtor has committed an act of bankruptcy. The Bankruptcy and Insolvency Act defines the conduct that constitutes an act of bankruptcy by a debtor (section 42) as follows:

- An assignment of assets to a trustee: If a debtor makes an assignment of his property to a trustee for the benefit of his creditors and the arrangement is not satisfactory to

---

[9] A person who defaults on a proposal may also be deemed to have made an assignment.

[10] Such an individual may, however, make a voluntary assignment. A corporation engaged in farming or fishing may be petitioned.

the creditors, they may cite the assignment as an act of bankruptcy and petition to have a bankruptcy order issued. They might choose to do so, for example, when the debtor has transferred his assets to a trustee who is not acceptable to them.

- A fraudulent transfer of assets to a third party other than a trustee: A transfer of property by a debtor in anticipation of bankruptcy in order to withhold assets from distribution to creditors is a fraudulent transfer. As we shall see when discussing "Powers and Duties of the Trustee" below, any attempt to deprive creditors of access to assets by transferring them to a third person (including the debtor's spouse or child) is void if the transfer takes place within a specified period prior to bankruptcy.

- A fraudulent preference: Any payment by a debtor that has the effect of settling the claim of one creditor in preference to the outstanding claims of other creditors is a fraudulent preference.

- An attempt by the debtor to abscond, with intent to defraud creditors.

- A failure to redeem goods seized under an execution issued against the debtor.[11] As discussed in Chapter 13, a creditor may sue a debtor, obtain judgment, and seek to satisfy the judgment by having the debtor's assets seized. When a debtor's assets are few, a seizure may well benefit the judgment creditor to the disadvantage of other creditors. Accordingly, if a debtor fails to take steps to prevent the sale of his property under an execution order, he commits an act that entitles his creditors to apply to the court for his bankruptcy. If they do so, all the debtor's property, including the property subject to the execution order, is put in the hands of a licensed trustee for distribution to all the creditors.[12]

- The presentation at a meeting of creditors of (a) a statement of assets and liabilities disclosing the debtor's insolvency, or (b) a written admission by the debtor that he is unable to pay his debts.

- An attempt to remove or hide any of his property, with intent to defraud creditors.

- Notice to any of the creditors that the debtor is suspending payment of his debts.

- A default in any proposal that the debtor has previously persuaded the creditors to accept as a means of forestalling bankruptcy proceedings.

- A failure to meet liabilities generally as they become due.

The most common of these acts of bankruptcy are failing to pay debts as they become due and failing to redeem goods seized under an execution.

ADMINISTRATION OF A BANKRUPT'S AFFAIRS

Powers and Duties of the Trustee

Once an assignment or bankruptcy order is made, the trustee takes possession of the assets of the bankrupt debtor and all books and documents relating to his affairs. She becomes in effect a temporary manager of the bankrupt debtor's business, subject to the supervision of inspectors appointed by the creditors. She may carry on the business or, alternatively, sell the assets. She can do such things as employ a lawyer, borrow further money for the business by pledging or mortgaging its remaining free (unsecured) assets, and negotiate with

---

[11] A debtor commits an act of bankruptcy if he permits an execution to remain unsatisfied for 15 days after seizure by the sheriff, until within five days of the time fixed for sale by the sheriff, or in a variety of other circumstances set out in section 42(1)(e).

[12] It is possible that, instead of petitioning for a bankruptcy order, all the debtor's major creditors may choose to obtain individual judgments and execution orders. In Ontario, the Creditors Relief Act, 2010, S.O. 2010, c. C.16, Sch. 4 provides for a scheme of distribution of the proceeds of sale among execution creditors.

creditors for the acceptance by them of specific assets in lieu of money settlement of their claims. She may even engage the bankrupt debtor himself to assist in the administration of the bankrupt estate. To do these things she must have specific authority from the inspectors (section 30). The principal duties of a trustee, however, are to recover all property that under bankruptcy law should form part of the debtor's estate, and to apply that property in satisfaction of the claims of creditors (sections 16(3), 25).

Recovery of Property   The trustee takes possession of those assets of the debtor that are in the debtor's possession and also seeks to recover any other assets, for example, by collecting debts owed to the debtor. As a general rule, the trustee cannot obtain a better title to property than the debtor himself possessed in that property. Consequently, the trustee's interest is subject to the claims of persons who own property that is in the possession of the debtor or of secured creditors who have interests in that property. The Personal Property Security Acts (PPSAs) have an exception to the general principle. If someone has leased personal property to the debtor and has failed to register that interest, the security interest may be ineffective and subordinate to the claim of the trustee.[13] As will be discussed further in later sections, some property (such as household goods) is exempt from seizure by the trustee.

In addition, there may be property that the debtor has disposed of and that by law should form part of his bankrupt estate and be available to satisfy the claims of creditors. For example, money collected for income tax, Canada Pension Plan, or employment insurance payments is deemed to be property held in trust for the government, and is not property of the debtor (section 67(3)). If a debtor has sold or disposed of assets for less than their market value, special rules apply so that a trustee may recover the property (sections 91–101.2).

Transfers at Undervalue   The term **transfer** refers to any sale, gift, trade, or disposition of property or supply of services by the debtor before becoming bankrupt. "Undervalue" means free or for payment that was obviously below fair market value. The intention of the rules is to prevent a person who is insolvent or on the verge of insolvency from prejudicing the claims of his creditors by giving his property away—usually to members of his family or to friends.

In general, any undervalue transfer[14] by a debtor, even to an unsuspecting good faith purchaser, that occurred within a year before his bankruptcy is void and the property or payment is recoverable by the trustee. In addition, the trustee may attack a transfer of property made as long as five years before the bankruptcy where the transfer was to a non-**arm's length** party—that is, a related or "knowing" purchaser. The trustee must show that at the date of the transfer the debtor was unable to pay his debts in full without the aid of such property and the transfer was done with the intent to defeat creditors (section 96).[15]

An undervalue transfer may also be attacked under provincial laws dealing with **fraudulent transfer**;[16] it is not unusual for a trustee in bankruptcy to pursue both kinds of remedies.

transfer   a gift, sale, or disposition of property made by a debtor before becoming bankrupt

arm's length   a transaction between persons who are not related or associated in any way

fraudulent transfer   a transfer of property by a debtor with the intention of putting that property out of the reach of creditors

---

[13] *Re Giffen*, [1998] 1 S.C.R. 91 considering the B.C. PPSA s. 20(1)(b); not followed in *Re Ouellet*, [2004] 3 S.C.R. 348 and *Lefebvre (Trustee) v. Tremblay*, [2004] 3 S.C.R. 326 at para. 40 because Quebec lacked a similar provision in its PPSA.

[14] The rule does not apply to property transferred in a genuine business transaction for good consideration (section 97); *Re Dowswell* (1999), 178 D.L.R. (4th) 193. Nor does it apply to transfers of property that would otherwise be exempt from execution, such as a RRIF; see, for example, *Royal Bank of Canada v. North American Life Assurance Co.* (1996), 132 D.L.R. (4th) 193 (S.C.C.). The trustee may also inquire into dividends paid or stock redemptions or purchases involving a company that goes bankrupt within a year (section 101).

[15] In practice, it is almost impossible for a trustee to establish the exact financial status of a bankrupt debtor at a time as long as a year or more before the bankruptcy.

[16] See, for example, Fraudulent Conveyances Act, R.S.B.C. 1996, c. 163; R.S.N.L. 1990, c. F-24; R.S.O. 1990, c. F.29; R.S.A. 2000, c. F-24; R.S.S. 1978, c. F-21.

A husband and wife had jointly owned their home since 1974. In 1978, the husband gave a personal guarantee to a bank in respect of a debt owed by the corporation of which he and his wife were the sole shareholders. In 1990, the husband transferred his half-interest in the home to his wife for $1. Shortly thereafter the bank demanded repayment of the debt and, when the husband was unable to meet the guarantee, it appointed a receiver. The husband died insolvent in 1991.

The bank successfully claimed that the transfer of the interest in the home was a fraudulent conveyance and was consequently void under the (Ontario) Fraudulent Conveyances Act. The bank was entitled to a 50 percent interest in the property.[17]

The Chans obtained a judgment against the Stanwoods for an amount exceeding $250 000 and were pressing for immediate payment. In an attempt to avoid the seizure of their family home and other assets, the Stanwoods consulted a lawyer, Davis, who recommended a complex scheme that involved the creation of a corporation with an elaborate share structure and voting rights. The home and assets were transferred to the corporation, but the Stanwoods remained in effective control of the corporation through their power to appoint "friendly" directors.

The Chans commenced proceedings under the (B.C.) Fraudulent Conveyances Act and were successful in having the transfer to the corporation set aside. Their claim for damages against the lawyer who devised the scheme failed. The court held that to advise someone to commit a breach of the Act is not a civil wrong.[18]

The provisions of the provincial legislation differ from those of the Bankruptcy and Insolvency Act in a number of respects, and the trustee may rely on the provincial Act to supplement the normal bankruptcy remedies.[19] In particular, it is not necessary to be an established creditor in order to bring proceedings under the Fraudulent Conveyances Acts to have a transaction set aside. Decisions have held that a claimant in a tort action (who had not yet obtained a judgment) could challenge a transfer of property to relatives designed to defeat the claim,[20] and that a wife could challenge a secret transfer of property by her husband to his children that would have the effect of depriving her of her rights under the Family Law Act.[21]

Preferences   A solvent debtor is entitled to pay his creditors in any order he pleases. He may choose to pay one creditor before he pays another—that is, to give preference to the claim of the first creditor over the second—perhaps because he depends upon the prompt services or delivery of goods from the first creditor. (Another reason is this: If the debtor is a corporation, the directors may have given personal guarantees of one or more of the debts.) By contrast, in bankruptcy the guiding principle is that creditors of the same class should be treated equally.

A debtor on the verge of bankruptcy is not permitted to unfairly favour certain creditors over others. The Act deals with this situation by providing that (a) a payment of money or a transfer of property to a creditor, (b) by an insolvent debtor, (c) within three months preceding bankruptcy, and (d) with a view to giving that creditor preference over other creditors, amounts to a **fraudulent preference** and is recoverable (section 95).

fraudulent preference   the payment of money or transfer of property to a creditor with a view to giving that creditor preference over other creditors

---

[17] *Bank of Montreal v. Bray* (1997), 36 O.R. (3d) 99; *Stone v. Stone* (2001) 55 O.R. (3d) 491. See also *XLO Investments Ltd. v. Hurontario Management Services* (1999), 170 D.L.R. (4th) 381 (Ont. C.A.) upholding trial judge's finding of fraudulent conveyance, cost order varied.

[18] *Chan v. Stanwood* (2002), 216 D.L.R. (4th) 625 (decided under previous legislation).

[19] *Flightcraft Inc. v. Parsons* (1999), 175 D.L.R. (4th) 642 (decided under previous legislation).

[20] *Hamm v. Metz* (2002), 209 D.L.R. (4th) 385.

[21] *Stone v. Stone, supra* n. 17. But see *Reisman v. Reisman*, 2012 ONSC 3148 (reorganization done of tax and estate planning purposes.

The time limit extends to 12 months where the creditor who received the preference is a related person or was not dealing at arm's length. The provisions are intended to nullify transactions that would otherwise defeat the legitimate claims of creditors. They do not invalidate payments made in good faith to creditors who were unaware of the impending bankruptcy, or other transfers of property such as the sale of inventory or other business assets in the normal course of business (section 97).[22] For more information on this topic, see the Companion Website.

CASE 29.3

Green Gables Manor Inc., a corporation operating a nursing home, made payments of $13 000 to each of its two controlling shareholders and directors. The payments were stated to be in respect of management fees owed to them. It also executed a general security agreement in their favour in respect of outstanding claims. The following day, a receiving order was granted, and Green Gables was declared bankrupt.

The trustee claimed repayment of the sums and a declaration that the security agreement was void. The court found that the two directors were "related" to the corporation for the purposes of the Bankruptcy and Insolvency Act, that the transactions represented a "preference," and that they should, accordingly, be set aside.[23]

Exempt Property   Not all the bankrupt's property is subject to seizure. For example, RRSPs (registered retirement savings plans) are **exempt** from bankruptcy seizure, save and except for the previous year's contribution. Provincial law may also exempt some property from seizure (section 67). Examples include household furnishings and appliances, tools of the bankrupt's trade, some farm property, and insurance policies, though these exemptions vary considerably from one province to another.

> **exempt**   property that is not subject to seizure by the trustee as a result of an exception in a federal or provincial statute

Payment of Claims

To rank as a claim against the bankrupt estate and share in distribution of the proceeds, all creditors must "prove" their debts. They do so by submitting declarations to the trustee outlining the details of their accounts with supporting evidence to substantiate the claims. The declaration states whether or not the claim is a secured or preferred claim. A provable claim is a debt or liability with a monetary value, owed to a creditor, which came into existence before the date of bankruptcy. Future and contingent claims are eligible but uncertain or unquantifiable claims may be denied by the trustee.[24] For more information on this topic, see the Companion Website.

Once the trustee has possession of the bankrupt's property, the duty is to use that property to satisfy the proven claims of creditors. That normally involves selling the property and distributing the cash proceeds among the creditors. In appropriate cases the trustee may distribute **liquidating dividends** (payments on account) to the creditors from time to time as required by the inspectors and as realization of the debtor's assets permits. In doing so she must, of course, be careful to take account of the claims of the secured and preferred creditors.

> **liquidating dividends**   payments made from time to time by a trustee in bankruptcy to creditors on account of the full amount due to them

Because the assets are almost always insufficient to satisfy all the claims in full, the priority of claims is important. A trustee must act with great care in the administration and liquidation of the debtor's affairs. She may be personally liable to creditors for losses caused

---

[22] *Orion Industries Ltd. v. Neil's General Contracting Ltd.*, 2013 ABCA 330

[23] *Re Green Gables Manor Inc.* (1998), 41 B.L.R. (2d) 299. Contrast *Sheraton Desert Inn Corp. v. Yung* (1998), 168 D.L.R. (4th) 126.

[24] Sections 121, 135; *Newfoundland and Labrador v. AbitibiBowater Inc.*, [2012] 3 SCR 443, 2012 SCC 67, at para 26, 34 (includes future or contingent claims).

them by her failure to pay the claims in the proper order of priority. The determination of priorities can be an extremely difficult matter, especially where the claims of secured creditors are involved. The trustee must determine whether a claim to a secured interest is effectively protected (for example, by registration under the PPSA).[25] Where there are two or more such claims, the trustee must determine their respective priority. That may prove especially difficult where the claims are made under different statutes, such as a provincial PPSA and the federal Bank Act.[26]

In such cases, it is normally advisable for the trustee to seek a ruling from the court.

super priority entitlement to be paid before secured creditors

Super Priority   **Super priority** entitles a creditor to have her claim paid before the claims of any secured creditor. The Bankruptcy and Insolvency Act gives specific creditors this status.

Unpaid Sellers   An unpaid seller has a right to repossess goods sold and delivered to a bankrupt in the 30 days preceding bankruptcy for use in the bankrupt's business (section 81.1). The supplier must make a demand within 15 days after bankruptcy, and the goods must still be in the possession of the purchaser, be identifiable, and be in the same condition as when sold. The claim ranks above any other claim to the goods, except that of a bona fide purchaser of the goods for value without notice of the supplier's right. A supplier who repossesses goods cannot subsequently claim against the bankrupt for any deficiency in respect of those goods.

Priority is also given to farmers, fishers, and aquaculturalists who have supplied their products to a bankrupt within 15 days of bankruptcy and have not been paid. The claims of such suppliers extend not only to the goods supplied but are also secured by a charge on the entire inventory of the purchaser. This charge ranks above any other claim against that inventory, except that of an unpaid seller of specific goods (section 81.2).

CASE 29.4

Thomson Electronics had supplied goods to Consumers Distributing, for which it had not been paid. Consumers Distributing was declared bankrupt, and Thomson claimed recovery of the goods that it had supplied in the preceding month. The goods were not in the possession of Consumers Distributing but were being stored in a warehouse belonging to Tibbett and Britten Inc., which was also a creditor of Consumers Distributing.

The court held that for section 81.1 to apply, the goods had to be in the actual physical possession of the bankrupt. Thomson's claim to recover the goods failed.[27]

current assets   cash or cash equivalent assets such as negotiable instruments, demand deposits, and accounts receivable

Wage Earners   The Act gives wage earners super priority for up to six months' unpaid wages (to a maximum of $2000) out of the **current assets** (liquid) of the debtor.[28] The priority extends to wages, commissions, salary, and compensation for services rendered, plus unremitted pension plan deductions. This claim ranks behind the unpaid seller but ahead of secured creditors. There is also a government-backed compensation scheme known as the Wage Earner Protection Program. Employees are entitled to claim up to $3000 (or four weeks) of arrears of wages from the fund.[29]

[25] See *Re Giffen, supra*, n.13.

[26] See e.g. *Royal Bank of Canada v. Sparrow Electric Corp.*, [1997] 1 S.C.R. 411; *Abraham v. Canadian Admiral Corp.* (1998), 39 O.R. (3d) 176; *Century Services Inc. v. Canada (Attorney General)*, [2010] 3 S.C.R. 379.

[27] *Thomson Consumer Electronics Canada, Inc. v. Consumers Distributing Inc.* (1999), 170 D.L.R. (4th) 115.

[28] *Supra*, n. 1, ss. 81.3, 81.4.

[29] Wage Earner Protection Program Act, S.C. 2005, c. 47.

Interim Financing Creditors   Sometimes it is necessary for an insolvent business to obtain credit while it tries to reorganize and survive as a going concern. Naturally, it is difficult to convince a lender to extend credit in such circumstances. A court may prioritize interim financing given during reorganization above any existing secured interest in an asset. The debtor and creditor must obtain permission of the court prior to making the loan. This type of financing is also known as **debtor-in-possession financing** (DIP) (section 50.6(3)).

debtor-in-possession financing   court-sanctioned secured loans advanced during reorganization and given priority over pre-existing secured creditors

Secured Creditors

Secured creditors rank behind unpaid sellers, agricultural suppliers, wage earners, and interim financing creditors in payment priority. The Act requires a secured creditor to give at least 10 days' notice to an insolvent person before enforcing her security (section 244) and contains provisions governing the conduct of a receiver, appointed by a secured creditor, insofar as that conduct relates to the administration of a bankrupt estate (sections 245–7).

Subject to these provisions, however, a secured creditor is entitled to enforce her security (seize the secured property) to obtain payment of what is owing. A secured creditor must pay to the trustee any surplus if the security she holds is worth more than the debt owing to her. When the trustee and secured creditor cannot agree on the value of the security, it may be necessary to sell it and pay the secured claim out of the proceeds (sections 127–34). The bankrupt estate is entitled to any surplus for the benefit of other creditors. When the value of the security is less than the secured debt, the creditor receives the full value of the security and, in addition, ranks as a general claim along with other unsecured creditors for the deficiency. When the trustee and secured creditor agree on the value of the secured assets without having to sell them, the creditor may accept the security in settlement of her account, either by paying any excess value to the trustee or by making a claim against the trustee as a general creditor for the deficiency.

Preferred Creditors

Out of the assets remaining after payment or settlement of priority and secured claims, the trustee must next pay the **preferred creditors**. Preferred creditors are listed in section 136 of the Act. The following is a summary of preferred claims, in their order of their priority.

preferred creditors   unsecured creditors whose claims are given preference over those of other unsecured creditors

1. When the bankrupt debtor is deceased, his reasonable funeral expenses and legal expenses related to his death.
2. Expenses and fees of the licensed trustee in bankruptcy and her legal costs.
3. A levy for the purpose of defraying the expense of the supervision of the Superintendent in Bankruptcy.
4. Up to six months' arrears of wages and pension deductions of employees of the bankrupt debtor to the extent of $2000 for each employee. This preference is available to satisfy remaining wages owed that were not paid under the super priority over current assets.
5. Spousal or child support arrears (s. 136 (d.1)); any tax refund owing to the debtor is exempt from seizure by the trustee if it is subject to a claim for arrears of spousal or child support.
6. Municipal taxes levied within the two years preceding bankruptcy.
7. Arrears of rent due to the landlord for a period of three months preceding bankruptcy.
8. The costs of the first execution or attachment creditor. (A creditor obtains an execution order against tangibles such as land or goods, and an attachment against choses in action such as accounts receivable or bank deposits.)
9. Indebtedness of the bankrupt under the Canada Pension Plan, the Employment Insurance Act, and the Income Tax Act for amounts required to be deducted from employees' salaries.
10. Claims for certain injuries sustained by employees not covered by workers' compensation.

General Creditors After settling the priority, secured, and preferred claims, the trustee pays the general creditors rateably to the extent of the funds remaining.

Deferred Creditors The BIA takes the claims of some creditors out of their usual class and delays their payment until after all other creditors. As noted above, non-arm's length creditors are deferred until after all other claims are paid (s. 137(1)). Similarly, silent partner loans (s. 139) and wages and compensation of officers and directors (s. 140) are deferred until after all other creditors are paid.

CHECKLIST

Priority of Payment of Claims

Claims against the property of a bankrupt debtor are paid in the following sequence:

1. Super priority claims
2. Secured creditors
3. Preferred creditors
4. General creditors
5. Deferred creditors

Duties of the Bankrupt Debtor

Following a receiving order or authorized assignment, the debtor must submit himself for examination by the official receiver to explain his conduct, the causes of his bankruptcy, and the disposition of his property. He must submit a sworn statement of his affairs to the trustee, together with a list of the names and addresses of his creditors and the security held by them, attend the first meeting of creditors, and supply the information they require. He must also hand over possession of his property to the trustee, cooperate with the trustee, and "aid to the utmost of his power in the realization of his property and the distribution of the proceeds among his creditors" (section 158(k)).[29A]

Bankruptcy Offences

A bankrupt debtor and any other person who commits an offence listed in the Act is liable to imprisonment or a substantial fine. These offences include failing to perform any of the duties considered above; making a fraudulent disposition of his property before or after bankruptcy; giving untruthful answers to questions put to him at an examination; concealing, destroying, or falsifying books or documents; and obtaining any credit or property by false representations before or after bankruptcy (section 198).

Discharge of the Bankrupt Debtor

An important object of bankruptcy legislation is to clear an honest but unfortunate debtor of outstanding debts and to leave him free to resume business life. The **discharge** of a bankrupt debtor usually cancels the unpaid portion of his debts remaining after the creditors receive their share of distribution, and gives the debtor a clean slate with which to start business again.

However, discharge does not cancel all debts. As discussed below, student loans are not automatically cancelled nor are income tax debts over $200 000. Debts arising from a

discharge a court order whereby a person who has been declared bankrupt ceases to have the status of a bankrupt person

---

[29A] Section 158(k), Bankruptcy and Insolvency Act, R.S.C., 1985, c. B-3.

child or spousal support order or the fraud of the bankrupt are not discharged; civil damage awards for intentionally inflicted bodily harm also survive.[30] Discharge is delayed for second-time bankrupts until after 24 or 36 months, depending upon their income. For more information on this topic, see the Companion Website.

Ethical Issue | Discrimination against Students

When a bankrupt person is discharged, the effect is normally to cancel or immediately discharge all his or her outstanding debts and to give him or her a fresh start. There are, however, some debts that are not cancelled (section 178). These include fines, penalties, damages for sexual assault, alimony, and student loans. The Canadian Federation of Students launched an unsuccessful challenge to this rule under the Charter.[31] As we have already noted, other debts to the government, such as personal income tax arrears, are also not automatically discharged.[32]

The 2007 amendments to the Bankruptcy and Insolvency Act softened but did not eliminate the harsh treatment of student loans. The new rule delays discharge of a student loan until seven years after completion of school (formerly 10 years), and students may apply to further reduce it to five years after completion of their studies for hardship reasons.

Questions to Consider

1. Do students deserve to be lumped together with criminals and "deadbeat" parents, as the *Toronto Star* put it? (April 3, 2004, at C2)

2. Are students (or ex-students) as a class entitled to the protection of the Charter?

3. What policy rationale justifies the different treatment of student loans?

Most debtors (who have completed mandatory counselling) are eligible for automatic discharge unless an objection is filed or tax arrears make up more than 75 percent of the debtor's unsecured debts. The chart below illustrates when an automatic discharge may be obtained under the amended BIA:

Automatic Discharge Availability			
Bankruptcy	**No Surplus**	**Surplus**	**75% of Unsecured Debts are Tax Arrears**
First	After 9 months	After 21 months	Hearing required
Second	After 24 months	After 36 months	Hearing required

One of the more important reasons a court may refuse or suspend the debtor's discharge is that his assets have proven to be insufficient to pay the unsecured creditors at least 50 cents on the dollar. He may still obtain a discharge, however, if he can show that he cannot reasonably be held responsible for this circumstance. Other reasons for refusing to give a discharge are the following:

- the bankrupt debtor neglected to keep proper books
- he continued to trade after he knew he was insolvent
- he failed to account satisfactorily for any loss or deficiency of assets
- he caused the bankruptcy by rash speculation or extravagant living
- within three months preceding bankruptcy he gave an undue preference to a creditor

---

[30] Section 178; *Gray (Re)* 2014 ONCA 236; *Dickerson v. 1610396 Ontario Inc.*, 2013 ONCA 653.

[31] *Chenier v. Canada (Attorney General)*, 2005 CanLII 23125 (Ont. Sup. Ct.).

[32] Section 172.1; see also Stephanie Ven-Ishai et al., "A Retrospective on the Canadian Consumer Bankruptcy System: 40 Years After the Tasse Report" (2011) 50 Can. Bus. L.J. 236 at 251–6.

- he was bankrupt or made a proposal to his creditors on a previous occasion
- he is guilty of any bankruptcy offence or has failed to perform his duties

Other related reasons are set out in the Act (section 173).[33]

Until obtaining his discharge, a bankrupt debtor is subject to a fine or imprisonment if, without disclosing his status, he obtains credit of $1000 or more for a purpose other than the supply of necessaries for himself and his family, or if he recommences business and fails to disclose to those with whom he deals that he is an undischarged bankrupt (section 199).

OTHER METHODS OF LIQUIDATION AND REORGANIZATION

Corporate Winding Up

There are, in addition to those under the BIA, a variety of ways in which the affairs of a solvent corporation may be wound up, but it is shareholders rather than the corporation or creditors who initiate the proceedings.

Each province has a separate statute or a part in its corporations act to provide a means of winding up solvent corporations.[35] The legislation may authorize the shareholders to appoint a liquidator (who may be a director, officer, or employee of the corporation) to wind up the affairs of the corporation without recourse to the court; alternatively, it may authorize them to apply to the court for a winding-up order and the appointment of a liquidator.

In addition, under the federal Winding-up and Restructuring Act,[36] the shareholders of a solvent, federally incorporated corporation may petition the court to issue a winding-up order. The court may issue a winding-up order if the capital of the corporation has been impaired to the extent of 25 percent, or if a substantial proportion of the shareholders petition for winding-up because of a lack of integrity or responsibility on the part of the corporation's management.

A corporation may also surrender its charter, apart from proceedings under either the Bankruptcy Act or a Winding-up Act. For example, the Canada Business Corporations Act permits dissolution, if a corporation has no property and no liabilities, by special resolution of the shareholders. "Articles of dissolution" are then sent to the director of the office that regulates federally incorporated corporations, and she issues a certificate of dissolution.[37] A corporation may wish to dissolve in this way when it has sold all its assets to another corporation and has distributed the proceeds to its shareholders, and when the purchasing corporation has assumed all its liabilities, with the consent of its creditors.

---

[33] In *Bank of Montreal v. Giannotti* (2000), 197 D.L.R. (4th) 266, the Ontario Court of Appeal refused a discharge to a bankrupt who had been "uncooperative, evasive and untruthful" about his financial affairs.

[34] *Michael Katz (Re)* 2013 ONSC 7426.

[35] See e.g. Corporations Act, C.C.S.M., c. C225, Part XVII; Business Corporations Act, R.S.O. 1990, c. B.16, Part XVI; Companies Winding-up Act, R.S.N.S. 1989, c. 82.

[36] R.S.C. 1985, c. W-11.

[37] R.S.C. 1985, c. C-44, s. 210.

The Companies' Creditors Arrangement Act

As discussed above, the Bankruptcy and Insolvency Act (BIA) provides an alternative to the formal liquidation of a debtor's estate by means of a "proposal." This allows the business to continue operating. For corporations, another method of avoiding liquidation is by means of a **compromise and arrangement** with the creditors, approved by the court, under the Companies' Creditors Arrangement Act (CCAA).[38] The CCAA and the BIA are distinct statutes that provide alternative complementary procedures, with many of their provisions being similar.

The CCAA allows a corporation in financial distress to seek court protection by way of a stay of BIA and creditor collection proceedings while it reorganizes its affairs in a way that may satisfy creditors. If the value of a corporation as a going concern exceeds its break-up value, a reorganization of its debts is usually preferable to the corporation itself, its creditors, and its employees. The mechanism is somewhat similar to that found in Chapter 11 of the U.S. Bankruptcy Code.

The purpose of the CCAA is to permit a corporation to restructure its affairs so that it can eliminate some of its debt and resume business in a leaner, more efficient form that will have a greater chance of returning to profitability. During the reorganization, the corporation's creditors are restrained from taking action (either enforcing collection of debts or forcing the debtor into bankruptcy). Creditors must work within the reorganization process. It is often complicated to determine which obligations must be honoured during restructuring and which may be stayed. For example, Nortel's obligation to make termination and severance payments to employees under the Ontario Employment Standards Act was stayed by the Ontario Court of Appeal until after CCAA restructuring.[39]

A relatively recent development has been the emergence of **vulture funds**—large investors who are prepared to purchase substantial portions of the debtor corporation's debts or its shares at a heavily discounted price, hoping that the reorganization will be successful. This development seems in some ways to be contrary to the true intention of the Act, since these investors are clearly far more concerned with realizing a quick profit on their investment than in securing the rehabilitation of the debtor. However, one advantage is that the process provides a market in which smaller creditors may sell their claims without having to wait for the reorganization to be completed.

There are some differences between the CCAA and the proposal procedures under the BIA. In particular, the CCAA applies only if the total creditor claims exceed $5 million. When a court grants a CCAA stay of bankruptcy and court proceedings (section 11.02), the existing management of the business continues to operate the business under the supervision of a court appointed **monitor** (section 11.7) who watches the management and prepares a report for the court and the Superintendent of Bankruptcy (section 23). The final arrangement must be approved by a two-thirds majority of the creditors.[40] A court may rule on and approve any controversial issues. Under the CCAA, judges have greater discretion and flexibility than under the BIA; courts tend to interpret the two statutes in a compatible and consistent way to discourage forum shopping.[41]

Arrangements may include protecting critical suppliers and interim financiers by granting priority in payment so that they will continue to supply the business during the restructuring phase.[42] As well, the arrangement often includes protection from liability for directors and officers so that they too will continue to manage the business during the

compromise and arrangement an agreement made by a debtor corporation with its creditors whereby arrangements are made for repayment of debts without liquidating the corporation

vulture funds large investors who purchase the debt or shares of a corporation in the course of its reorganization

monitor a person appointed to supervise the reorganization of a debtor corporation under the Companies' Creditors Arrangement Act

---

[38] R.S.C. c. C-36

[39] *Sproule v. Nortel Networks Corp*, 2009 ONCA 833.

[40] 40 CCAA, s. 6.

[41] *Century Services Inc. v. Canada (Attorney General)* 2010 SCC 60 at paras 47-63.

[42] CCAA, ss. 11.2, 11.4.

restructuring phase. Even with such immunity, disadvantaged groups of creditors often pursue oppression remedies.[43] As part of the CCAA restructuring process, directors may be removed from the board.[44]

BUILDERS' LIENS

Nature of Builders' Liens

A bailee who makes repairs or improvements on goods obtains a possessory lien on the goods for the value of her services. By contrast, when a person extends credit by performing work or supplying materials in the construction of a building or other structure affixed to land, it is physically impossible for him to exercise a possessory lien. In any event, under the law of real property, when goods are affixed permanently to land they become fixtures (part of the land): The supplier of the goods is not permitted to sever them from the property. In these circumstances, a creditor had no recourse at common law except to sue for the debt owing and obtain judgment and an order for execution against the land. However, additional protection is provided by statute.

builders' lien an interest that builders and others involved in construction work may have in a building as security for money owed to them for work done (also known as a mechanics' lien or a construction lien)

Contractors and Subcontractors In all provinces of Canada, persons who have extended credit in the form of goods and services to improve land now have a statutory remedy under **builders' lien** legislation. Although the title and wording of the acts vary from province to province, each act provides substantially the same protection for creditors. Its basic purposes are to give creditors who have provided work and material for the improvement of land an interest in the land as security for payment and "to prevent multiplicity of actions for small claims, in which the cost would be enormously out of proportion to and in excess of the sums claimed . . . ."[45]

The provisions of builders' lien acts operate in two rather different ways.

ILLUSTRATION 29.1

O Co. hires C. Co to build an apartment building on its land for an agreed price. C Co., in turn, subcontracts the specialized tasks of supplying and erecting the structural steel, installing the plumbing and heating systems and electrical wiring, and supplying and installing elevators to various firms specializing in these trades.

In Illustration 29.1, there are two types of contracts: a master contract between O Co., the owner of the property, and the main contractor, C Co.; and a series of subcontracts between the main contractor, C Co., and the various specialized trades. In respect to the master contract, O Co. is liable for the whole amount of the contract price as a contractual debt. C Co. has a builders' lien—that is, an interest in O Co.'s land and building as it is erected—for the total value of work and materials (to the maximum of the contract price) provided by C Co. and its subcontractors. In turn, the subcontractors and suppliers have a right of action against C Co. for the value of the work and materials supplied for the project under the terms of the subcontracts. There is, however, no privity of contract between the subcontractors and suppliers and O Co. Nevertheless, the legislation also gives liens against the land to the subcontractors and suppliers.

---

[43] Janis Sarra, "The Evolution of the Companies' Creditors Arrangement Act in Light of Recent Developments" (2011) 50 Can. Bus. L.J. 211 at 229–31.

[44] Ss. 11.5, 11.51; similar power exists under the BIA, ss. 64, 64.1

[45] *McPherson v. Gedge* (1883–4), 4 O.R. 246, at 257.

Holdback   The value of these liens is limited to a specified proportion of the price due from the owner, O Co., to the main contractor, C Co., under the master contract. This proportion, called a **holdback**, varies somewhat from province to province but is generally 10–20 percent.[46] Where the value of the work and materials exceeds the holdback, the subcontractors and suppliers have no security in the land for the excess sum.

O Co. fully protects itself against liens of the subcontractors and suppliers by retaining the holdback during construction and for a specified period afterward. If C Co. should become insolvent during this period, O Co. would pay the holdback into court for the benefit of the lienholders. The court would then supervise the payment of this money among the lienholders, and neither O Co. nor its land would be subject to their claims.

holdback   an amount that the owner who contracts for construction work may withhold from payments made to the principal contractor to protect against claims from subcontractors and suppliers

Who Is Protected?   A builders' lien is available only to creditors who participate directly as workers or supply material for use directly in the construction work.[47]

The courts have held that an architect who prepares the plans for a building comes within this definition and is entitled to a lien.[48] Some provincial statutes give a lien to a lessor who rents equipment for use on the contract site for the price of the rental of the equipment.[49] On the other hand, a party that sells tools, machinery, or general supplies to a contractor is not entitled to a lien against a building constructed with the use of the tools or machinery it has supplied; the tools and machinery remain the property of the contractor and can be used in other projects as well.[50] Where, however, a supplier delivers the goods directly to the building site, it obtains a lien immediately, whether the materials are eventually used in the structure or not.[51] The reason for this provision is that a supplier who delivers materials to the building site reasonably assumes that they will be used there and relies upon the property as security for his claim.

Suppliers of materials may, if they choose, waive their right of lien by contract. They may find an advantage in doing so when the effect is to persuade a mortgagee to lend additional funds for the completion of a project. The suppliers may then realize their claims out of the proceeds of a sale of the completed building. For more information on this topic, see the Companion Website.

Employees' Rights   The bargaining power of wage earners may be unequal to that of the builders and contractors who employ them, and these wage earners may not fully understand the nature of their rights. As a result, the various acts contain a provision that a term in a contract of employment waiving the employee's right of lien is void. However, in some provinces this provision does not apply to employees whose wages exceed a specified amount per day.

The acts give wage earners a priority for approximately one month's arrears of wages over all other liens derived through the same contractor or subcontractor.[52] This priority recognizes the fact that wages often provide the sole means of subsistence of wage earners, while suppliers of materials and lessors of equipment probably carry on business with several construction projects at once, and usually have larger capital funds to depend on if a single contractor or owner defaults in payment.

---

[46] See, e.g., Builders' Lien Act, S.B.C. 1997, c. 45, s. 4(1); Construction Lien Act, R.S.O. 1990, c. C.30, s. 1(1). (Subsequent references to these particular acts in footnotes will be simply to B.C. and Ont., followed by section number.)

[47] A land-use consultant engaged by a developer to advise on zoning issues was not entitled to a lien. His work contributed to the project as a whole, but did not constitute "work on" any particular improvement: *Kreuchen v. Park Savannah Development Ltd.* (1999), 171 D.L.R. (4th) 377.

[48] *Chaston Construction Corp. v. Henderson Land Holdings (Canada) Ltd.* (2002), 214 D.L.R. (4th) 405.

[49] Available in Ontario, Alberta, Newfoundland and Labrador, and Saskatchewan: see, e.g., Ont., ss. 1(1) and 14(1), supra n. 46.

[50] *Crowell Bros. v. Maritime Minerals Ltd.*, [1940] 2 D.L.R. 472.

[51] Supra n. 46, Ont., s. 15.

[52] *Ibid.*, B.C., s. 37; Ont., s. 81.

Procedures under Builders' Lien Legislation

Registration A builders' lien arises immediately upon work being done or materials being used in the improvement of property or (in some provinces) upon the supply of rented equipment for use on a contract site. The lienholder must register it against the title to the land. It may be registered during the performance of the work or services or supply of material or within a specified period of time (usually 45 days) after completion or abandonment of performance. If a lien is not registered within the time specified, it ceases to exist. Following registration, the lienholder must commence a legal action—usually within 90 days after the work has been completed or the materials have been placed or furnished, or after the expiry of the period of credit.[53] For this purpose, provinces have interpreted "completion of the contract" to mean "substantial performance of the contract."[54] Registration also gives a contractor or subcontractor a lien against the property itself.

In most of the provinces, an action brought by one lien claimant is deemed to be brought on behalf of all other lien claimants, and it is unnecessary even to name other lien claimants as participants, since they must be served with notice of the trial.[55]

Registration in the land registration system provides public notice of a lienholder's claim and establishes the lienholder's priority over unsecured creditors of the owner of the property and over subsequent mortgagees and purchasers of an interest in the property. A lien expires unless the lienholder brings an action to enforce the claim within the prescribed time and registers a certificate stating that the action has been started.

Lienholders' Rights A builders' lien does not give a lienholder the right to personally take possession of or to sell land and buildings to realize a claim. In fact, if the lienholder is a subcontractor and if the owner pays the statutory holdback into court, the lienholder's rights are limited to its share in this fund: It has no rights against the land and buildings of the owner. Even if an owner fails to pay the statutory holdback into court, the lienholder's claim against the land is limited to the amount the owner should have paid into court. To realize its claim against the land, a lienholder, whether a main contractor or a subcontractor, must first bring an action and obtain a court order appointing a trustee. The trustee then has the power to manage the property and to sell it for the benefit of the lienholder and other creditors.

If eventually the trustee does sell the property, she must pay the proceeds to satisfy, first, the claims for municipal taxes; second, those of mortgagees who have prior registered mortgages; third, lienholders' claims for wages, regardless of the order in which they filed their liens; fourth, all other lienholders' claims, regardless of the order in which they filed their liens; fifth, subsequent mortgagees or other persons who have a secured interest in the land; and, finally, if there are any proceeds left, claims of the general creditors of the owner. After all creditors are paid, any balance remaining belongs to the owner.

Progress Payments During the construction of a building and for the specified statutory period afterward, the owner may safely make progress payments to the contractor for all amounts except the statutory holdback.[56] However, if the owner receives notice from subcontractors or suppliers that liens are outstanding and unlikely to be paid by the contractor, she should cease payments to the contractor at once and ascertain the extent of the liens. If there is some doubt whether the holdback is sufficient to satisfy

---

[53] *Ibid.*, B.C., s. 14 (one year); Ont., s. 36.

[54] Construction Lien Act, R.S.O. 1990, Chapter C.30, B.C., s. 1; Ont., s. 2.

[55] *Ibid.*, Ont. ss. 50(3), 59.

[56] *Ibid.*, B.C., s. 6(3); Ont., s. 22(1).

the claims for liens, she should seek legal advice immediately; as soon as she has knowledge of these claims, she loses the protection of the Act to the extent that she continues to make payments to the contractor. On the other hand, she must not make the error of wrongfully withholding payment due to a solvent contractor because of an unfounded claim for a lien.

In some jurisdictions, all money received by contractors and subcontractors on account of the contract price is deemed to be trust funds held for the benefit of those who have performed work or services or furnished materials. The contractor or subcontractor, accordingly, cannot divert those funds to other purposes until all the claims against it are satisfied.[57]

Once the statutory period has elapsed and no claims have been registered, the owner may pay the holdback to the contractor and complete her obligations under the contract.

Practical Application of Builders' Liens

Mortgage Lenders   An owner of land usually finances a construction project by mortgaging the land to a mortgagee who advances the mortgage money as work progresses on the building. Some builders' lien laws require a mortgagee to withhold from the mortgage advances an amount equal to the sum that the owner should withhold from the contractor. Even if the Act does not have such requirements, it is sensible for a mortgagee to hold back.

Tenants   When a tenant contracts to have a building erected on his landlord's property or, perhaps more commonly, to have improvements made to existing buildings, a builders' lien is not enforceable against the landlord's interest in the property unless the lienholder can establish that the work was undertaken either expressly or impliedly at the request of the landlord.

Contractors Who Own the Land   Contractors construct buildings on their own land, especially residential buildings. If bad luck or mismanagement cause insolvency, his "subcontracts" with specialized trades are really main contracts with himself as owner. Accordingly, the land is subject to liability for the total value of the liens, and the holdback provisions do not apply. Often a builder will have obtained mortgage money on the land; the mortgagee will have priority over the lienholders for only the money already advanced to the builder before the liens arose.

OTHER STATUTORY PROTECTION OF CREDITORS

Provisions protecting the rights of creditors, or of particular types of creditors, are found in many statutes, in most of which creditor protection is merely incidental to the main aim of the statute. In addition to the measures discussed above, two other statutes merit a brief mention.

Bulk Sales Acts

All the common law provinces initially had a statute called the Bulk Sales Act, modelled on legislation commonly adopted in the United States. The purpose of the statute was to protect the creditors of a person making a "**bulk sale**"—that is, a sale of all, or substantially all, the inventory of a business or the fixtures and goods with which the business carried on. The statute called for notice to and consent by a creditor before a bulk sale would be effective. Most provinces have repealed their Bulk Sales Acts, apparently taking the view that with the adoption of comprehensive Personal Property Security Acts, the Bulk Sales Acts no longer served any useful purpose.

bulk sale   a sale of all or substantially all the assets of a business

---

[57] *Ibid.*, Ont., s. 8(1). See *Rudco Insulation Ltd. v. Toronto Sanitary Inc.* (1998), 42 O.R. (3d) 292.

The main exception to this trend has been Ontario, which still retains its Bulk Sales Act, although exemptions from the Act are often given.[58]

Business Corporations Acts

As noted in Chapter 26, a corporation's creditors may seek an "oppression remedy," provided in section 241 of the Canada Business Corporations Act (CBCA) and the various provincial acts. Although the primary intention behind the oppression remedy was to protect shareholder rights and interests, the CBCA[59] includes, in the definition of a "complainant" who may seek a remedy for oppression, the holder of a "security" of the corporation (which includes a debt obligation) and "any other person who, in the discretion of the court, is a proper person to make an application" under that part of the Act.

The remedy may be granted where the court is satisfied that the actions of a corporation have been oppressive or unfairly prejudicial to the interests of "any security holder, creditor, director, or officer" of the corporation.

In a number of cases, most notably in the Supreme Court of Canada's decision in *BCE Inc. v. 1976 Bondholders*, it has been held that creditors, both secured and unsecured, have standing to complain of oppression by the managers of their debtor corporation, and are entitled to seek any of the wide range of remedies that the court has discretion to order.[60]

To avoid claims of oppression, directors and officers must consider more than just the legal rights of creditors—they have a duty to consider the reasonable expectations of creditors before deciding on a course of action.[61] Usual commercial practice and past behaviour of management play a significant role in forming the reasonable expectations of creditors, and any departure from these should be done cautiously with due regard for the prejudicial effect on the creditor's interests.[62]

CASE 29.6

SCI Systems advanced money to GTL Co. in return for a promissory note for $800 000. GTL defaulted when the note became due, and SCI obtained a default judgment against GTL. GTL still failed to pay, claiming that it was unable to do so. SCI discovered that, shortly before the note became due, GTL paid dividends amounting to $850 000 to its three directors, who were also its sole shareholders, and also transferred to them other assets worth $250 000.

In an action under section 248 of the (Ontario) Business Corporations Act, the court held that the conduct of the directors had resulted in protecting the company from its payment obligation to SCI Systems. The acts of GTL Co.'s directors were oppressive to SCI, and the directors were personally liable for the full amount of the judgment.[63]

---

[58] R.S.O. 1990, c. B.14. Newfoundland and Labrador also has a Bulk Sales Act. *Mayfield Suites Hotel Mississauga Limited Partnership (Re)*, 2013 ONSC 7780 (suggesting Bulk Sales Act should be limited to situations where creditors will be paid in full, with other insolvency legislation picking up the slack for those cases where they will not. (para 17)).

[59] R.S.C. 1985, c. C-44, ss. 238, 241.

[60] *BCE Inc. v. 1976 Bondholders*, 2008 S.C.C. 69. See also *Sidaplex-Plastic Suppliers Inc. v. Elta Group Inc.* (1995), 131 D.L.R. (4th) 399; *Levy-Russell Ltd. v. Shieldings Inc.*, [1998] O.J. No. 3932; *First Edmonton Place Ltd. v. 315888 Alberta Ltd.*, [1988] A.J. No. 511 (Alta. Q.B.), aff'd [1989] A.J. No. 1021 (Alta C.A.). Section 241(3) of the Canadian Business Corporations Act empowers a court to make an order as it thinks fit upon a finding of oppression.

[61] *BCE Inc.*, *supra*, n. 60, at paras. 101–2.

[62] *BCE Inc.*, *supra*, n. 60, at paras 73–94.

[63] *SCI Systems, Inc. v. Gornitzki Thompson & Little Co.* (1997), 147 D.L.R. (4th) 300 varied only as to amount [1998] O.J. No. 2299 (Ont. Div. C.). The applicant also relied on the provisions of the Fraudulent Conveyances Act, R.S.O. 1990, c. F.29, and the Assignments and Preferences Act, R.S.O. 1990, c. A.33, but having found oppression, the court considered it unnecessary to deal with that issue. See also, *Far East Food Products Ltd. v. 1104742 Ontario Ltd.*, [2009] O.J. No. 1153 (Ont. S.C.).

Although the courts have occasionally warned that debt actions should not be routinely turned into oppression actions,[64] the practice of using the oppression remedy as a means of enforcing creditors' rights is growing rapidly. This trend is perhaps unfortunate, since it seems that the oppression remedy can be used to allow one creditor to gain an advantage over other creditors with competing claims, creditors who are not parties to the action and whose interests are not required to be considered by the court. It also adds yet another form of action to the already bewildering confusion of potentially conflicting creditors' remedies. In *BCE Inc. v. 1976 Bondholders*, the Supreme Court denied the bondholders' claim of oppression arising from the directors' decision to accept a buyout offer to privatize the company. The transaction was in the best interests of the company and necessary to remain financially viable, and conflicting stakeholder interests could not all be met.[65]

LIMITATIONS STATUTES

We noted in Chapter 12 that when a person has a right of action against someone who defaults payment on a debt or who is in breach of contract, she must begin an action within a prescribed period or lose the right to sue. In most provinces the usual limitation period is now two years.[66] A plaintiff must start court proceedings within the two-year period or lose the right to resort to the courts. Such limitations on actions are justified on the grounds that a person who fails to pursue a claim leaves the other party in a state of uncertainty that ought not to continue permanently, and because, as the years pass, it becomes more difficult to produce the evidence concerning the facts of the case.

The limitation period runs from the time that the claim is "discoverable." A right of action does not arise until there has been a breach or default. Thus, in a contract for the sale of goods on credit, the seller's right of action does not arise until the price becomes due and the buyer fails to pay. A trade account receivable often comprises a number of charges for goods or services invoiced at different times in the past and since paid in part. A customer (debtor) is entitled to specify the particular purchases against which a payment on account is to be applied, but in the absence of such instructions, the supplier (creditor) is entitled to treat each payment as discharging the oldest outstanding purchases and so keep the debt current.

The limitation period for an action for breach of contract starts over again if the debtor makes a part payment or delivers a written promise to pay. However, if the debtor makes a new promise to pay the debt, he is bound by that promise and may be sued upon it.

A debtor need not make an express promise to pay; his promise to pay may be implied from the circumstances of the part payment. Normally, a presumption of a new promise to pay arises from the mere fact of making a part payment or from a written acknowledgment of the debt, without other evidence to contradict the presumption.

Each province has a general limitations statute governing limitation periods for a number of different classes of actions, and limitation periods are often also prescribed in other statutes. The limitation periods vary considerably. For this reason, when considering starting an action or defending one under the provisions of a statute, a lawyer first checks to see if a limitation period might affect the rights of the parties.

---

[64] See *Royal Trust Corp. of Canada v. Hordo* (1993), 10 B.L.R. (2d) 86. A creditor does not have an automatic right to bring an action for an oppression remedy. The remedy is discretionary and should probably not be granted where ordinary bankruptcy proceedings provide a satisfactory resolution: see *C.C. Petroleum Ltd. v. Allen* (2003), 36 B.L.R. (3d) 244.

[65] 2008 S.C.C. 69, at paras. 61, 110–4.

[66] See e.g. Limitations Act, R.S.A. 2000, c. L-12, s. 3; Limitation Act, R.S.B.C. 1996, c. 266, s. 3; Limitations Act, S.O. 2002 c. 24, s. 4. In some provinces, the period for actions in contract is still six years; for example, Limitation of Actions Act, R.S.N.S. 1989, c. 258, s. 2(1)(e).

Strategies to Manage the Legal Risks

Businesses are both debtors and creditors. From a creditor perspective, the best strategy is to be careful when granting credit. Take advantage of the available public records of credit history, proposals, and bankruptcies. Search not only the corporate name of the debtor but also its directors and officers to determine if the current company is merely a fresh start after a bankrupt business. Ask for the personal guarantee of the principal where credit history is weak or unavailable. Take security in the goods provided; this will raise the priority of the debt in an eventual bankruptcy. Set up a control system to monitor lien periods for building supplies and limitation periods for all debts so the collection actions are commenced within the necessary legal time periods. If dealing with an insolvent debtor, seek super priority before extending further credit or continuing to supply.

From a debtor's perspective, consider carefully before personally guaranteeing the debts of the business; monitor accounts receivable so payments are made on time, and check credit history regularly to ensure that it properly reflects the position of the business. Take evasive action early by communicating with creditors and considering proposals or CCAA arrangements before bankruptcy is the only solution. Be careful not to mislead creditors as to the financial credibility of the company, as this is a bankruptcy offence and resulting debts are not discharged. Directors and officers may be personally liable if they do this.

Directors and officers of an insolvent corporation that is undertaking a BIA proposal or a restructuring under the CCAA should seek indemnification from liability either through director's liability insurance or a court-ordered preferred charge against the assets of the corporation. Such a charge ranks ahead of secured creditors. Of course, directors and officers must still act with due diligence in the best interests of the corporation as gross negligence or willful misconduct will not be indemnified.

When considering proposals under the BIA, arrangements under the CCAA or restructuring plans under business corporations legislation, directors and officers should be aware of their obligations to consider not only the legal rights of creditors but their reasonable expectations. Claims of oppression will follow any decision that unduly or unfairly prejudices the rights of a creditor. Due consideration of all interests and expectations balanced against the best interests of the corporation are management's best defence.

QUESTIONS FOR REVIEW

1. What objectives does the Bankruptcy and Insolvency Act seek to achieve?
2. What are the functions of the Superintendent of Bankruptcy, the Official Receiver, and the Trustee in Bankruptcy?
3. Distinguish between a bankrupt and an insolvent person.
4. How is a "consumer debtor" defined?
5. What is the difference between an assignment and a bankruptcy order?
6. What is the effect, in bankruptcy law, of a proposal?
7. Distinguish between an act of bankruptcy and a bankruptcy offence.
8. Distinguish between an arm's length and non-arm's length transaction preference.
9. What is a "transfer under value"?
10. What special right does an unpaid seller of goods have when the buyer is bankrupt?
11. What is a "preferred creditor"? What are the principal categories of preferred claims?
12. How does a bankrupt become "discharged"?

13. What is the aim of the Companies' Creditors Arrangement Act?
14. What is the purpose of a "holdback" under builders' lien legislation?
15. Whose interests are protected by a builders' lien?
16. How do the business corporations statutes protect creditors of corporations?

CASES AND PROBLEMS

1. Continuing Scenario

   Most of Ashley's Restaurant customers pay their accounts on a per visit basis. Credit is extended to only a few regular customers and some food services businesses that carry her bakery line. Bunch-A-Lunch is a lunch-truck sole proprietorship that carries Ashley's baked goods and is billed monthly. Its account has been in arrears for six months when Ashley receives a letter from a trustee in bankruptcy for Jason Bunch, the sole proprietor of Bunch-A-Lunch. The letter announces that Jason has made an assignment into bankruptcy and lists Ashley's Restaurant among his creditors. A prove claim form is enclosed. Upon further investigation, Ashley discovers that the bank has a PPSA security interest registered in the lunch truck; that Steven, the part-time driver who fills in for Jason, has not been paid in two months; and that the business has only been in operation for two years. This is a surprise to Ashley because Jason said that the business was 10 years old on the customer account application form he filled out for Ashley a year ago. What should Brendan, Ashley's lawyer, tell her about the bankruptcy process, where her claim would rank among other creditors, and whether her debt could survive the bankruptcy?

2. Leung was in serious financial difficulties. She owed $150 000 to Desert Rose Inc., in respect of a business venture. She also owed $100 000 to Kwan. She entered into an agreement with Kwan whereby she sold her house to Kwan for $500 000, which was approximately its fair market value. The debt of $100 000 was set off against the purchase price, and it was further agreed that Kwan would lease the house back to Leung for a period of two years at a rent of $30 000 a year. That sum of $60 000 was also set against the purchase price. The balance of $340 000 was paid on completion of the transfer and was mostly used by Leung to pay off debts to her other creditors.

   When Desert Rose sought to collect the debt owed to it, Leung was unable to pay. Does Desert Rose have grounds for impugning the transaction between Leung and Kwan?

3. On April 1, Greenfingers Garden Centre Ltd. was declared bankrupt as a result of a petition entered by the Agricultural Bank Ltd. The Bank was owed $250 000 by Greenfingers and had registered a security interest pursuant to a general security agreement that covered all of Greenfingers' inventory and other business assets.

   On the preceding March 1, Snow White Ornaments Inc. had supplied Greenfingers with 120 garden gnomes, to the value of $2500. On March 12, Bauer, a farmer, supplied a number of fruit trees to Greenfingers for $1000. And on March 15, Spreaders Inc. supplied Greenfingers with a quantity of bags of fertilizer for $800. None of them has been paid. Some of the trees and fertilizer, and almost all the gnomes, remain unsold.

   What claims do the respective creditors have?

4. Buckhouse Inc. is the owner of a large office building in the downtown area of a major Canadian city. It entered into a 10-year lease, at a monthly rental of $8000, with Justitia Ltd. As an inducement to enter into the lease, Buckhouse granted Justitia an 18-month rent-free period, a leasehold improvement allowance of $100 000, and a cash payment of $150 000.

   Justitia Ltd. is a corporation formed by two lawyers, Straight and Narrow, as a management company for their law practice. Straight and Narrow are the sole shareholders and directors of Justitia.

   The law practice occupied the premises for a period of 21 months, though Straight and Narrow never entered into a written lease with Justitia Ltd. At the end of that period, with rent having been paid for only three months, they moved out of the building and found other premises.

Justitia has ceased to pay rent to Buckhouse and, apart from the lease, has no assets. The inducement payment of $150 000 was paid out as a dividend to Straight and Narrow.

Does Buckhouse have any claim against Straight and Narrow?

5. The N.S.F. Manufacturing Co. Ltd. was adjudged bankrupt on a petition of its creditors, and the trustee in bankruptcy realized the following amounts from the sale of its business assets:

Cash in bank	$ 1 000
Accounts receivable	52 000
Inventories	25 000
Land and buildings	74 000
	$152 000

The liabilities of the business were as follows at the time of the receiving order:

Bank loan secured under section 427 of the Bank Act	$ 40 000
Trade accounts payable	65 000
Municipal taxes payable	5 000
Wages payable (five months at $3000 per month for one employee)	15 000
First mortgage on land and buildings	50 000
Second mortgage on land and buildings	25 000
	$200 000

The expenses of liquidation were $5000. The trustee's fee was $3000.

How many cents on the dollar should the general creditors receive? Show the order in which the trustee in bankruptcy made payments to the various types of creditors. Assume that all secured creditors had taken the necessary steps to protect their security.

6. Yorkville Construction Inc. was the main contractor on a large construction project on land owned by Mayfair Properties Ltd. Yorkville engaged Rodwell Ltd. to provide piping insulation services for the project. Yorkville received a series of payments from Mayfair under the contract, and used all the monies to pay its general overhead expenses, including advertising and promotion expenses, bank charges, insurance, lease payments on its vehicles, office rent, and utilities. It did not pay Rodwell for its work. Yorkville became insolvent.

Does Rodwell have any claim against (a) Mayfair or (b) the directors of Yorkville?

Additional Resources for Chapter 29 on the Companion Website

(www.pearsoncanada.ca/smyth)

In addition to pre- and post-tests, mini-cases, and application exercises, the Companion Website includes the following province-specific resources for Chapter 29:

- **Alberta:** Bankruptcy and Insolvency; Fraudulent Conveyances; Fraudulent Preferences
- **Atlantic Provinces:** Construction Liens; Fraudulent Conveyances and Preferences
- **British Columbia:** Builders' Liens; Collection Agents; Creditor Assistance Act; Debt Collection; Liens
- **Manitoba/Saskatchewan:** Builders' Liens; Exempt Property in Bankruptcy; Fraudulent Transfers and Conveyances
- **Ontario:** Assignment and Preferences; Bulk Sales; Construction Liens; Debt Collection Process; Fraudulent Conveyances; Limitation Periods

Chapter 30

International Business Transactions

— CANADIAN BUSINESS IN A GLOBAL ECONOMY

— LAW AND INTERNATIONAL BUSINESS

— FOREIGN TRADE

— FOREIGN INVESTMENT

— THE RESOLUTION OF INTERNATIONAL BUSINESS DISPUTES

— STRATEGIES TO MANAGE THE LEGAL RISKS

As previous chapters have identified, both law and business administration in Canada often involve international issues. Increasingly, the world is becoming a single giant marketplace in which businesses from different countries compete against and sometimes cooperate with each other. This chapter provides an overview of the legal framework within which international business is conducted, discussing various aspects of foreign trade, foreign investment, and the resolution of international business disputes.

We examine such questions as:

■ What are the common features of export contracts?

■ How are export contracts interpreted and enforced?

■ How do governments regulate international trade?

■ How is international trade affected and promoted by the World Trade Organization (WTO) and the North American Free Trade Agreement (NAFTA)?

■ What are the legal forms available to foreign investors?

■ How do governments regulate foreign investment?

■ In what ways does international law apply to investment?

■ How are international business obligations enforced by the courts?

■ What is the role of international commercial arbitration?

■ How are trade disputes resolved within NAFTA and the WTO?

CANADIAN BUSINESS IN A GLOBAL ECONOMY

For Canada, the international dimension of business is especially important. Canadian exports amount to approximately one-third of the nation's gross domestic product.[1] Canada ranks among the top 15 of the world's trading nations and is a major exporter of both goods and services. In 2012, its total exports amounted to $546.6 billion, and imports to $582.8 billion. To put these figures in perspective, one of the world's largest exporters, the United States, exports approximately three times as much merchandise as Canada, and Japan not even double.

Canada's largest trading partner is the United States, which takes over 70 percent of our exports and provides over 60 percent of our imports. In turn, Canada is one of the largest trading partners of the United States. The United States exports more to Canada than to any other trading partner and imports more from Canada than from anywhere else except the European Union and China.[2] Canada also has substantial trading relations with countries as diverse as China, the United Kingdom, Germany, Korea, Japan, the Netherlands, France, and Mexico.

Traditionally, Canada's strength was as an exporter of raw materials and minerals (and Canada remains among the world's largest exporters in these categories), as well as resource-based products, but Canada has become an important exporter of manufactured goods, chemicals, and transport and telecommunications equipment.

Perhaps of equal importance is the fact that, of the world's major industrialized economies, Canada ranks among the world's top 10 countries as both an exporter and importer of investment capital. By the end of 2012, total foreign direct investment (FDI) in Canada amounted to $633.9 billion, and Canadian FDI abroad to $711.6 billion.

LAW AND INTERNATIONAL BUSINESS

Historically, establishing international business operations was a progression for an existing business. First, a business marketed its products to the local community. Eventually, it expanded, creating substantial regional or national presence. At some stage, it found its first customer in another country and its operations became international. This is the **foreign trade** stage.

foreign trade   the buying and selling of goods and services between parties from different countries

As a business's foreign markets grew, a **foreign presence** was developed by appointing an agent in the other country or establishing a representative office there. Gradually, its activities might expand from simply seeking customers and providing information to supplying spare parts, repairs, and maintenance services. Eventually, the firm would commence other activities abroad, such as processing its products, labelling, packaging, or assembling components. Finally, the operations would develop into full-scale manufacturing, and a branch or subsidiary might be established. In this typical progression, the business graduated from foreign trade to **foreign investment** and became, by definition, a multinational enterprise.

foreign presence   placing representatives of a business in foreign markets

foreign investment   conducting operations in a foreign market

Two recent developments have altered the typical progression. First, the ecommerce revolution has allowed many new businesses to attract domestic and international customers at the same time. Launching a business online may mean that the very first customers

---

[1] Office of the Chief Economist of Foreign Affairs and International Trade Canada, Table 4-1, Canada's State of Trade and Investment Update 2013, http://www.international.gc.ca/economist-economiste/performance /state-point/state_2013_point/index.aspx?lang=eng#II. The statistics in this section are taken from the aforesaid report and the World Trade Organization's Canadian trade profile, http://stat.wto.org/CountryProfile /WSDBCountryPFView.aspx?Language=E&Country=CA (current to end of 2012, expressed in US $) and Statistics Canada, International investment position Table 376-0051 http://www.statcan.gc.ca/nea-cen/index-eng .htm (current to end of 2012, expressed in Can $).

[2] According to the WTO, China supplied 19.1 percent of the total imports to the United States in 2012, the European Union supplied 16.7 percent of total U.S. imports, and Canada was a close third at 14 percent. The United States sent 18.8 percent of its exports to Canada, the most to any country; second was the European Union, which received 17.1 percent.

of a new business could be international, accelerating the new business to the foreign trade stage. Second, access to cheap labour abroad has meant that many new ventures start with imported parts or even manufacture products abroad from the inception of the business. Therefore, in the current business environment, familiarity with international business issues is a necessity for even start-up businesses.

Foreign trade and foreign investment create a wide variety of legal relationships. There are contractual relationships of many different types—sale of goods and services, carriage of goods, bailment, insurance, agency, and employment. Questions arise regarding the law of negotiable instruments, intellectual property, partnerships and corporations, secured transactions, and creditors' remedies. There is an obvious complication: international business transactions, by definition, involve parties in two or more different countries—which country's law will apply to a transaction? This is a question of private law—the law that governs transactions between private parties such as a seller and a buyer of goods.

Virtually every government regulates foreign trade and investment to some extent. Therefore, international business also involves legal relationships between private persons or entities and governments. This raises questions of public law involving the foreign and domestic governments. Canada, like most developed nations, requires some domestic business behaviour abroad to conform to minimum domestic standards. For example, as discussed in Chapter 3, Canada's Corruption of Foreign Public Officials Act prohibits bribery of foreign government officials even when the practice is not prohibited by the foreign country.[3] For more information on this topic, see the Companion Website.

Finally, in an effort to open international markets for their businesses, governments often make bilateral agreements or multilateral agreements (such as the General Agreement on Tariffs and Trade [GATT], the North American Free Trade Agreement [NAFTA], and the International Convention for the Protection of Industrial Property). As a result, issues of **public international law**, involving relations between states, also arise. All proposed international treaties are debated in Parliament before Canada formally ratifies a treaty.[4]

Throughout this chapter we will refer to various **non-governmental organizations** (NGO) and super-governmental organizations (SGO) that work to establish common standards and laws around the world. Member countries of super-governmental organizations send government representatives to voice their positions and negotiate on their country's behalf. Examples include the World Trade Organization, the United Nations Commission on International Trade Law, and the Organisation for Economic Co-operation and Development. Some standards are introduced as codes of conduct, guiding principles, and suggested contractual language, with the hope that private business will voluntarily adopt them. Other times, treaties are negotiated or suggested legislative models are produced to influence governments as they implement domestic legislation. These organizations play a major role in the development of international business law.

public international law law involving relations between states

non-governmental organizations voluntary, non-profit associations of private entities working to influence policy, raise awareness, and effect change, such as the International Chamber of Commerce

FOREIGN TRADE

Export/Import Contracts

Export/import contracts are either contracts for the international sale of goods, or contracts for the supply of services abroad. Goods or services may be supplied in one of three main ways:

- The supplier may deliver directly to the customer in the other country.
- Delivery may be made through the supplier's own marketing organization established in the other country.

---

[3] S.C. 1998, c. 34, s. 3.

[4] Canada Treaty Information, http://www.treaty-accord.gc.ca/procedures.aspx.

■ The customer may accept delivery in the supplier's home country and himself arrange to ship the goods home.

The following discussion concentrates on the most common type of export transaction—contracts for the international sale of goods.

The Contract of Sale Much of the law of contract described earlier in this book applies equally to export contracts as it does to contracts with domestic parties. However, contracts with an international element present special problems due to the involvement of a customer in, and therefore the law of, another country.

Usually, the international sale of goods involves a number of parties and consists of several distinct though related contracts. In addition to the basic agreement for the sale of the goods, the parties normally arrange for the transportation of the goods, for their insurance during shipment, and, frequently, for the financing of the transaction. Carriers, insurers, banks, or finance houses may be involved as well as the buyer and seller. Since export transactions require special expertise, the parties commonly appoint specialist **export houses or freight forwarders** as agents to make the arrangements for shipment, insurance, and financing.

The Proper Law of the Contract An export contract by definition involves two or more countries. Which country's law governs the contract or a dispute arising under it? Why does it matter?

export houses or freight forwarders specialist firms that make the arrangements for shipment, insurance, and financing in export sales

A Canadian manufacturer sells goods to a Hungarian customer. The goods are to be shipped by a German airline, insured by a British insurance company, and financed by a Swiss bank.

Several contracts make up the entire transaction in Illustration 30.1, and each one might be governed by a different country's law. The laws of the different countries may not be the same with respect to the rights of unpaid vendors or carriers or implied terms of quality or fitness.

To determine which law applies—that is, the **proper law of the contract**—it is necessary to refer to a body of principles known as the **conflict of laws or private international law**. Canadian courts, and the courts of most other countries, hold that the proper law of the contract is the law that the parties intended to govern their relationship. The clearest method of establishing the proper law is for the parties themselves to name it in their contract.[5] A contract might state that it is subject to the law of Ontario or Michigan. The choice of law need not be that of the location of one of the parties or be related to the place where the contract is to be performed—sometimes the parties choose a "neutral" law.

If the contract does not expressly identify the proper law, a court will attempt to determine the intention of the parties first by considering the contract as a whole in light of the surrounding circumstances.[6] For example, if the contract states that any dispute is to be submitted to arbitration in a particular country, or that the courts of a particular country shall have jurisdiction, then it is probable that they also intended the law of that country to govern the contract.[7] An intention may also be inferred from the use of particular legal terminology or the form of the document. Where the court cannot draw such an inference, it will apply the system of law that it considers to be most closely

proper law of the contract the law of the country or jurisdiction by which the terms of a contract or disputes under it are to be interpreted and decided

conflict of laws or private international law the principles of law that apply to determine which country's laws govern a dispute involving private parties

---

[5] *Vita Food Products Inc. v. Unus Shipping Co. Ltd.*, [1939] A.C. 277.

[6] *Consolidated Bathurst Export Limited v. Mutual Boiler and Machinery Insurance Company*, [1980] 1 S.C.R. 888; *Herman v. Alberta (Public Trustee)*, 2002 ABQB 255.

[7] *Hamlyn & Co. v. Talisker Distillery*, [1894] A.C. 202.

connected with the contract. In making this determination, it will consider all the circumstances and pay special attention to such factors as the place where the contract was made, the place where it is to be performed, the subject matter of the contract, and the place of business of the parties.[8] For more information on this topic, see the Companion Website.

Contractual Terms Theoretically terms or expressions in import/export contracts may have different meanings in different legal systems, or to parties from different countries. In practice, the problem is not as severe as it might seem. Over time widely accepted standard terminology has evolved. The meaning of short forms, such as "FOB" and "CIF" discussed next, became largely standardized through continuous use. Eventually, use of a set of standard terms (known as **Incoterms**) adopted by the International Chamber of Commerce became standard commercial practice. The original Incoterms were first published in 1936, and the current version date is 2010.[9]

Another important development has been the publication and widespread adoption of standard form contracts, published by various trade associations and by international bodies such as the International Chamber of Commerce or the United Nations Economic Commission for Europe. Super-governmental organizations, such as the International Institute for the Unification of Private Law (**UNIDROIT**), the United Nations Commission on International Trade Law (**UNCITRAL**), and the Organisation for Economic Co-operation and Development (**OECD**) have encouraged the harmonization of national commercial laws or the adoption of uniform laws. For example, the 1980 Vienna Convention on Contracts for the International Sale of Goods, implemented in Canada in 1991,[10] standardized sale-of-goods terms and practices resulting in an international standard of interpretation. Canadian ecommerce legislation, discussed in Chapter 31, follows the template of the UNCITRAL model law. The process of harmonization is an ongoing one, continually evolving in order to support globalization.

The Documentation An export sale normally requires at least four documents:

- the contract of sale
- the bill of lading
- the insurance policy or certificate
- the invoice. For more information on this topic, see the Companion Website.

We have already discussed the contract of sale and bills of lading in Chapter 14, and insurance in Chapter 16. A bill of lading is an acknowledgment by the carrier that the goods have been delivered for shipment. It operates as a document of title to the goods, facilitating the financing of the transaction. The insurance policy, similarly, is evidence that the goods are insured against loss or damage during transit and is usually necessary in order to obtain financing.

In recent years these tangible forms of documentation have been replaced by computerized communications. NGOs such as the Comité Maritime International[11] have devised uniform sets of rules dealing with electronic data exchange for international maritime business transactions.

Incoterms a set of standard contractual terms adopted by the International Chamber of Commerce

UNIDROIT the International Institute for the Unification of Private Law, founded by the League of Nations in 1926 to harmonize laws; currently has 63 member states including Canada

UNCITRAL United Nations Commission on International Trade Law established by the United Nations General Assembly in 1966 to further harmonization and unification in international trade through conventions, model laws, and guidelines

OECD the Organisation for Economic Co-operation and Development, established in 1961, has 34 member countries including Canada, and promotes world trade and sustainable economic growth by setting standards for best practice

---

[8] *Imperial Life Assurance Co. of Canada v. Colmenares*, [1967] S.C.R. 443 at 448. See also *Pope & Talbot Ltd. (Re)*, [2009] B.C.J. No. 2248 at paras. 29–41.

[9] See http://www.iccwbo.org/incoterms/.

[10] International Sale of Goods Contracts Convention Act, S.C. 1991, c. 13. It has also been adopted by several of the provinces; see, for example, International Sale of Goods Act, S.N.S. 1988, c. 13; R.S.O. 1990, c. I.10.

[11] A non-governmental international non-profit organization devoted to the harmonization of maritime law: http://www.comitemaritime.org.

Shipment and Insurance   Terms describing transportation arrangements are an essential element of an export contract as transportation presents a significant risk of damage. Usually, the goods will be insured against loss or damage during transit, and either the buyer or the seller assumes responsibility for arranging insurance depending upon the travel arrangements. The contract price reflects whether it is the seller or the buyer who arranges and pays for shipment and insurance, and up to which stage of the journey. The parties may agree that the buyer will collect the goods from the seller's factory and make its own arrangements for transportation, or that the seller will deliver the goods to the buyer's premises in the other country, or that each will be responsible for some stage of the transportation. The specific arrangements for shipment may determine the point at which title to the goods, or the risk of loss, passes from the seller to the buyer.

Standard terms have evolved to describe the more common types of arrangements for shipment. Examples of these terms (with the corresponding Incoterm abbreviations) are

- EXW (ex works): the buyer picks up the goods from the seller's factory gate;
- FOB (free on board): the seller delivers the goods onto the buyer's carrier; if the carrier must load the freight then the FCA (free to carrier) and FAS (free alongside ship) acronyms apply, where the seller's duty is, respectively, to deliver to the first carrier (for example, where the goods are collected by the carrier and loaded into a container for shipment to a cargo terminal) and to deliver to a specified pier or warehouse at the port of shipment.
- CIF (cost, insurance, and freight): seller must arrange the carrier shipment and the buyer picks up the goods at the port of destination.[12]
- DDP (delivery duty paid): the seller delivers the goods to the buyer's location and pays all duty along the way.

The terms broadly correspond to the stages of shipment and the extent of the obligations undertaken by the seller. Figure 30.1 (below) illustrates the primary four contract types listed above.

Container shipping revolutionized the carriage of goods and triggered new legal terms, such as "full container load" (FCL) and "less than a full container load" (LCL). Where the consignment comprises a full container load, shipment may be made door to door in a sealed container. If there is less than a full container load, the goods are consolidated with the goods of other exporters in a "groupage container" and are loaded and separated at a container freight station. For more information on this topic, see the Companion Website.

EXW   FOB   CIF   DDP

Figure 30.1   Export Contracts

---

[12] Under a CFR (cost and freight) contract, the seller pays carriage, but the buyer arranges its own insurance.

Payment A key element in any contract of sale is the payment of the price. In an international contract, the currency used to define the price and to make payment should be named. The price may be defined in one currency but paid in some other currency. Generally, a seller does not mind in which currency the price is paid, so long as that currency is freely convertible. However, the price should be stated in a stable currency, especially if there is to be a substantial time lag between contract and payment; if the buyer's country imposes **exchange controls** or does not permit its currency to be freely converted—as is often the case in developing countries—the seller should also require actual payment to be made in a "hard" currency. An exporter or importer may also "hedge" against the risk of currency fluctuations by using a method of **foreign exchange risk management**, such as borrowing in foreign currency or taking an option to buy or sell foreign currency.

exchange controls restrictions on the conversion or export of currency

foreign exchange risk management methods of reducing the risk involved in currency fluctuations

Financing The time between the goods leaving the seller and reaching the buyer tends to be longer in international rather than domestic sales, and the amounts involved in international sales tend to be larger. A seller would like to receive payment as soon as its goods leave the factory or warehouse, whereas the buyer would prefer to postpone payment until the goods have been safely delivered. Accommodating both priorities normally requires the services of a banker.

Historically, the bill of exchange (see Chapter 19) was the most important method of payment in export sales. In recent years, other methods of financing have been adopted, the most important of which are the *collection arrangement* and the *letter of credit*. Under a **collection arrangement**, the seller employs the services of its bank to collect payment by depositing the documents with the bank and receiving credit for the price (less the bank's charges). By contrast, a buyer obtains a **letter of credit** from its bank and uses it to pay the seller.[13] More recently, banks and finance houses have developed other highly flexible methods of financing, such as non-recourse finance, factoring, and financial leasing, methods that require more detailed explanation and are beyond the scope of this book.

collection arrangement an arrangement whereby the seller employs the services of its bank to collect payment by depositing the documents with the bank and receiving credit for the price

letter of credit a document that the buyer of goods obtains from the bank and uses to pay the seller

Countertrade In its simplest form, **countertrade** is a form of barter. A seller agrees to accept, instead of money, payment in goods produced or procured by the buyer. Another increasingly common arrangement is for a corporation that sells machinery to a firm in a developing country to agree to accept part of that firm's production as the price; thus it might sell modern cutting and sewing equipment and receive finished clothing in return. The forms of countertrade are virtually unlimited, but countertrade involves greater risks than do simple sales, since the "seller" will have to find a way of disposing of the goods acquired in exchange. Further, parties should not assume that a good is exempt from government regulation: Certain products will be banned and import duties may attach to others.[14] For more information on this topic, see the Companion Website.

countertrade a form of barter, under which a seller agrees to accept payment in goods produced or procured by the buyer

Export and Import of Services Trade in services can take a number of forms. A buyer may come to a seller, as where a foreign tourist stays in a hotel or attends a concert in Canada. Transactions of this nature generally do not involve any element of foreign law. Or a seller might go to a buyer, as where a Canadian bank or insurance company opens a branch in another country to serve customers there. It is also possible for services to be transmitted to customers in other countries. Data, legal or financial advice, or technological expertise may be supplied to customers in other countries. Property in one country may be insured by an insurance company in another country. Banks may lend money to foreign clients. The value of Canadian service trade is much smaller than its trade in goods, reaching only $77.5 billion in exports and $105 billion in imports in 2012.[15]

---

[13] An alternative method is for the buyer to obtain a banker's guarantee.

[14] *UNCITRAL Legal Guide on International Countertrade Transactions*, United Nations, N.Y., 1993.

[15] *Supra*, n. 1.

Much of what has been said in relation to the international sale of goods applies equally to the provision of services—for example, the importance of determining the proper law of the contract and the problems of payment. Of particular importance in contracts involving the transfer of technology are the local rules governing the protection of intellectual property. A Canadian corporation that licenses a patent or a trademark or supplies "know-how" to an enterprise in another country will first want to ensure that its rights are protected by the laws of that country and that its trade secrets do not become public knowledge.

Intellectual Property Most developing nations are not members of the World Intellectual Property Organization discussed in Chapter 20 and do not integrate their intellectual property rules or standards with the developed world. Protection must be sought in the target country. China, for example, has a first-to-register system for trademarks,[16] and failure to register will mean loss of ability to protect a brand. There are also usually special rules for foreign companies seeking to register. Naturally, a business will want to convert its name, logo, or brand to a Chinese version that has meaning to the targeted consumer. As in Canada, copyrights do not have to be registered in China, but completing the optional registration process is recommended. Registration is not a guarantee of protection. Sometimes a developing nation lacks an effective or independent legal system, so enforcing a properly registered trademark against a resident may still be unsuccessful.[17] For added protection, import and export contracts should confirm the ownership of existing intellectual property, designate ownership of any new products, designs, etc., that are generated under the contract, and call for the safeguarding, return and nondisclosure of any confidential information, including product specifications, designs, or moulds, at the end of the contract.[18] The effectiveness of foreign intellectual property protection should be a consideration when entering a foreign market or designating the proper law of a contract.

Government Regulation of International Trade

Since foreign trade first began, governments have tried to regulate it by controlling exports and imports and imposing customs duties. Trade relations are a matter of national importance,[19] and although many countries, such as Canada and most of its major trading partners, are generally committed to the principle of free trade, they still maintain barriers that a would-be exporter must overcome. Governments want a reasonable positive **balance of trade** with other countries. Consequently, the tendency is to encourage exports and discourage imports.

balance of trade offset of value of exports against value of imports

Export Promotion Governments provide a variety of services to their own producers in order to assist them to compete in the global market. An important function of Canadian foreign affairs staff is to collect commercial information and disseminate it to Canadian business. More tangible support—mostly in the form of insurance, guarantees,

---

[16] Foreign Affairs and International Trade Canada, "Protecting Your Intellectual Property in China," www.tradecommissioner.gc.ca/eng/document.jsp?did=118683 (last visited December 30, 2014).

[17] See e.g. the Canadian Trade Commissioner Service, "Protecting your Intellectual Property in China," http://www.tradecommissioner.gc.ca/eng/document.jsp?did=96027; Craig Wong, "Investing in China Tricky Business at Best of Times, Experts Say," *The Record*, June 11, 2011 at C3; Voler Behr, "Development of a New Legal System in the People's Republic of China" (2006–07) 67 La. L. Rev. 1161.

[18] See, as an example where contractual term as to ownership of copyright influenced outcome, *Ann of Green Gables Licensing Authority Inc. v. Avonlea Traditions Inc.*, [2000] O.J. No. 740.

[19] As evidenced in Canada by the fact that the name of the foreign affairs department has been changed to "Foreign Affairs and International Trade Canada"; see http://www.international.gc.ca/international/index.aspx.

and financial services—is provided by Export Development Canada,[20] a Crown corporation credit agency owned by the Government of Canada whose purpose is to facilitate and develop Canada's export trade. Government support is especially important with respect to exports to less-developed countries, by providing loan guarantees and long-term credit. International aid programs may also provide indirect assistance to exporters. As will be discussed later, these promotional efforts must not violate trade treaties that guarantee equal treatment of domestic and foreign producers.

Export Controls Although the general policy of most countries is to encourage exports, restrictions upon exports remain common. Export controls in Canada date back to the Export Act of 1897,[21] which regulated the export of a number of commodities, notably lumber. The federal government introduced further controls for reasons of national security during the First World War, and created a more comprehensive system following the Second World War and the commencement of the Cold War in 1947 by the Export and Import Permits Act.[22] The Act introduced a system of licensing for exports of certain listed products and for most exports to listed countries. Among the listed products are armaments, munitions, and other strategic materials. Listed countries were mostly confined to members of the then communist bloc. Further regulations and other statutes have added to the lists both of products and of countries. Restrictions have been imposed on the export of certain types of cultural property and of some energy and agricultural products, and from time to time countries such as South Africa, Iran, Libya, and Iraq have joined the list of proscribed countries. Canada is also a member of the Wassenaar Arrangement under which 40 countries set restrictions on exports of high-tech products to communist and some other countries (Wassenaar Arrangement on Export Controls for Conventional Arms, Dual Use Goods and Technologies).[23] More recently, the Special Economic Measures Act[24] contains a general power to make orders and regulations restricting or prohibiting the exportation by Canadians of goods, whether from Canada or anywhere else in the world, to designated foreign states or to persons in such states.

An added problem, which has probably affected Canada more than any other country, has been the extraterritorial application of U.S. legislation. Such legislation is intended to prevent the re-export (from Canada and other countries) of products originating in the United States to countries such as Cuba, and also prohibits dealings with those countries by foreign subsidiaries of U.S. corporations. The so-called Helms-Burton law[25] carries the process still further, potentially rendering Canadian (and other) firms with investments in Cuba liable to penalties in U.S. courts. In response, the federal government amended the Foreign Extraterritorial Measures Act, rendering judgments under the Helms-Burton law unenforceable in Canada[26]. As of 2015, the U.S. is revising its position on Cuba.

Import Duties Customs duties on imports have been in existence almost as long as international trade itself. Originally these duties provided an important source of revenue for many countries but growth of other sources of government revenue, especially income tax, and the worldwide movement to tariff reduction have steadily reduced the fiscal importance of import duties. Now their most important function is to protect domestic products against competition from cheaper imports.

---

[20] EDC is governed by the Export Development Act, R.S.C. 1985, c. E-20. It reports to the federal government through the Minister of International Trade, SI/93-108.

[21] S.C. 1897, c. 17: now R.S.C. 1985, c. E-18.

[22] S.C. 1947, c. 17; now R.S.C. 1985, c. E-19.

[23] http://www.wassenaar.org.

[24] S.C. 1992, c. 17 (see especially section 4).

[25] The Cuban Liberty and Democratic Solidarity Act of 1996, 22 U.S.C. s. 6021–91.

[26] Foreign Extra-Territorial Measures Act, R.S.C. 1985, c. F-29, s. 7.1.

Two statutes contain most of Canada's import duty legislation—the Customs Act[27] and the Customs Tariff.[28] The first deals with the administration of the system by the Canada Revenue Agency and provides the basis for regulations that classify products and determine their dutiable value and country of origin. The Customs Tariff sets out the rates of duty (tariff) imposed on each category of products.

The setting of tariffs is no longer determined unilaterally by governments, but is largely regulated by international agreements, such as GATT and NAFTA, discussed next. For goods imported into Canada, various preferences are granted, notably for products coming from Commonwealth, Caribbean, and less-developed countries, and from our NAFTA partners, Mexico and the United States. Determining the "legal" origin of goods becomes very important, since goods may be manufactured in one country from raw material or components originating in another country, and may ultimately be destined for a third country.[29]

Import Restrictions

non-tariff barriers national rules, other than import duties, that restrict or prevent the importation of goods

With the decline in the importance of import duties over the years, the existence of **non-tariff barriers** has become more significant as an obstacle to international trade. Countries often impose restrictions on imports. Sometimes the restrictions are overt; in other instances they are less visible. By Canadian law, some goods (for example, narcotics) may not be imported at all; others may be imported only under licence and subject to particular conditions.

quotas restrictions on the quantities of goods that may be imported

Generally, Canada adopts a relatively liberal policy toward imports from other countries and adheres to the principles established by the GATT. Nevertheless, Canada does impose import **quotas**, or quantity restrictions, on certain products,[30] particularly textiles and agricultural products. A wide variety of other statutes impose restrictions on imports in order to protect public health, public safety, and the environment, and for other reasons of public policy. Other countries impose their own restrictions, and a Canadian manufacturer wishing to export its products must always check to ensure that the products will be allowed to enter the other country.

Frequently, national rules on the marketing of products are just as important as restrictions on importation. There is little point exporting products to a country if they cannot legally be resold there. National health and safety standards and labelling requirements must be complied with, and they are sometimes formulated in such a way that, although ostensibly applicable to domestic and imported products alike, in practice they discriminate against imports. For example most food products sold in Canada must be labelled in both French and English and described in metric units. For more information on this topic, see the Companion Website.

Dumping and Subsidies

dumping selling products abroad at prices below those charged on domestic sales

export subsidy the granting by governments of financial assistance to promote exports

The desire to promote exports, by producers themselves and by their governments, sometimes leads to two types of practices that are generally regarded as unfair—dumping and export subsidies. **Dumping** occurs when a firm sells goods abroad at prices lower than those at which similar goods sell in the domestic market. In effect, the firm uses the profits on its domestic sales to subsidize its exports and undercut its competitors. An **export subsidy** occurs when the government of a country provides special benefits, financial or otherwise, to its producers in order to assist them to export. Benefits

---

[27] R.S.C. 1985, c. 1 (2nd Supp.).

[28] S.C. 1997, c. 36.

[29] The dispute between Canada and the United States regarding the origin of Honda cars manufactured in Canada, using components made in Japan and sold in the United States, is a good example. See Frederic P. Cantin and Andreas F. Lowenfeld, "Rules of Origin, The Canada–U.S. FTA, and the Honda Case" (1993) 87(3) *American Journal of International Law* 375–90.

[30] See Export and Import Permits Act, R.S.C. 1985, c. E-19. Other restrictions are contained in the Customs Act and the Special Import Measures Act, R.S.C. 1985, c. S-15.

may take a wide variety of forms, such as reduced freight charges, income tax rebates, or unusually favourable credit terms or guarantees.

Dumping and export subsidies, by reducing the price of imported goods, confer a benefit on the consumers of the importing country. Not surprisingly, however, such practices are resented by domestic manufacturers of competing products. Where domestic competition exists and it appears that material injury has been or is likely to be caused to domestic producers of similar goods, importing countries often impose countermeasures to nullify the benefits of foreign subsidies. Countermeasures take the form of **anti-dumping duties and countervailing duties**, designed to increase the cost of imports by the amount of the margin of dumping or of the export subsidy. In Canada, such duties are imposed under the Special Import Measures Act[31]. Many Canadian exporters have encountered difficulties with the corresponding measures imposed by the United States.[32] We will return to this issue later, when considering the impact of the WTO and NAFTA on export subsidies, and the softwood lumber trade dispute.

anti-dumping duties and countervailing duties special duties imposed on imported products to counter the advantage obtained from dumping or export subsidies

The International Law of Trade

In theory, national governments are free to adopt whatever measures they choose to regulate imports into, and exports from, their own territories. Of course, other countries may retaliate. If Country A imposes restrictions on imports from Country B, it can hardly expect Country B to accept Country A's exports freely. The international law of trade is primarily based upon the principle of reciprocity, an approach generally followed in negotiating agreements between countries, sometimes bilaterally and sometimes on a multilateral basis. Canada is a party to many trade agreements that provide reciprocal access to domestic markets; the two most important are the General Agreement on Tariffs and Trade (GATT) and the North American Free Trade Agreement (NAFTA).

The GATT and the World Trade Organization (WTO)

The GATT is the principal document that formulates the rules for international trade. It came into force on January 1, 1948, with nine original members, one of which was Canada. It grew under supervision of the World Trade Organization to its 2014 membership of 160 countries including Russia, admitted in 2012.

After the Second World War, the multilateral trade agreement was negotiated—the GATT. Despite its title, the GATT was far more than just an "agreement." It had an administrative arm, its own secretariat (in Geneva), a council of members, and the capacity to establish tribunals (or panels) to adjudicate disputes between member countries. Over the years its scope was extended and its rules augmented by new agreements reached in a series of conferences or "rounds." The Uruguay Round commenced in 1986 and finally concluded in December 1993 with the creation of a new administrative organization, the WTO, which formally came into existence on January 1, 1995, to facilitate negotiation of new agreements and resolve disputes under existing agreements. WTO supersedes the GATT as an organization. The actual GATT agreement, however, remains in effect as the foundation of the trade rules, together with the various amendments and "side agreements" entered into over time. For more information on this topic, see the Companion Website.

Probably the most serious shortcoming of the GATT was that it applied only to the international trade in goods, and even then did not apply to most agricultural products or to textiles. The Uruguay Round extended GATT arrangements to include trade in some farm products, textiles, and some services, and to the protection of intellectual property

---

[31] R.S.C. 1985, c. S-15, s. 3.

[32] For an interesting example, see *IPSCO Inc. & IPSCO Steel Inc. v. United States & Lone Star Steel Co.* (1990) 899 F.2d 1192 (U.S. Court of Appeals), and the commentary by McConnell (1991), 70 Can. Bar Rev. 180.

rights. It also extended its application to include **trade-related investment measures** (TRIMs), and considerably strengthened the mechanisms available for the settlement of disputes. In 1997, further agreements were negotiated in relation to financial services, information technology, and telecommunications services. However, disagreements among WTO members still remain with respect to a number of sectors, in particular, agricultural products, cultural products, transportation services, electronic commerce, and environmental and labour standards.

In addition to providing a forum for negotiations and for the resolution of trade disputes, the most important functions of the GATT and WTO have been the harmonization of customs rules and the progressive reduction of customs duties. In addition, the GATT sets out a code of rules governing international trade and such matters as the transportation of goods, customs procedures, and valuation.

The fundamental principle that underlies the WTO is that of non-discrimination. That principle, in turn, has two elements: first, goods originating from one contracting state should not be treated more or less favourably than goods from another state—that is, all should receive **most-favoured-nation (MFN) treatment**;[33] second, goods from other member states should, once the appropriate tariff has been paid, be treated no less favourably than corresponding domestic goods—that is, they should receive **national treatment**. In accordance with these basic principles, the WTO generally prohibits quotas and other forms of non-tariff barriers, export subsidies, and, except under strict conditions, the imposition of anti-dumping duties and countervailing duties.

The GATT and WTO have had a two-way impact upon Canadian law and the laws of the other contracting states. First, membership imposes a positive duty to enact laws to implement the obligations agreed to within the framework of the organization. Therefore, Canada has implemented the GATT tariff schedule through the Customs Tariff. Second, there is a negative duty not to apply laws that are contrary to the obligations undertaken as a member. Consequently, insofar as Canada imposes anti-dumping and countervailing duties, it may do so only within the limits prescribed by the GATT. If Canada is found to be in breach of its WTO obligations, it is required to take the necessary steps to amend its legislation in order to comply.

CASE 30.1

The United States complained that Canada was in violation of the GATT by prohibiting or restricting the importation into Canada of certain American periodicals and magazines through discriminatory tax treatment of so-called split-run periodicals, and by applying favourable postage rates to certain Canadian periodicals. A WTO panel found that the Canadian measures were incompatible with the GATT. As a result, Canada was required to change its legislation.[34]

CASE 30.2

In 2002, the United States and New Zealand complained to the WTO that Canada was illegally subsidizing its dairy industry by allowing Canadian processors to buy lower-priced milk to manufacture cheese and other products for export under a scheme known as the Commercial Export Milk Program. A WTO panel concluded that the scheme amounted to an illegal subsidy; as a result, Canada agreed to discontinue the scheme.[35]

[33] By way of exception, reduced rates of duty are applied to many goods coming from less-developed countries.

[34] See United States v. Canada: Certain Measures Concerning Periodicals, WTO panel report WT/DS31/R, March 14, 1997.

[35] WTO panel report WT/DS103/33, May 15, 2003.

Canada filed a complaint against the European Communities' ban on imported seal products. Iceland and Norway joined in the complaint. In 2014 a WTO panel found that the regulations violated GATT in that it gave imported seal products less favourable treatment than domestic products. The appeal panel also found the special treatment of domestic seal products was unjustified.[36]

North American Free Trade

One exception to the MFN principle, allowed under WTO rules, permits the creation of regional **free trade areas**, within which customs duties may be eliminated entirely. The most important and best known of such areas is the European Union (EU), a customs and economic union of 28 European states (as of 2014). In 1988, another free trade area was created, with the signing of the Canada–United States Free Trade Agreement. This agreement, which came into force at the beginning of 1989,[37] provided for the phasing out of tariffs in trade between the two nations over a period of 10 years. Four years later, on December 17, 1992, the leaders of Canada, Mexico, and the United States signed the North American Free Trade Agreement (NAFTA), bringing into existence the world's largest free trade area, with more than 360 million consumers.[38] The NAFTA also contains a clause permitting other countries on the American continent to join, and at one point a Free Trade Area of the Americas (FTAA) was proposed.[39]

free trade areas groups of countries within which customs duties are eliminated

Although the NAFTA invokes similar principles to the WTO, including

- Non-discrimination,
- National treatment,
- Most favoured nation, and
- Fairness in tariffs, barriers, and subsidies,

in many respects it goes considerably further in liberalizing trade and investment:

- All tariffs on goods among the three countries are eliminated.
- Customs procedures are streamlined and user fees eliminated.
- Agricultural products are covered; import barriers, export subsidies, and domestic support on these products were phased out by 2008.
- Special rules apply to energy and natural resources, generally prohibiting export restrictions.
- Services, including financial services, are covered in the agreement, entitling providers to receive national treatment (or MFN treatment, if that is better).
- Government procurement—the purchase of goods and services by governments—is partly opened to foreign competition.
- Country of origin rules are specifically defined as origin impacts tariff classification or regional value content requirements.

---

[36] WTO panel report WT/DS400, Nov. 25, 2013 and WTO appeal report May 22, 2014.

[37] It takes effect in Canada by virtue of the Canada–United States Free Trade Agreement Implementation Act, S.C. 1988, c. 65.

[38] The NAFTA is implemented in Canada by the North American Free Trade Agreement Implementation Act, S.C. 1993, c. 44, and came into effect on January 1, 1994. The Canada–United States agreement is suspended during the operation of the NAFTA.

[39] Canada has also entered into bilateral free trade agreements with Honduras (2014), Panama (2013) Peru (2009), Chile (1997), Costa Rica (2002), and Israel (1997). See Foreign Affairs and International Trade Canada, Negotiations and Agreements, http://www.international.gc.ca/tradeagreementsaccordscommerciaux /agracc/index.aspx.

- All principal intellectual property rights—copyright, patents, and trademarks—are recognized and protected, and laws are to be harmonized to secure broadly equivalent protection in each country.[40]

- NAFTA is not restricted to trade in goods and services; it also contains provisions relating to investment (discussed later in this chapter). For more information on this topic, see the Companion Website.

Members may avoid NAFTA requirements if they can fit the activity into one of NAFTA's exceptions, which include:

- Cultural industries
- National security
- Taxation
- Health and safety

Other countries are also making FTAs. Central America, Chile, Mercosur, and Israel signed an FTA. Chile and China entered into an FTA on February 5, 2008. Canada has eight other FTAs, including one with the member states of the European Free Trade Association[41] and most recently with Honduras in 2014.

FOREIGN INVESTMENT

Forms of Foreign Investment

A distinction is commonly drawn between portfolio or capital investment and direct investment. Portfolio investment is essentially "passive" investment, normally in government or corporate bonds or stocks, shares, and securities. Foreign direct investment (FDI), by contrast, occurs as part of active business operations. It can be defined as

> investment made to acquire a lasting interest in an enterprise operating in an economic environment other than that of the investor, with the investor's purpose being to have an effective voice in the management of the enterprise.[42]

It may involve the acquisition of property, such as a factory or hotel, or of all or a substantial part of the shares[43] in an existing corporation in the host country. FDI may also involve the establishment of an entirely new business ("greenfield" investment), and also includes the reinvestment of earnings in the host country. For more information on this topic, see the Companion Website.

Normally, FDI is conducted through the establishment of

- a branch,
- a subsidiary, or
- a joint venture.

branch a business carried on by the owner in its own name at a location distinct from its head office

Where it establishes a **branch**, the investor carries on business in the host country in its own name, the foreign branch being an integral part of its global business, with the assets of the branch owned directly by the foreign investor. By contrast, a **subsidiary** is a separate

subsidiary a separate corporation owned or controlled by its "parent" corporation

---

[40] Canadian laws are not in complete conformity with the U.S. yet the Copyright Modernization Act discussed in Chapter 20 has moved Canada closer to the U.S.

[41] Member states of the EFTA are Iceland, Liechtenstein, Norway, and Switzerland. The European Free Trade Association is not to be confused with the European Union.

[42] United Nations, World Investment Directory 1992 (New York: UNCTC, 1992).

[43] To be classified as direct rather than capital (portfolio) investment, the acquisition must normally be of at least 10 percent of the shares of the host country corporation.

corporation, incorporated in the host country and owning assets there. The parent investor owns the shares in the subsidiary (or a majority of them), but not the assets. The distinction can sometimes be very important. For example, some countries do not allow foreign ownership of land, but permit a local corporation to do so, even if a majority of its shares are held by foreigners. One of Canada's largest private corporations is an example: Walmart Canada Corp. is a wholly owned subsidiary of the U.S. parent company, Wal-Mart Stores Inc.[44]

A **joint venture** is formed by two or more parties, at least one of which is normally from the host country. It can take the form either of a type of partnership (contractual joint venture) or of a jointly owned subsidiary corporation (equity joint venture). Canadian investors overseas generally prefer the subsidiary or equity joint venture forms, principally for tax reasons, and some host countries permit foreign investment only in those forms.

joint venture a form of business venture between two or more independent enterprises, or a corporation jointly owned by them

Government Regulation of Foreign Investment

A firm wishing to invest and carry on business in another country must, of course, comply with the laws of that country. For example, a foreign corporation that carries on business in Canada through a branch may be required by the laws of the province where the branch is located to obtain a licence and to register certain information.[45] If it wishes to incorporate a subsidiary in Canada, it may be required to have a certain number of directors who are resident Canadians.[46] In the same way, a Canadian firm seeking to establish a branch or subsidiary abroad will have to comply with the local laws. Some countries do not permit foreign corporations to conduct business through a branch. Others do not allow foreigners to own a majority of the shares in a domestic corporation, at least in some economic sectors, making a joint venture (with a local partner) the only feasible method of carrying on business.

Foreign investment is desirable because it brings much-needed capital into the economy, creates employment, opens up export markets, and introduces modern technology and management skills. On the other hand, some worry it may cause social and environmental damage, stifle the development of local business, and exert undue political influence. Consequently, countries seek both to attract foreign investment and to control it, by a mixture of incentives and restrictions. Inducements such as tax holidays may be offered, but at the same time foreign investors may be excluded from participating in certain activities (such as finance, communications, and transportation), forbidden to own real estate, or required to meet specific conditions such as creating jobs or utilizing domestic raw materials. Of course, such measures may violate NAFTA or GATT if applied to treaty partners.

Like many other countries, Canada requires that certain types of inward direct investment be reviewed and prior authorization be obtained from the Investment Review Division of Industry Canada.[47] The establishment of a new business is generally not reviewed; it requires only that Industry Canada be notified. The acquisition of "larger," existing Canadian businesses requires authorization[48] and must be "of significant benefit to

---

[44] This subsidiary is the biggest private corporation in Canada in 2013 with revenue over $23 billion. See *The Globe and Mail*, "Ranking of Canada's Biggest Private Companies," June 27, 2013.

[45] See, in Ontario, Corporations Information Act, R.S.O. 1990, c. C-39, and Extra-Provincial Corporations Act, R.S.O. 1990, c. E.27.

[46] See e.g. Canada Business Corporations Act, R.S.C. 1985, c. C-44, s. 105(3).

[47] Investment Canada Act, R.S.C. 1985, c. 28 (1st Supp.). Investment review responsibilities are assigned to Industry Canada under the direction of the Director of Investments (s. 6).

[48] General review limits are $5 million for direct investment, $50 million for indirect investment, and NAFTA review threshold is tied to Statistics Canada's Nominal Gross Domestic Product and is set at $354 million for 2014; see Industry Canada, Thresholds for Review, http://www.ic.gc.ca/eic/site/icalic.nsf/eng/h_lk00050.html.

Canada"; in practice, authorization is almost always granted. NAFTA and WTO members benefit from a much higher threshold value before review is required. In certain cases, the approval of provincial governments and of other bodies may also be required. For example, the 1999 takeover of MacMillan-Bloedel by the U.S. company Weyerhaeuser required the approval of the British Columbia and Ontario governments, the Canadian Competition Bureau, the Canadian Ministry for International Trade, and Investment Canada, in addition to court approval and the support of two-thirds of the MacMillan-Bloedel shareholders.

CASE 30.4

In 2010, a British–Australian company, BHP-Billiton, initiated a $38.6 billion takeover bid of the publicly traded Potash Corporation of Saskatchewan Inc., the world's largest fertilizer company. Approval of the deal was required under the Investment Canada Act, and although Industry Canada might have approved the deal with conditions, the government refused approval saying that the takeover was not in the best interests of Canada. As a result, the bid was withdrawn. The BBC reported that the decision was a political one taken because the Harper government was in a minority position and the Saskatchewan government and the majority of Saskatchewan people opposed the deal.[49]

A restrictive approach to foreign investment is taken in some sectors. All acquisitions or investments to establish a new business in cultural sectors such as book publishing and filmmaking are subject to review, regardless of the amount involved. A variety of federal and, in some cases, provincial statutes restrict foreign ownership of banking, financial, and telecom services, and businesses involved in insurance, transportation, fishing, oil, gas, and uranium. The existence of public monopolies—such as the post office, electricity, and liquor sales—further restricts the potential for foreign investment.

CONTEMPORARY ISSUE

BCE and the Ontario Teachers' Pension Fund

The Ontario Teachers' Pension Fund (OTPF) sought approval for a $51.7 billion purchase and privatization of BCE Inc., the country's largest telecommunications company and Bell Canada's parent. The proposal involved significant foreign investment through three private American equity partners, and therefore required the approval of many different agencies including the Canadian Radio-television and Telecommunications Commission (CRTC, for impact on telecommunications), the Competition Bureau (for market dominance issues), and Industry Canada (for foreign control issues).

Legislation requires that foreign control of telecom companies must not exceed 46.9 percent. The CRTC voiced a concern that future Canadian control of BCE should be protected. On March 27, 2008, the CRTC approved the deal on conditions including the following corporate governance provisions:

1. The number of directors must be fixed at 13.

2. Six Canadian directors must be nominated by Canadian investors, while non-Canadian investors may nominate only five.

3. The chairperson and CEO must be Canadian and cannot be the same person.

4. A second OTPF delegate must sit on the executive committee.

5. Independent programming committee members must be Canadians not affiliated with the non-Canadian investors.

---

[49] See BBC Mobile News, "BHP Billiton Abandons Takeover Bid for Canada's Potash," November 15, 2010, http://www.bbc.co.uk/news/business11754820; Dan Martin "Investment Canada Gives Potash Takeover Tentative Nod," *National Post—Financial Post*, November 1, 2010, http://financial post.com/news/Invesment+Canada+gives+Potash+takeover+tentative/3760213/story.html.

Foreign Investment and International Law

Certain types of investment rules clearly have an impact upon trade. If, in granting approval to a foreign investment, a host country attaches conditions (usually called **performance requirements**)—for example, that the investor must use local raw materials or components, or that it must export a stipulated percentage of its total production—those conditions will interfere with the investor's freedom to trade. The legality of such trade related investment measures (TRIMs) was considered by a panel of the GATT, in a complaint referred to it in 1982.[50] The United States, at the request of a number of American corporations that had invested in Canada, complained that conditions requiring the investors to buy components and materials from local Canadian sources were in effect imposing restrictions on the importation of similar goods. The panel upheld the complaint, ruling against Canada.

> **performance requirements** conditions attached by the host country in granting approval to a foreign investment

Probably the greatest fear of a potential foreign investor is that its assets might be expropriated by the host country government or nationalized without adequate compensation. **Expropriation** has been one of the more controversial issues in international law. Some industrialized countries would like to see expropriation entirely prohibited, whereas many developing countries consider the power to nationalize to be essential to their economic development. The United Nations supports a state's right to nationalize, expropriate, or transfer ownership of foreign-owned property, but declares that appropriate compensation must be paid.[51]

> **expropriation** a state's right to assume ownership of private property within its geographic borders

The 1985 convention establishing the Multilateral Investment Guarantee Agency, under the auspices of the World Bank, provides some protection against the consequences of expropriation, but probably of greater importance is the **bilateral investment protection treaty**, many of which have been entered into between capital-importing and capital-exporting countries. These treaties usually provide that foreign investment receive national treatment—that is, it should be treated no less favourably than a comparable domestic enterprise. It is usual to provide that a host country may not expropriate or nationalize the property of an investor from the other country "except for a public purpose, under due process of law, in a non-discriminatory manner," and that any such expropriation "must be accompanied by prompt, adequate, and effective compensation."[52]

> **bilateral investment protection treaty** a treaty entered into between two countries, whereby each country undertakes to protect investors from the other country and to give them certain rights

The NAFTA significantly relaxes the general rules of the Investment Canada Act for Mexican and U.S. investment in Canada. Performance requirements regarding such matters as exporting or local sourcing of goods or services are not permitted, and, as a general

---

[50] *United States v. Canada*: Administration of the Foreign Investment Review Act, report of February 7, 1984 (Case No. 108, GATT Doc. L/5308).

[51] United Nations Charter of Economic Rights and Duties of States, adopted December 12, 1974, GA Res. 3281 (xxix), UN GAOR, 29th Sess. Sup. No. 31 (1974) 50. Canada abstained from voting on this proposition.

[52] See e.g. Art. VI of the "Agreement between the Government of Canada and the Government of the Republic of Poland for the Promotion and Reciprocal Protection of Investments," signed in Warsaw on April 6, 1990 (Canada Treaty Series 1990, No. 43).

principle, investors are entitled to national treatment or to MFN treatment, if that is better.[53] Canadian investment in Mexico and the United States enjoys similar privileges and protection.

Ethical Issue **Weapons in Space**

In January 2008, MacDonald, Dettwiler and Associates Ltd., a British Columbia company involved in satellite technology, announced it would sell its space and satellite division to an American company, Alliance Techsystems, for $1.325 billion. The proposed sale drew immediate reaction because this division includes the "Canadarm" used on the space shuttle. Many Canadians consider the Canadarm a source of national pride. The Canadarm technology was developed by MacDonald, Dettwiler with the help of $430 million in grant money from the Canadian government.

To add to the controversy, Alliance Techsystems supplies arms such as land mines and cluster bombs to the U.S. military. Concern was expressed that the Canadarm, taxpayer-funded technology, might now be used to weaponize space and contravene Canada's position on the Mine Ban Treaty. Pursuant to the Investment Canada Act, the proposed sale required Industry Canada approval. On March 14, 2008, the Industry Minister stated that the sale would only be approved if there was a net benefit for Canada. In April 2008, the minister blocked the sale.

Questions to Consider

1. Could it be argued that there was a net benefit to Canada and should the possible use of the technology to weaponize space have been a factor in Industry Canada's decision?

2. Should government grants include conditions about future use or sale of the developments made using grant money?

Sources: Petti Fong, "Canadarm Sale Sparks Revolt," TheStar.com, January 18, 2008, www.thestar.com/news /canada/2008/01/18/canadarm_sale_sparks_revolt.html; Andrew Mayeda, et al., "Space sale of 'No net benefit' says Minister," *The National Post*, April 10, 2008, http://www. nationalpost.com/related/topics/Space+sale+benefit+says +minister/436123/story.html

---

THE RESOLUTION OF INTERNATIONAL BUSINESS DISPUTES

Like all other business activities, foreign trade and foreign investment can give rise to disputes. These may be based in private law, as, for example, between parties to an international contract for the sale of goods. Or disputes may be primarily about public or administrative law, between governments on the one hand and importers or investors on the other. In addition, questions of public international law may arise where it is alleged that one state is in breach of its treaty obligations to another. Disputes may be resolved before a national court, an arbitrator, or some form of international tribunal.

Courts

In principle, Canadian courts and those of most other countries are open to the world in the sense that there is no citizenship or residency requirement in order to sue or be sued in them. Still, a lawsuit may not be allowed to proceed in the location where it was started. Courts do not encourage "forum shopping"—that is, allowing a plaintiff to pick the location only because it is likely to view the claim favourably. There must be some connection to the location or the defendant must be present or consent. The level of connection varies by country; the following is a general overview of the Canadian approach.

---

[53] Sometimes a country imposes restrictions upon its own investors that do not apply to foreign investors. In such a case, MFN treatment may be more favourable than national treatment.

ILLUSTRATION 30.2

A Canadian manufacturer contracts to sell electrical equipment to a Korean construction company, with delivery to be made at a construction site in Saudi Arabia. The price is stated to be payable in Swiss francs. The manufacturer ships the equipment to Saudi Arabia, but the Korean company refuses to take delivery, claiming that the equipment does not meet the contract specifications.

The Canadian firm wishes to sue for the price; perhaps the Korean party will claim damages. But in which country should the action be brought? In Canada, Korea, Saudi Arabia, Switzerland, or perhaps somewhere entirely different? What if the contract stipulates that it is governed by the laws of New York State?

The question in Illustration 30.2 is one of jurisdiction.

Jurisdiction The question of whether a court will hear an action—that is, **assume jurisdiction** over a lawsuit—is decided by Canadian courts in a two-step analysis:

> **assume jurisdiction** hear the action; allow the lawsuit to proceed in the courts of that jurisdiction

1. First, the court decides whether the province where the lawsuit was started has jurisdiction at all (jurisdiction simpliciter).
2. Second, if jurisdiction exists, the court may be asked by the defendant not to hear the matter and to defer the lawsuit to a more appropriate foreign court (forum non conveniens).[54]

To establish jurisdiction in the first analysis if the defendant is not present or has not consented, the plaintiff must prove that the action has a "real and substantial connection" with the country or province in which the action was commenced. The real and substantial connection is established using objective factual connections between the location of the court and the action. The factual connecting factors may vary by province or depending upon the cause of action of the lawsuit. The Supreme Court has identified four connecting factors for tort actions:

- The defendant is resident in the jurisdiction.
- The defendant carries on business in the jurisdiction.
- The jurisdiction is the location where the tort occurred.
- A contract connected with the dispute was made in the jurisdiction.[55]

In a contract action, the location with jurisdiction is typically identified by a term of the contract; this contractual choice is almost always followed by the court.[56] When no forum selection clause exists, courts may consider the four factors above and have relied upon the following connecting factors in the past:

- a contract was to be performed there,
- damage from a breach of contract was sustained there,
- the dispute concerned property or goods situated there, or
- the contract stipulated that it should be governed by the laws of the country or province.

---

[54] *Club Resorts Ltd. v. Van Breda* [2012] SCC 17. There are two distinct processes with different tests to be applied.

[55] *Club Resorts Ltd. v. Van Breda* [2012] SCC 17 at para 64 Supreme Court specifically created tests for tort actions—it is not clear yet whether they also apply to contract or other actions: *Trillium v. General Motors* 2013 ONSC 2289; *Wang v. Lin* [2012] ONSC 3374; *Sears Canada Inc. v C&S Interior Designs Ltd.* [2012] ABQB 573.

[56] When there are multiple competing jurisdictions, courts have (rarely) ignored contractual choice of forum clauses in exceptional circumstances only: *Z.I. Pompey Industrie v. ECU-Line N.V.*, [2003] 1 S.C.R. 450; *Momentous.ca Corp. v. Canadian American Association of Professional Baseball Ltd.*, [2012] S.C.J. No.9.

British Columbia, Nova Scotia, Saskatchewan, and Yukon have passed legislation contemplating consideration of additional factors.[57]

As in Case 30.5 below, more than one country or province may have a real and substantial connection to the dispute, and therefore jurisdiction over it. If multiple lawsuits proceeded in different jurisdictions, conflicting outcomes could result. Therefore, in the second part of the analysis, a court may decline to exercise its jurisdiction, even though it might have a connection to the dispute, if the defendant proves that there is some other forum that is clearly more appropriate—this is the **forum non conveniens** principle.[58] Under this principle, criteria related to efficiency and fairness are used to pick the most appropriate of the multiple forums, such as:

forum non conveniens refusing to hear a proceeding because another jurisdiction is more appropriate or more closely connected to the matter

- the location of parties and witnesses;
- the cost of transferring to another jurisdiction or proceeding;
- the avoidance of multiple proceedings—that is, whether a foreign jurisdiction has already assumed jurisdiction;
- the avoidance of conflicting decisions;
- the ability to enforce any resulting judgment;
- the fair and efficient functioning of the Canadian legal system; and
- the relative strength of the connections of the two parties to each location.[59]

None of the described criteria is decisive on its own.

CASE 30.5

Van Breda, an Ontario resident, was seriously injured while vacationing at Club Resort in Cuba. The Club Resort vacation package was booked from the website of an Ontario web-based travel agency called Sport au Soleil. Although the resort was in Cuba, it was managed by a corporation in the Cayman Islands, and the management company hired Ontario professionals and Ontario tour operators, including Sport au Soleil, to advertise, promote, and obtain bookings for the resorts. Van Breda sued Sport au Soleil, Club Resort, and the management company in Ontario for negligence. The Resort claimed that Ontario did not have jurisdiction over the dispute and if it did Cuba was the more appropriate forum. The Supreme Court held that a real and substantial connection in a tort case could be demonstrated if the defendant was resident or carried on business in Ontario, the tort occurred in Ontario, or a contract connected to the action was made in Ontario. The Court found that the travel contract was made through the Ontario-based travel agency and therefore Ontario had jurisdiction. Cuba also had a real and substantial connection to the action as the tort occurred there. Applying fairness and efficiency principles to factors such as travel expense and transport issues for the Canadian-based paraplegic plaintiff and witnesses, the Supreme Court held that the Resort had not shown that Cuba was a clearly more appropriate forum than Ontario.[60]

Canadian courts take a holistic view of "appropriateness," considering all the relevant circumstances and will only defer if the other location is substantially, obviously, or clearly more appropriate. Even if actions are already under way in multiple jurisdictions, the Canadian approach is still to determine the most appropriate forum and not simply defer to the jurisdiction where the first action was started.[61] Rarely, parallel actions will be allowed

---

[57] Court Jurisdiction and Proceedings Transfer Act, S.B.C. 2003, c. 28, s. 56 (in force May 4, 2006); S.N.S. 2003, c. 2 (in force June 1, 2008); S.S. 1997, c. C-41.1 (in force March 1, 2004); these acts are based on the model law produced by the Uniform Law Conference of Canada.

[58] Club Resorts v. Van Breda, [2012] SCC 17 (SCC); Teck Cominco Metals Ltd. v. Lloyd's Underwriters, [2009] S.C.C. 11.

[59] Club Resorts Ltd., supra, n. 58.

[60] Club Resorts Ltd., supra, n. 58.

[61] Teck Cominco Metals, supra, n. 58, at para. 30.

to proceed in their respective jurisdictions. For more information on this topic, see the Companion Website.

The mining and smelting business of Teck Cominco Metals Ltd. in British Columbia was alleged to have caused waste to be discharged into the Columbia River, resulting in environmental damage to property in British Columbia and Washington State. A lawsuit was commenced in U.S. District Court. Teck notified its insurers, Lloyd's and Lombard, who denied coverage for a number of reasons including policy limits, and location of damage. Teck commenced an action in Washington against its own insurers, seeking an order that they must defend the company under the terms of the policy. Thereafter, the insurers commenced actions in British Columbia seeking an order that they did not have to defend the company. Teck brought an application to stay the B.C. proceedings under the forum non conveniens provisions of the B.C. legislation. The Supreme Court of Canada refused to stay the B.C. proceedings. Considering all the circumstances, the prior court action in Washington did not oust B.C.'s jurisdiction and the avoidance of multiple proceedings was just one factor among many to be considered. International jurisdictions should be viewed differently than interprovincial ones: "Blind acceptance of a foreign court's prior assertion of jurisdiction carries with it the risk of declining jurisdiction in favour of jurisdiction that is not more appropriate."[62]

Standing   Although parties need not be residents or citizens of a country in order to have access to its courts, some restrictions may apply. A foreign corporation that has not been licensed or registered in Canada cannot be a plaintiff in Canadian courts. Foreign plaintiffs without assets within the jurisdiction may be required to post **security for costs**. A further problem arises where the defendant is not present or does not have an establishment within the jurisdiction and cannot be served with the writ or originating process. Although courts may give leave to serve the defendant outside the jurisdiction, they are generally reluctant to grant judgments against absent defendants unless there is a very strong connection between the cause of action and the country concerned.

Choice of Law   We have already discussed the question of the proper law of the contract and the practice of identifying the choice of law in a contractual term. Sometimes the result is that the courts of one country apply the law of another. In Illustration 30.2, if the contract had stipulated that the law of New York was to apply, that clause might in itself be adequate reason for a Canadian court to decline jurisdiction to a Canadian plaintiff.[63] Even so, it might be possible for the Korean party to sue a Canadian defendant in a Canadian court for damages for non-performance, in which case the court would determine the rights of the parties according to New York law. For other types of actions, choice of law will be decided using a real and substantial connection analysis as described above.

Enforcement of Foreign Judgments   Even if a plaintiff persuades a court to accept jurisdiction in a dispute of an international nature and succeeds in obtaining a judgment against the defendant, the matter does not necessarily end there. Returning to our example in Illustration 30.2, a Canadian judgment against the Korean contractor, or a Korean judgment against the Canadian manufacturer, might be of little value if the losing party has no assets in the country where judgment is granted.

The question then arises of whether a foreign judgment may be enforced in Canada, and vice versa. This is another complex legal issue, often without a clear answer and dependent

security for costs   money deposited into the court in case an unsuccessful foreign plaintiff is ordered to pay the legal costs of the successful defendant

---

[62] The Supreme Court of Canada has ruled that, where the parties themselves have provided that disputes be referred to a particular forum, effect should normally be given to that agreement: *Z.I. Pompey Industrie v. Ecu-Line N.V. supra*, n. 56.

[63] The Supreme Court of Canada has ruled that, where the parties themselves have provided that disputes be referred to a particular forum, effect should normally be given to that agreement: *Z.I. Pompey Industrie v. Ecu-Line N.V. supra*, n. 56, Case 30.7.

upon the circumstances of each case. Canada has entered into treaties with trading parties agreeing to enforce their judgments, and provinces have passed legislation to enforce each other's judgments.[64] Still, there are limits. A foreign judgment debt will normally only be recognized so long as the foreign court was exercising proper jurisdiction according to the standards of the Canadian courts (the local "forum"): Did the foreign court properly assume jurisdiction over the dispute? As described above, the presence of the defendant, consent, or a "real and substantial connection" between the substance of the action and the country in which judgment was granted must exist;[65] the judgment must not be obtained by fraud; and the proceedings cannot offend against natural justice or public policy.[66]

CASE 30.7

Shore Boat Builders Ltd., a corporation incorporated in British Columbia, built a boat for Moses, a fisherman residing in Alaska. Moses later brought an action in an Alaska court, alleging that the boat was defective in a number of respects and claiming damages for breach of warranty. Shore considered that they had a good defence to the action since Moses had himself carried out certain modifications to the boat. However, on the advice of their lawyer, Shore did not enter an appearance in the Alaska proceedings. In default, judgment was given against Shore for damages of $58 000.

Moses then brought an action in British Columbia, claiming enforcement of the Alaska judgment. The British Columbia Court of Appeal held that the Alaska default judgment was enforceable. Shore had sold their product directly to an Alaska client; they therefore assumed the burden of defending their product in Alaska and could reasonably assume that they might be sued in Alaska in respect of that product. Alaska was the place where the loss was suffered and that was entitled to exercise jurisdiction.[67]

CASE 30.8

In 1981, the Beals bought a building lot in Florida for US $8000 from the Saldanhas, who were residents of Ontario. By mistake, the wrong lot was sold, and the Beals built a home on a lot they did not own. The Beals brought an action for damages, for breach of contract, in a Florida court.

The Saldanhas did not defend the action, apparently because they feared that the costs of defending the action, even if they won, would greatly exceed any award against them (which they did not expect would be much more than the $8000 paid for the land). In 1991, a Florida jury awarded triple compensatory damages of $210 000 and additional punitive damages of $50 000. The Beals sought to enforce the judgment in Ontario, by which time, with judgment interest at 12 percent and the fall in the

value of the Canadian dollar, the claim had risen to CDN $800 000.

The Ontario trial judge refused to enforce the judgment, holding that the Florida judgment had been obtained by fraud and that it would be contrary to public policy to enforce it in Ontario. On appeal, the Supreme Court of Canada ruled that the Florida judgment should be enforced. Since the land was situated in Florida, Florida had jurisdiction. Although there were some procedural features that would not have been allowed in Ontario (for example, the defendants were not notified of the actual amount claimed by the plaintiffs, merely that it exceeded $5000), there was no evidence of fraud or a denial of natural justice. International courtesy required that the Florida judgment be respected.[68]

---

[64] Most Canadian provinces have adopted legislation providing for the enforcement of foreign judgments on a reciprocal basis. However, only a few reciprocal agreements with other countries have been entered into, the ones with the United Kingdom being the most important; see, for example, Reciprocal Enforcement of Judgments (U.K.) Act, R.S.O. 1990, c. R.6.

[65] *Club Resorts Ltd., v. Van Breda*, surpa, n. 58, at para 16; Tanya Montestier, "Still A "Real and Substantial" Mess: The Law of Jurisdiction in Canada" (2013) 36 Fordham Int'l L.J. 397 at p. 457.

[66] *Morguard Investments Ltd. v. de Savoye* (1990), 76 D.L.R. (4th) 256. That case concerned the recognition by a British Columbia court of an Alberta judgment. However, the principles enunciated by the Supreme Court of Canada have subsequently been applied to judgments by foreign courts: *Beals v. Saldanha*, [2003] 3 S.C.R. 416; *Sincies Chiementin S.p.A. (Trustee) v. King*, [2010] O.J. No 5124 aff'd [2012] O.J. No. 4562 (O.A.C.).

[67] *Moses v. Shore Boat Builders Ltd.* (1993), 106 D.L.R. (4th) 654. Contrast *Brower v. Sunview Solariums Ltd.* (1998), 161 D.L.R. (4th) 575.

[68] *Beals v. Saldanha* (2003), 234 D.L.R. (4th) 1 (S.C.C.).

Commercial Arbitration

Sometimes a forum selection clause in an international contract chooses a private forum rather than the public courts. Arbitration, sometimes referred to as private justice, is an alternative dispute resolution process in which disputing parties select an independent neutral adjudicator to privately decide their dispute. The parties agree in advance to be bound by the decision of the arbitrator, with very limited rights to appeal. Parties design their own process through the selection of the arbitrator, the procedural rules, and the choice of law to be applied in determining the outcome. This control over the process, or **party autonomy** as it is often described, is considered a major benefit of arbitration.

party autonomy the parties' freedom to determine how their dispute will be resolved

The delays, costs, publicity, and uncertainties surrounding international litigation make binding arbitration attractive for resolution of any disputes arising in international commercial transactions. Rather than risk a dispute being heard before the "home" court of one party, parties usually insert an **arbitration clause** into the contract at the time of agreement. The arbitration clause designates the arbitrator, the location or forum, the choice of law to be applied, and the procedural rules to be followed. Sometimes it specifically names an arbitrator, but more commonly it nominates an organization that provides arbitration services such as the International Chamber of Commerce. There are now many private providers of international arbitration services located in all major commercial centres around the world. As part of an international trend, Canadian legislation and courts support a policy in favour of arbitration and generally refuse to assume jurisdiction over commercial disputes covered by a valid arbitration agreement.[69] Some provinces have limited the enforcement of standard form pre-dispute arbitration clauses involving consumers, but business-to-business agreements are routinely enforced, provided the dispute falls within the scope of the clause.[70]

arbitration clause a term in a commercial contract designating arbitration as the process for resolution of any disputes arising between the parties

One major advantage of arbitration, as opposed to litigation, is the ability to select an arbitrator with great experience in the specific area of the dispute, a right not available in the public courts. Other advantages are the non-public nature and confidentiality of the proceedings, which are especially important where the dispute concerns trade secrets, and usually costs are lower and decisions are speedier. Most modern commercial arbitration employs standard procedures, such as those adopted in the United Nations Commission on International Trade Law (UNCITRAL) model, which are generally better adapted to international disputes than regular court procedures.

Perhaps the greatest advantage of commercial arbitration, as opposed to litigation, lies in the relative ease with which awards may be enforced. Unlike litigation, arbitration is consensual: The parties to the original contract have agreed to submit any dispute to arbitration and to abide by the award. As a result, there is no valid reason for a court to refuse to enforce an arbitration award should one of the parties fail to comply with it. Canada has legislation, at both the federal and provincial levels, which implements the 1958 United Nations Convention on the Recognition and Enforcement of Foreign Arbitral Awards, and adopts the 1985 UNCITRAL Model Law on International Commercial Arbitration.[71]

---

[69] 1985 UNCITRAL Model Law on International Commercial Arbitration, UN doc. A/40/17, Ann. I (June 21, 1985; *Bisaillon v. Concordia University*, [2006] 1 S.C.R. 666; *Dell Computer Corp. v. Unions des consommateurs* [2007] SCC 34; *Seidel v. TELUS Communications* [2011] SCC 15. As noted in Chapter 2, courts and legislators are retreating from the policy in favour of arbitration in the area of consumer disputes.

[70] See, for example, Consumer Protection Act, 2002, S.O. 2002, c. 30, Sch. A, ss. 7–8; *Seidel v. TELUS*, 2011 S.C.C. 15 (interpreting ss. 3, 171 and 172 of the Business Practices and Consumer Protection Act, S.B.C. 2004, c. 2); Fair Trading Act, R.S.A. 2000, c. F-2, s. 16.

[71] Commercial Arbitration Act, R.S.C. 1985, c. 17 (2nd Supp.); United Nations Foreign Arbitral Awards Convention Act, R.S.C. 1985, c. 16 (2nd Supp.); International Commercial Arbitration Act: R.S.B.C. 1996, c. 233; R.S.O. 1990, c. I.9.

Disputes Involving Governments

Generally, governments cannot be compelled to appear as defendants before the courts of another country or to submit to arbitration. An individual or corporation that wishes to challenge the actions or decisions of a government—for example, the refusal of an import licence or the expropriation of an investment—may normally do so only in the courts of that country.

However, where a member state complainant alleges that a state is in breach of a treaty obligation owed to one or more other states, a number of procedures exist for the resolution of the dispute. Most often the treaty or convention designates a process to be followed for dispute resolution. For example, bilateral investment protection treaties usually provide that the parties agree to submit to binding arbitration any dispute concerning the expropriation of assets or payment of proper compensation, with such arbitration to be conducted by the International Centre for the Settlement of Investment Disputes or according to the UNCITRAL rules.[72] Most important from a Canadian perspective are the procedures provided for in the WTO and the NAFTA.

The GATT and WTO From its inception in 1948, the GATT contained a mechanism for the resolution of disputes between states that are parties to the agreement. The mechanism was revised and strengthened when the WTO was created in 1995.

Only states that are contracting parties (members) may raise a complaint against another contracting party. Private persons have no standing as such, though an individual or firm that has been injured by an action of a foreign government in violation of the GATT may request that its own government bring proceedings.

The WTO contains two types of proceedings for the settlement of disputes. There is provision for consultation between the parties and, if necessary, a conciliation procedure—essentially a negotiated diplomatic solution. Alternatively, a contracting state that considers that the proper operation of the rules is being "nullified or impaired" by the actions of another contracting state may request the WTO Council to appoint a panel to adjudicate the dispute. After hearing the submissions of the parties, the panel makes recommendations, which may require an offending state to remove a provision of law or an administrative practice found to be contrary to the rules or, in certain cases, to compensate an injured party. Under the WTO procedures, a panel decision may be appealed to a special appellate panel and a reasonable time is allowed for implementation of any compliance orders.

The overwhelming majority of disputes submitted to WTO panels involve at least one of four parties—Canada, the European Union, Japan, and the United States. Not surprisingly, considering the volume of trade between the two countries, disputes between Canada and the United States are common. Notable are those by the United States in respect of Canadian countervailing duties on grain corn and in respect of provincial rules on the marketing of alcoholic beverages, and by Canada against the United States in respect of countervailing duties on Canadian pork and on softwood lumber. The Canada–United States disputes concerning the Canadian treatment of "split-run" American magazines and the subsidies given to the Canadian dairy industry have already been mentioned (Cases 30.1 and 30.2), and adverse findings of the panel have led to changes in Canadian legislation. The following are examples of complaints filed:

- 2000—A WTO ruling on a U.S. complaint compelled Canada to change its rules on drug patents, increasing protection from 17 to 20 years.
- 2001—In a complaint by Brazil, a WTO panel found that Canada had provided export subsidies to aircraft manufactured by the Bombardier firm. (It also found Brazil guilty of subsidizing its manufacturer, Embraer.)

---

[72] See Settlement of International Investment Disputes Act S.C. 2008, c. 8. British Columbia, Newfoundland and Labrador, Ontario, and Saskatchewan have similar legislation.

- 2004—Canadian import duties on hormone-treated beef from the European Union (EU) were held to be no longer legitimate after the EU changed its rules following an earlier adverse panel ruling in which Canada had been a complainant.

- 2013—A WTO appeal panel agreed with Japan that a Canadian renewable energy generation program that paid private solar and wind producers for energy fed back into the public system (i.e., homeowner rooftop solar panels) violated Canada's WTO obligations because it required the use of equipment made in Ontario. Canada was ordered to reduce the amount of Ontario equipment required to qualify for the program by March 2014.

Canada files almost twice as many WTO complaints as are filed against it (33 as compared to 17, as at 2014); the following are successful examples:

- 2005—The WTO Appellate Panel ruled in Canada's favour in the infamous softwood lumber dispute against the United States. This dispute proceeded under both the WTO and NAFTA dispute resolution processes and is considered in the next section.[73]

- 2008—a continuation of the hormone-treated beef dispute resulted in a ruling upholding the Canadian and American retaliatory sanctions imposed against EU products as a result of the EU's continued improper restrictions on Canadian and American beef.

- 2008—a WTO panel held that Chinese import duties on Canadian, EU, and American automotive parts were illegal.

- 2013—a WTO appeal panel held that U.S. country of origin labelling requirements for beef and pork products violated the Technical Barriers to Trade Treaty by treating Canadian meat less favourably than domestic.

- 2014—as noted in Case 30.3, a WTO appeal panel upheld Canada's complaint about the EU's restriction on imported seal products.

NAFTA NAFTA offers three dispute resolution procedures depending upon the type of dispute operated by the NAFTA Secretariat:

- Chapter 20 is the primary process for disputes between governments about the application and interpretation of NAFTA,

- Chapter 19 is for disputes between governments about anti-dumping and countervailing duties, and most unusually,

- Chapter 11 is for complaints by investors (private business) against the host government

The processes in Chapters 19 and 20 are similar to those of the WTO, though the NAFTA has more effective implementation measures. When a dispute arises under both the NAFTA and the WTO, the complainant may choose under which set of procedures it should be settled.[74]

In the event of a dispute, Chapter 20 of the NAFTA provides for the holding of consultations at the request of either party. Should no mutually satisfactory agreement be reached, the dispute is then referred to a Free Trade Commission. If, in turn, the commission fails to find an acceptable solution, either party may request that the commission appoint an arbitral panel. A panel is composed of five members, two of whom are appointed by each

---

[73] Both sides had previously claimed victory in that dispute. In 2004, a WTO Panel ruled that the Canadian system of charging "stumpage fees" did constitute a subsidy, but that the U.S. method of calculating countervailing duties was improper.

[74] There are a few exceptions, where the NAFTA procedures must be used.

of the parties from lists of experts in trade law or practice, with a chairperson selected by agreement or by lot. The panel hears the submissions of the parties and produces a report, published by the commission. The parties must implement the report within 30 days; if a party fails to do so, an aggrieved party may withdraw benefits in retaliation. A party may appeal a panel decision to an Extraordinary Challenge Committee.

Chapter 19 disputes about the imposition of anti-dumping and countervailing duties occur frequently and are often more important, at least in financial terms, than the general disputes that are dealt with under Chapter 20. In particular, U.S. countervailing duties are widely perceived as constituting the most serious threat to Canadian exports.

Currently, each country applies its own anti-dumping and countervail laws, though in the longer term the parties are required to establish common rules on subsidies and on anti-competitive practices such as dumping. Under the NAFTA, the parties are entitled to ensure that the national laws are correctly applied. The nature of a complaint, consequently, is that the country imposing the anti-dumping or countervailing duty has incorrectly or improperly applied its own law. The complaint procedure has already been used on a number of occasions, most controversially in the softwood lumber case.

CASE 30.9

The softwood lumber dispute between Canada and the United States continued for over 20 years. In the United States, most forestry land is privately owned, whereas in Canada it is largely owned by the provinces, which grant long-term licences to lumber firms in return for the payment of "stumpage" rates. The United States claims that the Canadian system operates as a subsidy to Canadian lumber producers, who are then able to undercut their American competitors. At the request of the American lumber industry, the United States imposed countervailing duties on Canadian lumber. A Canadian complaint against those duties was upheld by a NAFTA panel in 1992 and confirmed on appeal two years later. Following fresh complaints from U.S. producers, new countervailing duties were imposed in 2002, leading to a fresh round of complaint procedures, both in the WTO and in NAFTA (under both Chapters 19 and 20).

Through decisions in September 2004 and March 2006, NAFTA tribunals again ruled that the countervailing duties were improper and should be refunded. In December 2005,

the WTO Appellate division also held that the U.S. countervailing duties were improperly collected, and Canada was entitled to take retaliatory measures. A separate arbitration was scheduled to determine the amount of retaliation. Canadian softwood lumber companies have paid approximately $3.7 billion in countervailing duties. Despite the many adverse trade rulings, the United States government did not revoke the duties.

Finally, in April 2006, the United States and the newly elected Canadian government arrived at a negotiated settlement. The agreement revoked the duties, provided for the return of at least 80 percent of the deposits collected since 2002, and ensured seven years of stability in the industry. The agreement was implemented in October 2006, and Export Development Canada began processing refunds. The Softwood Lumber Products Export Charge Act, 2006 received royal assent on December 14, 2006, by which time 98.9 percent of refunds had been paid to Canadian softwood lumber companies.[75]

NAFTA Chapter 11 Chapter 11, which deals with foreign investment, is unique and innovative. It provides a way in which Canadian, Mexican, and U.S. businesses that invest in another NAFTA country may sue the host government directly for infringement of the rights guaranteed by the agreement. NAFTA investor rights primarily protect firms from illegal expropriation by a government, but governments must also treat foreign investors no less favourably than domestic investors (national treatment). Businesses have used, or threatened to use, Chapter 11 to sue governments when their foreign operations have been affected by government policy measures that are "tantamount to expropriation"

---

[75] The agreement will refund more than $5 billion to Canadian companies. For a review of the history of the dispute, see the press releases issued by the Minister of International Trade on December 5, 2005; March 17, 2006; April 27, 2006; October 6, 2006; October 30, 2006; and December 14, 2006; available on the Foreign Affairs and International Trade Canada website (www.international.gc.ca).

decisions, when those measures make it effectively impossible for the firm to carry on its normal operations.[76] Several of the more controversial NAFTA tribunal rulings, or actions, involved challenges to environmental or health legislation:[77]

- 2000—A NAFTA tribunal ruled that Mexico had violated the agreement and ordered its government to pay $16.7 million to the U.S.–based Metalclad Corporation. The company had wanted to open a hazardous waste treatment and disposal site in central Mexico, but local government said the project violated environmental protection laws.

- 2000—S.D. Myers, a U.S. corporation, sued the Canadian government for $75 million because Canada banned the export of PCBs to the United States. The ban was subsequently lifted. The tribunal found in favour of the company on two counts of the complaint and awarded damages of $6 million.

- 2005—the Canadian-based company Methanex failed in its claim against the United States, which alleged that the state of California's decision to phase out the use of its gasoline additive, MTBE, cost the company $970 million. Methanex was ordered to pay the United States costs, valued at approximately $4 million.[78]

- 2007—Canada successfully defended a $160 million claim brought by UPS which alleged that Canada Post received preferential treatment due to its government ownership, especially from Canadian Border Services.[79]

- 2013—Eli Lilly commenced a $500 million claim against the Government of Canada alleging that the invalidation of two of its Canadian drug patents by the Federal Court violated Canada's NAFTA obligations, saying the negative court decisions amounted to an "expropriation" of exclusive rights. The action is ongoing and uses a private dispute between drug companies to highlight the differences between Canadian patent law and international intellectual property treaties.[80]

- 2013—Detroit International Bridge Company, owner of the Ambassador Bridge that connects Detroit and Windsor, filed a statement of claim alleging that the Government of Canada's plan to build a new government owned bridge between Detroit and Windsor, just 2.3 km from the Ambassador Bridge, undermines the financial feasibility of the Ambassador Bridge (and its planned expansion) by diverting traffic away from it and therefore amounts to discrimination in violation of NAFTA's national treatment obligation. This dispute is also ongoing.

NAFTA's arbitration tribunal proceedings have been criticized by consumer activists, on the grounds that they are mostly conducted in private. In Canada, the Canadian Union of Postal Workers and the Council of Canadians launched an unsuccessful legal challenge against the Chapter 11 tribunal process, claiming that the secrecy of the proceedings violates the Canadian Charter of Rights and Freedoms.[81]

---

[76] Most famous actions have been by Canadian softwood lumber manufacturers claiming damages as a consequence of the illegal U.S. countervailing duties.

[77] For an excellent review, see *Soloway* (2000) 33 C.B.L.J. 92.

[78] *Methanex Corporation v. United States of America*, www.state.gov/documents/organization/51052.pdf.

[79] *United Parcel Service of America, Inc. ("UPS") v. Government of Canada*, www.international.gc.ca/assets /tradeagreementsaccordscommerciaux/pdfs/MeritsAward24May2007.pdf.

[80] Eli Lilly Notice of Intent, NAFTA–Chapter 11–Investment, Government of Canada, Foreign Affairs, Trade and Development Canada website; see also *Eli Lilly Canada Inc. v. Novopharm limited*, 2011 FC 1288 *aff'd* 2012 FCA 232 (CanIII) leave to SCC denied 2013 CanLII 26762 (SCC).

[81] *Council of Canadians v. Canada (Attorney General)*, [2006] 277 D.L.R. (4th) 527 (O.A.C) leave to appeal to SCC denied [2007] S.C.C.A. No. 48. NAFTA received parliamentary approval as an international treaty, but this did not incorporate it into domestic law subject to the Charter.

Strategies to Manage the Legal Risks

First and foremost, Canadian businesses must address international issues early—at the initial stages of commencing business activities. The traditional model of waiting to develop an international presence until after a domestic market is established is no longer applicable in the internet era. Otherwise, a business could lose rights to valuable business assets. Do not assume that the laws of foreign jurisdictions are the same as Canada's—very often they are not. Intellectual property rights must be secured in the domestic and foreign customer, supplier, and creditor markets. Contracts should expressly specify intellectual property ownership, proper law of the contract, and choice of forum.

The regulations controlling access to foreign markets are complicated, and navigating them might be difficult for a small business operator. Government agencies are available to assist in this area, so contact with Economic Development Canada and the Canadian International Development Agency is beneficial. They may be able to access funding as well as information. Government assistance is also needed to obtain maximum benefits from GATT and NAFTA.

Canadian regulations also protect penetration of the domestic market, and businesses need to respect the controls on importing, as well as the limits on foreign investment. Major restructuring with foreign capital, merging with foreign companies, and dissolving a Canadian subsidiary by a foreign parent all require Industry Canada approval, which is discretionary. On a smaller scale, losing the income tax designation of a Canadian-controlled private corporation will have negative consequences for the taxation on dividends.

International business disputes are a natural consequence of doing business internationally and so they should be expected. Quick resolution before the business's brand is damaged is a typical business priority, and, in this light, arbitration should be considered as an alternative to court proceedings. It is often easier to get agreement to arbitration before any dispute arises (in the original contract between the parties) than after the parties are disagreeing over the dispute. One downside to arbitration is that appeal rights are limited, so outcomes are final.

Sometimes businesses ignore foreign court proceedings against them, especially if they have no assets in the subject jurisdiction. This is a mistake. Provided basic requirements are met, Canadian courts recognize and enforce foreign judgments, and a business will soon find its Canadian assets seized to satisfy the foreign order. Businesses should respond to and participate in every complaint process that is initiated against them.

QUESTIONS FOR REVIEW

1. Distinguish between foreign trade and foreign investment.
2. Distinguish between public international law and private international law.
3. What is meant by the "proper law of the contract"?
4. What are "Incoterms"? Give examples.
5. What documentation is usually involved in an international sale of goods?
6. What is the purpose of foreign exchange risk management?
7. How can services be exported?
8. In what ways do governments attempt to promote exports? Are export subsidies permissible?
9. What is meant by "non-tariff barriers"? Give examples.

10. What is dumping?

11. What are countervailing duties?

12. What is the relationship between the GATT and the WTO?

13. What are TRIMs?

14. Distinguish between most-favoured-nation treatment and national treatment.

15. Distinguish between portfolio (capital) investment and direct investment.

16. Distinguish between (a) a branch, (b) a subsidiary, and (c) a joint venture.

17. What are "performance requirements"?

18. What purposes are normally served by bilateral investment protection treaties?

19. What is "forum shopping"? Why is it considered objectionable?

20. What is meant by "forum non conveniens"?

21. What are the principal advantages of commercial arbitration as opposed to litigation?

22. How are disputes resolved within the WTO? Within the NAFTA?

23. Explain how the softwood lumber dispute demonstrates both the strengths and the weaknesses in the WTO and NAFTA dispute resolution processes.

24. In what way is Chapter 11 of the NAFTA novel?

CASES AND PROBLEMS

1. Continuing Scenario

Steven is a regular customer at Ashley's Toronto restaurant and loves Ashley's chocolate truffle cake so much that he wants it served at his company's sales convention being held at the Chateau Frontenac (CF) in Quebec City. He instructs the CF's caterer to buy enough cake for the 1000 attendees and get it to Quebec. CF sends an email to Ashley asking for a quote. Ashley replies, saying that that amount of cake will cost $10 000 and will need to be refrigerated during shipping. She tells CF that ABC Trucking Company has the appropriate truck. CF sends Ashley a purchase order for $10 000 worth of cake and instructs her to arrange for ABC to ship the cake to the hotel. Ashley does not notice the acronym DDP typed on the purchase order and her quote does not include the cost of shipping. Answer the following questions about the cake delivery.

   (a) If the cake is damaged due to the negligence of a crane operator while being loaded onto the refrigeration truck, is this Ashley's problem or the hotel's? Why? What difference would it make if "EKW" had been typed on the order?

   (b) If CF refused to pay for the cake because it was damaged, where should Ashely commence her lawsuit and why?

   (c) Should the law of Ontario or Quebec apply to this transaction?

   (d) What steps should Ashley take the next time she sends goods out of province?

2. XYZ Ltd., a large Canadian mining corporation, entered into an agreement three years ago with the government of the Republic of Utopia to develop the mining and processing of the rich zinc deposits in that country. A joint-venture corporation, Cantopia Ltd., was established (under the law of Utopia), in which XYZ held 49 percent of the shares and the government of Utopia held the remainder. XYZ invested $25 million in the project, in the form of machinery, technology, and capital to finance the operation of mines and smelters; the Utopian government's contribution to the project took the form of a lease, at nominal rent, of a large tract of land where valuable deposits had been discovered. It was agreed that Cantopia would mine the zinc, process it, and export it through XYZ's worldwide marketing organization. Profits would be shared proportionately, with 49 percent for XYZ and 51 percent for the government of Utopia.

   Recently, following a military coup, the new government of Utopia enacted a law requiring all mining enterprises to sell their total output to the newly established National Resources Corporation, wholly owned by the Utopian government, at prices to be established by a government agency. Under the prices established for zinc, it has become impossible for Cantopia to operate at a profit.

Are there any steps that XYZ can take to protect its investment?

3. Canadian production of widgets is almost entirely in the hands of three corporations—Altawidge Ltd., Ontwidge Ltd., and Scotiawidge Ltd. All three corporations export a substantial volume of their products to the United States.

Two years ago, as a result of increased competition from Malaysian widget producers, two of the Canadian corporations—Ontwidge and Scotiawidge—experienced financial difficulties. As a result, the governments of Ontario and Nova Scotia stepped in to help save the widget industry. They provided long-term, low-interest loans to the corporations and granted other benefits, such as research grants and exemption from property taxes. By contrast, Altawidge has received no government support, but has been able to compete with its rivals because its operations are more advanced technologically.

Recently, there have been complaints from widget producers in the United States that they have lost a substantial share of the American market to imports from Canada and Malaysia. They allege that widget production in both countries is heavily subsidized. As a result of these complaints, the U.S. Department of Commerce has introduced a countervailing duty of 17 cents for each widget imported from Canada. The effect of the duty is to make Canadian widgets more expensive in the United States than domestically produced widgets.

Altawidge has in turn complained that, whether or not the Nova Scotia and Ontario producers receive an improper subsidy, its own products enjoy no such benefit and should not be subjected to the duty.

Discuss the issues raised, and suggest what steps might be taken to resolve the dispute.

4. Maxrevs Ltd. is a corporation incorporated in Manitoba; it manufactures small gasoline-powered motors for use in a variety of power tools. It sells its motors directly to tool manufacturers throughout North America, and also sells in substantial quantities to wholesale dealers in motor parts and components. One of those dealers supplied a number of Maxrevs motors to Weed Eater manufacturer Snapper Inc., a corporation incorporated in Michigan.

Gonzalez, a resident of Texas, purchased a Snapper Weed Eater and subsequently sustained a severe injury to his leg and hand when the tool malfunctioned. He brought an action in a Texas court against both Snapper and Maxrevs. Although Maxrevs was served with notice of the proceedings, it did not enter an appearance and did not defend the action.

The Texas court found that the connection between the motor and the revolving blade was defective, and held Snapper liable. It also found that Maxrevs had been negligent in failing to provide adequate instructions for installation of its motors in tools of that kind and awarded damages against Maxrevs amounting to US $5 million.

Gonzalez has now filed a claim in the Manitoba court to enforce his judgment against Maxrevs. Is it likely that the Manitoba court will enforce the judgment?

Additional Resources for Chapter 30 on the Companion Website

(www.pearsoncanada.ca/smyth)

In addition to pre- and post-tests, mini-cases, and application exercises, the Companion Website includes the following province-specific resources for Chapter 30:

- **Alberta:** International Arbitration; Reciprocal Enforcement
- **Atlantic Provinces:** International Commercial Arbitration Act; Reciprocal Enforcement of Judgments
- **British Columbia:** Comity in the Enforcement of Foreign Judgments; International Arbitration; International Investment; Reciprocal Enforcement
- **Ontario:** Commercial Arbitration; Enforcement of Foreign Judgments; Inter-provincial Enforcement; Jurisdiction; Security for Costs

Chapter 31

Electronic Commerce

- ECOMMERCE
- ECOMMERCE AND THE LAW
- INTERNATIONAL ASPECTS OF ECOMMERCE
- STRATEGIES TO MANAGE THE LEGAL RISKS

Electronic commerce (ecommerce) is the most rapidly growing sector of the economy, along with information technology. Increasingly, business is being conducted through the internet and through other electronic means. Applying existing legal rules and principles to the new business environment raises challenging new legal issues.

In this chapter we examine such questions as:

- What is ecommerce?

- How is the law changing to accommodate the challenges of ecommerce?

- How are contracts made on the internet?

- What law governs those contracts?

- How are consumers protected in ecommerce transactions?

- How has the internet affected the law of defamation?

- How do trademark and copyright laws apply to the internet?

- Should government regulate ecommerce?

- Which courts have jurisdiction over internet disputes?

- To what extent is international cooperation necessary in order to regulate ecommerce?

ECOMMERCE

What Is Ecommerce?

electronic commerce (ecommerce)
the use of computer networks to facilitate commercial activities, including the production, distribution, sale, and delivery of goods and services

internet the interconnected logical networks that link computers worldwide

intranet closed systems linking specific users internal to a company or group; commonly used for data exchange

Electronic commerce (ecommerce) is broadly defined as "the delivery of information, products, services, or payments by telephone, computer, or other automated media."[1] More commonly, ecommerce refers to commercial activity that makes use of computer networks, including the **internet** or **intranet** systems.[2]

According to one report, "the Internet has done for electronic commerce what Henry Ford did for the automobile—converted a luxury for the few into a relatively simple and inexpensive device for the many."[3]

The Impact of Ecommerce on Business

Before 1995, ecommerce was almost nonexistent. Then firms such as Amazon.com, Cisco, and Dell began to use the internet extensively for commercial transactions. The worldwide volume of ecommerce grew from $28 billion in 1998 to more than $1 trillion by 2003. In Canada, the value of sales made via the internet reached $122 billion in 2012 (double the 2007 volume). More than 87 percent of Canadian businesses have internet access and 33% of businesses have integrated social media tools with their websites.[4] Business-to-business (B2B) transactions account for about two-thirds of all ecommerce. They include intranet activities—between branches of the same company or between related companies in a multinational group—and arm's-length transactions with other businesses involving internet supply of services or products, technical support, invoicing, or payment. Business-to-consumer (B2C) transactions most often involve electronic retailing where a consumer accesses a business website to purchase or license tangible or electronic goods or services. Canadians are among the most connected people in the world, with 79.2 percent of the population online.[5]

Ecommerce has changed the business world in three key areas:

- operational business practices
- cashless society
- surrounding business environment

electronic retailing (etailing)
the supply of tangible or electronic goods or services over the internet; supply of tangible goods involves a conventional mode of delivery; electronic goods are downloaded directly to the customer's computer

electronic transfer of funds
payment made through electronic (intangible) media such as telephone or internet rather than by cash or cheque; payment may take the form of credit card charges, debit of bank accounts, or even ecash, often through the business's website

Existing Business Practices Businesses are adapting all aspects of their operations to the online model. The hard-copy, tangible processes of the past are rapidly being replaced by the instantaneous movement of intangible bits of electronic data. The use of internet and intranet systems is transforming B2B and B2C relationships, as well as relationships with employees, government, and the public. As a result, businesses are supplying their products to customers through **electronic retailing (etailing)**, electronically monitoring their supply chain management and record keeping processes, and using **electronic transfer of funds** to bank, make payments, and collect accounts receivable online.

---

[1] "Electronic Commerce and Canada's Tax Administration: A Report to the Minister of National Revenue from the Minister's Advisory Committee on Electronic Commerce," Ottawa, April 1998.

[2] M. Fecenko and A. Huntley, *Ecommerce Corporate–Commercial Aspects* (Markham, ON: Lexis Nexis, 2003) at 3. The use of the internet raises other legal issues that are not related to ecommerce, as defined here. These are not considered in this chapter. For a comprehensive survey, see M. Geist, *Internet Law in Canada*, 3rd ed. (North York, ON: Captus Press, 2002).

[3] "The Economic and Social Impacts of Electronic Commerce: Preliminary Findings and Research Agenda" (Paris: OECD, 1998) at 10, www.oecd.org.

[4] Data from "Electronic Commerce in Canada," available from the Industry Canada website, http://e-com.ic.gc.ca.

[5] As of March 2011, there were 26 960 000 internet users in Canada: http://www.cia.gov.library/publications /the-world-factbook/geos/ca.html.

The internet is a natural advertising medium. Even those businesses not involved in etailing maintain websites as a form of advertising. Misleading online advertising may trigger criminal and/or civil liability under the Competition Act.[6]

Establishing a Website

A business website may be passive, seeking only to provide information, to advertise and market its products or services; or it may be active, to interact with others in the exchange of information or completion of sale transactions. Establishing a website involves several agreements. Generally, the business will:

- negotiate a website development agreement—Creating a website involves obtaining various development services (content, graphics, software, etc.) and raises intellectual property issues. Both confidentiality and the ownership of the intellectual property should be addressed in the agreement.

- negotiate a website-hosting agreement—once developed, the site must be installed and operated on a web server, usually operated by an internet service provider (ISP).

- negotiate an internet access agreement with the ISP—This agreement will have terms allowing the ISP to discontinue service for any behaviour it finds unacceptable. It will also have an exemption clause protecting the ISP from liability for service interruption and consent for release of private information for specific purposes.

- register a domain name[7] and protect the intellectual property associated with the website—this could involve trademark, copyright, and patents.

Additionally, if the site is active, it must be secure, and encryption services will be required. Privacy of collected information must be protected.

Cashless Society

In 2012, 47 percent of Canadians chose the internet as their primary banking tool. In the ecommerce marketplace, traditional banks are competing with **ecash**— online payment systems that enable the secure and anonymous transfer of money over the internet or other networks (including ewallets and **payment card networks**).[8] Ewallets are systems such as PayPal Inc., which store funds outside a financial institution for use online. Payment card networks include debit card systems (such as the Interac Association) that process point of sale demands for funds held in a financial institution. By 2003, Canadians were the highest per-capita users of debit cards in the world[9] and 70 percent of Canadians were ready to go cashless by 2012.[10] Ecash facilitates secure, small-value transactions that are not cost-effective when conventional credit cards are used. Smart cards with integrated circuit chips are replacing conventional magnetic credit and debit cards. Payment cards include *pay later* cards (traditional credit cards) *pay now* cards (debit cards) and *pay before* cards (pre-paid cards). The three forms of payment cards move between traditional banks regulated under the Bank Act and the Loans and Trust Companies Act, and payment card network systems regulated under the Payment Card Networks Act.[11]

ecash an online payment system that enables the anonymous transfer of money over the internet

payment card networks an electronic payment system used to accept, transmit, or process transactions made by payment card to transfer funds or information among issuer, user, and merchants

---

[6] Competition Act, R.S.C. 1985, c. C-34 is discussed in Chapter 3. The Competition Bureau has issued an Information Bulletin discussing the application of the Competition Act to representations made on the internet, available at www.competitionbureau.gc.ca.

[7] It may be necessary to register multiple domain names. See domain names under the heading "Intellectual Property."

[8] For background on Canadian payment systems, see Task Force for the Payments Systems Review, "Canadian Payments Landscape—Report," (September 2010), http://paymentsystemreview.ca/indes.php/resources/the-canadian -payment-system/index.html.

[9] *Ibid.*, Executive Summary; 94 percent of Canadians had debit cards in 2013.

[10] Paypal Canada Survey by Leger Marketing, http://www.newswire.ca/en/story/991907.

[11] Bank Act, S.C. 1991, c. 46; Loans and Trust Companies Act, S.C. 1991, c. 45; Payment Card Networks Act, S.C. 2010, c. 12, s. 1834.

As discussed in Chapter 19, payment law established for traditional banking focuses on cheques and negotiable instruments regulated under the Bills of Exchange Act. These laws seem insufficient as preauthorized debits, irrevocable payment messages, and immediate fund transfers gain popularity. The Canadian government is now regulating the growing number of electronic payment facilitators. In 2010, the Ministry of Finance introduced a Code of Conduct for the Credit and Debit Card Industry in Canada.[12] Two of its requirements are that credit and debit functions be on separate cards and that merchants be given 90 days' notice of fee increases. Also in 2010, the Payment Card Networks Act was passed, giving the responsibility for monitoring and regulating the payment card industry to the Financial Consumer Agency of Canada (FCAC).[13] FCAC also oversees prepaid cards, including the control of activation, maintenance, and dormancy fees.[14] Businesses that intend to issue "gift certificates" need to comply with these regulations.

Surrounding Business Environment The business environment is filled with new industries. Examples include internet service providers (ISPs), network infrastructure support and outsourcing, including data management and security, payments facilitators described above, and countless new online products and services. The global nature of the internet offers businesses access to customers and suppliers from around the world. Ecommerce is one of the major reasons why business has "gone global." Even small, local businesses are able to do business internationally via ecommerce, and the marketplace has expanded exponentially. Unfortunately, the explosion in ecommerce has also attracted abuse. Ecommerce increases concern about public safety, fraud, invasion of privacy, identity theft, money laundering, and tax evasion. Governments have responded with increased regulation, and businesses must protect themselves and their stakeholders with increased security and proactive measures.

The Impact of Ecommerce on the Law

Traditional legal principles involving contract, tort, intellectual property, and international law are adapting to meet ecommerce challenges. Privacy and consumer protection laws are stretching to cover online risks. Courts, legislatures, and the international community are creating new law in the form of case decisions, legislation, and international treaties.

Cases involving ecommerce issues are coming before the courts, and judges are reinterpreting long-held principles. Pressing issues require the immediate response of government. The federal government has the power to regulate the financial aspects of ecommerce under its banking power, and indeed all uses of the internet within Canada, under its general power to regulate intraprovincial communication.[15] In addition, provincial governments have power to regulate ecommerce under various constitutional categories including property and civil rights.[16] As a result, both federal and provincial governments have passed legislation addressing ecommerce issues.[17]

---

[12] Available on the Department of Finance Canada website: http://www.fin.gc.ca/n10/data/10-049_1-eng.asp.

[13] S.C. 2010, c. 12, s. 1834.

[14] Prepaid Payments Products Regulation SOR/2013-2009 (in force May 1, 2014)

[15] Constitution Act, 1867, s. 92(10)(a). Internet usage can constitute "broadcasting" under the Broadcasting Act, S.C. 1991, c. 11.

[16] Constitution Act, 1867, *ibid.*, s. 92 (13)(14).

[17] Initial support for self-regulation of the internet and ecommerce stemmed from its international usage and the belief that any attempt by one country to regulate ecommerce might simply result in business migrating to less restrictive regimes; see Geist, "The Reality of Bytes: Regulating Economic Activity in the Age of the Internet" (1998) 73 Wash. L. Rev. 521. Criminal use of the internet was always of greater concern. See the section in this chapter headed "Illegal Activities."

A consistent global approach to ecommerce law is considered best but both courts and legislatures face jurisdictional boundaries. Non-governmental organizations such as the Organisation for Economic Co-operation and Development (OECD), the World Trade Organization (WTO), the United Nations Commission on International Trade Law (UNCITRAL), and the World Intellectual Property Organization (WIPO) work toward standardization through international guidelines, treaties, conventions, and model laws. Member nations are encouraged to adopt domestic legislation consistent with international guidelines. Unfortunately, not all countries follow the international standards, and businesses face jurisdictional variation in ecommerce law.

ECOMMERCE AND THE LAW

Contract Law

Electronic commerce, like any other form of commerce, is principally about making contracts. Courts and legislatures have adapted traditional contract law principles to the ecommerce environment.

Formation of Contracts Key elements in the formation of a contract remain offer and acceptance. When does a contract come into existence in a typical ecommerce transaction?

ILLUSTRATION 31.1

Elektra visits her favourite online music store, clicks on "Browse," and chooses the classical music category. Following the website's instructions, she selects five songs, each time clicking on "Add this to my shopping basket." She then clicks on "Buy," types in her credit card details, and finally, clicks on "Confirm."

Has any contract been made? If so, when? Does the store's website constitute an offer to sell, or is it simply an advertisement or an invitation to treat?[18] Is the offer made when Elektra clicks on "Buy" or on "Confirm"? At what point is her order accepted by the store? Does that acceptance have to be communicated to Elektra before a contract comes into existence?[19]

These are some of the questions that arise in even the simplest type of ecommerce transaction. To answer these questions, courts refer to similar cases where communication has been by mail, phone, or fax. A business should design its website to spell out very clearly the legal consequences of clicking on each icon. It has become common for businesses to use a **web-wrap agreement**, or "click-wrap agreement," which requires the consumer to click on the appropriate box to indicate agreement with the non-negotiable standard terms of sale prepared in advance by the business.[20] These are the online versions of standard form contracts discussed in Chapter 6.

web-wrap agreement a website document setting out contractual terms, the acceptance of which is indicated by clicking on the appropriate icon (click-wrap agreements require the buyer to open the terms page before clicking acceptance of them)

CASE 31.1

A group of law students in Ontario entered into an agreement through the internet to subscribe to the Microsoft Network. In doing so, they were directed to the "membership rules," and before concluding the agreement they were

>

---

[18] See Chapter 6, under "The Nature of an Offer."

[19] See Chapter 6, under "Transactions between Parties at a Distance from Each Other."

[20] The use and validity of web-wrap agreements is discussed by Sigel, Ling, and Izenberg in a paper prepared for the Uniform Law Conference of Canada, www.ulcc.ca/en/cls.

Web-wrap agreements should be designed to ensure that all intended terms and conditions are brought to the attention of potential customers. In 2007, the Supreme Court of Canada stated that hyperlinks to "terms and conditions" must be visible, functional, and accessible.[22]

The Law Governing the Contract   Determining if and when a contract is made is of primary importance. But the moment when the contract is made may also determine where it is made, which in turn may determine the law that governs the transaction.[23]

ILLUSTRATION 31.2

Imagine an online consumer is a resident of British Columbia. The vendor is incorporated in Delaware. The website is operated through a server located in the Cayman Islands. On receiving the buyer's order, the server automatically notifies a warehouse in Alberta that the vendor uses to dispatch goods ordered by Canadian customers.

Is the contract governed by the laws of British Columbia, Delaware, the Cayman Islands, or Alberta? This is important because the law of the contract determines such matters as

- the capacity of the parties to contract;
- the legality of the contract;
- the formal requirements governing the contract;
- any terms that are to be implied;
- the effects of, and remedies for, breach of contract; and
- the applicability of consumer protection legislation.

Again, many of these questions can be answered by a clear statement of the law that is intended to govern, although consumer protection legislation in the customer's country may still apply, regardless of such a statement.[24]

Formal Requirements   As just noted, the law that governs a contract may impose certain formal requirements—for example (as noted in Chapter 10), some contracts must be in writing. Are electronic contracts "in writing"? Do electronic signatures constitute legal signatures? The federal government resolved these problems for individual-to-government

---

[21] *Rudder v. Microsoft Corp.*, [1999] O.J. No. 3778. See also *Kanitz v. Rogers Cable Inc.* (2002), 58 O.R. (3d) 299; *Wembley Marketing Ltd. v. ITEX Corp.*, [2008] O.J. No. 5194.

[22] *Dell Computer Corp. v. Union des consommateurs*, [2007] S.C.J. No. 43 (Q.L.), 2007 S.C.C. 34; in *Rogers Wireless Inc. v. Muroff*, 2007 S.C.C. 35 at para. 15 (citing *Dell* at para. 229), the Supreme Court accepted that internet consumers must have a certain level of computer competence.

[23] See Chapter 6, under "Determining the Jurisdiction Where a Contract Is Made." The place where a contract is made is one of a number of factors that may determine the law governing the contract: See Chapter 30, under "The Proper Law of the Contract."

[24] Consumer Protection Act, 2002, S.O. 2002, c. 30, Sch. A.

contracts in the Personal Information Protection and Electronic Documents Act (PIPEDA), enacted in 2000.[25]

This law adapts existing federal statutes and regulations to the electronic environment, allowing the use of electronic alternatives where the legislation requires paper copies, notice or communication of information or transactions (section 32), and it recognizes electronic documents and signatures.[26]

In Canada, the law of contract falls almost exclusively within provincial jurisdiction, so provincial legislation governs B2B and B2C electronic contracts.[27] It adapts contract law to the internet environment by addressing topics such as acceptance by clicking an icon, communication of acceptance, electronic signatures, and writing.

The provincial legislation is based upon the Uniform Electronic Commerce Act, a model statute prepared by the Uniform Law Conference of Canada in accordance with the principles of the United Nations model law.[28]

The Uniform Electronic Commerce Act says the following:

- Information in electronic form has legal effect or enforceability (s. 5).[29]

- Information in electronic form (with continued availability) satisfies a writing requirement (s. 7).[30]

- A legal signature of a person may be an electronic signature (s. 8).[31]

- An offer or the acceptance or any other part of contract formation may be in an electronic document or done by an electronic action such as touching or clicking on an appropriately designated icon or place on a computer screen or otherwise communicating electronically (unless otherwise agreed, s. 20).[32]

Consumer Protection Legislation   Consumer protection is primarily an area of provincial jurisdiction, although particular industries may also fall under federal protection, such as banking. In an attempt to offer Canadian consumers uniform online protection and provide international consistency, Industry Canada—together with the governments of Ontario, Alberta, and Quebec, and representatives of business—developed eight principles entitled "The Canadian Code of Practice for Consumer Protection in Electronic Commerce."[33] The principles incorporate the OECD Guidelines for Consumer Protection in the Content of Electronic Contracts.[34] The Industry Canada code of practice and the

---

[25] S.C. 2000, c. 5.

[26] See, especially, sections 41, 43, and 46.

[27] The relevant acts are the Electronic Commerce Act, S.N.L. 2001, c. E-5.2; S.N.S. 2000, c. 26; S.O. 2000, c. 17; R.S.P.E.I. 1988, c. E-4.1; Electronic Commerce and Information Act, C.C.S.M. 2000, c. E-55; Electronic Information and Documents Act, S.S. 2000, c. E-7.22; and Electronic Transactions Act, S.A. 2001, c. E-5.5; S.B.C. 2001, c. 10; S.N.B. 2001, c. E-5.5.

[28] The text of the Uniform Electronic Commerce Act is available from the Uniform Law Conference of Canada website: www.ulcc.ca.

[29] For corresponding provisions in the provincial legislation, *supra*, n. 27, see, for example, s. 3 (B.C.); s. 6 (N.S.); s. 4 (Ont.).

[30] See *ibid.*, s. 5 (B.C.); s. 8 (N.S.); s. 5 (Ont.).

[31] See *ibid.*, s. 11 (B.C.); s. 11 (N.S.); s. 11 (Ont.).

[32] See *ibid.*, s. 15 (B.C.); s. 21 (N.S.); s. 19 (Ont.).

[33] The Canadian Code of Practice for Consumer Protection in Electronic Commerce has three goals: equivalent protection, harmonization, and international consistency. The eight principles will be subject to periodic review and are available at http://cmcweb.ca/epic/site/cmc-cmc.nsf/eng/fe00064.html.

[34] The OECD consumer guidelines cover fair business practices, advertising, and marketing and are available at www.oecd.org/fr/sti/consommateurs/oecdguidelinesforconsumerprotectioninthecontextofelectroniccommerce1999 .html.

OECD guidelines reflect the developing international standards of consumer protection in online contracting.

Federal, provincial, and territorial consumer affairs representatives developed a model for B2C internet consumer protection legislation.[35] Some provinces have adopted consumer protection legislation based on the model law.[36] Protective measures include mandatory disclosure of terms, cancellation rights or cooling-off periods, and printable consumer copies.[37] Consumer protection laws may apply to transactions completed outside their specific jurisdiction. The Ontario legislation applies to all consumers located in Ontario, no matter where the vendor or the goods are based. Alberta's protections apply when either the consumer or vendor is a resident of Alberta, or the offer or acceptance is made in Alberta.[38] Quebec consumers are protected from waivers of Quebec authority.[39] An online vendor needs to be familiar with the specifics of the consumer protection laws in relevant jurisdictions.

CHECKLIST

Precautions to Be Taken by Vendors When Contracting Online

Where a website is to be used to sell goods and services, the trader should take the following precautions:

- Become familiar with the ecommerce and consumer protection laws of provinces, countries, or jurisdictions in which it intends to do business.

- Where necessary, customize contract terms for the specific jurisdiction.

- Design the website so that the terms of the contract are brought to the attention of customers before any contract is concluded. Ensure any hyperlinks are visible, easily accessible, and functional.

- State clearly which law and jurisdiction apply to any contracts formed.

- Avoid giving customers too much freedom to amend terms—use yes/no or accept/decline options wherever possible.

- Maintain full backups of all contracts made via web pages.

- Generate and forward a printable customer copy of the contract at the time of purchase.

Torts

The internet raises tort issues relating to damages, jurisdiction, and limitation periods, as well as issues about how and by whom a tort is committed. The tort most often associated with the internet is defamation. Courts have held that posting defamatory material on a

---

[35] Canada's Office of Consumer Affairs, Internet Sales Contract Harmonization Template, available at http://ic.gc.ca/eic/site/oca-bc.nsf/eng/ca01642.html.

[36] Consumer Protection and Business Practices Act, S.N.L. 2009, c. C-31.1, ss. 21V–21AF; Consumer Protection Act, 2002, S.O. 2002, c. 30, Sch. A, ss. 37–40; Consumer Protection Act, C.C.S.M. c. C200, ss. 127–35; Consumer Protection Act, S.S. 1996, c. C-30.1, ss. 75.5–75.91; Fair Trading Act, R.S.A. 2000, c. F-2, s. 42.

[37] See "Consumer Protection Rights in Canada in the Context of Electronic Commerce," Office of Consumer Affairs, August 31, 1998; M. Deturbide, *Consumer Protection Online* (Markham: Lexis Nexis Canada, 2006). The details of disclosure, notice, and cancellation protections are usually set out in the regulations rather than the legislation: Alberta Regulation 81/2001 (Internet Sales Regulation) passed pursuant to the Fair Trading Act, *ibid.* Particular industries may be subject to additional regulation: Alberta Regulation 246/2005 (Energy Marketing Regulation), Part 3: Internet Marketing Contracts.

[38] Section 2, Ontario Consumer Protection Act, 2002, *supra*, n. 24; Alberta Regulation 81/2001, s. 2 (Fair Trading Act).

[39] Article 3149 CCQ; (58.) Quebec law requires websites of firms whose place of business is in the province to be in the French language.

website or message board is publication for the purposes of libel, and constitutes "broadcasting" for purposes of libel and slander legislative notice or apology provisions.[40] The internet's ability to instantaneously reach a very large audience increases the size of damage awards.[41]

CASE 31.2

Fromm, a director of the Canadian Association of Free Expression Inc. (CAFÉ), posted nine comments on various websites complaining about W., an investigator with the Canadian Human Rights Commission (CHRC). He said W. was "a member of the thought police" and a "high priest of censorship" who abused his position with the CHRC. Fromm's posting triggered insulting responding posts. W. sued both Fromm and CAFÉ, who admitted making the postings as well as sending emails to a large distribution list. They

made no apology or retraction and argued fair comment as a defence. The trial judge found (and the Court of Appeal agreed) that the comments were defamatory and awarded general damages of $20 000 plus aggravated damages of $10 000. The court recognized that internet libel has global reach and the ability to instantaneously and irrevocably publish to a limitless audience. The fact that the comments were published literally to the world justified the award of aggravated damages.[42]

ISPs are an integral part of the ecommerce system. They have been described as the "gatekeepers" to the internet. Some anonymous internet posters mistakenly believe that they are not liable for defamatory comments because ISPs will keep their identities confidential. This is not always true—courts may order ISPs to release identifying information in some situations. Unfortunately for plaintiffs, ISPs may have only limited contact information. Still it can be valuable for service or notice purposes. For more information on this topic, see the Companion Website.

CASE 31.3

Brian Burke, former general manager of the Toronto Maple Leafs and Vancouver Canucks, started a defamation lawsuit against anonymous message board posters known only by their posting names. The message board administrators refused to provide the identity and residence of the

defendants. The British Columbia court gave Burke permission to serve notice of the lawsuits through the message board's personal message service which sends notification to users when logging into their accounts.[43]

Another common question is whether ISPs are themselves responsible for material placed on the internet through their servers. Who has committed the libel? Can the ISPs be considered to have "published" a libel? Courts generally take the view that ISPs are like a postal service or phone company and should not be responsible for any material transmitted by them.[44] ISPs are not considered parties to a tort so long as their activities are restricted

---

[40] *Janssen-Ortho Inc. v. Amgen Canada Inc.*, [2005] O.J. No. 2265 (dealing with an internet radio broadcast); *Bahlieda v. Santa* (2003), 233 D.L.R. (4th) 382 (ON. C.A.). In the context of the Ontario Libel and Slander Act, whether posting on the Internet was "broadcasting" was a triable issue and the Act requires written notice of intended legal action; see Chapter 3. See also *Warman v. Fromm*, [2007] O.J. No. 4754, aff'd [2008] O.J. No. 5043, leave to appeal denied [2009] S.C.C.A. No. 40; *Breeden v. Black* [2012] SCC 19.

[41] See e.g. *Barrick Gold Corporation v. Lopehandia* (2004), 71 O.R. (3d) 416 Ont. C.A.: damages were increased from $15 000 to $75 000 based on the "Internet factor." Publishing a libel in a limited number of personal emails is likely to be less harmful than posting it on a website: *Ross v. Holley*, [2004] O.J. No. 4643; *Newman v. Halstead*, (2006) B.C.J. No. 59. The recent popularity of blogs and social networks such as Facebook increase the likelihood of large defamation awards: *Newman v. Halstead*, [2006] BCSC 65.

[42] *Warman*, *supra*, n. 40. See also *Warman v. Grosvenor*, [2008] O.J. No. 4462.

[43] *Burke v. John Doe*, 2013 BCSC 964

[44] *Canadian Association of Internet Providers v. SOCAN* (2004), 240 D.L.R. (4th) 193 (S.C.C.). See also *Re Broadcasting Act*, [2010] F.C.J. No. 849 (FCA) where ISPs were found not to carry on (in whole or in part) a broadcasting undertaking (subject to the Broadcasting Act)—they merely provide end-users with access to broadcasting.

to the transmission of information.[45] Similarly, hyperlinks to another website containing defamatory content do not create a presumption that the first site has republished the defamatory content; hyperlinks are compared to footnotes—"they do not make the author of the footnotes a publisher of what the reader finds when the footnote is followed."[46] However, there could be liability if there is direct evidence of publication (members of the public following the link and reading the content), the defamatory content is commented upon, endorsed, or reproduced on the **linking or hyperlinking** site, or readers are encouraged to follow the link.[47]

Ecommerce can give rise to claims in tort in other ways. For example, many ecommerce services depend upon the use of sophisticated computer programs, which can go wrong—sometimes very wrong. In one case, an investor was awarded damages against a discount electronic trading broker when faults in the broker's data entry system caused the posting of multiple transaction records in the plaintiff's account and resulted in the plaintiff selling securities he did not own.[48] In another tort example, a student successfully sued Laurentian University for misrepresentations made on the university website.[49]

Intellectual Property

The general laws of intellectual property are covered in Chapter 20. However, ecommerce and the use of the internet create special challenges and opportunities for infringement. For example, although the components of a website may be quite standard or ordinary, the specific organization, presentation, and content of a website are often unique and attract both copyright and trademark protection. As well how the website operates maybe a patentable business method. In this section, we review intellectual property issues arising from new technology.

Trademarks A trademark is an identifiable feature used to distinguish one's goods or services from others; **infringement** is unauthorized use of a **trademark** or use of a confusingly similar mark. Infringement is actionable by the tort of **passing-off**, or under the Trademark Act, even when unintentional. The internet increases the probability of infringements, their seriousness, and the likelihood of detection. It is quite possible for two businesses in different countries, or in different jurisdictions within the same country, to have the same name or to have confusingly similar names. Prior to the internet this possible trademark infringement would likely have gone undetected.

linking or hyperlinking an electronic connection of one website to another website; links may be automatic or activated by the user, and the new website may replace the original website or open in its own frame or browser window

infringement violation of the rights of the owner of the intellectual property

trademark an identifiable feature that is used by a person for the purpose of distinguishing his goods or services from those of others

passing-off a common law tort involving the misrepresentation of goods, services, or a business in such a way as to deceive the public into believing that they are the goods, services, or business of some other person

ILLUSTRATION 31.3

Caitlin, the owner of the Enchanted Florist flower shop serving the greater Toronto area, creates a website to enable her customers to order flowers for delivery. On this website, she posts photographs of her flower arrangements and takes orders over the phone from regular customers with account numbers. A month later, Caitlin receives notice that shops in Halifax and Victoria—also named the Enchanted Florist—are claiming that she is infringing their trademarks.[50]

[45] The Supreme Court of Canada also ruled that the practice of "caching" information is "content neutral" and is simply a consequence of the improvement of internet technology and did not give rise to liability.

[46] *Crookes v. Wikimedia Foundation Inc.*, 2008 BCSC 1424, aff'd [2009] B.C.J. No. 1832 at paras. 18–20, 41, 59 aff'd *Crookes v. Newton* 2011 S.C.C. 47.

[47] *Ibid.*, paras. 59–72.

[48] *Robert v. Brokerage Services Inc.* (2001), 104 A.C.W.S. (3d) 988.

[49] *Olar v. Laurentian University* (2007), Carswell, Ont. 3595, aff'd [2008] O.J. No. 4623. The same representation was also contained in the hard copy of the university calendar.

[50] The example, with changes to the locations, is taken from Kalow, "From the Internet to Court: Exercising Jurisdiction Over World Wide Web Communications" (1997) 65 Fordham L. Rev. 2241.

Without the internet, each business would likely have been unaware of the other's existence. If litigation were pursued, the court would have to decide which of the parties was entitled to use the Enchanted Florist trademark, and whether it was entitled to sole use. This scenario presents another question. Which province's court should hear the dispute?

Of course, trademark infringement on the internet is not always accidental; sometimes the goal is to take advantage of the public's familiarity with the existing trademark.

CASE 31.4

Bell Actimedia Inc. produces and distributes trade and telephone directories in Canada, and provides business listings on the internet. It also owns the Canadian rights to the trademarks "Yellow Pages" and "Pages Jaunes." It learned that Globe Communications, a partnership registered in Quebec, had established a website with the address www.lespagesjaunes.com and was advertising itself as the "business directory of the French-speaking world."

Bell, which itself had registered several internet sites, including www.yellowpages.ca, www.canadayellowpages.com, www.pagesjaunes.ca, and www.pagesjaunescanada.com, sought an injunction to restrain Globe from using its "Pages Jaunes" trademark, alleging passing-off and unfair competition.

The Court held that Bell was entitled to the injunction sought; a prima facie case of infringement was made out, and Bell established that it would suffer irreparable harm if an injunction was not granted.[51]

In another case, owners of the "Yellow Pages" trademark obtained an award of damages against two corporations, one incorporated in Canada and the other in Nevada, for infringement of its mark (as well as of the "walking fingers" logo), by advertising their business directory service as "Canadian Yellow Pages on the internet" on their website, www.cdnyellowpages.com.[52]

CASE 31.5

The Software Guy was established in 2002 as an online retailer of business application software. In 2003 another firm, The Software King, started up a similar business, with a remarkably similar webpage. The two domain names were also very similar: www.thesoftwareguy.com and www.thesoftwareking.com. The proprietors of the two businesses had previously discussed setting up business together.

Software Guy sought an injunction to restrain Software King from using that name and from using text from its website.

The court dismissed the application. The names were confusingly similar because of the word "software," which is a generic term to which the applicant had no claim. As to the website, it seemed obviously pirated, even reproducing a grammatical error. However, there was a strong suggestion that the applicant had itself pirated the design from elsewhere. It was not the creator and had no copyright in the design.[53]

Unauthorized linking of websites may be trademark infringement if it suggests affiliation, endorsement, or sponsorship. Infringement is most likely when the link is opened in its own frame within a single browser window so that both websites are visible at the same time.

---

[51] *Bell Actimedia Inc. v. Puzo* (1999), 166 F.T.R. 202.

[52] *Tele-Direct (Publications) Inc. v. Canadian Business Online Inc.* (1998), 85 C.P.R. (3d) 332. There were also personal fines imposed on the director of the corporation which were subsequently varied: [200] F.C.J. No. 2.

[53] *Software Guy Brokers Ltd. v. Hardy*, [2004] B.C.J. No. 95.

Showmax Inc. intended to open a big-screen movie theatre. Its website contained an unauthorized link to a picture of an IMAX theatre from the IMAX website. The Federal Court found that the linkage incorrectly conveyed the impression that the two businesses were associated.[54]

domain name the registered internet address of a website

Domain Names

Trademark infringement sometimes results from confusingly similar internet addresses, or domain names.[55] A **domain name** has two or more parts, separated by dots. The part on the left is the most specific. The part on the right is the most general and is referred to as the "top-level domain." Historically, top-level domains were "generic," (gTLDs) such as commercial (.com), educational (.edu), or organizational (.org), or "national," such as Canada (.ca). Generic names are assigned by authorized registrars whose activities are supervised by the Internet Corporation for Assigned Names and Numbers (ICANN), a non-profit body established in 2000. National names are assigned by national authorities. In Canada, the ".ca" domain is controlled by the Canadian Internet Registration Authority (CIRA). In 2011, ICANN announced that it would "deregulate" gTLDs—any word in any language can follow the dot (for a significantly higher price than generic suffixes). The list of avalaible gTLDs will grow significantly. New top-level domains called strings are being released all the time (e.g., .coffee; .land), producing lots of new registrants who will issue names for their string. ICANN continues to supervise the expanded group of registrants.[56]

It is common for a business's domain name to include an existing trademark. Consequently, the use of an exclusive domain name may amount to the infringement of another's trademark. Businesses should register their domain names as trademarks, and the Canadian Intellectual Property Office is accepting such registrations, provided the generic or national portion (.com, .ca, etc.) is disclaimed. Examples of trademarked domain names are TSN.ca and GLOBALTV.COM.[57]

Canadian business corporations typically register in multiple gTLDs (.com, .ca, .eu). Registering a domain name in gTLD costs very little, so multiple registrations prevent imposters from buying the name and diverting traffic away from the business. Traffic to a site may determine its advertising value, and this might motivate imposters to choose domain names very similar to existing high traffic sites in hopes of diverting web traffic.[58] Deregulation will modify this practice—no one business is likely to pre-emptively register hundreds of domain names, and the new customized gTLDs will be expensive. This may mean more trademark infringement claims arising from the availability of similar domain names.

---

[54] *IMAX Corp. v. Showmax Inc.* (2000), 5 C.P.R. (4th) 81 (F.C.T.D.). It was also argued that linking infringed copyright. See also Fecenko, *supra*, n. 2, at 177.

[55] For a description of the evolution of the system and its legal implications, see Rebecca Gole, "Playing the Name Game: A Glimpse at the Future of the Internet Domain Name System" (1999) 51 Fed. Com. L. J. 403. See also Marc Watkins, "Government Regulation of the Dot-ca Domain Name Space" (2005) 2(1) Univ. of Ottawa L. & Tech. J. 145.

[56] See http://newgtlds.icann.org/en/program-status/delegated-strings.

[57] TSN.ca was registered by The Sports Network Inc. (TMA551540). The generic portions were disclaimed because they lack distinctiveness. GLOBALTV.COM was registered by Canwest Global Communications Corp. in 2000 (TMA597951) owned by Shaw Media Global Inc. (2013).

[58] In one trademark validity case, the court considered evidence of the number of website hits and advertising expenses: *Candrug Health Solutions Inc. v. Thorkelson*, [2007] F.C.J. No. 586 at para. 16, revrs'd [2008] F.C.J. 426. Another way to divert traffic and infringe trademark is to place a trademark in a "meta tag" used by search engines to compile search results. See Fecenko, *supra*, n. 2 at 175.

CASE 31.7

In 1995, ITV Technologies Inc., a British Columbia web-services provider, registered the domain name www.itv.net. WIC Television Ltd., an Edmonton-based television broadcaster since 1974, owned a number of stations throughout Canada. WIC owned several registered trademarks using the letters "ITV" and had registered a website with the domain name itv.ca. In 1996, WIC contacted ITV and asked it to stop using the ITV domain name.

Instead of waiting for WIC to sue for trademark infringement, ITV launched a pre-emptive strike and brought an action for an order expunging (removing) WIC's "ITV" trademarks, on the grounds that they were not registrable. WIC counterclaimed, alleging infringement of its trademarks and seeking an injunction.

After a nine-year court battle, both sides eventually lost.[59] There was nothing unlawful about WIC's marks, which were well-known and distinctive in Alberta, and there was no reason for them to be expunged. On the other hand, there was no evidence, or likelihood, of confusion between the products of the two companies, so the mark was not infringed.

In Case 31.7, the infringement of the trademark appears innocent, at least initially, with no intention to "steal" business. In other instances, there is an intention to derive a benefit from the use of another's well known trademark and to divert business away from the owner of the mark.[60] This type of passing-off succeeds because internet users, when trying to locate the website of a well known firm, will often guess about the address by trying the trade name plus ".com" or complete a general search and click on the first item.

CASE 31.8

The plaintiffs were the publishers of one of the oldest and most widely read newspapers in Saskatchewan. They also maintained a website, www.thestarphoenix.com, which reproduced the front page of their newspaper with the current day's lead stories and contained advertising paid for by their customers. The defendant created a website, www.saskatoonstarphoenix.com, that looked very much like the plaintiffs', but substituted his own advertising.

The court awarded damages to the plaintiffs. The defendant's actions amounted to passing-off. There was a misappropriation of the plaintiffs' goodwill, an intention to mislead the public, and actual or potential damage to the plaintiffs.[61]

Some other abuses of the domain name system have evolved. A U.S. court granted an injunction for trademark infringement in a case where an anti-abortion activist registered the domain name www.plannedparenthood.com in order to promote his views.[62] In British Columbia, an injunction and damages were granted against an individual using a domain name to redirect unsuspecting people to a website containing adult content.[63] Sometimes the intent is not to benefit from another's trademark but to damage it, for example, with registrations of (trademark)sucks.com. Sometimes these protest site registrations are held to be confusingly similar to the trademark and therefore infringing.[64] Other decisions have found them not confusing at all; it is obvious from the negative meaning of the word "sucks" that the two sites are not connected and free speech rights protect the operation

[59] *ITV Technologies, Inc. v. WIC Television Ltd.* (2003), 239 F.T.R. 203, aff'd [2005] F.C.J. No. 438 (F.C.A.).

[60] See also *Peinet Inc. v. O'Brien* (1995), 61 C.P.R. (3d) 334; *Molson Breweries v. Kuettner* (1999), 94 A.C.W.S. (3d) 550.

[61] *Saskatchewan Star Phoenix Group Inc. v. Noton*, [2001] S.J. No. 275.

[62] *Planned Parenthood v. Bucci* (1997), U.S. Dist. LEXIS 3338. Other examples are discussed in the article by Gole, *supra*, n. 55.

[63] *Law Society of British Columbia v. Canada Domain Name Exchange Corp.* (2004), 243 D.L.R. (4th) 746, aff'd (2005), 259 D.L.R. (4th) 171 (B.C.C.A.).

[64] See e.g. WIPO Decision No. D2005-0168 (*Air France v. Virtual Dates, Inc.*). The U.S. has legislation protecting against trademark dilution: Trademark Dilution Revision Act of 2006, 15 U.S.C § 114.

of a protest site.[65] Operators of protest sites should be equally concerned with liability for defamation.

One of the earliest internet issues was **cybersquatting**, where a person registers a domain name that includes a well known trademark or brand name, and then offers to sell the domain name to the owner of the mark for a high price. Such action constitutes a trademark infringement and usually results in the infringer having to relinquish the domain name and to pay court costs.[66] However, cybersquatters normally rely on the fact that the trademark owner may find it less expensive and more convenient simply to buy the domain name from the registrant. It is not clear if deregulation of gTLDs will launch a new round of cybersquatting for suffixes or whether the high cost of registration will discourage the practice.

cybersquatting the registration of a domain name containing the trademark of another person, with the intention of selling the domain name to the owner of the mark

---

CASE 31.9

A travel retailer had a website, located at www.itravel2000.com, and had registered the name "itravel" under the Ontario Business Names Act. It applied to the CIRA to register the .ca domain name, but was informed that the name had already been registered. The registrant was an individual who had no connection with the travel business, and had acquired the name with the sole purpose of selling it to the highest bidder.

On application by the travel retailer, an injunction was granted, preventing the defendant from using or selling the name.[67] If the CIRA complaints process had been used, a transfer of the domain name to the travel retailer could have been ordered.[68]

Domain name disputes may be resolved in the courts—for example, by actions for trademark infringement. Alternatively, in the case of generic names, ICANN has established an **alternative dispute resolution** policy, with a list of approved dispute resolution service providers, and CIRA has a similar process for names within the ".ca" domain.[69] The World Intellectual Property Office operates an arbitration and mediation centre. For more information on this topic, see the Companion Website.

alternative dispute resolution the use of private procedures such as arbitration and mediation to resolve disputes

---

CASE 31.10

Bill Cosby owned all the trademarks associated with the television show *Fat Albert and the Cosby Kids*, which was the basis for the December 2004 feature film entitled *Fat Albert*. Six months prior to the movie's release, Sterling Davenport registered the domain name fatalbert.org. After release of the movie, Davenport linked the domain name to a website selling sexually explicit products. Davenport had registered over 500 other domain names, often using celebrity names.

Bill Cosby filed an email complaint with the World Intellectual Property Office Arbitration and Mediation Center. Davenport never responded to the complaint, and the arbitrator found that the domain name was confusingly similar to the Cosby trademark, that Davenport registered the domain name in order to trade on Cosby's fame, and that both Davenport's registration and use of the domain name were done in bad faith. The arbitrator ordered that the domain name be transferred to Bill Cosby.[70]

---

[65] See, for example, *British Columbia Automobile Assn. v. Office and Professional Employees' International Union, Local 378*, [2001] B.C.J. No. 151 (copying a website design was found to be copyright infringement); WIPO Decision No. D2000-1104 (*Wal-Mart Stores, Inc. v. wallmartcanadasucks.com and Kenneth J. Harvey*).

[66] See e.g. *Panavision International Inc. v. Toeppen* (1996), U.S. Dist. LEXIS 19698. Mr. Toeppen reportedly registered some 240 names and then attempted to sell them for high fees. The U.S. has legislation on cybersquatting: Anticybersquatting Consumer Protection Act, 15 U.S.C. § 1125. In the U.K. see *British Telecommunications, plc v. One in a Million Ltd.*, [1998] E.W.J. No 954 (C.A.).

[67] *itravel2000.com Inc. v. Fagan* (2001), 197 D.L.R. (4th) 760.

[68] See e.g. CIRA Dispute No. 00239/13—americangirl.ca, http://www.cira.ca/legal/cdrp/dispute-resolution-decisions/.

[69] Details of the ICANN uniform domain-name dispute-resolution policy can be obtained from the ICANN website at http://www.icann.org/en/help/dndr/udrp/policy. For the CIRA dispute-resolution policy, see http://www.cira.ca/assets/Documents/Legal/Dispute/CDRPpolicy.pdf.

[70] WIPO Decision No. D2005-076, (*William H. Cosby, Jr. v. Sterling Davenport*), www.wipo.int/amc/en/domains/decisions/-html/2005/d2005-0756.html.

Copyright Copyright laws give the creator of a **work** the exclusive right to copy, produce, or distribute that work during the life of the author and for the 50 years thereafter. This monopoly applies to the publication, copying, and reproduction of materials on the internet or in email, in instant messaging, digitally, or in telecommunications. Anyone who copies, distributes, or uses a work without the owner's permission infringes the copyright and is liable for damages. The internet makes infringement of copyright, whether deliberate or unintentional, very easy.[71] The legal risk of infringement affects every business with a website or an employee with internet service.

work   an original published or unpublished literary, dramatic, musical, or artistic creation, including the title

In Canada, copyright law and policy are balanced between users' and owners' rights. No one set of rights is dominant. The Copyright Act contains the rules for use, infringement, and **royalty** collection for copyrighted material. The act is "technologically neutral"—copying in any form (print, telecommunication, or internet) is covered and royalties should not differ according to the medium used to deliver the work to the end user.[72] Many internet users incorrectly believe that when material is posted on a website, the author or owner consents to its being copied or reproduced. With some exceptions for "fair dealing,"[73] material posted on a website, and the site's design and visual appearance, cannot be copied or adopted without infringing the creator's copyright. A website is recognized as an artistic work, and merely linking websites may also infringe copyright because it associates the work with someone other than the creator. Businesses should clearly state the acceptable terms of use of material placed on their websites. Although not strictly required in Canada, it is prudent to give notice of copyright ownership by using the "©" symbol. For more information on this topic, see the Companion Website.

royalty   fee paid to the copyright owner for permission to copy the work

CASE 31.11

Sotramex, a firm specializing in cleaning up mining and forestry sites, prepared a technical description (written by one of its employees) to appear on the website of the International Centre for the Advancement of Environmental Technologies. A year or so later, Sorenviq, a competitor in the reforestation market, posted virtually identical content on its own website without acknowledging the true authorship.

The court found that the author's copyright had been infringed and ordered Sorenviq to remove the text from its website and pay $10 000 damages plus $5000 exemplary damages.[74]

The Copyright Act as amended in 2012 exempts some technical and private personal use copies from liability (section 29.22). Format shifting (moving material already purchased from one device to another), time shifting (recording material to be viewed later), and backing up computer programs are all allowed. Private use reproduction of musical works, performances, and sound recording is also allowed (sections 30.6, 80). The "YouTube exception" allows the use of copyrighted material to generate new content for noncommercial use (section 29.22).[75]

---

[71] For a basic review of the challenges that the internet has caused with respect to copyright, see Charlotte Waelde and Hector MacQueen, "Entertainment to Education: The Scope of Copyright" (2004) 3 I.P.Q. 259–83. The Supreme Court of Canada ruled, in the SOCAN case, *supra*, n. 44, that the practice of "caching" (that is, making temporary copies of webpages to speed up delivery) does not of itself constitute an infringement of copyright. Section 41.27 of the Copyright Act offers protection for search engines. Infringement may depend on whether the link is user activated, automatic, or "deep." For further discussion, see Geist (*supra*, n. 2), and IMAX, *supra*, n. 54.

[72] *Entertainment Software Association v. SOCAN* 2012 SCC 34 at para 9.

[73] The concept of "fair dealing" is discussed in Chapter 20 and includes research, private study, and news reporting: Copyright Act R.S.C. 1985, c. C-42, ss. 28–9 as amended.

[74] *Sotramex Inc. v. Sorenviq Inc.*, [1998] A.Q. No. 2241 (Quebec Superior Court—Civil Division).

[75] The nickname is developing because YouTube users often post their own video works merged with existing copyrighted sound recordings.

Some businesses whose main activity involves the supply of technological copyrightable works, such as software developers and music producers, have seen their industries transformed by internet copying. Reproduction and communication to the public are supposed to be the exclusive rights of the copyright owner. How are owners compensated if personal users copy for free?

First, the personal use exception for sound recordings does not apply if the copying is done for sale, rental, distribution, communication to the public, or performance in public (section 80(2)). Second, copyright owners are compensated through tariffs levied on the manufacturers of audio (nondigital) recording devices (section 82)[76] and businesses that distribute or facilitate the transmission of online material (section 70.13). The business incorporates the tariffs into the final price of its product.

The tariff model "taxes" infringing behaviour of *businesses* facilitating copying of works, sound recordings, or performances (sections 19, 70.1, 80). Individual creators assign the rights in their works to a "collective society." In turn, the society issues licences over the entire inventory for a fee.[77] It distributes the fees collected to the creators, after payment of the society's costs. The licence fee can be set by agreement with licensees or, more typically, by a tariff approved by the Copyright Board (section 70.15). The collective society's application to the Copyright Board will identify specific activity and businesses to be subject to the tariff. Those businesses receive notice and may oppose the imposition of the tariff. The Society of Composers, Authors and Music Publishers of Canada (SOCAN) is one collective; there are many others.[78]

A collective society can only request a fee or tariff for what would otherwise amount to an infringement of copyright. The fairness of the private-use exception depends upon revenue being generated by a fee or tariff at the distribution level. Balancing all the competing interests is a challenge. For example microSD memory cards are exempt from the audio recording levy because they are so widely used as components in many manufactured goods (e.g., smartphones) that the cost increases resulting from a tariff would negatively impact "ecommerce businesses and Canada's participation in the digital economy"[79] Many of the cases discussed in Chapter 20 are appeals of Copyright Board rulings on whether or not a tariff is appropriate in the circumstances. For internet tariffs, the analysis often focuses on whether the targeted activity is "communication to the public" and if so, whether infringement is excused by one of the fair dealing exceptions.[80]

ILLUSTRATION 31.4

(a) The Supreme Court of Canada denied SOCAN's request for a tariff on ISPs arising from transmission of copyrighted music. ISPs were merely intermediaries who provided the means of telecommunication; they were not communicators.[81]

(b) When SOCAN applied for a tariff on cell phone service providers who were allowing subscribers to download copyrighted music as ringtones, the Federal Court of Appeal held that the cell phone providers were

>

---

[76] The levy on the sale of each blank CD is 29 cents.

[77] Sections 2, 19, 70.1, 70.12.

[78] Canadian Private Copying Collective (CPCC) is an umbrella organization whose members include the collectives such as SOCAN, http://www.cpcc.ca/en/the-cpcc. It is responsible for the collection of the audio equipment levy. This levy was held not to apply to the sale of iPods or any digital recording devices because s. 82 only applies to audio equipment. *Apple Canada Inc. v. Canadian Private Copying Collective*, [2008] F.C.J. No. 5 (FCA).

[79] MicroSD Cards Exclusion Regulation (Copyright Act) SOR/2012-226, P.C. 2012-1370 Canada Gazette, Oct. 18, 2012.

[80] Copyright Act, R.S.C. 1985, c. C-42, ss. 3(1)(f), 80, 83.

[81] *Canadian Association of Internet Providers v. SOCAN*, (2004), 240 D.L.R. (4th) 193.

"communicating a musical work to the public" and a tariff was justified.[82] Ringtones were offered to the public even though they were individually copied.

(c) The Supreme Court denied SOCAN's request for a tariff on cell phone service providers who were offering prospective purchasers short free music previews. The behaviour was "communicating to the public" but was exempt under the fair dealing exception as consumer research—it actually promoted the purchase of music to the benefit of SOCAN.[83]

(d) SOCAN's request for a new tariff on online music providers for the individual streaming and downloading of music by its customers was allowed only for streaming. Downloading was not communicating (it was copying or reproducing and therefore already covered by an existing tariff equally applicable to any physical sale of music). Streaming was considered communication (a form of performance) not caught by any existing tariff.[84] "To the public" is not limited to mass or bulk communication but can arise from multiple individual transmissions of the same work that are user initiated.

Together, the foregoing SOCAN decisions support internet users' rights over the interests of collective societies and copyright owners.[85] However, the protection of owners' rights was not forgotten in the latest round of legislative amendments. Subject to a few exceptions, the legislation supports the owners' use of self-help measures such as **technical protection measures (TPMs)** and a **digital rights management system (DRMS)** to block unauthorized copying of their works.[86] Section 41.1 prohibits the circumvention of TPMs; the manufacture, import, or sale of technology for the purpose of circumvention; and the offering of services to assist in circumvention. Remedies for violation vary depending upon whether circumvention was intentional or knowing and whether the circumventer is a library, museum, or educational institution. In these latter cases, the only remedy available is an injunction (section 41.2). Tampering with a DRMS is also forbidden (section 41.22). The Act adds these activities to the existing criminal offences for copyright infringement with fines up to $1 000 000 and/or imprisonment for five years. For more information on this topic, see the Companion Website.

ISPs must also assist copyright owners in policing the internet for infringers. The 2012 reforms give ISPs the responsibility of notifying subscribers about allegations of infringements, however ISPs do not have to cut off the services of allegedly infringing subscribers, as is required in the U.S. (sections 41.25–41.27).[87]

The above described TPM, DRMT, and ISP measures were adopted to bring Canada into closer conformity with the World Intellectual Property Organization (WIPO) Internet Treaties, the WIPO Copyright Treaty (WCT), and WIPO Performances and Phonograms Treaty (WPPT). These treaties call for domestic legislation to create legal remedies for circumvention of TPMs or DRMS, impose obligations on ISPs, and entrench a copyright

technical protection measures (TPMs) access locks or use locks for electronic material. An access lock requires a password to access the work; a use lock blocks particular uses of the work such as copying

digital rights management system (DRMS) a system collecting data about the licensing, payment for, and authenticity of a work

---

[82] *Canadian Wireless Telecommunications Association, Bell Mobility Inc., and Telus Communications Company v. SOCAN*, [2008] F.C.J. No. 21, leave to SCC denied.

[83] *SOCAN v. Bell Canada* 2012 SCC 366

[84] *Rogers Communications Inc. v. SOCAN* 2012 SCC 35, [2012] 2 S.C.R. 283; *Entertainment Software Associations v. SOCAN* 2012 SCC 34, [2012] 2. S.C.R. 231.

[85] Daniel Gervais, The Internet Taxi: Collective Management of Copyright and the Making Available Right, after Pentalogy, in The Copyright Pentalogy—How the Supreme Court of Canada Shook the Foundations of Canadian Copyright Law, Micahel Geist, ed. (University of Ottawa Press, 2013).

[86] These measures are not without their critics. Access-to-information concerns have been raised because these systems do not distinguish between legal uses and infringing "conduct." See C.M. Correa, "Fair Use in the Digital Era," UNESCO INFOethics 2000, http://webworld.unesco.org/infoethics2000/papers.html#correa. For a discussion of other self-help efforts such as hacking, data poisoning, and defamation attacks launched against offenders, see Jennifer A. Chandler, "Technological Self-Help and Equality in Cyberspace" (2010) 56(1) McGill L.J. 39.

[87] Somewhat similar legislation has been enacted in the United States legislation to deal specifically with the liability of internet intermediaries for breach of copyright: Digital Millennium Copyright Act, 1998. Nathan Irving, "Copyright Law for the Digital World: An Evaluation of Reform Proposals" (2010) 10 Asper Rev. Int'l Bus. & Trade L. 1141.

holder's exclusive rights to make work available on the internet.[88] Canadian copyright laws are not as owner rights' friendly as the WIPO treaties. Canada is in the process of adopting anti-counterfeiting legislation as required in an international Anti-Counterfeiting Trade Agreement.[89] For more information on this topic, see the Companion Website.

Privacy

Concern is growing over the fact that organizations—government and business—have accumulated vast amounts of electronic information about private individuals that might be used for purposes not contemplated by the individual who originally supplied it. Electronic commerce greatly increases the amount of information that is made available, and, being in computerized form, that information is easily edited and transmitted. Data about data (known as metadata) can easily be sold to marketers and others. Failure to properly safeguard private information may expose a business to tort liability.

The Personal Information Protection and Electronic Documents Act (PIPEDA), which has already been referred to in the context of contract law and will be discussed in greater detail in Chapter 32, imposes restrictions on the use and misuse of personal information. The Act applies to every organization that collects, uses, or discloses personal information in the course of commercial activity. Organizations are required to develop and publish privacy policies. Probably its most important feature is the requirement to obtain an individual's consent to use or disclose information collected. In addition, individuals will have the right to inspect their personal information held by a company and to have it corrected. According to some critics, the Act does not go nearly far enough; individuals will usually be unaware that information about them is being used improperly. Proposed amendments to PIPEDA include adding an obligation to disclose any breach of privacy, and limiting protection offered to employees.[90] When a province has adopted its own privacy legislation, affected organizations may be exempt from the application of PIPEDA.[91]

Ethical Issue   Employee Technology Use

The internet is part of everyday business activity, and the majority of employees have access to the internet at work. In their personal lives, employees use the internet as a form of social networking and expression. Social networking sites allow members to chat, post biographical information, pictures, and personal opinions, and share all of this information with fellow members. Business is struggling with the level of acceptable personal internet use in the workplace.

Employers are concerned about issues such as wasted time, viruses, security, confidentiality, harassment, and infringing or illegal activity including downloading copyrighted material, gambling, and accessing pornography. Employers may be found vicariously liable for such behaviour.

A 2007 survey of employers conducted on behalf of the American Management Association reported that 66 percent of employers monitor employee internet activities, 43 percent

>

---

[88] The United States implemented the WIPO treaty provisions in 1998, *supra*, n. 87, and the European Union Copyright Directive, passed May 22, 2001, adopts WIPO treaty provisions.

[89] Bill C-56, 1st Sess., 41st Parl., Combating Counterfeit Products Act (2013).

[90] Section 29 required a review of PIPEDA five years after enactment. The findings of the review were reported to Parliament on May 2, 2007, and can be found at www.ic.gc.ca/epic/site/ecic-ceac.nsf/eng/gv00401.html. On August 1, 2007, the Privacy Commissioner issued guidelines for businesses to follow when a privacy breach occurs, available at www.priv.gc.ca/media/nr-c_/2007/nr-c_070801_e.asp; Bill C-29, 3rd Sess., 40th Parl. (2010) died when the Parliament was dissolved for the May 2011 election, was reintroduced Sept. 29, 2011, and remains stalled in the House of Commons.

[91] Personal Information Protection Act, S.A. 2003, c. P-6.5; Personal Information Protection Act, S.B.C. 2003, c. 63; An Act Respecting the Protection of Personal Information in the Private Sector, R.S.Q., c. P-39.1.

retain and review employee email, and 30 percent of employers have fired an employee for misuse of the internet.

Many employers have developed codes of conduct for technology use, but there is no uniform position on the use of social networking sites. Some employers have banned their use entirely, while others allow unlimited access.

Questions to Consider

1. Should employees access social networking sites while at work?

2. Should employers be entitled to monitor employee internet use?

3. When making employment decisions, should employers (or potential employers) make use of information available on potential employees' personal or social networking sites?

4. Should an employer have a say in what employees post after hours on personal sites?

Sources: American Management Association and The ePolicy Institute, 2007 Electronic Monitoring & Surveillance Survey, http://press.amanet.org/pressreleases/177/2007electronicm onitoringsurveillancesurvey; Virginia Galt, "Firms Develop Codes of Conduct to Curb Porn Surfing on Internet," *Globe and Mail*, July 19, 2004, B4; Virgina Galt, "Keyword for Workplace Messaging? Caution," *Globe and Mail*, October 7, 2006, B14; Dianne Stafford, "Employers Limiting Use of Internet by Staff," *National Post*, February 28, 2007, WK 7; Shelley McGill and Mark Baetz, "Technology Use Codes of Conduct: Is It a Choice Between Shaping the Organizational Culture and Effective Legal Enforcement?" (2012) 15(2) Empl. Rights & Empl. Policy J. 101.

Another privacy related issue is whether persons are, or should be, protected from electronic junk mail, or "spam." Arguably, spam constitutes an invasion of privacy and might be actionable under the common law of trespass. Spam can be a well intentioned marketing campaign or an unscrupulous attempt to sabotage or steal from the recipient. In one Ontario case, a firm brought an action against its ISP, seeking restoration of its internet service after the ISP had discontinued the service. The ISP disconnected service after complaints that the plaintiff firm had been sending out up to 200 000 unsolicited messages each day to promote the sale of its furniture. The court ruled that spam is a breach of "netiquette"—the internet's unwritten rules of conduct—and refused to order restoration.[92] Federal legislation regulates the use of spam.

INTERNATIONAL ISSUE

What to Do about Spam?

Spam, at one time considered to be a minor irritant, has become a major worldwide concern. In 2013, spam accounted for 70.7 percent of global email traffic and has spread to text messaging and social networking.[93] Time is wasted, hard-drive space is used up, computers can be paralyzed, and money is spent on special programs designed to block spam.

A substantial proportion of spam is intended to defraud. There can be few internet users who have not received a "Nigeria letter," offering millions of dollars in return for the temporary use of their bank accounts. Spam is also used to plant unwanted programs or viruses in the receiver's system.

Countries are adopting legislation to combat spam. Norway adopted legislation in 2001. The United Kingdom's

legislation, in place since 2003, has been criticized for exempting work addresses. The American CAN-SPAM Act has been denounced for being too soft on spammers. In 2014, Canada became the last of the G8 countries to implement anti-spam legislation. In addition, privacy legislation applies to spam because email addresses are considered personal information, and, therefore, use without consent is a privacy violation. The Criminal Code addresses unauthorized use of computers and fraudulent activities. Deceptive or misleading emails may be violations of the Competition Act.

In a widely reported case in April 2005, an American spammer, Jeremy Jaynes, became the first spammer to be convicted of violating anti-spam law and was sentenced to nine years in prison. Jaynes was alleged to have sent as

>

---

[92] *1267623 Ontario Inc. v. Nexx Online Inc.* (1999), 45 O.R. (3d) 40. It is normal for ISP contracts to include a "netiquette clause," so that the dissemination of spam would constitute a breach of the contract with the ISP.

[93] Kaspersky Internet Security Centre, http://www.usa.kaspersky.com (Jan. 8, 2014).

Canada's Anti-Spam Legislation (CASL)[95] prohibits sending (or permitting the sending of) a commercial electronic message to an electronic address without the consent of the recipient (section 6). The CRTC is in charge of a regulatory regime to enforce the prohibition, complete with offences and civil liability. The definitions of "electronic message" and "address" are sufficiently broad to capture emails, text messaging, tweeting, and webcam messaging, as well as voice mails. Even when permission is granted, the message must identify the sender with contact information and set out the mechanism to unsubscribe from further communications. Fines of up to $10 000 000 per violation may be imposed. Directors and officers are personally liable for their companies' infractions unless they can show due diligence. Employers are vicariously liable for violations committed by employees in the scope of their employment. Internet service providers are not liable as long as their involvement is restricted to supply of telecommunication services.

Businesses that rely on electronic communications as part of their marketing or advertising plan will have to adjust their mailing lists to fit within the business relationship exception. Consent is implied if

- the business transacted with the recipient within the last two years,
- the business and recipient were parties to a written contract that expired within the last two years, or
- the business received an inquiry from the recipient in the last six months (section 10(10)).

Consent is also implied if a person conspicuously publishes his electronic address without stating that he does not want to receive unsolicited commercial electronic messages. Businesses should add this disclaimer to all employee emails. Finally, damaged persons are given a statutory civil cause of action to sue the offender for damages.

An important sacrifice to privacy is incorporated into CASL. For the purposes of investigating compliance and violations, internet service providers may turn over information to authorities, including personal information (section 56). Spam violations may be investigated by the Privacy Commissioner or the Commissioner of Competition (where

---

[94] *Jaynes v. Commonwealth of Virginia*, Supreme Court of Virginia, 276 Va. 443, 666 S.E. 2d 303 (2008), cert. denied, 129 S. Ct. 1670 (2009). First judgment was withdrawn after successful petition for rehearing: 657 S.E. 2d 478 (2008).

[95] An Act to promote the efficiency and adaptability of the Canadian economy by regulating certain activities that discourage reliance on electronic means of carrying out commercial activities and to amend the Canadian Radio-television and Telecommunications Commission Act, the Competition Act, the Personal Information Protection and Electronic Documents Act, and the Telecommunications Act, S.C. 2010, c. 23 proclaimed in force July 1, 2014.

they amount to deceptive business practices discussed in Chapter 3), and these organizations may share personal information in pursuit of their common goals. For more information on this topic, see the Companion Website.

Illegal Activities

Spam is just one of the potentially damaging activities undertaken on the internet that is now prohibited by federal legislation. Identity theft and "phishing," the practices of using fraudulent emails and fake websites to induce recipients into disclosing personal financial data, are offences caught by CASL's prohibition of unsolicited emails. Spyware can secretly collect data and mount virus attacks; malware can disable computers, destroy files, and cause millions of dollars of damage. CASL restricts these practices by prohibiting the installation of computer programs into the receiver's computer without the express consent of the recipient (section 8). Some forms of hacking, such as "man in the middle" schemes, are banned by CASL's prohibition of redirecting electronic messages without express consent. All of these behaviours are offences subject to major fines, and directors and officers may face personal, civil, and vicarious liability.

The difficulty with CASL is that it applies to activities within Canada and, as we know, many illegal activities originate in other countries. The CRTC, the Privacy Commissioner, and the Commissioner of Competition are expressly authorized to share the results of their investigations, including personal information, with foreign organizations pursuing the same goals.

Many countries are concerned about the use of the internet to facilitate other activities, such as the dissemination of hate literature and child pornography. Pornography, in fact, is one of the most infamous sectors of ecommerce in financial terms. The internet provides an easy method of distribution and one that makes detection and prosecution extremely difficult. Another activity that, if not illegal, is often strictly regulated by governments, is gambling. Again, the internet provides a means of circumventing local laws by establishing offshore "virtual casinos" and betting offices. In 1998, a British company established what was claimed to be the first worldwide online betting service at www.sportingbet.com, based in the tax-haven island of Alderney. The principal attraction of offshore, online gambling—to both bookmakers and punters—is that it enables the taxes that governments often impose on gambling to be avoided, increasing profits and pay-outs. The objection—from the point of view of the rest of the population—is that it undermines what is often an important source of government revenue.

Perhaps the greatest concern that governments have with respect to ecommerce is tax evasion. In one study[96] of ecommerce prepared for the Canada Customs and Revenue Agency, tax administrators identified concerns, including evasion of sales taxes, income tax, and customs duties, as well as the difficulty of following an "audit trail" in online and ecash transactions.[97]

INTERNATIONAL ASPECTS OF ECOMMERCE

The international nature of the internet is one of the great potential advantages of ecommerce—and also the cause of many headaches for government officials, businesses, and their lawyers. Businesses are uncertain about which laws apply to their contracts and other activities, which courts have jurisdiction to resolve their disputes, and what liabilities they may be subject to. Governments are unsure to what extent they should attempt to regulate ecommerce, and even less sure whether such attempts would be effective. For example, if Canadian businesses are subjected to stricter privacy regulation than their American competitors, they may lose out in the race to develop ecommerce. However, the European Union's privacy

---

[96] "Electronic Commerce and Canada's Tax Administration."

[97] Canada Revenue Agency GST/HST Technical Information Bulletin B-090 explains the agency's position on GST and electronic commerce: www.cra-arc.gc.ca/E/pub/gm/b-090/b-090-e.pdf.

legislation bans foreign firms from conducting ebusiness in most of Europe unless those firms are subject to equally strict privacy rules at home. Therefore, Canada must draft legislation that is sufficiently strict to satisfy the Europeans, without losing out in the American market.

Jurisdiction

jurisdiction the right of a court to hear and resolve a dispute

Chapter 30 discussed the principles applied by courts to determine whether they have **jurisdiction** to hear a dispute with international aspects. It is simple to establish jurisdiction if the defendant lives in the jurisdiction or consents to it. If neither residence nor consent exists, the court will assume jurisdiction over a case when there is a "real and substantial connection" with the dispute or its parties. However, even when the court has jurisdiction, it may decide not to hear the dispute when there is a *clearly* more appropriate foreign jurisdiction that should deal with the lawsuit; this is the rule of "forum non conveniens."[98] These principles are complex even when applied to conventional business transactions that cross provincial, state, or national borders. Jurisdictional issues in the context of online transactions present an even greater challenge.[99] To quote from one study:

> Traditional rules relating to jurisdiction incorporate a notion of territoriality. But internet communications are not geographically dependent. The very origin of an email message may be unknown. Web site information cannot be confined to a target audience, but is disseminated simultaneously to a global market. It may affect individuals in many jurisdictions, all of which have their own particular laws.[100]

Jurisdiction over international contract disputes is often decided on "consent" based upon a choice of forum clause in the contract. However, tort actions typically lack consent and require a determination of real and substantial connection.[101] This connection is found by looking at a number of established factors including whether the tort is "committed" in the province or whether the defendant "carries on business" in the province. These connections are difficult to evaluate in the online context.

Where is an online business "carried on"? Sometimes, determining where the business operates is not even possible, since its web address does not necessarily indicate its physical location. This difficulty has led some provinces to assert jurisdiction over all its residents' consumer disputes.[102] That solution is not ideal. To do business internationally, a business would have to comply with the consumer laws of many different jurisdictions, some of which might regard a simple disclaimer of liability as ineffective. Also, a judgment against a foreign supplier might be useless if the supplier has no assets in the customer's country or if the judgment is not recognized in the business's country.

level-of-interactivity test a review of the features of a website to determine if it is active or passive; only active sites will be considered connected to the jurisdiction (also called the *active-versus-passive test*)

American courts[103] developed a **level-of-interactivity test** (also called an *active-versus-passive test*) to determine where an online business is being carried on; it identifies three levels of business activity:

1. where the out-of-state defendant is carrying on substantial business (actually and virtually) within the jurisdiction

---

[98] *Van Breda v. Club Resorts* [2012] SCC 17

[99] According to Professor Geist, "Lurking in the background of virtually every Internet law issue is the question of jurisdiction" (*supra*, n. 2, at 43).

[100] Ogilvy Renault, "Jurisdiction and the Internet: Are Traditional Rules Enough?" The study is reproduced on the website of the Uniform Law Conference of Canada at http://www.ulcc.ca/.

[101] *Van Breda v. Club Resorts* 2012 SCC 17.

[102] See the report "Consumer Protection Rights in Canada in the Context of Electronic Commerce," *supra*, n. 37. Also see the section on Consumer Protection, *supra*, nn. 33–36.

[103] *Zippo Manufacturing Co. v. Zippo Dot Com, Inc.* the plaintiff Pennsylvania corporation, manufacturer of the well-known brand of cigarette lighters, brought an action against a California corporation that provided an internet news service, for infringement of its "Zippo" trademark. (1997), 952 F. Supp. 1119 (W.D. Pa.).

2. where the defendant maintains an interactive site
3. where the defendant's site provides purely passive advertising

For level 1, there is jurisdiction where the business is being carried on; in level 3, there is no jurisdiction; level 2 remains an uncertain "grey area."[104] Some Canadian courts have used this level-of-interactivity test.[105] In 2012, the Supreme Court of Canada stated that carrying on business requires some kind of actual, not merely virtual, presence in the jurisdiction.

CASE 31.12

Van Breda, an Ontario resident, was seriously injured while vacationing at Club Resort in Cuba. The Club Resort vacation package was booked from the website of an Ontario web-based travel agency called Sport au Soleil. Although the resort was in Cuba, it was managed by a corporation in the Cayman Islands, and the management company hired Ontario professionals and Ontario tour operators, including Sport au Soleil, to advertise, promote, and obtain bookings for the resorts. Van Breda sued Sport au Soleil, Club Resort, and the management company in Ontario. The resort claimed that Cuba should have jurisdiction over the dispute. The Supreme Court held that carrying on business in the jurisdiction was one factor that could show a real and substantial connection to the jurisdiction but it required more than virtual presence or active advertising. The Court stopped short of defining what level of etrade was necessary to be carrying on business in the jurisdiction (para 87, 114). In the end it found that Ontario had a real and substantial connection to this action because the travel contract was made through the Ontario-based travel agency.[106]

Internet defamation actions demonstrate the difficulty with determining where an online tort is "committed." Typically defamation is committed where the defamatory statement is published—that is, where it is made available to be seen, heard, read, *downloaded*, or republished. But a defamatory statement posted on the internet could be read everywhere.[107] That would seem to suggest that a plaintiff alleging libel might sue anywhere in the world, choosing a jurisdiction where the law of defamation is most favourable and where damages are likely to be highest, acting as a *libel tourist*.

CASE 31.13

Bangoura had been employed by the United Nations and had worked in a number of African countries. After he retired, he settled in Ontario and became a Canadian citizen. The *Washington Post* published a story on its website alleging that Bangoura had been removed from his position with the UN Drug Control Programme because of a scandal that had occurred in Kenya.

Bangoura commenced a libel action against the *Post* in the Ontario Superior Court. The *Post* brought a motion to have the claim set aside on the grounds that the Ontario

>

---

[104] *Ibid.*, In *Zippo*, the California corporation was doing substantial business in Pennsylvania, and that the Pennsylvania courts were entitled to exercise jurisdiction. Contrast *Cybersell Inc. (Arizona) v. Cybersell Inc. (Florida)* (1997), US App. LEXIS 33871, where the Florida-incorporated defendant was found to be engaging solely in "passive" advertising in Arizona, and the Arizona court declined jurisdiction.

[105] *Braintech Inc. v. Kostiuk* (1999), 171 D.L.R. (4th) 46. See also *Pro-C Ltd. v. Computer City Inc.* (2000), 7 C.P.R. (4th) 193, revs'd [2001] O.J. No. 3600; *Wiebe v. Bouchard*, [2005] B.C.J. No. 73; *Desjean v. Intermix Media, Inc.* (2006), 57 C.P.R. (4th) 314, aff'd [2007] F.C.J. No. 1523 (F.C.A). In *Easthaven Ltd. v. Nutrisystem.com Inc.* (2001), 202 D.L.R. (4th) 560, discussed in Chapter 30, the Ontario Superior Court declined to accept jurisdiction in a dispute between a Barbados corporation and a Delaware corporation, where the only connection with Ontario was the fact that the domain name in question had been registered through an Ontario corporation.

[106] *Van Breda v. Village Resorts Ltd.*,[2010] O.J. No. 402, aff'd 2012 SCC 17 at para 87, 114. See also *Charron Estate v. Bel Air Travel Group Ltd.*, [2010] S.C.C.A. 114. The cases revise the factors relevant to determining the most convenient forum as set out in *Muscutt v. Courcelles* (2002), 60 O.R. (3d) 20 (Ont. C.A.).

[107] For an analysis of this problem, see Gosnell, "Jurisdiction on the Net: Defining Place in Cyberspace" (1998), 29 C.B.L.J. 345. Without evidence that someone in the jurisdiction downloaded or read the statement, the tort was not committed in the jurisdiction: *Crookes v. Yahoo*, 2007 BCSC 1325, aff'd [2008] B.C.J. No. 834.

court did not have jurisdiction. Initially, the court ruled that, even though the libel was published in Washington, D.C., injury was suffered by the plaintiff in Ontario, and the Ontario court could assume jurisdiction.[108] Reversing the trial court, the Court of Appeal held that the Washington court had jurisdiction; it was unreasonable to expect the newspaper to foresee that Bangoura would be a resident of Ontario three years later.[109]

Selecting the "clearly most appropriate" forum among multiple possibilities is done based on the values of fairness and efficiency. In the next case, the Supreme Court suggests that it is fair to pick the location where the most serious injury to reputation is suffered. Normally, that will be where the plaintiff lives, for that is where her reputation is harmed. Some level of foreseeability must be applied to this test; otherwise a defendant could again be sued anywhere.

CASE 31.14

Conrad Black started a defamation lawsuit in Ontario against 10 members of a special committee who prepared a report on his activities as director and chairman of Hollinger International, a publicly traded U.S. company. Only one of the defendants resided in Ontario. The report was very critical of Black's behaviour and of payments received by him. It was posted on the company's website and electronic press releases were sent to Ontario newspapers. The defendants challenged Ontario's jurisdiction. The Supreme Court held that Ontario had jurisdiction because the tort was committed in Ontario—the report was downloaded and republished by the Ontario newspapers. Repetition or republication constitutes new publication—the defendants anticipated republication when they sent the press releases. Ontario was the most appropriate forum because the most substantial harm to reputation occurred in Ontario. Black was a longtime resident of Ontario, his family resides in Ontario, and he made his newspaper reputation in Ontario. It was foreseeable to the defendants that damage would occur in Ontario as evidenced by press releases directed to Ontario media.[110]

Some provinces, including British Columbia, have adopted legislation that lists the relevant factors and process for consideration in first establishing that the province has jurisdiction and then selecting the most appropriate location from all other provinces, states, or countries with jurisdiction.[111]

Non-Governmental Organizations

Non-governmental organizations play an important role in building international harmony where conflicting laws exist. They work to build consensus among different governments; create model laws that governments can adopt in their own countries; and establish guidelines and codes of conduct for international behaviour.

The Organisation for Economic Co-operation and Development (OECD) is one such non-governmental organization. It has developed guidelines for domestic legislation in consumer protection, multinational corporate governance, bribery, and taxation.[112] The United Nations Committee on International Trade Law (UNCITRAL) produced model laws on international commercial arbitration and enforcement of foreign arbitral awards

---

[108] *Bangoura v. Washington Post* (2004), 235 D.L.R. (4th) 564. Although enforcement of an Ontario judgment might be a problem, Pitt, J., pointed out that a defamation action is often more about character vindication than about money. See also *Burke v. NYP Holdings Inc.* (2005), 48 B.C.L.R. (4th) 363 (B.C.S.C.).

[109] *Bangoura v. Washington Post* (2005), 258 D.L.R. (4th) 341; the Supreme Court of Canada refused leave to appeal.

[110] *Breedan v. Black*, 2012 SCC 19.

[111] Court Jurisdiction and Proceedings Transfer Act, S.B.C. 2003, c.28.

[112] OECD guidelines for regulation of multinational corporations are available at www.oecd.org.

that have been adopted by many countries.[113] The 2005 United Nations Convention on the Use of Electronic Communication in International Contracts addresses contract formation and jurisdiction issues. And, as has been noted, WIPO has multiple treaties addressing intellectual property law. Governments may choose to adopt these international standards completely, partially, or not at all. Although we are still a long way from international harmony in the regulation of ecommerce, progress is being made.

Strategies to Manage the Legal Risks

Many of the legal risks associated with ecommerce can be avoided with a well designed website and detailed contractual terms and conditions. Websites should be original, claim ownership in content, prohibit copying, and resist linking sites. Alternatively, disclaimers denying responsibility for linked content or third-party postings should be clearly displayed. Contract law enforces typical terms and conditions incorporated into a contract through an online click-wrap agreement. Therefore, including choice of law and forum provisions in addition to ADR clauses will reduce the jurisdictional problems for international disputes. Terms relating to ownership of intellectual property, restricted right to use or copy, and confidentiality will reduce intellectual property disputes. Exemption clauses and liquidated damage clauses will contain the size of damage awards—a necessary step because internet damages are often larger than those suffered in the physical world.

An online intellectual property strategy must address counterfeiting of electronic products as well as unauthorized use of marketing, communication, and business systems. Trademarks should be searched in all available databases, both domestically and internationally, before investment or promotion begins. Corresponding positive and negative domain names should be secured in popular generic top-level domains. Applying for the suffix should be considered. Patent protection of business methods should be obtained and copyright claimed in online visual, literary, and graphic work. As well as protecting the business's own IP, steps should be taken to ensure that employees do not infringe others' rights. A code of conduct for technology use can be a valuable tool. Particular attention should be paid to the new Canadian anti-spam legislation, as it restricts some traditional marketing practices, particularly the use of unsolicited emails. Consequences of violation can be quite severe, including personal liability for directors and officers.

QUESTIONS FOR REVIEW

1. What contracts are normally involved in establishing a business website?
2. What is a web-wrap agreement?
3. How has legislation addressed the formation of contracts made over the internet?
4. Why is it important to ascertain which legal system governs a contract?
5. Are internet service providers exposed to liability when users infringe copyright? Or violate anti-spam legislation?
6. What is ecash?
7. How can a domain name infringe some other person's trademark?
8. What are the legal consequences of violating Canada's anti-spam legislation?

---

[113] See Chapter 30; the United Nations created UNCITRAL to harmonize international trade law around the world.

9. What is the level-of-interactivity test?

10. What factors influence jurisdiction over an internet libel case?

11. How does Canada protect an individual's privacy in ecommerce transactions?

12. Why are non-governmental organizations important to ecommerce?

13. In what ways does the internet facilitate illegal activities?

14. What proposals are being made to reform the Copyright Act?

CASES AND PROBLEMS

1. Continuing Scenario

Jack was disappointed with his dining experience at Ashley's Restaurant. Jack was in town for a conference and made a reservation at Ashley's. When he arrived, he was advised that the guest dress code prohibited jeans; Jack protested that he had not been told this at the time of booking so he was allowed to dine but was seated at an out of the way table by the kitchen door. His meal was fine but he was still angry about his table location when he got home to Chicago after the conference. He decided to warn other diners so he logged on to an Ontario restaurant review website and registered under the name "foodie257." Jack gave a very negative review. He scored the food, service, and atmosphere as 1 out of a possible 10 points. In the comment section, he said "Ashley was rude and unprofessional," mistakenly believing that Ashley herself had acted as hostess and assigned his table. He went on to say that she had no skill in the restaurant business and her business would surely fail. He encouraged others to spread the word. Finally, he clicked the icon that said "share this review with friends" and sent it to all his social network friends. One of Ashley's regular diners saw the review and mentioned it to her. She was very upset and worried that other diners would see it.

   What obstacles will Ashley face if she tries to take legal action arising from this review?

2. On Saturday at 10:00 P.M., Jane (a resident of Manitoba) ordered a computer online from SMART Computers for $49 plus tax and delivery charges. Jane entered her credit card information and her email address, and clicked "BUY NOW." At 10:04 P.M., she received an email confirmation of her purchase showing a total credit card charge of $75. Jane placed the order after she was told by a friend that the SMART website mistakenly priced the computer at $49 instead of $449. Although SMART blocked the order page when it discovered the error on Friday, Jane successfully bypassed the block and also the webpages disclosing the terms and conditions of the sale. The order page indicated that the purchase was subject to terms and conditions, but there was no hyperlink to the terms. SMART refused to supply the computer, indicating that the computer was not available for $49. Jane started a breach of contract action in Manitoba. The terms and conditions stated that supply of the computer was subject to availability and that all disputes must be settled in the courts of Michigan in the United States.

   Consider the principles of offer, acceptance, consideration, and intention, and determine if there is a valid contract. If so, do the terms and conditions form part of the sale contract? What information will be important in order to determine the status of the contract and the terms and conditions?

3. Altanet Inc. is incorporated in Alberta and carries on the business of providing internet access and related services to its clients. In March 2007, it registered the domain name altanet.ca. One of its employees, O'Connor, developed a new technique for designing webpages for clients. He tried to persuade Altanet's management to adopt the technique, and, when they decided not to, he resigned from the corporation and decided to go into business on his own. In May 2007, he established a corporation, Rocky Netservices Inc., and registered the domain name alta.net.

   When Altanet's managers discovered the existence of the Rocky website, they wrote to O'Connor, alleging that he was attempting to pass his business off as that of Altanet in order to lure its clients away, and they demanded that he cease to use the domain name.

O'Connor replied that the two domain names were different and equally legitimate, that no similarity existed between the names of the two corporations, and that Altanet had no cause to complain about his using the new webpage technique since it had declined to adopt it when given the opportunity.

How should the ownership issues of domain name and website design be resolved?

4. Midas Prospecting Inc. is a corporation incorporated in British Columbia that is engaged in mineral exploration. Goldfinger, its CEO, lives in Vancouver.

From time to time, Goldfinger likes to search the internet for references to his company. One day, using his favourite search engine, Gargle, he discovered a story written by Sleaze, a university professor from New Zealand, published on the website of a little-known Australian journal that deals with environmental issues. The story, entitled "The Poisoners of Paraguay," alleged that Midas had discharged tonnes of cyanide into a river in Paraguay and that Goldfinger had managed to suppress the news by bribing that country's Minister of the Environment. Although there is evidence that some such event might have taken place, the story was clearly incorrect since neither Midas nor any other corporation with which it is associated has ever carried on operations in Paraguay.

The journal offered to publish a full retraction, and the offer was accepted by Goldfinger. Sleaze, however, insists that his story is substantially true and refuses to apologize.

Midas and Goldfinger have commenced an action for defamation in British Columbia against Sleaze, and against Gargle (which is based in California), which they claim has published the libel by providing the link to the story.

Consider (a) whether the B.C. court has jurisdiction to try the action and (b) whether the claim against Gargle has any validity.

For more cases and problems, see the Companion Website.

Additional Resources for Chapter 31 on the Companion Website

(www.pearsoncanada.ca/smyth)

In addition to pre- and post-tests, mini-cases, and application exercises, the Companion Website includes the following province-specific resources for Chapter 31:

- **Alberta:** Electronic Transactions
- **Atlantic Provinces:** Electronic Commerce Legislation
- **British Columbia:** Electronic Transactions
- **Manitoba/Saskatchewan:** Consumer Protection Act—Internet Agreement Legislation; Electronic Transactions
- **Ontario:** Amending Electronic Contracts; Consumer Protection Act; eCommerce Legislation

Chapter 32

Privacy

In this era of technological advancement, individual privacy is more and more difficult to protect. Privacy law is evolving to meet the new challenges and now regulates everyday business activities. A maze of overlapping federal and provincial privacy legislation imposes civil, regulatory, and even criminal liability on businesses that fail to protect the privacy of individuals.

In this chapter we examine such questions as:

- What aspects of a person's life are considered private?

- Is privacy a human right?

- What level of privacy should individuals expect?

- What provincial and federal regulatory regimes exist to supervise public-sector activities?

- What legislation governs private-sector personal information management?

- What laws govern privacy in the workplace?

- What concerns exist for personal information that is transferred to another country?

- How has tort law responded to invasion of privacy?

- How does criminal law address privacy issues?

PRIVACY

What Is Privacy?

Early legal scholars described privacy as "the right to be left alone" and considered it essential to a person's "autonomy, liberty, and integrity."[1] Modern **privacy** has three key dimensions: personal privacy, territorial or spatial privacy, and privacy of personal information.[2] **Personal privacy** involves issues of bodily integrity including surveillance, search, and seizure. **Territorial privacy** covers the protection of one's home, business, and other personal spaces (even laptops).[3] **Privacy of personal information** involves protection of the trail of information left behind as we live our daily lives and has three elements: secrecy, control, and anonymity. [4] Protection for personal information covers information about an individual and depends upon the nature of the information and the purpose for which it was made and obtained.[5] It extends beyond what is typically considered "personal and confidential." Relatively ordinary information can be used to identify us or reveal our personal habits, opinions, behaviours, beliefs, or characteristics. Controlling one's personal information is "intimately connected" to one's individual autonomy, dignity, and privacy.[6] For more information on this topic, see the Companion Website.

Participation in normal society means complete privacy is impossible. Privacy law and, to some extent, individuals themselves, determine how much privacy citizens will sacrifice. For example, how much private information is revealed on a personal website is entirely the individual's choice. Some people post pictures and blog about personal relationships, while others would never dream of such disclosure. On the other hand, residents are required by law to file a tax return containing very personal information. The law of privacy involves balancing the needs of society for freedom of expression with the individual's right to privacy. The law in this area is changing quite quickly and so we attempt only a general overview in this chapter.

Privacy as a Human Right

Government must respect people's privacy. In 1984, the Supreme Court of Canada declared that the right to privacy was a fundamental human right protected by section 8 of the Charter of Rights and Freedoms.[7] However, it held that the right to privacy was not absolute; individuals were only entitled to as much privacy as could reasonably be expected in the circumstance. This standard of protection, commonly referred to as the

privacy has three key dimensions: personal privacy, territorial or spatial privacy, and privacy of personal information

personal privacy the respect of bodily integrity free from unreasonable surveillance, search, and seizure

territorial privacy lack of intrusion in one's home, business, and other personal spaces

privacy of personal information the protection of the trail of information left behind as we go about our daily lives involving secrecy, control, and anonymity

---

[1] Alysia Davies, "Invading the Mind: The Right to Privacy and the Definition of Terrorism in Canada" (2006) 3(1) U. Ottawa Law & Tech. J. 249 at 261.

[2] The three aspects of privacy were first discussed in *R. v. Dyment*, [1988] 2 S.C.R. 417 and more recently in *R. v. Tessling*, [2004] 3 S.C.R. 432 and *R. v. Gamboc*, [2010] S.C.J. No. 55 and accepted again in *R. v. Spencer* 2014 SCC 43 at para 35 (although not mutually exclusive). The Federal Court of Appeal described privacy as connoting "concepts of intimacy, identity, dignity and integrity of the individual": *Canada (Information Commissioner) v. Canada (Transportation Accident Investigation & Safety Board)*, 2006 FCA 157 (C.A.), leave to appeal refused [2006] S.C.C.A. No. 259.

[3] *R. v. Cole* 2012 SCC 53 at paras. 1 – 3.

[4] *R. v. Spencer* 2014 SCC 43 at para 38.

[5] Teresa Scassa et al., "Privacy by the Wayside: The New Information Superhighway, Data Privacy and the Development of Intelligent Transportation Systems" (2011) 11 74 Sask. L.Rev. 117 at paras. 36, 46–51.

[6] *Alberta (Information and Privacy Commissioner) v. United Food and Commercial Workers, Local 401*, 2013 SCC 62, at para. 19.

[7] *Hunter v. Southam Inc.*, [1984] 2 S.C.R. 145; section 8 of the Charter protects against unreasonable search and seizure by government. Informational privacy depends upon the nature of the information and the purpose for which it is made—it is not confined to only personal and confidential information: *R. v. Gamboc, supra,* n. 2. *Alberta v. United Food, supra* n. 6.

reasonable expectation of privacy the subjective and objective assessment of reasonable privacy expectations in a given situation

reasonable expectation of privacy, requires a subjective and objective assessment of privacy expectations in each situation.

Section 7 of the Charter, dealing with life, liberty, and security of person, has also been interpreted as establishing constitutional authority for a right to privacy: "privacy is at the heart of liberty."[8] The combined effect of sections 7 and 8 is to limit the government's ability to interfere with an individual's privacy rights. Government invasion of privacy is acceptable only when no reasonable expectation of privacy exists or when, despite a reasonable expectation, the invasion itself is reasonable and the principles of **natural justice** are respected. The federal government and most provinces have enacted privacy legislation to protect individual privacy during public-sector activities.[9]

natural justice procedural fairness or due process

Federal and provincial human rights legislation prohibits private sector discrimination and harassment based on race, gender, religion, age, marital status, sexual orientation, ethnic origin, and disability.[10] Although privacy issues are not specifically addressed in the human rights legislation, the collection or use of personal information relating to a prohibited ground may lead to discriminatory or harassing behaviour. As a result, human rights and privacy complaints often arise out of the same circumstances.

Privacy and Technology

data shadows electronic records of the internet activity of a user

biometrics technological analysis of physical characteristics, such as fingerprints

cloud computing a server-focused computing system in which all processing and storage is done at the server level and users access the system over the internet from anywhere through a variety of devices

Technological advancements such as the internet, **data shadows**, digital cameras, **biometrics**, digital storage devices, and **cloud computing** pose serious threats to privacy.[11] The technological ability to collect, store, transmit, and alter personal information has transformed privacy risks. Also expanded is the ability to track movements, surveil subjects, and reveal findings to an expansive audience. Personal information may be used for obviously criminal purposes, such as identity theft, or more subtle activities such as targeted marketing or employment decisions. As early commentary colourfully describes, "The electronic computer is to privacy what the machine gun was to the horse cavalry."[12]

In addition to making violation of privacy interests much easier, technology has made protection of privacy rights much more difficult. Data flows freely across geographic borders. The creator, host, and user of a website could all be in different jurisdictions. Canadian laws protecting electronic personal information may be impossible to enforce if the website, its server, and/or its creator are located in different countries.

CASE 32.1

Lawson discovered that her personal information was being used by Accusearch Inc., an American company in the business of selling background checks and other tracing services. This use was without her consent, and she believed it violated the federal Personal Information Protection and Electronic Documents Act (PIPEDA).[13] She filed a complaint

>

---

[8] *R. v. Dyment, supra* n. 2, 427–8.

[9] See e.g. Privacy Act, R.S.C. 1985, c. P-21; Freedom of information and Protection of Privacy Act, R.S.O. c. F-31.

[10] Canadian Human Rights Act, R.S. 1985, c. H-6; Alberta Human Rights Act, R.S.A. 2000, c. A-25.5; British Columbia Human Rights Code, R.S.B.C. 1996, c. 210; The Human Rights Code, C.C.S.M., c. H-175; Human Rights Act, R.S.N.B. 2011, c. 171; Nova Scotia Human Rights Act, R.S.N.S. 1989, c. 214; Ontario Human Rights Code, R.S.O. 1990, c. H-19; Human Rights Act, R.S.P.E.I. 1988, c. H-12; Saskatchewan Human Rights Code, S.S. 1979, c. S-24.1; Human Rights Code, 2010, S.N.L. 2010, c. H-13.1.

[11] Scassa et al., *supra*, n. 5. *R. v. Spencer* 2013 SCC 43 at para 46.

[12] Dan Savantesson and Roger Clarke, "Privacy and consumer risks in cloud computing", (2010) 26(4) Computer Law & Security Review 391; McIsaac, Shields, and Klein, *The Law of Privacy in Canada* (Toronto: Thomson Carswell, 2007) at 1–4.2.

[13] S.C. 2000, c. 5, as amended.

with the Privacy Commissioner, who declined to investigate, stating that she lacked jurisdiction to investigate an American company. In reviewing this decision, the Federal Court held that the Privacy Commissioner was wrong; she did have jurisdiction to investigate. The complainant was Canadian, the source of the information was Canadian, the request for the background check originated in Canada, and the website displayed a Canadian presence with a ".ca" domain name. The court acknowledged that the non-resident status of the operator of the website might frustrate the success of the investigation, but that it should not be confused with a lack of jurisdiction.[14]

Privacy and Business

Governments are not the only institutions dealing with privacy-related issues. Businesses constantly collect, use, store, and transfer personal information about their employees, customers, consumers, suppliers, and competitors. Technology has enhanced an employer's ability to monitor employee conduct and customer behaviour through video surveillance, email and telephone monitoring, and key-card access systems. All of this means that privacy is also a private-sector concern. The Personal Information Protection and Electronic Documents Act (PIPEDA) is the primary piece of federal legislation regulating privacy issues in the private sector. Common law and criminal laws also expose businesses to liability for invasion of privacy.

INTERNATIONAL ISSUE

Outsourcing, Cloud Computing, and Transborder Data Flow

Outsourcing specialized operational tasks has become a common practice. When outsourcing involves the transfer of personal information, issues of security and privacy are raised. Customers may consent to the collection of personal data without realizing that their information could be shared with another company located halfway around the world and subject to different disclosure and protection rules. In recognition of international privacy concerns, the Organisation for Economic Co-operation and Development (OECD) created guidelines to enhance privacy protection during transborder data exchanges. Guideline 10 suggests that personal data should not be used or disclosed without the consent of the owner or authority of law.

Canadian outsourcing to the United States has become even more controversial since the enactment of the USA PATRIOT Act.[15] This legislation allows U.S. law-enforcement officials to obtain personal records or information from any source in the country without the data owner knowing. As a result, there have been several Canadian challenges of personal data outsourcing to the United States. In *B.C.G.E.U. v. British Columbia (Minister of Health)*, union members argued that the Ministry of Health was violating patients' rights to privacy under section 7 of the Charter by outsourcing physician billing data that contained personal patient information to a private U.S. company.[16] The B.C. Supreme Court disagreed, holding that as long as the contractual arrangement authorized under the Canada Health Act ensured that a reasonable expectation of privacy was protected, the practice was acceptable. Since then B.C., Nova Scotia, and Alberta passed legislation that restricts public (not private) sector transborder outsourcing.[17]

>

---

[14] *Lawson v. Accusearch Inc.*, 2007 FC 125 (F.C.); the Court agreed that PIPEDA did not have extraterritorial effect.

[15] Uniting and Strengthening America by Providing Appropriate Tools Required to Intercept and Obstruct Terrorism (USA PATRIOT) Act of 2001.

[16] *B.C.G.E.U. v. British Columbia (Minister of Health Services)*, 2005 BCSC 446 (S.C.), aff'd [2007] B.C.J. No. 650 (B.C.C.A.). See also Office of the Privacy Commissioner of Canada, Case Summary, #2007-365; Scassa et al., *supra*, n. 5, at para. 66.

[17] See Freedom of Information and Protection of Privacy Act (FOIPPA), R.S.B.C. 1996, c. 165, s. 30.1 (making it an offence to store, access, or disclose personal information outside Canada); R.S.A 2000, c. F-25, s. 92(3)(4). Nova Scotia passed similar legislation: Personal Information International Disclosure Act, S.N.S. 2006, c. 3. See also Freedom of Information and Protection of Privacy Act.

The Privacy Commissioner rejected a similar complaint against the Canadian Imperial Bank of Commerce.[18] The bank outsourced the processing of credit card transactions to an American company. The specific confidentiality and security provisions contained in the outsourcing agreement were approved by the Office of the Superintendent of Financial Institutions, and this satisfied the Commissioner. Both decisions turned on the specific terms of the outsourcing agreement and prior regulatory approval of the terms.

When considering sending sensitive information across the border and outsourcing to American firms, businesses should

- undertake a security analysis of the American company prior to contracting;
- inform the affected customer/data owner;
- include specific confidentiality, security, and reporting provisions in the outsourcing agreement;
- seek regulatory approval of the agreement, if available; and
- regularly audit the privacy practices of the outsourcing company.

Increased privacy concerns can be anticipated as the transnational public cloud computing industry replaces user owned software, desks, and laptops as the primary custodians of personal information. "By 2017, enterprise spending on cloud computing will amount to a projected $235.1 billion, triple the $78.2 billion spent in 2011 . . . [in 2014] global business spending for infrastructure and services related to the cloud will reach an estimated $174.2 billion, up 20 percent from the amount spent in 2013."[19]

Questions to Consider

1. If Canadian data is at greater risk of disclosure when transferred to the United States, why not ban all public and private outsourcing to the United States?

2. Are there certain types of information that should remain within Canadian borders?

3. How can personal information be protected when stored on a transnational cloud server?

Sources: Donna L. Davis, "Case Comment: Tracking Cross-border Data Flows: A Comment on *Lawson v. Accusearch Inc.*" (2007) 6(2) *Canadian Journal of Law and Technology* 119; "Frequently Asked Questions: USA PATRIOT Act Comprehensive Assessment Results," Treasury Board of Canada Secretariat, March 28, 2006, www.tbs-sct.gc.ca/pubs_pol/gospubs/TBM_128/usapa/faq_e.asp.

GOVERNMENT REGULATION OF PRIVACY

Privacy is the subject of a maze of regulation. There are federal and provincial statutes. Legislation of broad application sets general standards applicable to most public and private activities. Other legislation targets specific conduct such as telemarketing. Some statutes focus on particular industries such as healthcare or credit reporting. It is not the goal of this chapter to provide an exhaustive review of all privacy legislation. Instead, we focus on the statutes of general application addressing privacy of personal information, and specific conduct involving creation and collection, intentional or accidental disclosure, modification, and theft.

Regulation of Privacy in the Public Sector

In the public sector, privacy is protected by both federal and provincial legislative regimes. The federal legislation governs the conduct of the federal government, its agencies, and public institutions. Similarly, provincial legislation regulates the provincial government, agencies, and public institutions.

As noted, the Charter of Rights and Freedoms establishes constitutional protection of privacy and it, along with the Criminal Code, protects individual privacy during law-enforcement activities of government.

The collection, use, and disclosure of personal information by federal **government institutions** is regulated by the Privacy Act.[20] The definition of personal information covers

government institutions government departments and agencies listed in Schedule 1 of the Privacy Act

---

[18] Office of the Privacy Commissioner, PIPEDA Case Summary #313, October 19, 2005, http://www.priv.gc.ca/-cf-dc/2005/313_20051019_e.asp.

[19] Patrick Seitz, "Cloud Computing Sales to Triple by 2017, New Forecast Says" from Investor's Business Daily, [February 2, 2014] © [2014] Investor's Business Daily, Inc.. All rights reserved. Used by permission and protected by the Copyright Laws of the United States. The printing, copying, redistribution, or retransmission of this Content without express written permission is prohibited. http://news.investors.com/technology-click/021414-690137-amzn-goog-msft-battling-for-growing-cloud-market.htm.

[20] R.S.C. 1985, c. P-21.

recorded information about an identified individual. The Act also includes a non-exhaustive list of examples such as information about a person's educational, financial, medical, criminal, or employment history, and the personal opinions about the individual expressed by another person (section 3).

The **purpose of collection** must relate directly to an operating program or activity of the institution (section 4), and information should be obtained directly from the individual (section 5(1)) after disclosure of the purpose (section 5(2)). An institution need not comply with section 5 if to do so might compromise the purpose of collection or the accuracy of the information (section 5(3)). **Consent** of the individual is only required in order to use the information for a purpose other than the one for which it was collected (section 7).

purpose of collection a need for collecting personal information that must be related directly to an operating program or activity of the institution

consent approval of the person to whom the collected information relates

---

CASE 32.2

Bernard, an employee, who was not a member of the union but part of the bargaining unit represented by the union, objected to the federal government employer releasing his home contact information to the union as required under the collective agreement. The Supreme Court of Canada held that the union had a duty to keep all members of the bargaining unit informed (even non-union members) and that required contacting them—this was a legitimate need. The work contact information was not sufficient to meet this need and so access to home contact information was justified. The employer collected the information for the purpose of the administration of the employment relationship and sharing it with the union was consistent with this purpose. Therefore, sharing it without employee permission was allowed under s. 7 of the Privacy Act.[21]

The Privacy Act controls the disclosure of recorded personal information under its control (that is, under its administrative management). Society expects government to be open and transparent, so institutions have broad discretion to disclose information without the consent of the individual (section 8), including

■ for the purpose it was collected,

■ for any purpose in accordance with a statute,

■ in compliance with a subpoena or court order,

■ in legal proceedings involving the government,

■ to a regulatory investigative body,

■ for research or statistical purposes,

■ when the head of the institution believes that disclosure is in the public interest and the benefit clearly outweighs the invasion of privacy (with notice to the Privacy Commissioner section 8(5)),[22] and

■ to provincial or foreign governments investigating illegal activity.

Individuals are entitled to access their information held by a government and to have inaccuracies corrected (section 12). The institution must **retain** personal information for at least two years after its last use so that the individual has time to access it (section 4).[23] However, the right of access is complicated in the public sector, given the overriding

retain keep information available for subsequent access by the individual

---

[21] *Bernard v. Canada (Attorney General)* 2014 SCC 13.

[22] Public access to government records may be requested under the Access to Information Act, R.S.C. 1985, c. A-1. This statute allows the head of an institution to refuse public access to any record of personal information (s. 19). In one Supreme Court of Canada case, the privacy of personal information was given priority over the right of access: *H. J. Heinz Co. of Canada Ltd. v. Canada (Attorney General)*, [2006] 1 S.C.R. 441.

[23] Privacy Regulations, SOR/83-508, s. 4.

responsibilities associated with law enforcement, national security, and public confidence. Therefore, there are a number of exceptions to the right of access to personal information. Access may be refused if the information is

- contained in designated exempt data banks (section 18),
- obtained in confidence from another government (domestic or international) (section 19),
- injurious to federal–provincial relations (section 20),
- injurious to international affairs (section 21),
- prepared for or injurious to law enforcement or policing (section 22),
- obtained by the Privacy Commissioner (section 22.1),
- obtained as part of the Public Servants Disclosure Protection Act (section 22.2),
- about someone other than the individual (section 26),
- a threat to safety (section 25),
- subject to solicitor–client privilege, or
- medical in nature and access would not be in the best interests of the individual (section 28).

Compliance with the requirements of the Privacy Act is monitored by the Privacy Commissioner, who has the power to investigate and initiate complaints; compel written, oral, or documentary evidence; and assess whether or not the complaint is well founded.[24] After completion of a private investigation, a report of the findings, together with any corrective recommendations, is given to the head of the government institution under review and the complainant. Reports relating to a denial of access to personal information are reviewable by the Federal Court (section 41).

Government Transparency and Accountability

The Office of the Privacy Commissioner of Canada has identified a number of deficiencies in the current Privacy Act that reduce the transparency and accountability of the federal government. The following items are some of the changes that are recommended for immediate adoption:

- require an institution to meet a necessity or "needs" test before collecting personal information;
- expand the review powers of the Federal Court to include all privacy complaints, not just those involving a denial of access;
- give the Federal Court the power to award damages against offending institutions;
- allow the Privacy Commissioner to make public the reports of the privacy practices of government institutions; and
- strengthen the provisions governing the disclosure of personal information by the Canadian government to foreign states.[25]

The importance of the last recommendation is highlighted by the findings of Justice O'Connor during the Commission of Inquiry into the Actions of Canadian Officials in

---

[24] Two policies give guidance on compliance: the Policy on Privacy Protection (2008) and the Directive on Privacy Impact Assessment (2010); see Treasury Board of Canada Secretariat website (Policies), http://www.tbs-sct.gc.ca/pol/doc-eng.aspx?id=18308&section=text.

[25] Office of the Privacy Commissioner of Canada, "Privacy Act Reform," http://www.priv.gc.ca/parl/pa_r_e.asp (last visited June 1, 2014).

Relation to Maher Arar.[26] Justice O'Connor found that it was very likely that American authorities detained and deported Arar to Syria (where he was subsequently tortured) because of inaccurate information supplied to them by the RCMP. The Privacy Act expressly authorizes government institutions to share information with foreign governments investigating illegal behaviour.[27]

Ethical Issue Government Transparency and Accountability

A large part of the mission of the U.S. National Security Agency (NSA) is to track suspected terrorists and uncover terrorist plots against the United States. Senator Ron Wyden on the Senate Intelligence Committee was concerned about NSA tactics, and he was not alone. Edward J. Snowden, an NSA contractor, collected documents describing the NSA's wide-scale surveillance, interception, and collection of electronic written and oral communications, facial images, and fingerprints of Americans and foreigners located inside and outside the United States. The release of some documents to the press and publication of the NSA's practices by the *Guardian* and subsequently the *New York Times* shocked the world both as to the extent of NSA invasion of privacy and the lengths to which governments would go to keep the practices secret. The U.K. government pressured the *Guardian* newspaper to destroy computer hard drives and reporters and family were detained and questioned under terrorism laws. The *Guardian* enlisted the *New York Times* as a "safe haven" archive for the documents and partner in publication, believing it was beyond the reach of government suppression. Edward Snowden was charged with espionage by the U.S. government; he fled the country, eventually receiving temporary asylum in Russia, after his U.S. passport was revoked.

Questions to Consider

1. Under what circumstances should a government be permitted to use covert surveillance to collect and generate personal information about its citizens?

2. Should the standards be different for surveillance of non-citizens or those located outside the country?

3. Why are transparency and accountability important in government?

4. Was Snowden's collection and selective release of documents justified?

Sources: James Risen and Laura Poitras, "N.S.A. Collecting Millions of Faces From Web Images," *The New York Times*, Sunday, June 1, 2014, 1; Ryan Lizza, "The Political Scene: State of Deception, Why won't the President rein in the intelligence community," *The New Yorker*, December 16, 2013; CBC News Video, "Guardian Alleges Pressure by British Agents," http://www.cbc.ca/player/Embedded-Only/News/ID/2401978333/; "Inside the Mind of Edward Snowden," NBC News, http://www.nbcnews.com/feature/edward-snowden-interview.

CHECKLIST

Privacy Act

Government institutions dealing with personal information should

- ■ only collect information that directly relates to the operation of a government program or activity,
- ■ collect information directly from the individual,
- ■ keep information secure and up to date,
- ■ use or disclose information only for the purpose for which it was collected (with some exceptions),
- ■ obtain consent for any other use,
- ■ allow access to information by the individual (subject to broad exceptions), and
- ■ respond to complaints of individuals and recommendations of the Privacy Commissioner.

---

[26] Commission of Inquiry into the Actions of Canadian Officials in Relation to Maher Arar (Arar Commission): Report of Events Relating to Maher Arar (Ottawa: Canadian Government Publishing, 2006).

[27] Section 8(2)(f). See also Mutual Legal Assistance in Criminal Matters Act, R.S.C. 1985 (4th Supp.), c. 30.

Provincial Variation

The provinces have enacted legislation that deals with public-sector handling of personal information and access to information held by provincial agencies. Most provinces combine these topics into one "Freedom of Information and Protection of Privacy" (FIPPA) statute.[28] Some designate a provincial information and privacy commissioner (British Columbia, Alberta, Ontario, New Brunswick), while others leave supervision in the hands of the provincial ombudsman (Manitoba). It is beyond the scope of this chapter to review the specific variations among provinces, but some important distinctions from the federal legislation are as follows:

- British Columbia and Alberta: the Privacy Commissioner can make binding orders and comment on the privacy implications of proposed legislation.

- Ontario and Saskatchewan: separate legislation covers municipal governments.

- Ontario: the provincial Crown can be held liable for damages arising from negligent disclosure of a record.

- In addition, some provincial public sectors are regulated by specialized legislation.

Municipalities   As noted above, Saskatchewan and Ontario have separate privacy legislation covering municipal governments, boards, and agencies.[29] The form and substance of the municipal statutes mirror the FIPPA protection and access standards. Supervision of compliance is also managed by the provincial privacy commissioners.

The Saskatchewan Local Authority Freedom of Information and Protection of Privacy Act applies to boards of education, universities, colleges, and hospitals. The right of access under this Act has priority over confidentiality provisions. In Ontario, universities, colleges, boards of education, and hospitals fall under the provincial, not municipal, legislation.

Healthcare   Healthcare is an area of provincial jurisdiction involving both public-sector and private-sector stakeholders. For example, most hospitals are government institutions (already covered by FIPPA), while pharmacies and medical labs would be considered private-sector commercial activities (subject to private-sector legislation, as will be discussed later). Some (but not all) hospice, counselling, and support services are private-sector, not-for-profit organizations. All have access to very sensitive **personal health information** about individuals. Therefore, specific provincial legislation focusing on healthcare providers and custodians of health information exists to address the highly sensitive nature of this information. New Brunswick, Alberta, Manitoba, Saskatchewan, and Ontario have adopted legislation specifically addressing the protection of health information across all sectors of the healthcare industry (**PHIPA**).[30] Non-compliance with personal health legislation can result in fines ranging from

personal health information   information relating to the physical or mental health of an identifiable individual that is used or obtained primarily for the purpose of providing healthcare

PHIPA   Personal Health Information Protection Act (in Alberta and Saskatchewan, simply HIPA)

---

[28] British Columbia Freedom of Information and Protection of Privacy Act, *supra*, n. 17; Alberta Freedom of Information and Protection of Privacy Act, R.S.A. 2000, c. F-25; Saskatchewan Freedom of Information and Protection of Privacy Act, S.S. 1990–1, c. F-22.01; Manitoba Freedom of Information and Protection of Privacy Act, C.C.S.M., c. F175; Ontario Freedom of Information and Protection of Privacy Act, R.S.O. 1990, c. F.31; Nova Scotia Freedom of Information and Protection of Privacy Act, S.N.S. 1993, c. 5; Newfoundland Access to Information and Protection of Privacy Act, S.N.L. 2002, c. A-1.1; Prince Edward Island Freedom of Information and Protection of Privacy Act, R.S.P.E.I. 1988, c. F-15.01. Right to Information and Protection of Privacy Act, S.N.B. 2009, c. R-10.6.

[29] Saskatchewan Local Authority Freedom of Information and Protection of Privacy Act, S.S. 1990-91, c. L-27.1; Municipal Freedom of Information and Protection of Privacy Act, R.S.O. 1990, c. M-56.

[30] Personal Health Information Act, C.C.S.M., c. P-33.5; Health Information Act, R.S.A. 2000, c. H-5; Health Information Protection Act, S.S. 1999, c. H-0.021; Personal Health Information Protection Act, S.O. 2004, c. 3, Sch. A; Personal Health Information Privacy and Access Act, S.N.B. 2009, c. P-7.05. In other provinces, the privacy of health information is addressed through the standard federal and provincial public- or private-sector privacy statutes.

$50 000 in Manitoba to $500 000 for corporations in Saskatchewan. Organizations continue to be subject to general privacy legislation for non-health personal information such as financial or employment records. Classifying the type of information can be difficult.

Many individuals participating in the healthcare sector are licensed professionals bound by provincial legislation and also professional codes of ethics requiring confidentiality. Doctors, nurses, and pharmacists are just a few examples. Breach of confidentiality by these professionals triggers investigation and discipline by the professional licensing body.

CASE 32.3

The Ontario Divisional Court was asked to review the release of a nurse's occupational health records by the employer hospital. The records were released to the College of Nurses without her consent and used in an investigation of the nurse. The hospital identified the primary purpose of the record as employment. The court characterized the records as personal health information entitled to the protection of PHIPA. However, a PHIPA exception exists for release of information to a regulatory body.[31]

Naturally, both the legislation and professional standards make exceptions for non-consensual collection, use, and disclosure of personal health information when it is necessary for the effective delivery of health services or public safety. Individuals must be notified of disclosure.

Education   Education also falls under provincial jurisdiction and involves public- and private-sector participants. Privacy issues in this sector are regulated by multiple statutes:

- Public schools (elementary and secondary), boards, universities, and colleges are covered by the provincial Freedom of Information and Protection of Privacy Act(s) (FIPPA).

- Private schools (as private-sector commercial activities) are covered by PIPEDA.

- In Manitoba, school boards, universities, and colleges are subject to the Personal Health Information Act.[32]

- Both public and private schools (and boards) are subject to provincial education act(s) that regulate the use and disclosure of students' records.[33]

Ethical Issue   Privacy versus Security: The Virginia Tech Shooting

Seung Hui Cho, a student at Virginia Polytechnic Institute (Virginia Tech), walked into the West-Amber Johnston Hall co-ed residence at 7:15 A.M. on April 16, 2007, and started shooting. Police were called to the scene and proceeded with their investigation on the assumption that it was a domestic incident. Two hours later, after returning to his apartment to rearm, Cho entered the Norris Hall Engineering building, chained the doors shut, and continued his shooting spree. When it was all over, 33 people, including Cho, were dead and 23 others were injured.

Obviously, the primary responsibility for the shootings lies with Cho, but victims' families questioned the conduct of the school administrators. A subsequent investigation revealed that Cho was a deeply disturbed young man who struggled with mental illness his whole life. Problems

>

---

[31] *Hooper v. College of Nurses of Ontario*, 2006 CanLII 22656 (ON S.C.D.C.).

[32] Manitoba, *supra*, n. 30, s. 1.1.

[33] See e.g. the Ontario Education Act, R.S.O. 1990, c. E-2, s. 266.

surfaced in elementary and high school; school administrators became involved and Cho received treatment that
seemed to help. However, his medical history was not
passed on to Virginia Tech when Cho enrolled in postsec-
ondary education. Cho purchased his guns legally from a
registered firearms dealer who was also unaware of Cho's
mental condition. At Virginia Tech, some students and faculty expressed concern about Cho's violent writings, but no
action was taken.

Questions to Consider

1. Who is served by keeping medical information private?

2. Does keeping medical information secret further stigma-
tize the illness, or does it prevent discrimination?

Source: Marc Fisher, Richard Brusca, and Colin Ram, "A
Failure to Communicate: Did Privacy Laws Contribute to the
Virginia Tech Tragedy?"(2010) 17 Wash. & Lee J. C.R. & Soc.
Just. 141.

Regulation of Privacy in the Private Sector

Private-sector privacy is a matter of both federal and provincial legislative jurisdiction.
Federal jurisdiction stems from the general power over trade and commerce and the
interprovincial and international nature of data flow, as well as major privacy concerns
in key federally controlled industries such as banking and telecommunications.[34]
Provincial authority to regulate privacy stems from the property and civil rights power.
Therefore, separate from federal legislation, some provinces have enacted their own
comprehensive private-sector privacy legislation.

use (of personal information) any
access, change, or destruction of data
within the organization

disclosure (of personal information)
transfer of data to third parties outside
the organization

commercial activity any general
or particular activity performed or
stated in the objectives of an organization, that has a commercial aspect

PIPEDA As noted above, the Personal Information Protection and Electronic
Documents Act (PIPEDA) is the comprehensive private-sector federal legislation controlling the collection, **use**, and **disclosure** of personal information during a **commercial
activity** (section 4(1)(a)).[35] It applies to all persons, corporations, individuals, organizations, associations, partnerships, and trade unions operating in Canada that are not
already covered by the Privacy Act. However, if a province has adopted substantially
similar legislation, businesses covered by the provincial legislation will be exempt from
compliance with the federal statute. As discussed below, three provinces have taken
this step.

Enforcement The federal Privacy Commissioner monitors compliance with PIPEDA.
The Privacy Commission receives and investigates complaints, following which a report
must be issued. The commissioner lacks the power to make orders and functions in the
role of an ombudsman,[36] however any report may be reviewed by the Federal Court and
appropriate orders made. In addition, the commissioner may undertake research, educational initiatives, and audits of an organization to determine its level of PIPEDA compliance. The Act creates offences for destruction of requested information (section 8(8)),
whistle-blower retaliation (section 27.1), and obstruction of an investigation or audit
(section 28).

[34] The federal power over trade and commerce was defined by five questions: *General Motors of Canada Ltd. v. City
National Leasing* (1989), 58 D.L.R. (4th) 255 (S.C.C.). Section 7 of the Telecommunications Act empowers the
CRTC to take steps to protect the privacy of persons. The Bank Act does not have special privacy provisions, so
banks are governed by PIPEDA.

[35] The legislation was initiated to satisfy data protection requirements of European Union (EU Data Protection
Directive). The 1996 Model Code for the Protection of Personal Information developed by the Standards Council
of Canada served as the model for PIPEDA. Alberta's legislation was found to be overly broad and therefore in
violation of the Charter: *Alberta v. United Food, supra* n. 6 (freedom of expression was given priority over privacy).

[36] *Lavigne v. Canada (Office of the Commissioner of Official Languages)* 2002 SCC 53 at paras. 37-8: Stronger
enforcement power is one of the recommendations for reform: Office of the Privacy Commissioner of Canada,
"The Case for Reforming the Personal Information Protection and Electronic Documents Act" May 2013, http://
www.priv.gc.ca/parl2013/pipeda_r_201305_e.asp#toc4a.

A dismissed employee requested access to her employment file and complained to the Privacy Commissioner when the employer refused to make full disclosure. The Privacy Commissioner ordered production of all documents, even those for which solicitor–client privilege was claimed. Section 12 of PIPEDA gives the Commissioner power to order production in the same manner as a court. The Federal Court of Appeal overturned the production order and the Supreme Court of Canada agreed. It held that solicitor–client privilege was a fundamental part of the Canadian justice system, and PIPEDA (s. 12) does not confer a right of access to solicitor–client documents.[37]

Requirements PIPEDA covers **personal information** about an identifiable **individual** whether recorded or not, excluding the name, title, business address, or telephone number of an employee. Personal information includes information supplied to the organization, such as birth dates and marital status, and information created by the organization, such as employee identification numbers and performance evaluations. The legislation regulates the reasonable handling of personal information according to the following 10 guiding principles of the Canadian Standards Association Model Code:[38]

personal information recorded and unrecorded information about an identifiable individual, including that supplied by the individual and created by the organization

individual natural person, not a corporation

Principle 1: Accountability (Clause 4.1)

- *Policies and procedures*—organizations shall create, implement, and publicize internal policies and procedures that will assist in complying with PIPEDA.

- *Complaints process*—the policies must include a simple and accessible process for responding to and investigating complaints.

- *Compliance monitor*—every organization shall identify a person to be responsible for compliance with the Act.

- *Data transfers*—the organization is responsible for data transferred to third parties and must ensure its protection using contractual or other methods.

A bank customer complained to the Privacy Commissioner when a market research firm contacted her to participate in a survey. The surveyor revealed that her information was obtained from the bank's database. The bank hired the market research firm to survey on its behalf, and the firm subcontracted the telephone calling to a third party. The bank had a confidentiality agreement with the market research firm, but no agreement existed with the third party. The Privacy Commissioner found that the bank's confidentiality agreement "was deficient in that it made no provision for sub-contracting." The bank was in violation of the accountability principle.[39]

Principle 2: Identifying Purpose (Clause 4.2)

- *Collection*—an organization may only collect information that is necessary for an expressly identified purpose.

- *Communication*—the purpose of collection should be communicated to the data owner at time of collection but must be communicated before use.

- *Reasonableness*—the purpose must be one that a reasonable person would consider appropriate in the circumstances (section 5(3)).

---

[37] *Canada (Privacy Commissioner) v. Blood Tribe Department of Health*, 2008 S.C.C. 44.

[38] Model Code for the Protection of Personal Information, CAN/CSA Q830-96. It is incorporated into PIPEDA as a schedule: S.C. 2000, c. 5, Schedule 1. Sections 5 (1) and (2) require mandatory compliance with all obligations in the Schedule using the word "shall." When the word "should" is used, the Act considers the statement a recommendation.

[39] Office of the Privacy Commissioner of Canada, PIPEDA Case Summary #35, November 6, 2003, http://www.priv.gc.ca/cf-dc/2002/cf-dc_020110_02_e.asp.

Canadian Pacific Railway installed six video surveillance cameras in the mechanical facility of its Scarborough maintenance yard, focusing on entrances and exits. The railway posted signs warning of the security system and identifying the purpose of the cameras as protection against "theft, vandalism, unauthorized personnel, and incidents related." An employee alleged that the cameras were being used to track punctuality of employees and were a violation of PIPEDA. The Privacy Commissioner agreed that the use of the cameras was unreasonable (in contravention of section 5(3)). The Federal Court disagreed with the Commissioner and found the use of cameras reasonable for the identified purpose.[40]

In Case 32.6, the Court applied a four-part test to determine reasonableness:

(a) Is the measure demonstrably necessary to meet a specific need?

(b) Is it likely to be effective in meeting that need?

(c) Is the loss of privacy proportional to the benefit gained?

(d) Is there a less privacy-invasive way of achieving the same end?

Principle 3: Consent (Clause 4.3)

■ *Collection, use, and disclosure* require the knowledge and consent of the data owner.

■ *Meaningful consent* requires that the organization explain the purpose of the collection, use, or disclosure in understandable language prior to obtaining consent and once given, consent may be withdrawn.

■ *Exceptions*—section 7 describes situations when collection, use, or disclosure of data without knowledge or consent is acceptable.

■ *Reasonableness* (section 5(3)) may cure a lack of consent, but consent will not cure unreasonableness.

A credit bureau collected Social Insurance Numbers not from the data owners but from the data owners' banks. The data was to be used for identification purposes. The Privacy Commissioner held that this indirect collection was acceptable if the credit bureau received contractual confirmation from the banks that they had received all necessary consents from the data owners. Reliance upon the banks' consents was reasonable in the circumstances because a large volume of data was being processed on a daily basis.[41]

opt-out consent data-owner consent is implied from a failure to refuse consent

Consent is a very controversial issue because it can take so many forms and the requirements vary, given the circumstances and sensitivity of the information. Consent may be oral or written, express or implied. In particular, the popular practice of **opt-out consent**, considered a form of implied consent, has been the subject of much scrutiny.

Air Canada wanted to share Aeroplan member data with third parties for various marketing and surveying purposes, so it sent 60 000 of its 6 000 000 members a brochure describing five scenarios involving data sharing. Members

>

---

[40] *Eastmond v. Canadian Pacific Railway*, 2004 FC 852 at para. 127.

[41] Office of the Privacy Commissioner of Canada, PIPEDA Case Summary #194, July 16, 2003, http://www.priv.gc.ca/cf-dc/2003/cf-dc_030716_e.asp.

could check a box to "opt out" of the activity. When investigating complaints arising from this form of opt-out consent, the Privacy Commissioner found the following:

- It was unreasonable to imply consent after contacting only 1 percent of the membership.
- Express (not implied opt-out) consent was necessary for targeted marketing associated with the specific member's purchasing behaviour. This personal information was too sensitive for opt-out consent.
- A lack of confidentiality agreements with the third parties violated the accountability principle.

In consultation with the Privacy Commissioner's office, Air Canada redrew its information-sharing policy to exclude individualized member profiles, include confidentiality agreements, and identify an easy process for members to block the sharing of their data.[42]

Subsequent Privacy Commissioner reports recognized four criteria to determine if opt-out consent is acceptable in a particular circumstance:

- Personal information must be non-sensitive in nature and context.
- Information sharing must clearly define the precise limits of use or disclosure.
- The identified purpose must be clear, well defined, and brought to the attention of the data owner.
- An easy, inexpensive, and convenient process for withdrawing consent must be available and communicated to the data owner.[43]

CHECKLIST

Summary of Section 7 Exceptions to the Need for Consent

Section 7(1): Collection of information without consent must be

(a) in the interests of the owner and in a circumstance when consent cannot be obtained in a timely manner;

(b) for the purpose of investigating a breach of law where it is reasonable to believe consent would compromise accuracy or availability;

(c) for journalistic, literary, or artistic purposes;

(d) of publicly available information and specified in regulations; or

(e) in compliance with a legal obligation to disclose.

Section 7(2): Use of information without consent must be

(a) for the purpose of investigating a breach of law (committed or about to be committed);

(b) in an emergency that threatens the life, health, or security of an individual;

(c) for statistical or scholarly research or study;

(c.1) of information publicly available and specified in regulations; or

(d) of information collected under section 7(1)(a)(b) or (c).

Section 7(3): Disclosure without consent must be

(a) to a lawyer for the organization;

(b) for the purpose of collecting a debt owed by the individual to the organization;

---

[42] Office of the Privacy Commissioner of Canada, PIPEDA Case Summary #192, July 23, 2003, http://www.priv.gc.ca/cf-dc/2003/cf-dc_030723_01_e.asp.

[43] Office of the Privacy Commissioner of Canada, PIPEDA Case Summary #42, January 1, 2005, http://www.priv.gc.ca/cf-dc/2002/cf-dc_020320_e.asp.

Principle 4: Limiting Collection (Clause 4.4)

■ *Identified purpose*—only information necessary to fulfill the purpose may be collected.

■ Collection must use *fair and lawful means* without deception.

Principle 5: Limiting Use, Disclosure and Retention (Clause 4.5)

■ *Use and disclosure*—information shall be used or disclosed only for the identified purpose and with the consent of the data owner.

■ *Retention*—information may be kept for only as long as is necessary for the identified purpose.

■ *Destruction*—the organization shall have policies and guidelines governing the safe and secure destruction of the information.

CASE 32.9

A movie theatre chain offered accessibility equipment to assist disabled persons when viewing movies. The names, addresses, and phone numbers of people using the equipment were recorded on a sheet of paper held at the counter, and this information was sometimes verified against personal identification. The identified purpose of the collection was to allow follow-up with the patron if the equipment was returned damaged or not at all. The company believed this collection discouraged vandalism, damage, and theft.

An investigation by the Privacy Commissioner found that the collection was reasonable for the identified purpose; however, practices varied among specific theatres, and there were no policies with respect to safeguarding, retaining, or destroying the information. The breach of the retention and destruction requirements was remedied by implementing a policy of releasing the original record of the information to the patron when the equipment was returned in good repair.[44]

Principle 6: Accuracy (Clause 4.6)

■ Information must be *complete, accurate, and current.*

The challenge of this principle is that organizations are not to collect more information than required for their purpose—they cannot unnecessarily update personal information. This appears to conflict with the need for accuracy and currency. One solution is to clearly display the date up to which the information is accurate.

Principle 7: Safeguards (Clause 4.7)

■ *Security shall be appropriate* for the type of information and shall include physical, organizational, and technological measures.

[43A] Personal Information Protection and Electronic Documents Act, S.C. 2000, c. 5.

[44] Office of the Privacy Commissioner of Canada, PIPEDA Case Summary #304, June 20, 2005, http://www.priv.gc.ca/cf-dc/2005/304_20050607_e.asp.

- *Measures must protect* against theft, loss, unauthorized access, copying, or alteration.
- *Employee confidentiality* is one necessary component.

CASE 32.10

CIBC's privacy safeguards were found to be inadequate when it was discovered that loan applications containing personal information about applicants were being mistakenly faxed to unintended recipients in the United States and Quebec. Even more troubling was the fact that the misdirected faxes continued over several years (2001–04), even after the bank was repeatedly notified by the recipients. Eventually, one of the unintended recipients contacted the media. The interim efforts of the bank were deemed insufficient by the Privacy Commissioner because they did not involve retrieval of the customer data, confirmation of destruction, or notification of affected customers. In the wake of negative publicity and criticism from the Privacy Commissioner, CIBC banned all branch faxing across Canada pending the implementation of a new fax policy.[45]

Case 32.10 highlights an important gap in PIPEDA: It does not require an organization to notify an affected individual when a breach of privacy or security occurs. Despite calls for amendments to include breach notification, no change has been made at the time of publication.[46] In the CIBC case, the commissioner recommended implementation of an immediate notification mechanism as part of an effective safeguard policy. Proposed reform would require three notifications: the Privacy Commissioner, the affected individual, and other organizations that could reduce the risk of harm. In the case of hacked credit card information, this would mean notification of the holder of the card and the issuing credit card company.

Principle 8: Openness (Clause 4.8)

- *Availability*—information about policies and practices shall be available to the public.
- *Disclosure*—information about who has access to personal information shall be available to the public.

This principle is limited by the safeguard principle. Obviously, organizations are not required to publicize any part of their policies and practices that would compromise the effectiveness of the security.[47]

Principle 9: Access (Clause 4.9)

- *Accuracy*—a data subject shall have access to the recorded personal information and shall be able to dispute the accuracy of the record.
- *Correction*—the data subject is entitled to have the record corrected once the inaccuracy or incompleteness is established.

Despite this principle, individuals are not entitled to access information that is subject to solicitor–client privilege, doctor–patient confidentiality, or other legal proprietary interests. The safeguard principle requires that the organization confirm that the individual

---

[45] Office of the Privacy Commissioner of Canada, Incident Summary #2: CIBC's Privacy Practices Failed in Case of Misdirected Faxes, April 18, 2005, http://www.priv.gc.ca/cf-dc/incidents/2005/050418_01_e.asp.

[46] Breach notification was recommended during the five-year review of PIPEDA completed in 2007, and proposed in Bill C-29 (An Act to amend the Personal Information Protection and Electronic Documents Act), 3rd Sess., 40th Parl. (2010). The bill died when the Parliament was dissolved for the May 2011 election. "The Case for Reforming the Personal Information Protection and Electronic Documents Act," *supra* n. 36; Bill S-4 (Digital Privacy Act) 2nd Sess, 41st Parl. (2014) is currently before Parliament.

[47] Office of the Privacy Commissioner of Canada, PIPEDA Case Summary #183, July 10, 2003, http://www.priv.gc.ca/cf-dc/2003/cf-dc_030710_03_e.asp.

requesting the information is entitled to access it. Organizations are not entitled to charge the individual for access unless prior notice is given, and even then, the cost should be minimal.

Principle 10: Challenging Compliance (Clause 4.10)

- *Complaints process*—each organization must have an internal process to handle complaints.

In order to satisfy the Privacy Commissioner during any subsequent investigation or audit, a record of the internal investigation process and outcome should be maintained. Modifications made to privacy policies should be documented in order to establish responsiveness to concerns of the public.

Provincial Variation   Three provinces—British Columbia, Alberta, and Quebec—have passed provincial legislation acknowledged to be "substantially similar" to the federal statute.[48] Therefore, private-sector protection of personal information in these provinces is governed by the provincial statutes (not PIPEDA), with two key exceptions. First, federal agencies, works, and undertakings within the province still need to comply with PIPEDA. Second, extraprovincial transfer of the personal information continues to be governed by the federal legislation.

The provincial statutes broaden privacy protection to include not-for-profit activities and expand the authority of the provincial privacy commissioners to include order-making powers. They also extend protection to employees working in businesses within provincial constitutional jurisdiction, as discussed below. Finally, Alberta's legislation remedies the major gap in PIPEDA by requiring notification of any breach that poses a real risk of significant harm.[49] However, extending privacy protection too broadly has its risks—in 2013, the Supreme Court of Canada declared the Alberta Protection of Personal Information Act unconstitutional because it violated the Charter's protection of freedom of expression.

CASE 32.11

Complaints were filed with the Alberta Privacy Commissioner by people who were videoed and photographed crossing the picket line during a 305-day legal strike. Notices of surveillance were posted at the picket line. At first, it was held that the collection, use, and disclosure of the images violated Alberta's Personal Information Protection Act and should stop, but as the matter rose through the courts, ultimately to the Supreme Court of Canada, the provisions of the PIPA were found to be too broad and unreasonably suppressed the union's right to freedom of expression. PIPA was declared unconstitutional and the Alberta legislature was given 12 months to amend it. As at 2014, amendments are in progress.[50]

Specific Stakeholders

Employers and Employees   Privacy in the workplace involves balancing employees' reasonable expectations of privacy with the relevant business and property interests of the employer. Legislative protection varies depending upon the nature of the employment relationship. Personal information of public-sector employees is protected by the Privacy Act or its provincial equivalent. Private-sector employee information is protected

---

[48] Personal Information Protection Act, S.B.C. 2003, c. 63; Personal Information Protection Act, S.A. 2003, c. P-6.5; Act Respecting the Protection of Personal Information in the Private Sector, R.S.Q., c. P-39.1.

[49] Ibid. Alta., s. 34.1(1).

[50] Alberta (Information and Privacy Commissioner) v. United Food and Commercial Workers Union, Local 401, 2013 SCC 2013; Letter of Jill Clayton, Information and Privacy Commissioner of Alberta, December 20, 2013, available at www.oipc.ab.ca.

by PIPEDA if the employment is in a business within federal jurisdiction or crosses provincial boundaries. For employees of businesses within provincial jurisdiction, only British Columbia, Alberta, and Quebec (as described above) have legislation protecting their data. In other provinces, protection must be found in the employment contract, the collective agreement, or the common law.[51]

Countless privacy issues arise in the workplace. One of the most controversial is surveillance of employees by employers. Surveillance can take many forms: electronic, video, or observational tracking, and it can be **covert surveillance**, **disclosed surveillance**, or **consensual surveillance**. As Case 32.6 and Case 32.11 demonstrate, video surveillance of employees in the workplace is a controversial practice and will only be considered reasonable if it meets the Federal Court's four criteria described in relation to Case 32.6. Other forms of surveillance may still be too invasive, especially when surveillance is covert.

covert surveillance the employee is unaware of surveillance and has not consented to it

disclosed surveillance the employee is given advance notice of surveillance but does not consent to it

consensual surveillance the employee is aware of and consents to the surveillance

CASE 32.12

An employee filed a complaint after being terminated for cause associated with the employee's conduct during washroom visits. The complainant alleged that monitoring his washroom visits was a breach of privacy under PIPEDA.

After receiving a Health and Safety complaint about the "messy" condition of the men's washroom, the employer began secretly monitoring washroom visits. A log was kept by branch staff recording who used the washroom, when, and the condition in which it was left. Within three days, it was determined that the washroom only needed attention after visits by the complainant and the monitoring ceased.

The complainant was interviewed, issued a disciplinary letter, and warned that continued conduct would result in dismissal.

The Privacy Commissioner agreed that the covert surveillance was unreasonable in the circumstances (in violation of section 5(3)). Washrooms are places where a high expectation of privacy exists. The employer could not rely on the section 7 exceptions to the need for consent for an unreasonable invasion. The employer did not exhaust all less-invasive measures first.[52]

Case 32.12 suggests that employer surveillance practices should reflect that surveillance

- is a last resort,
- should be undertaken only after all other methods of collecting information have been unsuccessful, and
- should be limited to the least intrusive form possible.

Monitoring of employee email and internet use involves not only privacy but also property issues. The hardware, software, and network used in the workplace are company property, and communications using an employer's network could be considered by the recipient as communications from the employer. It is unlikely that any reasonable expectation of privacy exists when using a company asset.[53] The expectation of privacy is

---

[51] *International Association of Bridge, Structural, Ornamental and Reinforcing Iron Workers and Its Local 736 v. E.S. Fox Ltd.*, 2006 CanLII 468 (ON L.R.B.) at para. 14, aff'd 2006 CanLII 6007; *Re: McKesson Canada v. Teamsters Chemical Energy and Allied Workers Union, Local 424*, 136 L.A.C. (4th) 102; *Rodgers v. Calvert* (2004), 49 B.L.R. (3d) 53.

[52] Office of the Privacy Commissioner of Canada, PIPEDA Case Summary #379, May 21, 2008, http://www.priv.gc.ca/cf-dc/2007/379_20070404_e.asp.

[53] *Milson v. Corporate Computers Inc.*, [2003] W.W.R. 250 at paras. 40–1; *Camosun College v. CUPE*, [1999] B.C.C.A.A.A. No. 490 (an arbitrator upheld a dismissal based on the contents of an email sent using the employer's system). See also *Johnson v. Bell Canada*, 2008 FC 1086, suppl. reasons [2009] F.C.J. No. 1066, where personal emails about an employee saved in Bell's computer system were not subject to disclosure under PIPEDA because they were not business related. *R. v. Cole* 2012 SCC 53 the expectation of privacy is reduced by workplace policies and notices but not eliminated with respect to further disclosure to police.

reduced if the employer gives notice of the monitoring to the employee.[54] Common forms of notice include codes of conduct, privacy policies, and collective agreements.

CASE 32.13

Imperial Oil's dismissal of an employee for personal use of company email was upheld. The contents of the employee's emails could be considered sexist and racist and, therefore, violated the harassment policy of the employer. The employee was aware of Imperial Oil's technology-use policy, prohibiting personal use of the company's email system.[55]

Consumers   Most of the focus of private-sector legislation is on protection of personal information, but this is not the only area of concern for consumers and potential consumers. Spam and telemarketing have become a major intrusion on territorial privacy. Consumers are bombarded in their homes with unwanted emails and solicitation calls disguised as market surveys and free giveaways. Legislation has been adopted to curb these invasions. First, the federal Telecommunications Act was amended in 2005 to empower the Canadian Radio-television and Telecommunications Commission (CRTC) to establish a National Do Not Call List (DNCL).[56] Any telemarketers contacting consumers whose names are on the DNCL may be subject to fines of up to $15 000 per offending call. It is the obligation of the telemarketer to regularly check the list. Registered charities, political parties, and businesses with a pre-existing relationship with the consumer are exempt from the DNCL rules.

Other telemarketing controls implemented under the CRTC's authority to regulate telemarketers and its general responsibility for protecting privacy require that

- calls and faxes be confined to designated time periods such as 9:00 A.M. to 9:30 P.M. on weekdays,

- a consumer's request to not be called, when made during a telemarketing call, must be processed without further contact, and

- upon request, a telemarketer must provide a toll-free number that the consumer can call to speak to an employee of the telemarketer or client.[57]

Second, Canadian Anti-Spam legislation (CASL)[58] came into effect in 2014 and it prohibits sending unsolicited commercial electronic messages. The definition of "electronic" is so broad that it also covers telemarketing. As discussed in Chapter 31, CASL also makes installing a computer program without prior permission an offence. CASL is designed to combat spyware and phishing, tactics often used to steal personal information about the computer user. Legitimate businesses must adjust their marketing practices to fit within the CASL exceptions discussed below. Information collected in the course of a PIPEDA or CASL investigation may be shared between authorities.

---

[54] *Briar et al. v. Treasury Board* (2003), P.S.S.R.B. 3, summary, http://pslrb-crtfp.gc.ca/decisions/summaries/31092_e .asp (the system gave notice of monitoring at log-in). Covert monitoring requires reasonable cause. See Alberta Office of the Information and Privacy Commissioner, Parkland Regional Library, Review Number 3016, June 24, 2005, www.oipc.ab.ca/ims/client/upload/F2005-003.pdf.

[55] *Bhamre Employment Insurance Claim Appeal*, (September 23, 1998) CUB42012A. See also *Poliquin v. Devon Canada Corporation*, 2009 ABCA 216.

[56] S.C. 1993, c. 38, s. 41.1. Some provinces also regulate the conduct of telemarketers. See, for example, British Columbia Business Practices and Consumer Protection Act, Telemarketer Regulation 83/05.

[57] Canadian Radio-television and Telecommunications Commission, "Fact Sheet: New and Revised Unsolicited Telecommunications Rules," www.crtc.gc.ca/eng/INFO_SHT/t1030.htm.

[58] An Act to promote the efficiency and adaptability of the Canadian economy by regulating certain activities that discourage reliance on electronic means of carrying out commercial activities and to amend the Canadian Radio-television and Telecommunications Commission Act, the Competition Act, the Personal Information Protection and Electronic Documents Act, and the Telecommunications Act, S.C. 2010, c. 23.

Specific Businesses and Business Practices   Some private-sector businesses and business practices are subject to specific privacy regulation.

- Private investigators and security guards have specific privacy and confidentiality obligations.[59]

- Credit reporting agencies' disclosure of information is controlled by provincial consumer-protection legislation.[60]

- Airline and airline reservation system operators may be ordered to share passenger information with various government agencies in the interest of national security under the provisions of the Aeronautics Act.[61]

- Bulk emailing, a common promotional business practice, is now restricted by CASL. Businesses may only send unsolicited electronic commercial messages to an individual who has consented, has transacted with the business within the last two years, or has sent an inquiry to the business in the last six months. Directors and officers are personally liable for violations in addition to their corporations.

In sum, privacy issues are heavily regulated in both the private and public sectors. Businesses should familiarize themselves with the legislation that affects their industry before they develop a privacy policy.

CHECKLIST

Summary of Key Privacy Legislation

Legislation	Public Sector	Private Sector
Federal	● Charter of Rights and Freedoms	● Personal Information Protection and Electronic Documents Act (PIPEDA)
	● Criminal Code	● Telecommunications Act
	● Privacy Act	● Canadian Anti-Spam Legislation
Provincial	● Freedom of Information and Protection of Privacy (Acts)	● Personal Information Protection and Protection of Privacy (Acts) (B.C., Alta., Que.)
	● Municipal Freedom of Information and Protection of Privacy (Sask., Ont.)	● Education (Acts) (Alta., Man., Sask., and Ont.)
	● Education (Acts)	
	● Health Information Protection (N.B., Alta., Man., Sask., and Ont.)	

CIVIL LIABILITY

Failure to meet privacy obligations can give rise to civil liability in both contract and tort. As already noted, security obligations and confidentiality terms are standard in outsourcing contracts. In addition, employment contracts now commonly include

---

[59] See e.g. the Ontario Private Security and Investigative Services Act 2005, S.O. 2005, c. 34, O. Reg. 363/07.

[60] See e.g. the British Columbia Business Practices and Consumer Protection Act, S.B.C. 2004, c. 2, Part 6.

[61] R.S.C. 1985, c. A-2, s. 4.81.

confidentiality agreements. Consumer-protection laws imply privacy obligations into consumer agreements. Damages arising from any failure to comply with these terms may be recovered in a breach-of-contract action. As the following sections describe, tort liability is less clear.

Tort: Invasion of Privacy

Common Law Historically, the right to privacy was protected through property-based torts such as trespass, nuisance, and defamation. For example, the Alberta Supreme Court found that harassing collection calls so invaded the privacy of the debtor that an action in private nuisance was successful.[62] At present, the provinces disagree about whether an independent common law tort of invasion of privacy exists, separate from any property interest or statutory duties. Ontario became the first province to recognize a privacy tort when the Ontario Court of Appeal created the tort of intrusion on seclusion in 2011.[63] For more information on this topic, see the Companion Website.

CASE 32.14

A bank employee used her work computer to look up the personal banking records of her common-law spouse's former wife. The former wife sued for invasion of privacy and the bank employee defended, saying that there was no such tort. The Court of Appeal decided it was time to recognize the tort of intrusion on seclusion separate from any legislation. The tort occurs when the reckless or intentional conduct of the defendant invades the private affairs or concerns of the plaintiff without legal justification and a reasonable person would find the invasion "highly offensive causing distress, humiliation or anguish."[64] Importantly, proof of economic harm is not required.

Courts in British Columbia and Alberta have taken the opposite position; in 2009, the British Columbia Court of Appeal denied a claim for damages arising from common law tort of invasion of privacy,[65] saying "there is no common law claim for breach of privacy" the claim must be brought under the privacy legislation.[66]

---

willful invasion of privacy a person knew or should have known that her actions would invade the privacy of another

Statutory Cause of Action Alternatively, several provincial governments have created statutory causes of action. British Columbia, Manitoba, Saskatchewan, and Newfoundland and Labrador each have statutory causes of action for **willful invasion of privacy**.[67] The legislation includes a list of considerations to be taken into account when determining liability, including the nature of the action, the effect of the action, the relationship between the parties, the conduct of the parties, and any apology. In Manitoba, these factors are used to assess damages. Some situations are exempt from liability, including those where there is consent or the invasion is lawfully authorized or part of a lawful right of defence. Some provinces exempt news-gathering activities undertaken in the public interest. In addition, Canadian anti-spam legislation creates a civil cause of action for damage caused by breach.

---

[62] *Motherwell v. Motherwell* (1976), 73 D.L.R. (3d) 62 (Alta. C.A.).

[63] *Jones v. Tisge* 2012 ONCA 32; followed by *Hopkins v. Kay* 2014 ONSC 321; considered in Nova Scotia: *Trout Point Lodge Ltd. Handshoe*, 2012 NSSC 245 (para 55–65); *Condon v. Canada*, 2014 FC 250.

[64] *Jones, ibid.*, at para. 71.

[65] *Mohl v. University of British Columbia* 2009 BCCA 249. See as to Alberta: *Martin v. General Teamsters* 2011 ABQB 412; *Bank of Montreal v. Cochrane*, [2010] A.J. No. 1210.

[66] *Mohl, ibid.*, at para. 13.

[67] Privacy Act, R.S.B.C. 1996, c. 373, s. 1; Privacy Act, C.C.S.M., c. P125, s. 2; Privacy Act, R.S.S. 1978, c. P-24, s. 2; Privacy Act, R.S.N.L. 1990, c. P-22, s. 3.

Tort: Negligence

Protecting personal information is part of complying with privacy legislation and involves security measures. Inadequate security may allow internal or external unauthorized access to private information. As discussed in Chapter 4, the tort of negligence imposes liability when a duty of care is owed, the standard of care is not met, and damage is caused as a result. PIPEDA imposes a duty on businesses to protect personal information. If security measures are inadequate when compared to the reasonable efforts undertaken by other similar businesses, then liability will follow. This tort imposes liability on the custodian of the information, even when someone else actually accesses or misuses the information. Theft and unauthorized access are expected risks that must be secured against. In some circumstances, even breach of fiduciary duty could impose liability for improper use or disclosure of personal information.

CASE 32.15

In late 2006, TJX, the parent company of Winners and HomeSense stores, experienced one of the largest personal information security breaches in history, affecting approximately 45 million debit and credit cards (including Canadian customers). An intruder placed unauthorized software on the TJX computer system through a wireless connection based outside two stores in Florida. Using this connection, the intruder was able to access credit card information, driver's licence data, and provincial identification numbers. Upon investigation, the Privacy Commissioner found that

- it was not reasonable for TJX to collect driver's licence data and provincial identification numbers; and

- indefinite retention of the information unreasonably increased the risks to the customer, and although TJX had physical, administrative, and technical protection measures in place (locks, swipe cards, employee training,

and codes of conduct), its technical measures were below standard because

- it relied on a "weak" (wired equivalent) encryption protocol,

- the industry standard of Wi-Fi protected access was preferred in 2003 and required by September 2006, and

- the system was inadequately monitored.

Therefore, TJX was in breach of its obligations under PIPEDA.[68] Consumer class-action lawsuits were commenced in Canada and the United States alleging negligence associated with inadequate security. Terms of settlement of the lawsuits included providing consumers with identity theft insurance and credit report monitoring.[69] Banks also sued for costs associated with issuing new credit cards.

Security measures should include physical barriers, such as locks on doors; organization controls, including limiting those entitled to access material; and technological measures, including current encryption techniques.[70]

CRIMINAL LIABILITY

Criminal liability is a common way of dealing with privacy violations resulting in identity theft. General Criminal Code offences such as fraud (section 383) and impersonation (section 402) are effective measures to deal with the perpetrators of identity theft. Unauthorized intruders may be charged with unauthorized use of a computer (section 342.1), theft of telecommunications (section 326), mischief in relation to data (section 430(1.1)), or improper transfer of identity documents (s. 56.1)

---

[68] Office of the Privacy Commissioner of Canada and Office of the Information and Privacy Commissioner of Alberta, Report of an Investigation Into the Security, Collection and Retention of Personal Information: TJX Companies Inc./Winners Merchant International L.P., September 25, 2007, http://www.priv.gc.ca/cf-dc/2007/tjx_rep_070925_e.asp.

[69] Robert Westervelt, "TJX Should Have Had Stronger Wi-Fi Encryption, Say Canadian Officials," SearchSecurity.com, Sept. 25, 2007, http://searchsecurity.techtarget.com/news/article/0,289142,sid14_gci1273889,00.html.

[70] Scassa et al., *supra*, n. 5 at para. 86.

Sections 402.1 and 402.2 of the Criminal Code create specific offences for identity theft and identity fraud. Digital forms of identity information such as images, electronic signatures, and voice prints are included along with personal information such as names, addresses, credit card numbers, social insurance numbers, etc. Use, possession, sale, and transmission of the identity information are among the prohibited activities.

Part VI of the Criminal Code deals with invasion of privacy through the offence of willful interception of private communications (section 184). Private communications may be intercepted with the consent of either party involved, or with court authorization. What is considered a private communication is central to the offence, and this involves the concept of reasonable expectation. Most often these provisions are used in consideration of admissibility of criminal evidence and authorization of law enforcement interception.

CODES OF CONDUCT

The principles used as the basis for the federal Privacy Act were drawn from the Organisation for Economic Co-operation and Development guidelines. One of the motives behind the development of PIPEDA was the desire to meet the standards set by the European Directive on Protection of Data. Although Canada was not legally required to comply, the desire to do business with the European Union and to be perceived as a responsible government encouraged voluntary compliance.

The same motivation gives credibility to voluntary codes of conduct developed by industry associations and international organizations. In order to be respected and competitive within their industries, businesses comply with standards that may be more rigorous than those required by law. The Canadian Association of Internet Providers has a privacy code developed around the Canadian Standards Association's model code. The Canadian Bankers Association Privacy Code governs more than 50 domestic and foreign banks operating in Canada. The Insurance Bureau of Canada has a model personal information code available for use by its 120 member companies. The Canadian Marketing Association requires members to follow its code of seven privacy principles.[71]

As discussed earlier in the "Healthcare" section, certain professional associations govern the privacy practices of their members through professional codes of conduct or ethics. Violations trigger investigation and possible discipline by the self-regulating body. The Health Information Privacy Code of the Canadian Medical Association covers most of the physicians in Canada.

Strategies to Manage the Legal Risks

As this chapter demonstrates, privacy is a complicated legal issue involving a maze of provincial and federal legislation, voluntary codes of conduct, and potential civil or criminal liability. In order to develop effective and legally compliant privacy policies, a business should

- identify a person responsible for privacy within the organization;
- become familiar with the privacy legislation, industry standards, and codes of conduct applicable to its activities;
- complete an audit of the company's activities to determine

---

[71] All of the voluntary codes of conduct referred to in this section may be accessed through the Industry Canada website (Office of Consumer Affairs) or through the individual association websites.

- what personal information is collected, used, disclosed, and retained and for what purposes,
- what privacy risks exist, and
- what security measures and policies are currently in place;
- assess each type of information, practice, and risk based on
  - degree of sensitivity,
  - relevance to purpose,
  - invasiveness, and
  - seriousness of potential damage;
- develop and implement privacy policies and codes of conduct that comply with the legislation, meet or exceed industry standards, and reduce the likelihood of breach;
- develop a response protocol for privacy breaches that includes incident reporting, immediate containment of the breach, preservation of evidence, and notification of the affected individuals, police, or privacy commissioner (where relevant);
- educate and train employees; and
- communicate policies to relevant stakeholders, including customers, suppliers, and the public.

Finally, regular review and updating of policies and procedures is vital in our ever-changing technological environment.

QUESTIONS FOR REVIEW

1. What are the three key components of modern privacy?
2. What is the constitutional authority for declaring the right to privacy a human right?
3. What is the standard of protection that the Charter gives to privacy?
4. What federal legislation protects privacy in the public sector, and how is compliance monitored?
5. What federal legislation protects personal information held in the private sector, and what does this statute require businesses to do?
6. What test does a court apply to determine if a privacy-invasive activity is reasonable?
7. Does a common law tort of invasion of privacy exist in Canada?
8. How does inadequate security expose business to civil and possibly criminal liability?
9. What steps should be followed by a business considering outsourcing data processing to an American company?
10. How does the requirement of "consent" for collection, use, and disclosure of personal information differ in the public and private sectors?
11. What protection is available for employee personal information?

CASES AND PROBLEMS

1. Continuing Scenario

   Ashley's Restaurant always has a line-up of walk-in customers on Fridays and Saturdays. Approximately 50 percent of the tables are reserved. It is embarrassing when a reservation party does not show up and a waiting customer sees the table sit empty. Therefore, Ashley has a policy that requires the hostess to obtain a credit card number (plus expiry date) and a phone number with each reservation. This information is entered into the online reservation calendar beside the time slot. If the party does not appear, a $50.00 "no-show" charge is applied to their credit card.

Bill is standing beside the hostess station waiting for a table when Erin calls to make a reservation. The hostess opens the reservation system on the computer and enters the required information. Bill watches as the name, phone number, and credit card details are displayed on the screen in full view of all the customers in the line. A few hours later Erin's credit card is declined when she tries to buy gas because she has exceeded her limit. Apparently $14 000 of merchandise was fraudulently charged to her account between the time she made the reservation and the time she got gas. Discuss any possible potential liability for Ashley's Restaurant.

2. KDP Limited operates a pool-servicing business in Vancouver. In the summer, KDP has eight service vans on the road; each van has two employees, and 12 of the employees are students. It seems that fewer and fewer service calls are being completed each day, and the manager is concerned about productivity. The employees say it is the increased traffic in the city; it just takes longer to get to and from each call. It also seems that gas expenses are rising. The cost of gas is high and the vans are on average eight years old, so the manager is wondering whether more fuel-efficient vehicles should be leased.

Before making such a big investment, the manager decides to collect work-productivity information. He wonders if the vans are making unauthorized stops or not taking the most efficient routes to service calls. A GPS unit is installed in each van to track the start and stop times, speed, locations, routes taken, and mileage. The units cannot be turned off by the driver.

After secretly tracking each van for one week, it is discovered that Jim and Jeff, summer students operating van 3, are spending each afternoon at Jim's parents' backyard pool. They are dismissed. Jeff files a complaint with the Privacy Commissioner.

What should the Privacy Commissioner consider when investigating this complaint? Would your answer be different if the business were located in Winnipeg?

3. In 2005, Primtel Ltd., a wireless telephone company, decided to publish a telephone directory including all the telephone numbers of its subscribers except those numbers that were "unlisted." The directory was available to the public on the company's website. Customers were advised of the pending directory by way of an insert in the December 2004 billing. The fine print on the back of the insert advised those customers not wishing to appear in the directory to contact the company and arrange for "unlisted" status. Primtel charged an additional $2 per month fee for unlisted service.

Mary contracted with Primtel in 2002; at the time, she declined the unlisted option because of the additional fee. This was long before there was public access to her number online. She did not notice Primtel's bill insert, and, after receiving several annoying phone calls from a former boyfriend, she discovered that her phone number was available online. She complained to the Privacy Commissioner because she believed her private information had been disclosed without her consent.

What are the relevant rules relating to consent, and how should the Privacy Commissioner decide this case?

4. Ticketmarketer is a company that sells tickets online for concerts, plays, and sporting events. Payment is made by credit card, but purchasers are asked to provide their home address, phone number, and email. The company uses this information for verification of identity when tickets are picked up at the venue.

Joan is a marketing manager at Ticketmarketer and has started tracking what type of event each customer attends. She then uses the information for promotional purposes: Once repeat customers' preferences are identified, they receive advance notification of similar events by email.

Is there any privacy concern about this practice? If so, how should Joan revise the plan to become privacy compliant?

Glossary

Aboriginal peoples Canadian Indian, Inuit, and Métis peoples

absolute privilege complete immunity from liability for defamation

abuse of dominant position taking an unfair advantage of possessing a monopoly or dominant position in the marketplace

acceleration clause a provision whereby the full outstanding amount of a debt becomes immediately payable if the debtor defaults in making any installment payment

acceptance any conduct by the buyer in relation to the goods that amounts to recognition of an existing contract of sale

acceptor the drawee who consents to the bill of exchange by signing it together with the word "accepted" and the date

accommodation bill bill of exchange that contains an anomalous endorsement

accord and satisfaction a compromise between contracting parties to substitute a new contractual obligation and release a party from the existing one

act of bankruptcy a prescribed act of a debtor that must be proved before the debtor may be declared bankrupt

act of God the raging of the natural elements

action lawsuit

action for impeachment an action challenging the validity of a patent

actual authority the authority given expressly or impliedly to the agent by the principal

additional rent a tenant's proportionate share of maintenance costs, utilities, and taxes

adjudicate hear parties and deliver a decision with reasons

administrative law law about actions and operations of government administrators and administrative tribunals

administrator the personal representative of a person who dies intestate

admissible evidence evidence that is acceptable to the court

adverse possession the exclusive possession of land by someone who openly uses it like an owner and ignores the claims of other persons including the owner

advocate a barrister in Quebec

after-acquired property property acquired by the debtor after the debt has been incurred

age of majority the age at which a person is recognized as an adult according to the law of his or her province

agency agreement the agreement between principal and agent whereby the agent undertakes to act on behalf of the principal

agent a person acting for another person in contractual relations with third parties

agreement to sell a contract of sale in which the transfer of ownership in the goods is deferred to some future time

agreements in restraint agreements in restraint of trade, also known as non-competition agreements or restrictive covenants when they are included in a larger contract

alien non-citizen

alternative dispute resolution the use of private procedures such as arbitration and mediation to resolve disputes

amortization period length of time it should take to repay an entire debt with the specified payment schedule

annual general meeting the general meeting of shareholders that is required by law to be held each year to transact certain specified business

annual report the report on the business and affairs of the corporation, which the directors are required to present at the annual general meeting

anomalous endorsement an endorsement that is not added for the purpose of negotiating the instrument but as a guarantee to make it easier for the drawer to obtain credit on the bill

anticipatory breach an express repudiation that occurs before the time agreed for performance

anti-dumping duties and countervailing duties special duties imposed on imported products to counter the advantage obtained from dumping or export subsidies

apparent authority the authority that a third party is entitled to assume that the agent possesses

appellant the party who petitions for an appeal

appraisal remedy the right to have one's shares bought by the corporation at a fair price

appropriated designated as the subject matter of the contract

arbitration a form of ADR where a dispute is referred to an arbitrator who adjudicates the matter and the parties agree to be bound by the arbitrator's decision, although there may be a right to appeal to the courts

arbitration agreements contracts that require all disputes to be resolved in arbitration, not the courts

arbitration clause a term in a commercial contract designating arbitration as the process for resolution of any disputes arising between the parties

arbitration procedure the procedure in a rights dispute that binds the parties to accept the interpretation of the collective agreement by an arbitrator

arm's length a transaction between persons who are not related or associated in any way

articles of incorporation founding corporate document, often referred to as the charter or constitution of the corporation

assault the threat of violence to a person

assign transfer to another person outside the contract

assignee a third party to whom rights under a contract have been assigned

assignment the transfer by a party of its unperformed rights under a contract to a third party

assignment into bankruptcy a voluntary declaration of bankruptcy by the debtor

assignment of book debts security interest in the debtor's accounts receivable

assignor a party that assigns its rights under a contract to a third party

associated corporations corporations that are related either (a) vertically, as where one corporation controls the other (parent–subsidiary), or (b) horizontally, as where both corporations are controlled by the same person (affiliates)

assumed risk risk assumed by an employee in accepting a particular employment assumption agreement a contract between the mortgagee and the new purchaser in which the new purchaser agrees to comply with all the requirements in the original mortgage

assumption of the mortgage a subsequent purchaser takes over the responsibility of paying off the vendor's existing mortgage

attachment the moment in time when a debtor's property becomes subject to a security interest

attorney a lawyer in the United States, encompassing the roles of both barrister and solicitor

audit committee a group of directors responsible for overseeing the corporate audit and the preparation of financial statements; the committee has wider responsibilities in a distributing corporation

authorized capital the maximum number (or value) of shares that a corporation is permitted by its charter to issue

bailee party accepting possession of goods from a bailor

bailment possession of personal property without ownership

bailments for value contractual bailment

bailor owner or transferor of the goods

bait-and-switch advertising advertising a product at a bargain price but not supplying it in reasonable quantities

balance of trade offset of value of exports against value of imports

bankrupt a person who has made a voluntary assignment in bankruptcy or against whom a bankruptcy order has been made

bankruptcy order a court order made in proceedings instituted by creditors, whereby a debtor is declared bankrupt

bargain each party pays a price for the promise of the other

bargaining agent a union that has the exclusive right to bargain with the employer on behalf of the bargaining unit

bargaining unit a specified group of employees eligible to join the union

barrister a lawyer in England who accepts cases from solicitors and presents them in court, and also acts as consultant in complex legal issues

basic law a constitution that lists the founding legal principles accepted by the citizens of a country and that they regard as legitimate and binding

battery unlawful physical contact with a person

beneficial contracts of service contracts of employment or apprenticeship found to be for a minor's benefit

beneficial owner a person who, although not the legal owner, may compel the trustee to provide benefits to him

beneficiary a person who is entitled to the benefits of a trust or the person entitled to receive insurance monies

bid-rigging agreeing not to submit a bid or agreeing in advance what bids will be submitted in response to a call for bids or tenders

bilateral contract a contract where offeror and offeree trade promises and both are bound to perform later

bilateral investment protection treaty a treaty entered into between two countries, whereby each country undertakes to protect investors from the other country and to give them certain rights

bill of exchange a written order by one party to another party to pay a specified sum of money to a named party or to the bearer of the document

bill of lading a document signed by a carrier acknowledging that specified goods have been received by it for shipment

biometrics technological analysis of physical characteristics, such as fingerprints

board of directors the governing body of a corporation, responsible for the management of its business and affairs

bond a document evidencing a debt owed by a corporation

branch a business carried on by the owner in its own name at a location distinct from its head office

breach of contract a cause of action where a party to the contract claims that the other party has not fulfilled its promises

builders' lien an interest that builders and others involved in construction work may have in a building as security for money owed to them for work done (also known as a mechanics' lien or a construction lien)

building-scheme covenant a restrictive covenant that regulates land use over an entire neighbourhood or a shopping centre

bulk sale a sale of all or substantially all the assets of a business

burden the requirement that, unless a party can establish facts and law to prove its case, it will lose

business judgment rule courts will defer to the business decisions of directors and officers provided they are arrived at using an appropriate degree of prudence and diligence

bylaws the internal working rules of a corporation

calculation period stages at which accrued interest is added to principal

canon law law created by the Church, which had its own jurisdiction and courts in matters pertaining to itself, family law, and wills

case law a collection of individual cases decided by the courts that develop and shape legal principles

causation injury resulting from the breach of the standard of care

cause of action an event or set of events that gives rise to legal liability

caveat emptor let the buyer beware

certificate of incorporation a certificate that a corporation has come into existence

certificate of title summary of registered interests in a property, showing the owner and any mortgages, easements, or other interests held by others, which may be relied upon by the public

certification an acknowledgment by an administrative tribunal that a particular union commands sufficient membership to justify its role as exclusive bargaining agent for the employees

certification an undertaking by the bank to pay the amount of the cheque to its holder when later presented for payment

certification mark a special type of trademark used to identify goods or services that conform to a particular standard

chain of title the series of grants over the title search period that can be traced to the current owner (vendor)

charge a lien or encumbrance on land

chargee mortgagee

chargor mortgagor

chattel moveable personal property or goods; not land

chattel mortgage a mortgage of personal property

cheque a bill of exchange drawn against a bank and payable on demand

cheque truncation the physical movement of cheques is replaced by the electronic transfer of information

choses in action rights to intangible property such as patents, stocks, and contracts that may be enforced in the courts

choses in possession rights to tangible property that may be possessed physically

circumstantial evidence principle a prima facie case of negligence may be established by drawing reasonable inferences from the circumstances surrounding the product manufacture and failure

civil law the system of law involving a comprehensive legislated code, derived from Roman law that developed in continental Europe and greatly influenced by the Code Napoléon of 1804

civil liability responsibility arising from a breach of a private law, enforced through a lawsuit initiated by the victim

claim a statement of the features claimed to be new and in respect of which the applicant claims an exclusive right

class action an action in which an individual represents a group of possible plaintiffs and the judgment decides the matter for all members of the class at once

class rights special rights attached to a particular class of shares

closed mortgage a mortgage that does not permit early repayment of the debt without a substantial penalty

closed-shop agreement a collective agreement requiring all employees to be union members

cloud computing a server-focused computing system in which all processing and storage is done at the server level and users access the system over the internet from anywhere through a variety of devices

code of conduct a common standard of behaviour that may take the form of a values statement or a prescribed set of rules "often used by" a professional organization setting out the duties and appropriate standards of behaviour to be observed by its members

codified existing common law rules collected and put in statute form

codify set down and summarize in a statute the existing common law rules governing a particular area of activity

coercion improperly forced payment under protest

collateral agreement a separate agreement between the parties made at the same time as, but not included in, the written document

collateral security an interest in property of a debtor that gives a creditor the right to seize and sell it in the event of non-payment of the debt

collection arrangement an arrangement whereby the seller employs the services of its bank to collect payment by depositing the documents with the bank and receiving credit for the price

collective bargaining establishing conditions of employment by negotiation between an employer and the bargaining agent for its employees

collective rights society a society to which authors of musical and dramatic works assign performing and communication rights and which grants licences and collects fees

commercial activity any general or particular activity performed or stated in the objectives of an organization, that has a commercial aspect

commercial tenancies a lease of premises used for a business or non-residential purpose

commission agent one who sells on behalf of a principal to third parties and receives compensation through commissions

common carrier a business that holds itself out to the public as a transporter of goods for reward

common elements structures and areas external to a condominium unit, including communal facilities

common law the case-based system of law originating in England and covering most of the English-speaking world—based on the recorded reasons given by courts for their decisions

common law precedents developed over time from the decisions of many cases

common mistake a situation in which both parties believe the same misunderstanding or mistake about the contract

common share a share carrying no preferential right

community legal services or legal clinic a model of legal aid where legal services are delivered by community law offices with full-time staff lawyers and managed by boards elected by residents of the community

comparative value equal pay for work of equal value

compensation committee committee responsible for setting director and officer pay

compliance officer an employee that monitors regulatory and legislative requirements applicable to the business and ensures that the business complies

compromise and arrangement an agreement made by a debtor corporation with its creditors whereby arrangements are made for repayment of debts without liquidating the corporation

compulsory licence a licence granted to a person to work a patent without the consent of the owner of the patent

conciliation procedure bargaining with the help of a conciliation officer or board

concurrent powers overlapping powers of both levels of government to regulate the same activities

condition a major or essential term of the contract, the breach of which may relieve the injured party from further performance

condition precedent any set of circumstances or events that the parties stipulate must be satisfied or must happen before their contract takes effect

condition subsequent a future event that brings a promisor's liability to an end if it happens

conditional discharge the debtor is discharged under the original contract only if the negotiable instrument given in payment is honoured when presented

conditions essential terms of a contract

condominium corporation a corporation—whose members are the condominium owners—that is responsible for managing the property as a whole

condominium unit a unit in a multiple-unit development that may be owned in fee simple

conflict of interest a situation where a duty is owed to a client whose interests conflict with the interests of the profes- sional, another client, or another person to whom a duty is owed

conflict of laws or private international law the principles of law that apply to determine which country's laws govern a dispute involving private parties

consensual surveillance the employee is aware of and consents to the surveillance

consent approval of the person to whom the collected information relates

consequential damages secondary losses incurred by the non-breaching party that were foreseeable at the time of contracting consideration the price for which the promise of the other is bought

consignment the transfer of only possession of goods from one business to another for the purpose of offering for sale

conspiracies agreements or arrangements between competitors to lessen competition

constructive dismissal a substantial change to an employee's job that amounts to termination of the existing employment

constructive trust a trust relationship imposed by the court to prevent a party from being unjustly enriched by keeping property that should benefit another

construing interpreting

consumer an individual (not an organization) purchasing a product or service for personal, family, household, non-business purposes

consumer debtor an individual who is insolvent but whose aggregate debts do not exceed $75 000 (soon to be changed to $250 000)

consumers individuals who purchase goods and services from a business for their personal use and enjoyment

contempt of court a finding by a court that a person has willfully refused to obey a court order and therefore will be punished

contingency fee a fee paid for a lawyer's services only if the client is successful; there is no charge if the client is unsuccessful

contra proferentem a rule of contract interpretation that prefers the interpretation of a clause that is least favourable to the party that drafted the clause

contract a set of promises that the law will enforce

contractual joint venture a joint venture effected by agreement without the creation of any separate legal entity

contributory negligence a partial defence to a negligence action when the plaintiff's or another defendant's conduct also contributed to the injury

cooling-off period a time during which a consumer may cancel (rescind) a contract without any reason; length of the time period is set in provincial legislation

cooling-off period a time during which the employer cannot declare a lockout nor can the union begin a strike

corporate governance the rules governing the organization and management of the business and affairs of a corporation in order to meet its internal objectives and external responsibilities

corporate social responsibility a concept that suggests business decision makers consider ethical issues—including the interests of customers, employees, creditors, the public, and other stakeholders—in addition to legal and financial concerns

corporation a legal person formed by incorporation according to a prescribed legal procedure

costs funds paid by litigants to cover a portion of the government's expenses in maintaining the court system

counsel lawyer representing a plaintiff or defendant

counterclaim a claim by the defendant arising from the same facts as the original action by the plaintiff to be tried along with that action

countertrade a form of barter, under which a seller agrees to accept payment in goods produced or procured by the buyer

courts of chancery a system of courts under the king's chancellor and vice-chancellors developed from the hearing of petitions to the king—courts of equity

covenant a term, clause, or promise contained in a lease

covenant of quiet enjoyment a landlord's promise to do nothing to interfere with the tenant's possession and use of the premises

covenantor one who makes a covenant

covert surveillance the employee is unaware of surveillance and has not consented to it

criminal liability responsibility arising from commission of an offence against the government or society as a whole

criminal offences most serious offences that require proof of mental intent with penalties imposed by the courts

cumulative right the right of the holder of a preferred share to be paid arrears from previous years before any dividend is paid on the common shares

cumulative voting a method of electing directors by a form of proportional representation

current assets cash or cash equivalent assets such as negotiable instruments, demand deposits, and accounts receivable

cybersquatting the registration of a domain name containing the trademark of another person, with the intention of selling the domain name to the owner of the mark

damages a sum of money awarded as compensation for loss or injury

data shadows electronic records of the internet activity of a user

debenture an alternative term to describe a corporate bond

debtor-in-possession financing court-sanctioned secured loans advanced during reorganization and given priority over pre-existing secured creditors

deceit an intentional tort imposing liability when damage is caused by a false statement made with the intention of misleading another person

declaration of trust an agreement that establishes a trust and designates the trustees

deductible clause a clause requiring the insured to bear the loss up to a stated amount

deed a document under seal, which today is usually a small, red, gummed wafer

deed of conveyance a document under seal that transfers an interest in land from the owner to another party

defamation making an untrue statement that causes injury to the reputation of another person

demand draft a bill of exchange payable immediately upon presentation without any days of grace

demotion transferring an employee to a job with less responsibility and/or income potential

dependent agent an agent who acts exclusively, or mostly, for a single principal

deposit a sum of money paid by the buyer to the seller, to be forfeited if the buyer does not perform his or her part of the contract

derivative action proceedings brought by one or more shareholders in the name of the corporation in respect of a wrong done to the corporation

detrimental reliance the worsening of one's situation after acting upon false information

devices medical apparatus and test kits such as pregnancy tests

digital rights management system (DRMS) a system collecting data about the licensing, payment for, and authenticity of a work

digital rights management technology a system collecting data about the licensing, payment, use, and authenticity of a work

direct sales contract a contract formed at a place other than the business's place of business

directors' circular a document required to be issued to the shareholders by the board of directors when a takeover of a widely held corporation is proposed

disbarred expelled from the law society and deprived of the privilege of practising law

discharge a court order whereby a person who has been declared bankrupt ceases to have the status of a bankrupt person

discharge a contract cancel or end the obligations of a contract; make an agreement or contract inoperative

disclaimer an express statement to the effect that the person making it takes no responsibility for its accuracy

disclosed surveillance the employee is given advance notice of surveillance but does not consent to it

disclosure (of personal information) transfer of data to third parties outside the organization

discriminatory pricing where a seller makes a practice of discriminating between purchasers with respect to the price charged for goods or services

dishonour the failure by the party primarily liable to pay the instrument according to its terms

dismissal for cause dismissal without notice or further obligation by the employer when the employee's conduct amounts to breach of contract

distinguish identify a factual difference that renders a precedent inapplicable to the case before the court

distinguishing guise the shaping of goods or their containers, or a distinctive mode of wrapping or packaging

distress the right of the landlord to seize assets of the tenant found on the premises and sell them to realize arrears of rent

distributing corporation a corporation that issues its securities to the public; also referred to as an issuing corporation, reporting issuer, and publicly traded corporation

dividend a distribution to shareholders of a share of the profits of the corporation

doctrine of frustration the law excuses a party from performance when circumstances beyond the control of the parties have made performance impossible, pointless, or radically different from that contemplated by the parties

document under seal a covenant recorded in a document containing a wax seal, showing that the covenantor adopted the document as his act and deed

documents of record documents that a corporation is required to keep and make available to shareholders

domain name the registered internet address of a website

dominant tenement the piece of land that benefits from an easement

dower a widow's right to a life interest in one-third of the real property held by her husband in fee simple before his death

down payment a sum of money paid by the buyer as an initial part of the purchase price

drawee the party who is required to make payment on the bill of exchange

drawer the party who draws up the bill of exchange

drawing party the contracting party that prepared the agreement and/or the particular clause

dual offence an offence of the Competition Act that may be either a criminal or a regulatory offence, depending upon the seriousness of the conduct

due diligence defence establishing that an acceptable standard of care and skill was exercised by a director or officer

dumping selling products abroad at prices below those charged on domestic sales

duress actual or threatened violence or imprisonment as a means of coercing a party to enter into a contract

duty of care a relationship so close that one could reasonably foresee causing harm to the other

duty to account the duty of a person who commits a breach of trust to hand over any profits derived from the breach

duty to warn manufacturer's responsibility to make users aware of the risks associated with the use or misuse of the product

earnest a token sum or article given to seal a bargain—now a rare practice

easement a right enjoyed by one landowner over the land of another for a special purpose but not for occupation of the land

ecash an online payment system that enables the anonymous transfer of money over the internet

electronic commerce (ecommerce) the use of computer networks to facilitate commercial activities, including the production, distribution, sale, and delivery of goods and services

electronic retailing (etailing) the supply of tangible or electronic goods or services over the internet; supply of tangible goods involves a conventional mode of delivery; electronic goods are downloaded directly to the customer's computer

electronic transfer of funds payment made through electronic (intangible) media such as telephone or internet rather than by cash or cheque; payment may take the form of credit card charges, debit of bank accounts, or even ecash, often, through the business's website

endorse sign one's name on a negotiable instrument

endorsement written evidence of a change in the terms of a policy

entering (filing) an appearance filing notice of an intention to contest an action

entirety clause a term in a contract stating that the whole agreement is contained in the written documents and there are no other terms, conditions, representations, or warranties

enurement clause a clause in a contract that extends the rights and benefits to those inheriting from a party, succeeding the party, or taking an assignment from a party

equitable assignment an assignment other than a statutory assignment

equitable relief a discretionary remedy first developed by the courts of equity to undo an injustice

equitable remedies new remedies created by the courts of equity to address situations where money damages did not solve the problem

equity rules developed by the courts of equity as exceptions to existing rules of common law

equity joint venture a corporation formed, and jointly owned, by the parties to a joint venture for the purpose of carrying on the venture

equity of redemption the right of the mortgagor to redeem mortgaged land on payment of the debt in full

estates in time the right to exclusive possession of the land for a period of time

estopped prevented

examination for discovery process allowing either party to examine the other in order to narrow the issues

exchange controls restrictions on the conversion or export of currency

exclusive dealing where a supplier of goods makes it a condition that the buyer should deal only or primarily in the supplier's products

exclusive use clause a landlord's promise not to rent adjoining premises to any other entity in the same or competing business as the tenant

execution order an order that gives the sheriff authority to levy execution

executor the personal representative of a deceased person named in his or her will

executor or administrator legal representative of the estate of a dead person

exempt property that is not subject to seizure by the trustee as a result of an exception in a federal or provincial statute

exemption clause a clause in a contract that exempts or limits the liability of a party also known as an exclusion clause

exercise an option accept the offer contained in an option

expectation damages an amount awarded for breach of contract, based on expected benefits or profits

expert opinions opinions given by a person who purports to have specialized knowledge of a subject

export houses or freight forwarders specialist firms that make the arrangements for shipment, insurance, and financing in export sales

export subsidy the granting by governments of financial assistance to promote exports

express repudiation one of the contracting parties advises the other that it does not intend to perform as promised

expropriation a state's right to assume ownership of private property within its geographic borders

extinguish the title end the title of the owner and the owner's right to regain possession

factor a party who purchases drafts drawn on customers at a discount and then collects directly from the customer

false arrest causing a person to be arrested without reasonable cause

false imprisonment unlawfully restraining or confining another person

fault unjustifiable injurious conduct that intentionally or carelessly disregards the interests of others

federal paramountcy the principle that a federal law prevails over a conflicting provincial law

fee simple the interest in land closest to complete ownership

feudal law a system of land ownership rooted in sovereign ownership: land was handed down to lords who gave possession of parcels of land to lesser "royals" in exchange for military service and loyalty

fiduciary duty a duty imposed on a person who stands in a special relation of trust and loyalty to another

finance lease an arrangement where a third person provides credit financing, becomes the owner of the property, and leases it to the lessee

financial statements annual accounts that are required to be presented to the shareholders at the annual general meeting

financing statement the document summarizing the details of a security interest that is filed in order to protect that interest

firm collective reference to the partners in a partnership

fixed stored in a permanent or lasting form

fixed term a contract of employment with defined start and end dates

fixtures all things permanently attached to land are deemed part of the land

floating charge a form of mortgage on all the assets of a corporation other than those already specifically charged

foreclosure an order by a court ending the mortgagor's right to redeem within a fixed time

foreign exchange risk management methods of reducing the risk involved in currency fluctuations

foreign investment conducting operations in a foreign market

foreign presence placing representatives of a business in foreign markets

foreign trade the buying and selling of goods and services between parties from different countries

forfeiture to lose or forfeit to the landlord the balance of the term of a lease

format shifting transferring purchased material, such as music, from one of the owner's devices to another

forum non conveniens refusing to hear a proceeding because another jurisdiction is more appropriate or more closely connected to the matter

franchise agreement an agreement under which a franchisor grants to the franchisee a right to market the franchisor's products

fraudulent misrepresentation deceit

fraudulent preference the payment of money or transfer of property to a creditor with a view to giving that creditor preference over other creditors

fraudulent transfer a transfer of property by a debtor with the intention of putting that property out of the reach of creditors

free trade areas groups of countries within which customs duties are eliminated

freehold estate an interest in land that is indeterminate in time

fungible goods goods that may be replaced with different but identical goods

future goods goods that have not yet been produced

garnishee order an order requiring the debtor's employer to retain a portion of the debtor's wages each payday and surrender the sum to the creditor

general creditor a creditor that has no security other than the debtor's promise to pay

general damages damages to compensate for injuries that cannot be precisely expressed in monetary terms

general meeting of shareholders a formal meeting of shareholders at which they are able to vote on matters concerning the corporation

general partner a partner in a limited partnership whose liability is not limited

goods personal property, excluding both money and choses in action

goodwill the benefit and advantage of the good name, reputation, and connections of a business

government institutions government departments and agencies listed in Schedule 1 of the Privacy Act

gratuitous bailment a bailment where one party provides no consideration, or where there is no intention to create a contractual relationship

gratuitous promise a promise made without bargaining for or accepting anything in return

grievances disputes arising under the collective agreement

guarantee a promise to perform the obligation of another person if that person defaults

guarantor one who agrees to pay the debts of another person if that person defaults

guardian a person appointed to manage the affairs of a minor in the place of his or her parents

hearsay words attributed by a witness to a person who is not before the court

hire-purchase an agreement to lease an item of property with an option for the lessee to purchase it at the end of the stipulated term

holdback an amount that the owner who contracts for construction work may withhold from payments made to the principal contractor to protect against claims from subcontractors and suppliers

holder a party who acquires a negotiable instrument from the transferor

holder in due course a party who is not the original payee that acquires the cheque from that payee or a subsequent holder

holding out representing by words or conduct that a person is one's agent or has a particular authority

human rights recognized entitlements encompassing traditional freedoms associated with civil liberty and basic human necessities

illegal offends the public good or violates a statute

immediate parties the holder of an instrument and the party alleged to be liable on it who have had direct dealings with each other

implied term a term not expressly included by the parties in their agreement but which, as reasonable people, they would have included had they thought about it

implied term as to description it is implied that goods sold by description will conform to the description

implied term as to title it is implied that the seller has a right to sell the goods

implied term of fitness it is implied that the goods are of a type that is suitable for the purpose for which they are bought

implied term of merchantable quality it is implied that the goods are in reasonable condition and free from defects that would make them unsuitable for use

implied term that goods correspond with sample it is implied that, when a sample of the goods to be sold has been provided, the actual goods supplied will correspond to that sample in type and quality

Incoterms a set of standard contractual terms adopted by the International Chamber of Commerce

indefinite hiring a contract of employment for an undetermined length of time, with no expectation of termination or described end date

indemnity a promise by a third party to be primarily liable to pay the debt

indemnity or compensation a money award given as a supplement to rescission for loss sustained in performing a contract

independent agent an agent who carries on an independent business and acts for a number of principals

indeterminate liability inability to be determined so that the magnitude of liability cannot be reasonably predicted, anticipated, or planned for

individual natural person, not a corporation

indoor management rule the principle that a person dealing with a corporation is entitled to assume that its internal procedural rules have been complied with unless it is apparent that such is not the case

inducing breach of contract intentionally causing one party to breach his contract with another

infringement violation of the rights of the owner of the intellectual property

inherent vice a latent defect or dangerous condition of goods

in-house counsel a lawyer who provides legal services to a business as a full-time employee of the business

injunction a court order restraining a person from doing, or continuing to do, a particular act

injurious reliance loss or harm suffered by a promisee who, to his detriment, relied reasonably on a gratuitous promise

innkeeper a person or firm that maintains an establishment offering lodging to any member of the public

insider trading the use of confidential information relating to a corporation in dealing in its securities

insolvency having liabilities in excess of the realizable value of one's assets or being unable to pay one's debts as they fall due

insolvent unable to pay one's debts as they fall due or liabilities exceed realizable assets

insolvent person a person who is unable to meet (or has ceased to pay) his or her debts as they become due, or whose debts exceed the value of his or her realizable assets

inspector a person appointed by the court to investigate the affairs of a corporation

insurable interest genuine risk of loss that may be suffered from damage to the thing insured

insurance adjuster a person who appraises property losses

insurance agent an agent or employee of an insurance company

insurance broker an independent business that arranges insurance coverage for its clients

insurance policy the written evidence of the terms of a contract of insurance

interest dispute an employer and the union disagree about the particular terms to be included in the collective agreement

interests less than estates interests in land that do not give the right to exclusive possession

interlocutory injunction a temporary injunction preventing immediate harm from being done before the full trial of the matter

internet the interconnected logical networks that link computers worldwide

intestate when a person dies without leaving a will

intestate succession government rules that determine who gets the property of someone who dies without a will

intranet closed systems linking specific users internal to a company or group; commonly used for data exchange

invitee a person permitted by an occupier to enter premises for business purposes

inviting tenders seeking offers from suppliers

issued capital the shares that have been issued by a corporation

issuing commencing the lawsuit by filing a copy of the statement of claim with the court office job description a description of the responsibilities of a position, including objectives, qualifications, and supervisor

joint liability the situation where each of a number of persons is personally liable for the full amount of a debt

joint tenants concurrent holders, each of whom has a right of survivorship

joint venture a form of business venture between two or more independent enterprises, or a corporation jointly owned by them

judgment creditor a party who has obtained a court judgment for a sum of money

judgment debtor a party who has been ordered by the court to pay a sum of money

judicare a model of legal aid in which lawyers agree to be paid according to government fee schedules for serving clients who qualify for legal aid

jurisdiction the province, state, or country whose laws apply to a particular situation

jurisdiction the right of a court to hear and resolve a dispute

jurisdictional dispute two or more unions compete for the right to represent a particular group of employees

labour relations board an administrative tribunal regulating labour relations

land comprises the surface, all that is under the surface, including the minerals and oil, and everything above the surface, including buildings

land titles system a system of land registration where the land titles office brings all outstanding interests in the land up-to-date and certifies them as being correct

lapse the termination of an offer when the offeree fails to accept it within a specified time, or if no time is specified, then within a reasonable time

latent defect defect not readily apparent to an ordinary purchaser during an ordinary inspection

lease (1) an agreement where the owner of property allows another person to have possession and use of the property for a specific period in return for the payment of rent and (2) the agreement between landlord and tenant creating the leasehold interest

leaseback a financial arrangement enabling a business to buy a building and sell it to a financial institution that, in turn, gives a long-term lease of the property back to the business

leasehold an interest in land for a definite period of time

legal aid a system where the government pays for many legal services provided to low-income litigants

legal audit a review of each area, action, and interaction of the business to identify potential legal liability and legal compliance risks

legal capacity competence to bind oneself legally

legal liability responsibility for the consequences of breaking the law

legal person an entity recognized at law as having its own legal rights, duties, and responsibilities

legal risk business activities, conduct, events, or scenarios that could expose a business to any type of legal liability

legal risk management plan a plan developed by a business that identifies potential legal liability and provides preventive and remedial strategies

legal title an interest in land recognized by the common law

lessee the person who takes possession of the leased property; when applied to land the lessee is a tenant, the person to whom an interest in a leasehold estate is granted

lessor the owner of the leased property; when applied to land, known as a landlord being a grantor

let the loss fall where it lies the court will enforce the contract up to the moment of discharge—obligations due before the frustrating event remain; obligations arising after the frustrating event are discharged

letter of credit a document that the buyer of goods obtains from the bank and uses to pay the seller

letters patent a document incorporating a corporation, issued by the appropriate authority, and constituting the "charter" of the corporation

level-of-interactivity test a review of the features of a website to determine if it is active or passive; only active sites will be considered connected to the jurisdiction (also called the active-versus-passive test)

levy execution to seize and sell a debtor's chattels or arrange for a sale of his lands

libel written defamation

liberal approach to statutory interpretation statutory interpretation that considers the legislative intent, purpose, and history of the statute, as well as the context of the language

liberal approach to contractual interpretation an approach that looks to the intent of the parties and surrounding circumstances, and tends to minimize, but does not ignore, the importance of the words actually used

licence a right to use another's land for the benefit of a person

licensee a visitor (other than an invitee) who enters premises with the consent of the occupier

lien a right of a person in possession of property to retain that property until payment

life estate an estate in land that lasts for the life of one person

life tenant a holder of a life estate

limitation period the time period within which a right of action must be pursued or it is lost forever

limited liability the liability of shareholders is limited to the amount of their capital contributions

limited liability partnership a partnership in which non-negligent partners are not personally liable for losses caused by the negligence of a partner

limited partner a partner in a limited partnership whose liability is limited to the amount of his or her capital contribution

limited partnership a partnership in which some of the partners limit their liability to the amount of their capital contributions

linking or hyperlinking an electronic connection of one website to another website; links may be automatic or activated by the user, and the new website may replace the original website or open in its own frame or browser window

liquidated damages an amount agreed on to be paid in damages by a party to a contract if it should commit a breach

liquidating dividends payments made from time to time by a trustee in bankruptcy to creditors on account of the full amount due to them

listing agreement contract between the vendor and his real estate agent creating the obligation to pay commission

major breach a breach of the whole contract or of an essential term so that the purpose of the contract is defeated

maker the party who signs and delivers a promissory note

malicious prosecution causing a person to be prosecuted for a crime without an honest belief that the crime was committed mandatory injunction an order requiring a person to do a particular act

market restriction where a supplier makes it a condition that the buyer markets the product only within a prescribed area

material could reasonably be expected to influence or induce the decision of a party to enter into a contract

maturity date the end of the term when debt must be repaid

mediation a form of ADR where a neutral third party who is acceptable to both sides acts as a mediator, assisting the parties to reach a settlement

memorandum of association a document setting out the essential terms of an agreement to form a corporation

mens rea offences offences where the prosecution must establish a "guilty mind" on the part of the defendant

merchant law rules and trade practices developed by merchants in medieval trade guilds and administered by their own courts

merger the amalgamation of two or more businesses into a single business entity

minor breach a breach of a non-essential term of a contract or of an essential term in a minor respect

minor or infant a person who has not attained the age of majority according to the law of his or her province

miscarriage an injury caused by the tort of another person

mitigate duty to act reasonably and quickly to minimize the extent of damage suffered

mitigation action by the injured party to reduce the extent of loss caused by the other party's breach

monitor a person appointed to supervise the reorganization of a debtor corporation under the Companies' Creditors Arrangement Act

moral cause moral duty of promisor to perform his promise

moral rights the non-transferable rights of an author or creator to prevent a work from being distorted or misused

mortgage a loan contract that gives the lender an interest in the borrower's land as security for a debt

mortgage commitment document in which parties to a mortgage initially agree to borrow and lend

mortgagee a lender who accepts an interest in land as security for a loan

mortgagor a borrower who gives his lender an interest in his land as security for repayment of a debt

most-favoured-nation (MFN) treatment the principle that goods imported from one country should not be treated less favourably than those imported from any other country

mutual mistake a situation in which both parties believe a mistake exists in the contract but their understandings of the mistake are different

national treatment the principle that goods from another country should not be treated less favourably than domestic goods

natural justice procedural fairness or due process

necessaries essential goods and services

negative covenant a promise not to do something

negative option billing a practice of adding services and sending bills without request and relying upon the customer to cancel if they don't wish the service

negligence the careless causing of injury to the person or property of another

negligent misrepresentation an unintentional tort imposing liability when an incorrect statement is made without due care for its accuracy, and injury is caused

negotiability the special quality possessed by negotiable instruments as a distinct class of assignable contract

negotiable instrument a written contract containing a promise, express or implied, to pay a specific sum of money to a designated person or to "bearer"

negotiation the process of assigning a negotiable instrument

nemo dat quod non habet "no one can give what he does not have"

new trial a case sent back by the appeal court for retrial by the lower court

no par value shares shares that have no nominal value attached

no-fault insurance a system of compulsory insurance that eliminates fault as a basis for claims

nominating committee committee responsible for proposing and recruiting new directors

non est factum "it is not my doing"

non-governmental organizations voluntary, non-profit associations of private entities working to influence policy, raise awareness, and effect change, such as the International Chamber of Commerce

non-public purchasers purchasers that are not members of the general public, such as banks, insurance companies, and municipal corporations

non-tariff barriers national rules, other than import duties, that restrict or prevent the importation of goods

notary a solicitor in Quebec

notice advance warning that the employment relationship will end

notice to quit notice of an intention to bring the tenancy to an end

novation the parties to a contract agree to terminate it and substitute a new contract

occupier's liability a negligence tort imposing liability on occupants of land for harm suffered by visitors to the property

OECD the Organisation for Economic Co-operation and Development, established in 1961, has 34 member countries including Canada, and promotes world trade and sustainable economic growth by setting standards for best practice

offences of absolute liability offences where the absence of fault is no defence

offences of strict liability offences where there is a presumption of guilt unless the defendant can show that he or she took reasonable care

offer a description of a promise one party is willing to make, subject to the agreement of the other party

offeree the person to whom the offer is made

offeror the person making the offer

officers high-ranking members of a corporation's management team as defined in the bylaws or appointed by the directors, such as the president, vice-president, controller, chief executive officer, chief financial officer, general counsel, and general manager

official receiver a public official responsible for the supervision of bankruptcy proceedings

open mortgage a mortgage permitting repayment of the debt at any time without notice or bonus

operating lease a lease under which there is no intention to transfer ownership

opportunity cost the lost chance of making a similar contract with a different promisor

oppression remedy a statutory procedure allowing individual shareholders to seek a personal remedy if they have been unfairly treated

option a contract to keep an offer open for a specified time in return for a sum of money

opt-out consent data-owner consent is implied from a failure to refuse consent

ordinary resolution a resolution adopted by the general meeting and passed by a simple majority

outside counsel self-employed lawyers who work alone, in small partnerships, or in large national firms, and bill the business for services rendered

overholding tenant a tenant who remains on the premises without a new agreement with the landlord after the term of the lease expires

overrule declare an existing precedent no longer binding or effective

paid-up capital the shares that have been issued and fully paid for

par value a nominal value attached to a share at the time of issue

paralegal a non-lawyer who provides some form of legal service to the public

parallel pricing the practice, among competing firms, of adopting similar pricing strategies

parol evidence rule a rule preventing a party to a written contract from later using parol evidence to add to, subtract from, or modify the final written contract

part payment something tendered by the buyer and accepted by the seller after formation of the contract, to be deducted from the price

part performance performance undertaken in reliance on an oral contract relating to an interest in land, and accepted by the courts as evidence of the contract in place of a written memorandum

partial discharge a discharge of a definite portion of the mortgaged lands

participating right the right of a holder of a preferred share to participate in surplus profits or assets of the corporation in addition to the amount of the preferred dividend or redemption price

partnership the relationship between two or more persons carrying on a business with a view to profit

partnership agreement an agreement between persons to create a partnership and (usually) to set out the terms of the relationship

party and party costs an award that shifts some of the costs of litigation to the losing side according to a published scale of fees

party autonomy the parties' freedom to determine how their dispute will be resolved

passing-off a common law tort involving the misrepresentation of goods, services, or a business in such a way as to deceive the public into believing that they are the goods, services, or business of some other person

past consideration a gratuitous benefit previously conferred upon a promisor

patent agent a registered agent who pursues applications for patents on behalf of individual inventors

patent defect a defect discoverable by a purchaser during an ordinary inspection

pawnbroker a business that loans money on the security of pawned goods

payee the party named to receive payment on the bill of exchange

payment card networks an electronic payment system used to accept, transmit, or process transactions made by payment card to transfer funds or information among issuer, user, and merchants

payment in lieu of notice payment of the amount of compensation the employee would have earned during the reasonable notice period

penalty clause a term specifying an exorbitant amount for breach of contract, intended to frighten a party into performance

perfection the moment in time when a creditor's security interest becomes protected

performance requirements conditions attached by the host country in granting approval to a foreign investment

periodic tenancy a leasehold interest that renews itself automatically on the last day of the term for a further term of the same duration

personal health information information relating to the physical or mental health of an identifiable individual that is used or obtained primarily for the purpose of providing healthcare

personal information recorded and unrecorded information about an identifiable individual, including that supplied by the individual and created by the organization

personal insurance insurance against death, injury, or ill health of an individual

personal privacy the respect of bodily integrity free from unreasonable surveillance, search, and seizure

petitions requests to commence bankruptcy proceedings against a defaulting debtor

PHIPA Personal Health Information Protection Act (in Alberta and Saskatchewan, simply HIPA)

plaintiff the party that commences a private (civil) legal action against another party

pleadings documents filed by each party to an action providing information it intends to prove in court

pledge or pawn a bailment of personal property as security for repayment of a loan where possession passes to the bailee

postdate give a cheque a date later than the time when it is delivered to the payee

power of attorney a type of agency agreement authorizing the agent to sign documents on behalf of the principal

power of sale a right upon default to sell mortgaged land

predatory pricing where a seller temporarily reduces prices to an unreasonably low level with the aim of driving competitors out of business

pre-emptive right the right of a holder of shares to protect his percentage ownership in the company by buying the same percentage in any new issue of shares

preferred creditors unsecured creditors whose claims are given preference over those of other unsecured creditors

preferred shares shares carrying preferential rights to receive a dividend and/or to be redeemed on the dissolution of the corporation for a fixed price

pre-incorporation contract a purported contract made in the name of a corporation before it comes into existence

premium the price paid by the insured to purchase insurance coverage

prescription the creation of an easement over adjoining land through exercising a right continuously and openly

presents produces the instrument to the drawee bank, promisor, or maker principal the person on whose behalf the agent acts

principled exception allows third parties to rely upon a contractual exemption clause when the parties to the contract intended to include them, and their activities come within the scope of the contract and the exemption clause

priority a first, or prior, right to be repaid out of the debtor's assets

priority of registration priority of interests in real property is determined based on the order of registration in the public system

privacy has three key dimensions: personal privacy, territorial or spatial privacy, and privacy of personal information

privacy of personal information the protection of the trail of information left behind as we go about our daily lives involving secrecy, control, and anonymity

private companies corporations with a restricted number of shareholders prohibited from issuing their shares to the general public

private law law that regulates the relations between private persons and groups of private persons

private nuisance interference with an occupier's use and enjoyment of her land

private rights individual rights arising from private law

privilege the right of a professional to refuse to divulge information obtained in confidence from a client

privity of contract the relationship that exists between parties to a contract

privity of estate the relationship between tenant and landlord created by their respective interests in the land that passes to a transferee of the interest

probate the process of administering and settling the estate of a deceased person

procedural law rules that deal with how substantive rights and duties may be enforced

product defamation making false and damaging statements about the products of another person

product liability a negligence tort imposing liability on manufacturers for harm caused by defective products

professional corporation (PC) a special type of business corporation that may be formed by members of a profession

progressive employee discipline imposing increasingly serious consequences for each event of improper employee behaviour beginning with a warning and ending with dismissal

promisee a party who has the right to performance according to the terms of the contract

promisor a party who is under an obligation to perform a promise according to the terms of the contract

promissory estoppel or equitable estoppel the court's exercise of its equitable jurisdiction to estop a promisor from claiming that she was not bound by her gratuitous promise where reliance on that promise caused injury to the promisee

promissory note a written promise to pay a specified sum of money to another party at a fixed or determinable future time or on demand

proper law of the contract the law of the country or jurisdiction by which the terms of a contract or disputes under it are to be interpreted and decided

property (1) everything that is the subject of ownership or (2) the legal interest in a thing

property insurance insurance against damage to property

proposal a procedure whereby a debtor, by agreement with the creditors, reorganizes his or her affairs without being made bankrupt

prospectus the document that a corporation is required to publish when inviting the public to subscribe for its securities

proxy a person appointed to attend a general meeting of shareholders and to cast the votes of the shareholder appointing him or her

proxy form a form required to be circulated to shareholders before a general meeting, inviting them to appoint a proxy if they so wish

public international law law involving relations between states

public law law that regulates the conduct of government and the relations between government and private persons

public liability insurance insurance to cover damage to others caused by the business

public nuisance interference with the lawful use of public amenities

public offering selling shares to the public, which must be done in compliance with provincial securities regulations

public policy economic, social, and political considerations or objectives that are believed to be beneficial to society as a whole

publicly traded corporations corporations that issue shares to the public, also known as public corporations, widely held corporations, reporting issuers, and issuing corporations

punitive or exemplary damages damages awarded with the intention of punishing a wrongdoer

purchase lease a lease whereby ownership is intended to change hands at the end of the lease term

purchase-money security interest (PMSI) the interest that arises when goods purchased by a debtor are charged as security for a loan made to enable those actual goods being acquired

purpose of collection a need for collecting personal information that must be related directly to an operating program or activity of the institution

qualified privilege immunity from liability for defamation provided a statement was made in good faith

quantum meruit the fair amount a person deserves to be paid for benefit conferred

quasi-contract an obligation that may arise, not as a result of contractual relations, but because one party has received an unfair benefit at the expense of the other

quiet possession a warranty that there will be no interference with the lessee's possession or use of the asset

quotas restrictions on the quantities of goods that may be imported

ratification subsequent adoption by the proposed principal of a contract made by an agent acting without authority

ratifies acknowledges and promises to perform

real action an action to repossess an interest in land that had been interfered with

reasonable expectation of privacy the subjective and objective assessment of reasonable privacy expectations in a given situation

reasonable notice the acceptable length of notice of termination considering the nature of the contract, intentions of the parties, circumstance of the employment, and characteristics of the employee

rebut overcome

receiving order a court order to commence bankruptcy proceedings recognition dispute an employer refuses to recognize the union as the employees' bargaining agent

rectification correction of a written document to reflect accurately the contract made by the parties

redeem have the land reconveyed to the mortgagor

redeem reclaim the goods and continue with the conditional sale

regular on its face nothing appears out of order on the document itself

regulations administrative rules implemented by government as a result of authorization given in a statute

regulatory offences less serious offences created by government regulation through specialized legislation, agencies, and tribunals

regulatory or quasi-criminal liability responsibility arising from breaches of less serious rules of public law, often enforced through specialized regulatory tribunals set up by the government for specific purposes

relationship of master and servant the contractual relationship between an employer and an employee

reliance acting in a certain way because one believed the information received

reliance damages costs of expenditures and wasted effort reasonably made in preparation for performance

remainder the balance of a fee simple that goes to a third person at the end of a life estate

remainderman a person who holds the reversion or remainder in a fee simple

remote unrelated or far removed from the conduct

remote parties parties to an instrument who have not had direct dealings with one another

repossession the act of taking back possession of property that is in the possession of a defaulting debtor

representative action an action brought by one or more persons on behalf of a group having the same interest

repudiate reject or declare an intention not to be bound by

requisitions questions concerning claims against a seller's title to property

res judicata a case that has already been decided by a court and cannot be brought before a court again

rescind set aside; undo or revoke a contract and return the parties as nearly as possible to their original positions

rescission setting aside or rescinding a contract in order to restore the parties as nearly as possible to their pre-contract positions

reserve judgment postpone giving a decision after the hearing ends

residential tenancies a lease of premises used as living accommodation

residual powers powers that fall within federal jurisdiction because they are not expressly allocated to the provinces by the Constitution

respondent the party who defends on an appeal

responsible communication on matters of public interest a defence to defamation when the publication of the statement is in the public interest and was done responsibly

restitution an order to restore property wrongfully taken

restrictive covenant a term in restraint of trade, i.e., a promise not to carry on a competing business activity

restrictive covenant a covenant requiring the holder of the land to refrain from certain conduct or certain use of the land

resulting trust a trust relationship recognized when the conduct of the parties demonstrates the intention to hold property for the benefit of the other

retail sales sales of consumer goods by retail businesses, in the ordinary course of their business, to private individuals

retain keep information available for subsequent access by the individual

retainer the contract between a lawyer and client that describes the work that will be done and the fee that will be charged

reverse mortgage a form of mortgage under which no repayment is due until the mortgagor sells or dies

reversion the balance of a fee simple reserved to the grantor and her heirs at the end of a life estate

rider additional provisions attached to a standard policy of insurance

right of re-entry a landlord's remedy of evicting the tenant for failure to pay rent or breach of another major covenant

right of survivorship the right of a surviving tenant to the interest of a deceased joint tenant

right-of-way an easement that gives the holder a right to pass back and forth over the land of another in order to get to and from her own land

rights dispute an employer and the union differ in their interpretation of terms in an existing collective agreement

Roman law the system of law codified by the Eastern Roman Emperor Justinian in the 6th century

royal charter a special licence given by the Crown to form a corporation for the purpose of carrying on a particular activity

royalty fee paid to the copyright owner for permission to copy the work

royalty payments fees paid for permission to use another person's copyrighted material

rule of law established legal principles that treat all persons equally and that government itself obeys

rules of civil procedure the provincial regulations that set out the steps in a private lawsuit, including forms, fees, and timelines

sale-and-leaseback a transaction in which the owner of property sells it and immediately leases it back from the new owner

searching the title to examine the title to a piece of land

secured creditor a creditor that has collateral security in the form of a recognized claim against specified assets of the debtor

securities commission the statutory authority appointed to supervise the issue of securities to the general public, the operation of the securities industry, and the stock exchange

security agreements agreements that create a security interest, including chattel mortgages, conditional sales contracts, pledges, etc.

security for costs money deposited into the court in case an unsuccessful foreign plaintiff is ordered to pay the legal costs of the successful defendant

security interest an interest in goods, intangible property, or personal property that secures payment of a debt or performance of an obligation

security lease a purchase lease in which the lessor provides the credit

self-induced frustration a party willfully disables itself from performing a contract in order to claim that the contract has been frustrated senior officer a representative who plays an important role in establishing an organization's policies or is responsible for managing an important aspect of its activities, including the directors, the CEO, and the CFO of a corporation

servient tenement the land subject to the easement

serving providing a copy of the issued claim to each defendant

set aside rescind; undo or revoke a contract and return the parties as nearly as possible to their original positions

set off the right of a promisor to deduct an existing debt owed to him by the promisee

settlement an out-of-court procedure by which one of the parties agrees to pay a sum of money or perform an act in return for a waiver by the other party of all rights arising from the grievance

severance a procedure that turns a joint tenancy into a tenancy in common

severed removed from the contract

share a member's proportionate interest in the capital of a corporation

shareholder agreement an agreement between two or more shareholders that is distinct from the corporation's charter and bylaws

sight draft a bill of exchange payable "at sight"—three days of grace are allowed after presentation

slander spoken defamation

sole proprietorship an unincorporated business owned by a single individual

solicitor an "office" lawyer in England who interviews clients, carries on legal aspects of business and family affairs, and prepares cases for trial

solicitor–client fee payment for the time and expenses of a lawyer in preparing a case and representing the client in negotiations to settle or in court

solicitor–client privilege a client's right to have all communications with his or her lawyer kept confidential

special Acts of Parliament legislative acts creating a specific corporation

special damages damages to compensate for quantifiable injuries

special meeting any general meeting of shareholders other than the annual general meeting

special resolution a resolution of the general meeting required to be passed by a special (usually two-thirds) majority

specific goods goods in existence, identified and agreed upon as the subject matter of the sale

specific performance an order requiring a defendant to do a contracted-for act, usually to complete a transaction

specification the description of the invention, its use, operation, or manufacture

stakeholder a person or organization that manages a betting arrangement for a fee and redistributes winnings

stakeholders groups affected by the business activities of a corporation

standard form contract an offer prepared in advance by the offeror, including terms favourable to the offeror that cannot be changed by the offeree, but must be accepted as is or rejected in their entirety, also known as a contract of adhesion

standard of care the level of care that a person must take in the circumstances

standing the right to bring a lawsuit

standing offer an offer that may be accepted as needed from time to time

stare decisis to stand by a previous decision

stated capital account the amount received by a corporation for the issue of its shares

statement of adjustments a document setting out all the items—both credits and debits—that must be adjusted between the parties to arrive at the correct amount to be paid on closing

statement of defence a reply to a statement of claim, admitting facts not in dispute, denying other facts, and setting out facts in support of the defence

statute barred an action that may no longer be brought before a court because the party wishing to sue has delayed beyond the limitation period in the statute

statutes pieces of legislation passed by government

statutory assignment an assignment that complies with statutory provisions enabling the assignee to sue the other party without joining the assignor to the action

statutory damages damages a plaintiff may request instead of proving actual loss

stop payment an instruction from the drawer of a cheque to the bank not to pay the cheque

stoppage in transit the right of a seller to order a carrier not to deliver to the buyer

strict interpretation courts apply the provisions of a statute only where the facts of the case are covered specifically by the statute

strict liability liability that is imposed based upon causation regardless of fault

strict or plain-meaning approach an approach that restricts interpretation to the ordinary or dictionary meaning of a word

sub-bailee a person who receives a bailment of property from a bailee

subject to the equities subject to any rights or defences the promisor had against the original assignor

subordinate legislation law created by administrative agencies whose authority is granted by statute in order to carry out the purposes of the legislation

subrogation where one person becomes entitled to the rights and claims of another

subsidiary a separate corporation owned or controlled by its "parent" corporation

subsidiary promise an implied promise that the offeror will not revoke once the offeree begins performance in good faith and continues to perform

substantial performance performance that does not comply in some minor way with the requirements of the contract

substantive law the rights and duties that each person has in society

super priority entitlement to be paid before secured creditors

super-governmental organizations non-profit associations of governments from around the world working to find common approaches to international issues, such as the World Trade Organization or the United Nations

surrender abandonment of the premises by the tenant during the term of the lease

survey detailed drawing or map of the real property showing all the boundaries of the land and the location of all fixtures, encroachments, or overhangs

system of courts the organization of courts into a hierarchy that designates the responsibilities of the court and determines the importance of the precedent; the standard system has three levels: trial, appeal, and final appeal systemic discrimination discrimination that is pervasive throughout an employer's work force

takeover bid an offer by one corporation to acquire all or a substantial part of the shares of another corporation

technical protection measures (TPMs) access locks or use locks for electronic material. An access lock requires a password to access the work; a use lock blocks particular uses of the work such as copying

telemarketing the use of telephone communications for promoting the supply of a product or for promoting a business interest

tenancy from year to year a periodic tenancy that renews itself yearly

tenant's fixtures trade fixtures or any other fixtures attached for the convenience of the tenant or for the better enjoyment of the object

tenants in common concurrent holders of equal undivided shares in an estate

tender of performance an attempt by one party to perform according to the terms of the contract

term an interest in land for a definite period of time

term the time period during which an interest rate is fixed and principal lent

term certain a tenancy that expires on a specific day

term insurance personal insurance that provides coverage for a limited period only

territorial privacy lack of intrusion in one's home, business, and other personal spaces

third party a person who is not one of the parties to a contract but is affected by it

third-party liability liability to some other person who stands outside a contractual relationship

tied selling where a supplier makes it a condition that, to obtain one type of product, the buyer must also deal in other products of the supplier

time draft a bill of exchange payable within a stipulated period after the date stated on the instrument or after presentation

title holding ownership of a thing

title fraud fraudulent transfer or mortgaging of land by a non-owner

title insurance a policy of insurance that compensates the policy holder for defects in a title

tort a wrongful act causing harm to the person or property of another

trade fixture an object attached to the premises for the purpose of carrying on a trade or business

trademark an identifiable feature that is used by a person for the purpose of distinguishing his goods or services from those of others

trade-related investment measures national measures regulating investment that have an impact upon international trade

transfer under the land titles system, the equivalent of a grant; not required to be made under seal

transfer a gift, sale, or disposition of property made by a debtor before becoming bankrupt

trespass unlawful entering, or remaining, on the land of another without permission

trespasser one who enters without consent or lawful right on the lands of another or who, having entered lawfully, refuses to leave when ordered to do so by the owner

trust an arrangement that transfers property to a person who administers it for the benefit of another person

trust agreement the document that conveys property to a trustee to be used for the benefit of a third-party beneficiary

trust deed a document evidencing a mortgage on the property of a corporation

trustee a person or company who administers a trust

trustee in bankruptcy the person appointed to administer the property of a bankrupt

ultra vires beyond the powers and therefore void

unanimous shareholder agreement a shareholder agreement to which all shareholders are parties

unascertained goods goods that have not been set aside and agreed upon as the subject of a sale

UNCITRAL United Nations Commission on International Trade Law established by the United Nations General Assembly in 1966 to further harmonization and unification in international trade through conventions, model laws, and guidelines

unconscionable contracts contracts where there is unequal bargaining power between the parties and the powerful party gets an extremely advantageous deal

unconscionable terms terms agreed to by parties of unequal bargaining power that give an unfair advantage to the powerful party over the weaker party

undisclosed principal a contracting party who, unknown to the other party, is represented by an agent

undue influence the domination of one party over the mind of another to such a degree as to deprive the weaker party of the will to make an independent decision

unenforceable no court assistance or remedy is available to parties of the contract

unenforceable contract a contract that still exists for other purposes but neither party may obtain a remedy under it through court action

UNIDROIT the International Institute for the Unification of Private Law, founded by the League of Nations in 1926 to harmonize laws; currently has 63 member states including Canada

unilateral contract a contract in which the offer is accepted by performing an act or series of acts required by the terms of the offer

unilateral mistake a situation in which only one of the parties believes there is a mistake in the contract

unincorporated collectivity a group of persons that in most cases is not recognized by the courts and that may not sue or be sued

unitholders beneficiaries of an income trust

unjust enrichment an unfair benefit

unlawful interference with economic relations attempting by threats or other unlawful means to induce one person to discontinue business relations with another

unlawful means civil action available under common law

unperfected security interest a security interest that is not attached or perfected

unsecured creditor a creditor who has no security interest in any of the debtor's property

use (of personal information) any access, change, or destruction of data within the organization

utmost good faith a duty of disclosure owed when a special relationship of trust exists between the parties

vicarious liability the liability of an employer to compensate for torts committed by an employee during the course of his or her employment

vicarious performance a third party performs contractual obligations on behalf of the promisor who remains responsible for proper performance

void never formed in law

voidable the contract exists until set aside by a court; rights may pass to third parties before it is set aside

voidable contract a contract that may be rendered non-binding at the option of one of the parties

voluntary assumption of risk a defence to a negligence action when the plaintiff was aware of the risk and continued with the activity anyway

vulture funds large investors who purchase the debt or shares of a corporation in the course of its reorganization

wager an agreement between two persons in which each has some probability of winning or losing

waiver an agreement not to proceed with the performance of an existing contract

warranty a lesser or non-essential term that, when breached, does not relieve the injured party from performance

warranty of authority a person who purports to act as agent represents that she has authority to contract on behalf of the principal

waste damage to the premises that reduces its value

web-wrap agreement a website document setting out contractual terms, the acceptance of which is indicated by clicking on the appropriate icon (click-wrap agreements require the buyer to open the terms page before clicking acceptance of them)

willful invasion of privacy a person knew or should have known that her actions would invade the privacy of another

winding up the dissolution (or liquidation) of a corporation

without recourse no ability to claim against the endorser

work an original published or unpublished literary, dramatic, musical, or artistic creation, including the title

workers' compensation a scheme in which employers contribute to a fund used to compensate workers injured in industrial accidents regardless of how the accident was caused

World Intellectual Property Organization a specialized agency of the United Nations dedicated to harmonizing intellectual property laws and regimes worldwide

writ an ancient form required in order to take a grievance to court

wrongful detention the refusal by the seller to deliver goods whose title has passed to the buyer

Index

joint tenancy, 479–480
joint ventures, 572, 719
judge-made law. *see* case law
judges, 18
judgment creditors, 289
judgment debtors, 289
judgments, 289, 290
judicial review, 53
jurisdiction
    and contracts, 135, 137
    and corporations, 585–586
    and electronic commerce, 756–758
    in employee welfare legislation, 398
    federal/provincial powers, 49
    for international disputes, 723–725
    for trademarks, 450
jurisdictional disputes, 405
justice, 3, 41–42

K

know-how, 469–470
Kyoto Protocol, 652

L

labelling, 64–65
labour disputes, 405–406
labour law
    collective agreements, 404–405,
        406–407
    collective bargaining. *see* collective
        bargaining
    labour disputes, 405–406
labour relations board, 404
labour unions
    capacity to contract, 165–166
    collective bargaining. *see* collective
        bargaining
    and contracts, 165–166
    legal status of, 407–409
land. *see also* interests in land
    condominiums, 487–488
    contracts, 207–208
    defined, 476
    government regulation, 485–489
    leasehold estates, 487
    matrimonial home rights, 486–487
    use and development, 485–486
land law
    and privity of contract, 233–234
    Statute of Frauds, 207–208
land titles system, 492, 529–530
land use and development, 485–486
landlord and tenant. *see also* tenancy
    assignment, 503–504
    bankruptcy of tenant, 511
    checklist, 508
    classes of tenancies, 501–502
    covenants, 502–508, 519
    damages, 508–509, 511
    definite or ascertainable period, 501

discrimination, 519
distress, 509–510, 520
eviction, 509, 520
exclusive possession, 500–501
fitness for occupancy, 505
fixtures, 514–516
forfeiture, 512–513
injunction, 510, 511–512
insurance, 507
landlord's mortgagee, 517
lease registration, 517
leasebacks, 518
leasehold estates, 478–479, 487,
    500
legislation, 52, 208, 519–520
nature of relationship, 500
notice to quit, 513, 520
oral leases, 516
periodic tenancy, 501–502, 513
privity of contract, 516
privity of estate, 516
provision of services, 507
quiet enjoyment, 506
recovery of rent, 508–509
remedies of tenant, 511–512
remedies of the landlord, 508–511
renewal, 514
rent, 502–503
repairs, 505
residential tenancies, 518–520
restrictions on use of premises,
    504–505
sale of landlord's interest, 516–517
subletting, 504
surrender, 512
taxes, 507
tenancy at sufferance, 502
tenancy at will, 502
tenancy from year to year, 502
tenant in possession after expiration
    of fixed term, 513–514
term certain, 501
termination of tenancy, 512–514,
    520
terms for notice, 514
waste, 505
lapses, 128–129
latent defects, 543
law. *see also* legislation; specific types of law
    administrative law, 42
    and behaviour, 3–4
    and business, 4–5
    case law, 25–26
    choice of law, 725
    classifying, 22
    contract law. *see* contracts
    defined, 2
    electronic commerce, 738–755
    and ethics, 2–3
    and international business,
        706–707, 715, 721–722

    vs. justice, 3
    and morals, 2–3
    need for, 2
    private international law, 708
    private law, 2
    public law, 2
    role of, 2
    rule of, 2
    sources of, 10–11, 22, 24–26, 42
    tort law. *see* torts
lawsuits, 31–39
LCL, 710
learned intermediary, 92
leasebacks, 518
leasehold estates, 478–479, 487, 500
leases. *see also* landlord and tenant; leasing
    defined, 332, 500
    oil, gas, and mineral leases, 483–484
    oral leases, 516
    registration of, 517
    statutes, 208
lease-to-buy (LTB) leases, 335
lease-to-own, 333n
leasing
    as bailment, 332–333
    chattel leases, 333–334
    checklist, 336
    consent to assignment, 335–336
    costs payable by the lessee, 335
    duration, 335
    early termination—minimum pay-
        ment, 336
    ethics, 338
    fair-market-value (FMV) leases, 335
    finance leases, 334
    implied terms, 336–337
    insurance, 335
    leasehold estates, 478–479, 487, 500
    lease-to-buy (LTB) leases, 335
    lease-to-own, 333n
    legal risk management, 339
    lessees, 338
    lessors, 337–338
    operating leases, 333
    purchase options, 335
    purchases leases, 333–334
    real estate, 478–479
    reasons for, 334–335
    rights of the parties, 337–338
    sale-and-leaseback, 334
    security leases, 334
    sub-bailment, 335–336
    terms in, 335–337
    true leases, 333
legal advice, importance of, 198
legal aid, 35
legal audit, 5
legal capacity, 161
legal duty, 146–147
legal liability, 3
legal personality, 557

setting aside a contract (continued)
  undue influence, 196–198
  void and voidable contracts,
    186–188
settlement out of court, 38–39
severance, 316, 480
severed, 168
sex worker industry, 18
sexual orientation, 18
share capital, 591–592
shareholders
  annual reports, 620
  appraisal remedy, 622–623
  auditors, 620
  class rights, 617
  common shareholders, 593–594
  derivative action, 623
  vs. directors, 601
  directors' duties to, 608
  dividends, 617–618
  documents of record, 620
  duties of, 621
  financial rights, 617–619
  financial statements, 619
  information, right to, 619–621
  inspector, appointment of, 620–621
  legal risk management, 626
  loans to, 636
  majority rule, 621–622
  meetings, 616
  minority shareholders, 621–626
  oppression remedy, 624–625
  pre-emptive rights, 618–619
  preferred shareholders, 594
  in private corporations, 615
  proxies, 617
  in publicly traded corporations, 615
  rights of, 593–594, 615–621
  rights of second mortgagee, 626
  role of, 614–615
  shareholder agreements, 626–627
  surplus, distribution of, 618
  voting, 616–617
  winding up, 623–624
shares
  vs. bonds, 593
  class rights, 594
  common shares, 593
  defined, 592
  dividends, 617–618
  no par value shares, 592
  par value, 592
  preferred shares, 592
shark fins, 49
shipment, 710
sight drafts, 420
signatures, 209–210
silence, 130, 195–196
slander, 80
Small Claims Court, 28
smart cards, 737

social regulation, 48
social responsibility, 642
Society for Composers and Music
  Publishers (SOCAN), 458
Society of Composers, Authors and Music
  Publishers of Canada (SOCAN), 750
sole proprietorships, 553–554
solicitor–client fees, 35
solicitor–client privilege, 8, 117, 541
solicitors, 7
solvency test, 635
spam, 753–754
special Acts of Parliament, 584
special damages, 96
special endorsement, 427
special meetings, 616
special resolutions, 616
specific goods, 307
specific performance, 25, 311
specifications, 465
spouses, 197, 487n
stakeholders, 169, 633–634
standard form contracts, 126, 194, 312
standard of care
  and bailment, 326
  defined, 85
  for professionals, 112–113
  proving breach of, 91
  and public policy, 169–170
  and torts, 85, 88, 91, 112–113
standing, 31, 725
standing offers, 133
stare decisis, 24
stated capital account, 592
statement of adjustments, 544
statements of defence, 33
statute barred, 264
Statute of Frauds
  consequences, 210–211
  contracts covered by, 206–208
  guarantees, 206–207
  history of, 206
  international trends, 211–212
  land, 207–208
  part performance, 208
  and Sale of Goods Acts, 213
  written memorandum, 208–210, 211
statutes. see also legislation
  agreement legal by statute, 172–173
  agreements illegal by statute,
    171–172
  challenging, 16–17
  contracts affected by statute,
    168–173
  defined, 10
  described, 42–43
  Freedom of Information and
    Protection of Privacy (FIPPA)
    statute, 770
  general incorporation statutes,
    584–585

of limitation, 701
wording of, 168
statutory assignment, 239
statutory damages, 461
statutory easements, 480–481
statutory reform, 261, 402
stock exchange, 170
stockbrokers, 362
stop payments, 422
storage, 328
strict approach, 216
strict interpretation, 42
strict liability, 75, 76, 96, 610
strikes, 401, 404, 405, 406
student loans, 693
sub-bailees, 324
sub-bailment, 324, 335–336
subcontractors, 696
subject to the equities, 240, 424
subletting, 504
subordinate legislation, 42, 43–44
subrogation, 88, 352, 357
subsidiaries, 718
subsidiary promises, 136
subsidies, 714–715
substance vs. form, 205
substantial performance, 276
substantive law, 22
substituted agreement, 252–253
suing, 31–39
suitability and quality, 300–303
sum certain, 424
super priority, 690–691
super-governmental organizations,
  5, 707
Superior Trial Courts, 29
Supreme Court, 13–14, 18, 27, 29
surplus, distribution of, 618
surrender, 508, 512
Surrogate Courts, 29
surveillance, 779
surveys, 493–494
system of courts
  in Canada, 27–30
  Court of Appeal, 27
  courts of first instance, 26
  defined, 25
  in England, 25–26
  trial courts, 26
  in the U.S., 30
System of Electronic Disclosure by Insiders
  (SEDI), 640
System of Electronic Disclosure for
  Analysis and Retrieval (SEDAR), 640
systemic discrimination, 399

T
takeover bid, 641
takeovers, 641
tangible personal property, 236, 237, 296

EXPLANATION OF ABBREVIATIONS

Throughout the text and footnotes, references occur to reported decisions of the courts, to statutes, and to legal periodicals. Listed below are the abbreviations for frequently cited source materials.

Canada

REPORTS

A.J.	Alberta Journal
A.R.	Alberta Reports
Alta L.R.	Alberta Law Reports
B.C.J.	British Columbia Journal
B.L.R.	Business Law Reports
C.C.C.	Canadian Criminal Cases
C.C.E.L.	Canadian Cases on Employment Law
C.C.L.I.	Canadian Cases on the Law of Insurance
C.C.L.T.	Canadian Cases on the Law of Torts
C.E.L.R.	Canadian Environmental Law Reports
C.P.R.	Canadian Patent Reports
C.R.	Criminal Reports
C.S.	Cour Supérieure (Québec)
D.L.R.	Dominion Law Reports
D.T.C.	Dominion Tax Cases
Ex.C.R.	Exchequer Court Reports
F.C.	Federal Court Reports
F.T.R.	Federal Court Trial Reports
M.J.	Manitoba Journal
M.P.R.	Maritime Provinces Reports
N.B.R.	New Brunswick Reports
N.S.R.	Nova Scotia Reports
O.A.C.	Ontario Appeal Cases
O.A.R.	Ontario Appeal Reports
O.J.	Ontario Journal
O.L.R.	Ontario Law Reports
O.R.	Ontario Reports
O.W.N.	Ontario Weekly Notes
P.P.S.A C.	Personal Property Security Act Cases
S.C.R.	Supreme Court Reports
S.J.	Saskatchewan Journal
Sask.R.	Saskatchewan Reports
W.L.R.	Western Law Reports
W.W.R.	Western Weekly Reports

STATUTES

Revised Statutes of

R.S.A.	Alberta
R.S.B.C.	British Columbia
R.S.C.	Canada
R.S.M.	Manitoba
R.S.N.B.	New Brunswick
R.S.Nfld.	Newfoundland
R.S.N.S.	Nova Scotia
R.S.O.	Ontario
R.S.P.E.I.	Prince Edward Island
R.S.Q.	Quebec
R.S.S.	Saskatchewan

(Statutes for individual years are cited as S.A., S.B.C., S.C., S.M., S.N.B., S.Nfld., S.N.S., S.O., S.P.E.I., S.Q., S.S., respectively.)

S.O.R.	Statutory Orders and Regulations

PERIODICALS

C.B.L.J.	Canadian Business Law Journal
Can. Bar Rev.	Canadian Bar Review
Can. B.A.J.	Canadian Bar Association Journal
Osg.H.L.J.	Osgoode Hall Law Journal
UBC L. Rev.	University of British Columbia Law Review
U.T.L.J.	University of Toronto Law Journal

JUDGES

J.	Justice
J.A.	Justice of Appeal
JJ.	Justices
C.J.	Chief Justice
A.G.	Attorney-General

United Kingdom

REPORTS

All E.R.	All England Reports
E.R.	English Reports (Reprint)
I.R.	Irish Reports